Law of the European Union

Eleventh Edition

Law of the European Union

JOHN FAIRHURST

London School of Business and Management

PEARSON

Harlow, England • London • New York • Boston • San Francisco • Toronto • Sydney • Auckland • Singapore • Hong Kong
Tokyo • Seoul • Taipei • New Delhi • Cape Town • São Paulo • Mexico City • Madrid • Amsterdam • Munich • Paris • Milan

PEARSON EDUCATION LIMITED
Edinburgh Gate
Harlow CM20 2JE
United Kingdom
Tel: +44 (0)1279 623623
Web: www.pearson.com/uk

First published 1996 (print)
Second edition published under The Financial Times/Pitman Publishing imprint 1999 (print)
Third edition 2002 (print)
Fourth edition 2003 (print)
Fifth edition 2006 (print)
Sixth edition 2007 (print)
Seventh edition 2010 (print)
Eighth edition 2010 (print)
Ninth edition 2012 (print and electronic)
Tenth Edition 2014 (print and electronic)
Eleventh Edition 2016 (print and electronic)

© Pearson Professional Limited 1996 (print)
© Pearson Education Limited 1999, 2002, 2003, 2006, 2007, 2010 (print)
© Pearson Education Limited 2012, 2014, 2016 (print and electronic)

ISBN: 978-1-292-09033-7 (print)
           978-1-292-09035-1 (PDF)
           978-1-292-13028-6 (ePub)

British Library Cataloguing-in-Publication Data
A catalogue record for the print edition is available from the British Library

Library of Congress Cataloging-in-Publication Data
Names: Fairhurst, John, author.
Title: Law of the European Union / John Fairhurst.
Description: Eleventh edition. | New York : Pearson, 2016.
Identifiers: LCCN 2015044005 (print) | LCCN 2015044167 (ebook) | ISBN
  9781292090337 | ISBN 9781292130286 () | ISBN 9781292090351 ()
Subjects: LCSH: Law--European Union countries. | Courts--European Union
  countries. | European Union.
Classification: LCC KJE947 .F342 2016 (print) | LCC KJE947 (ebook) | DDC

10 9 8 7 6 5 4 3 2 1
20 19 18 17 16

Print edition typeset in 9/12pt StoneSerITCStd by Lumina Datamatics
Printed in Malaysia (CTP-PJB)

NOTE THAT ANY PAGE CROSS REFERENCES REFER TO THE PRINT EDITION

Brief contents

Contents

Part 1 Constitutional and administrative law of the European Union

Part 2 The free movement of persons and services, and freedom of establishment

Part 3 The free movement of goods

Part 4 Union competition law

Preface

Within this new edition I have included all legislative changes and recent judgments of the Court of Justice and the General Court. The format of this edition follows the same format as the previous edition.

Part 1 covers the Constitutional and Administrative Law of the European Union. Chapter 1 comprises an introduction to the European Communities and the European Union. This chapter contains a historical analysis of the evolution of the European Union. There is an update on the Union's protracted discussions for accession to the European Convention on Human Rights. Chapter 2 is devoted to the sources of Union law, including a commentary on general principles of law and fundamental rights. The rationale for this approach is that I prefer that learners have an understanding of such sources, principles and rights before embarking upon a consideration of the Union institutions (Chapter 3) and the decision-making process (Chapter 4). Chapter 3 has been updated to reflect the new composition of the European Parliament following the June 2014 elections and the appointment of the new Commission. There is a separate chapter on the Court of Justice of the European Union (which consists of the Court of Justice, the General Court and the specialised courts), together with its methods of interpretation (Chapter 5). Chapters 6–8 cover the preliminary ruling jurisdiction of the Court of Justice (Art 267 TFEU), direct actions against Member States (Arts 258–260 TFEU), and judicial review of acts of the Union institutions, respectively.

Chapter 9 examines the principles of supremacy of Union law over the national law of the Member States (including a commentary on its impact on the UK's traditional doctrine of parliamentary sovereignty), indirect effect, direct effect and state liability. Included in this chapter is a discussion of how these principles have been applied by UK courts. The final chapter of Part 1 (Chapter 10) explores the application of Union law in UK courts and the adaptation of remedies to the requirements of Union law.

The final three parts of the book (Parts 2–4) relate to three areas of substantive Union law: free movement of persons and services, and freedom of establishment (Part 2, Chapters 11–16); free movement of goods (Part 3, Chapters 17–18); and competition law (Part 4, Chapters 19–22). In each of these three parts, judgments of the Court of Justice and the General Court have been extracted to provide a deeper exposure to the methodology adopted by the Courts in the development of the Union's substantive law. New legislative developments have been incorporated throughout.

The EU's institutional websites provide a vast array of resources, including free full-text copies of legislation and judgments of the Court of Justice of the European Union. A number of the website addresses (URLs) have changed from those published in the last edition. This edition includes the updated URLs.

Updates to the book are available online at www.pearsoned.co.uk/legalupdates. This is an important feature given the dynamic nature of Union law. Whether you are a teacher or learner, I hope you find the time to access these online resources.

I would like to thank the following staff at Pearson Education for their support and guidance throughout this latest rewrite: Hannah Marston (Editor for Law) and Jennifer Sargunar (Senior Project Editor).

I have endeavoured to state the law as at 1 January 2016.

John Fairhurst
1 January 2016

Publisher's acknowledgements

We are grateful to the following for permission to reproduce copyright material:

Text

Box on page 169 from *Bulmer* v *Bollinger* [1974] 3 WLR 202; Boxes on page 271, page 304 from *Macarthys* Ltd v *Smith* [1979] ICR 785; Box on page 304 from *Macarthys* Ltd v Smith [1981] QB 180; Box on page 305 from *R* v *Secretary of State for Transport, ex parte Factortame* [1991] 1 AC 603 at 659; Box on pages 285–6 from *Foster* v *British Gas (No. 2)* [1991] 2 AC 306; Box on page 318 from *Woolwich Equitable Building Society* v *IRC* [1992] 3 WLR 366; Box on page 754 from *Garden Cottage Foods Ltd* v *Milk Marketing Board* [1984] AC 130.

Table of cases before the Court of Justice of the European Union (numerical)

Table of cases before national courts

Table of European Union Decisions

Table of European Union Treaties

Table of other Treaties, etc.

Table of European Union Regulations

Table of European Union Directives

Rules of Procedure of the Institutions of the European Union

Table of Statutes

List of abbreviations

AC	Appeal Cases
ACP	African Caribbean Pacific states
AJCL	American Journal of Comparative Law
AJIL	American Journal of International Law
All ER	All England Law Reports
Anglo-Am LRev	Anglo-American Law Review
BDMA	British Direct Mailing Association
BGC	British Gas Corporation
Bull EC	Bulletin of the European Communities
BYIL	British Yearbook of International Law
CAP	Common Agricultural Policy
CE	Compulsory Expenditure
CEE	Charge having an equivalent effect to a customs duty
CEN	European Committee for Standardisation
CENELEC	European Committee of Electrotechnical Standardisation
CFI	Court of First Instance
CFSP	Common Foreign and Security Policy
CJHA	Cooperation in Justice and Home Affairs
CLJ	Cambridge Law Journal
CLP	Current Legal Problems
CMLR	Common Market Law Reports
CML Rev	Common Market Law Review
COM	Common Organisation of the Market or Commission Document
COREPER	Committee of Permanent Representatives (*Comité des Représentants Permanents*)
Crim LR	Criminal Law Reports
DG	Directorate General
DSB	Dispute Settlement Board of the World Trade Organization (WTO)
EAGGF	European Agricultural Guidance and Guarantee Fund (often referred to as FEOGA – *Fonds européen d'orientation et de garantie agricole*)
EBL Rev	European Business Law Review
EC	European Community
ECB	European Central Bank
ECHR	European Convention on Human Rights
ECJ	European Court of Justice
ECLR	European Competition Law Review
ECL Rev	European Constitutional Law Review
ECOFIN	Council of Economic and Finance Ministers
ECR	European Court Reports
ECSC	European Coal and Steel Community

ECU	European Currency Unit
EEA	European Economic Area
EEC	European Economic Community
EELR	European Environmental Law Review
EESC	European Economic and Social Committee
EFTA	European Free Trade Association
EHRR	European Human Rights Reports Review
EIB	European Investment Bank
EIPL	European Intellectual Property Law
EJML	European Journal of Migration and Law
ELJ	European Law Journal
EL Rev	European Law Review
EMU	Economic and Monetary Union
EP	European Parliament
EPC	European Political Cooperation
EPL	European Public Law
ERDF	European Regional Development Fund
ESCB	European System of Central Banks
EU	European Union
Euratom	European Atomic Energy Community
FamLaw	Family Law
FAO	Food and Agriculture Organisation of the United Nations
FSR	Fleet Street Reports
FYRM	Former Yugoslav Republic of Macedonia
GATT	General Agreement on Tariffs and Trade
GmbH	Gesellschaft mit beschränkter Haftung (Plc)
GNP	Gross National Product
Harv Int LJ	Harvard International Law Journal
HarvLR or Harvard LR	Harvard Law Review
HRLJ	Human Rights Law Journal
IAT	Immigration Appeals Tribunal
IBL	International Business Lawyer
ICLQ	International and Comparative Law Quarterly
ICR	Industrial Cases Reports
IGC	Intergovernmental Conference
IndLJ	Industrial Law Journal
Int Lawyer	International Lawyer
IRLR	Industrial Relations Law Reports
JBL	Journal of Business Law
JCMS	Journal of Common Market Studies
JESP	Journal of European Social Policy
JHA	Justice and Home Affairs
JLIS	Journal of Law and Information Science
JLS	Journal of Law and Society
JPL	Journal of Planning and Environmental Law
JRC	Joint Research Centre
JSWL	Journal of Social Welfare Law (now JSWFL – Journal of Social Welfare and Family Law)

LIEI	Legal Issues of European Integration
LQR	Law Quarterly Review
MAFF	Ministry of Agriculture, Fisheries and Food
MCA	Monetary Compensatory Amount
MEP	Member of the European Parliament
MEQR	Measure having Equivalent Effect to Quantitative Restrictions
MGQ	Maximum Guaranteed Quantities
MLR	Modern Law Review
NATO	North Atlantic Treaty Organization
NCE	Non-Compulsory Expenditure
NILQ	Northern Ireland Legal Quarterly
NLJ	New Law Journal
OECD	Organisation for Economic Cooperation and Development
OJ	*Official Journal* of the European Communities
OJLS	Oxford Journal of Legal Studies
OLAF	European Anti-Fraud Office (Office Européen de Lutte Anti-Fraude)
PA	Public Administration
PL	Public Law
PPLR	Public Procurement Law Review
QB	Queen's Bench
QMV	Qualified Majority Voting
QRs	Quantitative Restrictions
SCA	Special Committee on Agriculture
SEA	Single European Act
SI	Statutory Instrument
SIRENE	Supplementary Information Request at the National Entry
SIS	Schengen Information System
SJ	Solicitors' Journal
SPUC	Society for the Protection of the Unborn Child
SRWT	Société Régionale Walloon du Transport
TEU	Treaty on European Union
TFEU	Treaty on the Functioning of the European Union
ToA	Treaty of Amsterdam
ToL	Treaty of Lisbon
ToN	Treaty of Nice
WHO	World Health Organization
WLR	Weekly Law Reports
WTO	World Trade Organization
Yale LJ	Yale Law Journal
YEL	Yearbook of European Law

Equivalences

For tables of equivalences as referred to in Article 5 of the Treaty of Lisbon, please refer to the document at the following web address: http://eur-lex.europa.eu/LexUriServ/LexUriServ.do?uri=OJ:C:2007:306:0202:0229:EN:PDF

(© European Union, http://eur-lex.europa.eu/, 1998-2015)

Part 1

Constitutional and administrative law of the European Union

1

An introduction to the European Communities and the European Union

Objectives

At the end of this chapter you should understand:

1. How and why the European Communities were established, and their aims and objectives.
2. How the European Union has evolved from its initial 6 Member States to 28 Member States and beyond.
3. How the Single European Act amended the founding Treaties.
4. What effect the Treaty on European Union had on the founding Treaties and how it established the European Union and its three pillars.
5. How the Treaty of Amsterdam amended the founding Treaties and the Treaty on European Union.
6. What effect the Treaty of Nice had on the founding Treaties and the Treaty on European Union.
7. How the Treaty of Lisbon amended the founding Treaties and the Treaty on European Union, including:
   - the renaming of the EC Treaty to the Treaty on the Functioning of the European Union (TFEU);
   - the renumbering of the TEU and TFEU;
   - the European Community's replacement and succession by the European Union, resulting in the merger of the three pillars of the European Union.
8. The legal status, within the context of EU law, of the European Convention on Human Rights and the European Court of Human Rights.
9. The purpose of the Treaty on Stability, Coordination and Governance.
10. The role of the European Free Trade Association and the relevance of the European Economic Area.

The post-war years

Objective 1

The **European Communities** came into existence in the aftermath of the Second World War, but the impetus for their creation, to a large extent, came from a desire not to repeat the mistakes made by the victorious powers in the inter-war years. The **Treaty** of Versailles of 1919 recognised the new nation-states of Central and Eastern Europe that had emerged following the collapse of the Austro–Hungarian and Ottoman empires. It also imposed heavy reparations on Germany, which the new Weimar Republic was unable to pay. The hyper-inflation that followed, and the crash of 1929, wiped out the savings of the large German middle class and pushed unemployment in Germany to more than 40 per cent of the labour force (Hobsbawm, 1994). The instability that this created led directly to the rise of the Nazi Party and the outbreak of the Second World War. It also gravely affected the economies of the other Western European powers. The UK, France and Italy, the victors who were the architects of Versailles, suffered almost as much as the vanquished from its consequences. Attempts at protecting national economies by tariff barriers were largely unsuccessful and did little more than maintain the economies of Western Europe in a state of stagnation until they were lifted by preparations for another world war. The experience of the inter-war years made clear beyond doubt that it was no longer possible for the states of Western Europe, including states like the UK and France which still had large colonial markets, to operate their national economies without regard to the effect on their immediate neighbours.

Another important lesson of the First World War and its aftermath was learned from the failure of linked defence treaties and the new League of Nations to avert war. The French, above all, grasped the importance of binding Germany's coal and steel industry, the sinews of its war machine, into a new political and economic alliance. At the same time, fear of the apparently expansionist Soviet Union that now occupied the whole of Eastern and Central Europe, including the former East Germany, impelled the democratic states of Western Europe and North America to come together in 1949 into the **North Atlantic Treaty Organization (NATO)**. The former West Germany did not join **NATO** until October 1954 (The Paris Agreements). The USA, instead of withdrawing from Europe as it had in 1919, was a founder member of NATO, the new defence organisation, and took a major part in European rehabilitation and reconstruction. Millions of dollars were poured into the former West Germany in grants and loans under the **Marshall Plan**, and it started on a rapid economic recovery. Other European states were also assisted under the Plan.

The recognition of the reality and, indeed, the need for mutual interdependence by Western European states, created a receptive atmosphere for resurgent ideas about European political unity. These were expressed with force and vision by Winston Churchill (the former UK Prime Minister) at Zurich in September 1946, when he proposed a 'sovereign remedy' to European tensions. He proposed the creation of 'a European family, or as much of it as we can', which would be provided with 'a structure under which it can dwell in peace, in safety and in freedom. We must build a kind of United States of Europe.' Although he did not envisage the UK becoming a member of this 'European family', he stated that the first step in its creation should be based on a partnership between France and Germany. This would have required an imaginative leap by the French, who were only just beginning to recover from German occupation and who had been the victims of three wars of aggression by Germany. The idea of European federation, based on a Franco–German partnership, was, however, taken up with enthusiasm by two French politicians, Jean Monnet and Robert Schumann, the former with responsibility for French economic planning and the latter as foreign minister.

In recognition of the Union's primary foundation objective – to secure peace throughout Europe – on 12 October 2012 the Union was awarded the Nobel Peace Prize for its contribution to the advancement of peace and reconciliation, democracy and human rights in Europe. The President of the **European Council** and the President of the **European Commission** issued the following joint statement:

It is a tremendous honour for the European Union to be awarded the 2012 Nobel Peace Prize. This Prize is the strongest possible recognition of the deep political motives behind our

Union: the unique effort by ever more European states to overcome war and divisions and to jointly shape a continent of peace and prosperity. It is a Prize not just for the project and the institutions embodying a common interest, but for the 500 million citizens living in our Union.

The first step in the construction of the new European order was the creation of the European Coal and Steel Community. The remainder of this chapter contains a sequential historical examination of the development of the European Communities and the **European Union (EU)**, from their humble beginnings through the establishment of the European Coal and Steel Community (with the participation of 6 Member States) to the establishment of the European Union (with the participation of 28 Member States). The rationale for this approach is to facilitate an understanding of how the EU has evolved to eventually replace and succeed the **European Community (EC)**, in order to appreciate how it might evolve in the future. A table of key dates and events is included towards the end of this chapter.

23 July 1952: the European Coal and Steel Community

On 9 May 1950, less than four years after Churchill made his Zurich speech, Robert Schumann (the former French Foreign Minister) stated that a united Europe was essential for the maintenance of world peace. He further stated that a European alliance was essential and that would require the century-old opposition between France and Germany to be eliminated. He proposed that the first stage on this road to European integration would require the whole of France and Germany's coal and steel production to be placed under one authority. His proposal provided that other countries within Europe could become members of the organisation which would be created.

France, Germany, Italy and the **Benelux countries** (Belgium, The Netherlands and Luxembourg) accepted the proposal in principle and negotiations started immediately. The UK was not a party to these negotiations, as it was not yet interested in joining the European family (at this time the UK still had strong connections with the Commonwealth). The negotiations progressed rapidly, and less than one year later, on 18 April 1951, the Treaty Establishing the **European Coal and Steel Community (ECSC)** was signed by these six countries in Paris. Because it was signed in Paris it is often referred to as the Treaty of Paris, however, its official title is 'The Treaty Establishing the ECSC'. **Ratification** of the Treaty by the six states was a mere formality.

Following ratification (i.e. approval), the Treaty entered into force on 23 July 1952, thus establishing the ECSC. This Treaty had a 50-year lifespan and therefore this Community came to an end on 23 July 2002. It was one of the three Communities which were collectively referred to as the European Communities; this is discussed further below.

Earlier in the discussion of the historical evolution of the European Communities, it was stated that European integration was necessary to ensure world peace. So how did the ECSC further this aim? Coal and steel were, in the 1950s, essential components in the production of arms and munitions. Thus, by depriving France and Germany of their independence in the production of these commodities, it was widely believed that future conflicts between France and Germany would be avoided. However, the Preamble to the Treaty made it quite clear that the long-term aims of the participants went a great deal further than the control of the production of coal and steel. The Treaty recognised that 'Europe can be built only through practical achievements which will first of all create solidarity, and through the establishment of common bases for economic solidarity'. The participants were 'resolved to substitute for age-old rivalries the merging of their essential interests; to create, by establishing an economic community, the basis for a deeper and broader community among peoples long divided by bloody conflicts' (Preamble). There was little UK enthusiasm for involvement, and successive UK governments (including the then Conservative administration under the Premiership of Winston Churchill) were prepared to support only the loosest association with their Continental neighbours. These fell far short of the aspirations of the six founding states and, for two decades, the UK remained on the sidelines of Community developments.

The ECSC Treaty created five institutions:

- an executive, called the High Authority;
- a Consultative Committee attached to the High Authority;
- a Special Council of Ministers;
- an Assembly;
- a Court of Justice.

The most striking thing about this new Community was the fact that it had legal personality. The High Authority was responsible for policy relating to the coal and steel industries in the Member States and had the power to make decisions directly affecting the economic agents in each country without regard to the wishes of the governments of those states. Investment in the coal and steel industries was influenced by the High Authority, though not subject to much control. Powers were reserved to regulate prices and production, but only if there were crises of shortage or over-production. There was also a social dimension to this Community: policies were to be framed for training, housing and redeployment. Competition was, at the same time, stimulated by rules on price transparency, as well as anti-trust laws which were modelled on those of the United States. These decisions were enforceable against the Member States in the new Court of Justice.

1 July 1958: the European Economic Community and the European Atomic Energy Community

Three of the founding states of the ECSC (Belgium, The Netherlands and Luxembourg) had already formed themselves into the **Benelux customs union**. From 1 January 1948, customs barriers were removed between Belgium, The Netherlands and Luxembourg, and a common customs tariff was agreed between them in relation to the outside world. The effect of this was that goods could freely pass between the three countries, with minimal formalities. Customs duties levied on goods originating within the three countries were abolished and goods entering from outside had a uniform customs tariff applied. In 1954 they also authorised the free flow of capital, which meant the freedom of investment and unrestricted transfer of currency between the three countries, and in 1956 they introduced the free movement of labour. The internal trade of these countries increased by 50 per cent between 1948 and 1956. This mini **common market** proved to be profitable to all three countries involved and its success whetted the appetites of neighbouring states and led to pressure to extend this experiment on a European scale.

This pressure created the political climate for a much more ambitious project. On 25 March 1957 the EEC Treaty was signed in Rome by the six founding states of the ECSC (and is often referred to as the **Treaty of Rome**), the aim being to establish a **European Economic Community (EEC)** in goods, persons, services and capital among these six states. The common market established by the EEC Treaty was, at the time, the biggest free trade area in the world. At the same time, the Treaty Establishing the European Atomic Energy Community (Euratom) was signed, providing for cooperation in the use of atomic energy. The UK participated in the initial negotiations for both Treaties but withdrew because it feared a loss of national sovereignty and damage to its favourable trading links with the Commonwealth. The EEC and Euratom Treaties came into force on 1 July 1958, following their ratification (i.e. approval) by the six states. This resulted in the existence of three Communities: EEC, ECSC and Euratom, which were collectively referred to as the European Communities. As stated above, the ECSC came to an end on 23 July 2002, and therefore from this date the EEC (later to be renamed the **EC**) and Euratom were collectively referred to as the European Communities.

The Preamble to the EEC Treaty set out the objective of the founding states:

> ... to lay the foundations of an ever closer union among the peoples of Europe ... to ensure the economic and social progress of their countries by common action to eliminate the barriers which divide Europe ... [to secure] the constant improvement of the living and working conditions of their peoples ... [and] to strengthen the unity of their economies and to ensure their harmonious development by reducing differences existing between various regions ... [and] by means of a common commercial policy, to [secure] the progressive abolition of restrictions on international trade.

The common market, which was created by the EEC Treaty, covered the whole economic field except those areas falling within the scope of the ECSC or Euratom. It involved the creation of a customs union, which required the abolition of all customs duties and quantitative restrictions in trade between the Member States, a **common external tariff**, and provisions for the free movement of persons, services and capital. These objectives reflected what had already largely been achieved in the Benelux states, the aim being to create, on a Community scale, economic conditions similar to those in the market of a single state; similar to the position in the UK where there is free movement of goods, persons, services and capital between England, Scotland, Wales and Northern Ireland.

As initially formulated, Art 3 EEC Treaty vested the Community with the power to pursue the following activities:

- the elimination, as between Member States, of customs duties and of quantitative restrictions on the import and export of goods, and of all other measures having equivalent effect;
- the establishment of a common customs tariff and a common commercial policy towards third countries (i.e. countries not within the Community);
- the abolition, as between Member States, of obstacles to the free movement of persons, services and capital;
- the adoption of a common agricultural policy;
- the adoption of a common transport policy;
- the creation of a Community competition policy;
- the approximation of the laws of the Member States to the extent required for the proper functioning of the common market;
- the association of overseas countries and territories in order to increase trade and promote economic development.

7

Article 3 empowered the Community (through its institutions) to pursue these *economic* activities and thus secure the four features of the common market discussed above: the free movement of goods, persons, services and capital.

The main institutions of the EEC – the Commission, the Council of Ministers, the Assembly and the Court of Justice – were modelled on those of the ECSC, and the Community had a similar legal structure.

In contrast, the object of Euratom was to develop nuclear energy, distribute it within the Community and sell the surplus to the outside world. For political reasons originally associated with France's nuclear weapons programme and, subsequently, as a result of widespread doubts about the safety and viability of nuclear power, Euratom never developed as originally envisaged. Euratom has, however, remained an important focus for research and the promotion of nuclear safety.

8 April 1965: merger of the institutions

Immediately after the EEC and Euratom Treaties were signed, agreement was reached to have only one Parliamentary Assembly and one Court of Justice for the ECSC, EEC and Euratom. For some time after the new Treaties came into effect, however, there remained separate Councils of Ministers and separate executive bodies – a High Authority in the case of the ECSC, and a Commission each for the EEC and Euratom.

On 8 April 1965, the simplification of the institutional structure of the Communities was completed by the signature of a Merger Treaty, the result of which was that there was thereafter one Council, one European Commission, one European Court of Justice and one Assembly (later to be renamed the European Parliament) for all three Communities.

1 July 1973: enlargement

Objective 2

See page 54 for more information on EFTA.

The UK's response to the creation of the EEC in 1958 was to propose a much looser 'free trade area'. This proposal was not welcomed by the Community, but in 1959 it resulted in the creation of a rival organisation, the **European Free Trade Association (EFTA)**, comprising Austria, Denmark, Norway, Portugal, Sweden, Switzerland and the United Kingdom. Although trade increased between these states, EFTA lacked the structure and coherence of the EEC, and its members' economies grew only modestly by comparison. By 1961, the UK government had realised that its failure to join the European Communities had been a mistake and, in that year, the Macmillan government applied for membership. After prolonged negotiations, the application, which needed the unanimous agreement of the Member States, was vetoed by the French President, General de Gaulle. The French were reluctant to accept the UK's membership because it was feared the UK would attempt to retain preferences for Commonwealth trade and also because the UK government was too close, politically, to the USA. France was afraid that the special relationship between the UK and the USA would obstruct French efforts to create a European defence community, free from US dominance. A further UK membership attempt was made by the government of Harold Wilson in 1967, but this was again vetoed by the French. In 1970, a third application was made by Edward Heath's government and on this occasion the application was successful. The **Treaty of Accession** was signed on 22 January 1972 and the UK, together with Denmark and Ireland, became members of the European Communities on 1 January 1973. Norway, which had participated in the accession negotiations, did not join, as a result of an adverse national referendum.

The Treaty of Accession bound the new Member States to accept the three Treaties and to accept the existing rules of the Communities. The UK Parliament, after a debate that split both the Conservative and Labour parties, enacted the European Communities Act 1972, which was intended to give effect to both present and future Community law in the UK. Divisions within the Labour Party about membership of the European Communities led the Labour government (which had been elected to office in 1974) to promise a referendum. This was held in 1975 and resulted in endorsement of continuing membership by a majority of almost 2:1.

1 January 1981: enlargement

Objective
2

Greece became a member of the European Communities on 1 January 1981, increasing the number of Member States to 10.

1 January 1986: enlargement

Objective
2

Portugal and Spain became members of the European Communities on 1 January 1986, increasing the number of Member States to 12.

1 July 1987: the Single European Act

Objective
3

The Single European Act (SEA) was a response to both the development and the lack of it in the three Communities. The **SEA** introduced the first major amendments to the founding Treaties. The SEA is *not* a UK Act of Parliament. It is a Treaty which was concluded between the Member States, the purpose of which was to amend the three founding Treaties: ECSC, EEC and Euratom. It was signed in February 1986 and came into force on 1 July 1987.

There now follows an overview of the main provisions of the SEA.

A European Union?

The Preamble to the SEA set out the Member States' commitment to transform relations as a whole between the Member States into a European Union; a Union which would have activities way beyond the solely economic sphere. Political cooperation between the Member States was considered to be of paramount importance in the creation of this European Union.

The SEA separated provisions relating to political cooperation from those relating to economic integration. Those provisions relating to economic integration were implemented by amending the founding EEC Treaty. However, in relation to political cooperation, those provisions were implemented outside the existing Treaty. It was provided for the representatives of the Member States (i.e. Prime Minister/President and Foreign Secretary) to meet regularly for the purpose of drawing up common political objectives (through a body referred to as the European Council).

Therefore, at one level (the economic level), policies were implemented through the structure of the EEC (having its own special methods of decision-making and enforcement), whereas political policies were developed outside this structure, through cooperation between the Member States; an **intergovernmental arrangement** which did not bind the Member States unless *all* the Member States were in agreement.

Amendments to the EEC Treaty

The main amendments made to the EEC Treaty are considered below.

Completing the internal market and new policy objectives

The Treaties came into force during the 1950s when concerns about war in Western Europe and mass unemployment were high. However, by the mid-1970s and early 1980s, these concerns tended to have given way to pressure for greater consumer protection and protection at work. There were also growing anxieties about the degradation of the natural environment. The response to these new concerns was initially tackled at national level, rather than Community level, which resulted in a whole range of different national standards for both goods and industrial production that seriously threatened the growth of a genuinely common market in goods and services. The development of a multiplicity of national standards was accompanied by a slowing down of the economies of all the Member States following the explosion of oil prices in 1973. Implementing the recommendations of the Commission's White Paper, *Completing the Internal Market* (1985), the SEA attempted to tackle this problem on two fronts. It extended the competence of the EEC to enable it to legislate for the whole area of the Community on the following:

- environmental matters;
- economic and social cohesion, including health and safety;
- consumer protection;
- academic, professional and vocational qualifications;
- public procurement (i.e. competition for public contracts);
- VAT (i.e. Value Added Tax, which is a tax levied internally on goods and services);
- excise duties and frontier controls;
- research and technological development.

It also aimed to give the completion of the common market a new boost by setting a target for creating a new internal market through removing all the remaining legal, technical and physical obstacles to the free movement of goods, persons, services and capital by 1 January 1993. This objective was set out in the former Art 8a of the EEC Treaty (added by the SEA), where the internal market was described as 'an area without internal frontiers in which the free movement of goods, persons, services and capital is ensured'. Article 8a EEC Treaty was renumbered Art 7a by the Treaty on European Union and Art 14 by the Treaty of Amsterdam. When the **Treaty of Lisbon (ToL)** came into force on 1 December 2009 (see below), Art 14 was replaced by Art 26 of the **Treaty on the Functioning of the European Union (TFEU)**.

The Treaty of Lisbon is discussed further at pages 24–48.

Increasing the European Parliament's legislative powers

Until 1979, members of the European Assembly were nominated by their national parliaments. The first direct elections to the newly named European Parliament took place in June 1979 (see Chapter 3), and the effect was that the Parliament became the only directly elected Community institution. It had, at the same time, only a consultative status in the legislative process (see Chapter 4). It was often said that the European Commission proposed legislation and the Council of Ministers disposed of it (i.e. adopted it). This situation generated pressure on the Member States to address the **'democratic deficit'** in the Communities' decision-making process. The SEA added a new **'cooperation procedure'** to the Treaties, giving the Parliament a more important role in the legislative process in four areas:

- prohibition of discrimination on the grounds of nationality (Art 12 EC Treaty, which has been replaced by Art 18 **of the Treaty on the Functioning of the European Union (TFEU)**, see below);
- the achievement of the free movement of workers (Art 40 EC Treaty, replaced by Art 46 TFEU);
- promotion of the right of establishment (Art 44 EC Treaty, replaced by Art 50 TFEU);
- measures for implementation of the internal market (Art 95 EC Treaty, replaced by Art 114 TFEU).

This new legislative procedure required the Council of Ministers to cooperate with the European Parliament. The Parliament would for the first time have a real input into the legislative process (being able to propose amendments). In addition to Parliamentary input, legislative measures in these four areas could be adopted by the Council by **'qualified majority'** rather than unanimity, thus overriding the objections of a Member State. The legislative process is considered in detail in Chapter 4.

1 November 1993: the Treaty on European Union

Objective 4 The next step in the constitutional development of the European Union was the adoption of the **Treaty on European Union (TEU)**, which was negotiated at Maastricht and signed on 7 February 1992. It came into force on 1 November 1993 once it had been ratified by the Member States. An overview of the main provisions is followed by a more substantive discussion of the key features of the **TEU**.

Overview

The TEU was intended to extend further the competencies of the Communities by creating two new **'pillars'** outside the legally binding, formal decision-making processes of the European Communities (the EC, ECSC and Euratom), which continued to exist. The two new 'pillars' of the European Union were: (i) Common Foreign and Security Policy (CFSP); and (ii) Cooperation in the fields of Justice and Home Affairs (JHA). These two pillars of the Union were really only intergovernmental in character and, like the foreign policy provisions of the SEA, created a broad framework for cooperation between the Member States rather than a process for the making of binding rules. The whole structure, which included the European Communities and the two new pillars, was called 'the European Union' (EU).

See Figure 1.1 on page 13 for a diagrammatic illustration of the structure of the EU.

Of more constitutional and legal significance were the amendments to the EEC Treaty. The EEC was renamed 'the European Community' (EC), giving legal recognition to the fact that the activities and competencies of the former 'economic' community ranged far beyond its original economic goals. The European Parliament's role in the legislative process was further strengthened by the introduction of the **co-decision procedure** which, for the first time, gave the Parliament the power to veto legislation in certain circumstances. The reunification of Germany in 1990 was reflected by an increased representation in the European Parliament, so that Germany now had the largest allocation of Members of the European Parliament (**MEPs**). It did not, however, gain any more votes in the qualified majority voting procedure within the Council of Ministers (see Chapter 4). A further institution was also created, the **Committee of the Regions**, with a role analogous to the **European Economic and Social Committee** (see Chapter 3).

The central economic feature of the TEU was the section designed to lead to **economic and monetary union (EMU)** in three stages. The UK and Denmark opted out of compulsory participation in the third stage. Sweden negotiated a similar opt-out when it joined the EU on 1 January 1995 (see below). The UK also refused to participate in the **Social Chapter**, which incorporated principles that had previously been agreed by the heads of government (excluding the UK) in Strasbourg in December 1989: the Community Charter of Fundamental Social Rights of Workers. Both of these opt-outs are considered in further detail below.

Some of the key features of the TEU are now considered.

The TEU provisions

The TEU consisted of the following seven *titles*:

- Title I: Common provisions (Arts A to F);
- Title II: Provisions amending the EEC Treaty (Art G);
- Title III: Provisions amending the ECSC Treaty (Art H);
- Title IV: Provisions amending the Euratom Treaty (Art I);
- Title V: Provisions on a Common Foreign and Security Policy (Arts J.1 to J.11);
- Title VI: Provisions on Cooperation in Justice and Home Affairs (Arts K.1 to K.9);
- Title VII: Final Provisions (Arts L to S).

Titles II, III and IV of the TEU simply amended the three founding Treaties (as previously amended by the SEA).

The European Union

Title I contained common provisions which set out the basic objectives of the TEU. This title did not amend the founding Treaties, but simply set out the basic aims and principles of the newly formed European Union (EU).

The three pillars of the European Union

Article A TEU provided for the establishing of a European Union:

> The Union shall be founded on the European Communities, supplemented by the policies and forms of cooperation established by this Treaty.

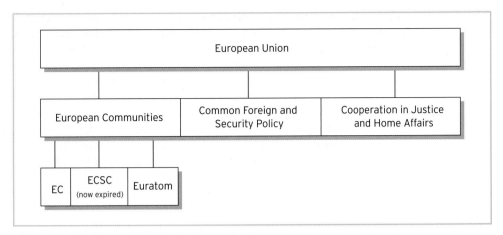

Figure 1.1   Structure of the European Union as at 1 November 1993

It followed from this that the EU was to be founded upon three pillars:

- The European Communities – EC, ECSC (now expired), Euratom;
- Common Foreign and Security Policy – Title V (Art J);
- Cooperation in Justice and Home Affairs – Title VI (Art K).

Figure 1.1 illustrates the structure of the European Union as at 1 November 1993.

Objectives of the European Union

Article B set out the objectives of the Union, some of which mirrored those contained in the founding Treaties as amended.

Protection of human rights

Article F(2) TEU provided that the Union would respect **fundamental rights** 'as guaranteed by the European Convention for the Protection of Human Rights and Fundamental Freedoms ... as general principles of Community law'.

However, Art L TEU provided that all the common provisions (which included Art F(2) TEU) were not justiciable by the European Court of Justice, i.e. the Court did not have the power to rule on their application or validity. Despite this, it was possible that the Court of Justice would take the common provisions into account, including Art F(2), when interpreting the founding Treaties, as amended. This is considered further below and in Chapter 2.

The two intergovernmental pillars

The second and third pillars of the Union, not being inserted into the amended founding Treaties, remained outside the formal structures of the European Communities. These two pillars, as previously mentioned, related to: (i) Common Foreign and Security Policy (CFSP); and (ii) Cooperation in Justice and Home Affairs (JHA).

Although intergovernmental in nature, and thus falling outside the formal Community structure, they did have a connection in that some of the Community institutions (in particular the Council of Ministers) played a part in policy development.

It was argued that, over a period of time, these two pillars would be subsumed into the formal Community structure. This would be achieved by amending the founding Treaties. If this happened, all Community institutions could play a part in developing these policy areas, perhaps with a greater role for the European Parliament. Germany's former Chancellor Kohl favoured this approach, which had already occurred in relation to the **single European currency policy**. Having initially been introduced by the SEA for development on an intergovernmental basis, the single European currency policy was subsequently incorporated into the formal EC structure (with its own special decision-making and enforcement powers) following amendments to the EC Treaty by the TEU. Economic and monetary policy was governed by Arts 98–124 EC Treaty (now replaced by Arts 119–144 TFEU).

Under the TEU, prior to its amendment by the Treaty of Amsterdam, the Court of Justice was excluded from exercising its powers in matters dealt with under these two pillars (except in certain *very limited* situations) – Art L TEU.

As its name suggests, the second pillar (Common Foreign and Security Policy) provided for joint foreign and security (i.e. defence) action by the Member States. This action would be taken by the Council acting *unanimously*. However, there was provision for the Council to provide that certain decisions could be adopted by a qualified majority vote (Art J.3, para 2 TEU). There was minimal involvement of the European Parliament and the Commission in the process. Article L TEU excluded the Court of Justice from ruling on these provisions.

The third pillar (Cooperation in Justice and Home Affairs) provided for cooperation in policy areas such as asylum, immigration, **'third country'** (i.e. non-EU) nationals, international crime (e.g. drug trafficking) and various forms of judicial cooperation. Action would again be taken by the Council of Ministers acting unanimously, with very limited provision for qualified majority voting (Art K.4, para 3 TEU). Once again there was little involvement of the European Parliament and the Commission, and Art L TEU excluded the Court of Justice from ruling on these provisions.

Amendments to the EEC Treaty

As discussed below, the EEC Treaty provisions were amended by the TEU to embrace tasks and activities which did not have a pure economic foundation. The TEU therefore amended the title of the EEC Treaty to the European Community Treaty (EC Treaty). From here on the EEC Treaty will be referred to as the EC Treaty (although as discussed below, when the **Treaty of Lisbon (ToL)** came into force on 1 December 2009, the EC Treaty was renamed the Treaty on the Functioning of the European Union (TFEU)).

The EC Treaty is the most important of the three founding Treaties. Amendments made to the EC Treaty by Art G (i.e. Title II) TEU were as follows:

- creation of a citizenship of the European Union (Art 17 EC Treaty, which has been replaced by Art 20 TFEU);
- common economic and monetary policy, with a timetable for the implementation of a common currency (Arts 98–124 EC Treaty, replaced by Arts 119–144 TFEU);
- adoption of the principle of **subsidiarity** (Art 5 EC Treaty, replaced by Art 5 TEU when the Treaty of Lisbon came into force);
- amendment of the decision-making process – extension of qualified majority voting for the adoption of Council Acts into new policy areas, and further powers given to the European Parliament;
- introduction of new areas of tasks and activities (the former Arts 2 and 3 EC Treaty were amended; these articles were replaced, in substance, by Art 3 TEU when the Treaty of Lisbon came into force).

Articles 2 and 3 EC Treaty, as amended by the TEU, extended the tasks and activities of the European Community beyond those with a purely economic base, now incorporating political and social goals. Article 2, for example, provided that the Community's tasks included the promotion of 'a high level of employment and of social protection, the raising of the standard of living and quality of life, and economic and social cohesion and solidarity'. This is indicative of the fact that the European Community now had tasks and activities which were not purely economic-based, hence its change of title from EEC to EC.

Protocols

Annexed to the EC Treaty, as amended by the TEU, were a number of **protocols**. Protocols formed part of the Treaty by virtue of Art 311 EC Treaty, which provided that:

> The protocols annexed to this Treaty by common accord of the Member States shall form an integral part thereof.

Two highly controversial protocols provided for the UK to opt out of certain Community policies which the UK government of the day found unacceptable: (i) social policy; and (ii) economic and monetary union.

Protocol on social policy

All Member States, except the UK, supported an amendment to the EC Treaty for greater Community competence to legislate in the area of social policy (e.g. employee protection rights). Margaret Thatcher was the UK Prime Minister, and her government objected to this proposal and would not compromise its position. Therefore, the UK agreed to a protocol which enabled the remaining Member States to enter into an agreement allowing them to have recourse to the Community institutions and Treaty procedures and mechanisms when adopting acts and decisions in the social policy area not otherwise covered by the Treaties. The *Agreement on Social Policy* was annexed to the protocol.

Following the election of a Labour government in the UK on 1 May 1997, it was announced that the UK would no longer retain its opt-out, and would take the necessary steps to be bound by the Agreement on Social Policy. This was put into effect by the Treaty of Amsterdam, which incorporated an amended version of the Agreement into the EC Treaty (see below).

Protocol on economic and monetary union: UK and Denmark

Under the SEA, economic and monetary policy, including working towards a single European currency, was introduced outside the formal structures of the Communities, to be dealt with on an intergovernmental basis. However, the TEU amended the EC Treaty to provide for this policy area (including a timetable for the introduction of a single European currency) to be dealt with under the formal structure of the Communities, thus making it more difficult for a recalcitrant Member State to block policy developments. The UK was not ready to sign up to full economic and monetary union, being somewhat cautious about agreeing to the single currency timetable. This protocol therefore provided the UK with an opt-out; the UK would not be:

> ... obliged or committed to move to the third stage of Economic and Monetary Union without a separate decision to do so by its Government and Parliament.

This protocol is often referred to as the UK's opt-out from the single currency, but it is more akin to an 'opt-in'. Denmark has a similar opt-out, provided for by the 'Protocol on certain provisions relating to Denmark'. Denmark rejected entry to the single currency in a referendum held on 28 September 2000, by a 53 per cent to 46 per cent majority. Sweden negotiated a similar opt-out to the UK and Denmark when it became a member of the EU on 1 January 1995 (see below). Sweden rejected entry to the single currency in a referendum held on 14 September 2003. The previous UK government (2005–2010) indicated its desire to join the single currency, provided the economic circumstances were favourable. The current UK government (2015–2020) will not take the UK into the single currency.

The third and final stage on the road to economic and monetary union required the Member States to decide which of them had met the criteria laid down in the Treaty for the forming of a common currency. The third stage started on 1 January 1999 (Art 121(4) EC Treaty, pre-Treaty of Amsterdam and Treaty of Lisbon). All Member States satisfied the criteria, except Greece. However, Greece was subsequently adjudged to have satisfied the economic criteria and joined the original 11 qualifying states.

19 Member States have now adopted the euro. See page 24 for the up-to-date position regarding membership of the single currency.

A European Central Bank was established, which set a common European interest rate for these 12 Member States. On 1 July 2002, national currencies in these 12 Member States ceased to be legal tender and all transactions are now completed in euros.

1 January 1995: enlargement

Objective 2

Three of the remaining EFTA members – Finland, Austria and Sweden – joined the European Union on 1 January 1995, increasing the number of Member States to 15. Norway, having once more successfully negotiated terms for entry, again failed to join after a second adverse national referendum.

1 May 1999: the Treaty of Amsterdam

Objective 5

The **Treaty of Amsterdam (ToA)** was agreed by the Member States in June 1997 and was formally signed by the Member States in Amsterdam on 2 October 1997. This Treaty was concluded on behalf of the UK by the Labour government elected to office on 1 May 1997, under the Premiership of Tony Blair. The Treaty came into force on 1 May 1999 once it had been ratified by the then 15 Member States. An overview of the main provisions is followed by a more substantive discussion of the key features of the Treaty.

Overview

It was anticipated that the **ToA** would take the first major steps towards restructuring the institutions of the European Union. This was widely seen as essential if the institutions, which had originally been set up for a European Community of six states, were to continue functioning effectively in an enlarged European Union. In the event, the Treaty achieved little in the way of institutional reform. A limit was set on the number of MEPs in the European Parliament, the powers of the President of the Commission were made more specific, and administrative support for the Council of Ministers was strengthened. The difficult decisions which further enlargement would inevitably bring were postponed. These decisions were partially addressed by the **Treaty of Nice (ToN)** and were further addressed by the Treaty of Lisbon (see below).

The ToA did, however, broaden the objectives of the EU, moving it further away from the narrow economic base of its early years. There were specific commitments to a number of important non-economic goals, with much more emphasis placed on the rights and duties of EU citizenship, and the EU's commitment to human and civil rights. Decisions within the EU were to be taken 'as openly as possible', and 'as closely as possible' to the citizen. The EU firmly proclaimed, in the common provisions of the revised TEU, that it was founded on respect for human rights, democracy and the rule of law, and respect for these principles was made an explicit condition of application for membership. Under a new Art 7 TEU, the rights of Member States could be suspended if the Council of Ministers determined that a Member State had been in 'serious and persistent breach' of its obligation to respect civil, political and human rights. Article 2 EC Treaty (which has been replaced by Art 8 TFEU) described equality between men and women as one of the principal objectives of the Community. Article 13 EC Treaty (now replaced by Art 19 TFEU) conferred power on the Community to legislate to combat discrimination based on sex, racial or ethnic origin, religion or belief, disability, age or sexual orientation. Environmental protection became one of the principal aims of the Community.

As discussed above, the TEU created a three-pillar structure for the Union, under which the European Communities (the EC, ECSC and Euratom) comprised the first pillar, Common Foreign and Security Policy (CFSP) the second pillar, and Cooperation in Justice and Home Affairs (JHA) the third pillar. Under the TEU, only the first pillar used the legally binding decision-making structures described in Chapter 4. Decisions made under the other two pillars were taken 'intergovernmentally' (i.e. politically) and they could not be enforced or challenged in the Court of Justice. The sharpness of this division between legally binding decisions and the political decision-making process was, unfortunately, blurred by the ToA. A large part of JHA (the third pillar) was brought within the framework of the Communities (the first pillar). Decisions in what remained of the third pillar (which was renamed 'Police and Judicial Cooperation in Criminal Matters') had a limited input from the European Parliament, and involvement by the Court of Justice was negligible. Decision-making in relation to the second pillar (CFSP) remained intergovernmental, outside the formal, legally binding Community decision-making structure.

Important changes were made to the decision-making structure of the Communities (the first pillar), giving the European Parliament greater powers to amend and block legislative proposals. Decision-making procedures are discussed in Chapter 4.

For anyone with any prior knowledge of EU law, the most obvious change brought about by the ToA was to renumber the provisions of the TEU and the EC Treaty. All the previously familiar landmarks disappeared (e.g. proceedings against Member States were now brought under Art 226 EC Treaty, and not under the former Art 169; references to the Court of Justice under what used to be Art 177 EC Treaty were now brought under Art 234). The wording of these provisions remained identical in most cases.

ToA provisions

The Treaty is divided into three parts:

- Part One (Arts 1–5) contains substantive amendments to, *inter alia*, the TEU and the EC Treaty.
- Part Two (Arts 6–11) contains provisions to simplify, *inter alia*, the TEU and the EC Treaty, including the deletion of lapsed provisions.
- Part Three (Arts 12–15) contains general and final provisions, including provisions to renumber articles of the TEU and the EC Treaty, see above.

Amendments made to the TEU by the ToA will be considered first, followed by those made to the EC Treaty.

Amendments to the TEU

The TEU articles were renumbered by the ToA. Amendments made will be considered under the relevant Titles of the TEU.

Title I – common provisions

The articles of Title I were renumbered from Arts A–F TEU to 1–7 TEU. The provisions themselves were also amended. In particular, Art 6(1) TEU (which has been renumbered Art 2 TEU by the Treaty of Lisbon) provided that:

> The Union is founded on the principles of liberty, democracy, respect for human rights and fundamental freedoms, and the rule of law, principles which are upheld by the Member States.

A new Art 6(3) TEU (now renumbered Art 4(2) TEU by the Treaty of Lisbon) provided that:

> The Union shall respect the national identities of its Member States.

A new Art 7 TEU was inserted, which provided for the Council of Ministers to suspend certain rights under the Treaty (including voting rights) of any Member State if the Council determined that the Member State had committed a 'serious and persistent breach' of the Art 6 TEU principles. As discussed above, Art 6(2) TEU (now renumbered Art 6(3) TEU by the Treaty of Lisbon) provided that:

> The Union shall respect fundamental rights as guaranteed by the European Convention of Human Rights and Fundamental Freedoms ... as general principles of Community law.

The former Art L TEU provided that all the common provisions (which included the former Art F(2)) were not justiciable by the Court of Justice. Article L TEU was renumbered Art 46 and was amended by the ToA to provide that Art 6(2) TEU *would* be justiciable by the Court of Justice. The Court could therefore explicitly take the Convention rights into account when interpreting and applying EU law.

Titles II, III, IV – amendments to the founding Treaties

The articles of Titles II, III and IV were simply renumbered from Arts G, H and I TEU to Arts 8, 9 and 10 TEU, respectively.

The three pillars of the European Union

As discussed above, the EU was founded upon three pillars:

1 The European Communities – EC, ECSC (now expired), Euratom;
2 Common Foreign and Security Policy (Title V);
3 Cooperation in Justice and Home Affairs (Title VI).

Figure 1.2 (page 19) illustrates the amended EU structure.

The major substantive change made by the ToA was to amend this structure and incorporate part of the third pillar (Justice and Home Affairs) into the EC Treaty, thus forming part of the first pillar. This is discussed further below, when considering the amendments made to the EC Treaty by the ToA.

Title V – common foreign and security policy

The articles of Title V were renumbered from J.1–J.11 TEU to Arts 11–28 TEU (now renumbered Arts 23–46 TEU by the Treaty of Lisbon). This remained the second pillar of the EU.

Although the ToA made some amendments to the main provisions of Title V, the role of the European Parliament did not change, and the exclusion of the Court of Justice from adjudicating on the provisions remained. The Secretary General of the Council of Ministers would now act as the 'High Representative' (i.e. the spokesperson) for the Common Foreign and Security Policy.

Title VI – police and judicial cooperation in criminal matters

The articles of Title VI were renumbered from K.1–K.9 TEU to Arts 29–42 TEU (these provisions were subsequently transferred into the Treaty on the Functioning of the European Union (TFEU) when the Treaty of Lisbon came into force on 1 December 2009; see below). This constituted the third pillar of the EU. As discussed above, the title of this third pillar changed from 'Cooperation in Justice and Home Affairs' to 'Police and Judicial Cooperation in Criminal Matters'. This was to reflect the fact that the provisions of the former third pillar relating to visas, asylum, immigration and other policies relating to the free movement of persons, were incorporated into the EC Treaty (Title VI EC Treaty).

This newly constituted third pillar stated the Union's objective as being able to 'provide citizens with a high level of safety within an area of freedom, security and justice' (Art 29 TEU), and to develop 'common action' among the Member States in the field of police and judicial cooperation and by preventing and combating racism and xenophobia.

Article 29 TEU stipulated that this would be achieved by:

> Preventing and combating crime, organised or otherwise, in particular terrorism, trafficking in persons and offences against children, illicit drug trafficking and illicit arms trafficking, corruption and fraud ...

The European Parliament was given an increased consultative role in the decision-making process and the Court of Justice generally had **jurisdiction** over most of the provisions.

Figure 1.2 illustrates the structure of the EU as at 1 May 1999, following the ToA's amendments to the third pillar.

Title VII – closer cooperation

This new title was inserted into the TEU by the ToA and contained three articles (Arts 43–45, which have been renumbered Art 20 TEU by the Treaty of Lisbon). These provisions enabled

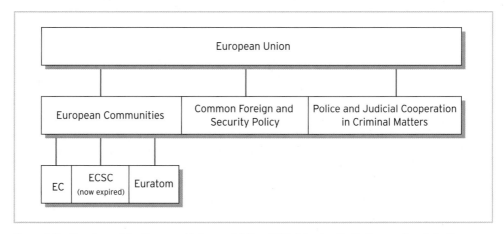

Figure 1.2   Structure of the European Union as at 1 May 1999, following the ToA's amendments to the third pillar

Member States to establish closer cooperation between themselves and to use the institutions, procedures and mechanisms of the TEU and EC Treaty. However, Art 43(c) TEU provided that these provisions could only be used as a 'last resort where the objectives of the ... Treaties could not be attained by applying the relevant procedures laid down therein'.

These provisions allowed flexibility in the future development of the European Communities and the European Union, recognising the right of Member States to 'opt out' from *new* policy initiatives not otherwise covered by the Treaties (this formalised the situation whereby the UK had opted out of the Social Policy Agreement and single European currency, for example).

A similar flexibility clause was inserted into the EC Treaty (Art 11 EC Treaty, which has now been replaced by Art 20 TEU and Arts 326–334 TFEU by the Treaty of Lisbon).

Title VIII – final provisions

The articles of Title VIII were renumbered from L–S TEU to Arts 46–53 TEU (now renumbered Arts 47–55 TEU by the Treaty of Lisbon). Article 49 TEU amended the procedure for the admission of new Member States. Applicant countries have to respect the fundamental principles set out in Art 6 TEU (now renumbered Art 2 TEU by the Treaty of Lisbon). The Council of Ministers would act unanimously after receiving the opinion of the Commission and the assent of the European Parliament.

Amendments to the EC Treaty

Article 2 EC Treaty was amended to include new tasks:

- promotion of equality between men and women;
- a high level of protection and improvement of the quality of the environment;
- promotion of a high degree of competitiveness;
- economic development which must be 'sustainable' as well as 'balanced and harmonious'.

Article 3 EC Treaty listed the activities of the Community which could be undertaken in order to achieve the tasks set out in Art 2. A new Art 3(2) EC Treaty provided that:

> In all the activities referred to in this Article, the Community shall aim to eliminate inequalities, and to promote equality, between men and women.

On 1 December 2009 when the Treaty of Lisbon came into force, Arts 2 and 3 EC Treaty were repealed and replaced, in substance, by Art 3 TEU.

The other main amendments to the EC Treaty by the ToA included:

- Article 11 EC Treaty (now replaced by Art 20 TEU and Arts 326–334 TFEU by the Treaty of Lisbon) inserted a flexibility clause similar to that in Title VII TEU (discussed above) allowing Member States to establish closer cooperation between themselves and to make use of the institutions, procedures and mechanisms laid down in the EC Treaty, provided the cooperation proposed did not, *inter alia*, 'concern areas which fall within the exclusive competence of the Community'.
- Article 13 EC Treaty (now replaced by Art 19 TFEU) provided a new non-discriminatory provision which conferred legislative competence on the Community to combat discrimination based on sex, racial or ethnic origin, religion or belief, disability, age or sexual orientation.

- Articles 61–69 EC Treaty (now replaced by Arts 67–81 TFEU) incorporated part of the former third pillar of the European Union that covered visas, asylum, immigration and other policies relating to the free movement of persons.
- Articles 125–130 EC Treaty (now replaced by Arts 145–150 TFEU) inserted a new title on employment.
- Articles 136–143 EC Treaty (now replaced by Arts 151–161 TFEU) incorporated an amended version of the Social Policy Agreement, which applied to *all* Member States. At Amsterdam the then newly elected UK Labour government agreed to end its opt-out.
- Titles XIII and XIV EC Treaty (now replaced by Titles XIV and XV TFEU) enhanced the provisions on public health and consumer protection, respectively.
- The decision-making process was amended to provide the European Parliament with a greater role in more policy areas.
- Minor amendments were made to the composition and/or role of some of the Community institutions.

1 February 2003: the Treaty of Nice

Objective 6

The **Treaty of Nice (ToN)** was agreed by the Member States in December 2000. It was formally signed by the Member States on 26 February 2001 but it could only come into force once it had been ratified by all the Member States. In a referendum during June 2001, the Irish electorate, by a majority of 54 per cent to 46 per cent, refused to ratify the Treaty. The other 14 Member States had already, or subsequently, ratified it. Ireland held a second referendum during October 2002, and this time there was a positive vote in favour of ratification (63 per cent to 37 per cent). Having now been ratified by the then 15 Member States, the Treaty came into force on 1 February 2003.

Below is an overview of the main amendments which the ToN made to the TEU and the EC Treaty.

Institutional reform

The main reason for the ToN was to reform the institutions, by amending the founding Treaties, in preparation for EU enlargement. The EC Treaty was amended to enable an enlarged membership of up to 27 Member States.

Fundamental rights

Article 7 TEU provided for the suspension of a Member State's Treaty rights if there had been a 'serious and persistent' breach of the Art 6(1) TEU principles (i.e. the principles of liberty, democracy, respect for human rights and fundamental freedoms, and the rule of law). The ToN amended Art 7 to provide that the suspension could be imposed if the Council of Ministers voted in favour by a four-fifths majority of its membership. Prior to the ToN it had required a unanimous vote by the Council. The role of the other institutions in this process remained unchanged.

Security and defence

Article 25 TEU (now renumbered Art 38 TEU by the Treaty of Lisbon) provided for the monitoring of the international situation within the areas covered by the second pillar

(Common Foreign and Security Policy), and the development of associated policies. In a meeting of the European Council, immediately prior to the meeting at which the ToN was agreed, a policy for the establishment of a European rapid reaction force was adopted. This 60,000-strong force would be used primarily for peace-keeping and emergency missions within the region.

Eurojust

Articles 29 and 31 TEU (now replaced by Arts 67, 82, 83 and 85 TFEU by the Treaty of Lisbon) were amended to provide that in the application of the third pillar (Police and Judicial Cooperation in Criminal Matters) there would be cooperation with, *inter alia*, the European Judicial Cooperation Unit (Eurojust). A declaration specified that Eurojust would comprise national prosecutors and magistrates (or police officers of equivalent competence) who were detached from each Member State.

Enhanced cooperation

Articles 43–45 TEU (now replaced by Art 20 TEU and Arts 326–334 TFEU by the Treaty of Lisbon) were substantially amended to better enable a minimum of eight Member States to establish closer cooperation between themselves and to use the institutions, procedures and mechanisms of the TEU and EC Treaty. Similar to the existing provisions, the amended provisions provided that closer cooperation could be undertaken only if it was 'aimed at furthering the objectives of the Union and the Community, at protecting and serving its interests'. This new provision also required that 'enhanced cooperation may be engaged in only as a last resort, when it has been established within the Council that the objectives of such cooperation cannot be attained within a reasonable period by applying the relevant provisions of the Treaties'.

New policies

A limited number of new policies were introduced, and some of the existing policies were refined. One new policy related to economic, financial and technical cooperation with third countries (i.e. non-EU countries) following the insertion of a new Art 181a EC Treaty (now replaced by Arts 212–213 TFEU by the Treaty of Lisbon). It was stated that this new policy would 'contribute to the general objective of developing and consolidating democracy and the rule of law, and to that of respecting human rights and fundamental freedoms'.

Decision-making process

Some **legal bases** for the adoption of secondary Community instruments (see Chapter 2), which originally required a unanimous vote by the Council of Ministers in order to be adopted, were amended to provide for their adoption by a qualified majority. In addition, the role of the European Parliament was enhanced within selected policy areas.

1 May 2004: enlargement

Objective
2

On 1 May 2004 membership of the European Union increased to 25, with the admission of ten new Member States:

- Cyprus (South)
- Czech Republic
- Estonia
- Hungary
- Latvia

- Lithuania
- Malta
- Poland
- Slovakia
- Slovenia

Political differences within Cyprus resulted in Northern Cyprus being excluded from membership. Cyprus has been divided between its Greek and Turkish Cypriot populations since 1974, when Turkey invaded the north of the island. The United Nations (UN) attempted to broker an agreement between the two sides to reunite the island, but no agreement was forthcoming. The UN therefore drafted its own agreement, which was voted on by the citizens from the north and south (in simultaneous referenda) on 24 April 2004. The Greek Cypriots rejected the agreement, whereas the Turkish Cypriots accepted it. Given the Greek Cypriots' rejection, the agreement was not concluded and the division between north and south remains. This being the case, only Southern Cyprus is a member of the European Union. However, accession negotiations with Turkey opened on 3 October 2005 (see below) and Turkey signalled an intent to recognise the Greek Cypriot southern part of the island. This intent may have a positive impact on future reunification negotiations.

Economic and monetary union

The 10 new Member States did not join the euro on 1 May 2004. They are only eligible to do so once they achieve the high degree of sustainable economic convergence with the euro area which is required for membership of the single currency. They need to fulfil the same convergence criteria which were applied to the existing euro area members, namely a high degree of price stability, sustainable government finances (in terms of both public deficit and public debt levels), a stable exchange rate and convergence in long-term interest rates.

There is no predefined-defined timetable for adoption of the euro by the new Member States. The levels of convergence required for membership are assessed by the Council of Ministers on a proposal from the Commission and on the basis of convergence reports by the Commission and the European Central Bank. These reports are produced at least every two years or at the request of a Member State seeking to join the euro.

On 11 July 2006, the Council adopted a decision allowing Slovenia to join the euro area on 1 January 2007. Slovenia became the first of the 10 new Member States to join. Slovenia was followed by Southern Cyprus and Malta who joined on 1 January 2008, Slovakia on 1 January 2009, Estonia on 1 January 2011, Latvia on 1 January 2015 and Lithuania on 1 January 2015. Nineteen Member States have now joined the euro. The UK, Denmark and Sweden continue to exercise their opt-out from the single European currency (see above). Following the global credit crunch in 2008, Greece has been experiencing severe economic problems, which may result in it eventually leaving the euro (see below).

1 January 2007: enlargement

Objective
2

On 25 April 2005, the then 25 Member States, together with Bulgaria and Romania, signed an Accession Treaty (OJ 2005 L 157/1), paving the way for Bulgaria and Romania's membership of the EU. Bulgaria and Romania became EU Member States on 1 January 2007, increasing the European Union from 25 to 27 Member States.

Economic and monetary union

Bulgaria and Romania did not join the euro on 1 January 2007. Similar to the 10 states which joined the EU on 1 May 2004, Bulgaria and Romania are only eligible to join the euro once they have achieved the high degree of sustainable economic convergence with the euro area which is required for membership of the single currency. As stated above, the euro has been adopted, and is currently in circulation, in the following 19 Member States:

- Austria
- Belgium
- Cyprus (South)
- Estonia
- Finland
- France
- Germany
- Greece
- Ireland
- Italy
- Latvia
- Lithuania
- Luxembourg
- Malta
- Netherlands
- Portugal
- Slovakia
- Slovenia
- Spain

1 December 2009: the Treaty of Lisbon

The proposed Constitutional Treaty

At the European Council meeting in Laeken on 14 and 15 December 2001, a declaration on the 'Future of the Union' was adopted (SN 300/1/01). This declaration provided for the establishment of a Convention on the Future of Europe, to work towards the adoption of a Constitution for the European Union.

The Convention formed the basis of an **Intergovernmental Conference (IGC)** during 2004 when the 'Future of the Union' was the subject of detailed discussion. This resulted in the text of a **Constitutional Treaty** being agreed at the meeting of the European Council on 18 June 2004, and the 'Treaty establishing a Constitution for Europe' was formally signed in Rome on 29 October 2004 (OJ 2004 C 310/1). The proposed Constitutional Treaty, if it had come into force, would have replaced the TEU and the EC Treaty.

The ratification process

The Constitutional Treaty could only come into force once it had been ratified by *all* the then 25 Member States. The ratification process varies from Member State to Member State. The ratification process in an individual Member State depends upon its constitutional requirements. Some Member States were constitutionally required to hold a referendum before being able to ratify the Treaty. Although the UK's constitution did not require a referendum to be held before the Treaty could be ratified, Tony Blair (the then UK Prime Minister) stated that he would hold a referendum. The UK's referendum was not scheduled to be held before 2006, because in the first half of 2005 the government was preoccupied with the May 2005 general election, and in the second half the UK held the presidency of the European Union's Council of Ministers.

On 29 May 2005, France held a referendum; 54.68 per cent rejected the Treaty. A few days later, on 1 June 2005, The Netherlands held a referendum; 61.7 per cent rejected the Treaty.

Despite the Treaty having been rejected by two Member States it was not officially abandoned. However, the UK stated that it was suspending the ratification process (i.e. no referendum would be held). Other Member States – Czech Republic, Denmark, Ireland and Portugal – postponed their scheduled referenda, while Poland and Sweden put the ratification process on hold.

Abandoned

At the meeting of the European Council on 16–17 June 2005, the Heads of State and Government agreed to come back to the issue of ratification in the first half of 2006 in order to make an overall assessment of the national debates launched as part of a 'period of reflection', and to agree on how to proceed.

At its meeting on 15–16 June 2006, the European Council stated that the 'period of reflection' had been useful in enabling the EU to assess the concerns and worries expressed in the course of the ratification process and that further work was needed before decisions on the future of the Constitutional Treaty could be taken.

This was an implicit admission that the Constitutional Treaty would *not* come into force in its current form.

The Council stated that the Presidency would present a report to the European Council during the first half of 2007, based on extensive consultations with the Member States. This report would contain an assessment of the state of discussion with regard to the Constitutional Treaty and would explore possible future developments.

At the European Summit held in Brussels on 21–23 June 2007, the proposed European Constitution was formally abandoned. It was decided to proceed with a new Reform Treaty which would *amend* the TEU and the EC Treaty, rather than *replace* them.

Ratification of the Treaty of Lisbon

The Reform Treaty, titled the Treaty of Lisbon (ToL), was signed by the representatives of the then 27 Member States on 13 December 2007 in Lisbon, Portugal. The ToL could only come into force once it had been ratified by each of the then 27 Member States. Although it had been anticipated that the ToL would come into force on 1 January 2009, because of ratification problems this was delayed until 1 December 2009.

Ratification by Ireland

The ratification process varies from Member State to Member State. Ireland was the only Member State constitutionally required to hold a referendum before being able to ratify the ToL. On 12 June 2008, Ireland held a referendum and 53.4 per cent rejected the Treaty.

Following Ireland's rejection of the ToL, the question to be answered was whether this would confine the ToL to the history books, or whether the EU would negotiate a compromise to enable Ireland to ask the Irish people to approve the ToL in a second referendum. The second scenario was always considered more likely.

At a meeting of the European Council, which concluded on 19 June 2008, it was decided to continue with the ratification process. Ireland was required to bring proposals forward to the December 2008 meeting of the European Council to enable it to ratify the Treaty. The ToL could not be amended without requiring all Member States to start the ratification process again. At the meeting of the European Council, which concluded on 12 December 2008, a compromise was reached whereby Ireland would agree to hold a second referendum.

The compromise with Ireland provided that all Member States would retain their Commissioner (the number of Commissioners would have been reduced from 1 November 2014; see below). Ireland also received guarantees on, for example, respect for the country's neutrality, and an acknowledgement that it had control over its own policies relating to direct taxation and abortion.

Ireland held a second referendum on 2 October 2009: 67.13 per cent voted in favour of the Treaty, with 32.87 per cent opposed. The Irish President (Mary McAleese) gave final approval to the Treaty on 16 October 2009.

Ratification by Poland and the Czech Republic

Ratification had been delayed in the Czech Republic while a legal challenge was pursued through the Czech courts. On 26 November 2008, the Czech Republic's highest court ruled that the ToL was consistent with the country's constitution, clearing the way for the Czech Parliament to approve the Treaty. However, the Czech Republic's President (Václav Klaus) refused to give final approval pending the outcome of the second Irish referendum. The Polish President (Lech Kaczyñski) likewise refused to give final approval.

Following the positive referendum vote in Ireland, Lech Kaczyñski approved the Treaty on 10 October 2009.

The position in the Czech Republic was more problematic. Although the ToL had been approved by both houses of the Czech Parliament, Václav Klaus continued to withhold his approval. He raised concerns about the implications for the Czech Republic once the Charter of Fundamental Rights of the European Union was given formal legal recognition by the ToL (see below). Article 6(1) TEU, as amended by the ToL, provides that the Union shall 'recognise the rights, freedoms and principles set out in the Charter of Fundamental Rights of the European Union'. The UK and Poland had already sought assurances that the Charter would not be indirectly incorporated into their national law. Article 1, Protocol No. 30 (which is annexed to the TEU and TFEU) provides as follows:

1 The Charter does not extend the ability of the Court of Justice of the European Union, or any court or tribunal of Poland or of the United Kingdom, to find that the laws, regulations or administrative provisions, practices or action of Poland or of the United Kingdom are inconsistent with the fundamental rights, freedoms and principles that it [i.e. the Charter] reaffirms.

2 In particular, and for the avoidance of doubt, nothing in Title IV of the Charter creates justiciable rights applicable to Poland or the United Kingdom except in so far as Poland or the United Kingdom has provided for such rights in its national law.

The European Council sought to secure the Czech Republic President's signature to the Treaty at its meeting held in Brussels on 29–30 October 2009. It was agreed that at the time of the conclusion of the next Accession Treaty a new Protocol would be added to both the TEU and TFEU to provide that Protocol No. 30 (which applies to the UK and Poland) will also apply to the Czech Republic. [Note: an Accession Treaty is adopted to admit new Member States to the European Union. The next Accession Treaty was concluded at the end of 2011 to pave the way for Croatia's entry to the EU on 1 July 2013 (see below).] This was sufficient to secure the support of the President of the Czech Republic.

A further complication arose following a second legal challenge on the compatibility of the Treaty with the Czech Constitution. The Czech Constitutional Court dismissed the application on 3 November 2009, and later the same day the Czech Republic President gave final approval to the ToL.

Having now been ratified by all the Member States, the ToL came into force on 1 December 2009.

The Treaty of Lisbon: introduction

Many of the changes which would have been implemented by the proposed Constitutional Treaty are replicated by the ToL. The changes introduced by the ToL are set out below.

Whereas the proposed Constitutional Treaty would have *replaced* the TEU and EC Treaty, the ToL *retains* and *amends* both these Treaties. The EC Treaty has been renamed the Treaty on the Functioning of the European Union (TFEU). The Union has replaced and succeeded the Community (Art 1 TEU). Throughout the TFEU, the word 'Community' has been replaced with the word 'Union'. The following terms are therefore no longer used: European *Community*; European *Communities*; or *Community* law. Reference is made solely to the European *Union* (or *Union*) and European *Union* law (or *Union* law).

The TEU and the TFEU constitute the Treaties on which the Union is founded (Art 1 TEU).

The articles within both the TEU and TFEU have been renumbered as part of a simplification exercise. As stated above, the ToA originally renumbered the provisions of the TEU and the EC Treaty when it came into force on 1 May 1999. The renumbering of both these Treaties by the ToL is therefore the second time this has occurred. Care must be taken when referring to EU case law, legislation and documents, to ensure that the old numbering (i.e. pre-ToA and pre-ToL) is distinguished from the numbering used post-ToA and post-ToL. The ToL renumbering came into effect when the ToL itself came into force (1 December 2009). For some time it will be necessary to be aware of both the old and new numbering. Subsequent chapters of this book are based on the post-ToL Treaty numbers but, where appropriate, there are cross-references to pre-ToL Treaty numbers.

Articles 1–7 Treaty of Lisbon

The ToL is divided into three parts:

- Article 1 amends the TEU;
- Article 2 amends the EC Treaty, and renames it the Treaty on the Functioning of the European Union (TFEU);
- Articles 3–7 contain the final provisions (e.g. Art 5(1) ToL concerns the renumbering of the TEU and the EC Treaty (which has been renamed the TFEU)).

The overview below considers some of the changes made by the ToL. Reference is made to the relevant Treaty provisions, as amended and renumbered by the ToL. The TEU and TFEU are collectively referred to as 'the Treaties' ((Art 1 TEU and Art 1(2) TFEU)).

The European Union: merger of the three pillars

The construction of the European Union (and its three pillars), as discussed above, was both complex and cumbersome. The ToL has therefore established a single European Union, which has replaced and succeeded the European Community (Art 1 TEU). The three pillars have been merged, although special procedures have been maintained in the fields of foreign policy, security and defence (see below). Reference is no longer made to the three pillars of the European Union.

The Union's objectives

The Union's objectives, set out in Art 3 TEU, are much more succinct than the combined objectives in the former Art 3 EC Treaty (in respect of the European Community) and the former Art 2 TEU (in respect of the EU). Article 3 TEU has, in substance, replaced both of these provisions. Article 3 TEU now provides that:

1 The Union's aim is to promote peace, its values and the well-being of its peoples.

2 The Union shall offer its citizens an area of freedom, security and justice without internal frontiers, in which the free movement of persons is ensured in conjunction with appropriate measures with respect to external border controls, asylum, immigration and the prevention and combating of crime.

3 The Union shall establish an internal market. It shall work for the sustainable development of Europe based on balanced economic growth and price stability, a highly competitive social market economy, aiming at full employment and social progress, and a high level of protection and improvement of the quality of the environment. It shall promote scientific and technological advance.

It shall combat social exclusion and discrimination, and shall promote social justice and protection, equality between women and men, solidarity between generations and protection of the rights of the child.

It shall promote economic, social and territorial cohesion, and solidarity among Member States.

It shall respect its rich cultural and linguistic diversity, and shall ensure that Europe's cultural heritage is safeguarded and enhanced.

4 The Union shall establish an economic and monetary union whose currency is the euro.

5 In its relations with the wider world, the Union shall uphold and promote its values and interests and contribute to the protection of its citizens. It shall contribute to peace, security, the sustainable development of the Earth, solidarity and mutual respect among peoples, free and fair trade, eradication of poverty and the protection of human rights, in particular the rights of the child, as well as to the strict observance and the development of international law, including respect for the principles of the United Nations Charter.

6 The Union shall pursue its objectives by appropriate means commensurate with the competences which are conferred upon it in the Treaties.

The Union's values, democratic principles and provisions having general application

Article 2 TEU provides that the Union is founded on:

... the values of respect for human dignity, freedom, democracy, equality, the rule of law and respect for human rights, including the right of persons belonging to minorities. These values are common to the Member States in a society in which pluralism, non-discrimination, tolerance, justice, solidarity and equality between women and men prevail.

Article 49 TEU provides that: 'Any European State which respects the values referred to in Article 2 and is committed to promoting them may apply to become a member of the Union.'

Democratic principles

Articles 9–12 TEU set out a number of democratic principles which regulate how the Union functions and operates. Given their importance they are set out in full.

Article 9 TEU sets out the principle of equality:

> In all its activities, the Union shall observe the principle of the equality of its citizens, who shall receive equal attention from its institutions, bodies, offices and agencies ...

Article 10 TEU establishes the principle of 'representative democracy':

1 The functioning of the Union shall be founded on representative democracy.

2 Citizens are directly represented at Union level in the European Parliament.
  Member States are represented in the European Council by their Heads of State or Government and in the Council by their governments, themselves democratically accountable either to their national Parliaments, or to their citizens.

3 Every citizen shall have the right to participate in the democratic life of the Union. Decisions shall be taken as openly and as closely as possible to the citizen.

4 Political parties at European level contribute to forming European political awareness and to expressing the will of citizens of the Union.

Article 11 TEU provides an enhanced consultative role for citizens and representative associations, including a 'citizens' petition for action':

1 The institutions shall, by appropriate means, give citizens and representative associations the opportunity to make known and publicly exchange their views in all areas of Union action.

2 The institutions shall maintain an open, transparent and regular dialogue with representative associations and civil society.

3 The European Commission shall carry out broad consultations with parties concerned in order to ensure that the Union's actions are coherent and transparent.

4 Not less than one million citizens who are nationals of a significant number of Member States may take the initiative of inviting the European Commission, within the framework of its powers, to submit any appropriate proposal on matters where citizens consider that a legal act of the Union is required for the purpose of implementing the Treaties.
  The procedures and conditions required for such a citizens' initiative shall be determined in accordance with the first paragraph of Article 24 of the Treaty on the Functioning of the European Union.

Article 24 TFEU provides that a Regulation will be adopted to set out the procedures and conditions of the European Citizens' Initiative (ECI). Regulation 211/2011 (OJ 2011 L 65/1) was subsequently adopted on 16 February 2011 and became applicable from 1 April 2012.

Article 11(4) TEU sets out the number of EU citizens who are needed to take the initiative: i.e. 'not less than one million citizens who are nationals of a significant number of Member States'. This has been made more specific in Regulation 211/2011. Article 2(1), Regulation 211/2011 provides that an ECI requires at least one million eligible signatories coming from a minimum of one-quarter of the EU Member States (i.e. at least seven Member States). In addition, Art 7(2), Regulation 211/2011 requires that in at least one-quarter of the Member States, signatories will comprise at least the minimum number of citizens set out in Annex I. This minimum number of citizens per Member State corresponds to the number of MEPs for the specific Member State, multiplied by 750. So, for example, for the 2014–2019 parliamentary term Estonia has six MEPs and therefore to comply with this requirement the minimum number of signatories from within Estonia will be 4,500 (i.e. 6 × 750).

Article 12 TEU provides national parliaments with an enhanced and explicit role in the functioning of the Union:

National Parliaments contribute actively to the good functioning of the Union:

(a) through being informed by the institutions of the Union and having draft legislative acts of the Union forwarded to them in accordance with the Protocol on the role of national Parliaments in the European Union;

(b) by seeing to it that the principle of subsidiarity is respected in accordance with the procedures provided for in the Protocol on the application of the principles of subsidiarity and proportionality;

(c) by taking part, within the framework of the area of freedom, security and justice, in the evaluation mechanisms for the implementation of the Union policies in that area, in accordance with Article 70 of the Treaty on the Functioning of the European Union, and through being involved in the political monitoring of Europol and the evaluation of Eurojust's activities in accordance with Articles 88 and 85 of that Treaty;

(d) by taking part in the revision procedures of the Treaties, in accordance with Article 48 of this Treaty;

(e) by being notified of applications for accession to the Union, in accordance with Article 49 of this Treaty;

(f) by taking part in the inter-parliamentary cooperation between national Parliaments and with the European Parliament, in accordance with the Protocol on the role of national Parliaments in the European Union.

Provisions having general application

Part One, Title II TFEU sets out a number of provisions which are stated to have 'general application':

● general consistency of policy (Art 7 TFEU);
● elimination of inequalities and promotion of equality between men and women (Art 8 TFEU);
● social protection (Art 9 TFEU);
● combating all forms of discrimination (Art 10 TFEU);
● the requirements of environmental protection (Art 11 TFEU);
● consumer protection (Art 12 TFEU);
● animal welfare (Art 13 TFEU);
● services of general economic interest (Art 14 TFEU);
● openness and transparency (Art 15 TFEU);
● protection of personal data (Art 16 TFEU);
● respect for churches and religious associations or communities (Art 17 TFEU).

As these provisions have general application, they will be applied by the Court of Justice of the European Union when interpreting and applying Union law.

Non-discrimination

With regard to the provision of general application, which seeks to combat all forms of discrimination (Art 10 TFEU), Art 18(1) TFEU (which has replaced the non-discrimination provision in the former Art 12 EC Treaty) specifically provides that:

Within the scope of application of the Treaties, and without prejudice to any special provisions contained therein, any discrimination on grounds of nationality shall be prohibited.

The former Art 12 EC Treaty has been applied extensively by the Court of Justice, particularly with regard to the Treaty provisions relating to Union citizenship and the free movement of persons (see Chapters 11–15). Article 18(1) TFEU is similarly applied by the Court.

Charter of Fundamental Rights of the European Union

The Charter of Fundamental Rights of the European Union was signed by the then 15 Member States during December 2000 at the meeting of the European Council held in Nice, France. The Charter combines in a single text the civil, political, economic, social and societal rights which had previously been laid down in a variety of international, European and national sources. It includes the following:

- rights of dignity (e.g. the right to life, and respect for private and family life);
- freedoms (e.g. freedom of assembly and of association);
- equality (e.g. respect for cultural, religious and linguistic diversity);
- solidarity (e.g. right of collective bargaining and action);
- citizens' rights (e.g. freedom of movement and residence);
- justice (e.g. presumption of innocence and right of defence).

Originally, the Charter was not legally binding. A Declaration annexed to the ToN provided that an Intergovernmental Conference would be held in 2004 to consider, *inter alia*, the status of the Charter. This resulted in the adoption of the proposed Constitutional Treaty and subsequently the adoption of the ToL.

The Charter, which was amended on 12 December 2007, is given legal recognition by the ToL. Article 6(1) TEU, as amended by the ToL, provides that the Union shall 'recognise the rights, freedoms and principles set out in the Charter of Fundamental Rights of the European Union'. The Charter therefore becomes an integral part of EU law, setting out the fundamental rights which every EU citizen can benefit from. However, it does not create fundamental rights which are of general application in national law. It only applies within the scope of EU law. A Declaration on the Charter (which was annexed to the Final Act of the Intergovernmental Conference which adopted the ToL) states that:

> The Charter of Fundamental Rights of the European Union, which has legally binding force, confirms the fundamental rights guaranteed by the European Convention for the Protection of Human Rights and Fundamental Freedoms as they result from the constitutional traditions common to the Member States.
>
> The Charter does not extend the field of application of Union law beyond the powers of the Union or establish any new power or task for the Union, or modify powers and tasks as defined by the Treaties.

The latter paragraph explicitly provides that the Charter does not introduce any new EU powers or tasks. As stated above, the UK and Poland sought reassurance that the Charter would not be indirectly incorporated into their national law. Article 1, Protocol No. 30 (which is annexed to the TEU and TFEU) provides that:

1 The Charter does not extend the ability of the Court of Justice of the European Union, or any court or tribunal of Poland or of the United Kingdom, to find that the laws, regulations or administrative provisions, practices or action of Poland or of the United Kingdom

are inconsistent with the fundamental rights, freedoms and principles that it [i.e. the Charter] reaffirms.

2 In particular, and for the avoidance of doubt, nothing in Title IV of the Charter creates justiciable rights applicable to Poland or the United Kingdom except in so far as Poland or the United Kingdom has provided for such rights in its national law.

As also stated above, in order to secure the Czech Republic President's signature to the ToL, it was agreed that at the time of the conclusion of the next Accession Treaty a new Protocol would be added to both the TEU and TFEU to provide that Protocol No. 30 (which only applied to the UK and Poland) would also apply to the Czech Republic. The next Accession Treaty was concluded at the end of 2011 to pave the way for Croatia's membership of the EU on 1 July 2013.

Objective 8	## The European Convention on Human Rights and Fundamental Freedoms (ECHR)

The ECHR's fundamental human rights which are applicable within the context of EU law are considered in further detail at pages 73–83.

The European Convention on Human Rights and Fundamental Freedoms (**ECHR**) was drafted in 1950 under the auspices of the Council of Europe, an international organisation originally composed of 21 Western European states, and now comprising 47 states. The ECHR (European Convention on Human Rights) is intended to uphold common political traditions of individual civil liberties and the rule of law. All the Member States of the EU are signatories.

It is important to distinguish the international structure created by the ECHR from the quite separate supranational institutions of the EU. The media often talks loosely about taking a case 'to Europe' without identifying whether the case is a human rights matter involving the ECHR and to be dealt with by the **European Court of Human Rights** in Strasbourg, or a matter of Union law to be referred to the Court of Justice in Luxembourg. Decisions made by the European Court of Human Rights are not legally binding on national courts, although they will be taken into account by these courts. Decisions of the Court of Justice are legally binding on all national courts. Decisions of the European Court of Human Rights may result in compensation being awarded against a state, in favour of a victim of human rights abuses, but such decisions are not binding on the state, and could (in legal theory) be ignored.

The Court of Justice, like national courts, takes account of the ECHR when interpreting and applying Union law. The TEU formally acknowledged the ECHR as forming part of the EU's fundamental principles. However, it has no application under Union law to matters outside the EU's legal competence. Although the ECHR was recognised by the TEU as an important source of Union law, it was only important when interpreting and applying *Union* law. Although this remains the case post-ToL, Art 6(2) TEU now provides that the Union will accede to the ECHR.

EU accession to the ECHR

Article 6(2) TEU provides that the Union will accede to the ECHR, although it states that 'such accession shall not affect the Union's competences as defined in the Treaties'. This means that accession to the ECHR will not extend the Union's powers and tasks. Application of the ECHR will be limited to those areas which come within the competence of the Union. Article 6(3) TEU further provides that the 'fundamental rights guaranteed by the European Convention of Human Rights and Fundamental Freedoms and as they result from the constitutional traditions common to the Member States, *shall constitute general principles of the Union's law*' [emphasis added]. This simply restates the previous position. However, once the Union accedes to the ECHR, EU law will have to be interpreted and applied in accordance with the ECHR, not simply as a 'general principle of the Union's law', but because: (i) the ECHR is directly applicable to the Union; and (ii) the Union is required (in international law) to adhere to the ECHR's provisions. Following accession to the ECHR, it will be possible for a decision of the Court of Justice to be contested by taking the case to the European Court of Human Rights in Strasbourg, claiming the Court of Justice has failed to correctly apply (or failed to apply) a provision of the ECHR.

Official ECHR accession talks started between the EU and the Council of Europe on 7 July 2010. The accession agreement was concluded by the Council of Europe and the European Council (acting unanimously) in late 2011. However, the European Parliament was also required to give its consent to the accession agreement. During 2012, the negotiations stalled. An ad hoc group, comprising members of the Council of Europe's Steering Committee for Human Rights (CDDH) and the EU, was established to provide some momentum to the negotiations. A draft agreement was concluded in April 2013. An opinion of the EU Court of Justice was sought on the compatibility of the draft agreement with EU treaties. Opinion 2/13 was delivered by the Court of Justice on 18 December 2014 and, because of problems it identified, the Court concluded that the draft agreement was not compatible with Union law. If the issues identified by the Court of Justice are satisfactorily resolved, through amendments to the draft agreement, the European Council must adopt a decision to authorise the signing of the accession agreement, acting unanimously. All Member States would then have to complete their internal procedure to ratify the agreement. The Union would then ratify the agreement and the Committee of Ministers of the Council of Europe would have to adopt it. It would then have to be ratified (i.e. approved) by all 47 contracting parties to the ECHR (including the individual Member States) in accordance with their respective constitutional requirements. It is safe to assume that the Union's accession to the ECHR will not take place in the foreseeable future.

The UK's Human Rights Act 1998

The ECHR was incorporated into the law of England, Wales, Scotland and Northern Ireland by the Human Rights Act 1998. All UK public bodies, including courts and tribunals, and even private bodies implementing public law, have to abide by the principles of the ECHR.

Therefore, ECHR rights may be applied either: (i) as a matter of Union law where they concern a measure within the competence of the Union; or (ii) under national law following the procedures set out in the Act where Union law is not involved. However, unlike the position of Union law, which has immediate primacy within the UK, if there is a clear conflict between a UK statute and one of the ECHR provisions then UK courts will only be able to make a 'declaration of incompatibility'. Ministers will then have to ensure that the offending legislation is amended to give full effect to the ECHR.

Relationship between the Union and the Member States

Article 4(2) TEU provides that the Union shall respect the 'equality of Member States before the Treaties as well as their national identities'. The Union will also respect the essential State functions of each Member State, which includes 'ensuring the territorial integrity of the State, maintaining law and order and safeguarding national security. In particular, national security remains the sole responsibility of each Member State' (Art 4(2) TEU).

Similar to the former Art 10 EC Treaty, Art 4(3) TEU provides that:

Pursuant to the principle of sincere cooperation, the Union and the Member States shall, in full mutual respect, assist each other in carrying out tasks which flow from the Treaties.

The Member States shall take any appropriate measure, general or particular, to ensure fulfilment of the obligations arising out of the Treaties or resulting from the acts of the institutions of the Union.

The Member States shall facilitate the achievement of the Union's tasks and refrain from any measure which could jeopardise the attainment of the Union's objectives.

Legal personality

Article 47 TEU provides that the Union shall have legal personality, enabling it to enter into international treaties and agreements on behalf of the Member States.

Union citizenship

Article 20 TFEU establishes Union citizenship, stating that Union citizens enjoy the rights, and are subject to the duties, provided for in the Treaties (Art 20(2) TFEU). Similar to the previous Arts 17 and 18 EC Treaty, Art 20(2) TFEU provides that 'These rights shall be exercised in accordance with the conditions and limits defined by the Treaties and by the measures adopted thereunder'.

Article 20(1) TFEU explicitly provides that 'Citizenship of the Union shall be additional to and not replace national citizenship'.

EU competences and the principle of conferral

Article 5(1) TEU provides that 'the limits of Union competences are governed by the principle of conferral'. This means the Union shall act 'only within the limits of the competences conferred upon it by the Member States in the Treaties to attain the objectives set out therein' (Art 5(2) TEU). The corollary is that 'Competences not conferred upon the Union in the Treaties remain with the Member States' (Art 5(2) TEU). The exercise of Union competences is also governed by 'the principles of subsidiarity and proportionality' (Art 5(1) TEU). This provision is complemented by a Protocol on the application of these two principles (Protocol No. 2, annexed to the TEU and TFEU), which incorporates an 'early-warning system' involving national parliaments in the monitoring of how subsidiarity is applied. National parliaments are informed of all new legislative initiatives, and if at least one-third are of the view that a proposal infringes the principle of subsidiarity then the Commission will have to reconsider the proposal.

Areas of exclusive competence, shared competence and actions to support, coordinate or supplement Member States' actions

The TFEU distinguishes between three categories of Union power:

- Areas of exclusive competence where only the EU may legislate and adopt legally binding acts. The Member States can only act if empowered to do so by the Union, or to implement Union acts. Article 3 TFEU provides that the EU has exclusive competence in the following areas:
  - customs union;
  - establishing competition rules necessary for the functioning of the internal market;

- monetary policy for the Member States whose currency is the euro;
- conservation of marine biological resources under the common fisheries policy;
- common commercial policy;
- conclusion of specific international agreements.

- Areas of shared competence where the EU and the Member States may legislate and adopt legally binding acts. The Member States can only exercise this shared competence if the EU has not exercised its competence to act, or if the EU has ceased to exercise its competence. Article 4 TFEU provides that the EU and the Member States have shared competence in the following principal areas:
  - internal market;
  - certain aspects of social policy;
  - economic, social and territorial cohesion;
  - agriculture and fisheries;
  - environment;
  - consumer protection;
  - transport;
  - trans-European networks;
  - energy;
  - area of freedom, security and justice;
  - certain aspects of common safety concerns in public health matters.

- Areas where the Union carries out actions to support, coordinate or supplement the actions of the Member States. Article 6 TFEU provides that this applies in the following areas:
  - protection and improvement of human health;
  - industry;
  - culture;
  - tourism,
  - education, vocational training, youth and sport;
  - civil protection;
  - administrative cooperation.

Particular cases which do not fit into this threefold general classification are dealt with separately. The following two areas, for example, are dealt with separately: coordination of economic and employment policies (Art 2(3) TFEU); and common foreign and security policy (Art 2(4) TFEU).

Legislative acts: ordinary legislative procedure and special legislative procedure

The power of legislative initiative rests with the Commission, 'except where the Treaties provide otherwise' (Art 17(2) TEU).

Article 289 TFEU provides that a legislative act can be adopted by the '**ordinary legislative procedure**' or a '**special legislative procedure**'. The ordinary legislative procedure, not surprisingly given its title, applies in the vast majority of cases. This procedure (which is set out in Art 294 TFEU) is practically a carbon copy of the former co-decision procedure; see Chapter 4.

The special legislative procedure refers to specific cases where the Treaties provide for the adoption of a regulation, **directive** or decision by the European Parliament with the Council's involvement, or by the Council with the participation of the Parliament (Art 289(2) TFEU).

General legislative power

Article 352 TFEU provides the Union with a general legislative power: 'If action by the Union should prove necessary ... to attain one of the objectives set out in the Treaties, and the Treaties have not provided the necessary powers, the Council ... shall adopt the appropriate measures' (Art 352(1) TFEU). Its scope appears wider than that of the former Art 308 EC Treaty, because Art 308 was confined to the internal market. However, the conditions under which Art 352 TFEU can be exercised are stricter in that, as well as requiring unanimity in the Council, the consent of the European Parliament must be obtained.

The institutional framework

Article 13(1) TEU provides that the Union shall have an 'institutional framework which shall aim to promote its values, advance its objectives, serve its interests, those of its citizens and those of the Member States, and ensure the consistency, effectiveness and continuity of its policies and actions'. The following seven Union institutions are recognised by Art 13(1) TEU:

- The European Parliament;
- The European Council;
- The Council;
- The European Commission (to be referred to as the 'Commission');
- The Court of Justice of the European Union;
- The European Central Bank;
- The **Court of Auditors.**

It should be noted that for the first time the European Council is treated as a Union institution in its own right.

Articles 13–19 TEU clarify the role of the Union institutions. Part Six, Title I TFEU contains the detailed provisions governing the institutions:

> **Institutional and Financial Provisions** (Arts 223–334 TFEU)
> *Title I*   *Institutional Provisions* (Arts 223–309 TFEU)
> Chapter 1   *The Institutions* (Arts 223–287 TFEU)
>   *Section 1*   *The European Parliament* (Arts 223–234 TFEU)
>   *Section 2*   *The European Council* (Arts 235–236 TFEU)
>   *Section 3*   *The Council* (Arts 237–243 TFEU)
>   *Section 4*   *The Commission* (Arts 244–250 TFEU)
>   *Section 5*   *The Court of Justice of the European Union* (Arts 251–281 TFEU)
>   *Section 6*   *The European Central Bank* (Arts 282–284 TFEU)
>   *Section 7*   *The Court of Auditors* (Arts 285–287 TFEU)

Changes which affect the institutions are discussed briefly below. These changes are considered in more detail in Chapters 3–5.

The European Parliament

The European Parliament has the power, jointly with the Council, to enact legislation and exercise the budgetary function, as well as exercise functions of political control and consultation as laid down in the Treaties (Art 14(1) TEU).

The European Parliament elects the President of the Commission on a proposal from the European Council (acting by qualified majority). The European Council is required to take into account the results of the elections of the European Parliament when deciding on who to propose (Art 17(7) TEU). The President, the High Representative of the Union for Foreign Affairs and Security Policy (see below), and the other members of the Commission are subject *as a body* to a vote of consent by the European Parliament, following which the European Council will appoint the Commission acting by a qualified majority (Art 17(7) TEU).

The number of MEPs is limited to 750 plus the President (Art 14(2) TEU). The Treaties do not make provision for the allocation of seats to each Member State, as was previously the case. However, Art 14(2) TEU provides that the European Council will adopt a decision, acting unanimously, on the initiative of the European Parliament and with its consent, to establish the total number of MEPs and the allocation of seats to each Member State. Under this new system, the allocation of seats to each Member State will be distributed among Member States according to 'degressive proportionality' (Art 14(2) TEU). Degressive proportionality in this context means that MEPs from more populous Member States represent more people than those from less populated Member States. No Member State will have fewer than 6 nor more than 96 MEPs (Art 14(2) TEU); see Chapter 3.

The European Council

The European Council is, for the first time, formally recognised as a Union institution (Art 13(1) TEU). The European Council provides the impetus for the Union's development and defines its political directions and priorities, but it does not exercise a legislative function (Art 15(1) TEU). The general rule regarding the adoption of decisions is consensus, except where the Treaties provide otherwise (Art 15(4) TEU).

The European Council is now led by a President with specific powers. The President is elected by a qualified majority of the European Council's members for a term of two-and-a-half years, renewable once (Art 15(5)–(6) TEU). The former Prime Minister of Belgium, Herman Van Rompuy, was elected to the post on 20 November 2009 and was subsequently elected for a second term. The former Prime Minister of Poland, Donald Tusk, was elected to the post for the period from 1 December 2014 to 31 May 2017. The President is not allowed to hold a national office at the same time as holding the Presidency (Art 15(6) TEU), and therefore Donald Tusk had to relinquish his role as Prime Minister of Poland. The President is required to 'ensure the external representation of the Union on issues concerning its common foreign and security policy, without prejudice to the powers of the High Representative of the Union for Foreign Affairs and Security Policy' (Art 15(6) TEU). Article 15(6) TEU also provides that the President of the European Council:

(a) shall chair it and drive it forward;
(b) shall ensure the preparation and continuity of the work of the European Council in cooperation with the President of the Commission, and on the basis of the work of the General Affairs Council;
(c) shall endeavour to facilitate cohesion and consensus within the European Council;
(d) shall present a report to the European Parliament after each of the meetings of the European Council.

The Council

Article 16(6) TEU provides for the Council to meet in different configurations. These configurations are determined by the European Council acting by a qualified majority (Art 236 TFEU). Article 16(6) TEU specifically provides for the creation of a Foreign Affairs Council.

The High Representative of the Union for Foreign Affairs and Security Policy (see below) presides over the Foreign Affairs Council (Art 18(3) TEU). The General Affairs Council, which is another configuration specifically mentioned in Art 16(6) TEU, ensures 'consistency in the work of the different Council configurations' (Art 16(6) TEU). All configurations, other than the Foreign Affairs Council, are presided over by one of the Council's Member State representatives, on the basis of a system of equal rotation (Art 16(9) TEU). The European Council, acting by a qualified majority, determines the Presidency of each configuration, other than that of Foreign Affairs (Art 236 TFEU).

In order to meet the requirement of transparency, Art 16(8) TEU provides that the Council shall meet in public when it deliberates and votes on a draft legislative act.

Qualified majority

Depending upon the specific Treaty provision, the Council may act by a qualified majority. On 1 November 2014, the formula for determining a qualified majority changed to one based on the 'double-majority' principle (i.e. a system based upon: (i) number of Member States; and (ii) population).

Article 16(4) TEU provides that this double- majority principle requires two thresholds to be achieved before a measure can be adopted: (i) the support of at least 55 per cent of the members of the Council (each Member State has one member) comprising at least 15 of them; and (ii) the support of Member States comprising at least 65 per cent of the population. In addition, a blocking minority must include at least four Member States, failing which the qualified majority will be deemed achieved. This provision prevents three or fewer of the larger Member States from being able to block a proposal. Article 238(2) TFEU provides a **derogation** from Art 16(4) TEU where the Council does not act on a proposal from either the Commission or the High Representative of the Union for Foreign Affairs and Security Policy. In this instance, the first threshold is increased, requiring the support of at least 72 per cent of the Member States. Article 238(3) TFEU sets out the qualified majority formula where not all Member States participate in the voting (e.g. where they are using the enhanced cooperation procedure (see below)).

A decision adopted by the Council has incorporated a revised 'Ioannina' compromise (see Chapter 4). This decision enables a small number of Member States, which is close to a blocking minority, to demonstrate their opposition to a proposed measure. From 1 November 2014 to 31 March 2017, if members of the Council representing either (i) three-quarters of the population; or (ii) at least three-quarters of the number of Member States, necessary to constitute a blocking minority under Art 16(4) TEU or 238(2) TFEU, indicate their opposition to the Council adopting an act by qualified majority, the Council has to delay adopting the act and must enter into further discussions. The Council is required to do all in its power, within a reasonable period of time, to find a satisfactory solution to address the concerns the Member States have raised. From 1 April 2017, this three-quarters requirement will be reduced to 55 per cent in both instances (i.e. either: (i) 55 per cent of the population; or (ii) at least 55 per cent of the number of Member States, necessary to constitute a blocking minority under Art 16(4) TEU or 238(2) TFEU).

Protocol No. 36, which is annexed to the TEU and TFEU, contains transitional arrangements which applied to qualified majority voting for the period to 31 October 2014 and which will apply during the period from 1 November 2014 to 31 March 2017. These arrangements will be discussed in Chapter 4; suffice to say at this stage that during the transitional period 1 November 2014 to 31 March 2017, when an act is to be adopted by qualified majority, a member of the Council may request that it be adopted in accordance with the system which applied until 31 October 2014, rather than the new double- majority system discussed above. Qualified majority is now the general rule for the adoption of decisions within the Council: 'The Council shall act by a qualified majority except where the Treaties provide otherwise' (Art 16(3) TEU). Unanimity remains in areas of direct taxation, social security, foreign policy and common security policy.

Where the TFEU, or Part V TEU, provides for the Council to act by unanimity, the European Council is empowered to adopt a decision, acting unanimously and after obtaining the consent of the European Parliament, authorising the Council to act by a qualified majority in the specified area or case (Art 48(7) TEU). This provision does not apply to decisions with military implications or those in the area of defence. The formal opposition of a single national parliament will be enough to block the decision to change from unanimity to qualified majority (Art 48(7) TEU). Previously, this change from unanimity to qualified majority could only be achieved by formally amending the Treaties.

Enhanced cooperation

Article 20 TEU provides for a system of 'enhanced cooperation', the detailed provisions of which are set out within Arts 326–334 TFEU. These provisions replace the former Arts 43–45 TEU and Art 11 EC Treaty, which were inserted into the Treaties by the ToN.

Enhanced cooperation requires the involvement of at least nine Member States (Art 20(2) TEU). It applies to the Union's non-exclusive competences (Art 20(1) TEU). Authorisation to proceed with enhanced cooperation is granted by a decision of the Council acting by a qualified majority, after obtaining the consent of the European Parliament, on a proposal from the Commission (Art 329(1) TFEU). With regard to the common foreign and security policy (see below), authorisation to proceed will be granted by a decision of the Council acting unanimously, after obtaining the opinion of: (i) the High Representative of the Union for Foreign Affairs and Security Policy; and (ii) the Commission. In this case, the European Parliament is simply informed (Art 329(2) TFEU). In both cases, the Council's decision authorising enhanced cooperation can only be adopted 'as a last resort when it has established that the objectives of such cooperation cannot be obtained within a reasonable period by the Union as a whole' (Art 20(2) TEU). Member States not participating in enhanced cooperation are able to take part in relevant Council meetings, 'but only members of the Council representing the Member States participating in enhanced cooperation shall take part in the vote' (Art 20(3) TEU and Art 330 TFEU). Acts adopted within the framework of enhanced cooperation will only bind the participating Member States (Art 20(4) TEU).

The enhanced cooperation procedure was used in 2011 by 25 of the then 27 Member States, Spain and Italy having refused to participate. The Council authorised the procedure to be used with a view to creating a single European patent (Council Decision 2011/167/EU). In *Spain and Italy* v *Council* (Joined Cases C-274/11 and C-295/11), Spain and Italy requested the Court of Justice to annul the Council's decision. The Court rejected this request.

Article 333(1) TFEU provides that where a provision of the Treaties which may be applied in the context of enhanced cooperation stipulates that the Council shall act unanimously, the Member States taking part in enhanced cooperation may, acting unanimously, change over to qualified majority voting. Article 333(2) TFEU provides that where a provision of the Treaties which may be applied in the context of enhanced cooperation stipulates that the Council shall adopt acts under a special legislative procedure, the Member States taking part in enhanced cooperation may, acting unanimously and after consulting the European Parliament, change over to the ordinary legislative procedure. However, these provisions do not apply to decisions having military or defence implications (Art 333(3) TFEU).

The Commission

The Commission's power of legislative initiative is clearly restated: 'Union legislative acts may only be adopted on the basis of a Commission proposal, except where the Treaties provide otherwise' (Art 17(2) TEU). Until 31 October 2014, the Commission consisted of one national from each Member State (Art 17(4) TEU). From 1 November 2014, the Commission consists of a number of members corresponding to two-thirds of the number of Member States, unless the European Council, acting unanimously, decides to alter this number. As discussed above, in order to satisfy the concerns of Ireland and to pave the way for the second Irish referendum on the ToL, the European Council made the necessary decision to revert to the previous composition. The Commission therefore continues to consist of one national from each Member State. If there had been a reduction in the number of Commissioners, the members would have been chosen on the basis of a system of 'strictly equal rotation between the Member States, reflecting the demographic and geographical range of all the Member States' (Art 17(5) TEU). The European Council would have set up the system, acting unanimously (Art 17(5) and Art 244 TFEU).

The political role of the President of the Commission, who is elected by the European Parliament (Art 14(1) TEU), has been reinforced. The role now includes:

- the appointment of Vice-Presidents, other than the High Representative (Art 17(6)(c) TEU);
- laying down guidelines within which the Commission is to work (Art 17(6)(a) TEU);
- deciding on the internal organisation of the Commission (Art 17(6)(b) TEU);
- the right to request the resignation of a Commissioner (Art 17(6) TEU).

The President is also involved in the appointment of the individual Commissioners: 'The Council, by common accord with the President-elect, shall adopt the list of the other persons whom it proposes for appointment as members of the Commission' (Art 17(7) TEU).

The High Representative of the Union for Foreign Affairs and Security Policy

Article 18 TEU provides for the appointment of the High Representative of the Union for Foreign Affairs and Security Policy. Although clearly not one of the EU institutions, it is an appropriate point to consider the High Representative. The High Representative is appointed by the European Council, acting by a qualified majority, with the agreement of the President of the Commission (Art 18(1) TEU). Federica Mogherini, the former Italian foreign minister, was appointed High Representative of the Union for Foreign Affairs and Security Policy from 1 November 2014, with the agreement of Jean-Claude Juncker, the newly elected President of the European Commission. He replaced Catherine Ashton, the UK's former European Commissioner for Trade.

The High Representative will:

- conduct the Union's common foreign and security policy (Art 18(2) TEU);
- chair the Foreign Affairs Council (Art 18(3) TEU);
- serve as one of the Vice-Presidents of the Commission (Art 18(4) TEU).

As a Vice-President of the Commission, the High Representative is subject to a collective vote of approval by the European Parliament (Art 17(7) TEU) and, possibly, a vote of censure (Art 234 TFEU and Art 17(8) TEU).

In this 'two-hatted' role (Commission–Council), the High Representative ensures the consistency of the Union's external action as a whole (Art 18(4)). The High Representative conducts the Union's common foreign and security policy, and common security and defence policy, contributing to policy development (Art 18(2) TEU). The High Representative is aided by a European External Action Service (Art 27(3) TEU). This Service consists of officials from relevant departments of the Council's General Secretariat and the Commission, as well as staff seconded from Member States' national diplomatic services (Art 27(3) TEU).

The Court of Justice of the European Union

Article 19(1) TEU provides that 'the Court of Justice, the General Court and specialised courts' shall be collectively referred to as the Court of Justice of the European Union. The former Court of First Instance has been renamed the General Court. The Court of Justice's competence has been broadened, particularly in the area of freedom, security and justice and certain aspects of foreign policy (see below).

Other institutions and advisory bodies

The provisions relating to the Union's other institutions (the European Central Bank and the Court of Auditors) and advisory bodies (the Committee of the Regions, and the European Economic and Social Committee) are contained solely within the TFEU.

Internal policies: area of freedom, security and justice

Of all the policies referred to as internal policies, it is in the area of freedom, security and justice that the ToL makes the most changes to the status quo, not least as a result of the removal of the distinction between measures covered by the former EC Treaty and those covered by the former 'third pillar', and the general application of co-decision (now referred to as the 'ordinary legislative procedure') and qualified majority voting (see above).

The Union's actions in the area of freedom, security and justice have been clarified. Such actions respect 'fundamental rights and the different legal systems and traditions of the Member States' (Art 67(1) TFEU).

Policy-making has been deepened: asylum and immigration policy are a common Union policy governed by the principles of solidarity and fair sharing of responsibility between Member States (Art 80 TFEU). This 'fair sharing of responsibility between Member States' includes the fair sharing of any financial implications (Art 80 TFEU).

It is with regard to judicial cooperation in criminal matters that the most innovative changes are found, above all because measures are adopted by qualified majority. Article 83(1) TFEU provides for the approximation of criminal legislation:

> The European Parliament and the Council may, by means of directives adopted in accordance with the ordinary legislative procedure, establish **minimum rules concerning the definition of criminal offences and sanctions in the areas of particularly serious crime with a cross-border dimension** resulting from the nature or impact of such offences or from a special need to combat them on a common basis … [emphasis added]

Article 83(1) refers to 'areas of particularly serious crimes with a cross-border dimension', and lists these as:

- terrorism;
- trafficking in human beings and sexual exploitation of women and children;

- illicit drug trafficking;
- illicit arms trafficking;
- money laundering;
- corruption;
- counterfeiting of means of payment;
- computer crime;
- organised crime.

The Council is empowered to adopt a decision, acting unanimously and after obtaining the European Parliament's consent, to extend this list to other crimes which meet the criteria set out in Art 83(1) TFEU.

In order to allay the fears of certain Member States, Art 83(3) TFEU provides a special 'emergency brake' procedure. If a Member State considers that a draft directive proposed under Art 83(1) may affect fundamental aspects of its criminal justice system, it has the power to request that the draft directive be referred back to the European Council. In this case, the ordinary legislative procedure will be suspended. Within a period of four months, if there is a consensus within the European Council, the proposal will be referred back to the Council and the suspension of the ordinary legislative procedure will be terminated so that the procedure can continue. However, if during this four-month period no consensus is reached within the European Council, if at least nine Member States want to establish enhanced cooperation on the basis of the draft directive, they will notify the European Parliament, the Council and the Commission accordingly. In such a case, authorisation to proceed will be deemed to have been granted, such that the provisions on enhanced cooperation will apply (see above).

The Court of Justice has a general role in monitoring the Union's activities in this area. However, Art 276 TFEU provides that:

> In exercising its powers regarding the provisions of Chapters 4 [judicial cooperation in criminal matters] and 5 [police cooperation] of Chapter V of Part Three relating to the area of freedom, security and justice, **the Court of Justice of the European Union shall have no jurisdiction to review the validity or proportionality of operations carried out by the police or other law-enforcement services of a Member State or the exercise of the responsibilities incumbent upon Member States with regard to the maintenance of law and order and the safeguarding of internal security.** [emphasis added]

The following provisions are illustrative of the complex system adopted for the development and implementation of policy and law in the area of freedom, security and justice:

- the definition by the European Council (and therefore by consensus) of strategic guidelines for legislative and operational planning, without European Parliament involvement (Art 68 TFEU);
- sharing the legislative initiative between the Commission and a quarter of the Member States (a Member State is no longer able to submit a proposal on its own) in the area of judicial cooperation in criminal matters and police cooperation (Art 76 TFEU);
- retaining unanimity in certain areas, particularly as regards cross-border aspects of family law (Art 81(3) TFEU) and all forms of police cooperation (Art 87(3) TFEU);
- the definition of a more prominent role for national parliaments, with particular regard to monitoring whether the principle of subsidiarity is being respected (Art 69 TFEU).

The following two provisions enable EU law to be further developed in the area of family law and serious crimes:

- measures which concern family law with cross-border implications may be adopted by the Council acting unanimously after consulting the European Parliament (Art 81(3) TFEU);
- the list of serious crimes for which a directive may lay down minimum rules may be extended by the Council, acting unanimously after obtaining the consent of the European Parliament (Art 83(1) TFEU); see above.

Finally, the Council is empowered to adopt a regulation, acting unanimously after obtaining the consent of the European Parliament, to establish a European Public Prosecutor's Office (Art 86(1) TFEU). If established, the European Public Prosecutor's Office will be responsible for combating offences which affect the Union's financial interests and to prosecute those responsible for such infringements (Art 81(1) and 81(2) TFEU). Article 81(4) TFEU provides that the remit of the European Public Prosecutor's Office can be extended to combating and prosecuting serious crime with a cross-border dimension, by means of a decision adopted unanimously by the Council after obtaining the consent of the European Parliament, and after having consulted the Commission. In 2013, a regulation was proposed by the Commission to establish the European Public Prosecutor's Office, but this regulation has not been adopted.

Protocol No. 21: UK and Ireland opt-out; Protocol No. 22: Denmark opt-out

Article 1 Protocol No. 21 (which is annexed to the TEU and TFEU) provides that the UK and Ireland will not take part in the adoption by the Council of any proposed measures relating to Title V of Part Three TFEU (i.e. all the TFEU provisions which relate to the area of freedom, security and justice). Article 2 provides that:

> In consequence of Article 1 ... none of the provisions of Title V of Part Three of the Treaty on the Functioning of the European Union, no measure adopted pursuant to that Title, no provision of any international agreement concluded by the Union pursuant to that Title, and no decision of the Court of Justice interpreting any such provision, measure or decision shall be binding upon or applicable in the United Kingdom or Ireland; and no such provision, measure or decision shall in any way affect the competences, rights and obligations of those States ...

Article 3(1) Protocol No. 21 provides that the UK or Ireland may notify the President of the Council in writing if they wish to take part in the adoption and application of any proposed measure under Title V of Part Three. If they notify the President within three months of the proposal or initiative being presented to the Council, they will be entitled to participate.

Protocol No. 22 provides Denmark with a similar opt-out.

External policies and action

It is in the area of external action that the ToL makes the most radical changes, more by means of institutional modifications, notably in the creation of the post of High Representative of the Union for Foreign Affairs and Security Policy (see above), than by improvement of procedures, which will remain practically unchanged. The role of the European Parliament in foreign policy has not changed fundamentally, although it now plays a more prominent role in common commercial policy and the conclusion of international agreements.

Articles 21 and 22 TEU set out general provisions which govern the Union's external action. Articles 23–46 TEU are specifically concerned with the Union's common foreign and security policy.

Article 21(1) TEU states that the Union's action on the international scene is guided by the following principles:

- democracy;
- the rule of law;
- the universality and indivisibility of human rights and fundamental freedoms;
- respect for human dignity;
- the principles of equality and solidarity;
- respect for the principles of the United Nations Charter and international law.

The Union will seek to develop relations and build partnerships with third countries (i.e. non-EU countries), and international, regional and global organisations which share the above principles, to promote multilateral solutions to common problems (Art 21(1) TEU).

Article 21(2) TEU provides that the Union will define and pursue common policies and actions, and work for a high degree of cooperation in all fields of international relations, in order to:

(a) safeguard its values, fundamental interests, security, independence and integrity;
(b) consolidate and support democracy, the rule of law, human rights and the principles of international law;
(c) preserve peace, prevent conflicts and strengthen international security, in accordance with the purposes and principles of the United Nations Charter, with the principles of the Helsinki Final Act and with the aims of the Charter of Paris, including those relating to external borders;
(d) foster the sustainable economic, social and environmental development of developing countries, with the primary aim of eradicating poverty;
(e) encourage the integration of all countries into the world economy, including through the progressive abolition of restrictions on international trade;
(f) help develop international measures to preserve and improve the quality of the environment and the sustainable management of global natural resources, in order to ensure sustainable development;
(g) assist populations, countries and regions confronting natural or man-made disasters;
(h) promote an international system based on stronger multilateral cooperation and good global governance.

Article 22(1) TEU provides that 'on the basis of the principles and objectives set out in Article 21, the European Council shall identify the strategic interests and objectives of the Union'. The European Council will make decisions on these strategic interests and objectives in relation to 'common foreign and security policy and to other areas of external action of the Union' (Art 22(1) TEU). The European Council will act unanimously on a recommendation from the Council; the Council will then formally adopt the decision (Art 22(1) TEU). Article 22(2) TEU provides that joint proposals may be submitted to the Council by the High Representative (with regard to common foreign and security policy) and the Commission (with regard to other areas of external action).

Common foreign and security policy

Some new legal bases have been introduced:

- a solidarity clause between Member States in the event of a terrorist attack or natural disaster (Art 222 TFEU);
- international agreements may be concluded with one or more states or international organisations in areas covered by the common foreign and security policy (Art 37 TEU).

Security policy has been modernised in a number of areas, in particular in the area of defence.

Article 24(2) TEU provides that:

Within the framework of the principles and objectives of its external action, the Union shall conduct, define and implement a common foreign and security policy, based on the development of mutual political solidarity among Member States, the identification of questions of general interest and the achievement of an ever-increasing degree of convergence of Member States' actions.

Article 26(1) TEU provides that:

The European Council shall identify the Union's strategic interests, determine the objectives of and define general guidelines for the common foreign and security policy, including for matters with defence implications. It shall adopt the necessary decisions.

Article 26(3) TEU provides that:

The common foreign and security policy shall be put into effect by the High Representative of the Union for Foreign Affairs and Security Policy and by the Member States, using national and Union resources.

Article 32 TEU provides that:

Member States shall consult one another within the European Council and the Council on any foreign and security policy of general interest in order to determine a common approach. Before undertaking any action on the international scene or entering into any commitment which could affect the Union's interests, each Member State shall consult the others within the European Council or the Council. Member States shall ensure, through the convergence of their actions, that the Union is able to assert its interests and values on the international scene. Member States shall show mutual solidarity.

Decisions relating to the common foreign and security policy are adopted by the European Council and the Council acting unanimously, except where otherwise provided (Art 31 TEU). It is not permissible to adopt legislative acts (Art 31 TEU). Any Member State, the High Representative, or the High Representative with the Commission's support, has the power to refer any question relating to the common foreign and security policy to the Council (Art 30(1) TEU).

Common security and defence policy

Article 42 TEU provides that:

1 The common security and defence policy shall be an integral part of the common foreign and security policy. It shall provide the Union with an operational capacity drawing on civil and military assets. The Union may use them on missions outside the Union for peace-keeping, conflict prevention and strengthening international security in

accordance with the principles of the United Nations Charter. The performance of these tasks shall be undertaken using capabilities provided by the Member States.

2   The common security and defence policy shall include the progressive framing of a common Union defence policy. This will lead to a common defence, when the European Council, acting unanimously, so decides. It shall in that case recommend to the Member States the adoption of such a decision in accordance with their respective constitutional requirements.

The policy of the Union in accordance with this Article shall not prejudice the specific character of the security and defence policy of certain Member States and shall respect the obligations of certain Member States, which see their common defence realised in the North Atlantic Treaty Organization (NATO), under the North Atlantic Treaty and be compatible with the common security and defence policy established within that framework.

3   Member States shall make civilian and military capabilities available to the Union for the implementation of the common security and defence policy, to contribute to the objectives defined by the Council. Those Member States which together establish multinational forces may also make them available to the common security and defence policy.

Member States shall undertake progressively to improve their military capabilities. The Agency in the field of defence capabilities development, research, acquisition and armaments (hereinafter referred to as 'the European Defence Agency') shall identify operational requirements, shall promote measures to satisfy those requirements, shall contribute to identifying and, where appropriate, implementing any measure needed to strengthen the industrial and technological base of the defence sector, shall participate in defining a European capabilities and armaments policy, and shall assist the Council in evaluating the improvement of military capabilities.

4   Decisions relating to the common security and defence policy, including those initiating a mission as referred to in this Article, shall be adopted by the Council acting unanimously on a proposal from the High Representative of the Union for Foreign Affairs and Security Policy or an initiative from a Member State. The High Representative may propose the use of both national resources and Union instruments, together with the Commission where appropriate.

5   The Council may entrust the execution of a task, within the Union framework, to a group of Member States in order to protect the Union's values and serve its interests. The execution of such a task shall be governed by Article 44.

6   Those Member States whose military capabilities fulfil higher criteria and which have made more binding commitments to one another in this area with a view to the most demanding missions shall establish permanent structured cooperation within the Union framework. Such cooperation shall be governed by Article 46. It shall not affect the provisions of Article 43.

7   If a Member State is the victim of armed aggression on its territory, the other Member States shall have towards it an obligation of aid and assistance by all the means in their power, in accordance with Article 51 of the United Nations Charter. This shall not prejudice the specific character of the security and defence policy of certain Member States.

Commitments and cooperation in this area shall be consistent with commitments under the North Atlantic Treaty Organization, which, for those States which are members of it, remains the foundation of their collective defence and the forum for its implementation.

Solidarity clause

As discussed above, Art 222 TFEU establishes a solidarity clause:

1 The Union and its Member States shall act jointly in a spirit of solidarity if a Member State is the object of a terrorist attack or the victim of a natural or man-made disaster. The Union shall mobilise all the instruments at its disposal, including the military resources made available by the Member States, to:

 (a) – prevent the terrorist threat in the territory of the Member States;
   – protect democratic institutions and the civilian population from any terrorist attack;
   – assist a Member State in its territory, at the request of its political authorities, in the event of a terrorist attack;

 (b) assist a Member State in its territory, at the request of its political authorities, in the event of a natural or man-made disaster.

2 Should a Member State be the object of a terrorist attack or the victim of a natural or man-made disaster, the other Member States shall assist it at the request of its political authorities. To that end, the Member States shall coordinate between themselves in the Council.

3 The arrangements for the implementation by the Union of the solidarity clause shall be defined by a decision adopted by the Council acting on a joint proposal by the Commission and the High Representative of the Union for Foreign Affairs and Security Policy. The Council shall act in accordance with Article 31(1) of the Treaty on European Union where this decision has defence implications. The European Parliament shall be informed.

   For the purposes of this paragraph and without prejudice to Article 240, the Council shall be assisted by the Political and Security Committee with the support of the structures developed in the context of the common security and defence policy and by the Committee referred to in Article 71; the two committees shall, if necessary, submit joint opinions.

4 The European Council shall regularly assess the threats facing the Union in order to enable the Union and its Member States to take effective action.

The Union and its neighbours

Article 8(1) TEU provides that the Union will develop a 'special relationship with neighbouring countries aiming to establish an area of prosperity and good neighbourliness, founded on the values of the Union and characterised by close and peaceful relations based on cooperation'. The Union is empowered to conclude specific agreements with the countries concerned, in order to achieve this special relationship (Art 8(2) TEU).

Union membership

Article 49 TEU sets out the conditions of eligibility, and the procedure, for accession to the Union. Any European State 'which respects the values referred to in Article 2 and is committed to promoting them' can apply to become a member of the Union. The application will be addressed to the Council, which will act unanimously after consulting the Commission and after obtaining the consent of the European Parliament, which will act by a majority of its component members. The conditions of admission and any amendments to the Treaties will be subject to agreement between the applicant state and the Member States. This agreement will require ratification by all the Member States in accordance with their constitutional requirements.

   Article 7 TEU provides for the suspension of certain rights resulting from Union membership, along similar grounds to those contained in the former Art 7 TEU (pre-ToL).

Article 50 TEU sets out, for the first time, the procedure for a Member State's voluntary withdrawal from the Union.

1 January 2013: the Treaty on Stability, Coordination and Governance

Objective 9

The EU concluded the Treaty on Stability, Coordination and Governance (TSCG) to tighten fiscal discipline in the Eurozone and deepen economic integration as a way to address the Eurozone's sovereign debt crisis. This new treaty constitutes an intergovernmental agreement outside the EU legal framework. This is because the UK vetoed its incorporation within the existing EU Treaties (i.e. the TEU and the TFEU). It is unclear how Union institutions such as the European Commission and the Court of Justice can be used to enforce what is, essentially, an international agreement among sovereign states.

The text of the treaty was finalised on 30 January 2012 and signed by the then 27 Member States (excluding the UK and the Czech Republic) on 2 March 2012. To come into force, the treaty required ratification by 12 of the 17 Eurozone members. Finland became the twelfth member to ratify the treaty on 21 December 2012. The treaty came into force on 1 January 2013.

1 July 2013: enlargement

Objective 2

At the end of 2011 all the Member States, together with Croatia, signed an Accession Treaty paving the way for Croatia's membership of the EU. This enabled Croatia to become an EU Member State on 1 July 2013, increasing the European Union from 27 to 28 Member States.

Future enlargement

In order to join the Union, each prospective Member State is required to fulfil the economic and political conditions known as the 'Copenhagen criteria' (which were adopted in 1993), according to which they must:

- be a stable democracy, respecting human rights, the rule of law, and the protection of minorities;
- have a functioning market economy;
- adopt the common rules, standards and policies that make up the body of EU law.

Turkey applied for EU membership as long ago as 14 April 1987, but its passage to entry has not been smooth. At its December 2004 meeting, the Council invited the Commission to present to the Council a proposal for a framework for negotiations with Turkey, on the basis set out below. Within the Commission's proposal, the Council was requested to agree on that framework with a view to opening negotiations on 3 October 2005. The framework for negotiations (which also applies to future candidate countries) is as follows:

The European Council agreed that accession negotiations with individual candidate states will be based on a framework for negotiations. Each framework, which will be established by the Council on a proposal by the Commission, taking account of the experience of the fifth enlargement process and of the evolving *acquis* [i.e. the total body of EU law accumulated so far], will address the following elements, according to own merits and specific situations and characteristics of each candidate state:

1 As in previous negotiations, the substance of the negotiations, which will be conducted in an Intergovernmental Conference (IGC) with the participation of all Member States on the one hand and the candidate State concerned on the other, where decisions require unanimity, will be broken down into a number of chapters, each covering a specific policy area. The Council, acting by unanimity on a proposal by the Commission, will lay down benchmarks for the provisional closure and, where appropriate, for the opening of each chapter; depending on the chapter concerned, these benchmarks will refer to legislative alignment and a satisfactory track record of implementation of the *acquis* as well as obligations deriving from contractual relations with the European Union.

2 Long transition periods, derogations, specific arrangements or permanent safeguard clauses, i.e. clauses which are permanently available as a basis for safeguard measures, may be considered. The Commission will include these, as appropriate, in its proposals for each framework, for areas such as freedom of movement of persons, structural policies or agriculture. Furthermore, the decision-taking process regarding the eventual establishment of freedom of movement of persons should allow for a maximum role of individual Member States. Transitional arrangements or safeguards should be reviewed regarding their impact on competition or the functioning of the internal market.

3 The financial aspects of accession of a candidate state must be allowed for in the applicable Financial Framework. Hence, accession negotiations yet to be opened with candidates whose accession could have substantial financial consequences can only be concluded after the establishment of the Financial Framework for the period from 2014 together with possible consequential financial reforms.

4 The shared objective of the negotiations is accession. These negotiations are an open-ended process, the outcome of which cannot be guaranteed beforehand. While taking account of all Copenhagen criteria, if the Candidate State is not in a position to assume in full all the obligations of membership it must be ensured that the Candidate State concerned is fully anchored in the European structures through the strongest possible bond.

5 In the case of a serious and persistent breach in a candidate state of the principles of liberty, democracy, respect for human rights and fundamental freedoms and the rule of law on which the Union is founded, the Commission will, on its own initiative or on the request of one-third of the Member States, recommend the suspension of negotiations and propose the conditions for eventual resumption. The Council will decide by qualified majority on such a recommendation, after having heard the Candidate State, whether to suspend the negotiations and on the conditions for their resumption. The Member States will act in the IGC in accordance with the Council decision, without prejudice to the general requirement for unanimity in the IGC. The European Parliament will be informed.

Parallel to accession negotiations, the Union will engage with every candidate state in an intensive political and cultural dialogue. With the aim of enhancing mutual understanding by bringing people together, this inclusive dialogue also will involve civil society.

Turkey

Accession negotiations between the EU and Turkey opened on 3 October 2005. An Accession Partnership was concluded on 23 January 2006 (Council Decision 2006/35/EC). The objective of the Partnership is to set out:

- priority areas which Turkey needs to address in preparation for accession;
- financial assistance guidelines for the implementation of these priority areas.

The accession negotiations were halted in June 2006 because of a trade dispute between Turkey and Southern Cyprus. The negotiations subsequently resumed in March 2007 but on 8 December 2009 the Commission decided to progress slowly with negotiations because Turkey was still refusing to open its ports and airports to Southern Cyprus.

On 10 October 2012, the European Commission adopted its Enlargement Package, which comprises a set of papers on the EU's policy on enlargement alongside an evaluation of progress towards EU membership for each country which is seeking membership. With regard to Turkey, the Commission stated that it had not yet met the EU's political and fundamental rights requirements, including those on freedom of expression. Turkey also needed to improve its relations with Southern Cyprus. On 30 October 2012, the Turkish Prime Minister (Recep Tayyip Erdoğan) said the Union would lose Turkey if it did not grant it membership by 2023.

Iceland

Iceland is a member of EFTA and the **European Economic Area (EEA)** EEA (see below). During the global credit crunch in 2008, Iceland suffered a severe financial crisis which pushed the country to the brink of bankruptcy. Iceland, which had never seriously considered EU membership before, applied for membership on 16 July 2009. On 24 February 2010 the Commission adopted its Opinion on Iceland's application (COM (2010) 62). Following the Commission's recommendation, the European Council opened accession negotiations with Iceland on 17 June 2010. Iceland's application was expected to progress smoothly through this accession procedure because of its membership of EFTA and the EEA. In May 2013, the Icelandic government took the decision to put the accession negotiations on hold, signalling an end to its proposed membership.

Former Yugoslav Republic of Macedonia

The Former Yugoslav Republic of Macedonia (FYRM) applied for EU membership on 22 March 2004 and was granted candidate-country status by the European Council on 17 December 2005. A European Partnership (the precursor to an Accession Partnership) was concluded between the EU and the FYRM on 30 January 2006 (Council Decision 2006/57/EC). During October 2009 the Commission made a recommendation that formal accession negotiations should be opened. However, since 2009 Greece and Bulgaria have vetoed the opening of membership discussions.

Montenegro

Montenegro applied for EU membership on 15 December 2008. On 9 November 2010 the Commission adopted its Opinion on Montenegro's application (COM (2010) 670). The Commission recommended that negotiations for Union accession should only be opened with Montenegro once it had achieved the necessary degree of compliance with the membership criteria. Sufficient progress was subsequently made and accession negotiations were opened on 29 June 2012.

Serbia

In June 2013 the European Council opened accession negotiations with Serbia. On 21 January 2014, the 1st Intergovernmental Conference took place, signalling the formal start of Serbia's accession negotiations.

Other potential members

The following countries are potential candidates for EU membership, when they meet the conditions:

- Albania – EU candidate status was granted on 27 June 2014;
- Bosnia and Herzegovina;
- Kosovo.

The Commission's website on enlargement is available at:

> http://ec.europa.eu/enlargement

Every autumn the Commission adopts a set of documents explaining EU policy on accepting new members:

- setting out the objectives and prospects for the coming year;
- assessing the progress made over past year by each country concerned.

The Enlargement Strategy and individual Progress Reports are available at:

> http://ec.europa.eu/enlargement/countries/strategy-and-progress-report

5 July 2015: Greece referendum

Following the global credit crunch in 2008, Greece experienced severe economic problems which resulted in Greece taking loans from the International Monetary Fund (IMF) and the **European Central Bank** (**ECB**). During June 2015, Greece defaulted on repayments of its loan to the IMF. The IMF and ECB refused to lend Greece any additional funds until Greece implemented further 'austerity reforms' to reduce its debt. The Greek government, which had been elected to office in January 2015 on an anti-austerity platform, called a referendum to enable the Greek people to vote on whether or not to accept the new austerity reforms proposed by the IMF and ECB. The referendum, which was held on 5 July 2015, resulted in the Greeks rejecting the new austerity reforms. Greece subsequently entered into new agreements with the IMF and ECB which prevented it from having to withdraw from the euro.

Key dates and events

23 July 1952	The European Coal and Steel Community (ECSC) Coal and Steel Community (ECSC) comes into force in the six founding Member States: France, (West) Germany, Italy and the Benelux countries (i.e. Belgium, The Netherlands and Luxembourg).

1 July 1958	The European Economic Community (EEC) and the European Atomic Energy Community (Euratom) come into force.
8 April 1965	Merger of the Community institutions.
1 January 1973	EU enlargement from six Member States to nine. The new Member States are Denmark, Ireland and the UK.
1 January 1981	EU enlargement from nine Member States to ten. The new Member State is Greece.
1 January 1986	EU enlargement from ten Member States to twelve. The new Member States are Portugal and Spain.
1 July 1987	The Single European Act (SEA) comes into force.
1 January 1993	The target date for completion of the internal market: 'an area without frontiers where the free movement of goods, persons, services and capital is ensured'.
1 November 1993	The Treaty on European Union (TEU) comes into force.
1 January 1995	EU enlargement from 12 Member States to 15. The new Member States are Austria, Finland and Sweden.
1 May 1999	The Treaty of Amsterdam (ToA) comes into force.
1 January 2002	The euro becomes legal tender in 12 Member States.
23 July 2002	The European Coal and Steel Community (ECSC) comes to an end.
1 February 2003	The Treaty of Nice (ToN) comes into force.
1 May 2004	EU enlargement from 15 Member States to 25. The new Member States are Cyprus (South), Czech Republic, Estonia, Hungary, Latvia, Lithuania, Malta, Poland, Slovakia and Slovenia.
1 January 2007	EU enlargement from 25 Member States to 27. The new Member States are Bulgaria and Romania.
1 January 2007	Slovenia joins the euro.
1 January 2008	Cyprus (South) and Malta join the euro.
1 January 2009	Slovakia joins the euro.
1 December 2009	The Treaty of Lisbon (ToL) comes into force.
1 January 2011	Estonia joins the euro.
1 January 2013	Treaty on Stability, Coordination and Governance (TSCG) comes into force.
1 July 2013	EU enlargement from 27 to 28 Member States. The new Member State is Croatia.
1 January 2014	Latvia joins the euro.
1 January 2015	Lithuania joins the euro.

A two-speed Europe?

The idea of a 'two-speed Europe' was much canvassed before the Amsterdam Intergovernmental Conference, at which the ToA was adopted. The concept of a 'two-speed Europe' meant that the states which were keen to embrace closer political and economic cooperation would be free to do so, while the other more reluctant states could follow at their own pace. To some extent, this had already happened in relation to economic and monetary union, with the UK, Denmark and Sweden negotiating opt-outs (see above).

The ToA went some way to formally recognising this kind of 'variable geometry'. Under the former Art 11 EC Treaty, the Council could authorise 'closer cooperation' between Member States. The Council would act on a proposal from the Commission. The ToN substantially amended this provision, and the former Arts 43–45 TEU established a system of 'enhanced cooperation'.

When the ToL came into force on 1 December 2009, it incorporated 'enhanced cooperation' into both the TEU and TFEU. Article 20 TEU provides for a system of 'enhanced cooperation', the detailed provisions of which are set out within Arts 326–334 TFEU.

See pages 34–36 for an explanation of the Union's non-exclusive competencies.

As discussed above, enhanced cooperation requires the involvement of at least nine Member States (Art 20(2) TEU). It only applies to the Union's non-exclusive competences (Art 20(1) TEU). Authorisation to proceed with enhanced cooperation is granted by a decision of the Council acting by a qualified majority, after obtaining the consent of the European Parliament, on a proposal from the Commission (Art 329(1) TFEU). With regard to the common foreign and security policy, authorisation to proceed may only be granted by a decision of the Council acting unanimously, after obtaining the opinion of: (i) the High Representative of the Union for Foreign Affairs and Security Policy; and (ii) the Commission. In this case, the European Parliament is simply informed (Art 329(2) TFEU). In both cases, the Council's decision authorising enhanced cooperation may only be adopted 'as a last resort when it has established that the objectives of such cooperation cannot be obtained within a reasonable period by the Union as a whole' (Art 20(2) TEU).

It is unlikely that the Commission will favour, or want to initiate, a process of separate development. There are two main reasons for this. First, a European Union in which there are different rules between the 'outer' and 'inner' areas will be extremely difficult to operate in practice. The Commission would not be in favour of having a body of rules which operates in different parts of the Union. Second, any further development of an 'inner core' of Member States, which is moving towards greater integration, will tend to accentuate what is already a tendency in the Union: the serious drift of commerce and industry towards the geographical centre of Western Europe. If Germany is in the 'inner core', because its economy is usually strong and it enjoys the largest market of all the Member States, businesses may tend to re-establish themselves nearer to the heart of Europe. Businesses from outside the Union seeking to circumvent the EU's external tariff wall may tend to look for locations in states which are in the inner core rather than in states on the periphery. For both these reasons, the Commission is likely to resist any further measures which may make the integration of Union markets more difficult rather than less difficult, which is likely to be the case if a body of rules is adopted which only applies within part of the Union.

UK referendum: in or out

Following the election to office of a majority conservative government in May 2015, by the end of 2017 a referendum will be held on the UK's continued membership of the European Union. Within the context of this referendum the UK government is negotiating reforms of the EU with the other 27 Member States, some of which may require amendments to the TEU and TFEU.

The European Economic Area

The remaining states within the European Free Trade Association (EFTA) continued to work together as a free trade area after the departure of Ireland, Denmark and the UK in 1973 (see above). On 2 May 1992, the then seven EFTA states, the EU and the Member States, signed an agreement to establish the European Economic Area (EEA). The EEA, which some initially saw as an alternative to full membership of the European Union, was intended to integrate the EFTA states *economically* into the Union without giving them a role in its institutions. The EEA gave the EFTA states access for their goods, persons, services and capital to the markets of the Union. Equally, the same facilities were granted by EFTA states in their territories to Member States of the EU. Only Switzerland refused to participate in the EEA, after a hostile national referendum. In this new trading area, all the *economic* rules of the EU apply, although the Member States of EFTA are not represented in any of the EU institutions and do not participate in the EU's decision-making process. Four bodies were established to coordinate the functioning of the EEA:

● The EEA Council;

● Joint Committee;

● Joint Parliamentary Committee;

● Consultative Committee.

The EEA came into effect on 1 January 1994. On 1 January 1995, three of the remaining EFTA members became full members of the EU, so that the EEA states now comprise the existing 28 EU Member States together with Iceland, Liechtenstein and Norway.

Summary

Now you have read this chapter you should be able to:

● Outline the aims and objectives of the European Communities, explaining how and why they came into existence.

● Evaluate the impact the following Treaties have had on the founding Treaties and the composition, role and function of the European Communities and the European Union:
  ● Single European Act;
  ● Treaty of European Union;
  ● Treaty of Amsterdam;
  ● Treaty of Nice.

● Explain how the Treaty of Lisbon amended the founding Treaties, with a specific reference to:
  ● the renaming of the EC Treaty to the Treaty on the Functioning of the European Union (TFEU);
  ● the renumbering of the TEU and TFEU;
  ● the European Community's replacement and succession by the European Union, resulting in the merger of the three pillars of the European Union;
  ● the legal status of the European Convention on Human Rights and the European Court of Human Rights, in the context of EU law.

- Explain the purpose of the Treaty on Stability, Coordination and Governance.
- Understand the nature of the European Free Trade Association and the European Economic Area in terms of their membership, reason for existence, role and relevance.

Reference

Hobsbawm, E. (1994) *Age of Extremes: The Short Twentieth Century*, Michael Joseph, Chapters 2, 3 and 8.

Further reading

Textbooks

Craig, P. and De Burca, G. (2011) *EU Law: Text, Cases and Materials* (5th edn), Oxford University Press, Chapter 1.

Foster, N. (2015) *Foster on EU Law* (5th edn), Oxford University Press, Chapter 1.

Steiner, J. and Woods, L. (2014) *EU Law* (12th edn), Oxford University Press, Chapter 1.

Weatherill, S. (2014) *Cases and Materials on EU Law* (11th edn), Oxford University Press, Chapter 1.

Journal articles

Baker, E. and Harding, C., 'From past imperfect to future imperfect? A longitudinal study of the third pillar' (2009) 34 EL Rev 25.

Barrett, G., '"The king is dead, long live the king": The recasting by the Treaty of Lisbon of the provisions of the Constitutional Treaty concerning national parliaments' (2008) 33 EL Rev 66.

Belling, V., 'Supranational fundamental rights or primacy of sovereignty?' (2012) 18 ELJ 251.

Boerger, A. and Rasmussen, M., 'Transforming European law: The establishment of the constitutional discourse from 1950 to 1993' (2014) 10 ECL Rev 199.

Cantore, C.M. and Martinico, G., 'Asymmetry or disintegration? A few considerations on the new Treaty on Stability, Coordination and Governance in the Economic and Monetary Union' (2013) 19 EPL 463.

Craig, P., 'The Treaty of Lisbon, process, architecture and substance' (2008) 33 EL Rev 137.

Dashwood, A., 'The United Kingdom in a re-formed European Union' (2013) 38 EL Rev 737.

Dougan, M., 'The Treaty of Lisbon 2007: Winning minds, not hearts' (2008) 45 CML Rev 617.

Doukas, D., 'The verdict of the German Federal Constitutional Court on the Lisbon Treaty: Not guilty, but don't do it again!' (2009) 34 EL Rev 866.

Elliott, M., 'Constitutional legislation, European Union law and the nature of the United Kingdom's contemporary constitution' (2014) 10 ECL Rev 379.

Goldoni, M., 'Reconstructing the early warning system on subsidiarity: The case for political judgment' (2014) 39 EL Rev 647.

Haukeland Fredriksen, H., 'Bridging the widening gap between EU treaties and the Agreement on the European Economic Area' (2012) 18 ELJ 868.

Hinarejos, A., 'Integration in criminal matters and the role of the Court of Justice' (2011) 36 EL Rev 420.

Kingston, S., 'Ireland's options after the Lisbon referendum: Strategies, implications and competing visions of Europe' (2009) 34 EL Rev 455.

Leczykiewicz, D., 'Constitutional conflicts and the third pillar' (2008) 33 EL Rev 230.

Leczykiewicz, D., '"Effective judicial protection" of human rights after Lisbon: Should national courts be empowered to review EU secondary law?' (2010) 35 EL Rev 326.

Lock, T., 'EU accession to the ECHR: Implications for the judicial review in Strasbourg' (2010) 35 ECL Rev 777.

Majone, G., 'Unity in diversity: European integration and the enlargement process' (2008) 33 EL Rev 457.

Messina, M., 'Strengthening economic governance of the European Union through enhanced cooperation: A still possible, but already missed, opportunity' (2014) 39 EL Rev 404.

Mitsilegas, V., 'The third wave of third pillar law. Which direction for EU criminal justice?' (2009) 34 EL Rev 523.

Organ, J., 'Decommissioning direct democracy? A critical analysis of Commission decision-making on the legal admissibility of European Citizens Initiative proposals' (2014) 10 ECL Rev 422.

Pech, L., '"A Union founded on the rule of law": Meaning and reality of the rule of law as a constitutional principle of EU law' (2010) 6 ECL Rev 359.

Schutze, R., 'Lisbon and the federal order of competences: A prospective analysis' (2008) 33 EL Rev 709.

Semmelmann, C., 'The European Union's economic constitution under the Lisbon Treaty: Soul-searching among lawyers shifts the focus to procedure' (2010) 35 ECL Rev 516.

Shuibhne, N.N., 'The reality of rights: From rhetoric to opt-out' (2009) 34 EL Rev 815.

Snell, J., '"European constitutional settlement", an ever closer Union, and the Treaty of Lisbon: Democracy or relevance?' (2008) 33 EL Rev 619.

Weiss, W., 'Human rights in the EU: Rethinking the role of the European Convention on Human Rights after Lisbon' (2011) 7 ECL Rev 64.

2

Sources of EU law (including general principles of law and fundamental rights)

Objectives

At the end of this chapter you should understand the nature and scope of the following sources of EU law:

1. The EU Treaties, in particular the Treaty on European Union (TEU) and the Treaty on the Functioning of the European Union (TFEU).
2. Secondary legislation made under the EU Treaties.
3. 'Soft law' comprising non-legally enforceable instruments, which may aid the interpretation and/or application of EU law.
4. Related Treaties made between the Member States.
5. International Treaties negotiated by the Union under powers conferred on it by the EU Treaties.
6. Decisions of the Court of Justice of the European Union (which includes the General Court).
7. General principles of law and fundamental rights upon which the constitutional laws of the Member States are based.

The sources of EU law

There are seven principal sources of EU law, each of which will be considered further within this chapter:

- The EU Treaties, in particular the Treaty on European Union (TEU) and the Treaty on the Functioning of the European Union (TFEU).
- **Secondary legislation** made under the EU Treaties.
- **'Soft law'** (i.e. non-legally enforceable instruments which may aid the interpretation and/or application of EU law).
- Related Treaties made between the Member States.
- International Treaties negotiated by the Union under powers conferred on it by the EU Treaties.
- Decisions of the Court of Justice of the European Union.
- General principles of law and fundamental rights upon which the constitutional laws of the Member States are based.

The EU Treaties

Objective
1

The principal EU Treaties are:

● the Treaty on European Union (TEU);

● the Treaty on the Functioning of the European Union (TFEU).

The TFEU was previously entitled the EC Treaty, having been renamed by the Treaty of Lisbon (ToL) when it came into force on 1 December 2009. The ToL amended the TEU and the TFEU. Article 1 TEU (as amended by the ToL) now provides that the TEU and the TFEU constitute the Treaties on which the Union is founded.

Prior to the ToL it was common to refer to the European Community in addition to the European Union. However, the ToL amended the TEU to provide that the Union replaces and succeeds the Community (Art 1 TEU). Throughout the TFEU, the word 'Community' has been replaced with the word 'Union'. The following terms are therefore no longer used: European *Community*; European *Communities*; or *Community* law. Reference is made solely to the European *Union* (or *Union*) and European *Union* law (or *Union* law).

The articles within both the TEU and TFEU have been renumbered by the ToL as part of a simplification exercise. The Treaty of Amsterdam (ToA) originally renumbered the provisions of the TEU and the EC Treaty when it came into force on 1 May 1999. The renumbering of the TEU and the TFEU by the ToL is therefore the second time this has occurred. Care must be taken when referring to EU case law, legislation and documents, to ensure that the old numbering (i.e. pre-ToA and pre-ToL) is distinguished from the numbering used post-ToA and post-ToL. The ToL renumbering came into effect on 1 December 2009. For some time it will be necessary to be aware of both the old and new numbering. Subsequent chapters of this book are based on the post-ToL Treaty numbers but, where appropriate, there are cross-references to pre-ToL Treaty numbers.

The TEU and the TFEU form the 'constitution' of the European Union and are therefore an important source of Union law. Although they do not purport to create the constitution of a federal state, in some respects they do have that effect. The TFEU has been interpreted in that way by the Court of Justice:

Opinion 1/91 on the Draft Agreement between the EEC and EFTA
[1991] ECR 6079

> The Court of Justice stated that:
>
> The EEC Treaty [renamed the EC Treaty by the TEU, and the TFEU by the ToL], albeit concluded in the form of an international agreement, nonetheless constitutes the constitutional charter of a Community [i.e. Union] based on the rule of law. As the Court of Justice has consistently held, the Community [i.e. Union] Treaties established a new legal order for the benefit of which the States had limited their sovereign rights, in ever wider fields, and the subjects of which comprised not only the Member States but also their nationals.
>
> The essential characteristics of the Community [i.e. Union] legal order which had thus been established were, in particular, its primacy over the law of Member States and the **direct effect** of a whole series of provisions which were applicable to their nationals and to the Member States themselves.

Although fulfilling many of the functions of a constitution for the Union, the EU Treaties still fall far short of creating a federal state. Even though EU law prevails in Member States, the Union depends on national courts and enforcement agencies to implement it. The EU Treaties most closely resemble a constitution in the way in which they define the competence of the Union itself, and each of its constituent parts and, to a lesser extent, the rights of its citizens. Although the Treaties do not contain a complete catalogue of citizens' rights, they do confer a number of rights which can be enforced directly in the national courts. Ultimately, the Court of Justice acts as guarantor of those rights and has, in fact, quite consciously used the doctrine of 'direct enforcement' (also referred to as 'direct effect') to empower citizens in their own courts and, if need be, against their own governments. A whole range of TFEU provisions have been held to create directly enforceable rights, among them:

- the right not to be discriminated against on grounds of nationality (Art 18 TFEU; previously Art 12 EC Treaty);
- the right to equal pay for work of equal value, regardless of gender (Art 157 TFEU; previously Art 141 EC Treaty);
- the right to seek work and remain as a worker in another Member State (Art 45 TFEU; previously Art 39 EC Treaty);
- the right to receive and provide services (Art 56 TFEU; previously Art 49 EC Treaty);
- the right not to be subjected to import taxes (Art 30 TFEU; previously Art 25 EC Treaty);
- the right to take action against another **undertaking** for breach of the competition rules (Art 102 TFEU; previously Art 82 EC Treaty; see *Garden Cottage Foods* **v** *Milk Marketing Board* [1984] AC 130).

This principle of direct enforcement/direct effect is considered in detail in Chapter 9.

The TEU and the TFEU

The TEU and the TFEU require further consideration. As the Court of Justice stated in *Opinion 1/91* (see above): '... the Community [i.e. Union] Treaties established a new legal order for the benefit of which the States had limited their sovereign rights, in ever wider fields'.

The Union's competences and the principle of conferral

The reference to 'ever wider fields' in *Opinion 1/91* refers, in part, to the limited nature of the Union's competences, in that the Union can act only in those policy areas where the Member States have given it the power to act through the TEU and the TFEU. It also recognises the fact that each time the EU Treaties have been amended the result has been that the powers of the Union have been enhanced through, for example, the inclusion of more policy areas.

Article 5(1) TEU provides that 'the limits of Union competences are governed by the principle of conferral'. This means the Union shall act 'only within the limits of the competences conferred upon it by the Member States in the Treaties to attain the objectives set out therein' (Art 5(2) TEU). The corollary is that 'Competences not conferred upon the Union in the Treaties remain with the Member States' (Art 5(2) TEU). The exercise of Union competences is also stated to be governed by 'the principles of subsidiarity and proportionality' (Art 5(1) TEU). This provision is complemented by a Protocol on the application of these two principles (Protocol No. 2, which is annexed to the TEU and TFEU), which incorporates an 'early-warning system' involving national parliaments in the monitoring of how subsidiarity is applied. National parliaments are informed of all new legislative initiatives and if at least one-third of them are of the view that a proposal infringes the principle of subsidiarity, the Commission will have to reconsider the proposal.

In order to understand the extent of the Union's legal competences it is essential to be familiar with the contents of the TEU and the TFEU. A useful starting point is to consider the index to both Treaties.

Index to the TEU

The index to the TEU, as amended, is as follows:

Preamble

Title I	**Common Provisions**
Title II	**Provisions on Democratic Principles**
Title III	**Provisions on the Institutions**
Title IV	**Provisions on Enhanced Cooperation**
Title V	**General Provisions on the Union's External Action and Specific Provisions on the Common Foreign and Security Policy**
	Chapter 1 *General provisions on the Union's external action*
	Chapter 2 *Specific provisions on the common foreign and security policy*
	Section 1 Common provisions
	Section 2 Provisions on the common security and defence policy
Title VI	**Final Provisions**

The full text of the TEU, as amended, is available at:

http://eur-lex.europa.eu/collection/eu-law/treaties.html

Index to the TFEU

The index to the TFEU, as amended, is as follows:

Preamble

Part One	**Principles**	
	Title I	*Categories and areas of Union competence*
	Title II	*Provisions having general application*
Part Two	**Non-discrimination and Citizenship of the Union**	
Part Three	**Union Policies and Internal Actions**	
	Title I	*The internal market*
	Title II	*Free movement of goods*
	Chapter 1	The customs union
	Chapter 2	Customs cooperation
	Chapter 3	Prohibition of quantitative restrictions between Member States
	Title III	*Agriculture and fisheries*
	Title IV	*Free movement of persons, services and capital*
	Chapter 1	Workers
	Chapter 2	Right of establishment
	Chapter 3	Services
	Chapter 4	Capital and payments

The full text of the TFEU, as amended, is available at:

http://eur-lex.europa.eu/collection/eu-law/treaties.html

Protocols, annexes and declarations

Both the TEU and TFEU are followed by a number of protocols, annexes and declarations. Protocols and annexes are given legal effect within the Union legal system by Art 51 TEU (previously Art 311 EC Treaty), which provides that:

> The Protocols and Annexes to the Treaties [i.e. the TEU and TFEU] shall form an integral part thereof.

Declarations may be legally effective within the Union legal system, if they are adopted by the Council (as most are). The agreement taken at the Edinburgh Summit, for example, following Denmark's rejection of the TEU in a referendum, is an example of a non-legally enforceable agreement. At this summit a decision and declaration on Denmark was taken, not by the Council, but by the heads of state and governments meeting within the European Council. This is more akin to an international agreement and does not form part of the Union legal system.

The Union's objectives

As discussed in Chapter 1, the Union's objectives, set out in Art 3 TEU, are much more succinct than the combined objectives in the former Art 3 EC Treaty (in respect of the former European Community) and the former Art 2 TEU (in respect of the European Union). Article 3 TEU, which replaced both of these provisions when the ToL came into force on 1 December 2009, provides that:

1 The Union's aim is to promote peace, its values and the well-being of its peoples.

2 The Union shall offer its citizens an area of freedom, security and justice without internal frontiers, in which the free movement of persons is ensured in conjunction with appropriate measures with respect to external border controls, asylum, immigration and the prevention and combating of crime.

3 The Union shall establish an internal market. It shall work for the sustainable development of Europe based on balanced economic growth and price stability, a highly competitive social market economy, aiming at full employment and social progress, and a high level of protection and improvement of the quality of the environment. It shall promote scientific and technological advance.

   It shall combat social exclusion and discrimination, and shall promote social justice and protection, equality between women and men, solidarity between generations and protection of the rights of the child.

It shall promote economic, social and territorial cohesion, and solidarity among Member States.

It shall respect its rich cultural and linguistic diversity, and shall ensure that Europe's cultural heritage is safeguarded and enhanced.

4 The Union shall establish an economic and monetary union whose currency is the euro.

5 In its relations with the wider world, the Union shall uphold and promote its values and interests and contribute to the protection of its citizens. It shall contribute to peace, security, the sustainable development of the Earth, solidarity and mutual respect among peoples, free and fair trade, eradication of poverty and the protection of human rights, in particular the rights of the child, as well as to the strict observance and the development of international law, including respect for the principles of the United Nations Charter.

6 The Union shall pursue its objectives by appropriate means commensurate with the competences which are conferred upon it in the Treaties.

Article 3 TEU sets out the broad objectives of the Union; objectives which include not only economic policies but also social and political policies. But how does the Union operate and function – is it run by the Member States?

The Union's institutional framework

The following seven Union institutions are established by Art 13(1) TEU:

- the European Parliament;
- the European Council;
- the Council;
- the European Commission (to be referred to as the 'Commission');
- the Court of Justice of the European Union;
- the European Central Bank;
- the Court of Auditors.

Articles 13–19 TEU clarify the role of the Union institutions. Part Six, Title I TFEU contains the detailed provisions governing the institutions. Together, these provisions constitute the Union's institutional framework. Article 13(1) TEU provides that, through the Union's institutional framework, the EU institutions shall aim to:

... promote its [i.e. the Union's] values, advance its objectives, serve its interests, those of its citizens and those of the Member States, and ensure the consistency, effectiveness and continuity of its policies and actions.

Each of these EU institutions must act within the powers granted to them under the EU Treaties. If any institution exceeds its powers as defined within the Treaties, any resultant act can be struck down as being *ultra vires*, i.e. in excess of its powers.

In the next three chapters it will be noted that in addition to these seven institutions, the Treaty provides for other named bodies to be established, and defines their role. Two such bodies are specifically referred to in Art 13(4) TEU: the European Economic and Social Committee, and the Committee of the Regions, both of which shall assist the European Parliament, the Council and the Commission.

Union policies

Part Three of the TFEU amplifies the broad Art 3 TEU objectives of the Union by setting out, in more detail, the substantive Union policies.

For example, Art 3(3) TEU provides that the Union shall establish an 'internal market'. Article 26(2) TFEU elaborates on this broad policy objective by stating that the internal market shall comprise 'an area without internal frontiers in which the free movement of goods, persons, services and capital is ensured in accordance with the provisions of the Treaties'. The more detailed provisions of the internal market are set out within Part Three of the TFEU. Part Three, Title IV TFEU governs the free movement of persons, services and capital. With regard to the free movement of persons, Part Three, Title IV, Chapter 1 TFEU contains four articles (Arts 45–48 TFEU) which are specifically concerned with the free movement of workers.

Article 45 TFEU defines the policy area of the free movement of workers in more detail, but it is still stated in quite broad terms. The first thing to note about Art 45 is that it is limited to the free movement of *workers*, not persons generally. Article 45 TFEU provides that:

1   Freedom of movement for workers shall be secured within the Union.

2   Such freedom of movement shall entail the abolition of any discrimination based on nationality between workers of the Member States as regards employment, remuneration and other conditions of work and employment.

3   It shall entail the right, subject to limitations justified on grounds of public policy, public security or public health:
    (a)   to accept offers of employment actually made;
    (b)   to move freely within the territory of Member States for this purpose;
    (c)   to stay in a Member State for the purpose of employment in accordance with the provisions governing the employment of nationals of that State laid down by law, regulation or administrative action;
    (d)   to remain in the territory of a Member State after having been employed in that State, subject to conditions which shall be embodied in regulations to be drawn up by the Commission.

4   The provisions of this Article shall not apply to employment in the public service.

Article 46 TFEU provides that the European Parliament and the Council shall issue directives or make regulations setting out the measures required to bring about the free movement of workers as defined in Art 45 TFEU. Article 46 TFEU provides that:

The European Parliament and the Council shall ... issue directives or make regulations setting out the measures required to bring about freedom of movement for workers, as defined in Article 45 ...

In many instances, the TFEU provides a framework of broad policies, which are to be supplemented by further *measures* to be adopted by certain Union institutions. In the case of Art 45, these further measures are in the form of directives and regulations, and the institutions which will adopt the directive or regulation are the European Parliament and the Council. The institutions and the legislative process will be considered further in the next three chapters. The measures which may be adopted are the next source of Union law.

Secondary legislation made under the EU Treaties

Objective
2

Article 288, para 1 TFEU (previously Art 249, para 1 EC Treaty) sets out the different types of Union legal acts:

To exercise the Union's competences, the institutions shall adopt regulations, directives, decisions, recommendations and opinions.

The consequences of the Union legal act depend upon its specific nature:

- *Regulations* shall have general application. They shall be binding in their entirety and directly applicable in all Member States (Art 288, para 2 TFEU).
- *Directives* shall be binding, as to the result to be achieved, upon each Member State to which they are addressed, but shall leave to the national authorities the choice of form and methods (Art 288, para 3 TFEU).
- *Decisions* shall be binding in their entirety. A decision which specifies those to whom it is addressed shall be binding only upon them (Art 288, para 4 TFEU).
- *Recommendations and opinions* shall have no binding force (Art 288, para 5 TFEU).

Article 288 TFEU provides that regulations, directives and decisions are 'binding' and are therefore legally enforceable. In contrast, Art 288 provides that recommendations and opinions have 'no binding force' and are therefore not legally enforceable. The former three legally enforceable measures are considered next, whereas the latter two are considered in the section entitled 'Soft law'.

Regulations

Article 288 TFEU provides that a regulation shall be binding upon all Member States and is *directly applicable* within all such states. Article 297(1) TFEU (previously Art 254 EC Treaty) provides that all legislative acts (which include regulations) must be published in the *Official Journal*, an official Union publication that consists of two related series and a supplement:

- **The L series (legislation)** contains all the legislative acts whose publication is obligatory under the Treaties, as well as other acts.
- **The C series (information and notices)** covers the complete range of information other than legislation.
- **The S series** is a supplement containing invitations to tender for public works and supply contracts.

The L and C series are published daily (except Sunday) and the supplement is published every day from Tuesday to Saturday. Being a legislative act, a regulation will be published in the L series. The regulation will be cited alongside a reference such as OJ 1990 L 257/13 (this is a reference for an EU regulation on the control of concentrations between businesses). The reference is decoded as: Year 1990, the L series of the *Official Journal*, issue number 257, page 13. The regulation enters into force on the date specified in the regulation, or – if there is no such date specified – on the twentieth day following its publication in the *Official Journal* (Art 288(1) TFEU (previously Art 191 EC Treaty)).

Issues of the *Official Journal* which have been published since 1998 are available at:

http://eur-lex.europa.eu/oj/direct-access.html

Directly applicable

As stated above, Art 288 TFEU provides that a regulation shall be *directly applicable*. Normally if a state enters into an agreement with another state, although that agreement may be binding in international law, it will only be effective in the legal system of that state if it is incorporated into national law in accordance with the state's constitutional requirements.

For example, if the UK entered into an agreement with France, in order for the agreement to be enforceable in UK courts an Act of Parliament would normally have to be enacted. The Act may incorporate (e.g. copy) the agreement into the relevant Act, or it may simply refer to the agreement and provide for it to be effective in the UK.

An EU regulation is an agreement made by an international body, the European Union. For the regulation to be incorporated into the national legal system, implementing legislation would have to be enacted by the national legislature. This would be very burdensome, because the Union adopts a vast number of regulations each year. The whole Union system would very quickly grind to a halt if a regulation had to be incorporated into the national law of each Member State before it was effective. Regulations, especially in the agricultural policy area, quite often require speedy implementation in order to have the desired effect. Such regulations would lose their effect if the Union had to await incorporation by each Member State into their respective national legal systems.

It is for this reason that Art 288 TFEU provides that a regulation shall be *directly applicable*. This means that EU regulations shall be taken to have been incorporated into the national legal system of each of the Member States automatically, and come into force in accordance with Art 297 TFEU (see above). They are binding on anyone coming within their scope throughout the whole of the European Union. They require no further action by Member States and can be applied by the courts of the Member States as soon as they become operative.

In the UK, the European Communities Act 1972 (as amended) provides for the direct applicability of EU regulations.

Directives

A directive differs from a regulation in that it applies only to those Member States to whom it is addressed, although normally a directive will be addressed to all the Member States. A directive sets out the result to be achieved, but leaves some choice to each Member State as to the form and method of achieving the end result. A directive will quite often provide a Member State with a range of options it can choose from when implementing the measure.

A directive is not directly applicable. It requires each Member State to incorporate the directive in order for it to be given effect in the national legal system. In the UK, this requires the enactment of an Act of Parliament or delegated legislation.

As stated above, Art 297(1) TFEU provides that all legislative acts (which include directives) must be published in the *Official Journal*. Directives will come into force on the date specified in the directive or, if no date is specified, on the twentieth day after publication in the *Official Journal* (Art 297(1) TFEU).

Regulation or directive?

Enabling the Union to legislate by means of either a regulation or a directive provides some flexibility. Very few Treaty articles provide that a specific instrument must be used.

This flexibility is necessary given the difference between the instruments. As discussed above, regulations are directly applicable in that they become part of the Member States' national legal systems just as they are. It is therefore necessary for a regulation to be precise and clear. Compare this to a directive, which is a much more flexible instrument. A directive sets out the result to be achieved, while leaving some degree of discretion to the Member State as to the choice of form and method for achieving that end result. However, despite this apparent flexibility, a directive may nevertheless contain very specific provisions, leaving very little discretion to the Member State.

Usually the EU institution empowered to propose an instrument is provided with some degree of flexibility as to the mode of instrument chosen, be it a regulation, a directive or some other instrument. However, some Treaty articles actually specify the mode of instrument. For example, Art 109 TFEU (previously Art 89 EC Treaty) provides that:

> The Council, on a proposal from the Commission and after consulting the European Parliament, may make any appropriate **regulations** for the application of Articles 107 and 108 ... [emphasis added]

Also, Art 115 TFEU (previously Art 94 EC Treaty) provides that:

> ... the Council shall, acting unanimously in accordance with a special legislative procedure and after consulting the European Parliament and the Economic and Social Committee, issue **directives** for the approximation of such laws, regulations or administrative provisions of the Member States as directly affect the establishment or functioning of the internal market. [emphasis added]

Decisions

Article 288 TFEU provides that a decision is binding in its entirety. Article 297(2) TFEU (previously Art 254(3) EC Treaty) provides that if a decision specifies those to whom it is addressed, such persons must be notified of the decision, and the decision will only take effect upon such notification. However, if a decision does not specify those to whom it is addressed, the decision must be published in the *Official Journal*, and it will take effect either on the date specified in the decision or, if there is no such date specified, on the twentieth day following its publication in the *Official Journal* (Art 297(2) TFEU).

The same can be said of decisions as can be said of regulations and directives, in that the Treaty articles are generally left open to allow the relevant institution to determine the actual mode of the instrument. However, some articles actually specify that the mode of the instrument shall be a decision. For example, Art 105(2) TFEU (previously Art 85(2) EC Treaty) provides that:

> If the infringement is not brought to an end, the Commission shall record such infringement of the principles in a reasoned **decision** ... [emphasis added]

Article 105(2) TFEU concerns infringement of Union competition rules.

Legal base

The relevant institution, so empowered by the Treaty, may choose the relevant mode for an instrument, unless the Treaty specifies that a particular mode must be used. Articles 45 and 46 TFEU relating to the free movement of workers were discussed above. Article 46 provides that:

> The European Parliament and the Council shall ... issue **directives or** make **regulations** setting out the measures required to bring about freedom of movement for workers, as defined in Article 45 ... [emphasis added]

The Council has adopted a number of directives and regulations pursuant to Art 46 TFEU. For example, Regulation 492/2011 of the European Parliament and the Council of 5 April 2011 on the freedom of movement for workers within the Union [OJ 2011 L 141/1].

Article 46 TFEU is said to be the *legal base* which empowers the Union institutions to adopt secondary legislation in relation to the policy of free movement of workers. Whenever the institutions seek to adopt secondary legislation, the institution which makes the proposal (more often than not the Commission) must find a relevant legal base within the Treaty. Without a legal base, the institutions are prevented from acting.

Soft law

Objective 3

Non-legally enforceable instruments which may aid the interpretation and/or application of Union law are referred to as 'soft laws' (Snyder, 1993). Such instruments may be referred to by the Court of Justice of the European Union when interpreting and/or applying Union law. One particular form of 'soft law' is considered further: recommendations and opinions.

Recommendations and opinions

Article 288 TFEU explicitly states that recommendations and opinions shall not have any binding force. However, the use of these two instruments may help clarify matters in a formal way. The former Art 211 EC Treaty empowered the Commission to formulate recommendations or deliver opinions on matters dealt with in the Treaty, not only where expressly provided for, but also whenever it considered it necessary. This has not been replicated in the TEU and the TFEU, as amended by the ToL. However, Art 17(1) TEU states that the Commission shall 'promote the general interest of the Union and take appropriate initiatives to that end'. This provision empowers the Commission to formulate recommendations or deliver opinions as appropriate, provided they 'promote the general interest of the Union'.

Although recommendations and opinions have no immediate legal force, they may achieve some legal effect as persuasive authority if they are subsequently referred to, and taken notice of, in a decision of the Court of Justice. National courts are bound to take them into account when interpreting Union measures, where they throw light on the purpose of the legislation: ***Grimaldi v Fonds des Maladies Professionnelles*** (Case C-322/88).

Related treaties made between the Member States

Objective 4

Treaties which are related to the original EU Treaties and which either amend or enlarge them are themselves a source of EU law. Within this category, as a source of law, are the Merger Treaties, the Single European Act, the Treaty on European Union, the Treaty of Amsterdam, the Treaty of Nice, the Treaty of Lisbon, the Treaty on Stability, Coordination and Governance, and the Treaties of Accession. A Treaty of Accession is necessary when the Union is enlarged. The last Accession Treaty was concluded in 2011 to pave the way for Croatia's membership on 1 July 2013. Like the original Treaties themselves, the Treaties of Accession have been held to confer directly enforceable rights on individuals (***Rush Portuguesa v Office National d'Immigration*** (Case C-113/89)).

International treaties negotiated by the Union under powers conferred by the EU Treaties

Objective 5

Article 47 TEU provides that the Union shall have legal personality, enabling it to enter into international treaties and agreements on behalf of the Member States.

This category includes not only multilateral treaties to which the Union is a party, such as the General Agreement on Tariffs and Trade (GATT), but Association Agreements concluded by the Union with individual states. The GATT agreement was held in *International Fruit* (Case 21–24/72) to be binding on the Union. The Court of Justice has also held that undertakings which complain to the Commission of illicit commercial practices which breach the Union's commercial policy instrument may rely upon the GATT as forming part of the rules of international law to which the instrument applies (*Fediol* (Case 70/87)).

The principle of direct enforceability (or direct effect) is considered on pages 274–292 and 303–305.

In *Kupferberg* (Case 104/81), the Court of Justice held that Art 21 of the EEC–Portugal Association Agreement was directly enforceable in the national courts. The principle of direct enforcement of such agreements has enabled the nationals of states which are parties to such agreements to enforce the agreement's provisions against Member States of the Union (the principle of direct enforcement is considered further in Chapter 9). In *Kziber* (Case C-18/90), the Court of Justice held that parts of the EEC–Morocco Cooperation Agreement are directly enforceable (see also, *Yousfi* v *Belgium* (Case C-58/93)).

Decisions of the Court of Justice of the European Union

Objective 6

Article 19(1) TEU, as amended by the ToL, provides that 'the Court of Justice, the General Court and specialised courts' shall be collectively referred to as the Court of Justice of the European Union. The former Court of First Instance has been renamed the General Court.

The jurisprudence (i.e. case law) of the Court of Justice of the European Union is a major source of law. It comprises not only all the formal decisions of the Court, but also the principles enunciated in its judgments and opinions. The Treaties and the implementing legislation do not, between them, contain an exhaustive statement of the relevant law, and much of the work of the Court of Justice of the European Union has been to put flesh on the legislative bones. The creative jurisprudence of the Court in particular, and its willingness to interpret measures in such a way as to make them effective, to achieve the *effet utile*, has done much to assist in the attainment of the general objectives of the EU Treaties.

The role of the Court of Justice of the European Union in developing Union law is discussed below and in Chapter 5.

Fundamental rights and general principles of law

Objective 7

Article 2 TEU states, unequivocally, that:

The Union is founded on the values of respect for human dignity, freedom, democracy, equality, the rule of law and respect for human rights, including the rights of persons belonging to minorities. These values are common to the Member States in a society in which pluralism, non-discrimination, tolerance, justice, solidarity and equality between men and women prevail.

The importance of these principles is emphasised by the powers conferred on the Council by Art 7(3) TEU to suspend, *inter alia*, the voting rights of any Member State found to be in breach.

Article 6(1) TEU, as amended by the ToL, provides that the Union shall recognise the rights, freedoms and principles set out in the Charter of Fundamental Rights of the European Union, which shall have the same legal value as the EU Treaties. Article 6(3) TEU, as amended by the ToL, further provides that fundamental rights 'as guaranteed by the European Convention for the Protection of Human Rights and Fundamental Freedoms and as they result from the constitutional traditions common to the Member States, shall constitute general principles of the Union's law'.

Where a fundamental right is recognised both by the Charter and by the European Convention on Human Rights (ECHR), the Charter provides that the right has the same meaning and scope as laid down by the ECHR. One of the rights recognised by the Charter (Art 50) and the ECHR (Art 4) is the fundamental right not to be tried or punished in *criminal* proceedings twice for the same offence. The following case is concerned with this prohibition on being punished twice. The Haparanda tingsrätt (Haparanda District Court, Sweden) was uncertain whether criminal proceedings for tax evasion could be brought against a defendant where a tax penalty had already been imposed upon him for the same acts of providing false information:

Åklagaren v *Åkerberg Fransson* (Case C-617/10)

Mr Åkerberg Fransson was self-employed. The Swedish tax authorities accused him of having infringed his declaration obligations with regard to tax in 2004 and 2005, which resulted in a loss of revenue from various taxes. The Swedish tax authorities imposed tax penalties for the 2004 and 2005 tax years.

In 2009 criminal proceedings were brought against Åkerberg Fransson in the Haparanda tingsrätt. The Public Prosecutor's Office accused him of having committed an offence of tax evasion (in respect of 2004 and 2005) punishable, under Swedish law, by a term of imprisonment of up to six years. The acts of providing false information which gave rise to those proceedings were the same as the acts that led to the tax penalties.

The Swedish court referred the case to the Court of Justice to determine whether the criminal charges against Åkerberg Fransson had to be dismissed on the ground that he had already been punished for the same acts.

The Court of Justice stated that the Charter only applies to the Member States when they are implementing Union law. Thus, fundamental rights guaranteed by the Charter must be complied with where national legislation falls within the scope of Union law. The Court explained that tax penalties and criminal proceedings for tax (VAT) evasion constituted implementation of a number of provisions of Union law which related to VAT. Therefore, the Charter applied and the prohibition on being punished twice, as set out in the Charter, was applicable to Åkerberg Fransson's situation.

The Court stated that a national court which is called upon to apply provisions of Union law is under a duty to give full effect to those provisions. If necessary, it should refuse to apply any conflicting provision of national legislation and it is not necessary for the court to request or await the prior setting aside of the national provision by legislative or other constitutional means.

However, the Court observed with regard to the principle which prevents a person from being punished twice that this principle does not preclude a Member State from imposing, for the same acts of evading declaration obligations in the field of VAT, a combination of tax penalties and criminal penalties. In order to ensure that all VAT revenue is collected and, in so doing, that the financial interests of the Union are protected, the Member States have freedom to choose the applicable penalties. These penalties may therefore take the form of administrative penalties, criminal penalties or a combination of the two. It is only if the tax penalty is criminal in nature and has become final within the meaning of the Charter that the principle preventing a person from being punished twice precludes criminal proceedings in respect of the same acts from being brought against the same person.

The Charter is considered next, followed by the Convention.

Charter of Fundamental Rights of the European Union

The Charter of Fundamental Rights of the European Union was signed by the then 15 Member States during December 2000 at the meeting of the European Council held in Nice, France. The Charter combines in a single text the civil, political, economic, social and societal rights which had previously been laid down in a variety of international, European and national sources. It includes the following:

- dignity (e.g. the right to life, and respect for private and family life);
- freedoms (e.g. freedom of assembly and of association);
- equality (e.g. respect for cultural, religious and linguistic diversity);
- solidarity (e.g. right of collective bargaining and action);
- citizens' rights (e.g. freedom of movement and residence);
- justice (e.g. presumption of innocence and right of defence).

Originally, the Charter was not legally binding. A Declaration annexed to the ToN provided that an Intergovernmental Conference would be held in 2004 to consider, *inter alia*, the status of the Charter. This resulted in the adoption of the proposed Constitutional Treaty and subsequently the adoption of the ToL.

The Charter, which was amended on 12 December 2007, is given legal recognition by the ToL. Article 6(1) TEU, as amended by the ToL, provides that the Union shall 'recognise the rights, freedoms and principles set out in the Charter of Fundamental Rights of the European Union'. The Charter is therefore an integral part of Union law, setting out the fundamental rights every Union citizen can benefit from. However, it does not create fundamental rights which are of general application in national law. It only applies within the scope of Union law. A Declaration on the Charter (which was annexed to the Final Act of the Intergovernmental Conference which adopted the ToL) states that:

> The Charter of Fundamental Rights of the European Union, which has legally binding force, confirms the fundamental rights guaranteed by the European Convention for the Protection of Human Rights and Fundamental Freedoms as they result from the constitutional traditions common to the Member States.
>
> The Charter does not extend the field of application of Union law beyond the powers of the Union or establish any new power or task for the Union, or modify powers and tasks as defined by the Treaties.

The latter paragraph explicitly provides that the Charter does not introduce any new EU powers or tasks. The UK and Poland sought reassurance that the Charter would not be indirectly incorporated into their national law. Article 1, Protocol No. 30 (which is annexed to the TEU and TFEU) provides that:

1 The Charter does not extend the ability of the Court of Justice of the European Union, or any court or tribunal of Poland or of the United Kingdom, to find that the laws, regulations or administrative provisions, practices or action of Poland or of the United Kingdom are inconsistent with the fundamental rights, freedoms and principles that it [i.e. the Charter] reaffirms.

2 In particular, and for the avoidance of doubt, nothing in Title IV of the Charter creates justiciable rights applicable to Poland or the United Kingdom except in so far as Poland or the United Kingdom has provided for such rights in its national law.

As discussed in Chapter 1, in order to secure the Czech Republic President's signature to the ToL, it was agreed that at the time of the conclusion of the next Accession Treaty a new Protocol would be added to both the TEU and TFEU to provide that Protocol No. 30 (which currently only applies to the UK and Poland) will also apply to the Czech Republic. The next Accession Treaty was concluded at the end of 2011 to pave the way for Croatia's entry to the EU on 1 July 2013.

The following case concerned a direct application by the Court of Justice of the Charter:

A, B, C v *Staatssecretaris van Veiligheid en Justitie* (Joined Cases C-148/13 to C-150/13)

Directives 2004/83 and 2005/85 establish, respectively, the minimum requirements that third-country nationals must fulfil in order to be able to claim refugee status, and the procedures for examining applications for asylum and the rights of applicants.

A, B and C were third-country nationals. They each lodged an application for asylum in The Netherlands, relying on their fear of persecution in their country of origin on account of their homosexuality. However, the competent authorities rejected their applications on the grounds that their sexual orientation had not been proven.

The three applicants appealed against those decisions. Hearing the dispute, the Raad van State (Council of State, The Netherlands) was uncertain whether there were any limits imposed by Union law as regards the verification of the sexual orientation of applicants for asylum. The Raad van State took the view that the mere fact of putting questions to an applicant for asylum could infringe the rights guaranteed by the Charter of Fundamental Rights of the European Union. The Raad van State referred the case to the Court of Justice for a **preliminary ruling** pursuant to Art 267 TFEU.

The Court of Justice stated that the declarations by an applicant for asylum as to his sexual orientation were merely the starting point in the process of assessment of the application and confirmation could be required.

However, the methods used by the competent authorities to assess the statements and the evidence submitted in support of applications for asylum **had to be consistent with Union law and, in particular, the fundamental rights guaranteed by the Charter, such as the right to respect for human dignity and the right to respect for private and family life.**

Furthermore, the assessment had to be made on an individual basis and must take account of the individual situation and personal circumstances of the applicant (including factors such as background, gender and age), in order for it to be determined whether the acts to which the applicant has been or could be exposed would amount to persecution or serious harm.

Against that background, the Court gave guidance as to the methods of assessment which could be used by national authorities to ensure compliance with Union law and the Charter.

The European Convention on Human Rights and Fundamental Freedoms (ECHR)

The ECHR is considered in further detail on pages 32–33.

The Court of Justice, like national courts, takes account of the European Convention on Human Rights and Fundamental Freedoms (ECHR) when interpreting and applying Union law. The TEU formally acknowledged the ECHR as forming part of the EU's fundamental principles. However, it has no application under Union law to matters outside the EU's legal competence. Although the ECHR was recognised by the TEU as an important source of Union law, it was only important when interpreting and applying *Union* law. Although this remains the case post-ToL, Art 6(2) TEU now provides that the Union will accede to the ECHR.

EU accession to the ECHR

Article 6(2) TEU provides that the Union will accede to the ECHR, although it states that 'such accession shall not affect the Union's competences as defined in the Treaties'. This means that accession to the ECHR will not extend the Union's powers and tasks. Application of the ECHR will be limited to those areas which come within the competence of the Union. Article 6(3) TEU further provides that the 'fundamental rights guaranteed by the European Convention of Human Rights and Fundamental Freedoms and as they result from the constitutional traditions common to the Member States, *shall constitute general principles of the Union's law*' [emphasis added]. This simply restates the previous position. However, once the Union accedes to the ECHR, EU law will have to be interpreted and applied in accordance with the ECHR, not simply as a 'general principle of the Union's law', but because: (i) the ECHR is directly applicable to the Union; and (ii) the Union is required (in international law) to adhere to the ECHR's provisions. Following accession to the ECHR, it will be possible for a decision of the Court of Justice to be contested by taking the case to the European Court of Human Rights in Strasbourg, claiming the Court of Justice has failed to correctly apply (or failed to apply) a provision of the ECHR.

Official ECHR accession talks started between the EU and the Council of Europe on 7 July 2010. The accession agreement was concluded by the Council of Europe and the European Council (acting unanimously) in late 2011. The European Parliament must also give its consent to the accession agreement. During 2012, the negotiations stalled. An *ad hoc* group, comprising members of the Council of Europe's Steering Committee for Human Rights (CDDH) and the EU, was established to provide some momentum to the negotiations. A draft agreement was concluded in April 2013. An opinion of the EU Court of Justice was sought on the compatibility of the draft agreement with EU treaties. Opinion 2/13 was delivered by the Court of Justice on 18 December 2014, and because of problems it identified the Court concluded that the draft agreement was not compatible with Union law. If the issues identified by the Court of Justice are satisfactorily resolved, through amendments to the draft agreement, the European Council will have to adopt a decision to authorise the signing of the accession agreement, acting unanimously. All Member States would then have to complete their internal procedure to ratify the agreement. The Union would then ratify the agreement and the Committee of Ministers of the Council of Europe would have to adopt it. It would then have to be ratified (i.e. approved) by all 47 contracting parties to the ECHR (including the individual Member States) in accordance with their respective constitutional requirements. It is safe to assume that the Union's accession to the ECHR will not take place in the foreseeable future.

General principles of law

In interpreting primary and secondary Union legislation, the Court of Justice of the European Union has developed a number of general principles of law, some based on the fundamental laws of the constitutions of the Member States, some based on principles of international law and some derived directly from the European Convention on Human Rights (ECHR). These general principles of law are also based on the rights, freedoms and principles set out in the Charter of Fundamental Rights of the European Union. The status of the Charter has been enhanced now that the Charter has been afforded legal recognition by the ToL through the amended Art 6(1) TEU.

Although the jurisdiction of the Court of Justice of the European Union is limited by Art 19(1) TEU (previously Art 220 EC Treaty) to the interpretation of the Treaties, this is to be done in such a way as to ensure that 'the law is observed'. This has been widely interpreted to mean not only the law established by the Treaties but 'any rule of law relating to the Treaty's application' (Pescatore, 1970).

The development and application of these general principles of Union law are considered further below. This is divided into two principal sections: (i) human rights; and (ii) other general principles of law.

Human rights

Article 6 TEU (as amended by the ToL) declares that:

1 The Union recognises the rights, freedoms and principles set out in the Charter of Fundamental Rights of the European Union ... which shall have the same legal value as the Treaties.

2 ...

3 Fundamental rights, as guaranteed by the European Convention for the Protection of Human Rights and Fundamental Freedoms and as they result from the constitutional traditions common to the Member States, shall constitute general principles of the Union's law.

The effect of Art 6 is to give formal recognition in the Treaty to what has been part of the jurisprudence of the Court of Justice of the European Union since *Stauder* (Case 29/69). In this case the Court of Justice declared that 'fundamental human rights are enshrined in the general principles of Community [i.e. Union] law and protected by the Court'. In *A v Commission* (Case T-10/93) the Court of First Instance (now the General Court) noted the commitment in what is now Art 6 TEU to respect the fundamental rights guaranteed by the ECHR and said, repeating the words of the Court of Justice in *ERT* (Case C-260/89), 'the Court draws inspiration from the constitutional traditions common to Member States and from the guidelines supplied by international treaties for the protection of human rights on which Member States have collaborated or of which they are signatories' (see, in particular, the judgment in *Nold v Commission* (Case 4/73)). The ECHR has special significance in that respect (see, in particular, *Johnston v Chief Constable of the Royal Ulster Constabulary* (Case 222/84)). It follows that, as the Court of Justice held in its judgment in *Wachauf v Germany* (Case 5/88), the Union cannot accept measures which are incompatible with observance of the human rights thus recognised and guaranteed.

What this means is that when there is a conflict between national law which is, for example, intended to implement Union law, but does so in such a way as to breach the Convention, the Court will rule that the national measure is contrary to Union law. In the *Johnston* case, national measures intended to prohibit sexual discrimination in Northern Ireland and to provide a remedy for those alleging discriminatory behaviour, were held contrary to Union law because the Court of Justice held that they did not give **complainants** an effective remedy as required by Art 13 ECHR. It must, however, be emphasised that the Court of Justice can only rule on compatibility between the ECHR and Union law in those areas of national law affected by Union law. It could not, for example, rule on the compatibility of a criminal trial in a Member State with the ECHR's provisions on fair process, if the trial was unrelated to any rules of Union law, even though the individual involved was an EU citizen (***Kremzow v Austria*** (Case C-299/95)). The Court of Justice defined the limits of its powers in the following case:

Demirel v Stadt Schwbisch Gmünd (Case 12/86)

> The Court of Justice held that it has:
>
> > ... no power to examine the compatibility with the European Convention on Human Rights of national legislation lying outside the scope of Community [i.e. Union] law.

The application of the ECHR and the development of the jurisprudence of fundamental rights has been a somewhat erratic process, depending very much on the types of cases which have come before the Court. Some provisions of the ECHR, particularly those relating to due process under Art 6 ECHR, have been discussed frequently by the Court, while others, such as those relating to the right to life, hardly at all. Fundamental rights have been drawn both from the ECHR and from the constitutions of the Member States: rights and freedoms recognised by national constitutions as being 'fundamental' both in the sense that they protect and promote the most essential human values, such as the dignity, the personality, the intellectual and physical integrity, or the economic and social well-being of the individual, and in the sense that they are inseparably attached to the person. The Court of Justice has emphasised its commitment to human rights in general on several occasions, over a period extending beyond 40 years, starting with ***Stauder*** (Case 29/69). However, until the Treaty on European Union came into force in 1993, there were no specific provisions for the protection of human rights as such in the Treaties. It is arguable that the Court has been reluctant to take on the protection of fundamental rights, and did so largely to protect the supremacy of its jurisdiction:

> Reading an unwritten bill of rights into Community [i.e. Union] law is indeed the most striking contribution the Court made to the development of a new constitution for Europe. This statement should be qualified in two respects. First ... that contribution was forced on the court from outside, by the German and, later, the Italian Constitutional Courts. Second, the court's effort to safeguard the fundamental rights of the Community [i.e. Union] citizens stopped at the threshold of national legislations.

(Mancini, 1989)

Even where a right is recognised by the Court as a 'fundamental' Union right, that recognition is not conclusive. The designation by the Court of a right as fundamental does not always mean that all other rules must give way before it. In some circumstances, one fundamental right may have to give way to another which the Court regards as even more important. Much will depend on the context in which the fundamental right is called upon, and the nature of the right itself. Some of the specific 'human' rights are now considered.

The right to property and the freedom to choose a trade or profession (Article 1 First Protocol ECHR; Articles 15 and 17 Charter of Fundamental Freedoms)

This right is contained in Art 1 of the First Protocol ECHR (and see ***Nold v Commission*** (Case 4/73)). The Court of Justice has declared 'The right to property is guaranteed in the

Community [i.e. Union] legal order' (**Hauer v Land Rheinland-Pfalz** (Case 44/79)). In the following case, the Court of Justice applied the principle of the right to property:

Wachauf (Case 5/88)

A German tenant farmer was deprived of his right to compensation under Regulation 857/84 for loss of a milk quota when his lease expired, as a result of the way in which the German government had interpreted the regulation. He argued that this amounted to expropriation without compensation. The case was referred to the Court of Justice, which held:

It must be observed that Community [i.e. Union] rules which, upon the expiry of the lease, had the effect of depriving the lessee, without compensation, of the fruits of his labour and of his investments in the tenanted holding would be incompatible with the requirements of the protection of fundamental rights in the Community [i.e. Union] legal order. Since those requirements are also binding on Member States when they implement Community [i.e. Union] rules, the Member States must, as far as possible, apply those rules in accordance with those requirements.

However, the Court of Justice held in **R v Ministry of Agriculture, ex parte Bostock** (Case C-2/92), that where a landlord 'inherited' the benefit of a milk quota, neither the milk quota scheme itself nor the Union principles of fundamental rights required a Member State to introduce a scheme for compensation for the outgoing tenant, nor did they confer directly on the tenant a right to such compensation.

In the following case, the Court affirmed that both the right to property and the freedom to pursue a trade or business formed part of the general principles of Union law:

Commission v Germany (Case C-280/93)

The Court of Justice stated that the two principles (i.e. the right to property and the freedom to pursue a trade or business) were not absolute, and:

... had to be viewed in relation to their social function. Consequently, the exercise of the right to property and the freedom to pursue a trade or profession could be restricted, particularly in the context of a common organisation of a market, provided that those restrictions in fact corresponded to objectives of general interest pursued by the Community [i.e. Union] and did not constitute a disproportionate and intolerable interference, impairing the very substance of the rights guaranteed.

In relation to access to a trade or profession, the principle of equality should ensure equal access to available employment and the professions between EU citizens and nationals of the host state (see **Thieffry** (Case 71/76)). In **UNECTEF v Heylens** (Case 222/86), the Court of Justice stated that 'free access to employment is a fundamental right which the Treaty confers individually on each worker of the Community [i.e. Union]'.

The right to carry on an economic activity (Articles 15 and 16 Charter of Fundamental Freedoms)

The right to carry on an economic activity is closely connected with the right to property. The Court has held that the right to property is guaranteed in the Union legal order. However, for example, it has also decided that a Union-imposed restriction on the planting of vines constitutes a legitimate exception to the principle, which is recognised in the constitutions of Member States (see **Hauer** (Case 44/79), **Eridania** (Case 230/78) and **S M Winzersett v Land Rheinland-Pfalz** (Case C-306/93)).

Freedom of trade

Procureur de la République v *Adbhu* (Case 240/83)

The Court of Justice stated that:

It should be borne in mind that the principles of free movement of goods and freedom of competition, together with freedom of trade as a fundamental right, are general principles of Community [i.e. Union] law of which the Court ensures observance.

The Court has held on several occasions that the right of goods to be allowed access to markets in other Member States under Art 34 TFEU (previously Art 28 EC Treaty) is, subject to the exceptions in Art 36 TFEU (previously Art 30 EC Treaty), a directly enforceable right. This decision elevates that right to a fundamental principle, in the face of which inconsistent Union and national legislation must generally give way (see Chapter 9). But the freedom to trade is not absolute, and may have to give way to the imperatives of the internal market (see *Commission* **v** *Germany*).

The right to an effective judicial remedy before national courts (Articles 6 and 13 ECHR; Article 47 Charter of Fundamental Freedoms)

The right to an effective judicial remedy before national courts has become one of the most developed fundamental principles in the jurisprudence of the Court of Justice, as illustrated in the following case:

Johnston v *Chief Constable of the RUC* (Case 222/84)

The RUC maintained a general policy of refraining from issuing firearms to female members of the force. The policy was defended on the ground, *inter alia*, that Art 53, Sex Discrimination (Northern Ireland) Order 1976 (SI 1976/1042 (NI 15)) permitted sex discrimination for the purpose of 'safeguarding national security or of protecting public safety or public order'. A certificate issued by the Secretary of State was to be 'conclusive evidence' that the action was necessary on security grounds. The complainant argued that the rule effectively barred her promotion, and that Directive 76/207 (which prohibited discrimination on grounds of sex in relation to conditions of employment) should take priority over national law. Article 6 of the Directive provided that complainants should be able to 'pursue their claims by judicial process'. On a reference to the Court of Justice, the Court held that the national tribunal had to be given enough information to determine whether or not the policy of the Chief Constable was objectively justified. This was necessary in the interests of effective judicial control:

The requirements of judicial control stipulated by that Article [Art 6 Dir 76/207] reflect a general principle of law which underlines the constitutional traditions common to the Member States. That principle is also laid down in Articles 6 and 13 of the European Convention on Human Rights and Fundamental Freedoms ... As the European Parliament, Council and Commission recognised in their joint declaration of 5 April 1977 (OJ 1977 C 103 p. 1) and as the Court has recognised in its own decisions, the principles on which the Convention is based must be taken into consideration in Community [i.e. Union] law.

The Court of Justice's approach in the above case was endorsed by the European Court of Human Rights in the following case:

Tinnelly & Sons Ltd and McElduff v UK (1999) 27 EHRR 249

With regard to similar Northern Ireland legislation permitting discrimination on religious grounds, the European Court of Human Rights declared that:

> The right of a court guaranteed by Article 6.1 ... cannot be replaced by the ***ipse dixit*** of the executive even if national security considerations constitute a highly material aspect of the case.

The principles of effective judicial control and effective remedies underlie several decisions relating to difficulties encountered by individuals in seeking to establish themselves in businesses and professions in other Member States. These principles require that sufficient reasons must be given for official decisions, to enable them to be challenged in court, should the need arise, as illustrated in the following case:

UNECTEF v Heylens (Case 222/86)

The Court of Justice stated that:

> Effective judicial review, which must be able to cover the legality of the reasons for the contested decision, presupposes in general that the court to which the matter is referred may require the competent authority to notify its reasons. But where, as in this case, it is more particularly a question of securing the effective protection of a fundamental right conferred by the Treaty on Community [i.e. Union] workers, the latter must also be able to defend that right under the best possible conditions and have the possibility of deciding, with a full knowledge of the relevant facts, whether there is any point in their applying to the courts. Consequently, in such circumstances the competent national authority is under a duty to inform them of the reasons on which its refusal is based, either in the decision itself or in a subsequent communication made at their request.

The right to due judicial process also involves a fair investigative process in accordance with the ECHR when the European Commission is investigating alleged breaches of competition law. In interpreting its investigative powers under the former Regulation 17/62 (which has been replaced by Regulation 1/2003 (OJ 2003 L 1/1); see Chapter 22), the Commission has to have regard to the ECHR and, in particular, the rights of the defence to be informed of the matters under investigation (see ***Hoechst v Commission*** (Case 46/87)). This principle has come to be known as 'equality of arms' (***Solvay SA v Commission*** (Case T-30/91)). The same principle entitles protection to be given to certain communications between the person under investigation and his lawyer (see ***Australia Mining & Smelting Ltd v Commission*** (Case 155/79)).

The protection of family life, home and family correspondence (Article 8 ECHR; Article 7 Charter of Fundamental Freedoms)

In ***National Panasonic*** (Case 136/79), the Court of Justice held that the principles of Art 8 ECHR were applicable to an investigation by the Commission of an alleged anti-competitive practice, but held that the exception in Art 8(2) ECHR justified the action taken by the Commission under the former Regulation 17/62 (which, as stated above, has been replaced by Regulation 1/2003).

In the following case, the applicant had applied for an appointment as a temporary member of the Commission's staff. He had agreed to undergo the normal medical examination but refused to be subjected to a test which might disclose whether or not he carried the AIDS virus:

X v *Commission* (Case C-404/92)

> The Court of Justice held that he was entitled to refuse the test:
>
> > The right to respect for private life, embodied in Art 8 ECHR and deriving from the common constitutional traditions of the Member States, is one of the fundamental rights protected by the legal order of the Community [i.e. Union]. It includes in particular a person's right to keep his state of health secret.

In *Digital Rights Ireland* and *Seitlinger and Others* (Joined Cases C-293/12 and C-594/12) the Court of Justice declared a directive invalid from the date on which the directive had entered into force because of the directive's incompatibility with, *inter alia,* Art 7 of the Charter.

The right of EU citizens in other Member States to have only those restrictions imposed on them as are necessary in the interests of national security or public safety in a democratic society (Article 2 Fourth Protocol ECHR)

This right has a wide application. The position of EU citizens in other Member States, in relation to their human rights, has been described in the most comprehensive terms by **Advocate General Jacobs** in the following case:

Christos Konstantinidis v *Stadt Altensteig-Standesamt* (Case C-168/91)

> Advocate General Jacobs stated that:
>
> > In my opinion, a Community [i.e. Union] national who goes to another Member State as a worker or a self-employed person under Articles 48, 52 or 59 of the [EC] Treaty [renumbered Articles 39, 43 or 49 EC Treaty by the ToA, and now Articles 45, 49 or 56 TFEU] is entitled ... to assume that, wherever he goes to earn his living in the European Community [i.e. Union], he will be treated in accordance with a common code of fundamental values, in particular those laid down in the European Convention on Human Rights. In other words, he is entitled to say *'civis Europeus sum'* and to invoke that status in order to oppose any violation of his fundamental rights.

This principle applies, *a fortiori*, following the creation of EU citizenship by Art 20 TFEU (previously Art 17 EC Treaty), because such citizenship carries with it, under Art 21 TFEU (previously Art 18 EC Treaty), a general right of residence anywhere in the Union, subject only to the limitations contained in the Treaty and in the implementing legislation (see Chapters 11–15).

Prohibition of discrimination on the grounds of sex in relation to pay and working conditions (Article 14 ECHR; Articles 21 and 23 Charter of Fundamental Freedoms)

The combating of discrimination and the promotion of equality between men and women is one of the principal objectives of the Union (Art 3(3) TEU and Art 8 TFEU). Article 157(1) TFEU (previously Art 141(1) EC Treaty) more specifically provides that 'Each Member State shall ensure that the principle of equal pay for male and female workers for work of equal value is applied'. Article 23 of the Charter of Fundamental Rights of the European Union provides that 'Equality between men and women must be ensured in all areas, including employment, work and pay'.

In *P/S and Cornwall County Council* (C-13/94), a case involving the dismissal of a transsexual, the Court of Justice held that the right not to be discriminated against on grounds of sex is 'simply the expression, in the relevant field, of the principle of equality, which is one of the fundamental principles of Community [i.e. Union] law'. However, since the Court was not prepared to regard cohabitees of the same sex as being in an 'equal' situation, the principle of equality did not apply to them (***Grant v South-Western Trains*** (Case C-249/96)). Despite this decision, the ToA's creation of a power for the Council to 'combat' discrimination on grounds of sexual orientation (Art 19 TFEU (previously Art 13 EC Treaty)), could well persuade the Court of Justice that the situation of same-sex couples is now an 'equal' situation. This argument is further strengthened now that the Charter of Fundamental Freedoms has, since 1 December 2009, been legally incorporated into Union law by Art 6(1) TEU. Article 21(1) of the Charter provides that 'Any discrimination based on any ground such as sex, race, colour, ethnic or social origin, genetic features, language, religion or belief, political or any other opinion, membership of a national minority, property, birth, disability, age or sexual orientation shall be prohibited'.

Pursuant to the former Art 13 EC Treaty (now Art 19 TFEU), the Council adopted Directive 2000/78 (OJ 2000 L 303/16), which establishes a general framework for equal treatment in employment and occupation. The directive, which had to be implemented by 3 December 2003, prohibits direct and indirect discrimination as regards access to employment and occupation on grounds of religion or belief, disability, age or sexual orientation. It applies to both the public and private sectors. Although the directive applies to EU and non-EU citizens, the prohibition does not cover national provisions relating to the entry into and residence of third-country (i.e. non-EU) nationals (Art 3(2)). The directive does not, therefore, extend the free movement provisions, *per se*, to non-EU citizens (see Chapter 11).

The following case concerned an application of Directive 2000/78:

Frédéric Hay v *Crédit Agricole Mutuel de Charente-Maritime et des Deux-Sèvres* (Case C-267/12)

At the time of the facts of the case, the relevant French legislation restricted marriage to persons of different sexes.

Hay was an employee of a company whose collective agreement granted certain benefits – days of special leave and a salary bonus – to employees on the occasion of their marriage. Hay, who had entered into a PACS arrangement (civil solidarity pact) with his same-sex partner, was refused those benefits on the ground that, under the collective agreement, they were granted only upon marriage.

Hay challenged that refusal before the French courts. The Cour de cassation (France), before which the case was brought at the highest level of appeal, referred the case to the Court of Justice pursuant to Art 267 TFEU to ascertain whether the difference in treatment for persons who had entered into a PACS arrangement with their same-sex partner constituted discrimination based on sexual orientation, which is prohibited under Directive 2000/78.

The Court of Justice examined whether persons who entered into a marriage and persons who, being unable to marry a person of their own sex, entered into a PACS arrangement, were in comparable situations for the purpose of the grant of the benefits in question. The Court stated in that regard that, like married persons, persons entering into a PACS arrangement commit, within a specific legal framework, to living a life together and to providing material aid and assistance to each other. The Court further stated that, at the time of the facts in the main proceedings, the PACS arrangement was the only possibility under French law for same-sex couples to procure legal status for their relationship which could be certain and effective against third parties.

The Court held that the situation of persons who marry and that of persons of the same sex who cannot enter into marriage and therefore conclude a PACS is comparable for the purpose of the grant of the benefits in question.

The Court also held that the collective agreement, which provided for paid leave and a bonus for employees who married whereas marriage was not possible for persons of the same sex, gave rise to direct discrimination based on sexual orientation against homosexual employees in a PACS arrangement. The fact that the PACS was not restricted only to homosexual couples did not change the nature of the discrimination against those couples who, unlike heterosexual couples, could not, at the material time, have legally entered into marriage.

The Court held that the unfavourable treatment of couples in PACS arrangements could not be upheld on the basis of any of the overriding reasons in the public interest provided for by Directive 2000/78, and therefore the disputed provision of the collective agreement was in breach of Union law.

Freedom of expression (Article 10 ECHR; Article 11 Charter of Fundamental Freedoms)

The right to freedom of expression has been considered on several occasions by the Court in the context of freedom to provide and receive services, and in relation to the establishment of businesses in other Member States. In the following case, the Court of Justice had to consider a challenge by an independent broadcasting company to the **monopoly** of the state broadcasting company:

Elleneki Radiophonia Tileorasi (ERT) (Case C-260/89)

Greek law forbade any party other than the state television company from broadcasting television programmes within Greek territory. The defendant company defied the ban and, when prosecuted, pleaded in their defence that the television monopoly was contrary both to Union law (in relation to, *inter alia*, the free movement of goods and services) and to Art 10 ECHR. The Greek government defended the television monopoly as a public policy derogation from the free movement of goods and services under the former Arts 46 and 55 EC Treaty (now Arts 52 and 62 TFEU). The Court of Justice accepted that these derogations were subject to the ECHR and said:

When a Member State invokes Articles 56 and 66 of the [EC] Treaty [renumbered Articles 46 and 55 EC Treaty by the ToA, and now Arts 52 and 62 TFEU] in order to justify rules which hinder the free movement of services, this justification, which is provided for in Community [i.e. Union] law, must be interpreted in the light of general principles of law, notably fundamental rights ... The limitations imposed on the power of Member States to apply the provisions of Articles 66 and 56 of the [EC] Treaty [now Arts 52 and 62 TFEU], for reasons of public order, public security and public health must be understood in the light of the general principles of freedom of expression, enshrined in Article 10 of the Convention. (para 45)

Access to information is an important corollary to the effective exercise both of freedom of expression (Art 10 ECHR and Art 11 Charter of Fundamental Freedoms) and of the right to know the basis of a decision under the general rules requiring a fair decision-making process. Article 296 TFEU (previously Art 253 EC Treaty) requires reasons to be given for all decisions by Union institutions. Article 169 TFEU (previously Art 152 EC Treaty) confers a right of information on consumers. Article 15(3) TFEU (previously Art 255(3) EC Treaty) confers a right of access for all EU citizens and those resident in the Union to documents produced by the Union institutions. This right of access is, however, subject to the rules made by each body. Article 42 of the Charter of Fundamental Freedoms explicitly states that any EU citizen has the right 'of access to documents of the institutions, bodies, offices and agencies of the Union, whatever their medium'. This right extends to any natural or legal person residing or having its registered office in a Member State. The Court of First Instance ((CFI), now renamed the General Court) has recognised that the policy decision of the Commission to make its documents available could be subject to its power to withhold documents on grounds of public security, international relations, monetary stability, court proceedings and investigations, but these limitations must be specifically justified in the case of each document, and interpreted strictly (***Van der Wal v Commission*** (Case T-83/96)). Article 15(3) TFEU provides for access to European Parliament, Council and Commission documents. Pursuant to the former Art 255 EC Treaty, Regulation 1049/2001 was adopted by the Council. This Regulation replaced Decision 94/90 with effect from 3 December 2001. Refusal to grant access must be based on one of the exceptions provided for in the Regulation and must be justified on the grounds that disclosure of the document would be harmful (see Chapter 3).

Regulation 1049/2001 is considered in further detail on pages 106–112.

Freedom of religion (Article 9 ECHR; Article 10 Charter of Fundamental Freedoms)

The question of religious discrimination came before the Court of Justice in the following case:

Prais v The Council (Case 130/75)

A woman of Jewish faith applied for a post as a Union official. She did not mention her faith in her application form, but when she was informed that she would have to sit a competitive examination on a particular day, she explained that she could not do so because it was an important Jewish festival. She asked to be able to take the examination on another day. She was refused, because the Council decided that it was essential for all candidates to sit the examination on the same day. The Court upheld the decision of the Council, because it had not been told, in advance, about the difficulty. The Court of Justice accepted, as did the Council, that freedom of religion was a general principle of Union law, but decided that it had not been breached in this case (see also Directive 2000/78 above).

Freedom of trade union activity including the right to join and form staff associations (Article 12 Charter of Fundamental Freedoms)

Union Syndicale v Council (Case 175/73) recognised the right to trade union membership. It is debatable if this extended to a right to engage in industrial action, although Art 28 of the Charter of Fundamental Freedoms provides that:

> Workers and employers, or their respective organisations, have, in accordance with Union law and national laws and practices, the right to negotiate and conclude collective agreements at the appropriate levels and, in cases of conflicts of interest, to **take collective action to defend their interests, including strike action**. [emphasis added]

Individuals benefiting from the protection of Union law are entitled to participate equally in trade unions and staff associations, and should not be penalised for taking part in legitimate trade union activity (see ***Rutili*** (Case 36/75) and ***Association de Soutien aux Travailleurs Immigrés*** (Case C-213/90)). This includes the right to vote and stand for office in such bodies (***Commission v Luxembourg*** (Case C-118/92)). The European Court of Human Rights, in ***Schmidt and Dahlstom*** (1979–80) 1 EHRR 632, held that the ECHR safeguards the freedom to protect the occupational interests of trade union members by trade union action, but leaves each state a free choice of the means to be used to this end. Article 8, Regulation 492/2011 (previously Art 8, Regulation 1612/68), which gives migrant workers equal rights with national workers as far as membership of trade unions and the election to office in them is concerned, refers only to 'the rights attaching' to such membership, without further elaboration. Article 12 of the Charter of Fundamental Freedoms further provides that:

1 Everyone has the right to freedom of peaceful assembly and to freedom of association at all levels, in particular in political, trade union and civic matters, which implies the right of everyone to form and to join trade unions for the protection of his or her interests.

2 Political parties at Union level contribute to expressing the political will of the citizens of the Union.

The UK's Human Rights Act 1998

See pages 269–272 for an explanation of the principle of supremacy of Union law.

In accordance with the principle of supremacy of Union law (see Chapter 9), the principles referred to in this chapter must be recognised and implemented by the courts of the UK as part of its national law.

The ECHR was incorporated into the law of England, Wales, Scotland and Northern Ireland by the Human Rights Act 1998. All public bodies (including courts and tribunals) and even private bodies implementing public law, will have to abide by the principles of the ECHR.

Therefore, ECHR rights may be applied either: (i) as a matter of Union law where they concern a measure within the competence of the Union; or (ii) under national law following the procedures set out in the Act where Union law is not involved.

Other general principles of law

Having considered some of the specific 'human rights' provisions, this section considers other general principles which have been embraced by the Court of Justice of the European Union when interpreting and applying Union law.

Proportionality

Proportionality is a general principle imported from German law, and is often invoked to determine whether a piece of subordinate legislation or an action purported to be taken under the Treaties goes beyond what is necessary to achieve the declared, lawful objects. It holds that 'the individual should not have his freedom of action limited beyond the degree necessary for the public interest' (***Internationale Handelsgesellschaft*** (Case 11/70)). This principle applies in relation to action by the Union in the sphere of legislation, to determine whether a regulation has, for example, gone beyond what is necessary to achieve the aim contained in the enabling Treaty provision, or whether a Union institution has exceeded the necessary action to be taken in relation to an infraction (i.e. breach) of Union law. It may thus be invoked to challenge fines imposed by undertakings found by the Commission to have breached the competition rules in Arts 101 and 102 TFEU (previously Arts 81 and 82 EC Treaty); see Chapter 22.

Article 5(1) TEU specifically provides that the use of EU competences is governed by the principle of proportionality. Article 5(4) TEU further provides that 'Under the principle of proportionality the content and form of Union action shall not exceed what is necessary to achieve the objectives of the Treaties'. Protocol No. 2, which is annexed to the TEU and the TFEU, concerns the application of the principles of subsidiarity and proportionality. Article 5(4) TEU specifically provides that the EU institutions shall apply the principle of proportionality as laid down in the Protocol.

The principle of proportionality is also applicable to action by Member States in relation to permitted derogations from Union law. While, for example, restrictions on imports from other Member States, and also other measures having an equivalent effect, are prohibited by Art 34 TFEU (previously Art 28 EC Treaty), an exception is permitted under Art 36 TFEU (previously Art 30 EC Treaty) in relation to action taken on the grounds of, *inter alia*, public health (see Chapter 18). A total ban on a product will in almost every case be disproportionate, while some sampling and testing, in proportion to the degree of the perceived risk, may be legitimate. Excessive action may constitute a disguised restriction on trade (***Commission v Germany (Re Crayfish Imports)*** (Case C-131/93)).

The principle of equality

Article 2 TEU provides that the Union is founded on:

> ... the values of respect for human dignity, freedom, democracy, equality, the rule of law and respect for human rights, including the right of persons belonging to minorities. These values are common to the Member States in a society in which pluralism, non-discrimination, tolerance, justice, solidarity and equality between women and men prevail.

The Union's objectives are set out in Art 3 TEU. Article 3(3) TEU provides that the Union:

> ... shall combat social exclusion and discrimination, and shall promote social justice and protection, equality between women and men, solidarity between generations and protection of the rights of the child.

Articles 9 to 12 TEU set out a number of democratic principles which regulate how the Union functions and operates. Article 9 TEU sets out the principle of equality:

> In all its activities, the Union shall observe the principle of the equality of its citizens, who shall receive equal attention from its institutions, bodies, offices and agencies ...

Article 8 TFEU provides that 'In all its activities, the Union shall aim to eliminate inequalities, and to promote equality, between men and women'. Article 10 TFEU further provides that 'In defining and implementing its policies and activities, the Union shall aim to combat discrimination based on sex, racial or ethnic origin, religion or belief, disability, age or sexual orientation'.

The TFEU includes three specific types of prohibition against discrimination:

- prohibition against discrimination on grounds of nationality under Art 19(1) TFEU (previously Art 12 EC Treaty);
- prohibition of discrimination between producers and consumers in relation to the operation of the Common Agricultural Policy under Art 40(2) TFEU (previously Art 34(2) EC Treaty);
- entitlement to equal pay for work of equal value for both men and women under Art 157 TFEU (previously Art 141 EC Treaty).

Article 19(1) TFEU (which, as stated above, replaces the non-discrimination provision in the former Art 12 EC Treaty) specifically provides that:

> Within the scope of application of the Treaties, and without prejudice to any special provisions contained therein, any discrimination on grounds of nationality shall be prohibited.

The former Art 12 EC Treaty has been applied extensively by the Court of Justice of the European Union, particularly with regard to the Treaty provisions relating to EU citizenship and the free movement of persons (see Chapters 11–15). Article 19(1) TFEU will undoubtedly be similarly applied by the Court.

The former Art 13 EC Treaty (now Art 19 TFEU) created a new power for the Council: 'within the limits of the powers conferred upon it by the Community [i.e. Union] ... [to] take appropriate action to combat discrimination based on sex, racial or ethnic origin, religion or belief, disability, age or sexual orientation'. Two directives have been adopted pursuant to the former Art 13 EC Treaty:

● Directive 2000/43 (OJ 2000 L 180/22) implements the principle of equal treatment between persons irrespective of racial or ethnic origin. The directive had to be implemented by 19 July 2003. The principle of equal treatment prohibits direct or indirect discrimination based on racial or ethnic origin (Art 1). It applies to EU and non-EU citizens and covers both public and private sectors in relation to employment, self-employment, education, social protection including social security and healthcare, social advantages, and access to and supply of goods and services (Art 3(1)). The prohibition of racial or ethnic discrimination does not, however, cover national provisions relating to the entry into and residence of third-country (i.e. non-EU) nationals (Art 13(2)). The directive does not, therefore, extend the free movement provisions *per se* to non-EU citizens (see Chapter 11).

● Directive 2000/78 (OJ 2000 L 303/16) establishes a general framework for equal treatment in employment and occupation, prohibiting direct and indirect discrimination as regards access to employment and occupation on grounds of religion or belief, disability, age or sexual orientation (see above).

The principle of equality has been recognised by the Court of Justice as one of general application and requires that comparable situations should not be treated differently unless such differentiation is objectively justified (*Graff* **v** *Hauptzollamt Köln-Rheinau* (Case C-351/92)). Besides the specific Treaty provisions, the Court of Justice has held that the fixing and collection of financial charges which make up the Union's own resources are governed by the general principle of equality (*Grosoli* (Case 131/73)), as is the allocation of Union tariff quotas by the Member States (*Krohn* (Case 165/84)).

The principle is also evident in the Court's requirement of equality of arms under which undertakings which are subject to investigation by the Commission for breach of competition law should have full knowledge of the allegations and evidence in the Commission's file (*Solvay SA* **v** *Commission* (Case T-30/91)).

Legal certainty and non-retroactivity

Legal certainty and **non-retroactivity** is a general principle of law familiar to all the legal systems of the Member States. In its broadest sense, it means that 'Community [i.e. Union] legislation must be unequivocal and its application must be predictable for those who are subject to it' (*Kloppenburg* (Case 70/81)). It means, for example, that the principle of the **indirect effect** of directives does not apply in relation to national provisions with criminal sanctions, because the need for legal certainty requires that the effect of national criminal law should be absolutely clear to those subject to it. In *Kolpinghuis Nijmegen* (Case 80/86), the Court of Justice stated that the national court's obligation to interpret domestic law to comply with Union law was 'limited by the general principles of law which form part of Community [i.e. Union] law, and in particular, the principles of legal certainty and non-retroactivity' (see Chapter 9).

The principle of indirect effect is explained in detail on pages 273–274 and 300–303.

The following case concerns the issue of national courts imposing penalties for breach of Union law. This case concerned an EU Regulation, whereas previous cases had been concerned with EU Directives:

X (Case C-60/02)

During November 2000, Rolex, a company which holds various trade marks for watches, applied in Austria for a judicial investigation to be opened against 'persons unknown', following the discovery of a consignment of counterfeit watches which persons unknown had attempted to transport from Italy to Poland, thus infringing its trade mark rights. Rolex asked for the goods to be seized and destroyed following that investigation. In July 2001 Tommy Hilfiger, Gucci and Gap likewise requested the opening of judicial investigations concerning imitation goods from China intended to be transported to Slovakia.

The Austrian court was faced with the following problem: the opening of a judicial investigation under the Austrian Code of Criminal Procedure required that the conduct complained of constituted a criminal offence. However, the court said, under the national law on the protection of trademarks only the import and export of counterfeit goods constituted a criminal offence. The mere transit across the national territory did not constitute a criminal offence. This interpretation of national law was disputed. The Austrian government, for example, was of the opinion that mere transit was a criminal offence under Austrian law.

The Austrian court referred a question to the Court of Justice on the compatibility of the Austrian law with Regulation 3295/94, which in the national court's view covered mere transit.

The Court of Justice held that the regulation applied to goods in transit from one non-member country to another, where the goods were temporarily detained in a Member State by the customs authorities of that state.

The Court stated that the interpretation of the scope of the regulation did not depend on the type of national proceedings (civil, criminal or administrative) in which that interpretation was relied on.

The Court then noted that there was no unanimity as to the interpretation to be given to the Austrian law on trademarks. The Austrian government and the claimant companies contested the view taken by the national court. In their opinion, mere transit was a criminal offence under Austrian law. That, said the Court, concerned the interpretation of national law, which was a matter for the national court, not the Court of Justice.

The Court of Justice stated that if the national court decided that the relevant provisions of national law did not in fact penalise mere transit contrary to the regulation, it would have to interpret its national law within the limits set by Union law, in order to achieve the result intended by the Union rule (see Chapter 9: principles of indirect effect and direct effect). In relation to the transit of counterfeit goods across the national territory, the Austrian court would have to apply the civil law remedies applicable under national law to the other offences, provided that they were effective and proportionate and constituted an effective deterrent.

The Court noted, however, that a particular problem arose where the principle of compatible interpretation was applied to criminal matters. As Regulation 3295/94 empowered Member States to adopt penalties for the conduct it prohibited (i.e. requiring the Member States to make an election as to the penalties it would impose), the Court's case law on directives had to be extended to it, according to which directives could not, of themselves and independently of a national law adopted by a Member State for their implementation, have the effect of determining or aggravating the liability in criminal law of persons who acted in contravention of their provisions.

The Court reached the conclusion that, if the national court considered that Austrian law did not prohibit the mere transit of counterfeit goods, the principle of non-retroactivity of penalties, which was a general principle of Union law, would prohibit the imposition of criminal penalties for such conduct, despite the fact that national law was contrary to Union law.

Legitimate expectation

Legitimate expectation is based on the concept that 'trust in the Community's [i.e. Union's] legal order must be respected' (**Deuka** (Case 5/75) *per* Advocate General Trabucchi). Under this principle, 'assurances relied on in good faith should be honoured' (**Compagnie Continentale v Council** (Case 169/73) *per* Advocate General Trabucchi). It is closely linked to the principle of legal certainty. The relationship between the two principles is illustrated in the following case:

Mulder (Case 120/86)

In order to stabilise milk production, Union rules required dairy farmers to enter into a five-year non-marketing agreement, in exchange for which they would receive a premium. In 1984, the Union introduced a system of milk quotas, under which milk producers would have to pay a levy on milk produced in excess of their quota in any one year. Those who had entered into the non-marketing agreement for 1983 were not allowed any quota, because there was no provision in the regulations for them to do so. Having suspended production for the non-marketing period, they were effectively excluded from subsequent milk production. A farmer excluded in this way challenged the validity of the regulations. The Court of Justice held that:

> ... where such a producer, as in the present case, has been encouraged by a Community [i.e. Union] measure to suspend marketing for a limited period in the general interest and against payment of a premium, he may legitimately expect not to be subject, upon the expiry of his undertaking, to restrictions which specifically affect him because he has availed himself of the possibilities offered by the Community [i.e. Union] provisions.

The principle of legitimate expectation seeks to ensure a fair process, although it cannot fetter the Union's freedom of action. The balance is not always easily struck, but the issues involved in doing so were applied in an English court by Sedley J in the following case:

R v *Ministry of Agriculture and Fisheries, ex parte Hamble Fisheries* [1995] 2 ALL ER 714

Sedley J stated that:

> The principle of legal certainty and the protection of legitimate expectation are fundamental to European Community [i.e. Union] law. Yet these principles are merely general maxims derived from the notion that the Community [i.e. Union] is based on the rule of law and can be applied to individual cases only if expressed in enforceable rules. Moreover, in most instances there are other principles which run counter to legal certainty and the protection of legitimate expectations; here the right balance will need to be struck. For instance, in the field of Community [i.e. Union] legislation the need for changes in the law can conflict with the expectation of those affected by such a change that the previous legal situation will remain in force ...

In the above case, the court decided that the legitimate expectation of the holders of fishing licences had not been infringed when the Ministry introduced a more restrictive fishing licensing policy to protect the remaining fish stocks allocated to the UK under the Union's quota system. The CFI (now the General Court) has held that operators in the Union's agricultural markets cannot have a legitimate expectation that an existing situation will prevail as the Union's intervention in these markets involves constant adjustments to meet changes in the economic situation (**O'Dwyer and Others** v **Council** (Cases T-466, 469, 473 and 477/93)).

Natural justice

Natural justice is a concept derived from English administrative law, but closely linked to the United States' 'due process'. It is sometimes used by the Court of Justice to mean no more than 'fairness', and is not always distinguishable from 'equity'. In the English administrative law sense, it implies two basic principles: (i) the right to an unbiased hearing; and (ii) the right to be heard before the making of a potentially adverse decision affecting the person concerned (see, for example, ***Ridge*** **v** ***Baldwin*** [1964] AC 40). In the following case, the Court of Justice referred to a general principle of good administration:

Kuhner (Case 33/79)

The Court of Justice stated the principle as:

> ... a general principle of good administration to the effect that an administration which has to take decisions, even legally, which cause serious detriment to the person concerned, must allow the latter to make known their point of view, unless there is a serious reason for not doing so.

The principle is explicit in relation to decisions affecting an individual's free movement rights on the grounds of public policy, public security and public health (Arts 27–32, Directive 2004/38), and implicit in other decisions affecting the exercise of those rights. It involves the right to be given full reasons for the decision in order that they may be challenged. The right to natural justice is thus closely linked to the right to an effective remedy, as stated by the Court of Justice in the following case:

Unectef v *Heylens and Others* (Case 222/86)

The Court of Justice stated that:

> 15. Where, as in this case, it is more particularly a question of securing the effective protection of a fundamental right conferred by the Treaty on Community [i.e. Union] workers, the latter must ... be able to defend that right under the best possible conditions and have the possibility of deciding, with a full knowledge of the relevant facts, whether there is any point in their applying to the courts.

Summary

Now you have read this chapter you should be able to:

- Explain the nature and scope of the different sources of EU law, including:
  - EU Treaties (in particular the Treaty on European Union (TEU) and the Treaty on the Functioning of the European Union (TFEU));
  - secondary legislation.
- Understand the nature of the following different forms of secondary EU legislation which may be adopted pursuant to Art 288 TFEU:
  - regulations;
  - directives;
  - decisions.

- Explain how soft law may be used as an aid to the interpretation and application of EU law.
- Understand the role the Court of Justice of the European Union plays in the creation and development of EU law.
- Evaluate how the decisions of the Court of Justice of the European Union have been influenced by fundamental rights and general principles of law.

References

Mancini, G.F., 'The making of a Constitution for Europe' (1989) 26 CML Rev 595.

Pescatore, P., 'Fundamental rights and freedoms in the system of the European Communities' (1970) AJIL 343.

Snyder, F., 'The effectiveness of European Community Law: Institutions, processes, tools and techniques' (1993) 56 MLR 19, 32.

Further reading

Textbooks

Craig, P. and De Burca, G. (2011) *EU Law: Text, Cases and Materials* (5th edn), Oxford University Press, Chapters 3–5.

Foster, N. (2015) *Foster on EU Law* (5th edn), Oxford University Press, Chapter 4.

Steiner, J. and Woods, L. (2014) *EU Law* (12th edn), Oxford University Press, Chapters 3 and 6.

Weatherill, S. (2014) *Cases and Materials on EU Law* (11th edn), Oxford University Press, Chapter 2.

Journal articles

Anagnostaras, G., 'Balancing conflicting fundamental rights: the Sky Osterreich paradigm' (2014) 39 EL Rev 111.

Bobek, M., 'Corrigenda in the Official Journal of the European Union: Community law as quicksand' (2009) 34 EL Rev 950.

Driessen, B., 'Delegated legislation after the Treaty of Lisbon: An analysis of Article 290 TFEU' (2010) 35 EL Rev 837.

Harpaz, G., 'The European Court of Justice and its relations with the European Court of Human Rights: The quest for enhanced reliance, coherence and legitimacy' (2009) 46 CML Rev 105.

Kral, R., 'National, normative implementation of EC regulations. An exceptional or rather common matter?' (2008) 33 EL Rev 243.

Leczykiewicz, D., '"Effective judicial protection" of human rights after Lisbon: Should national courts be empowered to review EU secondary law?' (2010) 35 EL Rev 326.

Leczykiewicz, D., 'Horizontal application of the Charter of Fundamental Rights' (2013) 38 EL Rev 479.

Lock, T., 'EU accession to the ECHR: Implications for the judicial review in Strasbourg' (2010) 35 ECL Rev 777.

Mancini, G.F., 'The making of a Constitution for Europe' (1989) 26 CML Rev 595.

Mendes, J., 'Delegated and implementing rule making: Proceduralisation and constitutional design' (2013) 19 ELJ 22.

Pescatore, P., 'Fundamental rights and freedoms in the system of the European Communities' (1970) AJIL 343.

Schutze, R., 'Lisbon and the federal order of competences: A prospective analysis' (2008) 33 EL Rev 709.

Semmelmann, C., 'The European Union's economic constitution under the Lisbon Treaty: Soul-searching among lawyers shifts the focus to procedure' (2010) 35 ECL Rev 516.

Snyder, F., 'The effectiveness of European Community law: Institutions, processes, tools and techniques' (1993) 56 MLR 19, 32.

Trstenjak, V. and Beysen, E., 'The growing overlap of fundamental freedoms and fundamental rights in the case-law of the CJEU' (2013) 38 EL Rev 293.

Van Bockel, B., 'New wine into old wineskins: The scope of the Charter of Fundamental Rights of the EU after Akerberg Fransson' (2013) 38 EL Rev 866.

Van Vooren, B., 'A case-study of "soft law" in EU external relations: The European Neighbourhood Policy' (2009) 34 EL Rev 696.

Weiss, W., 'Human rights in the EU: Rethinking the role of the European Convention on Human Rights after Lisbon' (2011) 7 ECL Rev 64.

3

Institutions and related bodies of the EU

Objectives

At the end of this chapter you should understand the composition, role and powers of:

1. The European Council.
2. The Commission.
3. The Council and COREPER.
4. The European Parliament.
5. The Court of Auditors.
6. The European Central Bank.
7. The advisory committees: the European Economic and Social Committee, and the Committee of the Regions.

The institutional framework

Article 13(1) TEU provides that the Union shall have an 'institutional framework which shall aim to promote its values, advance its objectives, serve its interests, those of its citizens and those of the Member States, and ensure the consistency, effectiveness and continuity of its policies and actions'. The following seven Union institutions are recognised by Art 13(1) TEU:

1 the European Parliament;
2 the European Council;
3 the Council;
4 the European Commission (to be referred to as the 'Commission');
5 the Court of Justice of the European Union;
6 the European Central Bank;
7 the Court of Auditors.

It should be noted that from 1 December 2009 (when the ToL came into force), the European Council is treated as a Union institution in its own right.

Article 13(2) TEU (previously Art 7(1) EC Treaty) further provides that each institution 'shall act within the limits of the powers conferred on it by the Treaties'. Each institution can, in other words, only act if it has been expressly authorised to do so by the EU Treaties. The Court of Justice has, by and large, been strict in limiting the activities of the other institutions to their specified functions, although (in the past) it has been more liberal when interpreting the powers of the European Parliament (*Les Verts* (Case 294/83); *Parliament v Council* (Case C-388/92)).

There are two other bodies expressly mentioned in Art 13(4) TEU (previously Art 7(2) EC Treaty), but which have only an advisory function in the decision-making process: the European Economic and Social Committee and the Committee of the Regions.

The role of each of the above institutions will be considered in turn in this chapter, except for the Court of Justice of the European Union (which will be considered in Chapter 5). Each institution has a defined role: (i) in the decision-making and law-making processes; (ii) in relation to adjudication; and/or (iii) in the audit of the Union's accounts.

The institutions do not fit easily into categories such as legislature, executive and judiciary. Although the Union performs legislative, executive and judicial functions, there is no formal 'separation of powers' doctrine in-built into the Union's constitution. The competence of each institution has not remained static; amendments to the founding Treaties have generally resulted in changes to the balance of power between these Union institutions: e.g. the European Parliament started off as a mere debating chamber with limited supervisory powers, but following the introduction of direct elections in 1979, subsequent amendments to the EU Treaties (by the SEA, TEU, ToA, ToN and ToL) have resulted in its powers being enhanced, at the cost of some of the other institutions. This shifting of the balance of powers will be explored throughout this and the following chapter.

Articles 13–19 TEU clarify the role of the Union institutions. Part Six, Title I TFEU contains the detailed provisions governing the institutions:

Part Six	**Institutional and Financial Provisions** (Arts 223–334 TFEU)
Title I	***Institutional Provisions*** (Arts 223–309 TFEU)
Chapter 1	The Institutions (Arts 223–287 TFEU)
	Section 1 The European Parliament (Arts 223–234 TFEU)
	Section 2 The European Council (Arts 235–236 TFEU)
	Section 3 The Council (Arts 237–243 TFEU)
	Section 4 The Commission (Arts 244–250 TFEU)
	Section 5 The Court of Justice of the European Union (Arts 251–281 TFEU)
	Section 6 The European Central Bank (Arts 282–284 TFEU)
	Section 7 The Court of Auditors (Arts 285–287 TFEU)
Chapter 2	Legal Acts of the Union, Adoption Procedures and Other Provisions (Arts 288–299 TFEU)
Chapter 3	The Union's Advisory Bodies (Arts 300–307 TFEU)
	Section 1 The Economic and Social Committee (Arts 301–304 TFEU)
	Section 2 The Committee of the Regions (Arts 305–307 TFEU)
Chapter 4	The **European Investment Bank** (Arts 308–309 TFEU)

The European Council

Objective
1

The provisions of the EU Treaties which govern the European Council are Art 15 TEU and Arts 235–236 TFEU. The European Council's website can be accessed at:

http://www.consilium.europa.eu

The European Council did not exist when the European Communities came into being on 1 January 1958. The European Council was created following a meeting of heads of state and government in Paris in 1974. It received formal recognition in the Single European Act (see Chapter 1).

The European Council (not to be confused with the Council, see below) is now formally recognised as a Union institution (Art 13(1) TEU). The European Council provides the impetus for the Union's development and defines its political directions and priorities, but it does not exercise a legislative function (Art 15(1) TEU). It is, essentially, a political forum in which the Member States' heads of state or government, meeting at least twice a year, together with its President and the President of the Commission, thrash out the political agenda for the Union in the ensuing months and years (Art 15(2)–(3) TEU). The Member States' heads of state or government may also be assisted at these meetings by one of their ministers (normally their foreign minister; Art 15(3) TFEU). These meetings are often referred to as European Summits. General programmes worked out in outline at these meetings are taken up and fleshed out by the Commission and may, in some cases, form the background to a whole raft of legislation or more detailed policy-making in such areas as the internal market and monetary policy. It is here also that discussions will take place on matters relating to the common foreign and security policy, and other areas of the Union's external action (Art 22(1) TEU). The European Council may invite the President of the European Parliament to speak at one of its meetings (Art 235(2) TFEU).

The general rule regarding the adoption of decisions by the European Council is consensus, except where the Treaties provide otherwise (Art 15(4) TEU). For example, Art 235(3) TFEU provides that the European Council shall act by a simple majority with regard to procedural questions and for the adoption of its Rules of Procedure. When a vote is taken, any member of the European Council can act on behalf of one other member (Art 235(1) TFEU). Abstention by members present at the meeting, or who are represented by another member, does not prevent the European Council from adopting an act which requires unanimity (Art 235(1) TFEU).

The subject matter of European Council meetings depends on a number of different factors but the following factors are relevant in determining what is discussed. The work of the European Council will depend, to some extent, on the political issues which currently preoccupy a majority of the heads of state or government. These might involve, for example, a foreign policy crisis, a run on the national currencies in the financial markets, or a major environmental disaster. To illustrate this point, the Copenhagen meeting of the European Council on 12 and 13 December 2002 considered the crises in Iraq and the Middle East; two declarations were adopted. At the meeting of the European Council on 11 and 12 December 2008, the Council was concerned with the global credit crunch. The Council approved a European Economic Development Plan to provide joint action across the EU to stimulate the Member States' economies. Other items will appear regularly on the Council's agenda, such as the general economic situation, the level of unemployment, and a review of the development of the internal market. The Commission will quite often be involved in bringing forward new policy initiatives. Major initiatives have started in this way, such as those leading to the adoption of the Social Charter at the Strasbourg Summit in 1989, and the programmes that led up to the signing of the TEU in 1992, the ToA in 1997, the ToN in 2000 and the ToL in 2008.

It is the task of the Commission to 'promote the general interest of the Union and take appropriate initiatives to that end' (Art 17(1) TEU, see below), but the European Council has also proved valuable for ensuring that Commission proposals are actually approved. Once they have been accepted by the European Council they are much more likely to be accepted by the Council of Ministers because they will, in principle at least, have been accepted by the heads of state or government of which the Council members are part.

The European Council is now led by a President with specific powers. The President is elected by a qualified majority of the European Council's members for a term of two-and-a-half years, renewable once (Art 15(5)–(6) TEU). The former Prime Minister of Belgium, Herman Van Rompuy, was elected to the post on 20 November 2009 and was subsequently elected for a second term which ended on 30 November 2014. The former Prime Minister of Poland, Donald Tusk, was elected to the post for the period from 1 December 2014 to 31 May 2017. The President is not allowed to hold a national office at the same time as holding the Presidency (Art 15(6) TEU), and therefore Donald Tusk had to relinquish his role as Prime Minister of Poland. The President is required to 'ensure the external representation of the Union on issues concerning its common foreign and security policy, without prejudice to the powers of the High Representative of the Union for Foreign Affairs and Security Policy' (Art 15(6) TEU). Article 15(6) TEU also provides that the President of the European Council:

(a) shall chair it and drive it forward;
(b) shall ensure the preparation and continuity of the work of the European Council in cooperation with the President of the Commission, and on the basis of the work of the General Affairs Council;
(c) shall endeavour to facilitate cohesion and consensus within the European Council;
(d) shall present a report to the European Parliament after each of the meetings of the European Council.

The Commission

Objective 2

The provisions of the EU Treaties which govern the Commission are Art 17 TEU and Arts 244–250 TFEU (previously Arts 211–219 EC Treaty). The Commission's website can be accessed at:

http://ec.europa.eu

The role of the Commission is set out in Art 17 TEU (previously Art 211 EC Treaty):

1 The Commission shall promote the general interest of the Union and take appropriate initiatives to that end. It shall ensure the application of the Treaties, and measures adopted by the institutions pursuant to them. It shall oversee the application of Union law under the control of the Court of Justice of the European Union. It shall execute the budget and manage programmes. It shall exercise coordinating, executive and management functions, as laid down in the Treaties. With the exception of the common foreign and security policy, and other cases provided for in the Treaties, it shall ensure the Union's external representation. It shall initiate the Union's annual and multiannual programming with a view to achieving interinstitutional agreements.

2 Union legislative acts may only be adopted on the basis of a Commission proposal, except where the Treaties provide otherwise. Other acts shall be adopted on the basis of a Commission proposal where the Treaties so provide.

This provision establishes the following eight primary roles for the Commission:

● to promote the general interest of the Union and take appropriate initiatives to that end;
● to ensure the application of the EU Treaties and the measures adopted by the institutions pursuant to the Treaties;

- to oversee the application of Union law under the control of the Court of Justice of the European Union;
- to execute the budget and manage programmes;
- to exercise coordinating, executive and management functions, as laid down in the EU Treaties;
- to ensure the Union's external representation, with the exception of the common foreign and security policy, and other cases provided for in the EU Treaties;
- to initiate the Union's annual and multiannual programming with a view to achieving inter-institutional agreements;
- to take part in the decision-making and legislative processes of the Union, as provided for in the EU Treaties.

Essentially, the Commission's function is to act as the executive of the Union and to see that Union policy is carried out, to formulate new policy and to draft legislation to give it effect, to police observance of Union rules (whether primary, in the form of Treaty provisions; or secondary, in the form of regulations, directives and decisions) and, to a lesser extent, to act as a legislative body in its own right. This latter function is largely related to the making (and enforcement) of detailed rules for the implementation of the Common Agricultural Policy.

Composition

15 Member States (pre 1 May 2004)

Following entry to the European Union of Austria, Finland and Sweden on 1 January 1995, the Commission consisted of 20 Commissioners (Art 156(1) Act of Accession, Art 30 Decision 95/1/EC OJ 1995 L 1/1; this was set out in the former Art 213 EC Treaty). The former Art 213 EC Treaty further provided that only nationals of the Member States were eligible as Commission members, and that the Commission must include at least one national of each of the Member States, with no more than two. Although the former Art 213 EC Treaty did not stipulate this, in practice the five largest Member States (France, Germany, Italy, Spain and the UK) each had two Commissioners appointed, with one each from the remaining ten Member States. Under the former Art 213 EC Treaty, the numbers could be increased by a unanimous vote of the Council of Ministers.

25 Member States (pre 1 January 2007)

Following the accession of the ten new Member States on 1 May 2004, the number of Commissioners increased. For a transitional period, ten new Commissioners were appointed, one from each of the ten new Member States. This increased the total number of Commissioners from 20 to 30 (there being two Commissioners from France, Germany, Italy, Spain and the UK).

Article 4 of the Protocol on EU Enlargement, which was attached to the ToN, provided that from 1 January 2005, the former Art 213(1) EC Treaty would be amended to provide that the Commission would include one national from each of the Member States. This amendment reduced the five larger Member States' representation from two to one.

Although the term of office of the transitional Commission had been due to expire on 31 December 2004, the Accession Treaty that was signed in Athens in April 2003 stipulated that the new Commission would take office on 1 November 2004, two months early (see below). However, the end of the transitional Commission was brought forward so that the operational difficulties of a 30-member Commission did not continue any longer than necessary. As it happened, political problems were encountered during the appointment process of the new Commission, which resulted in the transitional arrangement being continued until the new Commission took office on 22 November 2004 (see below).

27 Member States (from 1 January 2007)

Article 4 of the Protocol on EU Enlargement further provided that when the Union consisted of 27 Member States the former Art 213(1) EC Treaty would be further amended to provide that the number of members of the Commission would be smaller than the number of Member States. The number would be set by the Council acting unanimously. The members would be chosen according to a rotation system based on the principle of equality, the implementing arrangements for which would be adopted by the Council, again acting unanimously.

This never materialised. The Accession Treaty which provided for Bulgaria and Romania's entry into the EU included an Act setting out amendments to the founding Treaties. Article 45 of this Act provided that:

> A national of each new Member State [i.e. Bulgaria and Romania] shall be appointed to the Commission as from the date of accession. The new Members of the Commission shall be appointed by the Council, acting by qualified majority and by common accord with the President of the Commission, after consulting the European Parliament.
>
> The terms of office of the Members thus appointed shall expire at the same time as those of the Members in office at the time of accession.

Article 45 therefore provided for the number of Commissioners, following enlargement on 1 January 2007, to be increased from 25 to 27.

28 Member States (from 1 July 2013)

On 1 July 2013, the Union's membership increased from 27 to 28 Member States when Croatia became the latest member. Article 21 of the Accession Treaty provided for the appointment of a national of Croatia to the Commission from 1 July 2013 until 31 October 2014, increasing the number of Commissioners to 28.

28 Member States (from 1 November 2014)

Until 31 October 2014, the Commission consisted of one national from each Member State (Art 17(4) TEU). From 1 November 2014, the Commission consists of a number of members corresponding to two-thirds the number of Member States (i.e. 18 members, given there are 28 Member States), unless the European Council, acting unanimously, decides to alter this number. This number of members includes the President of the Commission and the High Representative of the Union for Foreign Affairs and Security Policy (Art 17(5) TEU). The members shall be nationals of the Member States, chosen on the basis of a system of 'strictly equal rotation between the Member States, reflecting the demographic and geographical range of all the Member States' (Art 17(5) TEU). The European Council will set up the system, acting unanimously (Art 17(5) and Art 244 TFEU).

However, as discussed in Chapter 1, in order to satisfy the concerns of Ireland, and to pave the way for the second Irish referendum for ratification of the ToL, the European Council agreed that it would make the necessary decision to revert to the current composition. As stated above, this required a unanimous decision by the European Council. The Commission therefore continues to consist of one national from each Member State.

Independence and integrity of the Commission

Article 17(3) TEU codifies the principle that the Commission will be independent and it will act with integrity, by providing that:

> ... The members of the Commission shall be chosen on the ground of their general competence and European commitment from persons whose independence is beyond doubt.
>
> In carrying out its responsibilities, the Commission shall be completely independent. Without prejudice to Article 18(2), the members of the Commission shall neither seek nor take instructions from any Government or other institution, body, office or entity. They shall refrain from any action incompatible with their duties or the performance of their tasks.

This principle of independence and integrity is further amplified by Art 245 TFEU (previously Art 213(2) EC Treaty), which provides that:

> The Members of the Commission shall refrain from any action incompatible with their duties. Member States shall respect their independence and shall not to seek to influence them in the performance of their tasks.
>
> The Members of the Commission may not, during their term of office, engage in any other occupation, whether gainful or not. When entering upon their duties they shall give a solemn undertaking that, both during and after their term of office, they will respect the obligations arising therefrom and in particular their duty to behave with integrity and discretion as regards the acceptance, after they have ceased to hold office, of certain appointments or benefits. In the event of any breach of these obligations, the Court of Justice may, on application by the Council acting by a simple majority or the Commission, rule that the Member concerned be, according to the circumstances, either compulsorily retired in accordance with Article 247 or deprived of his right to a pension or other benefits in its stead.

It is thereby provided that the Commission shall act in the general interests of the Union. The Commission members are not representatives of the Member States of their nationality.

The following case, decided by the Court of Justice in 2006, concerns the issue of whether or not a former Commissioner had breached the former Art 213(2) EC Treaty (now Art 245 TFEU), in failing to respect the obligations arising from her office as Commissioner:

Commission v *Edith Cresson* (Case C-432/04)

Cresson was a member of the Commission from 24 January 1995 to 8 September 1999, when the Commission left office, having resigned collectively on 16 March 1999. During her term of office at the Commission, Cresson's portfolio comprised science, research and development, human resources, education, training and youth, together with the Joint Research Centre (JRC).

When Cresson took up her functions, she sought to appoint one of her close acquaintances, Berthelot, a dental surgeon, as a 'personal adviser'. Because he was 66 years old, Berthelot could not be appointed as a member of a Commissioner's Cabinet, and Cresson was advised accordingly. Moreover, when Cresson took up office, her Cabinet was already fully staffed, as far as personal advisers were concerned. Cresson asked the administration to consider how it might be possible to appoint him. Berthelot was then engaged as a visiting scientist from September 1995 until the end of February 1997. Although appointment as a visiting scientist implies that the person concerned is mainly to work either in the JRC or the services dealing with research, Berthelot worked exclusively as a personal adviser to Cresson.

On the expiry of his contract on 1 March 1997, Berthelot was offered another visiting scientist's contract, for a period of one year expiring at the end of February 1998. His appointment as a visiting scientist thus lasted for a total period of two-and-a-half years, whereas the rules specify a maximum duration of 24 months. On 31 December 1997, Berthelot requested the termination of his contract from that date on medical grounds. His application was accepted.

Following a complaint by a Member of the European Parliament, a criminal investigation concerning Berthelot's file was opened in Belgium in 1999. In June 2004, the Chambre du conseil of the Tribunal de première instance de Bruxelles (Court of First Instance, Brussels) decided that no further action should be taken in the case, taking the view that there was no ground for continuing the criminal procedure.

At the same time, in January 2003 the Commission sent Cresson a statement of the complaints against her as regards the breach of her obligations as a Commissioner in relation to Berthelot's appointment. After hearing Cresson, the Commission brought an action before the Court of Justice based on the former Art 213 EC Treaty (now Art 245 TFEU).

The Court noted, first, that the former Art 213 EC Treaty required members of the Commission to respect the 'obligations arising [from their office]'. As there was nothing which restricted that concept, the Court stated that it was to be understood as extending not only to the duties of integrity and discretion expressly mentioned in that article, but also to all of the duties which arose from the office of member of the Commission, which included the obligation to be completely independent, to act in the general interest of the Union, and to observe the highest standards of conduct. Members of the Commission were obliged to ensure that the general interest of the Union took precedence at all times not only over national interests but also over personal ones.

However, the Court stated that while members of the Commission were under an obligation to conduct themselves in a manner which was beyond reproach, a breach of a certain gravity is required if a breach of the former Art 213(2) EC Treaty (now Art 245 TFEU) is committed.

The Court went on to hold that Cresson had acted in breach of the obligations arising from her office as a member of the Commission in relation to the appointment of Berthelot and the terms under which he worked. It essentially held that Berthelot's appointment constituted a circumvention of the rules relating to the appointment of members of a Cabinet and of visiting scientists.

Having regard to her personal involvement in that appointment, as it took place at her express request, after she had been informed that she could not recruit Berthelot to her Cabinet, Cresson was held responsible for that appointment and the circumvention of the rules it involved.

The Court held that in appointing a close acquaintance (Berthelot) as a visiting scientist, when he was not going to be engaged in the activities associated with that position, in order to allow him to undertake the role of personal adviser within her Cabinet, even though her Cabinet was fully staffed and even though Berthelot had passed the permitted age limit for performing that role, Cresson was liable for a breach of her obligations under the former Art 213(2) EC Treaty (now Art 245 TFEU).

The Court stated that the breach of the obligations arising from the office of member of the Commission calls, in principle, for the imposition of a penalty. However, the Court held that in this case the finding of the breach, of itself, constituted an appropriate penalty. The Court therefore decided not to impose on Cresson a penalty in the form of a deprivation of her right to a pension or other benefits.

Appointment

Article 17(7) TEU (previously Art 214 EC Treaty) provides for the appointment of the President and the other members. The European Council acting by a qualified majority propose to the European Parliament a candidate for President of the Commission. The European Council's proposal will be made 'taking into account the elections to the European Parliament and after having held the appropriate consultations' (Art 17(7) TEU). The President is elected by the European Parliament by a majority of its component members. If this majority is not forthcoming, then the European Council, again acting by a qualified majority, shall within one month propose a new candidate who shall be elected by the European Parliament following the same procedure (Art 17(7) TEU). The current Commission President is Jean-Claude Juncker. The three previous Presidents were José Manuel Barroso (whose period of office ended on 31 October 2014), Jacques Santer (who resigned on 15 March 1999) and Romano Prodi (whose period of office ended on 21 November 2004).

The President is also involved in the appointment of the individual Commissioners: 'The Council, by common accord with the President-elect, shall adopt the list of the other persons whom it proposes for appointment as members of the Commission' (Art 17(7) TEU).

The Commission comprises the President, the High Representative of the Union for Foreign Affairs and Security Policy (see below) and the other members. Article 17(7) TEU provides that the President, the High Representative and the other members of the Commission shall be subject *as a body* to a vote of consent by the European Parliament. On the basis of this consent the Commission shall be appointed by the European Council, acting by a qualified majority. The members are appointed for a renewable period of five years (Art 17(3) TEU).

It should be noted that the power of the European Parliament to veto the appointment of the Commission is only a power to block the appointment of the Commission as a body; it cannot block the appointment of an individual member (other than blocking the President's appointment). However, the Parliament may be able to negotiate a redistribution of portfolios to ensure that a member of which it disapproves does not have responsibility for a high-profile portfolio. The Parliament may threaten to veto the appointment of the whole Commission if its request is not met.

The period of office of the 2004–2009 Commission started on 22 November 2004. This was three weeks later than planned due to political problems which surfaced during the appointments process. During the European Parliamentary approval process, the Parliament opposed the appointment of Rocco Buttiglione (from Italy) because of his views on homosexuality and marriage. As stated above, the European Parliament cannot block the appointment of an individual member; it can only vote to block the appointment of the Commission as a whole. The Parliament felt so strongly about Buttiglione's appointment that it became clear they would vote against the appointment of the proposed Commissioners *en bloc*. At this stage, the Commission-elect was withdrawn. Franco Frattini (from Italy) took the place of Rocco Buttiglione. The President-elect also requested the replacement of Latvia's Ingridia Udre because of her views on EU taxation. He also reshuffled two portfolios. Following these changes, on 18 November 2004 the European Parliament approved the new appointments by 449 votes to 149, with 82 abstentions.

The current Commission took office on 1 November 2014, following the European Parliament's vote of consent.

Termination of office

Termination may occur by:

- expiry of the five-year period of office (Art 17(3) TEU (previously Art 214(1) EC Treaty));
- death (Art 246 TFEU (previously Art 215 EC Treaty));
- voluntary resignation (Art 246 TFEU (previously Art 215 EC Treaty)) – see ***Dalli v Commission*** (Case T-562/12);
- compulsory resignation pursuant to Art 17(6) TEU: 'A member of the Commission shall resign if the President so requests' – see ***Dalli v Commission*** (Case T-562/12);
- compulsory retirement pursuant to Art 247 TFEU (previously Art 216 EC Treaty): 'If any member of the Commission no longer fulfils the conditions required for the performance of his duties or if he is guilty of serious misconduct, the Court of Justice may, on application by the Council acting by a simple majority or the Commission, compulsorily retire him'; or
- compulsory *collective* resignation where the European Parliament passes a vote of no confidence pursuant to Art 17(8) TEU and Art 234 TFEU (previously Art 201 EC Treaty). Such a vote requires a two-thirds majority of the votes cast which must represent a majority of the total membership of the European Parliament. On 15 March 1999 the dominant socialist bloc of MEPs withdrew support for the President (Jacques Santer) and his 19 Commissioners following a damning report by an external fraud inquiry that charged them with losing political control over the Brussels executive. Their immediate resignation was demanded, and this was forthcoming. If they had not resigned, a vote of no confidence would have been carried and the President and Commissioners would have been legally required to resign.

Article 246 TFEU sets out the procedures which apply when a Commissioner's term of office comes to an end through death, resignation or compulsory retirement.

Role of the President

The ToA inserted a new paragraph into the former Art 219 EC Treaty providing that the 'Commission shall work under the political guidance of its President'. The President was therefore conferred authority to lead the Commission. The political role of the President of the Commission has been further reinforced by the ToL. Article 17(6) TEU, as amended by the ToL, provides that the President shall:

- lay down guidelines within which the Commission is to work;
- decide on the internal organisation of the Commission, ensuring it acts consistently, efficiently and as a collegiate body;
- appoint Vice-Presidents, other than the High Representative (see below), from among the members of the Commission;
- have the power to request the resignation of an individual Commissioner or the High Representative.

Article 248 TFEU empowers the President of the Commission to allocate areas of responsibility to individual members of the Commission, and to reshuffle such allocations during the Commission's term of office. Article 248 TFEU further provides that 'The Members of the Commission shall carry out the duties devolved upon them by the President under his authority'.

It will depend upon the President as to how influential and powerful he is. The former President Jacques Delors was a very influential and powerful leader, and contributed greatly to the future shaping of the Union. It was said that under Jacques Delors during the 1980s 'the office became a key focus of power, not just in the Commission, but in Europe as a whole. He gave the Commission a purpose and taught it to respond to his will' (Grant, 1994). Under a weak President, it becomes a fragmented bureaucracy, as demonstrated during Jacques Santer's period of office, which culminated in his resignation on 15 March 1999.

Structure

Each member of the Commission is responsible for one or more policy areas (portfolios), to be allocated by the President (Art 248 TFEU). Each member will be assisted by a small Cabinet of officials (similar to UK civil servants) whom he personally appoints. The Cabinet is headed by a Chef de Cabinet, who will liaise closely with the member.

The Commission itself is divided into a number of departments referred to as Directorates-General (DGs), and each DG is headed by a Director General who is individually responsible to the relevant member of the Commission. Each Directorate-General is further divided into a number of Directorates (usually between four and six), each headed by a Director. The Director is individually responsible to the relevant Director General. Each Directorate is further sub-divided into a number of Divisions each headed by a Head of Division who is individually responsible to the relevant Director (see Table 3.1).

Table 3.1 Structure of the Commission

Commission	Commissioner
Directorate-General	Director General
Directorate	Director
Division	Head of Division

Each Directorate-General used to be referred to by a number (e.g. DGI External Economic Affairs; DGV Employment, Industrial Relations and Social Affairs). However, in 1999 it was decided to label each DG with a clear name, in what was largely a symbolic change designed to facilitate understanding by outsiders. It was also announced that the number of DGs would be reduced from 42 to 36 and since has decreased further to 33. The website for the Directorates-General can be accessed at:

http://ec.europa.eu/about/ds_en.htm

There are approximately 38,000 staff employed by the Commission; a similar number to that employed by the local authority of a medium-sized European city.

The Commission acts as a collegiate body and decisions are made by a simple majority (Art 250 TFEU). Once taken, they bind the Commissioners (see Chapter 4). Although, as discussed above, the Commissioners are bound to act as a collegiate body on behalf of the Union rather than for the states from which they originate, it would be unrealistic to expect them to divest themselves of all political contacts with their national governments. Indeed, it would not be helpful to the Union for them to do so. They frequently use such contacts within the governments and civil services of Member States to promote Union policies, and to sound out the extent of support new legislation might secure in the European Parliament and the Council. Tensions do arise, however, when they appear to be too assiduous in promoting the policies of their own states.

Most Commissioners nevertheless see themselves as having a much freer hand in devising and promoting new policies. Unlike national politicians, they have no political platform to which they must adhere. They simply need to follow the very broad objectives established by the EU Treaties and, increasingly, by the European Council (see above). They need to promote a good working relationship with the European Parliament, although there will be few issues which will unite the Parliament sufficiently to secure the Commission's removal *en bloc*.

The Commission as initiator of changes in policy and legislation

In recent years the Commission has annually adopted a *Work Programme*. The Work Programme for 2015 was published on 16 December 2014 (COM (2014) 910 final) and it provides a useful indication of the Commission's priorities. The current Work Programme and related documents are available at:

> http://ec.europa.eu/atwork/key-documents

Although the Commission is often described as the Union's executive, that description does not do justice to its major policy-making role. Article 17(2) TEU explicitly states that:

> Union legislative acts may only be adopted on the basis of a Commission proposal, except where the Treaties provide otherwise. Other acts shall be adopted on the basis of a Commission proposal where the Treaties so provide.

The Work Programme referred to above is part of this process. The role of the Commission as the primary proposer of legislative acts has often been summarised by the *maxim* 'the Commission proposes and the Council disposes'. However, when considering the decision-making process this no longer accurately reflects the position, partly because of the increasingly important role of the European Council and partly because of the much enhanced role of the European Parliament (see Chapter 4). Directorates-General, assisted by a large number of specialist advisory committees drawn from the appropriate industrial, commercial and other sectors in the Member States, take an active part in drafting new provisions. This process has been particularly visible in the measures proposed to harmonise product standards, consumer safety measures, and health and safety at work measures in the internal market under Art 114 TFEU (previously Art 95 EC Treaty).

Policy initiation takes place at many levels within the Commission. Senior Commission officials who have moved from civil service posts within their Member States are often surprised by the extent to which they are enabled to bring forward their own policy initiatives. As there is no equivalent of a Cabinet with a political programme, either at Council or Commission level, there is much greater scope for even middle-ranking officials to bring forward proposals to implement the Work Programme.

The Commission also has an important external role, representing the Union in negotiations with other groups of states and trading organisations. This is specifically recognised by Art 207(3) TFEU (previously Art 133(3) EC Treaty), which provides that:

> Where agreements with one or more third countries [i.e. non-EU countries] or international organisations need to be negotiated and concluded, Article 218 shall apply, subject to the special provisions of this Article.
>
> The Commission shall make recommendations to the Council, which shall authorise it to open the necessary negotiations. The Council and the Commission shall be responsible for ensuring that the agreements negotiated are compatible with the internal Union policies and rules.

The Commission shall conduct these negotiations in consultation with a special committee appointed by the Council to assist the Commission in its task and within the framework of such directives as the Council may issue to it. The Commission shall report regularly to the special committee and to the European Parliament on the progress of negotiations.

Article 218 TFEU provides that:

1 Without prejudice to the specific provisions laid down in Article 207, agreements between the Union and third countries or international organisations shall be negotiated and concluded in accordance with the following procedure.

2 The Council shall authorise the opening of negotiations, adopt negotiating directives, authorise the signing of agreements and conclude them.

3 The Commission, or the High Representative of the Union for Foreign Affairs and Security Policy where the agreement envisaged relates exclusively or principally to the common foreign and security policy, shall submit recommendations to the Council, which shall adopt a decision authorising the opening of negotiations and, depending on the subject of the agreement envisaged, nominating the Union negotiator or the head of the Union's negotiating team.

4 The Council may address directives to the negotiator and designate a special committee in consultation with which the negotiations must be conducted.

5 The Council, on a proposal by the negotiator, shall adopt a decision authorising the signing of the agreement and, if necessary, its provisional application before entry into force.

6 The Council, on a proposal by the negotiator, shall adopt a decision concluding the agreement.

Except where agreements relate exclusively to the common foreign and security policy, the Council shall adopt the decision concluding the agreement:

(a) after obtaining the consent of the European Parliament in the following cases:
   (i) association agreements;
   (ii) agreement on Union accession to the European Convention for the Protection of Human Rights and Fundamental Freedoms;
   (iii) agreements establishing a specific institutional framework by organising cooperation procedures;
   (iv) agreements with important budgetary implications for the Union;
   (v) agreements covering fields to which either the ordinary legislative procedure applies, or the special legislative procedure where consent by the European Parliament is required.

   The European Parliament and the Council may, in an urgent situation, agree upon a time-limit for consent.

(b) after consulting the European Parliament in other cases. The European Parliament shall deliver its opinion within a time-limit which the Council may set depending on the urgency of the matter. In the absence of an opinion within that time-limit, the Council may act.

7 When concluding an agreement, the Council may, by way of derogation from paragraphs 5, 6 and 9, authorise the negotiator to approve on the Union's behalf modifications to the agreement where it provides for them to be adopted by a simplified procedure or by a body set up by the agreement. The Council may attach specific conditions to such authorisation.

8 The Council shall act by a qualified majority throughout the procedure.

However, it shall act unanimously when the agreement covers a field for which unanimity is required for the adoption of a Union act as well as for association agreements and the agreements referred to in Article 212 with the States which are candidates for accession. The Council shall also act unanimously for the agreement on accession of the Union to the European Convention for the Protection of Human Rights and Fundamental Freedoms; the decision concluding this agreement shall enter into force after it has been approved by the Member States in accordance with their respective constitutional requirements.

9   The Council, on a proposal from the Commission or the High Representative of the Union for Foreign Affairs and Security Policy, shall adopt a decision suspending application of an agreement and establishing the positions to be adopted on the Union's behalf in a body set up by an agreement, when that body is called upon to adopt acts having legal effects, with the exception of acts supplementing or amending the institutional framework of the agreement.

10 The European Parliament shall be immediately and fully informed at all stages of the procedure.

11 A Member State, the European Parliament, the Council or the Commission may obtain the opinion of the Court of Justice as to whether an agreement envisaged is compatible with the Treaties. Where the opinion of the Court is adverse, the agreement envisaged may not enter into force unless it is amended or the Treaties are revised.

Under Art 207(3) TFEU, and subject to the procedure set out within Art 218 TFEU, the Commission is empowered, subject to the necessary Council approval, to negotiate world trade agreements.

The Commission (through the High Representative of the Union for Foreign Affairs and Security Policy) represents the Union at a number of important international organisations. Article 220(2) TFEU provides that the High Representative and the Commission shall be instructed to implement Art 220(1) TFEU, which provides that:

The Union shall establish all appropriate forms of cooperation with the organs of the United Nations and its specialised agencies, the Council of Europe, the Organisation for Security and Cooperation in Europe and the **Organisation for Economic Cooperation and Development**.

The Union shall also maintain such relations as are appropriate with other international organisations.

The Commission is also the holder of Union funds and administers four special funds:

- the European Social Fund;
- the Cohesion Fund;
- the European Agricultural Guidance and Guarantee Fund;
- the European Regional Development Fund.

The European Social Fund is primarily concerned with expanding vocational training for workers in order to promote employment and occupational mobility (Arts 162 and 163 TFEU (previously Arts 146 and 147 EC Treaty)).

The Cohesion Fund was established in 1993 to provide financial support for projects in the fields of environment and trans-European networks in the area of transport infrastructure (Art 177 TFEU (previously Art 161 EC Treaty)). It was created as part of a process of transferring resources from some of the Union's wealthier states to those with less-developed economies. The four countries which initially benefited from the Cohesion Fund – those with Gross National Products (GNP) *per capita* at 90 per cent or less of the Union average – were Greece, Ireland, Portugal and Spain.

The European Agricultural Guidance and Guarantee Fund was set up to assist in the restructuring of national agricultural economies (Art 40(3) TFEU (previously Art 37 EC Treaty)).

The European Regional Development Fund is intended to help to redress the main regional imbalances in the Union through participation in the development of regions which are lagging behind economically (Art 176 TFEU (previously Art 160 EC Treaty)).

The Commission as 'Guardian of the Treaties'

The expression 'Guardian of the Treaties' is used to describe the Commission's role both as the keeper of the 'soul' of the Union, maintaining its course towards its declared aims of political and economic unity, and the more mundane, but equally important, role of ensuring that the Member States honour their obligation to give effect to the EU Treaties and the implementing legislation. This role is discharged both through political contact and, if need be, by the initiation of proceedings against Member States under Art 258 TFEU (previously Art 226 EC Treaty). The Commission is empowered by Art 258 TFEU to bring an action against a Member State which is acting in breach of Union law. This is a very important provision and is considered in greater detail in Chapter 7. The Commission will first of all ask the defaulting Member State for its own observations on the default. If the matter cannot be settled, the Commission will deliver a reasoned opinion. This will set out why the Commission considers the Member State to be in breach of Union law and what the Member State must do to remedy the situation. If the Member State still fails to act, the Commission may take proceedings against the Member State – such proceedings being brought before the Court of Justice. The action will be listed as *Commission v Member State*.

The Commission has another important policing and regulating function in relation to Arts 101 and 102 TFEU (previously Arts 81 and 82 EC Treaty). The preservation of a genuine internal market within the Union of goods, services and capital is dependent not just on the collaboration of governments in removing both visible and invisible barriers, but also on the exercise, by the Union, of substantial powers to prevent large private and state undertakings using **restrictive agreements** and other abuses of their dominant market position, to exclude Union-produced goods and services from domestic markets (see Chapters 20 and 21).

Access to Commission documents

The attitude towards openness and transparency has changed rapidly within all the Union institutions, including the Commission. A number of measures have been taken to open up the work of the Commission to public scrutiny, as a means of enabling citizens to take part in an informed way in the debate on the future of the Union. The Commission makes frequent use of Green Papers and White Papers. Green Papers are communications published by the Commission on a specific policy area. Primarily they are documents addressed to interested parties, organisations and individuals, who are invited to participate in a process of consultation and debate. In some cases they provide an impetus for subsequent legislation. White Papers, which often follow a Green Paper, are documents containing proposals for Union action in a specific area. While Green Papers set out a range of ideas presented for public discussion and debate, White Papers contain an official set of proposals in specific policy areas and are used as vehicles for their development. These documents can be accessed on the Europa website:

http://europa.eu/publications/official-documents

The vast catalogue of documents available on the Europa website has added to this openness and transparency.

In accordance with the wish expressed at several European Council meetings, the Commission adopted a decision on public access to Commission documents in February 1994. This implemented a joint code of conduct between the Commission and the Council. The general principle expressed in it was that the public should have the widest possible access to documents held by these two institutions, subject to public or private interests being protected (Commission Decision 94/90 of 8 February 1994 on public access to Commission documents).

The Treaty of Amsterdam amended the EC Treaty to include a new Art 255 (now Art 15 TFEU), which provides for access to documents of the European Parliament, Council of Ministers and Commission.

Article 15(3) TFEU now provides as follows:

> Any citizen of the Union, and any natural or legal person residing or having its registered office in a Member State, shall have a right of access to documents of the Union institutions, bodies, offices and agencies, whatever their medium, subject to the principles and the conditions to be defined in accordance with this paragraph.
>
> General principles and limits on grounds of public or private interest governing this right of access to documents shall be determined by the European Parliament and the Council, by means of regulations, acting in accordance with the ordinary legislative procedure.
>
> Each institution, body, office or agency shall ensure that its proceedings are transparent and shall elaborate in its own Rules of Procedure specific provisions regarding access to its documents, in accordance with the regulations referred to in the second subparagraph.
>
> The Court of Justice of the European Union, the European Central Bank and the European Investment Bank shall be subject to this paragraph only when exercising their administrative tasks.
>
> The European Parliament and the Council shall ensure publication of the documents relating to the legislative procedures under the terms laid down by the regulations referred to in the second subparagraph.

See pages 114–115 for the application of Regulation 1049/2001 to the Council of Ministers. Pursuant to the former Art 255 EC Treaty, Regulation 1049/2001 was adopted by the Council of Ministers. This Regulation replaced Decision 94/90 with effect from 3 December 2001. Refusal to grant access must be based on one of the exceptions provided for in the Regulation and must be justified on the ground that disclosure of the document would be harmful. Article 4 of the Regulation sets out the exceptions, for example:

1 The institutions shall refuse access to a document where disclosure would undermine the protection of:
  (a) the public interest, as regards:
    – public security
    – defence and military matters
    – international relations
    – the financial, monetary or economic policy of the Community or a Member State
  (b) privacy and the integrity of the individual, in particular in accordance with Community legislation regarding the protection of personal data.

2 The institutions shall refuse access to a document where disclosure would undermine the protection of:
  – commercial interests of a natural or legal person, including intellectual property
  – court proceedings and legal advice
  – the purpose of inspections, investigations and audits unless there is an overriding public interest in disclosure.

In the following case the Court of Justice overturned a decision of the Court of First Instance ((CFI) (now the General Court) on the ground that the exception in Art 4(1)(b) applied. The case concerned a disclosure by the Commission of minutes of a meeting in which the names of five persons were blanked out. The question was whether or not the Commission was legally obliged to disclose the identities of these five persons:

Bavarian Lager Co Ltd v *Commission* (Case C-28/08P)

A large number of operators of public houses and bars in the UK were bound by exclusive purchasing contracts requiring them to obtain supplies of beer from certain breweries. As a result, The Bavarian Lager Co Ltd, an importer of German beer, was not able to sell its product. Taking the view that British legislation did not sufficiently limit those exclusivity contracts, and thus constituted a measure having equivalent effect to a quantitative restriction on imports, the company lodged a complaint with the Commission in 1993.

The Commission decided to bring proceedings against the UK for failure to fulfil its obligations. On 11 October 1996, a meeting took place attended by representatives of the Commission's Directorate-General for the Internal Market and Financial Services, the UK Department of Trade and Industry and representatives of the Confederation des Brasseurs du Marché Commun. Bavarian Lager had asked to participate at that meeting, but the Commission had refused.

The UK amended the legislation in question, and the Commission decided, after the amended legislation came into force on 10 December 1997, to close the proceedings for failure to fulfil obligations.

Following a number of requests by Bavarian Lager based on Regulation 1049/2001, the Commission disclosed to it, *inter alia*, the minutes of the meeting of 11 October 1996, stating that the names of five persons who had attended that meeting had been blanked out, two of them having expressly objected to disclosure of their identity and the Commission having been unable to contact the three others. Bavarian Lager made a confirmatory request for the full minutes, containing the names of all the participants, which the Commission rejected by a decision of 18 March 2004.

The Commission took the view that Bavarian Lager had not established either an express and legitimate purpose or any need for such disclosure, as was required (so it argued) by the regulation on the protection of personal data (Regulation 45/2001), and that, therefore, the exception concerning the protection of private life, laid down by Regulation 1049/2001, applied. It further took the view that disclosure would compromise its ability to carry out investigations.

In Case T-194/04, Bavarian Lager applied to the Court of First Instance ((CFI) now the General Court) for the annulment of that decision. The CFI annulled the decision and the Commission appealed to the Court of Justice. The Court of Justice annulled the judgment of the CFI.

The Court of Justice stated that Regulation 1049/2001 establishes as a general rule that the public may have access to documents of the institutions, but lays down exceptions by reason of certain public and private interests.

In particular, its provision laying down an exception to the right of access to a document, in cases where disclosure would undermine the privacy and the integrity of the individual, establishes a specific and reinforced system of protection of a person whose personal data could, in certain cases, be communicated to the public.

Where a request based on Regulation 1049/2001 seeks to obtain access to documents including personal data, the provisions of the Data Protection Regulation (Regulation 45/2001) become applicable in their entirety. This includes the provisions: (i) requiring the recipient of personal data to establish the need for their disclosure; and (ii) conferring on the data subject the right to object, on compelling legitimate grounds relating to his particular situation, to the processing of data relating to him.

The Court of Justice held that the CFI was right to conclude that the list of participants in the meeting of 11 October 1996 appearing in the minutes of that meeting contained personal data, as the persons who participated in that meeting could be identified.

After stating that Bavarian Lager was able to have access to all the information concerning the meeting of 11 October 1996, including the opinions those contributing expressed in their professional capacity, the Court of Justice considered the issue of whether the Commission could grant access to the document containing the five names of participants at that meeting. The Court of Justice held that the Commission was right to verify whether the data subjects had given their consent to the disclosure of personal data concerning them.

In the absence of the consent of the five participants at the meeting of October 1996, the Commission sufficiently complied with its duty of openness by releasing a version of the document in question with their names blanked out.

The Court stated that Bavarian Lager had not provided any express and legitimate justification or any convincing argument to demonstrate the necessity for the personal data (i.e. the names) to be disclosed.

The Court of Justice therefore annulled the judgment of the CFI.

The following case concerned Art 4(2), Regulation 1049/2001 and the Commission's right to refuse access to a document where disclosure would risk undermining the protection of the purposes of inspections and investigations:

Commission v Technische Glaswerke Ilmenau (Case C-139/07P)

In December 1998, Germany notified the Commission of various measures designed to consolidate the financial position of Technische Glaswerke Ilmenau (TGI), including a partial waiver of payment and a bank loan. By decision of 12 June 2001, the Commission held that the waiver of payment constituted state aid incompatible with the internal market. An action for annulment of that decision brought by TGI was dismissed by the Union courts. In July 2001, the Commission opened a second formal investigation procedure in relation to aid granted by Germany to TGI, in particular the bank loan.

In March 2002, TGI applied for access to all the documents in the Commission's files regarding state aid cases concerning TGI. By decision of 28 May 2002, the Commission rejected the request for access, on the ground that disclosure of those documents would be likely to undermine the protection of the purposes of inspections and investigations.

TGI brought an action before the Court of First Instance ((CFI), now the General Court) seeking annulment of that Commission decision.

The CFI annulled the decision (in *Technische Glaswerke Ilmenau v Commission* (Case T-237/02)), accusing the Commission in particular of not examining the documents covered by the request for access in a concrete and individual manner. The Commission appealed against that judgment to the Court of Justice.

In its judgment, the Court of Justice stated that Union legislation is designed to confer on the public as wide a right of access as possible to documents of the institutions. However, that right of access is subject to certain limits based on reasons of public or private interest.

In this case, the Commission had refused TGI access to documents relating to procedures for reviewing state aid granted to it. The Commission invoked the exception to the right of access based on protection of the purposes of inspections and investigations. The Court of Justice confirmed that the documents of which disclosure was sought came within an activity of 'investigation', within the meaning of Regulation 1049/2001.

The Court also held that, in order to justify refusal of access to a document the disclosure of which has been requested, it is not sufficient for that document to fall within an activity excepted by the regulation. The institution concerned must also supply explanations as to how access to that document could specifically and effectively undermine such an activity. However, the Court stated that it is open to the Union institution concerned to base its decisions in that regard on general presumptions which apply to certain categories of documents, as considerations of a generally similar kind are likely to apply to requests for disclosure relating to documents of the same nature.

As regards procedures for reviewing state aid, such a general presumption may arise from the fact that those procedures are open solely *vis-à-vis* the Member State responsible for the granting of the aid. Interested parties other than the Member State responsible for granting the aid do not have a right under those procedures to consult the documents on the Commission's administrative file.

Therefore, the Court of Justice concluded that the CFI erred in its interpretation of the regulation concerning access to documents by failing to recognise the existence of a general presumption according to which disclosure of the documents on the administrative file would, in principle, undermine the protection of the purposes of inspections and investigations. The Court of Justice annulled the CFI's judgment and, ruling on the dispute itself, dismissed the action for annulment brought by TGI before the CFI.

The following case concerned Art 4(2), Regulation 1049/2001 and the Commission's right to refuse access to a document where disclosure would risk undermining the protection of legal advice:

Sweden v *Mytravel and Commission* (Case C-506/08P)

This case formed part of a dispute originating in 1999, when MyTravel (then called Airtours), a UK tour operator, informed the Commission of a planned **merger** with its competitor First Choice in order to obtain a decision authorising that operation. Authorisation was refused on the ground that it was incompatible with the single market. Following the action brought by MyTravel, the Commission's decision was annulled by a judgment of the General Court of 6 June 2002.

The Commission then established a working group comprising officials of the Directorate-General for Competition ('DG Competition') and the legal service in order to consider whether it was appropriate to bring an appeal against that judgment and to assess the implications of that judgment for merger control procedures and in other areas. The report of the working group was presented to the Commissioner responsible for competition prior to the expiry of the period allowed for bringing an appeal against the judgment of the General Court.

MyTravel made a request to the Commission for access to the report, to the documents relating to its preparation and the documents contained in the file relating to the merger, on which the report was based.

By two separate decisions, the Commission refused to communicate those documents on the ground that: (i) their disclosure would undermine, in particular, the decision-making process and the protection of legal opinions; and (ii) there was no overriding public interest in disclosure.

By judgment of 9 September 2008, the General Court dismissed the action by MyTravel against those decisions on the ground that the Commission was entitled to refuse access to the documents requested in so far as their communication could have undermined the protection of the decision-making process of the institution and the protection of legal advice. Subsequently, Sweden decided to apply to the Court of Justice to have that judgment of the General Court set aside.

The Court of Justice stated that some of the documents concerned fell within the context of the administrative functions of the Commission. That administrative activity did not require as extensive an access to documents as that concerning the legislative activity of an institution of the Union. However, that did not in any way mean that such an activity escaped the rules laid down by the access to documents legislation.

That legislation provides for exceptions which derogate from the principle that the public should have the widest possible access to documents, and those exceptions must therefore be interpreted and applied strictly. **The Court considered that, where an institution decided to refuse access to a document it had been requested to communicate, it must, in principle, explain how disclosure of that document could specifically and effectively undermine the protected interest – in particular protection of the decision-making process of the institution and the protection of legal advice – upon which it was relying in the particular case.**

With regard to the exception for protecting the decision-making process of the institution, the Court noted that MyTravel introduced its request for access after the expiry of the time-limit for appealing against the judgment of the General Court which had annulled the Commission decision concerning the merger in question. The Court of Justice analysed all of the documents concerned and concluded that the General Court should have required the Commission to indicate the specific reasons why it considered that the disclosure of certain documents at issue would seriously undermine the decision-making process of that institution, even though the procedure to which those documents related was closed.

With regard to the exception for protecting legal advice, the General Court took the view that the disclosure of internal notes of the Commission's legal service would risk communicating to the public internal discussions between DG Competition and the legal service on the lawfulness of the 1999 decision (which declared the concentration operation in question incompatible with the single market), which could call into question the lawfulness of future decisions in the same sector. The Court of Justice stated that openness contributes to conferring greater legitimacy on the institutions in the eyes of European citizens and increasing their confidence in them by allowing divergences between various points of view to be openly debated.

The Court of Justice held that the Commission misapplied both the exception for protecting its decision-making process and the exception for protecting legal advice. The Court of Justice set aside the judgment of the General Court and annulled the two decisions of the Commission.

In *Unión de Almacenistas de Hierros de España* v *Commission* (Case T-623/13), the General Court held that documents exchanged between the Commission and a national competition authority in proceedings concerning an infringement of EU competition rules were not, in principle, accessible to the public. This was because: (i) disclosure could undermine the protection of commercial interests of the undertakings concerned (Art 4(2)); and (ii) there was a need to protect the national competition authority's investigation activities (Art 4(2)).

In the following case, the CFI (now the General Court) clarified the conditions governing the treatment by the institutions of a request for access to a large number of documents:

VKI v *Commission* (Case T-2/03)

The Verein für Konsumenteninformation (VKI), an association for Austrian consumers, had made a request to the Commission for access to its administrative file in a competition procedure that had resulted in a decision censuring eight Austrian banks for their participation in a **cartel** (known as the 'Lombard Club'). The Commission refused that request in its entirety and the VKI brought an action for annulment of that refusal before the CFI (renamed the General Court).

The CFI stated that the purpose of the concrete, individual examination the institution must in principle undertake in response to a request for access is to enable the institution in question to assess: (i) the extent to which an exception to the right of access is applicable; and (ii) the possibility of partial access. The CFI held that such an examination may not therefore be necessary if it is obvious that access must be refused or, on the contrary, granted.

In this case, the CFI found that the exceptions relied on by the Commission did not necessarily apply to the whole of the Lombard Club file and that, even in the case of the documents to which they may apply, they may concern only certain passages in those documents. Consequently, **the Commission was bound, in principle, to carry out a concrete, individual examination of each of the documents referred to in the request, in order to determine whether any exceptions applied or whether partial access was possible.**

However, the CFI added that **derogation from that obligation to examine the documents may be permissible in exceptional cases where the administrative burden entailed by a concrete, individual examination of the documents proves to be particularly heavy, thereby exceeding the limits of what may reasonably be required. In such a situation, the institution is obliged to try to consult with the applicant in order to: (i) ascertain or to ask him to specify his interest in obtaining the documents in question; and (ii) consider specifically whether and how it may adopt a measure less onerous than a concrete, individual examination of the documents. The institution nevertheless remains obliged, against that background, to prefer the option which, whilst not itself constituting a task which exceeds the limits of what may reasonably be required, remains the most favourable to the applicant's right of access.**

In this case, it was not apparent from the contested decision that the Commission considered specifically and exhaustively the various options available to it in order to take steps which would not impose an unreasonable amount of work on it but would, on the other hand, increase the chances that the applicant might receive access to the documents concerned, at least in respect of part of its request. As a result, the CFI annulled the Commission's decision.

Article 4(4), Regulation 1049/2001 provides that an institution which is requested to disclose a document originating from a third party has to consult the third party with a view to assessing whether one of the exceptions provided for by the Regulation is applicable, unless it is clear that the document is or is not to be disclosed. Article 4(5) provides that a Member State may request the institution not to disclose a document originating from that Member State without its prior agreement.

In *Messina* v *Commission* (Case T-76/02) the Court of First Instance ((CFI), now the General Court) examined whether the Commission could lawfully refuse access to documents which were in its possession but which had been drawn up by the Italian authorities. The CFI pointed out in this regard that the institutions may be required, in appropriate cases, to communicate documents originating from third parties, including, in particular, the Member States. The CFI noted, however, that the Member States are subject to special treatment inasmuch as Art 4(5), Regulation 1049/2001 confers on a Member State the power to request an institution not to disclose documents originating from that state without its prior agreement. In this case the Italian authorities had opposed communication to the applicant of the documents emanating from them, and therefore the Commission had been entitled to reject the application for access.

The same issue arose in the following case:

IFAW Internationaler Tierschutz-Fonds v *Commission* (Case T-168/02)

Germany had refused to agree to the disclosure to the applicant of certain documents originating from the German authorities, and therefore the Commission refused to disclose them to that applicant. On an application for annulment of the decision refusing access, the CFI (renamed the General Court) upheld that decision. Pointing out that the Member States are in a different position from that of other third parties, the CFI observed that a Member State has the power to request an institution not to disclose a document originating from it and the institution is obliged not to disclose it without its 'prior agreement'. That obligation imposed on the institution to obtain the Member State's prior agreement, which is clearly laid down in Art 4(5), Regulation 1049/2001, would risk becoming a dead letter if the Commission was able to decide to disclose that document despite an explicit request not to do so from the Member State concerned. Thus, where a request is made by a Member State under that provision, the institution is obliged not to disclose the document in question.

Documents on this transparency policy are available at:

> http://ec.europa.eu/transparency/access_documents

The High Representative of the Union for Foreign Affairs and Security Policy

Article 18 TEU provides for the appointment of the High Representative of the Union for Foreign Affairs and Security Policy. Although clearly not one of the EU institutions, it is an appropriate point to consider the High Representative. The High Representative is appointed by the European Council, acting by a qualified majority, with the agreement of the President of the Commission (Art 18(1) TEU). Federica Mogherini, the former Italian foreign minister, was appointed High Representative of the Union for Foreign Affairs and Security Policy from 1 November 2014, with the agreement of Jean-Claude Juncker, the newly elected President of the European Commission. He replaced Catherine Ashton, the UK's former European Commissioner for Trade.

The High Representative:

- conducts the Union's common foreign and security policy (Art 18(2) TEU);
- chairs the Foreign Affairs Council (Art 18(3) TEU);
- serves as one of the Vice-Presidents of the Commission (Art 18(4) TEU).

As a Vice-President of the Commission, the High Representative is subject to a collective vote of approval by the European Parliament (Art 17(7) TEU) and, possibly, a vote of censure (Art 234 TFEU and Art 17(8) TEU).

In this 'two-hatted' role (Commission–Council), the High Representative ensures the consistency of the Union's external action as a whole (Art 18(4)). The High Representative conducts the Union's common foreign and security policy, and common security and defence policy, contributing to policy development (Art 18(2) TEU). The High Representative is aided by a European External Action Service (Art 27(3) TEU), which consists of officials from relevant departments of the Council's General Secretariat and the Commission, as well as staff seconded from Member States' national diplomatic services (Art 27(3) TEU).

The Council

Objective 3

The provisions of the EU Treaties which govern the Council are Art 16 TEU and Arts 237–243 TFEU (previously Arts 202–210 EC Treaty). The Council's website can be accessed at:

http://www.consilium.europa.eu

The EU Treaties refer to the Council, although some commentators refer to the Council of Ministers.

Composition

The Council consists of a representative of each Member State at ministerial level 'who may commit the government of the Member State in question and cast its vote' (Art 16(2) TEU (previously Art 203 EC Treaty)). The Council is therefore made up of politicians from the Member States who are authorised to bind the Member State they represent. The membership will vary according to the matter under discussion within the specialised Council meetings (referred to as 'configurations', see below).

Article 16(6) TEU provides for the Council to meet in different configurations. These configurations are determined by the European Council acting by a qualified majority (Art 236 TFEU). Article 16(6) TEU specifically provides for the creation of a Foreign Affairs Council. The High Representative of the Union for Foreign Affairs and Security Policy (see above) presides over the Foreign Affairs Council (Art 18(3) TEU). The General Affairs Council, which is another configuration specifically mentioned in Art 16(6) TEU, ensures 'consistency in the work of the different Council configurations' (Art 16(6) TEU). Although Member States are normally represented by the senior minister from the relevant department, this may not always be possible and there are occasions when Council meetings comprise ministers of different levels of seniority.

President of the Council

The office of President of the Council is held in turn by each Member State for a period of six months in the order decided by the Council acting unanimously. The handover of the chair of the Council of the EU takes place from each rotating Presidency to the next one on 1 January or 1 July each year. Following the Council Decision of 1 January 2007, the order of rotating presidencies was determined up until 2020.

In order to achieve coherence and effectiveness of Council work towards implementing the Union's objectives, it was decided in 2007 to establish the idea of a group of presiding countries. In particular, three consecutive Presidencies (the so-called 'Trio' presidency) coordinate their objectives for an 18-month period and prepare a common programme which presents these objectives.

Each rotating Presidency ensures the smooth functioning of the Council, represents the EU in international conferences, organises meetings and sets the agenda for the Council, COREPER and other Council preparatory bodies. The Presidency also promotes policy decisions, acting as an honest broker, aiming at reaching consensus among the 28 Member States, in a way that always supports the EU interests. The Presidency has the opportunity to formulate, in cooperation with EU institutions, the decisions taken by the Council on the basis of the dossiers that are inherited by previous Presidencies as well as the forthcoming proposals. However, the Presidency can focus on certain important issues, which may define the identity of the Presidency.

Team presidencies

The ToL, which came into force on 1 December 2009, introduced the concept of team presidencies for the Council configurations. All configurations, other than the Foreign Affairs Council, are presided over by one of the Council's Member State representatives, on the basis of a system of equal rotation (Art 16(9) TEU). The European Council, acting by a qualified majority, determines the Presidency of each configuration, other than that of Foreign Affairs (Art 236 TFEU).

The President of a particular configuration is responsible for preparing the agenda for Council meetings, so that holding the presidency provides an opportunity for Member States to ensure that issues that are of importance to them are placed at the top of the agenda.

Function

The function of the Council is set out in Art 16(1) TEU (previously Art 202 EC Treaty) in very broad terms:

> The Council shall, jointly with the European Parliament, exercise legislative and budgetary functions. It shall carry out policy-making and coordinating functions as laid down in the Treaties.

Decision-making remains the central role of the Council and the different methods of decision-making are considered in detail in Chapter 4. Despite the increasingly important role of the European Parliament, particularly following amendments made to the EU Treaties by the ToL, in the overwhelming majority of cases the Council is the place where final decisions will be made. Discussions in the Council have previously been held in secret. However, in order to meet the requirement of transparency, Art 16(8) TEU now provides that the Council will meet in public when it deliberates and votes on a draft legislative act.

As stated above, the former Art 255 EC Treaty (now Art 15 TFEU) confers a right of access to all Council documents for all citizens of the Union, and any natural or legal person residing or having its registered office in a Member State. This has been implemented by Regulation 1049/2001, which came into effect on 3 December 2001. Refusal to grant access must be based on one of the exceptions provided for in the Regulation and must be justified on the ground that disclosure of the document would be harmful.

In the following case, the Court of Justice overturned a decision of the CFI (now the General Court) relating to access to legal advice given to the Council with regard to legislative questions:

Sweden and Turco v Council (Joined Cases C-39/05 AND C-52/05)

On 22 October 2002, Turco submitted a request to the Council for access to the documents appearing on the agenda of the 'Justice and Home Affairs' Council meeting, including an opinion of the Council's legal service on a proposal for a directive laying down minimum standards for the reception of applicants for asylum in Member States.

The Council refused to disclose the document, on the grounds that the advice of its legal service deserved particular protection because it was an important instrument which enabled the Council to be sure of the compatibility of its acts with Union law, and that disclosure of its legal service's opinions could create uncertainty regarding the legality of legislative acts adopted further to those opinions. The Council was of the view that in the circumstances there was no overriding public interest that would permit disclosure of the document. The principle of transparency and openness of the decision-making process relied upon by Turco did not, according to the Council, constitute a relevant criterion in so far as it would apply to all documents of its legal service, making it practically impossible for the Council to refuse access to any opinion under Regulation 1049/2001.

In *Turco v Council* (Case T-84/03), Turco asked the CFI to annul the Council's decision, but it declined to do so on the ground that disclosure of legal opinions such as that in question could give rise to lingering doubts as to the lawfulness of legislative acts to which such advice related and could also compromise the independence of the opinions of the Council's legal service. The CFI held that the overriding public interest in disclosure must be distinct from the principles underlying Regulation 1049/2001, in particular the principle of openness relied on by Turco.

Sweden and Mr Turco appealed to the Court of Justice.

In its judgment, the Court pointed out that **the examination undertaken by the Council before disclosing a document must be carried out in three stages: (i) it must satisfy itself that, over and above the way a document is described, that document does indeed concern legal advice; (ii) it must examine whether disclosure of the parts of the document in question would undermine the protection of legal advice; and (iii) it must ascertain whether there is any overriding public interest justifying disclosure.**

With regard to the second stage, the Court stated that the exception relating to legal advice in Regulation 1049/2001 is aimed at protecting an institution's interest in seeking frank, objective and comprehensive advice. The Court stated that the Council's general and abstract submission that disclosure could lead to doubts as to the lawfulness of a legislative act was not sufficient to establish that the protection of legal advice would be undermined, because it is precisely openness in this regard that contributes to greater legitimacy and confidence in the eyes of European citizens. Similarly, the Court stated that the independence of the Council's legal service would not be compromised by disclosure of legal opinions where there was no reasonably foreseeable and not purely hypothetical risk of that institution's interest in seeking frank, objective and comprehensive advice being undermined.

The Court stated that the disclosure of documents containing the advice of an institution's legal service on legal questions arising when legislative initiatives are being debated increases transparency and strengthens the democratic right of European citizens to scrutinise the information which has formed the basis of a legislative act.

The Court concluded that Regulation 1049/2001 imposes, in principle, an obligation to disclose the opinions of the Council's legal service relating to a legislative process. There are, however, exceptions to that principle as regards opinions given in the context of a legislative process, where the subject matter is of a particularly sensitive nature or where the opinion has a wide scope and goes beyond the context of the legislative process. In such a case, the institution concerned must give a detailed statement of reasons for refusing disclosure.

The Court of Justice set aside the CFI's judgment and annulled the Council's decision refusing Mr Turco access to the legal opinion in question.

COREPER

COREPER , which is the French acronym for the **Committee of Permanent Representatives**, plays an important role in providing continuity during the inevitable absences of relevant ministers from the Council. The Committee consists of senior national officials who are permanently located in Brussels. The Committee was originally established by Art 4 of the Merger Treaty in 1965, but it was formally integrated into the Union's decision-making structure by the former Art 207 EC Treaty (now Art 16(7) TEU and Art 240(1) TFEU). Article 16(7) TEU now provides that 'A Committee of Permanent Representatives of the Governments of the Member States shall be responsible for preparing the work of the Council'. Article 240(1) TFEU provides that 'A committee consisting of the Permanent Representatives of the Governments of the Member States shall be responsible for preparing the work of the Council and for carrying out the tasks assigned to it by the latter. The Committee may adopt procedural decisions in cases provided for in the Council's Rules of Procedure'.

The Committee operates on two levels: COREPER I, which consists of the ambassadors from the Member States who are seconded to the Union in Brussels, and COREPER II, which is staffed by the ambassadors' deputies. The primary task of COREPER is to prepare items for discussion at Council meetings and it will be assisted in this by a wide range of specialist advisory committees. If the text of a policy statement or legislation can be agreed before the meeting, it will be tabled in Part A of the Council agenda, where it will normally be adopted without further discussion. More difficult, controversial items, on which agreement has not been possible, will appear in Part B of the agenda. In these cases the issue may, subject to the appropriate legal base, have to be decided by a qualified majority vote (see Chapter 4). Now that Art 16(8) TEU requires the Council to meet in public when it deliberates and votes on a draft legislative act, each Council meeting is divided into two parts, dealing respectively with deliberations on Union legislative acts and non-legislative activities.

The European Parliament

Objective
4

The provisions of the EU Treaties governing the European Parliament are Art 14 TEU and Arts 223–234 TFEU (previously Arts 189–201 EC Treaty). The European Parliament's website can be accessed at:

http://www.europarl.europa.eu

The EC Treaty, as it was originally drawn in 1957, included provision for 'an Assembly' whose task was to 'exercise the advisory and supervisory powers' conferred upon it. The Assembly is now called 'The European Parliament' and the words 'advisory and supervisory' have disappeared. The Parliament, which in 1979 became a directly elected body, 'shall, jointly with the Council, exercise legislative and budgetary functions. It shall exercise functions of political control and consultation as laid down in the Treaties' (Art 14(1) TEU). Originally, its members were drawn from nominees from the national parliaments, but now it is the only directly elected institution in the Union. Article 14(3) TEU states that 'The members of the European Parliament shall be elected for a term of five years by direct universal suffrage in a free and secret ballot'. However, the name 'Parliament' is somewhat misleading. It shares a number of important features with national parliaments and has considerable influence but it falls short of being a real, sovereign parliament as would be understood in the UK. The principal difference is that it lacks the power both to initiate legislation and to impose taxes. Its powers have increased, however, and are likely to continue to do so following the changes to decision-making made by the SEA, TEU, ToA, ToN and ToL. The rationale for the increase in Parliament's powers has been to counter the argument that the Union was democratically deficient because its only directly elected body had no real powers.

Composition

Members of the European Parliament (MEPs) are elected on different variants of proportional representation. Prior to the June 1999 election, UK MEPs were elected by the first-past-the-post system as used for general elections (except in Northern Ireland where MEPs had previously been elected by a system of proportional representation). The UK Labour Party, which was elected to government following a landslide general election victory on 1 May 1997, had stated in its manifesto that: 'We have long supported a proportional voting system for election to the European Parliament'. The European Parliamentary Elections Act 1999 was duly enacted and was in force in time for the June 1999 MEP elections. The Act divided the UK into electoral regions, with MEPs being elected by a regional list system. The electorate votes either for *a registered party* (e.g. Labour, Conservatives, etc. – i.e. a closed party list system) or *an individual candidate* who stands as an independent. The first seat is allocated to the party or individual candidate with the greatest number of votes. The second and subsequent seats are allocated in the same way, but the number of votes given to a party to which one or more seats have already been allocated is divided by the number of seats allocated *plus one*.

Northern Ireland uses a different system, which is the same as that used for elections to the Northern Ireland Assembly.

2009–2014 European Parliamentary term

If the Treaty of Lisbon (ToL) had come into force prior to the European Parliament elections in June 2009, the EU Treaties would have been amended to enable a decision to be made, prior to these elections, which would have specified the total number of MEPs and the allocation of seats to each Member State.

Because the ToL was not in force when the June 2009 elections to the European Parliament took place, the total number of MEPs was restricted to 736, distributed in accordance with the former Art 190(2) EC Treaty. However, at its December 2008 meeting, the European Council adopted a declaration as follows:

> In the event that the Treaty of Lisbon enters into force after the European elections of June 2009, transitional measures will be adopted as soon as possible, in accordance with the necessary legal procedures, in order to increase, until the end of the 2009–2014 legislative period, in conformity with the numbers provided for in the framework of the IGC which approved the Treaty of Lisbon, the number of MEPs of twelve Member States for which the number of MEPs was set to increase. Therefore, the total number of MEPs will rise from 736 to 754 until the end of the 2009–2014 legislative period. The objective is that this modification should enter into force, if possible, during the year 2010.

Once the ToL came into force, a decision was made to increase the number of MEPs from 736 to 754. The additional 18 MEPs were elected for the remainder of the 2009–2014 parliamentary term. Article 19(1) of the Accession Treaty, which paved the way for Croatia's EU membership, provided for an additional 12 MEPs from Croatia, bringing the total number to 766 from 1 July 2013. This increase was expressly stipulated to be 'By way of derogation from Article 2 of the Protocol on transitional provisions ... and by way of derogation from the maximum number of seats provided for in ... Article 14(2) of the TEU'.

2014–2019 European Parliamentary term

The elections for the 2014–2019 European Parliamentary term were held during June 2014. The number of MEPs was reduced from 766 to 751, to comply with Art 14(2) TEU.

The allocation of seats to each Member State for the 2009–14 European Parliamentary term is as follows (alphabetically) (Table 3.2) and numerically (Table 3.3)

Table 3.2 Allocation of seats to each Member State for the 2014–19 European Parliamentary term (alphabetical)

Member State	Representatives	Member State	Representatives
Austria	18	Latvia	8
Belgium	21	Lithuania	11
Bulgaria	17	Luxembourg	6
Croatia	11	Malta	6
Cyprus	6	Netherlands	26
Czech Republic	21	Poland	51
Denmark	13	Portugal	21
Estonia	6	Romania	32
Finland	13	Slovakia	13
France	74	Slovenia	8
Germany	96	Spain	54
Greece	21	Sweden	20
Hungary	21	UK	73
Ireland	11		
Italy	73	**Total**	**751**

Table 3.3 Allocation of seats to each Member State for the 2014–19 European Parliamentary term (numerical)

Member State	Representatives	Member State	Representatives
Germany	96	Bulgaria	17
France	74	Denmark	13
Italy	73	Finland	13
UK	73	Slovakia	13
Spain	54	Croatia	11
Poland	51	Ireland	11
Romania	32	Lithuania	11
Netherlands	26	Latvia	8
Belgium	21	Slovenia	8
Czech Republic	21	Cyprus	6
Greece	21	Estonia	6
Hungary	21	Luxembourg	6
Portugal	21	Malta	6
Sweden	20		
Austria	18	**Total**	**751**

Protocol on the Privileges and Immunities of the European Union

MEPs enjoy protection under the Protocol on the Privileges and Immunities of the European Union. In particular, by reason of this immunity, Art 8 of the Protocol provides that MEPs may not be subject to any form of inquiry, detention or legal proceedings in respect of opinions expressed or votes cast by them in the performance of their duties.

When legal proceedings are brought against an MEP on account of opinions he has expressed or votes he has cast, it falls within the exclusive jurisdiction of the national court hearing the case to determine the case taking into account this immunity.

In the following case, criminal proceedings were brought before the Tribunale di Isernia (District Court, Isernia) against Mr Patriciello, an MEP. He was charged with the offence of making false accusations against a public official in the performance of his duties. It was alleged that, in the course of an altercation in a public car-park, he wrongfully accused a police officer of illegal conduct by asserting that the officer had falsified evidence relating to car parking offences:

Aldo Patriciello (Case C-163/10)

In 2009, acting in response to Patriciello's request, the European Parliament, taking the view that he had acted in the general interest of his constituents (Art 6(3) of the Rules of Procedure of the European Parliament), decided to defend that MEP's immunity.

The Italian court referred the case to the Court of Justice to enable the Court to define the tests relevant for determining whether a statement, made by an MEP outside the precincts of the European Parliament and giving rise to prosecution in his Member State of origin for the offence of making false accusations, constitutes 'an opinion expressed in the performance of his parliamentary duties' and may, on that ground, enjoy immunity.

The Court of Justice noted that the extent of the immunity in respect of opinions expressed or votes cast by MEPs in the performance of their parliamentary duties must be established on the basis of EU law alone. The immunity granted to MEPs is intended to protect their freedom of expression and their independence. It is therefore a bar to the bringing of any judicial proceedings in respect of those opinions or votes. It follows that if the substantive conditions for recognition of immunity have been met, immunity may not be waived by the European Parliament and the national court called upon to apply it is bound to dismiss the action brought against the MEP concerned.

The Court then made it clear that although parliamentary immunity essentially covers statements made within the precincts of the European Parliament, **it is not impossible that a statement made beyond those precincts may also amount to an opinion expressed in the performance of parliamentary duties. Whether or not it is such an opinion must therefore be determined having regard to its character and content, not to the place where it was made.**

The Court stated that parliamentary immunity is closely linked to freedom of expression, which is an essential foundation of a pluralist, democratic society reflecting the values on which the Union is based. Furthermore, this freedom constitutes a fundamental right guaranteed by the Charter of Fundamental Rights of the European Union which has the same legal value as the Treaties. The Court noted that it is also affirmed in the European Convention for the Protection of Human Rights and Fundamental Freedoms.

On the basis of those findings, the Court stated that the concept of an 'opinion' capable of attracting immunity must be understood in a wide sense to include remarks that, by their content, correspond to assertions amounting to subjective appraisal. **In order to enjoy immunity, an opinion must be connected with parliamentary duties.**

The Court held that recognition of immunity is capable of definitively preventing prosecutions for criminal offences and therefore denying the persons damaged by those offences of any judicial remedy, even of preventing their obtaining compensation for the damage suffered.

Having regard to those consequences, the Court stated that **immunity may be granted only if the connection between the opinion expressed and parliamentary duties is direct and obvious.**

It is for the Italian court to determine whether such a link is obvious in this particular case – i.e. whether the statement made by the MEP could be regarded as the expression of an opinion in the performance of parliamentary duties.

The Court stated, however, that having regard to the descriptions of the circumstances and the content of the allegations made by Patriciello, the latter's statements appeared to be far removed from his duties as an MEP. In the circumstances they were hardly capable of presenting a direct link to a general interest of concern to citizens.

Moreover, the Court noted that the European Parliament's decision to defend immunity was no more than an opinion without any binding effect on national courts.

Finally, if, having regard to the interpretation provided by this judgment, the national court decided not to follow the opinion of the European Parliament, EU law does not place the national court under any particular obligation as regards the reasons given for its decision.

Article 9 of the Protocol further provides that during sessions of the European Parliament, MEPs enjoy, *inter alia*, in the territory of their State, the immunities accorded to members of their national parliament. This is a matter of MEPs' privilege, which may be lifted in certain cases by the European Parliament. The following case concerned the application of Arts 8 and 9 of the Protocol:

Bruno Gollnisch v *Parliament* (Joint cases T-346/11 and T-347/11)

Bruno Gollnisch was an MEP and was also President of the Front National group of the Rhône-Alpes (France) regional council. On 3 October 2008, that group issued a press release. Following a complaint from the International League against Racism and Anti-Semitism (LICRA), the French authorities opened a judicial inquiry on 22 January 2009 for incitement to racial hatred.

On 14 June 2010, during a plenary session, the President of the European Parliament announced he had received a request from Gollnisch for defence of his immunity under the Protocol. The request was referred to the Legal Affairs Committee of the European Parliament for it to be examined.

The French authorities subsequently requested a waiver of Gollnisch's parliamentary immunity, in order to pursue the investigation of the complaint.

On 10 May 2011, the European Parliament adopted two decisions: (i) to waive Gollnisch's immunity; and (ii) not to defend his immunity.

Gollnisch brought an action before the General Court seeking annulment of those two decisions and for compensation for the non-material damage he claimed to have suffered.

The General Court rejected both actions brought by Gollnisch.

The General Court reiterated that the rules on immunity of MEPs, established by the Protocol, sought to protect the freedom of expression and the independence of MEPs and that parliamentary privilege included, in principle, protection from judicial proceedings (Arts 8 and 9 of the Protocol).

The General Court clarified the distinction between *waiver* of immunity and *defence* of immunity within the meaning of the Protocol. *Defence* of immunity only covered the case where there had been no request for the waiver of an MEP's immunity, but his privilege, which was to be inferred from provisions of the national legislation of the Member State of origin of the MEP, was compromised *inter alia* by actions of the national police or judicial authorities.

The General Court stated that in *Patriciello* (Case C-163/10), the Court of Justice had held that an MEP's opinion (in the broadest sense) was only covered by immunity if it had been expressed 'in the performance of [his duties]', thus implying the requirement of a link between the opinion expressed and the performance of the parliamentary duties. That link had to be direct and obvious.

However, in the present case, the General Court noted that the statement set out in the press release, allegedly made by Gollnisch, concerned the manner in which the President and Director General of services of the Rhône-Alpes regional council reacted to a request from the intelligence services seeking to obtain information in relation to certain civil servants. It was not disputed that the statement was drafted by the spokesperson of the Front National group, of which Gollnisch was President. It was also not disputed that, during a press conference which took place in Lyon, Gollnisch confirmed that the press release had been drafted by persons authorised to speak in the name of the elected representatives of the political group concerned within the regional council. Those facts directly concerned the duties carried out by the applicant acting in his capacity as regional councillor and President of the Front National group. Consequently, there was no link between the statement allegedly made by Gollnisch and his duties as MEP nor, *a fortiori*, a direct and obvious link between the statement at issue and his duties as an MEP.

The Parliament could not therefore be criticised, having regard to the circumstances of the present case and to France's application, for having lifted the immunity of Gollnisch so as to allow the French authorities to pursue their investigation on the basis of the Protocol.

In the same way, the General Court held that the Parliament considered correctly that the judicial investigation initiated in France had not been brought with the intention of causing damage to his political activity as a MEP. The judicial proceedings had not been brought by a political opponent but by an association authorised under French law to bring proceedings against exponents of written or oral racist or anti-Semitic statements. In addition, the proceedings did not concern either historical matters or acts carried out during an electoral campaign and further, there was no evidence to show that the manifest purpose of the proceedings was to make an example out of him.

The obligation for the Parliament to examine, with care and impartiality, all the pertinent elements of the present case had been met.

Finally, the General Court stated that Gollnisch had failed to show a breach of the principle of sound administration. The same was true in relation to the principle of equal treatment, as Gollnisch had been unable to show that he had been the subject of different treatment in comparison with that usually reserved for MEPs in comparable situations.

Consequently, the General Court dismissed the applications and the subsidiary application for compensation.

Political groups

MEPs are elected for a term of five years (Art 14(3) TEU). They stand as members of national political parties, but sit within broad political rather than national groupings in the European Parliament. As at 1 December 2015 the political groups were represented within the European Parliament as follows (Table 3.4):

Table 3.4 European Parliament political groups as at 1 December 2015

Political Party	Number of seats
European People's Party (Christian Democrats)	216
Progressive Alliance of Socialists and Democrats (includes UK Labour Party MEPs)	190
European Conservatives and Reformists (includes UK Conservative MPs)	75
Alliance of Liberals and Democrats for Europe (includes UK Liberal Democrat MEPs)	70
European United Left/Nordic Green Left	52
Greens/European Free Alliance	51
Europe of Freedom and Direct Democracy Group	45
Europe of Nations and Freedom	39
Others (unattached and vacant seats) plus the President	15
Total	**751**

The number of MEPs attached to each of the official political parties is available at:

http://www.europarl.europa.eu/meps/en/crosstable.html

Article 10(4) TEU (previously Art 191 EC Treaty) states that 'Political parties at European level contribute to forming European political awareness and to expressing the political will of citizens of the Union'.

Political activity in the European Parliament largely takes place through the groups. The European Parliament's Rules of Procedure were amended on 30 November 2009. The latest version of the Rules (January 2015) are practically unchanged from the November 2009 amended version. Prior to the November 2009 amendments, Rule 29(2) related to the formation of political parties within the Parliament:

A political group shall comprise Members elected in at least one-fifth of the Member States. The minimum number of Members required to form a political group shall be twenty.

The effect of this provision was that a political group could only be formed if it included at least 20 MEPs from at least 6 Member States.

The Identity, Tradition and Sovereignty Group was a far-right political group, with 23 MEPs attached to it. However, following an inter-group row during November 2007 between an Italian MEP (Alessandra Mussolini, the granddaughter of the Italian wartime Fascist dictator) and five Romanian MEPs, the five Romanian MEPs withdrew from the group. This led to the political group's collapse because it fell below the minimum needed to form a political group. The row had escalated when it was reported that Mussolini commented that 'Breaking the law has become a way of life for Romanians'. Her comment followed the expulsion of a number of Romanians from Italy after a Romanian gypsy was arrested for the murder of an Italian naval officer.

The European Parliament's Rules of Procedure were amended on 30 November 2009. Rule 32(2) of the Rules of Procedure (January 2015 version) now governs the formation of political parties within the Parliament:

A political group shall comprise Members elected in at least **one-quarter** of the Member States. The minimum number of Members required to form a political group shall be **25**. [emphasis added]

There are a number of reasons why groups have developed. Primarily they are formed to provide mutual ideological support and identification. In addition, there are organisational benefits, including funds for administrative and research purposes which are better deployed in support of groups than for individuals. There are also advantages in the conduct of Parliamentary business that stem from group status, as the Parliament arranges much of its business around the groups. Although non-attached members are not formally excluded, and indeed are guaranteed many rights under the Rules of Procedure, they can, in practice, be disadvantaged in the distribution of committee chairmanships or in the preparation of the agendas for plenary sessions (i.e. meetings of the full Parliament).

A section of the Parliament's website is set aside for the political groups, each of which publishes a plethora of information. The website for the political groups can be accessed at:

http://www.europarl.europa.eu/aboutparliament

The following case, which came before the CFI (now the General Court), concerned 29 formerly unattached MEPs who sought to form a group (and therefore receive the financial and organisational benefits bestowed upon groups):

Jean Claude Martinez, Charles De Gaulle, Front National, Emma Bonino, Marco Pannella, Marco Cappato, Gianfranco Dell'Alba, Benedetto Della Vedova, Olivier Dupuis, Maurizio Turco, Lista Emma Bonino v *European Parliament* (Joined Cases T-222/99, T-327/99 and T-329/99)

Twenty-nine MEPs informed the President of the European Parliament (as required under Rule 29(4) of the Rules of Procedure (now Rule 32(1))) of the formation of their group: Technical Group of Independent Members – Mixed Group. The 'rules of constitution' for this new group declared that:

> ... the individual signatory members affirm their total independence of one another. And hence: freedom to vote independently both in committee and plenary session; each member shall refrain from speaking on behalf of the Members of the group as a whole; the purpose of meetings of the group shall be to allocate speaking time and to settle any administrative and financial matters concerning the group; and the Bureau of the group shall be made up of the representatives of the individual members.

At the time, Rule 29(1) (now Rule 32(1)) provided that 'members may form themselves into groups according to their political affinities'. Having been through various Parliamentary procedures, on 13 September 1999 the Parliament determined that Rule 29(1) should be interpreted such that 'the formation of a group which openly rejects any political character and all political affiliation between its Members is not acceptable within the meaning of this Rule'. Given the new group's constitution, which guaranteed its members total independence, the Parliament resolved to dissolve the group. Members of the group issued proceedings before the CFI (now the General Court) contesting these decisions. The Court dismissed the applications.

The above case provides that political groups within Parliament must share some common ideological platform and must work together within Parliament. If that is not the case then Parliament can refuse to recognise the group and thus prevent it from being provided with the financial and organisational benefits bestowed upon groups. In the above case it did seem quite clear that the group members shared very little in common, were not prepared to work together within the Parliament, and were simply forming the group so that they could take advantage of the benefits. Rule 226(5) of the Rules of Procedure provides that 'Uncontested interpretations and interpretations adopted by Parliament shall be appended in italic print as explanatory notes to the appropriate Rule or Rules'. Rule 32(1) now includes the following explanatory note:

Parliament need not normally evaluate the political affinity of members of a group. In forming a group together under this Rule, the Members concerned accept by definition that they have political affinity. Only when this is denied by the Members concerned is it necessary for Parliament to evaluate whether the group has been constituted in accordance with the Rules.

Article 224 TFEU provides that the European Parliament and the Council shall lay down the regulations governing political parties at European level and in particular the rules regarding their funding.

Parliamentary meetings

The Parliament holds plenary sessions (i.e. all MEPs congregating together in one chamber) in Strasbourg, committee meetings in Brussels and is serviced by staff located in Luxembourg. A new building was erected in Brussels for full Parliamentary sessions but the European Council meeting in Edinburgh in December 1992 confirmed that the Parliament would remain in Strasbourg. A new Parliament building was opened in Strasbourg in December 1999 to ensure that the chamber could accommodate all the MEPs. Enlargement of Union membership, and the resultant increase in the number of MEPs, meant that the previous chamber was too small. A decision by the Parliament to increase the number of plenary sessions held in Brussels was struck down by the Court of Justice in October 1997 (*France* v *European Parliament* (Case C-345/95)). MEPs and officials will continue to live a highly peripatetic existence, largely because the Parliament is a major employer and the Member States cannot agree on a single, permanent site for it. Indeed, Protocol No. 6, which is annexed to the TEU and the TFEU, confirms the split location for the Parliament:

> The European Parliament shall have its seat in Strasbourg where the 12 periods of monthly plenary sessions, including the budget session, shall be held. The periods of additional plenary sessions shall be held in Brussels. The Committees of the European Parliament shall meet in Brussels. The General Secretariat of the European Parliament and its departments shall remain in Luxembourg.

Except in August, the Parliament sits for one week in each month in Strasbourg. It occasionally sits for additional periods to discuss special items, such as the budget. Between the monthly part-sessions, two weeks are set aside for meetings of the Parliamentary committees, and one week for meetings of the political groups.

Full details of the Parliamentary agenda and post-session report are available on the Parliament's website at:

http://www.europarl.europa.eu/plenary

Committee meetings

The Parliament has a large range of specialist committees. Some are permanent, while others are *ad hoc* (i.e. set up to consider a particular matter). The committees cover such matters as Internal Market and Consumer Protection; Economic and Monetary Affairs; Employment and Social Affairs; Transport and Tourism; Budgets; Foreign Affairs.

Much of Parliament's legislative groundwork will be conducted in committee. When Parliament receives a request from the Council or Commission for an opinion, approval or assent, the request will be sent to the relevant committee for a report to be prepared for full debate and vote in the chamber. The committee will appoint a member to be responsible for preparing the report. This person is called the **'Rapporteur'**. The Rapporteur will lead the debate when the report of the committee comes before the full Parliament (i.e. when the Parliament sits in plenary session in Strasbourg).

The committees follow legislative and policy matters in detail and, as they usually meet *in camera* (i.e. the public are excluded from their meetings unless invited to attend by the Chairperson), they are given confidential information, both by Commission officials and by the independent experts and representatives of pressure groups who appear before them.

Powers of the Parliament

There are three main powers exercised by the Parliament:

- participation in the legislative processes of the Union;
- acting as the budgetary authority;
- supervision of the Commission.

In addition to these formal powers, the Parliament takes an active part in the political life of the Union, commissioning reports and passing resolutions on social and political issues, human rights, defence and foreign policy and on many other matters. It can, however, do little more than express a view on the issues about which the majority of MEPs are concerned.

Article 225 TFEU (previously Art 192 EC Treaty) provides that the European Parliament, acting by a majority of its component members, may:

> ... request the Commission to submit any appropriate proposal on matters on which it considers that a Union act is required for the purposes of implementing the Treaties. If the Commission does not submit a proposal it shall inform the European Parliament of the reasons.

The European Parliament approves the admission of new Member States (Art 49 TEU). Parliament has the power to set up a temporary *Committee of Inquiry* to 'investigate ... alleged contraventions or maladministration in the implementation of Union law' (Art 226 TFEU (previously Art 193 EC Treaty)), and to appoint a *Parliamentary Ombudsman* to investigate complaints about any of the other Union institutions, except the Court of Justice of the European Union acting in its judicial role (Art 228 TFEU (previously Art 195 EC Treaty)). Emily O'Reilly is the current European Ombudsman. The Ombudsman can investigate complaints against the Union institutions of maladministration, which includes such matters as unfairness, discrimination, abuse of power, lack or refusal of information or unnecessary delay. The Ombudsman's website can be accessed at:

http://www.ombudsman.europa.eu

The role of Parliament in the decision-making process is discussed in Chapter 4.

The budget

In relation to the budget, the Parliament has an important function, which it shares with the Council. The Union's budget is drafted by the Commission and placed before the Council and the European Parliament before 1 September each year. This is necessary because the Union's financial year runs from 1 January to 31 December (Art 313 TFEU). The budget is divided into two parts: compulsory expenditure (CE) and non-compulsory expenditure (NCE). CE relates to those items where the expenditure is required by the

EU Treaties, primarily the Common Agricultural Policy, which usually absorbs around 50 per cent of the total budget, whereas NCE covers such items as social and regional policy, research and aid to non-EU countries in Central and Eastern Europe.

Prior to the ToL, Parliament had wide powers to amend NCE items, but its powers to modify CE items were more limited under the former Art 272 EC Treaty. Parliament could, however, acting by a majority of its members, representing a two-thirds majority of the votes actually cast, reject the whole of the draft budget and ask for a new draft to be submitted to it (former Art 272(8) EC Treaty). If that occurred, the Union institutions had to continue on a month-by-month basis, spending no more than one-twelfth per month of the previous year's budget until a new budget was approved (former Art 273 EC Treaty).

Following amendments made by the ToL, the European Parliament's role in the budgetary process has been enhanced. Article 314(4) TFEU provides that the European Parliament may amend any part of the draft budget, irrespective of whether the item concerns CE or NCE. The Parliament adopts amendments by a majority of its component members (Art 314(4)(c) TFEU). If this occurs, a meeting of the Conciliation Committee is convened, comprising members of the Council and the European Parliament. The aim of this Committee is to seek agreement between the members on a joint text (Art 314(5) TFEU). Ultimately, if a joint text cannot be agreed, the Commission is required to submit a new draft budget (Art 314(8) TFEU).

Supervision of the Commission

There is close and continuous contact between the Commissioners and the European Parliament. Although Commissioners are not members of the Parliament, they frequently take part in debates where legislation is under discussion, and they will often attend the specialist committees of the Parliament to deal with detailed points arising from Commission proposals. Commissioners have the right to attend the European Parliament and to be heard (Art 230 TFEU (previously Art 197 EC Treaty)).

Commissioners have a duty to respond, orally or in writing, to questions put to them by the European Parliament or its members (Art 230 TFEU (previously Art 197 EC Treaty)). Since 1974, this has become formalised into a Westminster-type Question Time which is held at each part-session at times decided by Parliament (Rule 129, Rules of Procedure, January 2015). Outside these part-sessions, there are regular exchanges between the Commission, the various Parliamentary Committees and individual MEPs.

Parliament has the right to dismiss the Commission *en bloc* under Art 17(8) TEU and Art 234 TFEU (previously Art 201 EC Treaty). Although it has never done so, as discussed above, it effectively forced Jacques Santer's Commission from office when Parliament threatened to use its censuring powers. The Commission accepted defeat and resigned, rather than face the humiliation of a certain defeat.

The powers of the Parliament have been reinforced by the requirement that the new Commission (i.e. the President, the High Representative of the Union for Foreign Affairs and Security Policy, and the other members of the Commission) is subject to a vote of consent by the Parliament (Art 17(7) TEU (previously Art 214(2) EC Treaty)). Prior to taking up office in 1995, individual Commissioners in the Santer administration were subjected to intensive questioning in American-style appointment committees. As a result of this questioning, Padraig Flynn, the Commissioner for Social Affairs, gave up the chair of the Commission's women's rights committee to the President of the Commission, Jacques Santer. As discussed above, the 2004–2009 Commission's period of office started on

22 November 2004. This was three weeks later than planned, due to political problems which surfaced during the appointments process. During the European Parliamentary approval stage, the Parliament opposed the appointment of Rocco Buttiglione (from Italy). Franco Frattini (from Italy) took the place of Rocco Buttiglione. The President-elect also requested the replacement of Latvia's Ingridia Udre, and reshuffled two portfolios. Following these changes, the European Parliament approved the appointments.

The current Commission took office on 1 November 2014, following the European Parliament's vote of consent.

As previously discussed, the Commission's Work Programme is put together and implemented in close conjunction with Parliament, and there is a considerable coincidence of interest to both the Commission and Parliament in developing Union-wide policies. Where these fail to materialise, it is often as a result of the more nationally orientated policies of the Member States, reflected in the Council.

Enlargement of the powers of the European Parliament

The most obvious difference between the European Parliament and national parliaments is its inability to initiate legislation.

As discussed in Chapter 4, although Parliament has at a minimum, in most cases, the right to be consulted, such consultation may mean no more than the right to comment on a draft prepared by the Commission. Under some Treaty provisions there is no right of consultation at all, although Commission and Council practice is, nonetheless, to seek Parliament's views. In other cases, especially in relation to decisions in the field of economic and monetary policy, Parliament has no more than the right to be informed of the decision reached by the Council (Art 121(2) TFEU (previously Art 99(2) EC Treaty), and Art 126(11) TFEU (previously 104(11) EC Treaty)). Even where Parliament's opinion must be sought, there remains considerable scope for rejection of its views by the Council, provided that Parliament's opinion is properly considered by the Council.

It was widely felt that these limitations were inappropriate for the only democratically elected institution in the Union. The role of Parliament in the legislative process has been strengthened following amendments to the EU Treaties by the SEA, TEU, ToA, ToN and ToL. Most recently, the 'ordinary legislative procedure' was introduced by the ToL and it is modelled on the former co-decision procedure. This procedure, which now applies in the vast majority of cases, empowers the Parliament to put forward amendments to a legislative proposal and ultimately to block the Council from adopting the legislative proposal (see Chapter 4).

There is, arguably, a 'democratic deficit' in relation to Parliament's inability to dismiss individual Commissioners and to make Ministers accountable to Parliament for their decisions in the Council. Although Council documents are now available after meetings, and Council deliberations on legislative acts are now open to the public (Art 16(8) TEU), the meetings of the Council generally take place in more or less complete secrecy. There is considerable support, largely among MEPs, for a Minister from the Council to be required to attend the Parliamentary debate and to report back to the Parliament at the conclusion of the ministerial meeting. Although there is some support for these proposals in Germany and The Netherlands, the UK government has remained firmly opposed to them, on the grounds that they would further undermine the powers of the UK Parliament to which national ministers are, in the last resort, solely accountable.

Court of Auditors

The Court of Auditors was established by an amendment to the Treaties in 1975 (second Budgetary Treaty 1975). It is not, strictly speaking, a court, but more an audit commission. It is responsible for the external audit of the general budget of the Union. The internal audit is the responsibility of the Financial Controller of each institution.

The Court came into being partly as a result of the desire of some of the newer Member States to establish more effective audit arrangements and partly as a result of the desire of the European Parliament to have greater power in the financial affairs of the Union. An independent audit body is seen by the European Parliament as an important part in establishing greater financial control. It had, initially, the status of a separate body but, since the TEU came into effect in 1993, it has been classed as one of the Union institutions (Art 13(1) TEU).

The Court consists of 28 full-time members, one from each Member State (Art 285 TFEU (previously Art 246 EC Treaty)). The Council, after consulting the European Parliament, adopts the list of 28 members drawn up in accordance with the proposals made by each Member State (Art 286(2) TFEU (previously Art 247(2) EC Treaty)). The members shall be chosen from 'among persons who belong or have belonged in their respective States to external audit bodies or who are especially qualified for this office. Their independence must be beyond doubt' (Art 286(1) TFEU (previously Art 247(2) EC Treaty)). The Court of Auditors' website can be accessed at:

http://www.eca.europa.eu

The European Central Bank

Article 13(1) TEU recognises the European Central Bank (ECB) as one of the Union institutions. It is linked to the establishment of a European System of Central Banks. The ECB was initially set up as part of the progression towards economic and monetary union. The ECB can enact legislation, impose fines, submit opinions and be consulted within its field of operation (Arts 282–284 TFEU (previously Arts 105, 106, 107 and 110 EC Treaty)). The ECB's website can be accessed at:

http://www.ecb.europa.eu

The European Economic and Social Committee (EESC)

The European Economic and Social Committee (EESC) was established by the former Art 257 EC Treaty to assist the Council and the Commission in an advisory capacity. The Committee originally consisted of 'representatives of the various categories of economic and social activity, in particular, representatives of producers, farmers, carriers, workers, dealers, craftsmen, professional occupations and representatives of the general public'. The ToN amended Art 257 EC Treaty to provide that the Committee would consist of 'representatives of the various economic and social components of organised civil society, and in particular representatives of producers, farmers, carriers, workers, dealers, craftsmen, professional occupations, consumers and the general public'. Consumers were explicitly included for the first time. The ToL further amended this provision, and now Art 300(2)

TFEU provides that the Committee shall consist of 'representatives of organisations of employers, of the employed, and of other parties representative of civil society, notably in socio-economic, civic, professional and cultural areas'. The Committee's website can be accessed at:

http://www.eesc.europa.eu

The Council adopts the list of members drawn up in accordance with proposals made by each Member State. Before adopting the list, the Council has to consult with the Commission, and it may additionally obtain the opinion of European bodies which are representative of the various economic and social sectors and of civil society to which the Union's activities are of concern (Art 302 TFEU (previously Art 259 EC Treaty)).

Members are appointed for a period of five years and they may be reappointed (Art 302 TFEU (previously Art 259 EC Treaty)). Seats are allocated according to the relative population of each Member State. Article 301 TFEU provides that the number of members of the EESC shall not exceed 350.

Members of the Committee shall not be bound by any mandatory instructions, and they shall be 'completely independent in the performance of their duties, in the Union's general interest' (Art 300(4) TFEU).

Function of the Committee

The European Economic and Social Committee (EESC) is not recognised by Art 13(1) TEU as one of the Union institutions, although it is mentioned in Art 13(4) TEU. A requirement in Art 24 of the Merger Treaty that the Council consult 'other institutions' when adopting or amending staff regulations was held not to apply to the EESC (*Adam v Commission* (Case 828/79)). Article 304 TFEU (previously Art 262 EC Treaty) provides that the EESC must be consulted by the European Parliament, the Council or the Commission where the Treaties so provide; in other cases consultation is at the discretion of those institutions. When the Committee is consulted, it responds by the submission of an opinion to the relevant institutions (Art 304 TFEU). These institutions can, if they wish, impose a deadline for the submission of an opinion, but this must not be less than one month (Art 304 TFEU). Failure to deliver an opinion cannot prevent further action by the institutions. The Committee also has the right to submit opinions on its own initiative where it considers such action appropriate (Art 304 TFEU). Opinions of the EESC are prepared by a section designated by the Chairperson and then discussed and adopted at plenary sessions of the full Committee held during the last seven days of the month (Title II, EESC's Rules of Procedure). Although the Committee's opinions are not legally binding, the expertise of the Committee's membership does mean that they carry considerable weight with the institutions. Where the EU Treaties require consultation with the EESC, failure to do so could lead to the annulment of a measure by the Court of Justice of the European Union, on the basis of failure to meet an essential procedural requirement (see Chapter 8).

The Committee of the Regions

The Committee of the Regions, like the EESC, is not recognised by Art 13(1) TEU as one of the Union institutions, although it is mentioned in Art 13(4) TEU. It was intended to represent a move towards more region-orientated decision-making, and to create 'an ever closer union among the peoples of Europe', as required by Art 1 TEU. The Committee's website can be accessed at:

http://cor.europa.eu

Members are appointed for a period of five years and they may be reappointed (Art 302 TFEU (previously Art 259 EC Treaty)). Seats are allocated according to the relative population of each Member State. Article 305 TFEU (previously Art 263 EC Treaty) provides that the number of members of the Committee of the Regions shall, like the EESC, not exceed 350.

The members were previously representatives of regional and representative bodies in the Member States. The former Art 263 EC Treaty (now Art 300 TFEU) was amended by the ToN to provide that the Committee shall consist of 'representatives of regional and local bodies *who either hold a regional or local authority electoral mandate or are politically accountable to an elected assembly'* (emphasis added). Members therefore need to have an electoral mandate to represent citizens at a local level. No member of the Committee shall at the same time be a Member of the European Parliament (Art 305 TFEU).

Where a member's mandate comes to an end, their membership of the Committee shall automatically terminate (Art 305 TFEU).

Function of the Committee

Prior to the ToL, the Committee's basic role was comparable to the EESC, its principal role being to deliver opinions on legislation when consulted by the European Parliament, the Council or the Commission. It issues own-initiative opinions in appropriate cases (Art 307 TFEU). The Committee's members are not bound by mandatory instructions, and members are completely independent in the performance of their duties 'in the Union's general interest' (Art 300(4) TFEU).

Following the ToL coming into force on 1 December 2009, the Committee has been given the power to challenge legislative proposals it considers to be in breach of the subsidiarity principle (the principle that decisions should be taken as closely as possible to the citizens). This power is established by Art 8, Protocol No. 2 which is attached to the TEU and TFEU. It only applies if the legal base for a legislative proposal requires consultation with the Committee. The President of the Committee of the Regions, or the Committee's member who is responsible for drawing up the draft opinion, may propose that an action be brought before the Court of Justice. This proposal will be considered by the full Committee, which will decide on the proposal by a majority of the votes cast. If such a decision is adopted, the action shall be brought before the Court of Justice by the President on behalf of the Committee.

See pages 150–153 for a discussion of the subsidiarity principle.

Summary

Now you have read this chapter you should be able to:

- Name the institutions of the Union established by Art 13(1) TEU.

- Outline the composition, role and powers of each Union institution and explain the difference between the European Council and the Council.

- Discuss the respective roles of the President of the European Council, and the High Representative of the Union for Foreign Affairs and Security Policy.

- Understand the composition, role and powers of the Union advisory bodies.

Reference

Grant, C., 'The House that Jacques Built', *Independent*, 29 June 1994.

Further reading

Textbooks

Craig, P. and De Burca, G. (2011) *EU Law: Text, Cases and Materials* (5th edn), Oxford University Press, Chapter 2.

Foster, N. (2015) *Foster on EU Law* (5th edn), Oxford University Press, Chapter 2.

Steiner, J. and Woods, L. (2014) *EU Law* (12th edn), Oxford University Press, Chapter 2.

Journal articles

Alemanno, A., 'Unpacking the principle of openness in EU law: Transparency, participation and democracy' (2014) 39 EL Rev 72.

Amtenbrink, F. and Van Duin, K., 'The European Central Bank before the European Parliament: Theory and practice after ten years of monetary dialogue' (2009) 34 EL Rev 561.

Driessen, B., 'The Council of the European Union and access to documents' (2005) 30 EL Rev 675.

Grant, C., 'The house that Jacques built', *Independent*, 29 June 1994.

Heliskoski, J. and Leino, P., 'Darkness at the break of noon: The case law on Regulation No. 1049/2001 on access to documents' (2006) 43 CML Rev 735.

Kaeding, M. and Hardacre, A., 'The European Parliament and the future of comitology after Lisbon' (2013) 19 ELJ 382.

Kranenborg, H., 'Access to documents and data protection in the European Union: On the public nature of personal data' (2008) 45 CML Rev 1079.

Pech, L., '"A Union founded on the rule of law": Meaning and reality of the rule of law as a constitutional principle of EU law' (2010) 6 ECL Rev 359.

Tsadiras, A., 'Rules of institutional "flat sharing": The European Ombudsman and his national peers' (2008) 33 EL Rev 101.

Tsadiras, A., 'The European Ombudsman's remedial powers: An empirical analysis in context' (2013) 38 EL Rev 52.

Tsadiras, A., 'Unravelling Ariadne's thread: The European Ombudsman's investigative powers' (2008) 45 CML Rev 757.

4

The decision-making process

Objectives

At the end of this chapter you should understand:

1. The respective roles of the Union's institutions and national parliaments within the Union's legislative process.

2. The importance of choosing the appropriate legal base when adopting secondary Union legislation, and how this choice of legal base impacts upon the voting systems used in the Council of Ministers.

3. The legislative process, including:
   - the ordinary legislative procedure;
   - the special legislative procedure;
   - other procedures.

4. The relevance of the principle of subsidiarity to the Union's decision-making process, and the role of national parliaments in enforcing the application of this principle.

Decision-making within the Union

Decision-making is central to the effective functioning of the Union. Decisions made by Union institutions may relate to the implementation of a policy, such as enlargement of the Union, or the adoption of a trade agreement with other states, or they may be part of a number of different legislative programmes. The type of process will be determined by the subject matter of the decision, as interpreted (normally) by the Commission. The Commission (because it is normally empowered to make the proposal) will then choose the appropriate *legal base* in the EU Treaties (see below). That choice will determine which institutions and other bodies will be involved in the process, the voting system used in the Council and the extent to which the European Parliament will be able to influence the content of the measure and, in some cases, whether it is approved at all. Although, as discussed in Chapter 3, the European Council plays an increasingly important role in setting policy goals, the task of translating those goals into specific policy decisions and legislation still belongs almost exclusively to the Commission. The European Parliament does have the power under Art 225 TFEU (previously Art 192 EC Treaty) to suggest new areas for legislation, but the decision on whether or not to bring forward such legislation and in what form is for the Commission alone. Apart from a few exceptional situations where the Council may act on its own initiative, and in the case of foreign and security policy (Arts 23–46 TEU), in most cases the EU Treaties provide that the Council shall act on a proposal from the Commission. This is confirmed by Art 17(2) TEU, which provides that the power of legislative initiative rests with the Commission 'except where the Treaties provide otherwise'.

Dialogue between the Commission, Council and European Parliament

Objective 1

The virtual monopoly the Commission enjoys over the legislative process could cause serious problems. If the Commission submits no proposals, the Council is paralysed and the progress of the Union comes to a halt, whether in the field of the internal market, agriculture, transport, commercial policy or the environment. However, except for a period of relative stagnation during the economic crisis of the 1970s, the Commission has always been active in promoting the development of the Union through a series of legislative programmes. As discussed in Chapter 3, the Commission outlines its annual Work Programme each year. This programme provides a framework of policy and legislative objectives. The Commission then brings forward a series of proposals within that programme. Once a proposal is lodged, a dialogue begins between Commission officials and the representatives of the Council in COREPER. This will continue until the legislation has passed through all its stages and the Council has finally approved it. Where the legislative process requires involvement of the European Parliament, the Commission will similarly open a dialogue with the Parliament.

See page 116 for further discussion of COREPER.

Legislative proposals

Legislative proposals may result from the implementation of a wide programme of action, such as that laid down in the plans for the internal market, or in response to particular circumstances calling for specific legislation. The appropriate Directorate General – assisted by one of the Commission's advisory committees – will prepare the first draft, which will initially be approved by the appropriate Commissioner holding the relevant portfolio. The views of these advisory committees, which will contain representatives of industrial, commercial and social interests in Member States, are not in any sense binding on the Commission. The Commission, voting as a collegiate body on a simple majority basis, will then consider the proposal.

EU competences and the principle of conferral

Article 5(1) TEU provides that 'the limits of Union competences are governed by the principle of conferral'. This means the Union shall act 'only within the limits of the competences conferred upon it by the Member States in the Treaties to attain the objectives set out therein' (Art 5(2) TEU). The corollary is that 'Competences not conferred upon the Union in the Treaties remain with the Member States' (Art 5(2) TEU).

The TFEU distinguishes between three categories of Union power:

1   Areas of *exclusive* competence where only the EU may legislate and adopt legally binding acts. The Member States can only act if empowered to do so by the Union, or to implement Union acts. Article 3 TFEU provides that the EU has exclusive competence in the following areas:

- customs union;
- establishing competition rules necessary for the functioning of the internal market;
- monetary policy for the Member States whose currency is the euro;
- conservation of marine biological resources under the common fisheries policy;
- common commercial policy;
- conclusion of specific international agreements.

2   Areas of *shared* competence where the EU and the Member States may legislate and adopt legally binding acts. The Member States can only exercise this shared competence if the EU has not exercised its competence to act, or if the EU has ceased to exercise its competence. Article 4 TFEU provides that the EU and the Member States have shared competence in the following principal areas:

- internal market;
- certain aspects of social policy;
- economic, social and territorial cohesion;
- agriculture and fisheries;
- environment;
- consumer protection;
- transport;
- trans-European networks;
- energy;
- area of freedom, security and justice;
- certain aspects of common safety concerns in public health matters.

3   Areas where the Union carries out actions to *support, coordinate or supplement* the actions of the Member States. Article 6 TFEU provides that this applies in the following areas:

- protection and improvement of human health;
- industry;
- culture;
- tourism;
- education, vocational training, youth and sport;
- civil protection;
- administrative cooperation.

Particular cases which do not fit into this threefold general classification are dealt with separately, for example: (i) coordination of economic and employment policies (Art 2(3) TFEU); and (ii) common foreign and security policy (Art 2(4) TFEU).

Legal base

Objective 2

Before the Commission considers drafting a proposal, it must ensure that it has the necessary competence to act, i.e. it must find a *legal base* within the relevant Treaty. Articles 45 and 46 TFEU (previously Arts 39 and 40 EC Treaty) were discussed in Chapter 2, and it was noted that the Commission is empowered to propose legislative acts in relation to the free movement of workers. The extent of this power is set out in Art 46 TFEU and must not be exceeded, i.e. 'The European Parliament and the Council shall … issue directives or make regulations setting out the measures required to bring about freedom of movement for workers, as defined in Article 45 ...'. If it is exceeded, the resulting instrument may be struck down by the Court of Justice, as being *ultra vires*; i.e. in excess of power (see below).

General legislative power

Article 352 TFEU provides the Union with a *general* legislative power if no *specific* power has been provided by the Treaties: 'If action by the Union should prove necessary ... to attain one of the objectives set out in the Treaties, and the Treaties have not provided the necessary powers, the Council ... shall adopt the appropriate measures' (Art 352(1) TFEU). Its scope appears wider than that of the former Art 308 EC Treaty, because Art 308 was confined to the internal market. However, the conditions under which Art 352 TFEU can be exercised are stricter in that, as well as requiring unanimity in the Council, the consent of the European Parliament must be obtained.

Voting procedures

The Commission

Decisions by the Commission on whether or not to adopt a proposal are taken by a simple majority of its members (Art 250 TFEU). Although the appropriate Director General will initiate a proposal, the Commission as a body has no power to delegate approval of the details of that proposal to an individual Commissioner. The Court of Justice made the position clear in the following case:

Commission v *Basf and Others* (Case C-137/92)

The Court of Justice stated that:

> The functioning of the Commission is governed by the principle of collegiate responsibility. The principle of collegiate responsibility is based on the equal participation of the Commissioners in the adoption of decisions, from which it follows in particular that decisions should be the subject of collective deliberation and that all the members of the college of Commissioners should bear collective responsibility at political level for all decisions adopted.

The European Parliament: 2014–2019 Parliamentary term

Except as otherwise provided in the Treaties, the European Parliament acts by a *majority of the votes cast* (Art 231 TFEU (previously Art 198 EC Treaty)). This is sometimes referred to as a simple majority, so that abstentions by MEPs within the chamber, and MEPs not present, are not taken into account. However, some Treaty articles provide for something more than an absolute majority of the votes cast. For example, Art 225 TFEU provides that 'The European Parliament may, acting by *a majority of its component members ...*' (emphasis added). There are 751 MEPs and therefore a minimum of 376 votes are required. Article 234 TFEU (a censure motion against the Commission) requires a 'two-thirds majority of the votes cast, representing a majority of the component Members of the European Parliament'. The second limb of this is similar to that under Art 225 TFEU, in that there have to be at least 376 votes in favour. However, the first limb provides an additional hurdle to be overcome: of the votes cast, there must be a two-thirds majority in favour. To illustrate this (based on 751 MEPs), on a vote under Art 234 TFEU, if 630 MEPs voted, with 400 in favour and 230 against, although the second limb would have been satisfied, the first limb would not have been (because the majority in favour is less than two-thirds of the votes cast). If 360 MEPs vote, with 250 in favour and 110 against, although this time the first limb has been satisfied, the second limb has not (because, based on 751 MEPs, a minimum of 376 votes in favour is required).

A quorum exists when one-third of the component MEPs are present in the Chamber (Rule 168(2), Rules of Procedure, January 2015): based on 751 MEPs, at least 251 MEPs must be present in the Chamber. However, all votes are valid whatever the number of voters unless the President of the Parliament, acting on a request made by at least 40 MEPs, ascertains that, at the moment of voting, the quorum is not present. In that case, the vote is placed on the agenda of the next sitting (Rule 168(3), Rules of Procedure). The right to vote is a personal right and MEPs are required to cast their votes individually and in person (Rule 177). Although members of the European Council, Council and Commission have the right to attend debates of the European Parliament and to participate in the discussion, they have no right to vote (Art 230 TFEU (previously Art 197 EC Treaty)).

The Council

The EU Treaties provide for three voting methods in the Council:

- simple majority;
- qualified majority;
- unanimity.

Prior to the ToL, the former Art 205(1) EC Treaty provided that simple majority voting was the system to be used unless otherwise provided in the Treaty. However, the Treaty almost invariably provided for some other system. Following the ToL, qualified majority has now become the general rule for the adoption of decisions within the Council: 'The Council shall act by a qualified majority except where the Treaties provide otherwise' (Art 16(3) TEU).

Simple majority

Under the 'simple majority' voting system, one vote is allocated to each Member State, and the decision is simply made in favour of the largest number of votes cast. It is largely used for the establishment of sub-committees of the Council and for procedural matters.

Qualified majority

Until 31 October 2014

Previous to 31 October 2014, qualified majority voting (QMV) was a system of voting which was weighted according to the population size of the Member State. Article 3(3), Protocol No. 36 (which is annexed to the TEU and the TFEU, and which was amended by Art 20 of the Accession Treaty, paving the way for Croatia's EU membership), provided that for acts of the European Council and of the Council requiring a qualified majority, members' votes would be weighted as follows alphabetically (Table 4.1) and numerically (Table 4.2):

Table 4.1 QMV Member State vote allocation up until 31 October 2014 (alphabetical)

Member State	QMV allocation	Member State	QMV allocation
Austria	10	Latvia	4
Belgium	12	Lithuania	7
Bulgaria	10	Luxembourg	4
Croatia	7	Malta	3
Cyprus	4	Netherlands	13
Czech Republic	12	Poland	27
Denmark	7	Portugal	12
Estonia	4	Romania	14
Finland	7	Slovakia	7
France	29	Slovenia	4
Germany	29	Spain	27
Greece	12	Sweden	10
Hungary	12	UK	29
Ireland	7		
Italy	29	**Total**	**352**

Table 4.2 QMV Member State vote allocation up until 31 October 2014 (numerical)

Member State	QMV allocation	Member State	QMV allocation
France	29	Sweden	10
Germany	29	Croatia	7
Italy	29	Denmark	7
UK	29	Finland	7
Poland	27	Ireland	7
Spain	27	Lithuania	7
Romania	14	Slovakia	7
Netherlands	13	Cyprus	4
Belgium	12	Estonia	4
Czech Republic	12	Latvia	4
Greece	12	Luxembourg	4
Hungary	12	Slovenia	4
Portugal	12	Malta	3
Austria	10		
Bulgaria	10	**Total**	**352**

Article 3(3), Protocol No. 36 (as amended by Art 20 of the Accession Treaty, which paved the way for Croatia's EU membership), further provided that:

> Acts shall be adopted if there are at least 260 votes in favour representing a majority of the members where, under the Treaties, they must be adopted on a proposal from the Commission. In other cases decisions shall be adopted if there are at least 260 votes in favour representing at least two-thirds of the members.

In order for an act to be adopted by qualified majority, two thresholds had to be satisfied: (i) at least 260 votes had to be cast in favour; and (ii) a majority of Member States had to vote in favour in respect of a Commission proposal and two-thirds otherwise.

Article 3(3), Protocol No. 36, further provided that:

A member of the European Council or the Council may request that, where an act is adopted by the European Council or the Council by a qualified majority, a check is made to ensure that the Member States comprising the qualified majority represent at least 62% of the total population of the Union. If that proves not to be the case, the act shall not be adopted.

From 1 November 2014

On 1 November 2014, the formula for determining a qualified majority changed to one based on the 'double-majority' principle (i.e. a system based upon: (i) number of Member States; and (ii) population).

Article 16(4) TEU provides that this double-majority principle requires two thresholds to be achieved before a measure can be adopted: (i) the support of at least 55 per cent of the members of the Council, comprising at least 15 of them; and (ii) the support of Member States comprising at least 65 per cent of the population. In addition, a blocking minority must include at least four Member States, failing which the qualified majority will be deemed achieved. This provision will prevent three or fewer of the larger Member States from being able to block a proposal. Article 238(2) TFEU provides a derogation from Art 16(4) TEU where the Council does not act on a proposal from either the Commission or the High Representative of the Union for Foreign Affairs and Security Policy. In this instance, the first threshold is increased, requiring the support of at least 72 per cent of the Member States. Article 238(3) TFEU sets out the qualified majority formula where not all Member States participate in the voting (e.g. where they are using the enhanced cooperation procedure (see below)).

A decision adopted by the Council incorporates a revised 'Ioannina' compromise (see below). This decision enables a small number of Member States, which is close to a blocking minority, to demonstrate their opposition to a proposed measure. From 1 November 2014 to 31 March 2017, if members of the Council representing either: (i) three-quarters of the population; or (ii) at least three-quarters of the number of Member States necessary to constitute a blocking minority under Art 16(4) TEU or 238(2) TFEU, indicate their opposition to the Council adopting an act by qualified majority, the Council has to delay adopting the act and enter into further discussions. The Council is required to do all in its power, within a reasonable period of time, to find a satisfactory solution to address the concerns the Member States have raised. From 1 April 2017, this three-quarters requirement will be reduced to 55 per cent in both instances (i.e. either: (i) 55 per cent of the population; or (ii) at least 55 per cent of the number of Member States, necessary to constitute a blocking minority under Art 16(4) TEU or 238(2) TFEU).

Protocol No. 36, which is annexed to the TEU and TFEU, contains transitional arrangements which apply to QMV for the period from 1 November 2014 to 31 March 2017. During this period, when an act is to be adopted by qualified majority, a member of the Council may request that it be adopted in accordance with the system which applied until 31 October 2014 (see above), rather than the new double-majority system discussed above.

Unanimity

Unanimity is reserved for the most important decisions, or those for which Member States are least prepared to pool their national sovereignty. Although this effectively gives Member States a veto, that veto must be exercised for a measure to be blocked. Abstention by Members present or represented does not prevent the adoption of an act which requires unanimity (Art 238(4) TFEU (previously Art 205(3) EC Treaty)). Unanimity is, for example, required for the admission of new Member States (Art 49 TEU), and for approval of any other matter within the competence of the Union for which the Treaty does not provide a legal base (Art 352 TFEU, see above).

The Luxembourg Accord

The Luxembourg Accord (which is also referred to as the Luxembourg Compromise) was the result of an impasse between France and the other Member States in relation to farm prices in 1965. The decision had to be determined, under the Treaty, by the Council acting by a qualified majority. The French insisted on the right to secure a unanimous decision in cases such as this, where a vital national interest was at stake. The other Member States could not agree. France then remained absent from all but technical meetings of the Council for seven months, and important decision-making in the Union virtually drew to a halt. The Accord was negotiated in a reconvened meeting of the Council in January 1966. The three points that emerged from this meeting, as far as voting procedures were concerned, are as follows:

1 Where, in the case of decisions which may be taken by majority vote on a proposal of the Commission, very important interests of one or more partners are at stake, the members of Council will endeavour, within a reasonable time, to reach solutions which can be adopted by all the members of the Council while respecting their mutual interests and those of the Union.

2 With regard to the preceding paragraph, the French delegation considers that where very important interests are at stake the discussion must be continued until unanimous agreement is reached.

3 The six delegates note that there is a divergence of views on what should be done in the event of a failure to reach complete agreement.

The six delegations concluded by observing that the divergence noted in point 3 did not prevent the Union's work from being resumed in accordance with the normal procedure. There are a number of things to be said about the Accord. In the first place, the title 'Accord' is inappropriate. There was, in fact, no agreement, only an agreement to disagree. Secondly, the Accord has no standing in law. In so far as it purports to amend the voting procedure laid down by the Treaty in certain circumstances, it cannot be effective. Changes to the text and substance of the EU Treaties have to be carried out in the appropriate form, after consultation with the European Parliament and the Commission. This was not done in the case of the Accord. The Commission has never accepted that the Accord has any validity, and has disassociated itself from it (Bull EC 5 1982, p. 8).

Pierre Pescatore, a former judge of the Court of Justice, has described the Accord as 'a mere press release', without the least force of law (Pescatore, 1987 at p. 13). The Court of Justice has stated (but not in the context of the Accord) that 'the rules regarding the manner in which the Community [i.e. Union] institutions arrive at their decisions [i.e. by a qualified majority vote or by unanimity] are laid down in the Treaty and are not at the disposal of the Member States or of the institutions themselves' (*United Kingdom* v *Council* (Case 68/86)). There is no *general* right to veto proposed legislation. What there has been is a willingness, in some cases where Member States appear to be in difficulties in relation to a domestic political situation, to refrain from pressing to a qualified majority vote where the EU Treaties authorise it.

The Accord has undoubtedly encouraged Member States to reach a compromise wherever possible. The formal invocation of the Accord has been rare, and has not always achieved the desired result. In 1982, for example, when the UK sought to block the adoption of an agricultural price package in order to put pressure on the other Member States to agree to a reduction of the UK's contributions, its purported 'veto' was ignored and a vote was taken. However, in 1985, Germany invoked the Accord to forestall an increase in cereal prices, and was successful. It is significant that no Member State which has been overridden, following an appeal to the Accord, has ever taken the decision to the Court of Justice. Recent changes to the EU Treaties have tended to increase the use of QMV and reduce the use of unanimity. It is likely, therefore, that appeals to vital national interests under the Accord will become even rarer than at present.

The Ioannina Declaration

Some recognition was shown early in 1994, of the continuing need to take into account the genuine difficulties of some Member States when a qualified majority vote is to be taken. Under a declaration made in March 1994 at the Ioannina Summit, if members of the Council representing a total of between 23 and 26 votes indicated their intention to oppose the adoption by the Council of a decision by a qualified majority vote, then the Council was committed to do all in its power to reach – within a reasonable time, and without infringing the obligatory time limits in the former Arts 251 and 252 EC Treaty procedures – a satisfactory solution that could be adopted by at least 68 votes (out of the then 87 votes). The former Art 251 EC Treaty is now Art 294 TFEU, and the former Art 252 EC Treaty has been repealed; see below.

This did no more than provide an opportunity to delay a qualified majority vote, but could not prevent one from being held, because the new Treaty time limits had still to be respected. However, unlike the Luxembourg Accord, the Declaration had the force of law. It was intended to continue to apply until the amendments to the EU Treaties following the Intergovernmental Conference of 1996 came into effect, but it was continued by the Treaty of Amsterdam until the 2004 enlargement of the Union (Declaration 50, ToA). Although the Declaration was given legal effect by a Decision of the Council of Ministers, its vagueness must have meant that it was most unlikely to have been the subject of litigation before the Court of Justice. Following the re-weighting of votes in the Council, the Treaty of Nice brought the Ioannina Declaration to an end.

However, as stated above, a decision adopted by the Council now incorporates a revised 'Ioannina' compromise. This decision enables a small number of Member States, which is close to a blocking minority, to demonstrate their opposition to a proposed measure which may be adopted by a qualified majority. From 1 November 2014 to 31 March 2017, if members of the Council representing either: (i) three-quarters of the population; or (ii) at least three-quarters of the number of Member States necessary to constitute a blocking minority under Art 16(4) TEU or 238(2) TFEU, indicate their opposition to the Council adopting an act by qualified majority, the Council has to delay adopting the act and enter into further discussions. The Council is required to do all in its power, within a reasonable period of time, to find a satisfactory solution to address the concerns the Member States have raised. From 1 April 2017, this three-quarters requirement will be reduced to 55 per cent in both instances (i.e. either: (i) 55 per cent of the population; or (ii) at least 55 per cent of the number of Member States, necessary to constitute a blocking minority under Art 16(4) TEU or 238(2) TFEU).

The legislative process

The power of legislative initiative rests with the Commission, 'except where the Treaties provide otherwise' (Art 17(2) TEU).

Legal acts and legislative acts

Article 288 TFEU provides that regulations, directives and decisions constitute 'legal acts' of the EU. Article 289(3) TFEU provides that 'legal acts [i.e. regulations, directives and decisions] adopted by *legislative procedure* shall constitute *legislative acts*' (emphasis added). There are two legislative procedures prescribed by the TFEU: (i) the 'ordinary legislative procedure' (Art 289(1) TFEU); and (ii) the 'special legislative procedure' (Art 289(2) TFEU). Therefore, a regulation, directive or decision adopted by either the ordinary or special legislative procedure will constitute a legislative act. As will be discussed below, in a few cases the EU Treaties make provision for regulations, directives and decisions to be adopted using some other procedure. Because the procedure used is neither the ordinary nor special legislative procedure, the resultant act is a 'legal act' although it is not categorised as a 'legislative act' pursuant to Art 289(3) TFEU.

The practical impact of the differentiation between a legal act which is a legislative act and one which is not, is that the EU Treaties contain additional provisions which apply solely to legislative acts. For example, Art 290 TFEU allows a legislative act to incorporate a power of delegation, which if exercised will enable the Commission to adopt non-legislative acts of general application:

1 A legislative act may delegate to the Commission the power to adopt non-legislative acts of general application to supplement or amend certain non-essential elements of the legislative act.

   The objectives, content, scope and duration of the delegation of power shall be explicitly defined in the legislative acts. The essential elements of an area shall be reserved for the legislative act and accordingly shall not be the subject of a delegation of power.

2 Legislative acts shall explicitly lay down the conditions to which the delegation is subject; these conditions may be as follows:
   (a) the European Parliament or the Council may decide to revoke the delegation;
   (b) the delegated act may enter into force only if no objection has been expressed by the European Parliament or the Council within a period set by the legislative act.
   For the purposes of (a) and (b), the European Parliament shall act by a majority of its component members, and the Council by a qualified majority.

3 The adjective 'delegated' shall be inserted in the title of delegated acts.

The ordinary legislative procedure, not surprisingly given its title, applies in the vast majority of cases. This procedure is practically a carbon copy of the former co-decision procedure (Art 294 TFEU (previously Art 251 EC Treaty)); see below.

The special legislative procedure refers to specific cases where the Treaties provide for the adoption of a regulation, directive or decision by the European Parliament with the Council's involvement, or by the Council with the participation of the European Parliament (Art 289(2) TFEU).

There now follows a detailed discussion of the ordinary legislative procedure, followed by the special legislative procedure, and concluding with other legal acts adopted using neither procedure (and therefore constitute mere EU legal acts, rather than legislative acts).

The ordinary legislative procedure: Article 294 TFEU

The TEU introduced the co-decision procedure, providing the European Parliament with substantial new powers of amendment and, ultimately, a veto. This procedure was subsequently simplified and much extended by the ToA (and to a more limited extent by the ToN). The ToL renamed the co-decision procedure the ordinary legislative procedure and, as stated above, it applies in the vast majority of cases. The ordinary legislative procedure is set out in Art 294 TFEU (previously Art 251 EC Treaty).

The ordinary legislative procedure must be applied wherever the legal base provides that an act shall be adopted 'in accordance with the ordinary legislative procedure' (Art 294(1) TFEU). For example, Art 46 TFEU provides that:

> The European Parliament and the Council shall, **acting in accordance with the ordinary legislative procedure** ... issue directives or make regulations setting out the measures required to bring about freedom of movement for workers, as defined in Article 45 ... [emphasis added].

The ordinary legislative procedure starts with the Commission submitting a proposal to the European Parliament and the Council (Art 294(2) TFEU).

First reading

The Parliament adopts its position at first reading and communicates it to the Council (Art 294(3) TFEU). There are then two possibilities:

- If the Council approves the Parliament's position, the Council, acting by a qualified majority, shall adopt the act concerned. The wording of the act will correspond to the position of the Parliament (Art 294(4) TFEU); or

- If the Council does not approve the Parliament's position, the Council, acting by a qualified majority, shall adopt its position and communicate its position to the Parliament (Art 294(5) TFEU). The Council shall inform the Parliament fully of the reasons why it adopted its own position at first reading (Art 294(6) TFEU). This will obviously include reasons as to why the Council has rejected the Parliament's position. The Commission shall also inform the Parliament fully of its position (Art 294(6) TFEU).

Second reading

Within three months of the Council's position being communicated to the European Parliament, if the Parliament either fails to take a decision, or approves the Council's position, the Council will be deemed to adopt the act in accordance with its position (Art 294(7)(a) TFEU). Alternatively, within this three-month period, Parliament may:

- by *a majority of its component members* reject the Council's position, in which case the act is deemed *not* to have been adopted; i.e. a veto (Art 294(7)(b) TFEU); or

- by *a majority of its component members*, propose amendments to the Council's position (Art 294(7)(c) TFEU).

Following the June 2014 Parliamentary elections a 'majority of the European Parliament's component members' equated to 376, because there are 751 MEPs.

If amendments have been proposed by the European Parliament, the amended text is forwarded to both the Council and the Commission. The Commission then delivers an opinion on the Parliament's amendments (Art 294(7)(c) TFEU). The Council will adopt one of three positions:

- accept all amendments;
- reject all amendments; or
- accept some amendments and reject others.

Within three months of receiving the Parliament's amended text, the Council has two options:

- the Council approves *all* the amendments of the Parliament acting: (i) by a qualified majority if the Commission has also accepted all the amendments; (ii) by unanimity if the Commission has rejected all the amendments; or (iii) by a mixture of the two if the Commission has accepted some (qualified majority) and rejected others (unanimity). In this case the act is deemed to have been adopted (Art 294(8)(a) and 294(9) TFEU); or
- the Council does not approve all the amendments. In this case, the President of the Council, in agreement with the President of the European Parliament, shall convene a meeting of the Conciliation Committee within six weeks (Art 294(8)(b) TFEU).

Conciliation Committee

The Conciliation Committee consists of an equal number of members of the Council or their representatives and the European Parliament (Art 296(10) TFEU). Their task is to agree a joint text on the basis of the positions of the Council and the European Parliament at second reading (Art 296(10) TFEU). This joint text will be reached by the Council representatives acting by a qualified majority and the Parliament representatives acting by a majority. The Commission takes part in the discussions and 'shall take all necessary initiatives with a view to reconciling the positions of the European Parliament and the Council' (Art 296(11) TFEU). There are two possible outcomes. If, within six weeks of being convened, the Conciliation Committee:

- approves a joint text, then the act will be adopted in accordance with the joint text within six weeks of such approval, by the Parliament acting by a majority of the votes cast (i.e. simple majority), and the Council acting by a qualified majority (Art 296(13) TFEU). The act will be deemed not adopted if approval is not obtained from either institution; or
- does not approve a joint text, then the act is deemed not to have been adopted (Art 296(12) TFEU).

There are provisions in Art 296 TFEU for the above periods of three months and six weeks to be extended by one month and two weeks, respectively, at the initiative of the European Parliament or the Council (Art 296(14) TFEU).

It should be appreciated that this is a very complicated and cumbersome procedure, and it is necessary to understand that this is a reflection of the competing interests between the three institutions involved in the legislative process. The European Parliament demands more powers, but the Council resists such demands. However, Art 296 TFEU has shifted some power from the Council to the Parliament because now the Parliament can actually veto a proposal, although the Parliament cannot demand that its amendments be accepted.

The Parliament ultimately either has to accept the proposal in totality or reject it in totality. It is therefore a negative power rather than a true (positive) legislative power.

The Art 296 TFEU procedure can be seen to be a balancing act of competing interests. The Commission will resist any inroad into its role as policy initiator and developer. Article

296 has made an inroad into the Commission's territory because if a Conciliation Committee is set up the Council and the Parliament can agree a joint text by qualified majority and simple majority, respectively. This joint text may amend the Commission's proposal. The joint text (if agreed) can then be adopted by the whole Council acting by a qualified majority and the Parliament acting by a majority of the votes cast.

While the Art 296 procedure is an important development in the evolution of the European Parliament's legislative powers it should be noted that:

- it only involves an ultimate power to veto;
- the Parliament must cooperate with the Council in order to seek its agreement to amendments (or at least seek a qualified majority if the matter proceeds to a Conciliation Committee);
- it is limited to certain policy areas, although the policy areas have been substantially extended by amendments made by the ToA and ToN, and further extended by the ToL such that it is now referred to as the ordinary (or normal) legislative procedure.

Figure 4.1 comprises a flowchart setting out the application of the Art 294 TFEU ordinary legislative procedure.

Special legislative procedure

As stated above, although the 'ordinary legislative procedure' applies in the vast majority of cases, Art 289 TFEU provides that a legislative act can also be adopted by a 'special legislative procedure'.

The special legislative procedure refers to specific cases where the Treaties provide for the adoption of a regulation, directive or decision: (i) by the European Parliament with the Council's involvement; or (ii) by the Council with the participation of the European Parliament (Art 289(2) TFEU). The difference between the two is that the former will require the act to be adopted jointly by the Parliament and the Council, whereas the latter simply requires consultation with Parliament. The legal base will detail the exact role of each institution, together with the voting procedure (in the case of the Council, the voting procedure is qualified majority unless otherwise stated (Art 16(3) TEU)).

An example of a legal base where the special legislative procedure provides for the adoption of a legislative act by the European Parliament with the Council's involvement is Art 86(1) TFEU, which provides that:

> In order to combat crimes affecting the financial interests of the Union, the Council, by means of regulations adopted in accordance with a special legislative procedure, may establish a European Public Prosecutor's Office from Eurojust. The Council shall act unanimously after obtaining the **consent** of the European Parliament. [emphasis added]

An example of a legal base where the special legislative procedure provides for the adoption of a legislative act by the Council with the participation of the European Parliament is Art 64(3) TFEU, which provides that:

> ... only the Council, acting in accordance with a special legislative procedure, may unanimously, and after **consulting** the European Parliament, adopt measures ... [emphasis added]

Under a special legislative procedure such as that provided for by Art 64(3) TFEU, which simply requires Parliament's 'participation', measures are proposed by the Commission, the Parliament is consulted and delivers an opinion, and the Council makes the final

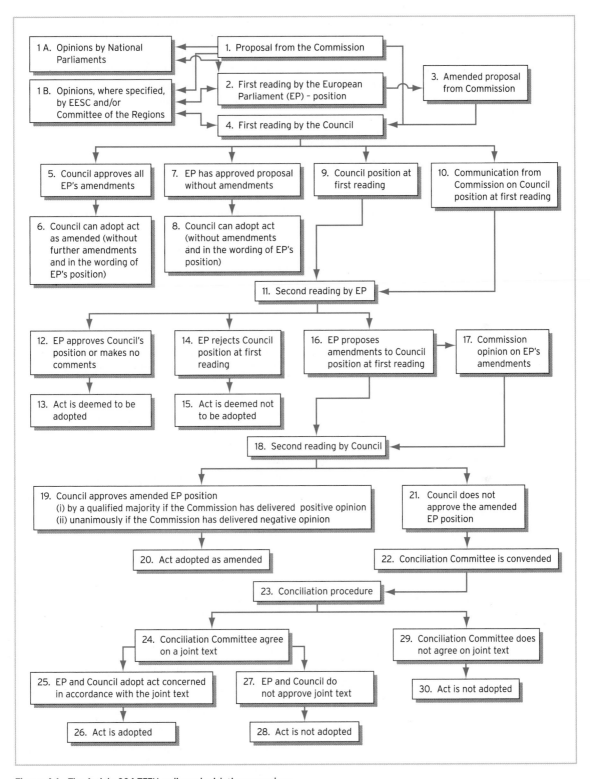

Figure 4.1 The Article 294 TFEU ordinary legislative procedure

decision. The opinion will be prepared by the Rapporteur of one of the Parliament's specialist committees (see Chapter 3). Its preparation follows the hearing of evidence by the Committee from specialist advisers, interested individuals and organisations, and members of the officials of the Directorate General originally responsible for drafting the proposal. Although the Council is not required to follow the opinion of Parliament, the consultation must be genuine. Parliament must have a proper opportunity to respond to the proposal. This was recognised as an essential procedural requirement by the Court of Justice in the following case:

Roquette Frères v Council (Case 138/79)

The Court of Justice stated that:

> The consultation provided for in ... the Treaty is the means which allows the Parliament to play an actual part in the legislative process of the Community [i.e. Union]. Such power represents an essential factor in the institutional balance intended by the Treaty. Although limited, it reflects at Community [i.e. Union] level the fundamental principle that the peoples should take part in the exercise of power through the intermediary of a representative assembly. Due consultation of the Parliament in the cases provided for by the Treaty therefore constitutes an essential formality disregard of which means that the measure concerned is void. (at p. 3360)

This principle was further developed to require re-consultation when a measure on which Parliament had already given an opinion was subsequently changed. In **European Parliament v Council** (Case C-65/90) the Court of Justice said that further consultation was required unless the amendments essentially corresponded to the wishes already expressed by the Parliament. In **European Parliament v Council** (Case C-388/92) the Court of Justice held that the obligation to re-consult arose 'on each occasion when the text finally adopted, viewed as a whole, departs substantially from the text on which Parliament has already been consulted'. On that basis the Court found that the Council had disregarded the prerogatives of Parliament and annulled Regulation 2454/92. However, consultation is a two-way process. Where Parliament wilfully fails to respond it cannot subsequently complain that its views have not been taken into account, as illustrated in the following case:

European Parliament v Council (Case C-65/93)

The Council had informed the Parliament of the urgent need for approval of draft regulations on tariff preferences relating to agricultural products to be made under the former Art 43 EC Treaty (which was renumbered Art 37 EC Treaty by the ToA, and is now Art 43 TFEU). Having agreed to deal with the draft regulations as a matter of urgency, Parliament then decided to adjourn discussion of them for reasons wholly unconnected with their content. The draft regulations were subsequently adopted by the Council without having received Parliament's opinion. The Parliament sought to annul the regulations on the ground of failure to consult. The Court of Justice rejected the application:

> ... Inter-institutional dialogue, on which the consultation procedure in particular is based, is subject to the same mutual duties of sincere cooperation as those which govern relations between Member States and the Community [i.e. Union] institutions. By adopting that course of action [adjournment of consideration of the draft regulation] the Parliament failed to discharge its obligation to cooperate sincerely with the Council ... In those circumstances the Parliament is not entitled to complain of the Council's failure to await its opinion before adopting the contested regulation ...

Although the Council should not come to a final decision without giving the Parliament an opportunity to respond, it does not have to suspend all discussion until it receives that opinion (*European Parliament v Council* (Case C-417/93)).

Other procedures

As stated above, in a few cases the EU Treaties provide for legal acts to be adopted using a procedure other than the ordinary or special legislative procedure. Because the procedure used is neither the ordinary nor special legislative procedure, the resultant act is a 'legal act' although it is not categorised as a 'legislative act' pursuant to Art 289(3) TFEU (see above).

Commission acting alone

The Commission is, in very limited policy areas, empowered by the EU Treaties to enact legislation. One example is Art 106(3) TFEU (previously Art 86(3) EC Treaty), which provides that:

> The Commission shall ensure the application of the provisions of this Article and shall, where necessary, address appropriate directives or decisions to Member States.

This article is concerned with the role of the state in relation to public bodies or other bodies, to which the state has granted special or exclusive rights (e.g. privatised utility companies, such as water, gas, electricity, etc.).

Council and Commission acting alone

The EU Treaties empower the Council to adopt a Commission proposal without any involvement of any other institution, in a very limited number of policy areas. For example, Art 31 TFEU provides as follows:

> Common Customs Tariff duties shall be fixed by the Council on a proposal from the Commission.

The involvement of national parliaments

Objective 4

Article 12 TEU now provides as follows:

> National Parliaments contribute actively to the good functioning of the Union:
>
> (a) through being informed by the institutions of the Union and having draft legislative acts of the Union forwarded to them in accordance with the Protocol on the role of national Parliaments in the European Union;
>
> (b) by seeing to it that the principle of subsidiarity is respected in accordance with the procedures provided for in the Protocol on the application of the principles of subsidiarity and proportionality;
>
> (c) by taking part, within the framework of the area of freedom, security and justice, in the evaluation mechanisms for the implementation of the Union policies in that area, in accordance with Article 70 of the Treaty on the Functioning of the European Union, and through being involved in the political monitoring of Europol and the evaluation of Eurojust's activities in accordance with Articles 88 and 85 of that Treaty;
>
> (d) by taking part in the revision procedures of the Treaties, in accordance with Article 48 of this Treaty;

(e) by being notified of applications for accession to the Union, in accordance with Article 49 of this Treaty;

(f) by taking part in the inter-parliamentary cooperation between national Parliaments and with the European Parliament, in accordance with the Protocol on the role of national Parliaments in the European Union.

Article 12 TEU establishes the interaction between the Union institutions and national parliaments particularly with regard to the national parliaments' role in the legislative procedure and the application of the principle of subsidiarity (see below). Protocol No. 1, which is annexed to the TFEU and TEU, specifically refers to the role of national parliaments. Protocol No. 2 refers to the application of the principles of subsidiarity and proportionality. Each of these Protocols is set out in full below. National parliaments will have eight weeks to examine draft European legislative acts. If one-third of the national parliaments (one-quarter in the field of Justice and Home Affairs) oppose a draft, the Commission must review it. If over half of all national parliaments oppose an act subject to the ordinary legislative procedure, the European legislator (a majority of the European Parliament or 55 per cent of the votes in the Council) must decide whether or not to proceed with the legislative process. National parliaments may also take a case to the Court of Justice if they consider that a legislative act is contrary to the principle of subsidiarity.

Protocol No. 1 provides as follows:

TITLE I
INFORMATION FOR NATIONAL PARLIAMENTS

ARTICLE 1

Commission consultation documents (green and white papers and communications) shall be forwarded directly by the Commission to national Parliaments upon publication. The Commission shall also forward the annual legislative programme as well as any other instrument of legislative planning or policy to national Parliaments, at the same time as to the European Parliament and the Council.

ARTICLE 2

Draft legislative acts sent to the European Parliament and to the Council shall be forwarded to national Parliaments.

For the purposes of this Protocol, 'draft legislative acts' shall mean proposals from the Commission, initiatives from a group of Member States, initiatives from the European Parliament, requests from the Court of Justice, recommendations from the European Central Bank and requests from the European Investment Bank for the adoption of a legislative act.

Draft legislative acts originating from the Commission shall be forwarded to national Parliaments directly by the Commission, at the same time as to the European Parliament and the Council.

Draft legislative acts originating from the European Parliament shall be forwarded to national Parliaments directly by the European Parliament.

Draft legislative acts originating from a group of Member States, the Court of Justice, the European Central Bank or the European Investment Bank shall be forwarded to national Parliaments by the Council.

ARTICLE 3

National Parliaments may send to the Presidents of the European Parliament, the Council and the Commission a reasoned opinion on whether a draft legislative act complies with the principle of subsidiarity, in accordance with the procedure laid down in the Protocol on the application of the principles of subsidiarity and proportionality.

If the draft legislative act originates from a group of Member States, the President of the Council shall forward the reasoned opinion or opinions to the governments of those Member States.

If the draft legislative act originates from the Court of Justice, the European Central Bank or the European Investment Bank, the President of the Council shall forward the reasoned opinion or opinions to the institution or body concerned.

ARTICLE 4

An eight-week period shall elapse between a draft legislative act being made available to national Parliaments in the official languages of the Union and the date when it is placed on a provisional agenda for the Council for its adoption or for adoption of a position under a legislative procedure. Exceptions shall be possible in cases of urgency, the reasons for which shall be stated in the act or position of the Council. Save in urgent cases for which due reasons have been given, no agreement may be reached on a draft legislative act during those eight weeks. Save in urgent cases for which due reasons have been given, a ten-day period shall elapse between the placing of a draft legislative act on the provisional agenda for the Council and the adoption of a position.

ARTICLE 5

The agendas for and the outcome of meetings of the Council, including the minutes of meetings where the Council is deliberating on draft legislative acts, shall be forwarded directly to national Parliaments, at the same time as to Member States' governments.

ARTICLE 6

When the European Council intends to make use of the first or second subparagraphs of Article 48(7) of the Treaty on European Union, national Parliaments shall be informed of the initiative of the European Council at least six months before any decision is adopted.

ARTICLE 7

The Court of Auditors shall forward its annual report to national Parliaments, for information, at the same time as to the European Parliament and to the Council.

ARTICLE 8

Where the national Parliamentary system is not unicameral, Articles 1 to 7 shall apply to the component chambers.

TITLE II
INTERPARLIAMENTARY COOPERATION

ARTICLE 9

The European Parliament and national Parliaments shall together determine the organisation and promotion of effective and regular interparliamentary cooperation within the Union.

ARTICLE 10

A conference of Parliamentary Committees for Union Affairs may submit any contribution it deems appropriate for the attention of the European Parliament, the Council and the Commission. That conference shall in addition promote the exchange of information and best practice between national Parliaments and the European Parliament, including their special committees. It may also organise interparliamentary conferences on specific topics, in particular to debate matters of common foreign and security policy, including common security and defence policy. Contributions from the conference shall not bind national Parliaments and shall not prejudge their positions.

Subsidiarity

Following an amendment made to the EC Treaty by the TEU, there was recognition of a national dimension to the decision-making process (the principle of subsidiarity, set out in the former Art 5 EC Treaty). Although subsidiarity was not a new concept for the Union, the TEU made it a central criterion to be applied by the Commission when it proposed new legislation.

At the Edinburgh European Council Meeting of October 1993, it was decided that the Commission should consult more widely before proposing legislation and should include in the recitals to any new measure its justification for initiating the measure, under the subsidiarity principle. If legislation had to be made at Union level, directives were to be preferred to regulations, and 'framework directives' (allowing Member States considerable leeway in the manner of implementation) were to be preferred to specific and detailed directives.

As part of the process of implementing the new subsidiarity principle, the Commission embarked on a so-called 'bonfire of measures' and the abandonment of some legislative programmes, with a view to the policies they were intended to implement being carried out at national level. It announced the withdrawal of proposals for more than 15 directives, including proposals on the liability of suppliers of services, minimum standards for the keeping of animals in zoos, speed limits for motor vehicles and maximum alcohol levels for vehicle drivers (Bull EU 6 1994, p. 26).

Subsidiarity was again discussed at the Amsterdam Conference in 1997 and some attempt was made to build the principle into the decision-making process. A Protocol added to the ToA provided that:

> Subsidiarity is a dynamic concept and should be applied in the light of the objectives set out in the Treaty. It allows Community [i.e. Union] action within the limits of its powers to be expanded where circumstances so require, and conversely, to be restricted or discontinued where it is no longer justified.

The Protocol required every proposed piece of Union legislation to state how it complied with the principle of subsidiarity and proportionality and why 'a Community [i.e. Union] objective can be better achieved by the Community [i.e. Union]'. Essentially, Member States retained powers only in those areas where the Treaties conferred no powers on the Union, or where the Union had general powers in a given area but had not yet chosen to act. Once it did act, its measures prevailed over national rules, and it had exclusive competence.

Following the ToL coming into force on 1 December 2009, Art 5 TEU governs the principle of subsidiarity and provides as follows:

1 The limits of Union competences are governed by the principle of conferral. The use of Union competences is governed by the principles of subsidiarity and proportionality.

2 Under the principle of conferral, the Union shall act only within the limits of the competences conferred upon it by the Member States in the Treaties to attain the objectives set out therein. Competences not conferred upon the Union in the Treaties remain with the Member States.

3 Under the principle of subsidiarity, in areas which do not fall within its exclusive competence, the Union shall act only if and in so far as the objectives of the proposed action cannot be sufficiently achieved by the Member States, either at central level or at regional and local level, but can rather, by reason of the scale or effects of the proposed action, be better achieved at Union level.

The institutions of the Union shall apply the principle of subsidiarity as laid down in the Protocol on the application of the principles of subsidiarity and proportionality. National Parliaments ensure compliance with the principle of subsidiarity in accordance with the procedure set out in that Protocol.

4   Under the principle of proportionality, the content and form of Union action shall not exceed what is necessary to achieve the objectives of the Treaties.

The institutions of the Union shall apply the principle of proportionality as laid down in the Protocol on the application of the principles of subsidiarity and proportionality.

Article 4(1) TEU further provides that 'In accordance with Article 5, competences not conferred upon the Union in the Treaties remain with the Member States'.

Protocol No. 2, which is annexed to the TEU and TFEU, relates to application of the principles of subsidiarity and proportionality. Protocol No. 2 provides as follows:

ARTICLE 1

Each institution shall ensure constant respect for the principles of subsidiarity and proportionality, as laid down in Article 5 of the Treaty on European Union.

ARTICLE 2

Before proposing legislative acts, the Commission shall consult widely. Such consultations shall, where appropriate, take into account the regional and local dimension of the action envisaged. In cases of exceptional urgency, the Commission shall not conduct such consultations. It shall give reasons for its decision in its proposal.

ARTICLE 3

For the purposes of this Protocol, 'draft legislative acts' shall mean proposals from the Commission, initiatives from a group of Member States, initiatives from the European Parliament, requests from the Court of Justice, recommendations from the European Central Bank and requests from the European Investment Bank for the adoption of a legislative act.

ARTICLE 4

The Commission shall forward its draft legislative acts and its amended drafts to national Parliaments at the same time as to the Union legislator.

The European Parliament shall forward its draft legislative acts and its amended drafts to national Parliaments.

The Council shall forward draft legislative acts originating from a group of Member States, the Court of Justice, the European Central Bank or the European Investment Bank and amended drafts to national Parliaments.

Upon adoption, legislative resolutions of the European Parliament and positions of the Council shall be forwarded by them to national Parliaments.

ARTICLE 5

Draft legislative acts shall be justified with regard to the principles of subsidiarity and proportionality. Any draft legislative act should contain a detailed statement making it possible to appraise compliance with the principles of subsidiarity and proportionality. This statement should contain some assessment of the proposal's financial impact and, in the case of a directive, of its implications for the rules to be put in place by Member States, including, where necessary, the regional legislation. The reasons for concluding that a Union objective can be better achieved at Union level shall be substantiated by qualitative and, wherever possible, quantitative indicators. Draft legislative acts shall take account of the need for any burden, whether financial or administrative, falling upon the Union, national governments, regional or local authorities, economic operators and citizens, to be minimised and commensurate with the objective to be achieved.

ARTICLE 6

Any national Parliament or any chamber of a national Parliament may, within eight weeks from the date of transmission of a draft legislative act, in the official languages of the Union, send to the Presidents of the European Parliament, the Council and the Commission a reasoned opinion stating why it considers that the draft in question does not comply with the principle of subsidiarity. It will be for each national Parliament or each chamber of a national Parliament to consult, where appropriate, regional parliaments with legislative powers.

If the draft legislative act originates from a group of Member States, the President of the Council shall forward the opinion to the governments of those Member States.

If the draft legislative act originates from the Court of Justice, the European Central Bank or the European Investment Bank, the President of the Council shall forward the opinion to the institution or body concerned.

ARTICLE 7

1 The European Parliament, the Council and the Commission, and, where appropriate, the group of Member States, the Court of Justice, the European Central Bank or the European Investment Bank, if the draft legislative act originates from them, shall take account of the reasoned opinions issued by national Parliaments or by a chamber of a national Parliament.

   Each national Parliament shall have two votes, shared out on the basis of the national Parliamentary system. In the case of a bicameral Parliamentary system, each of the two chambers shall have one vote.

2 Where reasoned opinions on a draft legislative act's non-compliance with the principle of subsidiarity represent at least one-third of all the votes allocated to the national Parliaments in accordance with the second subparagraph of paragraph 1, the draft must be reviewed. This threshold shall be a quarter in the case of a draft legislative act submitted on the basis of Article 76 of the Treaty on the Functioning of the European Union on the area of freedom, security and justice.

   After such review, the Commission or, where appropriate, the group of Member States, the European Parliament, the Court of Justice, the European Central Bank or the European Investment Bank, if the draft legislative act originates from them, may decide to maintain, amend or withdraw the draft. Reasons must be given for this decision.

3 Furthermore, under the ordinary legislative procedure, where reasoned opinions on the non-compliance of a proposal for a legislative act with the principle of subsidiarity represent at least a simple majority of the votes allocated to the national Parliaments in accordance with the second subparagraph of paragraph 1, the proposal must be reviewed. After such review, the Commission may decide to maintain, amend or withdraw the proposal.

   If it chooses to maintain the proposal, the Commission will have, in a reasoned opinion, to justify why it considers that the proposal complies with the principle of subsidiarity. This reasoned opinion, as well as the reasoned opinions of the national Parliaments, will have to be submitted to the Union legislator, for consideration in the procedure:

   (a) before concluding the first reading, the legislator (the European Parliament and the Council) shall consider whether the legislative proposal is compatible with the principle of subsidiarity, taking particular account of the reasons expressed and shared by the majority of national Parliaments as well as the reasoned opinion of the Commission;

   (b) if, by a majority of 55% of the members of the Council or a majority of the votes cast in the European Parliament, the legislator is of the opinion that the proposal is not compatible with the principle of subsidiarity, the legislative proposal shall not be given further consideration.

ARTICLE 8

The Court of Justice of the European Union shall have jurisdiction in actions on grounds of infringement of the principle of subsidiarity by a legislative act, brought in accordance with the rules laid down in Article 263 of the Treaty on the Functioning of the European Union by Member States, or notified by them in accordance with their legal order on behalf of their national Parliament or a chamber thereof.

In accordance with the rules laid down in the said Article, the Committee of the Regions may also bring such actions against legislative acts for the adoption of which the Treaty on the Functioning of the European Union provides that it be consulted.

ARTICLE 9

The Commission shall submit each year to the European Council, the European Parliament, the Council and national Parliaments a report on the application of Article 5 of the Treaty on European Union. This annual report shall also be forwarded to the Economic and Social Committee and the Committee of the Regions.

Treaty amendments

Prior to the ToL coming into force, amendments to the EU Treaties required the unanimous approval of all Member States, following which the amendments would take effect once the proposed amendments had been ratified by all Member States according to their specific constitutional requirements. Article 48(1) TEU now provides that 'The Treaties may be amended in accordance with an ordinary revision procedure. They may also be amended in accordance with simplified revision procedures'. The ordinary revision procedure is similar to the pre-ToL procedure. The simplified revision procedure is a new concept. In particular, Art 48(7) TEU now provides as follows:

> Where the Treaty on the Functioning of the European Union or Title V of this Treaty provides for the Council to act by unanimity in a given area or case, the European Council may adopt a decision authorising the Council to act by a qualified majority in that area or in that case. This subparagraph shall not apply to decisions with military implications or those in the area of defence.
>
> Where the Treaty on the Functioning of the European Union provides for legislative acts to be adopted by the Council in accordance with a special legislative procedure, the European Council may adopt a decision allowing for the adoption of such acts in accordance with the ordinary legislative procedure.

The appropriate legal base

In almost every case, as the initiator of the legislative process, the choice of legal base is made by the Commission. It is not always clear, especially in relation to proposals which touch on a number of different activities, which Treaty provision, and hence which decision-making process, is appropriate. Article 5(2) TEU (previously Art 5 EC Treaty) provides that 'Under the principle of conferral, the Union shall act only within the limits of the competences conferred upon it by the Member States in the Treaties to attain the objectives set out therein. Competences not conferred upon the Union in the Treaties remain with the Member States.'

When legislating, the Commission is bound to give reasons for its proposal, the legal base on which it is made, and the process through which it passed, including the institutions and other bodies which participated in the decision (Art 296 TFEU; previously Art 253 EC).

This information is normally contained in the preamble to the measure. Prior to the SEA, the choice of legal base rarely gave rise to controversy. However, subsequently there were some disputes, largely either because Member States contested the competence of the Union to legislate at all or because a legal base was chosen allowing for a qualified majority vote within the Council of Ministers, when some Member States demanded a base requiring unanimity and therefore the opportunity to block the measure by exercising their national veto (see above). This, however, is less likely following the ToL coming into force because the vast majority of legal bases are governed by the ordinary legislative process.

Defects in the legal base may be one of three types:

- the Union's lack of competence;
- an institution's lack of competence;
- inappropriate Treaty provision for the subject matter of the legislation.

The Court of Justice has not yet found that a proposed action is without a legal base, but some challenges have been successful. In *Germany* v *Commission* (Case 281/85) Germany, France, The Netherlands and the UK sought to annul a decision made by the Commission in relation to migration policy from non-Member States. The Court of Justice held that the Commission did have the power to consult with Member States on the impact of third-country (i.e. non-EU) immigration on the employment market, and how this was affecting Union workers, but that it did not have the power to make a binding measure restricting the way in which Member States could regulate immigration into their territories from outside the Union. The Commission will generally choose the legal base offering the best chance of approval for a measure, if there is at least an arguable alternative:

Commission v *Council (Generalised Tariff Preferences)* (Case 45/86)

The Court of Justice stated that:

> The choice of a legal base for a measure may not depend simply on an institution's conviction as to the objective pursued but must be based on objective factors which are amenable to judicial review.

In the following case a conflict arose between the Council on the one hand, and the Parliament and the Commission on the other, as to the choice of the appropriate legal base:

Commission v *Council* (Case C-300/89)

The Commission (supported by the Parliament) applied to the Court of Justice for the annulment of Directive 89/428 on procedures for harmonising the programmes for the reduction and elimination of pollution caused by waste from the titanium dioxide industry. The Commission had proposed that the directive should be based on the former Art 100a EC Treaty (now Art 114 TFEU), which provided for the Council to act by a qualified majority in cooperation with the Parliament. However, despite the Parliament's objections, the Council adopted the directive on the basis of environmental policy, pursuant to the former Art 130s EC Treaty. This article provided at the time (but see, now, Art 192 TFEU) that decisions in Council should be taken unanimously, and only after consultation with the Parliament. The Court decided that the appropriate legal base was the former Art 100a EC Treaty, which provided that decisions should be taken by qualified majority in Council, in cooperation with the European Parliament. Although the directive had the dual objectives of environmental protection and the removal of distortions of competition by establishing harmonised production conditions, it was not possible to have recourse to two legal bases, and the unanimity rule in the former Art 130s EC Treaty was incompatible with the cooperation procedure in the former Art 130a EC Treaty. The decision of the Court of Justice has a strong political flavour:

> [20] The very purpose of the cooperation procedure, which is to increase the involvement of the European Parliament in the legislative process of the Community [i.e. Union] would thus be jeopardised. As the Court stated in its judgment in *Roquette Frères v Council* (Case 138/79) and *Maizena v Council* (Case C-139/79), para. 34, that participation reflects a fundamental democratic principle that the peoples should take part in the exercise of power through the intermediary of a representative assembly.

The Commission has continued to show a preference for articles for which QMV is the appropriate procedure in the Council of Ministers. The following case is an example in the field of higher education:

European Parliament v Council (Case C-295/90)

The Court of Justice had decided in *Gravier v City of Liège* (Case 293/83) that the former Art 128 EC Treaty, which contained some fairly general provisions on the promotion of a common vocational training policy, created a directly enforceable right of access to vocational training in other Member States. As a Treaty right, it was to be delivered in accordance with the principles of equality contained in the former Art 7 EC Treaty (now Art 19(1) TFEU).

The former Arts 7 and 128 EC Treaty were, therefore, taken as the basis for a new directive on student mobility (Directive 90/366). Article 7 provided for measures to eliminate discrimination on grounds of nationality to be decided by a qualified majority vote, and it was on this basis that the measure was proposed. The Council of Ministers substituted the former Art 235 EC Treaty (now Art 352 TFEU) as the legal base, on the grounds thatas the former Art 128 EC Treaty contained no voting procedure, the residual voting system in Art 235 (a unanimous vote) was more appropriate. Although the directive was unanimously approved by the Council of Ministers, its legal base was challenged by the Parliamentbecause it did not want to see a **precedent** established of unanimous decision-making in relation to future educational measures. The Court of Justice upheld the challenge on the basis that the measure was, fundamentally, about equal access to vocational training, and that the former Art 7 EC Treaty, which required only a qualified majority vote, was the proper legal base. The Court ordered that the directive be annulled and a new measure be proposed with the former Art 7 EC Treaty as the legal base.

As stated above, now that the ToL has come into force, such conflict will become less pronounced because the majority of legislative acts will be adopted under the 'ordinary legislative procedure' set out in Art 294 TFEU (see above). However, Art 352 TFEU provides the Union with a *general* legislative power if no *specific* power has been provided by the Treaties: 'If action by the Union should prove necessary ... to attain one of the objectives set out in the Treaties, and the Treaties have not provided the necessary powers, the Council … shall adopt the appropriate measures' (Art 352(1) TFEU). The procedures under which this general legislative power can be exercised are different from those of the ordinary legislative procedure, because in addition to requiring unanimity in the Council, the consent of the European Parliament must be obtained.

Summary

Now you have read this chapter you should be able to:

- Compare and contrast the respective roles of the Union's institutions and national parliaments within the Union's legislative process.
- Understand the importance of choosing the appropriate legal base when adopting secondary Union legislation, and discuss how this choice of legal base impacts upon the voting systems used in the Council of Ministers.
- Explain the legislative process, including:
  - the ordinary legislative procedure;
  - the special legislative procedure;
  - other procedures.
- Understand and evaluate the relevance of the principle of subsidiarity to the Union's decision-making process, and the role of national parliaments in enforcing the application of this principle.

Reference

Pescatore, P., 'Some Critical Remarks on the Single European Act' (1987) 24 CML Rev 9.

Further reading

Textbooks

Craig, P. and De Burca, G. (2011) *EU Law Text, Cases and Materials* (5th edn), Oxford University Press, Chapter 5.

Foster, N. (2015) *Foster on EU Law* (5th edn), Oxford University Press, Chapter 4.

Steiner, J. and Woods, L. (2014) *EU Law* (12th edn), Oxford University Press, Chapter 3.

Toth, A.G. (1994) 'A Legal Analysis of Subsidiarity', in O'Keefe, D. and Twomey, P. (eds) *Legal Issues of the Maastricht Treaty*, Chancery Publications.

Weatherill, S. (2014) *Cases and Materials on EU Law* (11th edn), Oxford University Press, Chapter 2.

Journal articles

Alemanno, A., 'Unpacking the principle of openness in EU law: Transparency, participation and democracy' (2014) 39 EL Rev 72.

de Ruiter, R. and Neuhold, C., 'Why is fast track the way to go? Justifications for early agreement in the co-decision procedure and their effects' (2012) 18 ELJ 536.

Driessen, B., 'Delegated legislation after the Treaty of Lisbon: An analysis of Article 290 TFEU' (2010) 35 EL Rev 837.

Kiiver, P., 'The early-warning system for the principle of subsidiarity: The national parliament as a Conseil d'Etat for Europe' (2011) 36 EL Rev 98.

Klamert, M., 'Conflicts of legal basis: No legality and no basis but a bright future under the Lisbon Treaty' (2010) 35 EL Rev 497.

Obradovic, D. and Alonso Vizcaino, J.M., 'Good governance requirements concerning the participation of interest groups in EU consultations' (2006) 43 CML Rev 1049.

Pliakos, A., 'Who is the ultimate arbiter? The battle over judicial supremacy in EU law' (2011) 36 EL Rev 109.

Semmelmann, C., 'The European Union's economic constitution under the Lisbon Treaty: Soul-searching among lawyers shifts the focus to procedure' (2010) 35 ECL Rev 516.

The Court of Justice of the European Union

Objectives

At the end of this chapter you should understand:

1. The composition and role of the Court of Justice, with particular reference to judges and Advocates General.

2. The structure of the Court of Justice and how it reaches a judgment.

3. The various methods of interpretation used by the Court of Justice, and how these methods differ from those used by the UK judiciary.

4. The composition, role and powers of the General Court.

5. The role of the specialised courts.

6. How the Court of Justice's jurisdiction is defined and the various heads of jurisdiction.

Introduction

Article 13(1) TEU (previously Art 7(1) EC Treaty) establishes the Union institutions. In addition to the European Parliament, European Council, Council, Commission, European Central Bank and Court of Auditors (which were considered in Chapter 3), Art 13(1) TEU also established, as a Union institution, the Court of Justice of the European Union. Article 19(1) TEU provides that 'The Court of Justice of the European Union shall include the Court of Justice, the General Court and specialised courts'.

The Court of Justice of the European Union should not be confused with the European Court of Human Rights, which is not a Union institution and does not have jurisdiction to adjudicate on Union law. The European Court of Human Rights has jurisdiction to adjudicate on breaches of the ECHR. All Member States are signatories to the ECHR, and Art 6(2) TEU provides that the Union will accede to the ECHR (see Chapter 1). The Court of Justice of the European Union is permanently in session in Luxembourg and vacations are fixed according to the workload. The European Court of Human Rights sits in Strasbourg.

The Court of Justice of the European Union plays a pivotal role in the Union. Some of the legal principles which govern the way the Union functions are not found in the Treaty or the legislative acts made under it, but they are to be found in the case law of the Court. This has been considered in Chapter 2 and is considered further in Chapter 9.

Statute of the Court of Justice of the European Union

The Court of Justice of the European Union is itself governed by the TEU and TFEU, and the Statute of the Court of Justice of the European Union, which is appended to the TEU and TFEU as a protocol (Protocol No. 3). The Statute annexed to the TEU and TFEU has the title: 'Protocol on the Statute of the Court of Justice of the European Union'. This new Statute came into effect when the Treaty of Lisbon came into force on 1 December 2009. A consolidated version of the Statute was published on 1 July 2013. Article 254, para 6 TFEU provides that 'Unless the Statute of the Court of Justice of the European Union provides otherwise, the provisions of the Treaties relating to the Court of Justice shall apply to the General Court'. The full text of the Statute is available at:

http://curia.europa.eu/jcms/jcms/Jo2_7031/

Rules of Procedure of the Court of Justice of the European Union

Detailed effect is given to the Statute by the Court's Rules of Procedure. There are separate Rules of Procedure for the Court of Justice and the General Court.

Article 253, para 6 TFEU (previously Art 245, para 3 EC Treaty) provides that 'The Court of Justice shall establish its Rules of Procedure. Those Rules shall require the approval of the Council'. The Council will act by a qualified majority (Art 16(3) TEU now specifies that the Council acts by a qualified majority unless the Treaties provide otherwise; see Chapter 4).

Article 254, para 5 TFEU provides that 'The General Court shall establish its Rules of Procedure in agreement with the Court of Justice. Those Rules shall require the approval of the Council'.

The procedures applying to specialised courts will be determined when such a court is established (Art 257 TFEU).

New Rules of Procedure for the Court of Justice came into force on 1 November 2012. These Rules were amended on 18 June 2013 to pave the way for Croatia's membership of the Union from 1 July 2013.

Chapter structure

Within this chapter each of the three courts (Court of Justice, General Court and specialised courts) will be considered separately. Immediately following the section on the Court of Justice, there is a discussion of the doctrine of precedent and a consideration of whether the Court is bound by such doctrine. This is followed by a consideration of the Court's methods of interpretation. Towards the end of the chapter there is an explanation of the jurisdiction of the Court of Justice of the European Union, and how this is divided (and shared) between the Court of Justice, the General Court and the specialised courts.

The Court of Justice

Members

Objective 1

Article 19 TEU (previously Art 221 EC Treaty) provides that the Court of Justice will consist of one judge from each Member State. There are therefore 28 judges.

Similar to the former Art 222 EC Treaty, Art 252 TFEU provides for eight Advocates General and also provides for this number to be increased by the Council acting unanimously, at the request of the Court of Justice. A Declaration (Number 38) is annexed to the TEU and TFEU. This Declaration provides that if the Court of Justice requests the number of Advocates General to be increased to 11, Poland will be allocated a 'permanent' Advocate General. France, Germany, Italy, Spain and the UK already have a permanent Advocate General. A rotation system would be applied for the remaining five Advocates General.

Article 253 TFEU (previously Art 223 EC Treaty) provides that both judges and Advocates General:

> ... shall be chosen from persons whose independence is beyond doubt and who possess the qualifications required for appointment to the highest judicial offices in their respective countries or who are jurisconsults of recognised competence.

The requirements for these appointments are therefore not intended to be confined to those who have made a career in the courts and are destined for, or already sit, on the bench in their Member State. Appointments may also be made from the ranks of distinguished academic lawyers or 'jurisconsults of recognised competence'.

While Art 253 TFEU follows the principle of independence set out in the former Art 223 EC Treaty, Art 253 TFEU also provides that judges and Advocates General are appointed by common accord of the governments of the Member States 'after consultation of the panel provided for in Article 255'. This panel comprises seven persons chosen from among for-

See pages 173–175 for a discussion of the General Court.

mer members of the Court of Justice and the General Court, members of national supreme courts and lawyers of recognised competence, one of whom is proposed by the European Parliament (Art 255 TFEU). The purpose of the panel is to give an opinion on the candidates' suitability to perform their duties.

A new judge is required to take an oath to perform his duties impartially and conscientiously and to preserve the secrecy of the deliberations of the Court. He also signs a solemn declaration to behave with integrity and discretion in relation to the acceptance of benefits after he has left office (Arts 2 and 4 Statute of the Court of Justice). Judges may not hold any political or administrative office (Art 4 Statute). They may not follow any other occupation, paid or unpaid, during their period of office unless exemption is exceptionally granted by the Council acting by a simple majority (Art 4 Statute).

Article 253 TFEU (previously Art 223 EC Treaty) provides for the appointments to be for a renewable six-year term. Appointment and reappointment of the judges and Advocates General is staggered, taking place every three years. Article 253 TFEU, for example, states that: 'Every three years there shall be a partial replacement of the Judges ... in accordance with the conditions laid down in the Statute of the Court of Justice of the European Union'. Article 9 of the Statute provides that: 'When, every three years, the Judges are partially replaced, fourteen judges shall be replaced'.

It has been argued that this necessity to seek reappointment could threaten the impartiality of the judiciary, because if a particular judge acts against the interests of the Member State of his nationality it is likely he would not be nominated for reselection. Accordingly, there may be pressure on the judge to be sympathetic to national issues. This argument may be rejected because the Court delivers one judgment, and therefore it is impossible for a Member State to ascertain the actual views of their nominee (see below). The same, however, could not be said of Advocates General, the role of whom is considered below.

President and Vice-President of the Court

Article 254 TFEU (previously Art 223 EC Treaty) provides for the election by the judges of a President for a term of three years, which may be renewed.

The President directs the judicial business and administration of the Court. Thus he presides at hearings of the full court, fixes and extends time limits for lodging pleadings, documents, etc., and usually deals with interlocutory applications (i.e. applications within the course of the proceedings, prior to the full hearing). As stated above, the appointments panel will act 'on the initiative of the President' (Art 255 TFEU).

Article 15(1) of the Rules of Procedure provides for the President to designate a **Judge-Rapporteur** to each case before the Court. The function of the Judge-Rapporteur is to manage the case throughout its progression through the Court's system. The Judge-Rapporteur is responsible for drafting the final judgment.

Article 13 of the Statute provides that the Council (acting unanimously) may provide for the appointment of Assistant Rapporteurs to assist the Judge-Rapporteur. These assistants will be legally qualified persons and shall be appointed by the Council.

Article 8(4) of the Rules of Procedure provides for the election of a Vice-President. Article 10 of the Rules of Procedure sets out the responsibilities of the Vice-President.

Advocates General

The title 'Advocate' is something of a misnomer, because the Advocate General represents no one and does not present a case on anyone's behalf. Although not a judge, the Advocate General enjoys equal status with the judges. Article 10(1) of the Rules provides for the Court to designate a First Advocate General for a period of one year, after hearing the Advocates General. Once the President has assigned a Judge-Rapporteur to a case, the First Advocate General assigns an Advocate General to the case (Art 16(1), Rules). Thus each case will have one Judge-Rapporteur and one Advocate General.

Article 252 TFEU (previously Art 222 EC Treaty) prescribes the role of the Advocate General as being:

> . . . to make, in open court, reasoned submissions on cases which, in accordance with the Statute of the Court of Justice of the European Union, require his involvement.

The various Court stages are considered below. Once all the formal stages have been completed, but before the judges deliberate upon their judgment, the Advocate General will prepare his personal opinion as to the decision the Court should reach, which he will deliver in open court. He is an independent adviser to the Court.

Article 20 of the Statute provides that, after hearing the Advocate General assigned to a particular case, if the Court considers that the case raises no new point of law, it may decide to determine the case without a submission (i.e. Opinion) from the Advocate General. During the period 2006–2014 the percentage of judgments delivered by the Court of Justice without an Advocate General's Opinion was as follows:

2006	2007	2008	2009	2010	2011	2012	2013	2014
33%	44%	41%	52%	50%	46%	53%	48%	33%

The recommendation in the Opinion is not binding on the Court, or on the parties, and the Court is free to follow it or not, as it chooses. However, in spite of their non-binding nature, the Opinions of Advocates General carry considerable weight on account of the very high standard of legal analysis they contain and they are frequently cited in the Court as well as in legal writing as persuasive sources of authority.

The Opinion is fully reasoned. It normally deals with every aspect of the case, and will generally be much longer and more wide-ranging than the judgment of the Court. It will usually attempt to set the case in a broader context than the issues which divide the parties. It will set out the relevant facts and any applicable legislation (e.g. Treaty articles, regulations, directives, etc.), the issues that have been raised will be discussed, there will be a full review of any relevant past case law of the Court, and it will conclude with a recommendation for a solution which the Court may adopt.

An Opinion that is particularly persuasive may strongly influence the Court, especially if it suggests creating a new principle or departing from a previous decision of the Court. In the vast majority of cases, judgments of the Court will follow the Opinion. However, for example, in **Paola Faccini Dori v Recreb SRL** (Case C-91/92) the Court did not follow the Advocate General's Opinion. In this case the Advocate General recommended a departure from existing case law of the Court, which the Court was not minded to depart from.

The reasoning of the Court's judgment may not be as clear and fully argued as the Advocate General's Opinion, due to the fact that the Court must reach a single judgment. The Opinion therefore may be persuasive in future cases on broadly the same theme. The Opinion is published together with the judgment in the European Court Reports (the official Union law reports, abbreviated to ECR) and both are available at:

> http://curia.europa.eu/en/content/juris

Registrar

Article 253 TFEU (previously Art 223 EC Treaty) provides that:

> The Court of Justice shall appoint its Registrar and lay down the rules governing his service.

The Rules provide for the Registrar to be appointed for a six-year renewable term (Art 18(4), Rules).

The Registrar heads the Registry, which is responsible for the filing of documents, distribution of documents to relevant parties, etc. The Registrar is also responsible for the administration of the Court of Justice, and is directly responsible to the President of the Court.

Chambers

Article 251 TFEU provides as follows:

> The Court of Justice shall sit in chambers or in a Grand Chamber, in accordance with the rules laid down for that purpose in the Statute of the Court of Justice of the European Union.
> When provided for in the Statute, the Court of Justice may also sit as a full court.

Article 16 of the Statute provides that the Court shall form chambers of three or five judges. The Grand Chamber consists of 15 judges and will be presided over by the President of the Court (Art 27(1), Rules). The Grand Chamber shall sit whenever a Member State or Union institution that is a party to the proceedings so requests. After hearing the Advocate General, the Court may decide to refer the case to the full Court, if it considers the case to be of exceptional importance.

Article 16 of the Statute provides that the Court shall sit as a full Court where cases are brought to it pursuant to:

- Art 228(2) TFEU (previously Art 195(2) EC Treaty) – dismissal of the Ombudsman;
- Art 245(2) TFEU (previously Art 213(2) EC Treaty) – compulsory retirement of a Commission member, or removing his right to a pension or other benefits, on the ground of his breach of his obligations under Art 247 TFEU (previously Art 213 EC Treaty);

- Art 247 TFEU (previously Art 216 EC Treaty) – compulsory retirement of a Commission member on the ground that he no longer fulfils the conditions required for the performance of his duties or he is guilty of serious misconduct; or

- Art 286(6) TFEU (previously Art 247(7) EC Treaty) – compulsory retirement of a member of the Court of Auditors, or removing his right to a pension or other benefits, on the ground that he no longer fulfils the requisite conditions or meets the obligations arising from his office.

Article 17 of the Statute provides that decisions of the court shall be valid only when an uneven number of its members are sitting in the deliberations. It further provides that chambers consisting of three or five judges shall be valid only if they are taken by at least three judges, those of the Grand Chamber are valid only if at least nine judges are sitting, and those of the full Court are valid only if at least 15 judges are sitting.

Of the cases brought to a close during the period 2006–2014, the distribution of cases between the formations of the Court of Justice was as follows:

	2006	2007	2008	2009	2010	2011	2012	2013	2014
Full court and Grand Chamber	57	51	66	41	71	63	48	52	55
Chambers (5 judges)	278	249	272	283	288	300	283	366	340
Chambers (3 judges)	108	154	124	166	132	177	180	197	228
President	1	2	7	5	5	4	12	5	1
Total	**444**	**456**	**469**	**495**	**496**	**544**	**523**	**620**	**624**

These statistics clearly indicate that the majority of cases brought before the Court of Justice are heard by a five-judge chamber.

Language

The case may be conducted in any one of the Union's official languages (there are 23), and it may also be conducted in Irish (Art 36, Rules). It is for the applicant to choose the language (Art 37(1), Rules). This is overridden by Art 37(1)(a)–(c) of the Rules. For example, Art 37(1)(a) provides that if the defendant is a Member State, the language of the case shall be conducted in the official language of that Member State. If the Member State has more than one official language, the applicant may choose between them. References for a preliminary ruling pursuant to Art 267 TFEU (previously Art 234 EC Treaty; see Chapter 6) shall be conducted in the language of the referring national court (Art 37(3), Rules).

The Court itself will use French as its working language. This is despite a majority of citizens of the Member States now speaking English rather than French. French was chosen as the working language of the Court because when the first Community (the ECSC, which expired on 23 July 2002) was created by the six founding Member States, French was the official language of three of them (France, Belgium and Luxembourg).

Procedure of the Court

Objective 2

The rules concerning the procedure of the Court are laid down in the Statute of the Court and the Rules of Procedure (see above). The new Rules of Procedure which came into force on 1 November 2012 were amended on 18 June 2013 to pave the way for Croatia's membership of the Union from 1 July 2013. These new Rules have amended and clarified the Court's procedure.

Article 53(1) of the Rules of Procedure provides that the procedure before the Court shall consist of a written part and an oral part, except where the Rules provide for some other procedure.

Article 53(4) of the Rules provides that a case may be dealt with under an expedited procedure. Originally, the expedited procedure had only been available in a reference for a preliminary ruling pursuant to Art 267 TFEU (see below and Chapter 6).

Article 53(5) of the Rules provides that a reference for a preliminary ruling may be dealt with under an urgent procedure (see Chapter 6).

The Court's process is essentially inquisitorial. Unlike an English adversarial process, the procedure of the Court, after the initiation of the case by one or more of the parties, is Court-led. The Court can request the parties to provide documents and statements; witnesses are heard at the instigation of the Court. Their evidence is part of the investigation by the Judge-Rapporteur and not, as in an English case, part of the oral hearing. The procedure in a direct action (as opposed to a reference under Art 267 TFEU, which is considered in Chapter 6) generally has the following stages:

1 written proceedings;

2 preliminary report;

3 measures of organisation and measure of inquiry;

4 oral hearing;

5 Advocate General's opinion;

6 judgment.

These stages are now considered in further detail.

Written proceedings

Article 20 of the Statute provides that:

> The written procedure shall consist of the communication to the parties and to the institutions of the Communities [i.e. Union] whose decisions are in dispute, of applications, statements of case, defences and observations, and of replies, if any, as well as of all papers and documents in support or of certified copies of them.

Direct actions are initiated by the applicant filing an application (this is known as a 'pleading') at the Court's registry in accordance with Art 21 of the Statute. At this stage, the case may be assigned to a chamber or Grand Chamber, and a Judge-Rapporteur and Advocate General will be appointed. Articles 123 and 124 of the Rules require the Registrar to serve the application on the defendant and any Union institution affected, following which the defendant has two months within which to lodge his defence, if any (this is also known as a 'pleading').

After the close of pleadings, the defendant can argue separately that the application is not admissible, e.g. he may argue that the proceedings were not issued within any relevant time-limit. The Court may hear this application at this stage and, if successful, the action will be struck out. Alternatively, the Court may decide to hear the argument as to admissibility at the substantive hearing (i.e. the hearing of the main application).

Preliminary report

When the written part of the procedure is concluded, Art 59(1) of the Rules provides that the President will fix a date for the Judge-Rapporteur to present a preliminary report to the general meeting of the Court.

This preliminary report will contain advice on whether any of the following should be undertaken:

- measures of organisation of procedure;
- measures of inquiry.

Article 60 of the rules provides that the report will also contain advice on the formation of the Court to which the case should be referred (e.g. to a Chambers of three or five judges).

In addition, the report will also contain the Judge-Rapporteur's proposals as to whether to dispense with the Advocate General's Opinion pursuant to Art 20 of the Statute.

Measures of organisation and measures of inquiry

Article 61 of the Rules provides that the Court may invite the parties (or other interested persons referred to in Art 23 of the Statute) to answer certain questions in writing or to answer the questions at the actual hearing.

Article 62 of the Rules provides that the Judge-Rapporteur or the Advocate General may request the parties (or other interested persons referred to in Art 23 of the Statute) to submit information relating to the facts, documents or other particulars. They may also submit questions to be addressed at the hearing.

With regard to the measures of inquiry, Art 63(1) of the Rules provides that the Court shall decide in its general meeting whether a measure of inquiry is necessary. If it does decide a measure of inquiry is necessary, Art 64(1) of the Rules provides that the Court will, after hearing the Advocate General, prescribe the measures of inquiry that it considers appropriate by means of an order setting out the facts to be proved.

Article 64(2) of the Rules provides that the following measures of inquiry may be adopted:

- the personal appearance of the parties;
- a request for information and production of documents;
- oral testimony;
- the commissioning of an expert's report;
- an inspection of the place or thing in question.

Article 65(1) of the Rules provides that the task of undertaking the inquiry itself shall be entrusted to the Judge-Rapporteur if the formation of the Court does not undertake the inquiry itself. The Advocate General shall take part in the measures of inquiry (Art 65(2)) and the parties are entitled to attend (Art 65(3)).

Oral hearing

Articles 76–85 of the Rules govern the procedural aspects associated with the oral procedure.

Article 76(2) of the Rules provides that the Court may decide not to hold an oral hearing. The Judge-Rapporteur, upon hearing the Advocate General, will make a request to the Court to dispense with the oral hearing. The Court may decide to dispense with the oral hearing if it considers it has sufficient information to give a ruling. This will enable the Court to give rulings within a shorter period of time.

If an oral hearing takes place, the President of the Court will fix the date for the public hearing. Previous to 1 November 2012, a report for the hearing was prepared by the Judge-Rapporteur. However, this is no longer required.

See pages
161–162 for
further discussion
of Opinions of
Advocates General.

The oral proceedings are brief compared to those in an English court in a contested action. They consist of the addresses by counsel for the parties followed by the Opinion of the Advocate General (see below). Addresses by counsel tend to be quite brief. They are expected to have lodged a copy of their submission before the hearing, and will normally use their address to emphasise their strongest arguments and to attack the weakest points in those of their opponents. The judges will quite frequently challenge points made, but the cut and thrust of forensic debate is somewhat blunted by the need for instant translation by interpreters as the argument proceeds.

Advocate General's Opinion

Article 82(1) of the Rules provides that if an oral hearing takes place the Advocate General's Opinion shall be delivered after the close of that hearing. This is subject to Art 20 of the Statute, which provides that after hearing the Advocate General assigned to the case, the Court can decide to determine the case without an Advocate General's Opinion if the Court considers that the case raises no new point of law.

If applicable, the Advocate General's Opinion will be delivered in open court at some future date. Although he takes no part in the discussions between the judges which precede the judgment, his Opinion will have a significant influence on their decision. The Court has held that it is not open to the parties to submit written observations in response to the Advocate General's Opinion (*Emesa Sugar (Free Zone) NV v Aruba* (Case C-17/98)). Immediately after delivery of the Opinion the Court goes into deliberation.

Judgment

Articles 86 to 92 of the Rules govern the procedural aspects associated with the delivering of a judgment. Judgment is always reserved by the Court, i.e. it goes into secret deliberation and will deliver its judgment in open court at some future date. This is necessary because a single judgment is delivered. The deliberation may be lengthy, taking many weeks (or months) to conclude.

A draft judgment will be prepared by the Judge-Rapporteur. This draft will form the basis of the deliberation. It may be necessary to go through the judgment sentence by sentence, voting on individual sentences. The votes of the judges are taken in ascending order of seniority; this is to ensure that the younger judges do not merely follow their seniors. The judgment may be short on reasons, or it may include differing (maybe conflicting) reasons, in order to obtain the necessary majority. It will be recalled (from above) that Art 17 of the Statute provides that a judgment will be valid only if an uneven number of judges sit in on the deliberation.

The deliberation will be conducted in French, and the judgment will be drafted in French, then translated into the language of the hearing (the authentic version of the judgment) once agreed.

Expedited hearing

As stated above, Art 53(4) of the Rules provides that a case may be dealt with under an expedited procedure. Originally, the expedited procedure had only been available in a reference for a preliminary ruling pursuant to Art 267 TFEU (see Chapter 6). With regard to a direct action, Art 133(1) of the Rules provides as follows:

> At the request of the applicant or the defendant, the President of the Court may, where the nature of the case requires that it be dealt with within a short time, after hearing the other party, the Judge-Rapporteur and the Advocate General, decide that a case is to be determined pursuant to an expedited procedure derogating from the provisions of these Rules.

The expedited procedure provides for truncated written and oral procedures to enable the court to deliver its judgment in a shorter period of time.

Publication of judgments

The formal ruling of the judgment (the 'operative part') is published in the *Official Journal*. Prior to May 2004, the whole of the judgment together with the Advocate General's Opinion would be published in the official European Court Reports (ECR). The reports are published in each of the official languages. They are not published in Irish because it is not one of the official languages. The series of reports are distinguished by colour, the UK version being purple.

The correct mode of citation is for the case number to precede the title, followed by the year of publication of the judgment in square brackets, the abbreviation ECR, and ending with the page number of the report – e.g. Case 20/59 *Italy* v *High Authority* [1960] ECR 423.

Since the Court of First Instance (CFI) was established (renamed the General Court by the ToL, see below), cases before that court are prefixed with a capital letter 'T' (from the French version of 'Tribunal') and those of the Court of Justice by 'C'. From 1990, the volumes of law reports are divided into two sections, so that the page number is now preceded by the numeral 'I' for cases before the Court of Justice and the numeral 'II' for cases before the CFI/General Court: e.g. Case C-79/89 *Brown Boveri* v *Hauptzollamt Mannheim* [1991] ECR I-1853. The two sections may be bound in two separate volumes depending upon the number of cases reported.

Due to the fact that judgments are always drafted in French, the bound French volume will usually be available six months following the end of the month to which it relates. There are 11 monthly paperback volumes: no judgments are delivered in August. They will subsequently be bound into one yearly volume. Following certain changes at the Court of Justice (for example, it decided not to publish the Report for the Hearing in all the official languages) the printed volumes are usually available in all languages quite soon after publication of the French version.

Judgments are available from the Court's Registry (at a charge) on the day of the judgment, or very shortly thereafter. Judgments (and Opinions of Advocates General) are now available (free of charge) at:

http://curia.europa.eu/en/content/juris

An alternative means of accessing the Court's case law is through electronic and online databases such as LexisNexis. There are several independent unofficial law reports, e.g. the Common Market Law Reports (CMLR). The advantage of these reports is that, because they employ their own translators, a case may appear in them before it appears in the official ECR. However, the cases published are selective. The judgments may omit the Advocate General's Opinion and will rarely include the Report for the Hearing. The downside is that their translations may differ from the version of the official report (ECR). Some important cases may also be reported in the domestic law reports, e.g. All ER, Weekly Law Reports. When conducting research or litigation, it is always advisable to refer to the ECRs; alternatives should be used only if the official report is not available.

The selective publication of judgments from May 2004

During early 2004 the Court of Justice reviewed its methods of work, in order to make them more efficient and to counteract the expanding average length of proceedings. The result was the adoption of a series of measures put into practice progressively from May 2004.

The Reports for the Hearing drawn up by the Judge-Rapporteur are now drafted in a shorter and more summary form and contain only the essential elements of the case. Where the procedure in a case, in accordance with the Rules of Procedure, does not require an oral hearing, a report of the Judge-Rapporteur is no longer produced.

The Court also re-examined its practice of publishing judgments in the ECR. Two factors were identified at the centre of the problem:

- it was found that the volume of the Reports, which exceeded 12,000 pages in 2002 and 13,000 pages in 2003, was liable to compromise the accessibility of the case law;
- all judgments published in the Reports necessarily had to be translated into all the official languages of the Union, which represented a substantial workload for the Court's translation department.

Given that not all the judgments it delivers are equally significant from the point of view of the development of Union law, the Court decided to adopt a policy of *selective publication* of its decisions in the ECR.

In an initial stage, as regards direct actions and appeals, judgments are no longer published in the Reports if they come from a chamber of three judges or five judges if, pursuant to the last paragraph of Art 20 of the Statute, the case is decided without an Opinion of the Advocate General. It will, however, be open to the chamber giving judgment to decide to publish such a decision in whole or in part in exceptional circumstances. Texts of the decisions not published in the Reports are accessible in electronic form in the language or languages available. The Reports are available electronically at:

http://www.curia.europa.eu/en/content/juris

The Court decided not to extend this new practice to references for a preliminary ruling, in view of their importance for the interpretation and uniform application of Union law in all the Member States (see Chapter 6).

This reduction in the workload of the Court's translation department following the adoption of the selective publication policy was already apparent in 2004. The total saving as a result of selective publication amounted in 2004 to approximately 20,000 pages.

Precedent

The doctrine of precedent (***stare decisis***) does not apply to the Court of Justice. However, the Court generally follows its own previous decisions. This is necessary for the sake of legal certainty. Nonetheless, faced with a very persuasive Advocate General's Opinion, the Court may be persuaded to deviate from its past case law (e.g. to develop a new Union legal principle). The Court may, of its own volition, depart from its own previous case law, for example on policy grounds.

An example of a departure from its past case law is illustrated in the following case:

Criminal Proceedings against Keck and Mithouard (Cases C-267 and 268/91)

The Court of Justice held that:

14 ... the Court considers it necessary to re-examine and clarify its case law on this matter ...
16 ... contrary to what has previously been decided ...

It is usual for lawyers to cite previous case law when arguing a point of law before the Court. Indeed, the Advocate General in his Opinion, and the Court in its judgment, will generally refer to previous cases. It may be difficult, if not impossible, to extract a ***ratio decidendi*** (i.e. principle of law applied to the facts) from the judgment because of the style of the Court's single judgment.

Methods of interpretation

Objective 3

The task of the Court of Justice of the European Union is stated as being to '... ensure that in the interpretation and application of the Treaties the law is observed' (Art 19 TFEU (previously Art 220 EC Treaty)). The sources of law to which the Court has to give effect are diverse (and are considered in detail in Chapter 2). Many of the Treaty provisions, and some of the implementing legislation, are expressed in the broadest terms, and the Court of Justice plays a crucial role in developing the law and constitution of the Union.

The methods of interpretation the Court of Justice employs when interpreting Union law, whether it is a provision of the Treaty, a regulation, a directive, etc., are considered further below. This 'European way' of interpretation is totally different from that employed by the English judiciary. This was recognised by Lord Denning, sitting in the English Court of Appeal, in the following case:

Bulmer v *Bollinger* [1974] 3 WLR 202

Lord Denning stated that:

> The [EC] Treaty [renamed the TFEU] is quite unlike any of the enactments to which we have become accustomed ... It lays down general principles. It expresses its aims and purposes. All in sentences of moderate length and commendable style. But it lacks precision. It uses words and phrases without defining what they mean. An English lawyer would look for an interpretation clause, but he would look in vain. There is none. All the way through the Treaty there are gaps and lacunae. These have to be filled by the judges, or by regulations or directives.
>
> It is the European way ... Seeing these differences, what are the English courts to do when they are faced with a problem of interpretation? They must follow the European pattern. No longer must they argue about the precise grammatical sense. They must look to the purpose and intent ... They must divine the spirit of the Treaty and gain inspiration from it. If they find a gap, they must fill it as best they can ... These are the principles, as I understand it, on which the European Court acts.

The approach of Lord Denning in the above case has its source in s 3(1), European Communities Act 1972, a UK Act of Parliament, which provides:

> For the purposes of all legal proceedings any question as to the meaning or effect of any of the Treaties, or as to the validity, meaning or effect of any Community [i.e. Union] instrument, shall be treated as a question of law (and, if not referred to the European Court, be for determination as such in accordance with the principles laid down by and any relevant decision of the European Court or any court attached thereto).

The 'principles laid down by ... the European Court' is wide enough to include the Court of Justice's method of interpretation. The European Communities Act 1972 was enacted by the UK Parliament to enable the UK to become a Member State of the European Union with effect from 1 January 1973.

The Court employs the following four separate methods of interpretation:

- literal;
- historical;
- contextual;
- teleological.

It has emerged that the last two (and the last one in particular) are most often employed by the Court of Justice, these two being novel to the English legal system. The four methods of interpretation are now considered.

Literal interpretation

This rule is commonly used by the English judiciary when interpreting national legislation. You begin with the words of the text and give them their natural, plain meaning. The Court of Justice may refuse to employ this method, even where the words of the measure in question appear to be perfectly clear (see, e.g., **Commission v Council** (Case 22/70)).

Literal interpretation may be more difficult for the Court of Justice to apply because of the lack of interpretation sections in the relevant legislative measure. It will therefore be left to judicial interpretation to develop the meanings of certain words and phrases. Examples of words and phrases from the TFEU which have required interpretation include:

- 'charges having equivalent effect' (Arts 28 and 30 TFEU (previously Arts 23 and 25 EC Treaty));
- 'worker' and 'public policy' (Art 45 TFEU (previously Art 39 EC Treaty));
- 'abuse of a dominant position' (Art 102 TFEU (previously Art 82 EC Treaty)).

For an explanation of the meaning of 'directly applicable' see pages 65–66. Secondary legislation may be drafted more specifically (especially regulations which are to be directly applicable as they stand (see Chapter 2)). Nevertheless, the Court of Justice may apply one of the other methods rather than the literal method.

Historical interpretation

Historical interpretation requires a consideration of the subjective intention of the author of the text. This will involve an examination of the preliminary debates. This may be equated with the English **mischief rule**, where the judge seeks to establish the legislative intent, i.e. to ascertain why the legislation was enacted; what its purpose was conceived to be at the time of enactment.

Historical interpretation is occasionally used by the Court of Justice. Generally the Court is not prepared to examine records of debates. With regard to regulations, directives and decisions, Art 296 TFEU (previously Art 253 EC Treaty) provides that the reasons on which they are based must be given, i.e. the reasons as to why they have been enacted. These reasons will be contained in the preamble. The Court of Justice may be guided by these historical reasons in ascertaining the legislative intention of the relevant Union institutions. They are occasionally referred to in judgments of the Court of Justice, as illustrated in the following case:

Markus v *Hauptzollamt Hamburg-Jonas* (Case 14/69)

The Court of Justice held that:

> ... according to the seventh recital of the preamble to the regulation in question ... the eighth recital of the same preamble states ... It must therefore be assumed that the authors of the first paragraph of Article 16 intended ... The solution is confirmed by the penultimate recital of the preamble to the said regulation according to which ...

Contextual interpretation

This method is extensively used by the Court of Justice when interpreting the EU Treaties and secondary legislation. It involves placing the provision within its context and interpreting it in relation to the other provisions. A particular paragraph of a directive or regulation, for example, must be considered not in isolation, but within the context of the whole instrument. When interpreting an article of the TEU or TFEU the Court of Justice may have regard to 'the general scheme of the Treaty as a whole', as illustrated in the following case:

Commission v *Luxembourg and Belgium* (Cases 2 and 3/62)

The Court of Justice was considering the former Art 12 EC Treaty (which was subsequently replaced by Art 25 EC Treaty; and is now Art 30 TFEU), which provides that:

> Customs duties on imports and exports and charges having equivalent effect shall be prohibited between Member States. This prohibition shall also apply to customs duties of a fiscal nature.

The Court of Justice held that:

> The position of those Articles [former Arts 9 and 12 EC Treaty (now Arts 28 and 30 TFEU)] towards the beginning of that Part of the Treaty dealing with the 'Foundations of the Community' [i.e. 'Foundations of the Union'] – [former] Article 9 [now Art 28 TFEU] being placed at the beginning of the Title relating to 'Free Movement of Goods' and [former] Article 12 [now Art 30 TFEU] at the beginning of the section dealing with the 'Elimination of Customs Duties' – is sufficient to emphasise the essential nature of the prohibitions which they impose.

The Court, relying upon the 'general scheme' of these provisions and of the Treaty as a whole, went on to state that there was:

> ... a general intention to prohibit not only measures which obviously take the form of the classic customs duty but also all those which, presented under other names or introduced by the indirect means of other procedures, would lead to the same discriminatory or protective results as customs duties.

In the above case, the Court of Justice gave a wide interpretation to the general words 'charges having equivalent effect', whereas an English court may have applied the *ejusdem generis* rule to limit its scope: i.e. where specific categories are followed by general words, then the general words are limited to the context of the specific categories. The Court of Justice used the general expression as a catch-all provision, looking at the specific provision in context and in relation to the Treaty as a whole, the aim of which is to abolish all restrictions on the free movement of goods.

Teleological interpretation

When applying this method of interpretation, the Court will interpret the provision in question in furtherance of the aims and objectives of the Union as a whole. As discussed in Chapter 1, the EU Treaties set out a broad programme rather than a detailed plan. The preamble to the Treaties and some of the introductory articles (e.g. Art 3 TEU) set out the broad aims and objectives of the Union in very general terms. When interpreting the Treaties or other Union legislation, the Court of Justice may be guided by these overarching aims and objectives (the grand scheme), thus adopting a teleological approach.

Therefore, the contextual approach considers a specific section of a legal instrument in the context of all the sections of that instrument, whereas the teleological approach goes outside the actual instrument and considers the whole purpose, the aims and objectives, of the Union.

The Court has become accustomed to interpreting Union law teleologically, by reference to the broad policy objectives of the EU Treaties, rather than, as would an English court, by the meaning of the words before it and their immediate context. It was, for example, accepted that the European Parliament had the right to bring an action for annulment against the Council or Commission, although only Member States, the Council and affected individuals had specifically been given such a right in the former Art 230(1) EC Treaty (now Art 263 TFEU). The Court of Justice held that not to imply such a right for the Parliament would deprive it of the legal means with which to protect its privileges against incursions by the other institutions (*Parliament v Council* (Case C-70/88)). The former Art 230 EC Treaty was subsequently amended by the TEU to give the Parliament the right to take such action to protect its prerogatives. The Court also extended the right of free movement of workers to those looking for work, even though the former Art 39 EC Treaty (now Art 45 TFEU) appeared to confer the right only on those to whom an offer of work had actually been made. The Court of Justice considered that the object of the Treaty to secure the free movement of labour would not be achieved if only those with an offer of employment from another Member State were enabled to move (*Procureur du Roi v Royer* (Case 48/75)). In these, and in many other matters, the Court has used its interpretative powers to put flesh on the bones of Treaty provisions, and to do so in such a way as to facilitate the effective development of the Union.

Underlying these decisions is what can only be described as the policy of the Court. All national courts have unstated policy objectives, such as the maintenance of the rule of law or the discouragement of anti-social behaviour. The law will be interpreted as far as possible to achieve those ends. The Court's objectives are more clearly discernible. Broadly, the Court's policies could be said to consist of strengthening the Union's structure, increasing the scope and effectiveness of Union law and enhancing the powers of the Union institutions.

The Court's policy of securing greater effectiveness for Union law is achieved partly by interpreting the law in such a way that it achieves the broader objectives of the EU Treaties, even if this has to be done, in some cases, by ignoring the express words of Union legislation. It can also be seen in the doctrine of the direct effect of directives under which the measures originally intended to bind only the Member States have become the means by which individuals can secure their rights in national courts (see Chapter 9). In pursuit of the same policy objectives, remedies in national courts, which were originally seen as being of purely national concern and beyond the competence of the Court, are now judged by the Court in terms of their effectiveness to secure the implementation of Union law. If they are not effective, they must be set aside and an effective remedy provided: *R v Secretary of State for Transport, ex parte Factortame (No. 2)* (Case C-213/89); see Chapter 10.

Article 263 TFEU is considered in detail at pages 248–261.

The General Court

To cope with the great increase in the work of the Court of Justice, the SEA provided for the creation of a Court of First Instance (CFI) to be attached to the Court of Justice (former Art 225 EC Treaty). When the ToL came into force on 1 December 2009, the CFI was renamed the General Court (Art 19(1) TEU).

As discussed above, the General Court has its own Rules of Procedure. The latest version came into force on 1 July 2015.

The number of cases completed by the General Court (previously the CFI) during the period 2006 to 2014 is shown in Table 5.1:

Table 5.1 Cases completed by the General Court 2006–2014

2006	2007	2008	2009	2010	2011	2012	2013	2014
436	397	605	555	527	714	688	702	814

Article 50 of the Statute provides that the General Court may sit in chambers of three or five judges. The Rules of Procedure can determine when the General Court may sit in plenary session or even be constituted by a single judge. As with the Court of Justice, a Grand Chamber can be established. The number of cases completed by the president, a single judge, chambers of three or five judges, the Grand Chamber, or (since 2007) the Appeal Chamber during the period 2006 to 2014 is shown in Table 5.2.

Table 5.2 Cases completed by the president, a single judge, chambers of three or five judges, the Grand Chamber, or (since 2007) the Appeal Chamber during the period 2006–2014

	2006	2007	2008	2009	2010	2011	2012	2013	2014
President	19	16	52	50	54	56	50	40	48
Single judge	7	2	0	0	3	0	0	0	0
Chambers (5 judges)	55	52	17	29	8	25	9	8	16
Chambers (3 judges)	355	318	510	445	423	604	592	596	699
Grand Chamber	0	2	0	0	2	0	0	0	0
Appeal Chamber	–	7	26	31	37	29	37	58	51
Total	**436**	**397**	**605**	**555**	**527**	**714**	**688**	**702**	**814**

Jurisdiction

Article 256 TFEU replaced the former Art 225 EC Treaty, providing as follows:

1 The General Court shall have jurisdiction to hear and determine at first instance actions or proceedings referred to in Articles 263, 265, 268, 270 and 272, with the exception of those assigned to a specialised court set up in Article 257 and those reserved in the Statute for the Court of Justice. The Statute may provide for the General Court to have jurisdiction for other classes of action or proceeding.

Decisions given by the General Court under this paragraph may be subject to a right of appeal to the Court of Justice on points of law only, under the conditions and within the limits laid down by the Statute.

2 The General Court shall have jurisdiction to hear and determine actions or proceedings brought against decisions of the specialised courts.

Decisions given by the General Court under this paragraph may exceptionally be subject to review by the Court of Justice, under the conditions and within the limits laid down by the Statute, where there is a serious risk of the unity or consistency of Union law being affected.

3   The General Court shall have jurisdiction to hear and determine questions referred for a preliminary ruling under Article 267, in specific areas laid down by the Statute.

Where the General Court considers that the case requires a decision of principle likely to affect the unity or consistency of Union law, it may refer the case to the Court of Justice for a ruling.

Decisions given by the General Court on questions referred for a preliminary ruling may exceptionally be subject to review by the Court of Justice, under the conditions and within the limits laid down by the Statute, where there is a serious risk of the unity or consistency of Union law being affected.

Article 256(3) TFEU simply re-enacted the former Art 225(3) EC Treaty, with regard to cases referred by a national court for a preliminary ruling pursuant to Art 267 TFEU (previously Art 234 EC Treaty). The Statute has not made provision for the General Court to have jurisdiction to hear Art 267 TFEU cases.

Article 256(2) TFEU provides a limited right of appeal from decisions of the specialised courts (previously referred to as judicial panels, see below).

Article 256(1) TFEU provides the General Court with jurisdiction in the following categories of case:

- Article 263 TFEU – acts of the Union institutions;
- Article 265 TFEU – failure of the Union institutions to act;
- Article 268 TFEU – compensation for damage pursuant to the second and third paragraphs of Art 340 TFEU;
- Article 270 TFEU – staff cases;
- Article 272 TFEU – pursuant to an arbitration clause contained in a contract concluded by or on behalf of the Union.

Article 256(1) TFEU excludes from the above categories those cases assigned to a specialised court (see below), and also those reserved to the Court of Justice within the Statute. Article 51 of the Statute reserves to the Court of Justice certain types of case brought by a Member State pursuant to Arts 263 and 265 TFEU.

Article 256(1) further provides that the Statute may expand the General Court's jurisdiction to other categories of case.

Article 62 of the Court's Statute provides that in the cases provided for in Art 256(2) and (3) TFEU, if the Court of Justice's First Advocate General considers that there is a serious risk of the unity or consistency of Union law being affected, he may propose that the Court of Justice review the decision of the General Court. The proposal by the First Advocate General must be made within one month of delivery of the General Court's decision. Within one month of receiving the proposal, the Court of Justice has to decide whether or not to review the decision.

Membership of the General Court

Article 19 TEU provides that the General Court shall include at least one judge from each Member State. Article 254 TFEU provides for the exact number of judges of the General Court to be determined by the Statute. Article 48 of the Statute provides that the General

Court shall consist of 28 judges. During 2015 the Court of Justice of the European Union proposed that, by 2017, the number of judges should be increased to 56. This proposal was made because of the General Court's increasing case load and the consequential delays in dealing with cases. This proposal has been approved in principle by the Council of the European Union.

Article 254 TFEU requires members of the General Court to 'possess the ability required for appointment to *high* judicial office' [emphasis added]. This is the same requirement as that for membership of the Court of Justice, and deviates from the former position in Art 224 EC Treaty, which provided that members of the former CFI must possess the ability required for appointment to 'judicial office'.

Article 19(2) TEU provides that judges of the General Court will be appointed by common accord of the governments of the Member States for six years. Article 254 TFEU further provides that they shall be appointed by common accord 'after consultation of the panel provided for in Article 255'. This is identical to appointment of judges and Advocates General to the Court of Justice under Art 253 TFEU. The panel under Art 255 TFEU comprises seven persons chosen from among former members of the Court of Justice and the General Court, members of national supreme courts and lawyers of recognised competence, one of whom is proposed by the European Parliament. The purpose of the panel is to provide an opinion on the candidates' suitability to perform the duties.

Specialised courts

Objective 5

As discussed above, Art 257 TFEU empowers the European Parliament and the Council to establish 'specialised courts' – this is a renaming of the former judicial panels which were established by the Council, acting unanimously, under the former Art 225a EC Treaty.

Decisions of a specialised court are subject to a right of appeal on points of law (and in certain circumstances matters of fact) to the General Court (Art 257 TFEU). Article 256(2) TFEU provides that the Court of Justice may exceptionally review a decision of the General Court (where the General Court has acted as a court of appeal from a specialised court) if there is a serious risk of the unity or consistency of Union law being affected. The members of the specialised courts are appointed by the Council, acting unanimously (Art 257 TFEU).

EU Civil Service Tribunal

As discussed above, the former Art 225a EC Treaty provided for judicial panels to be set up by the Council, acting unanimously. On 2 November 2004 the Council adopted Decision 2004/752 establishing the European Union Civil Service Tribunal (OJ 2004 L 333/7).

The General Court was in favour of this reform because of the special nature of this field of litigation and the workload anticipated as a result of application of the provisions of new Staff Regulations. This tribunal had jurisdiction to hear disputes involving the EU civil service (i.e. staff cases), in respect of which jurisdiction was previously exercised by the General Court. As discussed above, judicial panels have been replaced by specialised courts. The EU Civil Service Tribunal continues to exist, but as a specialised court. The practical effect of this change is negligible. The provisions relating to the Tribunal's composition, jurisdiction, etc. are contained in an Annex to the Court's Statute. The number of cases completed by the tribunal during the period 2006–2014 is shown in Table 5.3:

Table 5.3 Cases completed by the tribunal during the period 2006–2014

2006	2007	2008	2009	2010	2011	2012	2013	2014
50	150	129	155	129	166	121	184	152

Of the 152 cases completed during 2014, one was decided by the full court, 139 by a chamber of three judges, four by a single judge and eight by the President.

The jurisdiction of the Court of Justice of the European Union

Besides the general function of ensuring that Union law is observed, the Court of Justice, the General Court and the specialised courts have a number of other tasks. As the Courts, like the other Union institutions, can act only within the limits of their powers, they have jurisdiction only if jurisdiction has been expressly conferred upon them (Art 13(2) TEU (previously Art 7 EC Treaty)). This means that the Courts have, unlike English courts, no 'residual' or 'inherent' powers and, consequently, cannot hear cases not expressly falling within their jurisdiction. It has, for example, been held that judicial protection cannot be afforded to private individuals who might otherwise be deprived of all legal redress at both national and Union level, since there is no express provision authorising them to do so (*Schlieker* v *HA* (Case 12/63)). The Court of Justice has also ruled that, in hearing appeals from the General Court, it has no jurisdiction to review the facts established by the General Court (*John Deere Ltd* v *Commission* (Case C-7/95)). However, the Court of Justice has shown some flexibility in ruling on cases which it might, hitherto, have refused to adjudicate (*Imm Zwartveld* (Case 2/88); *Dzodzi* v *Belgium* (Case C-297/88)).

The main heads of jurisdiction for the Court of Justice are as follows:

- to give preliminary rulings under Art 267 TFEU (previously Art 234 EC Treaty) at the request of a national court or tribunal (see Chapter 6);

- to establish whether or not a Member State has failed to fulfil an obligation under the Treaty. Actions for this purpose may be brought by the Commission under Art 258 TFEU (previously Art 226 EC Treaty), or by a Member State under Art 259 TFEU (previously Art 227 EC Treaty) (see Chapter 7);

- to exercise unlimited jurisdiction with regard to penalties in actions brought by the Commission under Arts 260(2) and 261 TFEU (previously Arts 228(2) and 229 EC Treaty) (see Chapter 7);

- to review the legality of an act, or of a failure to act, of the EU institutions, at the request of Member States, the European Parliament, the Council or the Commission (Arts 263 and 264 TFEU (previously Arts 230 and 231 EC Treaty)); (see Chapter 8);

- to grant compensation for damage caused by Union institutions in actions brought by Member States, and natural and legal persons under Arts 268 and 340 TFEU (previously Arts 235 and 288 EC Treaty) (see Chapter 8);

- to act as a Court of Appeal from the General Court under Art 256(1) TFEU (previously Art 225(1) EC Treaty).

The jurisdiction of the General Court and the specialised courts has been considered above.

Summary

Now you have read this chapter you should be able to:

- Explain the role of the Court of Justice with regard to the interpretation and application of Union law.
- Outline the membership composition of the Court of Justice.
- Assess the Court of Justice's role in the development of Union law.
- Explain how the Court of Justice interprets Union law through the use of the following methods of interpretation:
  - literal;
  - historical;
  - contextual;
  - teleological.
- Understand how a UK court's approach to interpretation differs from that of the Court of Justice.
- Explain the role of the General Court with particular reference to its membership composition, jurisdiction and powers.
- Explain the role of the specialised courts.
- Identify the main heads of jurisdiction of the Court of Justice.

Further reading

Textbooks

Craig, P. and De Burca, G. (2011) *EU Law: Text, Cases and Materials* (5th edn), Oxford University Press, Chapter 2.

Foster, N. (2015) *Foster on EU Law* (5th edn), Oxford University Press, Chapter 2.

Steiner, J. and Woods, L. (2014) *EU Law* (12th edn), Oxford University Press, Chapter 2.

Journal articles

Barnard, C., 'The PPU: Is it worth the candle? An early assessment' (2009) 34 EL Rev 281.

Bobek, M., 'Legal reasoning of the Court of Justice of the EU' (2014) 39 EL Rev 418.

De la Serre, E.B. and Sibony, A., 'Expert evidence before the EC courts' (2008) 45 CML Rev 941.

Derlén, M., 'Multilingual interpretation of CJEU case law: Rule and reality' (2014) 39 EL Rev 295.

Grimmel, E., 'Judicial interpretation or judicial activism? The legacy of rationalism in the studies of the European Court of Justice' (2012) 18 ELJ 518.

Hadroušek, D. and Smolek, M., 'Solving the European Union's General Court' (2015) 40 EL Rev 188.

Harpaz, G., 'The European Court of Justice and its relations with the European Court of Human Rights: The quest for enhanced reliance, coherence and legitimacy' (2009) 46 CML Rev 105.

Hinarejos, A., 'Integration in criminal matters and the role of the Court of Justice' (2011) 36 EL Rev 420.

Reestman, J-H. and Claes, M., 'For history's sake. On Costa v ENEL, Andre Donner and the external secret of the Court of Justice's deliberations' (2014) 10 ECL Rev 191.

Shuibhne, N.N., 'A court within a court: Is it time to rebuild the Court of Justice?' (2009) 34 EL Rev 173.

6

Preliminary ruling jurisdiction of the Court of Justice (Article 267 TFEU)

Objectives

At the end of this chapter you should understand:

1. The purpose of the Art 267 TFEU preliminary ruling procedure.

2. The scope of 'national courts and tribunals' within Art 267.

3. The types of question a national court is empowered to refer to the Court of Justice under Art 267.

4. How to distinguish between the national courts and tribunals that have a *discretion* to refer a question to the Court of Justice under Art 267 from those that are under an *obligation* to make a referral.

5. Why a national court or tribunal may not consider it *necessary* to make a reference to the Court of Justice under Art 267, with a particular reference to the doctrines of precedent and acte clair.

6. The role of the national court once a referral to the Court of Justice under Art 267 has been made.

Introduction to the Court of Justice's preliminary ruling jurisdiction

Objective 1

National courts perform a crucial role in administering and applying Union law. The Court of Justice has developed an important body of case law on the application of directly enforceable Union provisions in the courts of Member States (see Chapter 9), but it depends on the national courts to cooperate with it to make those provisions effective, as the Court intimated in the following case:

Simmenthal (Case 106/77)

The Court of Justice stated that:

> A national court which is called upon, within the limits of its jurisdiction, to apply provisions of Community [i.e. Union] law is under a duty to give full effect to those provisions, if necessary refusing of its own motion to apply any conflicting provisions of national legislation, even if adopted subsequently, and it is not necessary for the court to request or await the prior setting aside of such provisions by legislative or other constitutional means.

There is a clear danger that, given the disparate national legal traditions of the Member States, Union law will develop differently in the national courts. If this were to happen, individuals and businesses would be operating under different rules and many of the benefits of an open Union and a genuine internal market would be lost. The Union has, therefore, a fundamental interest in ensuring that its law has the same meaning and effect in all the Member States. The only effective way of doing this is to provide that ultimate authority for deciding the meaning of Union law should reside in one court. That court is, of course, the Court of Justice. The best way to ensure the harmonious development of Union law would have been to have established the Court of Justice as a final Court of Appeal on matters of Union law. That course seemed to constitute too direct a challenge to the supremacy of national legal systems, and was rejected by the founders of the Union. They opted, instead, for a system of references by national courts. Article 267 TFEU (previously Art 234 EC Treaty), which establishes the preliminary reference procedure, is the only provision of the Treaty that expressly acknowledges the enforcement role of the courts of the Member States.

Jurisdiction

Article 19 TEU and Arts 251–281 TFEU set out the provisions that apply to the Court of Justice of the European Union. Article 19(1) TEU provides that:

> The Court of Justice of the European Union shall include the Court of Justice, the General Court and specialised courts ...

The Statute of the Court of Justice of the European Union came into force at the same time as the ToL (1 December 2009). The Statute is annexed to the TEU and TFEU as a Protocol (Number 3). A consolidated version of the Statute was published on 1 July 2013. Article 253 TFEU provides that the Court of Justice shall adopt its Rules of Procedure, which will require the approval of the Council acting by a qualified majority. New Rules of Procedure for the Court of Justice came into force on 1 November 2012. These Rules were amended on 18 June 2013 to pave the way for Croatia's membership of the Union from 1 July 2013.

Article 256(3) TFEU re-enacts the former Art 225(3) EC Treaty with regard to cases referred by a national court for a preliminary ruling pursuant to Art 267 TFEU (previously Art 234 EC Treaty). Article 256(3) TFEU provides as follows:

> The General Court shall have jurisdiction to hear and determine questions referred for a preliminary ruling under Article 267, in specific areas laid down by the Statute.
>
> Where the General Court considers that the case requires a decision of principle likely to affect the unity or consistency of Union law, it may refer the case to the Court of Justice for a ruling.
>
> Decisions given by the General Court on questions referred for a preliminary ruling may exceptionally be subject to review by the Court of Justice, under the conditions and within the limits laid down by the Statute, where there is a serious risk of the unity or consistency of Union law being affected.

The Statute has not made provision for the General Court to have jurisdiction to hear and determine Art 267 TFEU cases. Only the Court of Justice has such jurisdiction. However, the Statute sets out the conditions for review by the Court of Justice, if the General Court is provided with jurisdiction to hear and determine Art 267 TFEU cases.

Article 62 of the Statute provides that:

In the cases provided for in Article 256(2) and (3) of the Treaty on the Functioning of the European Union, where the First Advocate General considers that there is a serious risk of the unity or consistency of Union law being affected, he may propose that the Court of Justice review the decision of the General Court.

The proposal must be made within one month of delivery of the decision by the General Court. Within one month of receiving the proposal made by the First Advocate General, the Court of Justice shall decide whether or not the decision should be reviewed.

Article 62b of the Statute of the Court of Justice provides that:

... In the cases provided for in Article 256(3) of the Treaty on the Functioning of the European Union, in the absence of proposals for review or decisions to open the review procedure, the answer(s) given by the General Court to the questions submitted to it shall take effect upon expiry of the periods prescribed for that purpose in the second paragraph of Article 62. Should a review procedure be opened, the answer(s) subject to review shall take effect following that procedure, unless the Court of Justice decides otherwise. If the Court of Justice finds that the decision of the General Court affects the unity or consistency of Union law, the answer given by the Court of Justice to the questions subject to review shall be substituted for that given by the General Court.

The need for jurisdictional reform has primarily been due to the fact that the majority of cases which come before the Court of Justice are cases referred by national courts pursuant to Art 267 TFEU. This has impacted upon the effective operation of the Court, although over recent years there has been a reduction in the length of time taken before a judgment is delivered by the Court of Justice in cases referred to it pursuant to Art 267.

The number of cases referred to the Court of Justice under Art 267 TFEU and which were completed, together with the *total* number of cases completed by the Court, during the period 1999–2014, are shown in Table 6.1.

Table 6.1 Cases completed by the Court of Justice 1999–2014

Year	Number of Art 267 TFEU cases completed by the Court of Justice	Total number of cases completed by the Court of Justice
1999	192	395
2000	268	526
2001	182	434
2002	241	513
2003	233	494
2004	262	665
2005	254	574
2006	266	546
2007	235	570
2008	301	567
2009	259	588
2010	339	574
2011	388	638
2012	386	595
2013	413	620
2014	476	624

The length of time taken for a judgment to be delivered in cases referred to the Court of Justice under Art 267 TFEU has been on a steady decline since 2004, such that in 2014 the length of time was 15.0 months (the shortest period for over 20 years) (Table 6.2).

Table 6.2 Time taken for a judgment to be delivered in cases referred to the Court of Justice under Art 267 TFEU

Year	Length of time for Art 267 TFEU judgment to be delivered	Year	Length of time for Art 267 TFEU judgment to be delivered
1999	21.2 months	2007	19.3 months
2000	21.6 months	2008	16.8 months
2001	22.7 months	2009	17.1 months
2002	24.1 months	2010	16.1 months
2003	25.5 months	2011	16.4 months
2004	23.5 months	2012	15.7 months
2005	20.4 months	2013	16.3 months
2006	19.8 months	2014	15.0 months

Special forms of procedure

From 1 July 2000, the Court's Statute and Rules of Procedure have provided a simplified procedure for certain types of case referred to it under Art 267 TFEU, and in other situations have provided an accelerated procedure. Since early 2008, the Court's Statute and Rules of Procedure have provided an urgent preliminary ruling procedure. Each of these special forms of procedure will be considered further.

Simplified procedure

The simplified procedure may be applied to those questions referred to the Court which are identical to questions that have been answered previously, where the answer to the question can be clearly deduced from existing case law and where the answer admits of no reasonable doubt. Article 99 of the Rules provides that:

> Where a question referred to the Court for a preliminary ruling is identical to a question on which the Court has already ruled, where the reply to such a question may be clearly deduced from existing case-law or where the answer to the question referred for a preliminary ruling admits of no reasonable doubt, the Court may at any time, on a proposal from the Judge-Rapporteur and after hearing the Advocate General, decide to rule by reasoned order.

During the period 2005–2014 the Court of Justice made a number of orders pursuant to the simplified procedure, bringing the following number of cases to a close (Table 6.3).

Table 6.3 Orders made pursuant to the simplified procedure

2005	2006	2007	2008	2009	2010	2011	2012	2013	2014
29	21	18	39	22	24	30	26	33	31

This has undoubtedly had an effect on reducing the average time taken to deliver a judgment in Art 267 TFEU proceedings (see above).

Accelerated (or expedited) procedure

Article 105(1) of the Rules provides an accelerated procedure, as follows:

At the request of the referring court or tribunal or, exceptionally, of his own motion, the President of the Court may, where the nature of the case requires that it be dealt with within a short time, after hearing the Judge-Rapporteur and the Advocate General, decide that a reference for a preliminary ruling is to be determined pursuant to an expedited procedure derogating from the provisions of these Rules.

If the accelerated procedure is applied, Art 105(2) provides that the date for the hearing shall be fixed immediately, thus enabling the court to deliver its judgment in a shorter period of time.

Although use of the accelerated procedure was requested on a number of occasions during the period 2004 to 2007 in relation to Art 267 TFEU proceedings, the requirement of exceptional urgency was not satisfied in any case. During 2008 it was requested eight times and the requirement of exceptional urgency was satisfied (for the first time ever) in two cases. During the period 2009–2014 the Court of Justice received the following number of requests for use of the accelerated procedure (Table 6.4):

Table 6.4 Requests made and granted for use of the accelerated procedure

	2009	2010	2011	2012	2013	2014
Number of requests made for use of the accelerated procedure	5	12	13	5	14	12
Number of cases in which the requirement for 'exceptional urgency' was satisfied	0	4	2	2	0	2

Urgent preliminary ruling procedure

The urgent preliminary ruling procedure enables questions relating to the area of freedom, security and justice that are referred for a preliminary ruling to be dealt with expeditiously and appropriately. After establishing that existing procedures, including the accelerated procedure under Art 105 of the Rules of Procedure, were not capable of ensuring that these categories of case would be dealt with sufficiently expeditiously, the Court proposed the creation of this new procedure in order to be able to decide such cases within a particularly short time and without delaying the handling of other cases pending before the Court.

The procedure is contained in Art 23a of the Statute and Art 107 of the Rules. The principal features of the urgent preliminary ruling procedure are apparent from the differences between it and the ordinary and accelerated preliminary ruling procedures. First, the written procedure is limited to the parties to the main proceedings, the Member State from which the reference is made, the European Commission and the other EU institutions if a measure of theirs is at issue. The parties and all the interested persons referred to in Art 23 of the Statute will be able to participate in an oral procedure, where they can express a view on the written observations that have been lodged. Second, cases subject to the urgent preliminary ruling procedure will, as soon as they arrive at the Court, be assigned to a Chamber of five Judges specially designated for this purpose. Finally, the procedure in these cases will, for the most part, be conducted electronically.

The urgent preliminary procedure was applied for the first time in *PPU* (Case C-195/08). In this case, the Court of Justice delivered its judgment on 11 July 2008, clarifying the law relating to the return of a child wrongly retained in another Member State. During 2008, the procedure was requested in six cases and the designated chamber decided that the conditions under Art 107 of the Rules were satisfied in three cases. This new procedure enabled the Court to complete these three cases in an average period of 2.1 months. During the period 2008–2014 the procedure was applied as shown Table 6.5.

Table 6.5 Requests made and granted for use of the urgent preliminary procedure

	2008	2009	2010	2011	2012	2013	2014
Number of cases in which the procedure was requested	6	3	6	5	5	5	6
Number of cases in which the procedure was applied	3	2	5	2	4	2	4
Average time period to complete each case	2.1 months	2.5 months	2.1 months	2.5 months	1.9 months	2.2 months	2.2 months

Determining a case without an Opinion of the Advocate General

As discussed in Chapter 5, Art 20 of the Statute provides that, after hearing the Advocate General assigned to a particular case, if the Court considers that the case raises no new point of law, it may decide to determine the case without a submission (i.e. Opinion) from the Advocate General. This provision will apply to cases referred to the Court of Justice for a preliminary ruling pursuant to Art 267 TFEU, in addition to other categories of case.

References from national courts under Article 267 TFEU

Objective 2

See page 200 for a flowchart illustrating the Art 267 TFEU procedure.

Article 267 TFEU (previously Art 234 EC Treaty) envisages a partnership role between the Court of Justice and the national court, with jurisdiction divided between the Court of Justice, which interprets the law, and the national courts which apply it. It must be emphasised that Art 267 references have a different function from an appeal. In an appeal, the initiative lies with the parties, and if the appeal is successful the appellate court can substitute its own decision for that of the lower court. In a reference, however, it is the lower (national) court itself which takes the decision to refer the case. The Court of Justice rules on the issues raised, but it is then for the lower (national) court to apply the ruling of the Court of Justice to the facts of the case before it. Ultimately, the national court will make the final decision. The objective of the reference procedure is to retain the independence of the national courts, while at the same time preventing 'a body of national case law not in accord with the rules of Community [i.e. Union] law from coming into existence in any Member State' (*Hoffmann La Roche* v *Centrafarm* (Case 107/76)). It must, however, be emphasised that in many instances the national court will be able to give judgment *without* making a reference to the Court of Justice. National courts do so throughout the European Union, quite properly, in many cases each day.

Article 267 TFEU provides:

The Court of Justice of the European Union shall have jurisdiction to give preliminary rulings concerning:

(a) the interpretation of the Treaties;
(b) the validity and interpretation of acts of the institutions, bodies, offices or agencies of the Union.

Where such a question is raised before any court or tribunal of a Member State, that court or tribunal may, if it considers that a decision on the question is necessary to enable it to give judgment, request the Court of Justice to give a ruling thereon.

Where any such question is raised in a case pending before a court or tribunal of a Member State against whose decisions there is no judicial remedy under national law, that court or tribunal shall bring the matter before the Court.

If such a question is raised in a case pending before a court or tribunal of a Member State with regard to a person in custody, the Court of Justice of the European Union shall act with the minimum of delay.

The wording of Art 267 TFEU is very similar to that of the former Art 234 EC Treaty, with the exception of the 'acts' upon which the Court of Justice may provide preliminary rulings. Also, for the first time, Art 267 TFEU explicitly requires the Court to act 'with the minimum of delay' if the case relates to a person who is in custody. This is understandable given the length of time it normally takes for the Court to provide its judgment (see above).

What matters can be the subject of a reference under Article 267 TFEU?

Objective 3

Article 267 TFEU refers to two types of provision which can be the subject of a reference to the Court of Justice for a preliminary ruling:

- interpretation of the Treaties;
- the validity and interpretation of acts of the institutions, bodies, offices or agencies of the Union.

The most common of these are now considered.

Interpretation of the Treaties

'Interpretation of the Treaties' covers the TEU, the TFEU, the amending Treaties and the Treaties of Accession, the last normally being made expressly subject to Art 267 TFEU. In the case of the UK's entry to the European Union, this was achieved by Art 1(3) of the Treaty of Accession of 1972 (***Department of Health and Social Security* v *Barr and Montrose Holdings Ltd.*** (Case C-355/89)).

There are some policy areas in both the TEU and TFEU where the Court of Justice has either limited jurisdiction or no jurisdiction, and therefore the power to interpret such provisions within an Art 267 referral will likewise be limited.

Prior to the ToL coming into force, the construction of the European Union (and its three pillars), as discussed in Chapter 1, was both complex and cumbersome. When the ToL came into force on 1 December 2009, it established a single European Union, which replaced and succeeded the European Community (Art 1 TEU). The former three pillars of the European Union were merged even though special procedures were maintained in the fields of foreign policy, security and defence. Reference is no longer to be made to the three pillars of the European Union.

Title V, Chapter 2, Sections 1 and 2, Arts 23–46 TEU relate to the Common Foreign and Security Policy. Title V, Chapter 4, Arts 82–86 TFEU relate to Judicial Cooperation in Criminal Matters. Title V, Chapter 5, Arts 87–89 relate to Police Cooperation. Article 24(1) TEU provides that 'The Court of Justice of the European Union shall not have jurisdiction with respect to these provisions [which relate to the common foreign and security policy]'. Similarly, Art 276 TFEU provides that:

In exercising its powers regarding the provisions of Chapters 4 [judicial cooperation in criminal matters] and 5 [police cooperation] of Chapter V of Part Three [of the TFEU] relating to the area of freedom, security and justice, **the Court of Justice of the European Union shall** have no jurisdiction to review the validity or proportionality of operations carried out by the police or other law-enforcement services of a Member State or the exercise of the responsibilities incumbent upon Member States with regard to the maintenance of law and order and the safeguarding of internal security. [emphasis added]

Validity and interpretation of acts of the institutions of the Union

See pages 64–68 for a full explanation of 'Union acts'.

'Acts of the institutions, bodies, offices or agencies of the Union' includes not only legally binding acts, such as regulations, directives and decisions, but also opinions and recommendations where these are relevant to the interpretation of Union law by the courts of Member States: *Frecassetti* (Case 113/75); *Grimaldi v Fonds des Maladies Professionnelles* (Case C-322/88). In *Deutsche Shell AG v Hauptzollamt Hamburg* (Case C-188/91), the Court of Justice held that 'arrangements' made by a joint committee responsible for implementing a convention on a common transit policy between the EU and EFTA formed 'part of the Community [i.e. Union] legal order'. The Court noted that the fact that a Union legal measure lacked compulsory effect did not exclude the Court from giving a legal ruling on it, because national courts were obliged to take it into account when interpreting the Convention.

In the *Deutsche Shell* case the Court of Justice emphasised that it did not have jurisdiction under what is now Art 267 TFEU to give a ruling on the compatibility of a national measure with Union law. However, it does in fact come very close to doing so. Characteristically, it will describe the national measure in hypothetical terms and state that, if there was such a measure, it would not be compatible with Union law! Although the Court can only give a ruling on the interpretation (and validity – see below) of *Union* law, it has been prepared to rule on the meaning of *national* provisions which are not intended to implement Union law but which are based on the wording of a Union provision: *Gmurzynska-Bscher* (Case C-231/89).

The Court has the power to give preliminary rulings which relate to the *validity* of Union acts in addition to their interpretation. However, it should be noted that the Court does not have the power to question the validity of the Treaties. 'Validity' relates to the question of whether or not the Union act is void (i.e. of no effect). A Union act may, for example, have been made *ultra vires* (where, for example, the opinion of the European Parliament has not been obtained despite the relevant Treaty article requiring this). Consider the following scenario: a levy is imposed by a regulation; the regulation may provide for the levy to be collected by a national agency. An individual may be sued when he refuses to pay the levy. In his defence he may argue that the regulation is not valid because a procedural step in the legislative process has not been followed. The national court may refer the matter to the Court of Justice pursuant to Art 267 to ascertain if the regulation (i.e. a Union act) is valid. The Court of Justice will make the ruling and pass the case back to the national court. The national court will then apply the law as determined by the Court of Justice. If the Court of Justice rules that the regulation is invalid, the national court will be obliged to rule in favour of the defendant. As will be discussed in Chapter 8, this indirect way of challenging the validity of a Union act may be a much more effective mechanism than the restricted power to challenge such an act directly under Art 263 TFEU (previously Art 230 EC Treaty).

Which courts or tribunals are able to refer?

Objective 4

Depending on the status of the court or tribunal, some *may*, while others *must*, refer to the Court of Justice questions of interpretation of the Treaties or interpretation/validity of Union acts. Before discussing the issue of which courts and tribunals have a *discretion* to refer, and which are under an *obligation* to make a referral, it is necessary to ascertain which courts or tribunals should consider the possibility of a reference under Art 267. Article 267 refers to 'any court or tribunal of a Member State' so that, at first glance, it would appear that references can only be made by courts and tribunals within the state's judicial structure. However, the essential elements to determine the status of the body in relation to Art 267 are its power to make legally binding decisions, its independence from the parties and the recognition of its decision-making function by the state. To be able to make references under Art 267 it will have to satisfy all these criteria. An arbitrator, although conferred with a power by contract to make legally binding decisions on the parties, and also being independent of the parties, lacks the official state recognition to make his decisions 'judicial' in character, and he cannot, therefore, make a reference under Art 267 (***Nordsee v Reederei Mond*** (Case 102/81)). However, an arbitration board or a disciplinary body which is recognised by the state as having a function in making legally binding decisions in relation to an industry or a professional body may well be a 'court or tribunal' for the purpose of Art 267, as illustrated in the following case:

Broekmeulen v Huisarts Registratie Commissie (Case 246/80)

A Netherlands' body called the Appeals Committee for General Medicine heard appeals from the Netherlands' body responsible for registering persons seeking to practise medicine in The Netherlands. Without registration, it was practically impossible to practise. Both of these bodies were established by the Royal Netherlands Society for the Promotion of Medicine, a private association, but were recognised indirectly in some Netherlands' legal provisions. The Appeals Committee was not a court or tribunal under Netherlands' law. It followed an adversarial procedure and allowed legal representation.

The applicant was a national of The Netherlands and had qualified in Belgium. He wanted to practise in The Netherlands and applied for registration. This was refused and he appealed. The case was referred to the Court of Justice pursuant to the former Art 177 EC Treaty (now Art 267 TFEU (previously Art 234 EC Treaty)) and the question arose whether the Appeals Committee was a 'court or tribunal of a Member State'. If it was not, then the Court of Justice would not have jurisdiction to give a preliminary ruling. The Court of Justice stated that:

17. In order to deal with the question of applicability in the present case of Article 177 of the Treaty [now Article 267 TFEU], it should be noted that it is incumbent upon Member States to take the necessary steps to ensure within their own territory the provisions adopted by the Community [i.e. Union] institutions are implemented in their entirety. If, under the legal system of a Member State, the task of implementing such provisions is assigned to a professional body acting under a degree of governmental supervision, and if that body, in conjunction with the public authorities concerned, creates appeal procedures which may affect the exercise of rights granted by Community [i.e. Union] law, it is imperative, in order to ensure the proper functioning of Community [i.e. Union] law, that the Court should have an opportunity of ruling on issues of interpretation and validity arising out of such proceedings.

18. As a result of all the foregoing considerations and in the absence, in practice, of any right of appeal to the ordinary courts, the Appeals Committee, which operates with the consent of the public authorities and with their cooperation, and which, after an adversarial procedure, delivers decisions which are recognised as final, must, in a matter involving the application of Community [i.e. Union] law, be considered as a court or tribunal of a Member State within the meaning of Article 177 of the Treaty [now Art 267 TFEU]. Therefore, the Court has jurisdiction to reply to the question asked. [emphasis added]

In **Walter Schmid** (Case C-516/99), the Court of Justice held that the Fifth Appeal Chamber of the regional finance authority for Vienna (Austria) was not a 'court or tribunal' within the scope of Art 267 TFEU, because it was not independent. The Chamber was established to enable taxpayers to resolve any dispute with the tax authority. However, the tax authority personnel would sit as adjudicators (together with others not employed by the tax authority). The adjudicators who were not employed by the tax authority were nevertheless selected by the authority, and they did not have a sufficient period of tenure to detach themselves closely enough from the tax authority.

The concept of 'court or tribunal' was at issue in the following case:

De Coster v Collège des Bourgmestres et Échevins de Watermael-Boitsfort (Case C-17/00)

A dispute arose between De Coster and the Collège, when the Collège levied a municipal charge on De Coster in respect of his satellite dish. He contended, *inter alia*, that this tax breached the former Art 49 EC Treaty (now Art 56 TFEU) because it was a restriction on the free movement of services (i.e. the freedom to receive television programmes coming from other Member States). The Collège decided to refer the case to the Court of Justice pursuant to the former Art 234 EC Treaty (now Art 267 TFEU) for a preliminary ruling. The first question before the Court was whether or not the Collège was a 'court or tribunal'. The Court stated that:

9. First of all, the question of whether the Collège juridictionnel de la Région de Bruxelles-Capitale should be considered to be a national court or tribunal for the purposes of Article 234 EC [now Art 267 TFEU] must be examined.

10. It is settled case-law that in order to determine whether a body making a reference is a court or tribunal for the purposes of Article 234 EC [now Art 267 TFEU], which is a question governed by Community [i.e. Union] law alone, the Court takes account of a number of factors, such as whether the body is established by law, whether it is permanent, whether its jurisdiction is compulsory, whether its procedure is *inter partes*, whether it applies rules of law and whether it is independent (see, in particular, Case C-54/96 *Dorsch Consult* [1997] ECR I-4961, para. 23 and the case law cited therein, and Joined Cases C-110/98 to C-147/98 *Gabalfrisa and Others* [2000] ECR I-1577, para. 33).

11. In the case of the Collège juridictionnel de la Région de Bruxelles-Capitale, Article 83d(2) of the Law of 12 January 1989 concerning the Brussels institutions (Moniteur belge of 14 January 1989, p. 667), states:

    The judicial functions which in the provinces are exercised by the permanent deputation are exercised in respect of the territory referred to in Article 2(1) by a board of 9 members appointed by the Council of the Brussels-Capital Region on the proposal of its government. At least three members must come from the smallest linguistic group.

    The members of this board are subject to the same rules on ineligibility as those which apply to the members of the permanent deputations in the provinces.

    In proceedings before the board, the same rules must be respected as those which apply when the permanent deputation exercises a judicial function in the provinces.

12. It is thus established that the Collège juridictionnel de la Région de Bruxelles-Capitale is a permanent body, established by law, that it gives legal rulings and that the jurisdiction thereby invested in it concerning local tax proceedings is compulsory.

13. However, the Commission maintains that no assurance can be gained from examination of Article 83d of the Law of 12 January 1989 that the procedure followed before the Collège juridictionnel is inter partes, or that the latter exercises its functions completely independently and impartially in applications by taxpayers challenging taxes charged them by the municipal councils. In particular, the Commission raises the question of whether the Collège juridictionnel is independent of the executive.

14. Regarding the requirement that the procedure be *inter partes*, it must first be noted that that is not an absolute criterion (**Dorsch Consult**, paragraph 31, and **Gabalfrisa**, paragraph 37, both cited above).

15. Secondly, it must be noted that in the present case Article 104a of the Provincial Law of 30 April 1836, a provision inserted by the Law of 6 July 1987 (Moniteur belge of 18 August 1987, p. 12309), and the Royal Decree of 17 September 1987 concerning the procedure before the permanent deputation when it exercises a judicial function (Moniteur belge of 29 September 1987, p. 14073), both of which are applicable to the Collège juridictionnel de la Région de Bruxelles-Capitale by virtue of Article 83d(2) of the Law of 12 January 1989, indicate that the procedure followed before the latter is indeed *inter partes*.

16. Article 104a of the abovementioned Provincial Law and Article 5 of the Royal Decree of 17 September 1987 indicate that a copy of the application is sent to the defendant, who has 30 days in which to submit a reply (which is then sent to the applicant), that the preparatory inquiries are adversarial, that the file may be consulted by the parties and that they may present their oral observations at a public hearing.

17. As to the criteria of independence and impartiality, it must be noted that there is no reason to consider that the Collège juridictionnel does not satisfy such requirements.

18. First, as is clear from Article 83d(2) of the Law of 12 January 1989, it is the Conseil de la Région de Bruxelles-Capitale that appoints the members of the Collège juridictionnel and not the municipal authorities whose tax decisions the Collège juridictionnel is, as in the main proceedings, required to examine.

19. Secondly, it is apparent *inter alia* from the Belgian Government's answers to the questions put to it by the Court that members of the Collège juridictionnel may not be members of a municipal council or of the staff of a municipal authority.

20. Thirdly, Articles 22 to 25 of the Royal Decree of 17 September 1987 establish procedure for challenging appointment which is applicable to the members of the Collège juridictionnel by virtue of Article 83d(2) of the Law of 12 January 1989, and which is to be based on reasons essentially identical to those which apply in the case of members of the judiciary.

21. Finally, it appears from the explanations provided by the Belgian Government at the request of the Court that appointments of members of the Collège juridictionnel are for an unlimited period of time and cannot be revoked.

22. It is clear from the above that the Collège juridictionnel de la Région de Bruxelles-Capitale must be considered to be a court or tribunal for the purposes of Article 234 EC [now Art 267 TFEU]; accordingly, the reference for a preliminary ruling is admissible. [emphasis added]

In the above case, the Court of Justice held that the Collège was a 'court or tribunal' for the purpose of the former Art 234 EC Treaty (now Art 267 TFEU), such that the Court could provide the Collège with a preliminary ruling. Paragraph 10 of the Court's judgment sets out some of the factors which the Court will take into account when determining this question (i.e. whether the body is established by law, whether it is permanent, whether its jurisdiction is compulsory, whether its procedure is *inter partes*, whether it applies rules of law and whether it is independent).

A national court determining an appeal against an arbitration award, not according to law but according to what is 'fair and reasonable', may be regarded as a 'court or tribunal' for the purpose of Art 267 TFEU (*Municipality of Almelo and Others* v *Energiebedvijf NV* (Case C-394/92)). A court delivering an advisory 'opinion' may likewise be a 'court or tribunal' for the purpose of Art 267. In *Garofalo and Others* v *Ministero della Sanità and Others* (Joined Cases C-69–79/96) an opinion delivered by the Italian Consiglio del Stato to the Italian President, although not binding on him, was held to be a proper subject for a reference under Art 267. In the UK, besides references from magistrates' courts, crown courts and county courts, there have also been references from VAT tribunals, employment tribunals and the social security commissioners.

Admissibility

In the following case, the Court of Justice had an opportunity to clarify its case law on the admissibility of a reference for a preliminary ruling where the circumstances of the dispute in the main proceedings are confined to a single Member State:

Salzmann (Case C-300/01)

The Court of Justice noted that the referring court was seeking an interpretation of Union law for the purpose of determining the scope of rules of national law which refer to it. The Court cited its own case law in that connection, according to which: (i) it is for the national courts alone to determine, having regard to the particular features of each case, both the need to refer a question for a preliminary ruling and the relevance of such a question (*Guimont* (Case C-448/98), para 22, and *Reisch* (Joined Cases C-515/99, C-519/99 to C-524/99 and C-526/99 to C-540/99), para 25); and (ii) it is only in the exceptional case, where it is quite obvious that the interpretation of Union law sought bears no relation to the facts or the purpose of the main action, that the Court refrains from giving a ruling (*Konle* (Case C-302/97), para 33, and *Angonese* (Case C-281/98), para 18). However, the Court pointed out that a situation where national law requires that a national be allowed to enjoy the same rights as those which nationals of other Member States would derive from Union law in the same situation does not correspond to such an exceptional case. Moreover, the Court held that:

> ... where, in relation to purely internal situations, domestic legislation adopts solutions which are consistent with those adopted in Union law in order, in particular, to avoid discrimination against foreign nationals, it is clearly in the Union interest that, in order to forestall future differences of interpretation, provisions or concepts taken from Union law should be interpreted uniformly, irrespective of the circumstances in which they are to apply' (para 34).

What is the appropriate stage in the proceedings for a reference to be made?

A reference to the Court of Justice may be made at any stage in the proceedings, even before a full hearing, either during the interim stage (i.e. a hearing on a preliminary matter before the full hearing) or where the case is being dealt with in the absence of one of the parties (*Simmenthal* v *Amministrazione delle Finanze dello Stato* (Case 70/77); *Balocchi* v *Ministero delle Finanze dello Stato* (Case C-10/92)). The Court does, however, think it desirable that an *inter partes* hearing (i.e. a hearing where all the parties are invited to take part) takes place before the reference, if that is possible (***Eurico Italia Srl* v *Ente Nazionale Risi*** (Case C-332/92)).

The Court of Justice will not hear arguments that the national court or tribunal should not, under national law, have made the reference (***Reina* v *Landeskreditbank Baden-Württemberg*** (Case 65/81)). However, the Court does expect the case to have reached a stage at which the relevant facts have been established and the issues identified on which the assistance of the Court is required:

Irish Creamery Milk Suppliers Association v *Ireland* (Case 36/80)

The Court of Justice stated that:

> It might be convenient, in certain circumstances, for the facts in the case to be established and for questions of purely national law to be settled at the time the reference is made to the Court of Justice so as to enable the latter to take cognisance of all the features of fact and of law which may be relevant.

In ***Telemarsicabruzzo SpA*** (Joined Cases C-320–322/90), the Court refused to give a ruling, stating that the need to give a practical interpretation of Union law requires the national court to define the factual and legal framework in which the questions arose, or that at least it explains the factual assumptions on which those questions are based. Neither had been done in this case. In ***Venntveld*** (Case C-316/93), however, although all the relevant facts were not included, the Court held that there was sufficient information in the case file and in the pleadings to give a preliminary ruling.

In the following case, the Court of Justice held inadmissible a question referred to it to enable the referring court to decide whether the legislation of another Member State is in accordance with Union law:

Bacardi-Martini and Cellier des Dauphins (Case C-318/00)

The Court observed that, when such a question is before it, the Court must display special vigilance and 'must be informed in some detail of [the referring court's] reasons for considering that an answer to the question is necessary to enable it to give judgment' (para. 46). The Court pointed out, *inter alia*, that where the national court has confined itself to repeating the argument of one of the parties, without indicating whether and to what extent it considers that a reply to the question is necessary to enable it to give judgment, and, as a result, the Court does not have the material before it to show that it is necessary to rule on the question referred, that question is inadmissible.

A discretion to refer

Article 267, para 2 TFEU provides that:

> Where such a question is raised before any court or tribunal of a Member State, that court or tribunal **may**, if it considers that a decision on the question is necessary to enable it to give judgment, request the Court of Justice to give a ruling thereon. [emphasis added]

It contemplates a situation in which the national court or tribunal considers that it is 'necessary' to refer a question to the Court of Justice to enable it to give judgment in the case. In such a case, it *may* refer the question to the Court. The question to be referred must relate to one of the matters considered above (e.g.: (i) interpretation of the Treaties; or (ii) the validity or interpretation of a regulation, directive or decision). Therefore, before the discretion to refer arises, the national court must be of the view that 'a decision on the question is *necessary* in order to enable it to give judgment' [emphasis added]; see below. The decision on whether or not to make a reference is essentially a matter for the national court, as explained by the Court of Justice in the following case:

Dzodzi v *Belgium* (Joined Cases C-297/88 and C-197/89)

The Court of Justice stated that:

> In the context of the division of judicial functions between national courts and the Court of Justice, provided for by Article 177 [replaced by Art 234 EC Treaty, and now Art 267 TFEU], the Court of Justice gives preliminary rulings without, in principle, needing to enquire as to the circumstances which led to the national court submitting questions to it ... The only exception to that principle would be in cases in which it appeared that the procedure provided for in Article 177 [now Art 267 TFEU] had been abused and where the question submitted sought, in reality, to lead the Court of Justice to make a ruling on the basis of an artificial dispute, or where it is obvious that the provision of Community [i.e. Union] law submitted to the Court of Justice could not be applied.

In the above case, the Court of Justice allowed a reference where the national court needed a ruling to determine a question of national law in an area of law that was outside the competence of the Union but which had been based on Union law.

Although the national court has the discretion to assess the need for a reference, it should explain how it has come to the conclusion that a reference is necessary, so that the Court of Justice can be satisfied that it has the jurisdiction to deal with the matter (*Foglia* v *Novello (No. 2)* (Case 244/80)). Once it is satisfied that it has the jurisdiction to deal with a reference, the Court is, in principle, bound to give a ruling. It cannot refuse to do so on the basis that, if its ruling were to have the effect of annulling a Union or national provision, this would create a 'legal vacuum' in a Member State. It then would be for the national court to interpret national law in such a way as to fill any gap (*Gmurzynska* (Case C-231/89); *Helmig and Others* (Joined Cases C-399, 409 and 425/92 and C-34, 50 and 78/93)). However, the national court does have 'the widest discretion' (*Rheinmühlen* (Case 166/73), paras 3 and 4). The power to make a reference arises 'as soon as the judge perceives either of his own motion or at the request of the parties that the litigation depends on a point referred to in the first paragraph of Art 177 [replaced by Art 234 EC Treaty, and now Art 267 TFEU]'. Even if the national judge decided that it was 'necessary' to make a referral, he has a total discretion whether or not to do so (see below).

If one of the parties to the national proceedings withdraws from them, the Court of Justice cannot continue to deliver a judgment on the reference, because such a judgment would then no longer be 'necessary' for the outcome of the case (*Teres Zabala Erasun and Others* v *Instituto Nacional de Empleo* (Joined Cases C-422–424/93)). Even if a superior national court has decided the issue, the lower court is not precluded from making a reference by national rules. Although the national court has a discretion to refer if it is a lower court and where its decisions are subject to appeal (see below), it has little real discretion in cases where its decision depends on the disputed *validity* of a Union act. It has itself no power to declare the Union act invalid, so it has no choice but to refer the matter to the Court of Justice for a ruling on its validity (*Foto-Frost* (Case 314/85)).

An obligation to refer

Article 267, para 3 TFEU provides that:

> Where any such question is raised in a case pending before a court or tribunal of a Member State against whose decisions there is no judicial remedy under national law, that court or tribunal **shall** bring the matter before the Court. [emphasis added]

Therefore, a court or tribunal which satisfies the above criteria has no discretion; it is *required* to refer the case to the Court of Justice for a preliminary ruling. The criteria are as follows:

- no judicial remedy under national law;
- where any such question is raised;
- a decision on the question is necessary to enable it to give judgment.

Each of these criteria will now be considered.

'No judicial remedy under national law'

The concept of 'no judicial remedy under national law' clearly includes the situation where there can be no further appeal. This situation may arise if the national court is, like the UK Supreme Court, the highest in the hierarchy of courts. The UK Supreme Court replaced the judicial functions of the House of Lords from 1 October 2009. It may also arise in specific cases where no appeal is possible from a court which is very low in the hierarchy. In some jurisdictions, for example, there may be no appeal where the amount claimed or the value of the goods concerned is below a certain figure. In the landmark case of *Costa v ENEL* (Case 6/64), the amount claimed was less than £2. There was no appeal from the magistrate's decision because of the smallness of the sum. The magistrate was therefore obliged to refer the question before him to the Court of Justice under what is now Art 267 TFEU. In *Parfums Christian Dior BV v Evora BV* (Case C-337/95), The Netherlands' Court of Appeal (the Hoge Raad) had the power to refer a question on trade mark law to the Benelux Court, the highest court for points of law affecting the **Benelux Agreement**. The Court of Justice held that, if the Hoge Raad decided *not* to refer the case to the Benelux Court, it was *obliged* to refer the case to the Court of Justice. If it did refer the case to the Benelux Court, the Benelux Court was itself, as the ultimate court *in that case*, obliged to refer the matter to the Court of Justice.

In the following case, the Court of Justice was directly required to consider the application of what is now Art 267 TFEU to the Swedish District Court:

Kenny Roland Lyckeskog (Case C-99/00)

The Swedish District Court had referred the case to the Court of Justice, asking the court whether it came within the third paragraph of the former Art 234 EC Treaty (now Art 267 TFEU), because an appeal from its decision to the Swedish Supreme Court would only apply if the Supreme Court declared that the appeal was admissible. The Court of Justice stated that decisions of a national court which can be challenged before a supreme court are not decisions of a 'court or tribunal of a Member State against whose decisions there is no judicial remedy under national law' within the meaning of the former Art 234 EC Treaty (now Art 267 TFEU). The fact that examination of the merits of such appeals is subject to a declaration of admissibility by the Swedish Supreme Court does not have the effect of depriving the parties of a judicial remedy. Therefore, because there was an appeal to the Supreme Court, the District Court did not come within the scope of the third paragraph of the former Art 234 EC Treaty (now Art 267 TFEU), even though the Supreme Court could refuse to hear the appeal (if it held the appeal to be inadmissible).

The question arises as to the impact the above case has on the English legal system. In the English legal system a litigant whose case comes before the Court of Appeal can request leave (i.e. permission) to appeal to the UK Supreme Court if he loses the case. If the Court of Appeal refuses leave to appeal, the litigant can then request it from the Supreme Court, but the Supreme Court could also refuse leave. According to the judgment of the Court of Justice in the above case, in these circumstances the Court of Appeal *would not* be considered to be a court 'against whose decisions there is no judicial remedy'. However, if the **Parfums Christian Dior BV v Evora BV** case is applied the outcome may be different. If both the Court of Appeal and the Supreme Court refuse leave to appeal, in these circumstances the Court of Appeal *would* be considered to be a court 'against whose decisions there is no judicial remedy'.

Within the English legal system, the term 'judicial remedy' is wide enough to include applications for judicial review. Even when, for example, there is no appeal from the Immigration Appeal Tribunal, its decisions are subject to judicial review and may subsequently be referred to the Court of Justice in the course of those judicial review proceedings (see, for example, **R v Immigration Appeal Tribunal, ex parte Antonissen** (Case C-292/89)). In such a case, it would appear that there is no obligation on the tribunal to refer and an English tribunal has, in fact, refused to refer a case because it held that it was not obliged to do so because of the availability of judicial review of its decisions (**Re A Holiday in Italy** [1975] 1 CMLR 184 (National Insurance Commissioner)). This would seem to be compatible with the Court of Justice's decision in **Lyckeskog** (Case C-99/00).

Having considered the scope of 'no judicial remedy under national law', the other two criteria are now considered.

'Where any such question is raised'

This was considered above, and includes a question relating to: (i) the interpretation of the Treaties; or (ii) the validity or interpretation of a Union act (e.g. a regulation, directive or decision).

'A decision on the question is necessary to enable it to give judgment'

There is no express reference to this criterion in Art 267, para 3 TFEU, although there is such a reference in Art 267, para 2 TFEU. However, in the following case the Court of Justice stated that it is also applicable to the third paragraph:

CILFIT (Case 283/81)

The Court of Justice stated that:

> 10 ... it follows from the relationship between the second and third paragraphs of Article 177 [which was replaced by Art 234 EC Treaty, and is now Art 267 TFEU] that the courts or tribunals referred to in paragraph 3 have the same discretion as any other national court or tribunal to ascertain whether a decision on a question of Community [i.e. Union] law is necessary to enable them to give judgment.

The issue of necessity to make a referral is considered in further detail below.

To conclude this section, a court or tribunal which satisfies the above three criteria has no discretion; it must refer the question to the Court of Justice for a preliminary ruling.

Is it necessary to make the referral?

Objective 5

As discussed above, a court or tribunal will have a discretion (pursuant to Art 267, para 2 TFEU) or be under an obligation (pursuant to Art 267, para 3 TFEU) to refer a case to the Court of Justice for a preliminary ruling only if it 'considers a decision on the question to be *necessary* to enable it to give judgment' [emphasis added]. There may be a number of reasons why the court or tribunal does not consider it *necessary* to have the question answered by the Court of Justice. Two of these reasons are now considered further: (i) the development of precedent; and (ii) the doctrine of *acte clair*.

The development of precedent

Not every question concerning the interpretation of Union law which is relevant to the outcome of a case requires a reference under Art 267 TFEU. In Chapter 5 it was stated that the doctrine of precedent does not apply to the Court of Justice, but the Court generally follows its own previous decisions for the sake of legal certainty. This has been acknowledged by the Court of Justice in the following case:

CILFIT (Case 283/81)

> The Court of Justice stated that:
>
> ... the authority of an interpretation under Article 177 [now Art 267 TFEU] already given by the Court may deprive the obligation of its purpose and thus empty it of its substance. Such is the case when the question raised is materially identical with a question which has already been the subject of a preliminary ruling in a similar case.

In the above case, the Court of Justice held that it may not be *necessary* to make a referral to it because the question may already have been answered in a previous case (e.g. the Court of Justice may already have interpreted the relevant Treaty article). However, a national court can refer any question on interpretation or validity, whether or not the Court of Justice has ruled on the point. The case before the national court may raise some new fact or argument. However, if it does not raise any new fact or argument, the Court may, in its ruling, simply restate the substance of the earlier case, as it did in the following case:

Da Costa (Cases 28–30/62)

> The Court of Justice held that:
>
> The questions of interpretation posed in this case are identical with those settled [in the case of **Van Gend en Loos**] and no new factor has been presented to the Court. In these circumstances the Tariefcommissie must be referred to the previous judgment.

In the above case, it would appear that the Court of Justice is actively encouraging national courts to apply the Court's previous decisions. A system of precedent has therefore emerged by default. As discussed above, Art 99 of the Court's Rules of Procedure provides for a simplified procedure. This procedure will be applied to those questions referred to the Court which are identical to questions that have been answered previously, where the answer to the question can be clearly deduced from existing case law and where the answer admits of no reasonable doubt. This further supports the notion that the Court is informally bound by the doctrine of precedent. The following case lends additional support to this suggestion:

International Chemical Corporation (Case 66/80)

The Court of Justice had previously ruled in a former Art 177 EC Treaty referral (which was replaced by Art 234 EC Treaty, and is now Art 267 TFEU) that Regulation 563/76 was invalid. This case concerned the regulation's validity. The Italian court hearing the case referred the matter to the Court of Justice asking whether the previous decision that the regulation was invalid applied only to that particular case, or whether it was effective in any subsequent litigation. The Court of Justice held that the purpose of the former Art 177 EC Treaty (now Art 267 TFEU) was to ensure that Union law was applied uniformly by national courts. Uniform application did not only concern the interpretation of Union law, it also concerned the validity of a Union act. The Court said that in the previous case, the ruling that the regulation in question was void was addressed to the national court making the reference. **However, as it was declared to be void, any other national court could like-wise regard the act as void for the purpose of a judgment which it had to give.**

In the following case the Court of Justice applied this principle when it was called upon to interpret a measure (rather than decide on its validity):

Kühne & Heitz (Case C-453/00)

The Court of Justice stated that in view of the obligation on all the authorities of the Member States to ensure observance of Union law, and also of the retroactive effect inherent in interpretative judgments, **a rule of Union law which has been interpreted on the occasion of a reference for a preliminary ruling must be applied by all State bodies within the sphere of their competence, even to legal relationships which arose or were formed before the Court gave its ruling on the request for interpretation.**

With regard to compliance with that obligation, the Court stated that account must be taken of the demands of the principle of legal certainty, which is one of the general principles of Union law.

It should be noted, however, that the Court of Justice is the sole arbitrator upon the validity of an act of the Union institutions. To decide otherwise would put the objective of uniform application of Union law at risk. It is not open to a national court to declare an act of the Union (e.g. a regulation or directive) to be void, unless the Court of Justice has decided this in an earlier judgment (see ***Firma Foto-Frost*** (Case 314/85)).

An interesting situation arose in the following case, which was decided by the English Court of Appeal:

R v Secretary of State for the Home Department, ex parte A [2002] EWCA Civ 1008, unreported

In judicial review proceedings, the English High Court thought that it was necessary to make a referral to the Court of Justice pursuant to the former Art 234 EC Treaty (now Art 267 TFEU), because it concerned interpretation of Union law. The claimant challenged this decision to refer the case to the Court of Justice, and the Court of Appeal held that a judgment of the Court of Justice in 2000 had made it perfectly clear the interpretation which should be placed on the Union law provisions; it therefore followed that it was not necessary to make the referral.

The doctrine of *acte clair*

In *CILFIT* (Case 283/81), the Court of Justice held that a court which is bound by the mandatory reference provisions in what is now Art 267, para 3 TFEU is not obliged to refer a case if the answer to a question of interpretation of Union law is 'so obvious as to leave no scope for any reasonable doubt' (para 16). This situation of an apparently transparent interpretative point is normally referred to in Union law as *acte clair*. In the following case, the Court described the circumstances in which a reference should be made:

CILFIT (Case 283/81)

The Court of Justice stated that:

16. Finally, the correct application of Community [i.e. Union] law may be so obvious as to leave no scope for reasonable doubt as to the manner in which the question raised is to be resolved. Before it comes to the conclusion that such is the case, the national court or tribunal must be convinced that the matter is equally obvious to the Courts of the other Member States and to the Court of Justice. Only if those conditions are satisfied, may the national court or tribunal refrain from submitting the question to the Court of Justice and take upon itself the responsibility for resolving it.

17. However, the existence of such a possibility must be assessed on the basis of the characteristic feature of Community [i.e. Union] law and the particular difficulties to which its interpretation gives rise.

18. To begin with, it must be borne in mind that Community [i.e. Union] legislation is drafted in several languages and that the different language versions are equally authentic. An interpretation of a provision of Community [i.e. Union] law thus involves a comparison of the different language versions.

19. It must also be borne in mind, even where the different language versions are entirely in accord with one another, that Community [i.e. Union] law uses terminology which is peculiar to it. Furthermore, it must be emphasised that legal concepts do not necessarily have the same meaning in Community [i.e. Union] law and in the law of the various Member States.

20. Finally, every provision of Community [i.e. Union] law must be placed in its context and interpreted in the light of the provisions of Community [i.e. Union] law as a whole, regard being had to the objectives thereof and to its state of evolution at the date on which the provision in question is to be applied. [emphasis added]

The methods of interpretation used by the Court of Justice are explained in further detail on pages 169–172.

The approach adopted by the Court of Justice when interpreting Union law has been considered in Chapter 5; suffice to say at this point the Court of Justice does not interpret such law literally, but generally favours a contextual or teleological approach. Quite often the interpretation of the Court could not have been predicted. Hence, although the Court has given permission to national courts to apply the doctrine of *acte clair*, the national court must do so with the utmost caution.

A court bears an onerous responsibility in declining to refer a question which, by virtue of the lack of possibility for further appeal or review of its decisions, it ought *prima facie* to refer. In the following case, an English judge recognised the advantages enjoyed by the Court of Justice in this context:

Customs and Excise Commissioners v *Samex* [1983] 3 CMLR 194

Bingham J stated that:

> ... [the Court of Justice] has a panoramic view of the Community [i.e. Union] and its institutions, a detailed knowledge of the treaties and of much subordinate legislation made under them, and an intimate familiarity with the functioning of the Community market [i.e. internal market] which no national judge denied the collective experience of the Court of Justice could hope to achieve.

Other English courts have not been so mindful of their limitations. *R v London Boroughs Transport Committee, ex parte Freight Transport Association* [1991] 3 All ER 915 involved the interpretation of directives on vehicle brake construction and the powers of national authorities to impose further restrictions on vehicles. The House of Lords (the judicial functions of which are now exercised by the UK Supreme Court) refused to make a reference despite the issues being complex. Lord Templeman noted that 'no plausible grounds had been advanced for a reference to the European Court'. The refusal to refer was criticised, and one of the parties made a complaint to the Commission about the refusal. This case is not, however, indicative of a general unwillingness to refer cases by the Supreme Court, as the *Factortame* and the equal treatment cases demonstrate (*R v Secretary of State for Transport, ex parte Factortame (No. 1)* (Case C-221/89); *R v Secretary of State for Transport, ex parte Factortame (No. 2)* (Case C-213/89); *Webb v EMO Cargo* [1993] 1 WLR 49; *R v Secretary of State for Employment, ex parte EOC* [1995] 1 CMLR 345). There is, however, historical evidence of a reluctance to refer by English courts and tribunals, not least because of the time such references take (see, for example: *Johnson v Chief Adjudication Officer* [1994] 1 CMLR 829; *Gould and Cullen v Commissioners of Customs and Excise (VAT Tribunal)* [1994] 1 CMLR 347; *R v Ministry of Agriculture, Fisheries and Food, ex parte Portman Agrochemicals Ltd* [1994] 1 CMLR 18). As discussed above, there is one situation in which *any* national court *must* refer a question to the Court of Justice. If 'a national court (even one whose decision is still subject to appeal) intends to question the validity of a Community [i.e. Union] act, it *must* refer the question to the Court of Justice' [emphasis added] (*Foto-Frost v Hauptzollamt Lübeck-Ost* (Case 314/85)).

Interim measures

It can take up to two years before a decision on a reference under Art 267 TFEU is available from the Court of Justice. However, as discussed above, over recent years the Court of Justice has become more efficient in determining such cases. The Court of Justice has jurisdiction under Art 279 TFEU (previously Art 243 EC Treaty) to 'prescribe any interim measures' and will sometimes do so where the legality of a Union act is being challenged under Art 263 TFEU (previously Art 230 EC Treaty; see Chapter 8). Under Art 267 TFEU, the validity of any act of the institutions may be raised in a reference. The following questions need to be addressed:

- Can the Union act whose validity is being challenged be suspended by the national court pending the outcome of the reference?
- Will the Court of Justice suspend it?
- Should national courts suspend national legislation which is alleged to conflict with Union law or which implements a Union act whose validity is disputed?

The Court of Justice may use its power under Art 279 TFEU to order a Member State to cease pursuing a course of conduct which *prima facie* breaches Union law, and which is requested by a party to the proceedings (*Commission v UK (Re Nationality of Fishermen)* (Case 246/89R); *Commission v Germany* (Case C-195/90)). This will normally be an interim measure in the course of Art 258 TFEU (previously Art 226 EC Treaty) proceedings against a Member State (see Chapter 7). Alternatively, national courts may be required to suspend a provision of national law which, arguably, conflicts with Union law (see *Factortame*, above). Although the criteria for granting interim relief are national, presumptions about the validity of primary national law should not act as a bar to its interim suspension.

The position with regard to the suspension of national measures implementing a provision of Union law, the validity of which is challenged, was discussed by the Court of Justice in the following case:

Zückerfabrik Süderdithmarschen v *HZA Itzehoe* (Case C-143/88)

The Court of Justice declared that, to enable the former Art 234 EC Treaty (now Art 267 TFEU) references to work effectively, national courts must have the power to grant interim relief in the situation where a national measure is disputed on the grounds of the validity of the Union act on which it is based, on the same grounds as when the compatibility of a national measure with Union law is contested. However, the national court has to be careful before doing so:

> Where a national court or tribunal has serious doubts about the validity of a Community [i.e. Union] act on which a national measure is based, it may, in exceptional circumstances, temporarily suspend application of the latter measure or grant other interim relief with respect to it. It must then refer the question of validity to the Court of Justice, stating the reasons for which it considers that the Community [i.e. Union] act is not valid.

National courts can apply national criteria when deciding, in the particular circumstances, whether or not to grant suspensory relief, but the national measures must be effective in providing the necessary remedies to protect rights conferred by Union law (*Factortame (No. 2)* (Case C-213/89)) and to prevent 'irreparable damage' to the person seeking relief, pending the outcome of the reference (*Atlanta Fruchthandelsgesellschaft GmbH* v *Bundesamt für Ernährung und Forstwirtschaft* (Case C-465/93)).

Interpretation or application

Objective 6

Article 267 TFEU empowers the Court of Justice to interpret Union law, but not to apply it to the facts of a case. The application of the law to the facts is the role of the national court. The national court, if it considers a decision of the Court of Justice is necessary in order for it to give a judgment, will refer the matter to the Court of Justice requesting an answer to a given question (or series of questions) which concerns the interpretation or validity of Union law. The Court of Justice answers the question(s) and sends the case back to the national court for the national court to apply the law to the facts of the case. However, this distinction may become blurred in practice, as illustrated in the following case:

Cristini (Case 32/75)

Article 7(2), Regulation 1612/68 (which has now been replaced by Art 7(2), Regulation 492/2011) provides that a Union worker who is working in another Member State is entitled to the same 'social advantages' as workers of that Member State (see Chapter 12). Large French families were allowed reduced fares on the French railways. The question referred to the Court of Justice by the French court was whether this was a 'social advantage' within the meaning of the regulation and thus should be available to large families of all Member State nationals working in France. The Court of Justice stated that it was not empowered to decide the actual case, as its duty is simply to interpret the provision of the regulation in question. The Court, however, went on to hold that the concept of 'social advantage' included this type of fare reduction offered by the French Railways.

In the above case, the Court of Justice not only interpreted Union law, but also applied it to the particular facts. However, to be fair to the Court, in answering the national court's question it would have been difficult for the Court of Justice to have done anything else.

Figure 6.1 comprises a flowchart which illustrates how the Art 267 TFEU preliminary ruling jurisdiction of the Court of Justice is applied.

Summary

Now you have read this chapter you should be able to:

- Explain how the Art 267 TFEU preliminary ruling procedure seeks to ensure the harmonious development of Union law.
- Distinguish between the Art 267 TFEU procedure and an appeal.
- Describe the scope of 'national courts and tribunals' within the context of Art 267 TFEU.
- Outline the different types of question which may be the subject of a reference from a national court or tribunal to the Court of Justice pursuant to Art 267 TFEU.
- Identify when a national court or tribunal has an *obligation* to refer a question to the Court of Justice (pursuant to Art 267, para 3 TFEU).
- Identify when a national court or tribunal has a *discretion* to refer a question to the Court of Justice (pursuant to Art 267, para 2 TFEU).
- Assess how the doctrines of precedent and *acte clair* impact upon the decision of a national court or tribunal to make a reference to the Court of Justice pursuant to Art 267 TFEU.
- Assess the extent to which the Court of Justice not only interprets Union law but applies it to the facts of an individual case, and discuss whether this is a role which, under Art 267 TFEU, falls within the sole jurisdiction of the national court or tribunal which referred the case.

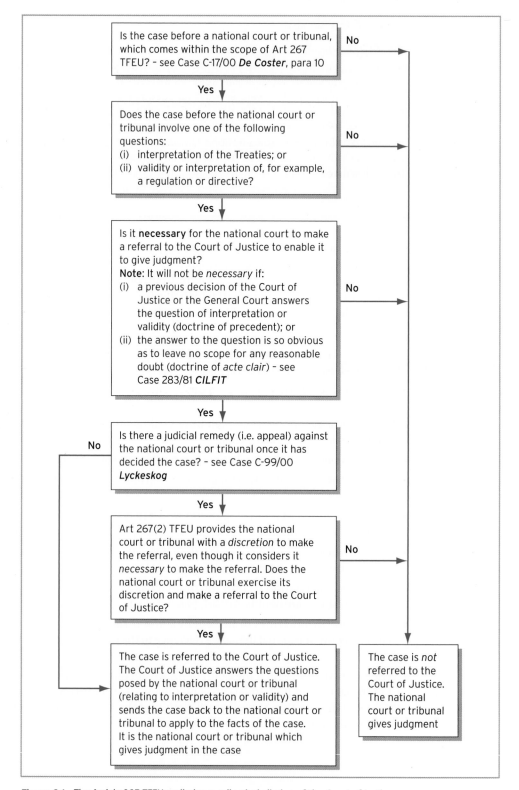

Figure 6.1 The Article 267 TFEU preliminary ruling jurisdiction of the Court of Justice

Further reading

Textbooks

Craig, P. and De Burca, G. (2011) EU Law: Text, Cases and Materials (5th edn), Oxford University Press, Chapter 13.

Foster, N. (2015) Foster on EU Law (5th edn), Oxford University Press, Chapter 6.

Steiner, J. and Woods, L. (2014) EU Law (12th edn), Oxford University Press, Chapter 10.

Weatherill, S. (2014) Cases and Materials on EU Law (11th edn), Oxford University Press, Chapter 7.

Journal articles

Arnull, A., 'The Law Lords and the European Union: Swimming with the incoming tide' (2010) 35 EL Rev 57.

Barnard, C., 'The PPU: Is it worth the candle? An early assessment' (2009) 34 EL Rev 281.

Bobek, M., 'Landtova, Holubec, and the problem of an uncooperative court: Implications for the preliminary rulings procedure' (2014) 10 ECL Rev 54.

Bobek, M., 'Learning to talk: Preliminary rulings, the courts of the Member States and the Court of Justice' (2008) 45 CML Rev 1611.

Broberg, M., 'Acte clair revisited: Adapting the acte clair criteria to the demands of the times' (2008) 45 CML Rev 1383.

Broberg, M. and Fenger, N., 'Preliminary references as a right – but for whom? The extent to which preliminary references decisions can be subject to appeal' (2011) 36 EL Rev 276.

Broberg, M. and Fenger, N., 'Variations in member states' preliminary references to the Court of Justice – are structural factors (part of) the explanation?' (2013) 19 ELJ 488.

Dyevre, A., 'If you can't beat them, join them: The French Constitutional Council's first reference to the Court of Justice' (2014) 10 ECL Rev 154.

Kilbey, I., 'Financial penalties under Article 228(2) EC: Excessive complexity?' (2007) 44 CML Rev 743.

Póltorak, N., '*Ratione temporis* application of the preliminary rulings procedure' (2008) 45 CML Rev 1357.

7

Direct actions against Member States (Articles 258–260 TFEU)

Objectives

At the end of this chapter you should understand:

1. The interaction between the Commission's power under Art 258 TFEU and that of a Member State under Art 259 TFEU.

2. The Art 258 TFEU procedure.

3. The nature of the Commission's discretion on whether to initiate action against a defaulting Member State.

4. The purpose of a reasoned opinion, the powers available to a Member State to challenge a defective opinion, the different forms of breach of Union law and whether or not the Commission can continue to pursue an action under Art 258 TFEU if a defaulting Member State remedies the breach.

5. Any defences which a Member State can rely upon to justify a breach of Union law.

6. The Court of Justice's power to impose a lump sum and/or penalty payment on a defaulting Member State, pursuant to Art 260(2) TFEU, and the enhanced power to impose a lump sum or penalty payment under Art 260(3) TFEU where the Member State's breach of Union law relates to non-implementation of a directive.

The obligation of Member States under the Treaties

Member States have a general duty, under Art 4(3) TEU (previously Art 10 EC Treaty), to 'take any appropriate measure, general or particular, to ensure fulfilment of the obligations arising out of the Treaties or resulting from the acts of the institutions of the Union. The Member States shall facilitate the achievement of the Union's tasks and refrain from any measure which could jeopardise the attainment of the Union's objectives'. The obligation to observe Union law extends beyond the Treaties and secondary legislation to agreements made by the Union with other states under Art 218 TFEU (previously Art 300(1) EC Treaty; *SZ Sevince* (Case 192/89), para 13; First EEA Case Opinion 1/94). This positive duty to do what is required of them both under the Treaties and under legislation enacted by the EU institutions is underpinned by a negative obligation within Art 4(3) TEU to 'refrain from any measure which could jeopardise the attainment of the Union's objectives'. The Commission shall ensure 'the application of the Treaties, and of measures adopted by the institutions pursuant to them' (Art 17(1) TEU (previously Art 211 EC Treaty)).

The principle of 'direct effect' is fully explained at pages 274–292 and 303–305.

The obligation to observe Union law binds, as shall be seen in the discussion on the direct enforcement of directives (referred to as the principle of 'direct effect'), not only the state, but organs and emanations of the state (see Chapter 9). Those organs include government departments, state-funded and regulated agencies providing public services, state governments in federal systems (the *Länder*, for example, in Germany), local authorities (*Costanzo* (Case 103/88); *Johnston* v *RUC* (Case 222/84)), and the courts. All are, potentially, the subject of enforcement proceedings, although the actual defendant in each case will be the state itself.

In some cases where action is required, lack of Commission resources may limit or delay its response to unlawful action or inaction by Member States. A more appropriate response than a Commission initiative may be reliance by individuals on the direct enforcement of Treaty and other Union acts in the courts of the offending Member State (see Chapter 9). However, despite the liberal interpretation of the Treaties and the secondary legislation by the Court of Justice, not every Union provision is sufficiently precise and unconditional to be directly enforceable. In addition, individuals may not have the means to start proceedings or to obtain the evidence to prove a breach. Action by individuals in the courts of the state alleged to have breached Union law does not preclude action by the Commission in the Court of Justice. For example, in 1977 the UK government banned the importation of main crop potatoes. A Dutch potato exporter challenged this by applying for a declaration in the English High Court that the ban breached the former Art 28 EC Treaty (now Art 34 TFEU). A reference was made to the Court of Justice under the former Art 234 EC Treaty (now Art 267 TFEU) which confirmed that the ban was indeed unlawful (*Meijer* v *Department of Trade* (Case 118/78)). A parallel case was also brought by the Commission in the Court of Justice under what is now Art 258 TFEU (*Commission* v *UK* (Case 231/78)).

Action by the Commission: Article 258 TFEU

Objective 1

If an individual is unable or unwilling to commence proceedings in relation to the alleged breach, there may be no practical alternative to action by the Commission. The Commission has the power to commence proceedings. Where Member States fail to implement Union law, or fail to eliminate obstacles to its implementation, it can take the necessary action under Art 258 TFEU (previously Art 226 EC Treaty):

> If the Commission considers that a Member State has failed to fulfil an obligation under the Treaties, it shall deliver a reasoned opinion on the matter after giving the State concerned the opportunity to submit its observations.
>
> If the State concerned does not comply with the opinion within the period laid down by the Commission the latter may bring the matter before the Court of Justice of the European Union.

Action by another Member State: Article 259 TFEU

As an alternative to Art 258 TFEU, action can be commenced by other Member States under Art 259 TFEU (previously Art 227 EC Treaty):

> A Member State which considers that another Member State has failed to fulfil an obligation under the Treaties may bring the matter before the Court of Justice of the European Union.

Before a Member State brings an action against another Member State for an alleged infringement of an obligation under the Treaties, it shall bring the matter before the Commission.

The Commission shall deliver a reasoned opinion after each of the States concerned has been given the opportunity to submit its own case and its observations on that of the other party's case both orally and in writing.

If the Commission has not delivered an opinion within three months of the date on which the matter was brought before it, the absence of such opinion shall not prevent the matter from being brought before the Court of Justice.

Member States have shown a marked reluctance to use Art 259 TFEU (and the former Art 227 EC Treaty). Although Member States have quite frequently brought breaches of Union law to the attention of the Commission, it could be politically damaging for a Member State to take action all the way to the Court of Justice. The increased use of QMV has made the governments of Member States more aware of the need to retain the goodwill of fellow states. A very public confrontation in the Court of Justice is not likely to be regarded as helpful. In fact, only four cases have proceeded to judgment in the life of the Union: *France* v *UK* (Case 141/78), *Belgium* v *Spain* (Case C-388/95), *Spain* v *United Kingdom* (Case C-145/04) and *Hungary* v *Slovakia* (Case C-364/10). For this reason, any action in the Court of Justice that results from a complaint to the Commission about the failure of a Member State to meet its obligations is likely to be brought by the Commission under Art 258 TFEU.

Nevertheless, Art 259 TFEU can be usefully employed by a Member State to focus the Commission's mind to take action under Art 258. During 1999, when the Union lifted a worldwide ban on UK beef (which had originally been imposed for health reasons), France refused to allow UK beef to be imported and sold in France. The UK informed the Commission that it intended to take action against France under what is now Art 259 TFEU. The Commission, which had been involved in negotiations with France in an attempt to resolve the dispute, eventually decided to take action against France under what is now Art 258 TFEU, and thus prevent the UK from taking its own independent action under what is now Art 259 TFEU. The case eventually came before the Court of Justice and France was held to be in breach of the Treaty (*Commission* v *France* (Case C-1/00)). France eventually lifted its ban.

The stages of Article 258 TFEU proceedings

The administrative stage

Objective 2

Figure 7.1, at page 213, illustrates the Art 258 TFEU procedure.

Suspected breaches of Union law generally come to the notice of the Commission as a result of the complaints of individuals or businesses affected by the breach. The first stage is usually an informal inquiry by letter to the government of the Member State concerned to ascertain the relevant facts. Member States have a legal duty to cooperate with Commission investigations into alleged breaches by them (*Commission* v *Spain* (Case C-375/92)).

In *Greece* v *Commission* (Case 240/86), the Commission was investigating the possible breach by Greece of certain Treaty articles relating to the free movement of goods. The Commission requested certain information, which Greece refused to give. Accordingly, the Commission could not ascertain whether Greece was in breach of the Treaty provisions. The Commission initiated proceedings against Greece under what is now Art 258 TFEU, alleging that Greece was in breach of its duty under what is now Art 4(3) TEU because of its failure to cooperate with the Commission. The Court of Justice held that Greece was in breach of what is now Art 4(3) TEU.

Therefore, if the Commission requires information from a Member State to enable it to ascertain if that Member State is in breach of its Union law obligations, it will have to pursue Art 258 TFEU proceedings for breach of Art 4(3) TEU if the Member State refuses to cooperate. If successful, the Member State will have to 'take the necessary measures to comply with the judgment of the Court' (Art 260(1) TFEU; previously Art 228(1) EC Treaty) and thus hand the information over. If this information discloses a breach, the Commission will have to start fresh Art 258 TFEU proceedings with regard to this breach.

Commission's discretion or obligation?

Objective
3

Article 258 TFEU provides that:

> ... If the Commission **considers** ... it **shall** deliver a reasoned opinion ... [the Commission] **may** bring the matter before the Court of Justice of the European Union. [emphasis added]

The Commission does not have to carry out a formal investigation, but it does at least have to 'consider' whether or not there may have been a breach of Union law. Where the Commission does consider there has been a breach, it must, after giving the Member State an opportunity to submit observations on the suspected breach, deliver a reasoned opinion to the government of the state concerned; see below. The reasoned opinion will often follow prolonged correspondence between the Member State and the Commission. The Commission will have to decide, at some stage in its discussions with (or, in some cases, non-cooperation by) Member States, whether or not to proceed to the delivery of a formal opinion which will stipulate a date by which the necessary remedial action should have taken place. The Commission may decide to take no further action if it considers the breach is not serious and that its resources would be better applied to other infractions.

It would seem that the Commission does have a discretion, but it also has a duty under Art 258 TFEU. It must consider the possibility of whether or not there has been a breach and it must take the most appropriate action. This may be to decide not to commence proceedings. Advocate General Roemer gave some indication of the appropriate considerations the Commission should have in mind in the following case:

Commission v *France* (Case 7/71)

Advocate General Roemer said that it might be justifiable not to start formal proceedings where: (i) there is a possibility that an amicable settlement may be achieved if formal proceedings are delayed; (ii) the effects of the violation are only minor; (iii) there is a major political crisis which could be aggravated if proceedings are commenced in relation to relatively minor matters; and (iv) there is a possibility that the Union provision in issue might be altered in the near future. The Advocate General commented that Member States resent proceedings being brought against them and the Commission is not always anxious, on this account alone, to take action.

Many breaches of Union law go on for years without being remedied. For example, the UK government failed to implement Directive 64/221 for more than 20 years after it had been held to have been in default in *Van Duyn* (Case 41/74). In 1996 the French government was again before the Court of Justice for failing to amend its Code du Travail Maritime, 22 years after the Court in *Commission* v *France (Re French Merchant Seamen)* (Case 167/73) had held that the Code breached the former Arts 12 and 39 EC Treaty (now Arts 18 and 45 TFEU); *Commission* v *France* (Case C-334/94), and see *Commission* v *Belgium* (Case C-37/93) which concerned similar restrictions on Belgian ships. Some of the cases in which action has not been taken involve immigration and social issues, which tend to be more politically sensitive.

Despite the embarrassment Art 258 TFEU proceedings may occasionally cause to Member States, the Commission is regularly using them in over 2,000 cases each year; see *32nd Annual Report on Monitoring the Application of Union Law* (2014), which is available at:

> http://ec.europa.eu/atwork/applying-eu-law/infringements-proceedings/
> annual-reports

The reasoned opinion

Objective
4

If the Commission decides that a violation of Union law has occurred, it must record the infringement in a reasoned opinion or decision served on the offending Member State. In arriving at that opinion the Commission must take into account the replies to its inquiries from the state and any defences which may have been advanced. The Court of Justice has said that an opportunity to submit such observations before a reasoned opinion is served is an essential procedural requirement. A failure to observe it may invalidate the whole process (**Commission v Italy** (Case 31/69), para 13).

Types of infringement

A large number of infringements concern either the failure to implement directives or a failure to implement them properly, or to observe their terms when implemented. Other infringements may involve direct breaches of Treaty provisions. Whether or not there is an infringement will often depend on the nature and effect of national legal provisions and of the administrative steps taken to give effect to the Union provision. It is on these legal and factual issues that many disputes with the Commission over implementation occur. A few examples will serve to indicate the diversity of the actions brought by the Commission under what is now Art 258 TFEU and the issues involved.

In **Commission v UK** (Case C-337/89) proceedings were brought by the Commission against the UK for failing to legislate to implement Directive 80/778 to ensure that water used for food production met the maximum nitrate levels in the directive. The UK government argued that most food production was carried out with water from the domestic supply and that legislation was not necessary. The Court of Justice upheld the Commission's view that, in the absence of a specific derogation in the directive, all water used for food production should be made to comply. However, in **Commission v Belgium** (Case C-376/90), the Court rejected the Commission's interpretation of Directive 80/836/Euratom, which required the adoption of national laws protecting the general public and workers against specified levels of ionising radiation. The Commission considered that Member States were not allowed to fix different dose limits from those laid down in the directive, even if they were stricter than those specified. The Court disagreed, holding that the directive only laid down maximum exposure levels and Belgium was not, therefore, in breach for enacting lower permitted exposure levels.

It will also be a breach by the Member State if, while implementing the directive, it does not provide an effective remedy or uses means which cannot be relied upon by individuals in the national courts. Directive 77/187 protects employees who are employed by an undertaking which is transferred to a new owner. The Directive had been implemented in the UK by the Transfer of Undertakings (Protection of Employment) Regulations 1981 (SI 1981/1794) and, *inter alia*, provided for consultation with employee representatives. The UK's implementing regulations, however, provided no means for recognising such employee representatives. Effectively, in the UK the duty to consult could be negated by the employer's refusal to recognise employee representatives, and there was no effective remedy for this failure to consult. The Court of Justice held that where a Union directive does not specifically provide any penalty for an infringement, what is now Art 4(3) TEU requires the Member States to guarantee the application and effectiveness of Union law. For that purpose, while the choice of penalties remains within the discretion of the Member State, it must ensure in particular that infringements of Union law are penalised under conditions, both procedural and substantive, which are analogous to those applicable to infringements of national law of a similar nature and importance and which, in any event, make the penalty effective, proportionate and dissuasive (***Commission v UK*** (Case C-382/92), para 55).

Contents of the opinion

The opinion must set out the Union provision and specific details of the breach, together with a response to the Member State's arguments that it has complied or its justification for not having complied, and it must detail the steps to be taken by the Member State to correct its infringement. The opinion has to be more fully reasoned than a legislative act under Art 296 TFEU (previously Art 253 EC Treaty; ***Commission v Germany (Re Brennwein)*** (Case 24/62) and ***Commission v Italy*** (Case C-439/99)).

Time-limit

The Commission must set a time-limit within which the Member State must end its violation. The Court of Justice has held that a Member State must be given a 'reasonable period of time' within which to comply with the opinion and thus negate the Commission's power to institute proceedings before the Court of Justice (***Commission v Ireland*** (Case 74/82)).

It is normal practice for a Member State to be given at least two months to respond to a reasoned opinion, but a shorter period might be permissible in certain cases. In the case of the French ban on British beef (see above), the Commission issued a letter of formal notice to France on 16 November 1999. The Commission gave France only two weeks to explain its action. Following the expiry of this two-week period a reasoned opinion was served on France, giving an equally short period within which to lift the ban, after which proceedings were issued in the Court of Justice (***Commission v France*** (Case C-1/00)).

Effect of complying with the reasoned opinion

If a Member State complies with the reasoned opinion within the time-limit laid down, the Commission does not have the power to bring the matter before the Court of Justice. This in effect gives the Member State a period of grace within which it is protected from the threat of legal proceedings. If the Commission does subsequently bring proceedings, it has the obligation of proving that the violation was not ended before the expiry of the time-limit (***Commission v Belgium*** (Case 298/86)). In the following case, the Court of Justice articulated the effect of complying with, and not complying with, the reasoned opinion:

Commission v Italy (Case 7/61)

The Court of Justice stated:

It is true that the second paragraph of [the former] Article 169 [which was replaced by Art 226 EC Treaty, now Art 258 TFEU] gives the Commission the right to bring the matter before the Court only if the State concerned does not comply with the Commission's opinion within the period laid down by the Commission, the period being such as to allow the State in question to regularise its position in accordance with the provisions of the Treaty.

> However, if the Member State does not comply with the opinion within the prescribed period, there is no question that the Commission has the right to obtain the Court's judgment on that Member State's failure to fulfil the obligations flowing from the Treaty.

This was reaffirmed by the Court of Justice in **Commission v Italy** (Case C-439/99), where part of the proceedings was ruled inadmissible by the Court because Italy had partially complied with the reasoned opinion within the time period laid down in the opinion.

Failure to implement a directive

If a Member State fails to implement a directive within the time-limit stipulated in the directive, once this time-limit has expired the Commission may move swiftly against the defaulting Member State. If it has still failed to implement it by the date specified in the reasoned opinion, the Commission may take enforcement action in the Court of Justice irrespective of whether the Member State subsequently implements the directive. However, if the directive has been implemented within the time period laid down within the reasoned opinion, no further action can be taken pursuant to Art 258 TFEU.

Take as an example the case of the Working Time Directive 93/104 (OJ 1993 L 307/18) which should have been implemented by all Member States by 23 November 1996. The UK failed to implement it on time. The directive provides rights for individual workers (e.g. four weeks' paid annual leave, minimum daily and weekly rest periods and a 48-hour maximum working week, all of which are subject to certain exceptions and derogations). A relatively short breach by the UK would have an enormous impact on an indeterminate number of workers. The UK eventually implemented the directive by the Working Time Regulations 1998 (SI 1998/1833) which came into force on 1 October 1998 (almost two years after the date stipulated in the directive). The Commission had taken no action against the UK under what is now Art 258 TFEU. Even if it had taken action, provided the UK had implemented the directive before the time-limit laid down in the reasoned opinion had expired, the UK could not have been brought before the Court of Justice. A sceptic could therefore argue that a Member State may view the period from the date of implementation specified in the directive, to expiry of the reasoned opinion, as an extra period of time within which to implement the directive (although see Chapter 9 for the development of principles by the Court of Justice, which in certain situations empower citizens to enforce their Union law rights in national courts, and ultimately to claim damages from the state if loss has been suffered due to the Member State's breach of Union law; also see the discussion below on the Commission's enhanced power under Art 260(3) TFEU, which was introduced when the ToL came into force on 1 December 2009). The following case further illustrates this point:

Commission v UK (Cases C-382 and 383/92)

The Acquired Rights Directive 77/187 (OJ 1977 L 61/27) had been implemented in the UK by delegated legislation: the Transfer of Undertakings (Protection of Employment) Regulations 1981 (SI 1981/1974). The aim of the directive was, *inter alia*, to ensure that when a business or part of a business was transferred to another party (e.g. sold), the employees would continue in the employment of the new employer on the same conditions as before (i.e. same hours of work, pay, etc.). Any dismissal connected with the transfer would be unlawful.

Article 1, Directive 77/187 provided it would apply to an 'undertaking, business or part of a business'. This was transposed into Regulation 2(1) of the UK regulations as applying to an undertaking, which would include any trade or business 'but not including any undertaking … which is not in the nature of a commercial venture'.

The English courts held that a local authority was not 'in the nature of a commercial venture', because it was not a profit-making organisation, and therefore the regulations did not apply. Accordingly, where part of a local authority's activities was transferred to a private contractor, because the regulations did not apply, the employees could be dismissed lawfully, or those re-employed could have their pay reduced, etc. Therefore, where, following a competitive tender, responsibility for refuse collection was transferred to a private contractor, the employees affected were the former local authority refuse collectors.

Following subsequent rulings of the Court of Justice on the interpretation of the directive, it became clear that the directive applied in these circumstances and therefore the UK had incorrectly implemented the directive by providing that it would not apply to undertakings 'not in the nature of a commercial venture' (see, for example, *Dr Sophie Redmond Stichting Foundation* v *Bartol and Others* (Case C-29/91)).

The Commission initiated former Art 226 EC Treaty (now Art 258 TFEU) proceedings against the UK once the time-limit specified in the reasoned opinion had expired. Although the UK had remedied the breach by the time the matter reached the Court of Justice, the Court nevertheless held that the UK was in breach of its obligations under the Treaty, i.e. to implement the directive correctly by the date of implementation specified in the directive.

When the ToL came into force on 1 December 2009, a new provision (Art 260(3) TFEU) was introduced. Article 260(3) TFEU provides as follows:

> When the Commission brings a case before the Court pursuant to Article 258 on the grounds that the Member State concerned has failed to fulfil its obligation to notify measures transposing a directive adopted under a legislative procedure, it may, when it deems appropriate, specify the amount of the lump sum or penalty payment to be paid by the Member State concerned which it considers appropriate in the circumstances.
>
> If the Court finds that there is an infringement it may impose a lump sum or penalty payment on the Member State concerned not exceeding the amount specified by the Commission. The payment obligation shall take effect on the date set by the Court in its judgment.

This new provision provides that if the Commission brings Art 258 TFEU proceedings before the Court of Justice against a Member State which has failed to implement a directive, if the Commission considers it appropriate it may specify a lump sum or penalty payment which the Member State should be required to pay (see below for further discussion on the imposition of lump sum and penalty payments for a breach of Art 260(1) TFEU). If the Court subsequently finds the Member State to be in breach of its Union law obligations, it can impose the lump sum or penalty payment on the Member State, but the amount must not exceed that specified by the Commission. This new financial penalty provision will go some way to addressing the previous deficiency in the procedure when used against a Member State which has flagrantly failed to implement a directive.

Three of the first cases to come before the Court of Justice with regard to the application of Art 260(3) TFEU are: *Commission v Poland* (Case C-245/12), *Commission v Poland* (Case C-544/12) and *Commission v Poland* (Case C-320/13). The Commission requested that the Court of Justice impose penalty payments on Poland, pursuant to Art 260(3) TFEU, because of Poland's failure to notify the Commission of the measures it had taken to transpose specified directives into national law. In Case C-245/12 the Commission specified that the Court impose a daily penalty payment of 93,492 euros from the day on which judgment was delivered, in Case C-544/12 a payment of 75,003 euros and in Case C-320/13 a payment of 61,380 euros. Although the Commission subsequently withdrew the proceedings because Poland implemented the directives (after the proceedings had been issued), these cases illustrate the potency of this new provision.

Altering the subject matter

When the case comes before the Court of Justice, the Commission cannot rely on matters which have not been included in the reasoned opinion (*Commission v Belgium* (Case 186/85), para 13).

In the following case, the Court of Justice held that this applies even if both parties consent:

Commission v Italy (Case 7/69)

After the date for complying with a reasoned opinion which had been served on Italy had expired, the Commission started enforcement proceedings in the Court of Justice. After starting these proceedings, Italy amended its law in an attempt to comply with the reasoned opinion, but the Commission still considered Italy to be in breach of Union law. The two parties agreed that the Court of Justice should decide whether the new Italian law complied with Union obligations, rather than adjudicate on Italy's initial breach.

The Court of Justice refused to consider this question. The nature of the proceedings could not be altered, even by consent. The subject matter of the Commission's complaint had changed significantly since it had issued the reasoned opinion, the issuing of which is a compulsory part of the Art 258 TFEU procedure. The proceedings (as set out in the reasoned opinion) only concerned a default existing at the time the proceedings were initiated. What transpired afterwards was irrelevant for the current proceedings. If the Commission wished to have the new law tested, the full Art 258 TFEU proceedings must be started afresh, i.e. formal letter, reasoned opinion and enforcement proceedings.

Disclosure of draft reasoned opinion

In the following case, the Court of First Instance ((CFI), now the General Court) held that the European Commission was not obliged to disclose a draft reasoned opinion which it subsequently decided not to serve on a Member State because it was satisfied with the action taken by that Member State to remedy the alleged breach of Union law:

Bavarian Lager Company Ltd v *Commission* (Case T-309/97)

The CFI (renamed the General Court) stated that:

> The Joint Code of Conduct concerning access to Council and Commission documents (OJ 1993 L 340/4) laid down the general principle that the public was to have the widest access to documents held by the Commission and the Council, and on the basis of that and Case T-105/95 *UK* v *Commission* [1997] ECR II-313, the applicant [Bavarian Lager Company Ltd] asserted that it had a right to access to the document in issue [i.e. the draft reasoned opinion].
>
> The grounds which could be relied on by a Community [i.e. Union] institution to reject an application for access were listed in the Code of Conduct which provided, *inter alia*:
>
> 'The institutions will refuse access to any documents where disclosure could undermine the protection of the public interest (public security … inspections and investigations) …'
>
> It was on that exception that the Commission grounded its refusal.
>
> The applicant classified the document to which it sought access as a reasoned opinion, but that was wrong in fact and in law.
>
> The document was in fact a draft reasoned opinion drawn up by Commission staff after the members of the Commission had decided to deliver a reasoned opinion.
>
> In view of the decision to suspend the procedure, that document was in the end never signed by the Commissioner responsible or communicated to the Member State.
>
> The procedure initiated under Article 169 [which was replaced by Art 226 EC Treaty, and is now Art 258 TFEU] thus only got as far as the stage of inspection and investigation and never reached the stage where the Commission delivered a reasoned opinion, and the 'opinion' remained a purely preparatory document.
>
> The Member States were entitled to expect confidentiality from the Commission during investigations which could lead to an infringement procedure, and the disclosure of documents relating thereto, during the negotiations between the Commission and the Member State concerned, could jeopardise the purpose of the infringement procedures: to enable the Member State to comply of its own accord with the requirements of the Treaty or, if appropriate, to justify its position.
>
> The safeguarding of that objective warranted, under the heading of the protection of the public interest, the refusal of access to a preparatory document relating to the investigation stage of the Article 169 [now Art 258 TFEU] procedure.

The CFI dismissed the application.

The judicial stage

Objective
5

The Commission does not have to commence proceedings immediately on the expiry of the period specified in its opinion. In one case it waited six years before commencing proceedings (***Commission* v *Germany*** (Case C-422/92)). It is envisaged that the Commission may wish to give the offending state more time to take the necessary remedial action (***Commission* v *France*** (Case 7/71), para 5).

Member States have attempted to rely upon a number of defences to justify their breaches of Union law, but the Court has not, generally, been receptive. In relation to non-transposition of directives, it is frequently argued either that there has been a shortage of parliamentary time or, alternatively, that transposition is not necessary because the terms of the directive are, in fact, observed and conflicting national legislative provisions are not adhered to. The first defence was resolutely disposed of by the Court of Justice in the following case:

Commission v Belgium (Case 77/69)

Belgium had imposed a discriminatory tax on wood which violated Art 95 EC Treaty (which was replaced by Art 90 EC Treaty, and is now Art 110 TFEU; see Chapter 17). A draft law to amend the tax scheme had been laid before the Belgian Parliament, but had fallen when the Parliament was dissolved. The Belgian government argued that these were matters out of its control and it had been prevented from legislating by *force majeure*. The Court of Justice was curt in its dismissal of the argument:

> The obligations arising from Article 95 [now Art 110 TFEU] of the Treaty devolve upon States as such and the liability of a Member State under Article 169 [which was replaced by Art 226 EC Treaty, and is now Art 258 TFEU] arises whatever the agency of the State whose action or inaction is the cause of the failure to fulfil its obligations, even in the case of a constitutionally independent institution. The objection raised by the defendant cannot therefore be sustained. [paras 15 and 16] [see also *Commission v Belgium* (Case 1/86)].

Nor is the fact that the requirements imposed by a directive are difficult to meet accepted as a defence, as illustrated in the following case:

Commission v UK (Case C-56/90)

The UK attempted to justify its failure to take all necessary measures to ensure that bathing beaches in Blackpool and Southport met the environmental and health standards set by Directive 76/160 by arguing that implementation was made more difficult by local circumstances. The Court of Justice stated that, even assuming that absolute physical impossibility to carry out the obligations imposed by the directive might justify failure to fulfil them, the UK had not established such impossibility in this case.

Nor can Member States qualify their obligations imposed by directives in response to the demands of 'special' local circumstances or particular economic or social interest groups. In ***Commission v Hellenic Republic*** (Case C-45/91), the Greek government attempted to justify its failure to implement a directive on the safe disposal of toxic waste because of 'opposition by the local population'. The Court commented that it had consistently held that a Member State cannot rely on an internal situation to justify disregard of its obligations. Similar defences relating to local conditions have been advanced, and rejected, in two Art 258 TFEU proceedings following the failure of Member States to implement Directive 79/409 on the protection of wild birds (***Commission v Netherlands (Re Protection of Wild Birds)*** (Case 339/87); ***Commission v Spain*** (Case C-355/90)).

In ***Commission v Greece*** (Case C-105/91), the Greek government defended its admittedly unlawful and discriminatory tax on foreign vehicles by arguing that the Greek vehicles concerned constituted no more than 10 per cent of the internal demand and that there was no manifest discrimination. The Court of Justice rejected the defence on the ground that it had consistently held that a Member State was guilty of a failure to fulfil its obligations under the Treaty regardless of the frequency or the scale of the infringement. The defence that a directive or regulation is observed in practice or 'administratively' where there are conflicting national provisions has also been rejected by the Court of Justice on a number of occasions (***Commission v Italy*** (Case 166/82); ***Commission v Germany (Re Nursing Directives)*** (Case 29/84); ***Commission v UK (Re Tachographs)*** (Case 128/78)). However, the use of existing, legally binding provisions of national law may be acceptable if they provide an effective means of implementing the directive. Such legislation may,

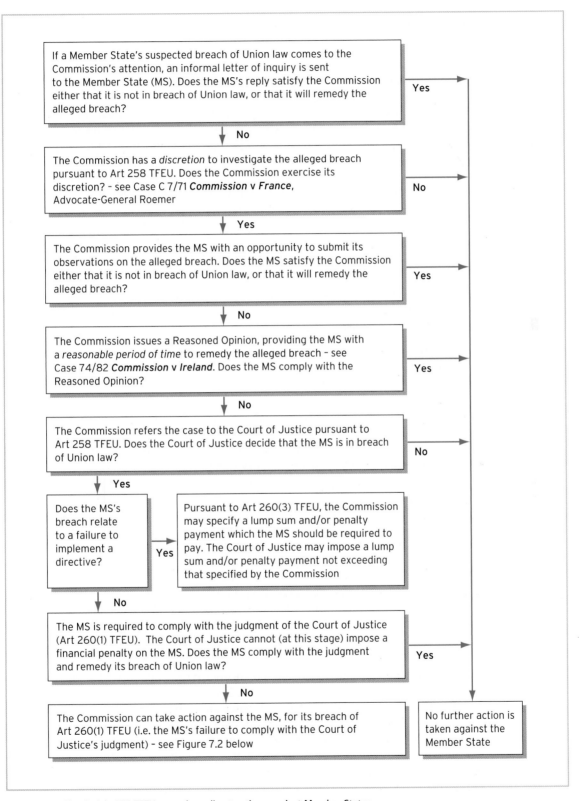

Figure 7.1 The Article 258 TFEU procedure: direct actions against Member States

therefore, provide a defence to non-implementation (**Commission v Netherlands** (Case C-190/90)). Individuals must, nonetheless, be able to rely on a text of national law that accurately reflects their rights and on which they can rely in the event of a judicial challenge (**Commission v France** (Case 167/73)). For this reason, a Union obligation cannot be implemented by the government of a Member State simply by accepting assurances from the bodies affected that they will meet the terms of the Union provision. It is suggested, therefore, that **R v Secretary of State for the Environment, ex parte Friends of the Earth** [1994] 2 CMLR 760, in which Schiemann J held that an undertaking from water authorities given to the Secretary of State that they would meet Union requirements on water quality was an acceptable way of meeting the UK's Union obligations, is probably wrongly decided; this case was decided by an English court, not the Court of Justice.

Figure 7.1 comprises a flowchart which illustrates the application of the Art 258 TFEU procedure: direct actions against Member States.

Pecuniary penalty: Article 260 TFEU

Objective 6

Once judgment has been given against a Member State, failure to observe the terms of that judgment will constitute a breach of Art 260(1) TFEU (previously Art 228(1) EC Treaty). Article 260 TFEU provides:

The Article 260 TFEU procedure is illustrated in a flowchart at page 222

1 If the Court of Justice of the European Union finds that a Member State has failed to fulfil an obligation under the Treaties, the State shall be required to take the necessary measures to comply with the judgment of the Court.

2 If the Commission considers that the Member State concerned has not taken the necessary measures to comply with the judgment of the Court, it may bring the case before the Court after giving that State the opportunity to submit its observations. It shall specify the amount of the lump sum or penalty payment to be paid by the Member State concerned which it considers appropriate in the circumstances.

   If the Court finds that the Member State concerned has not complied with its judgment it may impose a lump sum or penalty payment on it.

   This procedure shall be without prejudice to Article 259.

3 When the Commission brings a case before the Court pursuant to Article 258 on the grounds that the Member State concerned has failed to fulfil its obligation to notify measures transposing a directive adopted under a legislative procedure, it may, when it deems appropriate, specify the amount of the lump sum or penalty payment to be paid by the Member State concerned which it considers appropriate in the circumstances.

   If the Court finds that there is an infringement it may impose a lump sum or penalty payment on the Member State concerned not exceeding the amount specified by the Commission. The payment obligation shall take effect on the date set by the Court in its judgment.

Article 260(3) TFEU has been considered above. Article 260(1) and (2) TFEU are now considered.

Following a judgment of the Court of Justice pursuant to Art 258 TFEU, the Member State is obliged to take the necessary measures to give effect to the Court's judgment (Art 260(1) TFEU). This may require national legislation being implemented, amended or repealed to remedy the Member State's breach of Union law. If the Member State fails to comply with the judgment it will be in breach of its Art 260(1) TFEU duty. The Commission is then empowered by Art 260(2) TFEU to initiate fresh enforcement proceedings for breach of Art 260(1). Under the former Art 228(2) EC Treaty (which has been replaced by Art 260(2) TFEU), the three Art 226 stages had to be applied: (i) administrative stage; (ii) reasoned opinion; and (iii) referral to the Court of Justice. Under Art 260(2) TFEU there is no explicit requirement to issue a reasoned opinion before the Commission refers the case to the Court of Justice, thus streamlining the procedure.

If the Commission decides to make a referral to the Court of Justice, the Commission recommends a lump sum and/or penalty payment which should be imposed against the defaulting Member State. However, this is only a recommendation; the Court of Justice will levy any amount it wishes. There is no upper limit.

Prior to the TEU, the former Art 228(2) EC Treaty (which has been replaced by Art 260(2) TFEU) carried no sanction. All the Court of Justice was empowered to do was to make a declaration that a Member State was acting in breach of its Union law obligations. The incorporation of financial sanctions into the former Art 228 EC Treaty procedure strengthened the Commission's hand in ensuring that Member States complied with their Union law obligations. However, the Commission will still seek to resolve the conflict informally; it will explore every possible avenue before initiating Court proceedings.

On 8 January 1997 the Commission agreed a procedure with regard to recommending to the Court the use of penalties (OJ 1997 C 63/2). It started with a basic penalty of 55 euros per day, which would be multiplied by factors to account for the gravity of the breach, the length of time it had lasted and the relative wealth of the state. For example, the UK would face a minimum daily penalty of 90,000 euros and a maximum of 537,500 euros. France and Germany have larger economies and therefore would face increased penalties, while Italy would be liable to a slightly lower penalty.

As stated above, Art 260(2) TFEU is worded similarly to the former Art 228(2) EC Treaty except that under Art 260(2) TFEU there is no explicit requirement to issue a reasoned opinion before the Commission brings proceedings before the Court of Justice. This should be taken into account when considering cases which concern the application of the former Art 228(2) EC Treaty.

In the following case, the Court of Justice imposed a financial penalty on Greece in proceedings initiated by the Commission under what is now Art 260(2) TFEU, and the Court commented upon the Commission's pecuniary penalty guidelines:

Commission v Hellenic Republic (Case C-387/97)

Greece had failed to fulfil its obligations under Art 4, Directive 75/442 on waste (OJ 1975 L 194/39) and Art 5, Directive 78/319 on toxic and dangerous waste (OJ 1978 L 84/43), whereby Member States had to take measures to ensure that, respectively, waste and toxic and dangerous waste were disposed of without endangering human health and harming the environment. In addition, Greece had failed to comply with Art 6, Directive 74/442 and Art 12, Directive 78/319, whereby the competent authorities were required to draw up plans in relation to waste disposal.

The Commission brought proceedings under the former Art 169 EC Treaty (which was replaced by Art 226 EC Treaty, and is now Art 258 TFEU), which culminated in the judgment in Case C-45/91, given on 7 April 1992.

After further communications between the Commission and the Greek government between 1993 and 1996, the Commission issued a reasoned opinion to the effect that, by continuing not to draw up or implement requisite waste disposal plans, Greece had failed to comply with the 1992 judgment. The Commission therefore brought an action under the former Art 171(2) EC Treaty (which was replaced by Art 228(2) EC Treaty, and is now Art 260(2) TFEU).

In its judgment, the Court of Justice concluded that it had not been proved that Greece had failed to comply with the judgment in Case C-45/91 in relation to Art 5, Directive 78/319, but in other respects that judgment had not been complied with.

The Court of Justice stated that the former Art 171(2) EC Treaty (now Art 260(2) TFEU) did not specify the period within which a judgment had to be complied with, but the importance of immediate and uniform application of Union law meant that the process of compliance had to be initiated at once and completed as soon as possible.

In the absence of provisions in the Treaty, the Court stated that the Commission could adopt guidelines for determining how the lump sums or penalty payments which it intended to propose to the Court were calculated, so as in particular to ensure equal treatment between the Member States. The Court of Justice then referred to the Commission's guidelines and continued:

> The Commission's suggestion that account should be taken both of the gross domestic product of the Member State concerned, and of the number of votes in the Council, appeared appropriate in that it enabled that State's ability to pay to be reflected while keeping the variation between Member States within a reasonable range.
>
> Those suggestions could not bind the court but were a useful point of reference.
>
> First, since the principal aim of penalty payments was that the Member State should remedy the breach of obligations as soon as possible, a penalty payment had to be set that was appropriate to the circumstances and proportionate both to the breach which had been found and to the State's ability to pay.
>
> Second, the degree of urgency that the Member State should fulfil its obligations could vary in accordance with the breach.
>
> In that light, and as the Commission had suggested, the basic criteria which were to be taken into account in order to ensure that penalty payments had coercive force and Community [i.e. Union] law was applied uniformly and effectively were, in principle, the duration of the infringement, its degree of seriousness and the ability of the Member State to pay.
>
> In applying those criteria, regard should be had in particular to the effects of the failure to comply on private and public interests, and to the urgency of getting the Member State to fulfil its obligations.
>
> In the present case, having regard to the nature of the breaches of obligations, which continued to the present day, a penalty payment was the means best suited to the circumstances.
>
> The duration of the infringement was considerable, as was its degree of seriousness and in particular the effect on private and public interests, given, *inter alia*, that the failure to comply with the obligation in Article 4 of Directive 75/442 could, by the very nature of that obligation, directly endanger human health and harm the environment.

In the above case, the Court of Justice ordered Greece to pay to the Commission, into the account of 'EC [i.e. EU] own resources', a penalty payment of 20,000 euros for each day of delay in implementing the measures necessary to comply with the judgment in Case C-45/91 from delivery of the present judgment (i.e. 4 July 2000) until the judgment in Case C-45/91 had been complied with. Interestingly, the Court only applied the daily penalty from the date of the current judgment (i.e. 4 July 2000) and not 'a reasonable period' after its initial judgment when it had been held that Greece was in breach of its Union law obligations (i.e. 7 April 1992). Nevertheless, the potency of the Art 260 TFEU (and its predecessor, Art 228 EC Treaty) is clearly amplified in the above case.

In the following case, an action was brought before the Court of Justice pursuant to what is now Art 260(2) TFEU, for France's failure to fulfil its obligations under what is now Art 260(1) TFEU:

Commission v *France* (Case C-304/02)

It was alleged that France had failed to comply with the judgment of 11 June 1991 in ***Commission* v *France*** (Case C-64/88), in which it had been found that France had failed to fulfil its obligations under regulations concerning fishing and the control of fishing activities.

The Court held that France had not taken all the necessary measures to comply with the judgment in ***Commission* v *France*** (Case C-64/88).

In relation to the financial penalties which could be imposed on France and in the light of the Advocate General's Opinion of 29 April 2004, the Court raised the issue of: (i) its ability to impose a lump sum penalty, although the Commission had requested a penalty payment; and (ii) its right to impose both a lump sum penalty and a penalty payment. The Court of Justice reopened the oral procedure because there had been no argument in the proceedings on these two issues.

In relation to the possibility of imposing both a penalty payment and a lump sum, the Court observed that the former Art 228(2) EC Treaty (now Art 260(2) TFEU) has the objective 'of inducing a defaulting Member State to comply with a judgment establishing a breach of obligations and thereby of ensuring that Community [i.e. Union] law is in fact applied'. The Court considered the measures provided for by that provision (the lump sum and the penalty payment) to pursue the same objective. **The purpose of a penalty payment is to induce a Member State to put an end as soon as possible to a breach of obligations which, in the absence of the measure, would tend to persist (persuasive effect), while the lump sum 'is based more on assessment of the effects on public and private interests of the failure of the Member State concerned to comply with its obligations, in particular where the breach has persisted for a long period since the judgment which initially established it' (deterrent effect). The Court concluded that where the breach of obligations has continued for a long period and is inclined to persist, it is possible to have recourse to both types of penalty. Therefore, the conjunction 'or' in the former Art 228(2) EC Treaty (now Art 260(2) TFEU), 'may ... have an alternative or a cumulative sense and must therefore be read in the context in which it is used'. The Court stated that the fact that both measures were not imposed in previous cases could not constitute an obstacle, if imposing both measures appeared appropriate, regard being had to the circumstances of the case. Thus, 'it is for the Court, in each case, to assess in light of its circumstances the financial penalties to be imposed', as the Court is not bound by the Commission's suggestions.**

Finally, the Court considered its discretion as to the financial penalties that can be imposed. When a penalty payment is to be imposed on a Member State in order to penalise non-compliance with a judgment establishing a breach of obligations, it is for the Court to set the penalty payment so that it is appropriate to the circumstances and proportionate both to the breach that has been established and to the ability to pay of the Member State concerned. For that purpose, the basic criteria which must be taken into account in order to ensure that penalty payments have coercive force and Union law is applied uniformly and effectively are, in principle, the duration of the infringement, its degree of seriousness and the ability of the Member State concerned to pay. In applying those criteria, regard should be had in particular to the effects of failure to comply on private and public interests and to the urgency of getting the Member State concerned to fulfil its obligations.

The Court found that France's breach of obligations had persisted over a long period and imposed a dual financial penalty:

(i) A **penalty payment** of 57,761,250 euros for each period of six months from delivery of the current judgment at the end of which the judgment in ***Commission* v *France*** (Case C-64/88) had not yet been fully complied with;

(ii) A **lump sum penalty** of 20,000,000 euros.

The above case clearly establishes the principle that the Court of Justice can impose both a penalty payment **and** a lump sum penalty. A penalty payment is imposed to persuade the defaulting Member State to comply with the judgment, whereas a lump sum penalty is imposed to deter all Member States from breaching their Union law obligations.

In *Commission v France* (Case C-177/04), the Court of Justice levied a penalty payment on France which was greater than that which had been recommended by the Commission. The Court agreed with the coefficients the Commission had used relating to the seriousness of the breach, France's gross domestic product and its number of votes in the Council. However, the Court disagreed with the coefficient the Commission had used relating to the duration of the infringement. The Court stated that for the purpose of calculating this coefficient, regard is to be had to the period between the Court's first judgment and the time at which it assesses the facts, not the time at which the case is brought before it.

Subsequently, in *Greece v Commission* (Case C-369/07), the Court of Justice imposed both a penalty payment and lump sum penalty on Greece. The Court stated that Greece's failure to fulfil its Union law obligations (to comply with the Court's previous judgment) had lasted for more than four years. The Court imposed upon Greece a periodic penalty payment of 16,000 euros per day of delay in implementing its judgment of four years previous, counting from one month after the delivery of the present judgment, allowing Greece to demonstrate that it had ended the failure to fulfil its Union obligations. The Court stated that the application of the two penalties was based on the capability of each to fulfil its own objective and depended on the circumstances of each case. The amount of the lump sum payment had to be determined by reference to the persistence of the failure to fulfil obligations (since the *first judgment* establishing that failure) and to the public and private interests in question. The Court levied on Greece a lump sum penalty payment of 2 million euros.

The Court has also imposed both a lump sum penalty and a periodic penalty upon Spain (*Commission v Spain* (Case C-610/10)).

In *Commission v Ireland* (Case C-279/11 and C-374/11) the Court imposed both a lump sum penalty and a periodic penalty upon Ireland. However, the Court reduced the amount the Commission had recommended because Ireland's ability to pay had, to a certain degree, been diminished as a result of the economic crisis which started in Ireland during 2008. This economic crisis gripped the whole of the EU, but it affected some countries more than others. Ireland had to secure substantial financial assistance from the EU, the European Central Bank and the IMF.

In *Greece v Commission* (Case C-407/09), the Court of Justice did not impose a penalty payment on Greece following the Commission's withdrawal of its request. The Commission withdrew its request because Greece had remedied the default two months after the Commission had issued proceedings. However, the Commission did not withdraw its request for the imposition of a lump sum and the Court ordered Greece to pay a lump sum of 3 million euros.

In the following case, despite Italy's breach of what is now Art 260(1) TFEU, the Court of Justice decided *not* to impose a penalty payment which had been suggested by the Commission:

Commission v Italy (Case C-119/04)

In 1995 Italy adopted a law to reform foreign-language teaching. The post of 'foreign-language assistant' was abolished and replaced by that of 'linguistic associate'. Following that law's entry into force, the Commission received several complaints from former foreign-language assistants that, in the conversion to linguistic associate, their length of service as assistants had not been taken into account for the purposes of pay and social security. The Commission therefore instigated legal proceedings against Italy.

On 26 June 2001, in *Commission v Italy* (Case C-212/99), the Court of Justice found that Italy had failed to fulfil its obligations under the provisions of the former EC Treaty guaranteeing freedom of movement for workers, by not guaranteeing recognition of the acquired rights of former foreign-language assistants in six Italian universities, even though such recognition was guaranteed to Italian nationals.

Believing that Italy had still not complied with that judgment, on 4 March 2004, the Commission commenced the present action (C-119/04) against Italy, requesting that the Court find Italy in breach of the judgment of June 2001 and impose a penalty payment of 309,750 euros per day from the date of judgment in the present case until Italy had complied.

The case was decided by the Court in July 2006. The Court held that, by not ensuring, at the date of expiry of the period prescribed in the reasoned opinion, recognition of the rights acquired by former assistants who had become associates and linguistic experts, even though such recognition was guaranteed to all national workers, Italy had failed to take all the measures necessary to comply with the judgment of 26 June 2001 in *Commission v Italy* (Case C-212/99) and had therefore failed to fulfil its obligations under the EC Treaty.

However, in view of the fact that the breach of obligations no longer persisted on the date of the Court's examination of the facts, the Court rejected the Commission's application for the imposition of a penalty payment.

The case of *Commission v France* Case (C-304/02) has been considered above. In Case C-304/02 the Court of Justice held that France's failure to comply with the Court's judgment in *Commission v France* (Case C-64/88) had persisted over a long period. The Court imposed a dual financial penalty:

(i) a **penalty payment** of 57,761,250 euros for each period of six months from delivery of the judgment in Case C-304/02 at the end of which the judgment in Case C-64/88 had not yet been fully complied with;

(ii) a **lump sum penalty** of 20,000,000 euros.

The Commission subsequently sent France a decision (Decision C (2006) 659 Final) on 2 March 2006 requesting payment of the periodic penalty (i.e. 57,761,250 euros for each period of six months from delivery of the Court's judgment in Case C-304/02 until the Court's judgment in Case C-64/88 had been complied with). France requested the General Court to annul that decision or, alternatively, to reduce the amount of the periodic penalty. In the following case, the General Court rejected France's application:

France v Commission (T-139/06)

The General Court confirmed that the Commission was competent to require the payment of the periodic penalty imposed by the Court.

In effect, in its second judgment, delivered in 2005, the Court of Justice had clearly determined the rights and obligations of France. The Court had equally fixed the lump sum fine, payable immediately (a sanction for the past infringement), and the periodic penalty payment (a sanction for any future infringement) which was subject to a six-monthly finding by the Commission as to the absence of full compliance with the 1991 judgment.

The Court of Justice had, therefore, given the Commission the power to make this finding autonomously. As such, the Commission was competent to recover, in its capacity as authorising officer, the periodic penalty payment to be paid by France to the Commission into the 'Union own resources' account.

Furthermore, the General Court rejected France's argument that its rights of defence were violated. According to the General Court, the criteria to be used to determine whether the 1991 judgment had been fully implemented were determined by the Court of Justice in 2005. These criteria were further explained by the Commission in July 2005 in a meeting with the French authorities and also in a note of 28 September 2005. France therefore had two opportunities to make known its views regarding these criteria. Consequently, if the Commission was required to cooperate with the Member States so as to facilitate the application of Union law, this dialogue should, in principle, have taken place within the time limits fixed by the Court.

Finally, the General Court ruled that France had not shown that the Commission's decision was vitiated by an error of assessment or that the Commission had exceeded its powers.

The General Court held that the infringements that led the Court to rule that France had failed to fulfil its obligations under EU law continued during the latter half of 2005 and the beginning of 2006. As a consequence, the Commission, when adopting its decision, did not determine that there was a new infringement but rather that there was an absence of any significant change to the infringements found by the Court in its two judgments. The periodic penalty was thus payable.

The General Court concluded that the full amount of the periodic penalty must be paid. Even on the assumption that the information provided by France could be considered to show an improvement in the situation, it nevertheless remained that as of 1 March 2006 France had not fully implemented the Court's judgment of 11 June 1991. The Commission, bound by the 2005 judgment, was not able to reduce the amount and the efforts made by France were not such as to excuse the infringements.

This aspect was considered further by the Court of Justice in the following case:

Commission v Portugal (Case C-292/11P)

By judgment of 14 October 2004 (**Commission** v **Portugal** (Case C-275/03)), the Court of Justice held that Portugal had failed to fulfil its obligations by not repealing its national legislation which made the award of damages to persons injured by a breach of Union law, in the field of public procurement, conditional on proof of fault or fraud.

Taking the view that Portugal had failed to comply with that judgment, the Commission brought a fresh action seeking imposition of a penalty payment. By its judgment of 10 January 2008 (**Commission** v **Portugal** (Case C-70/06)) the Court of Justice held that Portugal had not complied with its first judgment of 2004, as the Portuguese legislation had not been repealed by the end of the period prescribed by the Commission. The Court accordingly ordered Portugal to pay to the Commission a penalty payment of 19,392 euros for each day of delay in implementing the measures necessary to ensure compliance with the first judgment of 2004, with effect from the date of delivery of the second judgment, 10 January 2008.

On 31 December 2007 (i.e. a few days before the 2008 judgment was delivered), Portugal adopted Law No 67/2007, which repealed the national legislation in question and put in place a new system of compensation for damage caused by the State. That law came into force on 30 January 2008. The Commission, however, took the view that this new law did not constitute an adequate and complete measure to ensure compliance with the 2004 judgment. In order to avoid prolonging the dispute, Portugal subsequently adopted Law No 31/2008 amending Law No 67/2007, while maintaining that Law No 67/2007 contained all the measures necessary to ensure compliance with the 2004 judgment. Law No 31/2008 came into force on 18 July 2008.

In the context of the proceedings for recovery of the penalty payment set by the Court of Justice, the Commission took the view that Law No 67/2007 did not constitute adequate compliance with the 2004 judgment. In its view, Portugal had complied with that judgment only when it adopted Law No 31/2008. Accordingly, in its decision of 25 November 2008, the Commission determined that the daily penalty payment was payable up to 17 July 2008, the day before Law No 31/2008 came into force.

Portugal then brought an action before the General Court against that decision of the Commission. By judgment of 29 March 2011 (*Portugal v Commission* (Case T-33/09)), the General Court annulled the decision. It held that the assessment of the content of new legislation adopted by a Member State with a view to complying with a judgment of the Court of Justice delivered pursuant to Art 260(2) TFEU comes in all cases within the exclusive jurisdiction of the Court of Justice and must, if there is a disagreement between the Commission and that Member State, be the subject of a fresh procedure.

The Commission appealed the decision of the General Court and brought the current case before the Court of Justice to have that judgment of the General Court set aside.

The Court of Justice dismissed the Commission's appeal.

The Court noted that **the procedure under Art 260 TFEU** which was intended to induce a defaulting Member State to comply with a judgment establishing a failure to fulfil obligations **must be regarded as a special judicial procedure for the enforcement of the Court's judgments and, in other words, as a method of enforcement.** Therefore, the Commission's review of the measures adopted by that Member State for the purpose of complying with such a judgment and the recovery of any sums owed had to be carried out having regard to the scope of the failure to fulfil obligations, as defined by the Court of Justice.

In the present case, **it was clear both from the operative part of the 2004 judgment and from that of the 2008 judgment that the failure to fulfil obligations established by the Court related to the failure to repeal national legislation. The Commission, however, took the view that Law No 67/2007, repealing the national legislation at issue, did not ensure proper compliance with the 2004 judgment. The Court considered that, in doing so, the Commission formed a view on the issue of the conformity of the new Portuguese law with Union law, even though that Portuguese law introduced a system of liability distinct from that of the repealed legislation and which the Court of Justice could not have examined beforehand. However, the Commission's power of appraisal, in the context of compliance with a judgment of the Court of Justice, cannot be exercised in a manner which is prejudicial to the Court's exclusive jurisdiction to rule on the conformity of national legislation with EU law.**

Likewise, as was pointed out in the judgment under appeal, **the General Court also cannot itself give a ruling on the Commission's assessment as to whether compliance with a judgment establishing a failure to fulfil obligations can be achieved through a national practice or national legislation which has not previously been examined by the Court of Justice. Were it to do so, the General Court would, inevitably, be required to make a ruling as to whether that practice or national legislation was in conformity with Union law, thereby encroaching on the exclusive jurisdiction of the Court of Justice in that regard.**

It followed that, in the case where there is a difference between the Commission and the Member State concerned as to whether a national practice or national legislation which the Court of Justice has not examined beforehand is appropriate for ensuring compliance with such a judgment, the Commission cannot, by adopting a decision, resolve such a difference itself and draw from this the necessary inferences for the calculation of the penalty payment.

An action for annulment may, admittedly, be brought against such a decision before the General Court, the judgment of which may be the subject of an appeal to the Court of Justice. However, the analysis that the General Court would carry out in such proceedings would place unwarranted restrictions on the possibility for the Court of Justice to reconsider findings of fact on which the General Court based its analysis, as the Court of Justice is not entitled to review such findings of fact in appeal proceedings.

It therefore follows that, in the judgment under appeal, the General Court did not unduly limit the powers of the Commission in the verification of compliance by Portugal with the 2008 judgment or, consequently, its own jurisdiction in relation to the review of the Commission's assessment in that regard.

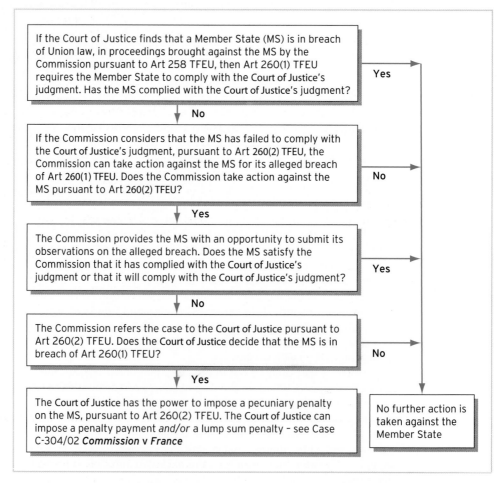

Figure 7.2 The Article 260(2) TFEU procedure: imposition of a financial penalty on a Member State which fails to comply with Article 260(1) TFEU

Figure 7.2 comprises a flowchart illustrating the application of the Art 260(2) TFEU procedure: imposition of a financial penalty on a Member State which fails to comply with Art 260(1) TFEU.

Failure to implement an EU directive

The case of *Commission v Italy* (Case C-119/04), see above, can be contrasted with that of *Commission v France* (Case C-121/07). In *Commission v France* (Case C-419/03), the Commission took action against France under what is now Art 258 TFEU for its failure to implement Directive 2001/118. This Directive, which concerns the deliberate release into the environment of genetically modified organisms (GMOs), should have been implemented by 17 October 2002. On 15 July 2004, in Case C-419/03, the Court of Justice held that France was in breach of its Union law obligation to implement the Directive. France failed to comply with this judgment and therefore the Commission issued proceedings before the Court of Justice pursuant to what is now Art 260(2) TFEU; *Commission v France* (Case C-121/07). The Commission proposed that France be ordered to pay both a penalty payment and a lump sum payment. However, before the Court of Justice gave judgment, France implemented the directive. The Commission therefore informed the Court of Justice that its request to order France to pay a penalty payment was devoid of purpose (in line with the Court's judgment in *Commission v Italy* (Case C-119/04), see above) but that it wanted to continue with its request that France be ordered to pay a lump sum payment:

Commission v *France* (Case C-121/07)

The Court of Justice stated that the reference date for assessing whether there had been a failure to comply with its judgment in Case C-419/03 was February 2006 (i.e. the date specified by the Commission in its reasoned opinion as the date by which France was required to comply with the Court's judgment). By this date, France had failed to take any steps to comply with the Court's judgment in Case C-419/03.

The Court considered that the imposition of a penalty payment was not necessary because by June 2008 France had fully transposed the directive. However, the Court of Justice ordered France to pay a lump sum payment of 10 million euros.

The Court stated that an order for the payment of a lump sum is not made automatically, and it depends on the specific details of the breach and the approach adopted by the Member State concerned. In this particular case, the Court stated that France's unlawful conduct in the GMO sector was of such a nature as to require the adoption of a dissuasive measure, such as a lump sum payment. The Court also noted the considerable length of time for which the breach persisted after its initial judgment in Case C-419/03 was delivered on 15 July 2004. Also relevant to its decision to order France to pay the lump sum, was its assessment that this was a serious breach of Union law; the objective of the Directive was to approximate the laws, regulations and administrative provisions of the Member States on the placing on the market and deliberate release into the environment of GMOs, to protect human health and the environment and to facilitate the free movement of goods.

As stated above, since the ToL came into force on 1 December 2009, Art 260(3) TFEU now provides that if the Commission brings Art 258 TFEU proceedings before the Court of Justice against a Member State which has failed to implement a directive, if the Commission considers it appropriate it may specify a lump sum or penalty payment which the Member State should be required to pay. If the Court subsequently finds the Member State to be in breach of its Union law obligations, it can impose the lump sum or penalty payment on the Member State, but the amount must not exceed that specified by the Commission. This provision applies during the initial Art 258 TFEU proceedings. It will go some way to addressing the deficiency in the previous procedure when used against a Member State which has flagrantly failed to implement a directive.

Interim measures

Breaches of Union law may occur inadvertently or intentionally. In the former case, Member States will normally take remedial action when the breach is brought to their attention by the Commission. In the latter case, Member States may risk action by the Commission when they are confronted by internal political pressures they cannot, or will not, resist. They will often do so in the hope that, by the time the Commission commences proceedings, a solution can be found and the illegal action can be terminated. Such considerations appear to have motivated the French government in the ban it imposed on the import of lamb and mutton from other Member States, principally the UK (***Commission v France (Re Sheepmeat)*** (Case 232/78)). Similar considerations seem, at least, to have been in the mind of the French government during 1999 when it refused to lift the ban on the sale of UK beef. A worldwide ban had earlier been imposed by the Union in response to concerns about UK beef being affected by Bovine Spongiform Encephalopathy (BSE) or 'mad cow disease'. When the ban was lifted during 1999 the French refused to comply, and the Commission issued proceedings against France under what is now Art 258 TFEU (***Commission v France*** (Case C-1/00), see above).

Given that several years may elapse between the initial complaint to the Commission and the hearing before the Court of Justice, the Commission, in circumstances where continuing damage is being caused while the case is processed, may apply to the Court for interim relief. Interim relief may be granted by the Court under Art 279 TFEU (previously Art 243 EC Treaty), which simply states:

> The Court of Justice of the European Union may in any cases before it prescribe any necessary interim measures.

The speed of the relief available is demonstrated by ***Commission v Ireland*** (Case 61/77R). In this case, Ireland had introduced fisheries conservation measures which the Commission regarded as contrary to the Treaty. The Commission commenced proceedings under what is now Art 258 TFEU and, at the same time, made an application for an interim order requiring Ireland to suspend the operation of the legislation. Only nine days later the Court gave judgment. It doubted the validity of the Irish legislation on grounds of discrimination and, after several adjournments to promote a settlement, ordered the Irish government to suspend the measures within five days. The following case also concerned the conservation of diminishing fishing stocks:

Commission v *UK* (Case C-246/89R)

The UK government, concerned about fishing vessels from other Member States operating in UK waters under UK 'flags of convenience' to gain access to UK fishing quotas, enacted the Merchant Shipping Act 1988. The Act confined the issue of fishing licences to companies registered in the UK and whose owners or shareholders were UK nationals or were ordinarily resident in the UK. The Act was clearly discriminatory under the former Art 7 EC Treaty (which was replaced by Art 12 EC Treaty, and is now Art 18 TFEU), and it was an obstacle to establishment under the former Art 43 EC Treaty (now Art 49 TFEU). The UK government argued that the measures were necessary to protect the UK fishing quota. Pending the hearing of the case, could the Spanish shipowners who had challenged the licensing system continue to fish? The Court of Justice noted that the owners of the vessels were suffering heavy losses while their ships remained idle, and would soon have to sell them under very adverse conditions. *Prima facie*, the companies had a right to continue in business and, given the urgency of the situation, the Court ordered the UK to suspend the relevant provisions of the Merchant Shipping Act 1988. The Court of Justice subsequently found that there was unlawful discrimination (*Factortame* (Case C-221/89)).

The following case concerned Germany's imposition of a new tax on heavy goods vehicles with a view to encouraging greater use of water transport on the country's inland waterways:

Commission v *Germany* (Case C-195/90R)

The German tax, which was to be imposed largely for environmental reasons, was to take effect on 1 July 1990. The Commission applied for what was, in effect, an *ex parte* interim order from the President of the Court of Justice, which was ordered on 28 June 1990, pending the full hearing of the interim application. Under the Court's Rules of Procedure, applicants need to state grounds indicating: (i) a *prima facie* case establishing the breach of the law alleged; and (ii) urgency and the need for the interim measures.

On the law allegedly infringed, the Commission argued that the new German tax breached the 'standstill' provisions of the former Art 72 EC Treaty (now Art 92 TFEU), which were intended to protect the present position until a common Union transport policy was adopted under the former Art 70 EC Treaty (now Art 90 TFEU). It also breached the former Art 90 EC Treaty (the prohibition against discriminatory taxation, which is now Art 110 TFEU, see Chapter 17), as the charge, although payable by all vehicles of the appropriate weight, was offset in relation to German vehicles by a reduction in German vehicle tax. The Court of Justice accepted that these arguments constituted a sufficiently strong case to meet the first requirement of the rules of procedure, but were the circumstances sufficiently urgent for interim relief? The Court had previously determined that the urgency of an application for an interim measure was to be assessed in the light of the extent to which an interim order was necessary to avoid serious and irreparable damage (*Commission* v *Greece* (Case C-170/94R)). The Commission argued that the new German tax would disrupt its attempts to create a common transport policy and would drive a number of carriers out of business before the full proceedings could be heard. The German government insisted that if the tax was suspended it would suffer irreparable damage in the loss of tax, which could not be recovered subsequently if the tax was found to be lawful in the main proceedings. The Court accepted the Commission's argument of the need to protect the *status quo* and the need to avoid irreparable damage to transport undertakings. The German government could hardly be said to be suffering a loss to its exchequer, because the tax had never existed before. The interim order to suspend the operation of the new tax was, therefore, confirmed.

Subsequently, an application for interim relief arose out of the award of contracts to replace old buses in Belgium and the alleged breach of the procedures laid down in Directive 90/531 by the Société Régionale Walloon du Transport (SRWT). The contract had been awarded (wrongly, the Commission maintained) and the delivery of the first buses was due to take place before the full hearing could take place. The Commission argued that there was a risk of serious and irreparable damage, in that the award of the contract and the first deliveries would confront the Commission with a *fait accompli*, and would create the conditions for a serious and immediate threat to the Union legal order. The Court agreed that the failure to comply with a directive applicable to a public contract constituted a serious threat to the Union legal order, and that a declaration at the conclusion of the proceedings under what is now Art 258 TFEU could not cancel the damage suffered. However, the Court felt that an application for interim relief should be pursued with due diligence. The Commission had taken more than two months to apply for relief after one of the unsuccessful tenderers had informed it of the situation. The formal contract was, in the meantime, concluded. The Commission's application for interim relief was refused (***Commission v Belgium*** (Case C-87/94)).

Other direct actions against Member States

The power of the Commission to take cases directly to the Court of Justice where a Member State has granted aid to an undertaking in breach of Art 107 TFEU (previously Art 87 EC Treaty) will be considered in Chapter 19. Failure to abolish the offending aid within the time specified will entitle the Commission to proceed without giving a reasoned opinion as required under Arts 258 and 259 TFEU.

There are also special powers given to the Commission under Art 114(9) TFEU (previously Art 95(9) EC Treaty) to enable it to bring Member States before the Court of Justice without going through the Art 258 TFEU procedure in cases where a Member State has used its power to derogate from a **harmonising directive** on grounds of major needs, or protection of the environment or the working environment. This could apply if the Commission believes that the Member State is using its power of derogation improperly.

Summary

Now you have read this chapter you should be able to:

- Explain the function of the Art 258 TFEU procedure, and understand the circumstances in which the Commission may commence proceedings against a Member State.

- Explain the purpose of Art 259 TFEU and identify why a Member State may be reluctant to initiate action pursuant to it.

- Outline the following matters which occur during the course of Art 258 TFEU proceedings:
  - investigation of the alleged breach by the Commission;
  - submission of a Member State's observations on the alleged breach to the Commission;
  - the Commission's issue of a reasoned opinion setting out details of the alleged breach;

- the Member State's compliance (or otherwise) with such reasoned opinion within a reasonable period of time;
- the Commission's referral of the case to the Court of Justice if the Member State fails to comply with such reasoned opinion;
- if the breach by the Member State relates to the non-implementation of a Union directive, the power of the Court of Justice to impose a lump sum or penalty payment on the defaulting Member State pursuant to Art 260(3) TFEU;
- a Member State's obligation to comply with a judgment of the Court of Justice (pursuant to Art 260(1) TFEU);
- the Commission's power to take action pursuant to Art 260(2) TFEU if a Member State fails to comply with the judgment of the Court of Justice.
- Understand the purpose of Art 260(2) TFEU and the circumstances in which the Court of Justice may impose a lump sum and/or penalty payment on a Member State which has failed to comply with a judgment of the Court of Justice pursuant to Art 260(1) TFEU.

Further reading

Textbooks

Craig, P. and De Burca, G. (2011) *EU Law: Text, Cases and Materials* (5th edn), Oxford University Press, Chapter 12.

Foster, N. (2015) *Foster on EU Law* (11th edn), Oxford University Press, Chapter 7.

Steiner, J. and Woods, L. (2014) *EU Law* (12th edn), Oxford University Press, Chapter 11.

Weatherill, S. (2014) *Cases and Materials on EU Law* (11th edn), Oxford University Press, Chapter 4.

Journal articles

Jack, B., 'Article 260(2) TFEU: An effective judicial procedure for the enforcement of judgments?' (2013) 19 ELJ 404.

Kilbey, I., 'The interpretation of Article 260 TFEU (ex 228 EC)' (2010) 35 EL Rev 370.

Smith, M., 'Enforcement, monitoring, verification, outsourcing: The decline and decline of the infringement process' (2008) 33 EL Rev 777.

Wennerås, P., 'A new dawn for Commission enforcement under Articles 226 and 228 EC: General and persistent infringements, lump sums and penalty payments' (2006) 43 CML Rev 31.

8

Judicial review of acts of Union institutions

Objectives

At the end of this chapter you should understand:

1. The range of Union acts that can be reviewed by the Court of Justice of the European Union pursuant to Art 263 TFEU, and be able to compare and contrast the conditions that apply to a 'privileged applicant' and a 'non-privileged applicant'.

2. The four grounds for review under Art 263 TFEU.

3. How an indirect challenge to a Union act could be pursued under Arts 277 and 267 TFEU.

4. The power under Art 265 TFEU to challenge a Union institution's failure to act.

5. How the Court of Justice of the European Union applies the rules relating to a claim for damages against a Union institution for unlawful acts, pursuant to Art 340 TFEU.

Legality of Union acts: Article 263 TFEU

Objective 1

Although the Union does not have a formal constitution, the TEU and TFEU confer specific powers and duties on each of the institutions and establish what the Court of Justice has, on a number of occasions, referred to as 'a new legal order' (***Opinion 1/91*** [1991] ECR I-6079). Each of the institutions has a limited competence and must carry out its functions in the way specified in the Treaties and according to general principles of Union law (Art 13 TEU (previously Art 7(1) EC Treaty)).

If an institution exceeds its powers or uses them unlawfully, its acts may be subject to review by the Court of Justice under Art 263 TFEU (previously Art 230 EC Treaty). Article 263 TFEU provides:

> The Court of Justice of the European Union shall review the legality of legislative acts, of acts of the Council, of the Commission and of the European Central Bank, other than recommendations and opinions, and of acts of the European Parliament and of the European Council intended to produce legal effects *vis-à-vis* third parties. It shall also review the legality of acts of bodies, offices or agencies of the Union intended to produce legal effects *vis-à-vis* third parties.

It shall for this purpose have jurisdiction in actions brought by a Member State, the European Parliament, the Council or the Commission on grounds of lack of competence, infringement of an essential procedural requirement, infringement of the Treaties or of any rule of law relating to their application, or misuse of powers.

The Court shall have jurisdiction under the same conditions in actions brought by the Court of Auditors, by the European Central Bank and by the Committee of the Regions for the purpose of protecting their prerogatives.

Any natural or legal person may, under the conditions laid down in the first and second paragraphs, institute proceedings against an act addressed to that person or which is of direct and individual concern to them, and against a regulatory act which is of direct concern to them and does not entail implementing measures.

Acts setting up bodies, offices and agencies of the Union may lay down specific conditions and arrangements concerning actions brought by natural or legal persons against acts of these bodies, offices or agencies intended to produce legal effects in relation to them.

The proceedings provided for in this Article shall be instituted within two months of the publication of the measure, or of its notification to the plaintiff, or, in the absence thereof, of the day on which it came to the knowledge of the latter, as the case may be.

Article 263 TFEU is substantially the same as the former Art 230 EC Treaty, although there are some subtle differences, which will be discussed throughout this chapter. The case law considered within this chapter is almost exclusively based on the former Art 230 EC Treaty. The former Art 230 EC Treaty provided:

The Court of Justice shall review the legality of acts adopted jointly by the European Parliament and the Council, of acts of the Council, of the Commission and of the European Central Bank, other than recommendations and opinions, and of acts of the European Parliament intended to produce legal effects *vis-à-vis* third parties.

It shall for this purpose have jurisdiction in actions brought by a Member State, the Council or the Commission on grounds of lack of competence, infringement of an essential procedural requirement, infringement of this Treaty or of any rule of law relating to its application, or misuse of powers.

The Court shall have jurisdiction under the same conditions in actions brought by the European Parliament, by the Court of Auditors and by the ECB for the purpose of protecting their prerogatives.

Any natural or legal person may, under the same conditions, institute proceedings against a decision addressed to that person or against a decision which, although in the form of a regulation or a decision addressed to another person, is of direct and individual concern to the former.

The proceedings provided for in this Article shall be instituted within two months of the publication of the measure, or of its notification to the plaintiff, or, in the absence thereof, of the day on which it came to the knowledge of the latter, as the case may be.

The constituent parts of Art 263 TFEU (and the former Art 230 EC Treaty) raise five issues:

1 When is an action barred by lapse of time?
2 What type of Union act may be reviewed?
3 Who may challenge such an act, i.e. who has, in the language of English administrative law, the **locus standi** to mount a challenge?
4 What are the grounds for challenge?
5 What are the consequences of an annulment?

There now follows a consideration of these five issues.

Article 263 TFEU: time limits

Article 263, para 6 TFEU provides that proceedings should be instituted within two months of:

- the date of publication of the measure; or
- notification of the measure to the applicant; or, in the absence thereof
- the day on which the measure came to the knowledge of the applicant.

This is identical to the wording of the former Art 230, para 5 EC Treaty. Therefore the case law decided under this former provision is directly relevant to Art 263, para 6 TFEU.

The third criterion, i.e. the day on which the measure came to the knowledge of the applicant, is subsidiary to the first and second criteria of publication or notification of the measure. Moreover, if the third criterion applies, the period for bringing an action can begin to run only from the moment when the applicant acquires precise knowledge of the content of the decision in question and of the reasons on which it is based in such a way as to enable him to exercise his right of action. It is for the party who has knowledge of a decision to request the whole text thereof within a reasonable period. Accordingly, the Court of First Instance ((CFI), now the General Court) held in **COBB v Commission** (Case T-485/04) that where an applicant requests communication of a decision excluding eligible expenditure under a programme implemented under the European Regional Development Fund (ERDF) more than four months after becoming aware of it, a reasonable time is exceeded.

In the following case, the CFI had an opportunity to add an important rider to the application of these principles in a case concerning litigation on state aid:

Olsen v Commission (Case T-17/02)

The applicant contested a Commission decision authorising state aid paid to a Spanish competitor. Its action was lodged just over six months after Spain, the only addressee of the contested decision, was notified of it. As the applicant was not the addressee of the contested decision, the CFI (now the General Court) held in its judgment that the criterion of notification of the decision was not applicable to it. As to whether, in this case, the criterion of publication or that of the day on which a measure came to the knowledge of an applicant was applicable, the CFI cited the case law according to which, with regard to measures which are published in the *Official Journal*, the criterion of the day on which a measure came to the knowledge of an applicant was not applicable; in such circumstances it was the date of publication which marked the starting point of the period prescribed for instituting proceedings (Case C-122/95 *Germany v Council* [1998] ECR I-973, at para 39).

In the area of state aid, decisions by means of which the Commission, after a preliminary examination, finds that no doubts are raised as to the compatibility with the internal market of a notified measure and decides that the measure is compatible with the common market, are to be the subject of a summary notice published in the *Official Journal* (Regulation 659/99). The summary notice includes a reference to the website of the Secretariat General of the Commission and the statement that the full text of the decision in question, from which all confidential information has been removed, can be found there, in the authentic language version or versions. The CFI held that the fact that the Commission gives third parties full access to the text of a decision placed on its website, combined with publication of a summary notice in the *Official Journal* enabling interested parties to identify the decision in question and notifying them of this possibility of access via the Internet, must be considered to be publication for the purposes of the former Art 230, para 5 EC Treaty (now Art 263, para 6 TFEU). In this case, the applicant could legitimately expect that the contested decision would be published in the *Official Journal*. Olsen's subsequent appeal to the Court of Justice was dismissed (Case C-320/05P).

The two-month period expires at the end of the day in the last month which bears the same number as the day of the occurrence of the event which caused time to start running (*Misset* v *Council* (Case 152/85)). So, for example, if the measure had been published in the *Official Journal* on 2 February 2014, the two-month period would expire at midnight on 2 April 2014. The CFI has held that where an applicant lets the time- limit expire for bringing an action against a decision unequivocally affecting his interests, he cannot start time running again by asking the institution to reconsider its decision and then start proceedings against the confirmation of the decision (*Cobrecaf SA* v *Commission* (Case T-514/93)). The expiry of the period of time allowed for bringing proceedings will not be fatal if the applicant can rely on Art 45 of the Statute of the Court, which provides:

> ... No right shall be prejudiced in consequence of the expiry of the time- limit if the party concerned proves the existence of unforeseeable circumstances or of *force majeure*.

The Court of Justice has, however, shown reluctance in allowing applications outside the statutory time limits. Time limits do not apply where the issue of the legality of a Union act is raised in proceedings under Art 267 TFEU (previously Art 234 EC Treaty); see below. However, a national court cannot refer a case under Art 267 TFEU to the Court of Justice if the applicant could have challenged the Union act within the time- limit under Art 263 TFEU, but failed to do so (*TWD Deggendorf* (Case C-188/92)); see Chapter 6.

Article 263 TFEU: reviewable acts

Not every act of a Union institution may be reviewed. Under the former Art 230, para 1 EC Treaty, *prima facie* it was only those acts the former Art 249 EC Treaty (now Art 288 TFEU) defined as legally binding – i.e. regulations, directives and decisions – which were subject to review. Opinions and recommendations were not reviewable. However, other acts not specified in the former Art 249 EC Treaty (now Art 288 TFEU) were treated by the Court of Justice as subject to review. Article 263, para 1 TFEU (which replaced Art 230, para 1 EC Treaty) has been rewritten to accommodate the case law of the Court of Justice, and in particular to include as reviewable those Union acts which are 'intended to produce legal effects *vis-à-vis* third parties', and to extend the range of acts to include those of 'bodies, offices or agencies of the Union intended to produce legal effects *vis-à-vis* third parties'. The case law considered below concerned the former Art 230, para 1 EC Treaty; this case law is directly relevant to the rewritten Art 263, para 1 TFEU.

In *Commission* v *Council* (Case 22/70), the Court of Justice held that a resolution passed by the Council to participate in a European Transport Agreement was reviewable under the former Art 230 EC Treaty. The Court refused to interpret the former Art 249 EC Treaty (now Art 288 TFEU) restrictively, and declared that 'an action for annulment must ... be available in the case of all measures adopted by the institutions, whatever their nature and form, which are intended to have legal effects'. In the following case, the Court of Justice emphasised that the determining factor is whether or not an act has legal consequences, no matter how it has been arrived at:

IBM v Commission (Case 60/81)

The Court of Justice stated that:

> In order to ascertain whether the measures in question are acts within the meaning of Article 173 [which was replaced by Art 230 EC Treaty, and is now Art 263 TFEU] it is necessary ... to look to their substance. According to the consistent case law of the Court any measure the legal effects of which are binding on, and capable of affecting the interests of, the applicant by bringing about a distinct change in his legal position is an act or decision which may be the subject of an action under Article 173 [now Art 263 TFEU] for a declaration that it is void. However, the form in which such acts or decisions are cast is, in principle, immaterial as regards the question whether they are open to challenge under that article.

It is, however, often difficult to distinguish between form and substance. An act may not have any legal consequence precisely because it has not been adopted in the form required. In *Air France* v *Commission* (Case T-3/93) the Commissioner responsible for competition policy, Sir Leon Brittan, had issued a press statement about the merger between Dan Air and British Airways, declaring that it would not result in a sufficient concentration of air transport to have a Union dimension. Air France's attempt to challenge this press statement failed at the first hurdle, because the statement had not been adopted by the whole Commission and did not have the *form* of a legal act. It could, therefore, have no legal consequences (see also *Nefarma* v *Commission* (Case T-113/89)).

As it was originally written, the former Art 230 EC Treaty made no mention of measures adopted by the European Parliament. Despite this, the Court of Justice held in *Parti Ecologiste ('Les Verts')* v *European Parliament* (Case 294/83) that measures adopted by the Parliament intended to have legal effects *vis-à-vis* third parties were subject to annulment under the former Art 230 EC Treaty (see also *Luxembourg* v *European Parliament* (Case C-213/88)). The Court of Justice has also held that a declaration made by the President of the Parliament at the conclusion of the debate by Parliament on the Union's budget has the character of a legal act and is also subject to annulment (*Council* v *Parliament* (Case 34/86); *Council* v *European Parliament* (Case C-284/90)). This situation should be contrasted with that in the following case which likewise concerned whether a declaration of the President of the Parliament was a measure open to challenge:

Le Pen v Parliament (Case T-353/00)

The declaration of the President of the Parliament stated that, in accordance with Art 12(2) of the Act concerning the election of representatives to the Parliament by direct universal suffrage, annexed to the Council Decision of 20 September 1976, 'the ... Parliament takes note of the notification of the French government declaring the disqualification of Mr Le Pen from holding office'. The CFI (now the General Court) held that the declaration was not open to challenge. In its judgment, the CFI stated that the intervention of the European Parliament under the first subparagraph of Art 12(2) of the abovementioned Act was restricted to taking note of the declaration, already made by the national authorities, that the applicant's seat was vacant. The CFI accordingly held that the declaration of the President of the Parliament was not intended to produce legal effects of its own, distinct from those of the decree dated 31 March 2000 of the French Prime Minister stating that the applicant's ineligibility brought to an end his term of office as a representative in the European Parliament.

Le Pen's appeal to the Court of Justice was dismissed (Case C-208/03P).

Measures taken by the Parliament affecting third parties were made specifically subject to review as a result of amendments made to the former Art 230, para 1 EC Treaty by the TEU; Art 263, para 1 TFEU contains a similar right of review.

A measure adopted by the Court of Auditors has also been held to be reviewable under the former Art 230 EC Treaty (***Maurissen and others v Court of Auditors*** (Cases 193 and 194/87)). A decision by the Commission to close the file on a complaint alleging breach of the former Art 82 EC Treaty (now Art 102 TFEU) has also been held to be a 'decision' reviewable under the former Art 230 EC Treaty (***SFEI and Others v Commission*** (Case C-39/93P)).

Although the acts of the Council are reviewable, it has been held that the representatives of the Member States must be acting *as* the Council for what is now Art 263 TFEU to apply. In ***Parliament v Council*** (Cases C-181/91 and C-248/91), the Parliament attempted to challenge a decision made at a Council meeting granting special aid to Bangladesh. The Court of Justice held that acts adopted by representatives of the Member States acting not as members of the Council but as representatives of their governments amounted to the collective exercise of the competencies of the Member States. They were not, therefore, acts of the Council and were not, consequently, subject to review by the Court of Justice.

Some acts are specifically excluded from review. There are some policy areas in both the TEU and TFEU where the Court of Justice of the European Union has either limited jurisdiction or no jurisdiction.

Prior to the ToL coming into force, the construction of the European Union (and its three pillars), as discussed in Chapter 1, was both complex and cumbersome. When the ToL came into force on 1 December 2009, it established a single European Union, which replaced and succeeded the European Community (Art 1 TEU). The former three pillars of the European Union were merged even though special procedures were maintained in the fields of foreign policy, security and defence. Reference is no longer to be made to the three pillars of the European Union.

Title V, Chapter 2, Sections 1 and 2, Arts 23–46 TEU relate to the Common Foreign and Security Policy. Title V, Chapter 4, Arts 82–86 TFEU relate to Judicial Cooperation in Criminal Matters. Title V, Chapter 5, Arts 87–89 relate to Police Cooperation. Article 24(1) TEU provides that 'The Court of Justice of the European Union shall not have jurisdiction with respect to these provisions [which relate to the common foreign and security policy]'. Similarly, Art 276 TFEU provides that:

> In exercising its powers regarding the provisions of Chapters 4 [judicial cooperation in criminal matters] and 5 [police cooperation] of Chapter V of Part Three [of the TFEU] relating to the area of freedom, security and justice, **the Court of Justice of the European Union shall have no jurisdiction to review the validity or proportionality of operations carried out by the police or other law-enforcement services of a Member State or the exercise of the responsibilities incumbent upon Member States with regard to the maintenance of law and order and the safeguarding of internal security**. [emphasis added]

The former Art 230 EC Treaty was likewise subject to similar exclusions. In the context of the former Art 230 EC Treaty, the Court, however, decided that it does have jurisdiction to determine the *scope* of such exclusions (see, for example, ***Svenska Journalistforbundet v Council of European Union*** (Case T-174/95)).

Continuing the theme of acts which are not subject to review, in the following case the CFI (now the General Court) held that decisions by the Commission to commence legal proceedings against certain American cigarette manufacturers before a federal court in the USA did not constitute measures that were open to challenge:

Philip Morris International and Others v *Commission* (Joined Cases T-377/00, T-379/00, T-380/00, T-260/01 and T-272/01)

The CFI (now the General Court) held that a decision to bring court proceedings does not in itself alter the legal position in question, but has the effect merely of opening a procedure whose purpose is to achieve a change in that position through a judgment. While noting that the commencement of legal proceedings may give rise to certain consequences by operation of law, the CFI held that their commencement does not in itself determine definitively the obligations of the parties to the case and that this determination results only from the judgment of the court. The CFI stated that this finding applies both to proceedings before the Union Courts and to proceedings before courts of the Member States and even of non-member countries, such as the United States.

Philip Morris International's appeal to the Court of Justice was dismissed (Case C-131/03P).

The CFI (now the General Court) has held that where, in the context of an action for annulment, the contested measure is *negative* it must be appraised in the light of the nature of the request to which it constitutes a reply.

In particular, the refusal by a Union institution to withdraw or amend a measure may constitute a decision whose legality may be reviewed under what is now Art 263 TFEU, only if the measure which the Union institution refuses to withdraw or amend could itself have been contested under that provision (***Institouto N. Avgerinopoulou and Others v Commission*** (Case T-139/02), and ***Comunidad Autónoma de Andalucía v Commission*** (Case T-29/03)).

In ***Comunidad Autónoma de Andalucía v Commission***, the European Anti-Fraud Office (OLAF) issued a final report following an external investigation. OLAF forwarded the report to the competent Spanish authorities in accordance with Art 9, Regulation 1073/1999. The CFI (now the General Court) held that a letter from the Director -General of OLAF, informing the applicant that it was not possible to investigate its complaint directed against the final report, could not be regarded as a decision against which proceedings could be brought. This was due to the fact that the report did not constitute a measure producing binding legal effects such as to affect the applicant's interests; rather, it was a recommendation or an opinion which lacked binding legal effects.

Competition law cases

In the field of Union competition law, a number of cases have concerned the issue of whether or not the act is reviewable. In ***Coe Clerici Logistics v Commission*** (Case T-52/00), a letter from the Commission refusing to act on an undertaking's complaint based on the former Arts 82 and 86 EC Treaty (now Arts 102 and 106 TFEU) was not, in principle, a measure against which an action for annulment could be brought. After recalling that the exercise of the Commission's power conferred by the former Art 86(3) EC Treaty to assess the compatibility of state measures with the Treaty rules was not coupled with an obligation on the part of the Commission to take action, the CFI (now the General Court) held that legal or natural persons who request the Commission to take action under the former Art 86(3) do not, in principle, have the right to bring an action against a Commission decision not to use the powers which it has under that article. However, as the applicant relied at the hearing on the judgment in ***max.mobil v Commission*** (Case T-54/99), the CFI added that 'if the contested act, in so far as it concerns infringement of Art 82 EC [now Art 102 TFEU] in conjunction with Art 86 EC [now Art 106 TFEU], must be classified as a decision rejecting a complaint' as referred to in *max.mobil* v *Commission*, the applicant should be regarded as entitled to bring his action. The question as to the admissibility of the action did not affect the outcome of the dispute because the CFI held on the merits that the action was unfounded.

However, the Court of Justice subsequently reversed the decision of *max.mobil* v *Commission* on appeal, which undoubtedly means that the CFI (now the General Court) would have decided the question of admissibility in *Coe Clerici Logistics* v *Commission* differently:

Commission v T-Mobile Austria GMBH (Case C-141/02P)

[Note: max.mobil had become T-Mobile Austria GmbH prior to the appeal.]
The Court of Justice held that the CFI (now the General Court) had erred in declaring max.mobil's action was admissible and therefore held that the judgment had to be set aside.

The case gave the Court an opportunity to be more specific about the scope of its decision in *Bundesverband der Bilanzbuchhalter* v *Commission* (Case C-107/95P), according to which the Commission is empowered to determine, using the powers conferred on it by the former Art 90(3) EC Treaty (which was replaced by Art 86(3) EC Treaty, and is now Art 106(3) TFEU), that a given state measure is incompatible with the rules of the Treaty and to indicate what measures the state to which a decision is addressed must adopt in order to comply with its obligations under Union law. It observed that it followed from that judgment that individuals may, in certain circumstances, be entitled to bring an action for annulment against a decision the Commission addresses to a Member State on the basis of the former Art 90(3) EC Treaty (now Art 106(3) TFEU) if the conditions laid down in the fourth paragraph of the former Art 173 EC Treaty (which was replaced by Art 230, para 4 EC Treaty, and is now Art 263, para 4 TFEU) are satisfied. The Court held, however, that it follows from the wording of the former Art 90(3) EC Treaty and from the scheme of that article as a whole that **the Commission is not obliged to bring proceedings within the terms of those provisions, as individuals cannot require the Commission to take a position in a specific sense.** It held that the fact that max.mobil had a direct and individual interest in annulment of the Commission's decision to refuse to act on its complaint was not such as to confer on it a right to challenge that decision; nor could the applicant claim a right to bring an action pursuant to Regulation No. 17 (now Regulation 1/2003), which is not applicable to the former Art 90 EC Treaty (now Art 106 TFEU; see Chapter 22). According to the Court, that finding was not at variance with the principle of sound administration or with any other general principle of Union law. **No general principle of Union law requires that an undertaking be recognised as having standing before the Union courts to challenge a refusal by the Commission to bring proceedings against a Member State on the basis of Art 90, para 3 EC Treaty (now Art 106, para 3 TFEU).**

The orders of the CFI (now the General Court) in *Commerzbank* v *Commission* (Case T-219/01), *Dresdner Bank* v *Commission* (Case T-250/01) and *Reisebank* v *Commission* (Case T-216/01) resulted from challenges to decisions of the hearing officer which had been made pursuant to Art 8, Commission Decision 2001/462. Article 8 relates to the terms of reference of hearing officers in certain competition proceedings. By those decisions, several banks which were subject to administrative investigation to establish their participation in an arrangement contrary to the former Art 81 EC Treaty (now Art 101 TFEU) had been refused access to information relating to the circumstances which had led to the hearing officer terminating some of the administrative procedures initiated against other banks. In each of the three cases the CFI held that the decision of the hearing officer in itself produced only limited effects, characteristic of a preparatory measure in the course of an administrative procedure initiated by the Commission, and could not therefore justify the action being admissible before that procedure had been completed. It followed that any infringement of rights of defence by the refusal, capable of rendering the administrative procedure unlawful, could properly be pleaded only in an action brought against the final decision finding that the former Art 81 EC Treaty (now Art 101 TFEU) had been infringed.

Finally, in the field of state aid, the CFI (now the General Court) had the opportunity to clarify the case law concerning the ability to challenge decisions to initiate the formal investigation procedure envisaged in the former Art 88(2) EC Treaty (now Art 108(2) TFEU). The CFI distinguished between cases which concerned the provisional classification of *new* aid and that of *existing* aid. Decisions initiating the formal examination procedure with regard to measures that have been provisionally classified as *new* aid have previously been held to have independent legal effects *vis-à-vis* the final decision for which they are a preparatory step (see judgments in ***Government of Gibraltar* v *Commission*** (Joined Cases T-195/01 and T-207/01), ***Territorio Histórico de Guipúzcoa and Others* v *Commission*** (Joined Cases T-269/99, T-271/99 and T-272/99) and ***Territorio Histórico de Álava and Others* v *Commission*** (Joined Cases T-346/99, T-347/99 and T-348/99)). This can be contrasted with the decision initiating the formal examination procedure which gave rise to the order in ***Forum 187* v *Commission*** (Case T-276/02), in which the Belgian scheme at issue – the coordination centres scheme – was classified as a scheme of *existing* aid. The CFI held that such a decision does not produce any independent legal effects and, as such, did not constitute a challengeable measure.

Article 263 TFEU: who may apply for review?

There are two categories of applicant:

1 Specified Union institutions and Member States – referred to as a 'privileged applicant'.

2 Any natural or legal person – referred to as a 'non-privileged applicant'.

Different rules apply depending upon whether the applicant is privileged or non-privileged. It is much more difficult to prove standing for a non-privileged applicant.

Privileged applicants

Article 263, para 2 TFEU confers specific and unlimited rights of challenge on Member States, the European Parliament, the Council of Ministers and the Commission. Under the former Art 230, para 2 EC Treaty, the European Parliament was not included as one of the Union institutions with a specific and unlimited right of challenge (the Parliament's power was limited to a right of challenge to enable it to protect its prerogatives). In ***Regione Siciliana* v *Commission*** (Case C-417/04), the Court of Justice gave consideration to the concept of a 'Member State' within the context of what is now Art 263, para 2 TFEU. The Court stated that an action by a local or regional entity cannot be treated in the same way as an action by a Member State. The term 'Member State' within the meaning of what is now Art 263 TFEU only includes government authorities of the Member States. However, the Court stated that, on the basis of that article, a local or regional entity may, to the extent that it has legal personality under national law, institute proceedings on the same terms as a 'non-privileged applicant' (see below).

Under Art 263, para 3 TFEU, the Court of Auditors, the European Central Bank and the Committee of the Regions have more limited rights of challenge to enable them to protect their prerogatives.

Non-privileged applicant

Article 263, para 4 TFEU provides:

> Any natural or legal person may ... institute proceedings against an act addressed to that person or which is of direct and individual concern to them, and against a regulatory act which is of direct concern to them and does not entail implementing measures.

Under Art 263, para 4 TFEU, a non-privileged applicant is empowered to challenge the legality of a Union act in three cases:

- an *act* addressed to the applicant;
- an *act* addressed to another person which is of *direct and individual concern* to the applicant;
- a *regulatory act* which is of *direct concern* to the applicant, and which does not entail implementing measures.

In contrast, the former Art 230, para 4 EC Treaty limited the right of challenge by a non-privileged applicant. A non-privileged applicant could only challenge the legality of a specified act in the following three cases:

- a *decision* addressed to the applicant;
- a *decision* addressed to another person which is of *direct and individual concern* to the applicant;
- a *decision* in the form of a regulation which is of *direct and individual concern* to the applicant.

The right to challenge an 'act' addressed to the applicant under Art 263 TFEU is broader than the right to challenge a 'decision' addressed to the applicant under the former Art 230 EC Treaty, because potentially the 'act' could include not only a decision, but a regulation or directive. In any event, its scope is relatively straightforward. An applicant to whom an act is addressed is empowered to challenge the legality of the act before the Court of Justice of the European Union, within the time limits specified in Art 263 TFEU (see above). Many decisions which were subject to challenge by individuals under the former Art 230, para 4 EC Treaty had been adopted by the Commission in relation to Union competition law, and they were challenged by individuals and companies to whom the decision was addressed.

In contrast to an 'act' addressed to the applicant, the latter two rights of challenge set out in Art 263, para 4 TFEU are not as straightforward.

If the measure the individual is seeking to have reviewed is 'a regulatory act which ... does not entail implementing measures' under Art 263, para 4 TFEU, then in order to have standing an individual will only need to show 'direct concern' rather than 'direct *and individual* concern'. The precise scope of what constitutes a 'regulatory act' will require clarification by the Court of Justice, because this was not previously included in the former Art 230, para 4 EC Treaty. However, the case law below relating to direct concern will assist in determining the scope of 'regulatory act'.

The right to challenge an 'act' addressed to another person which is of direct and individual concern to the applicant under Art 263, para 4 TFEU is broader than the right to challenge a 'decision' addressed to another person which is of direct and individual concern to the applicant under the former Art 230, para 4 EC Treaty. Such an 'act' could potentially include not only a decision, but a regulation (or directive), and therefore it automatically covers the final type of reviewable act set out in the former Art 230, para 4 EC Treaty (i.e. a decision in the form of a regulation, which is of direct and individual concern to the applicant). This part of the former Art 230, para 4 EC Treaty (i.e. a decision, or a decision in the form of a regulation, which is of direct and individual concern to the applicant) has produced a catalogue of litigation. This case law is of direct relevance to Art 263, para 4 TFEU and is considered further below. First, however, there follows is a discussion about whether or not the applicant has a legal interest in bringing the proceedings, because this is a precursor to the issue of direct and individual concern.

Legal interest in bringing proceedings

An action for annulment brought by a natural or legal person is admissible only in so far as the applicant has a legal interest in seeing the contested measure annulled. Although a legal interest in bringing proceedings is not expressly required by Art 263 TFEU (or the former Art 230 EC Treaty), the applicant must prove that he has such an interest in bringing proceedings. The CFI (now the General Court) stated that this is an essential and fundamental prerequisite for any legal proceedings in the context of what is now Art 263 TFEU (*Schmitz-Gotha Fahrzeugwerke v Commission* (Case T-167/01)) and that, in the absence of a legal interest in bringing proceedings, it is unnecessary to examine whether the contested act is of direct and individual concern to the applicant (*Olivieri v Commission and European Agency for the Evaluation of Medicinal Products* (Case T-326/99)).

That interest must be a vested and present interest and is assessed as at the date when the action is brought. If the interest which an applicant claims concerns a future legal situation, he must demonstrate that the prejudice to that situation is already certain (*NBV v Commission* (Case T-138/89), at para 33). Such an interest is not established by an applicant who seeks the annulment of an act addressed to a Member State ordering it to recover state aid from various companies where, contrary to the applicant's assertions, the act does not impose any joint and several obligation on him to repay the contested aid (*Schmitz-Gotha Fahrzeugwerke*).

The following case concerned a future legal situation, but on its particular facts the CFI (now the General Court) held that there was a vested and present interest in bringing proceedings:

MCI v Commission (Case T-310/00)

The applicant (MCI) had notified the Commission of an agreement it had entered into with Sprint, for the two companies to merge. During the Commission's investigations, MCI informed the Commission that it was abandoning the proposed merger. The Commission refused to regard this as amounting to a formal withdrawal of the notified agreement, and went on to adopt a decision prohibiting the proposed merger.

The CFI (now the General Court) held that MCI had an interest in obtaining the annulment of this decision. The CFI added that, as long as the Commission decision continued to stand, MCI was prevented by law from merging with Sprint, at least in the configuration and under the conditions put forward in the notification, should it again have the intention to do so. The fact that the undertaking did not necessarily have that intention, or that it would perhaps not carry it out, was a purely subjective circumstance that could not be taken into account when assessing its legal interest in bringing proceedings for the annulment of a measure which, unquestionably, produced binding legal effects such as to affect its interests by bringing about a distinct change in its legal position.

Although the applicant's interest in bringing proceedings must be assessed as at the time when the application is lodged, in the following case the CFI (now the General Court) decided otherwise:

First Data v *Commission* (Case T-28/02)

The applicants contested a decision by which the Commission opposed, on the basis of the former Art 81 EC Treaty (now Art 101 TFEU), certain rules governing membership of a bank card scheme. Those rules were withdrawn after the action was brought so that, in the view of the CFI (now the General Court), the applicants' interest in bringing proceedings, in so far as it had any, had ceased to exist.

The CFI held that the Court could dismiss the proceedings if the applicant (who initially had a legal interest in bringing proceedings) had lost all personal interest in having the contested decision annulled due to an event which occurred **after** that application was lodged.

The facts of the above case gave the CFI (now the General Court) an opportunity to apply the established principle that an interest in bringing proceedings cannot be assessed on the basis of a future, hypothetical event. In particular, if it is claimed that the interest concerns a future legal situation, the applicant must demonstrate that the prejudice to that situation is already certain (***NBV*** v ***Commission***, at para 33).

The CFI (now the General Court) applied these principles in the following cases:

Gruppo Ormeggiatori del porto di Venezia and others v *Commission* (Joined Cases T-228/00, T-229/00, T-242/00, T-243/00, T-245/00 to T-248/00, T-250/00, T-252/00, T-256/00 to T-259/00, T-267/00, T-268/00, T-271/00, T-275/00, T-276/00, T-281/00, T-287/00 and T-296/00), *Sagar* v *Commission* (Case T-269/00) and *Gardena Hotels and Comitato Venezia Vuole Vivere* v *Commission* (Case T-288/00)

The CFI (now the General Court) declared the actions inadmissible because of a lack of a legal interest in bringing the proceedings. The actions were brought by Italian undertakings contesting a Commission decision declaring certain aid to firms incompatible with the internal market. Raising an absolute bar to proceeding of its own motion, **the CFI found that the applicants had no legal interest in bringing proceedings on the basis essentially of the decision of Italy not to proceed to recover the aid from the applicants.** To substantiate their interest in bringing proceedings the applicants confined themselves to citing future and uncertain circumstances, namely the possibility that the Commission would make a different assessment from that made by Italy and would require it to recover the alleged aid from the applicant undertakings.

Accordingly, because it was only in the future and uncertain event of a Commission decision calling into question Italy's implementing decision that their legal position would be affected, **the applicant undertakings had not demonstrated that there was a vested, present interest in seeking the annulment of the contested decision.** Moreover, even in that event, the applicant undertakings would not thereby be deprived of any effective legal remedy, given the possibility they had of bringing actions in the national courts against any decisions of the competent national authority requiring them to return the alleged aid.

In the following case, the CFI (now the General Court) applied the case law on 'interest in bringing proceedings' and declared the action inadmissible:

Sniace v Commission (Case T-88/01)

The CFI (now the General Court) declared as inadmissible the action brought by Sniace contesting a decision of the Commission declaring aid it had received incompatible with the internal market. Sniace disputed the classification of the aid as state aid in the decision, claiming that it affected it adversely, in particular because of the risk of legal action and certain effects on its relations with the credit institution which granted the aid. The Court dismissed the action on the basis that the applicant had no legal interest in bringing proceedings, citing the case law mentioned above according to which **if the interest upon which an applicant relies concerns a future legal situation, he must demonstrate that the prejudice to that situation is already certain** (*NBV v Commission*). The CFI held that the applicant had not shown that: (i) the alleged risk of legal proceedings was, in this case, vested and present; nor (ii) that the classification as state aid could entail the obligation to notify the Commission in future of any measure adopted by that credit institution in favour of the applicant; nor (iii) that the damage, which, according to the applicant, resulted from the conduct of the administrative procedure, could be linked to the classification as state aid in the contested decision.

Sniace's appeal to the Court of Justice was dismissed (Case C-260/05P).

The CFI has also held that an applicant does not have a legal interest in bringing proceedings where he seeks the annulment of a Commission decision granting marketing authorisation for a medicinal product and it is established that the scientific information forwarded by him to the European Agency for the Evaluation of Medicinal Products has: (i) justified the reopening of the assessment procedure; and (ii) been examined and taken into account under that procedure (***Olivieri v Commission and European Agency for the Evaluation of Medicinal Products*** (Case T-326/99)).

An act addressed to another person which is of direct and individual concern to the applicant; and a regulatory act which is of direct concern to the applicant and which does not entail implementing measures

As discussed above, Art 263, para 4 TFEU limits access to challenge by a non-privileged applicant. Other than an act which is addressed to the applicant, a non-privileged applicant can only challenge the legality of a specified act in two cases:

- an *act* addressed to another person which is of **direct and individual concern** to the applicant;
- a *regulatory act*, which is of **direct concern** to the applicant, and which does not entail implementing measures.

In contrast, the former Art 230, para 4 EC Treaty limited the right of challenge by a non-privileged applicant. Other than a decision which is addressed to the applicant, a non-privileged applicant could only challenge the legality of a specified act in two cases:

- a *decision* addressed to another person which is of **direct and individual concern** to the applicant;
- a *decision* in the form of a regulation, which is of **direct and individual concern** to the applicant.

If the measure the individual is seeking to have reviewed is 'a regulatory act which ... does not entail implementing measures' under Art 263, para 4 TFEU, then in order to have standing, an individual will only need to show 'direct concern' rather than 'direct and individual concern'. As stated above, the precise scope of what constitutes a 'regulatory act' will require clarification by the Court of Justice because this was not previously included in the former Art 230, para 4 EC Treaty. However, the case law below relating to direct concern is relevant to this new provision, and there will be further discussion as to its possible scope below.

The Court considers the issue of *direct concern* and *individual concern* as two separate issues, both of which have to be satisfied in the case of 'an act addressed to another person'.

Direct concern

With regard to 'direct concern', in the following cases the CFI (now the General Court) denied the *locus standi* of employees' representatives to challenge Commission decisions approving mergers which were likely to result in redundancies:

Comité Centrale d'Enterprise de la Société Générale des Grandes Sources and Others v Commission and Comité Centrale d'Enterprise de la Société Anonyme Vittel and Others v Commission (CASE T-96/92)

> The CFI (now the General Court) held that the employee representatives had standing to challenge the decisions of the Commission only in so far as the proposed mergers affected rights of representation of the employee organisations concerned. The CFI was not satisfied that redundancies were an inevitable consequence of the mergers. Even if they were, the effect on the *representatives* of the redundancies would 'only be of an indirect nature' and they did not, therefore, have standing to challenge the decisions.

Even individuals who the Court acknowledged ought to have been consulted as a matter of good environmental practice before a decision was made were held not to have standing to challenge the decision when it was made because the regulation did not give them a *right* to challenge it: *Associazone Agricoltori di Rovigo v Commission* (Case C-142/95).

The following cases concerned Regulation 2004/2003, which governs political parties within the European Parliament and the rules regarding their funding:

Bonde and Others v Parliament and Council (Case T-13/04), *Bonino and Others v Parliament and Council* (Case T-40/04) *and Front National and Others v Parliament and Council* (Case T-17/04)

> The CFI (now the General Court) held that Members of Parliament acting in their own name (and not on behalf of the party to which they belong) were not directly concerned by Regulation 2004/2003 because, *inter alia*, the economic consequences of that Regulation did not affect their legal position but only their factual situation. Conversely, in the *Bonino* and *Front National* cases, the CFI held that the Regulation, which creates a status for political parties at European level, directly affected certain political groupings. First, the creation of an advantageous legal status from which some political groupings could benefit while others were excluded from it was likely to affect equality of opportunity between political parties. Second, decisions on the financing of political parties taken in accordance with the criteria established by the contested Regulation came within the limited discretion of the competent authority. Such decisions were thus purely automatic in nature deriving solely from the contested Regulation without the application of other intermediary rules.
>
> The applicants' appeal to the Court of Justice was dismissed (Case C-338/05P).

So far as concerns the circumstances in which an applicant is regarded as directly concerned by the measure whose annulment he seeks, in each of the cases considered below the CFI (now the General Court) recalls that a Union measure is of direct concern to an individual if:

(i)   the measure directly affects the legal situation of the person concerned;
(ii) the measure leaves no discretion to the addressees who are entrusted with the task of implementing the measure, implementation being purely automatic and resulting from Union rules without the application of other intermediate rules.

In *Institouto N. Avgerinopoulou and Others v Commission* (T-139/02) and *Regione Siciliana v Commission* (Case T-341/02), the CFI (now the General Court) dismissed both applications for lack of direct interest because the national authorities had a *discretion* in implementing the contested measures.

In the following case, the CFI (now the General Court) clarified certain details of the application of the criterion of direct concern where decisions are adopted relating to aid granted by the ERDF. This judgment marked a certain development in relation to previous decisions made in slightly different contexts (see *SLIM Sicilia v Commission* (Case T-105/01)):

Regione Siciliana v Commission (Case T-341/02)

The applicant disputed a decision relating to the cancellation of ERDF aid granted to Italy and then paid to the applicant for the construction of a dam. The Commission argued that the decision was not of direct concern to the applicant as the Member States formed a screen between the Commission and the final beneficiary of the assistance. However, the CFI (now the General Court) dismissed that plea of inadmissibility, citing case law to the effect that for a person to be directly concerned by a measure that was not addressed to him, the measure had to directly affect the individual's legal situation and its implementation had to be purely automatic, resulting from Union rules alone to the exclusion of other intermediate rules (see *P Dreyfus v Commission* (Case C-386/96), at para 43).

With regard, first of all, to the alteration of the applicant's legal situation, the CFI held that the contested decision had the initial direct and immediate effect of changing the applicant's financial situation by depriving it of the balance of the assistance remaining to be paid by the Commission and requiring it to repay the sums paid by way of advances. As regards the criterion that the contested decision should be automatically applicable, the CFI observed that the contested decision automatically produced legal effects on the applicant as a result of Union law alone, and the national authorities enjoyed no discretion in their duty to implement the decision. The CFI dismissed the argument that the national authorities could in theory decide to release the applicant from the financial consequences that the contested decision entailed for it directly. A national decision providing funding of that magnitude would remain extraneous to the application in Union law of the contested decision. Its effect would be to put the applicant back in the situation it occupied before the contested decision was adopted, by bringing about in its turn a second alteration of the applicant's legal situation which was changed in the first place, and automatically, by the contested decision.

[Note, the CFI ruled Regione Siciliana's action as inadmissible on other grounds. Regione Siciliana's appeal to the Court of Justice was dismissed (Case C-417/04P).]

Individual concern

In the following case, the Court of Justice established a test which would be applied in future cases to ascertain whether the applicant was 'individually concerned' with the measure:

Plaumann & Co v *Commission* (Case 25/62)

Following a request to it from some German importers of clementines, the German government requested the Commission to grant it permission to suspend the collection of taxes on imports of clementines into Germany from non-Member States. The Commission refused the request in a letter addressed to the German government (i.e. a decision addressed to the government). The applicant was an importer of clementines who sought to challenge the legality of the decision. The Court of Justice had to consider whether the decision which was addressed to another person (i.e. the German government) was of direct and individual concern to the applicant. **The Court of Justice adopted the following highly restrictive test to ascertain if the applicant was individually concerned by the decision addressed to the German government:**

> **Persons other than those to whom a decision is addressed may only claim to be individually concerned if that decision affects them by reason of certain attributes which are peculiar to them or by reason of circumstances in which they are differentiated from all other persons and by virtue of these factors distinguishes them individually just as in the case of the person addressed.** In the present case the applicant is affected by the disputed Decision as an importer of clementines, that is to say, by reason of a commercial activity which may at any time be practised by any person and is not therefore such as to distinguish the applicant in relation to the contested Decision as in the case of the addressee. For these reasons the present action for annulment must be declared inadmissible. [emphasis added]

The ***Plaumann*** test has been cited in a number of later cases and should therefore be considered to be authoritative. The test can be stated as follows:

> The applicant must be differentiated from all other persons, and by reason of these distinguishing features singled out in the same way that the initial addressee was singled out.

In ***Plaumann***, the applicant failed, because in applying the test to the facts of the case, the Court of Justice held that the applicant practised a commercial activity (i.e. importing of clementines) which could be carried on by any other person in the future. He did not belong to a *closed -class* of persons on the date of the decision. Although the ***Plaumann*** test is very difficult to satisfy, in the following joined cases, the CFI (now the General Court) held that the applicants belonged to a closed -class of persons on the date of the decision, and therefore they were individually concerned with the decision:

Boyle and Others v *Commission* (Joined Cases T-218/03 to T-240/03)

This case concerned a Commission decision addressed to Ireland rejecting a request to increase the objectives of the Multiannual guidance programme for the Irish fishing fleet ('MAGP IV').

The CFI (now the General Court) held that although the applicants, who were owners of vessels belonging to the Irish fishing fleet, were not the addressees of the decision, they were nonetheless concerned by it. The request for an increase made by Ireland was made up of all of the individual requests of owners of vessels, including the applicants' requests. **Although the decision was addressed to Ireland, it applied to a series of identified vessels and had therefore to be considered to be a series of individual decisions, each affecting the legal situation of the owners of those vessels.** The number and identity of the vessel-owners in question were fixed and ascertainable even before the date of the contested decision and the Commission was in a position to know that its decision affected solely the interests and positions of those owners. **The contested decision thus concerned a closed group of identified persons at the time of its adoption, whose rights the Commission intended to regulate.** The factual situation thus created therefore characterised the applicants by reference to all other persons and distinguished them individually in the same way as an addressee of the decision.

The application of the ***Plaumann*** test is open to severe criticism; the Court not being concerned with economic reality. First, the fact that the sector of the market (e.g. importing clementines) may be dominated exclusively by one person or a few persons, may realistically prevent other persons entering that particular sector of the market. This has, in the past, been ignored by the Court of Justice. Second, the application of the test may make it virtually impossible for an individual to succeed. The Court of Justice will nearly always be able to say that the applicant does not have distinguishing features because any other person *may*, in the future, take on such distinguishing features.

The ***Plaumann*** test was applied in the following case:

A E Piraiki-Patraiki v Commission (Case 11/82)

The applicants were Greek exporters of yarn to France. They contested a Commission decision which allowed France to impose a quota system on the amount of yarn that could be imported into France from Greece during the period November 1981 to January 1982. The Court of Justice quoted the *Plaumann* test and then continued:

12. The applicants argue that they fulfil the conditions set out above since they are the main Greek undertakings which produce and export cotton yarn to France. They argue that they therefore belong to a class of traders individually identifiable on the basis of criteria having to do with the product in question, the business activities carried on and the length of time during which they have been carried on. In that regard the applicants emphasise that the production and export to France of cotton yarn of Greek origin requires industrial and commercial organisation which cannot be established from one day to the next, and certainly not during the short period of application of the decision in question.

13. That proposition cannot be accepted. It must be pointed out that the applicants are affected by the decision at issue only in their capacity as exporters to France of cotton yarn of Greek origin. The decision is not intended to limit the production of those products in any way, nor does it have such a result.

14. As for the exportation of those products to France, **that is clearly a commercial activity which can be carried on at any time by any undertaking whatever.** It follows that the decision at issue concerns the applicants in the same way as any other trader actually or potentially finding himself in the same position. The mere fact that the applicants export goods to France is not therefore sufficient to establish that they are individually concerned by the contested decision. [emphasis added]

In the following case, the Court of Justice held that there was an exception to the general restrictive principle, provided the decision concerned a set of past events:

Alfred Toepfer and Getreide-Import Gesellschaft v *Commission* (Cases 106 and 107/63)

The applicants were importers of grain. They applied to the German authorities on 1 October 1963 for an import licence. On this date the duty on such imports was zero. However, Germany had requested the Commission to raise the duty with immediate effect. To comply with this request, the Commission, in a decision addressed to the German authorities, confirmed that all applications made on 1 October would be rejected and that duty would be imposed from 2 October. The applicants sought to have this decision annulled. The Court of Justice held the applicant had standing because:

... the only persons concerned by the said measures were importers who had applied for an import licence during the course of the day of 1 October 1963. The number and identity of these importers had already become fixed and ascertainable before 4 October, when the contested decision was made. The Commission was in a position to know that its decision affected the interests and the position of the said importers alone.

The factual situation thus created differentiates the said importers, including the applicants, from all other persons and distinguishes them individually just as in the case of the person addressed.

Therefore the objection of inadmissibility which has been raised is unfounded and the applications are admissible.

Similar to the *Piraiki-Patraiki* case above, some of the Greek exporters had already entered into contracts for the export of cotton yarn to France on the date the decision to impose quotas was made. Accordingly, the Court of Justice held that such exporters satisfied the test in so far as they could show that:

17. ... before the date of the contested decision they had entered into contracts with French customers for the delivery of cotton yarn from Greece during the period of application of that decision.

Some greater flexibility has, however, been shown by the CFI (now the General Court) in allowing a journalist to apply for the annulment of a decision refusing access to documents without requiring him to show a special interest above others affected by the refusal (*Svenska Journalist-forbundet* v *Council of the European Union* (Case T-174/95)). Also, individuals who have complained that the conduct of an undertaking infringes the former Art 82 EC Treaty (now Art 102 TFEU), where the Commission refuses to investigate the complaint, will have standing to challenge that refusal (*Demo-Studio Schmidt* v *Commission* (Case 210/81); compare, *Lord Bethell* v *Commission* (Case 246/81)).

In the following cases, the CFI (now the General Court) considered the issue of 'individual concern' where the applicant is an association of undertakings (e.g. a group of companies):

Bundesverband der Nahrungsmittel- und Speiseresteverwertung and Kloh v *Parliament and Council* (Case T-391/02) *and Schmoldt and Others* v *Commission* (Case T-264/03)

The CFI (now the General Court) held that where a legal person bringing an action for annulment is an association of undertakings (e.g. a group of companies), it may, when it has taken part in the procedure leading to the adoption of the contested measure, be granted standing in at least three kinds of circumstances:

1. where a legal provision expressly grants it a series of procedural powers;

2. where the association itself is distinguished individually because its own interests as an association are affected, in particular because its negotiating position has been affected by the measure whose annulment is being sought;

3. where it represents the interests of undertakings which would themselves be entitled to bring proceedings.

In these cases, the CFI refused to accept that the applicant associations had occupied a clearly circumscribed position as negotiator which was intimately linked to the subject-matter of the contested measure.

A more flexible application of the 'individual concern' test

The CFI (now the General Court) and Court of Justice have reconsidered past case law, and addressed the issue of whether or not the strict application of the test, with regard to 'individual concern', should be relaxed. In *Jégo-Quéré et Cie SA* v *Commission* (Case T-177/01), the CFI decided that there should be a departure from application of the *Plaumann* test:

> a natural or legal person is to be regarded as individually concerned by a Community [i.e. Union] measure of general application that concerns him directly if the measure in question affects his legal position, in a manner which is both definite and immediate, by restricting his rights or imposing obligations on him. The number and position of other persons who are likewise affected by the measure, or who may be so, are of no relevance in that regard.

However, this judgment received a swift rebuff from the Court of Justice less than three months later:

Unión de Pequeños Agricultores v *Council of the European Union (supported by the Commission)* (Case C-50/00P)

The Unión had applied for the partial annulment of a regulation pursuant to the former Art 230 EC Treaty (now Art 263 TFEU). The CFI rejected the application and the Unión appealed to the Court of Justice. The Court of Justice held as follows:

40. By Article 173 [which was replaced by Art 230 EC Treaty, and is now Art 263 TFEU] and Article 184 [which was replaced by Art 241 EC Treaty and is now Art 277 TFEU], on the one hand, and by Article 177 [which was replaced by Art 234 EC Treaty, and is now Art 267 TFEU], on the other, the Treaty has established a complete system of legal remedies and procedures designed to ensure judicial review of the legality of acts of the institutions, and has entrusted such review to the Community [i.e. Union] Courts (see, to that effect, *Les Verts* v *Parliament*, paragraph 23). Under that system, where natural or legal persons cannot, by reason of the conditions for admissibility laid down in the fourth paragraph of Article 173 of the Treaty [now Art 263, para 4 TFEU], directly challenge Community [i.e. Union] measures of general application, they are able, depending on the case, either indirectly to plead the invalidity of such acts before the Community [i.e. Union] Courts under Article 184 of the Treaty [now Art 277 TFEU] or to do so before the national courts and ask them, since they have no jurisdiction themselves to declare those measures invalid (see Case 314/85 *Foto-Frost* [1987] ECR 4199, paragraph 20), to make a reference to the Court of Justice for a preliminary ruling on validity.

41. Thus it is for the Member States to establish a system of legal remedies and procedures which ensure respect for the right to effective judicial protection.

42. In that context, in accordance with the principle of sincere cooperation laid down in Article 5 of the Treaty [which was replaced by Art 10 EC Treaty], national courts are required, so far as possible, to interpret and apply national procedural rules governing

the exercise of rights of action in a way that enables natural and legal persons to chal-lenge before the courts the legality of any decision or other national measure relative to the application to them of a Community [i.e. Union] act of general application, by pleading the invalidity of such an act.

43. As the Advocate General has pointed out in paragraphs 50 to 53 of his Opinion, it is not acceptable to adopt an interpretation of the system of remedies, such as that favoured by the appellant, to the effect that a direct action for annulment before the Community [i.e. Union] Court will be available where it can be shown, following an examination by that Court of the particular national procedural rules, that those rules do not allow the individual to bring proceedings to contest the validity of the Community [i.e. Union] measure at issue. Such an interpretation would require the Community [i.e. Union] Court, in each individual case, to examine and interpret national procedural law. That would go beyond its jurisdiction when reviewing the legality of Community [i.e. Union] measures.

44. Finally, it should be added that, according to the system for judicial review of legality established by the Treaty, a natural or legal person can bring an action challenging a regulation only if it is concerned both directly and individually. Although this last con-dition must be interpreted in the light of the principle of effective judicial protection by taking account of the various circumstances that may distinguish an applicant individu-ally (see, for example, Joined Cases 67/85, 68/85 and 70/85 *Van der Kooy* v *Commis-sion* [1988] ECR 219, paragraph 14; *Extramet Industrie* v *Council*, paragraph 13, and *Codorniu* v *Council*, paragraph 19), such an interpretation cannot have the effect of setting aside the condition in question, expressly laid down in the Treaty, without going beyond the jurisdiction conferred by the Treaty on the Community [i.e. Union] Courts.

45. While it is, admittedly, possible to envisage a system of judicial review of the legality of Community [i.e. Union] measures of general application different from that established by the founding Treaty and never amended as to its principles, it is for the Member States, if necessary, in accordance with Article 48 [T]EU to reform the system currently in force.

46. In the light of the foregoing, the Court finds that the Court of First Instance did not err in law when it declared the appellant's application inadmissible without examining whether, in the particular case, there was a remedy before a national court enabling the validity of the contested regulation to be examined.

In the above case, the Court of Justice held that the pre-*Jégo-Quéré* case law was correct, and that to depart from this case law would be to depart from the Treaty provisions. If the Member States sought to extend the rights of individuals to challenge Union measures, then that could only come about by an amendment to the Treaty. The CFI's judgment in *Jégo-Quéré* was overruled. The Court of Justice subsequently reversed the CFI's judgment when *Jégo-Quéré* came before it on appeal from the CFI (Case C-263/02P).

Regulatory act which does not entail implementing measures

An interesting comment made by the Court of Justice at para 45 in the above case may pro-vide some guidance on the possible scope of 'regulatory act' within Art 267, para 4 TFEU. As discussed above, if the measure the individual is seeking to have reviewed is 'a regula-tory act which … does not entail implementing measures' under Art 263, para 4 TFEU, then in order to have standing, an individual will only need to show 'direct concern' rather than 'direct *and individual* concern'. At para 45 of the above case the Court of Justice recog-nised that 'it is, admittedly, possible to envisage a system of judicial review of the legality of Community [i.e. Union] measures of general application different from that established by the founding Treaty'. However, the Court recognised that this would require the Treaty to be amended. When the ToL came into force on 1 December 2009, Art 263, para 4 TFEU contained this new provision relating to 'regulatory act' and the above case law may assist in ascertaining its precise scope. Ultimately, however, this question can only be resolved by decisions of the General Court and the Court of Justice.

Competition cases

In the field of state aid, actions mainly seek the annulment either of: (i) a decision taken without opening the formal investigation procedure referred to in the former Art 88(2) EC Treaty (now Art 108(2) TFEU); or (ii) a decision taken at the end of that procedure (see Chapter 19). As those decisions are addressed to the Member State concerned, it is for the undertaking, which is not the addressee, to show that that measure is of *direct and individual concern* to it.

In its judgment in *Commission* v *Aktiongemeinschaft Recht und Eigentum* (Case C-78/03P), the Court of Justice held that:

- an action for the annulment of a decision taken on conclusion of the preliminary phase of examination of aid under the former Art 88(3) EC Treaty (now Art 108(3) TFEU), brought by a person who is concerned within the meaning of the former Art 88(2) EC Treaty (now Art 108(2) TFEU), where he seeks to safeguard the procedural rights available to him under the latter provision, is admissible (i.e. he has direct and individual concern in the decision);

- where an applicant calls in question the merits of the decision appraising the aid as such or a decision taken at the end of the formal investigation procedure, an action for annulment of such a decision is admissible only if he succeeds in establishing that he has a particular status within the meaning of the judgment in *Plaumann* v *Commission* (see above).

In *Air One* v *Commission* (Case T-395/04), the CFI (now the General Court) clarified the application of that distinction where the Commission took a decision without initiating the formal review procedure. In this case, the applicant, an Italian airline company, complained to the Commission alleging that the Italian authorities granted unlawful aid to the air carrier Ryanair in the form of reduced prices for the use of airport and ground-handling services. The applicant also called upon the Commission to order Italy to suspend those aid payments. In so far as this was an action for failure to act (see below), the CFI needed to establish the admissibility of an action brought by the applicant for annulment of at least one of the measures the Commission could have adopted on conclusion of the preliminary procedure for examination of aid. To that end the CFI applied the case law of the Court of Justice and it clarified the definition of 'sufficient relationship of competition' for an undertaking to be considered a competitor of the recipients of aid and, therefore, concerned within the meaning of the former Art 88(2) EC Treaty (now Art 108(2) TFEU). The CFI held that the action was admissible. It was sufficient to establish that the applicant and the recipient of aid jointly operate, directly or indirectly, an international airline and that the applicant aims to develop scheduled passenger transport services from or to Italian airports, *inter alia* regional airports, in relation to which it may be in competition with the recipient.

In *Danske Busvognmaend* v *Commission* (Case T-157/01), a trade association representing the interests of the majority of Danish bus companies was recognised by the CFI (now the General Court) as having the status of a 'party concerned', on the ground that when it made a complaint to the Commission its interventions influenced the course of the administrative procedure and that at least some of its members were in competition with the undertaking which benefited from the disputed aid.

In *Kronofrance v Commission* (Case T-27/02), the CFI (now the General Court) held that the applicant, who had pleaded the failure to open the formal investigation procedure, was a 'party concerned' in light of its status as a competitor, a status established by having regard to the identity of the products manufactured by it with those of the undertaking benefiting from the aid and to the fact that their sales areas overlapped.

In *Thermenhotel Stoiser Franz and Others v Commission* (Case T-158/99), the CFI (now the General Court) held that hotel operators in a tourist resort in the Province of Styria (Austria) were entitled to challenge the legality of a Commission decision declaring the public financing of the construction of a luxury hotel in the same resort to be compatible with the internal market. The CFI observed that the applicants were direct competitors of the hotel receiving the aid in question and that they were recognised as having this status in the contested decision.

In the last three of the above cases it was held that the applicant undertakings were, in their capacity as parties concerned within the meaning of the former Art 88(2) EC Treaty (now Art 108(2) TFEU), individually concerned by the decisions that the aid was compatible with the internal market. It should be noted, with regard to the extent of the review of the pleas, that in one instance the CFI (now the General Court) regarded the pleas for annulment in their entirety as seeking to establish that the Commission had unlawfully failed to open the formal investigation procedure (*Thermenhotel Stoiser Franz*), whereas in another instance it annulled the decision approving the grant of aid on its merits (*Danske Busvognmaend*).

Where the contested decision has been adopted at the end of the formal investigation procedure provided for by the former Art 88(2) EC Treaty (now Art 108(2) TFEU), it is not sufficient, in order for an undertaking to be distinguished individually in the same way as the addressee of the decision, that it has the status of a 'party concerned'. According to the case law, such a decision is of individual concern to the undertakings which were at the origin of the complaint which led to that procedure and whose views were heard and determined the conduct of the procedure, provided that their position on the market is *substantially affected* by the aid which is the subject of that decision.

Applying these criteria, the CFI (now the General Court) held that the Austrian company Lenzing was individually concerned by a Commission decision concerning the state aid granted by Spain to the company Sniace, because Lenzing, a competitor of the recipient company: (i) was at the origin of the complaint that led to the opening of the procedure and participated actively in the procedure; and (ii) provided information such as would show that its position on the market was substantially affected by the contested decision, for instance information concerning the characteristics of the market in question, namely a very limited number of producers, fierce competition and significant production surpluses (*Lenzing v Commission* (Case T-36/99) – Spain appealed the CFI's judgment, but this appeal was dismissed by the Court of Justice (*Spain v Lenzing* Case C-525/04P)).

Conversely, in *Deutsche Post and DHL v Commission* (Case T-358/02) the CFI (now the General Court) found that Deutsche Post and DHL International, two companies operating on the Italian market in postal services which were open to competition, had not played an active role during the administrative procedure which preceded the adoption of the decision relating to state aid granted by Italy in favour of Poste Italiane. It therefore examined whether the measure authorised by that decision was nevertheless liable to affect significantly their position on the market in question and concluded, in the absence of sufficient proof of the magnitude of the prejudice to their position on the market, that this was not the case.

This was likewise the situation in the following case (which has been considered above):

Sniace v Commission (Case T-88/01)

Sniace disputed a Commission decision which found measures adopted for the benefit of Lenzing Lyocell, an Austrian company, to be compatible with the internal market. The CFI (now the General Court) raised of its own motion the question of the applicant's standing to bring proceedings over that decision and, in particular, the question whether it was of individual concern to it in the light of the criteria defined for the first time by the Court of Justice in its judgment *COFAZ and Others v Commission* (Case 169/84), at para 25. According to those criteria, in the field of state aid, not only the undertaking in receipt of the aid but also the undertakings competing with it which have played an active role in the procedure initiated pursuant to the former Art 88(2) EC Treaty (now Art 108(2) TFEU) in respect of an individual grant of aid are recognised as being individually concerned by the Commission decision closing that procedure, provided that their position on the market is substantially affected by the aid which is the subject of the contested decision. That was not the position in this case. First, the applicant played only a minor role in the course of the administrative procedure, as it lodged no complaint nor any observations which had a significant impact on the conduct of the procedure. Second, analysis of the physical characteristics, the price and the manufacturing processes of the products sold by the applicant and Lenzing Lyocell did not lead the CFI to find that they were in direct competition, as the applicant did not establish that the contested decision was capable of significantly affecting its position on the market.

Sniace's appeal to the Court of Justice was dismissed (Case C-260/05P).

The following case concerned Union merger law, and likewise deviated from the 'normal' rules relating to non-privileged applicants. The General Court held that consumer associations have the right to be heard, in the context of the administrative procedure before the Commission relating to a merger investigation, subject to compliance with two conditions:

Association belge des consommateurs test-achats ASBL v Commission (Case T-224/10)

The Association belge des consommateurs test-achats (ABCTA) is a non-profit organisation which has as its main objective the protection of consumer interests and, in particular, of consumer interests in Belgium. With c. 350,000 individual members, it is the largest consumer association in Belgium.

In June 2009, ABCTA learned that Électricité de France (EDF) had announced its intention to acquire exclusive control of Segebel SA, a holding company whose only asset was a 51 per cent shareholding stake in SPE SA, the second largest electricity operator in Belgium after the incumbent operator Electrabel SA, which was controlled by GDF Suez SA. At the material time, the French State held 84.6 per cent of the shares in EDF. The French State held a minority shareholding interest of 35.91 per cent in GDF Suez.

On 23 June 2009, ABCTA sent a letter to the European Commission expressing its concerns about the merger at issue. It requested the Commission to consider the negative consequences for competition which, it claimed, would be brought about as a result of the French State's shareholding in EDF and GDF Suez, particularly on the Belgian markets for gas and electricity. In July 2009, the Commission replied to ABCTA that its observations would be taken into account in the analysis of the merger at issue.

On 23 September 2009, EDF notified the merger at issue to the Commission. On 30 September 2009, a notification notice was published in the *Official Journal* of the European Union, inviting interested third parties to submit their observations. ABCTA did not react to that notification.

On 12 November 2009, the Commission adopted: (i) a decision (Decision C 2009/8954) by which it rejected a request from the competent Belgian authorities for partial referral of the merger investigation (the non-referral decision); and (ii) a decision (Decision C 2009/9059) by which it declared the merger at issue to be compatible with the internal market (the clearance decision).

ABCTA applied to the General Court to have those two Commission decisions annulled.

The application for annulment of the clearance decision

The Court observed that a natural or legal person may institute proceedings against a decision addressed to another person only if that decision was of direct and individual concern to the former. However, it followed from the Court's case -law that, for Commission decisions relating to the compatibility of a merger with the internal market, the *locus standi* of third parties concerned by a merger must be assessed differently depending on whether they: (i) relied on defects affecting the substance of those decisions ('first category' of interested third parties); or (ii) submitted that the Commission infringed procedural rights granted to them by the acts of Union law governing the monitoring of mergers ('second category' of interested third parties).

So far as concerned the first category, it was necessary for those third parties to be individually concerned by the contested decision. In other words, the decision at issue had to affect those third parties by reason of certain attributes which were peculiar to them or by reason of a factual situation which differentiated them from all other persons and thereby distinguished them individually in the same way as the addressee. ABCTA, however, did not come within the first category as it was not individually concerned by the Commission decision.

So far as concerned the second category, the Court stated that, according to EU law, consumer associations enjoyed a procedural right to be heard, in the context of the administrative procedure before the Commission relating to a merger investigation, subject to compliance with two conditions: (i) the merger had to relate to goods or services used by final consumers; and (ii) an application to be heard by the Commission during the investigation procedure had to actually have been made in writing by the association.

While the Court found that ABCTA satisfied the first condition – the merger at issue being likely to have effects, at least secondary effects, on consumers – that association did not, however, satisfy the second condition.

In that regard, the Court pointed out that the steps third parties were required to follow in order to be involved in a merger investigation procedure had to be taken following the formal notification of the merger. That would make it possible, in the interest of third parties, to avoid the situation in which such requests were made by them before the Commission had determined the purpose of the merger investigation procedure, at the time of notification of the transaction at issue.

Furthermore, that meant that the Commission did not have to separate systematically, from among the requests received, those which concerned transactions attributable only to abstract hypotheses, or even to mere hearsay, from those which concerned transactions resulting in a notification. The opposite scenario would be inconsistent with the need for rapid action which characterised the EU rules on merger investigation.

In the present case, ABCTA had asked the Commission to be heard in the context of the merger investigation procedure two months prior to notification of the merger. However, that fact could not make up for the non-renewal of that application or for the lack of any initiative on the part of ABCTA, once the economic transaction envisaged by EDF and Segebel, of which ABCTA had prior knowledge, had in fact become a duly notified merger and thus set in motion the procedure in the context of which ABCTA wished to be heard.

The application for annulment of the non-referral decision
According to settled case -law, a third party concerned by a merger was entitled to challenge, before the General Court, the Commission's decision to uphold a national competition authority's referral request.

By contrast, the Court held that interested third parties were not entitled to challenge a non-referral decision by which the Commission rejected a request for referral brought by a national authority.

The procedural rights and judicial protection that EU law conferred on those third parties were not in any way jeopardised by the non-referral decision. Quite to the contrary, that decision ensured for third parties concerned by a concentration with a Union dimension that: (i) the merger would be assessed by the Commission in the light of EU law; and (ii) the General Court would be the judicial body having jurisdiction to deal with any action against the Commission's decision bringing the procedure to an end.

Consequently, the General Court dismissed the action as being inadmissible.

Decisions in the form of regulations: regulatory acts which do not entail implementing measures?

Under the former Art 230, para 4 EC Treaty, an individual could challenge the legality of a regulation provided it was in reality a decision which was of direct and individual concern to him. While this is not explicitly required within the context of Art 263, para 4 TFEU (because it now refers to an 'act' rather than a 'decision'), the cases decided under the former provision are included here because they may be relevant to future decisions on the scope of 'act' under Art 263, para 4 TFEU. Further, they could also be relevant to the scope of 'regulatory act' under Art 263, para 4 TFEU.

The test which the Court of Justice applied in this situation has been just as stringent as that applied in the *Plaumann* case (above), as illustrated in the following case:

Calpak SpA and Società Emiliana Lavorazione Frutta SpA v *Commission* (Cases 789 and 790/79)

Under the terms of a regulation, aid was to be granted to the producers of pears calculated on the basis of the average production over the previous three years. A later regulation provided that aid would now be assessed on the basis of one marketing year in which production was low. The applicants – who were pear producers – challenged the legality of the latter regulation, claiming it was in fact a decision, and argued that because they belonged to a closed class of persons (i.e. they were readily identifiable by the Commission on the date the regulation was passed), they therefore had the necessary standing. The Court of Justice held as follows [emphasis added]:

6. The Commission's main contention is that as the disputed provisions were adopted in the form of regulations, their annulment may only be sought if their content shows them to be, in fact, decisions. But in the Commission's view the provisions in question, which lay down rules of general application, are truly in the nature of regulations within the meaning of Article 189 of the Treaty [which was replaced by Art 249 EC Treaty, and is now Art 288 TFEU] ...

7. The second paragraph of Article 173 [which was replaced by Art 230 EC Treaty, and is now Art 263 TFEU] empowers individuals to contest, *inter alia*, any decision which, although in the form of a regulation, is of direct and individual concern to them. The objective of that provision is in particular to prevent the Community [i.e. Union] institutions from being in a position, merely by choosing the form of a regulation, to exclude an application by an individual against a decision which concerns him directly and individually; it therefore stipulates that the choice of form cannot change the nature of the measure.

8. By virtue of the second paragraph of Article 189 of the Treaty [now Art 288 TFEU] **the criterion for distinguishing between a regulation and a decision is whether the measure is of general application or not** ...

9. A provision which limits the granting of production aid for all producers in respect of a particular product to a uniform percentage of the quantity produced by them during a uniform period is by nature a measure of general application within the meaning of Article 189 of the Treaty [now Art 288 TFEU]. **In fact the measure applies to objectively determined situations and produces legal effects with regard to categories of persons described in a generalised and abstract manner.** The nature of the measure as a regulation is not called in question by the mere fact that it is possible to determine the number or even the identity of the producers to be granted the aid which is limited thereby.

10. Nor is the fact that the choice of reference period is particularly important for the applicants, whose production is subject to considerable variation from one marketing year to another as a result of their own programme of production, sufficient to entitle them to an individual remedy. Moreover, the applicants have not established the existence of circumstances such as to justify describing that choice ... as a decision adopted specifically in relation to them and, as such, entitling them to institute proceedings under the second paragraph of Article 173 [now Art 263 TFEU].

11. It follows that the objection raised by the Commission must be accepted as regards the applications for the annulment of the provisions in the two regulations in question.

Paragraph 9 of the above judgment is particularly important, as it demonstrates the very restrictive nature of the test. A regulation is the correct form of Union instrument (rather than a decision) provided it applies to 'objectively determined situations and produces legal effects with regard to persons described in a generalised and abstract manner'. It could be possible for the Commission to draft a regulation in such terms in almost every situation, thus ensuring the regulation could not be challenged by an aggrieved individual pursuant to the former Art 230 EC Treaty (although it may constitute either an 'act' or a 'regulatory act' pursuant to Art 263, para 4 TFEU; see above).

The Court of Justice has made an exception in relation to a regulation which applies to a completed set of past events. For example, in **International Fruit Company BV v Commission** (Cases 41–44/70), the Court held that the regulation in question applied to a closed category of persons on the date the regulation was passed, i.e. those who had made import applications in the previous week. Accordingly, an action to challenge the regulation by a person falling within this class was admissible.

Also, in the case of anti-dumping regulations, the Court has accepted the standing of a company to challenge a regulation of a general character (**Codorniu** (Case C-309/89)). If the regulation is intended to affect a specific group of undertakings, it may be 'a conglomeration of individual decisions ... under the guise of a regulation', and those affected may have the status to challenge it (**International Fruit Co v Commission** (Case 41/70)).

As discussed above, if the measure the individual is seeking to have reviewed is 'a regulatory act which ... does not entail implementing measures' under Art 263, para 4 TFEU, then in order to have standing, an individual will only need to show 'direct concern' rather than 'direct and individual concern'. It is possible that the above scenarios may be the type of 'regulatory act' which the drafters of the new provision had in mind.

Article 263 TFEU: the legal basis for a challenge

Objective 2

Article 263, para 2 TFEU (and the former Art 230, para 2 EC Treaty) provides four possible bases (i.e. grounds) for a challenge. These are:

- lack of competence;
- infringement of an essential procedural requirement;
- infringement of the Treaty or any rule of law relating to its application;
- misuse of powers.

These are not mutually exclusive and two or more may be cited together in an application for judicial review. Each of these four grounds will now be considered in more detail.

Lack of competence

This corresponds in English law to *substantive ultra vires* – a body can only do that which it is authorised to do by law. A number of challenges have been mounted on the grounds that the Commission has chosen the wrong legal base for the proposal of a legislative act (see *Commission v Council (Re Titanium Dioxide Waste)* (Case C-300/89)). In *Germany, France, Netherlands, Denmark and the UK v Commission* (Cases 281, 283–285, 287/85), the Commission had adopted a decision under what is now Art 153 TFEU under which Member States were required to consult with the Commission on measures relating to the integration of workers from states outside the Union. The Court of Justice held that the social policy objects of what is now Art 153 TFEU were confined to measures that affected migrants from other Member States, and did not extend, as this decision purported to do, to measures affecting only migrants from states outside the Union.

There are not a great many challenges which are successful on this basis, but the following two cases are examples of where such challenges *were* successful:

The concept of legal base is considered in detail at pages 67–68 and 134–135.

France v Commission (Case C-327/91)

The Commission had concluded an agreement with the USA to promote cooperation and coordination and to lessen the possibility of conflict between the parties in the application of their competition laws. The case concerned the competence of the Commission to conclude the agreement. In a challenge by the French government, the Court held that the Commission did not have the competence to do so. Under the former Art 228 EC Treaty (before amendment by the TEU) the Commission had the power to negotiate agreements with states outside the Union or with international organisations, but they had to be concluded by the Council.

Laboratoires Servier v *Commission* (Case T-147/00)

> The CFI (now the General Court) annulled a Commission decision withdrawing marketing authorisation for certain medicinal products, on the basis of a ground relating to a matter of public policy raised by it of its own motion. The CFI observed that the lack of competence of an institution which has adopted a contested measure constitutes a ground for annulment for reasons of public policy, which must be raised by the Union judicature of its own motion. The decision of the CFI was appealed to the Court of Justice; the appeal was dismissed (Case C-156/03P).

The relationship between the power of the Union judicature to raise a ground of its own motion and the existence of a public policy interest underlying the ground was confirmed in *Strabag Benelux* v *Council* (Case T-183/00), para 37 and in *Henkel* v *OHIM – LHS (UK)* (Case T-308/01), para 34.

Infringement of an essential procedural requirement

This is probably the most oft-cited basis of challenge and is equivalent in English law to *procedural ultra vires*. It comprises breaches of both formal procedural requirements laid down in the Treaties and in secondary legislation, and the more informal rules of fairness required by general principles of Union law (see Chapter 2). The most important general procedural requirement in the Treaties is that laid down in Art 296 TFEU (previously Art 253 EC Treaty), under which secondary legislation must state the reasons on which it is based. The CFI (now the General Court) emphasised the importance of this provision in the following case:

Eugénio Branco Ld v *Commission* (Case T-85/94)

> The CFI (now the General Court) stated that:
>
> > According to a consistent line of case law, the purpose of the obligation to state the reasons on which an individual decision is based is to enable the Community [i.e. Union] judicature to review the legality of the decision and to provide the person concerned with sufficient information to make it possible to ascertain whether the decision is well founded or whether it is vitiated by a defect which may permit its legality to be contested. The extent of that obligation depends on the nature of the measure in question and on the context in which it was adopted.

In the above case, and two similar previous cases, the Court annulled Commission decisions withdrawing approval or partial support of projects financed by the European Social Fund. Besides the obligation imposed by what is now Art 296 TFEU, there was also a breach of the requirement imposed by Art 6(1), Regulation 2950/83 under which the Commission, before deciding to suspend, reduce or withdraw fund aid, had to give the relevant Member State the opportunity to comment (*Consorgan Lda* v *Commission* (Case C-181/90); *Socurte Ld and Others* v *Commission* (Cases T-432, 434/93)).

Breach of a procedural requirement may be so fundamental that the decision or other measure may be void *ab initio*, i.e. the decision will be held to have never existed. This issue arose in the following case:

Commission v BASF AG and Others (Case C-137/92P)

The CFI had dismissed as inadmissible actions for annulment of a measure that purported to have been taken by the Commission under the former Art 81 EC Treaty (now Art 101 TFEU) on the ground that the measure was 'non-existent'. The Court of Justice allowed an appeal. The Court stated that acts of the Union institutions are presumed to be lawful and accordingly produce legal effects, even if they are tainted by irregularities, until such time as they are annulled or withdrawn. However, it held that there are some acts so tainted by irregularity, whose gravity is so obvious, that they cannot be tolerated by the Union legal order. They must be treated as having no legal effect, even provisional. The Court said that such a conclusion, with all its potentially serious consequences, should be reached only in 'quite extreme circumstances'. In this case, both the operative part of the decision and the reasons for it had been adopted by a single Commissioner and three of the texts of the decision in the relevant languages had never been seen by the full Commission, contrary to the Commission's Rules of Procedure. It constituted a breach of an essential procedural requirement and was consequently annulled by the Court. The decision of the Commission had not, however, been 'non-existent'.

Infringement of the Treaty or any rule relating to its application

There is an obvious overlap between Art 296 TFEU, the need to give reasons, procedural requirements, and the general principles of fairness and natural justice which are fundamental principles of Union law. In addition there are also the rights set out in the ECHR, together with the principles of non-discrimination, proportionality, legitimate expectation, respect for property rights and equal treatment (see Chapter 2). These latter rights and principles are not absolute and may, in appropriate circumstances, have to give way to restrictions imposed in the interest of the common organisation of the internal market, 'provided that those restrictions in fact correspond to objectives of general interest pursued by the Community [i.e. Union], and do not constitute a disproportionate and intolerable interference, impairing the very substance of the rights guaranteed' (***Germany v Commission (Re Banana Market)*** (Case C-280/93)).

Misuse of powers

This ground for challenge stems from the French *détournement de pouvoir*. This is the equivalent, in English administrative law, of using a power for an improper or illegitimate purpose. As the power is itself lawful, a challenger must prove a subjective matter, the purpose for which it has been used (***Netherlands v High Authority*** (Case 6/54)). As outsiders are not privy to the reasons for institutional decisions unless they are made public, most of the few successful cases have relied on published documents, or the reasons given under what is now Art 296 TFEU, which indicate that the institution has misunderstood the purpose for which a power has been conferred on it (***Giuffrida v Council*** (Case 105/75)).

The UK's challenge to the Working Time Directive: a case study

In 1990, the Commission proposed a directive to regulate working time, under the health and safety provisions of the former Art 118a EC Treaty (which was replaced by Art 137 EC Treaty, and is now Art 153 TFEU (OJ 1990 C 254/4)). The legislative procedure which applied to the former Art 118a empowered the Council to adopt the proposal acting by a qualified majority (see Chapter 4). The Working Time Directive 93/104 was adopted by the Council, acting by a qualified majority, on 23 November 1993, with an implementation date of 23 November 1996 (OJ 1993 L 307/18). Eleven of the then 12 Member States voted in favour. The UK abstained and indicated that it would challenge the legality of the directive.

On 8 March 1994 the UK brought an action under what is now Art 263 TFEU for the annulment of the directive and, in the alternative, the annulment of specific parts of the directive including, *inter alia*, the second sentence of Art 5 of the directive. The second sentence of Art 5 provided that the minimum weekly rest period should 'in principle include Sunday'. In *UK v Council of the European Union* (Case C-84/94), in support of its action, the UK relied on four pleas:

1 the legal base of the directive was defective;

2 breach of the principle of proportionality;

3 misuse of powers;

4 infringement of essential procedural requirements.

Defective legal base

The main thrust of the UK's argument centred around the first plea that the directive was not concerned with the improvement of the health and safety of workers and therefore should not have been adopted under the former Art 118a (now Art 153 TFEU). It was contended that the correct legal base was either the former Art 100 EC Treaty (which was replaced by Art 94 EC Treaty, and is now Art 115 TFEU) or the former Art 235 EC Treaty (which was replaced by Art 308 EC Treaty, and is now Art 352 TFEU), which at the time both required unanimity within the Council of Ministers.

The former Art 100 EC Treaty empowered the Council of Ministers to adopt directives which directly affected the establishment or functioning of the internal market, by a *unanimous* vote. The former Art 100a EC Treaty derogated from the former Art 100 in that it empowered the Council of Ministers to adopt directives which directly affected the establishment or functioning of the internal market by a *qualified majority* while specifically excluding provisions 'relating to the rights and interests of employed persons'.

The UK first argued that provisions which related to the rights and interests of employed persons and which directly affected the internal market would, as a general rule, have to be enacted under the former Art 100. The Court of Justice rejected this submission. It held that the former Art 118a was a more specific legal base than the former Arts 100 and 100a and this was confirmed by the actual wording of the former Art 100a(1) which stated that its provisions applied 'save where otherwise provided in this Treaty'. Therefore the more specific legal base of the former Art 118a was to be preferred.

Second, the UK argued that a strict interpretation of the former Art 118a EC Treaty only permitted the adoption of directives with a genuine and objective link to the health and safety of workers and which therefore related to physical conditions and risks at the workplace. This did not apply to measures concerning, in particular, weekly working time (Art 6 of the Directive), paid annual leave (Art 7) and rest periods (Arts 4 and 5), whose connection with the health and safety of workers was tenuous. The UK's alternative plea was for the annulment of these specific provisions. This was also rejected by the Court of Justice, which held that a broad scope was to be given to health and safety. This was supported by reference to the Constitution of the World Health Organization (to which all the Member States belong), in which 'health' is defined as 'a state of complete physical, mental and social well-being which does not consist only in the absence of illness or infirmity'. The UK additionally argued that the reference to the adoption of 'minimum requirements' in the former Art 118a(2) empowered the Council of Ministers only to adopt measures which were at a level acceptable to all Member States, and which constituted a minimum benchmark. This was similarly rejected by the Court. The reference to 'minimum requirements' enabled Member States to adopt more stringent measures than those contained in the directive, as confirmed by the former Art 118a(3).

Third, it was argued by the UK that the former Art 118a did not empower the Council to adopt directives which dealt with the question of health and safety in a 'generalised, unspecific and unscientific manner'. The UK supported this argument with reference to previous directives which had been adopted under the former Art 118a, which covered specific areas of activity. The Court likewise rejected this argument. Past practice of the Council could not create a precedent binding on the Union institutions with regard to the correct legal base. In any event, the Health and Safety Framework Directive 89/391 (OJ 1989 L 183/1), which had been adopted under the former Art 118a, had a general, unspecific scope.

The Court of Justice concluded that 'where the principal aim of the measure in question is the protection of the health and safety of workers, [the former] Art 118a must be used, albeit such a measure may have ancillary effects on the establishment and functioning of the internal market'.

Having set out the legal rationale for the adoption of a directive under the former Art 118a, the Court examined whether, in the particular circumstances of this case, the Working Time Directive had been properly adopted under this article. The Court noted that the approach taken by the directive, viewing the organisation of working time essentially in terms of the favourable impact it may have on the health and safety of workers, was apparent from its preamble. While it could not be denied that the directive might affect employment, its essential and overriding objective was one of health and safety. However, the Court did not accept that choosing Sunday as the weekly rest day (Art 5, second sentence) was more closely connected to the health and safety of workers than any other day of the week. The Court therefore upheld this part of the UK's alternative claim. The second sentence of Art 5, which could be severed from the other provisions of the directive, was annulled.

With regard to the former Art 235 EC Treaty, the Court of Justice simply noted that the article could be used as the legal base for a measure only where no other Treaty provision conferred on the Union institutions the necessary power to adopt it; this was not the case here.

Breach of the principle of proportionality

First, the UK argued that not all measures which may 'improve' the level of the health and safety protection of workers constitute minimum requirements. This was rejected by the Court of Justice, which reiterated the point made above that the concept of 'minimum requirements' does not limit Union action to the lowest level of protection provided by the various Member States, but means a Member State can adopt provisions more stringent than those of the directive.

Second, it was argued by the UK that the application of the principle of proportionality would require the directive's objective of safeguarding the health and safety of workers to be attained by measures which were less restrictive and involved fewer obstacles to the competitiveness of industry and the earning capacity of individuals. The Court held that the Council, acting as legislature, must be allowed a wide discretion where it was making social policy choices and was required to carry out complex assessments. The Court would only rule the measure to be disproportionate if the exercise of the Council's discretion had been vitiated by manifest error or misuse of powers, or if it had manifestly exceeded the limits of its power. This could not be proven and was therefore rejected by the Court.

Third, the UK argued that a measure could only be proportionate if it complied with the principle of subsidiarity. It was for the Union institutions to demonstrate that the aims of the directive could be better achieved at Union level rather than national level. The Court held that it had been demonstrated that Union action was necessary to adopt minimum requirements with the objective of raising the level of the health and safety protection of workers.

Misuse of powers

Misuse of powers is defined by the Court of Justice as the adoption of a measure with the exclusive or main purpose of achieving an end other than that stated, or evading a procedure specifically prescribed by the Treaty. The Court had already held that the former Art 118a EC Treaty was the appropriate legal base and therefore this plea was also dismissed.

Infringement of essential procedural requirements

The UK argued that the directive was inadequately reasoned because there was a failure to demonstrate a connection between the health and safety of workers and the provisions of the directive. Many of the provisions were concerned with improving the living and working conditions of workers, or the internal market, rather than the health and safety of workers. This was rejected. The various recitals in the preamble to the directive clearly reasoned the connection between the provisions and the health and safety of workers. There was no necessity to include in the preamble specific references to scientific material justifying the adoption of the various provisions.

Consequences of annulment

Under Art 264 TFEU (previously Art 231 EC Treaty):

> If the action is well founded, the Court of Justice of the European Union shall declare the act concerned to be void.
>
> However, the Court shall, if it considers this necessary, state which of the effects of the act which it has declared void shall be considered as definitive.

Under Art 266 TFEU (previously Art 233 EC Treaty):

> The institution whose act has been declared void or whose failure to act has been declared contrary to the Treaties shall be required to take the necessary measures to comply with the judgment of the Court of Justice of the European Union.
>
> This obligation shall not affect any obligation which may result from the application of the second paragraph of Article 340.

As decisions and other acts having legal consequences will affect only single undertakings or individuals or groups of undertakings, the Court of Justice, if it finds the decision or other act to be void, will declare it to be void from the moment of delivery of the judgment. It can, of course, declare an act non-existent, but, as can be seen in the *BASF Case* (Case C-137/92), it is reluctant to do this because of the disruption this may cause to actions which may have been based on the assumption that the act was valid. Article 264, para 2 TFEU enables the Court to declare part of an act void. In the case of Union legislation, it will frequently declare that, for example, the provisions of an annulled directive or regulation will remain effective until a new regulation is adopted (see, for example, the Court of Justice's declaration on annulling Directive 90/366 on students' rights in *European*

Parliament v *Council* (Case C-295/90), and on Council Regulation 2454/92 on transport undertakings operating in other Member States in *European Parliament* v *Council* (Case C-388/92)).

Article 266 TFEU requires the institution concerned to take the necessary remedial action to correct the failure which has been established by the judgment of the Court. There is no time-limit for this, but the Court of Justice has held that such steps should be taken within a reasonable period from the date of the judgment (*European Parliament* v *Council* (Case 13/83)).

Indirect challenge to a Union act under Articles 277 and 267 TFEU

Objective 3

The legality of a Union act may become an issue in proceedings in which the object is not the Union act itself but some action of an institution which purports to be based upon it. The issue can be raised only if it is relevant to the proceedings (*Italy* v *Commission* (Case 32/65)). Attacks on the legality of Union acts in this way are normally called indirect challenges and they may result in the judicial review of the legality of Union acts long after the time has passed for an application for review under Art 263 TFEU. The issue of legality may arise before both the Court of Justice and the General Court at Union level, or in national courts. Where it arises at Union level it is subject to the rules laid down in Art 277 TFEU (previously Art 241 EC Treaty), which provides:

> Notwithstanding the expiry of the period laid down in Article 263, sixth paragraph, any party may, in proceedings in which an act of general application adopted by an institution, body, office or agency of the Union is at issue, plead the grounds specified in Article 263, second paragraph, in order to invoke before the Court of Justice of the European Union the inapplicability of that act.

The first point to note is that an indirect challenge in this way is only available in relation to 'an act of general application' (this is undoubtedly targeted at EU Regulations, as was explicitly the case under the former Art 241 EC Treaty) and cannot, therefore, be used in relation to other Union acts having legal effect. Second, the effect of the former Art 241 EC Treaty was limited to proceedings brought before the Court of Justice (*Wöhrmann* v *Commission* (Case 31/62)). Although Art 277 TFEU excludes an indirect challenge to other acts having legal effect, this rule may, in some cases, be circumvented where the issue arises in a national court. The question of the legality of the Union measure may then be raised, as already noted in connection with time limits under Art 263 TFEU, in the national court and referred to the Court of Justice under Art 267 TFEU (previously Art 234 EC Treaty). The operation of Art 267 TFEU is examined in Chapter 6. The relevant part of that article enables national courts to ask for a preliminary ruling, *inter alia*, in relation to 'the validity … of acts of the institutions … of the Union'.

See pages 183–200 for a detailed discussion of Art 267 TFEU.

If a national body purports to act on the basis of, for example, a decision or a directive which is invalid, a party to the proceedings may ask the national court to refer the question of the validity of that measure to the Court of Justice pursuant to Art 267 TFEU. Such a reference will be necessary if the issue arises, because national courts have no power themselves to rule on the validity of a Union measure (*Foto-Frost* v *HZA Lübeck-Ost* (Case 314/85)). An important restriction on that principle is, however, the rule laid down by the Court in *TWD Deggendorf* (Case C-188/92). In that case the Court of Justice held that no indirect challenge to a Commission decision could be made under what is now Art 267 TFEU where the party had been informed of the Commission decision and could 'without doubt' have challenged it directly before the Court under what is now Art 263 TFEU, but had not done so.

Challenging a failure to act: Article 265 TFEU

Institutions may act unlawfully not only by exceeding or abusing their powers, but also by failing to carry out a duty imposed on them by the Treaty or some other provision having legal effect. This form of inaction may result in proceedings brought under Art 265 TFEU (previously Art 232 EC Treaty):

> Should the European Parliament, the European Council, the Council, the Commission or the European Central Bank, in infringement of the Treaties, fail to act, the Member States and the other institutions of the Union may bring an action before the Court of Justice of the European Union to have the infringement established. This Article shall apply, under the same conditions, to bodies, offices and agencies of the Union which fail to act.
>
> The action shall be admissible only if the institution, body, office or agency concerned has first been called upon to act. If, within two months of being so called upon, the institution, body, office or agency concerned has not defined its position, the action may be brought within a further period of two months.
>
> Any natural or legal person may, under the conditions laid down in the preceding paragraphs, complain to the Court that an institution, body, office or agency of the Union has failed to address to that person any act other than a recommendation or an opinion.

Standing to challenge a failure to act

The position of 'privileged' applicants (i.e. Member States and institutions) that can bring proceedings under Art 265 TFEU irrespective of any particular interest, and 'non-privileged' applicants (i.e. legal and natural persons) that need to establish a special interest, is the same under Art 265 TFEU as in relation to challenges under Art 263 TFEU (see above). The Court has, in fact, stated that 'in the system of legal remedies provided for by the Treaty, there is a close relationship between the right of action given in [Art 263 TFEU] ... and that based on [Art 265 TFEU]' (*European Parliament* v *Council (Re Transport Policy)* (Case 13/83)).

Scope for challenge

There have not been many successful actions brought on this basis. Many of the duties conferred on the institutions are, in reality, 'powers', whereby the institution has a discretion about whether, and how, to exercise that 'duty'. To satisfy Art 265 TFEU, the institution generally only needs to have addressed the issue and defined its position. In the case of natural or legal persons, if the only outcome of the institution's deliberations will be an opinion or a recommendation, a failure to produce either is not a failure which can be dealt with by Art 265 TFEU. Where there is a clear duty to act, as imposed on the Commission by Art 105(1) TFEU (previously Art 85(1) EC Treaty) in relation to breaches of Arts 101 and 102 TFEU (previously Arts 81 and 82 EC Treaty), a statement by the Commission that it is not going to respond to a complaint might give grounds for an action under Art 265 TFEU, after the appropriate warning has been given. For example, in *Ladbroke Racing (Deutschland) GmbH* v *Commission* (Case T-74/92), Ladbroke had complained to the

Commission about a denial of access for the televising of horse racing, alleging a breach of the former Arts 81 and 82 EC Treaty (now Arts 101 and 102 TFEU) by German and French companies in the horse racing and communications businesses. After deciding to investigate the complaint in December 1990, the Commission had still not defined its position on the alleged breach of the former Art 82 EC Treaty (now Art 102 TFEU) by June 1992, when it was formally requested to do so. The CFI found that there was a breach following the instigation of proceedings under what is now Art 265 TFEU. The Commission could have either initiated the procedure for establishing a breach of the former Art 82 EC Treaty, dismissed the complaint in a formal letter to the complainant, or made a reasoned decision not to pursue the complaint on the ground of a lack of Union interest. It had, however, done none of these things. If there is a refusal to pursue an investigation, it may in itself constitute a decision which is best challenged under Art 263 TFEU (previously Art 230 EC Treaty); *SFEI and Others* v *Commission* (Case C-39/93P), see above. It should be noted that the enforcement procedures, in relation to Union competition law, have changed following the coming into force of Regulation 1/2003 (see Chapter 22).

The difficulty of launching a successful action under Art 265 TFEU is illustrated by the *Transport Policy* case ((Case 13/83), see above) concerning the former Arts 70 and 71 EC Treaty (now Arts 90 and 91 TFEU) that require the Council to adopt a common transport policy for the Union. More than 20 years after the Treaty had come into force no such policy had been adopted, and the Parliament brought proceedings against the Council for failure to act under what is now Art 265 TFEU, after a number of requests had been made to the Council for progress in this area. The Court of Justice agreed that the Council had been 'called upon to act, by the Parliament, as required by [Art 265 TFEU] … and had produced equivocal replies as to what, if any, action it proposed to take'. The requirement in the former Arts 70 and 71 EC Treaty was not sufficiently precise, however, to amount to an enforceable obligation. Other cases have failed because the Court decided that all that was required was an opinion (*Chevally* v *Commission* (Case 15/70)), or because the decision the applicant required was not to be addressed to him (*Lord Bethell* v *Commission* (Case 246/81)).

Claims for damages against Union institutions for unlawful acts: Article 340 TFEU

Objective 5

Article 266 TFEU (previously Art 233 EC Treaty) specifically preserves the question of non-contractual liability as a separate issue from the legality or otherwise of institutional acts. As in English law, the fact that a public body has acted unlawfully does not, *per se*, mean that the body concerned is under a duty to compensate those adversely affected by its action, although a court does have the power to order the payment of compensation at the conclusion of an application for judicial review. Whether or not damages are payable under Union law depends on the way in which the Court has interpreted the provisions of Art 340 TFEU. Article 340 TFEU provides:

> The contractual liability of the Union shall be governed by the law applicable to the contract in question.
>
> In the case of non-contractual liability, the Union shall, in accordance with the general principles common to the laws of the Member States, make- good any damage caused by its institutions or by its servants in the performance of their duties.

> Notwithstanding the second paragraph, the European Central Bank shall, in accordance with the general principles common to the laws of the Member States, make good any damage caused by it or by its servants in the performance of their duties.
>
> The personal liability of its servants towards the Union shall be governed by the provisions laid down in their Staff Regulations or in the Conditions of Employment applicable to them.

The liability of Union institutions in contract will generally be governed by the law of the Member State where the institution is situated. Liability in non-contractual matters (tort, in English law) is governed by Art 340, para 2 TFEU, which provides that:

> In the case of non-contractual liability, the Union shall, in accordance with the general principles common to the laws of the Member States, make good any damage caused by its institutions or by its servants in the performance of their duties.

This provision is substantially the same as the former Art 288, para 2 EC Treaty (which was replaced by Art 340, para 2 TFEU).

The Court of Justice laid down some basic rules for liability in the following case:

Lütticke v *Commission* (Case 4/69)

The Court of Justice stated that there must be actual damage to the claimant and a causal link between the damage and the alleged unlawful conduct of the institution. Fault is not an essential element in liability, in the sense that the institution does not have to be conscious of any wrongdoing. The only type of fault that need be established is an unlawful act by the relevant institution. Where there is a positive duty to do something, there must be an omission to do it and where there is a discretion, it must have been exercised in an unlawful way. The wrongdoing- is likely to have been the result of carelessness, failure to make appropriate inquiries or the giving of misleading information. The conduct giving rise to a claim under the former Art 288 EC Treaty (now Art 340 TFEU) will usually amount to no more than *faute de service* or poor administrative practice causing loss to the claimant. The scope for liability is much wider than under English law, however, and institutions can be liable for wrongful legislative acts.

This liability was, however, limited by the so-called ***Schöppenstedt formula*** (***Zückerfabrik Schöppenstedt v Council*** (Case 5/71)). Under this formula the Court held that 'the Community [i.e. Union] does not incur liability on account of a legislative measure which involves choices of economic policy unless a sufficiently serious breach of a superior rule of law for the protection of the individual has occurred' (see ***HNL v Council and Commission*** (Case 83/77), para 4; ***Unifruit Hellas v Commission*** (Case T-489/93)).

The Court of Justice has subsequently extended the requirement of a 'sufficiently serious breach' to all cases for damages under what is now Art 340 TFEU, unless there is a particular justification for a departure from this requirement:

Bergaderm and Goupil v *Commission* (Case C-352/98P)

The Court of Justice stated as follows:

39. The second paragraph of Article 215 of the Treaty [which was replaced by Art 288 EC Treaty, and is now Art 340 TFEU] provides that, in the case of non-contractual liability, the Community [i.e. Union] is, in accordance with the general principles common to the

laws of the Member States, to make good any damage caused by its institutions or by its servants in the performance of their duties.

40. The system of rules which the Court has worked out with regard to that provision takes into account, *inter alia*, the complexity of the situations to be regulated, difficulties in the application or interpretation of the texts and, more particularly, the margin of discretion available to the author of the act in question (Joined Cases C-46/93 and C-48/93 *Brasserie du Pêcheur* and *Factortame* [1996] ECR I-1029, paragraph 43).

41. **The Court has stated that the conditions under which the State may incur liability for damage caused to individuals by a breach of Community [i.e. Union] law cannot, in the absence of particular justification, differ from those governing the liability of the Community [i.e. Union] in like circumstances.** The protection of the rights which individuals derive from Community [i.e. Union] law cannot vary depending on whether a national authority or a Community [i.e. Union] authority is responsible for the damage (*Brasserie du Pêcheur* and *Factortame*, paragraph 42).

42. **As regards Member State liability for damage caused to individuals, the Court has held that Community [i.e. Union] law confers a right to reparation where three conditions are met: the rule of law infringed must be intended to confer rights on individuals; the breach must be sufficiently serious; and there must be a direct causal link between the breach of the obligation resting on the State and the damage sustained by the injured parties** (*Brasserie du Pêcheur* and *Factortame*, paragraph 51).

43. As to the second condition, as regards both Community [i.e. Union] liability under Article 215 of the Treaty [now Art 340 TFEU] and Member State liability for breaches of Community [i.e. Union] law, **the decisive test for finding that a breach of Community [i.e. Union] law is sufficiently serious is whether the Member State or the Community [i.e. Union] institution concerned manifestly and gravely disregarded the limits on its discretion** (*Brasserie du Pêcheur* and *Factortame*, paragraph 55; and Joined Cases C-178/94, C-179/94, C-188/94, C-189/94, C-190/94 *Dillenkofer and Others* v *Germany* [1996] ECR I-4845, paragraph 25).

44. Where the Member State or the institution in question has only considerably reduced, or even no, discretion, the mere infringement of Community [i.e. Union] law may be sufficient to establish the existence of a sufficiently serious breach (see, to that effect, Case C-5/94 *Hedley Lomas* [1996] ECR I-2553, paragraph 28). [emphasis added]:

The scope of state liability is considered in detail at pages 292–300.

In the above case, the Court of Justice reviewed its case law establishing Member States' liability for damage caused to individuals by a breach of Union law (referred to as state liability or *Francovich* **damages**, see Chapter 9). At para 41 the Court stated that 'the conditions under which the state may incur liability for damage caused to individuals by a breach of Community [i.e. Union] law cannot, in the absence of particular justification, differ from those governing the liability of the Community [i.e. Union] in like circumstances'. For the Union to incur non-contractual liability for an unlawful act, three conditions therefore have to be satisfied:

(i) the rule of law infringed must be intended to confer rights on individuals;
(ii) the breach of that rule of law must be sufficiently serious;
(iii) there must be a direct causal link between the breach of the obligation resting on the Union institution and the damage sustained by the injured party.

The issue of 'sufficiently serious breach' has subsequently been considered by the CFI (now the General Court) in the following case:

Afrikanische Frucht-Compagnie and Internationale Fruchtimport Gesellschaft Weichert & Co v Commission (Joined Cases T-64/01 and T-65/01) and *Cantina sociale di Dolianova and Others v Commission* (Case T-166/98)

> The CFI (now the General Court) stated that as regards the requirement that the breach must be sufficiently serious, the decisive test for finding that there has been such a breach is whether the Member State or the Union institution concerned **manifestly and gravely disregarded the limits on its discretion**. Where the Member State or the institution in question has only considerably reduced discretion, or even no discretion at all, the mere infringement of Union law may be sufficient to establish the existence of a sufficiently serious breach.

The expression 'rule of law intended to confer rights on individuals' has been analysed on several occasions by the CFI (now the General Court). For instance, it has been held that the aim of the rules applicable to the system of the division of powers between the various Union institutions is to ensure that the balance between the institutions provided for in the Treaty is maintained and not to confer rights on individuals. Accordingly, any unlawful delegation of the Council's powers to the Commission is not such as to incur liability (*Afrikanische Frucht-Compagnie and Internationale Fruchtimport Gesellschaft Weichert & Co v Commission*).

It has also been held, by reference to the case law of the Court of Justice, that infringement of the obligation to state reasons is not such as to give rise to the liability of the Union (*Afrikanische Frucht-Compagnie and Internationale Fruchtimport Gesellschaft Weichert & Co v Commission*).

On the other hand, in its judgment in *Cantina sociale di Dolianova and Others v Commission*, the CFI (now the General Court) held that the prohibition on unjust enrichment and the principle of non-discrimination were intended to confer rights on individuals. The breach by the Commission of those principles was held to be sufficiently serious.

Liability for a lawful act

In the case of non-contractual liability under Art 340 TFEU, the Union has, in accordance with the general principles common to the laws of the Member States, to make good any damage caused by its institutions or by its servants in the performance of their duties. In a series of judgments the CFI (now the General Court), sitting as a Grand Chamber, expressly recognised that the Union could incur liability even in the absence of unlawful conduct:

FIAMM and FIAMM Technologies v Council and Commission (Case T-69/00), *Laboratoire du Bain v Council and Commission* (Case T-151/00), *Groupe Fremaux and Palais Royal v Council and Commission* (Case T-301/00), *CD Cartondruck v Council and Commission* (Case T-320/00), *Beamglow v Parliament and Others* and *Fedon & Figli and Others v Council and Commission* (Case T-383/00)

> In 1993, the Council adopted Regulation 404/93 introducing for the Member States common rules for the import of bananas (the COM for bananas). This Regulation contained preferential provisions for bananas from certain African, Caribbean and Pacific States. Following complaints lodged by certain states, the Dispute Settlement Board (DSB) of

the World Trade Organization (WTO) held that the Union regime governing the import of bananas was incompatible with the WTO agreements. In 1998 the Council therefore adopted a regulation amending that regime. As the United States took the view that the new regime was still not compatible with the WTO agreements, it requested, and obtained, authorisation from the DSB to impose increased customs duty on imports of Union products appearing on a list drawn up by the United States' authorities. Six companies established in the EU brought proceedings before the CFI (now the General Court) claiming compensation from the Commission and the Council for the damage alleged to have been suffered by them because the United States' retaliatory measures applied to their exports to the United States.

In its judgment, the CFI (now the General Court) first held that the Union could not incur liability in this case for unlawful conduct. However, it held that **where it has not been established that conduct attributed to the Union institutions is unlawful, that does not mean that undertakings which, as a category of economic operators, are required to bear a disproportionate part of the burden resulting from a restriction of access to export markets, can in no circumstances obtain compensation by virtue of the Union's non-contractual liability.** National laws on non-contractual liability allow individuals, albeit to varying degrees, in specific fields and in accordance with differing rules, to obtain compensation in legal proceedings for certain kinds of damage, even in the absence of unlawful action by the perpetrator of the damage. **Where the damage caused by the conduct of the Union institution is not shown to be unlawful, the Union can incur non-contractual liability if the following conditions are met: (i) actual damage is sustained; (ii) there is a causal link between that damage and the conduct of the Union institution; and (iii) the damage in question is of an unusual and special nature.**

This was the first time that the Court has held that the Union could incur non-contractual liability in the absence of unlawful conduct on the part of its bodies, other than in a purely hypothetical case. In this case, the CFI held that the condition requiring the applicants to have sustained damage was satisfied. That was also true of the condition relating to the causal link between that damage and the conduct of the institutions. The withdrawal of concessions in relation to the Union, which took the form of the increased customs duties on imports, was to be regarded as a consequence resulting objectively, in accordance with the normal and foreseeable operation of the WTO dispute settlement system which was accepted by the Union, from the retention in force by the defendant institutions of a banana import regime incompatible with the WTO agreements. Thus, the conduct of the defendant institutions necessarily led to the adoption of the retaliatory measure, and 'must be regarded as the immediate cause of the damage suffered by the applicants following imposition of the United States' increased customs duty'. Conversely, the applicants had not succeeded in proving that they sustained unusual damage – damage which exceeded the limits of the economic risks inherent in operating in the sector concerned. The possibility of tariff concessions being suspended is among the vicissitudes inherent in the current system of international trade and, accordingly, has to be borne by every operator who decides to sell his products on the market of one of the WTO members. The CFI therefore dismissed the six actions.

Likewise in the following case, the CFI (now the General Court) has acknowledged that the Union may incur liability in the absence of unlawful conduct:

Galileo v *Commission* (Case T-279/03)

The CFI (now the General Court) recalled that **Union liability in the absence of unlawful conduct could only arise if there was unusual and special damage. Damage is held to be unusual if it exceeds the limits of the economic risks inherent in operating in the sector concerned.** In this case, the CFI held that the damage caused by a Union institution's use of a term to designate a project could not be regarded as exceeding the limits of the risks inherent in the use by the applicants of the same term in respect of their trade marks, given that, by reason of the characteristics of the term chosen (inspired by the first name of the renowned Italian mathematician, physicist and astronomer), the proprietor of the trade mark voluntarily exposed himself to the risk that someone else could legally give the same name to one of its projects.

Remedies

The Court has not developed a comprehensive set of principles concerning the type and extent of damages which may be recovered, but certain rules have emerged in the case law. Actual financial loss that results from the unlawful action by the Commission may be recovered, but it must be established that this results directly from the unlawful conduct (***Dumortier Frères* v *Council*** (Case 64/76)). The Court has also awarded damages for shock, disturbance and uneasiness, in Union staff cases (***Algera* v *Common Assembly*** (Case 7/56)).

Difficulties may arise where a national authority has acted on what subsequently transpires to have been an unlawful act by a Union institution. Who is liable? Should the injured party sue the institution which promulgated the unlawful act, or the national institution which implemented it, or both? Where the claimant's loss has occurred as a result of being obliged to pay money under an unlawful act, and he is claiming restitution, he will be expected to claim in the national courts against the national institution (***Vreugdenhil* v *Commission*** (Case C-282/90)). Where there is no remedy in the national courts, claims can be brought against the relevant Union institution in the Court of Justice (***Krohn* v *Commission*** (Case 175/84), paras 24–29).

In the following case, the CFI (now the General Court) reiterated the principle of the autonomy of remedies:

Holcim (France) v *Commission* (Case T-86/03)

The CFI (now the General Court) held that where an applicant could have brought an action for annulment or for failure to act against an act or abstention allegedly causing it loss, but failed to do so, the failure to exercise such remedies does not in itself make the action for damages time-barred. On the question of autonomous remedies this case also allowed the CFI to clarify the scope of the case law according to which an action for damages is inadmissible where it actually seeks the withdrawal of an individual decision which has become definitive. That case law concerns 'the exceptional case where an application for compensation is brought for the payment of an amount precisely equal to the duty which the applicant was required to pay under an individual decision, so that the application seeks in fact the withdrawal of that individual decision' (see, for example, *Krohn* v *Commission* (Case 175/84), at para 33). The CFI made clear that this case law was relevant only where the alleged damage results solely from an individual administrative measure which has become definitive and which the person concerned could have contested in an action for annulment. In this case the loss alleged by the applicant did not result from an individual administrative measure which the applicant could have contested, but from the wrongful failure of the Commission to take a measure necessary to comply with a judgment. The action was therefore held admissible.

Summary

Now you have read this chapter you should be able to:

- Explain the range of Union acts which may be judicially reviewed by the General Court or the Court of Justice pursuant to Art 263 TFEU.

- Outline the conditions which are applied to determine whether a 'privileged' applicant has the standing to challenge the legality of a Union act, and compare and contrast such conditions with those which are applied to determine a 'non-privileged' applicant's standing.

- Explain the four grounds upon which a Union act may be challenged:
  - lack of competence;
  - infringement of an essential procedural requirement;
  - infringement of the Treaties or any rule of law relating to their application;
  - misuse of powers.

- Understand how Arts 277 and 267 TFEU may be utilised to enable an indirect challenge to be made against a Union act.

- Discuss the extent of the power to challenge a Union institution's failure to act, pursuant to Art 265 TFEU.

- Explain how the Court of Justice of the European Union applies the rules relating to a claim for damages against a Union institution for unlawful acts, pursuant to Art 340 TFEU.

Further reading

Textbooks

Craig, P. and De Burca, G. (2011) *EU Law: Text, Cases and Materials* (5th edn), Oxford University Press, Chapters 14 to 16.

Foster, N. (2015) *Foster on EU Law* (11th edn), Oxford University Press, Chapter 7.

Steiner, J. and Woods, L. (2014) *EU Law* (12th edn), Oxford University Press, Chapters 12 to 14.

Weatherill, S. (2014) *Cases and Materials on EU Law* (11th edn), Oxford University Press, Chapter 8.

Journal articles

Balthasar, S., '*Locus standi* rules for challenges to regulatory acts by private applicants: The new Art 263(4) TFEU' (2010) 35 EL Rev 542.

Bergstrom, C.F., 'Defending restricted standing for individuals to bring direct actions against "legislative" measures' (2014) 10 ECL Rev 481.

Kornezov, A., 'Shaping the new architecture of the EU system of judicial remedies: Comment on Inuit' (2014) 39 EL Rev 251.

Pliakos, A., 'Who is the ultimate arbiter? The battle over judicial supremacy in EU law' (2011) 36 EL Rev 109.

Temple Lang, J. and Raferty, C., 'Remedies for the Commission's failure to act in "comitology" cases' (2011) 36 EL Rev 264.

Thies, A., 'The impact of general principles of EC law on its liability regime towards retaliation victims after FIAMM' (2009) 34 EL Rev 889.

Tridimas, T. and Gari, G., 'Winners and losers in Luxembourg: A statistical analysis of judicial review before the European Court of Justice and the Court of First Instance (2001–2005)' (2010) 35 EL Rev 131.

9

Principles of supremacy, indirect effect, direct effect and state liability

Objectives

At the end of this chapter you should understand:

1. What is meant by 'the supremacy of Union law', and its impact on UK constitutional law.

2. The *Marleasing* interpretative obligation and how UK courts and tribunals have applied this obligation.

3. The principle of direct effect, how to apply the test for ascertaining whether a provision of Union law is capable of having direct effect, and the rule that 'generally' excludes directives from having horizontal direct effect.

4. The principle of state liability established by the Court of Justice in *Francovich* and how this principle has developed.

The supremacy of Union law

Objective 1

Nowhere in the Treaty is there a reference to the supremacy of Union law over the national law of the Member States. However, the Court of Justice has consistently held that this principle of supremacy is implied in the Treaty. The Court addressed this issue of supremacy in the following case:

Flaminio Costa v *Enel* (Case 6/64)

In an oft-quoted statement, the Court of Justice stated that:

> By creating a Community [i.e. Union] of unlimited duration, having its own institutions, its own personality, its own legal capacity and capacity of representation on the international plane and, more particularly, real powers stemming from a limitation of sovereignty or a transfer of powers from the States of the Community [i.e. Union], **the Member States have limited their sovereign rights, albeit within limited fields, and have thus created a body of law which binds both their nationals and themselves.** [emphasis added]

Although this principle of supremacy has never been explicitly set out within a Treaty, when the ToL came into force on 1 December 2009, Declaration 17 stated as follows:

> The Conference recalls that, in accordance with well settled case law of the Court of Justice of the European Union, the Treaties and the law adopted by the Union on the basis of the Treaties have primacy over the law of Member States, under the conditions laid down by the said case law.
>
> The Conference has also decided to attach as an Annex to this Final Act the Opinion of the Council Legal Service on the primacy of EC law [i.e. Union law] as set out in 11197/07 (JUR 260):
>
> *Opinion of the Council Legal Service of 22 June 2007*
>
> It results from the case-law of the Court of Justice that primacy of EC law [i.e. Union law] is a cornerstone principle of Community law [i.e. Union law]. According to the Court, this principle is inherent to the specific nature of the European Community [i.e. European Union]. At the time of the first judgment of this established case-law (***Costa/ENEL***, 15 July 1964, Case 6/64) there was no mention of primacy in the treaty. It is still the case today. The fact that the principle of primacy will not be included in the future treaty shall not in any way change the existence of the principle and the existing case-law of the Court of Justice.

The principle of EU supremacy and UK constitutional law

The incorporation of Union law into UK domestic law was implemented by the enactment of the European Communities Act 1972. This Act has been amended subsequently, most recently on 1 December 2009 by the European Union (Amendment) Act 2008. The 2008 Act gave effect to the ToL and more specifically changed the terminology used throughout the 1972 Act, replacing all references to 'Community' with 'Union'.

The effect of s 2(1) of the 1972 Act is that all provisions of Union law which are enforceable in the UK – either indirectly through an **interpretative obligation** which requires national courts to interpret national law in such a way as to avoid a conflict with Union law (i.e. the principle of indirect effect, see below), or through a right of direct enforcement of Union law in the national courts (i.e. the principle of direct effect, see below) – are given the force of law in UK courts and tribunals. This applies to Union law made both before and *after* the coming into force of the Act. Section 2(4) provides that:

> ... any enactment passed **or to be passed** ... shall be construed and have effect subject to the foregoing provisions of this section. [emphasis added]

The 'foregoing provisions' includes 2(1), which provides for the incorporation of the interpretative obligation (i.e. the principle of indirect effect, see below) and the right to directly enforce EU law in national courts (i.e. the principle of direct effect, see below). Section 2(4) therefore amounts to a statement that UK Acts of Parliament passed *or to be passed* shall be construed and have effect subject to the principles of indirect effect and direct effect (see below).

There are *three* interpretations of the above:

1 UK legislation shall only be effective in so far as it is consistent with Union legislation, no matter how clearly the statute states that the Act of Parliament was to have effect notwithstanding any Union law to the contrary. This view is clearly adopted by the Court of Justice (see e.g. ***Costa* v *ENEL***, above). The view of the Court of Justice is that Union law is supreme and should be given precedence.

2 The traditional doctrine of UK parliamentary sovereignty, as affirmed in **Vauxhall Estates Ltd v Liverpool Corpn** [1932] 1 KB 733 and **Ellen Street Estates v Minister of Health** [1934] 1 KB 590, incorporates the doctrine of implied repeal and provides that if a later statute is inconsistent with s 2(4), s 2(4) should be impliedly repealed to the extent of that inconsistency. Those advocating this approach would refuse to give effect to s 2(4), insisting that UK legislation always, by implication, repeals an earlier legislative provision with which it is inconsistent.

3 Section 2(4) is in effect a rule of interpretation. It is assumed that the UK Parliament, in enacting legislation, intends to legislate consistently with Union law. Therefore if the UK Parliament wishes to act inconsistently, it should state its intention expressly in an Act of Parliament.

This third approach was favoured by the UK's Court of Appeal in the following case:

Macarthys Ltd v Smith [1979] ICR 785

Lord Denning stated:

> If ... our legislation is deficient or is inconsistent with Community [i.e. Union] law by some oversight of our draftsmen then it is our bounden duty to give priority to Community [i.e. Union] law. Such is the result of ss. 2(1) and (4) of the European Communities Act 1972 ... Thus far I have assumed that our Parliament, whenever it passes legislation, intends to fulfil its obligations under the Treaty. If the time should come when our Parliament deliberately passes an Act with the intention of repudiating the Treaty or any provision in it or intentionally of acting inconsistently with it *and says so in express terms* then I should have thought that it would be the duty of our courts to follow the statute of our Parliament. I do not however envisage such a situation.

This third approach is based on the premise that the UK Parliament has partially surrendered its sovereignty by enacting the 1972 Act, thus providing for the application of Union law in the UK courts. This can be seen as a limited surrender because the UK Parliament could expressly repeal the 1972 Act; the 1972 Act is not entrenched. The UK would thus withdraw from the Union and the UK Parliament would regain its full sovereignty.

The **Factortame** litigation provides an illustration of the way in which the UK courts have dealt with conflicts between national legislation and Union law. In **Factortame Ltd v Secretary of State for Transport** [1990] 2 AC 85, during a judicial review application the question arose of whether the Merchant Shipping Act 1988, and regulations made pursuant to it, deprived the applicants of their rights under Union law. The Divisional Court referred the substantive matter to the Court of Justice under what is now Art 267 TFEU for a preliminary ruling. Pending the Court of Justice's ruling, the Divisional Court granted an interim injunction restraining enforcement of the Act. The Court of Appeal allowed the Secretary of State's appeal against the grant of the interim injunction and the applicants appealed to the House of Lords (the judicial functions of which are now exercised by the Supreme Court).

The House of Lords held that under UK law there was no power to grant an interim injunction against the Crown, but it referred the matter to the Court of Justice for a preliminary ruling as to whether there was a power to grant such an injunction under Union law.

In 1990 the Court of Justice held that there was such a power. The matter was referred back to the House of Lords for them to apply the Court's preliminary ruling. In **Factortame Ltd v Secretary of State for Transport (No. 2)** [1991] 1 AC 603 the House of Lords considered the ruling of the Court of Justice and applied the following principles to the question of whether or not to grant an interim injunction:

- the balance of convenience;
- whether damages would be an adequate remedy;
- the importance of upholding the law of the land and the obligation on certain authorities to enforce the law;
- the fact that the challenge was *prima facie* so firmly based as to justify so exceptional a course.

On the facts of the case, the House of Lords granted the interim injunction.

On 25 July 1991 the Court of Justice (Case C-221/89) held that the 1988 Act conflicted with Union law. On 2 October 1991 the Divisional Court (in an unreported decision) granted the appropriate declaration, in effect refusing to enforce the 1988 Act against the applicants. If the traditional doctrine of Parliamentary sovereignty had been applied, the 1988 Act would have impliedly repealed those provisions of the earlier legislation which were inconsistent with it (i.e. s 2(4), European Communities Act 1972).

Article 258 TFEU: ineffective means of enforcement

As discussed in Chapter 7, Art 258 TFEU (previously Art 226 EC Treaty) expressly provides a mechanism for **infraction proceedings** to be initiated by the Commission against a defaulting Member State to ensure the state complies with its Union law obligations. The weakness in the former Art 226 EC Treaty procedure was that, as initially formulated, there was no provision for imposing a penalty on a defaulting Member State; it proved ineffective in dealing with a recalcitrant Member State. However, as discussed in Chapter 7, following amendments made to the former Art 226 EC Treaty (now Art 258 TFEU) by the TEU, if a Member State fails to comply with a declaration made by the Court of Justice that it is in breach of Union law, the Commission may take action against that state under the former Art 228(2) EC Treaty (now Art 260(2) TFEU). In this instance the Court of Justice can impose a financial penalty (a penalty payment and/or a lump sum penalty) on the defaulting Member State.

When the ToL came into force on 1 December 2009, a new provision (Art 260(3) TFEU) was introduced. Article 260(3) TFEU provides that if the Commission brings Art 258 TFEU proceedings before the Court of Justice against a Member State which has failed to implement a directive, if the Commission considers it appropriate it may specify a lump sum or penalty payment which the Member State should be required to pay. If the Court subsequently finds the Member State to be in breach of its Union law obligations, it can impose the lump sum or penalty payment on the Member State, but the amount must not exceed that specified by the Commission.

While the power to impose a financial penalty has strengthened the Art 258 TFEU procedure, a continuing weakness with Art 258 TFEU is that the rights of individuals are not sufficiently safeguarded (e.g. a compensation order cannot be made against a defaulting Member State in favour of an aggrieved individual). The UK, for example, may have failed to implement a directive or may have implemented it incorrectly. With regard to employment-related directives, the purpose of such directives is to provide protection for employees. Breach of such a directive may have a significant impact upon an indeterminate number of workers. The fact that the UK may be brought before the Court of Justice will be of little comfort to this group of persons who had been deprived of their rights under Union law. The fact that Union law is considered by the Court of Justice to be supreme is irrelevant. It does not repair the possible damage suffered by them, unless they can enforce Union law in the courts of the Member States.

The impact on individuals can be illustrated by considering the Working Time Directive 93/104 (OJ 1993 L 307/18), which should have been implemented by all Member States by 23 November 1996. The UK failed to implement it on time. The directive provides rights for individual workers, for example paid annual leave, minimum daily and weekly rest periods and a 48-hour maximum working week, all of which are subject to certain exceptions and derogations. A relatively short breach by the UK could have had an enormous impact on an indeterminate number of workers. The UK implemented the directive by the Working Time Regulations 1998 (SI 1998/1833), which came into force on 1 October 1998 (almost two years after the date stipulated in the directive). The Commission took no action against the UK under what is now Art 258 TFEU. Even if it had taken action, provided the UK implemented the directive before expiry of the time-limit laid down in the reasoned opinion, the UK could not have been brought before the Court of Justice. In addition, if the Court had ruled against the UK, it would not have had the power to award compensation to those workers whose rights had been infringed by the UK's failure to implement the directive.

See pages 202–214 for further discussion of the Art 258 TFEU reasoned opinion and the effect of the time-limit.

Development of Union law principles

In an attempt to address the problem of ineffective individual rights, the Court of Justice developed principles whereby an aggrieved national of a Member State would be afforded rights based upon Union law which could, in certain circumstances, be enforced in the courts of Member States. These rights are enshrined in the three principles of indirect effect, direct effect and state liability (also referred to as *Francovich* damages).

These principles have been established by the Court of Justice following referrals to it from national courts pursuant to what is now Art 267 TFEU; see Chapter 6. These three principles are considered further.

The principle of indirect effect

Objective
2

In the following case, the Court of Justice adopted a novel approach to enable the claimant to indirectly enforce an incorrectly implemented directive:

Harz v Deutsche Tradax (Case 79/83)

Germany had incorrectly implemented Directive 76/207 on equal employment rights, because German law provided only nominal compensation whereas the directive required proper compensation to be available (see *Marshall (No. 2)* (Case C-271/91)). The case was referred to the Court of Justice by the (West) German Labour Court.

The Court's starting point was the former Art 10 EC Treaty (now Art 4(3) TEU): the obligation of Member States to take all appropriate measures to give effect to Union law. The Court of Justice stated that this obligation 'is binding on all the authorities of Member

States including, for matters within their jurisdiction, the courts. It follows that, in applying the national law ... **national courts are required to interpret their national law in the light of the wording and the purpose of the directive** in order to achieve the result referred to in the third paragraph of Art 189 EC Treaty [which was replaced by Art 249 EC Treaty, and is now Art 288 TFEU]' (para 26) [emphasis added]. The national court was therefore under an obligation to 'interpret' the national law on sexual discrimination in such a way that there was no limit on proper compensation to which injured parties were entitled. On this basis, the German court which had referred the case could award proper compensation to Harz.

The above case concerned the interpretation of legislation which had been put into place to implement the directive in question. It was questionable whether this new interpretative obligation was confined to cases where the Member State had implemented the directive but had done so incorrectly. In the following case, the Court of Justice held that it was not confined to such cases:

Marleasing SA v *La Comercial SA* (Case C-106/89)

A Spanish court was confronted with a national law on the constitution of companies which conflicted with Directive 68/71. The directive had not been implemented in Spain. The Court of Justice, nevertheless, held that:

> ... in applying national law, whether the provisions concerned **pre-date** or post-date the directive, the national court asked to interpret national law is bound to do so in every way possible in the light of the text and the aims of the directive to achieve the results envisaged by it and thus comply with Article 189(3) of the Treaty [now Art 288, para 3 TFEU]. [emphasis added]

See page 308 for a flowchart relating to the principle of indirect effect.

The above judgment provides that, for example, a national court could be required to 'interpret' a provision of national law that preceded a directive by many years, and which had been enacted with quite different considerations in mind, 'in the light of the text and the aims of the directive'. The extent of this interpretative obligation has caused particular challenges for UK courts. These are considered below. The Court of Justice has made it clear that the courts of Member States should act on the presumption that relevant national legislation, whether passed before or after the relevant directive, was intended to implement it. However, whether this is in fact possible, in the light of the wording of the national provision, is essentially a matter of interpretation by those courts (***Wagner Miret*** (Case 334/92)).

There is one exception to the obligation to interpret national law in conformity with an unimplemented directive. That is where the national measure, which ought to be interpreted in this way, imposes criminal liability. The Court of Justice held in ***Arcaro*** (Case C-168/95) that no obligation could be imposed on an individual by an unimplemented directive. Nor could there be any liability in criminal law of persons who act in contravention of that directive's provisions. The Court of Justice has, however, held that a person can be convicted of a driving offence in a national court, even where that conviction rests upon evidence obtained under national legislation made in breach of a Union directive (***Lemmens*** (Case C-226/97)).

The principle of direct effect

Objective 3

The national court may be unable to interpret national law to avoid a conflict with Union law. To address this weakness with the principle of indirect effect, in the following case the Court of Justice developed the principle of direct effect:

Van Gend en Loos v *Nederlandse Administratie der Belastingen* (Case 26/62)

Van Gend en Loos had imported ureaformaldehyde from Germany into The Netherlands. It had been charged a customs duty. This breached the rules on the free movement of goods between Member States, and in particular the former Art 12 EC Treaty (which was replaced by Art 25 EC Treaty, and is now Art 30 TFEU). Van Gend en Loos issued proceedings in a Netherlands' court, claiming reimbursement of the customs duty from The Netherlands' government. The court referred the question of whether or not the claimant could rely on the former Art 12 EC Treaty (now Art 30 TFEU) in the national court to the Court of Justice. The Court of Justice first of all addressed the general question of whether Treaty provisions could confer directly effective rights on individuals, and held as follows:

> The Community [i.e. Union] constitutes a new legal order of international law for the benefit of which the States have limited their sovereign rights, albeit within limited fields, and the subjects of which comprise not only the Member States but also their nationals. **Independently of the legislation of Member States, Community [i.e. Union] law therefore not only imposes obligations on individuals but is also intended to confer on them rights which become part of their legal heritage. These rights arise not only where they are expressly granted by the Treaty, but also by reason of obligations which the Treaty imposes in a clearly defined way upon individuals as well as upon Member States** and upon institutions of the Community [i.e. Union]. [emphasis added]

Effective supervision

Prior to **Van Gend en Loos**, if the national court was unable to interpret national law to avoid a conflict with Union law, the accepted method of enforcement was, as stated above, for the Commission to issue infraction proceedings against the defaulting Member State under what is now Art 258 TFEU. However, even if such proceedings proved successful, this would have been of no assistance to Van Gend en Loos. It would not have resulted in the repayment to it of the customs duty levied in breach of Union law. The Court of Justice accordingly dismissed the suggestion (by Belgium, The Netherlands and (West) Germany) that, because there existed machinery under what is now Art 258 TFEU to bring offending states before the Court of Justice, this must preclude the possibility of the use of Treaty provisions before national courts:

Van Gend en Loos v *Nederlandse Administratie der Belastingen* (Case 26/62)

The Court of Justice stated that:

> ... the argument based on Articles 169 and 170 of the Treaty [which were replaced by Arts 226 and 227, and are now Arts 258 and 259 TFEU] put forward by the three Governments ... is misconceived. The fact that these Articles of the Treaty enable the Commission and the Member States to bring before the Court a State which has not fulfilled its obligations does not mean that individuals cannot plead these obligations, should the occasion arise, before a national court, any more than the fact that the Treaty places at the disposal of the Commission ways of ensuring that obligations imposed upon those subject to the Treaty are observed, precludes the possibility, in actions between individuals before a national court, of pleading infringement of these obligations ... The vigilance of individuals concerned to protect their rights amounts to an effective supervision in addition to the supervision entrusted by Articles 169 and 170 [now Arts 258 and 259 TFEU] to the diligence of the Commission and of the Member States.

In this landmark judgment, the Court of Justice created the principle of direct effect, which was based upon the premise that the Treaty created rights for citizens of Member States which, if enforced by them in the courts of the Member States, would provide an additional supervisory function to that already contained in what are now Arts 258 and 259 TFEU.

The scope of direct effect

See page 309 for a flowchart relating to the principle of direct effect.

The Court of Justice, in establishing the general principle of direct effect, limited its scope only to those provisions which were *sufficiently precise and unconditional*. This has been applied quite flexibly by the Court and has resulted in articles of the Treaty and provisions of directives being held to be directly effective by the Court in circumstances where a national court could have been excused from coming to the opposite conclusion.

Before considering the three forms of Union legislation (EU Treaties, regulations and directives) separately, the following examples give an indication of the Court of Justice's approach in determining whether or not a provision is *sufficiently precise and unconditional*.

Sufficiently precise

The following two cases illustrate the Court of Justice's approach in determining whether or not a provision is 'sufficiently precise'.

In *Van Duyn* v *Home Office* (Case 41/74) (see below) the Court of Justice held that Art 3(1) of the Residence and Public Policy, Security and Health Directive 64/221 (OJ Sp. Ed. 1964 850/64 p. 117), which provides that 'measures taken on the grounds of *public policy* or of *public security* shall be based exclusively on the personal conduct of the individual concerned' (emphasis added), was sufficiently precise to be capable of having direct effect, despite the fact that the scope of 'public policy' and 'public security' would require determination by the Court. Directive 64/221 has since been replaced by Directive 2004/38.

Similarly, in *Defrenne* v *SABENA* (Case 43/75) the Court of Justice held that what is now Art 157 TFEU – which sets out a principle that men and women 'should receive equal pay for equal work' – was sufficiently precise to be capable of having direct effect despite the fact that the scope of 'equal pay' and 'equal work' would likewise have to be determined by the Court.

Unconditional

A Union provision is 'unconditional' if it is not subject, in its implementation or effects, to any additional measure by either the Union institutions or Member States.

In *Van Gend en Loos* v *Administratie der Belastingen* (Case 26/62), the former Art 12 EC Treaty (which was replaced by Art 25 EC Treaty, and is now Art 30 TFEU) was held by the Court of Justice to be unconditional because the former Art 12 EC Treaty imposed a negative obligation on Member States to 'refrain from introducing between themselves any new customs duties on imports and exports ... and from increasing those which they already apply in their trade with each other'. It was not qualified by any reservation on the part of the Member States which would make its implementation conditional upon a positive legislative measure being enacted under national law.

This case can be contrasted with *Costa* v *ENEL* (Case 6/64), where the Court of Justice held, *inter alia*, that the former Art 102 EC Treaty (which was replaced by Art 97 EC Treaty, and is now Art 117 TFEU) was not unconditional. The former Art 102 EC Treaty provided that, where a Member State intended to adopt or amend its laws in such a way that there was a reason to fear this might cause distortion of the conditions of competition in the internal market, there was an obligation of prior consultation between the Member State and the Commission. It was held that this was *not* unconditional because it was subject to additional measures in the form of 'prior consultation' and therefore was not capable of having direct effect.

Treaty articles

As a general principle, treaties and international agreements are not capable, in international law, of conferring rights on individuals in the courts of their own state. However, as discussed above, the Court of Justice has developed the principle of direct effect to provide otherwise with regard to Union law (*Van Gend en Loos v Nederlandse Administratie der Belastingen* (Case 26/62)).

The principle of direct effect was established in *Van Gend en Loos* but its application was still unclear. Certain Treaty provisions were to be enforceable against Member States, provided that the obligations imposed were 'sufficiently precise' and 'unconditional'. These were necessary preconditions, because many Treaty provisions are set out in the most general terms and do not appear to impose a commitment to do anything. Sometimes they express no more than a statement or an aspiration. For example, Art 10(4) TEU (previously Art 191 EC Treaty) provides that 'Political parties at European level contribute to forming European political awareness and to expressing the will of citizens of the Union'. Following *Van Gend en Loos*, and largely on the basis of the chance appearance of appropriate cases before it, the Court of Justice has developed its criteria for determining whether particular Treaty provisions have direct effect, and if so, against whom.

In *Van Gend en Loos* the Court had found that the former Art 12 EC Treaty (which was replaced by Art 25 EC Treaty, and is now Art 30 TFEU) was directly effective against the state. It had reached this position to some extent, at least, on the basis that the state had entered into a commitment when it signed the Treaty. That commitment was owed not only to the other Member States as parties, but also to its own citizens as actual or potential beneficiaries of the Treaty. However, the decision did not resolve the status of Treaty provisions between private citizens. Could a private citizen rely on an article of the Treaty, provided that it was sufficiently precise and unconditional, against another private citizen or undertaking? The Court did not give an unequivocal reply to this question until 13 years later in the following case:

Defrenne v Sabena (Case 43/75)

An air stewardess made a claim against her employer for equal pay to that received by male stewards. The former Art 119 EC Treaty (which was replaced by Art 141 EC Treaty, and is now Art 157 TFEU) provided that 'Each Member State shall during the first stage ensure and subsequently maintain the application of the principle that men and women should receive equal pay for equal work'. Belgium had not enacted legislation to bring this about. The issue was whether the claimant could rely on the former Art 119 EC Treaty (now Art 157 TFEU) in her national court. The case was referred to the Court of Justice on a reference under the former Art 177 EC Treaty (which was replaced by Art 234 EC Treaty, and is now Art 267 TFEU) (see Chapter 6).

The Court of Justice dismissed the suggestion that the wording of the article confined the obligation to the Member State itself, and held as follows:

[35] In its reference to 'Member States', Article 119 [now Art 157 TFEU] is alluding to those States in the exercise of all those of their functions which may usefully contribute to the

> implementation of the principle of equal pay ... Thus ... this provision is far from merely referring the matter to the powers of the national legislative authorities. Therefore, the reference to 'Member States' in Article 119 cannot be interpreted as excluding the intervention of the courts in the direct application of the Treaty ... **Since Article 119 is mandatory in nature, the prohibition on discrimination between men and women applies not only to the action of public authorities, but also extends to all agreements which are intended to regulate paid labour collectively, as well as to contracts between individuals.** [emphasis added]

The effect of the above judgment was, therefore, that what is now Art 157 TFEU could be used between individuals in relation to a contract of employment. Some articles of the Treaty could thus be vertically effective (i.e. directly enforceable by private individuals/undertakings against the state, as in **Van Gend en Loos**) or both vertically and horizontally effective (i.e. directly enforceable by private individuals/undertakings against the state, *and* by private individuals/undertakings against other private individuals/undertakings) according to their wording and the context. In subsequent years the Court held that what is now Art 18 TFEU, prohibiting discrimination on grounds of nationality, was both vertically and horizontally effective. This was the situation in the following case:

Walrave and Koch v *Association Union Cycliste Internationale* (Case 36/74)

The Court of Justice held that:

> ... prohibition of such discrimination does not only apply to the acts of public authorities, but extends likewise to rules of any other nature aimed at regulating in a collective manner gainful employment and the provision of services.

Other Treaty provisions have also been held to be both horizontally and vertically effective, including:

- Articles 34 and 35 TFEU (previously Arts 28 and 29 EC Treaty) – prohibiting the imposition of restrictions on the export and import of goods: **Dansk Supermarked** (Case 58/80);

- Article 45 TFEU (previously Art 39 EC Treaty) – free movement of workers: **Donà v Mantero** (Case 13/76);

- Articles 49 and 50 TFEU (previously Arts 43 and 49 EC Treaty) – the right of establishment of businesses and professions and the right to provide services: **Thieffry v Paris Bar Association** (Case 71/76);

- Articles 101 and 102 TFEU (previously Arts 81 and 82 EC Treaty) – the prohibition of restrictive agreements and the abuse of a monopoly position: **Brasseries de Haecht** (Case 48/72); **Marty** (Case 37/79).

The accumulation of case law in relation to a number of these provisions has resulted in a subtle change in the terminology of the Court of Justice. In the jurisprudence of the Court, many of these Treaty provisions, especially those relating to freedom of movement, have come to be regarded not merely as directly effective Treaty provisions at the suit of individuals in national courts, but also as *fundamental rights* of EU citizens. The principle of direct effect is regarded as fundamentally important to the development of the Union. As a judge of the Court of Justice has declared:

Without direct effect, we should have a very different Community [i.e. Union] today – a more obscure, more remote Community [i.e. Union] barely distinguishable from so many other international organisations whose existence passes unnoticed by ordinary citizens. (Mancini and Keeling, 1994)

Regulations

See pages 65–66 for further discussion on EU Regulations and the concept of direct applicability.

The EC Treaty provides in Art 288, para 2 TFEU (previously Art 249, para 2 EC Treaty) that 'A regulation shall have general application. It shall be binding in its entirety and directly applicable in all Member States'. The reference to 'directly applicable' means that domestic legislation is not required in order to incorporate a regulation into national law. Union regulations are thus part of UK law without any further need of implementation. Indeed, any attempt at express incorporation is illegal, unless it is explicitly or implicitly required by the regulation itself (***Fratelli Variola SpA v Amministrazione Italiana delle Finanze*** (Case 34/73)). Whether or not a directly applicable measure is 'directly effective' (i.e. is capable of creating individual rights which a national court must recognise) will depend on the terms of the regulation; it must be 'sufficiently precise and unconditional' (see above). In practice, many are directly effective and are a fruitful source of individual rights (see, for example, Regulation 492/2011 on employment rights of migrant workers, and Regulation 883/2004 on social security benefits for those employed and self-employed in other Member States; see also Chapters 12 and 14). Regulations which are 'sufficiently precise and unconditional' will be both vertically and horizontally effective (i.e. directly enforceable by private individuals/undertakings against the state, *and* by private individuals/undertakings against other private individuals/undertakings).

Directives

Implementation of directives

Directives were not originally seen as being capable of creating directly effective rights. In contrast to regulations, they are not described as having direct applicability. Article 288, para 3 TFEU (previously Art 249 EC Treaty) provides that:

> A directive shall be binding, as to the result to be achieved, upon each Member State to which it is addressed, but shall leave to the national authorities the choice of form and methods.

Unlike regulations, directives are not directed at the world at large but at Member States. In the case of Treaty articles, this did not deter the Court from finding that individuals could also be bound by them (see *Defrenne*, above). However, unlike Treaty articles, directives are always conditional. They depend, under Art 288 TFEU, on the Member State giving effect to them. They have, since the inception of the Treaty, been a form of legislative subsidiarity, giving the Member State the option of the way in which it will implement the directive in order to meet the Union's objectives. The problem, as it became clear to both the Commission and the Court of Justice, was that Member States either simply did not implement directives by the date required, or implemented them in such a way as to fail, in whole or in part, to achieve their objectives.

Implementation does not mean that a directive must be directly transposed into national law. The Court described the Member States' obligations in the following case:

Commission v Germany (Re Nursing Directives) (Case 29/84)

The Court of Justice stated:

The implementation of a directive does not necessarily require legislative action in each Member State. In particular, the existence of general principles of constitutional and administrative law may render the implementation by specific legislation superfluous, provided, however, that those principles guarantee that the national authorities will, in fact, apply the directive fully, and where the directive is intended to create rights for individuals, the legal position arising from those principles is sufficiently clear and precise, and the persons concerned are made fully aware of their rights, and, where appropriate, are afforded the possibility of relying upon them before national courts. (para 23)

Although legislation may not always be necessary in relation to directives which are not intended to confer rights on individuals, the vast majority have either that intention, or at least that effect if implemented. In such cases, the issue of circular letters, urging a change of policy or a change in administrative practice, will not constitute implementation. Such practices, which may alter from time to time at the whim of the authority, and be quite unknown to the ordinary citizen, completely lack the certainty and transparency which Union law demands (**Commission v Belgium** (Case 102/79)).

A failure to implement a directive, or to correctly implement it, often results in a complaint by interested individuals and groups to the relevant Directorate -General in the Commission. This will usually be followed by protracted correspondence between the Commission and the offending state. If this is unsuccessful, formal Art 258 TFEU (previously Art 226 EC Treaty) proceedings may be instituted by the Commission before the Court of Justice. A financial penalty can be imposed on the Member State by the Court of Justice if the Member State has *failed to implement* the directive (Art 260(3) TFEU). However, if the Member State has *incorrectly implemented* the directive, and fails to comply with the Court's judgment (i.e. it does not remedy the breach by correctly implementing the directive), new proceedings can be brought by the Commission against the defaulting Member State for a breach of Art 260(1) TFEU (a failure to comply with a judgment of the Court of Justice) and in this instance a financial penalty can be imposed on the Member State by the Court of Justice (Art 260(2) TFEU; see Chapter 7). The process, from first complaint to judgment, may take several years. Enforcement procedures, given the limited resources of the Commission, can only be a partial solution to the problem. Until all Member States have implemented a directive, however, those states which fail to do so may gain an unfair competitive advantage. Many directives, for example those aimed at enhancing workers' rights, can significantly increase business costs. In addition, individuals may be deprived of rights the Union law has sought to provide them with. It is this situation to which the Court of Justice responded in its approach to unimplemented (or incorrectly implemented) directives.

Direct effect of directives

It is clear from the wording of Art 288 TFEU (and the former Art 249 EC Treaty) that directives were not to be directly applicable in the same way as regulations. They required Member States to act to give the directives effect in their territories. However, in *Grad* (Case 9/70), in a case turning on the effect of a regulation, the Court suggested that a directive might have some effect in a state where it had not been implemented by the due date. In the following case, the Court of Justice took its first important step towards recognising the direct effect of a directive:

Van Duyn v *Home Office* (Case 41/74)

The claimant in the case, Van Duyn, a Dutch national, was a member of the Church of Scientology. She wished to enter the UK to work at the headquarters of the organisation. She was refused leave to enter. The UK government had decided some years previously that the Church of Scientology was an undesirable organisation, although no steps had been taken against it, except to publicise the government's view.

In this case, *prima facie*, Van Duyn, as a worker, had a right of entry under the former Art 39 EC Treaty (now Art 45 TFEU). That right was, and remains, subject to the right of the host state to exclude and expel on public policy and public security grounds. The limits of the powers of the host state to derogate from its Treaty obligation on these grounds, and the extent of the procedural rights of those affected by such a decision, were set out in the former Directive 64/221 (which has been repealed and replaced by Directive 2004/38). In particular, Art 3(1), Directive 64/221 provided that a decision should be based 'exclusively on the personal conduct of the individual concerned'. Van Duyn argued that membership of an organisation could not be 'personal conduct' under Art 3(1). The UK government maintained that its power to refuse entry could not be limited in this way, because the UK had not yet implemented Directive 64/221 (it remained unimplemented for 20 years; see Chapter 16). The case was referred to the Court of Justice under the former Art 177 EC Treaty (which was replaced by Art 234 EC Treaty, and is now Art 267 TFEU). The Court refused to accept the position taken by the UK government, and held as follows:

> The UK observes that, since Article 189 [which was replaced by Art 249 EC Treaty, and is now Art 288 TFEU] of the Treaty distinguishes between the effects ascribed to regulations, directives and decisions, it must therefore be presumed that the Council, in issuing a directive rather than making a regulation, must have intended that the directive should have had an effect other than that of a regulation and accordingly that the former should not be directly applicable ... However ... it does not follow from this that other categories of acts mentioned in that article can never have similar effects. It would be incompatible with the binding effect attributed to a directive by Article 189 [now Art 288 TFEU] to exclude, in principle, the possibility that the obligation which it imposes may be invoked by those concerned. In particular, where the Community [i.e. Union] authorities have, by directive, imposed on Member States the obligation to pursue a particular course of conduct, the useful effect of such an act would be weakened if individuals were prevented from relying on it before their national courts and if the latter were prevented from taking it into consideration as an element of Community [i.e. Union] law.

The guiding principle adopted by the Court of Justice in the above case is that of ensuring the *effet utile* (i.e. the useful effect) of a measure in the territories and courts of Member States. In addition to this guiding principle is another (implied) principle referred to as the equitable doctrine of estoppel, or the doctrine of the impermissibility of reliance on one's own turpitude.

This principle is referred to as the equitable doctrine of estoppel, or the continental doctrine of the impermissibility of reliance on one's own turpitude. Application of this principle prevents a Member State from defending itself against a claim by an individual by raising as a defence its own failure to implement a directive (Advocate General Van Gerven in **Barber** (Case C-262/88)). Once the deadline for implementing a directive has passed, and not before (see **Ratti** (Case 148/78)), an individual may enforce the directive against the government of the state which has failed to implement it. The directive is therefore *vertically* effective.

Not every directive is, however, effective in this way. As the Court said in **Van Duyn**, 'it is necessary to examine in every case, whether the nature, general scheme and wording of the provision in question are capable of having direct effects'; i.e. are the provisions 'unconditional and sufficiently precise?' (**Becker** (Case 8/81)).

Directives: sufficiently precise and unconditional

The fact that a directive requires Member States to perform a positive act to implement it does not in itself prevent it from being capable of being unconditional.

For example, the Court of Justice held in **Francovich v Republic of Italy** (Cases C-6 and 9/90) that in the case of employment-related directives in general, in order to be sufficiently precise and unconditional, it is necessary to be able to:

- identify the persons who are entitled to the right;
- ascertain the content of that right;
- identify the person/body liable to provide that right.

A similar approach was adopted by the Court of Justice in **Kampelmann v Landschafts-verband Westfalen-Lippe** (Cases C-253–258/96) in which it was held that Art 2(2)(c), Directive 91/583 (OJ 1991 L 288/32), which imposed an obligation on employers to inform their employees of the conditions applicable to their contract or employment relationship, was sufficiently clear and precise to be capable of having direct effect.

The **Francovich** case (see below and later in the chapter) concerned Directive 80/987 (OJ 1980 L 283/23), which sought to protect employees on their employers' insolvency:

Francovich v Republic of Italy (Cases C-6/90 & 9/90)

The persons entitled to the rights under Directive 80/987 were employees (Art 2(2) of the directive refers to national law for the definition of the terms 'employee' and 'employer'). The Court of Justice held this was sufficiently precise to allow a national judge to ascertain whether an applicant had the status of employee under national law and whether the applicant was excluded from the scope of the directive under the specific exclusions set out therein.

The content of the right was more problematic. In implementing the directive, the Member State was given a number of choices, which included, *inter alia*:

- choice of date from which the payment of wages would accrue. As a result Member States could limit the payment of wages to periods of three months or eight weeks; and
- a discretion to set a liability ceiling so that payment of wages would not exceed a certain sum.

Given these legislative choices it would appear that the directive was not unconditional or sufficiently precise. However, the Court of Justice held that it was possible to calculate the *minimum* guarantee provided for by the directive which would impose the least burden on the body liable to provide the benefit (i.e. the 'guarantee institution'). With regard to the discretion to set a liability ceiling, the Court of Justice held that this discretion would not be available, however, unless the Member State had actually implemented the directive and taken advantage of the derogation in its implementing legislation.

The identity of the person/body liable to provide the benefit was subject to the Member State making a legislative choice as to whether the body should be public or private, and whether it would be publicly or privately funded. Under the directive, Member States enjoyed a wide discretion with regard to the functioning and financing of the 'guarantee institution'. The Member State had to identify the institution which would be liable to provide the benefit. The Court of Justice held this provision was not sufficiently precise or unconditional and therefore the directive was not capable of having direct effect.

Vertical effect: the state

As discussed above, the Court of Justice held that if a directive was 'sufficiently precise and unconditional' then it could be enforced against the state (i.e. **vertical direct effect**). It was not until 1986 in the following case that the Court explicitly stated that directives could *not* be enforced against private individuals and legal persons (although, see below on this issue):

Marshall v Southampton Area Health Authority (Case 152/84)

The Court of Justice declared that a directive could only be directly enforced against the state. After considering the effect of the third paragraph of the former Art 189 EC Treaty (which was replaced by Art 249 EC Treaty, and is now Art 288 TFEU), the Court stated (at paras 46 and 48) that:

> a Member State which has not adopted the implementing measures required by the directive within the prescribed period may not plead, as against individuals, its own failure to perform the obligations which the directive entails ... According to Article 189 [now Art 288 TFEU] ... the binding nature of a directive ... exists only in relation to 'each Member State to which it is addressed'. It follows that a directive may not of itself impose obligations on an individual and that a provision of a directive may not be relied upon as such against such a person. [emphasis added]

In the above case, the Court of Justice's reasoning for distinguishing between vertical and horizontal effect was based upon the fact that what is now Art 288 TFEU does not provide for directives to bind individuals and therefore it would be unfair for the Court to give them such an effect. The Court of Justice, however, was anxious to prevent a Member State from defending an action on the basis of its own wrongdoing.

So, if the directive is sufficiently precise and unconditional, the individual can enforce the unimplemented directive against 'the state'. But what constitutes 'the state'? Under Art 4(3), para 2 TEU (previously Art 10 EC Treaty), the obligation to implement Union law binds the Member States: 'The Member States shall take any appropriate measure, general or particular, to ensure fulfilment of the obligations arising out of the Treaties or resulting from the acts of the institutions of the Union.' The Court of Justice has been prepared to give 'Member State' a broad interpretation. Initially, it referred to the state exercising various functions and it was not necessary that it should be engaged in activities normally carried on by (or associated with) the state, such as operating immigration controls, collecting taxes, enforcing public health measures. In addition, directives were enforceable against the state when it was, for example, simply acting as an employer, as further illustrated in the *Marshall* case:

Marshall v Southampton Area Health Authority (Case 152/84)

The claimant was employed by the Health Authority. She wished to retire at 65, the same age as her male colleagues. The rules of the authority required her to retire at the age of 60. She was dismissed on the grounds of her age at 62, and brought proceedings against the Authority on grounds of sex discrimination. Discrimination on grounds of sex in relation to conditions of employment is prohibited by Directive 76/207. The UK's Sex Discrimination Act 1975, which had been enacted to implement the directive while it was still in draft form, contained an exception, allowing differential male and female retirement ages. There was no such exception in the directive. To that extent, therefore, the UK had failed to correctly implement the directive. The question to be determined was whether Marshall could enforce the directive against the Health Authority. The Court of Justice, on a referral under the former Art 177 EC Treaty (which was replaced by Art 234 EC Treaty, and is now Art 267 TFEU), held that she could:

> Where a person involved in legal proceedings is able to rely on a directive as against the State, he may do so regardless of the capacity in which the latter is acting, whether employer or public authority. In either case it is necessary to prevent the State from taking advantage of its own failure to comply with Community [i.e. Union] law.

In the above case, the Court of Justice added that it was for the national courts to determine the status of a body for the purpose of determining whether or not a directive could be directly enforced against it. It has, however, continued to give guidance. It decided in **Costanzo v Comune di Milano** (Case 103/88) that 'the state' included 'all organs of the administration, including decentralised authorities such as municipalities'. How 'decentralised' a body could be, and still be bound, was still to be determined by the Court of Justice.

Vertical effect: emanation of the state

In the following case, the Court of Justice addressed the issue of how 'decentralised' a body could be, and still be bound by an unimplemented or incorrectly implemented directive:

Foster v *British Gas* (Case C-188/89)

The UK House of Lords (the judicial functions of which are now exercised by the Supreme Court) requested a preliminary ruling from the Court of Justice, pursuant to the former Art 177 EC Treaty (which was replaced by Art 234 EC Treaty, and is now Art 267 TFEU), on the question of whether the British Gas Corporation (BGC) was, at the material time, a body of such a type that individuals could directly enforce a directive against it in the national courts and tribunals. At the material time, BGC had not been privatised (it was privatised on 24 August 1986 by the UK Gas Act 1986). Foster was employed by BGC and was made to retire at the age of 60. This was in line with company policy which required women to retire at the age of 60 and men at the age of 65. As discussed above, under English law (the Sex Discrimination Act 1975, which was in force at the material time) although it was unlawful for any employer to discriminate against a woman employed in Great Britain 'by dismissing her or subjecting her to any other detriment', this did not apply to 'provisions in relation to death or retirement'. Foster therefore sought to rely upon the Equal Treatment Directive (Council Directive 76/207) which did not allow discriminatory retirement ages.

In the *Marshall* case, the Court of Justice interpreted the Equal Treatment Directive as meaning that such a general policy of discriminatory retirement ages constituted discrimination on grounds of sex, contrary to the directive, which could be relied upon against a state authority. Foster's application to an employment tribunal was dismissed on the ground that the BGC was not a state authority within the meaning of *Marshall* and therefore the directive could not be relied upon against it. This decision was subsequently confirmed by both the Employment Appeal Tribunal and the Court of Appeal. The question of 'state authority' was critical to the outcome of the case, hence the House of Lords' referral of such question to the Court of Justice.

The Court of Justice (at para 18) stated that:

> ... the Court has held in a series of cases that unconditional and sufficiently precise provisions of a directive could be relied on against organisations or bodies which were subject to the authority or control of the State or had special powers beyond those which result from the normal rules applicable to relations between individuals. [emphasis added]

The Court of Justice (at para 20) developed a test to be applied to ascertain if the body against whom a directive was sought to be enforced was an *emanation of the state*:

> ... a body, whatever its legal form, which has been made responsible, pursuant to a measure adopted by the State, for providing a public service under the control of the State and has for that purpose special powers beyond those which result from the normal rules applicable in relations between individuals is included in any event among the bodies against which the provisions of a directive is capable of having direct effect may be relied upon. [emphasis added]

The three **Foster** criteria, established by the Court of Justice at para 20 in the above case, for determining whether a body is an 'emanation of the state' can be summarised as:

- provision of a public service;
- under state control;
- having special powers.

It should be noted that at para 18 in the above case the Court of Justice provided 'emanation of the state' with a potentially far wider scope.

The Court of Justice returned the case to the House of Lords (the judicial functions of which are now exercised by the Supreme Court) for the test to be applied to the facts of the case:

Foster v British Gas (No. 2) [1991] 2 AC 306

Lord Templeman was of the view that there was no justification for a narrow or strained construction of the Court of Justice's ruling (at p. 315, paras E–F). He further stated (at p. 315, paras G–H):

> I decline to apply the ruling of the European Court of Justice, couched in terms of broad principle and purposive language characteristic of Community [i.e. Union] law, in a manner which is ... sometimes applied to an enactment of the UK ... I can find no warrant in the present circumstances for the limited and speculative approach of [British Gas plc] and have no means of judging whether the relevant provisions of the Directive are enforceable against the BGC save by applying the plain words of the ruling of the European Court of Justice.

Lord Templeman reviewed the regulatory provisions under the UK Gas Act 1972 whereby the Secretary of State was authorised to make regulations and whereby the BGC was obliged to develop and maintain a gas supply for the UK (see s 2, Gas Act 1972) and he concluded (at p. 313, para F):

> Thus the BGC was a body which was made responsible pursuant to a measure adopted by the State [i.e. the Gas Act 1972] for providing a public service.

He further held (at p. 314, para B) that the BGC performed its public service under the control of the state:

> The BGC was not independent, its members were appointed by the State; the BGC was responsible to the minister acting on behalf of the State, and the BGC was subject to directions given by the Secretary of State.

Under s 29, Gas Act 1972 the BGC was afforded a monopoly for the supply of gas. This was sufficient for it to satisfy the Court's third criterion that the BGC had conferred upon it 'special powers beyond those which result from the normal rules applicable in relations between individuals' (at p. 314, para D).

The House of Lords held that the BGC satisfied the three criteria established by the Court of Justice and therefore the BGC was an 'emanation of the state' against which the directive could be enforced. The inconsistent provisions of the Sex Discrimination Act 1975 would be overridden.

Soon after the Court of Justice's decision in **Foster**, three cases which concerned the concept of 'emanation of the state' and the application of the **Foster** test came before the UK courts.

The first case was factually similar to the **Marshall** and **Foster** cases:

Doughty v Rolls-Royce Plc [1992] CMLR 1045

Ms Doughty was compulsorily retired at age 60, in accordance with company policy that women retire at 60 whereas men retire only at 65. As considered above, such discrimination was, at the material time, expressly permitted under English law. Doughty sought to rely upon the Equal Treatment Directive. The question before the Court of Appeal was whether or not Rolls-Royce was an emanation of the state. Lord Justice Mustill gave the leading judgment with which Lady Justice Butler-Sloss and Sir John Megaw agreed.

Mustill LJ quoted extensively from the employment tribunal's findings of fact as to the nature of Rolls-Royce, which at the material time had not been privatised (see p. 1048, para 8). All of Rolls-Royce's shares were held on behalf of the Crown; the ultimate power in relation to the company and its business rested with the shareholder (i.e. the Crown) by virtue of its ability to pass resolutions in General Meeting. In December 1980 a 'Memorandum of Understanding with Rolls-Royce – Relationship with Government' was issued. This provided that the government had three separate roles in its relationship with Rolls-Royce:

- that of 100 per cent shareholder;
- that of principal customer for the development and production of military engines; and
- that of its overall sponsorship of the aerospace industry.

The employment tribunal held that Rolls-Royce was an emanation of the state because as 100 per cent shareholder the state had the power to require the directors to alter the contracts of employment of the company's employees so as to comply with the directive.

This decision was reversed by the Employment Appeal Tribunal ([1987] IRLR 447), which held that the crucial question was whether or not Rolls-Royce could be said to be an organ or agent of the state carrying out a state function (see paras 11–12).

The appeal to the Court of Appeal was heard after the decisions of the Court of Justice and the House of Lords in **Foster**. Mustill LJ stated that the **Foster** test was not intended to be an exhaustive statement for determining the status of the entity, but, nevertheless, it was Mustill LJ's opinion that in a case factually similar to **Foster**, the test:

... must always be the starting point and will usually be the finishing point. If all the factors identified by the Court are present it is likely to require something very unusual to produce the result that an entity is not to be identified with the State. Conversely, although the absence of a factor will not necessarily be fatal, it will need the addition of something else, not contemplated by the formula ... (para 24) [emphasis added]

Mustill LJ went on to examine whether or not the three *Foster* criteria were satisfied. He accepted that the second criterion, requiring the service to be provided under the control of the state, was satisfied. However, he stated that if this point had been crucial to the outcome it would have required detailed examination. He stated that with regard to this criterion, the relevant question was whether the public *service* (rather than the *body* providing the service) was under the state's control. He concluded that the other two criteria were not satisfied: Rolls-Royce could not be said to have been made responsible for providing a public service, pursuant to a measure adopted by the state, nor was there any evidence that Rolls-Royce possessed or exercised any 'special powers'.

Accordingly, *Doughty* could not enforce the directive against Rolls-Royce, because Rolls-Royce was deemed not to be an emanation of the state.

The second case centred on the question of whether the provisions of the Collective Redundancies Directive 92/129 could be enforced directly against the privatised company, South West Water:

Griffin and Others v *South West Water Services Ltd* [1995] IRLR 15

The English High Court first considered the question of whether South West Water (SWW) was an emanation of the state. It was common ground between the parties that the correct approach was to consider whether the three *Foster* criteria were fulfilled. Blackburne J relied upon Mustill LJ's dicta in *Doughty* that the *Foster* criteria must be the starting point and would usually be the finishing point. In deciding the question, Blackburne J conducted a detailed examination of the powers and duties conferred upon the newly privatised SWW and of the control to which it was subject.

It was common ground between the parties that the first criterion, the 'public service' condition, and the third criterion, the 'special powers' condition, were fulfilled. The crucial question was whether or not the second criterion, the 'state control' condition, was satisfied. Blackburne J, as did Mustill LJ in *Doughty*, made it clear (at para 94) that:

The question is not whether the body in question is under the control of the State, but whether the public service in question is under the control of the State ... It is also irrelevant that the body does not carry out any of the traditional functions of the State and is not an agent of the State ... It is irrelevant too that the State does not possess day-to-day control over the activities of the body.

The question therefore was whether or not the public services of water and sewerage provision performed by SWW were under the control of the state. There were a whole number of powers available to the Secretary of State and the Director General of Water Services to conclude that the public service of water and sewerage provision performed by SWW were under the control of the state, thus fulfilling the 'control' condition (see paras 96–110).

The three *Foster* criteria being satisfied, SWW was an emanation of the state, a body against which the directive was capable of being enforced.

It should be noted that, as discussed above, the directive could therefore be directly enforced, provided the provisions of the directive were *sufficiently precise and unconditional*. In the above case, the High Court decided that the relevant provisions were *not* sufficiently precise and unconditional and therefore the directive could not be enforced against SWW.

The following is the third and final case:

National Union of Teachers and Others v *The Governing Body of St Mary's Church of England (Aided) Junior School and Others* [1997] IRLR 242

The individual applicants had been employed at a school which had been closed down, following which a new school was established under the control of a temporary governing body. The applicants were not re-employed. It was argued by the applicants that the Acquired Rights Directive 77/187 applied automatically to transfer their contracts of employment and therefore their dismissals were unlawful. It was common ground that, at the material time, English law would not assist the applicants.

To determine whether the governing body was an emanation of the state, the employment tribunal applied the *Foster* test and concluded that it did not satisfy the 'special powers' criterion. The directive could therefore not be directly enforced against the governing body because it was not an emanation of the state. The appeal to the Employment Appeal Tribunal ([1995] ICR 317) was dismissed. The Court of Appeal unanimously allowed the appeal. The leading judgment was delivered by Schiemann LJ.

Schiemann LJ quite correctly recognised that the Court of Justice had not established a test which should be applied to all situations. Although each party to the case had relied upon the *Foster* test, he stated that:

> It is clear from the wording of paragraph 20 [of the Court's judgment in *Foster*] and in particular the words 'is included among' that the formula there used was not intended to be an exclusive formula.

The governing body relied heavily upon the Court of Appeal's decision in *Doughty*, and in particular on Mustill LJ's observation that in a case of the same general type as *Foster*, the test formulated by the Court of Justice would always be the starting point and would usually be the finishing point. However, Schiemann LJ was of the view that this case was not of the same general type as that of *Foster*:

> That case and *Rolls-Royce* were both concerned with commercial undertakings in which the Government had a stake. The present case is not concerned with any commercial undertaking but rather with the provision of what would generally in the Community [i.e. Union] be regarded as the provision of a public service.

He said that the Employment Appeal Tribunal was wrong in applying the *Foster* test as if it was a statutory definition. Even though the parties had relied upon the test, Schiemann LJ did not think it was appropriate to apply it in a similar fashion to the Appeal Tribunal. Nevertheless, in view of the parties' submissions, he made his own observations on the application of the three *Foster* criteria to the particular facts.

The first two criteria, 'public service' provision and 'state control', were fulfilled. However, he was not satisfied that the governing body had 'special powers'. Despite this reservation, he held that the governing body was an emanation of the state. He was no doubt influenced by the financial benefit accruing to the local education authority if the appeal was dismissed:

> The financial position is that the failure to transpose the Directive will, if the present appeal is dismissed, have the effect of allowing the local education authority and the State to

benefit from the failure to transpose the Directive. The *Rolls-Royce* case indicates that the mere fact that some incidental benefit may arise to the State from a failure to implement a directive does not necessarily bring the doctrine of vertical effect into play. In the present case the benefit is direct to the local education authority, as is conceded because of the provisions of s 46 of the Education Reform Act 1988, and the local education authority, as is further conceded, is an emanation of the State for the purposes of the doctrine of direct vertical effect. [emphasis added]

Section 46, Education Reform Act 1988 provided that local education authorities were responsible for redundancy payments. The nature of the service being provided and the fact that the body providing the service was financially dependent upon the local education authority were indicative of the outcome of the case. Schiemann LJ quite correctly departed from a strict application of the *Foster* test, preferring to address the question on the basis that the state should not benefit from its own failure to implement a directive.

The Court of Justice subsequently delivered a judgment which considered the *Foster* test further:

Kampelmann v Landschaftsverband Westfalen-Lippe (Cases C-253–258/96)

The Court of Justice held that, in accordance with its *Foster v British Gas* judgment:

46. ... a directive ... may ... be relied on against organisations or bodies which are subject to the authority or control of the State **OR** have special powers beyond those which result from the normal rules applicable to relations between individuals, such as local or regional authorities **OR** other bodies which, irrespective of their legal form, have been given responsibility by the public authorities and under their supervision, for providing a public service. [emphasis added]

Although in the above case the Court of Justice stated that this judgment was in line with its *Foster* judgment (i.e. para 46 of the *Kampelmann* judgment is almost identical to para 18 of the *Foster* judgment, with one important exception), in the operative part of *Foster* the three criteria were stated to be cumulative, whereas in the *Kampelmann* judgment the Court of Justice set out the criteria as alternatives. If this had been subsequently reaffirmed by the Court of Justice as a departure from *Foster*, then the bodies and organisations against which a directive may be capable of having direct effect could have been extended. However, this would have required the Court to explicitly depart from its previous reasoning as to why a directive should only be enforceable vertically (i.e. to prevent a Member State profiting from its own failure to implement (or correctly implement) a directive). The Court of Justice subsequently considered the concept of 'emanation of the state' in the following case, and made no reference to its *Kampelmann* judgment:

Rieser Internationale Transporte GmbH v Autobahnen- und Schnellstraßen-Finanzierungs-AG (Asfinag) (Case C-157/02)

With regard to enforcement of a directive against an 'emanation of the state', the Court of Justice held as follows:

22. It ought to be borne in mind that the Court has consistently held (Case 8/81 *Becker* [1982] ECR 53, paragraphs 23 to 25, and Case C-188/89 *Foster and Others* [1990] ECR I-3313, paragraph 16) that where the Community [i.e. Union] authorities have, by means

of a directive, placed Member States under an obligation to adopt a certain course of action, the effectiveness of such a measure would be diminished if persons were prevented from relying upon it in proceedings before a court and national courts were prevented from taking it into consideration as an element of Community [i.e. Union] law. Consequently, a Member State which has not adopted the implementing measures required by the directive within the prescribed period may not plead, as against individuals, its own failure to perform the obligations which the directive entails. Thus, wherever the provisions of a directive appear, as far as their subject-matter is concerned, to be unconditional and sufficiently precise, those provisions may, in the absence of implementing measures adopted within the prescribed period, be relied upon as against any national provision which is incompatible with the directive or in as so far the provisions define rights which individuals are able to assert against the State.

23. The Court has further held (Case 152/84 *Marshall* [1986] ECR 723, paragraph 49, and *Foster and Others*, cited above, paragraph 17) that where a person is able to rely on a directive as against the State he may do so regardless of the capacity in which the latter is acting, whether as employer or as public authority. In either case it is necessary to prevent the State from taking advantage of its own failure to comply with Community [i.e. Union] law.

24. **A body, whatever its legal form, which has been made responsible, pursuant to a measure adopted by the State, for providing a public service under the control of the State and has for that purpose special powers beyond those which result from the normal rules applicable in relations between individuals is included in any event among the bodies against which the provisions of a directive capable of having direct effect may be relied upon** (*Foster and Others*, paragraph 20, and Case C-343/98 *Collino and Chiappero* [2000] ECR I-6659, paragraph 23).

25. It is clear from the information contained in the order for reference that the Austrian State is the sole shareholder in Asfinag. It has the right to check all measures taken by that company and its subsidiaries and at any time to demand information about their activities. It is entitled to impose objectives with regard to the organisation of traffic, safety and construction. Every year Asfinag is required to draw up a plan for the maintenance of the motorways and expressways and to submit to the State the calculation of the costs involved. Furthermore, every year within the periods necessary for the drawing-up of the State's budget, it must present to the State calculations with the estimated costs of planning, constructing, maintaining and managing motorways and national expressways.

26. In addition, the order for reference makes it clear that Asfinag is not entitled of its own authority to fix the amount of the tolls to be levied. That amount is fixed by law. Paragraphs 4 and 8 of the law known as the Asfinag Law (BGBl. 1982/591) provide that the amount of the payment must be fixed by the Bundesminister für Wirtschaftliche Angelegenheiten (Federal Minister for Economic Affairs) in concert with the Bundesminister für Finanzen (Federal Minister for Finance), according to certain criteria including, *inter alia*, the type of vehicle.

27. Those facts clearly show that Asfinag is a body to which, pursuant to an act adopted by the public authorities, the performance of a public-interest service (namely: the constructing, planning, operating, maintaining and financing of motorways and expressways in addition to the levying of tolls and user charges), has been entrusted, under the supervision of those public authorities, and which for that purpose possesses special powers beyond those resulting from the normal rules applicable in relations between individuals.

28. According to the decisions cited in paragraph 24 above, such a body, whatever its legal form, is included among those against which the provisions of a directive capable of having direct effect may be relied upon.

> 29. In consequence, the answer to be given to the first question must be that, when contracts are concluded with road users, the provisions of a directive capable of having direct effect may be relied upon against a legal person governed by private law where the State has entrusted to that legal person the task of levying tolls for the use of public road networks and where it has direct or indirect control of that legal person. [emphasis added]

In the above case, the Court of Justice, at para 24, set out the *Foster* criteria as being cumulative. The Court did not refer to the *Kampelmann* judgment. The Court then applied the three criteria to the facts of the case, at paras 25–27. The Court concluded, at para 28, that in the case of a company which had been entrusted by Austria to levy toll charges for the use of public roads, and where Austria had direct or indirect control of the toll-levying company, the three *Foster* criteria were satisfied. Such a company was therefore an emanation of the state against which a directive (which was sufficiently precise and unconditional) could be enforced. The above case would suggest that the Court of Justice had not deliberately departed from the *Foster* case in *Kampelmann*, and it has undoubtedly confirmed that the *Foster* criteria will be applied cumulatively in the future.

Horizontal effect

The following case concerned the question of whether or not a Union directive could have horizontal direct effect:

Paola Faccini Dori v Recreb SRL (Case C-91/92)

The issue before the Court of Justice was whether Miss Faccini Dori could rely upon an unimplemented directive in the national (Italian) court against a private company (which was not an emanation of the state).

On 9 February 1994 the opinion of Advocate General Lenz was delivered at a sitting of the full Court. The Advocate General recognised that the Court of Justice had consistently held that directives could not have direct effect in relations between individuals, and that for reasons of legal certainty this should be maintained with regard to situations in the past. However, as regards the future, the Advocate General was of the opinion that those provisions of a directive which are sufficiently precise and unconditional should have direct effect; for future cases the Union should recognise that directives may be directly effective both vertically and horizontally.

As discussed in Chapter 5, the Court of Justice is not bound by the doctrine of precedent and accordingly could have departed from its own previous decisions. However, for the sake of legal certainty the Court generally follows and builds upon its own previous case law. The Court of Justice rejected the Advocate General's opinion. The Court stated that ever since the *Marshall* case it had been held that a directive could not of itself impose obligations on an individual. Accordingly, a directive could not be relied upon against such an individual.

Although the above judgment would appear to have settled the issue, certainly for the foreseeable future, on occasion the Court of Justice has implicitly allowed horizontal direct enforcement, provided no particular obligation was placed on the defendant. For example, in *CIA Security International v Signalson and Securitel* (Case C-194/94) a directive required the Commission to be notified of certain technical regulations. This was effectively not implemented by the relevant Member State. The claimant sought to rely on the directive to relieve him from an obligation, without it imposing an obligation on the defendant under the directive, and the Court of Justice allowed this. In effect the Court allowed the claimant to directly enforce the directive horizontally.

In **Criminal Proceedings against Rafael Ruiz Bernáldez** (Case C-129/94), Spain had a law requiring drivers of vehicles to have a valid motor insurance policy. However, Spanish law, contrary to a directive, provided that an insurance company was not liable to compensate a third party victim of a driver who was under the influence of alcohol at the time of the accident. The Court of Justice held that the unimplemented directive should apply, thus indirectly imposing an obligation on the insurance company. The practical effect, once again, was to allow the directive to be directly enforced horizontally, although the Court of Justice did not explicitly state this to be the case.

The principle of state liability

Objective 4

The possibility of taking action against the state for failing to implement a directive was first considered in the following case:

Francovich and Bonifaci v Republic of Italy (Cases C-6/90 and 9/90)

An Italian company went into liquidation, leaving Francovich and other employees with unpaid arrears of salary. Directive 80/987 required Member States to set up a compensation scheme for employees in these circumstances, but Italy had not established one. Francovich therefore sought compensation from the Italian government. The case was referred to the Court of Justice. The Court was asked: (i) whether the directive had direct effect; (ii) whether the Member State was liable for the damage arising from its failure to implement the directive; and (iii) to what extent it was liable for damages for violation of its obligations under Union law.

The Court decided that the directive was insufficiently precise to have direct effect (see above). However, it emphasised that the Treaty created a legal order which was binding upon Member States and citizens. The *effet utile* (i.e. the useful effect) of Union law would be diminished if individuals were not able to obtain damages after suffering loss incurred because of a violation of Union law by a Member State. There was an implied obligation under the former Art 5 EC Treaty (which was replaced by Art 10 EC Treaty, and is now Art 4(3) TEU) to compensate individuals affected by such a violation. The Court held that, in cases such as this, where there was a violation of the state's obligation to implement Union law under the former Art 189 EC Treaty (which was replaced by Art 249 EC Treaty, and is now Art 288 TFEU), there was a right to compensation from the state, provided the following three conditions were satisfied:

- The result which had to be attained by the directive involved rights conferred on individuals.
- The content of those rights could be identified from the provisions of the directive.
- There was a causal link between the failure by the Member State to fulfil its obligations and the damage suffered by the person affected.

The Court did not decide how the extent of liability was to be determined, as this was to be a matter for national law. National procedures had, however, 'to ensure the full protection of rights which individuals might derive from Community [i.e. Union] law'. In this particular case, the failure of Italy to implement the directive in question had already been established by the Court.

Generally, there will not be a defence to simple non-implementation because, whatever practical difficulties there may be, the obligation to implement is strict (***Commission v Belgium*** (Case 1/86)).

See page 310 for a flowchart relating to the principle of state liability.

The Court has developed the concept of state liability and entitlement to damages in a number of subsequent judgments.

Legislative acts

The following joined cases concerned directly effective Treaty articles that had been breached:

Brasserie du Pêcheur v *Germany* and *R* v *Secretary of State for Transport, ex parte Factortame Ltd and Others* (Cases C-46 and 48/93)

The former case concerned a pre-existing German law which breached the former Art 30 EC Treaty (which was replaced by Art 28 EC Treaty, and is now Art 34 TFEU), and the latter a UK Act of Parliament which was enacted in breach of, *inter alia*, the former Art 52 EC Treaty (which was replaced by Art 43 EC Treaty, and is now Art 49 TFEU). The claimants sought damages against the respective states for the legislature's breach of Union law. The national courts referred a number of questions to the Court of Justice for a preliminary ruling pursuant to the former Art 177 EC Treaty (which was replaced by Art 234 EC Treaty, and is now Art 267 TFEU).

The first question in both cases concerned whether or not the *Francovich* principle of state liability would oblige Member States to make-good damage caused to individuals by a breach of Union law by the state legislature, no matter what form that breach took. In assessing this question, the Court of Justice initially stated that it was irrelevant that the breach concerned a directly effective Treaty article and that it was irrelevant which organ of state was responsible for the breach:

> 31. ... the Court held in *Francovich and Others*, at paragraph 35, that the principle of State liability for loss and damage caused to individuals as a result of breaches of Community [i.e. Union] law for which it can be held responsible is inherent in the system of the Treaty.
> 32. It follows that that principle holds good for any case in which a Member State breaches Community [i.e. Union] law, whatever be the organ of the State whose act or omission was responsible for the breach.

The Court of Justice then gave consideration to the conditions under which state liability may be incurred. Reiterating its *Francovich* judgment, the Court stated that:

> 38. Although Community [i.e. Union] law imposes State liability, the conditions under which that liability gives rise to a right to reparation depend on the nature of the breach of Community [i.e. Union] law giving rise to the loss and damage.

In examining the facts of the two cases, the Court of Justice stated that the national legislatures had a wide discretion in the relevant fields of activity. Where there was such a wide discretion, three conditions had to be met in order to incur state liability (at para 51):

● the rule of law infringed must be intended to *confer rights on individuals*;
● the breach must be *sufficiently serious*;
● there must be a *direct causal link* between the breach of the obligation resting on the state and the damage sustained by the injured parties.

293

The former Arts 30 and 52 EC Treaty (now Arts 34 and 49 TFEU) are directly effective and therefore the first condition was satisfied *per se*. It is the second condition which is the most interesting. The Court of Justice stated that the decisive test for finding that a breach of Union law is sufficiently serious is whether the Member State 'manifestly and gravely disregarded the limits on its discretion' (at para 55). The Court of Justice then set out a number of factors which may be taken into consideration by the national court when assessing whether or not there was such a manifest and grave disregard by the Member State of the limit on its discretion:

56. The factors which the competent court may take into consideration include the clarity and precision of the rule breached, the measure of discretion left by that rule to the national or Community [i.e. Union] authorities, whether the infringement and the damage caused was intentional or involuntary, whether any error of law was excusable or inexcusable, the fact that the position taken by a Community [i.e. Union] institution may have contributed towards the omission, and the adoption or retention of national measures or practices contrary to Community [i.e. Union] law. [emphasis added]

57. On any view, a breach of Community [i.e. Union] law will clearly be sufficiently serious if it has persisted despite a judgment finding the infringement in question to be established, or a preliminary ruling or settled case law of the Court on the matter from which it is clear that the conduct in question constituted an infringement.

The *Factortame* case returned to the UK court for it to apply the three conditions of state liability. The case reached the House of Lords (*R v Secretary of State for Transport, ex parte Factortame Ltd and Others (No. 5)* [1999] 3 WLR 1062). The House of Lords (the judicial functions of which are now exercised by the Supreme Court) held that the adoption of legislation which was discriminatory on the ground of nationality in respect of the registration of UK fishing vessels, in breach of clear and unambiguous rules of Union law, was *sufficiently serious* to give rise to liability in damages to individuals who suffered loss as a consequence. Factortame would then have to prove its losses (i.e. prove that there was a *direct causal link* between the breach and the damage they had sustained).

Legislative act: incorrect implementation of a directive

The following case concerned the incorrect implementation of a directive by the UK, a situation in which a Member State does not enjoy a wide discretion. Article 288, para 3 TFEU requires a Member State to implement a directive within the time period laid down:

R v HM Treasury, ex parte British Telecommunications plc (Case C-392/93)

The Court of Justice (at para 39) restated the three conditions in the previous joined cases. Where a Member State acts in a field in which it has a wide discretion in the taking of legislative decisions, for the defaulting Member State to incur liability:

the rule of law infringed must be intended to confer rights on individuals; the breach must be sufficiently serious; and there must be a direct causal link between the breach … and the damage sustained.

The Court of Justice held (at para 40) that this restrictive approach was equally applicable to the facts of this case, where the UK had incorrectly transposed a directive. Once again the Court stated that it was for the national court to determine whether or not there was a **sufficiently serious breach**. However, because the Court of Justice had all the necessary facts before it, it went on to advise the national court as to the determination of the factual situation.

In the *Brasserie du Pêcheur* and *Factortame* joined cases, the Court of Justice held (at para 56) that one of the relevant factors was the clarity and precision of the rule breached. In this case the directive was imprecisely worded and was reasonably capable of bearing the interpretation given to it by the UK. Moreover, the UK had acted in good faith (at para 43). The Court of Justice noted that this interpretation was shared by other Member States and 'was not manifestly contrary to the wording of the directive or to the objective pursued by it' (at para 43).

Additionally, there had been no case law from the Court of Justice to guide the UK. The Commission had not questioned the UK's implementing legislation. In those circumstances, the Court of Justice held that the breach could not be regarded as sufficiently serious.

Executive act: breach of the Treaty

The following case again involved the UK courts:

R v Ministry of Agriculture, Fisheries and Food, ex parte Hedley Lomas (Ireland) Ltd (Case C-5/94)

The UK Ministry of Agriculture refused licences for the exporting of livestock to Spain for slaughter because it was of the view that Spain was acting contrary to Directive 74/557, which concerns the stunning of animals before slaughter. Unlike the previous cases, this involved an act of the executive rather than an act of the legislature. The Court of Justice held that the refusal by the Ministry was a quantitative restriction contrary to the former Art 34 EC Treaty (which was replaced by Art 29 EC Treaty, and is now Art 35 TFEU), which could not be justified under the former Art 36 EC Treaty (which was replaced by Art 30 EC Treaty, and is now Art 36 TFEU). The UK was therefore in breach of Union law.

In reaching its judgment, the Court of Justice restated that part of its judgment in *Brasserie du Pêcheur* and *Factortame*, where it held that in a field in which a Member State has a wide discretion to make legislative choices, a defaulting Member State will incur liability where three conditions are satisfied:

> 25. ... the rule of law infringed must be intended to confer rights on individuals; the breach must be sufficiently serious; and there must be a direct causal link between the breach of the obligation resting on the State and the damage sustained by the injured parties.

In an attempt to impose a common standard for state liability throughout the Union, the Court of Justice held that:

> 26. Those three conditions are also applicable in the circumstances of this case.

This was despite the fact that the breach did not involve a legislative act and despite the fact that the Member State did not enjoy a wide discretion. Although the Court of Justice introduced the three conditions in order to impose a uniform test for state liability throughout the Union, it acknowledged that the concept of 'sufficiently serious breach' will vary, depending upon the facts of the case. With regard to this particular case, the Court of Justice stated:

> 28. ... where, at the time when it committed the infringement, **the Member State** in question was not called upon to make any legislative choices and **had only considerably reduced, or even no, discretion, the mere infringement of Community** [i.e. Union] **law may be sufficient to establish the existence of a sufficiently serious breach.** [emphasis added]

Failure to implement a directive: *Francovich* revisited

The next case concerned Germany's failure to transpose Directive 90/314/EEC:

Dillenkofer and Others v *Federal Republic of Germany* (Joined Cases C-178, 179 and 188–190/94)

This case was factually similar to *Francovich*. In *Francovich* the Court of Justice did *not* make it a condition that the breach of Union law must be sufficiently serious in order for state liability to be incurred. However, in this case, the Court of Justice stated that this was a condition, but by the very nature of the breach (i.e. a complete disregard of the Member State's obligation under the former Art 189, para 3 EC Treaty (which was replaced by Art 249, para 3 EC Treaty, and is now Art 288, para 3 TFEU)) the breach was sufficiently serious *per se* (i.e. automatically).

National courts: failure to apply Union law

The following case is important because it extended the principle of state liability to 'courts of last instance':

Köbler (Case C-224/01)

A German national had worked as an ordinary professor in an Austrian university for ten years. He applied for a special length-of-service increment, which was normally paid to professors with 15 years' experience exclusively at Austrian universities, arguing that he had completed the requisite length of service if the duration of his service in universities of other Member States was taken into consideration. After it had referred a question on this point for a preliminary ruling, the Austrian court took account of the judgment in *Schöning-Kougebetopoulou* (Case C-15/96). In this case, the Court of Justice had held that the provisions of Union law on freedom of movement for workers within the Union precluded a clause in a collective agreement which applied to the public service of a Member State, which provided for promotion on grounds of seniority for employees of that service after eight years' employment in a salary group determined by that agreement, without taking any account of previous periods of comparable employment completed in the public service of another Member State. The Austrian court then withdrew the question it had referred for a preliminary ruling and, without referring a second question to the Court of Justice, confirmed that the refusal of the application of the person concerned was justified, on the ground that the special length-of-service increment was a loyalty bonus, which objectively justified a derogation from the Union law provisions on freedom of movement for workers.

Köbler then brought an action for damages before the referring court for breach of Union law. In its preliminary ruling the Court of Justice confirmed that **the principle, stated in particular in *Brasserie du Pêcheur* and *Factortame* (Cases C-46/93 and C-48/93), where Member States are obliged to make-good damage caused to individuals by infringements of Union law for which they are responsible, applies in cases where the alleged infringement stems from a decision of a court adjudicating at last instance where the rule of Union law infringed is intended to confer rights on individuals, the breach is sufficiently serious and there is a direct causal link between that breach and the loss or damage sustained by the injured parties.** The Court of Justice made clear that, as regards the second condition, in order to determine whether the infringement is sufficiently serious when the infringement at issue stems from a decision of a court, the competent national court, taking into account the specific nature of the judicial function, must determine whether that infringement is manifest. Finally, it added that it is for the legal system of each Member State to designate the court competent to determine disputes relating to that reparation.

Although it is generally for the national courts to consider the abovementioned criteria, the Court of Justice took the view that it had available to it all the material facts enabling it to establish whether the conditions necessary for liability to be incurred by the Member State concerned were fulfilled. **As regards the existence of a sufficiently serious breach, the Court of Justice held that an infringement of Union law does not have the requisite manifest character for liability under Union law to be incurred by a Member State for a decision of one of its courts adjudicating at last instance, where: (i) Union law does not expressly cover the point of law at issue, no reply was to be found to that question in the Court's case law and that reply was not obvious; and (ii) the infringement was not intentional but was the result of an incorrect reading of a judgment of the Court.**

The applicant did not succeed in the above case, because the Court of Justice held that the Austrian court's infringement of Union law was not 'sufficiently serious'. The Court of Justice stated that in a case where the infringement concerns the decision of a court of last instance (i.e. a court from which there is no appeal (e.g. the Supreme Court in the UK)), in order to establish that the infringement is 'sufficiently serious' it must be determined whether or not the infringement is *manifest*. This decision quite clearly affords national courts a degree of protection. The necessity to show that the infringement is manifest will be an onerous task.

The following case further develops the principles established in ***Köbler***:

Traghetti del Mediterraneo SpA v *Italy* (Case C-173/03)

In 1981, the maritime transport company 'Traghetti del Mediterraneo' (TDM) brought proceedings against a competing company, Tirrenia di Navigazione, before the Tribunale di Napoli. TDM sought compensation for the damage that its competitor had allegedly caused it through its policy of low fares on the maritime cabotage market between mainland Italy and the islands of Sardinia and Sicily, which had been made possible by public subsidies.

TDM submitted in particular that the conduct in question constituted unfair competition and abuse of a dominant position, which was prohibited by the former Art 82 EC Treaty (now Art 102 TFEU).

The action for compensation was dismissed by all the Italian courts which had heard the case: at first instance, the Tribunale di Napoli, then, on appeal, the Corte d'appello di Napoli and the Corte Suprema di Cassazione (the Supreme Court). Taking the view that the judgment of the latter court was founded on an incorrect interpretation of the Union rules, the administrator of TDM, which had in the meantime been put into liquidation, brought proceedings against Italy before the Tribunale di Genova. That action sought compensation for the damage suffered by TDM as a result of the errors of interpretation committed by the supreme court (the court of last instance in this case) and of the breach of its obligation to make a reference for a preliminary ruling to the Court of Justice.

In those circumstances, the Tribunale di Genova asked the Court of Justice whether Union law and, in particular, the principles laid down by the Court in the ***Köbler*** judgment preclude national legislation such as the Italian law which: (i) excludes all liability of a Member State for damage caused to individuals by an infringement of Union law committed by a national court adjudicating at last instance, where that infringement is the result of an interpretation of provisions of law or of an assessment of the facts and evidence carried out by that court; and (ii) also limits such liability solely to cases of intentional fault and serious misconduct on the part of the court.

The Court of Justice observed that the principle that a Member State is obliged to make-good damage caused to individuals as a result of breaches of Union law for which it is responsible applies to any case in which a Member State breaches Union law, whichever is the authority of the Member State whose act or omission was responsible for the breach.

The Court then noted that the essential role played by the judiciary in the protection of individuals' rights under Union law would be weakened if individuals could not, under certain conditions, obtain compensation for damage caused by an infringement of Union law attributable to a court of a Member State adjudicating at last instance. In such a case, individuals must be able to rely on state liability in order to obtain legal protection of their rights.

The Court stated that the interpretation of provisions of law and the assessment of facts and evidence constitute an essential part of judicial activity and may lead, in certain cases, to a manifest infringement of the applicable law.

To exclude any possibility that state liability may be incurred where the infringement allegedly committed by the national court relates to its interpretation of provisions of law or its assessment of facts or evidence would amount to depriving the principle of state liability of all practical effect and lead to a situation where individuals would have no judicial protection if a national court adjudicating at last instance committed a manifest error in the exercise of those activities of interpretation or assessment.

With regard to the limitation of state liability solely to cases of intentional fault and serious misconduct on the part of the court, the Court of Justice pointed out that state liability for damage caused to individuals by reason of an infringement of Union law attributable to a national court adjudicating at last instance may be incurred in the exceptional case where that court has manifestly infringed the applicable law.

Such manifest infringement is to be assessed, *inter alia*, in the light of a number of criteria, such as: (i) the degree of clarity and precision of the rule infringed; (ii) whether the error of law was excusable or inexcusable; and (iii) the non-compliance by the court in question with its obligation to make a reference for a preliminary ruling. A manifest infringement is presumed where the decision involved is taken in manifest disregard of the case law of the Court of Justice on the subject.

Accordingly, the Court of Justice held that although it remains possible for national law to define the criteria relating to the nature or degree of the infringement which must be met before state liability can be incurred for an infringement of Union law attributable to a national court adjudicating at last instance, under no circumstances may such criteria impose requirements stricter than that of a manifest infringement of the applicable law.

Consequently, the Court of Justice held that the limitation of state liability solely to cases of intentional fault and serious misconduct on the part of the court is contrary to Union law if such a limitation were to lead to exclusion of liability of the Member State concerned in other cases where a manifest infringement of the applicable law was committed.

The following case also concerned the Italian courts and the application of the principles established in *Köbler*:

Commission v Italy (Case C-379/10)

The Commission claimed that an Italian statute on compensation for damage caused in the exercise of judicial functions and the civil liability of judges was incompatible with EU law with regard to the liability of Member States for an infringement of EU law by one of their courts adjudicating at last instance.

The Commission alleged that Italy had made it impossible for the state to be held liable for damage caused to individuals where the infringement of EU law came about as a result of the way such a court had interpreted provisions of law or assessed the facts and evidence, and that, in other cases where the issue was not the interpretation of provisions of law or the assessment of facts and evidence, it had limited the cases where state liability could be incurred to those involving intentional fault or gross negligence.

The Court stated that the Italian statute excluded, in a general manner, state liability in respect of the interpretation of law and the assessment of facts or evidence.

As the Court had already ruled in *Köbler*, EU law precludes such general exclusion of state liability for damage caused to individuals as a result of an infringement of EU law attributable to a court adjudicating at last instance, where the infringement in question resulted from an interpretation of provisions of law, or an assessment of facts or evidence, carried out by that court.

Moreover, the Court of Justice stated that Italy had not established that the Italian legislation was interpreted by the Italian courts as merely imposing a limit on state liability and not as ruling it out altogether.

The Court pointed out that a Member State is required to make-good any damage caused to individuals as a result of an infringement of EU law by state bodies, where three conditions are met: (i) the rule of EU law infringed confers rights on the individuals; (ii) the infringement is sufficiently serious; and (iii) there is a direct causal link between the breach of the obligation on the state and the damage sustained by the individual.

The same conditions apply as regards state liability for damage which had been caused by a decision of a national court against which there was no possibility of appeal (i.e. a court of last instance). Thus, a 'sufficiently serious breach of a rule of EU law' would arise where the national court had manifestly infringed the applicable law. National law may define the nature or the degree of a breach resulting in state liability but on no account could it impose stricter requirements.

The Court of Justice held that it had been sufficiently demonstrated by the Commission that the condition, laid down in the Italian statute, requiring 'gross negligence', as interpreted by the Italian Court of Cassation, amounted to the imposition of requirements stricter than those entailed by the condition requiring a 'manifest infringement of the applicable law'. Italy, however, had not succeeded in establishing that the interpretation of that statute by the Italian courts was consistent with the case law of the Court.

In conclusion, the Court held that, in so far as it ruled out the possibility of the state incurring liability for an infringement of EU law by a court whose decision was not open to appeal, where the infringement came about as a result of the way in which that court had interpreted provisions of law or assessed the facts or evidence, and in so far as it limited state liability in this connection to cases involving intentional fault or gross negligence, the Italian legislation was incompatible with the general principle of the liability of Member States for a breach of EU law.

Conclusion

The ***Dillenkofer*** and ***Köbler*** cases complete the post-***Francovich*** case law in so far as it has established that the conditions relating to state liability are fixed no matter what the nature of the breach and irrespective of the organ of the state which is responsible for the breach. This ensures uniform application of the principle throughout the Member States. It will be for the national court to determine whether or not the breach is, on its facts, sufficiently serious. As evidenced in the cases discussed, this may be a difficult question to answer and the factors to be taken into consideration will vary depending upon the particular circumstances of the case. In *Brasserie du Pêcheur* and *Factortame* the Court set out, at paras 56–57, some factors to be taken into account when determining this question with regard to legislative acts. However, the Court of Justice determined that fault, i.e. intention or negligence, is not in itself one of the conditions which it is necessary to satisfy in order for state liability to be established. Two other cases applying the principle of state liability are: *Denkavit and Others* (Cases C-283, 291 & 292/94); and *Brinkmann Tabakfabriken GmbH v Skatteministeriet* (Case C-319/96).

Application of the principles of indirect effect and direct effect in UK courts

Indirect effect

Objective 2

Where legislation has been enacted to implement a directive, the courts have shown themselves capable of creative interpretation, on the basis that Parliament would have intended that the legislation be interpreted in conformity with the directive, even if it had been misunderstood at the time of enactment:

Litster v Forth Dry Dock [1989] 2 WLR 634

The House of Lords (the judicial functions of which are now exercised by the Supreme Court) had to consider Directive 77/187, which was intended to protect workers dismissed in connection with a business transfer. The directive had been implemented in the UK by the Transfer of Undertakings (Protection of Employment) Regulations 1981 (SI 1981/1794). The UK regulations protected employees who had been dismissed immediately before the transfer of the undertaking.

In this case the employees had been dismissed one hour before the transfer. On a literal interpretation of the regulations the employees were not employed immediately before the transfer, and therefore they could not rely on the regulations. However, several decisions of the Court of Justice had held that workers dismissed prior to the transfer, but for a reason connected with the transfer, would (for the purposes of the directive) be treated as having been employed by the undertaking at the time when it took place. The House of Lords decided that it was the duty of the UK court to give the UK regulations 'a construction which accords with the decisions of the European Court upon the corresponding provisions of the directive to which the regulation was intended to give effect' (Lord Keith). Accordingly, the House of Lords read into the regulations 'or would have been so employed if he had not been unfairly dismissed', and the dismissed employees were held to come within the scope of the regulations.

The House of Lords (the judicial functions of which are now exercised by the Supreme Court) took a different line in the following case:

Duke v GEC Reliance [1988] 2 WLR 359

The case turned on the legality of different retirement ages for men and women, the same point as in **Marshall** and **Foster**, above. In this case, however, the employer was a private undertaking, and the question of vertical direct effect could not arise. The question before the court was whether it had an obligation to interpret the Sex Discrimination Act 1975 in accordance with the Equal Treatment Directive dated 9 February 1976. The House of Lords decided that it did not. Parliament had passed the Act in the belief that it was entitled to have discriminatory retirement ages even when the directive (which was then in draft format) came into effect. Lord Templeman stated that:

> Of course a UK court will always be willing and anxious to conclude that UK law is consistent with Community [i.e. Union] law. Where an Act is passed for the purpose of giving effect to an obligation imposed by a directive or other instrument a British court will seldom encounter difficulty in concluding that the language of the Act is effective for the intended purpose. But the construction of a British Act of Parliament is a matter of judgment to be determined by British courts and to be derived from the language of the legislation considered in the light of the circumstances prevailing at the date of the enactment ... It would be most unfair to the **respondent** to distort the construction of the Sex Discrimination Act 1975 in order to accommodate the Equal Treatment Directive 1976 as construed by the European Court of Justice in the 1986 **Marshall** case.

The above decision has been criticised. Lord Slynn, a former Lord Advocate and English Lord of Appeal, has expressed the anxiety of UK judges on the issue:

> I find it difficult to say that a statute of 1870 must be interpreted in the light of a 1991 directive. If the former is in conflict with the latter, it is not for the judges to strain language but for Governments to introduce new legislation. (Slynn, 1992, p. 124)

Although this observation is consistent with UK constitutional principles, it not consistent with the judgment of the Court of Justice in **Simmenthal** (Case 106/77):

> Every national court must, in a case within its jurisdiction, apply Community [i.e. Union] law in its entirety and protect rights which the latter confers on individuals and must accordingly set aside any provision of national law which may conflict with it, whether prior or subsequent to the Community [i.e. Union] rule.

The application of the principle by the UK, post-**Marleasing**, is usefully illustrated by the approach adopted by the House of Lords (the judicial functions of which are now exercised by the Supreme Court) in the following case:

Webb v Emo Cargo (UK) Ltd (No. 2) [1995] IRLR 647

Webb was employed to cover for Stewart while she was on maternity leave. Webb later discovered that she herself was pregnant and that she would not be able to provide the requisite cover during Stewart's maternity leave. EMO Cargo dismissed Webb who subsequently made a complaint that she had been discriminated against on grounds of sex. Section 1(1), Sex Discrimination Act 1975 ('the 1975 Act') states that:

> A person discriminates against a woman in any circumstances relevant for the purposes of ... this Act if –
>
> (a) on the ground of her sex he treats her less favourably than he treats or would treat a man ...

Section 5 of the 1975 Act provides that:

> 3. A comparison of the cases of persons of different sex or marital status under sections 1(1) or 3(1) . . . must be such that the relevant circumstances in the one case are the same, or not materially different, in the other.

Section 6(2) further provides that:

> It is unlawful for a person, in the case of a woman employed by him at an establishment in Great Britain, to discriminate against her –
>
> . . .
>
> (b) by dismissing her, or subjecting her to any other detriment.

An employment tribunal dismissed her complaint. It held that the correct approach was to compare the treatment of Webb with that which would have been accorded to a man in comparable circumstances. If a man had told his employer that he would be absent from work for a similar period, there is very little doubt that likewise he would have been dismissed. Accordingly, Webb's dismissal was not on the ground of her sex (under s 1(1) of the 1975 Act) and she was not treated less favourably than EMO Cargo would have treated a man.

The Employment Appeal Tribunal ([1990] IRLR 124) dismissed Webb's appeal, as did the Court of Appeal ([1992] IRLR 116). The Court of Appeal stated that it was necessary to determine whether a man with a condition as nearly comparable to that of Webb (i.e. pregnancy) which had the same practical effect upon his ability to do the job would, or would not, have been dismissed; this was an application of s 5(3) of the 1975 Act.

On Webb's appeal to the House of Lords ([1993] IRLR 27), Lord Keith of Kinkel held (at para 8) that there was no direct application of a gender-based criterion:

> If [Ms Webb's] expected date of confinement had not been so very close to that of Valerie Stewart she would not have been dismissed. It was her expected non-availability during the period when she was needed to cover for Valerie Stewart which was the critical factor.

Lord Keith discussed the application of s 5(3) of the 1975 Act to ascertain whether it was legitimate to compare the non-availability of a man for medical reasons. He concluded that the relevant circumstance for the purpose of s 5(3) was the expected unavailability at the material time. The precise reason (i.e. pregnancy) was not relevant, nor was it relevant that this reason was a condition only capable of affecting women, therefore (at para 11):

> . . . on a proper construction of the relevant provisions of the 1975 Act the dismissal did not . . . constitute direct unlawful discrimination.

However, the *Marleasing* **interpretative obligation** was acknowledged by Lord Keith, who stated (at para 21) that it applied:

> Whether the domestic legislation came after or, as in this case, preceded the Directive.

Directive 76/207 (the Equal Treatment Directive) applies to the same area of activity, sex discrimination, as the 1975 Act. Article 2(1) provides that:

> For the purposes of the following provisions, the principle of equal treatment shall mean that there shall be no discrimination whatsoever on grounds of sex either directly or indirectly by reference in particular to marital or family status.

Article 5(1) provides that:

> Application of the principle of equal treatment with regard to working conditions, including the conditions governing dismissal, means that men and women shall be guaranteed the same conditions without discrimination on grounds of sex.

Lord Keith thought it was necessary to refer the matter to the Court of Justice for a preliminary ruling, pursuant to the former Art 177 EC Treaty (which was replaced by Art 234 EC Treaty, and is now Art 267 TFEU), to ascertain if, on the facts of the case, there was a breach of the directive. If there was, then the House of Lords would be required to decide if the 1975 Act could be construed in such a way as to accord with the Court's decision.

The Court of Justice (Case C-32/93) held (at para 29) that Webb's dismissal contravened the directive:

> Article 2(1) read with Article 5(1) of Directive 76/207 precludes dismissal of an employee who is recruited for an unlimited term with a view, initially, to replacing another employee during the latter's maternity leave and who cannot do so because, shortly after recruitment, she is found herself to be pregnant.

The Court of Justice was clearly influenced by the fact that Webb was not simply taken on to cover for the maternity leave. She was initially employed some months prior to Stewart's expected maternity leave, in order that she could be trained. It was intended to retain her following Stewart's return to work. The Court of Justice decided that the contract of employment was for an unlimited duration rather than for a specific period directly related to the length of Stewart's maternity leave. The case was then referred back to the House of Lords ((No. 2) [1995] IRLR 647), where Lord Keith observed (at para 11) that:

> The ruling of the European Court proceeds on an interpretation of the broad principles dealt with in Articles 2(1) and 5(1) of the Directive 76/207/EEC. Sections 1(1)(a) and 5(3) of the Act of 1975 set out a more precise test of unlawful discrimination and the problem is how to fit the terms of that test into the ruling.

What the House of Lords was seeking to ascertain (at para 2) was whether it was:

> ... possible to construe the relevant provisions of the Act of 1975 so as to accord with the ruling of the European Court.

Lord Keith held (at para 11) that it was possible to interpret s 5(3) in such a fashion:

> in a case where a woman is engaged for an indefinite period, the fact that the reason why she will be temporarily unavailable for work at a time when to her knowledge her services will be particularly required is pregnancy is a circumstance relevant to her case, being a circumstance which could not be present in the case of a hypothetical man.

The House of Lords held that Webb's dismissal constituted direct sex discrimination contrary to the 1975 Act and remitted the case back to the employment tribunal for compensation to be assessed.

The application of **Marleasing** was possible in the above case because it did not involve *distorting* the meaning of the Act, an Act which preceded the directive. The Act was simply interpreted purposively by the House of Lords (the judicial functions of which are now exercised by the Supreme Court) in order to accord with the wording and purpose of the directive.

Clearly, the **Duke** case and those cases subsequent to it are not in conflict with this decision. In these cases, Parliament had expressly permitted the discriminatory retirement ages complained of. To have decided otherwise would have required the court to *distort* the clear wording of the Sex Discrimination Act 1975.

Direct effect: the provisions of the EU Treaties

Objective
3

Under the law and practice within the UK, the EU Treaties, like any other Treaty, are effective in the UK only after they have been incorporated into the UK's legal system, and they will be effective only to the extent of their incorporation (**Blackburn v Attorney-General** [1971]

2 All ER 1380 at 1382; Lord Denning MR). The UK's accession to the European Union was given effect in national law by the European Communities Act 1972. The 1972 Act has been subsequently amended, most recently by the European Union (Amendment) Act 2008 (which made the necessary changes to the 1972 Act to give effect to the ToL when it came into force on 1 December 2009). The implementation of Union rights will, therefore, depend on the extent to which Union law has been fully incorporated by the 1972 Act, and the extent to which UK courts are prepared to interpret national law in conformity with Union obligations (*R v Secretary for Foreign and Commonwealth Office, ex parte Rees-Mogg* [1994] 1 CMLR 101 (QBD)).

Section 2(1), European Communities Act 1972 provides that only those provisions which 'in accordance with the Treaties are **without further enactment** to be given legal effect … shall be … enforced, allowed, and followed' in UK courts (emphasis added). Section 3(1) of the 1972 Act further provides that:

> For the purposes of all legal proceedings any question as to the meaning or effect of any of the Treaties, or as to the validity, meaning or effect of any EU instrument, shall be treated as a question of law and, if not referred to the European Court, be for determination as such in accordance with the principles laid down by and any relevant decision of the European Court.

Under s 2(1), UK courts have not had any difficulty in giving effect to Treaty provisions or regulations, because 'in accordance with the Treaties' both are to be given legal effect without further legislative enactment. Thus, in the following case, the directly effective provisions of what is now Art 157 TFEU on equal pay were held to prevail over the Equal Pay Act 1970:

Macarthys Ltd v *Smith* [1981] QB 180

The Court of Appeal held that it was bound to give effect to the former Art 119 EC Treaty (now Art 157 TFEU) because it was directly effective. Lord Denning expressed the position in this way:

> The provisions of Article 119 of the EEC Treaty [now Art 157 TFEU] take priority over anything in our English statute on equal pay which is inconsistent with Article 119. **That priority is given by our law. It is given by the European Communities Act 1972 itself.** (at 200–1) [emphasis added]

There was no difficulty where the legislation of the UK Parliament could be construed in accordance with Union law. The problem came where national law had been enacted after UK membership in a way that clearly conflicted with a directly effective Treaty provision:

Macarthys Ltd v *Smith* [1979] ICR 785

Lord Denning stated that:

> If the time should come when our Parliament deliberately passes an Act with the intention of repudiating the Treaty or any provision in it – and says so in express terms then I should have thought that it would be the duty of our courts to follow the statute of our Parliament. (at 789)

When the House of Lords was confronted with the Merchant Shipping Act 1988, which had been enacted to prevent Spanish fishermen from 'quota hopping' into UK fishing areas, the moment seemed to have arrived. It was fairly clear that these measures discriminated on grounds of nationality against the right of Spanish fishing businesses to establish themselves in the UK in accordance with two directly effective provisions: former Arts 7 and 52 EC Treaty (which were replaced by Arts 12 and 43 EC Treaty, and are now Arts 18 and 49 TFEU). Following a reference to the Court of Justice, the House of Lords (the judicial functions of which are now exercised by the Supreme Court) was, however, prepared to hold the Act to be without effect to the extent of the conflict. 'It is the duty of a UK court', said Lord Bridge in his speech, 'when delivering final judgment, to override any rule of national law found to be in conflict with any directly enforceable rule of Community [i.e. Union] law' (*R* v *Secretary of State for Transport, ex parte Factortame* [1991] 1 AC 603 at 659).

Direct effect: directives

United Kingdom courts have experienced some difficulty with directly enforcing directives. As discussed above, *prima facie*, directives are not directly applicable, and so do not fall into that category of Union provisions which, without further enactment, are to be given legal effect under s 2(1), European Communities Act 1972. However, where they have been held by the Court of Justice to create directly enforceable rights they have been applied vertically against emanations of the state by UK courts, following references to the Court of Justice, as in *Marshall* and *Foster* v *British Gas* (see above). However, as discussed above, UK courts have had some difficulty in determining the scope of 'state emanation' (see *Doughty*, *Griffin* and *NUT*, above).

Despite this difficulty with state emanation, where UK courts have determined that a directive can be enforced against the state or an emanation of the state, they have complied fully with the principle. The House of Lords (the judicial functions of which are now exercised by the Supreme Court) has gone as far as to hold that parts of the Trade Union and Labour Relations Act 1978 were incompatible with a directly effective directive (Directive 76/207) in *Equal Opportunities Commission* v *Secretary of State for Employment* [1994] 1 All ER 910.

Unimplemented directives: a continuing problem

The approach adopted by the Court of Justice to individuals affected by the non-implementation of directives was, as discussed above, a pragmatic response to a perceived problem of inequality between Member States. Those states which failed to implement directives on time might actually enjoy an advantage over those states which had shouldered the burden the directive had imposed. Individuals in the non-implementing state would be deprived of the benefits the directive was intended to confer upon them. Despite the increase in Art 258 TFEU proceedings, bringing defaulting Member States before the Court is slow and is only a partial solution to the problem (see Chapter 7). Even if it achieves belated implementation of the directive, it cannot provide compensation to those individuals who have been deprived of its beneficial effect. The principle of indirect effect requires national courts to interpret national law, wherever possible, in such a way as to avoid a conflict with Union law. As the national court may decide that it is not possible to interpret the national law to avoid a conflict with Union law, the creation of the doctrine of vertical direct effect (i.e. the right to enforce the directive against the defaulting Member State) and a gradual enlargement of that right by the Court so that enforcement is now possible against a whole range of state or state-sponsored bodies, has provided a valuable weapon in the hands of intended beneficiaries.

Although in Marshall and Faccini Dori the Court of Justice failed to grasp the nettle and give directives **horizontal direct effect** between individuals, this has been partly mitigated by the development of the interpretative obligation of indirect effect. However, application of the principle of indirect effect depends very much on the willingness of national courts to engage in creative interpretation of national legislation. At the present time the Court seems reluctant, as it demonstrated in **Wagner Miret** (Case C-334/92), to be more specific in defining the nature of the national court's interpretative obligation. The Court of Justice has made it clear that it expects individuals who are unsuccessful in persuading a national court to give it interpretative effect, or who cannot establish the vertical direct effect of a directive, to claim damages against their own Member State. This will involve a direct claim against the Member State for its failure to implement, on the basis of the Court's decisions in **Brasserie du Pêcheur** and **Factortame** (Cases C-46 and 48/93). It may, as in **Faccini Dori**, require the individual to commence a whole new legal action after having failed to establish the interpretative effect of the directive against another individual.

However, a claim against a Member State cannot be regarded as a wholly satisfactory substitute for the enforcement of a directive against those who were intended to be bound by it. The Member State may have believed, in good faith, that it had taken all necessary steps to implement the directive, and it may be hard to establish that the breach was 'sufficiently serious'. Even if this can be established, damages may not constitute a satisfactory remedy for, say, the failure to set up an area of environmental protection, as required by an unimplemented directive. The losers may be the local community as a whole rather than an individual and it may be impossible to establish any causal link, as required by **Francovich**, between the failure to implement the directive and any specific loss suffered by an individual. These difficulties will probably remain unless and until the Court accepts that unimplemented directives may have horizontal as well as vertical direct effect.

Enforcement of a directive in the national courts: the correct approach

Objectives 2–4

The Court of Justice has reaffirmed its approach to the application of the principles of indirect effect, direct effect and state liability in a number of cases. The approach was reaffirmed in the following case, which concerned the application of the Working Time Directive 93/104 (which was codified by Directive 2003/88):

Maribel Dominguez v Centre Informatique du Centre Ouest Atlantique, Préfet de la région Centre (C-282/10)

With regard to the principle of indirect effect, the Court of Justice held as follows:

24. ... the court has consistently held that when national courts apply domestic law **they are bound to interpret it, so far as possible, in the light of the wording and the purpose of the directive concerned in order to achieve the result sought by the directive** and consequently comply with the third paragraph of Article 288 TFEU. This obligation to interpret national law in conformity with European Union law is inherent in the system of the Treaty on the Functioning of the European Union, since it permits national courts, for the matters within their jurisdiction, to ensure the full effectiveness of European Union law when they determine the disputes before them ...

25. It is true that this principle of interpreting national law in conformity with European Union law has certain limitations. Thus the obligation on a national court to refer to the content of a directive when interpreting and applying the relevant rules of domestic law is limited by general principles of law and it cannot serve as the basis for an interpretation of national law **contra legem** ... [emphasis added]

With regard to the principle of direct effect, the Court of Justice stated as follows:

32. In the event that such an interpretation is not possible, it is necessary to consider whether … [the Directive] has a direct effect and, if so, whether … [the claimant] may rely on that direct effect against … [the defendants] in the main proceedings, in particular her employer … in view of … [her employer's] legal nature.

33. In that regard, it is clear from the settled case-law of the Court that, whenever the provisions of a directive appear, so far as their subject-matter is concerned, to be **unconditional and sufficiently precise**, they may be relied upon before the national courts by individuals **against the State** where the latter has failed to implement the directive in domestic law by the end of the period prescribed or where it has failed to implement the directive correctly …

…

37. … the Court has consistently held that a directive cannot of itself impose obligations on an individual and cannot therefore be relied on as such against an individual (see, *inter alia*, Case C91/92 *Faccini Dori* [1994] ECR I-3325, paragraph 20; Case C192/94 *El Corte Inglés* [1996] ECR I-1281, paragraph 15; C403/01 *Pfeiffer and Others* [2004] ECR I8835, paragraph 108; and Case C555/07 *Kücükdeveci* [2010] ECR I-365, paragraph 46).

38. It should also be recalled however that, where a person is able to rely on a directive not as against an individual but as against the State he may do so regardless of the capacity in which the latter is acting, whether as employer or as public authority. **In either case it is necessary to prevent the State from taking advantage of its own failure to comply with European Union law** (see, *inter alia*, Case 152/84 *Marshall* [1986] ECR 723, paragraph 49; Case C188/89 *Foster and Others* [1990] ECR I3313, paragraph 17; and Case C343/98 *Collino and Chiappero* [2000] ECR I-6659, paragraph 22).

39. **Thus the entities against which the provisions of a directive that are capable of having direct effect may be relied upon include a body, whatever its legal form, which has been made responsible, pursuant to a measure adopted by the State, for providing a public service under the control of the State and has for that purpose special powers beyond those which result from the normal rules applicable in relations between individuals** (see, *inter alia*, **Foster and Others**, paragraph 20; *Collino and Chiappero*, paragraph 23; and Case C356/05 *Farrell* [2007] ECR I-3067, paragraph 40). [emphasis added]

With regard to the principle of state liability, the Court of Justice stated as follows:

42. … it should be borne in mind that even a clear, precise and unconditional provision of a directive seeking to confer **rights or impose obligations on individuals cannot of itself apply in proceedings exclusively between private parties** (see *Pfeiffer and Others*, paragraph 109).

43. In such a situation, the party injured as a result of domestic law not being in conformity with European Union law can nonetheless rely on the judgment in Joined Cases C6/90 and C9/90 *Francovich and Others* [1991] ECR I-5357 in order to obtain, if appropriate, compensation for the loss sustained. [emphasis added]

It should be noted that in the above case, the Court of Justice stated that indirect effect (i.e. the interpretative obligation) should be applied by the national court before direct effect. If the national court can interpret national law to comply with Union law, the principle of direct effect becomes irrelevant. It is only necessary to consider the principle of direct effect if the national court determines that it is 'not possible' to interpret the national law in such a way.

When considering a case relating to the enforcement of an EU directive in the national courts, the following issues should be considered in this order:

1 Is the directive indirectly effective: will the national courts comply with their *Marleasing* interpretative obligation and interpret national law in such a way as to comply with the wording and purpose of the directive? If it is not indirectly effective, then:

2 Is the directive directly enforceable: (i) has the directive's date for implementation expired; **and** (ii) is it sufficiently precise and unconditional; **and** (iii) is it being enforced against the state or an emanation of the state? If it is not directly effective, then:

3 Is it possible to claim *Francovich* damages from the state because of the state's failure to implement (or correctly implement) the directive?

Obviously it will only be necessary to consider the principles of indirect effect and direct effect if the directive has not been implemented by the Member State or if the directive has been implemented incorrectly. If the directive has been correctly implemented then the national implementing legislation can be applied (in the UK this will either be through an Act of Parliament or delegated legislation).

The flowcharts in Figures 9.1 to 9.3 illustrate the above approach.

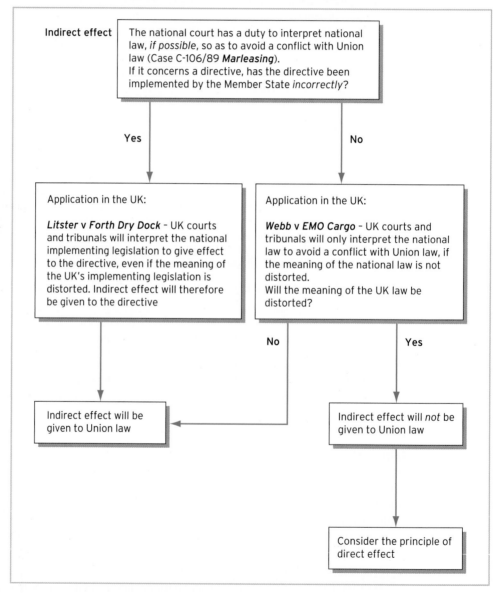

Figure 9.1 The principle of indirect effect

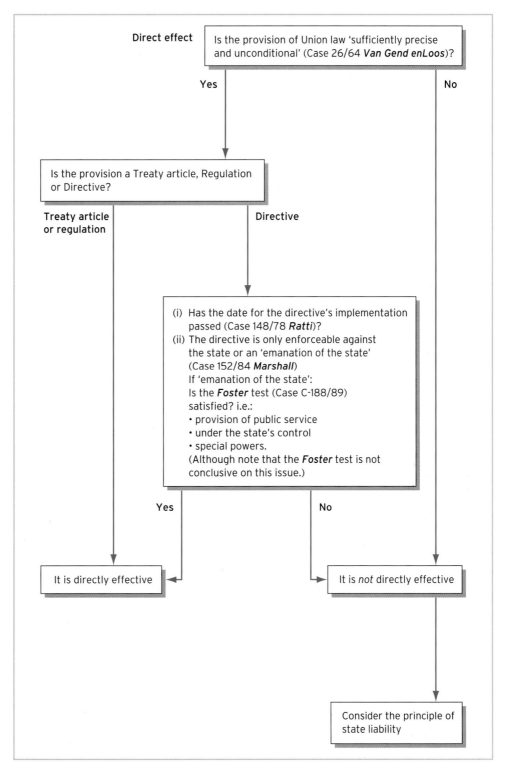

Figure 9.2 The principle of direct effect

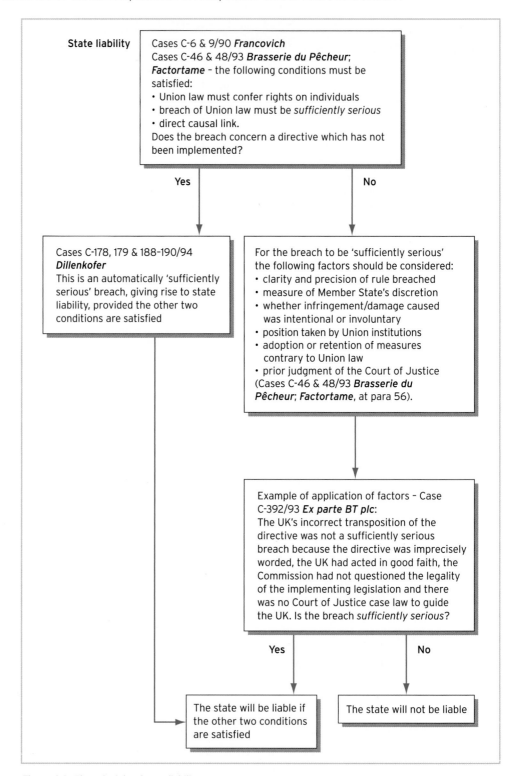

Figure 9.3 The principle of state liability

Summary

Now you have read this chapter you should be able to:

- Explain the concept of 'supremacy of Union law' and discuss its impact on UK constitutional law.
- Explain the concept of indirect effect, and discuss how English courts and tribunals have applied the interpretative obligation established by the Court of Justice in its *Marleasing* judgment.
- Outline what is meant by the principle of direct effect of Union law.
- Explain how the Court of Justice determines whether a provision of Union law is capable of having direct effect.
- Evaluate the distinction between horizontal direct effect and vertical direct effect.
- Explain the rationale for the Court of Justice's decision that directives are generally only capable of having vertical direct effect.
- Evaluate the principle of state liability, established by the Court of Justice in *Francovich*, and discuss how this principle has evolved through subsequent judgments of the Court.

References

Mancini, G.F. and Keeling, D.T., 'Democracy and the European Court of Justice' (1994) 57 MLR 175.

Slynn, G. (1992) *Introducing a New Legal Order*, Sweet & Maxwell, p. 124.

Further reading

Textbooks

Craig, P. and De Burca, G. (2011) *EU Law: Text, Cases and Materials* (5th edn), Oxford University Press, Chapters 7 to 9.

Foster, N. (2015) *Foster on EU Law* (5th edn), Oxford University Press, Chapters 5 and 6.

Steiner, J. and Woods, L. (2014) *EU Law* (12th edn), Oxford University Press, Chapters 4, 5, 7, 8 and 9.

Weatherill, S. (2014) *Cases and Materials on EU Law* (11th edn), Oxford University Press, Chapters 3, 5 and 6.

Journal articles

Albors-Llorens, A., 'The direct effect of EU directives: Fresh controversy or a storm in a teacup? Comment on Portgas' (2014) 39 EL Rev 851.

Anagnostaras, G., 'The quest for an effective remedy and the measure of judicial protection afforded to putative Community law rights' (2007) 32 EL Rev 727.

Arnull, A., 'The Law Lords and the European Union: Swimming with the incoming tide' (2010) 35 EL Rev 57.

Arnull, A., 'The principle of effective judicial protection in EU law: An unruly horse?' (2011) 36 EL Rev 51.

Craig, P.P., 'The legal effect of Directives: Policy, rules and exceptions' (2009) 34 EL Rev 349.

Dougan, M., 'When worlds collide! Competing visions of the relationship between direct effect and supremacy' (2007) 44 CML Rev 931.

Doukas, D., 'The verdict of the German Federal Constitutional Court on the Lisbon Treaty: Not guilty, but don't do it again!' (2009) 34 EL Rev 866.

Elliott, M., 'Constitutional legislation, European Union law and the nature of the United Kingdom's contemporary constitution' (2014) 10 ECL Rev 379.

Fredriksen, H.H., 'State liability in EU and EEA law: The same or different?' (2013) 38 EL Rev 884.

Granger, M-P.F., 'National applications of *Francovich* and the construction of a European administrative ius commune' (2007) 32 EL Rev 157.

Havu, K., 'Horizontal liability for damages in EU law – the changing relationship of EU and national law' (2012) 18 ELJ 407.

Leczykiewicz, D., '"Effective judicial protection" of human rights after Lisbon: Should national courts be empowered to review EU secondary law?' (2010) 35 EL Rev 326.

Leczykiewicz, D., 'Horizontal application of the Charter of Fundamental Rights' (2013) 38 EL Rev 479.

Lenaerts, K. and Corthaut, T., 'Of birds and hedges: The role of primacy in invoking norms of EU law' (2006) 31 EL Rev 287.

Nassimpian, D., '… And we keep on meeting: (de)fragmenting state liability' (2007) 32 EL Rev 819.

Pescatore, P., 'The doctrine of "direct effect": An infant disease of Community law' (2015) 40 EL Rev 135.

Phelan, W., 'Can Ireland legislate contrary to European Community law?' (2008) 33 EL Rev 530.

Pliakos, A., 'Who is the ultimate arbiter? The battle over judicial supremacy in EU law' (2011) 36 EL Rev 109.

Reestman, J-H. and Claes, M., 'For history's sake. On Costa v ENEL, Andre Donner and the external secret of the Court of Justice's deliberations' (2014) 10 ECL Rev 191.

Richards, C., 'The supremacy of Community law before the French Constitutional Court' (2006) 31 EL Rev 499.

Szydlo, M., 'Contracts beyond the scope of the EC procurement directives – who is bound by the requirement for transparency?' (2009) 34 EL Rev 720.

10

Applying EU law in the English courts and adapting English remedies to the requirements of EU law

Objectives

At the end of this chapter you should understand:

1. How EU law is applied in English courts and how English courts have adapted remedies to ensure compatibility with EU law.

The Union approach to legal remedies

Objective 1

Some consideration was given in Chapter 9 to the approach of English courts towards the enforcement of unimplemented or incorrectly implemented directives, and that approach is complicated by the UK's unique concept of parliamentary sovereignty and the less distinctive, but equally difficult, separation of powers between legislature and judiciary. The same problems are apparent when the prospective claimant seeks an appropriate avenue for the enforcement of a right derived from Union law or the redress of a wrong resulting from its breach in the courts of England and Wales.

The effectiveness of remedies in national courts has become an increasing preoccupation of the Court of Justice, and the Court has moved from its original position on national remedies. In **Comet v Produktschap voor Siergewassen** (Case 45/76), it held that the remedy to deal with a breach of Union law should be 'no less effective' than that available to protect a right derived from national law and should not make it 'impossible in practice' to obtain relief. This comparative standard with a very low irreducible minimum does not fully take into account the deficiencies of national legal remedies, which may place all kinds of obstacles in the path of a claimant seeking to enforce a Union right. Although the way in which national courts operate is, in theory at least, outside the competence of Union law, the practical effects of deficiencies in national legal systems have led the Court of Justice to put an increasing emphasis on the duty of cooperation in Art 4(3) TEU (previously Art 10 EC Treaty), and the extent to which it binds national courts. Consequently, the Court of Justice took a stronger line in **R v Secretary of State for Transport, ex parte Factortame (No. 2)** (Case C-213/89). In this case, the House of Lords (the judicial function of which is now exercised by the Supreme Court) had declared that national law did not allow an interim order against the Crown to suspend the operation of the Merchant

Shipping Act 1988. The Court of Justice held that the national court must 'set aside' any national rule which precluded it from granting interim relief. In *Johnston v Chief Constable of the RUC* (Case 222/84), the Court of Justice specifically adopted Art 13 of the ECHR as a fundamental principle of Union law. Article 13 ECHR provides that:

> Everyone whose rights and freedoms as set forth in this Convention are violated shall have an effective remedy before a national authority notwithstanding that the violation has been committed by persons acting in an official capacity.

See Chapter 6 for a full discussion of the Art 267 TFEU procedure.

In the following case, the English Court of Appeal referred the case to the Court of Justice for a preliminary ruling pursuant to what is now Art 267 TFEU:

Courage v *Cohan* (Case C-453/99)

The claimant had entered into a contract with the defendant. The contract was void because it was in breach of Union competition law (the former Art 85 EC Treaty (which was replaced by Art 81 EC Treaty, and is now Art 101 TFEU)). The claimant was suing the defendant for breach of this contract. English law prevented a party to an illegal contract from recovering damages from the other side. However, the Court of Justice held that a party to a contract which was liable to restrict or distort competition within the meaning of the former Art 85 EC Treaty (now Art 101 TFEU) was able to rely on the breach of that provision in order to obtain relief from the other contracting party. The Court further held that the former Art 85 EC Treaty (now Art 101 TFEU) precluded the English rule under which a party to a contract was barred from claiming damages for loss caused by performance of that contract on the sole ground that the claimant was a party to that contract. However, the Court held that Union law does not preclude national law from denying a party who is found to **bear significant responsibility** for the distortion of competition the right to obtain damages from the other contracting party. Under a principle which is recognised in most of the legal systems of the Member States and which the Court has applied in the past, a litigant should not profit from his own unlawful conduct, where this is proven.

The effect of the Court's judgment in the *Factortame* case (above) is that there is now a necessary implication in Union law that 'an appropriate legal remedy must be created if one does not exist' (Advocate General Mischo in *Francovich v Italy* (Cases C-6/90 and 9/90)). Union legislation may also prescribe the type of remedy and the amount of damages that should be awarded (see, for example, Directives 93/37 and 93/38 on public procurement contracts). Some directives may specify the bodies or types of bodies which should have the standing to challenge decisions infringing the directive (see, for example, Directive 93/12 on unfair consumer contract terms). Some directives make specific requirements as to penalties, with a view to ensuring that national implementing legislation contains real deterrent sanctions (see, for example, Directive 92/59 on product safety and Directive 89/592 on insider dealing). Where there is no penalty prescribed by Union law, the Court has held that national law should provide a penalty that is 'effective, proportionate and dissuasive' (*Commission v UK* (Case C-382/92)).

Public law remedies: judicial review

The obligation to implement Union law in the UK falls primarily on the government and the various agencies it has chosen to carry out the functions of public administration. In English law, all bodies which exercise public powers, whether conferred by statute or common law, and whether public or private in origin, are subject to control and review by the courts (*Council of Civil Service Unions v Minister for the Civil Service* [1985] AC 374; *R v Panel on Takeovers and Mergers, ex parte Datafin plc* [1987] QB 815). In relation to Union law, that process of control and review extends to decisions made about the implementation of Union law. If the decision relates to the exercise of a power conferred on a subordinate body to legislate by way of delegated legislation, the court may intervene to prevent an abuse of those delegated legislative powers (*R v HM Treasury, ex parte Smedley* [1985] QB 657). If, conversely, the decision is by Parliament itself on the scope and content of primary legislation then the decision on whether or not to legislate, and in what form, is not subject to any control or review by the courts (*Blackburn v Attorney-General* [1971] 1 WLR 1037; *R v Secretary of State for Foreign and Commonwealth Affairs, ex parte Rees-Mogg* [1993] 3 CMLR 101).

It is now accepted by the English courts that they are able to rule on the compatibility of English law with Union law (*Factortame Ltd v Secretary of State for Transport* [1989] 2 All ER 692). The appropriate remedy in such a case is a declaration setting out the extent of the incompatibility (*R v Secretary of State for Employment, ex parte EOC* [1994] 2 WLR 409). Although a court in judicial review proceedings has the power to award damages, previously they could only be awarded where they would be available in an ordinary *private* action (e.g. breach of contract, etc.) This position was affected by the decision of the House of Lords (the judicial functions of which are now exercised by the Supreme Court) in *R v Secretary of State for Transport, ex parte Factortame and Others (No. 5)* [1999] 3 WLR 1062, where the House of Lords held that the UK's breach of Union law was 'sufficiently serious', rendering the UK government liable to the claimants for all losses which flowed from the breach. This was an application of the *Francovich* principle of state liability (Cases C-6/90 and 9/90); see Chapter 9.

Claims in tort against the state

As discussed in Chapter 9, the Court of Justice has held on many occasions that, subject to Treaty provisions being sufficiently precise and unconditional, such provisions could create rights which were enforceable at the suit of individuals in the courts of Member States (*Van Gend en Loos* (Case 26/62)). The application of this doctrine in relation to those Treaty provisions found to be directly effective has to be worked out in the national courts according to substantive and procedural national rules. In English law, where damages are claimed, this has meant that the breach of Union law has had to be recognised either as a new tort or incorporated within the bounds of an old one.

The principle of direct effect is explained in detail at pages 274–292 and 303–305.

In *Bourgoin v Ministry of Agriculture, Fisheries and Food (MAFF)* [1985] 3 All ER 385, the proceedings arose out of a ban imposed by the Ministry on the importation of turkeys from France in the run-up to Christmas 1981. The ban was imposed, ostensibly, on animal health grounds, but in *Commission v UK* (Case 40/82) the Court of Justice held that the real reason behind the ban was a desire to protect the home market from foreign competition. It was not, therefore, justified under the former Art 30 EC Treaty (now Art 36 TFEU). Bourgoin was an importer who suffered considerable loss by the action of the UK government. He brought an action in damages, claiming infringement of the former Art 28 EC Treaty (now Art 34 TFEU) as a breach of statutory duty, breach of an innominate tort, or for misfeasance in public office. The Court of Appeal held, by a majority, that the only appropriate remedy was judicial review and that damages would not be available. Although the House of Lords (the judicial functions of which are now exercised by the Supreme Court) had held, in ***Garden Cottage Foods Ltd v Milk Marketing Board*** [1984] AC 130, that a breach of the former Art 82 EC Treaty (now Art 102 TFEU) gave rise to a claim for breach of statutory duty, a breach of the former Art 28 EC Treaty (now Art 34 TFEU) by a public authority was different. The former Art 28 EC Treaty did not confer private rights, simply a right to ensure that a public duty was performed. That duty could be enforced in judicial review proceedings and, in accordance with general principles of administrative law, damages would not normally be available. Following the judgment of the Court of Justice in ***Brasserie du Pêcheur SA v Germany*** ((Case 46/93), see Chapter 9) this view was no longer valid. The question to be determined by the national court is whether or not the breach in question is 'sufficiently serious' and, if it is, whether there is a sufficient causative link between the breach and the damage suffered.

It is now clear, as a matter of English law, that a person who argues that he has suffered a loss as a result of a breach of a public law duty will not be compelled to proceed by way of judicial review, with its highly restrictive three-month time- limit for the commencement of proceedings. Provided that he can show a particular loss, he does not need to prove a breach of a duty giving rise to a claim in tort, or the existence of a contract to bring a private action (***Roy v Kensington and Chelsea and Westminster FPC*** [1992] 1 AC 624). A person who has suffered loss as a result of a breach by a public body of a Treaty provision or a legally binding act of the institutions of the Union, and who can satisfy the criteria laid down by the Court of Justice in ***Brasserie du Pêcheur***, will be able to succeed in the English courts (see the view expressed ***obiter*** by Lord Goff in ***Kirklees MBC v Wickes*** [1993] AC 227).

See pages 293–300 for a discussion of the criteria laid down by the Court of Justice in the *Brasserie du Pêcheur* case.

Claims in tort between private individuals for breaches of Treaty provisions

Individuals who have suffered loss as the result of a breach of a directly effective provision of the Treaty will be able to claim damages against another individual who has caused that loss. This is clearly the case in relation to what is now Art 102 TFEU (***Garden Cottage Foods v Milk Marketing Board*** [1984] AC 130). Damages may also be awarded by English courts for breach of what is now Art 101 TFEU (***H.J. Banks and Co Ltd v British Coal Corporation*** (Case C-128/92); ***MTV Europe v BMG Records (UK) Ltd*** [1995] 1 CMLR 437). Individuals are also clearly entitled to damages for discriminatory treatment at work in breach of Art 157 TFEU, or on grounds of nationality under Art 18 TFEU. An individual might, for example, wish not only to secure equal treatment, but also to obtain damages where national law precluded them. As can be seen in ***Defrenne v SABENA*** (Case 43/75), an individual may make such a claim for compensation for loss of equal pay simply on the basis of the Treaty provision (see ***Macarthys Ltd v Smith*** (Case 129/79)).

Any national limitations on the extent of compensation payable in cases of sex discrimination should not be observed where they prevent the claimant from being adequately compensated for the damage suffered. Although the decision in ***Marshall v Southampton and South-West Hampshire Area Health Authority (No. 2)*** (Case 271/91) was limited to the interpretation of Art 6, Directive 76/207 in relation to the amount of damages payable, the principles laid down are wide enough to cover other claims against the state and emanations of the state (see Woolridge and D'Sa, 1993). This view is supported by the Court of Justice's decision in the following case:

Commission v UK (Case C-382/92)

The Court of Justice held that the UK's implementation of Directives 77/187 (Transfer of Undertakings) and 75/129 (Consultation on Redundancy) did not provide sufficient compensation for workers affected by a breach of the rules by the employer. The Court held that the compensation payable under the Employment Protection Act 1975, which purported to implement Directive 75/129, was potentially so little as to deprive the measure of its practical effect:

Where a Community [i.e. Union] directive does not specifically provide any penalty for an infringement or refers for that purpose to national laws, regulations and administrative provisions, Article 5 of the Treaty [which was replaced by Art 10 EC Treaty, and is now **Art 4(3) TEU**] requires the Member States to take all measures necessary to guarantee the application and effectiveness of Community [i.e. Union] law. For that purpose, while the choice of penalties remains within their discretion, they must ensure in particular that infringements of Community [i.e. Union] law are penalised under conditions, both procedural and substantive, which are analogous to those applicable of a similar nature and which, in any event, make the penalty **effective, proportionate and dissuasive.** [emphasis added]

In the above case, although the Court of Justice was speaking of 'penalties', it is clear from the circumstances of the case that it had in mind both criminal sanctions and civil damages which could, in appropriate circumstances, be punitive in nature. It is apparent from the emphasised words that the Court has now moved on from merely requiring equivalent remedies. Where the national remedy is not effective, the remedy for the breach of Union law should be 'effective, proportionate and dissuasive'. This principle will apply whether or not the defendant is the state, an emanation of the state or a private individual or undertaking.

Union law as the basis for a claim in contract, a defence in breach of contract proceedings, and for claims in quasi-contract

Union law may be used to found, or assist in, a claim for breach of contract in English courts. Under Art 157 TFEU (previously Art 141 EC Treaty), for example, discriminatory provisions in collective agreements are made unlawful and any contract, therefore, which incorporates the terms of such a discriminatory agreement will be void in so far as it offends against Art 157 TFEU (*Defrenne* v *SABENA* (above)). Union law may also be used as a defence to a claim for breach of contract. If an individual is sued for breach of a contract which, for example, infringes the prohibition on restrictive agreements in Art 101(1) TFEU (previously Art 81(1) EC Treaty), he may raise the issue of validity of the agreement under Union law as a defence (*Brasserie de Haecht* v *Wilkin* (Case 23/67); *Society of Lloyds* v *Clementson* [1995] 1 CMLR 693).

In *Amministrazione delle Finanze* v *San Giorgio* (Case 199/82), the Court of Justice decided that an individual was entitled to recover charges that had been levied on him contrary to a directly effective provision of Union law. The right of recovery was a necessary adjunct to the right to equal treatment. National law should, therefore, enable individuals who have been wrongly taxed or charged in this way to recover the payments they have made. So, for example, an EU citizen in receipt of educational services must not be charged a different fee from home students (*Gravier* v *City of Liège* (Case 293/83)), nor may importers be levied tax at a rate which exceeds that payable in respect of home-pro-duced goods of the same kind (Art 110 TFEU (previously Art 90 EC Treaty)). When this happens, the individuals affected should be able to recover the sums overpaid.

The rule laid down by the Court of Justice in **San Giorgio** conflicted with an established rule of English law that a person who has paid money under a mistake of fact can generally recover it, but a person who has paid money under a mistake of law cannot, generally, do so (D'Sa, 1994). However, mistake of law is narrowly construed so that, for example, a payment made on the basis of a misunderstanding about a rule of foreign law is regarded as a mistake of fact. Union law is not 'foreign law', of course, because it is incorporated into English law and must be treated as a question of law and not fact (**R v Goldstein** [1983] 1 CMLR 252). In the following case, the House of Lords (the judicial functions of which are now exercised by the Supreme Court) narrowed the rule further, so that money paid to a public body in response to an unlawful demand on the basis of a mistake of law will now be recoverable:

Woolwich Equitable Building Society v IRC [1992] 3 WLR 366

Referring to the right of recovery in relation to money wrongfully paid under Union law, Lord Goff of Chievely remarked:

At a time when Community [i.e. Union] law is becoming increasingly important, it would be strange if the right of the citizens to recover overpaid charges were to be more restricted under domestic law than it is under Community [i.e. Union] law.

A similar extension of Union principles into the wider application of the common law fol-lowed the decision of the Court of Justice in **Factortame** that interim orders should bind the Crown, when the House of Lords subsequently held that such orders were available even in cases not involving Union law (**Re M** [1994] 1 AC 377).

Union law as a defence in criminal proceedings

Many of the landmark decisions of Union law have been made by the Court of Justice on references from national courts during the course of criminal proceedings. In **Procureur du Roi v Dassonville** (Case 8/74), the defendant was prosecuted for selling Scotch whisky without supplying purchasers with a certificate of origin. The Court held that the legisla-tion under which he was prosecuted was incompatible with the former Art 28 EC Treaty (now Art 34 TFEU) and as a consequence the national court would, therefore, have been obliged to dismiss the charge against him. Similarly, the defendants in **R v Henn and Darby** (Case 34/79) were able to raise in their prosecution a potential breach of the former Art 28 EC Treaty (now Art 34 TFEU), although the Court of Justice held that the UK legisla-tion was justifiable under the former Art 30 EC Treaty (now Art 36 TFEU).

In the English courts, so-called Euro-defences have been successfully raised in criminal proceedings for 'overstaying', contrary to the Immigration Act 1971. In **R v Pieck** (Case 157/79) the charge against the defendant had to be dismissed because the requirement imposed on the defendant to obtain 'leave' for his continuing residence was held to be contrary to the rights of residence conferred on him by the former Art 39 EC Treaty (now Art 45 TFEU; see also **R v Kirk** (Case 63/83)). Also, where Union law provides a defence in an unimplemented directive, the defendant may rely upon it (**Pubblico Ministero v Ratti** (Case 148/78)). Conversely, prosecutors cannot rely on an unimplemented directive to interpret the criminal law in such a way as to secure a conviction. This offends against the Union principle of legal certainty and non-retroactivity (***Officier van Justitie v Kolping-huis Nijmegen BV*** (Case 80/86)).

Euro-defences, using the former Art 28 EC Treaty (now Art 34 TFEU), were relied upon by businesses prosecuted under the Shops Act 1950, until this avenue was finally closed by the Court of Justice in ***Stoke-on-Trent and Norwich City Councils v B&Q*** (Case C-169/91). Prosecutions are, in any event, unlikely to be pursued following the liberalisation of Sunday trading in England and Wales by the Sunday Trading Act 1994. The scope for the use of the former Art 28 EC Treaty (now Art 34 TFEU) to defeat prosecutions under national laws aimed at consumer protection has also been considerably diminished by the decision of the Court of Justice to exclude from the scope of the former Art 28 EC Treaty (now Art 34 TFEU) 'selling arrangements' which are unlikely to affect trade between states, in ***Keck and Mithouard*** (Cases C-267 and 268/91); see Chapter 18.

Summary

Now you have read this chapter you should be able to:

- Explain how EU law is applied in English courts.
- Evaluate how English courts have adapted national remedies to ensure they are compatible with the principles of EU law.

References

D'Sa, R. (1994) *European Community Law and Civil Remedies in England and Wales*, Sweet & Maxwell, Chapters 9 and 10, pp. 46–58.

Woolridge, F. and D'Sa, R., 'Damages for breaches of Community directives: The decision in Marshall (No. 2)', (1993) 4 EBL Rev 255.

Further reading

Textbooks

Craig, P. and De Burca, G. (2011) *EU Law: Text, Cases and Materials* (5th edn), Oxford University Press, Chapter 7 to 9.

Foster, N. (2015) *Foster on EU Law* (5th edn), Oxford University Press, Chapter 6.

Steiner, J. and Woods, L. (2014) *EU Law* (12th edn), Oxford University Press, Chapters 4, 5, 7, 8 and 9.

Journal articles

Anagnostaras, G., 'The incomplete state of Community harmonisation in the provision of interim protection by the national courts' (2008) 33 EL Rev 586.

Arnull, A., 'The Law Lords and the European Union: Swimming with the incoming tide' (2010) 35 EL Rev 57.

Arnull, A., 'The principle of effective judicial protection in EU law: An unruly horse?' (2011) 36 EL Rev 51.

Leczykiewicz, D., '"Effective judicial protection" of human rights after Lisbon: Should national courts be empowered to review EU secondary law?' (2010) 35 EL Rev 326.

Part 2

The free movement of persons and services, and freedom of establishment

11

European Union citizenship and free movement rights

At the end of this chapter you should understand:

1. Which provisions of the EU Treaties relate to the free movement of workers, freedom of establishment and the free movement of services and the relevance of Art 26(2) and the European Economic Area Agreement to the free movement of persons.

2. How Directive 2004/38 has consolidated the Union law provisions relating to entry and residence.

3. The nature of EU citizenship within the context of Art 21(1) TFEU, and the rights which are derived from EU citizenship.

4. The limited rights of free movement for non-EU citizens.

5. The Schengen *acquis* and the UK's participation in the Schengen arrangements.

Introduction to the free movement of persons

Objective 1

The free movement of persons has been a cornerstone of the European Union since its inception. That freedom was not, initially, an entitlement for citizens of Member States to move anywhere in the Union for any purpose, but was linked to a number of specific economic activities:

- Articles 45–48 TFEU (previously Arts 39–42 EC Treaty) – workers.
- Articles 49–54 TFEU (previously Arts 43–48 EC Treaty) – rights of establishment.
- Articles 56–62 TFEU (previously Arts 49–55 EC Treaty) – services.

Each of these Treaty provisions has been elaborated by detailed secondary legislation. The rights of individuals and undertakings in the three principal categories are examined in more detail in Chapter 12 (workers) and Chapter 13 (services and establishment).

Free movement rights must be seen in the context of four important developments of recent years. The first of these are the measures taken to create the internal market which shall, under Art 26(2) TFEU (previously Art 14(2) EC Treaty), 'comprise an area without internal frontiers in which the free movement of goods, persons, services and capital is ensured in accordance with the provisions of the Treaties'. Although Art 26(2) TFEU

The principle of direct effect is considered further at pages 274–292 and 303–305.

creates a commitment for the Union to remove border restrictions, it is not clear whether the provision has direct effect. In *R v Secretary of State for the Home Department, ex parte Flynn* [1995] 3 CMLR 397, McCullough J held that it did not match the criteria for having direct effect. It imposed no obligation on Member States, 'let alone one which is clear and precise'. He therefore refused a claim by the applicant, an EU citizen, that he had been unlawfully detained for questioning at Dover. This decision was subsequently upheld in the Court of Appeal; although note that this was a decision of an English court and not the Court of Justice.

See pages 8 and 54 for further commentary on EFTA and the EEA.

The second development is the European Economic Area (EEA) Agreement, which came into effect on 1 January 1994. Under the EEA Agreement all the free movement rights enjoyed under the EU Treaties were extended to the remaining states of EFTA (currently Iceland, Liechtenstein and Norway, but not including Switzerland). European Union citizens and their families, and citizens of the participating EFTA states and their families, enjoy the full free movement rights of the Treaty and of the implementing legislation in all the territories of the EU and the participating EFTA states.

The third development is the adoption of Directive 2004/38, which sets out the rights of entry and residence which apply across the whole range of persons exercising their right of free movement: tourists, work-seekers, workers, the self-employed, providers and recipients of services and retired persons. The directive merges, into a single instrument, all the legislation on the right of entry and residence for EU citizens and their family members (which includes non-EU family members). It introduces a general right of residence of up to three months for all EU citizens without any conditions or formalities other than the requirement to hold a valid identity card or passport. The scope of this directive is considered in detail below.

The fourth development is the creation of EU citizenship by the Treaty on European Union (Art 20 TFEU (previously Art 17 EC Treaty)).

An overview of the right of free movement for persons is discussed briefly below. There will be a detailed discussion of such rights in Chapters 12 and 13 in the context of the free movement of workers, work-seekers, providers and recipients of services, and those establishing themselves in another Member State (e.g. the self-employed). Following this overview there is a detailed exploration of the provisions of Directive 2004/38, followed by a commentary on EU citizenship. This is followed by a discussion of the free movement rights of non-EU citizens, which are additional to those set out within Directive 2004/38. This Chapter concludes with a brief consideration of the **Schengen** *acquis* and its integration into the EU.

Free movement rights

In the early days of the Union, freedom of movement was seen as the means by which labour and skills shortages in one Member State could be met out of a surplus of labour and skills in another. That approach was subsequently modified, both in later implementing legislation and by decisions of the Court of Justice. The Court has interpreted the EU Treaties and the implementing provisions generously. The application of the former Art 39(3)(a) EC Treaty (now Art 45(3)(a) TFEU), which appears to confer a right to go to another Member State only on those able to 'accept offers of employment **actually made**' (emphasis added), to work-seekers is perhaps one of the most remarkable examples of creative interpretation (*Procureur du Roi v Royer* (Case 48/75)); see Chapter 12. Although until the 1990s each of the free movement rights depended on a specific economic activity, the Court has tended to develop a body of general principles applicable to all those exercising free movement rights. Directive 2004/38 (which replaced, *inter alia*, Directive 90/364) creates a general right of entry and residence for up to three months (see below).

Most importantly, all free movement rights are directly effective and enforceable in the courts of Member States as fundamental rights (see Chapter 9). The entry or residence of those exercising them is not dependent upon any consent or leave given by the host Member State. Provided that an individual is engaged in an activity which confers Union rights of entry or residence, or comes within the scope of the general right of residence (for up to three months) set out in Directive 2004/38, the host Member State cannot terminate that right of residence (*R v Pieck* (Case 157/79)). There are exceptions to rights of entry and residence in cases where the individual constitutes a threat to public policy, public security or public health under Arts 45(3) and 52(1) TFEU (previously Arts 39(3) and 46(1) EC Treaty) and Directive 2004/38. These powers of Member States to derogate from individual rights of free movement have, however, been interpreted strictly by the Court (see *Adoui and Cornuaille v Belgian State* (Cases 115 and 116/81), and Chapter 15).

As free movement rights are fundamental rights, the Court of Justice has held that they must be transparent in national legislation. Incompatible provisions of national law which, for example, exclude the employment of foreign nationals, even though they are not, in practice, applied in the case of EU citizens, must be amended to make it absolutely clear that EU citizens enjoy equal access (*Commission v France (Re French Merchant Seamen)* (Case 167/73)). It is not sufficient that Union rights should be enjoyed by virtue of administrative concessions. Those enjoying such rights must be made aware of them and, should the need arise, be able to rely upon them before a court of law (*Commission v Germany (Re Nursing Directives)* (Case 29/84)).

Decisions affecting the exercise by an individual of free movement rights should set out the reasons for them, to enable an effective legal challenge to be made. The procedures for challenging any denial of such rights, whether on the basis of public policy, public security or public health, under Directive 2004/38 (see Chapter 15), or on any other ground, should follow the Union principles of fairness and be compatible with the European Convention on Human Rights (*UNECTEF v Heylens and Others* (Case 222/86)). The provisions of the Convention are now directly applicable to the exercise of Union rights (Art 6(3) TEU (previously Art 6(2) TEU)). Failure to deliver these rights can give rise to a claim in damages against the Member State concerned.

Non-discrimination on grounds of nationality (Art 18 TFEU (previously Art 12 EC Treaty)) is another fundamental principle of Union law that is important in the exercise of free movement rights. The detailed provisions of Regulation 492/2011 (previously Regulation 1612/68) relating to equal access to employment and to other benefits enable the worker and his family to integrate into the host Member State, but there is no parallel legislation relating to the self-employed and to those providing and receiving services. Decisions of the Court of Justice relating to access to housing and the criminal process, which have been secured for workers under the former Arts 7(2) and 9, Regulation 1612/68 (now Arts 7(2) and 9, Regulation 492/2011), have, however, been achieved for the self-employed and the recipients of services by a creative use of Art 18 TFEU; see *Commission v Italy* (Case 63/86) and *Cowan v Le Trésor Public* (Case 186/87). Article 18 TFEU does, however, apply only to matters covered by the EU Treaties and any aspect of an individual's life which may affect his entry into or residence in another Member State as a beneficiary of Union law (unless, as discussed below, the Court applies Art 18 TFEU in conjunction with the EU citizenship provisions, to confer an independent right to be treated without discrimination in all matters).

The free movement rights will also be enhanced by measures adopted pursuant to Art 19 TFEU (previously Art 13 EC Treaty). Article 19 TFEU is the legal base for the adoption of measures to 'combat discrimination based on sex, racial or ethnic origin, religion or belief, disability, age or sexual orientation', provided such measures do not exceed the powers of the Union as conferred upon it by the EU Treaties. In other words, measures can be adopted to combat discrimination provided they are in furtherance of the existing powers of the Union.

Pursuant to what is now Art 19 TFEU, the Council adopted Directive 2000/43 (OJ 2000 L 180/22), which implemented the principle of equal treatment between persons irrespective of racial or ethnic origin. The directive had to be implemented by 19 July 2003. The principle of equal treatment prohibits direct or indirect discrimination based on racial or ethnic origin (Art 1). It applies to EU and non-EU citizens and covers both public and private sectors in relation to employment, self-employment, education, social protection including social security and healthcare, social advantages, and access to and supply of goods and services (Art 3(1)). The prohibition of racial or ethnic discrimination does not, however, cover national provisions relating to the entry into and residence of third-country (i.e. non-EU) nationals (Art 13(2)). The directive does not, therefore, extend the free movement provisions *per se* to non-EU citizens (see below).

Again pursuant to what is now Art 19 TFEU, the Council adopted Directive 2000/78 (OJ 2000 L 303/16) which establishes a general framework for equal treatment in employment and occupation. The directive had to be implemented by 3 December 2003. The directive prohibits direct and indirect discrimination as regards access to employment and occupation on grounds of religion or belief, disability, age or sexual orientation. It applies to both the public and private sectors. As with Directive 2000/43, this directive applies to EU and non-EU citizens, but likewise, the prohibition does not cover national provisions relating to the admission and residence of third-country (i.e. non-EU) nationals (Art 3(2)). The directive does not, therefore, extend the free movement provisions, *per se*, to non-EU citizens (see below).

See Case C-267/12 at pages 80–81 which relates to an application of Directive 2000/78 by the Court of Justice.

Directives 2000/43 and 2000/78 have been implemented in the UK by the Equality Act 2006 (as subsequently amended) and secondary legislation.

Although discrimination in relation to both employment and self-employment is generally prohibited, restrictions on the employment of EU nationals in 'the public service' are permitted by Art 45(4) TFEU (previously Art 39(4) EC Treaty). There are similar provisions relating to the self-employed, who may be refused participation in activities which 'are connected, even occasionally, with the exercise of official authority' (Art 51 TFEU (previously Art 45 EC Treaty)). There is no definition in the Treaties or the secondary legislation of either 'the public service' or 'the exercise of official authority', but both exceptions have been narrowly interpreted by the Court of Justice. The mere fact that the employer is the state is not conclusive; it is the nature of the employment which is the determining factor (**Lawrie-Blum v Land Baden-Württemberg** (Case 66/85); see Chapters 12 and 13).

To benefit from Union free movement rights, a person must be, or have been, a migrant in some sense or other. A person who has not left his own state, and does not intend to do so, cannot be a beneficiary (**Iorio** (Case 298/84)). However, this may change in relation to family reunification. Article 79(2)(a) TFEU (previously Art 63(3)(a) EC Treaty) enables measures to be adopted on immigration policy concerning the 'conditions of entry and residence, and standards on the issue by Member States of long-term visas and residence permits, including those for the purpose of family reunification'. Pursuant to Art 79(2)(a) TFEU, a directive has been proposed which would apply to EU citizens who do not exercise their free movement rights. The aim of the proposed directive is to avoid discriminating between EU citizens who exercise their free movement rights and those who do not. In order to achieve this, it is necessary to provide for the family reunification of EU citizens residing in countries of which they are nationals to be governed by the rules of Union law relating to free movement. The proposed directive would provide that an EU citizen who had not exercised his free movement rights in another Member State would have the right to have specified family members installed with him. This right would override any less generous national provisions. However, it is unlikely that the proposed directive will be adopted in the foreseeable future. In the meantime, an EU citizen can be a worker or a self-employed person *vis-à-vis* his own state if he works in another Member State for a period of time and then returns home. He may then enjoy the family rights of a Union migrant against his own state, which will override the more restrictive national provisions (***Morson v Netherlands*** (Case 35/82); ***R v IAT and Surinder Singh*** (Case C-370/90)). A person who has not left his own state may still benefit from free movement rights if, for example, he has arranged employment in another Member State, or wishes to establish a business there. Subject to the public policy, public security or public health exceptions, he cannot be prevented from leaving (Art 4(1), Directive 2004/38; see below and Chapters 12, 13 and 15).

Directive 2004/38: right of entry and residence

Objective 2

Chapters 12 and 13 include a detailed consideration of the substantive provisions of the EU Treaties and secondary legislation relating to the free movement of workers, work-seekers, providers and recipients of services, and those establishing themselves in another Member State (e.g. the self-employed). Directive 2004/38 (which relates to an EU citizen's right of entry and residence in a Member State of which they are not a national) is considered here in detail because the directive, which had to be transposed into national law by 30 April 2006, sets out the rights of entry and residence which apply across the whole range of persons exercising their right of free movement, for example tourists, students, retired persons, work-seekers, workers, the self-employed, and providers and recipients of services. The directive merges into a single instrument all the legislation on the right of entry and residence for EU citizens and their family members (which includes non-EU family members). The following nine directives were repealed: Directives 64/221, 68/360, 72/194, 73/148, 75/34, 75/35, 90/364, 90/365 and 93/96. Regulation 1251/70 was subsequently repealed by Regulation 635/2006, and Regulation 1612/68 was subsequently repealed and replaced by Regulation 492/2011. The purpose of the new directive is to simplify the law. It sets out to reduce to the bare minimum the formalities which EU citizens and their family members must complete in order to exercise their right of residence. There now follows a comprehensive review of the full range of rights of entry and residence set out within the directive.

Scope

The directive is designed to regulate:

- the conditions under which EU citizens and their families exercise their right to move and reside freely within the Member States;
- the right of permanent residence;
- restrictions on the abovementioned rights on grounds of public policy, public security or public health.

Family members

Article 3(1) provides that the Directive applies to all EU citizens exercising their right to move to, or reside in, a Member State other than that of which they are a national, and to 'family members' who accompany or join them. Article 2(2) defines 'family members' as the EU citizen's:

(a) spouse;

(b) registered partner, if the legislation of the host Member State treats registered partnerships as equivalent to marriage;

(c) direct descendants (i.e. children, grandchildren, etc.) who are under the age of 21 or who are dependants, and those of the spouse or partner as defined above;

(d) dependent direct relatives in the ascending line (i.e. parents, grandparents, etc.), and those of the spouse or partner as defined above.

This definition of 'family members' (which includes third-country nationals) has a broader scope than the former definition set out in Art 10, Regulation 492/2011 (previously Art 10(1), Regulation 1612/68).

In addition to family members (as defined by Art 2(2)), Art 3(2) provides that the host Member State shall, in accordance with its national legislation, 'facilitate' entry and residence for the following persons:

(a) any other family members (whether or not they are EU citizens) who are dependants or members of the household of the EU citizen having the primary right of residence, or where serious health grounds strictly require the personal care of the family member by the EU citizen;

(b) the partner with whom the EU citizen has a durable relationship, which is duly attested.

The host Member State is required to undertake an extensive examination of the personal circumstances of such persons and shall justify any denial of entry or residence (Art 3(2)).

Spouses: separate accommodation

In the following case, the Court of Justice was faced with the question of whether or not a spouse of an **EU worker** could still come within the scope of the former Art 10(1), Regulation 1612/68 (now Art 2(2), Directive 2004/38) if they separated and were no longer living together:

Diatta v *Land Berlin* (Case 267/83)

The applicant was a Senegalese (i.e. non-EU) national who had married a French national. Both were resident and working in Berlin (Germany). They later separated, moved into separate accommodation and she intended to divorce him. She applied for an extension to her residence permit. This was refused on the ground that she was no longer a family member of an EU worker. She challenged this refusal and the national court referred the case to the Court of Justice for a preliminary ruling pursuant to what is now Art 267 TFEU (previously Art 234 EC Treaty). The former Art 11, Regulation 1612/68, provided the member of an EU worker's family with the right to take up any activity as an employed person throughout the territory of the Member State concerned, notwithstanding her nationality (Art 11, Regulation 1612/68 has been repealed and replaced by Art 23, Directive 2004/38). The Court was asked whether a migrant worker's family had to live permanently with the EU worker in order to qualify for a right of residence, or whether Art 11, Regulation 1612/68 gave a separate and independent right of residence. The Court of Justice held as follows:

18. In providing that a member of a migrant worker's family has the right to install himself with the worker, **Article 10 of the Regulation does not require that the member of the family in question must live permanently with the worker, but, as is clear from Article 10(3), only that the accommodation which the worker has available must be such as may be considered normal for the purpose of accommodating his family. A requirement that the family must live under the same roof permanently cannot be implied.**

19. In addition, such an interpretation corresponds to the spirit of Article 11 of the Regulation [Art 11, Regulation 1612/68 has been repealed and replaced by Art 23, Directive 2004/38], which gives the member of the family the right to take up any activity as an employed person throughout the territory of the Member State concerned, even though that activity is exercised at a place some distance from the place where the migrant worker resides.

20. It must be added that the marital relationship cannot be regarded as dissolved so long as it has not been terminated by the competent authority. It is not dissolved merely because the spouses live separately, even where they intend to divorce at a later date. [emphasis added]

In the above case, the Court of Justice did not decide that the family members had a separate and distinct right of residence, because the family's right to reside in the host Member State was linked to that of the EU worker. However, the Court held that there was no necessity for them to live under one roof. To decide otherwise would have conflicted with the right given to family members by the former Art 11, Regulation 1612/68 to work within the host Member State, notwithstanding their nationality. Article 11, Regulation 1612/68 has been repealed and replaced by Art 23, Directive 2004/38. Article 23, Directive 2004/38 provides that 'irrespective of nationality, the family members of a Union citizen who have the right of residence or the right of permanent residence in a Member State shall be entitled to take up employment or self-employment there'. In *Diatta*, the EU worker was working in Berlin in Germany. If his spouse had decided to exercise her rights under the former Art 11, Regulation 1612/68 (now Art 23, Directive 2004/38) and work in Munich in Germany, then quite clearly she would have needed to have separate accommodation because it would be practically impossible to commute between Berlin and Munich on a daily basis.

Divorce, annulment and termination of registered partnership

Directive 2004/38 has made provision, for the first time, for the family members' retention of the right of residence in the event of divorce, annulment of marriage or termination of registered partnership. In the case of EU family members, divorce, annulment of marriage or termination of partnership does not affect the family member's right of residence (Art 13(1)). However, in the case of non-EU family members, retention of the right of residence is restricted (Art 13(2)). This is discussed in more detail below.

Dependants

In *Centre Public d'Aide Sociale de Courcelles v Lebon* (Case 316/85) the Court of Justice held that the status of 'dependant' did not require an objective assessment as to the *need* for support, but required an assessment of the facts to ascertain whether the worker was *actually providing support* for the family member. This support could be financial or non-financial. The following case concerned the right of entry and residence of a dependant over the age of 21:

Reyes v *Migrationsverket* (Case C-423/12)

Directive 2004/38 extends the right of all EU citizens to move and reside freely within the territory of the Member States to the members of their family, whatever their nationality. Family members include, in particular, direct descendants who are less than 21 years old or direct descendants who are dependent on the EU citizen.

Ms Reyes, who was born in 1987 and is a Philippines citizen, was left in the care of her maternal grandmother when she was three years old, because her mother had moved to Germany to work. Ms Reyes' mother obtained German citizenship. Ms Reyes was brought up by her maternal grandmother for her entire childhood and adolescence. She studied for two years at high school and four years at college from ages 17 to 23. After having undertaken training involving work experience, she qualified as a nursing assistant. After her exams, she helped her sister to look after her sister's children. Ms Reyes' mother remained in close contact with her family in the Philippines throughout that time by sending money each month to support them and pay for their studies and visiting them each year. Ms Reyes had never held a job and nor had she applied for any allowances from the Philippines social security authorities.

In 2009, the mother of Ms Reyes moved to Sweden to live with a Norwegian citizen whom she married in 2011. Since 2009, Ms Reyes' stepfather, who had resources in the form of a retirement pension, regularly sent money to the Philippines to Ms Reyes and other members of his wife's family.

In 2011, Ms Reyes entered the Schengen area. She applied for a residence permit in Sweden as a family member of her mother, on whom she claimed that she was dependent. Her application was rejected since she had not proved that the money which was indisputably transferred to her by her mother and her partner had been used to supply her basic needs in the form of board and lodging and access to healthcare in the Philippines. Nor had she shown how her home country's social insurance and security system could assist a citizen in her situation. However, she did show that she held qualifications from her country of origin and that she had also carried out work experience there. Furthermore, she had been economically dependent on her grandmother throughout her childhood and adolescence.

The Migrationsöverdomstolen (Administrative Court of Appeal for Immigration matters, Stockholm), before which the case was pending, referred the case to the Court of Justice to ascertain whether a Member State could require that, in order to be regarded as being dependent and thus to come within the definition of 'family member' set out in that provision, a direct descendant who was 21 years old or older had to show that he had tried without success to find employment or to obtain subsistence support from the authorities of the country of origin and/or otherwise had tried to support himself. It also asked whether, in interpreting the term 'dependant', any significance attached to the fact that a family member was deemed to be well placed to obtain employment and in addition intended to start work in the Member State.

In its judgment, the Court stated that, **in order for a direct descendant, who was 21 years old or older, of an EU citizen to be regarded as a 'dependant' of that citizen, the existence of a situation of real dependence had to be established. In order to determine the existence of such dependence, the host Member State had to assess whether, having regard to his financial and social conditions, the descendant in question was not in a position to support himself. The need for material support had to exist in the State of origin of that descendant or the State whence he came at the time when he applied to join that citizen. However, there was no need to determine the reasons for that dependence or therefore for the recourse to that support.**

The fact that an EU citizen regularly, for a significant period, paid a sum of money to that descendant, which was necessary in order for him to support himself in the State of origin, was such as to show that the descendant was in a real situation of dependence *vis-à-vis* that citizen. That descendant could not be required, in addition, to establish that he had tried without success to find work or obtain subsistence support from the authorities of his country of origin and/or otherwise tried to support himself.

The requirement for such additional evidence, which would not be easy to provide in practice, would likely make it excessively difficult for that descendant to obtain the right of residence in the host Member State. Furthermore, it was not excluded that this requirement could have obliged that descendant to take more complicated steps, such as trying to obtain various certificates stating that he had not found any work or obtained any social allowance, than that of obtaining a document of the competent authority of the State of origin or the State from which the applicant came attesting to the existence of a situation of dependence. The Court had already held that such a document could not constitute a condition for the issue of a residence permit.

The Court therefore concluded that **Union law precluded a Member State from requiring a direct descendant, who was 21 years old or older, in order to be regarded as dependent and thus come within the definition of a 'family member' of an EU citizen, to show that he had tried unsuccessfully to obtain employment or to obtain subsistence support from the authorities of his country of origin and/or otherwise to support himself.**

The Court added that **the situation of dependence had to exist, in the country from which the family member concerned came, at the time when he applied to join the EU citizen on whom he was dependent. The fact that a family member – due to personal circumstances such as age, education and health – was deemed to be well placed to obtain employment, and in addition intended to start work in the Member State, did not affect the interpretation of the requirement in that provision that he be a 'dependant'.**

Right of exit and entry (Articles 4 and 5)

All EU citizens have the right to leave or enter another Member State by virtue of having a valid identity card or valid passport (Arts 4(1) and 5(1)). Under no circumstances can an entry or exit visa be required (Arts 4(2) and 5(1)).

'Family members' who do not have the nationality of a Member State (i.e. non-EU family members) may be subject to an entry visa requirement under Regulation 539/2001; residence cards will be deemed equivalent to visas (Art 5(2)); see *Sean Ambrose McCarthy and Others* v *Secretary of State for the Home Department* (Case C-202/13).

Where the EU citizen or their family member do not have the necessary travel documents, the host Member State must afford them every facility to obtain the requisite documents or to have them sent (Art 5(4)). Once installed with the principal beneficiary, the spouse or other family member is entitled to access to employment and equal treatment as if he was an EU citizen (*Gül* v *Regierungspräsident Düsseldorf* (Case 131/85)).

Article 5(5) provides that the host Member State may require each person travelling to, or residing in, another Member State to register their presence in the country within a reasonable and non-discriminatory period of time. Failure to comply with this requirement may make the person liable to a proportionate and non-discriminatory sanction.

General right of residence for up to three months (Article 6)

Article 6(1) provides that EU citizens shall have the right of residence in another Member State for a period of up to three months without any conditions or formalities other than the requirement to hold a valid identity card or passport (or a valid passport in the case of non-EU family members).

Article 6(2) provides that 'family members' who do not have the nationality of a Member State (i.e. non-EU family members) enjoy the same rights as the EU citizen whom they have accompanied or joined.

The host Member State may require the persons concerned to register their presence in the country within a reasonable and non-discriminatory period of time (Art 5(5), see above).

Article 14(1) provides that EU citizens and their family members shall have the right of residence under Art 6, 'as long as they do not become an *unreasonable* burden on the social assistance system of the host Member State' (emphasis added). Expulsion shall not be an automatic consequence if an EU citizen or his family members have recourse to the host Member State's social assistance system (Art 14(3)). Article 14(4) further provides that (other than in accordance with the provisions relating to restrictions on the right of entry and residence on grounds of public policy, public security or public health) an expulsion order cannot be issued against an EU citizen or his family members, if:

(i)   the EU citizen is a worker or self-employed person in the host Member State; or
(ii) the EU citizen entered the host Member State to seek employment and provided he can supply evidence that he is continuing to seek work and has a genuine chance of being employed.

Right of residence for more than three months (Article 7)

The right of residence for more than three months remains subject to certain conditions. Article 7(1) provides that EU citizens have the right to reside in another Member State, for a period exceeding three months, if they:

(a) are engaged in an economic activity in the host Member State (on an employed or self-employed basis);

(b) have comprehensive sickness insurance and sufficient resources for themselves and their family members to ensure they do not become a burden on the social assistance system of the host Member State during their stay. Article 8(4) provides that Member States may not specify a minimum amount of resources they deem sufficient, but they must take account of the personal situation of the person concerned. The amount of minimum resources cannot be higher than the threshold below which nationals of the host Member State become eligible for social assistance, or, if this does not apply, higher than the minimum social security pension paid by the host Member State;

(c) are following a course of study, including vocational training, at a public or private institution which is accredited or financed by the host Member State. The student must have comprehensive sickness insurance and assure the Member State, by a declaration or equivalent means, that they have sufficient resources for themselves and their family members to ensure that they do not become a burden on the social assistance system of the host Member State during their stay. Article 8(3) provides that Member States may not require the declaration to refer to any specific amount of resources; or

(d) are a 'family member' of an EU citizen who falls into one of the above categories.

The following case concerned an EU citizen who was claiming to have a right of residence under Art 7(1)(b) and who was seeking to claim certain social assistance benefits:

Elisabeta Dano, Florin Dano v *Jobcenter Leipzig* (Case C-333/13)

In Germany, foreign nationals who entered the country in order to obtain social assistance or whose right of residence arose solely out of the search for employment were excluded from benefits by way of basic provision ('Grundsicherung'), which were intended in particular to cover the recipients' subsistence costs.

Two Romanian nationals, Ms Dano and her son Florin, brought proceedings before the Social Court, Leipzig (Germany), against Jobcenter Leipzig, which refused to grant them benefits by way of basic provision; for Ms Dano, subsistence benefit ('existenzsichernde Regelleistung') and, for her son, social allowance ('Sozialgeld'), as well as a contribution to accommodation and heating costs. Ms Dano did not enter Germany in order to seek work there and, although she was requesting benefits by way of basic provision that were only for jobseekers, it was apparent from the case -file that she was not seeking employment. She had not been trained in a profession and had not worked in Germany or Romania. She and her son had been residing in Germany since at least November 2010, and they lived in the home of Ms Dano's sister, who provided for them. Ms Dano received, for her son, child benefit amounting to €184 per month and an advance on maintenance payments of €133 per month. Those benefits were not at issue in the present case.

The Social Court, Leipzig, referred the case to the Court of Justice to ascertain whether for the purpose of having access to certain social benefits (such as German benefits by way of basic provision), nationals of other Member States could claim equal treatment with nationals of the host Member State only if their residence complied with the conditions of Directive 2004/38.

The Court of Justice stated that, under the directive, the host Member State was not obliged to grant social assistance during the first three months of residence.

Where the period of residence was longer than three months but less than five years (the period which was at issue in the present case), one of the conditions the directive laid down for a right of residence was that economically inactive persons had to have sufficient resources of their own (Art 7(1)(b)). The directive thus sought to prevent economically inactive Union citizens from using the host Member State's welfare system to fund their means of subsistence. A Member State therefore had the possibility of refusing to grant social benefits to economically inactive Union citizens who exercised their right to freedom of movement solely in order to obtain another Member State's social assistance, even though they did not have sufficient resources to claim a right of residence. In this connection, each individual case had to be examined without taking account of the social benefits claimed. Accordingly, the Court held that Directive 2004/38 and Regulation 883/2004 on the coordination of social security systems did not preclude domestic legislation which excluded nationals of other Member States from entitlement to **certain 'special non-contributory cash benefits'** (such as the benefits at issue in this case, which the Social Court, Leipzig, had classified as 'special non-contributory cash benefits'), although they were granted to nationals of the host Member State who were in the same situation, in so far as those nationals of other Member States did not have a right of residence under the directive in the host Member State.

Finally, the Court stated that Regulation 883/2004 did not govern the conditions for the grant of special non-contributory cash benefits. That competence lay with national legislatures, and therefore they also had competence to define the extent of the social cover provided by that type of benefit. Consequently, when the Member States laid down the conditions for the grant of special non-contributory cash benefits and the extent of such benefits, they were not implementing EU law, and the Charter of Fundamental Rights of the EU was therefore not applicable.

So far as concerned Ms Dano and her son, the Court stated that they did not have sufficient resources and thus could not claim a right of residence in Germany under Directive 2004/38. Therefore, they could not invoke the principle of non-discrimination laid down by the directive and by Regulation 883/2004.

Jobcenter Berlin Neuköln v *Nazifa, Sonita, Valentina and Valentino Alimanovic* (Case C-67/14) has subsequently come before the Court of Justice (although the judgment of the Court has not yet been delivered). The facts are different to those of ***Dano*** because in this case the EU citizen had been seeking work for over 3 months, having previously been employed in the host Member State. The Advocate General stated that because the EU citizen was seeking work and had previously been employed in the host Member State, it would be a breach of the principle of equal treatment to automatically exclude him from entitlement to social assistance benefits without allowing him to demonstrate the existence of a genuine link with the host Member State.

Article 7(2) provides that the right of residence also applies to family members who are not nationals of a Member State (i.e. non-EU family members), who are accompanying or joining an EU citizen in the host Member State, provided that such EU citizen satisfies the conditions set out in (a), (b) or (c) above.

In the case of students, there is a limitation on the family members who may accompany or join them. Article 7(4) provides that only the spouse/registered partner and dependent children shall have the right of residence as family members of the student. Dependent direct relatives in the ascending lines, and those of his spouse/registered partner, shall have their entry and residence facilitated (in accordance with Art 3(2), see above).

Residence permits are abolished for EU citizens. However, Arts 8(1) and 8(2) provide that Member States may require EU citizens to register with the competent authorities within a period of not more than three months as from the date of arrival. A registration certificate will be issued immediately (Art 8(2)). For the registration certificate to be issued, Art 8(3) provides that Member States may only require the following documentation:

(a) in the case of an EU citizen to whom Art 7(1)(a) applies (i.e. a worker or self-employed person), a valid identity card or passport, and confirmation of engagement from the employer or a certificate of employment, or proof of their self-employed status;

(b) in the case of an EU citizen to whom Art 7(1)(b) applies (i.e. a citizen having sufficient resources and comprehensive sickness insurance), a valid identity card or passport, proof of comprehensive sickness insurance, and proof that they have sufficient resources for themselves and their family members not to become a burden on the social assistance system of the host Member State during their period of residence; or

(c) in the case of an EU citizen to whom Art 7(1)(c) applies (i.e. a student), a valid identity card or passport, proof of enrolment at an accredited institution, proof of comprehensive sickness insurance, and a declaration (or equivalent means) that they have sufficient resources for themselves and their family members not to become a burden on the social assistance system of the host Member State during their period of residence.

Article 8(5) provides that registration certificates will be issued to family members who are nationals of a Member State (i.e. EU family members); this is subject to the production of specified documentation. This provision also applies to other EU family members whose entry and residence to the host Member State shall be facilitated in accordance with Art 3(2).

Article 9 applies to family members who are not nationals of a Member State (i.e. non-EU family members). Such family members must apply for a residence card not more than three months from their date of arrival (Art 9(2)). A residence card is valid for at least five years from its date of issue, or for the envisaged period of residence of the EU citizen if this is less than five years (Art 11(1)). Article 10(2) sets out the documentation required before a residence card will be issued. This provision also applies to other non-EU family members whose entry and residence to the host Member State shall be facilitated in accordance with Art 3(2). Article 11(2) provides that the validity of a residence card shall not be affected by:

(i)   temporary absences of up to six months a year;
(ii) absences of a longer period for compulsory military service; or
(iii) one absence of up to 12 months for important reasons (e.g. pregnancy and childbirth, serious illness, study or vocational training, or a posting in another Member State or a third country (i.e. non-EU country)).

In the following case, the Court of Justice considered whether Irish legislation was contrary to Directive 2004/38. The Irish legislation in question provided that a third-country (i.e. non-EU) national who was a family member of an EU citizen, could only reside with or join that citizen in Ireland if he was already lawfully resident in another Member State:

Metock and Others v *Minister for Justice, Equality and Law Reform* (Case C-127/08)

The Irish legislation transposing Directive 2004/38 provided that a national of a third country who was a family member of a Union citizen could reside with or join that citizen in Ireland only if he was already lawfully resident in another Member State. The question of the compatibility of the Irish legislation with the directive was raised in four cases pending before the High Court of Ireland. In each of those cases a third-country national arrived in Ireland and applied for asylum. In each case the application was refused. While resident in Ireland those four persons married citizens of the Union who did not have Irish nationality but were resident in Ireland. None of the marriages was a marriage of convenience.

After the marriage, each of the non-EU spouses applied for a residence card as the spouse of a Union citizen. The applications were refused by the Minister for Justice on the ground that the spouse did not satisfy the condition of prior lawful residence in another Member State.

Actions were brought against those decisions in the High Court, which referred the cases to the Court of Justice (pursuant to the former Art 234 EC Treaty (now Art 267 TFEU)). Guidance was requested on whether: (i) a condition of prior lawful residence in another Member State was compatible with the directive; and (ii) whether the circumstances of the marriage and the way in which the non-EU spouse of the Union citizen entered the Member State concerned had consequences for the application of the directive.

The Court of Justice stated that, as regards family members of a Union citizen, the application of the directive was not conditional on their having previously resided in a Member State. The directive applied to all Union citizens who moved to or resided in a Member State other than that of which they were a national, and to their family members who accompanied them or joined them in that Member State. The definition of family members in the directive did not distinguish according to whether or not they had already resided lawfully in another Member State.

The Court stated that its judgment in *Akrich* (Case C-109/01) had to be reconsidered. In *Akrich*, the Court ruled that, in order to benefit from the rights of entry into and residence in a Member State, the non-EU spouse of a Union citizen had to be lawfully

335

resident in a Member State when he moved to another Member State in the company of a Union citizen. The Court stated that this was wrong, and the benefit of such rights could not depend on prior lawful residence of the spouse in another Member State.

The Court emphasised that if Union citizens were not allowed to lead a normal family life in the host Member State then the exercise of the freedoms they were guaranteed by the Treaty would be seriously obstructed, because they would be discouraged from exercising their rights of entry into and residence in that Member State.

The Minister for Justice and several Member States argued that to interpret the directive in the fashion adopted by the Court would have serious consequences by bringing about a great increase in the number of persons able to benefit from a right of residence in the Union. The Court stated that only the family members of a Union citizen who had exercised his right of freedom of movement could benefit from the rights of entry and residence under the directive. Moreover, the Member States could refuse entry and residence on grounds of public policy, public security or public health, the refusal being based on an individual examination of the particular case. It added that the Member States could also refuse, terminate or withdraw any right conferred by the directive in the case of abuse of rights or fraud, such as marriages of convenience.

The Court held that a non-EU spouse of a Union citizen who accompanied or joined that citizen could benefit from the directive, irrespective of when and where their marriage took place and of how that spouse entered the host Member State.

The Court stated that the directive did not require that the Union citizen must already have founded a family at the time when he moved, in order for his family members who were nationals of non-member countries to be able to enjoy the rights established by the directive. The Court further stated that it made no difference whether nationals of non-member countries who were family members of a Union citizen had entered the host Member State before or after becoming family members of that citizen. The host Member State was, however, entitled to impose penalties, in compliance with the directive, for entry into and residence in its territory in breach of the national rules on immigration.

The following two cases (which were considered together by the Court of Justice) concerned the refusal of the Netherlands' authorities to grant a right of residence to a third-country national who was a family member of an EU citizen; the EU citizen was a national of The Netherlands:

O., B., S. and G. v Minister voor Immigratie, Integratie en Asiel (Cases C-456/12 and C-457/12)

Case C-456/12: Mr O. and Mr B

Case C-456/12 concerned the refusal to grant a right of residence where the EU citizen returned to the Member State of which he was a national, after short periods of residence in another Member State with the family member in question.

In 2006, O., a Nigerian national, married a Netherlands' national and from 2007 to April 2010 he lived in Spain. During that period, O.'s wife resided for two months with her husband in Spain and regularly spent time with O. in the form of holidays in Spain.

B., a Moroccan national, lived from December 2002 with his partner who had Netherlands' nationality. In 2005, B. moved to Belgium and lived in an apartment rented by his partner. His partner resided with B. in Belgium every weekend. In April 2007, B. returned to Morocco and in July 2007 B. married the Netherlands' national in question.

As O. and B. were family members of EU citizens, the referring court asked whether EU law, in particular Art 21 TFEU and Directive 2004/38, granted such third-country nationals a right of residence in the Member State of which the citizens in question were nationals.

The Court stated that **Art 21 TFEU and Directive 2004/38 did not confer any autonomous right on third-country nationals. Any rights conferred on third-country nationals were rights derived from the exercise of freedom of movement by an EU citizen.**

The Court further stated that **Directive 2004/38 did not confer any derived right of residence on third-country nationals who were family members of an EU citizen residing in the Member State of which he was a national. Directive 2004/38 applied only where a citizen moved or resided in a Member State other than that of which he was a national.**

With regard to the question as to whether Art 21 TFEU granted such a derived right of residence, the Court explained that a refusal to allow a derived right of residence for a family member of an EU citizen who was a third-country national, could interfere with the EU citizen's freedom of movement under that provision. An EU citizen could be discouraged from leaving his Member State of origin because he was uncertain whether he would be able to continue, on returning to that Member State, a family life which he had created or strengthened in another Member State. **However, such an obstacle would arise only where the residence in the host Member State had been genuine, that is to say where it satisfied the requirements of Directive 2004/38 relating to a right of residence for a period of longer than three months.**

It followed that, where an EU citizen had, pursuant to and in conformity with the provisions of Directive 2004/38 relating to a right of residence for a period of longer than three months, genuinely resided in another Member State and, during that genuine residence, a family life had been created and strengthened in that Member State, the effectiveness of Art 21 TFEU required that the citizen's family life in the host Member State could continue on returning to his Member State of origin. This implied that, in such a case, a derived right of residence was allowed for the family member who was a third-country national.

The conditions for granting such a derived right of residence, based on Art 21 TFEU should not, in principle, be more strict than those provided for by Directive 2004/38 for the grant of a derived right of residence to a third-country national who was a family member of an EU citizen where that citizen had exercised his right of freedom of movement by becoming established in a Member State other than the Member State of which he was a national. Even though Directive 2004/38 did not cover the return of the EU citizen to the Member State of which he was a national, it had to be applied by analogy given that in both cases it was the EU citizen who was the reference point for the grant of a derived right of residence to a third-country national who was a member of his family.

As regards the question whether the cumulative effect of various short periods of residence in the host Member State could create a derived right of residence for a family member of an EU citizen who was a third-country national on the citizen's return to his Member State of origin, the Court stated that only a period of residence satisfying the conditions of Directive 2004/38 relating to a right of residence for a period of longer than three months would give rise to such a right of residence. The Court stated that, even when considered together, short periods of residence (such as weekends or holidays spent in a Member State other than that of which the citizen is a national) did not satisfy those conditions.

The court also stated that B. acquired the status of family member of an EU citizen after his partner's residence in the host Member State. A third-country national, who had not had, at least during part of his residence in the host Member State, the status of family member of an EU citizen, was not entitled to a derived right of residence in that Member

State pursuant to Directive 2004/38. Accordingly, that third-country national was also unable to rely on Art 21 TFEU for the grant of a derived right of residence on the return of the EU citizen to the Member State of which he was a national.

In the light of all the foregoing, the Court held that where an EU citizen had, pursuant to and in conformity with the provisions of Directive 2004/38 relating to a right of residence for a period of longer than three months, created or strengthened a family life with a third-country national during genuine residence in a Member State other than that of which he was a national, the provisions of that directive applied by analogy where that EU citizen returned, with the family member in question, to his Member State of origin.

Case C-457/12: Ms S. and Ms G

Like Case C-456/12, Case C-457/12 concerned the refusal of Netherlands' authorities to grant a right of residence to a family member of an EU citizen of Netherlands' nationality. However, unlike Case C-456/12, the Union citizens in question had not resided with a family member in a Member State other than that of which they were nationals.

S. is a Ukrainian national. She claimed a right of residence with her son-in-law who is a Netherlands' national. S. submitted that she took responsibility for caring for her grandson. Her son-in-law resided in The Netherlands but travelled to Belgium at least once a week in the course of his work for an employer established in The Netherlands.

G., a Peruvian national, married a Netherlands' national in 2009. The latter resided in The Netherlands but worked for an undertaking established in Belgium. He travelled daily between The Netherlands and Belgium for his work.

In that context, the Raad van State asked the Court of Justice whether EU law conferred a derived right of residence on a third-country national who was a family member of an EU citizen, where that citizen resided in the Member State of which he was a national but regularly travelled to another Member State in the course of his professional activities.

The Court confirmed that, in the situations at issue in Case C-457/12, the EU citizens came within the scope of freedom of movement for workers guaranteed by Art 45 TFEU. Any EU citizen who, under an employment contract, worked in a Member State other than that of their place of residence came within the scope of Art 45 TFEU.

The Court stated that the effectiveness of the right to freedom of movement for workers could require that a derived right of residence be granted under Art 45 TFEU to a third-country national who was a family member of the worker – an EU citizen – in the Member State of which the latter was a national.

The Court stated that it was therefore for the referring court to determine whether, in each of the situations at issue in Case C-457/12, the grant of a derived right of residence to the third-country national in question who was a family member of an EU citizen was necessary to guarantee the citizen's effective exercise of the rights guaranteed by Art 45 TFEU. According to the Court, the fact that the third-country national in question took care of the EU citizen's child could be a relevant factor to be taken into account when examining whether the refusal to grant a right of residence to that third-country national could discourage the EU citizen from effectively exercising his rights under Art 45 TFEU. However, the mere fact that it could appear desirable that the child be cared for by the third-country national who was the direct relative in the ascending line of the EU citizen's spouse was not sufficient in itself to constitute such a dissuasive effect.

Article 45 TFEU therefore conferred a derived right of residence on a third-country national who was the family member of an EU citizen in the Member State of which that citizen was a national, where the citizen resided in that Member State but regularly travelled to another Member State as a worker within the meaning of that provision, if the refusal to grant such a right of residence discouraged the worker from effectively exercising his rights under Art 45 TFEU, which it was for the referring court to determine.

The following case concerned a third-country national who was seeking a residence card on the basis of him 'residing' with his spouse and/or his daughter (both of whom were EU citizens):

Iida v *Stadt Ulm* (Case C-40/11)

Iida, a Japanese national, had been married to a German national since 1998. He had lived in Ulm (Germany) since 2005, where he had a permanent job. Their daughter was born in 2004 in the United States, and she had German, Japanese and American nationality. The spouses separated in 2008, but they had not divorced. Ilda's wife went to live in Vienna (Austria) with her daughter. The spouses jointly exercised parental responsibility for their daughter.

Iida visited his daughter in Vienna one weekend a month, and she spent most of her holidays with her father in Ulm. Iida obtained a right of residence in Germany in connection with family reunion and because of being employed. Extending his residence permit was a matter of discretion, and therefore **Iida applied for a residence card as a family member of an EU citizen on the basis of Directive 2004/38. The German authorities refused to grant him one.**

The Verwaltungsgerichtshof Baden-Württemberg (Higher Administrative Court, Baden-Württemberg) asked the Court of Justice whether EU law allowed a third-country national exercising parental authority over his child, who was an EU citizen, to remain in the child's Member State of origin (Germany) in order to maintain regular personal relations, where the child had moved to another Member State (Austria).

The Court noted that Iida could, on application and regardless of his family situation, be granted the status of long-term resident within the meaning of Directive 2003/109. He had resided legally in Germany for more than five years and appeared to have sufficient resources to support himself and to have sickness insurance.

However, **the Court held that Iida could not claim a right of residence as a family member of an EU citizen on the basis of Directive 2004/38. Under this Directive, such a right presupposed that the direct relative in the ascending line was dependant on the child. Iida did not satisfy that condition, as it was his daughter who was dependent on him.**

Moreover, **while Iida could be regarded as a family member of his spouse, from whom he was separated but not divorced, he did not satisfy the condition laid down by the directive of having accompanied or joined her in a Member State other than that of which she was a national.**

The Court also stated that Iida could not base a right of residence directly on the TFEU by referring to the EU citizenship of his daughter or his spouse.

The Court pointed out that Iida had always lived in Germany in accordance with national law, without the absence of a right of residence under EU law having discouraged his daughter or his spouse from exercising their right of freedom of movement by moving to Austria.

Moreover, even after their move, Iida could not be granted a right of residence in Germany on another legal basis, without it being necessary to rely on his daughter and his spouse's EU citizenship.

Finally, Iida could not rely on the Charter of Fundamental Rights of the European Union, which lays down a right to respect for private life and certain rights of the child. As Iida did not satisfy the conditions of Directive 2004/38 and had not applied for a right of residence as a long-term resident within the meaning of Directive 2003/109, his situation showed no connection with EU law, so that the Charter of Fundamental Rights of the European Union did not apply.

Article 7(3) provides that an EU citizen shall retain the status of worker or self-employed person in the host Member State in the following circumstances:

(a) he is temporarily unable to work as the result of an illness or accident;

(b) he is in duly recorded involuntary unemployment after having been employed for more than one year and has registered as a jobseeker with the relevant employment office in the host Member State;

(c) he is in duly recorded involuntary unemployment after completing a fixed-term employment contract of less than a year *or* after having become involuntarily unemployed during the first 12 months *and* has registered as a jobseeker with the relevant employment office in the host Member State. In this case, the status of worker shall be retained for not less than six months; or

(d) he embarks on vocational training. Unless he is involuntarily unemployed, the retention of the status of worker shall require the training to be related to the previous employment.

Article 12(1) provides that if an EU citizen dies or departs from the host Member State, his EU family members shall not have their right of residence affected. In the case of a non-EU family member, their right of residence shall not be affected if the EU citizen dies provided that the non-EU family member has been residing in the host Member State as a family member for at least one year before the EU citizen's death (Art 12(2)).

Article 12(3) provides that if an EU citizen dies or departs from the host Member State, if his children reside in the host Member State and are enrolled at an educational establishment, then his children and the parent who has actual custody of the children (whether or not they are EU citizens) shall have the right to reside in the host Member State until the children have completed their studies.

Article 13 governs a family member's right of residence following divorce, annulment of marriage or termination of partnership. In the case of EU family members, divorce, annulment of marriage or termination of partnership does not affect the family member's right of residence (Art 13(1)). However, in the case of non-EU family members, retention of the right of residence is restricted. Article 13(2) provides that there shall be no loss of the right of residence where:

(a) prior to the start of the divorce or annulment proceedings or termination of the registered partnership, the marriage or registered partnership had lasted at least three years, including one year in the host Member State;

(b) by agreement between the spouses or the registered partners, or by court order, the spouse or partner who is a non-EU national has custody of the EU citizen's children;

(c) this is warranted by particularly difficult circumstances, such as having been a victim of domestic violence while the marriage or registered partnership was subsisting; or

(d) by agreement between the spouses or registered partners, or by court order, the spouse or partner who is a non-EU national has the right of access to a minor child, provided that the court has ruled that such access must be in the host Member State, and for as long as is required.

Article 14(2) provides that EU citizens and their family members shall have the right of residence under Arts 7, 12 and 13 'as long as they meet the conditions set out therein'; expulsion shall not be an automatic consequence if an EU citizen or his family members have recourse to the host Member State's social assistance system (Art 14(3)). Article 14(4) further provides that (other than in accordance with the provisions relating to restrictions on the right of entry and residence on grounds of public policy, public security or public health) an expulsion order cannot be issued against an EU citizen or his family members if:

(i) the EU citizen is a worker or self-employed person in the host Member State; or
(ii) the EU citizen entered the host Member State to seek employment and provided he can provide evidence that he is continuing to seek work and has a genuine chance of being employed.

Procedural safeguards (Article 15)

Article 15(1) provides that the procedures set out in Arts 30 and 31 (see below) will apply by analogy to all decisions restricting free movement of EU citizens and their family members on grounds other than public policy, public security or public health.

Expiry of the identity card or passport on the basis of which the persons concerned entered the host Member State and were issued with a registration certificate or residence card shall not constitute a ground for expulsion from the host Member State (Art 15(2)).

Right of permanent residence (Article 16)

EU citizens acquire the right of permanent residence in the host Member State after a five-year period of continuous legal residence (Art 16(1)), provided that an expulsion decision has not been enforced against them (Art 21). This right of permanent residence is no longer subject to any conditions. The same rule applies to non-EU family members who have lived with an EU citizen in the host Member State for five years (Art 16(2)), and again provided that an expulsion decision has not been enforced against them (Art 21). Article 16(3) provides that continuity of residence shall not be affected by:

(i)   temporary absences not exceeding six months a year;
(ii) absences of a longer period for compulsory military service; or
(iii) one absence of up to 12 months for important reasons (e.g. pregnancy and childbirth, serious illness, study or vocational training, or a posting in another Member State or a third country).

The following two cases (which were considered together by the Court of Justice) related to how terms of imprisonment should be treated when considering lengths of residency for the purpose of the above provisions:

Onuekwere v Secretary of State for the Home Department and *Secretary of State for the Home Department v G* (Cases C-378/12 and C-400/12)

Case C-378/12
By his marriage to an Irish citizen who had exercised her right of freedom of movement and residence in the United Kingdom, Onuekwere, a Nigerian national, obtained a residence permit valid for five years in that Member State. During his residence in the UK as a family member of an EU citizen, Onuekwere was sentenced on several occasions by the UK courts for various offences and was imprisoned for a total period of three years and three months.

Onuekwere subsequently requested a permanent residence card, alleging in particular that, as his wife had acquired the right of permanent residence, he also had to be granted that right. In addition, he claimed that the total duration of his residence in the UK (periods in prison included) far exceeded the duration of five years required for the grant of that right. Moreover, he pointed out that, even if the periods spent in prison were not counted for that purpose, the sum of the periods not including the stays in prison was greater than five years.

His request for a permanent residence card having been dismissed, Onuekwere brought an action before the Upper Tribunal (Immigration and Asylum Chamber), London (United Kingdom). That tribunal referred the case to the Court of Justice to ascertain whether periods in prison and periods of a duration of less than five years which preceded and followed the imprisonment of an applicant had to be taken into account for the purposes of the acquisition of a permanent residence permit.

The Court of Justice stated, first, that a third-country national, who was a family member of a Union citizen who had exercised his right of free movement and residence, could only count the periods he had spent with that citizen for the purposes of the acquisition of a right of permanent residence. As a consequence, the periods during which he had not resided with that citizen because of his imprisonment in the host Member State could not be taken into account for that purpose.

Furthermore, the Court stated that the EU legislature made the acquisition of the right of permanent residence subject to the integration of the person concerned in the host Member State. Such integration was based not only on territorial and temporal factors but also on qualitative elements, relating to the level of integration in the host Member State. In that regard, the Court stated that the imposition of a prison sentence by the national court was such as to show the non-compliance by the person concerned with the values expressed by the society of the host Member State in its criminal law. Accordingly, the taking into consideration of periods of imprisonment for the purposes of the acquisition of the right of permanent residence would clearly be contrary to the aim pursued by the directive in establishing that right of residence.

Finally, for the same reasons, the Court held that **the continuity of residence of five years was interrupted by periods of imprisonment in the host Member State. As a consequence, the periods which preceded and followed the periods of imprisonment could not be added up to reach the minimum period of five years required for the acquisition of a permanent residence permit.**

Case C-400/12

Ms G., a Portuguese national, had resided in the UK since 1998, acquiring a right of permanent residence in 2003. In 2009, she was sentenced by the UK courts to 21 months' imprisonment for having abused one of her children. Furthermore, while she was still in prison, the United Kingdom authorities ordered that she be deported from the UK on grounds of public policy and public security.

Ms G. contested the expulsion order before the UK courts, contending in particular that, having resided in the UK for more than 10 years, she benefited from the highest level of protection which EU law reserved to EU citizens as regards expulsion. The Upper Tribunal (Immigration and Asylum Chamber), London (United Kingdom), before which the dispute had been brought, referred the case to the Court of Justice to ascertain whether, despite her imprisonment, Ms G. could benefit from that enhanced protection against expulsion.

The Court of Justice stated, first, that unlike the requisite period for acquiring a right of permanent residence, which began when the person concerned commenced lawful residence in the host Member State, **the 10-year period of residence necessary for the grant of the enhanced protection against expulsion had to be calculated by counting back** from the date of the decision ordering that person's expulsion. Furthermore, the Court stated that **this period of residence must, in principle, be continuous.**

Secondly, as regards the link between the integration of a person in the society of the host Member State and his imprisonment, the Court held that, for the same reasons as those put forward in the judgment delivered in Case C-378/12, **periods of imprisonment could not be taken into consideration for the purposes of the calculation of the 10-year period of residence.**

Finally, the Court stated that **periods in prison, in principle, interrupted the continuity of the period of residence necessary for the grant of the enhanced protection.** Nevertheless, the Court stated that, in order to determine the extent to which the non-continuous nature of the period of residence prevented the person concerned from enjoying enhanced protection, an overall assessment had to be made of his situation. As part of that overall assessment which was required for determining whether the integrating links between the person concerned and the host Member State had been broken, the national authorities should take into account the relevant considerations of his imprisonment. Similarly, in the context of that overall assessment, the national authorities should take into consideration the fact that the person concerned, such as Ms G., had resided in the host Member State during the 10 years prior to imprisonment.

Once granted, the right of permanent residence is lost only in the event of more than two successive years' absence from the host Member State (Arts 16(4) and 20(3)).

Article 17 recognises the right of permanent residence for EU citizens who are workers or self-employed persons and for their family members, before the five-year period of continuous residence has expired, subject to certain conditions being met. Article 17 applies to cases where the EU citizen:

(i)   has reached retirement age;
(ii) has become permanently incapable of working; or
(iii) lives in the host Member State but works in another Member State.

Article 17 also provides that the family members of an EU worker or self-employed person have the right of permanent residence if the EU worker or self-employed person dies before acquiring the right of permanent residence. This right, which applies to family members of whatever nationality, is subject to the following conditions:

(a) the worker or self-employed person had, at the time of death, resided continuously on the territory of that Member State for two years;

(b) the death resulted from an accident at work or an occupational disease; or

(c) the surviving spouse lost the nationality of that Member State following marriage to the worker or self-employed person.

Articles 12 and 13 were considered above. Of relevance to permanent residence are the following provisions.

Article 12(1) provides that if an EU citizen dies or departs from the host Member State, his family members who are nationals of a Member State shall not have their right of residence affected. However, before acquiring the right of permanent residence, the persons concerned must meet the conditions set out in Art 7(1)(a), (b), (c) or (d); see above. In the case of a non-EU family member, their right of residence shall not be affected if the EU citizen dies provided that the non-EU family member has been residing in the host Member

State as a family member for at least one year before the EU citizen's death (Art 12(2)). However, before acquiring the right of permanent residence, the persons concerned must meet the conditions set out in Art 7(1)(a), (b) or (d) (*note: category (c) does not apply to this situation*). Article 18 provides that the family members to whom Art 12(2) apply, who satisfy the conditions set out in Art 12(2), shall acquire the right of permanent residence after legally residing in the host Member State for a period of five consecutive years; this is without prejudice to Art 17 (see above).

Article 13 governs a family member's right of residence following divorce, annulment of marriage or termination of partnership. In the case of EU family members, divorce, annulment of marriage or termination of partnership does not affect the family member's right of residence (Art 13(1)). However, before acquiring the right of permanent residence, the persons concerned must meet the conditions set out in Art 7(1)(a), (b), (c) or (d); see above. In the case of non-EU family members, retention of the right of residence is restricted. Article 13(2) sets out the circumstances in which there shall be no loss of the right of residence (see above). In this situation, however, before acquiring the right of permanent residence, the persons concerned must meet the conditions set out in Art 7(1)(a), (b) or (d). Article 18 provides that the family members to whom Art 13(2) applies, who satisfy the conditions set out in Art 13(2), shall acquire the right of permanent residence after legally residing in the host Member State for a period of five consecutive years; this is without prejudice to Art 17 (see above).

EU citizens entitled to permanent residence will be issued with a document certifying such residency (Art 19(1)). Article 20(1) provides that non-EU family members who are entitled to permanent residence will be issued with a residence card, renewable automatically every ten years. The application for a permanent residence card has to be submitted before the residence card expires (Art 20(2)). The residence card must be issued no more than six months after the application is made (Art 20(1)). Failure to apply for a permanent residence card may render the person concerned liable to proportionate and non-discriminatory sanctions (Art 20(2)).

Article 21 provides that continuity of residence may be attested by any means of proof in use in the Member State.

Common provisions on the right of residence and right of permanent residence

Article 22 provides that the right of residence and right of permanent residence shall cover the whole territory of the host Member State. Territorial restrictions can only be imposed if the same restrictions apply to the host Member State's nationals. Family members, irrespective of their nationality, are entitled to engage in an economic activity on an employed or self-employed basis (Art 23).

EU citizens qualifying for the right of residence or the right of permanent residence, and the members of their family, benefit from equal treatment with host-country nationals in the areas covered by the Treaty (Art 24(1)). However, for the first three months of residence, or while the EU citizen is exercising his right to reside while seeking work under Art 14(4)(b), the host Member State is not obliged to grant entitlement to social assistance to persons other than employed or self-employed workers and the members of their family (Art 24(2)). Equally, host Member States are not required to provide maintenance aid (i.e. student grants or student loans) to persons with a right of residence who have come to the country in question to study (Art 24(2)).

Article 25(1) provides that under no circumstances can possession of a registration certificate, etc., be made a precondition for the exercise of a right or the completion of an administrative formality. Entitlement to rights may be attested by any other means of proof, where such documentation is not available. Article 25(2) further provides that all the documents listed in Art 25(1) shall be issued free of charge or for a charge which does not exceed that imposed on nationals for the issuing of a similar document.

If a Member State requires their own nationals to carry an identity card, then the host Member State can require non-nationals to carry their registration certificate or residence card. The host Member State may impose the same sanction as those imposed on their own nationals if a non-national fails to comply (Art 26).

Restrictions on the right of entry and the right of residence on grounds of public policy, public security or public health

EU citizens or members of their family may be refused entry to, or expelled from, the host Member State on grounds of public policy, public security or public health (Art 27(1)). Under no circumstances may an expulsion decision be taken on economic grounds (Art 27(1)). Measures taken on the grounds of public policy or public security must comply with the principle of proportionality and must be based on the personal conduct of the individual concerned; previous criminal convictions do not automatically justify such measures (Art 27(2)). The personal conduct must represent a genuine, present and sufficiently serious threat which affects one of the fundamental interests of society (Art 27(2)).

Article 27(3) provides that in order to ascertain whether the person concerned represents a danger to public policy or public security, the host Member State, if it considers it essential, may request the Member State of origin or other Member States to provide information concerning any previous police record the person concerned may have. The request is to be made by the host Member State:

(i)   when issuing the registration certificate;
(ii) if there is no registration system, no later than three months from the date of the person's arrival in the host Member State or date the person reported his presence in the host Member State as provided for in Art 5(5); or
(iii) when issuing the residence card.

Such enquiries must not be made as a matter of routine. The Member State consulted should provide its reply within two months.

A person who is expelled from a Member State on grounds of public policy, public security or public health shall have the right to re-enter the Member State which issued him with a passport or identity card, even if the document is no longer valid, or if the nationality of the holder is in dispute (Art 27(4)).

Article 28(1) provides that before taking an expulsion decision on grounds of public policy or public security, the host Member State must assess a number of factors such as the period for which the individual concerned has been resident, his age, state of health, family and economic situation, degree of social and cultural integration in the host Member State and the extent of his links with the country of origin. Only for serious grounds of public policy or public security can an expulsion decision be taken against an EU citizen or his family members, if the EU citizen or his family members have acquired the right of permanent residence in the host Member State (Art 28(2)). In addition, an expulsion decision may not be taken against an EU citizen or his family members who have resided in the host country for ten years or if he is a minor, unless the decision is based on imperative grounds of public security, and, in the case of a minor, provided that expulsion is necessary for the best interests of the child (Art 28(3)).

Article 29 is concerned with the restriction on the right of entry and residence on the ground of public health. The only diseases which can justify restricting the right of entry and residence are:

(i) those with epidemic potential as defined by the relevant instruments of the World Health Organization (WHO);
(ii) other infectious diseases or other contagious parasitic diseases if they are subject to protection provisions applying to nationals of the host Member State (Art 29(1)).

Article 29(2) provides that diseases occurring after a three-month period from the date of arrival shall not constitute grounds for expulsion from the host Member State. A Member State can require the person concerned to undergo a medical examination, which must be provided free of charge, if there are serious indications that a medical examination is necessary; such medical examinations must not be carried out as a matter of routine (Art 29(3)). The person concerned by a decision refusing leave to enter or reside in a Member State on the ground of public policy, public security or public health must be notified in writing of that decision, in such a way that they are able to comprehend its content and the implications for them (Art 30(1)). The grounds for the decision must be given precisely and in full, unless this is contrary to the interests of state security (Art 30(2)), and the person concerned must be informed of the appeal procedures available to them (Art 30(3)). Except in cases of urgency, the subject of such decision must be allowed at least one month in which to leave the Member State (Art 30(3)).

Article 31 sets out the procedural safeguards which apply if a decision is taken against a person's right of entry and residence on the grounds of public policy, public security or public health. Article 31 provides as follows:

1 The persons concerned shall have access to judicial and, where appropriate, administrative redress procedures in the host Member State to appeal against or seek review of any decision taken against them on the grounds of public policy, public security or public health.

2 Where the application for appeal against or judicial review of the expulsion decision is accompanied by an application for an interim order to suspend enforcement of that decision, actual removal from the territory may not take place until such time as the decision on the interim order has been taken, except:
   - where the expulsion decision is based on a previous judicial decision; or
   - where the persons concerned have had previous access to judicial review; or
   - where the expulsion decision is based on imperative grounds of public security under Article 28(3).

3 The redress procedures shall allow for an examination of the legality of the decision, as well as of the facts and circumstances on which the proposed measure is based. They shall ensure that the decision is not disproportionate, particularly in view of the requirements laid down in Article 28.

4 Member States may exclude the individual concerned from their territory pending the redress procedure, but they may not prevent the individual from submitting his/her defence in person, except when his/her appearance may cause serious troubles to public policy or public security or when the appeal or judicial review concerns a denial of entry to the territory.

Persons excluded from a Member State on grounds of public policy or public security can apply for the exclusion order to be lifted after a reasonable period, and in any event after a maximum of three years, by putting forward arguments to establish that there has been a material change in the circumstances which justified the decision ordering their exclusion (Art 32(1)). The Member State concerned is required to reach a decision on such application within six months of its submission (Art 32(1)). The person applying for the lifting of the exclusion order does not have a right of entry into the Member State concerned while the application is being considered (Art 32(2)).

An expulsion order cannot be issued by a Member State as a penalty or legal consequence of a custodial penalty, unless the requirements of Arts 27–29 (see above) are complied with (Art 33(1)). Where an expulsion order is issued under this provision, and where it is enforced more than two years after it was issued, the Member State is required to check that the individual concerned is a current and genuine threat to public policy or public security, and the Member State shall assess whether there has been any material change in circumstances since the expulsion order was issued (Art 33(2)).

EU citizenship

Objective
3

Article 20 TFEU (which is substantially the same as the former Art 17 EC Treaty) provides that:

1   **Citizenship of the Union is hereby established**. Every person holding the nationality of a Member State shall be a citizen of the Union. Citizenship of the Union shall be additional to and not replace national citizenship.

2   Citizens of the Union shall enjoy the rights and be subject to the duties provided for in the Treaties. They shall have, *inter alia*:
    (a) the right to move and reside freely within the territory of the Member States;
    (b) the right to vote and to stand as candidates in elections to the European Parliament and in municipal elections in their Member State of residence, under the same conditions as nationals of that State;
    (c) the right to enjoy, in the territory of a third country in which the Member State of which they are nationals is not represented, the protection of the diplomatic and consular authorities of any Member State on the same conditions as the nationals of that State;
    (d) the right to petition the European Parliament, to apply to the European Ombudsman, and to address the institutions and advisory bodies of the Union in any of the Treaty languages and to obtain a reply in the same language.

These rights shall be exercised in accordance with the conditions and limits defined by the Treaties and by the measures adopted thereunder. [emphasis added]

Article 21(1) TFEU (which is practically unchanged from the former Art 18(1) EC Treaty) provides as follows:

Every citizen of the Union shall have the right to move and reside freely within the territory of the Member States, **subject to the limitations and conditions laid down in the Treaties and by the measures adopted to give them effect**. [emphasis added]

The emphasised words of Art 21(1) TFEU would seem to make it clear that EU citizenship does not bring any new free movement rights into being but formally attaches the existing rights, with all the qualifications and exceptions, to the new citizenship. The most that might have been said about EU citizenship and free movement is that possession of such citizenship raises a presumption of a right of entry or residence, which would have to be rebutted by the host Member State if those rights were to be refused or terminated. The

Treaty envisages that the existing rights form the basis for further development, because it authorises the adoption of further measures 'to give them effect' (Art 21(1)). The scope of EU citizenship was a central issue in the following case, which was decided by an English court, not the Court of Justice:

R v Secretary of State for the Home Department, ex parte Vitale and Do Amaral [1995] ALL ER (EC) 946

The applicants, both EU citizens, were resident in the UK and had been in receipt of income support for a number of months. They had not found work and, in the view of the Department of Employment, they were not seeking work. They were therefore asked to leave the country. They argued that, irrespective of the truth of the allegations, they were entitled to remain simply as EU citizens. Judge J rejected this argument:

... [Article 21(1) TFEU] provides two distinct rights, the right to move freely within the territory and the right to reside freely. Neither right is free-standing nor absolute. It is expressly and unequivocally subject to the limitations and conditions contained in the Treaty. Moreover it is clear from the provisions in ... [Article 21(2) TFEU] and, more significantly ... [Article 25 TFEU], that provisions may be adopted in due course 'to strengthen or add to the rights laid down' in the part of the Treaty devoted to 'citizenship'. In effect, therefore, the existence of limitations and the potential for extending the rights of citizens are acknowledged in ... [Article 25 TFEU] as well as ... [Article 21 TFEU]. So ... [Article 21 TFEU] does not provide every citizen of the Union with an open-ended right to reside freely within every Member State.

This decision of the English Divisional Court was upheld by the Court of Appeal ([1996] All ER (EC) 461). The limited scope of what is now Art 21(1) TFEU received some support from the Court of Justice in the following case:

Kremzow v Austria (Case C-299/95)

The claimant argued that, as an EU citizen, he was entitled to the protection of Union law in relation to criminal proceedings which had been brought against him. The Court of Justice held, on a reference from the national court, that the mere fact of his EU citizenship was 'not a sufficient connection with Community [i.e. Union] law to justify the application of Community [i.e. Union] provisions'.

The Court of Justice was, however, subsequently prepared to hold that an EU citizen who had been *permitted* by the host state to remain there (where she had no right to remain under Union law) was entitled, as an EU citizen, to equal treatment in relation to welfare and other benefits in line with nationals of the host state. It left open the question of whether a person who is no longer exercising their free movement rights could still enjoy an independent right of residence as an EU citizen (***Sala v Freistaat Bayern*** (Case C-85/96)).

One of the rights conferred by the Treaty is that contained in Art 18 TFEU, which is practically unchanged from the former Art 12 EC Treaty and provides as follows:

Within the scope of application of the Treaties, and without prejudice to any special provisions contained therein, any discrimination on grounds of nationality shall be prohibited.

The European Parliament and the Council, acting in accordance with the ordinary legislative procedure, may adopt rules designed to prohibit such discrimination.

In the following case, the Court of Justice applied this non-discriminatory provision (Art 18 TFEU) alongside the EU citizenship provisions, which enabled it to elevate the status of EU citizenship:

Grzelczyk v Centre Public d'aide sociale d'Ottignies-Louvain-la-Neuve (Case C-184/99)

A student of French nationality paid his own way throughout his first three years of full-time studies at a Belgian university by taking on minor jobs and obtaining credit. At the start of his fourth and final year he applied for a Belgian social security benefit known as minimum subsistence allowance (minimex). His application was refused on the ground that under the relevant Belgian legislation a non-Belgian applicant was only eligible if *inter alia* Regulation 1612/68 applied to him. Regulation 1612/68 has been repealed and replaced by Regulation 492/2011, which came into force on 16 June 2011. This Regulation is considered further in Chapter 12; it is applicable to 'workers' not 'students'. If he had been Belgian then he would have been entitled to the benefit, notwithstanding the fact that he was not a worker within the scope of Regulation 1612/68 (now Regulation 492/2011). The Belgian tribunal had doubts as to whether the national legislation was compatible with the former Arts 12 and 17 EC Treaty (now Arts 18 and 20 TFEU). The tribunal therefore referred the case to the Court of Justice for a preliminary ruling pursuant to the former Art 234 EC Treaty (now Art 267 TFEU). The Court of Justice held that:

29. It is clear from the documents before the Court that a student of Belgian nationality, though not a worker within the meaning of Regulation No 1612/68 [now Regulation 492/2011], who found himself in exactly the same circumstances as Mr Grzelczyk would satisfy the conditions for obtaining the minimex. The fact that Mr Grzelczyk is not of Belgian nationality is the only bar to its being granted to him. It is not therefore in dispute that the case is one of discrimination solely on the ground of nationality.

30. Within the sphere of application of the Treaty, such discrimination is, in principle, prohibited by . . . [Article 18 TFEU]. In the present case . . . [Article 18 TFEU] must be read in conjunction with the provisions of the Treaty concerning citizenship of the Union in order to determine its sphere of application.

31. Union citizenship is destined to be the fundamental status of nationals of the Member States, enabling those who find themselves in the same situation to enjoy the same treatment in law irrespective of their nationality, subject to such exceptions as are expressly provided for.

. . .

36. The fact that a Union citizen pursues university studies in a Member State other than the State of which he is a national cannot, of itself, deprive him of the possibility of relying on the prohibition of all discrimination on grounds of nationality laid down in . . . [Article 18 TFEU].

37. As pointed out in paragraph 30 above, in the present case that prohibition must be read in conjunction with . . . [Article 21(1) TFEU], which proclaims 'the right to move and reside freely within the territory of the Member States, subject to the limitations and conditions laid down in this Treaty and by the measures adopted to give it effect'.

38. As regards those limitations and conditions, it is clear from Article 1 of Directive 93/96 [which has been repealed and replaced by Directive 2004/38] that Member States may require of students who are nationals of a different Member State and who wish to exercise the right of residence on their territory, first, that they satisfy the relevant national authority that they have sufficient resources to avoid becoming a burden on the social assistance system of the host Member State during their period of residence, next, that they be enrolled in a recognised educational establishment for the principal purpose of

following a vocational training course there and, lastly, that they be covered by sickness insurance in respect of all risks in the host Member State.

39. Article 3 of Directive 93/96 [which has been repealed and replaced by Directive 2004/38] makes clear that the directive does not establish any right to payment of maintenance grants by the host Member State for students who benefit from the right of residence. On the other hand, there are no provisions in the directive that preclude those to whom it applies from receiving social security benefits.

40. As regards more specifically the question of resources, Article 1 of Directive 93/96 [which has been repealed and replaced by Directive 2004/38] does not require resources of any specific amount, nor that they be evidenced by specific documents. The article refers merely to a declaration, or such alternative means as are at least equivalent, which enables the student to satisfy the national authority concerned that he has, for himself and, in relevant cases, for his spouse and dependent children, sufficient resources to avoid becoming a burden on the social assistance system of the host Member State during their stay (see paragraph 44 of the judgment in Case C-424/98 *Commission* v *Italy* [2000] ECR I-4001).

. . .

46. It follows from the foregoing that . . . [Articles 18 and 20 TFEU] preclude entitlement to a non-contributory social benefit, such as the minimex, from being made conditional, in the case of nationals of Member States other than the host State where they are legally resident, on their falling within the scope of Regulation No 1612/68 [now Regulation 492/2011] when no such condition applies to nationals of the host Member State. [emphasis added]

In the above case, the Court of Justice (at paras 29–30) stated that because it was clear that a student who was Belgian but otherwise in the same circumstances as the applicant would be entitled to minimex, the case was one of discrimination solely on the ground of nationality which, in principle, was prohibited by what is now Art 18 TFEU. The Court further stated at para 30 that what is now Art 18 TFEU had to be read in conjunction with the Treaty provisions on EU citizenship (what is now Art 20 TFEU), to determine its sphere of application. The Court then went on to say that EU citizenship was destined to be the fundamental status of nationals of the Member States, enabling those who found themselves in the same situation to enjoy the same treatment in law irrespective of their nationality, subject to some exceptions as are expressly provided for (para 31).

The Court noted that Directive 93/96 (which has been replaced by Directive 2004/38) requires Member States to grant a right of residence to student nationals of a Member State who satisfy certain requirements. Although Art 3 of this Directive makes clear that there is no right to payment of maintenance grants by the host Member State for students who benefit from this right of residence, it contains no provision precluding those to whom it applies from receiving social security benefits. The Court therefore held that what are now Arts 18 and 20 TFEU precluded Belgium from making entitlement to minimex conditional on the applicant (Mr Grzelczyk) coming within the scope of Regulation 1612/68 (i.e. being an 'EU worker') when no such condition applied to Belgian nationals (Regulation 1612/68 has been repealed and replaced by Regulation 492/2011).

The *Grzelczyk* case clearly raised the profile and status of EU citizenship. Due to the fact that the applicant had a right of residence under Union law as a student, the Court held that as an EU citizen he was entitled to be treated in the same way as a national with regard to the payment of social security benefits; an application of the non-discriminatory provision (Art 18 TFEU). It was unclear whether this would pave the way for the Court of Justice to extend its scope to others (e.g. work-seekers). *Grzelczyk* could be distinguished from that of, for example, a work-seeker because it could be argued that a student is contributing to the economy of the host Member State whereas a work-seeker is not necessarily doing so. In any event in *Grzelczyk* the Court stated that its judgment did not prevent a Member State from:

(i) taking the view that a student who had recourse to social assistance was no longer fulfilling the conditions of his right of residence; or

(ii) taking measures, within the limits imposed by Union law, to either withdraw his residence permit or refuse to renew it.

But in no case, the Court said, could such a measure become the automatic consequence of a student who was a national of another Member State having recourse to the host Member State's social security system (see paras 40–45). If the Court did extend this case to, for example, work-seekers, such that they were entitled to claim social security benefits under the same terms as a national, it would therefore be open to a Member State to determine that the work-seeker no longer satisfied the conditions relating to his right of residence. The right of a work-seeker to claim a social security benefit has since been considered by the Court of Justice in two cases: *Collins* (Case C-138/02) and *Ioannidis* (Case C-258/04); see Chapter 12.

Directive 2004/38 (relating to the right of entry and residence) was subsequently adopted and had to be transposed into national law by 30 April 2006. Article 6(1), Directive 2004/38 provides that EU citizens shall have the right of residence in another Member State for a period of up to three months; this will therefore include work-seekers (see Chapter 12). Article 14(1), Directive 2004/38 further provides that EU citizens and their family members shall have the right of residence under Art 6, 'as long as they do not become an *unreasonable* burden on the social assistance system of the host Member State' (emphasis added). Expulsion shall not be an automatic consequence if an EU citizen or his family members have recourse to the host Member State's social assistance system (Art 14(3), Directive 2004/38).

The principle of EU citizenship and non-discrimination developed by the Court of Justice in *Grzelczyk* was subsequently applied by the Court in *Marie-Nathalie D'Hoop* v *Office national de l'emploi* (Case C-224/98) and *Garcia Avello* (Case C-148/02).

EU citizenship has influenced the development of the law relating to the free movement of workers and work-seekers, the freedom to provide and receive services, and the freedom of establishment. This is considered further in Chapters 12 and 13. The following cases relate to how the concept of EU citizenship has influenced the development of the law relating to the free movement of persons who are not exercising one of these fundamental freedoms.

In the following case, the Korkein oikeus (Supreme Court, Finland) referred a question on the interpretation of what is now Art 21 TFEU to the Court of Justice for a preliminary ruling:

Pusa (Case C-224/02)

Pusa, a Finnish national, was in receipt of an invalidity pension in Finland. Pusa owed money to Osuuspankkien Keskinäinen Vakuutusyhtiö (OKV), and OKV sought an 'attachment' on Pusa's invalidity pension to enable deductions to be made from his pension automatically; these deductions would be paid to OKV.

The case concerned the calculation of the amount which OKV should be authorised to debit from Pusa's pension (i.e. the amount of the 'attachment'). The Finnish law on enforcement provided that part of remuneration was excluded from attachment, that part being calculated from the amount which remained after compulsory deduction at source of income tax in Finland. The problem in this case lay in the fact that Pusa was resident in Spain and he was subject to income tax there. In accordance with the provisions of a double taxation agreement, he was not subject to any deduction at source in Finland. The part of his pension subject to attachment was therefore calculated on the basis of the gross amount of the pension, which would not have been the case if he had continued to reside in Finland.

The Finnish Supreme Court asked the Court of Justice whether such a situation was compatible with the freedom of movement and residence guaranteed to EU citizens by the EU Treaties.

The Court stated that within all the Member States an EU citizen must be granted the same treatment in law as that accorded to the nationals of those Member States who find themselves in the same situation. The Court stated that if the Finnish law on enforcement had to be interpreted to mean that it did not allow the tax paid by the person concerned in Spain to be taken into account, that difference of treatment would result in Pusa being placed at a disadvantage by virtue of exercising his right to move and reside freely in the Member States, as guaranteed under the former Art 18 EC Treaty (now Art 21 TFEU). The Court stated that precluding all consideration of the tax payable in the Member State of residence could not be justified in the light of the legitimate objectives pursued by such a law of preserving the creditor's right to recover the debt due to him and preserving the debtor's right to a minimum subsistence income.

Consequently, the Court held that:

Community [i.e. Union] law in principle precludes legislation of a Member State under which the attachable part of a pension paid at regular intervals in that State to a debtor is calculated by deducting from that pension the income tax pre-payment levied in that State, while the tax which the holder of such a pension must pay on it subsequently in the Member State where he resides is not taken into account at all for the purposes of calculating the attachable portion of that pension (para 48) [emphasis added].

However, the Court considered that:

Community [i.e. Union] law does not preclude such national legislation if it provides for tax to be taken into account, where taking the tax into account is made subject to the condition that the debtor prove that he has in fact paid or is required to pay within a given period a specified amount as income tax in the Member State where he resides (para 48) [emphasis added].

The Court said that this is only the case:

. . . to the extent that: (i) the right of the debtor to have tax taken into account is clear from that legislation; (ii) the rules for taking tax into account guarantee the right to obtain an annual adjustment of the attachable portion of his pension to the same extent as if the tax had been deducted at source in the Member State which enacted that legislation; and (iii) the rules do not have the effect of making it impossible or excessively difficult to exercise that right (para 48).

The next case was quite novel – the former Art 18 EC Treaty (now Art 21 TFEU) was successfully relied upon to enable a Chinese national to reside in the UK on the basis that she was the carer of her newborn child who had acquired Irish nationality:

Zhu and Chen (Case C-200/02)

Mr and Mrs Chen were Chinese nationals and parents of a first child born in China. They wanted to have a second child but came up against China's birth control policy, the 'one child policy', which imposed financial penalties on couples who gave birth to more than one child. They therefore decided that Mrs Chen would give birth abroad. Their second child was born in September 2000 in Belfast, Northern Ireland (Northern Ireland is part of the UK). The choice of the place of birth was no accident. The law of Ireland (which is not part of the UK) allowed any person born in the island of Ireland (which for this purpose includes Northern Ireland) to acquire Irish nationality. The child therefore acquired Irish nationality. However, because she did not meet the requirements laid down by the relevant UK legislation, she did not acquire UK nationality. After the birth, Mrs Chen moved to Cardiff (Wales) with her child, and applied for a long-term residence permit for herself and her child, which was refused. Mrs Chen appealed and the appellate authority referred a question to the Court of Justice on the lawfulness of that refusal, pointing out that:

(i)   the mother and child provided for their needs;
(ii) they did not rely on public funds and there was no realistic possibility of their becoming so reliant;
(iii) they were insured against ill health.

The Court said that **the capacity to be the holder of rights guaranteed by the EU Treaties and by secondary law on the free movement of persons did not require that the person concerned had attained the age prescribed for the acquisition of legal capacity to exercise those rights personally. Moreover, the enjoyment of those rights could not be made conditional on the attainment of a minimum age.**

As regards the child's right of residence, the Court recalled that the former Art 18 EC Treaty (now Art 21 TFEU) has direct effect. Purely as a national of a Member State, and therefore an EU citizen, she could rely on the right of residence laid down by that provision. However, this was subject to the limitations and conditions imposed, in particular, by Art 1(1), Directive 90/364, which allows Member States to require that the persons concerned have sickness insurance and sufficient resources (Directive 90/364 has since been replaced by Directive 2004/38, see below). The Court found that the child had sickness insurance and sufficient resources, and therefore satisfied Art 1(1), Directive 90/364. The fact that the sufficient resources of the child were provided by her mother and she had none herself was immaterial; a requirement as to the origin of the resources could not be added to the requirement of sufficient resources.

Finally, with regard to the fact that Mrs Chen went to Ireland with the sole aim of giving her child the nationality of a Member State, in order then to secure a right of residence in the UK for herself and her child, the Court stated that it was for each Member State to define the conditions for the acquisition and loss of nationality. A Member State could not restrict the effects of the grant of the nationality of another Member State by imposing an additional condition for the recognition of that nationality with a view to the exercise of the fundamental freedoms provided for in the Treaty.

With regard to the mother's right of residence, the Court noted that the former Directive 90/364 (now Directive 2004/38) recognises a right of residence for 'dependent' relatives in the ascending line of the holder of the right of residence, which assumed that material support for the family member was provided by the holder of the right of residence. In the present case, the Court stated the position was exactly the opposite. Mrs Chen could not thus be regarded as a 'dependent' relative of her child in the ascending line. However, **where a child was granted a right of residence by the former Art 18 EC**

> Treaty (now Art 21 TFEU) and the former Directive 90/364 (now Directive 2004/38), the parent who was the carer of the child could not be refused the right to reside with the child in the host Member State, as otherwise the child's right of residence would be deprived of any useful effect.

The above case was applied by the Court of Justice in *Ruiz Zambrano* v *Office national de l'emploi* (Case C-34/09). The Court of Justice held that EU citizenship requires a Member State to allow third-country nationals who are parents of a child who is a national of that Member State to reside and work there, where a refusal to do so would deprive the child of the rights attaching to the status of EU citizenship.

The following case concerned a migrant student's right to a maintenance loan at a preferential rate of interest:

Bidar (Case C-209/03)

The Court of Justice examined whether the conditions for granting student support in England and Wales complied with Union law. In England, the state provided students with a loan at a preferential rate of interest to cover maintenance costs. The loan was repayable after the student completed his studies, provided he was earning in excess of a certain sum. A national of another Member State was eligible to receive such a loan if he was 'settled' in the UK and had been resident there throughout the three-year period preceding the start of the course. However, under English law a national of another Member State could not, in his capacity as a student, obtain the status of being settled in the UK.

Dany Bidar, a young French national, had completed the last three years of his secondary education in the UK, living as a dependent of a member of his family without ever having recourse to social assistance. He was refused financial assistance to cover his maintenance costs, which he applied for when he started a course in economics at University College London, on the grounds that he was not settled in the UK for the purposes of UK law. He brought proceedings before the English High Court, which referred three questions to the Court of Justice for a preliminary ruling.

The first of those questions sought to determine whether assistance such as that at issue in the present case was outside the scope of the Treaty, in particular the former Art 12 EC Treaty (now Art 18 TFEU). It should be noted that the Court had earlier held in *Lair* (Case 39/86) and *Brown* (Case 197/86) that assistance given to students for maintenance and for training was in principle outside the scope of the Treaty for the purposes of the former Art 12 EC Treaty (now Art 18 TFEU); see Chapter 12. In the present case, the Court held that the former Art 12 EC Treaty (now Art 18 TFEU) had to be read in conjunction with the provisions on EU citizenship and noted that an EU citizen lawfully resident in the territory of the host Member State could rely on the former Art 12 EC Treaty (now Art 18 TFEU) in all situations which came within the scope *ratione materiae* of Union law, in particular those involving the exercise of the right to move and reside within the territory of the Member States, as conferred by the former Art 18 EC Treaty (now Art 21 TFEU). In the case of students who moved to another Member State to study there, there was nothing in the text of the Treaty to suggest that they lost the rights the Treaty conferred on EU citizens. The Court added that **a national of a Member State who lived in another Member State where he pursued and completed his secondary education, without it being objected that he did not have sufficient resources or sickness insurance, enjoyed a right of residence on the basis of the former Art 18 EC Treaty (now Art 21 TFEU) and Directive 90/364 (now Directive 2004/38, see below)**. With regard to *Lair* and *Brown*, the Court stated that as judgment had been given in those cases the TEU had introduced EU citizenship and inserted a chapter devoted to education and training into the Treaty. **In the light of those factors, it had to be held that this type of financial assistance came within the scope of the Treaty for the purposes of the prohibition of discrimination laid down in the former Art 12 EC Treaty (now Art 18 TFEU).**

The Court then considered whether, where the requirements for granting assistance were linked to the fact of being settled or to residence and where these requirements were likely to place nationals of other Member States at a disadvantage, the difference in treatment between them and nationals of the Member State concerned could be justified. The Course stated that it was permissible for Member States to ensure that the granting of social assistance did not become an unreasonable burden. **In the case of assistance covering the maintenance costs of students, it was thus legitimate to seek to ensure a certain degree of integration by checking that the student in question had resided in the host Member State for a certain length of time.** However, a link with the employment market, as in the case of allowances for persons seeking employment which were at issue in *D'Hoop* (Case C-224/98) and *Collins* (Case C-138/02), could not be required.

In principle, a requirement that an applicant should be settled in the host Member State could therefore be allowed. However, in so far as it precluded any possibility for a student who was a national of another Member State to obtain the status of settled person, and hence to receive the assistance even if he had established a genuine link with the society of the host Member State, the legislation in question was incompatible with the former Art 12 EC Treaty (now Art 18 TFEU).

The above case was applied by the Court of Justice in *Förster v Hoofddirectie van de Informatie Beheer Groep* (Case C-158/07). In the *Förster* case, the Dutch body which administered educational maintenance grants adopted a policy rule which provided that a student from the European Union must have been lawfully resident in The Netherlands for an uninterrupted period of at least five years before claiming a maintenance grant. The Court of Justice held that this period was appropriate for the purpose of evidencing that the applicant was integrated into the society of the host Member State. The Court did not consider this condition was excessive.

The following joined cases were similar to the above two in that they also concerned an educational maintenance grant. However, in these joined cases the maintenance grant was provided by the EU citizen's home state (Germany) to facilitate a period of study within another Member State:

Morgan v Bezirksregierung Köln and *Iris Bucher v Landrat des Kreises Düren* (Joined Cases C-11/06 and C-12/06)

Having completed her secondary education in Germany, Morgan, a German national, moved to the UK where she worked for a year as an au pair before commencing her university studies (in the UK), for which she applied to the German authorities for a grant. Her application was rejected because, under German legislation, the grant was subject to the condition that the course of study should constitute a continuation of education or training pursued for at least one year in a German establishment.

Bucher, who is also a German national, lived with her parents in Bonn (Germany) until she decided to move to Düren, a German town on The Netherlands border, and pursue a course of study in The Netherlands town of Heerlen. Bucher applied to the authorities in Düren for a grant, which she was refused on the ground that she was not 'permanently' resident near a border as required by the German legislation.

The administrative court in Aachen, before which both students brought actions, asked the Court of Justice (pursuant to the former Art 234 EC Treaty (now Art 267 TFEU)) whether freedom of movement for EU citizens precluded the condition that studies abroad had to be a continuation of education or training pursued for at least one year in Germany. If the reply to that question was in the affirmative, the national court stated that it would also uphold Bucher's action.

In its judgment, the Court of Justice stated that **where a Member State provided for a system of education or training grants which enabled students to receive such grants if they pursued studies in another Member State it had to ensure that the detailed rules for the award of those grants did not create an unjustified restriction on freedom of movement.**

On account of the personal inconvenience, additional costs and possible delays it entailed, **the twofold obligation to have attended an education or training course for at least one year in Germany and to continue only that same education or training in another Member State was liable to discourage EU citizens from leaving Germany in order to pursue studies in another Member State. It therefore constituted a restriction on freedom of movement for EU citizens.**

Justification for the restriction on freedom of movement

A number of arguments were submitted to the Court seeking to justify the condition of a first stage of studies in Germany.

The Court recognised that the objective of ensuring that students completed their courses in a short period of time could constitute a legitimate aim in the context of the organisation of the education system. However, the Court held that the first-stage studies condition in Germany was inappropriate for achieving that objective.

The Court held that **the requirement of continuity** between the studies in Germany and those pursued abroad was not proportionate to the objective of enabling students to determine whether they had made 'the right choice' in respect of their studies. That requirement **could prevent students from pursuing**, in another Member State, **education or training different from that pursued in Germany**. As regards education or training courses in respect of which there were no equivalents in Germany, the students concerned were obliged to choose between foregoing the planned education or training course and losing entitlement to an education or training grant.

The Court stated that, **in principle, a Member State was entitled**, in order to ensure that education or training grants to students wishing to study in other Member States did not become an unreasonable burden which could have consequences for the overall level of assistance granted by that State, **to grant such assistance only to students who had demonstrated a certain degree of integration into the society of that State. However, the first-stage studies condition was too general and exclusive in that it unduly favoured an element which was not necessarily representative of the degree of integration into the society of that Member State at the time the application for assistance was made.**

The Court also rejected the argument that the first-stage studies condition was necessary to prevent duplication of the assistance granted by different Member States. It observed that that condition was in no way intended to prevent or take account of any duplication. It could not therefore be claimed that the requirement of a first stage of studies in Germany was appropriate or necessary, by itself, to ensure that those grants were not duplicated.

The Court concluded that **the restriction on freedom of movement could not be justified by the reasons put forward.**

The German legislation which was applicable in the above case was amended in 2008. The new legislation provided that students could obtain a maintenance grant for their studies in another Member State for one year. To be eligible to receive a grant for a period of more than one year, the student had to show he had permanently resided in Germany for at least three years prior to commencing his studies. The compatibility of this new legislation with Union law was considered by the Court of Justice in *Prinz* v *Region Hannover* and *Seeberger* v *Studentenwerk Heidelberg* (Case C-523/11). The Court of Justice stated that while it may be legitimate for a Member State to grant assistance to students who have demonstrated a sufficient degree of integration into German society, the condition of three years' permanent residency was too general and exclusive and went beyond what was necessary to achieve the objective. The residency condition risked excluding students who were sufficiently connected with German society but who did not have a three-year uninterrupted period of residence.

At issue in the following case was whether a residence condition was compatible with what is now Art 21 TFEU:

Tas-Hagen and Tas (Case C-192/05)

This case concerned legislation on the award of benefits to civilian war victims which required the person concerned to be resident on national territory at the time at which the application was submitted.

The Court of Justice held that a benefit to compensate civilian war victims came within the competence of the Member States, although they had to exercise that competence in accordance with Union law.

With regard to the residence condition, the Court stated that it could deter exercise of the freedoms accorded by the former Art 18 EC Treaty (now Art 21 TFEU) and therefore constitute a restriction on those freedoms. It stated that the condition could be justified in principle by the desire to limit the obligation of solidarity with war victims to those who had links with the population of the state concerned during and after the war. The condition of residence demonstrated the extent to which those persons were connected to its society. However, while noting the wide margin of appreciation enjoyed by the Member States with regard to benefits that were not covered by Union law, the Court held that a residence condition could not be a satisfactory indicator of that connection when it was liable to lead to different results for persons resident abroad whose degree of integration was in all respects comparable. **The Court therefore held that a residence criterion based solely on the date on which the application for the benefit was submitted was not a satisfactory indicator of the degree of attachment of the applicant to the society which was demonstrating its solidarity with him and therefore failed to comply with the principle of proportionality.**

The next case provided the Court of Justice with the opportunity to clarify the limits of the material scope of the EU Treaties with regard to EU citizenship:

Schempp (Case C-403/03)

In Germany, income tax legislation provided that maintenance payments to a divorced spouse was deductible (thus reducing a person's income tax liability). That advantage was also granted where recipients (the divorced spouse in this case) had their principal or habitual residence in another Member State, provided that taxation of the recipient's maintenance payments was proved by a certificate from the tax authorities of that other

Member State. Egon Schempp, a German national resident in Germany, was refused the deduction of maintenance payments made to his former spouse resident in Austria, because Austrian tax law excluded the taxation of maintenance payments.

When a question was referred to it from the Bundesfinanzhof (Federal Finance Court, Germany) for a preliminary ruling on whether the German system complied with the former Arts 12 and 18 EC Treaty (now Arts 18 and 21 TFEU), the Court considered first of all whether such a situation came within the scope of Union law. The governments which had submitted observations contended that Schempp had not made use of his right of free movement, and the only external factor was the fact that Schempp was paying maintenance in another Member State. **The Court observed that EU citizenship was not intended to extend the material scope of the Treaty to internal situations which had no link with Union law.** However, the situation of a national of a Member State who had not made use of the right to free movement could not, for that reason alone, be assimilated to a purely internal situation. Here, the exercise by Schempp's former spouse of a right conferred under Union law to move freely to, and reside in, another Member State had an effect on his right to deduct in Germany, so **there was no question of it being an internal situation with no connection with Union law.**

The Court then considered, with regard to the principle of non-discrimination, whether Schempp's situation could be compared with that of a person who was paying maintenance to a former spouse resident in Germany and was entitled to deduct the maintenance payments made to her. The Court held that this was not the case. The Court stated that the unfavourable treatment of which Schempp complained derived from the difference between the German and Austrian tax systems with regard to the taxing of maintenance payments. It was settled case law that the former Art 12 EC Treaty (now Art 18 TFEU) is not concerned with any disparities in treatment which may result from differences existing between the various Member States, so long as they affect all persons subject to them in accordance with objective criteria and without regard to their nationality.

As regards the application of the former Art 18 EC Treaty (now Art 21 TFEU), the Court found that the German legislation did not in any way obstruct Schempp's right to move to and reside in other Member States. The transfer of his former spouse's residence to Austria did entail tax consequences for him. However, the Court observed that the Treaty offered no guarantee to an EU citizen that transferring his activities to a Member State other than that in which he previously resided would be neutral as regards taxation. Given the disparities in the tax legislation of the Member States, such a transfer could be to the citizen's advantage in terms of indirect taxation or not, according to the circumstances. That principle applied *a fortiori* to a situation where the person concerned had not himself made use of his right of free movement, but claimed to be the victim of a difference in treatment following the transfer of his former spouse's residence to another Member State.

Likewise, in the following case the Court of Justice held that there was no breach of the former Art 18 EC Treaty (now Art 21 TFEU):

De Cuyper (Case C-406/04)

The Court of Justice examined the compatibility of Belgian legislation on unemployment with the freedom of movement and residence conferred on EU citizens by the former Art 18 EC Treaty (now Art 21 TFEU).

Under Belgian legislation, unemployed persons over 50 years of age, although no longer obliged to remain available for work, were subject to a residence requirement. The Court of Justice reiterated the point that the right of residence of EU citizens was not unconditional, but was conferred subject to the limitations and conditions laid down by the Treaty and by the measures adopted to give it effect.

The Court found that the Belgian legislation placed certain Belgian nationals at a disadvantage simply because they had exercised their freedom of movement and residence, and was thus a restriction on the freedoms conferred by Art 18 EC Treaty (now Art 21 TFEU). It accepted, however, that the restriction was justified by objective considerations of public interest independent of the nationality of the persons concerned. The Court stated that a residence condition reflected the need to monitor the employment and family situation of unemployed persons by allowing inspectors to check whether the situation of a recipient of the unemployment allowance had undergone changes which could have an effect on the benefit granted. The Court also noted that the specific nature of monitoring with regard to unemployment justified the introduction of arrangements that were more restrictive than for other benefits and that more flexible measures, such as the production of documents or certificates, would mean that the monitoring would no longer be unexpected and would consequently be less effective.

The above cases demonstrate that, when determining the scope of an EU citizen's right of free movement, the Art 21(1) TFEU right of EU citizens to move and reside freely within the territory of the Member States and the anti-discriminatory Art 18 TFEU provision must be taken into consideration. In some situations these two provisions will be of fundamental importance to the outcome of the case.

Other rights derived from EU citizenship

The creation of EU citizenship is part of a broader programme of enhancement of individual political and social rights in the European context. The EU Treaties and secondary legislation adopted pursuant to the Treaties confer other benefits on EU citizens in addition to the general right of residence. Article 20(2) TFEU (previously Art 17(2) EC Treaty) sets out some of the rights afforded to EU citizens (these rights are dealt with in detail in the EU Treaties):

Citizens of the Union shall enjoy the rights and be subject to the duties provided for in the Treaties. They shall have, *inter alia*:

(a) the right to move and reside freely within the territory of the Member States;
(b) the right to vote and to stand as candidates in elections to the European Parliament and in municipal elections in their Member State of residence, under the same conditions as nationals of that State;
(c) the right to enjoy, in the territory of a third country in which the Member State of which they are nationals is not represented, the protection of the diplomatic and consular authorities of any Member State on the same conditions as the nationals of that State;
(d) the right to petition the European Parliament, to apply to the European Ombudsman, and to address the institutions and advisory bodies of the Union in any of the Treaty languages and to obtain a reply in the same language.

These rights shall be exercised in accordance with the conditions and limits defined by the Treaties and by the measures adopted thereunder.

As discussed above, Directive 2004/38 has established a general, but limited, right of entry and residence (for up to three months) for all those holding the nationality of a Member

State. Extended rights of residence (for over three months) are, under Directive 2004/38, primarily linked to persons engaged in an economic activity and to persons who are financially self-sufficient. Chapters 12 and 13 will examine who comes within the scope of persons who are engaged in an economic activity (i.e. workers (and work-seekers), providers and recipients of services, and those establishing themselves in another Member State (e.g. the self-employed)), and the benefits attaching to such persons.

Free movement rights of non-EU citizens

Objective 4

Directive 2004/38 provides EU citizens with the right to move to, or reside in, a Member State other than that of which they are a national. Family members (which includes non-EU family members) also have the right to accompany or join them. The provisions of Directive 2004/38 have been considered in detail above. There now follows a consideration of the other free movement rights afforded to non-EU citizens.

As discussed above, under the EEA Agreement nationals of Iceland, Liechtenstein and Norway enjoy the full range of free movement rights.

Nationals of other third countries (i.e. non-EU citizens) can enjoy a number of important (although less extensive) free movement rights under Treaties made with it. For example, limited rights are enjoyed by the beneficiaries of Association Agreements made with the Union. Such agreements have been held by the Court of Justice to be directly effective (*Kupferberg* (Case 104/81)). The rights in these cases are normally limited to equal treatment in employment and social security after admission, but they do not entitle the beneficiaries to enter. Such rights have been recognised in this way under the EC–Turkey Agreement (*Kus* v *Landeshauptstadt Wiesbaden* (Case C-237/91); *Eroglu* v *Baden-Württemberg* (Case C-355/93)), and under the EC–Morocco Cooperation Agreement (*Bahia Kziber* v *ONEM* (Case C-18/90); *Yousfi* v *Belgium* (Case C-58/93)). There are other agreements with *inter alia* Tunisia and Algeria, which contain provisions that could be used by nationals of those states while working in the Union.

The following case gave the Court of Justice an opportunity to rule, for the first time, on the effects of a partnership agreement between the European Union and a non-Member State:

Simutenkov (Case C-265/03)

Igor Simutenkov was a Russian national who had a residence permit and a work permit in Spain. He was employed as a professional football player under an employment contract entered into with Club Deportivo Tenerife, and he held a federation licence as a non-EU player issued by the Spanish Football Federation.

According to the Federation's rules, in competitions at national level clubs could field only a limited number of players from countries which did not belong to the European Economic Area. Simutenkov requested that his licence be replaced by a licence as an EU player, basing his application on the EC–Russian Federation Partnership Agreement, which, in relation to working conditions, prohibited discrimination of a Russian national based on nationality. The Federation rejected Simutenkov's application. The Spanish court dealing with the case referred a question to the Court of Justice for a preliminary ruling in order to ascertain whether the rules of the Spanish Football Federation were compatible with the agreement.

Having established that the principle of non-discrimination laid down by Art 23(1) of the EC–Russia Partnership Agreement could be relied on by an individual before the national courts, the Court of Justice considered the scope of that principle.

It stated that **the agreement established, for the benefit of Russian workers lawfully employed in the territory of a Member State, a right to equal treatment in working conditions of the same scope as that which nationals of Member States were recognised as having under the EU Treaties. That right precluded any limitation based on nationality.**

The Court also stated that the limitation based on nationality did not relate to specific matches between teams representing their respective countries but applied to official matches between clubs and thus to the essence of the activity performed by professional players. Such a limitation was therefore not justified on sporting grounds.

The Court of Justice accordingly held that Art 23(1) of the EC–Russian Federation Partnership Agreement precluded the application to a professional sportsman of Russian nationality, who was lawfully employed by a club established in a Member State, of a rule drawn up by a sports federation of that state which provided that in competitions organised at national level, clubs could field only a limited number of players from countries which were not parties to the European Economic Area Agreement.

Other third-country nationals (i.e. non-EU citizens) may benefit from Union free movement rights in a different way. Undertakings established in one Member State have the right to go to another, either to provide a service or to become established there (Arts 49 and 56 TFEU (previously Arts 43 and 49 EC Treaty)). To enable the undertaking to carry out its activities in the host Member State it is entitled to take its workforce with it whatever their nationality. Such employees should be admitted without any requirement of a work permit in the host Member State and should be entitled to remain there until the business of the undertaking is complete. On this basis, the French immigration authorities have been obliged to allow non-EU workers employed by Portuguese and Belgian companies to work without any further restrictions than those already imposed in the state of origin of the undertaking (*Rush Portuguesa Lda* (Case C-113/89); *Van der Elst* v *OMI* (Case C-43/93)). This right is conferred on the undertaking rather than on the worker and if challenged should, in principle, have to be asserted by the undertaking in the courts of the Member State. However, Advocate General Tesauro, in his opinion in *Van der Elst* (above), described the workers in the *Rush Portuguesa* case as having a *derived* right in relation to entry and employment, although he did not argue that it could be asserted by them personally (p. 3813). Somewhat surprisingly, the UK's Immigration Appeal Tribunal has held that the right of the employing company in the UK can be the subject of an application for judicial review by the *employee* (*Pasha* v *Home Office* [1993] 2 CMLR 350).

Third-country nationals (i.e. non-EU citizens) given leave to enter any Member State may be issued with an EU visa and be able to travel anywhere in the EU for a period of up to three months. The visa may be issued by any Member State, but it is in a standard form for use in all the Member States (Art 79(2) TFEU, Regulation 1683/95, OJ 1995 L 164). In addition, such nationals will benefit from Directive 2000/43 prohibiting discrimination on grounds of racial or ethnic origin, and Directive 2000/78 prohibiting direct and indirect discrimination as regards access to employment and occupation on grounds of religion or belief, disability, and age or sexual orientation (see above). Directive 2003/86 (OJ 2003 L 251/12) provides a right to family reunification for the benefit of third-country nationals who are residing lawfully within a Member State (i.e. those who hold a residence permit valid for at least one year in a Member State, and who are genuinely able to stay long term). This directive, which was adopted pursuant to what is now Art 79(2)(a) TFEU, had to be implemented by 3 October 2005; the directive does not apply to the UK, Ireland and Denmark. The directive will be applied by the Court of Justice in *K and A* (Case C-153/14). The Court will determine the legality of the following two requirements imposed by The Netherlands in respect of a non-EU national who is intending to join his non-EU family members who are residing lawfully in The Netherlands:

(i) passing an examination which tests the non-EU national's knowledge of the country and its language;
(ii) the payment of an examination fee.

Following on from the adoption of Directive 2003/86, the Council subsequently adopted Directive 2003/109 (OJ 2004 L 16/44), also pursuant to what is now Art 79(2)(a) TFEU. Directive 2003/109 provides a right to 'long-term resident status' for third-country nationals who are long-term residents of a Member State. This directive had to be implemented by 23 January 2006; the directive does not apply to the UK, Ireland and Denmark. In the following case, the Court of Justice held that a Member State cannot impose excessive and disproportionate charges for the grant of residence permits issued pursuant to Directive 2003/109:

Commission v Netherlands (Case C-508/10)

In The Netherlands, with the exception of Turkish nationals, third-country nationals who requested a residence permit pursuant to Directive 2003/109 were liable to pay a charge which varied from €188 to €830. The Court of Justice pointed out that no provision of the directive fixed the amount of the charges which Member States could impose for the issue of residence permits. However, whilst it was undisputed that Member States enjoyed a margin of discretion in that respect, it was not unlimited.

Therefore, while it was open to Member States to make the issue of residence permits under Directive 2003/109 subject to the levying of charges, **the level of those charges should not have either the object or the effect of creating an obstacle to the obtaining of the rights conferred by that directive, otherwise both the objective of integration and the spirit of that directive would be undermined.**

In that respect, the Court of Justice stated that the amounts of the charges claimed by The Netherlands varied within a range in which the lowest amount was about seven times higher than the amount to be paid to obtain a national identity card. Even if Dutch citizens and third-country nationals and the members of their families were not in identical situations, such a variation illustrated the disproportionate nature of the charges claimed.

The Court of Justice held that those excessive and disproportionate charges were liable to create an obstacle to the exercise of the rights conferred by the directive. As a consequence, by applying them to third-country nationals – those who seek long-term resident status in The Netherlands and those who have already acquired that status in another Member State – who were seeking authorisation for them and members of their family to be able to reside there, The Netherlands had failed to fulfil its obligations under the directive.

In the following case, the Court of Justice held that EU law precluded national or regional legislation which treated third-country nationals who were long-term residents differently from EU citizens with regard to the allocation of funds for housing benefits:

Servet Kamberaj v Istituto per L'edilizia sociale della Provincia autonoma di Bolzano, Giunta della provincia autonoma di Bolzano, Provincia autonoma di Bolzano (Case C-571/10)

Mr Kamberaj, an Albanian national, had resided in Italy since 1994. As the holder of a residence permit for an indefinite period, he received 'housing benefit' from 1998 to 2008.

Housing benefit was allocated to: (i) EU citizens (whether Italian or not); and (ii) third-country nationals and stateless persons, provided that those third-country nationals and stateless persons had resided permanently and lawfully in Italy for at least five years and had worked there for at least three years. From 2009, different methods were used to allocate those funds to those two categories, depending on whether the persons concerned were EU citizens or third-country nationals.

The Social Housing Institute ('IPES') rejected Kamberaj's application for benefit in respect of 2009, on the ground that the budget intended for third-country nationals was exhausted. Kamberaj asked the Tribunale di Bolzano to find that this rejection decision amounted to discrimination contrary to Directive 2003/109.

The Tribunale di Bolzano referred the case to the Court of Justice to ask whether this mechanism for allocation of the funds for housing benefit – which treated third-country nationals who were long-term residents less favourably than EU citizens – was compatible with EU law.

The Court stated that the effect of applying different multipliers to the allocation of funds was to disadvantage the category of third-country nationals, as the budget available to satisfy their demands for housing benefit was smaller than that for EU citizens (whether Italian or not) and was therefore likely to be used up more quickly than theirs.

According to the Court, **a third-country national who had acquired the status of a long-term resident in a Member State was in a comparable situation, with regard to housing benefit, to that of an EU citizen (whether Italian or not), with the same economic need.**

The Court assessed the scope of Directive 2003/109, with regard to the equal treatment of third-country nationals who were long-term residents and nationals of the Member State of residence in the fields of social security, social assistance and social protection. As the EU legislature wished to respect the differences between the Member States, those concepts were defined by national law, subject however to compliance with EU law. It followed that it was for the national court to assess whether housing benefit came within the scope of the fields covered by Directive, taking into account both the integration objective pursued by the Directive and the provisions of the Charter of Fundamental Rights.

Under Art 11(4), Directive 2003/109, Member States could limit the application of equal treatment in respect of social assistance and social protection to core benefits. Those benefits – which include minimum income support, assistance in case of illness, pregnancy, parental assistance and long-term care – had to be granted equally to nationals of the Member State concerned and to third-country nationals who were long-term residents in accordance with the modalities of allocation determined by the legislation of that Member State.

The concept of core benefits had to be interpreted in conformity with the principles of the Charter of Fundamental Rights (Art 34), which recognises and respects the right to social and housing assistance so as to ensure a decent existence for all those who lack sufficient resources. Thus, the national court had to establish whether the housing benefit in question was a core benefit, taking into consideration its objective, its amount, the conditions subject to which it was granted and the place of that benefit in the Italian system of social assistance.

The Court held that EU law precluded a national or regional law which – when the funds for the housing benefit were allocated – provided for different treatment for third-country nationals and nationals of the Member State in which they resided, in so far as the housing benefit came within the scope of one of the three fields covered by the principle of equal treatment provided for under Directive 2003/109. This was for the national court to determine.

The Schengen *acquis* and its integration into the European Union

Objective 5

During the 1980s, a debate opened up about the meaning of the concept of 'free movement of persons'. Some Member States felt that this should apply to EU citizens only, which would involve keeping internal border checks in order to distinguish between EU citizens and non-EU citizens. Others argued in favour of free movement for everyone, which would mean an end to internal border checks altogether. As the Member States found it impossible to reach an agreement, France, Germany, Belgium, Luxembourg and The Netherlands decided in 1985 to create a territory without internal borders. This became known as the 'Schengen area'. Schengen is the name of the town in Luxembourg where the first agreements were signed. This intergovernmental cooperation expanded to include 13 countries in 1997, following the signing of the Treaty of Amsterdam, which (on 1 May 1999) incorporated into EU law: (i) the decisions taken since 1985 by Schengen group members; and (ii) the associated working structures. When the Treaty of Lisbon came into force on 1 December 2009, Protocol No. 19 provided for the integration of the Schengen *acquis* into the framework of the European Union. Protocol No. 19 provides as follows:

ARTICLE 1

The . . . [28 Member States of the EU, excluding Ireland and the UK] shall be authorised to establish closer cooperation among themselves in areas covered by provisions defined by the Council which constitute the Schengen *acquis*. This cooperation shall be conducted within the institutional and legal framework of the European Union and with respect for the relevant provisions of the Treaties.

ARTICLE 2

The Schengen *acquis* shall apply to the Member States referred to in Article 1, without prejudice to Article 3 of the Act of Accession of 16 April 2003 or to Article 4 of the Act of Accession of 25 April 2005. The Council will substitute itself for the Executive Committee established by the Schengen agreements.

ARTICLE 3

The participation of Denmark in the adoption of measures constituting a development of the Schengen *acquis*, as well as the implementation of these measures and their application to Denmark, shall be governed by the relevant provisions of the Protocol on the position of Denmark.

ARTICLE 4

Ireland and the United Kingdom of Great Britain and Northern Ireland may at any time request to take part in some or all of the provisions of this *acquis*.

The Council shall decide on the request with the unanimity of its members referred to in Article 1 and of the representative of the Government of the State concerned.

ARTICLE 5

1　Proposals and initiatives to build upon the Schengen *acquis* shall be subject to the relevant provisions of the Treaties.

　　In this context, where either Ireland or the United Kingdom has not notified the Council in writing within a reasonable period that it wishes to take part, the authorisation referred to in Article 329 of the Treaty on the Functioning of the European Union shall be deemed to have been granted to the Member States referred to in Article 1 and to Ireland or the United Kingdom where either of them wishes to take part in the areas of cooperation in question.

2　Where either Ireland or the United Kingdom is deemed to have given notification pursuant to a decision under Article 4, it may nevertheless notify the Council in writing, within three months, that it does not wish to take part in such a proposal or initiative. In that case, Ireland or the United Kingdom shall not take part in its adoption. As from the latter notification, the procedure for adopting the measure building upon the Schengen *acquis* shall be suspended until the end of the procedure set out in paragraphs 3 or 4 or until the notification is withdrawn at any moment during that procedure.

3　For the Member State having made the notification referred to in paragraph 2, any decision taken by the Council pursuant to Article 4 shall, as from the date of entry into force of the proposed measure, cease to apply to the extent considered necessary by the Council and under the conditions to be determined in a decision of the Council acting by a qualified majority on a proposal from the Commission. That decision shall be taken in accordance with the following criteria: the Council shall seek to retain the widest possible measure of participation of the Member State concerned without seriously affecting the practical operability of the various parts of the Schengen *acquis*, while respecting their coherence. The Commission shall submit its proposal as soon as possible after the notification referred to in paragraph 2. The Council shall, if needed after convening two successive meetings, act within four months of the Commission proposal.

4　If, by the end of the period of four months, the Council has not adopted a decision, a Member State may, without delay, request that the matter be referred to the European Council. In that case, the European Council shall, at its next meeting, acting by a qualified majority on a proposal from the Commission, take a decision in accordance with the criteria referred to in paragraph 3.

5　If, by the end of the procedure set out in paragraphs 3 or 4, the Council or, as the case may be, the European Council has not adopted its decision, the suspension of the procedure for adopting the measure building upon the Schengen *acquis* shall be terminated. If the said measure is subsequently adopted any decision taken by the Council pursuant to Article 4 shall, as from the date of entry into force of that measure, cease to apply for the Member State concerned to the extent and under the conditions decided by the Commission, unless the said Member State has withdrawn its notification referred to in paragraph 2 before the adoption of the measure. The Commission shall act by the date of this adoption. When taking its decision, the Commission shall respect the criteria referred to in paragraph 3.

ARTICLE 6

The Republic of Iceland and the Kingdom of Norway shall be associated with the implementation of the Schengen *acquis* and its further development. Appropriate procedures shall be agreed to that effect in an Agreement to be concluded with those States by the Council, acting by the unanimity of its Members mentioned in Article 1. Such Agreement shall include provisions on the contribution of Iceland and Norway to any financial consequences resulting from the implementation of this Protocol.

A separate Agreement shall be concluded with Iceland and Norway by the Council, acting unanimously, for the establishment of rights and obligations between Ireland and the United Kingdom of Great Britain and Northern Ireland on the one hand, and Iceland and Norway on the other, in domains of the Schengen *acquis* which apply to these States.

ARTICLE 7

For the purposes of the negotiations for the admission of new Member States into the European Union, the Schengen *acquis* and further measures taken by the institutions within its scope shall be regarded as an *acquis* which must be accepted in full by all States candidates for admission.

Development of the Schengen area

The first agreement between the five original group members was signed on 14 June 1985. A further Convention was drafted and signed on 19 June 1990. When this Convention came into effect in 1995, it abolished the internal borders of the signatory states and created a single external border where immigration checks for the Schengen area were carried out in accordance with a single set of rules. Common rules regarding visas, asylum rights and checks at external borders were adopted to allow the free movement of persons within the signatory states without disturbing law and order.

Accordingly, in order to reconcile freedom and security, this freedom of movement was accompanied by so-called 'compensatory' measures. This involved improving coordination between the police, customs and the judiciary and taking necessary measures to combat problems such as terrorism and organised crime. In order to make this possible, an information system known as the **Schengen Information System (SIS)** was set up to exchange data on people's identities and descriptions of objects which were either stolen or lost.

The Schengen area was extended to include every Member State except for the UK and Ireland (Article 5, Protocol No. 19, which is annexed to the TEU and TFEU; see above). Denmark has reserved the power to determine whether future decisions will apply to it (Article 4, Protocol No. 22, which is annexed to the TEU and TFEU; see below).

Measures adopted by Schengen group members

Among the main measures are:

- the removal of checks at common borders, replacing them with external border checks;
- a common definition of the rules for crossing external borders and uniform rules and procedures for controls there;
- separation in air terminals and ports of people travelling within the Schengen area from those arriving from countries outside the area;
- harmonisation of the rules regarding conditions of entry and visas for short stays;
- coordination between administrations on surveillance of borders (liaison officers and harmonisation of instructions and staff training);
- the definition of the role of carriers in measures to combat illegal immigration;
- requirement for all non-EU nationals moving from one country to another to lodge a declaration;
- the drawing up of rules for asylum seekers (Dublin Convention, replaced in 2003 by the Dublin II Regulation);
- the introduction of cross-border rights of surveillance and hot pursuit for police forces in the Schengen states;

- the strengthening of legal cooperation through a faster extradition system and faster distribution of information about the implementation of criminal judgments;
- the creation of the **Schengen Information System (SIS)**.

The Schengen *acquis* comprises these measures, together with:

(i)   the agreement signed on 14 June 1985;
(ii) the Convention implementing that agreement, signed on 19 June 1990;
(iii) the decisions and declarations adopted by the Executive Committee set up by the 1990 Convention;
(iv) the steps taken in order to implement the 1990 Convention by the authorities on whom the Executive Committee conferred decision-making powers;
(v)   the subsequent protocols and accession agreements.

The Schengen Information System (SIS)

An information network was set up to allow all border posts, police stations and consular agents from Schengen group Member States to access data on specific individuals or on vehicles or objects which had been lost or stolen.

Member States supply the network through national networks (N-SIS) connected to a central system (C-SIS), and this is supplemented by a network known as SIRENE (Supplementary Information Request at the National Entry).

See pages 22, 23 and 48 for a list of the new Member States which joined the EU in 2004, 2007 and 2013.

The Member States that joined the European Union on 1 May 2004, 1 January 2007 and 1 July 2013 are bound by the entire Schengen *acquis*. Following the SIS-II becoming operational on 9 April 2013 (see below), border controls have been abolished for all Member States, other than Bulgaria, Croatia, Cyprus and Romania (in addition to the UK and Ireland which, as discussed above, have opted out). Bulgaria and Romania will fully operate the SIS for the purpose of external border controls once a decision to lift internal border checks comes into force. Croatia and Cyprus have a temporary derogation from joining the Schengen area.

The second-generation Schengen Information System (SIS-II)

The Schengen Information System (SIS) was not designed, and therefore lacked the capacity, to operate in more than 15 or so countries. It was therefore necessary to develop a new second-generation Schengen Information System (SIS-II) to enable the new and future Member States to use the system, and to take account of the latest developments in information technology. The SIS-II became operational on 9 April 2013.

The participation of Denmark

As stated above, although Denmark has signed the Schengen Agreement, it can choose whether or not to apply any new decisions. Article 4, Protocol No. 22 (which is annexed to the TEU and TFEU) provides:

> 1   Denmark shall decide within a period of six months after the Council has decided on a proposal or initiative to build upon the Schengen *acquis* covered by this Part, whether it will implement this measure in its national law. If it decides to do so, this measure will create an obligation under international law between Denmark and the other Member States bound by the measure.

2   If Denmark decides not to implement a measure of the Council as referred to in para-
    graph 1, the Member States bound by that measure and Denmark will consider appropri-
    ate measures to be taken.

The participation of Ireland and the United Kingdom

In accordance with Article 5, Protocol No. 19 (which is annexed to the TEU and TFEU), Ireland and the UK can take part in all or some of the Schengen arrangements if the Schengen
group Member States and the government representative of the country in question vote
unanimously in favour within the Council (see above).

In March 1999 the UK asked to take part in some aspects of Schengen, namely police and
judicial cooperation in criminal matters, the fight against drugs and the Schengen Information System (SIS). A Council Decision approving the request by the UK was adopted
on 29 May 2000 (OJ 2000 L 131). Ireland asked to take part in some aspects of Schengen,
broadly corresponding to the aspects covered by the UK's request, in June 2000. The Council adopted a decision approving Ireland's request on 28 February 2002 (OJ 2002 L 64). The
Commission had issued opinions on the two applications, stressing that the partial participation of the two Member States should not have the effect of reducing the consistency of
the *acquis* as a whole.

After evaluating the conditions that must precede implementation of the provisions
governing police and judicial cooperation, the Council decided on 22 December 2004 that
this part of the Schengen *acquis* could be implemented by the UK (OJ 2004 L 395).

The following joined cases concerned a refusal by the Council to allow the UK to take
part in the adoption of two regulations concerning the Schengen *acquis*. Although this case
concerned a previous Protocol, the principles apply equally to the current Protocol No. 19:

UK v Council (Case C-77/05 and Case C-137/05)

According to the Protocol integrating the Schengen *acquis* into the framework of the
European Union, Ireland and the United Kingdom may at any time request to take part in
some or all of the provisions of the *acquis*. If the UK and/or Ireland do not notify their wish
to take part in the adoption of a measure to build upon the Schengen *acquis*, the other
Member States are free to adopt the measure without the participation of those countries.
A decision of 29 May 2000 listed the provisions of the Schengen *acquis* in which the UK
was to participate, and provided that the UK was deemed irrevocably to have notified its
wish to take part in all proposals and initiatives based on those provisions.

On 11 February 2004 the UK informed the Council of its intention to take part in the
adoption of the regulation establishing the Frontex Agency (Regulation 2007/2004).

On 19 May 2004 the UK informed the Council that it also intended to take part in the
adoption of the regulation establishing standards for security features and biometrics in
passports (Regulation 2252/2004).

Despite those notifications the UK was not allowed to take part in the adoption of those
two regulations, on the ground that they constituted developments of provisions of the
Schengen *acquis* in which the UK did not take part. Both regulations were adopted without the UK's participation.

The UK claimed that the Council's refusal to allow it to take part in the adoption of the
regulations was in breach of the Schengen Protocol. The UK brought two actions before
the Court of Justice. The UK considered that its right to take part in the adoption of such
measures was independent of whether or not it took part in the provisions of the Schengen *acquis* on which the measure was based.

The Court considered that the provision in the Schengen Protocol on the participation of the UK and Ireland in existing measures and the provision making it possible for those Member States to take part in the adoption of new measures had to be read together, not independently, even though they related to two different aspects of the Schengen *acquis*.

The Court held that it followed from the use of the words 'proposals and initiatives to build upon the Schengen *acquis*' in those provisions that the measures in question were based on the Schengen *acquis*, of which they constituted merely an implementation or further development.

Logically, such measures had to be consistent with the provisions they implemented or developed. The participation of a Member State in their adoption therefore presupposed that it had accepted the area of the Schengen *acquis* which was the context of the measure to be adopted or of which it was a development.

In those circumstances, the Court concluded that the possibility of the UK and Ireland taking part in the adoption of a new measure in connection with the Schengen *acquis* was applicable only to proposals and initiatives to build upon an area of the *acquis* in which those countries had already been authorised to take part.

The Court held that in the present case, the UK had not accepted the area of the Schengen *acquis* which was the context of the regulations in question, and therefore the Council was right to refuse to allow the UK to take part in the adoption of those measures.

Associated countries: Iceland, Liechtenstein, Norway and Switzerland

Iceland, Liechtenstein, Norway and Switzerland are associate members of the Schengen area and operate the SIS.

Summary

Now you have read this chapter you should be able to:

- Understand why Art 26(2) TFEU is relevant to the free movement of persons.

- Identify the provisions of the EU Treaties which are relevant to the free movement of workers, freedom of establishment and the free movement of services.

- Explain how the European Economic Area Agreement impacts upon the Union law provisions on the free movement of persons.

- Explain how Directive 2004/38 has consolidated the Union law provisions relating to entry and residence.

- Understand the nature of EU citizenship within the context of Art 21(1) TFEU and the rights which are derived from EU citizenship.

- Identify the limited rights of free movement for non-EU citizens.

- Explain the Schengen *acquis* and the extent of the UK's participation in the Schengen arrangements.

Further reading

Textbooks

Barnard, C. (2013) *The Substantive Law of the EU: The Four Freedoms* (4th edn), Oxford University Press, Chapter 12.

Craig, P. and De Burca, G. (2011) *EU Law: Text, Cases and Materials* (5th edn), Oxford University Press, Chapter 23.

Foster, N. (2015) *Foster on EU Law* (5th edn), Oxford University Press, Chapter 9.

Steiner, J. and Woods, L. (2014) *EU Law* (12th edn), Oxford University Press, Chapter 21.

Weatherill, S. (2014) *Cases and Materials on EU Law* (11th edn), Oxford University Press, Chapter 15.

Journal articles

Currie, S., 'Accelerated justice or a step too far? Residence rights of non-EU family members and the court's ruling in Metock' (2009) 34 EL Rev 310.

Dautricourt, C. and Thomas, S., 'Reverse discrimination and free movement of persons under Community law: All for Ulysses, nothing for Penelope?' (2009) 34 EL Rev 433.

de Mars, S., 'Economically inactive EU migrants and the United Kingdom's National Health Service: Unreasonable burdens without real links?' (2014) 39 EL Rev 770.

Dougan, M., 'Cross-border educational mobility and the exportation of student financial assistance' (2008) 33 EL Rev 723.

Fahey, E., 'Interpretative legitimacy and the distinction between "social assistance" and "work seekers allowance": Comment on Cases C-22/08 and C-23/08 Vatsouras and Koupatantze' (2009) 34 EL Rev 933.

Hardy, J., 'The objective of Directive 2003/86 is to promote the family reunification of third country nationals' (2012) 14 EJML 439.

Kocharov, A., 'What intra-Community mobility for third-country nationals?' (2008) 33 EL Rev 913.

Kochenov, D., 'The right to have what rights – EU citizenship in need of clarification' (2013) 19 ELJ 502.

Kochenov, D. and Plender, R., 'EU citizenship: From an incipient form to an incipient substance? The discovery of the Treaty text' (2012) 37 EL Rev.

Koutrakos, P., 'Visa-free travel: Foreign policy in the making' (2009) 34 EL Rev 669.

Magnússon, S. and Hannesson, Ó. Í., 'Towards integration and equality for third-country nationals? Reflections on Kamberaj' (2013) 38 EL Rev 248.

Meloni, A., 'The Community code on visas: Harmonisation at last?' (2009) 34 EL Rev 671.

O'Brien, C., 'Real links, abstract rights and false alarms: The relationship between the ECJ's "real link" case law and national solidarity' (2008) 33 EL Rev 643.

O'Leary, S., 'Equal treatment and EU citizens: A new chapter on cross-border educational mobility and access to student financial assistance' (2009) 34 EL Rev 612.

Reynolds, S., 'Exploring the "intrinsic connection" between free movement and the genuine enjoyment test: Reflections on EU citizenship after Iida' (2013) 38 EL Rev 376.

Skovgaard-Petersen, H., 'There and back again: Portability of student loans, grants and fee support in a free movement perspective' (2013) 38 EL Rev 783.

Sorensen, K.E., 'Reconciling secondary legislation with the Treaty rights of free movement' (2011) 36 EL Rev 339.

Spaventa, S., 'Seeing the wood despite the trees? On the scope of Union citizenship and its constitutional effects' (2008) 45 CML Rev 13.

Staver, A., 'Free movement and the fragmentation of family reunification rights' (2013) 15 EJML 69.

Thym, D., 'When Union citizens turn into illegal immigrants: The Dano case' (2015) 40 EL Rev 249.

Wiesbrock, A., 'Free movement of third-country nationals in the European Union: The illusion of inclusion' (2010) 35 EL Rev 455.

12

Free movement of workers

Objectives

At the end of this chapter you should understand:

1. The provisions of the EU Treaties which established the free movement of workers.

2. The meaning and scope of 'EU worker'.

3. The provisions of Directive 2004/38 which apply to require the abolition of restrictions to movement and residence of EU workers and their families and which provide a right for workers and their families to remain in a Member State, having been employed there.

4. The provisions of Regulation 492/2011 (previously Regulation 1612/68) and how they have been applied by the Court of Justice of the European Union.

5. The application of the 'employment in the public service' exception.

6. How the transitional arrangements have impacted upon the right of free movement for EU citizens who are nationals of one of the countries which became a Member State of the EU on 1 May 2004, 1 January 2007 or 1 July 2013.

Introduction to the free movement of workers

Objective
1

The free movement of workers is of great economic and social importance to the Union. Although the right to move to other Member States in an employed capacity was originally seen as no more than an economic function whereby a surplus of labour and skills in one part of the Union could meet a shortage in another, the worker was soon recognised in the Union's legislation, and in the decisions of the Court of Justice, as more than merely a unit of labour. The right to move under what is now Art 45 TFEU (previously Art 39 EC Treaty) was seen as 'a fundamental right' which was to be 'exercised in freedom and dignity' (Preamble, Regulation 492/2011 (previously Regulation 1612/68)). Advocate General Trabucchi in *Mr and Mrs F v Belgian State* (Case 7/75) stated that 'The migrant worker is not to be viewed as a mere source of labour, but as a human being'.

The exercise of the migrant worker's rights is to be facilitated in the workplace and in the broader social context of the host Member State. The implementing legislation and the jurisprudence of the Court of Justice is directed at securing the worker's departure from his

See pages
274–292 and
303–305 for an
explanation of
the principle of
direct effect.

state of origin and his entry, residence and integration, in the widest sense, into the economic and social fabric of the host Member State. Article 45 TFEU is directly effective, not only at the instance of the worker but also, the Court of Justice has held, by his employer (***Clean Car Autoservice GmbH v Landeshauptmann von Wien*** (Case C-350/96)). Consideration begins with Art 45 TFEU and the rights of EU workers. Article 45 TFEU applies to EU citizens who are working within the territory of a Member State. The Court of Justice has held that workers employed on gas-drilling platforms at sea, on the continental shelf adjacent to a Member State, are as a rule subject to EU law (***Salemink v Raad van bestuur van het Uitvoeringsinstituut Werknemersverzekeringen*** (C-347/10)).

Article 45 TFEU (which is practically unchanged from the former Art 39 EC Treaty) provides as follows:

1 Freedom of movement for workers shall be secured within the Union.

2 Such freedom of movement shall entail the abolition of any discrimination based on nationality between workers of the Member States as regards employment, remuneration and other conditions of work and employment.

3 It shall entail the right, subject to limitations justified on grounds of public policy, public security or public health:
   (a) to accept offers of employment actually made;
   (b) to move freely within the territory of Member States for this purpose;
   (c) to stay in a Member State for the purpose of employment in accordance with the provisions governing the employment of nationals of that State laid down by law, regulation or administrative action;
   (d) to remain in the territory of a Member State after having been employed in that State, subject to conditions which shall be embodied in regulations to be drawn up by the Commission.

4 The provisions of this Article shall not apply to employment in the public service.

The importance of the principles of free movement and of non-discrimination have been emphasised time and again by the Court of Justice. In relation to non-discrimination, Art 45 TFEU sets out the general Art 18 TFEU anti-discrimination principle, but specifically in relation to workers. Article 18 TFEU (the wording of which is practically unchanged from the former Art 12 EC Treaty) provides as follows:

Within the scope of application of the Treaties, and without prejudice to any special provisions contained therein, any discrimination on grounds of nationality shall be prohibited ...

Secondary legislation

Article 46 TFEU provides for secondary legislation to be adopted to bring about the freedoms as defined in Art 45 TFEU. Article 46 TFEU (which is practically unchanged from the former Art 40 EC Treaty) provides as follows:

The European Parliament and the Council shall, acting in accordance with the ordinary legislative procedure and after consulting the Economic and Social Committee, issue directives or make regulations setting out the measures required to bring about freedom of movement for workers, as defined in Article 45, in particular:

(a) by ensuring close cooperation between national employment services;
(b) by abolishing those administrative procedures and practices and those qualifying periods in respect of eligibility for available employment, whether resulting from national

legislation or from agreements previously concluded between Member States, the maintenance of which would form an obstacle to liberalisation of the movement of workers;

(c) by abolishing all such qualifying periods and other restrictions provided for either under national legislation or under agreements previously concluded between Member States as imposed on workers of other Member States conditions regarding the free choice of employment other than those imposed on workers of the State concerned;

(d) by setting up appropriate machinery to bring offers of employment into touch with applications for employment and to facilitate the achievement of a balance between supply and demand in the employment market in such a way as to avoid serious threats to the standard of living and level of employment in the various regions and industries.

Several directives and regulations have been adopted under the former Art 40 EC Treaty (now Art 46 TFEU), the most important of which are discussed later in this Chapter.

Reverse discrimination

The rights of free movement, which are conferred on workers and their families by the abovementioned Treaty provisions and secondary legislation, will apply only to 'EU workers'.

The provisions do not prohibit discrimination in a totally 'internal' situation: i.e. national workers cannot claim rights in their own Member State which workers who are nationals of other Member States could claim there. In *R v Saunders* (Case 175/78), the Court of Justice held that because there was no factor connecting Saunders with any of the situations envisaged by Union law, Saunders could not rely upon what is now Art 45 TFEU to challenge a binding-over order which effectively excluded her from part of the national territory. There was a similar outcome in the following case:

Morson and Jhanjan v Netherlands (Cases 35 and 36/82)

Two Dutch nationals were working in their home state, The Netherlands. They wanted to bring their parents (Surinamese (i.e. non-EU) nationals) into the Netherlands to live with them. Had they been members of any other EU country, working in The Netherlands, their parents would have been covered by Directive 2004/38 (which replaced Art 10, Regulation 1612/68). Under Directive 2004/38, which is considered below, the parents would have been able to join their children. However, their children were nationals working in their own Member State, who had not exercised their right of free movement within the Union, and therefore Union law did not apply: i.e. it was a totally internal situation.

This was confirmed by the Court of Justice in *Land Nordrhein-Westfalen v Uecker; Jacquei v Land Nordrhein-Westfalen* (Cases C-64 and 65/96).

However, in the following case the facts were different, which enabled the Court of Justice to draw the opposite conclusion:

R v Immigration Appeal Tribunal and Surinder Singh, ex parte Secretary of State for the Home Department (Case-370/90)

An Indian national married a UK national. They both worked in Germany before returning to the UK some years later. The UK argued that the spouse's right to re-enter the UK derived from national law, not Union law (i.e. it was an internal situation). The Court of Justice considered the period of work in another Member State, and stated as follows:

19. A national of a Member State might be deterred from leaving his country of origin in order to pursue an activity as an employed or self-employed person as envisaged by the Treaty in the territory of another Member State if, on returning to the Member State of which he is a national in order to pursue an activity there as an employed or self-employed person, the conditions of his entry were not at least equivalent to those which he would enjoy under the Treaty or secondary law in the territory of another Member State.

20. He would in particular be deterred from so doing if his spouse and children were not also permitted to enter and reside in the territory of his Member State of origin under conditions at least equivalent to those granted them by Community [i.e. Union] law in the territory of another Member State.

In the above case the Court of Justice held that the Union law provisions on the free movement of workers can be relied upon by a worker against the Member State of which he is a national *provided* he has resided and been employed in another Member State. This has been reconfirmed by the Court of Justice in *Terhoeve v Inspecteur van de Belastingdienst Particulieren/Ondernemingen Buitenland* (Case C-18/95). In *O., B., S. and G. v Minister voor Immigratie, Integratie en Asiel* (Cases C-456/12 and C-457/12), which is considered in full in Chapter 11, the Court of Justice stated that the EU citizen must have been legally resident in another Member State for longer than 3 months in order to be able to rely upon Union law against the Member State of which he is a national.

As discussed in Chapter 11, pursuant to the former Art 63(3)(a) EC Treaty (now Art 79(2)(a) TFEU), a directive has been proposed to apply to EU citizens who do not exercise their free movement rights. The aim of the proposed directive is to avoid discriminating between EU citizens who exercise their free movement rights and those who do not. In order to achieve this, it is necessary to provide for the family reunification of EU citizens residing in countries of which they are nationals to be governed by the rules of Union law relating to free movement. The proposed directive would provide that an EU citizen who had not exercised his free movement rights in another Member State would have the right to have specified family members installed with him. This right would override any less generous national provisions. However, it is unlikely that the proposed directive will be adopted within the foreseeable future.

The following case concerned a couple who were German nationals, employed in Germany but resident in France. The issue was whether they could rely upon what is now Art 45 TFEU to allow them to offset losses on their French home against their income tax liability in Germany:

Ritter-Coulais (Case C-152/03)

The Court of Justice held that the situation of Mr and Mrs Ritter-Coulais, who worked in a Member State (i.e. Germany) other than that of their actual place of residence (i.e. France), fell within the scope of the former Art 39 EC Treaty (now Art 45 TFEU). The Court stated that although the German tax legislation (which prohibited the offsetting of losses incurred on foreign residences) was not specifically directed at non-residents, it was apparent that non-residents were more likely to own a home outside the national territory and were also more likely to be nationals of other Member States. The Court held that this less favourable treatment was contrary to the former Art 39 EC Treaty (now Art 45 TFEU).

Equal treatment and the abolition of discrimination

As discussed above, Art 45(1) TFEU provides that freedom of movement for workers shall be secured within the Union. It entails the abolition of any discrimination based on nationality in relation to access to employment, remuneration and other conditions of work (Art 45(2) TFEU). As discussed in Chapter 11, two anti-discrimination directives will have an impact on, *inter alia*, EU citizens exercising their free movement rights. Article 19 TFEU (previously Art 13 EC Treaty) is the legal base for the adoption of measures to 'combat discrimination based on sex, racial or ethnic origin, religion or belief, disability, age or sexual orientation', provided such measures do not exceed the powers of the Union as conferred upon it by the EU Treaties. In other words, measures can be adopted to combat discrimination provided they are in furtherance of the existing powers of the Union.

See pages 67–68 and 134–135 for an explanation of what is meant by 'legal base'.

Pursuant to what is now Art 19 TFEU, the Council adopted Directive 2000/43 (OJ 2000 L 180/22), which implemented the principle of equal treatment between persons irrespective of racial or ethnic origin. The directive had to be implemented by 19 July 2003. The principle of equal treatment prohibits direct or indirect discrimination based on racial or ethnic origin (Art 1). It applies to EU and non-EU citizens and covers both public and private sectors in relation to employment, self-employment, education, social protection including social security and healthcare, social advantages, and access to and supply of goods and services (Art 3(1)). The prohibition of racial or ethnic discrimination does not, however, cover national provisions relating to the admission and residence of third-country (i.e. non-EU) nationals (Art 13(2)). The directive does not, therefore, extend the free movement provisions *per se* to non-EU citizens.

See Case C-267/12 at pages 80–81 which relates to an application of Directive 2000/78 by the Court of Justice.

Again pursuant to what is now Art 19 TFEU, the Council adopted Directive 2000/78 (OJ 2000 L 303/16), which establishes a general framework for equal treatment in employment and occupation. The directive had to be implemented by 3 December 2003. The directive prohibits direct and indirect discrimination as regards access to employment and occupation on grounds of religion or belief, disability, age or sexual orientation. It applies to both the public and private sectors. As with Directive 2000/43, this directive applies to EU and non-EU citizens, but likewise, the prohibition does not cover national provisions relating to the admission and residence of third-country (i.e. non-EU) nationals (Art 3(2)). The directive does not, therefore, extend the free movement provisions *per se* to non-EU citizens.

Rights of a worker

Although the exercise of workers' rights may be made subject to national rules relating to public policy, public security or public health (as limited by the provisions of Directive 2004/38; see Chapter 15), Art 45 TFEU provides that an EU worker should have the right to:

- accept offers of employment actually made;
- move freely within the territory of Member States for this purpose;
- stay in a Member State for the purpose of employment;
- remain in the territory of a Member State after having been employed in that state.

Implementing legislation has given detailed effect to these provisions. Directive 2004/38 defines the rights of workers and the obligations of the immigration authorities of Member States in relation to entry and residence (see Chapter 11). Directive 2004/38 also contains detailed provisions on rights of retirement in the state where the worker has been employed and confers a right of retirement on workers in Member States other than those where the person has been employed (see Chapter 11). Regulation 492/2011 (which repealed and replaced Regulation 1612/68) deals with matters relating to equal access to employment, equality of terms of employment, housing, education and social rights (see below). Regulation 883/2004 (which repealed and replaced Regulation 1408/71) ensures that workers who are entitled to contributory and related benefits continue to enjoy them in the host Member State and on return to their home state (see Chapter 14). All of these provisions create directly effective rights.

Scope of the term 'worker'

Objective 2

The range of rights accruing under Art 45 TFEU and the secondary legislation is dependent upon the person coming within the scope of the term 'worker'. However, neither the TFEU nor the secondary legislation defines 'worker', and so the Court of Justice has been left to elaborate upon its meaning. In the following case, which is also discussed below, the Court of Justice provided some clarification:

Lawrie-Blum v *Land Baden-Württemberg* (Case 66/85)

The Court of Justice stated that:

> Objectively defined, a 'worker' is a person who is obliged to provide services for another in return for monetary reward and who is subject to the direction and control of the other person as regards the way in which the work is to be done. (para 14)

This is a classic definition and simply distinguishes an employee (i.e. a person who performs under a contract *of service*) from one who is self-employed, an independent contractor (i.e. a person who performs under a contract *for services*).

In a series of cases which have come before the Court of Justice, it has further considered the question of the scope of 'worker'. In *Hoekstra (née Unger)* v *Bestuur der Berijfsvereniging voor Detailhandel en Ambachten* (Case 75/63) the Court held that the activities which confer EU worker status are a matter of Union law. It is therefore for the Court to determine its meaning and scope. Had this not been the case, the result could have been an unequal application of the provisions throughout the Union, e.g. Germany's definition might not have been the same as the UK's, which might not have been the same as Greece's, etc.

In the following case, the question before the Court of Justice was whether the concept of 'worker' within the meaning of Art 45 TFEU includes a part-time employee who earns less than the minimum required for subsistence as defined under national law:

Levin v *Staatssecretaris van Justitie* (Case 53/81)

Mrs Levin was a British national married to a South African national. She was refused a residence permit by The Netherlands' authorities because it was claimed that she was not a 'worker' within the scope of what is now Art 45 TFEU (previously Art 39 EC Treaty). She challenged the refusal before the national courts, which referred the matter to the Court of Justice pursuant to what is now Art 267 TFEU (previously Art 234 EC Treaty). The Court was asked to explain the concept of 'worker' for Union law purposes, and in particular whether it included an individual who worked part-time and earned an income less than the minimum required for subsistence as defined under national law. The Court stated that there was no definition of 'worker' within the Treaty or secondary legislation and that its scope was a matter of Union law:

11. ... [T]he terms 'worker' and 'activity as an employed person' may not be defined by references to the national laws of the Member States but have a Community [i.e. Union] meaning. If that were not the case, the Community [i.e. Union] rules on the free movement of workers would be frustrated, as the meaning of those terms could be fixed and modified unilaterally, without any control by the Community [i.e. Union] institutions, by national laws which would thus be able to exclude at will certain categories of persons from the benefit of the Treaty.

...

13. In this respect it must be stressed that these concepts define the field of application of one of the fundamental freedoms guaranteed by the Treaty and, as such, may not be interpreted restrictively.

...

15. An interpretation which reflects the full scope of these concepts is also in conformity with the objectives of the Treaty which include, according to Articles 2 and 3, the abolition, as between Member States, of obstacles to freedom of movement for persons, with the purpose *inter alia* of promoting throughout the Community [i.e. Union] a harmonious development of economic activities and a raising of the standard of living. Since part-time employment, although it may provide an income lower than that considered to be the minimum required for subsistence, constitutes for a large number of persons an effective means of improving their living conditions, the effectiveness of Community [i.e. Union] law would be impaired and the achievement of the objectives of the Treaty would be jeopardised if the enjoyment of rights conferred by the principle of freedom of movement for workers were reserved solely to persons engaged in full-time employment and earning, as a result, a wage at least equivalent to the guaranteed minimum wage in the sector under consideration.

...

17. It should however be stated that whilst part-time employment is not excluded from the field of application of the rules on freedom of movement for workers, those rules cover only the pursuit of effective and genuine activities, to the exclusion of activities on such a small scale as to be regarded as purely marginal and ancillary. It follows both from the statement of principle of freedom of movement for workers and from the place occupied by the rules relating to that principle in the system of the Treaty as a whole that those rules guarantee only the free movement of persons who pursue or are desirous of pursuing an economic activity. [emphasis added]

In the above case, as in **Hoekstra**, the Court of Justice made it clear that it is for the Court, *not* the Member States, to define the term 'worker'. The Court then went on to consider at para 15 whether or not part-time work was sufficient to bring somebody within the scope of 'EU worker' for Union law purposes. The Court stated that it was important to understand that part-time work was not only a valuable contribution to the economies of the Member States, but it also contributed to the raising of living standards for the individual employees concerned. The fact the work was part-time should not affect Mrs Levin's status as an 'EU worker'.

The Court stated at para 17 that the part-time work must constitute an 'effective and genuine' economic activity which must not be on such a small scale as to be 'purely marginal and ancillary'. This is the test to be applied to ascertain if the person is an 'EU worker'. The Court concluded that the intention of the applicant was irrelevant. It was irrelevant that the applicant had taken up an economic activity in order to obtain a residence permit provided that, in the words of para 17, such economic activity was 'effective and genuine' and not on such a small scale as to be 'purely marginal and ancillary'.

This was a very important case, clarifying that part-time workers could be covered by the Union law provisions on free movement of workers. It did not matter if the worker chose to supplement his income from other sources. This was taken a step further in the following case, which involved a music teacher whose income was below the minimum level of subsistence, and who therefore claimed social security benefits to supplement her income:

Kempf v *Staatssecretaris van Justitie* (Case 139/85)

A German national was living and working in the Netherlands as a music teacher. She gave 12 lessons a week. Her application for a residence permit was refused. She challenged this refusal and the national court referred the case to the Court of Justice pursuant to what is now Art 267 TFEU (previously Art 234 EC Treaty). It was argued by the Netherlands and Denmark that work providing an income below the minimum level of subsistence was not 'effective or genuine' if the person undertaking the work claimed social security benefits. If it was not 'effective or genuine' then the person would not come within the scope of EU worker and therefore could not benefit from the rights under the Treaty or secondary legislation. The Court of Justice held as follows:

> 14. ... In that regard, it is irrelevant whether those supplementary means of subsistence are derived from property or from the employment of a member of his family, as was the case in *Levin*, or whether, as in this instance, they are obtained from financial assistance drawn from the public funds of the Member State in which he resides, provided that the effective and genuine nature of his work is established. [emphasis added]

In the above case, the Court of Justice once again reiterated the test to be applied in order to ascertain whether or not a person comes within the scope of EU worker: i.e. the pursuit of an economic activity which is effective and genuine, and which is not on such a small scale as to be purely marginal or ancillary.

In *Lawrie-Blum* (see above), the Court held that a trainee teacher qualified as an EU worker even though her remuneration was only nominal. The fact that the salary was less than a teacher's full salary was immaterial. What mattered was the genuinely economic nature of the work in question, and the receipt of some remuneration.

The Court of Justice has not laid down any criteria as to how much, or how little, or what kind of work, is 'effective and genuine' and not 'purely marginal and ancillary', although some guidance can be gained from the cases.

In *Steymann* v *Staatssecretaris van Justitie* (Case 196/87), the individual was engaged in maintenance and repair work for a religious community. He received his keep (i.e. accommodation, meals, etc.), but no wages. Despite the fact that his reward was 'in kind' rather than monetary, the Court of Justice held that he came within the scope of EU worker.

In *Bettray* v *Staatssecretaris van Justitie* (Case 344/87), however, the person concerned was engaged in paid work as part of a form of therapy. It was, therefore, ancillary. The following case involved a socio-occupational reintegration programme:

Trojani (Case C-456/02)

A destitute French national had been given accommodation in a Salvation Army hostel in Brussels (Belgium) where, in return for his board and lodging and a small amount of pocket money, he performed a variety of jobs for about 30 hours per week as part of a personal socio-occupational reintegration programme. The question arose of whether he could claim a right of residence as a worker, a self-employed worker or a person providing or receiving services within the terms of the former Arts 39, 43 and 49 EC Treaty (now Arts 45, 49 and 56 TFEU) respectively. If not, could he benefit from that right by direct application of the former Art 18 EC Treaty (now Art 21 TFEU) in his capacity merely as an EU citizen (see Chapter 11)?

The Tribunal du Travail de Bruxelles (Labour Court, Brussels) referred the case to the Court of Justice.

On the issue of the right of residence as a worker, the Court of Justice pointed out the Union scope of the concept of EU worker. The essential feature of an employment relationship was that for a certain period of time a person performed services for and under the direction of another person in return for which he received remuneration. Neither the *sui generis* nature of the employment relationship under national law, nor the level of productivity of the person concerned, the origin of the funds from which the remuneration was paid or the limited amount of that remuneration could have any consequence in that regard. The Court found that, in this case, the constituent elements of any paid employment relationship – the relationship of subordination and payment of remuneration – were present: the benefits in kind and in cash the Salvation Army provided for Trojani constituted the consideration for the services he performed for and under the direction of the hostel. However, it remained to be determined whether those services were real and genuine or whether, on the contrary, they were on such a small scale as to be regarded as purely marginal and ancillary, with the result that the person concerned could not be classified as a worker. In that connection the Court left it to the national court to determine whether those services were real and genuine. It did, however, provide some guidelines: the national court had, in particular, to ascertain whether the services performed were capable of being treated as forming part of the normal labour market, regard being had to the status and practices of the hostel, the content of the social reintegration programme, and the nature and details of performance of the services.

Surprisingly small amounts of work can be regarded as sufficient to come within the scope of EU worker. In ***Raulin v Netherlands Ministry for Education and Science*** (Case C-357/89), the person claiming EU worker status had been on an 'on call' contract for a period of eight months. During that period she only actually worked for a total of 60 hours. Nonetheless, the Court of Justice held that the brevity of her employment period did not exclude her from coming within the scope of EU worker. This principle was subsequently reaffirmed by the Court of Justice in ***Ninni-Orasche*** (Case C-413/01).

In view of the broad scope which has been given by the Court of Justice to EU worker, some Member States have expressed concern that EU nationals from Member States with less generous welfare benefit provisions would migrate to those with more generous provisions (this is discussed further below). However, Member States have a number of options available to them in this regard. One of them, in relation to part-time workers, is to provide that benefits will only be available to national and non-national workers who are 'available for full-time work'.

Work-seekers

Not every individual wishing to go to another Member State to work will already have arranged employment. Before Directive 2004/38 came into force and introduced a general right of residence of up to three months for EU citizens (see below), if a literal interpretation had been applied to Art 45(3) TFEU, work-seekers would not seem to have qualified for a right of free movement, because the beneficiaries of Art 45(3) TFEU are described as those in a position 'to accept offers of employment actually made'. However, in the following case the Court of Justice delivered a remarkably creative judgment:

Procureur du Roi v *Royer* (Case 48/75)

The Court of Justice held that:

... the right of nationals of a Member State to enter the territory of another Member State and reside there for the purposes intended by the Treaty – in particular to look for or pursue an occupation or activities as employed or self-employed persons, or to rejoin their spouse or family – is a right conferred directly by the Treaty, or, as the case may be, by the provisions adopted for its implementation.

Although in the above case the Court of Justice decided that work-seekers were entitled to enter another Member State to look for work, it did not give any indication as to how long that right should continue. For a number of years it was thought that the appropriate period was three months, partly because that was the limit of the entitlement to payment of unemployment benefit under the former Regulation 1408/71 (which has been repealed and replaced by Regulation 883/2004; see Chapter 14), and partly because the Council of Ministers had made a declaration to that effect at the time of approval of Regulation 1612/68 (now Regulation 492/2011) and the former Directive 68/360 (see the opinion of Advocate General Lenz in ***Centre Public d'Aide Sociale*** v ***Lebon*** (Case C-316/85)). The Court of Justice rejected both bases for limiting the rights of residence of work-seekers. In ***R*** v ***Immigration Appeal Tribunal, ex parte Antonissen*** (Case C-292/89), the Court said that there was 'no necessary link between the right to unemployment benefit in the Member State of origin and the right to stay in the host State' (para 20). The Council of Ministers' declaration had 'no legal significance', as it was not part of any binding legislative provision (para 18). The way seemed clear for an unequivocal statement by the Court of Justice on how long an individual may look for work in another Member State. The Court's response to that question only marginally clarified the issue:

R v *Immigration Appeal Tribunal, ex parte Antonissen* (Case C-292/89)

Antonissen was a Belgian national who came to the UK in 1984 to find work. He did not find work. In 1987 the Secretary of State decided to deport him, following his conviction and imprisonment for a drug-related offence. He sought judicial review of the decision and the case was referred to the Court of Justice. The relevant issue here concerned the length of time a person could stay in the territory of another Member State while seeking work. The Court of Justice held as follows:

16. In that regard, it must be pointed out in the first place that the effectiveness of ... [Article 45 TFEU] is secured in so far as Community [i.e. Union] legislation or, in its absence, the legislation of a Member State gives persons concerned a reasonable time in which to apprise themselves, in the territory of the Member State concerned, of offers of employment corresponding to their occupational qualifications and to take, where appropriate, the necessary steps in order to be engaged.

...

21. In the absence of a Community [i.e. Union] provision prescribing the period during which Community [i.e. Union] nationals seeking employment in a Member State may stay there, a period of six months, such as that laid down in the national legislation at issue in the main proceedings, does not appear in principle to be insufficient to enable the persons concerned to apprise themselves, in the host Member State, of offers of employment corresponding to their occupational qualifications and to take, where appropriate, the necessary steps in order to be engaged and, therefore, does not jeopardise the effectiveness of the principle of free movement. However, if after the expiry of that period the person concerned provides evidence that he is continuing to seek employment and that he has genuine chances of being engaged, he cannot be required to leave the territory of the host Member State. [emphasis added]

In the above case the Court of Justice held that EU nationals could enter another Member State to seek work, and that they could stay there for a *reasonable period of time* while they sought work (para 16). The Court stated that (in the context of the UK legislation existing at the material time) six months was a *reasonable period of time* to allow a person seeking work to find employment. This did not mean that a period of less than six months would not be reasonable. At the end of para 21 the Court declared that even if work has not been found at the end of this period, the EU national cannot be deported if he can show that he is still seeking work and he has genuine chances of finding work.

The Court of Justice subsequently decided, in **Commission v Belgium** (Case C-344/95), that the period of *three months* provided by Belgium to EU nationals to find work was also reasonable, provided that it could be extended if the work-seeker was looking for work and had a genuine chance of finding work.

Work-seekers are entitled to entry and limited rights of residence but not the full range of benefits enjoyed by those who have full EU worker status, unless EU citizenship can be relied upon to extend the range of benefits; see Chapter 11.

Directive 2004/38

Objective
3

Article 6(1), Directive 2004/38 now provides that EU citizens shall have the right of residence in another Member State for a period of up to three months without any conditions or formalities other than the requirement to hold a valid identity card or passport. A work-seeker would therefore be able to rely on this provision. With regard to social assistance, Art 24(2) provides that for the first three months of residence, or while the EU citizen is exercising his right to reside while seeking work under Art 14(4)(b), the host Member State is not obliged to grant entitlement to social assistance to persons other than employed or self-employed workers and the members of their family. EU citizens qualifying for this right of residence benefit from equal treatment with host-country nationals in the areas covered by the Treaty (Art 24(1)).

The worker's family

It is not only the worker who will derive benefits from Union law, but also the family of the worker. However, the rights of the family are dependent upon the worker's status as an EU worker (see above). Although the worker has to be an EU national, the family of the worker does not. The scope of 'family members' is governed by Art 2(2) Directive 2004/38 (see Chapter 11). Article 3(1) provides that Directive 2004/38 applies to all EU citizens exercising their right to move to, or reside in, a Member State other than that of which they are a national, and to 'family members' who accompany or join them. In addition to 'family members' as defined in Art 2(2), Art 3(2) provides that the host Member State shall, in accordance with its national legislation, 'facilitate' entry and residence for other defined family members (see Chapter 11).

The exercise of workers' rights

Directive 2004/38 has altered the legislative provisions relating to the exercise of workers' rights in relation to departure from the home state, entry into the host Member State, residence rights and residence permits, and penalties for non-compliance with administrative formalities. The Directive repealed and replaced a number of directives, including Directive 68/360. The changes introduced by Directive 2004/38 are considered in Chapter 11.

Loss of EU worker status on cessation of employment

As discussed above, a person retains EU worker status as long as he continues in employment. However, that status is not automatically lost when a person ceases to work. The provisions of the Treaties and the implementing legislation (prior to the adoption of Directive 2004/38) give little guidance on how long EU worker status is retained after cessation of employment. Article 45(3)(d) TFEU refers to the right 'to remain in the territory of a Member State after having been employed in that State, subject to conditions which shall be embodied in regulations to be drawn up by the Commission'. This was generally taken to mean the right to remain after retirement, or when the worker had become incapable of employment. Regulation 1251/70 was made to this effect. However, the Court of Justice in *Lair* v *University of Hannover* (Case 39/86) referred to what is now Art 45(3)(d) TFEU in more general terms, saying that 'migrant workers are granted certain rights linked to their status of worker even when they are no longer in the employment relationship'. It did not, however, indicate for how long that status might continue.

As the right of residence is not dependent on the possession of a residence permit, it was assumed that the provisions of the former Art 7(1), Directive 68/360 which excluded the loss of a residence permit, except in the event of 'voluntary' unemployment, applied no less to someone who had no such permit (Directive 68/360 has been repealed and replaced by Directive 2004/38). This was the view of the UK Immigration Appeal Tribunal in *Lubbersen* v *Secretary of State for the Home Department* [1984] 3 CMLR 77.

The concept of EU citizenship is further explored at pages 347–359 (Chapter 11).

In the following case, the issue before the Court of Justice was whether or not EU citizenship could be relied upon to assist a migrant worker who no longer had a right of residence:

Baumbast and R v *Secretary of State for the Home Department* (CASE C-413/99)

The Court of Justice held that:

A citizen of the European Union who no longer enjoys a right of residence as a migrant worker in the host Member State can, as a citizen of the Union, enjoy there a right of residence by direct application of Article 18(1) EC [now Art 21(1) TFEU]. The exercise of that right is subject to the limitations and conditions referred to in that provision, but the competent authorities and, where necessary, the national courts must ensure that those limitations and conditions are applied in compliance with the general principles of Community [i.e. Union] law and, in particular, the principle of proportionality.

In the above case, the Court of Justice held that what is now Art 21(1) TFEU, which provides every EU citizen with the right to move and reside freely within the territory of the Member States, grants a right of continued residence to an EU worker within the host Member State, even after the EU worker has ceased working. Under Art 21(1) TFEU this right is 'subject to the limitations and conditions laid down in the Treaties and by the measures adopted to give them effect'. It was therefore unclear as to what this right actually amounted to, but it was an important development, and built upon the recent case law of the Court of Justice relating to EU citizenship; see Chapter 11. The Court did not address the issue of whether or not the status of EU worker was retained (in addition to the right to residence).

The concept of 'voluntary' unemployment has had little attention from the Court of Justice, except in the context of the availability of 'social advantages' to those who retain EU worker status (Art 7(2), Regulation 492/2011, which repealed and replaced Regulation 1612/68 when it came into force on 16 June 2011, see below). In connection with obtaining access to educational 'social advantages', the Court has held that a worker will retain his status as an EU worker, even though he has voluntarily left that employment to take up a vocational course, provided there is a link between the course and his previous employment (*Raulin* (Case C-357/89), para 21). In *Ninni-Orasche* (Case C-413/01), the Court of Justice held that an EU worker who had been employed in the host Member State for a fixed term (which had been set at the outset) would not be considered voluntarily unemployed when that fixed term expired. In this case, the EU worker had been employed for a fixed term of two-and-a-half months, and the worker had applied for a study grant from the host Member State when that fixed term expired.

A worker who does become voluntarily unemployed may become a work-seeker (*Tetik* v *Land Berlin* (Case C-171/95)).

Directive 2004/38

Directive 2004/38 now sets out the circumstances in which an EU citizen will retain the status of worker (or self-employed person). Article 7(3) provides that an EU citizen shall retain the status of worker or self-employed person in the host Member State in the following circumstances:

- he is temporarily unable to work as the result of an illness or accident;
- he is in duly recorded involuntary unemployment after having been employed for more than one year and has registered as a jobseeker with the relevant employment office in the host Member State;

- he is in duly recorded involuntary unemployment after completing a fixed-term employment contract of less than a year or after having become involuntarily unemployed during the first 12 months and has registered as a jobseeker with the relevant employment office in the host Member State. In this case, the status of worker shall be retained for not less than six months; or

- he embarks on vocational training. Unless he is involuntarily unemployed, the retention of the status of worker shall require the training to be related to the previous employment.

The following case concerned the above provision:

Jessy Saint Prix v *Secretary of State for Work and Pensions* (Case C-507/12)

In the United Kingdom, income support was a benefit granted to certain categories of people whose income did not exceed a defined amount. Women who were pregnant or who had recently given birth could be eligible for that benefit, in particular during the period surrounding childbirth. However 'people from abroad' (that is, claimants who were not habitually resident in the UK) were not entitled to that benefit, unless they acquired the status of worker within the meaning of Directive 2004/38.

Jessy Saint Prix is a French national who entered the UK on 10 July 2006 where she worked, mainly as a teaching assistant, from 1 September 2006 until 1 August 2007. At the beginning of 2008 Ms Saint Prix took up agency positions, working in nursery schools. On 12 March 2008, already nearly six months pregnant, Ms Saint Prix stopped that work because the demands of caring for young children had become too strenuous. The claim for income support made by Ms Saint Prix was refused by the UK authorities on the grounds that Ms Saint had lost her status as a worker. On 21 August 2008, three months after the birth of her child, Ms Saint Prix resumed work.

Called upon to examine whether Ms Saint Prix was entitled to income support, the Supreme Court of the United Kingdom referred the case to the Court of Justice to ascertain whether a woman who gave up work, or seeking work, because of the physical constraints of the late stages of pregnancy and the aftermath of childbirth was a 'worker' for the purposes of EU law.

The Court of Justice stated that a woman in the situation of Ms Saint Prix could retain the status of 'worker'. In support of its reasoning, the Court noted that an EU citizen who no longer pursued an activity could still retain the status of worker in specific cases set out within Art 7(3), Directive 2004/38: temporarily unable to work, involuntary unemployment or vocational training. The Court observed that the directive did not list exhaustively the circumstances in which a migrant worker who was no longer in employment may nevertheless continue to benefit from the status of being a worker. In any event, the directive, which expressly sought to facilitate the exercise of the rights of an EU citizen to move and reside freely within the territory of the Member States, could not, by itself, limit the scope of the concept of worker within the meaning of the TFEU. The Court stated that this was clear from the case-law of the Court that classification as a worker within the meaning of the TFEU, and the rights deriving from such status, did not necessarily depend on the actual or continuing existence of an employment relationship.

In those circumstances, the fact that the physical constraints of the late stages of pregnancy and the immediate aftermath of childbirth required a woman to give up work during the period needed for recovery did not in principle deprive her of the status of 'worker'. The fact that she was not actually available on the employment market of the host Member State for a few months did not mean that she had ceased to belong to that market during that period, provided she returned to work or found another job within a reasonable period after confinement. Otherwise, an EU citizen would be deterred from exercising their right to freedom of movement if they risked losing their status as workers in the host Member State.

The Court held that, in order to determine whether the period that had elapsed between childbirth and starting work again could be regarded as reasonable, the national court should take account of all the specific circumstances of the case and the national rules on the duration of maternity leave.

Article 12(1), Directive 2004/38 provides that if an EU citizen dies or departs from the host Member State, his EU family members shall not have their right of residence affected. In the case of a non-EU family member, their right of residence shall not be affected if the EU citizen dies provided that the non-EU family member has been residing in the host Member State as a family member for at least one year before the EU citizen's death (Art 12(2)).

Article 12(3) provides that if an EU citizen dies or departs from the host Member State, if his children reside in the host Member State and are enrolled at an educational establishment, then his children and the parent who has actual custody of the children (whether or not they are EU citizens) shall have the right to reside in the host Member State until the children have completed their studies.

Article 13 governs a family member's right of residence following divorce, annulment of marriage or termination of partnership (see Chapter 11).

Article 14(2) provides that EU citizens and their family members shall have the right of residence under Arts 7, 12 and 13 'as long as they meet the conditions set out therein'. Expulsion shall not be an automatic consequence if an EU citizen or his family members have recourse to the host Member State's social assistance system (Art 14(3)). Article 14(4) further provides that (other than in accordance with the provisions relating to restrictions on the right of entry and residence on grounds of public policy, public security or public health) an expulsion order cannot be issued against an EU citizen or his family members if:

(i)   the EU citizen is a worker or self-employed person in the host Member State; or

(ii) the EU citizen entered the host Member State to seek employment and he can provide evidence that he is continuing to seek work and has a genuine chance of being employed.

Equal access to employment, housing, education and social rights under Regulation 492/2011

Objective 4

Regulation 492/2011 repealed and replaced Regulation 1612/68 when it came into force on 16 June 2011. The provisions of Regulation 492/2011 are practically identical to the former Regulation 1612/68.

Equal access to employment

Regulation 492/2011 provides a wide range of directly enforceable rights designed to enable the migrant worker to obtain employment, and to provide the means:

... by which workers are guaranteed the possibility of improving their living and working conditions and promoting their social advancement ... The right of freedom of movement, in order that it may be exercised, by objective standards, in freedom and dignity, requires that equality of treatment be ensured in fact and in law in respect of all matters relating to the actual pursuit of activities as employed persons and to eligibility for housing, and also that obstacles to the mobility of workers be eliminated, in particular as regards the conditions for the integration of the worker's family into the host country.

(Preamble)

Articles 1, 3 and 4, Regulation 492/2011 (previously Arts 1, 3 and 4, Regulation 1612/68) require equal treatment in relation to applications for employment by those entitled to free movement rights and prohibit national quotas and other systems of limiting access to employment by foreign nationals. Where these exist, it is not sufficient for the Member State to issue instructions that they are not to be applied in relation to EU citizens. They must be repealed or amended so that EU workers are fully aware of their right to have access to that type of employment. In *Commission v France (Re French Merchant Seamen)* (Case 167/73), the Court held that a quota system excluding foreign deck officers from French ships, under the Code Maritime, was unlawful under both the former Arts 1–4, Regulation 1612/68 (now Arts 1–4, Regulation 492/2011) and what is now Art 18 TFEU. The Court refused to accept an assurance that it was not enforced against EU nationals. Individuals needed to be able to see a clear statement of their rights in the national legislation. The Court came to a similar decision in relation to the reservation of seamen's jobs for Belgian nationals (*Commission v Belgium* (Case C-37/93)). The same principle of transparency was applied by the Court in relation to nursing posts in the German health service (*Commission v Germany (Re Nursing Directives)* (Case 29/84), para 23). The only exception to this rule is the right given to Member States by Art 45(3) TFEU to exclude EU nationals from the public service. This exception is, however, very narrowly construed by the Court of Justice (see below). It is permissible to make a knowledge of the state's national language a precondition of appointment, provided that it is necessary for the type of post to be filled. This may be so, even if it is a language which the applicant will not be required to use to carry out the job. In *Groener v Minister of Education* (Case 379/87), the Court of Justice held that a requirement of Irish law that teachers in vocational schools in Ireland should be able to speak Irish was permissible under the former Art 3(1), Regulation 1612/68 (now Art 3(1), Regulation 492/2011) because of the national policy to maintain and promote the national language as a means of sustaining national education and culture.

Under Regulation 492/2011, EU work-seekers are entitled to receive the same assistance as that offered to national workers from the state's employment offices (Art 5). Recruitment should not depend on medical, vocational and other criteria which are discriminatory on grounds of nationality (Art 6). The Court of Justice has held that refusal by a government department in one Member State to take into account the employment experience of a job applicant in the government service of another Member State amounted to unlawful discrimination (*Schöning-Kougebetopoulo v Hamburg* (Case C-15/96)). Those entitled to Union free movement rights are also entitled to equal access to any form of employment on an equal basis, even that requiring official authorisation (*Gül v Regierungspräsident Düsseldorf* (Case 131/85)). The only exception to this is in relation to the public service under Art 45(4) TFEU.

The general prohibition on discrimination contained in Art 45(2) TFEU covers not only measures that directly impact on the rights of access to employment, but any conditions that may make the engagement of EU workers more difficult or result in their employment on less favourable terms, as illustrated in the following case:

Allué and Coonan v *Università Degli Studi di Venezia* (Case 33/88)

The applicants challenged national legislation under which foreign- language assistants' contracts at Italian universities were limited to one year, where no such limitation applied to other university teachers' contracts. There was evidence that about a quarter of those affected were from other Member States. On a preliminary reference under what is now Art 267 TFEU (previously Art 234 EC Treaty) the Court of Justice held that, while it was permissible to adopt measures 'applying without distinction in order to ensure the sound management of universities', such measures had to 'observe the principle of proportionality'. It concluded that the limitation constituted 'an insecurity factor' and was precluded by what is now Art 45(2) TFEU (previously Art 39(2) EC Treaty).

Under Art 7(1) and (4), Regulation 492/2011 (previously Art 7(1) and (4), Regulation 1612/68), EU workers are entitled to the same treatment in relation to all conditions of employment, including pay, dismissal, reinstatement and re-employment, and they should benefit equally from the terms of any collective agreement negotiated with the management. The former Art 7(1), Regulation 1612/68 was at issue in the following case:

Köbler (Case C-224/01)

A Member State's national legislation provided a special length-of-service increment to university professors who had carried on that role for at least 15 years with a university in that state, the universities being under state control. The national legislation did not allow periods completed at a university in other Member States to be taken into account. The Court of Justice held that such a regime was likely to impede the free movement of workers, given that it constituted a loyalty bonus. The Court of Justice stated that such a loyalty payment could be deemed compatible with Union law if it was imposed because of a pressing public interest reason which was capable of justifying the obstacle to free movement. Although the Court accepted that the objective of the bonus was to reward workers' loyalty in the context of a policy concerning research or university education, and such an objective constituted a pressing public interest reason, the Court held that the obstacle this would present to the free movement provisions could not be justified. A loyalty bonus, which did not allow for like service within the state universities of other Member States to be taken into account, therefore breached the former Art 7(1), Regulation 1612/68 (now Art 7(1), Regulation 492/2011) and Art 45 TFEU (previously Art 39 EC Treaty).

The following case was an Art 267 TFEU reference to the Court of Justice by a German court:

Merida (Case C-400/02)

In Germany, a collective agreement which applied to civilians employed by foreign armed forces stationed in Germany provided, *inter alia*, for the payment by the German state of 'interim assistance' to those workers whose contract of employment had been terminated. Merida, a French resident who worked until 1999 for the French forces stationed in Baden-Baden, Germany, received that allowance with effect from that time.

However, the method by which it was calculated induced him to bring an action against the German state. The allowance was calculated on the basis of remuneration from which German wage tax had been notionally deducted, even where, as in Merida's case, the remuneration was subject to tax in his country of residence, i.e. France, under a double taxation agreement between the two countries. The German Bundesarbeitsgericht (Federal Labour Court) asked the Court of Justice whether the method of calculation in question was compatible with the former Art 39 EC Treaty (now Art 45 TFEU).

Apart from the former Art 39 EC Treaty (now Art 45 TFEU), in order to reply to the question submitted, the Court of Justice referred to the prohibition of discrimination set out in the former Art 7(4), Regulation 1612/68 (now Art 7(4), Regulation 492/2011). The Court stated that, unless it was objectively justified and proportionate to its aim, a provision of national law was indirectly discriminatory if it was intrinsically liable to affect migrant workers more than national workers and if there was a consequent risk that it would place the former at a particular disadvantage. The Court went on to hold that the notional deduction of German wage tax, in order to determine the basis of assessment of the interim allowance, placed frontier workers such as Merida at a disadvantage. While application of that method of assessment ensured that German residents would, for the first year following the end of their contract of employment, receive an income equivalent to that of an active worker, this was not the case with regard to French residents whose allowance, in the same way as their remuneration, was subject to tax in France.

With a view, however, to justifying the manner in which the disputed method of assessment was applied to frontier workers, the German government put forward grounds of simplified administration and limitation of financial charges. The Court unequivocally dismissed those objections, which could not in any event justify non-compliance with the obligations under the Treaties.

Article 7(1), Regulation 492/2011 also provides EU workers with a right to participate equally in trade unions and staff associations, and the workers should not be penalised for taking part in legitimate trade union activities (***Rutili v Minister of the Interior*** (Case 36/75); ***Association de Soutien aux Travailleurs Immigrés*** (Case C-213/90)). Restrictive contractual provisions which inhibit their re-employment in other Member States may breach Art 45 TFEU even if they are applied by a sporting body, such as a football association, which is not an emanation of the state, and which applies the rules to all employees of that category, irrespective of nationality (***Donà v Mantero*** (Case 13/76) and ***Bosman*** (Case C-415/93)).

The following case expands upon the above case law and considers the issue of **objective justification**:

Olympique Lyonnais Sasp v *Olivier Bernard and Newcastle United FC* (Case C-325/08)

At the material time, the Professional Football Charter of the Fédération française de football contained rules applicable to the employment of football players in France. According to the Charter, '*joueurs espoir*' were football players between the ages of 16 and 22 employed as trainees by a professional club under a fixed-term contract. At the end of the period of training, the Charter obliged a *joueur espoir* to sign his first professional contract with the club that trained him, if the club required him to do so.

In 1997, Olivier Bernard signed a *joueur espoir* contract with Olympique Lyonnais for three seasons. Before that contract was due to expire, Olympique Lyonnais offered him a professional contract for one year. Bernard refused to sign that contract and signed a professional contract with Newcastle United FC, an English football club.

Olympique Lyonnais sued Bernard, seeking an award of damages against him and Newcastle United of over 50,000 euros, equivalent to the salary Bernard would have received over one year if he had signed the contract offered by Olympique Lyonnais.

The Cour de cassation, before which a final appeal was brought, asked the Court of Justice whether the principle of freedom of movement for workers permitted the clubs which provided the training to prevent or discourage their *joueurs espoir* from signing a professional contract with a football club in another Member State in as much as the signature of such a contract might give rise to an order to pay damages.

The Court stated that Bernard's gainful employment constituted an economic activity and, as such, was subject to Union law. The Court noted that the Charter had the status of a national collective agreement aimed at regulating gainful employment and, as such, also came within the scope of Union law.

The Court then held that the rules at issue, which required a *joueur espoir* to sign a professional contract with the club which trained him, or to be liable in damages, was likely to discourage that player from exercising his right of free movement. Consequently, **those rules were a restriction on freedom of movement for workers.**

However, the Court had already held in the *Bosman* case, that in view of the considerable social importance of sporting activities and in particular football in the European Union, the objective of encouraging the recruitment and training of young players had to be accepted as legitimate.

In considering whether a system which restricted the freedom of movement of such players was suitable to ensure that the said objective was attained and did not go beyond what was necessary to attain it, account had to be taken of the specific characteristics of sport in general, and football in particular, and of their social and educational function.

In the Court's view, the prospect of receiving training fees was likely to encourage football clubs to seek new talent and train young players.

The Court stated that **a scheme providing for the payment of compensation for training where a young player, at the end of his training, signed a professional contract with a club other than the one which trained him could, in principle, be justified by the objective of encouraging the recruitment and training of young players. However, such a scheme had to be capable of actually attaining that objective and be proportionate to it,** taking due account of the costs borne by the clubs in training both future professional players and those who would never play professionally.

The Court held that it followed that **the principle of freedom of movement for workers did not preclude a scheme which, in order to attain the objective of encouraging the recruitment and training of young players, guaranteed compensation to the club which provided the training if, at the end of his training period, a young player signed a professional contract with a club in another Member State. This was subject to the proviso that the scheme was suitable to ensure the attainment of that objective and did not go beyond what was necessary to attain it.**

With regard to the French scheme at issue in the main proceedings, the Court noted that it was characterised by the payment to the club which provided the training, not of compensation for training, but of damages, to which the player concerned would be liable for breach of his contractual obligations and the amount of which was unrelated to the real training costs incurred by the club. The damages in question were not calculated in relation to the training costs incurred by the club providing that training but in relation to the total loss suffered by the club. Therefore, the Court held **the French scheme went beyond what was necessary to encourage the recruitment and training of young players and to fund those activities.**

The 'public service' exception

Although, as a general rule, Member States are not entitled to restrict access to any type of employment on grounds of nationality (Arts 18 and 45(3) TFEU, and Arts 1, 3, 4 and 6, Regulation 492/2011), there is one important exception. Under Art 45(4) TFEU, the right of equal access 'shall not apply to employment in the public service'. The term 'public service' is not defined in the Treaty or the implementing legislation. The Commission issued a notice in 1988 which indicated its view of a number of occupations in public employment which do not fall within the Art 45(4) TFEU exception. This included posts in public health care, teaching in state education, non-military research, and public bodies involved in the administrative services. This was a far from exhaustive list, which did not have the force of law. The scope of Art 45(4) TFEU has primarily been left to be determined by the Court of Justice. The Court has sought to limit its application, in order to give the widest employment opportunities to EU workers.

In the following case, Advocate General Mayras offered a definition in his Opinion which has largely been adopted in subsequent judgments of the Court of Justice:

Sotgiu v *Deutsche Bundespost* (Case 152/73)

Advocate General Mayras stated as follows:

It is clear ... that for the interpretation of ... [Article 45(4) TFEU] the concept of employment in the public service cannot be defined in terms of the legal status of the holder of the post. A Community [i.e. Union] interpretation which would allow a uniform application of the exception provided for by this provision requires us therefore to have resort to factual criteria based on the duties which the post held within the administration entails and the activities actually performed by the holder of the post.

The exception will only be applicable if this person possesses a power of discretion with regard to individuals or if his activity involves national interests – in particular those which are concerned with the internal or external security of the State. [emphasis added]

In the following case, the Court of Justice elaborated on the two central criteria proposed by Advocate General Mayras:

Commission v *Belgium* (Case 149/79)

The Court of Justice held that what is now Art 45(4) TFEU (previously Art 39(4) EC Treaty):

... **removes from the ambit of ... [Article 45(1)–(3) TFEU] a series of posts which involve direct or indirect participation in the exercise of powers conferred by public law and duties designed to safeguard the general interests of the State or of other public authorities.** Such posts in fact presume on the part of those occupying them the existence of a special relationship of allegiance to the State and reciprocity of rights and duties which form the foundation of the bond of nationality. [emphasis added]

In the above case the Court of Justice adopted a somewhat looser definition than that offered by Advocate General Mayras. Instead of the limitation applying to a person with a power of discretion over individuals, the Court held that it applied to posts participating in the exercise of such powers. In other words, all those who acted under the instructions of the person vested with the public powers would be included in the exception. On this basis, the Court seems to have accepted that the posts of head technical office supervisor, principal supervisor, works supervisor, stock controller and night-watchman within the municipalities of Brussels and Auderghem fell within the exception. It is clear that a person with specific statutory powers, such as an environmental health officer, a registrar of births and deaths and a police officer, would all occupy posts falling within the exception relating to the exercise of public powers. In relation to national security and allegiance, appointments with the defence ministry dealing with issues relating to national defence would fall within the 'allegiance' aspect of the exception. Some posts, such as a police officer at a defence establishment, would seem to fall within both.

The essential factor is the nature of the work, not the status of the employer or of the worker, as illustrated in the following case:

Lawrie-Blum v *Land Baden-Württemberg* (Case 66/85)

The applicant was a trainee teacher employed by the Ministry of Education, with the status of a civil servant. The local state government argued that she came within the exception in the former Art 39(4) EC Treaty (now Art 45(4) TFEU), because she performed 'powers conferred by public law', including the preparation of lessons, the awarding of marks, and participation in the decision of whether or not pupils should move to a higher class. The Court of Justice rejected this argument. It held that the exception in the former Art 39(4) (now Art 45(4) TFEU) had to be construed in such a way as to limit its scope to what was strictly necessary for safeguarding the interests which that provision allowed Member States to protect.

Access to posts could not be limited simply because the host Member State designated such workers as civil servants (**Bleis v Ministère de l'Education Nationale** (Case C-4/91)). To allow that would be to accept the power of the Member States to determine who fell within the exception of Art 45(4) TFEU. The derogation permitted by Art 45(4) TFEU applies only to access to employment. It does not apply to the terms of employment once access has been permitted. It would not therefore be permissible for national and EU citizens to be engaged in the same work but on different contractual terms or conditions (**Sotgiu v Deutsche Bundespost** (Case 152/73); **Allué and Coonan v Università di Venezia** (Case 33/88)).

The Court did not elaborate in **Lawrie-Blum** on the special qualities of public employment to which Art 45(4) TFEU is applicable, except to repeat, almost verbatim, its formulation in **Commission v Belgium** (above). It added that 'Those very strict conditions are not fulfilled in the case of a trainee teacher, even if he does in fact take the decisions described by the [government of] Baden-Württemberg' (para 28). Undoubtedly, senior officers in the government's Education Service would take major public policy decisions affecting education. The Court did not make it clear at what level the Art 45(4) TFEU exception would start to apply.

In the following case, the Court of Justice had to interpret Art 45(4) TFEU in relation to provisions of German and Spanish law which restricted, to nationals of the relevant Member State:

(i)   employment as master of a vessel used in small-scale maritime shipping;

(ii) employment as master and chief mate on merchant navy ships.

Anker and Others (Case C-47/02) *and Colegio de Oficiales de la Marina Mercante Española* (Case C-405/01)

The Court of Justice stated that the concept of public service within the meaning of the former Art 39(4) EC Treaty (now Art 45(4) TFEU) covered posts which involved direct or indirect participation in the exercise of powers conferred by public law and duties designed to safeguard the general interests of the state or of other public authorities. This was a repeat of the formulation in *Commission v Belgium* (above). The Court then went on to consider the posts at issue in this case. It held that the rights conferred on those holding the posts (i.e. the master of the ship) were connected to the maintenance of safety and to the exercise of police powers. These powers went beyond the requirement merely to contribute to maintaining public safety by which any individual was bound. The master of the ship also had certain auxiliary duties in respect of the registration of births, marriages and deaths. The Court pointed out that the fact that masters were employed by a private natural or legal person was not, as such, sufficient to exclude the application of the former Art 39(4) EC Treaty (now Art 45(4) TFEU) because in order to perform the public functions which were delegated to them, masters acted as representatives of public authority in the service of the general interests of the flag state.

The Court pointed out that the derogation had to be limited to what was strictly necessary for safeguarding the general interests of the Member State concerned, which would not be imperilled if the public law rights were only exercised sporadically or even by nationals of other Member States. Therefore, the Court of Justice concluded that the former Art 39(4) EC Treaty (now Art 45(4) TFEU) had to be construed as allowing a Member State to reserve the posts at issue for its own nationals only if the rights under powers conferred by public law granted to persons holding such posts were in fact exercised on a regular basis and did not represent a very minor part of their activities.

The public service in the UK

Until May 1991, all Civil Service posts in the UK were unavailable to all EU nationals, with the exception of Irish citizens who were not classified as aliens under the Aliens Employment Act 1955. The 1955 Act provided some limited exceptions, but it was far too sweeping to comply with Art 45(4) TFEU, as interpreted by the Court of Justice in *Commission v Belgium* (above). The European Communities (Employment in the Civil Service) Order 1991 (SI 1991/1221) was brought into effect to enable EU citizens and their families to have access to Civil Service posts in accordance with Union law. It did not specify the posts which were to be opened up, but an internal Civil Service Circular (GC/378) listed a large number of jobs which would be open to EU citizens. The list included bookbinders, catering staff, civil researchers, cleaners, dentists, porters, plumbers, teachers, translators and typists. However, the post of curator in such museums as the National Gallery, the Tate Gallery, and the National Galleries of Scotland all remained closed to EU citizens. The Circular acknowledged that the criteria for identifying posts that came within what is now Art 45(4) TFEU according to the concept of powers conferred by public law were difficult to apply in the UK, where the concept did not have the same meaning as in other Member States. Nevertheless, many of the posts which were still stated to be unavailable – such as that of clerical officer in the Department of Health and museum curators – were clearly not within the narrow core of state activities envisaged by the Court of Justice in *Commission v Belgium* (above). Special restrictions imposed on access by Irish nationals to the Civil Service in Northern Ireland were held by the High Court of Northern Ireland in

Re Katherine Colgan and Others [1997] 1 CMLR 53 to be unlawful, disproportionate and not justified by what is now Art 45(4) TFEU.

Under the European Communities (Employment in the Civil Service) Order 1991, about 97,000 (18 per cent) of all posts within the UK civil service were reserved for UK nationals only. The European Communities (Employment in the Civil Service) Order 2007 amended the 1991 Order, and this new Order achieved a reduction in the number of posts reserved for UK nationals throughout the Civil Service to something less than 5 per cent of the total number of posts in the Civil Service. In terms of numbers, this meant that (approximately) a further 70,000 posts were made available to non-UK nationals.

Social advantages

Objective 4

Article 7(2), Regulation 492/2011 (previously Art 7(2), Regulation 1612/68) provides simply that the EU worker 'shall enjoy the same social and tax advantages as national workers'. This provision has been a fruitful source of rights for EU workers and their families. 'Social advantages' has been given the broadest of interpretations by the Court of Justice:

Ministère Public v *Even and Onpts* (Case 207/78)

The Court of Justice stated that:

'social advantages' were all those advantages which, whether or not [they] are linked to a contract of employment, are generally granted to national workers, primarily because of their objective status as workers or by virtue of the mere fact of their residence on the national territory and the extension of which to workers who are nationals of other Member States therefore seems suitable to facilitate their mobility. [emphasis added]

In his opinion in the following case, Advocate General Mancini also emphasised that the equal treatment provisions of the former Regulation 1612/68 (now Regulation 492/2011) are not confined to the employment relationship:

Gül v *Regierungspräsident Düsseldorf* (Case 131/85)

Advocate General Mancini stated that:

The migrant worker is not regarded by Community [i.e. Union] law – nor is he by the internal legal systems – as a mere source of labour but is viewed as a human being. In this context the Community [i.e. Union] legislature is not concerned solely to guarantee him the right to equal pay and social benefits in connection with the employer–employee relationship, it also emphasised the need to eliminate obstacles to the mobility of the worker ... [and see *Mr and Mrs F* v *Belgium* (Case 7/75), Opinion of A-G Trabucchi] (at p. 1579)

Adopting an approach of facilitating the removal of obstacles, and assisting the worker in the process of integrating into the social fabric of the Member State, the Court has held a very diverse range of benefits to come within the scope of 'social advantages', as illustrated in the following case:

Fiorinin (née Cristini) v *SNCF* (Case 32/75)

SNCF, the French railway company, offered a fare reduction to large families of French nationality. Cristini, an Italian national resident in France and the widow of an Italian national who had worked in France, was refused the reduction card on the basis of nationality. SNCF argued that the former Art 7(2), Regulation 1612/68 (now Art 7(2), Regulation 492/2011) covered only advantages connected with the contract of employment. The national court made a reference to the Court of Justice under what is now Art 267 TFEU (previously Art 234 EC Treaty). It should be noted that Cristini was entitled to remain in France under what is now Art 17(4), Directive 2004/38 (see below) as the spouse of a deceased worker. By Art 24(1), Directive 2004/38 all EU citizens residing in the territory of the host Member State 'shall enjoy equal treatment with the nationals of that Member State within the scope of the Treaty. The benefit of this right shall be extended to family members who are not nationals of a Member State and who have the right of residence or permanent residence'. The Court of Justice held as follows:

12. ... [T]he reference to 'social advantages' in Article 7(2) cannot be interpreted restrictively.

13. It therefore follows that, in view of the equality of treatment which the provision seeks to achieve, the substantive area of application must be delineated so as to include all social and tax advantages, whether or not attached to the contract of employment, such as reduction in fares for large families.

14. It then becomes necessary to examine whether such an advantage must be granted to the widow and children after the death of the migrant worker when the national law provides that, at the request of the head of the family, each member of the family shall be issued with an identity card entitling him or her to the reduction.

15. If the widow and infant children of a national of the Member State in question are entitled to such cards provided that the request has been made by the father before his death, the same must apply where the deceased father was a migrant worker and a national of another Member State.

16. It would be contrary to the purpose and the spirit of the Community [i.e. Union] rules on freedom of movement for workers to deprive the survivors of such a benefit following the death of the worker whilst granting the same benefit to the survivors of a national.

...

19. Accordingly the answer to the question should be that Article 7(2) of Regulation (EEC) No 1612/68 [now Art 7(2), Regulation 492/2011] of the Council must be interpreted as meaning that the social advantages referred to by that provision include fare reduction cards issued by a national railway authority to large families and that this applies, even if the said advantage is only sought after the worker's death, to the benefit of his family remaining in the same Member State. [emphasis added]

In the above case, the Court of Justice held that 'social advantages' under Art 7(2) do not have to be connected with the worker's contract of employment (para 13). In **Inzirillo v Caisse d'Allocations Familiales de l'Arrondissement de Lyon** (Case 63/76), the applicant was an Italian, working in France, who had been refused a disability allowance for his adult son. It was argued that the former Art 7(2), Regulation 1612/68 (now Art 7(2), Regulation 492/2011) was not applicable because the allowance was not a social advantage to the worker (as provided for in Art 7(2)) but rather to his son. The Court of Justice held that offspring were covered by the former Art 10(1), Regulation 1612/68 (now Art 2(2)(c), Directive 2004/38) and that an allowance for disabled adults which a Member State awarded to its own nationals constituted a social advantage to a non-national in a case like this.

In *Mutsch* (Case 137/84), the applicant was a German national working in Belgium. He was charged with a criminal offence. In that part of Belgium, German-speaking Belgian nationals were allowed to have proceedings conducted in German. Mutsch was denied this right as a non-Belgian citizen, but the Court of Justice held that he was entitled to this facility as a 'social advantage' under Art 7(2).

Netherlands v *Reed* (Case 59/85) was considered above with regard to family members, but it provides an interesting illustration of how Art 7(2) may come to the aid of a worker when other provisions may not assist. The case concerned a UK national who travelled to the Netherlands to live with her long-term partner, who was also a UK national working in The Netherlands. The Court of Justice held that 'spouse' within the former Art 10(1), Regulation 1612/68 (now Art 2(2)(a), Directive 2004/38) only referred to a married relationship. However, the problem was resolved by relying upon the former Art 7(2), Regulation 1612/68 (now Art 7(2), Regulation 492/2011) on the specific facts of the case. In Dutch law, a foreigner who had a stable relationship with a working national was treated as that person's spouse. The Court held that this constituted a 'social advantage' within Art 7(2), as it would further the policy of free movement of persons. This situation is now covered by Art 2(2)(b), Directive 2004/38 which includes within the scope of family members a 'registered partner' if the legislation of the host Member State treats registered partnerships as equivalent to marriage.

The tax advantages referred to in the former Art 7(2), Regulation 1612/68 were held in *Biehl* (Case C-175/88) and *Schumacher* (Case C-279/93) to require that different rates of tax payable by residents and non-residents could not be applied to workers from other Member States.

The following case considered the scope of the former Art 7(2), Regulation 1612/68 (now Art 7(2), Regulation 492/2011):

Commission v *Netherlands* (Case C-542/09)

Funding for higher education studies in the Netherlands was available to students who were aged between 18 and 29 years old and who were either nationals of the Netherlands or any other Member State of the European Union. To receive funding for higher education pursued outside The Netherlands, students had to be eligible for funding for higher education in the Netherlands and had to additionally have resided lawfully in the Netherlands for at least three out of the six years preceding enrolment at an educational establishment abroad. This condition, known as the '3 out of 6 years' requirement, applied irrespective of the student's nationality.

The Commission brought an action before the Court of Justice against The Netherlands, claiming that the '3 out of 6 years' requirement constituted indirect discrimination against migrant workers and members of their families, prohibited by Art 45 TFEU and contrary to the former Art 7(2), Regulation 1612/68 (now Art 7(2), Regulation 492/2011).

The Court pointed out that assistance granted for maintenance and education in order to pursue university studies evidenced by a professional qualification constituted a social advantage for the purposes of the former Regulation 1612/68 (now Regulation 492/2011). For the migrant worker, study finance granted by a Member State to the children of workers constituted a social advantage for the purpose of that Regulation, where the worker continued to support the child.

In that respect, the Court noted that the principle of equal treatment prohibited not only direct discrimination on grounds of nationality but also all indirect forms of discrimination which, through the application of other criteria of differentiation, led to the same result. That was the position in the case of a measure which required a specified period of residence, in that it primarily operated to the detriment of migrant workers and frontier workers who were nationals of other Member States, in so far as non-residents were usually non-nationals.

The Court therefore held that the '3 out of 6 years' residence requirement created inequality in treatment as between Netherlands' workers and migrant workers residing in the Netherlands or employed there as frontier workers. **Such an inequality constituted unlawful indirect discrimination, unless it was objectively justified**.

With regard to objective justification, the Court rejected the argument of the Netherlands that the residence requirement was necessary in order to avoid an unreasonable financial burden which could have consequences for the very existence of the assistance scheme. The Court pointed out that the objective of avoiding an unreasonable financial burden could not be regarded as an overriding reason relating to the public interest, capable of justifying the unequal treatment between Netherlands' workers and workers from other Member States.

The Netherlands also claimed that, given that the national legislation at issue was intended to encourage students to pursue studies outside The Netherlands, the requirement ensured that the portable funding was available solely to those students who, without it, would pursue their education in The Netherlands. By contrast, the first instinct of students who did not reside in the Netherlands would be to study in the Member State in which they were resident and, accordingly, mobility would not be encouraged.

The Court noted that **the objective of encouraging student mobility was in the public interest and constituted an overriding reason relating to the public interest, capable of justifying a restriction of the principle of non-discrimination on grounds of nationality.** The Court pointed out, however, that legislation which was liable to restrict a fundamental freedom guaranteed by the Treaty, such as freedom of movement for workers, could be justified only if it was appropriate for attaining the legitimate objective pursued and did not go beyond what was necessary in order to attain that objective.

In that context, the Netherlands claimed that the legislation at issue had the merit of encouraging student mobility and pointed to the enrichment brought by studies outside the Netherlands, not only to the students but also to the Netherlands' society and its employment market. Accordingly, the Netherlands expected that students who received funding under that scheme would return to the Netherlands after completing their studies in order to reside and work there.

The Court acknowledged that those aspects tended to reflect the situation of most students and that the residence requirement was therefore appropriate for attaining the objective of promoting student mobility. However, the Court stated that the Netherlands should at least have shown why they opted for the '3 out of 6 years' rule, prioritising length of residence to the exclusion of all other representative elements.

By requiring specific periods of residence in the territory of the Member State concerned, the '3 out of 6 years' rule accorded most importance to an element which was not necessarily the sole element representative of the actual degree of attachment between the concerned party and that Member State. In consequence, **the Court of Justice held that the Netherlands had failed to establish that the residence requirement did not go beyond what was necessary to attain the objective sought by that legislation.**

The following case also concerned funding for higher education studies, but this time with regard to the child of a cross-border worker:

Giersch and Others v *Luxembourg* (Case C-20/12)

Luxembourg granted financial aid, in the form of a grant and a loan, in order to promote higher education studies by students in its territory or in the territory of any other state. That aid was granted to students holding Luxembourg nationality or the nationality of another Member State, who were resident in Luxembourg when they were about to embark on higher education studies. Thus, the children of cross-border workers, who usually resided in a country bordering upon Luxembourg, were not entitled to the aid.

A number of children of cross-border workers to whom financial aid had been denied contested the lawfulness of their exclusion from the category of beneficiaries of the aid before the Luxembourg courts. The tribunal administratif (Luxembourg), before which those disputes were brought, referred the case to the Court of Justice to ask whether the Luxembourg legislation relating to the grant of that aid was compatible with the principle of the freedom of movement of workers.

The Court of Justice stated that aid granted in order to finance the university studies of the child of a migrant worker constituted, for that worker, a social advantage which had to be granted to him under the same conditions as those applying to national workers. The Court made clear in that regard that the principle of equal treatment could not be limited to migrant workers residing in a host Member State but had to extend to cross-border workers who, while employed as a worker in that Member State, resided in another Member State. In addition, where the social advantage was granted directly to the child of a migrant worker, that child could himself rely on the principle of equal treatment.

The Court further held that **the condition of residence required by Luxembourg legislation amounted to indirect discrimination on grounds of nationality in so far as it was liable to operate mainly to the detriment of nationals of other Member States, as non-residents were in the majority of cases foreign nationals.** In that context, the Court stated that such discrimination could not be justified by budgetary considerations, as the application and the scope of the principle of non-discrimination on grounds of nationality could not depend on the state of the public finances of the Member States.

The Court nevertheless considered that **the condition of residence was appropriate for attaining the objective pursued by Luxembourg of promoting higher education studies and of significantly increasing the proportion of Luxembourg residents who held a higher education degree.** Students who were resident in Luxembourg when they were about to embark on their higher education studies would be more likely than non-resident students to settle in Luxembourg and become integrated in the Luxembourg labour market after completing their studies, even if those studies were undertaken abroad.

However, the Court held that **the system of financial aid in question was too exclusive in nature. By imposing a prior condition of residence by the student in Luxembourg territory, the law favoured an element which was not necessarily the sole representative element of the actual degree of attachment of the person concerned to Luxembourg.**

Thus, it was possible that a non-resident student could also have an attachment to Luxembourg sufficient to make it reasonably probable that he would return to settle in Luxembourg and make himself available to the labour market of that Member State. That would be the case where that student resided alone or with his parents in a Member State which bordered Luxembourg and where, for a significant period of time, his parents had worked in Luxembourg and lived near to that Member State.

The Court pointed out in that regard that **less restrictive measures were available which would make it possible to attain the objective sought by the Luxembourg legislature. For example, where the aid granted consisted of a loan, a system of financing which made the grant of that loan, or even the outstanding balance thereof, or its non-reimbursement,** conditional on the student who received it returning to Luxembourg after his studies abroad in order to work and reside there, would be better adapted to the special situation of the children of cross-border workers. In addition, in order to avoid 'study grant forum shopping' and to ensure that the cross-border worker parent of the student had a sufficient link with Luxembourg society, the financial aid could be made conditional on that parent having worked in Luxembourg for a certain minimum period of time.

Finally, the risk of duplication with equivalent financial aid paid in the Member State in which the student resides, with or without his parents, could be avoided by taking that aid into account in the grant of the aid paid by Luxembourg.

In those circumstances, the Court held that the contested Luxembourg legislation went beyond what was necessary to attain the objective pursued by the legislature. Therefore, that legislation was contrary to the principle of the freedom of movement for workers.

Retaining EU worker status

The advantages to which migrant workers are entitled will continue even after they have ceased employment, provided that they retain their EU worker status. Thus, a worker who is not voluntarily unemployed can claim payments of 'social assistance' from the host Member State. He is excluded from claiming them as social security benefits under Art 3(5), Regulation 883/2004 (see Chapter 14). However, the Court held in *Scrivner and Cole v Centre Public d'Aide Sociale de Chastre* (Case 122/84) that 'a social benefit guaranteeing a minimum means of subsistence in a general manner' constituted a social advantage. In this case, the applicant was therefore entitled to the Belgian payment, minimex, despite the fact that national rules restricted it to Belgian citizens. Similarly, a person who loses his job and takes up an educational course is entitled to an educational grant as a social advantage (*Lair v University of Hannover* (Case 39/86)). This will be the case even if the worker gives up his job voluntarily, provided that there is a link between the job and the course that is undertaken (*Raulin* (Case C-357/89), paras 18 and 22).

In the following case, the Court of Justice sought to address the issue of retention of EU worker status, following the worker's departure from the host Member State after his employment had ceased:

Ghislain Leclere, Alina Deaconescu v *Caisse Nationale des Prestations Familiales* (Case C-43/99)

Leclere (a Belgian national) received an invalidity pension from a Member State (Luxembourg) in which he used to work, but in which he did not reside. He was a frontier worker, living in Belgium and travelling to Luxembourg every day to work. Following an accident at work he became entitled to an invalidity pension. The pension therefore became payable while he had the status of EU worker. However, he was attempting to claim a benefit from the Luxembourg authorities for a child he had after his employment had ended. This was refused on the ground that he no longer resided there. The Court of Justice held as follows:

> A person receiving an invalidity pension who resides in a Member State other than the State providing his pension is not a worker within the meaning of Article 7 of Regulation 1612/68/EEC [now Art 7(2), Regulation 492/2011] and does not enjoy rights attaching to that status unless they derive from his previous professional activity.

In the above case the Court of Justice held that it does not follow that Leclere retains the status of EU worker within the meaning of the former Regulation 1612/68 (now Regulation 492/2011). The Court stated that he was protected by what are now Art 45 TFEU and Regulation 492/2011 against any discrimination affecting rights he had acquired during his former employment but, because he was no longer employed and was not resident in Luxembourg, he could not claim to acquire new rights which had no links with his former occupation. This case clears up the issue of former EU workers who are no longer resident in the host Member State.

In *Ninni-Orasche* (Case C-413/01), the Court of Justice held that an EU worker who had been employed in the host Member State for a fixed term (which had been set at the outset) would not be considered voluntarily unemployed when that fixed term expired. In this case, the EU worker had been employed for a fixed term of two-and-a-half months, and had applied for a study grant from the host Member State when that fixed term expired.

Directive 2004/38

Article 7(3), Directive 2004/38 provides that an EU citizen shall retain the status of worker or self-employed person in the host Member State in the following circumstances:

(a) he is temporarily unable to work as the result of an illness or accident;

(b) he is in duly recorded involuntary unemployment after having been employed for more than one year and has registered as a jobseeker with the relevant employment office in the host Member State;

(c) he is in duly recorded involuntary unemployment after completing a fixed-term employment contract of less than a year *or* after having become involuntarily unemployed during the first 12 months *and* has registered as a jobseeker with the relevant employment office in the host Member State. In this case, the status of worker shall be retained for no less than six months; or

(d) he embarks on vocational training. Unless he is involuntarily unemployed, the retention of the status of worker shall require the training to be related to the previous employment.

Limits of Article 7(2)

The former Art 7(2), Regulation 1612/68 (now Art 7(2), Regulation 492/2011) has been held to cover all social advantages whether or not they are actually linked to the employment, and even where they are only of indirect benefit to the worker himself. But the Court of Justice has made it clear that Art 7(2) can be invoked only where the advantage is actually of some direct or indirect benefit to the worker, and not just to a family member or dependant, as illustrated in the following case:

Centre Public d'aide Sociale de Courcelles v *Lebon* (Case 316/85)

The Court of Justice stated as follows:

12. However, the members of a worker's family, within the meaning of Article 10 of Regulation No 1612/68 [now Art 2(2), Directive 2004/38] qualify only indirectly for the equal treatment accorded to the worker himself by Article 7 of Regulation No 1612/68

> [now Art 7, Regulation 492/2011]. Social Benefits such as the income guaranteed to old people by the legislation of a Member State (see the judgment of 12 July 1984 in Case 261/83 *Castelli* v *ONPTS* [1984] ECR 3199) or guaranteeing in general terms the minimum means of subsistence operate in favour of members of the worker's family only if such benefits may be regarded as a social advantage, within the meaning of Article 7(2) of Regulation No 1612/68 [now Art 7(2), Regulation 492/2011], for the worker himself.

The Court of Justice was faced with a sensitive issue in the following case:

Ministère Public v *Even and ONPTS* (Case 207/78)

Even was a French national working in Belgium. He received an early retirement pension from the Belgian authorities. A percentage was deducted from the pension based upon the number of years early he had received the pension. This rule was applied to all recipients, except Belgian nationals who were in receipt of a Second World War service invalidity pension granted by an Allied nation. Even was in receipt of a French war service pension and pleaded the principle of equality of treatment between nationals and non-nationals to claim the benefit of an early retirement pension without any deduction. The national court referred the matter to the Court of Justice for a preliminary ruling under what is now Art 267 TFEU (previously Art 234 EC Treaty). The Court of Justice held as follows:

22. It follows from all its provisions and from the objective pursued that **the advantages which this regulation extends to workers who are nationals of other Member States are all those which, whether or not linked to a contract of employment, are generally granted to national workers primarily because of their objective status as workers or by virtue of the mere fact of their residence on the national territory** and the extension of which to workers who are nationals of other Member States therefore seems suitable to facilitate their mobility within the Community [i.e. Union].

23. … The main reason for a benefit such as that granted by the Belgian national legislation in question to certain categories of national workers is the services which those in receipt of the benefit have rendered in wartime to their own country and its essential objective is to give those nationals an advantage by reason of the hardships suffered for that country.

24. Such a benefit, which is based upon a scheme of national recognition, cannot therefore be considered as an **advantage granted to a national worker by reason primarily of his status of worker** or resident on the national territory and for that reason does not fulfil the essential characteristics of the 'social advantages' referred to in Article 7(2) of Regulation No 1612/68 [now Art 7(2), Regulation 492/2011]. [emphasis added]

In the above case, the Court of Justice, at para 22, set out three factors to be taken into account when deciding whether a worker is entitled to a particular benefit in a host Member State under Art 7(2):

- status as an EU worker;
- residence on national territory; and
- suitability of the benefit in facilitating worker mobility within the Union.

In the above case, the Court held that the benefit, which was linked to wartime military service, was not suitable to facilitate the free movement of workers, and therefore did not constitute a 'social advantage' (para 24). This is not surprising given the sensitive nature of what the Court was being asked to adjudicate upon. The following case has a similar theme to that of *Ministère Public* v *Even and ONPTS*, and the Court of Justice reached a similar conclusion:

Baldinger (Case C-386/02)

The Austrian Law on Compensation for Prisoners of War, adopted in 2000, provided for the grant of a monthly financial benefit to former prisoners of war, subject to the condition that the recipient was an Austrian national. The question referred to the Court of Justice for a preliminary ruling asked whether such legislation was compatible with the provisions governing the free movement of workers. In this case, the allowance in question had been refused to a former Austrian national who had been a prisoner of war in Russia from 1945 to 1947, but who had acquired Swedish nationality in 1967, at the same time forfeiting his Austrian nationality.

The Court examined the legislation in question in the light of the former Regulation 1408/71 (now Regulation 883/2004), the former Regulation 1612/68 (now Regulation 492/2011) and the former Art 39(2) EC Treaty (now Art 45(2) TFEU).

With regard to the former Regulation 1408/71 (now Regulation 883/2004; see Chapter 14), the Court stated that an allowance of this kind was excluded from its scope as it was covered by Art 4(4), which provided that the Regulation did not apply to 'benefit schemes for victims of war or its consequences'.

The Court found that the allowance in question was provided to former prisoners of war who proved that they had undergone a long period of captivity, in testimony of national gratitude for the hardships which they had endured and was thus paid as a *quid pro quo* for the service they had rendered to their country.

The Court reasoned along identical lines with regard to the former Regulation 1612/68 (now Regulation 492/2011) that **an allowance of the kind in issue in the case was excluded from the scope of that Regulation as it did not come within the category of advantages granted to national workers principally because of their status as workers or national residents and, as a result, did not fulfil the essential characteristics of the 'social advantages' referred to in the former Art 7(2), Regulation 1612/68 (now Art 7(2), Regulation 492/2011).**

The Court finally reached the same conclusion with regard to the former Art 39(2) EC Treaty (now Art 45(2) TFEU), which covers conditions of employment, remuneration and other working conditions. That provision, the Court ruled, could not cover compensatory allowances linked to service rendered in wartime by citizens to their own country and the essential aim of which was to provide those citizens with a benefit because of the hardships which they had endured for that country.

In the above case, the Court of Justice held that the benefit payable to former prisoners of war did not constitute a 'social advantage' within the context of the former Art 7(2), Regulation 1612/68 (now Art 7(2), Regulation 492/2011), because it did not fulfil the essential characteristics of 'social advantage'.

The following case concerned national legislation which required spouses of migrant workers who were nationals of other Member States to have resided in the territory of that Member State for four years before they became entitled to apply for indefinite leave to remain, but which required residence of only 12 months for the spouses of persons who were settled in that territory:

Kaba v *Secretary of State for the Home Department* (Case C-356/98)

Kaba, a Yugoslav national, married a French national who found work in the UK in April 1994. In 1996 Kaba applied for indefinite leave to remain in the UK, but was refused on the ground that paragraph 255 of the Immigration Rules 1994 was not satisfied because his wife (an EU national) had only remained in the UK as an EU worker for one year and ten months and not the required four years. After four years, Kaba's wife was entitled to apply for indefinite leave to remain in the UK, as the spouse of an EU worker. However, Kaba challenged this refusal, maintaining there was discrimination, contrary to the former Art 7(2), Regulation 1612/68 (now Art 7(2), Regulation 492/2011). This was based upon the fact that if Kaba's wife had been a UK citizen then he would have been eligible for indefinite leave to remain in the UK after just one year, rather than the four-year requirement which applied to the spouse of an EU worker. The national court referred the matter to the Court of Justice, which held as follows:

> The relevant Community [i.e. Union] rules conferred on the spouses of migrant workers who were nationals of other Member States a right of residence co-extensive with that accorded to those workers.
>
> However, in seeking to remain in the UK, K was applying, in his capacity as the spouse of a migrant worker, for a more extensive right of residence than that conferred on the migrant worker herself.
>
> Even if such a right constituted a social advantage within Article 7(2) of Regulation 1612/68 [now Art 7(2), Regulation 492/2011], there was still the question whether legislation such as that in issue constituted discrimination contrary to that provision.
>
> The equal treatment rule laid down in Article 7 prohibited not only overt discrimination but also all covert forms of discrimination which, by the application of other distinguishing criteria, led to the same result.
>
> It was true that where rules made the grant of an advantage subject to the requirement that the beneficiary be present and settled in national territory, that condition was more easily met by national workers than by workers who were nationals of other Member States but, as Community [i.e. Union] law stood at present, the right of nationals of a Member State to remain in another Member State was not unconditional.
>
> For example ... [Article 21 TFEU], while granting citizens of the Union the right to move freely within the Member States, expressly referred to the limitations and conditions laid down in the Treaty and the measures adopted to give it effect. Accordingly, the Member States were entitled to rely on any objective difference there might be between their own nationals and those of other Member States, when they laid down the conditions under which leave to remain indefinitely in their territory was to be granted to the spouses of such persons.
>
> In particular, they were entitled to require the spouses of persons who did not themselves enjoy an unconditional right of residence to be resident for a longer period than that required for the spouses of persons who already enjoyed such a right, before granting the same right to them.
>
> Once leave to remain indefinitely had been granted, no condition could be imposed on the person to whom such leave had been granted, and therefore the authorities must be able, when the application was made, to require the applicant to have established sufficiently enduring links with the state.

In the above case the Court of Justice held that the legislation in question did not constitute discrimination contrary to the former Art 7(2), Regulation 1612/68 (now Art 7(2), Regulation 492/2011). The Court therefore did not need to decide whether or not this would otherwise have been a social advantage within Art 7(2).

This case came back before the Court of Justice in **Kaba** (Case C-466/00). The Court was asked to rule on whether its reply would have been different had the Court taken into consideration the fact that the situation of those two categories of person (i.e. national worker and EU worker) were comparable in all respects under UK law, except with regard to the period of prior residence which was required for the purpose of being granted indefinite leave to remain in the UK. The Court held that this made no difference to its previous decision. The Court stated that the right of residence of an EU worker is subject to the condition that the person remains a worker or a person seeking employment, unless he derives that right from other provisions of Union law. An EU worker's situation is *not* comparable to that of a national who is not subject to any restriction regarding the period for which he may reside within the territory of that Member State. A national would not, during his stay, need to satisfy any condition comparable to those laid down by the provisions of Union law, which grant EU workers a right of residence in another Member State. The Court held that because the rights of residence of these two categories of persons (i.e. EU worker and national worker) are not in all respects comparable, the same holds true with regard to the situation of their spouses, particularly so far as concerns the question of the duration of the residence period on completion of which they may be given indefinite leave to remain in the UK.

Article 16, Directive 2004/38 now sets out the right of permanent residence for an EU worker and his family members. EU citizens acquire the right of permanent residence in the host Member State after a five-year period of continuous legal residence (Art 16(1)), provided that an expulsion decision has not been enforced against them (Art 21). This right of permanent residence is not subject to any conditions. The same rule applies to non-EU family members who have lived with an EU citizen in the host Member State for five years (Art 16(2)), and again provided that an expulsion decision has not been enforced against them (Art 21).

Social advantages for work-seekers

Access to social advantages is conditional upon the acquisition of EU worker status. A person who has never worked in the host Member State will not be eligible, as illustrated in the following case:

Centre Public d'aide Sociale de Courcelles v *Lebon* (Case 316/85)

The applicant, a French national living in Belgium, claimed minimex. She lived with her father, also French, who was a retired EU worker. She no longer satisfied the 'family member' provisions of the former Art 10, Regulation 1612/68 (now Art 2(2)(c), Directive 2004/38) because she was over the age of 21 and no longer dependent upon her father. She had never found employment. The Court of Justice held in this case that, as she was no longer dependent, she was not entitled to a social advantage as a member of his family, and could not claim such an advantage as a work-seeker in her own right:

It must be pointed out that the right to equal treatment with regard to social and tax advantages applies only to workers. Those who move in search of employment qualify for equal treatment only as regards access to employment in accordance with ... [Article 45 TFEU] and Articles 2 and 5 of Regulation No 1612/68 [Arts 2 and 5, Regulation 492/2011].

The following two cases concerned a work-seeker's right to claim a social security benefit. In both cases 'EU citizenship' influenced the Court's judgment:

Collins (Case C-138/02)

In the UK, the grant of a 'jobseeker's allowance' to persons seeking employment was subject to the applicants satisfying one of the following conditions:

(i)   was habitually resident in the UK; or
(ii) was a worker for the purposes of the former Regulation 1612/68 (now Regulation 492/2011);
(iii) had a right to reside in the UK pursuant to the former Directive 68/360 (now Directive 2004/38).

Brian Collins was born in the United States and had dual American and Irish nationality. Having spent one semester in the UK in 1978 as part of his university studies and having worked for ten months in 1980 and 1981 on a part-time and casual basis in bars and the sales sector, he returned to the UK in 1998 for the purpose of seeking employment. He applied for a jobseeker's allowance but was refused on the grounds that he did not satisfy one of the three conditions above.

Three questions were referred to the Court of Justice for a preliminary ruling. The first two concerned the regulation and the directive, while the third asked whether there could be some provision or principle of Union law capable of assisting the applicant in his claim.

On the question of whether Collins was a worker within the terms of the former Regulation 1612/68 (now Regulation 492/2011), the Court took the view that, as 17 years had elapsed since he had last been engaged in an occupational activity in the UK, Collins did not have a sufficiently close connection with the employment market in that Member State. The situation of Collins, the Court ruled, was comparable to that of any person seeking his first employment. The Court pointed out in this regard that a distinction had to be drawn between persons looking for work in the host Member State without having previously worked there and those who had already entered the employment market in that Member State. While the former benefit from the principle of equal treatment only as regards access to employment, the latter could, on the basis of the former Art 7(2), Regulation 1612/68 (now Art 7(2), Regulation 492/2011), claim the same social and tax advantages as national workers (see Chapter 12). The Court took the view that Collins was not a worker in the sense in which that term covers persons who had already entered the employment market.

With regard to whether Collins was entitled to reside in the UK pursuant to the former Directive 68/360 (now Directive 2004/38), the Court first pointed out that the Treaty itself conferred a right of residence, which could be limited in time, on nationals of Member States who were seeking employment in other Member States. The right to reside in a Member State conferred by the former Directive 68/360 was reserved for nationals who were already employed in that Member State. Collins was not in that position and he could not rely on the directive.

The Court of Justice concluded by examining the UK legislation in the light of the fundamental principle of equal treatment. Nationals of one Member State who were seeking employment in another Member State came within the scope of the former Art 39 EC Treaty (now Art 45 TFEU) and were thus entitled to benefit from the right to equal treatment set out in the former Art 39(2) EC Treaty (now Art 45(2) TFEU). However, the Court held that in principle this did not extend the right of equal treatment to benefits of a financial nature such as the jobseeker's allowance. Equality of treatment with regard to social and financial benefits applied only to persons who had already entered the employment market, while others specifically benefited from it only as regards access to employment. The Court considered, however, that in view of the establishment of EU citizenship and the interpretation in the case law of the right to equal treatment enjoyed by EU citizens, it was no longer possible to exclude a benefit of a financial nature intended to facilitate access to employment in the labour market of a Member State, from the scope of the former Art 39(2) EC Treaty (now Art 45(2) TFEU). In the present case, the residence condition imposed by the UK legislation was likely to be more easily satisfied by UK nationals. It could be justified only if it was based on objective considerations that were independent of the nationality of the persons concerned and proportionate to the legitimate aim of the national law. It was, the Court pointed out, legitimate for the national legislature to seek to ensure that there was a genuine link between an applicant for the allowance and the employment market, in particular by establishing that the person concerned was, for a reasonable period, genuinely seeking work. However, if it was to be proportionate, a period of residence required for that purpose could not exceed what was necessary in order to enable the national authorities to be satisfied that the person concerned was genuinely seeking work.

Ioannidis (Case C-258/04)

The Court of Justice was required to examine the case of a Greek national who arrived in Belgium in 1994 after completing his secondary education in Greece and having obtained recognition of the equivalence of his certificate of secondary education. After a three-year course of study in Liège (Belgium), he obtained a graduate diploma in physiotherapy and then registered as a jobseeker. He went to France to follow a paid training course from October 2000 to June 2001 and then returned to Belgium, where he submitted an application for a 'tideover allowance', an unemployment benefit provided for under Belgian legislation for young people seeking their first job. His application was refused because he did not fulfil the relevant requirements at that time, which were that he should have:

(i)   completed his secondary education in Belgium; or
(ii) pursued education or training of the same level and equivalent thereto in another Member State and been the dependent child of a migrant worker (for the purposes of the former Art 39 EC Treaty (now Art 45 TFEU)) who was residing in Belgium.

The Cour du travail de Liège (Higher Labour Court, Liège) referred a question to the Court of Justice regarding the compatibility of the Belgian system with Union law.

The Court of Justice observed that nationals of a Member State seeking employment in another Member State came within the scope of the former Art 39 EC Treaty (now Art 45 TFEU) and therefore enjoyed the right to equal treatment laid down in the former Art 39(2) EC Treaty (now Art 45(2) TFEU).

The remainder of the Court's judgment drew on case law set out in recent judgments delivered by the Court, in particular those in *D'Hoop* (Case C-224/98) and *Collins* (Case C-138/02).

The Court of Justice observed that in *Collins* it held that, in view of the establishment of EU citizenship and the interpretation of the right to equal treatment enjoyed by EU citizens, it was no longer possible to exclude a benefit of a financial nature intended to facilitate access to employment in the labour market of a Member State, from the scope of the former Art 39(2) EC Treaty (now Art 45(2) TFEU). In addition, the Court had already found in *D'Hoop* that the tideover allowances provided for by the Belgian legislation were social benefits, the aim of which was to facilitate, for young people, the transition from education to the employment market. Ioannidis was therefore justified in relying on the former Art 39 EC Treaty (now Art 45 TFEU) to claim that he could not be discriminated against on the basis of nationality as far as the grant of a tideover allowance was concerned. The condition that secondary education must have been completed in Belgium could be met more easily by Belgian nationals and could therefore place nationals of other Member States at a disadvantage.

As for possible justification of that difference in treatment, the Court again referred to *D'Hoop*, in which it held that although it was legitimate for the national legislature to wish to ensure that there was a real link between the applicant for a tideover allowance and the geographic employment market concerned, a single condition concerning the place where completion of the secondary education diploma was obtained was too general and exclusive in nature and went beyond what was necessary to attain the objective pursued. Finally, as regards the fact that the Belgian legislation afforded a right to a tideover allowance to an applicant if he had obtained an equivalent diploma in another Member State and if he was the dependent child of a migrant worker who was residing in Belgium, the Court considered, by converse implication, that a person who pursued higher education in a Member State and obtained a diploma there, having previously completed secondary education in another Member State, may well be in a position to establish a real link with the employment market of the first Member State, even if he was not the dependent child of a migrant worker residing in that Member State. The Court noted that, in any event, dependent children of migrant workers who were residing in Belgium derive their right to a tideover allowance from the former Art 7(2), Regulation 1612/68 (now Art 7(2), Regulation 492/2011), regardless of whether there was a real link with the employment market (see above).

Directive 2004/38

As discussed in Chapter11, Art 14(1), Directive 2004/38 provides that EU citizens and their family members shall have the right of residence under Art 6, 'as long as they do not become an *unreasonable* burden on the social assistance system of the host Member State' (emphasis added). Expulsion shall not be an automatic consequence if an EU citizen or his family members have recourse to the host Member State's social assistance system (Art 14(3)). Article 14(4) further provides that (other than in accordance with the provisions relating to restrictions on the right of entry and residence on grounds of public policy, public security or public health) an expulsion order cannot be issued against an EU citizen or his family members if, *inter alia*, the EU citizen entered the host Member State to seek employment and provided he can supply evidence that he is continuing to seek work and has a genuine chance of being employed.

With regard to social assistance, Art 24(2) provides that for the first three months of residence, or while the EU citizen is exercising his right to reside while seeking work under Art 14(4)(b), the host Member State is not obliged to grant entitlement to social assistance to persons other than employed (or self-employed) workers and the members of their family (see Chapter 11).

Education and vocational training

EU workers are entitled, by virtue of Art 7(3), Regulation 492/2011 (previously Art 7(3), 1612/68), to equal access to vocational schools and retraining centres. Article 10, Regulation 492/2011 (previously Art 12, Regulation 1612/68) also provides that EU workers' children are to be admitted to the host Member State's 'general educational, apprentice-ship and vocational training courses under the same conditions as nationals of that State, if such children are residing in its territory'. The former Art 12, Regulation 1612/68 (now Art 10, Regulation 492/2011) has received a greater degree of attention by the Court of Justice.

Neither the Treaty nor any implementing measures define the former Art 12 (now Art 10) meaning of 'vocational training', but the Court of Justice in *Gravier v City of Liège* (Case 293/83) said that 'any form of education which prepares for a qualification for a par-ticular profession, trade or employment or which provides the necessary skills for such a profession, trade or employment is vocational training whatever the age and level of the pupil or student'. The applicant's course in *Gravier* – strip cartoon design – clearly fell into that category. In the following case, the Court of Justice held that whether all or part of a course was 'vocational' was for the national court to decide on the facts:

Blaizot (Case 24/86)

The Court of Justice held that academic work at university level was not excluded, pro-vided either the final academic examination gave the required qualification for a particular trade, profession or employment, or:

the studies in question provide specific training and skills ... [which] ... the student needs for the pursuit of a profession, trade or employment, even if no legislative or administrative provisions make the acquisition of that knowledge a prerequisite for that purpose. (para 19)

Despite the need for a course of study with at least some career-orientated skills, the Court, in *Lair v University of Hannover* (Case 39/86), did not appear to doubt that a course in Romance and Germanic languages, that had no immediate vocational orientation, was nonetheless a 'vocational training course' (see Flynn, 1988).

The entitlement to equal access includes non-discrimination in relation to course fees (*Gravier*, above), so that, on any distinctions drawn by the host Member State between 'home' and 'foreign' students, EU citizens and their families exercising free movement rights should be classified as 'home' students. In addition, equal access applies not only to courses in the host Member State, but also to courses in other states, where the host state assists its own nationals in relation to attendance at foreign universities and colleges (*Matteucci* (Case 235/87)).

The educational rights of EU workers' children extend to a right to be admitted to the host Member State's primary and secondary schooling system, as well as to vocational courses in further and higher education (*Casagrande* (Case 9/74)).

In the following case, the Court of Justice held that the child of an EU worker had the right to go to school and pursue further education in the host Member State. This right, once exercised, will continue to apply to the child even if the worker has left the host Member State and has lost their EU worker status. This applies irrespective of whether or not the child is an EU citizen.

Baumbast and R v Secretary of State for the Home Department (Case C-413/99)

The Court of Justice held that:

Children of a citizen of the European Union who have installed themselves in a Member State during the exercise by their parent of rights of residence as a migrant worker in that Member

> State are entitled to reside there in order to attend general educational courses there, pursu-
> ant to Article 12 of Regulation (EEC) No 1612/68 [now Art 10, Regulation 492/2011] ... The
> fact that the parents of the children concerned have meanwhile divorced, the fact that only
> one parent is a citizen of the Union and that parent has ceased to be a migrant worker in the
> host Member State and the fact that the children are not themselves citizens of the Union are
> irrelevant in this regard.

Consistent with this judgment, the Court of Justice had earlier stated in **Brown v Secretary of State for Scotland** (Case 197/86) that Brown did not have any rights under the former Art 12, Regulation 1612/68 (now Art 10, Regulation 492/2011) because he was born after his parents had ceased to work and reside in the host Member State (i.e. his parents had lost their EU worker status before Brown had been born).

In the **Baumbast** case, the Court of Justice went one step further:

Baumbast and R v Secretary of State for the Home Department (Case C-413/99)

The Court of Justice stated that:

> Where children have the right to reside in a host Member State in order to attend general
> education courses pursuant to Article 12 of Regulation No 1612/68 [now Art 10, Regulation
> 492/2011], that provision must be interpreted as entitling the parent who is the primary carer
> of those children, irrespective of his nationality, to reside with them in order to facilitate the
> exercise of that right notwithstanding the fact that the parents have meanwhile divorced
> or that the parent who has the status of citizen of the European Union has ceased to be a
> migrant worker in the host Member State.

In the above case the Court of Justice decided that where the child was exercising the right to attend general educational courses, the parent who had primary care of the child had the right to reside with the child, even if this parent did not have EU worker status, and irrespective of whether or not this parent was an EU citizen.

In the following case, the Court of Justice confirmed that **Baumbast** was still good law following the coming into force of Directive 2004/38:

London Borough of Harrow v Ibrahim (Case C-310/08) and Teixeira v London Borough of Lambeth (Case C-480/08)

The Court of Appeal of England and Wales, which was hearing these two cases, asked the Court of Justice:

(i) whether the interpretation of the former Art 12, Regulation 1612/68 (now Art 10, Reg-
     ulation 492/2011) adopted in the *Baumbast* judgment was applicable following the
     entry into force of Directive 2004/38;
(ii) whether the right of residence of the person who was the child's primary carer was
     now subject to the conditions laid down by the Directive for the exercise of the right
     of residence, especially the requirement that the parent must have sufficient resources
     not to become a burden on the social assistance system.

In its judgments, the Court pointed out that the former Art 12, Regulation 1612/68 (now
Art 10, Regulation 492/2011) allowed the child of a migrant worker to have an independent right of residence in connection with the right of access to education in the

host Member State. Before the entry into force of Directive 2004/38, when Art 10, Regulation 1612/68 concerning the right of residence was still in force, the right of access to education laid down by the former Art 12, Regulation 1612/68 (now Art 10, Regulation 492/2011) was not conditional on the child retaining, throughout the period of education, a specific right of residence under the former Art 10, Regulation 1612/68. Once the right of access to education had been acquired, the right of residence was retained by the child and could no longer be called into question. The former Art 12, Regulation 1612/68 (now Art 10, Regulation 492/2011) required only that the child had lived with at least one of his parents in a Member State while that parent resided there as a worker. That article had to be applied independently of the provisions of Union law, which expressly govern the conditions of exercise of the right to reside in another Member State.

That independence was not called into question by the entry into force of the new Directive 2004/38. The Court pointed out that the former Art 12, Regulation 1612/68 (now Art 10, Regulation 492/2011) was not repealed or even amended by Directive 2004/38, unlike other articles of the regulation. Furthermore, the legislative history of the Directive showed that it was designed to be consistent with the *Baumbast* judgment.

The Court observed that **the grant of the right of residence for the children and the parent was not conditional on self-sufficiency.** That interpretation was supported by Directive 2004/38, which provided that the departure or death of the citizen did not entail the loss of the right of residence of the children or the parent.

Consequently, the Court held that the right of residence of a parent who was the primary carer for a child of a migrant worker, where that child was in education in the host Member State, was not conditional on that parent having sufficient resources not to become a burden on the social assistance system of the host Member State.

On a separate point, the Court held that the right of residence of such parent ended when the child reached the age of majority, unless the child continued to need the presence and care of that parent in order to be able to pursue and complete his education in the host Member State.

Maintenance grants and loans

The issue of access to higher education maintenance grants came before the Court of Justice in **Brown v Secretary of State for Scotland** (Case 197/86). The Court of Justice held that although access to education in terms of admission fees and admission criteria came within the scope of the Treaties (and thus within the prohibition against discrimination under what is now Art 18 TFEU), access to educational grants was not. Brown argued in the alternative that he was an EU worker and therefore had an independent right to an education grant as a social advantage under the former Art 7(2), Regulation 1612/68 (now Art 7(2), Regulation 492/2011):

Brown v Secretary of State for Scotland (Case 197/86)

Brown, who was a French national of Anglo-French origin, had applied for a discretionary grant from the Scottish Education Department to attend an electrical engineering course at Cambridge. Prior to the commencement of the course, he had obtained employment with an engineering company in Edinburgh for eight months. This job was described as 'pre-university industrial training'. Although he did not qualify for a grant under the Scottish regulations, he argued that he was entitled to receive one as a social advantage in his capacity as an EU worker, under the former Art 7(2), Regulation 1612/68 (now Art 7(2), Regulation 492/2011). The case was referred to the Court of Justice under what is now Art 267 TFEU. The Court of Justice held as follows:

> [a person who] enters into an employment relationship in the host State for a period of eight months with a view to subsequently taking up university studies there in the same field of activity ... is to be regarded as a worker within the meaning of Article 7(2) of Regulation 1612/68 [now Art 7(2), Regulation 492/2011].

That should have concluded the issue, but the Court then added (at para 27):

> it cannot be inferred from that finding that a national of a Member State will be entitled to a grant for studies in another Member State by virtue of his status as a worker where it is established that he acquired that status exclusively as a result of his being accepted for admission to university to undertake the studies in question. In such circumstances, **the employment relationship, which is the only basis for the rights deriving from Regulation No. 1612/68 [now Regulation 492/2011], is merely ancillary to the studies to be financed by the grant.** [emphasis added]

As discussed previously, where the employment is 'ancillary' to some other purpose (e.g. 'therapy' as in the case of *Bettray* (Case 344/87), above), the individual may not be regarded as an EU worker under either Art 45 TFEU or Art 7(2), Regulation 492/2011 (previously Art 7(2), Regulation 1612/68), for the purpose of social advantages. On that basis, the Court of Justice, and the Advocate General could well have concluded that Brown was not an EU worker at all. His entitlement to social advantages would not, therefore, have arisen, as in the case of *Lebon*, above. The Court, however, decided to hold that he was both an EU worker and at the same time disentitled to the social advantages to which such workers would normally be entitled in these circumstances.

EU citizenship is considered in depth at pages 347–359 (Chapter 11). The nature of EU citizenship was considered by the Court of Justice in the following case (see Chapter 11), the outcome of which necessitates a reassessment of the *Brown* judgment:

Grzelczyk v Centre Public d'Aide Sociale d'ottignies-Louvain-la-Neuve (Case C-184/99)

One of the rights conferred by the Treaty is that contained in Art 18 TFEU (previously Art 12 EC Treaty), which provides that 'Within the scope of application of the Treaties ... any discrimination on grounds of nationality shall be prohibited'. In this case, Grzelczyk, a student of French nationality paid his own way throughout his first three years of full-time studies at a Belgian university by taking on minor jobs and obtaining credit. At the start of his fourth and final year he applied for a Belgian social security benefit known as minimum subsistence allowance (minimex). His application was refused on the ground that under the relevant Belgian legislation a non-Belgian applicant was only eligible if, *inter alia*, the former Regulation 1612/68 (now Regulation 492/2011) applied to him; but it is applicable to 'workers' not 'students'. If he had been Belgian then he would have been entitled to the benefit, notwithstanding the fact that he was not a worker within the scope of the former Regulation 1612/68 (now Regulation 492/2011). The Belgian tribunal had doubts as to whether the national legislation was compatible with the former Arts 12 and 17 EC Treaty (now Arts 18 and 20 TFEU). The tribunal therefore referred the case to the Court of Justice for a preliminary ruling pursuant to what is now Art 267 TFEU.

The Court of Justice stated that as it was clear that a student who was Belgian but otherwise in the same circumstances as the applicant would be entitled to minimex, the case was one of discrimination solely on the ground of nationality which, in principle, was prohibited by the former Art 12 EC Treaty (now Art 18 TFEU); at paras 29–30. The Court further stated at para 30 that the former Art 12 EC Treaty had to be read in conjunction with the Treaty provisions on EU citizenship (the former Art 17 EC Treaty; now Art 20 TFEU), to determine its sphere of application. The Court then went on to say that EU citizenship was destined to be the fundamental status of nationals of the Member States, enabling those who found themselves in the same situation to enjoy the same treatment in law irrespective of their nationality, subject to some exceptions as were expressly provided for (para 31).

The Court noted that Directive 93/96 required Member States to grant the right of residence to student nationals of a Member State who satisfied certain requirements (Directive 93/96 has since been repealed and replaced by Directive 2004/03). Although Art 3 of this Directive made it clear that there was no right to payment of maintenance grants by the host Member State for students who benefited from the right of residence, it contained no provision precluding those to whom it applied from receiving social security benefits. The Court therefore held that the former Arts 12 and 17 EC Treaty (now Arts 18 and 20 TFEU) precluded Belgium from making entitlement to minimex conditional on the applicant (Mr Grzelczyk) coming within the scope of the former Regulation 1612/68 (i.e. being an EU worker) when no such condition applied to Belgian nationals.

Due to the fact that the applicant had a right of residence under Union law as a student, the Court held that as an EU citizen he was entitled to be treated the same as a national would be with regard to the payment of social security benefits; an application of the non-discriminatory Art 12 EC Treaty (now Art 18 TFEU) provision.

However, the Court in this case stated that its judgment did not prevent a Member State from: (i) taking the view that a student who had recourse to social assistance was no longer fulfilling the conditions of his right of residence; or (ii) taking measures, within the limits imposed by Union law, to either withdraw his residence permit or refuse to renew it. But in no case, the Court said, could such a measure become the automatic consequence of a student who was a national of another Member State having recourse to the host Member State's social security system (see paras 40–45).

The principle of EU citizenship and non-discrimination developed by the Court of Justice in *Grzelczyk* has been subsequently applied by the Court in *Marie-Nathalie D'Hoop* v *Office national de l'emploi* (Case C-224/98); see Chapter 11.

In the *Brown* case, with regard to the former Art 7(2), Regulation 1612/68 (now Art 7(2), Regulation 492/2011), the Court of Justice held that Brown was to be regarded as an EU worker, but because his work was linked to his studies (i.e. pre-course training) he only gained his EU worker status because of his studies and therefore he was not allowed to claim a maintenance grant under Art 7(2). Directive 93/96 expressly provided for the exclusion of maintenance grants for any student who benefited from the right of residence under the directive. However, arguably, Brown's right to residence had arisen because of his status as an EU worker rather than as a student. The Court of Justice further stated that the non-discriminatory rule in the former Art 12 EC Treaty (now Art 18 TFEU) did not apply to provide assistance for maintenance and training to students. In *Grzelczyk* the Court stated that *Brown* was decided before EU citizenship had been introduced. Although the *Grzelczyk* case may not assist students to claim maintenance grants (because of their exclusion under the former Art 3, Directive 93/96; and now excluded under Art 24(2),

Directive 2004/38) this case could assist students, such as Brown, to have recourse to the host Member State social security system on the same terms as nationals.

As described above, in **Ninni-Orasche** (Case C-413/01), the Court of Justice held that an EU worker who had been employed in the host Member State for a fixed term (which had been set at the outset) would not be considered voluntarily unemployed when that fixed term expired. In this case, the EU worker had been employed for a fixed term of two-and-a-half months, and the worker had applied for a study grant from the host Member State when that fixed term expired. As EU worker status was retained, the right to a study grant came within the scope of the former Art 7(2), Regulation 1612/68 (now Art 7(2), Regulation 492/2011).

Directive 2004/38: free movement of students

As discussed in Chapter 11, Art 7(1), Directive 2004/38 provides that EU citizens have the right to reside in another Member State, for a period exceeding three months, if *inter alia* they are following a course of study, including vocational training, at a public or private institution which is accredited or financed by the host Member State. The student must have comprehensive sickness insurance and assure the Member State, by a declaration or equivalent means, that they have sufficient resources for themselves and their family members to ensure that they do not become a burden on the social assistance system of the host Member State during their stay. Article 8(3) provides that Member States may not require the declaration to refer to any specific amount of resources. EU citizens qualifying for the right of residence or the right of permanent residence under Directive 2004/38, and the members of such EU citizens' families, benefit from equal treatment with host-country nationals in the areas covered by the Treaty (Art 24(1)). However, for the first three months of residence, the host Member State is not obliged to grant entitlement to social assistance to persons other than employed (or self-employed) workers and the members of their family (Art 24(2)). Equally, host Member States are not required to provide maintenance aid (i.e. student grants or student loans) to persons with a right of residence who have come to the country in question to study (Art 24(2)).

Family rights: a summary

Directive 2004/38 confers extensive family rights on the EU worker. Although much of this section has been discussed in Chapter 11, it is useful to reconsider the basic rights relating to family members of an EU worker.

An EU worker may be accompanied by, or be joined by: (i) his spouse or registered partner (if the host Member State's legislation recognises registered partnerships as equivalent to marriage); (ii) their descendants who are under the age of 21 or who are dependent (this applies to the descendants of the EU worker and, separately, those of his spouse/registered partner); and (iii) his own dependent direct relatives in the ascending line and those of his spouse (Art 2(2); Art 6(2); and Art 7(1)(d)). Dependent children, grandchildren, and even great-grandchildren have the right to install themselves with the worker. The same applies to the parents and grandparents of both the EU worker and his spouse/registered partner, if dependent. Other family members not coming within the ascending or descending lines, such as aunts, uncles, nephews and nieces, should have their entry 'facilitated' if: (i) they are dependent on the worker; (ii) they are members of the worker's household; or (iii) serious health grounds strictly require the worker to provide the family member with personal care; the same applies to the 'partner' of the worker provided they have a 'durable relationship' which is duly attested (Art 3(2); Art 6(2); and Art 7(1)(d)). Where a person has the right to have their entry 'facilitated', the host Member State is required to undertake an extensive examination of the personal circumstances of such persons and shall justify any denial of entry or residence (Art 3(2)). In the case of family members who are not nationals of a Member State, it is permissible that they should obtain an entry visa before being admitted, unless they have been issued with a residence card under the directive, in which case the residence card will suffice (Art 5(2)). In cases where a visa is required, Member States should grant such persons 'every facility to obtain the necessary visas'; the visa shall be issued free of charge (Art 5(2)).

There should be no need to prove the relationship at the point of entry, although Art 5(5) provides that the host Member State may require each person travelling to, or residing in, another Member State to register their presence in the country within a reasonable and non-discriminatory period of time. Failure to comply with this requirement may make the person liable to a proportionate and non-discriminatory sanction.

If the worker is resident in the host Member State for no longer than three months, the family members will have the right of entry and residence without any conditions or formalities other than the requirement to hold a valid identity card or passport (Art 6(1)); in the case of non-EU family members only a passport will suffice (Art 6(2)).

If the worker is resident in the host Member State for longer than three months, a registration certificate will be issued to family members who are nationals of a Member State (i.e. EU family members); this is subject to the production of specified documentation (Art 8(5)). This provision also applies to other EU family members whose entry to and residence in the host Member State is facilitated in accordance with Art 3(2); see above. In the case of family members who are not nationals of a Member State (i.e. non-EU family members), such family members must apply for a residence card not more than three months from their date of arrival (Art 9(2)). A residence card is valid for at least five years from its date of issue, or for the envisaged period of residence of the worker if this is less than five years (Art 11(1)). Article 10(2) sets out the documentation required before a residence card will be issued. This provision also applies to other non-EU family members whose entry and residence to the host Member State shall be facilitated in accordance with Art 3(2). Article 11(2) provides that the validity of a residence card shall not be affected by:

(i) temporary absences of up to six months a year;
(ii) absences of a longer period for compulsory military service; or
(iii) one absence of up to 12 months for important reasons (e.g. pregnancy and childbirth, serious illness, study or vocational training, or a posting in another Member State or a third country).

Much of the case law of the Court of Justice prior to Directive 2004/38 will remain relevant, but there are exceptions. While the rights of residence of spouses do not depend on their continuing cohabitation, in *Diatta v Land Berlin* (Case 267/83) the Court of Justice held that the right of residence subsisted as long as the marriage continued, irrespective of whether or not the parties to the marriage were still together. Once the marriage was dissolved, the spouse's right of residence in that capacity would appear to have been terminated. However, Directive 2004/38 now provide s for the retention of the right of residence by family members in the event of divorce, annulment of marriage or termination of registered partnership. In the case of EU family members, divorce, annulment of marriage or termination of partnership does not affect the family member's right of residence (Art 13(1)). However, in the case of non-EU family members, retention of the right of residence is restricted. Article 13(2) provides that there shall be no loss of the right of residence where:

(a) prior to the start of the divorce or annulment proceedings or termination of the registered partnership, the marriage or registered partnership had lasted at least three years, including one year in the host Member State;

(b) by agreement between the spouses or the registered partners, or by court order, the spouse or partner who is a non-EU national has custody of the EU citizen's children;

(c) this is warranted by particularly difficult circumstances, such as having been a victim of domestic violence while the marriage or registered partnership was subsisting; or

(d) by agreement between the spouses or registered partners, or by court order, the spouse or partner who is a non-EU national has the right of access to a minor child, provided that the court has ruled that such access must be in the host Member State, and for as long as is required.

Article 12(1) provides that if an EU citizen dies or departs from the host Member State, his EU family members shall not have their right of residence affected. In the case of a non-EU family member, their right of residence shall not be affected if the EU citizen dies provided that the non-EU family member has been residing in the host Member State as a family member for at least one year before the EU citizen's death (Art 12(2)).

The EU worker's children have the right to be admitted to the host Member State's primary and secondary schooling system, as well as to vocational courses in further and higher education, pursuant to Art 10, Regulation 492/2011 (previously Art 12, Regulation 1612/68; see *Casagrande* (Case 9/74)). In ***Baumbast and R v Secretary of State for the Home Department*** (Case C-413/99) the Court held that the child of an EU worker had the right to go to school and pursue further education in the host Member State, and that this right, once exercised, would continue to apply to the child even if the worker had left the host Member State and had lost his EU worker status. This applied irrespective of whether or not the child is an EU citizen. The Court additionally held that where the child was exercising the right to attend general educational courses, the parent who had primary care of the child had the right to reside with the child, even if this parent did not have EU worker status, and irrespective of whether or not this parent was an EU citizen. Article 12(3), Directive 2004/38, provides that if an EU citizen dies or departs from the host Member State, if his children reside in the host Member State and are enrolled at an educational establishment, then his children and the parent who has actual custody of the children (whether or not they are EU citizens) shall have the right to reside in the host Member State until the children have completed their studies.

Family free movement rights derive directly from Union law. They apply not only to EU citizens who work in other Member States in relation to those states, but also in relation to their own state when they have returned to it after having worked in another Member State. In ***R v Immigration Appeal Tribunal and Surinder Singh*** (Case C-370/90), the Court of Justice held that a national of a Member State who has gone to another Member State in order to work there as an employed person under what is now Art 45 TFEU, and returns to establish himself as a self-employed person in the territory of the Member State of which he is a national, has the right to return to that state under the same conditions as are laid down by the former Regulation 1612/68 (now Regulation 492/2011) or Directive 2004/38.

Members of the family have a right to work in the host Member State. Under Art 23, Directive 2004/38, all family members who have the right of residence in a Member State are entitled to take up employment or self-employment there, even if they are not nationals of any Member State (i.e. non-EU family members).

EU family members acquire the right of permanent residence in the host Member State after a five-year period of continuous legal residence (Art 16(1)), provided that an expulsion decision has not been enforced against them (Art 21). This right of permanent residence is no longer subject to any conditions. The same rule applies to non-EU family members who have lived with an EU citizen in the host Member State for five years (Art 16(2)), and again provided that an expulsion decision has not been enforced against them (Art 21).

Article 17 recognises the right of permanent residence for EU citizens who are workers or self-employed persons, and for their family members, before the five-year period of continuous residence has expired, subject to certain conditions being met (see below).

Housing provisions

The entry of family members used to be conditional upon the EU worker having available for them 'housing considered as normal for national workers in the region where he is employed' (Art 10(3), Regulation 1612/68). This condition was operative only at the time of the family's entry. An attempt by the German authorities to make access to reasonable housing provisions a precondition for the renewal of a residence permit was held by the Court of Justice in *Re Housing of Migrant Workers: EC Commission v Germany* (Case 249/86) to be unlawful. The reference to adequate housing in Art 10(3) related only to the 'installation' of the worker's family. The Court emphasised the importance of family reunion, as guaranteed by Art 8 of the European Convention on Human Rights, and the need to 'facilitate ... the integration of the worker and his family into the host Member State without any difference in treatment in relation to nationals of that State' (paras 10 and 11). Perhaps for this reason, Directive 2004/38, which repealed and replaced Art 10, Regulation 1612/68, makes no reference to a need for the EU worker to have such housing available for his family members.

The need for equal treatment in the housing field is dealt with in Art 9, Regulation 492/2011 (previously Art 9, Regulation 1612/68). Under this provision, the worker 'shall enjoy all the rights and benefits accorded to national workers in matters of housing, including ownership of the housing he needs'. If his family remained in the country from which he came, they shall be considered for this purpose as residing in the region where he is working. On this basis, the EU worker is entitled to be treated, both for the purpose of applications for public housing and the purchase of a private house, as having his family with him. The Court of Justice held in *Commission v Germany* (above) that the acquisition of housing solely to secure a residence permit could be penalised if the family then moved into less suitable accommodation, but that any penalty should fall short of measures leading to expulsion (para 14).

Right of permanent residence under Directive 2004/38

As discussed in Chapter 11, Art 7, Directive 2004/38, provides a right of residence for more than three months. This provision has been considered above with regard to EU workers and students, but the right also extends to EU citizens who have comprehensive sickness insurance and sufficient resources for themselves and their family members to ensure that they do not become a burden on the social assistance system of the host Member State during their stay (Art 7(1)(a)).

EU citizens acquire the right of permanent residence in the host Member State after a five-year period of continuous legal residence (Art 16(1)), provided that an expulsion decision has not been enforced against them (Art 21); see Chapter 11.

Article 17 recognises the right of permanent residence for EU citizens who are workers or self-employed persons, and for their family members, before the five-year period of continuous residence has expired, subject to certain conditions being met; see Chapter 11. Article 17 also provides that the family members of an EU worker or self-employed person have the right of permanent residence if the EU worker or self-employed person dies before acquiring the right of permanent residence.

Articles 12 and 13 are relevant to the right of permanent residence. Article 12(1) provides that if an EU citizen dies or departs from the host Member State, his family members who are nationals of a Member State shall not have their right of residence affected; see Chapter 11. Article 13 governs a family member's right of residence following divorce, annulment of marriage or termination of partnership; see Chapter 11.

May 2004 enlargement – transitional arrangements

Objective 6

Following enlargement on 1 May 2004, transitional periods limited the free movement of workers from the new Member States to the pre-2004 Member States. These transitional periods were set out in the Accession Treaty. The transitional arrangements which apply to Bulgaria and Romania (which became Member States on 1 January 2007) and Croatia (which became a Member State on 1 July 2013) are considered below.

For the first two years following the accession of the new Member States (i.e. until 30 April 2006), access to the labour markets of pre-2004 Member States depended on national measures and policies, as well as bilateral agreements. From 1 May 2004, the UK decided to allow the free movement of worker provisions to apply to all EU citizens within the UK (i.e. the UK opted *not* to restrict access to its labour market, although it required such workers to register with the Workers Registration Scheme within 30 days of starting work). Ireland and Sweden also allowed full free movement.

At the end of the first two years the Commission was required to draft a report on the functioning of the transitional arrangements. The Commission's report was published on 8 February 2006 (COM (2006) 48 final). This report informed a review by the Council of Ministers.

Member States were required to notify the Commission as to their intention for the next period of up to three years either to continue with national measures, or to allow free movement of workers. Free movement of workers had to be in place after five years (i.e. by 1 May 2009) unless a pre-2004 Member State was authorised by the Commission to continue to apply national measures for a further two years (i.e. until 30 April 2011). The Commission could only grant authorisation if the Member State making the request was experiencing serious disturbances within its labour market. This requirement had to be objectively justified. Germany and Austria were authorised by the Commission to continue to apply national measures for a further two years (and the UK continued to require registration with the Workers Registration Scheme within 30 days of starting work). Since 1 May 2011, seven years after accession, there has been complete freedom of movement for workers from the pre-2007 Member States.

January 2007 enlargement – transitional arrangements

Bulgaria and Romania became Member States on 1 January 2007. The pre-2007 Member States were authorised to adopt transitional arrangements limiting Bulgarian and Romanian citizens' free movement rights for a period of up to seven years. These transitional arrangements were similar to those which originally applied to the states which joined the EU on 1 May 2004. From 1 January 2014, seven years after accession, there has been complete freedom of movement for workers from Bulgaria and Romania.

July 2013 enlargement – transitional arrangements

Croatia became a Member State on 1 July 2013. Transitional arrangements will limit Croatian citizens' free movement rights for a period of up to seven years. From 1 July 2020, seven years after accession, there will be complete freedom of movement for workers from Croatia.

Details of the transitional arrangements adopted by Member States are made available through the Commission's Job Mobility Portal:

http://ec.europa.eu/social/main.jsp?catId=466&langId=en

Summary

Now you have read this chapter you should be able to:

- Identify the provisions of the TFEU which relate to the free movement of workers.
- Evaluate how the Court of Justice has, through its case law, defined the concept and scope of 'EU worker'.
- Understand how the 'employment in the public service' exception is applied by the Court of Justice.
- Explain the provisions of Directive 2004/38, which relate to the abolition of restrictions to movement and residence of EU workers and their families and which provide a right for workers and their families to remain in a Member State having been employed there.
- Explain how the provisions of Regulation 492/2011 (previously Regulation 1612/68) are applied by the Court of Justice.
- Understand the purpose and effect of the transitional arrangements which relate to the right of free movement of an EU citizen who is a national of one of the Member States which acceded to the EU in 2004, 2007 and 2013.

Reference

Flynn, J., 'Vocational training in Community law and practice' (1988) 8 YEL 59.

417

Further reading

Textbooks

Barnard, C. (2013) *The Substantive Law of the EU: The Four Freedoms* (4th edn), Oxford University Press, Chapter 9.

Craig, P. and De Burca, G. (2011) *EU Law: Text, Cases and Materials* (5th edn), Oxford University Press, Chapter 21.

Foster, N. (2015) *Foster on EU Law* (5th edn), Oxford University Press, Chapter 9.

Steiner, J. and Woods, L. (2014) *EU Law* (12th edn), Oxford University Press, Chapters 22 and 23.

Weatherill, S. (2014) *Cases and Materials on EU Law* (11th edn), Oxford University Press, Chapter 13.

Journal articles

Currie, S., 'Accelerated justice or a step too far? Residence rights of non-EU family members and the court's ruling in Metock' (2009) 34 EL Rev 310.

Dautricourt, C. and Thomas, S., 'Reverse discrimination and free movement of persons under Community law: All for Ulysses, nothing for Penelope?' (2009) 34 EL Rev 433.

Dougan, M., 'Cross-border educational mobility and the exportation of student financial assistance' (2008) 33 EL Rev 723.

Downward, P., Parrish, R., Pearson, G. and Semens, A., 'An assessment of the compatibility of UEFA's home grown player rule with article 45 TFEU' (2014) 39 EL Rev 493.

Fahey, E., 'Interpretive legitimacy and the distinction between "social assistance" and "work seekers allowance": Comment on Case C-22/08 and C-23/08 *Vatsouras* and *Koupatantze*' (2009) 34 EL Rev 933.

Kocharov, A., 'What intra-Community mobility for third-country nationals?' (2008) 33 EL Rev 913.

Koutrakos, P., 'Visa-free travel: Foreign policy in the making' (2009) 34 EL Rev 669.

O'Brien, C., 'Real links, abstract rights and false alarms: The relationship between the ECJ's "real link" case law and national solidarity' (2008) 33 EL Rev 643.

O'Leary, S., 'Equal treatment and EU citizens: A new chapter on cross-border educational mobility and access to student financial assistance' (2009) 34 EL Rev 612.

Peers, S., 'EC immigration law and EC association agreements: Fragmentation or integration?' (2009) 34 EL Rev 628.

Pijetlovic, K., 'Another classic of EU sports jurisprudence: Legal implications of Olympique Lyonnais *v* Olivier Bernard and Newcastle United FC (C-325/08)' (2010) 35 EL Rev 857.

Staver, A., 'Free movement and the fragmentation of family reunification rights' (2013) 15 EJML 69.

13

Free movement of providers and recipients of services, and freedom of establishment

Objective 1

Objectives

At the end of this chapter you should understand:

1. Which provisions of the TFEU apply to the free movement of providers and recipients of services and the freedom of establishment.

2. The application of Art 56 TFEU on the free movement of providers and recipients of services, the scope for restrictions to be objectively justified, and the provisions and scope of Directive 2006/123 (the 'Services Directive').

3. How Art 56 TFEU has been applied to remove obstacles to the freedom of establishment.

4. The scope of Directive 2004/38 with regard to the conferring of a general right of residence and which enables a person to remain within a Member State having pursued a self-employed activity there.

5. The application of Art 18 TFEU and Art 24, Directive 2004/38 establishing the right of equal treatment for those exercising their free movement rights as providers and recipients of services and their Union law rights of establishment.

6. How Art 49 TFEU is applied in respect of qualifications and training and to analyse the impact on Art 49 of the harmonisation directives and the two general directives which have been repealed and replaced by Directive 2005/36.

The TFEU and Directive 2004/38

When the ToL came into force on 1 December 2009, the former Arts 43, 49, 50 and 54 EC Treaty were replaced by Arts 49, 56, 57 and 61 TFEU, respectively. The wording of each of these four new provisions is practically unchanged from the former EC Treaty provisions.

Individuals may wish to move to another Member State to engage in a business or profession in a self-employed capacity. Article 49 TFEU (previously Art 43 EC Treaty) provides for the freedom of establishment:

> Within the framework of the provisions set out below, restrictions on the freedom of establishment of nationals of a Member State in the territory of another Member State shall be prohibited. Such prohibition shall also apply to restrictions on the setting-up of agencies,

419

branches or subsidiaries by nationals of any Member State established in the territory of any Member State.

Freedom of establishment shall include the right to take up and pursue activities as self-employed persons and to set up and manage undertakings, in particular companies or firms within the meaning of the second paragraph of Article 54, under the conditions laid down for its own nationals by the law of the country where such establishment is effected, subject to the provisions of the Chapter relating to capital.

'Establishment' is not defined in the Treaty or the implementing legislation. However, Art 49 TFEU requires the abolition of restrictions on the freedom of establishment of nationals of a Member State in the territory of another Member State. Freedom of establishment includes the right of individuals and companies to set themselves up in business in a Member State (a permanent or settled place of business). It covers the self-employed and in addition the practising of a profession or trade (e.g. lawyer, doctor, vet) on a permanent or semi-permanent basis. Naturally, a person may seek to practise a profession in another Member State in an employed capacity (i.e. as an EU worker), and therefore the Union law provisions relating to workers will apply (see Chapter 12) in addition to those of establishment, which relate to recognition of the profession or trade.

Articles 56 and 57 TFEU (previously Arts 49 and 50 EC Treaty) provide for the abolition of restrictions on individuals to provide services in a Member State other than that in which they are established. Article 56 TFEU (previously Art 49 EC Treaty) provides that:

Within the framework of the provisions set out below, restrictions on freedom to provide services within the Union shall be prohibited in respect of nationals of Member States who are established in a Member State other than that of the person for whom the services are intended.

The European Parliament and the Council, acting in accordance with the ordinary legislative procedure, may extend the provisions of the Chapter to nationals of a third country who provide services and who are established within the Union.

Article 57 TFEU (previously Art 50 EC Treaty) provides that:

Services shall be considered to be 'services' within the meaning of the Treaties where they are normally provided for remuneration, in so far as they are not governed by the provisions relating to freedom of movement for goods, capital and persons.

'Services' shall in particular include:

(a) activities of an industrial character;
(b) activities of a commercial character;
(c) activities of craftsmen;
(d) activities of the professions.

Without prejudice to the provisions of the Chapter relating to the right of establishment, the person providing a service may, in order to do so, temporarily pursue his activity in the Member State where the service is provided, under the same conditions as are imposed by that State on its own nationals.

Article 57 TFEU provides that services shall be considered to be 'services' within the meaning of the Treaty 'where they are normally provided for remuneration'. Article 57 lists such services as including activities of an industrial and commercial character, activities of craftsmen and activities of the professions. This is, however, far from being an exhaustive list. The person providing the service 'may, in order to do so, temporarily pursue his activity in the Member State where the service is provided'. This is 'without prejudice to the provisions of the Chapter relating to the right of establishment'. There is, in fact, a close link to the right of establishment. The right to provide the service confers a right of residence as long as the service is provided. If the service provider wishes to provide that service in the host Member State on a long-term basis then Art 49 TFEU will apply, and he may become established in that state. The crucial element that differentiates the service provider from the established business is the process of 'setting up'. This may involve anything from leasing or buying business premises, to acquiring a licence to run a company in the host Member State (see *Steinhauser v City of Biarritz* (Case 197/84) and *R v Secretary of State for Transport, ex parte Factortame* (Case C-213/89)). The Court of Justice referred to 'establishment' in the *Factortame* case as 'the actual pursuit of an economic activity through a fixed establishment for an indefinite period' (para 20).

With regard to services, Art 61 TFEU provides as follows:

> As long as restrictions on freedom to provide services have not been abolished, each Member State shall apply such restrictions without distinction on grounds of nationality or residence to all persons providing services within the meaning of the first paragraph of Article 56.

Article 18 TFEU (previously Art 12 EC Treaty), the Treaty's general anti-discrimination provision, has been applied by the Court of Justice when determining cases relating to the freedom of establishment and the provision and receipt of services.

None of the Treaty provisions confers a right to go to another Member State to *receive* services, but the former Directive 73/148 was more wide-ranging than the former Arts 43, 49 and 50 EC Treaty (now Arts 49, 56 and 57 TFEU). It provided for the abolition of restrictions on the movement and residence of:

(a) nationals of a Member State established or seeking to establish themselves in another Member State in order to pursue activities as self-employed persons or who were seeking to provide services in that state;

(b) nationals of Member States seeking to go to another Member State *as recipients of services*.

Directive 73/148 has been repealed and replaced by Directive 2004/38. Article 6, Directive 2004/38 establishes the right for all EU citizens and their family members to reside in another Member State for a period of up to three months without any conditions or formalities, other than the requirement to hold a valid identity card or passport (only a passport will suffice in the case of non-EU family members). This general right of residence for up to three months will clearly be applicable to both providers and recipients of services. Article 7, Directive 2004/38 creates a right of extended residence (for more than three months) for EU citizens and their family members who, *inter alia*, are economically self-sufficient.

The scope of the Treaty provisions and Directive 2004/38 in relation to: (i) the providers of services; (ii) the recipients of services; and (iii) the right of establishment, are considered below.

Providers of services

Objective
2

Article 56 TFEU is directly effective (see, e.g., *Van Binsbergen* (Case 33/74)). However, in the following case the Court of Justice held that what is now Art 56 TFEU will not apply to a totally internal situation:

Peter Jägerskiöld v Torolf Gustafsson (Case C-97/98)

On 29 May 1997 Gustafsson (G) fished with a spinning rod in waters belonging to Jäger-skiöld (J) in the township of Kimoto in Finland. Two days earlier, on 27 May 1997, G had paid the fishing licence fee provided for in Finnish law, which allowed him to practise that type of fishing even in private waters.

J brought an action before the national court for a declaration that G could not, without his permission, fish with a rod in his waters, notwithstanding the fact that G had paid the fishing licence fee provided for by Finnish law. In support of his action, J argued that the Finnish law, on which the right to fish with a rod was based, was contrary to the Union rules concerning the free movement of goods or to those relating to the freedom to provide services. The Court held that the provisions relating to the free movement of goods did not apply, but those relating to the freedom to provide services did apply. However, the Court of Justice continued:

> . . . concerning the provisions of the Treaty relating to the freedom to provide services, it is sufficient to observe that these provisions are not applicable to activities which are confined in all respects within a single Member State.

> **The legal proceedings pending before the Tingsratt are between two Finnish nationals, both established in Finland, concerning the right of one of them to fish in waters belonging to the other situated in Finland.**

> Such a situation does not present any link to one of the situations envisaged by Community [i.e. Union] law in the field of the free provision of services. [emphasis added]

Remuneration

Article 57 TFEU provides that services will come within the scope of the Treaty if they are 'normally provided for remuneration'. The Court of Justice considered the essential characteristic of remuneration in the following case:

Belgium v Humbel (Case 263/86)

The Court of Justice said that 'the essential characteristic of remuneration is that it constitutes the countervailing financial advantage for the services in question and is normally fixed between the supplier and the recipient of the service'. The Court held, on this basis, that courses of study provided in the framework of a national educational system were not provided for remuneration. The situation was not affected by the fact that students had to pay a registration fee or some other charge. By establishing and maintaining a national educational system, 'the State does not intend to engage in activities for which remuneration is received, but is fulfilling its duty to its people in the social, cultural and educational fields' (paras 17 and 18).

Education can, however, constitute a service if it is provided by a private body on a commercial basis (see *Luisi and Carbone v Ministero del Tesoro* (Case 286/83)). The services are, therefore, either of a commercial character, or they are, at least, provided in exchange for money or money's worth.

In contrast, in *Geraets-Smits v Stichting Ziekenfonds* and *Peerbooms v Stichting CZ Groep Zorgverzekeringen* (Case C-157/99), the Court of Justice held that the fact that hospital medical treatment is financed directly by sickness insurance funds on the basis of agreements and pre-set scales of fees does not remove such treatment from the sphere of services within the meaning of Art 57 TFEU. Article 57 TFEU does not require the service to be paid for by those to whom the service is provided. The Court stated that the essential characteristic of remuneration lies in the fact that it constitutes consideration for the service in question.

The Court of Justice has also held that there must be an *economic* link in order to come within the provisions of the Treaty:

SPUC v *Grogan* (Case C-159/90)

Ireland had a restriction on the publication of information about the provision of abortion in other Member States (abortion was illegal in Ireland; and subject to one very specific exception, it continues to remain illegal). A Students' Union in Dublin provided information about abortion services which were lawfully available in London. This practice was challenged before the Irish Courts by the Society for the Protection of Unborn Children (SPUC). The matter was referred by the national court to the Court of Justice pursuant to what is now Art 267 TFEU (previously Art 234 EC Treaty).

The Court of Justice held that the provision of abortion could constitute a service. However, the Court held that because the Students' Union was not distributing the information **on behalf of the economic operators** (i.e. the clinics providing the service (abortions)), Ireland could restrain its activity. The Students' Union had no economic link with the clinics – it was not being paid.

The above case may have been decided differently had the clinics themselves been advertising their services, because clearly there would have been an *economic link*, or if the Students' Union had been acting as the agent of the clinics (and was being paid). This case was also politically sensitive given that abortion was illegal under Ireland's constitution. There could therefore have been strong policy considerations for the Court's decision.

Meaning of 'service'

The Court of Justice considered the meaning of 'service' in the following case:

Schindler (Case C-275/92)

The undertakings concerned were agents of four local state lotteries in Germany. They sent letters from the Netherlands to the UK enclosing application forms with invitations to participate in the German lotteries. The letters were confiscated by Customs and Excise on the grounds that they infringed national legislation on lotteries and gaming. The Court of Justice held that the letters were not 'goods', so the restrictions did not fall to be considered under the former Art 29 EC Treaty (now Art 35 TFEU). The Court then went on to determine whether or not they were a 'service'.

The Court decided that they were a service. The services provided by the operators of the lottery enabled purchasers of tickets to participate in a game of chance with the hope of winning, by arranging for that purpose for the stakes to be collected, the draws to be organised, and the prizes for winnings to be ascertained and paid out. The services were 'normally provided for remuneration', represented by the price of the lottery ticket. They were cross-border, as they were offered in a Member State other than that in which the lottery operator was established.

The Court of Justice reached a similar conclusion in relation to the offer of financial services by telephone to potential recipients in another state (*Alpine Investments BV* v *Minister van Financiën* (Case C-384/93)), and similarly in relation to the provision of insurance (*Safir* v *Skattemyndigheten i Dalarnas Lan* (Case C-118/96); *Skandia and Ramstedt*

(Case C-422/01)). As previously discussed, in *Geraets-Smits v Stichting Ziekenfonds* and *Peerbooms v Stichting CZ Groep Zorgverzekeringen* (Case C-157/99), the Court of Justice held that *medical activities* came within the scope of what is now Art 57 TFEU and there was no need to distinguish between care provided in a hospital environment and care provided outside such an environment.

In *Konsumentombudsmannen (KO) v Gourmet International Products AB (GIP)* (Case C-405/98) the Court of Justice held that the Treaty provisions on freedom to provide services precluded a prohibition on the advertising of alcoholic beverages because it had a particular effect on the cross-border supply of advertising space, given the international nature of the advertising market in the category of products to which the prohibition related. Such a prohibition (i.e. the *advertising* of goods) therefore constitutes a restriction on the freedom to provide services within the meaning of what is now Art 56 TFEU. The Court, however, held that such a restriction may be justified by the protection of public health, which is a ground of general interest recognised by Art 52 TFEU, and which is applicable to the provision of services in accordance with Art 62 TFEU. This is discussed further within Chapter 15. Restrictions may also be objectively justified by overriding reasons in the general interest, provided the rules are applied to all persons and undertakings operating in the territory of the Member State where the service is provided (see below).

Providers of services and their workers

Services may be provided by sole traders, companies or partnerships. If the providers are companies, they do not need to be owned or controlled by nationals of the Member State in which they are based, nor do the employees of the company providing a service in another Member State have to be EU citizens. The service provider should be able to operate in other Member States without restriction, as illustrated in the following case:

Van der Elst v OMI (Case C-43/93)

The claimant operated a demolition company which was established in Belgium. He employed a number of foreign workers, many of them from Morocco. They had work permits and were lawfully employed in Belgium. The company was engaged to carry out a demolition contract in France. Foreign employees were not permitted by the French authorities to work on the contract without French work permits. The national court referred the case to the Court of Justice under what is now Art 267 TFEU (previously Art 234 EC Treaty). The Court of Justice held that the Belgian undertaking was providing a service under what are now Arts 56 and 57 TFEU (previously Arts 49 and 50 EC Treaty). The question before the Court was whether the company could transfer its workforce to France to service the demolition contract.

The Court of Justice held that where a service was being provided pursuant to what are now Arts 56 and 57 TFEU (previously Arts 49 and 50 EC Treaty), the provider of the service had the right to post its workforce in the host Member State, irrespective of the workforce's nationality. Any attempt to impose further controls on its workforce would amount to an unlawful restriction on the provision of services. The imposition of further work permit requirements would, the Court said, amount to the duplication of the procedures the company had already gone through in its home state.

Directive 96/71, which was subsequently adopted, concerns the posting of workers within the context of the provision of services, i.e. where an individual/undertaking provides services in another Member State, and the service provider sends his own workers to the host

Member State. The following case relates to the rules which may be enacted by Member States with regard to the employment of workers posted from another Member State, in the light of Directive 96/71:

Commission v Germany (Case C-341/02)

The Commission brought an action against Germany for failure to fulfil its Treaty obligations, and questioned the compatibility with Directive 96/71 of the method applied by Germany for the purpose of comparing the minimum wage fixed by national German provisions with the remuneration which was actually paid by an employer established in another Member State.

In its action, the Commission criticised Germany for not recognising, as constituent elements of the minimum wage, all of the allowances and supplements paid by employers established in other Member States to their employees in the construction industry who had been posted to Germany, with the exception of a bonus which was granted to workers in that industry. According to the Commission, the failure to take these allowances and supplements into account resulted – by reason of the different methods of calculating remuneration in other Member States – in higher wage costs for employers established in other Member States, who were thus prevented from offering their services in Germany. While the Commission acknowledged that the host Member State was allowed to determine, under Directive 96/71, the minimum rate of pay, the fact nonetheless remained that the host Member State could not, in comparing that rate and the wages paid by employers established in other Member States, impose its own payment structure.

The German government contested that argument, contending that hours worked outside the normal working hours (i.e. overtime) had a greater economic value than normal working hours and that the bonuses relating to such hours should not be taken into account in the calculation of the minimum wage.

The Court of Justice began by taking note that the parties were in agreement that – in accordance with Directive 96/71 – account need not be taken, as component elements of the minimum wage, of the following: (i) payment for overtime; (ii) contributions to supplementary occupational retirement pension schemes; (iii) the amounts paid in respect of reimbursement of expenses actually incurred by reason of the posting; and (iv) flat-rate sums calculated on a basis other than that of the hourly rate. **It was the gross amounts of wages that must be taken into account**.

The Court then stated that, in the course of the proceedings, Germany had adopted and proposed a number of amendments to its rules, which the Court considered appropriate for removing several of the inconsistencies between German law and the directive. These included, *inter alia*, the taking into account of allowances and supplements paid by an employer which, in the calculation of the minimum wage, did not alter the relationship between the service provided by the worker and the consideration he received in return, and the taking into account, under certain conditions, of the bonuses in respect of the 13th and 14th salary months. However, those amendments were made after the expiry of the period laid down in the reasoned opinion, i.e. too late to be taken into consideration by the Court. Therefore, the Court had to declare that Germany had failed to fulfil its obligations.

Finally, the Court observed that it was entirely normal that, if an employer required a worker to carry out additional work or to work under particular conditions, compensation had to be provided to the worker for those additional services without it being taken into account for the purpose of calculating the minimum wage. Directive 96/71 did not require that such forms of compensation, which, if taken into account in the calculation of the minimum wage, altered the relationship between the service provided and the consideration received in return, be treated as elements of the minimum wage. The Court accordingly dismissed the Commission's action on that point.

The following case also concerned posted workers:

Commission v Germany (Case C-244/04)

Germany's Law on Aliens governed the posting of employed persons who were non-EU nationals. That law provided that foreigners who intended to reside for more than three months on German territory and to pursue paid employment had to be in possession of a specific residence visa. Thus, undertakings which sought to provide services in Germany had to ensure that their workers from non-Member States obtained a visa from the German diplomatic representation in the Member State where the undertaking was established. As regards the detailed rules for the issue of that visa, a circular laid down that the German diplomatic representation had to satisfy itself, in advance, that the worker had been employed for at least a year by the undertaking which intended to effect the posting.

The Commission brought this action against Germany pursuant to the former Art 226 EC Treaty (now Art 258 TFEU), because of Germany's alleged breach of the Union law provisions on the freedom to provide services.

The Court of Justice held that a prior check could make it more difficult, or even impossible, to exercise the freedom to provide services through posted workers who were non-EU nationals, and thus constituted a breach of the Treaty provisions. The Court also held that the requirement of at least a year's prior employment by the undertaking effecting the posting constituted a restriction on the freedom to provide services.

Consequently, the Court of Justice concluded that Germany had infringed the provisions on the freedom to provide services.

Directive 96/71 provides that the terms and conditions of employment guaranteed to workers posted to the host Member State are to be laid down by law, regulation or administrative provision and/or, in the construction sector, by collective agreements or arbitration awards which have been declared universally applicable.

Swedish law on the posting of workers sets out the terms and conditions of employment falling within the matters listed in Directive 96/71, save for minimum rates of pay. Swedish law is silent on remuneration, the determination of which in Sweden is traditionally entrusted to labour and management by way of collective negotiations. Under Swedish law, trade unions are entitled to have recourse to collective action, under certain conditions, which is aimed at forcing any employer both to enter into negotiations on pay and to sign a collective agreement. The following case concerned Directive 96/71, the Swedish law relating to the Directive and the right of trade unions to take collective action (note: this case also considers the issue of objective justification, which is considered in detail in the subsequent section):

Laval un Partneri Ltd v Svenska Byggnadsarbetareförbundet and Others (Case C-341/05)

In May 2004, Laval un Partneri Ltd ('Laval'), a Latvian company, posted workers from Latvia to work on building sites in Sweden. Latvia is a member of the EU. The work was carried out by a subsidiary, L&P Baltic Bygg AB ('Baltic Bygg').

In June 2004, Laval and Baltic Bygg, on the one hand, and the Swedish building and public works trade union, Svenska Byggnadsarbetareförbundet (SB), on the other, began negotiations with a view to determining the rates of pay for the posted workers and to Laval's signing the collective agreement for the building sector. However, the parties were unable to reach an agreement. In September and October, Laval signed collective agreements with the Latvian building sector trade union, to which 65 per cent of the posted workers were affiliated.

On 2 November 2004, SB began collective action in the form of a blockade of all Laval's sites in Sweden. The Swedish electricians' trade union joined in with a sympathy action, the effect of which was to prevent electricians from providing services to Laval. None of the members of those trade unions were employed by Laval. After work had stopped, Baltic Bygg was declared bankrupt and the posted workers returned to Latvia.

The Arbetsdomstolen, before which Laval brought proceedings, *inter alia*, for a declaration as to the lawfulness of the collective action and for compensation for the damage suffered, asked the Court of Justice if Union law precluded trade unions from taking collective action in the circumstances described above.

The Court pointed out that Directive 96/71 did not allow the host Member State to make the provision of services in its territory conditional on the observance of terms and conditions of employment, which went beyond the mandatory rules for minimum protection. As regards the matters referred to in Directive 96/71, the latter expressly laid down the degree of protection which undertakings established in other Member States had to guarantee, in the host Member State, to the workers posted to the territory of the latter.

The Court accepted that the right to take collective action had to be recognised as a fundamental right which formed an integral part of the general principles of Union law the observance of which the Court ensured, but stated that the exercise of that right could be subject to certain restrictions. The fundamental nature of the right to take collective action was not such as to render Union law inapplicable to such action.

In this case, the Court pointed out that the right of trade unions of a Member State to take collective action, by which undertakings established in other Member States could be forced into negotiations with the trade unions of unspecified duration in order to ascertain minimum wage rates and to sign a collective agreement – the terms of which went beyond the minimum protection guaranteed by Directive 96/71 – was liable to make it less attractive, or more difficult, for such undertakings to carry out construction work in Sweden, and therefore constituted a restriction on the freedom to provide services.

A restriction on the freedom to provide services could be justified only if it pursued a legitimate objective compatible with the Treaty and was justified by overriding reasons of public interest. If that was the case, it had to be suitable for securing the attainment of the objective it pursued and not go beyond what was necessary in order to attain it.

In that regard, the Court pointed out that the right to take collective action for the protection of the workers of the host State against possible social dumping could constitute an overriding reason of public interest. In that context, the blockading of sites by a trade union of the host Member State which was aimed at ensuring that workers posted in the framework of a transnational provision of services had their terms and conditions of employment fixed at a certain level, came within the objective of protecting workers.

However, as regards the specific obligations, the obstacle which that action formed could not be justified with regard to such an objective.

As regards the negotiations on pay which the trade unions sought to impose, by way of collective action, on undertakings established in another Member State which posted workers temporarily to their territory, the Court emphasised that Union law did not prohibit Member States from requiring such undertakings to comply with their rules on minimum pay by appropriate means.

However, collective action could not be justified with regard to the public interest objective of protecting workers where the negotiations on pay formed part of a national context characterised by a lack of provisions, of any kind, which were sufficiently precise and accessible that they did not render it impossible or excessively difficult in practice for such an undertaking to determine the obligations with which it was required to comply as regards minimum pay.

Finally, the Court stated that national rules which failed to take into account collective agreements to which undertakings that post workers to Sweden were already bound in the Member State in which they were established, gave rise to discrimination against such undertakings, in so far as under those national rules they were treated in the same way as national undertakings which had not concluded a collective agreement.

The Court stated that it followed from the Treaty that such discriminatory rules could be justified only on grounds of public policy, public security or public health.

The application of those rules to foreign undertakings which were bound by collective agreements to which Swedish law did not directly apply was intended to:

(i) allow trade unions to take action to ensure that all employers active on the Swedish labour market paid wages and applied other terms and conditions of employment in line with those usual in Sweden;

(ii) create a climate of fair competition, on an equal basis, between Swedish employers and entrepreneurs from other Member States.

As none of the considerations constituted grounds of public policy, public security or public health, the Court held that such discrimination could not be justified.

Objective justification

As with the free movement of workers, if a restriction on the freedom to provide services is found to exist, the Member State can seek to justify it on grounds of public policy, public security or public health (Art 52 TFEU), which is applicable by reason of Art 62 TFEU. This is considered in Chapter 15.

As discussed in the above case, the freedom to provide services may also be restricted by rules which are justified by overriding reasons in the general interest, provided the rules are applied to all persons and undertakings operating in the territory of the Member State where the service is provided. The restriction will not be justified if the reason for the restriction is safeguarded by the rules to which the provider of the service is subject in the Member State where he is established (see, in particular, *Commission* v *Italy* (Case C-180/89), and *Commission* v *Greece* (Case C-198/89), para 18). This objective justification defence will only apply to restrictions which are indirectly discriminatory or to those which are non-discriminatory. It is similar to the application of the '*Cassis* rule of reason' relating to the free movement of goods (see Chapter 18).

The *Cassis* rule of reason is fully discussed at pages 623–641.

The nature of the defence was discussed by the Court of Justice in the following case, which concerned a restriction that the provider of the service must satisfy a residence requirement:

Van Binsbergen v Bestuur van de Bedrijfsvereniging voor de Metaalnijverheid (Case 33/74)

A national of the Netherlands acted as legal adviser to the applicant in relation to legal proceedings before a Netherlands' court. The legal adviser moved to Belgium during the course of the proceedings and was told that he could no longer represent the applicant, because under Netherlands' law only persons established in the Netherlands could act as legal advisers. The national court referred the matter to the Court of Justice under what is now Art 267 TFEU (previously Art 234 EC Treaty) to determine whether or not the

Netherlands' rule was compatible with what is now Art 56 TFEU (previously Art 49 EC Treaty). It was undoubtedly indirectly discriminatory because it would be more difficult for a non-national to satisfy than a national. The Court of Justice held that this restriction was contrary to what is now Art 56 TFEU because it was excessive. However, the Court acknowledged that not every restriction would be incompatible with what is now Art 56 TFEU:

12. However, taking into account the particular nature of the services to be provided, specific requirements imposed on the person providing the service cannot be considered incompatible with the Treaty where they have as their purpose the application of professional rules justified by the general good – in particular rules relating to the organisation, qualifications, professional ethics, supervision and liability – which are binding upon any person established in the State in which the service is provided, where the person providing the service would escape from the ambit of those rules by being established in another Member State.

. . .

14. In accordance with those principles, the requirement that persons whose functions are to assist the administration of justice must be permanently established for professional purposes within the jurisdiction of certain courts or tribunals cannot be considered incompatible with the provisions of . . . [Articles Arts 56 and 57 TFEU], where such requirement is objectively justified by the need to ensure observance of professional rules of conduct connected, in particular, with the administration of justice and with respect for professional ethics.

The above case established that for an indirectly discriminatory or non-discriminatory restriction to the provision of a service to be compatible with Art 56 TFEU the restriction must:

1 be adopted in pursuance of a legitimate public interest, which is not incompatible with Union aims (some of these Union aims are set out at para 12 above (e.g. observance of professional ethics));

2 be equally applicable to persons established within the Member State and which would be avoided if the person providing the service was established in another Member State;

3 be objectively justified. This involves an application of the **proportionality test**, i.e.:

- is there a 'genuine need' for the restriction;
- is the restriction appropriate to achieve the aim of such 'genuine need';
- could the aim of such 'genuine need' which is being pursued by the restriction, be satisfied by other, less restrictive means?

In **Van Binsbergen**, the Court of Justice held that the public interest in the proper administration of justice could be achieved by a less restrictive means (i.e. it did not satisfy the proportionality test). Rather than a *place of residence* within the jurisdiction, an *address for service* within the jurisdiction could have been imposed.

The Court of Justice further defined the scope of the objective justification defence in the following case:

Criminal Proceedings against Webb (Case 279/80)

Webb was the manager of a company established in the UK and which was licensed by the UK authorities to act as an agent for the supply of manpower. The company was paid to recruit temporary technical staff for employment by a business located in the Netherlands. Webb was prosecuted for having supplied workers without the necessary licence issued by the Netherlands' authorities. The case was referred to the Court under what is now Art 267 TFEU (previously Art 234 EC Treaty) to consider the compatibility of the licence requirement with what is now Art 56 TFEU (previously Art 49 EC Treaty). In this case, the service being provided was the provision of manpower (from the UK to the Netherlands). The restriction to the freedom to provide services, which was under challenge, was the Netherlands' licence requirement. The Court of Justice held as follows:

> 17. In Cases 110 and 111/78 *Van Wesemael* [1979] ECR 35, the Court held that, regard being had to the particular nature of certain services, specific requirements imposed on the provider of the services cannot be considered incompatible with the Treaty where they have as their purpose the application of rules governing such activities. However, **the freedom to provide services is one of the fundamental principles of the Treaty and may be restricted only by provisions which are justified by the general good and which are imposed on all persons or undertakings operating in the said State in so far as that interest is not safeguarded by the provisions to which the provider of the service is subject in the Member State of his establishment.**
>
> . . .
>
> 20. Such a measure would be excessive in relation to the aim pursued, however, if the requirements to which the issue of a licence is subject coincided with the proofs and guarantees required in the State of establishment. In order to maintain the principle of freedom to provide services **the first requirement is that in considering applications for licences and in granting them, the Member State in which the service is to be provided may not make any distinction based on the nationality of the provider of the services or the place of his establishment; the second requirement is that it must take into account the evidence and guarantees already furnished by the provider of the services for the pursuit of his activities in the Member State of his establishment.** [emphasis added]

In the above case, the Court of Justice (at para 20) set out three conditions which needed to be satisfied in order for the restriction to be objectively justified. The three conditions (similar to those established by the Court in *Van Binsbergen*) are that the restriction must:

1 pursue a justified aim;

2 be equally applicable to nationals, non-nationals and those established within and outside the Member State alike;

3 not be any more restrictive or burdensome than is necessary (i.e. an application of the proportionality test).

This approach was followed by the Court of Justice in the following case:

Questore di Verona v *Diego Zenatti* (Case C-67/98)

Italian law made it a criminal offence to conduct or organise games of chance and prohibited the organisation of games or betting, which were reserved to the state or to organisations holding a state concession. Betting licences were granted by the state to two organisations, which were required to serve to promote sporting activities through investments in sports facilities, especially in the poorest regions and in the peripheral areas of large cities, and to support equine sports and the breeding of horses. The restriction was intended to satisfy social policy concerns (relating to the harmful effects of gambling) and the concern to prevent fraud. These two organisations could authorise other persons and bodies who could offer appropriate safeguards.

Mr Zenatti (Z) had acted as an intermediary in Italy for the London company SSP Overseas Betting Ltd (SSP), a licensed bookmaker. Z ran an information exchange for the Italian customers of SSP in relation to bets on foreign sports events. He would send to London, by fax or internet, forms which had been filled in by customers, together with bank transfer forms. He would receive faxes from SSP for transmission to the same customers. Action was taken against Z because he had not been licensed to provide such a service in Italy, and he was ordered by the national court to cease the activity. The Italian court referred the case to the Court of Justice pursuant to what is now Art 267 TFEU (previously Art 234 EC Treaty), to consider whether the restriction was compatible with the Union law provisions on the freedom to provide services. The Court of Justice held as follows:

> The Italian legislation, inasmuch as it prohibits the taking of bets by any person or body other than those which may be licensed to do so, applies without distinction to all operators who might be interested in such an activity, whether established in Italy or in another Member State.
>
> However, such legislation constitutes an obstacle to the freedom to provide services.
>
> **The Court thus verifies whether that restriction on the freedom to provide services is permissible under the exceptions expressly provided for by the Treaty or is justified, in accordance with the case law of the Court, by overriding reasons relating to the public interest.**
>
> The legislation at issue in the main proceedings pursues objectives similar to those pursued by the UK legislation on lotteries, as identified by the Court in *Schindler*, since it seeks to prevent such gaming from being a source of private profit, to avoid risks of crime and fraud and the damaging individual and social consequences of the incitement to spend which it represents and to allow it only to the extent to which it may be socially useful as being conducive to the proper conduct of competitive sports.
>
> **Those objectives must be considered together. They concern the protection of the recipients of the service and, more generally, of consumers as well as the maintenance of order in society and have already been held to rank among those objectives which may be regarded as constituting overriding reasons relating to the public interest. Moreover, measures based on such reasons must be suitable for securing attainment of the objectives pursued and not go beyond what is necessary to attain them.**
>
> Determination of the scope of the protection which a Member State intends providing in its territory in relation to lotteries and other forms of gambling falls within the margin of appreciation which the Court recognised as being enjoyed by the national authorities. It is for those authorities to consider whether, in the context of the aim pursued, it is necessary to prohibit activities of that kind, totally or partially, or only to restrict them and lay down more or less rigorous procedures for controlling them.
>
> The provisions adopted must be assessed solely in the light of the objectives pursued by the national authorities of the Member State concerned and of the level of protection which they seek to ensure.
>
> The fact that the games in issue are not totally prohibited is not enough to show that the national legislation is not in reality intended to achieve the public-interest objectives at which it is purportedly aimed, which must be considered as a whole. Limited authorisation of gambling on the basis of special or exclusive rights granted or assigned to certain bodies, which has the advantage of confining the desire to gamble and the exploitation of gambling within controlled channels, of preventing the risk of fraud or crime in the context of such exploitation, and of using the resulting profits for public-interest purposes, likewise falls within the ambit of those objectives.
>
> **However, such a limitation is acceptable only if, from the outset, it reflects a concern to bring about a genuine diminution in gambling opportunities and if the financing of social activities through a levy on the proceeds of authorised games constitutes only an**

> incidental beneficial consequence and not the real justification for the restrictive policy adopted. Even if it is not irrelevant that lotteries and other types of gambling may contribute significantly to the financing of benevolent or public-interest activities, that motive cannot in itself be regarded as an objective justification for restrictions on the freedom to provide services.
>
> It is for the national court to verify whether, having regard to the specific rules governing its application, the national legislation is genuinely directed to realising the objectives which are capable of justifying it and whether the restrictions which it imposes do not appear disproportionate in the light of those objectives. [emphasis added]

In the above case, the Court of Justice held that the Union provisions on the freedom to provide services do not prevent national legislation reserving to certain bodies the right to take bets on sporting events, provided that the legislation is justified by social policy objectives which are intended to limit the harmful effects of such activities and if the restrictions it imposes are not disproportionate in relation to those objectives. The Court further held that where a contribution is made from the profits of the authorised provider to benevolent activities, this contribution should constitute only an *incidental beneficial concern*. It should not be the real justification for the restriction. The justification must be based on overriding reasons relating to the public interest (e.g. confining the desire to gamble; preventing the risk of fraud or other criminal activity).

The Court of Justice had to adjudicate on betting over the internet in *Gambelli* (Case C-243/01). The Court held that Italian legislation, which made it punishable as a criminal offence, without a concession or licence from the state, to collect, accept, register or transmit proposed bets, particularly on sporting events via the internet, was contrary to what are now Arts 49 and 56 TFEU. However, the Court held that the restriction could be objectively justified on moral, religious and/or cultural grounds. In deciding whether or not the restriction was objectively justified, consideration could be given to the morally and financially harmful consequences for the individual and society. Following on from this case, *Liga Portuguesa de Futebol Profissional (CA/LPFP) and Bwin International Limited v Departamento de Jogos da Santa Casa da Misericórdia de Lisboa* (Case C-42/07) concerned the grant, by Portugal, of the sole and exclusive right to operate lotteries, lotto games and sporting bets over the internet. The body to which this sole and exclusive right was granted was a non-profit-making organisation which operated under the strict control of the Portuguese authorities. Portugal claimed its objective was to prevent the operation of such activities over the internet for fraudulent and criminal purposes. This sole and exclusive right was challenged. The Court of Justice reaffirmed that because of the specific features associated with the offering of games of chance (i.e. gambling) over the internet, a prohibition may be objectively justified on the grounds of combating fraud and crime. Similar decisions were reached by the Court of Justice in the following cases, which regulated games of chance: *Sporting Exchange v Minister van Justitie and Ladbrokes Betting & Gaming* and *Ladbrokes International v Stichting de Nationale Sporttotalisator* (Case C-203/08 and Case C-258/08); *Criminal proceedings against Otto Sjöberg and Anders Gerdin* (Joined Cases C-447/08 and C-448/08); and *Zeturf Ltd v Premier ministre* (Case C-212/08).

On the facts of the following cases, the Court of Justice held that a public monopoly for the organisation of sporting bets and lotteries could *not* be objectively justified, because the regulation at issue did not limit games of chance in a consistent and systematic manner:

Winner Wetten GmbH v *Bürgermeisterin der Stadt Bergheim* (Case C-409/06); *Markus Stoss and Others* v *Wetteraukreis* and *Kulpa Automatenservice Asperg GmbH and Others* v *Land Baden-Württemberg* (Joined Cases C-316/07, C-358/07 to C-360/07, C-409/07 and C-410/07); and *Carmen Media Group Ltd* v *Land Schleswig-Holstein and Others* (Case C-46/08)

In Germany, jurisdiction over gambling was divided between the federal State and the Länder. In most of the Länder, there was a regional monopoly for the organisation of sporting bets and lotteries, while the organisation of bets on horse racing and the operation of gaming machines and casinos were entrusted to duly authorised private operators.

By the treaty on lotteries in Germany (Lotteriestaatsvertrag), which came into force on 1 July 2004, the Länder created a uniform framework for the organisation of games of chance, apart from casinos. Following a judgment of the Budesverfassungsgericht (German Federal Constitutional Court), that treaty was replaced by the treaty on games of chance in Germany (Glücksspielstaatsvertrag), which entered into force on 1 January 2008. The latter treaty prohibited all organisation or intermediation of public games of chance on the internet.

The present cases, which came before various German courts, were referred to the Court of Justice for a preliminary ruling. The Court of Justice was asked to rule on the compatibility of the German rules on games of chance with Union law.

Joined Cases C-316/07, C-358/07 to C-360/07, C-409/07 and C-410/07 prohibited intermediaries from offering sporting bets organised by Austrian, Maltese and UK betting companies. Those companies held authorisations to organise sporting bets in their respective countries.

Case C-46/08 concerned the rejection of an application of the Carmen Media Group for authorisation to offer sporting bets in Germany via the internet. Carmen Media Group held an 'off-shore' licence in Gibraltar (where it is established), authorising it to organise bets only outside Gibraltar.

Case C-409/06 concerned a dispute between an intermediary for sporting bets, acting on behalf of a Maltese betting company and the German authorities.

The Court of Justice held that the German rules on sporting bets constituted a restriction on the freedom to provide services (and the freedom of establishment). Nevertheless, the Court stated that **such a restriction could be justified by imperative reasons in the public interest, such as preventing incitement to squander on gambling and combating gambling addiction**. However, the national measures for attaining those objectives had to be suitable and had to be limited to the restrictions necessary for that purpose.

In that regard, the Court considered that, with a view to channelling the desire to gamble and the operation of games into a controlled circuit, Member States were free to establish public monopolies. In particular, such a monopoly was likely to overcome the risks connected with the gaming industry more effectively than a system under which private operators were authorised to organise bets subject to compliance with the relevant legislation.

The Court stated that the fact that some games of chance were subject to a public monopoly whilst others were subject to a system of authorisations issued to private operators could not, in itself, call into question the consistency of the German system as those games had different characteristics.

However, the Court of Justice held that the German courts were right to take the view that **the German rules did not limit games of chance in a consistent and systematic manner** for the following two reasons: (i) the holders of public monopolies carried out intensive advertising campaigns with a view to maximising profits from lotteries, thereby departing from the objectives justifying the existence of those monopolies; and (ii) with regard to games of chance such as casino games and automated games, which did not fall within the public monopoly but carried a greater risk of addiction than games which were subject to that monopoly, the German authorities carried out or tolerated policies designed to encourage participation in those games. In such circumstances, **the preventive objective of that monopoly could no longer be pursued, so that the monopoly ceased to be justifiable.**

The Court of Justice noted, however, that Member States had a broad discretion in determining the level of protection against the dangers emanating from games of chance. In the absence of any Union harmonisation in the matter, Member States were not required to recognise authorisations issued by other Member States in that area. For the same reasons, and having regard to the risks posed by games of chance on the internet in comparison with traditional games of chance, Member States could also prohibit the offering of games of chance on the internet.

Two subsequent cases concerning games of chance, which centred around the issue of objective justification, are: *Criminal proceedings against Jochen Dickinger and Franz Ömer* (Case C-347/09); and *Stanleybet International Ltd and Others* v *Ypourgos Oikonomias kai Oikonomikon and Others* (Joined Cases C-186/11 and C-209/11).

HIT and HIT LARIX v *Bundesminister für Finanzen* (Case C-176/11) concerned Austrian legislation which required prior authorisation for the advertising of casinos which were located in another Member State. The Court of Justice held that such legislation, which restricted the freedom to provide services, was justified by the objective of protecting the population against the risks connected with games of chance. Given that objective, the Court held that it did not appear to constitute an excessive burden for the operators of foreign casinos and was accordingly capable of complying with the principle of proportionality.

The above cases considered the issue of objective justification in the context of games of chance. The following cases consider the issue of objective justification in various other contexts.

FKP Scorpio Konzertproduktionen (Case C-290/04) concerned national legislation under which a procedure of retention of tax at source was applied to payments made to providers of services not resident in the Member State in which the services were provided, whereas payments made to resident providers of services were not subject to a retention. The Court of Justice held that the obligation on the recipient of services to make a retention if he is not to incur liability was a breach of what is now Art 56 TFEU. It constituted indirect discrimination because the non-residency rule would apply primarily to non-nationals. The Court held, however, that such legislation was justified by the need to ensure the effective collection of income tax from persons established outside the Member State of taxation and constituted a means which was proportionate to the objective pursued.

In *Duomo Gpa Srl and Others* v *Comune di Baranzate and Others* (Joined Cases C-357/10 to C-359/10), Italy awarded contracts to third parties for the collection of taxes. To be considered for a contract, a private company required a fully paid-up share capital of 10 million euros. The only ground of justification put forward for this requirement was the need to protect public authorities against possible non-performance by the contractor, in the light of the high overall value of the contracts awarded. In practice, the contractors, by first collecting the tax revenue, would hold and deal with millions of euros which they were required to pay over to the public authorities. The Court of Justice did not rule out the possibility that such an objective could constitute an overriding reason in the public interest. However, it noted that a restriction of the fundamental freedoms could only be justified if the relevant measure was appropriate for ensuring the attainment of the legitimate objective pursued and did not go beyond what was necessary to attain that objective. According to the national court which had referred the case to the Court of Justice, other provisions were capable of providing adequate protection for public authorities (e.g. proof of the contractor's technical and financial capacity, creditworthiness and solvency and/ or the application of minimum thresholds for share capital that varied depending on the value of the contracts actually awarded to the contractor). Consequently, the Court held that, as the Italian provision went beyond the objective of protecting the public authorities against non-performance by the contractor, it contained disproportionate, and therefore unjustified, restrictions of the fundamental freedoms.

The three *Van Binsbergen* conditions were applied by the Court of Justice in ***Commission v France*** (Case C-262/02). This case concerned a French regulation that French broadcasters could only transmit sporting events taking place in another Member State if any advertising for alcoholic beverages was removed. The French sought to justify the restriction on public health grounds. The Court of Justice held that although the French regulation was in breach of what is now Art 56 TFEU, it was objectively justified and it was proportionate.

The case of ***Football Association Premier League and Others* v *QC Leisure and Others*; *Karen Murphy* v *Media Protection Services Ltd*** (Cases C-403/08 and C-429/08) concerned the grant of the exclusive right to broadcast live English Premier League football games. The English Football Association Premier League granted broadcasters the exclusive right on a territorial basis. In the agreement, the broadcaster was required to encrypt its signal and only to transmit the encrypted signal to subscribers, in order to prevent access to subscribers outside the territory. The agreement prohibited the broadcaster from supplying decoder cards to persons outside the territory. The Court of Justice held that the prohibition on the import, sale or use of decoder cards to persons outside the territory was contrary to the freedom to provide services and could not be justified either in light of the objective of protecting **intellectual property rights** or by the objective of encouraging the public to attend football stadiums.

The *Van Binsbergen* case made it clear (at para 20) that the proportionality test requires that any restrictions imposed by the Member State in which the provider is established should be taken into consideration, as it may duplicate the restrictive measures. For example, where a licence is required, both Member States may have licensing requirements. Therefore the licence requirement of the Member State in which the service is to be provided may not be necessary. This is illustrated in the following case:

Jean-Claude Arblade, Arblade & Fils SARL; Bernard Leloup, Serge Leloup, Sofrage SARL (Cases C-369 and 376/96)

The Court of Justice had to decide whether a company established within the Union, which provided services in another Member State and posted its own workforce in the host Member State for the duration of the contract, had to comply with the host state's social legislation designed to safeguard the rights of workers (e.g. a requirement that certain social and labour documents had to be kept). The Court held that this constituted a restriction on the freedom to provide services within the meaning of the former Art 49 EC Treaty (now Art 56 TFEU). However, it held that the restriction could be justified (and would therefore be compatible with the Treaty obligations) if it was necessary in order to safeguard, effectively and by appropriate means, the overriding public interest the social protection of workers represented. Nevertheless, the Court stated that the national court would also have to assess whether the objective of the host state's legislation was satisfied by legislation the service provider had to comply with in his home Member State, in which case the restriction could not be justified. The Court of Justice stated that this would be the case where:

> . . . the undertaking is already subject, in the Member State in which it is established, to obligations which are comparable, as regards their objective of safeguarding the interests of workers, to those imposed by the legislation of the host Member State, and which relate to the same workers and the same periods of activity.

While the Court is reluctant to recognise new 'overriding interests in the general interest', it will, in exceptional circumstances, accept that such interests enable a Member State to impose a total ban on the import of the service in question, even when it is permitted, within strict limitations, in the Member State imposing the ban (*Schindler*, above).

The case of *Geraets-Smits v Stichting Ziekenfonds* and *Peerbooms v Stichting CZ Groep Zorgverzekeringen* (Case C-157/99 – see below) considered the application of objective justification in the context of recipients of services, and therefore it is considered in the next section.

Recipients of services

Article 56 TFEU expressly refers to the freedom to provide services but does not mention the recipient. However, secondary legislation does acknowledge the recipient: the former Directive 64/221 protected the position of a recipient of services who resided in or travelled to another Member State for that purpose; the former Art 1(b), Directive 73/148 required the abolition of restrictions on the movement and residence of nationals wishing to go to another Member State as recipients (as well as providers) of services. These two directives were repealed and replaced by Directive 2004/38, which, as discussed above, creates a general right of entry and residence for up to three months for all EU citizens and their family members without any conditions or formalities, other than the requirement to hold a valid identity card or passport, or, in the case of non-EU family members, a passport (Art 6). Article 7, Directive 2004/38 creates a right of extended residence in excess of three months for EU citizens and their family members who, *inter alia*, are **economically self-sufficient** (i.e. who have sufficient resources for themselves and their family members not to become a burden on the social assistance system of the host Member State during their period of residence and have comprehensive sickness insurance cover in the host Member State).

In the following case, the Court of Justice held that the Treaty provisions cover the recipients of services:

Luisi and Carbone v Ministero del Tesoro (Cases 286/82 and 26/83)

The applicants were Italian nationals who were prosecuted for attempting to export more than the legal maximum of Italian currency for use abroad. They argued that they had exported it for use within the Union to pay for services as tourists and to purchase medical treatment. They further argued that the currency restrictions were contrary to Union law.

The Court was asked whether the restrictions were covered by the rules on the payment for services covered by what are now Arts 123, 56 and 57 TFEU (previously Arts 107, 49 and 50 EC Treaty). The Court of Justice held as follows:

10. By virtue of . . . [Article 56 TFEU], restrictions on freedom to provide such services are to be abolished in respect of nationals of Member States who are established in a Member State other than that of the person for whom the service is intended. In order to enable services to be provided, the person providing the services may go to the Member State where the person for whom it is to be provided is established or else the latter may go to the State in which the person providing the service is established. Whilst the former case is expressly mentioned in the third paragraph of . . . [Article 57 TFEU], which permits the person providing the service to pursue his activity temporarily in the Member State where the service is provided, the latter case is the necessary corollary thereof, which fulfils the objective of liberalising all gainful activity not covered by the free movement of goods, persons and capital.

. . .

16. It follows that the freedom to provide services includes the freedom, for the recipient of services, to go to another Member State in order to receive a service there, without being obstructed by restrictions, even in relation to payments and that tourists, persons receiving medical treatment and persons travelling for the purposes of education or business are to be regarded as recipients of services. [emphasis added]

In the above case, the Court of Justice held that tourism itself was a service which was covered by what is now Art 56 TFEU. In *Cowan v Le Trésor Public* (Case 186/87), the Court of Justice declared that tourists were entitled to full equal treatment under what is now Art 18 TFEU, and that equal treatment included access to the criminal process and to national provisions on criminal injuries compensation. In addition, leisure activities pursued by recipients of services from other Member States must not be subject to discriminatory treatment (*Commission v Greece* (Case C-62/96); *Commission v Spain* (Case C-45/93); *Commission v Italy* (Case C-388/01)). Equal treatment under Art 18 TFEU, within the context of Art 56 TFEU, is considered in more detail below.

Recipients of services were, like providers, entitled to remain in the host Member State only for as long as the service was received. However, given the breadth of the concept of 'services', it would seem that any EU citizen or national of an EEA state could remain in another Member State for as long as he was paying for a service. He could, for example, be paying for accommodation out of his own resources. As long as he was relying exclusively on his own resources, however modest, he was providing 'remuneration' and would seem to be entitled to remain under Arts 56 and 57 TFEU; and see *Belgium v Humbel* (Case 263/86). Article 7, Directive 2004/38 now makes this explicitly clear. As discussed above, Art 7 creates a right of extended residence (for more than three months) for EU citizens and their family members who, *inter alia*, are economically self-sufficient.

Objective justification

As discussed above in the context of providers of services, the freedom to provide services may be restricted by rules which are justified by overriding reasons in the general interest. The following case concerned the application of objective justification within the context of recipients of services:

Geraets-Smits v *Stichting Ziekenfonds and Peerbooms* v *Stichting CZ Groep Zorgverzekeringen* (Case C-157/99)

This case concerned two citizens of the Netherlands who were resident there. Payment for medical treatment was made by the appropriate sickness insurance fund. The fund holder reached agreements with providers within the Netherlands for the payment of particular hospital and medical services. Although a person could go to *another* Member State to receive medical services, the Netherlands' legislation provided that this was subject to prior authorisation which would only be granted if: (i) the proposed treatment was among the benefits for which the sickness insurance scheme assumed responsibility, which meant that the treatment had to be regarded as 'normal in the professional circles concerned'; and (ii) the treatment abroad was necessary in terms of the medical condition of the person concerned, which supposed that adequate care could not be provided without undue delay by a care provider which had entered into an agreement with the sickness insurance fund in the Netherlands.

The facts of the case were that Geraets-Smits (the first applicant) left the Netherlands to seek treatment in Germany for Parkinson's disease. Her application to the sickness insurance fund was rejected because: (i) the treatment she received was not regarded as 'normal treatment within the professional circles concerned' because the specific type of treatment she received in Germany was not considered any better than that she would have received in the Netherlands; and (ii) satisfactory and adequate treatment was available in the Netherlands at an establishment which had an agreement with the sickness insurance fund.

Peerbooms (the second applicant) left the Netherlands to seek treatment in Austria when he fell into a coma following a road accident. His application was also refused by the sickness insurance fund on the same grounds that Geraets-Smits's application was refused.

The national court referred the case to the Court of Justice pursuant to what is now Art 267 TFEU (previously Art 234 EC Treaty).

The Court of Justice stated that Member States had the power to organise their social security schemes (in this case medical insurance funds) and to determine the conditions concerning the right or duty to be insured with a social security scheme. However, Member States had to comply with Union law when exercising this power.

Medical activities came within the scope of the former Art 50 EC Treaty (now Art 57 TFEU). The fact that the national legislation at issue was social security legislation did not exclude the application of the former Arts 49 and 50 EC Treaty (now Arts 56 and 57 TFEU). When considering the two conditions (established by national legislation) which were applied by the sickness insurance funds, the former Art 49 EC Treaty (now Art 56 TFEU) precluded the application of any national rules which had the effect of making the provision of services between Member States more difficult than the provision of services purely within one Member State. The Court held that the necessity to obtain prior authorisation which would only be granted if the two conditions were satisfied deterred, or even prevented, insured persons from applying to providers of medical services established in another Member State and therefore constituted, both for insured persons and service providers, a barrier to the freedom to provide services.

The Court then had to determine whether or not these conditions could be objectively justified.

The Court recognised that, as regards the objective of maintaining a balanced medical and hospital service open to all, that objective, even if intrinsically linked to the method of financing the social security system, could also fall within the derogations on grounds of public health under what is now Art 52 TFEU (previously Art 46 EC Treaty), in so far as the objective contributed to the attainment of a high level of health protection. The

Court also stated that what is now Art 52 TFEU (previously Art 46 EC Treaty) permitted Member States to restrict the freedom to provide medical and hospital services in so far as the maintenance of treatment capacity or medical competence on national territory was essential for the public health, and even the survival, of the population.

The Court stated that it was necessary to determine whether the national legislation at issue in these proceedings could actually be justified in the light of these overriding reasons and, in such a case, to ensure that: (i) they did not exceed what was objectively necessary for that purpose; and (ii) the same result could not be achieved by less restrictive rules. This was an application of the proportionality test.

With regard to the prior authorisation requirement, the Court held that this did not breach Union law. However, the two conditions which were attached to the grant of such authorisation had to be justified with regard to the overriding considerations considered above, and had to also satisfy the requirement of proportionality.

With regard to the condition that the proposed treatment was 'normal', the Court noted that in applying this condition the Netherlands' sickness insurance funds only considered what was 'normal' within medical circles in the Netherlands. Although the Court stated that it was open to a Member State to limit its costs by excluding certain products or hospital and medical treatments from reimbursement under its social security scheme, the Court held that in determining what was 'normal', consideration had to be given to wider international medical views, i.e. it was necessary to consider what was normal according to the state of international medical science, and medical standards which were generally accepted at international level.

With regard to the condition concerning the 'necessity' of the proposed treatment, the Court held that this was justified provided that the condition was construed to the effect that authorisation to receive treatment in another Member State may be refused on that ground only if the same or equally effective treatment could be obtained without undue delay from an establishment with which the insured person's sickness insurance fund had contractual arrangements.

In the following case, the Court of Justice reaffirmed its position in *Smits* and *Peerbooms*, with regard to the following two conditions: (i) making repayment of medical expenses incurred in a Member State other than that of affiliation subject to a requirement of prior authorisation; and (ii) providing that such prior authorisation will only be issued in the case of medical necessity. The Court proceeded to consider the issue of objective justification:

Müller-Fauré and van Riet (C-385/99)

In order to establish whether or not the national legislation requiring prior authorisation was objectively justified, the Court distinguished between *hospital care* and *non-hospital care*. With regard to *hospital care*, making repayment of medical expenses subject to prior acceptance of financial responsibility by the national social security system in cases where such care was provided in a Member State other than that of affiliation was, in the Court's view, a measure both reasonable and necessary. This did not compromise the planning of such care operated through the system of health service agreements (*Smits* and *Peerbooms*). That planning was designed to ensure that there was sufficient and permanent accessibility to a balanced range of high-quality hospital treatment and to control costs, preventing, as far as possible, any wastage of financial, technical and human resources. The Court did, however, go on to hold that, for the system of prior authorisation to be capable of operating, the conditions placed on the granting of such authorisation had to be justified and satisfy the requirement of proportionality. Similarly, a scheme of prior administrative authorisation could not legitimise discretionary decisions taken by the national authorities which were liable to negate the effectiveness of Union law provisions on the freedom to provide services. Such a scheme therefore had to be based on objective, non-discriminatory criteria which were known in advance, in such a way as to circumscribe the exercise of the national authorities' discretion, so that it was not used arbitrarily (*Smits* and *Peerbooms*).

Finally, still following *Smits* and *Peerbooms*, the Court held that the condition which specified that the treatment had to be 'necessary' could be justified under the former Art 49 EC Treaty (now Art 56 TFEU) provided it was interpreted as meaning that prior authorisation could be refused only where treatment which was the same or equally effective for the patient could be obtained without undue delay, within the state of affiliation, from an establishment with which the insured person's sickness insurance fund had an agreement.

With regard to *non-hospital care*, the Court held that the information in the documents brought before it for assessment did not demonstrate that removing the requirement for prior authorisation would cause cross-border movements of patients so large as to seriously undermine the financial stability of the social security system and thereby threaten the overall level of public health protection. Furthermore, such care was generally provided near to the place where the patient resided, in a cultural environment which was familiar to him and which allowed him to build up a relationship of trust with the doctor treating him. Those factors were likely to limit any possible financial impact on the national social security system in question of removing the requirement for prior authorisation in respect of care provided in foreign practitioners' surgeries. Bearing in mind that it was for the Member States alone to determine the extent of the sickness cover available to insured persons, and finding that, in this case, the actual amount in respect of which reimbursement was sought was relatively small (para 106), the Court concluded that removing the requirement for prior authorisation issued by sickness funds to their insured persons, so as to enable them to benefit from such healthcare provided in a Member State other than the state of affiliation, was not likely to undermine the essential features of the sickness insurance scheme in question. The system requiring such prior authorisation for *non-hospital care* was therefore incompatible with the former Art 49 EC Treaty (now Art 56 TFEU).

In the above case, the Court of Justice distinguished between *hospital care* and *non-hospital care*. In the case of *hospital care*, the Court held that the restrictions imposed by national legislation (requiring prior authorisation etc.) were *prima facie* compatible with Union law, provided such restrictions were necessary and proportionate. However, in the case of *non-hospital care*, the Court held that such restrictions were incompatible with Union law because they could not be objectively justified *per se*.

In the following case, the Court of Justice referred to its judgments in *Smits* and *Peerbooms*, and *Müller-Fauré* and *van Riet*, in the context of restrictions imposed on persons seeking to travel to another Member State to seek hospital treatment (i.e. hospital care):

Inizan (Case C-56/01)

The Court of Justice was required to consider whether a national system established by the former Art 22(1)(c)(i) and (2), Regulation 1408/71 (now Regulation 883/2004) was compatible with the former Arts 49 and 50 EC Treaty (now Arts 56 and 57 TFEU). This system:

(i) required that the competent social security institution give prior authorisation before assuming financial responsibility for benefits-in-kind provided to the affiliated person on its behalf by the institution where the affiliated person was staying;

(ii) made the grant of such authorisation subject to conditions.

The Court examined the compatibility with the former Art 22(1)(c)(i) and (2), Regulation 1408/71 (now Regulation 883/2004) and the former Arts 49 and 50 EC Treaty (now Arts 56 and 57 TFEU), of the conditions for granting prior authorisation for the reimbursement of care costs incurred in a Member State other than the affiliated person's state of residence.

With regard to the former Regulation 1408/71 (now Regulation 883/2004), the Court considered the condition which stipulated that the treatment the patient intended to undergo in a Member State other than that in which he resided must not be capable of being given to him within the time normally necessary for obtaining the treatment in question in the Member State of residence, taking account of his current state of health and the probable course of the disease. The Court held that this was not fulfilled whenever it appeared that an identical course of treatment, or one with the same degree of effectiveness for the patient, could be obtained in time in the Member State of residence.

In assessing whether that was the case, the competent institution was required to take into account all the circumstances of each particular case, paying due regard not only to the medical situation of the patient at the time authorisation was applied for and, where appropriate, to the degree of his pain or the nature of his disability, which might, for example, make it impossible or excessively difficult to work, but also to his previous history (*Smits* and *Peerbooms*, and *Müller-Fauré* and *van Riet*).

With regard to the former Arts 49 and 50 EC Treaty (now Arts 56 and 57 TFEU), the Court repeated its findings in *Smits* and *Peerbooms*, and *Müller-Fauré* and *van Riet*. It thus held that those findings did not preclude legislation of a Member State which: (i) made reimbursement of the cost of hospital care provided in a Member State other than that in which the insured person's sickness fund was established, conditional upon prior authorisation by that fund; and (ii) made the grant of that authorisation subject to the condition that the insured person could not receive the treatment appropriate to his condition within the territory of the Member State where the fund was established. However, authorisation could be refused on that ground only if treatment which was the same or equally effective for the patient could be obtained without undue delay in the territory of the Member State in which he resided.

In the above case, national legislation required an 'insured person' to obtain prior authorisation before travelling to another Member State to receive hospital care. The national legislation stated that such authorisation would only be granted if the 'insured person' could not receive appropriate treatment within his home Member State. The Court of Justice held that authorisation could only be refused if the appropriate treatment (which had to be the same or equally effective to that which the insured person was seeking in the other Member State), was available in the insured person's home Member State 'without undue delay'.

The following case considered the same issue of travelling to another Member State to receive medical treatment, and whether restrictions imposed could be objectively justified:

Commission v *France* (Case C-512/08)

Provisions of the French Social Security Code made reimbursement in respect of planned medical treatment, which would be received *outside of a hospital setting* in another Member State, subject to prior authorisation by the competent French institution if that treatment required the use of *major medical equipment*. The Commission took action against France, arguing that this was contrary to the freedom to provide services.

The 'major medical equipment' included, for example, nuclear magnetic resonance imaging or spectrometry apparatus used to detect and treat, in particular, cancer and certain cerebral palsies.

The Court stated that medical services supplied for consideration came within the scope of the freedom to provide services, and there was no need to distinguish treatment provided in a hospital environment from treatment provided outside such an environment (i.e. the Court treated both as coming within the scope of 'hospital care').

The Court further stated that the freedom to provide services included the freedom for the recipients of services, including persons in need of medical treatment, to go to another Member State in order to receive those services there without being hampered by restrictions. The prior authorisation required under French legislation for reimbursement in respect of medical treatment involving the use of major medical equipment was capable of deterring, or even preventing, persons insured under the French system from applying to providers of medical services established in another Member State. This therefore constituted a restriction on the freedom to provide services.

However, regardless of the setting, hospital or otherwise, in which it was installed and used, the Court of Justice stated that it had to be possible for the major medical equipment (exhaustively listed in the Public Health Code) to be the subject of planning policy with particular regard to quantity and geographical distribution. This would help ensure a rationalised, stable, balanced and accessible supply of up-to-date treatment. It would also avoid, as far as possible, any waste of financial, technical and human resources, because of the high cost of purchasing and using the equipment necessary for detecting and treating cancer.

Consequently, having regard to the dangers both to the organisation of public health policy and to the balance of the financial social security system, the requirement of prior authorisation for that type of treatment was a justified restriction.

The Court noted, however, that a prior authorisation scheme had to be based on objective, non-discriminatory criteria known in advance, to ensure that the exercise of the national authorities' discretion was not used arbitrarily. Such a system had to be based on a procedural system which was easily accessible and capable of ensuring that a request for authorisation would be dealt with objectively and impartially within a reasonable time. It also had to be possible for refusals to grant authorisation to be challenged in judicial proceedings.

Commission v *Portugal* (Case C-255/09) came before the Court of Justice shortly after the Court had given judgment in *Commission* v *France* (Case C-512/08). Portuguese legislation provided for the reimbursement of non-hospital medical care which was 'highly specialised' if this could not be provided in Portugal. Reimbursement was subject to a threefold prior authorisation: (i) a detailed medical report in favour of the treatment; (ii) approval of that report by the medical director of the hospital service; and (iii) the consent of the Director General for Hospitals. For other non-hospital medical care, Portuguese law provided no possibility of reimbursement. The Court held that Portuguese law breached the Treaty provisions on the freedom to provide services in so far as: (i) prior authorisation was required for 'highly specialised' non-hospital treatment, where such treatment did not involve the use of major and costly equipment; and (ii) there was no possibility of reimbursement for all other non-hospital treatment (e.g. consultation with a general practitioner or dentist), where such treatment did not involve the use of major and costly equipment.

In order to facilitate the free movement of 'insured persons' seeking to exercise their Union law rights to travel to another Member State to seek medical treatment, the E112 scheme was introduced across the EU. It is now referred to as the S2 scheme. Under the S2 scheme, the authorising Member State will issue the insured person with an S2 form. This provides proof to the medical services within the host Member State that the insured person has received the necessary authorisation. Application of the former E112 (now S2) scheme was one of the issues that arose in the following case:

R, on the application of Yvonne Watts v Bedford Primary Care Trust and the Secretary of State for Health (Case C-372/04)

Under Union law, the former E112 (now S2) scheme enabled an application to be made for authorisation to travel abroad in order to receive treatment there. That authorisation could not be refused where the treatment in question was normally available in the Member State of residence but could not be provided there in the individual case without undue delay. The health insurance fund was then required to reimburse the cost of treating the patient.

Suffering from arthritis of the hips, Mrs Watts applied to the Bedford PCT (the primary healthcare fund for Bedford, England) for authorisation to undergo surgery abroad under the former E112 scheme. In that context, a consultant saw her in October 2002 who classified her case as 'routine', which meant a wait of one year for surgery. The Bedford PCT refused to issue Mrs Watts with an E112 form (now an S2 form) on the ground that treatment could be provided to the patient 'within the government's NHS Plan targets' and therefore 'without undue delay'. Mrs Watts lodged an application with the High Court for judicial review of the decision refusing authorisation.

Following deterioration in her state of health, she was re-examined in January 2003 and was listed for surgery within three or four months. Bedford PCT repeated its refusal but in March 2003 Mrs Watts underwent a hip replacement operation in France for which she paid £3,900. She therefore continued with her application in the High Court, claiming in addition reimbursement of the medical fees incurred in France. The High Court dismissed the application on the ground that Mrs Watts had not had to face undue delay after the re-examination of her case in January 2003. Both Mrs Watts and the Secretary of State for Health appealed against that judgment. In those circumstances, the Court of Appeal referred to the Court of Justice questions on the scope of the former Regulation 1408/71 (now Regulation 883/2004) and the Treaty provisions concerning the freedom to provide services.

The scope of the former Regulation 1408/71 (now Regulation 883/2004); see Chapter 14

The Court of Justice stated that under the former Regulation 1408/71 (now Regulation 883/2004), the competent institution issued prior authorisation for reimbursement of the cost of the treatment provided abroad only if it could not be provided within the time normally necessary for obtaining the treatment in question in the Member State of residence.

The Court stated that, in order to be entitled to refuse to grant authorisation on the ground of waiting time, the competent institution had to establish that the waiting time, arising from objectives relating to the planning and management of the supply of hospital care, did not exceed the period which was acceptable in the light of an objective medical assessment of the clinical needs of the person concerned in the light of his medical condition and the history and probable course of his illness, the degree of pain he was in and/or the nature of his disability at the time when the authorisation was sought.

Furthermore, the setting of waiting times should be done flexibly and dynamically, so that the period initially notified to the person concerned could be reconsidered in the light of any deterioration in his state of health occurring after the first request for authorisation.

In the present case, the Court stated that it was for the referring court to determine whether the waiting time invoked by the competent body of the NHS exceeded a medically acceptable period in the light of the patient's particular condition and clinical needs.

The scope of the freedom to provide services
The Court held that in a situation in which a person whose state of health necessitates hospital treatment goes to another Member State and there receives the treatment in question for which payment is made, comes within the scope of the provisions on freedom to provide services regardless of the way in which the national system operates with which that person is registered and from which reimbursement of those services is subsequently sought.

The Court stated that the system of prior authorisation which governed the reimbursement by the NHS of the cost of hospital treatment provided in another Member State deterred or even prevented the patients concerned from applying to providers of hospital services established in another Member State and constituted, both for those patients and for service providers, an obstacle to the freedom to provide services.

However, the Court considered that such a restriction could be justified in the light of overriding reasons. It held that, from the perspective of ensuring that there was sufficient and permanent access to high-quality hospital treatment, controlling costs and preventing – as far as possible – any wastage of financial, technical and human resources, the requirement that the assumption of costs by the national system of hospital treatment provided in another Member State be subject to prior authorisation appeared to be a measure which was both necessary and reasonable.

Nevertheless, the conditions attached to the grant of such authorisation had to be justified in the light of the overriding considerations mentioned above and had to satisfy the requirement of proportionality. The regulations on the NHS did not set out the criteria for the grant or refusal of the prior authorisation necessary for reimbursement of the cost of hospital treatment provided in another Member State, and therefore did not circumscribe the exercise of the national competent authorities' discretionary power in that context. The lack of a legal framework in that regard also made it difficult to exercise judicial review of decisions refusing to grant authorisation.

The Court held in that regard that, where the delay arising from such waiting lists appeared to exceed an acceptable period in the individual case concerned, having regard to an objective medical assessment of all the circumstances of the situation and the patient's clinical needs, the competent institution could not refuse authorisation on the grounds of: (i) the existence of those waiting lists; (ii) an alleged distortion of the normal order of priorities linked to the relative urgency of the cases to be treated; (iii) the fact that the hospital treatment provided under the national system in question was free of charge; (iv) the duty to make available specific funds to reimburse the cost of treatment provided in another Member State; and/or (v) a comparison between the cost of that treatment and that of equivalent treatment in the Member State of residence.

Consequently, the competent authorities of a national health service, such as the NHS, had to provide mechanisms for the reimbursement of the cost of hospital treatment in another Member State to patients to whom that service was not able to provide the treatment required within a medically acceptable period.

The mechanism for reimbursement

The Court held that the patient who was granted authorisation to receive hospital treatment in another Member State (the state of treatment), or received a refusal to authorise which was unfounded, was entitled to reimbursement by the competent institution of the cost of the treatment in accordance with the provisions of the legislation of the state of treatment, as if he was registered in that state.

Where there is no provision for reimbursement in full, there is an obligation on the competent institution to place the patient in the position he would have been in had the national health service with which he was registered been able to provide him free of charge, within a medically acceptable period, with treatment equivalent to that which he received in the host Member State. This requires the competent institution to reimburse the patient the difference between: (i) the cost of that equivalent treatment in the state of residence up to the total amount invoiced for the treatment received in the host Member State; and (ii) the amount reimbursed by the institution of that state pursuant to the legislation of that state, where the first amount was greater than the second. Conversely, where the cost charged in the state of treatment was higher than the cost of comparable treatment in the Member State of residence, the competent institution was only required to cover the difference between the cost of the hospital treatment in the two Member States up to the cost of the same treatment in the state of residence.

As regards the travel and accommodation costs, as the obligation on the competent institution exclusively concerns the expenditure connected with the healthcare received by the patient in the Member State of treatment, they should be reimbursed only to the extent that the legislation of the Member State of residence imposed a corresponding duty on its national system where the treatment was provided in a local hospital covered by that system.

Details of the S2 (previously the E112) scheme, as applied within the UK, are available on the Department of Health's website, at:

http://www.nhs.uk/NHSEngland/Healthcareabroad/plannedtreatment

The following case concerned the right of EU citizens to use 'coffee-shops' in the Netherlands:

Josemans v *Burgemeester van Maastricht* (Case C-137/09)

Under the 1976 Law on opium (Opiumwet 1976), the possession, dealing, cultivation, transportation, production, import and export of narcotic drugs, including cannabis and its derivatives, were prohibited in the Netherlands. The Netherlands applied a policy of tolerance with regard to cannabis. That policy was reflected, *inter alia*, in the establishment of 'coffee-shops', the main activities of which were the sale and consumption of cannabis. The local authorities could authorise such establishments in compliance with certain criteria. In a number of coffee-shops, non-alcoholic beverages and food were also sold.

To reduce drug tourism, and even to prevent it, the Municipal Council of Maastricht inserted a residence criterion in the General Maastricht Municipal Regulation. This residence criterion prohibited any coffee-shop owner from providing admission to the coffee-shop of persons who did not have their actual place of residence in the Netherlands.

Josemans ran the 'Easy Going' coffee-shop in Maastricht. Following two reports attesting that persons who were not resident in the Netherlands had been admitted to it, the Burgemeester van Maastricht (Mayor of Maastricht) temporarily closed the coffee-shop.

Josemans lodged an objection against that decision. He submitted that the legislation at issue in the main proceedings constituted unjustified unequal treatment of EU citizens and that, more specifically, people who were not resident in the Netherlands were denied the opportunity to buy non-alcoholic beverages and food in coffee-shops, which was contrary to Union law.

It was against this background that the Raad van State (Council of State), before which the dispute was brought, made a reference for a preliminary ruling to the Court of Justice.

The Court of Justice stated that **the harmfulness of narcotic drugs, including those derived from hemp, such as cannabis, was generally recognised and that there was a prohibition in all the Member States on marketing them,** with the exception of strictly controlled trade for use for medical and scientific purposes.

As the release of narcotic drugs into the economic and commercial channels of the Union was prohibited, a coffee-shop proprietor could not rely on the freedoms of movement or the principle of non-discrimination in so far as concerned the marketing of cannabis.

As regards the activity of marketing non-alcoholic beverages and food in such establishments, the Mayor of Maastricht submitted that this activity was altogether secondary to the sale of cannabis and could not have any bearing on the outcome of the main proceedings.

The Court did not accept that argument and held that the freedoms of movement could validly be relied on by such a proprietor in those circumstances.

According to the Court, the marketing of non-alcoholic beverages and food in coffee-shops constituted a catering activity. Consequently, the rules at issue had to be examined in the light of the freedom to provide services.

The Court stated that there was a restriction on the exercise of the freedom to provide services in so far as the proprietors of coffee-shops were not entitled to market lawful goods to persons residing in other Member States and those persons were precluded from enjoying such services.

That restriction was, however, justified by the objective of combating drug tourism and the accompanying public nuisance.

The rules were intended to put an end to the public nuisance caused by the large number of tourists wanting to purchase or consume cannabis in the coffee-shops in the municipality of Maastricht. According to the information provided by the Mayor of Maastricht, the 14 coffee-shops in the municipality attracted around 10,000 visitors per day (c. 3.9 million visitors per year). Of those visitors, 70 per cent were not resident in the Netherlands.

The Mayor of Maastricht stated that the problems associated with the sale of 'soft' drugs which arose in Maastricht (the various forms of public nuisance and crime, the increasing number of illegal premises selling drugs, including 'hard' drugs) had been exacerbated by drug tourism.

The Court stated that combating drug tourism and the accompanying public nuisance was part of combating drugs. It concerned both the maintenance of public order and the protection of the health of citizens, at Member State level and at Union level.

Those objectives constituted a legitimate interest which, in principle, justified a restriction of the obligations imposed by Union law, even under a fundamental freedom such as the freedom to provide services.

The Court stated that a prohibition on admitting non-residents to coffee-shops constituted a measure capable of substantially limiting drug tourism and, consequently, of reducing the problems it caused.

With regard to the possibility of adopting measures which were less restrictive of the freedom to provide services, the Court stated that other measures implemented to combat drug tourism and the accompanying public nuisance had proved to be insufficient and ineffective in the light of the objective pursued.

As for the possibility of granting non-residents access to coffee-shops whilst refusing to sell cannabis to them, the Court pointed out that it was not easy to control and monitor with accuracy that the product was not served to or consumed by non-residents. Furthermore, there was a danger that such an approach would encourage the illegal trade in or the resale of cannabis by residents to non-residents inside coffee-shops.

Furthermore, the Court observed that the rules in question did not preclude a person who was not resident in the Netherlands from going, in the municipality of Maastricht, into other catering establishments in order to consume non-alcoholic beverages and food. There were more than 500 such establishments.

Directive 2006/123: the Services Directive

Directive 2006/123 (OJ 2006 L 376/36), the 'Services Directive' was adopted on 12 December 2006 and had to be implemented by 28 December 2009. The directive incorporates four main objectives for creating an internal services market:

- to ease freedom of establishment for providers and the freedom of provision of services in the EU;
- to strengthen rights of recipients of services as users of the latter;
- to promote the quality of services; and to establish effective administrative cooperation among the Member States.

The directive establishes a general legal framework which favours freedom of establishment for providers as well as the free movement of services, while guaranteeing a superior level of quality.

The aims of Directive 2006/123

The directive aims to maximise the benefits of the internal market for citizens, consumers and businesses. There are still barriers hindering service providers from establishing themselves in other Member States or trading across borders. The directive seeks to achieve the following:

1 Businesses will be able to establish themselves anywhere in the EU. Service providers will be able to obtain information and complete administrative formalities through single points of contact in each Member State. This will speed up authorisation and reduce costs. So, for example, a business wishing to build and run a hotel or a store in another Member State will no longer have to deal with several different authorities at national, regional and local level. A service provider will be able to complete all formalities to set up a business online. This will avoid the expense and inconvenience of multiple visits to authorities in the Member State into which they intend to provide services. Authorisation schemes in Member States will be clearer, more transparent, less restrictive and non-discriminatory.

2 Businesses will find it easier to provide services across borders. Service providers will be free to provide their services across borders into other Member States, except where prohibited by Member State requirements that are non-discriminatory, proportionate and necessary for reasons relating to public policy, public security, public health and the protection of the environment.

(i) It will be possible to provide services in a Member State without having to be established there. Currently a business has to have a permanent presence to provide certain types of services. Removing a requirement to establish will make it possible for more businesses to offer services on a temporary or occasional basis. Activities covered by an establishment requirement in some Member States include many tourism-related services, e.g. mountain guides, yacht and sailing boat hire, ski instructors, etc.

(ii) Businesses will no longer be required by a Member State to take on a particular legal form in order to provide services into that territory.

3 Consumers will be properly protected. Consumers will benefit from better information on businesses and the services they offer. They will know more about price and quality. It will not be possible to discriminate against consumers on grounds of residence or nationality. All EU citizens will enjoy the same rights wherever they live. For example, museums will not be able to charge non-residents higher prices, and organisers of sports events such as marathons will not be allowed to charge non-residents higher participation fees.

4 Supervision will be improved due to more effective cross-border cooperation between authorities. Member States will have to step up administrative cooperation between them to ensure improved and effective supervision of service providers without duplication. This will be underpinned by a new electronic system allowing for the direct and efficient exchange of information between Member States.

Scope

The directive establishes a general legal framework for any service provided for economic return (with the exception of excluded sectors) while taking the specific nature of certain activities or professions into account. The following services are excluded:

- non-economic services of general interest;
- financial services (including those such as banking, credit, insurance and re-insurance, occupational or personal pensions, securities, investment funds and payments);
- electronic communication services with respect to matters covered by directives;
- transport services, including port services;
- services of temporary work agencies;
- healthcare services;
- audiovisual services;
- gambling;
- activities which are connected with the exercise of official authority;
- certain social services (relating to social housing, childcare and aid for persons in need);
- private security services;
- services provided by notaries and bailiffs, who are appointed by an official act of government.

Administrative simplification

The directive requires the Member States to examine and, if need be, simplify the procedures and formalities applicable to accessing a service activity and to exercise them. In particular, the directive includes:

- putting in place points of single contact at which a provider may complete all the necessary formalities to fulfil various duties;
- the obligation to make this possible online.

Removing legal and administrative barriers to the development of service activities

To ease freedom of establishment, the directive:

- includes the obligation to evaluate the compatibility of the authorisation schemes in light of the principles of non-discrimination and proportionality and to maintain certain principles regarding the conditions and procedures of authorisation applicable to service activities;
- repeals certain legal requirements that remain in the legislation of some Member States and which are no longer justifiable, such as requirements on nationality;
- contains the obligation to evaluate the compatibility of other legal requirements in light of the principles of non-discrimination and proportionality.

Easing the freedom to provide temporary cross-border services

To improve the free provision of services, the directive stipulates that the Member States must guarantee freedom of access to the service activity and the freedom to exercise such activity throughout their territory. The Member State to which the service provider moves to become established may only enforce its own requirements in as much as these are non-discriminatory, proportional and justified for reasons of public order, public safety, public health or environmental protection.

The directive also provides for a certain number of significant derogations from the principle, as regards, for example, professional qualifications, secondment and services of general economic interest.

Strengthening consumer rights as service users

Within the framework of protecting the rights of recipients, the directive:

- affirms the right of recipients to use the services of other Member States;
- establishes the right of recipients to obtain information on the rules applicable to providers, whatever their location may be, and on the services offered by a service provider.

Ensuring service quality

In this area, the directive aims to:

- strengthen the quality of services by encouraging, for example, voluntary certification of activities or drawing up quality charters;
- encourage European codes of conduct to be drawn up, in particular by professional bodies or associations.

Establishing effective administrative cooperation among the Member States

In order to facilitate the establishment and free movement of services throughout the EU, the directive:

- lays down a legal obligation requiring the Member States to cooperate with the relevant authorities of other Member States in order to ensure efficient control of service activities in the Union while avoiding a multiplication of monitoring (this includes an alert mechanism between Member States);
- constitutes the basis for developing an electronic system for the exchange of information between Member States, which is vital for establishing effective administrative cooperation between them.

Canvassing by members of a regulated profession

In the following case, the Court of Justice held that Directive 2006/123 prohibits a national rule which forbids canvassing by qualified accountants:

Société fiduciaire nationale d'expertise comptable v Ministre du Budget, des Comptes publics et de la Fonction publique (Case C-119/09)

The French Code of professional conduct and ethics of qualified accountants forbid them to engage in any 'canvassing', i.e. any unsolicited contact with third parties with a view to offering their services.

Société fiduciaire applied to the Conseil d'État (France) for the annulment of the regulatory code on the ground that the prohibition it imposed was contrary to the Services Directive 2006/123.

The Conseil d'État referred a question to the Court of Justice on the interpretation of the Services Directive, asking whether the Member States could prohibit the members of a regulated profession from engaging in canvassing.

The Court stated that it was clear that in adopting Directive 2006/123 the EU legislature's intention was: (i) to put an end to total prohibitions on the members of a regulated profession from engaging in commercial communications whatever their form; and (ii) to remove prohibitions on one or more forms of commercial communication, e.g. advertising, direct marketing or sponsorship.

However, the Member States retained the right to lay down prohibitions relating to the content or methods of commercial communications as regards regulated professions, provided that the rules laid down were justified and proportionate for the purposes of ensuring the independence, dignity and integrity of the profession, as well as professional secrecy.

The Court considered the scope of the concept of 'canvassing' in order to determine whether it constituted 'commercial communication' which, under Directive 2006/123, a Member State could not prohibit generally and absolutely.

As there was no EU definition of the concept of 'canvassing', the Court interpreted it as a form of communication of information intended to seek new clients, which involved personal contact between the provider and a potential client, in order to offer services to the targeted potential clients. It could, therefore, be classified as direct marketing. Therefore, canvassing constituted commercial communication within the meaning of the directive.

> Consequently, the Court held that the prohibition on any canvassing by qualified accountants could be regarded as a total prohibition of commercial communications, prohibited by Directive 2006/123.
>
> The Court held that the French prohibition had to be regarded as a total prohibition on commercial communications and constituted, therefore, a restriction on the freedom to provide cross-border services. Indeed, that prohibition could affect professionals from other Member States more, by depriving them of an effective means of penetrating the French market.

Information relating to Directive 2006/123 is available at:

http://ec.europa.eu/growth/single-market/services/services-directive

The provision of services and rights of establishment

There is a close link between the provision of services by the self-employed and undertakings, and the establishment of businesses in another Member State: one frequently precedes the other. Thus, provisions under Arts 49–54 TFEU (previously Arts 43–48 EC Treaty) dealing with establishment, particularly the preliminaries to becoming established, will often overlap with the provision of services. Article 49 TFEU (previously Art 43 EC Treaty) provides that freedom of establishment includes:

> . . . the right to take up and pursue activities as self-employed persons and to set up and manage undertakings, in particular companies or firms . . . under the conditions laid down for its own nationals by the law of the country where such establishment is effected.

'Companies or firms' means companies and firms constituted under civil or commercial law, including cooperative societies, and other legal persons governed by public or private law, except for those which are non-profit-making (Art 54 TFEU (previously Art 48 EC Treaty)). Although the inclusive term 'other legal persons' would seem to exclude the English partnership, as this has no legal personality, this is not in fact the case. The rights both to the provision of services and to establishment belong to both natural and legal persons. In practice, it does not matter whether a partnership enjoys the right to set up branches in another Member State by virtue of being a 'legal person' or a collection of 'natural persons', provided that both have their registered office, central administration or principal place of business within the EU.

Article 49 TFEU draws a distinction between nationals of Member States and those already established in the territory of a Member State. Each state defines its own nationals, thereby affording them the benefits enjoyed by EU citizenship (see Chapter 11). However, an undertaking which does not have its principal office in the EU can set up agencies and branches in other Member States, provided it is established in one of the Member States.

Obstacles to establishment

Objective 3

The former Art 54 EC Treaty (which was replaced by Art 44 EC Treaty, and is now Art 50 TFEU) provided for the drawing up of a general programme for the abolition of restrictions on freedom of establishment within the Union. The Council and Commission sought to give priority treatment to activities where freedom of establishment made a particularly valuable contribution to the development of production and trade, abolishing administrative procedures and practices forming obstacles to establishment, and enabling nationals of Member States to acquire and use land and buildings. Existing necessary safeguards for the operation of businesses and the professions would be harmonised and coordinated.

The General Programme made under the former Art 54 EC Treaty (now Art 50 TFEU) was approved in December 1961. Title III of the Programme called for the abolition of discriminatory measures which could impair access to non-wage-earning activities of EU nationals. The measures to be abolished included the following:

- Provisions which made access to a non-wage-earning activity conditional upon the issue of an official authorisation or the issue of a document, such as a foreign merchant's card or a foreign professional's card.

- The imposition of taxes or other charges which would make access to a business or profession in another Member State more difficult and costly. In *Hayes* v *Kronenberger* (Case C-323/95), for example, the Court of Justice held that a requirement that foreign litigants from other Member States pay a sum as security for costs in court proceedings, in circumstances where local nationals were not required to do so, was discriminatory and was liable to have an adverse effect on trade in goods and services between Member States.

- Provisions which barred or limited membership in companies, particularly with regard to the activities of their members.

- Restrictions imposed on foreign nationals in relation to entry into various commercial and other contracts, the right to tender or participate in public works contracts, to borrow and have access to various forms of credit, and to have access to loans and grants provided by state agencies.

To give effect to the programme, the Commission drew up a wide range of directives which were intended to facilitate access to a great variety of activities, including itinerant traders, film producers, hairdressers and the providers of gas, water and electricity services. Some of these required specific periods of academic training and practical experience, while others simply required a period of self-employment and a certificate of good character (compare the provisions in Directive 86/653 on self-employed commercial agents with Directive 87/540 on carriers of goods by waterway). It was thought, initially, that until an appropriate directive was in place, national measures would continue to apply and, in many cases, would have the effect of excluding EU nationals from participating in the relevant business or occupation. The right to equality of opportunity provided in Art 49 TFEU in relation to establishment and Art 57 TFEU in relation to the provision of services relates to the conditions for establishment and self-employment in the host Member State. These may, in many instances, be more difficult for EU nationals to satisfy, despite their overt application to local nationals and EU nationals on the same terms.

In *Reyners* v *Belgian State* (Case 2/74), the Court of Justice held that what is now Art 49 TFEU was directly effective. This case concerned a Dutch citizen who had been born and educated in Belgium. He was resident in Belgium, and held a doctorate in Belgian law. He was excluded from legal practice in Belgium because he was not a Belgian. The Court of Justice held that this restriction was incompatible with what are now Arts 18 and 49 TFEU.

The right of establishment and the right to provide services have been described by the Court of Justice as 'fundamental rights', and the Court has been active in asserting that businesses and the self-employed should have access to activities in Member States without hindrance, or direct or indirect discrimination, even where there were no implementing Union measures. The difficulty in many of these cases is that perfectly proper national measures to protect consumers and users of professional services, or to achieve other legitimate objectives, have been used by practitioners to exclude competitors from other Member States. The Court has often had to judge whether a national measure could be objectively justified, or whether it operated as an unlawful restriction. In **Commission v Italy (Re Freedom of Establishment)** (Case 168/85), the Court of Justice held that national provisions on tourism, the operation of pharmacies and access to the occupation of journalism, which denied access to those not holding Italian nationality, were incompatible with what are now Arts 45, 49 and 56 TFEU. It was not sufficient that instructions should be issued disapplying them to EU citizens. They had to be repealed.

In the following case, the Court of Justice was required to determine whether Union law precluded provisions contained in Italian and German legislation which provided that only pharmacists may own and operate a pharmacy:

Commission v Italy; Apothekerkammer des Saarlandes and Others
(Cases C-171/07 and C-172/07)

The Court of Justice held that legislation which provided that only pharmacists could own and operate a pharmacy constituted a restriction on, *inter alia*, the freedom of establishment. However, this restriction could be justified by the objective of ensuring that the provision of medicinal products to the public was reliable and of good quality.

The Court stated that where there was uncertainty as to the existence or extent of risks to human health, it was important that a Member State should be able to take protective measures without having to wait until the reality of those risks became fully apparent. Furthermore, a Member State could take measures that reduced, as far as possible, a public-health risk – this more specifically included a risk to the reliability and quality of the provision of medicinal products to the public.

In this context, the Court drew attention to the very particular nature of medicinal products, whose therapeutic effects distinguished them substantially from other goods; if medicinal products were consumed unnecessarily or incorrectly, they could cause serious harm to health.

The Court held that because Member States had the power to determine the level of protection of public health, they could require that medicinal products be supplied by pharmacists.

The Court observed that although a pharmacist, like other persons, would pursue the objective of making a profit, it was presumed that a pharmacist would operate the pharmacy not with a purely economic objective, but also from a professional viewpoint. His private interest connected with the making of a profit was thus tempered by his training, by his professional experience and by the responsibility which he owed, given that any breach of the rules of law or professional conduct undermined not only the value of his investment but also his own professional existence.

The Court then observed that non-pharmacists, by definition, lacked training, experience and responsibility equivalent to those of pharmacists. Accordingly, they did not provide the same safeguards as pharmacists.

The Court held that a Member State could therefore take the view, in the exercise of its discretion, that the operation of a pharmacy by a non-pharmacist could represent a risk to public health, in particular to the reliability and quality of the supply of medicinal products at retail level.

The following case concerned a Spanish law which made the setting-up of a new pharmacy conditional upon prior administrative authorisation:

José Manuel Blanco Pérez and María del Pilar Chao Gómez v *Consejería de Salud y Servicios Sanitarios, Principado de Asturias* (Joined Cases C-570/07 and C-571/07)

In Spain, national legislation made the setting- up of a new pharmacy conditional upon prior administrative authorisation. That legislation was implemented by the Autonomous Communities, which set specific criteria for the licensing of new pharmacies.

In 2002, Asturias (Spain) decided to launch a call for applications with a view to issuing new pharmacy licences. That decision was based on the Asturian decree regulating pharmacies and pharmaceutical services. This established a licensing system which limited the number of pharmacies in an area by reference to the population of that area. Only one pharmacy could be opened, as a rule, per unit of 2,800 inhabitants and a supplementary pharmacy could not be opened until that threshold had been exceeded, that pharmacy being established for the fraction above 2,000 inhabitants. Furthermore, the system prohibited the opening of a pharmacy within 250 metres of another pharmacy. The decree also set out criteria for making a selection from among pharmacists competing for a licence, with points awarded on the basis of their professional and teaching experience.

José Manuel Blanco Pérez and María del Pilar Chao Gómez, both qualified pharmacists, wanted to open a new pharmacy in Asturias, without having to comply with the territorial planning rules as per the Asturian decree. Consequently, they brought an action against the call for applications launched by Asturias and against that decree.

Uncertain whether the Asturian decree was compatible with the principle of the freedom of establishment, the Tribunal Superior de Justicia de Asturias (Spain), before which the proceedings were brought, referred the case to the Court of Justice for a preliminary ruling.

The conditions linked to population density and the minimum distance between pharmacies
The Court of Justice held that the conditions, established by the Asturian decree, linked to population density and the minimum distance between the pharmacies (that is to say, a minimum number of 2,800 inhabitants per pharmacy and a minimum distance of 250 metres between pharmacies) constituted a restriction on the freedom of establishment. However, the Court observed that such measures could be justified, provided that the following four conditions were satisfied:

(i)   the measures had to apply in a non-discriminatory manner;
(ii) they had to be justified by overriding reasons relating to the general interest;
(iii) they had to be appropriate for attaining the objective pursued;
(iv) they had not to go beyond what was necessary for attaining that objective (i.e. an application of the proportionality test).

The Court found that the conditions linked to population density and the minimum distance between pharmacies in the region applied without discrimination on grounds of nationality.

The Court held that **the objective of the demographic and geographical restrictions laid down by the Asturian decree was to ensure that the provision of medicinal products to the public was reliable and of good quality. Accordingly, that objective constituted an overriding reason relating to the general interest and was capable of justifying national legislation such as that at issue in the main proceedings.**

The Court considered that the Asturian legislation was appropriate to the attainment of that objective. The Court considered that, if that field was wholly unregulated, it was not inconceivable that pharmacists would become concentrated in the areas considered to be attractive, so that certain other less attractive areas would suffer from a shortfall in the number of pharmacists needed to ensure a pharmaceutical service which was reliable and of good quality.

Nevertheless, the Court examined the consistency of the Asturian legislation in the light of the objective of ensuring that the provision of medicinal products to the public was reliable and of good quality. In this respect, the Court observed that the uniform application of the basic '2,800 inhabitants' and '250 metres' rules fixed by the Asturian decree could well be unsuccessful in ensuring adequate access to pharmaceutical services in areas which had certain special demographic features. First, if the '2,800 inhabitants' rule were uniformly applied in certain rural areas where the population was generally scattered and less numerous, certain inhabitants would find themselves beyond reasonable reach of a pharmacy and would thus be denied adequate access to pharmaceutical services. Secondly, in certain densely populated areas, the strict application of the '250 metres' rule could well give rise to a situation in which more than 2,800 inhabitants lived inside the perimeter laid down for a single pharmacy.

In so doing, the Court observed that the Asturian decree implemented the national legislation. However, the Court pointed out that the national legislation provided for certain adjustment measures to address these issues. In those circumstances, the Court stated that it was for the national court to determine whether, in any geographical area with special demographic characteristics, the competent authorities made use of the power conferred by the national legislation.

Finally, the Court stated that the Asturian legislation did not go beyond what was necessary to attain the objective of ensuring that the provision of medicinal products to the public was reliable and of good quality.

The Court held, therefore, that the conditions linked to population density and the minimum distance between pharmacies were not in breach of the freedom of establishment, provided that the basic '2,800 inhabitants' and '250 metres' rules did not, in any geographical area which had special demographic features, prevent the establishment of a sufficient number of pharmacies to ensure adequate pharmaceutical services. This was a matter for the national court to ascertain.

The selection criteria for licensees for new pharmacies established by the Asturian decree
The Court stated that the freedom of establishment requires that the criteria applicable in the context of an administrative authorisation scheme should not be discriminatory.

On that issue, the Court observed that, under the Asturian decree, a further 20 per cent was to be added to a candidate's 'score' for professional qualifications and professional experience obtained within Asturias. Under that legislation, where several candidates scored an equal number of points, licences were to be granted in accordance with an order of priority in which precedence was given to certain categories of candidate. Among those categories, in third place, was that of pharmacists who had pursued their professional activities within Asturias. The Court stated that those two criteria could be met more easily by pharmacists from the Member State concerned, who more often pursued their economic activities on the national territory, than by pharmacists who were nationals of other Member States, who more frequently pursued those activities in another Member State. The Court concluded, therefore, that those two selection criteria were discriminatory and hence precluded by the freedom of establishment.

Marcello Costa and *Ugo Cifone* (Joined Cases C-72/10 and C-77/10) concerned Italian legislation which provided that the collection and management of bets could only be engaged in by the holder of a licence. In 2006 a significant number of new licences were put out to tender. One of the requirements was that a minimum distance had to be observed between the new outlets and those for which a licence had been awarded following a previous tendering procedure. The Court of Justice held that the effect of the minimum distance measure was to protect the market position acquired by operators which were already established, to the detriment of new licence holders who were compelled to open premises in less commercially attractive locations than those occupied by the former. Italy sought to justify such unequal treatment on two grounds: (i) the purported aim of the measure was to prevent consumers who lived close to betting establishments from being exposed to an excess of supply; this was rejected by the Court because the betting and gaming sector in Italy had long been marked by a policy of expanding activity with the aim of increasing tax revenue; and (ii) the objective of the legislation was to counter the risk that consumers living in less-well-served areas might opt for clandestine betting or gaming. The Court pointed out that the means used in order to achieve the purported objective had to be consistent and systematic. In this case, the rules on minimum distances were imposed not on licence holders already established on the market, but only on new licence holders. This meant that the only operators to be placed at a disadvantage would be the new licence holders. In any event, the Court stated that a national system which required minimum distances between outlets would be justifiable only if it did not have as its true objective the protection of the market position of the existing operators. This was a matter for the national court to determine. Moreover, it was for the national court to determine whether the obligation to observe minimum distances, which precluded the establishment of additional outlets in densely-populated areas, was really an appropriate way of attaining the purported objective and whether it actually resulted in new operators choosing to set up in less populated areas, thereby ensuring nationwide coverage.

In the following case, a UK court referred questions to the Court of Justice for a preliminary ruling in relation to the interpretation of what are now Arts 49 and 54 TFEU, and the question of objective justification:

Marks & Spencer (Case C-446/03)

Marks & Spencer, a company resident in the UK, was the principal trading company of a retail group specialising in the sale of off-the-peg clothing, food, homeware and financial services. It had subsidiaries in the UK and in a number of other Member States, including Germany, Belgium and France. In 2001 it ceased trading in continental Europe because of losses incurred from the mid-1990s. On 31 December 2001 the French subsidiary was sold to a third party, while the German and Belgian subsidiaries ceased operating.

In 2000 and 2001, Marks & Spencer submitted claims to the UK tax authorities for group tax relief in respect of the losses incurred by the German, Belgian and French subsidiaries. United Kingdom tax legislation (the Income and Corporation Taxes Act 1988 (ICTA)) allowed the parent company of a group, under certain circumstances, to effect an offset between its profits and losses incurred by its subsidiaries. However, those claims were rejected on the ground that the rules governing group relief did not apply to subsidiaries not resident or trading in the UK. Marks & Spencer appealed against that refusal to the Special Commissioners of Income Tax, which dismissed the appeal. Marks & Spencer then brought an appeal before the English High Court, which decided to stay proceedings and to refer questions to the Court of Justice for a preliminary ruling. The national court was uncertain whether the UK provisions, which prevented a UK-resident parent company from deducting from its taxable profits the losses it had incurred in other Member States by its subsidiaries established there, although they allowed it to deduct losses incurred by a resident subsidiary, were compatible with the former Arts 43 and 48 EC Treaty (now Arts 49 and 54 TFEU) on the freedom of establishment.

The Court of Justice recalled that, although direct taxation came within the competence of Member States, national authorities had to exercise that competence consistently with Union law.

The Court held that the UK legislation constituted a restriction on freedom of establishment, in breach of the former Arts 43 and 48 EC Treaty (now Arts 49 and 54 TFEU), in that it applied different treatment for tax purposes to losses incurred by a resident subsidiary from that applied to losses incurred by a non-resident subsidiary. This would deter parent companies from setting up subsidiaries in other Member States.

However, **the Court acknowledged that such a restriction could be permitted if it pursued a legitimate objective compatible with the Treaty and was justified by imperative reasons in the public interest** (i.e. the restriction could be objectively justified). It was necessary, in such a case, that its application be appropriate to ensuring the attainment of the objective thus pursued and not go beyond what was necessary to attain it.

The Court set out the relevant objective criteria relied upon by Member States and analysed whether the UK legislation justified the differing treatment applied by it. The criteria put forward were:

(i) protection of a balanced allocation of the power to impose taxation between the various Member States concerned, so that profits and losses were treated symmetrically in the same tax system;

(ii) the fact that the legislation provided for avoidance of the risk of double use of losses which would exist if the losses were taken into account in the Member State of the parent company and in the Member State of the subsidiaries;

(iii) escaping the risk of tax avoidance which would exist if the losses were not taken into account in the Member State where the subsidiary was established, because otherwise the losses which accrued to a group of companies could be transferred to the companies established in the Member States which applied the highest rates of taxation and in which the tax value of the losses was the highest.

The Court held in the light of those criteria that the UK legislation pursued legitimate objectives which were compatible with the Treaty and constituted overriding reasons in the public interest.

However, the Court held that the UK legislation did not comply with the principle of proportionality and went beyond what was necessary to attain the objectives pursued where: (i) the non-resident subsidiary had exhausted the possibilities available in the Member State where it was established of having the losses taken into account for the accounting period concerned by the claim for relief and also for previous accounting periods; and (ii) there was no possibility for the foreign subsidiary's losses to be taken into account in the Member State where it was established for future periods either by the subsidiary itself or by a third party, in particular where the subsidiary had been sold to that third party.

Consequently, the Court of Justice held that where, in one Member State, the resident parent company demonstrated to the tax authorities that those conditions were fulfilled, it was contrary to the freedom of establishment to preclude the possibility for the parent company to deduct from its taxable profits in that Member State the losses incurred by its non-resident subsidiary.

In *Test Claimants in the FII Group Litigation v Commissioners of Inland Revenue and The Commissioners for Her Majesty's Revenue and Customs* (Case C-35/11), the Court of Justice held that the differential tax treatment which was applied to share dividends received by a company, which varied depending on whether such dividend was received from a resident company or non-resident company, constituted a restriction on the freedom of establishment.

The central issue in the following case was whether the measure taken was disproportionate:

Criminal proceedings against Engelmann (Case C-64/08)

Austrian legislation established a **State monopoly** state monopoly over games of chance, with the effect that the right to organise and operate them was reserved to the state. The federal law in force was intended to regulate games of chance with a view to their supervision and to enable the state to derive the maximum amount of revenue from them.

The Federal Minister for Finance was permitted to grant a total of 12 concessions, entitling their holders to organise and operate gaming establishments. **The concessionaire had to be a public limited company having its seat in Austria and was subject to supervision by the ministry**. The organisation of games of chance without authorisation could give rise to criminal proceedings.

At the time, the 12 concessions were held by a single company, Casinos Austria AG. They were granted and renewed without a public tendering procedure.

Engelmann, a German national, operated two gaming establishments in Austria without previously having applied for a concession from the Austrian authorities. By a judgment at first instance, he was found guilty of unlawfully organising games of chance and ordered to pay a fine of 2,000 euros. Engelmann appealed to the Landesgericht Linz (Regional Court, Linz, Austria). The Austrian court referred questions to the Court of Justice for a preliminary ruling on the compatibility of the Austrian legislation with the freedom of establishment (and the freedom to provide services).

The Court of Justice stated that the obligation on persons holding concessions to operate gaming establishments to have its seat in Austria constituted a restriction on the freedom of establishment. That obligation discriminated against companies which had their seat in another Member State and prevented those companies from operating gaming establishments in Austria through an agency, branch or subsidiary.

With regard to the possibility of justifying that restriction in the interest of preventing those activities from being carried out for criminal or fraudulent purposes, the Court held that **the categorical exclusion of operators whose seat was in another Member State was disproportionate**, as it went beyond what was necessary to combat crime. There were various less restrictive measures available to monitor the activities and accounts of such operators. In addition, any undertaking established in a Member State could be supervised and could have sanctions imposed on it, regardless of the place of residence of its managers. There was nothing to prevent supervision being carried out on the premises of the establishments in order to prevent any fraud being committed by the operators against consumers.

With regard to the grant of the concessions, the Court considered that limiting the number of concessions could be justified by the need to limit opportunities for gambling. The grant of concessions for a duration of 15 years could also be justified having regard to the concessionaire's need to have a sufficient length of time to recoup his investments.

However, the absence of a competitive procedure when the concessions were granted to Casinos Austria AG did not comply with the freedom of establishment (and the freedom to provide services). The Court stated that the obligation of transparency required the concession-granting authority to ensure a degree of publicity sufficient to enable a service concession to be opened up to competition and the impartiality of the award procedures to be reviewed. That obligation was a condition which had to be met before a Member State could exercise its right to award licences to operate casinos, irrespective of the method of selecting operators. The grant of a concession, in the absence of any transparency, to an operator located in the Member State of the awarding authority constituted difference in treatment to the detriment of operators located in other Member States. The latter operators had no real possibility of manifesting their interest in obtaining the concession in question. Such a difference in treatment was contrary to the principle of equal treatment and the prohibition of discrimination on grounds of nationality, and constituted indirect discrimination on grounds of nationality prohibited by Union law.

Provisions which are less direct than national restrictions may also infringe the rights conferred by Arts 49, 56 and 57 TFEU. In a series of cases brought by the Commission under the former Art 226 EC Treaty (now Art 258 TFEU), local restrictions on the operation of insurance services were challenged in the Court of Justice. In each of the four Member States concerned, insurance undertakings were required to conduct their business in those states through individuals already established and authorised to practise there (***Commission v Denmark*** (Case 252/83); ***Commission v France*** (Case 220/83); ***Commission v Germany*** (Case 205/84); ***Commission v Ireland*** (Case 206/84)). The Court accepted that, in the state of Union law prevailing at the time, the authorisation and licensing of insurance services was still a matter of the law of the host Member State. However, in operating its national system, the host Member State could not duplicate equivalent statutory conditions which have already been satisfied in the Member State where the business has originally been established.

The Court of Justice has held that until such time as national rules on company taxation are harmonised throughout the Union, it is permissible for a Member State to impose a restriction on companies, so that they cannot move their principal place of business without the consent of the national tax authorities (***R v HM Treasury, ex parte Daily Mail and General Trust plc*** (Case 81/87)). The retention of national company taxation rules should not, however, allow Member States to operate discriminatory tax rules which operate as a barrier to the establishment of branches of foreign undertakings in their territories (***R v IRC, ex parte Commerzbank AG*** (Case C-330/91)). A similar principle applies, pending the adoption of a common visa policy, in the case of companies which operate in other Member States and employ third-country (i.e. non-EU) nationals (***Van der Elst*** (Case C-43/93)). Although such national rules may be accepted by the Court of Justice, they will be acceptable only if they meet the qualifications laid down by the Court in the ***Gebhard*** case (Case C-55/94). National measures liable to hinder or make less attractive the exercise of the fundamental freedoms guaranteed by the Treaty must fulfil four conditions:

1 they must be applied in a non-discriminatory manner;
2 they must be justified by imperative requirements in the general interest;
3 they must be suitable for securing attainment of the objective which they pursue;
4 they must not go beyond what is necessary to attain the objective.

The TFEU emphasises the presumption in favour of freedom of establishment and the right to provide services in other Member States by stating that 'the Union and the Member States . . . shall take care that such services operate on the basis of principles and conditions, particularly economic and financial conditions, which enable them to fulfil their missions' (Art 14 TFEU).

Rights of entry and residence: Directive 2004/38

Objective 4

As discussed in Chapter 11, Directive 2004/38 concerns the right of EU citizens to move and reside freely within the Member States. The provisions of the directive which are relevant to the freedom of establishment, and the free movement of providers and recipients of services, are briefly discussed below; see Chapter 11 for a detailed commentary.

General right of residence for a period up to three months (Article 6)

Article 6(1) provides that EU citizens shall have the right of residence in another Member State for a period of up to three months without any conditions or formalities other than the requirement to hold a valid identity card or passport (or a valid passport in the case of non-EU family members).

Article 6(2) provides that 'family members' who do not have the nationality of a Member State (i.e. non-EU family members) enjoy the same rights as the EU citizen whom they have accompanied or joined.

Article 14(1) provides that EU citizens and their family members shall have the right of residence under Art 6, 'as long as they do not become an *unreasonable* burden on the social assistance system of the host Member State' (emphasis added). Expulsion shall not be an automatic consequence if an EU citizen or his family members have recourse to the host Member State's social assistance system (Art 14(3)). Article 14(4) further provides that (other than in accordance with the provisions relating to restrictions on the right of entry and residence on grounds of public policy, public security or public health) an expulsion order cannot be issued against an EU citizen or his family members, if, *inter alia*, the EU citizen is a self-employed person in the host Member State.

This general right of residence will be of particular relevance to those exercising the Union law rights to provide and receive services, whereas the extended right of residence provided by Art 7 (see below) will be of particular relevance to those exercising their Union law rights of establishment. The extended right of residence will also be of relevance to those exercising their Union law rights to receive services, because such residence will apply to the economically self-sufficient (Art 7(1)(b)).

Right of residence for more than three months (Article 7)

The right of residence for more than three months remains subject to certain conditions. Article 7(1) provides that EU citizens have the right to reside in another Member State, for a period exceeding three months, if *inter alia* they:

- are engaged in an economic activity in the host Member State (on an employed or self-employed basis) (Art 7(1)(a)); or

- have comprehensive sickness insurance and sufficient resources for themselves and their family members to ensure they do not become a burden on the social assistance system of the host Member State during their stay. Article 8(4) provides that Member States may not specify a minimum amount of resources they deem sufficient, but they must take account of the personal situation of the person concerned. The amount of minimum resources cannot be higher than the threshold below which nationals of the host Member State become eligible for social assistance, or, if this does not apply, higher than the minimum social security pension paid by the host Member State (Art 7(1)(b)).

Article 7(2) provides that the right of residence also applies to family members who are not nationals of a Member State (i.e. non-EU family members), who are accompanying or joining an EU citizen in the host Member State, provided that such EU citizen satisfies the conditions set out in Art 7(1)(a) or (b) above.

Article 7(3) provides that an EU citizen shall retain the status of worker or self-employed person in the host Member State in the following circumstances:

(a) he is temporarily unable to work as the result of an illness or accident;

(b) he is in duly recorded involuntary unemployment after having been employed for more than one year and has registered as a jobseeker with the relevant employment office in the host Member State;

(c) he is in duly recorded involuntary unemployment after completing a fixed-term employment contract of less than a year *or* after having become involuntarily unemployed during the first 12 months *and* has registered as a jobseeker with the relevant employment office in the host Member State. In this case, the status of worker shall be retained for not less than six months; or

(d) he embarks on vocational training. Unless he is involuntarily unemployed, the retention of the status of worker shall require the training to be related to the previous employment.

Article 12(1) provides that if an EU citizen dies or departs from the host Member State, his EU family members shall not have their right of residence affected. In the case of a non-EU family member, their right of residence shall not be affected if the EU citizen dies provided that the non-EU family member has been residing in the host Member State as a family member for at least one year before the EU citizen's death (Art 12(2)).

Article 12(3) provides that if an EU citizen dies or departs from the host Member State, if his children reside in the host Member State and are enrolled at an educational establishment, then his children and the parent who has actual custody of the children (whether or not they are EU citizens) shall have the right to reside in the host Member State until the children have completed their studies.

Article 13 governs a family member's right of residence following divorce, annulment of marriage or termination of partnership.

Article 14(2) provides that EU citizens and their family members shall have the right of residence under Arts 7, 12 and 13 'as long as they meet the conditions set out therein'. Expulsion shall not be an automatic consequence if an EU citizen or his family members have recourse to the host Member State's social assistance system (Art 14(3)). Article 14(4) further provides that (other than in accordance with the provisions relating to restrictions on the right of entry and residence on grounds of public policy, public security or public health), an expulsion order cannot be issued against an EU citizen or his family members, if, *inter alia*, the EU citizen is a self-employed person in the host Member State.

Right of permanent residence (Article 16)

EU citizens acquire the right of permanent residence in the host Member State after a five-year period of continuous legal residence (Art 16(1)), provided that an expulsion decision has not been enforced against them (Art 21). The same rule applies to non-EU family members who have lived with an EU citizen in the host Member State for five years

(Art 16(2)), and again provided that an expulsion decision has not been enforced against them (Art 21).

Once granted, the right of permanent residence is lost only in the event of more than two successive years' absence from the host Member State (Arts 16(4) and 20(3)).

Article 17 recognises the right of permanent residence for EU citizens who are self-employed persons, and for their family members, before the five-year period of continuous residence has expired, subject to certain conditions being met. Article 17 also provides that the family members of EU citizens who are self-employed persons have the right of permanent residence if the EU worker or self-employed person dies before acquiring the right of permanent residence (subject to the specified conditions; see Chapter 11).

Article 12(1) provides that if an EU citizen dies or departs from the host Member State, his family members who are nationals of a Member State shall not have their right of residence affected. However, before acquiring the right of permanent residence, the persons concerned must meet the conditions set out in Art 7(1)(a), (b) or (d). In the case of a non-EU family member, their right of residence shall not be affected if the EU citizen dies provided that the non-EU family member has been residing in the host Member State as a family member for at least one year before the EU citizen's death (Art 12(2)). Before acquiring the right of permanent residence, such non-EU family members must likewise meet the conditions set out in Art 7(1)(a), (b), or (d). Article 18 provides that the family members to whom Art 12(2) applies, who satisfy the conditions set out in Art 12(2), shall acquire the right of permanent residence after legally residing in the host Member State for a period of five consecutive years; this is without prejudice to Art 17 (see above).

Article 13 governs a family member's right of residence following divorce, annulment of marriage or termination of partnership.

The Treaty provisions

In the following case, the Court of Justice considered the right of residence of a spouse who was a non-EU citizen, married to a national of a Member State established in his host Member State, but who provided services to persons established in other Member States. The non-EU citizen had to rely directly on the former EC Treaty (now TFEU) provisions because the relevant directives did not apply to this situation (and arguably Directive 2004/38 does not apply):

Mary Carpenter v *Secretary of State for the Home Department* (Case C-60/00)

Mary Carpenter was a national of the Philippines (i.e. a non-EU national). She was given leave to enter the UK as a visitor for six months. She overstayed that leave and failed to apply for an extension of her stay, as she was required to do under UK law. She later married a UK national (Peter Carpenter). Mr Carpenter ran a business selling advertising space in journals and offered various services to the editors of those journals. His business was established in the UK, but a large proportion of the business was conducted with advertisers in other Member States. Mr Carpenter travelled to those other Member States for the purpose of his business. Mrs Carpenter applied for leave to remain as the spouse of a UK national but her application was refused. A deportation order was made against her.

Mrs Carpenter appealed. She argued that she had a right under Union law to remain in the UK. She argued that because her husband's business required him to travel around the EU, providing and receiving services, her presence within the UK made it easier for him to do this because she could look after his children from his first marriage. If she was deported she argued that it would restrict Mr Carpenter's right to provide and receive services under the former Art 49 EC Treaty (now Art 56 TFEU). The appeal tribunal referred the case to the Court of Justice, for a preliminary ruling pursuant to the former Art 234 EC Treaty (now Art 267 TFEU). The Court of Justice held as follows:

> Article 49 EC [now Art 56 TFEU] read in the light of the fundamental right to respect for family life, is to be interpreted as precluding, in certain circumstances such as those in the main proceedings, a refusal, by the Member State of origin of a provider of services established in that Member State, who provides services to recipients established in other Member States, of the right to reside in its territory to that provider's spouse, who is a national of a third country.

In the above case, the Court of Justice held that there was a Union dimension because Mr Carpenter was providing services within other Member States. The provision of services was a fundamental right and was to be interpreted and applied in accordance with the rights set out within the European Convention for the Protection of Human Rights. The Court held that if Mrs Carpenter was deported, then this would interfere with the exercise by Mr Carpenter of his right to provide services under what is now Art 56 TFEU because his right to respect for his family life within the meaning of Art 8 of the European Convention on Human Rights would have been infringed; this would also infringe Art 7 of the Charter of Fundamental Rights of the European Union. The Court therefore held that what is now Art 56 TFEU prevented Mrs Carpenter's deportation.

Equal treatment

Objective 5

The scope of 'social advantages' under Art 7(2), Regulation 492/2011 is considered at pages 393–406.

The self-employed, and the providers and recipients of services, do not have the benefit of Art 7(2), Regulation 492/2011 (previously Art 7(2), Regulation 1612/68) relating to social advantages, because the regulation applies only to workers. On the face of it, this is an important difference, as social advantages have played an important part in the jurisprudence of the Court in relation to the integration of workers and their families into the host Member State (see Chapter 12). There are no equivalent provisions in Directive 2004/38, and its beneficiaries are obliged to look to Art 18 TFEU to be put on an equal footing with nationals. The Court has considerably mitigated the difference by a creative application of Art 18 TFEU, as is illustrated in the following cases.

In *Commission* v *Italy (Re Housing Aid)* (Case 63/86), the Court of Justice held that Italian law contravened what is now Art 18 TFEU, where the law in question confined a discounted mortgage facility to Italian nationals. The following case subsequently came before the Court of Justice:

Cowan v Le Trésor Public (Case 186/87)

> Mr Cowan, a British citizen, was assaulted in the exit of a Metro station while he was visiting Paris (France) as a tourist (i.e. the recipient of services (see above)). He was held to be entitled to the same rights in relation to criminal injuries compensation as a French national. The Court of Justice confined itself to considering the availability of the compensation scheme to non-French nationals. On the same basis that it had decided that equal access to the criminal process was a necessary precondition to the vindication of the rights of the worker in the criminal process (and could thus be seen to be a 'social advantage') in *Mutsch* (Case 137/84), the Court decided that the criminal injuries scheme should be similarly available to Cowan.

Presumably the Court of Justice would have come to the same conclusion in the above case if his attackers had been identified and his application had been for legal aid to bring proceedings against them for assault.

In *Commission v Spain* (Case C-45/93), the Court of Justice held that the principle of equal treatment extended to the right of visitors from other EU states to free admission to museums, where this facility was available to Spanish nationals (see also *Commission v Italy* (Case C-388/01)). In this case, the visitors could rely upon what is now Art 18 TFEU, because while visiting other EU states they were considered to be the recipients of services (see above), thus coming within the scope of what is now Art 56 TFEU.

In *Gravier v City of Liège* (Case 293/83), the Court of Justice held that Ms Gravier was exercising a Union right to receive education. In the course of exercising such a right, she was entitled to benefit from what is now Art 18 TFEU. On that basis she should receive equal treatment in relation to payment of the university admission fee, the *minerval*, so that she would have to pay only the same amount as 'home' students (see also *Commission v Belgium (Re University Fees)* (Case C-47/93)).

Although the Court of Justice has enthusiastically applied what is now Art 18 TFEU to enable an individual to overcome obstacles, either overt or covert, to the exercise of rights conferred by what are now Arts 49, 56 and 57 TFEU, it has been more reluctant to do so when the obstacle relates to the individual's shortage of resources. The Court held that the right to equal treatment in relation to access to vocational education did not extend to financial assistance to enable an individual to go to another Member State and receive a grant to support himself while at a vocational school or on a vocational course. Such a right did not exist under what was then Art 128 EC Treaty, nor under what is now Art 18 TFEU (see *Lair v University of Hannover* (Case 39/86)). Indeed, the right to receive education as a 'service' under Art 56 TFEU depends on the individual providing 'remuneration' for it (*Humbel* (Case 263/86), paras 8–13). With regard to equal treatment, Art 24(1), Directive 2004/38 provides that EU citizens qualifying for the right of residence or the right of permanent residence and the members of their family benefit from equal treatment with host-country nationals in the areas covered by the Treaty.

The 'official authority' exception

As with Art 45 TFEU, the rights of entry and residence of those entering to provide and receive services are subject to the right of the host Member State to derogate on grounds of public policy, public security or public health (Arts 52(1) and 62 TFEU). The scope of these provisions will be examined in Chapter 15. In addition, the rights enjoyed by virtue of Arts 49, 56 and 57 TFEU 'shall not apply . . . to activities . . . connected, even occasionally, with the exercise of official authority' (Art 51 TFEU). Like the public service exception in Art 45(4) TFEU, 'the exercise of official authority' is not defined in the Treaty. Its scope was considered by the Court of Justice in the following case:

Reyners v Belgian State (Case 2/74)

Reyners, the defendant, argued that the profession of *avocat* (i.e. lawyer) was exempted from the chapter of the Treaty on rights of establishment because it sometimes involved the exercise of official authority. The Court of Justice rejected the idea that an *avocat*, despite his occasional official duties, was necessarily concerned with the exercise of official authority:

> An extension of the exception allowed by . . . [Article 51 TFEU] to a whole profession would be possible only in cases where such activities were linked with that profession in such a way that freedom of establishment would result in imposing on the Member State concerned the obligation to allow the exercise, even occasionally, by nationals of functions appertaining to official authority. This extension is on the other hand not possible when, within the framework of an independent profession, the activities connected with the exercise of official authority are separable from the professional activity in question taken as a whole. (paras 46 and 47)

The 'exercise of official authority' would seem to be analogous to the exercise of 'public service' under Art 45(4) TFEU (*Commission v Belgium* (Case 149/79); see above, Chapter 12), and will be just as narrowly construed by the Court of Justice (see, for example, *Commission v Greece* (Case C-306/89) in which road traffic experts were held not to come within the scope of the exception in what is now Art 51 TFEU; and *Commission v Italy* (Case C-272/91) where the provision of computer services for the state lottery was likewise held not to come within the scope of the exception in what is now Art 51 TFEU).

Professional qualifications

Objective
6

Freedom of establishment includes the right of individuals to practise a profession or trade (e.g. lawyer, doctor and vet) on a permanent or semi-permanent basis. Naturally, a person may seek to practise a profession in another Member State in an employed capacity (i.e. as an EU worker), and therefore the Union law provisions relating to workers will apply (see Chapter 12) in addition to those of establishment which relate to recognition of the profession or trade. Freedom of establishment with regard to professional qualifications was addressed by the Union through:

(i) specific harmonising directives, which have been repealed and replaced by Directive 2005/36;
(ii) Directive 89/48 (the Mutual Recognition of Diplomas Directive), which has also been repealed and replaced by Directive 2005/36;
(iii) Directive 92/51 (the Recognition of Diplomas for other Professional Activities), which has also been repealed and replaced by Directive 2005/36;
(iv) case law of the Court of Justice.

Specific harmonising directives

The lack of common qualifications in the Union, and unwillingness to recognise diplomas and other qualifications from other Member States, proved a major obstacle to the exercise of free movement rights, especially for those with specialist skills. The problem was addressed by the General Programme, which resulted in the production of a whole range of harmonising directives relating to a wide range of activities (e.g. GPs, nurses, vets). The harmonising directives provided that if the professional satisfied the conditions set out within the directive, then recognition of the profession was guaranteed throughout the Union. The harmonising directives have been repealed and replaced by Directive 2005/36 (see below).

Directive 89/48: mutual recognition of diplomas

Little progress was made in relation to other traditional professions. It is generally accepted that in professions such as law, accountancy, banking and insurance the public needs to be protected against those who might misrepresent their skills and qualifications. To protect both public and professionals, many such professions are regulated by law. Regulation will cover matters such as education and training, professional conduct and disciplinary proceedings. In some Member States the regulatory process is entirely in the hands of government. In the UK and Ireland it is largely in the hands of professional bodies, operating within a statutory framework. Individuals and undertakings providing financial services will also work within a framework of self-regulation and state regulation, the trend in the UK during the 1980s and 1990s being towards self-regulation and deregulation. From the point of view of the consuming public, the self-regulation process by professionals has sometimes been seen to be as much concerned with the protection of professionals from competition as with protection of the public from abuse. It could also be perceived in an internal market as a covert form of **protectionism** in relation to the delivery of professional services by citizens of other Member States.

The reluctance of national professional bodies to agree harmonised standards for particular occupations led the Commission to adopt a new approach in 1985, following publication of the White Paper on the internal market. That approach acknowledged the need:

> . . . to provide a rapid response to the expectations of nationals of Community [i.e. Union] countries who hold higher-education diplomas awarded on completion of professional education and training issued in a Member State other than that in which they wish to pursue their profession.

> (Preamble to Directive 89/48)

The new approach involved both general educational criteria and the mutual recognition of educational diplomas and relevant practical experience. Directive 89/48 opened the way for entry into professional practice in other Member States for a whole new range of activities. In the UK these occupations included: actuaries, auditors, barristers, chiropodists, dieticians, physiotherapists, optometrists, civil engineers, marine architects, town planners, solicitors and teachers. Directive 89/48 has been repealed and replaced by Directive 2005/36. This is a consolidating directive (i.e. it mirrors the provisions in Directive 89/48 and the other directives it has replaced) and therefore the provisions of Directive 89/48, and its application, are relevant to Directive 2005/36.

The former Directive 89/48 (as amended by Directive 2001/19) was essentially a 'residual' directive, in the sense that it did not apply to professions which were the subject of a separate harmonising directive establishing arrangements for the mutual recognition of diplomas by Member States (Art 2). It applied to 'regulated professional activity', that is, 'a professional activity, in so far as the taking up or pursuit of such an activity or one of its modes of pursuit in a Member State is subject, directly or indirectly by virtue of laws, regulations or administrative provisions, to the possession of a diploma' (Art 1). Beneficiaries of the directive were those who could show the following:

- possession of a diploma indicating that the holder had the professional qualifications required for the taking up or pursuit of a regulated profession in one of the Member States in a self-employed capacity or as an employed person;
- completion of a post-secondary course of at least three years' duration, or of an equivalent duration part-time, at a university or establishment of higher education or another establishment of similar level;

- where appropriate, that the holder of the diploma had successfully completed the professional training required in addition to the post-secondary course.

The host Member State could also require the holder of the diploma to provide evidence of professional experience of not more than four years where the period of education and training fell short by more than one year compared to that required in the host Member State. Where the education and training received by the individual in his home state differed substantially from that required in the host Member State, or where there was a substantial mismatch between the regulated activities in the home and host Member States, the host Member State could require the holder of the diploma either to complete an adaptation period of not more than three years, or to take an aptitude test. Except in those cases where the holder would need a precise knowledge of the law of the host Member State to carry on the profession, the choice of whether to undergo an adaptation period or an aptitude test belonged to the diploma holder.

The former Directive 89/48 was considered by the Court of Justice in the following case:

Burbaud (Case C-285/01)

A Portuguese national was refused admission to the hospital managers' corps of the French civil service on the ground that it was first necessary to pass the entrance examination of the Ecole Nationale de la Santé Publique (the French National School of Public Health, the ENSP). The Court of Justice first analysed whether the duties performed by the members of the corps fell within the scope of the former Directive 89/48. The Court held that confirmation of passing the ENSP final examination could be regarded as a diploma. Its equivalence to the qualification awarded to Burbaud by a Lisbon school should be ascertained by the national court. The Court held that if it transpires that the diplomas were awarded on completion of equivalent education or training, the directive precluded the French authorities from making the access of a Portuguese national to the profession of manager in a public hospital subject to the condition that she complete the ENSP course and pass its final examination. A method of recruitment which did not allow for account to be taken of specific qualifications in the field of hospital management of candidates who were nationals of other Member States placed them at a disadvantage which was liable to dissuade them from exercising their rights, as workers, to freedom of movement. While such an obstacle to a fundamental freedom guaranteed by the Treaty could be justified by an objective in the general interest, such as selection of the best candidates in the most objective conditions possible, it was a further condition that the restriction did not go beyond what was necessary to achieve that objective. The Court held that requiring candidates who were properly qualified to pass the ENSP entrance examination had the effect of downgrading them, which was not necessary to achieve the objective pursued and which could not therefore be justified in the light of the Treaty provisions. The Court therefore concluded that such an examination was incompatible with the Treaty provisions.

In the following case, the Commission brought an action against Greece for non-compliance with the former Directive 89/48:

Commission v Greece (Case C-274/05)

The Commission complained that Greece had systematically refused to recognise diplomas which had been obtained following education and training provided within the framework of 'homologation agreements' (also referred to as 'franchise agreements').

Under these agreements, education and training provided by a private body in Greece was homologated by an authority (normally a university) of another Member State, which awarded the diploma on the basis of a prior agreement between the two establishments.

The Court stated that the general system for the recognition of higher education diplomas was based on the mutual trust that Member States had in the professional qualifications that they awarded. That system did not involve recognition of a diploma for its intrinsic value, but established a presumption that the qualifications of a person entitled to pursue a regulated profession in one Member State were sufficient for the pursuit of that profession in the other Member States. It was for the competent authorities awarding the diplomas alone to verify, in the light of the rules applicable in their professional education and training systems, the conditions necessary for their award and the nature of the establishment in which the holder received his education and training. By contrast, **the host Member State could not examine the basis on which the diplomas had been awarded.**

The Court rejected Greece's approach – which was to apply its own rules (as the Member State in which the education and training were received) – as that would have the effect of treating persons who received education and training of an equivalent quality differently, that is to say, depending on the Member State in which they undertook their education and training. The Court also noted that the education and training should not necessarily have been received in a university or in a higher education establishment.

The Court therefore declared that, by failing to recognise the diplomas awarded by the competent authorities of another Member State following education and training provided in Greece within the framework of a homologation agreement, Greece had infringed the Union rules on recognition of diplomas.

The following case also concerned the application of the former Directive 89/48:

Consiglio degli Ingegneri v Ministero della Giustizia, Marco Cavallera (Case C-311/06)

The pursuit of the profession of engineer in both Italy and Spain was conditional on possession of a university diploma and registration in the register of the relevant professional body. In addition, the Italian system, unlike that in Spain, provided for a state examination which a candidate had to pass in order to be entitled to pursue the profession.

Cavallera, an Italian national, was the holder of a mechanical engineering qualification awarded in 1999 by the University of Turin (Italy) after three years' education and training.

In 2001 he applied for, and obtained, homologation (i.e. approval) in Spain of his Italian qualification, allowing him to accede to the regulated profession. On the basis of the certificate of homologation, Cavallera enrolled in the register of one of the 'colegios de ingenieros técnicos industriales' in Catalonia (Spain), in order to be entitled to pursue in Spain the regulated profession of industrial technical engineer, specialising in mechanical engineering.

Cavallera did not work professionally outside Italy and did not follow any course of study or take any examinations under the Spanish education system. Likewise, he did not take the state examination provided for under Italian legislation for the purpose of being entitled to pursue the profession of engineer.

In 2002, on application by Cavallera, the Italian Ministero della Giustizia (Ministry of Justice) recognised the validity of the Spanish certificate for the purpose of his enrolment in the register of engineers in Italy.

The Consiglio Nazionale degli Ingegneri (National Council of Engineers) challenged that decision, arguing that, under the former Directive 89/48 and the relevant national legislation, the Italian authorities could not recognise Cavallera's Spanish certificate, because such recognition would have the effect of exempting him from the state examination required under Italian law.

The Consiglio di Stato (the Italian court of final instance) referred the case to the Court of Justice pursuant to the former Art 234 EC Treaty (now Art 267 TFEU) to determine whether the former Directive 89/48 could be relied on by Cavallera for the purpose of gaining access to the profession of engineer in Italy.

The Court stated that, according to the actual definition in the former directive itself, a 'diploma' excluded a certificate issued by a Member State if that certificate: (i) did not attest to any education or training covered by the education system of that Member State; and (ii) was not based on either an examination taken or professional experience acquired in that Member State. The application of the former directive in such circumstances would be tantamount to allowing a person who had merely obtained a qualification in the Member State in which he studied, which did not in itself provide access to that regulated profession, nonetheless to gain access to that profession, even though the homologation certificate obtained elsewhere provided no evidence that the holder had acquired an additional qualification or professional experience. That would be contrary to the principle, enshrined in the former directive, that Member States reserve the option of fixing the minimum level of qualification necessary to guarantee the quality of services provided within their territory.

The former Directive 89/48 was implemented in the UK by the European Communities (Recognition of Professional Qualifications) (First General System) Regulations 2005 (SI 2005/18). Under these regulations, professional bodies were obliged to recognise the qualifications of other Union professionals, to provide full reasons where this was not done in individual cases, and to set up an independent appeal tribunal before which any refusal of recognition could be challenged. The European Communities (Recognition of Professional Qualifications) Regulations 2007 (SI 2007/2781) have implemented those parts of Directive 2005/36 which apply: (i) to the 'general system' professions (i.e. those covered by the former Directive 89/48); and (ii) universally across all professions.

With regard to the establishment of lawyers, Directive 98/5 was adopted at the end of 1997, the aim of which is to make it easier for lawyers to practise in other Member States. The directive, which had to be implemented by March 2000:

- permits EU lawyers to be established under their home title in another Member State;
- requires them to register with an appropriate regulatory body in the host state;
- gives them a right to representation within the host regulatory body;
- subjects them to the rules and regulatory regime of the host regulatory body;
- offers them a 'fast track' to requalification as a lawyer of the host state.

Directive 98/5 has been implemented in the UK by the European Community (Lawyer's Practice) Regulations 2000 (SI 2000/1119), as amended, which came into force on 22 May 2000. Directive 98/5 has not been affected by Directive 2005/36. The following case, which concerned Directive 98/5, was decided by the Court of Justice:

Wilson v *Ordre des avocats du barreau du Luxembourg and Commission* v *Luxembourg* (Cases C-506/04 and C-193/05)

In order to practise the profession of lawyer in Luxembourg, Luxembourg law set down a condition that a lawyer had to 'be proficient in the language of statutory provisions as well as the administrative and court languages', and required a prior test of that knowledge.

Graham Wilson, a UK national, was a barrister. He was a member of the Bar of England and Wales and had practised the profession of lawyer in Luxembourg since 1994. In 2003, Wilson refused to attend an oral hearing with the Bar Council in order to assess his linguistic knowledge. As a consequence, the Bar Council refused to register him on the register of lawyers practising under their home-country professional title.

Wilson challenged that decision by bringing an action for annulment before a court in Luxembourg, which referred the case to the Court of Justice, seeking guidance on whether Directive 98/5 allowed the host Member State to make the right of a lawyer to practise his profession on a permanent basis in that Member State under his home-country professional title subject to a test of his proficiency in the languages of that Member State.

The Court of Justice stated that the directive aimed to facilitate the exercise of the fundamental freedom of establishment for lawyers, and that it precluded a prior test of linguistic knowledge. Only a certificate attesting to registration with the competent authority of the home Member State was necessary in order to be registered with a Bar in the host Member State. To compensate for the exclusion of this prior testing, rules of professional conduct existed to ensure the protection of consumers and the proper administration of justice. Therefore, subject to disciplinary sanctions, a European lawyer had to respect those rules of both the home Member State and those of the host Member State. Among those obligations was the duty of a lawyer not to handle cases which required linguistic knowledge that he did not possess.

Furthermore, according to the directive, a European lawyer who wanted to join the profession of the host Member State had to show that he had effectively and regularly pursued an activity for a period of at least three years in the law of that Member State.

The Court concluded that the directive precluded a national law which made registration of a European lawyer with the Bar of the host Member State subject to a language test.

In parallel to this case, the Commission also brought an action against Luxembourg for its failure to fulfil obligations, taking the view that three national measures were contrary to the directive:

(i) Registration on the Bar register following an oral test to assess linguistic knowledge

Luxembourg relied on the proper administration of justice to justify the existence of that provision, but the Court of Justice observed, as in Wilson's case, that the directive did not provide for any condition other than that the lawyer had to produce a certificate attesting to registration in the home Member State, and concluded that the Luxembourg provision which made registration of a European lawyer with the competent national authority subject to a prior test of linguistic knowledge was contrary to the directive.

(ii) The prohibition on European lawyers accepting service on behalf of companies in Luxembourg

The Court noted the principle that European lawyers were entitled to pursue the same professional activities as lawyers practising under the professional title of the host Member State, subject to the exceptions provided for by the directive. The activity of accepting service on behalf of companies was not included in those exceptions. Member States were not authorised to provide in their national law for other exceptions to that principle.

(iii) The obligation to produce each year a certificate from the home Member State

The Court observed that that obligation was an unjustified administrative burden which was contrary to the directive, as the latter already enshrined a principle of mutual assistance, according to which the competent authority of the home Member State had to notify the competent authority of the host Member State when disciplinary proceedings were initiated against a European lawyer.

On those three grounds, the Court of Justice declared that Luxembourg had failed to fulfil its Union obligations.

The following case concerned Directive 98/5:

Angelo Alberto Torresi and Pierfrancesco Torresi v *Consiglio dell'Ordine degli Avvocati di Macerata* (Joined Cases C-58/13 and C-59/13)

The purpose of Directive 98/5 is to facilitate practice of the profession of lawyer on a permanent basis (in a self-employed or salaried capacity) in a Member State other than that in which the professional qualification was obtained, although the profession can be practised only under the home-country professional title. The directive provides that the competent authority of the Member State where the lawyer is established is to register the lawyer upon presentation of a certificate attesting to his registration with the competent authority in the Member State where the lawyer obtained his title.

After two Italian nationals (Mr Angelo Alberto Torresi and Mr Pierfranco Torresi) had obtained university law degrees in Italy, they each obtained a university law degree in Spain. On 1 December 2011 they were registered as lawyers in the register of the Ilustre Colegio de Abogados de Santa Cruz de Tenerife (Bar of Santa Cruz de Tenerife, Spain). On 17 March 2012 they submitted applications to the Bar Council of Macerata (Italy) for their registration in the 'special section of the lawyers' register' (in accordance with Art 3, Directive 98/5). That section covered lawyers who had a title issued in a Member State other than Italy, but who were established in Italy (Art 3(2), Directive 98/5).

As the Bar Council of Macerata did not issue a decision within the period prescribed, Angelo Alberto Torresi and Pierfranco Torresi brought actions before the Consiglio Nazionale Forense (the National Bar Council in Italy; 'CNF') seeking a decision on their applications for registration. They claimed that under the legislation in force the registrations applied for were subject to a single condition, namely the presentation of 'a certificate attesting to registration with the competent authority in the home Member State' (in this case, Spain). As that condition was met in this case, Angelo Alberto Torresi and Pierfranco Torresi considered that they should have been registered.

The CNF argued that it was not open to Angelo Alberto Torresi and Pierfranco Torresi to rely on the directive on the establishment of lawyers if the acquisition of the title in Spain had no other purpose than to circumvent Italian law governing access to the profession of lawyer and thereby constitute an abuse of the right of establishment. The CNF therefore sought to ascertain from the Court of Justice whether the competent authorities of a Member State may refuse, on the ground of an abuse of rights, registration in the register of lawyers to nationals of that Member State who, after obtaining a university degree in that Member State, had travelled to another Member State in order to acquire there the professional qualification of lawyer and had subsequently returned to the first Member

State with a view to practising the profession there under the title obtained in the second Member State.

The Court of Justice stated that, in order to facilitate the practice of the profession of lawyer on a permanent basis in a Member State other than that in which the professional qualification was obtained, Directive 98/5 set up a mechanism for the mutual recognition of the professional titles of migrant lawyers wishing to practise under their home-country title. The EU legislature thereby sought to put an end to the differences in national rules on conditions for registration which gave rise to inequalities and obstacles to freedom of movement. The directive therefore undertakes a complete harmonisation of the conditions applicable to the right of establishment of lawyers.

The Court had previously ruled in *Commission v Luxembourg* (Case C-193/05) and *Wilson* (Case C-506/04) that the presentation of a certificate attesting to registration in the home Member State was the only condition to which registration of the person concerned in the host Member State could be subject, enabling him to practise in the latter Member State under his home-country professional title.

The Court stated that rules of EU law could not be relied on for abusive or fraudulent ends and, that a Member State was entitled to take any measures necessary to prevent its nationals from improperly circumventing its national legislation. In that regard, the Court stated that a finding of abuse required an objective element (namely, despite formal observance of the conditions laid down by EU rules, the purpose of those rules had not been achieved) and a subjective element (namely, it had to be apparent that there was an intention to obtain an improper advantage).

That said, the Court held that, in a single market, the right of EU citizens to choose the Member State in which they wished to acquire their professional title and the Member State in which they intended to practise their profession was inherent in the exercise of the fundamental freedoms guaranteed by the Treaties.

The fact that a national of a Member State who had obtained a university degree in that State travels to another Member State, in order to acquire there the title of lawyer, and subsequently returned to his Member State in order to practise there the profession of lawyer under the professional title obtained in the other Member State, was the realisation of one of the objectives of the directive and did not constitute an abuse of the right of establishment.

Nor did the fact that the submission of the application for registration in the register of lawyers took place soon after the professional title was obtained in the host Member State constitute an abuse of rights, as there was no requirement in the directive that there be a period of practical experience in the home Member State.

The Court held that it did not constitute an abuse where a national of a Member State who holds a university degree travelled to another Member State in order to acquire the professional qualification of lawyer in the host Member State and subsequently returned to his Member State in order to practise there.

Directive 92/51: recognition of diplomas for other professional activities

The former Directive 89/48 only applied to regulated professional activities where the holder had completed at least three years in higher education. There remained a large residual category of many professional and other activities for which some further education was required, but which did not fall within the scope of the former Directive 89/48. A further directive was therefore approved in 1992. Directive 92/51 (which was subsequently amended by Directive 2001/19) dealt with the remaining areas of professional education and training and applied to holders of diplomas, which showed either that the holder had successfully completed a post-secondary course of at least a year or the equivalent on a part-time basis, entry to which was on the same basis as entry into university or higher education, or that the holder had been successful in completing one of the recognised education and training courses listed in the directive. Similar to the former Directive 89/48, the host Member State could require the diploma holder to complete an adaptation period of not more than three years or to take an aptitude test (Art 4(1)(b)).

Directive 92/51 has been repealed and replaced by Directive 2005/36 (see below).

Directive 2005/36: the recognition of professional qualifications

Directive 2005/36 on the recognition of professional qualifications (OJ 2005 L 255/22) was adopted on 7 September 2005 and had to be transposed into national law by 20 October 2007. The provisions of the directive are considered in further detail below.

Scope

The directive applies to all EU citizens seeking to practise a 'regulated profession' in a Member State other than that in which they obtained their professional qualifications, on either a self-employed or employed basis (Art 2(1)).

At a legislative level, the directive forms part of the process of legislative consolidation aimed at combining the three general system directives (Directives 89/48, 92/51 and 99/42) in a single text along with 12 sectoral directives (i.e. 93/16, 77/452, 77/453, 78/686, 78/687, 78/1026, 78/1027, 80/154, 80/155, 85/432, 85/433 and 85/384) covering the seven professions of doctor, nurse, dental practitioner, veterinary surgeon, midwife, pharmacist and architect. The consolidation of these 15 directives resulted in their repeal on 20 October 2007 (Art 62). The directive has subsequently been amended by Directive 2013/55, which has an implementation date of 18 January 2016 (see below).

The specific directives on the provision of services and establishment of lawyers (i.e. Directives 77/249 and 98/5) are not covered by this exercise, as they concern the recognition not of professional qualifications but of the authorisation to practise. Recognition of lawyers' qualifications was previously governed by Directive 89/48, and is thus now covered by Directive 2005/36.

Allowing Member State nationals the freedom to provide services and the right of establishment

The recognition of professional qualifications enables beneficiaries to gain access in host Member States to the professions in which they are qualified, and to practise under the same conditions as nationals of that Member State in cases where these professions are regulated.

The directive makes a distinction between 'freedom to provide services' and 'freedom of establishment' on the basis of criteria identified by the Court of Justice: duration, frequency, regularity and continuity of the provision of services. Title II, Arts 5–9 relate to freedom to provide services, and Title III, Arts 10–52 relate to freedom of establishment.

Articles 5–9: facilitating temporary and occasional provision of cross-border services

Nationals of a Member State who are legally established in a given Member State may provide services on a temporary and occasional basis in another Member State under their original professional title without having to apply for recognition of their qualifications. However, if service providers relocate outside of their Member State of establishment in order to provide services, they must also provide evidence of two years' professional experience if the profession in question is not regulated in that Member State.

The host Member State may require the service provider to make a declaration prior to providing any services on its territory and renew it annually, including the details of any insurance cover or other means of personal or collective protection with regard to professional liability. The host Member State may also require that the first application be accompanied by certain documents listed in the directive, such as proof of the nationality of the service provider, of their legal establishment, and of their professional qualifications.

If the host Member State requires *pro forma* registration with the competent professional association, this must occur automatically upon the competent authority that received the prior declaration forwarding the applicant's file to the professional organisation or body. For professions which have public health or safety implications and do not benefit from automatic recognition, the host Member State may carry out a prior check of the service provider's professional qualifications within the limits of the principle of proportionality.

In cases where the service is provided under the professional title of the Member State of establishment or under the formal qualification of the service provider, the competent authorities of the host Member State may require service providers to furnish the recipient of the service with certain information, particularly with regard to insurance coverage against the financial risks connected with any challenge to their professional liability.

The competent authorities shall ensure the exchange of all information necessary for complaints by a recipient of a service against a service provider to be correctly pursued. The host Member State may also ask the Member State of establishment for information regarding the service provider's legal establishment, good conduct, and the absence of any penalties for professional misconduct. With regard to both the temporary provision of services and permanent establishment in another Member State, the directive provides for the proactive exchange of information relating to any serious circumstances which arose when the individual in question was established on their territory and which are liable to have consequences for the pursuit of the professional activities concerned. This exchange of information must, at any rate, be carried out in compliance with existing legislation on data protection.

Articles 10–52: improving the existing systems of recognition for the purpose of permanent establishment in another Member State

In the context of the provision of cross-border services, 'freedom of establishment' is the framework which applies when a professional enjoys the effective freedom to become established in another Member State in order to conduct a professional activity there on a stable basis. With respect to establishment, the directive comprises the three former systems of recognition:

1   *Chapter I, Arts 10–15: general system for the recognition of professional qualifications.* This system applies as a fall-back to all the professions not covered by specific rules of recognition and to certain situations where the migrant professional does not meet the conditions set out in other recognition schemes. This general system is based on the principle of mutual recognition, without prejudice to the application of compensatory measures if there are substantial differences between the training acquired by the migrant and the training required in the host Member State. The compensatory measure may take the form of an adaptation period or an aptitude test. The choice between one or other of these tests is up to the migrant unless specific derogations exist.

2   *Chapter II, Arts 16–20: system of automatic recognition of qualifications attested by professional experience.* The industrial, craft and commercial activities listed in the directive are subject, under the conditions stated, to the automatic recognition of qualifications attested by professional experience.

3   *Chapter III, Arts 21–49: system of automatic recognition of qualifications for specific professions.* The automatic recognition of training qualifications, on the basis of coordination of the minimum training conditions, covers the following professions: doctors, nurses responsible for general care, dental practitioners, specialised dental practitioners, veterinary surgeons, midwives, pharmacists and architects.

The three systems of recognition of qualifications, which are applicable in the context of establishment, are set out and examined in detail below.

Chapter I, Articles 10–15: general system for the recognition of professional qualifications

When, in a host Member State, access to, or pursuit of, a profession is regulated (i.e. subject to possession of specific professional qualifications), the competent authority in the host Member State allows access to, and pursuit of, the profession in question under the same conditions as for nationals, provided that the applicant holds a training qualification obtained in another Member State which attests to a level of training at least equivalent to the level immediately below that required in the host Member State.

When, on the other hand, in the Member State of the applicant, access to a profession is not subject to possession of specific professional qualifications, the applicant should, in order to be able to gain access to the profession in a host Member State which does regulate that profession, provide proof of two years' full-time professional experience over the preceding ten years on top of the qualification.

The directive distinguishes between five levels of professional qualification:

(i)   attestation of competence which corresponds to general primary or secondary education, attesting that the holder has acquired general knowledge, or an attestation of competence issued by a competent authority in the home Member State on the basis of a training course not forming part of a certificate or diploma, or of three years' professional experience;

(ii)   a certificate which corresponds to training at secondary level, of a technical or professional nature or general in character, supplemented by a professional course;

(iii)   a diploma certifying successful completion of training at post-secondary level of a duration of at least one year, or professional training which is comparable in terms of responsibilities and functions;

(iv) a diploma certifying successful completion of training at higher or university level of a duration of at least three years and less than four years;

(v) a diploma certifying successful completion of training at higher or university level of a duration of at least four years.

On an exceptional basis, other types of training can be treated as coming within one of the five levels.

The host Member State can make recognition of qualifications subject to the applicant completing a compensation measure (aptitude test or adaptation period of a maximum of three years) if:

1 the training is one year shorter than that required by the host Member State; or

2 the training received covers substantially different matters to those covered by the evidence of formal training required in the host Member State; or

3 the profession, as defined in the host Member State, comprises one or more regulated professional activities which do not exist in the corresponding profession in the applicant's home Member State, and that difference consists of specific training which covers substantially different matters from those completed by the migrant.

The host Member State must, in principle, offer the applicant the choice between an adaptation period and an aptitude test. The host Member State can only derogate from this requirement in the cases specifically provided for, or with the Commission's authorisation.

The directive provides for representative professional associations at both national and European level to establish 'common platforms' by determining measures to compensate for the substantial differences identified between the training requirements in at least two-thirds of the Member States, and in all the Member States which regulate that profession. That is, the platform must make it possible to provide adequate guarantees as to the level of qualification. If such a platform is likely to make the recognition of professional qualifications easier, the Commission may submit it to the Member States and adopt an implementing measure. Once this implementing measure has been adopted, the Member States shall waive the imposition of compensatory measures on applicants who meet the platform's conditions.

Chapter II, Articles 16–20: system of automatic recognition of qualifications attested by professional experience in certain industrial, craft and commercial activities

By including the classes of professional activity covered by the former 'transitional' directives (i.e. Directives 64/222, 64/427, 68/364, 68/366, 68/368, 70/523, 75/368, 75/369, 82/470 and 82/489, which had already been consolidated by Directive 99/42) and reducing the number of types of recognition to three, this directive aims to continue the objective of simplifying the legislation which sets the key conditions for the recognition of professional experience.

The elements taken into consideration for the recognition of professional experience are the duration and form of professional experience (in a self-employed or employed capacity) in the reference sector. Previous training is also taken into consideration and may reduce the amount of professional experience required. All previous training should, however, be proven by a certificate recognised by the Member State or judged by a competent professional body to be fully valid.

The pursuit of professional activities referred to in list I of Annex IV (which refers to various sectors ranging from the textile industry through to the chemical industry, via the oil industry, printing, manufacturing industry, and construction) is subject to the following conditions (Table 13.1):

Table 13.1 Conditions attaching to professional activities referred to in list I of Annex IV

Years of professional experience in a self-employed capacity	Years of professional experience in an employed capacity	Previous training
6	–	–
3	–	3
4	–	2
3	5	–
–	5 in an executive position (except hairdressing establishments)	3

With regard to the pursuit of the professional activities referred to in list II of Annex IV (which refers to numerous sectors ranging from the manufacture of transport equipment to activities allied to transport, postal services and telecommunications and photographic studios) the directive lays down the following conditions (Table 13.2):

Table 13.2 Conditions attaching to professional activities referred to in list II of Annex IV

Years of professional experience in a self-employed capacity	Years of professional experience in an employed capacity	Previous training
5	–	–
3	–	3
4	–	2
3	5	–
–	5	3
–	6	2

With regard to the pursuit of the professional activities referred to in list III of Annex IV (which refers to numerous sectors ranging from restaurants and hotels to personal, community and recreation services, and others) the directive lays down the following conditions (Table 13.3):

Table 13.3 Conditions attaching to professional activities referred to in list III of Annex IV

Years of professional experience in a self-employed capacity	Years of professional experience in an employed capacity	Previous training
3	–	–
2	–	Unspecified duration
2	3	–
–	3	Unspecified duration

Chapter III, Articles 21–49: system of automatic recognition of qualifications for the professions of doctor, nurse, dentist, veterinary surgeon, midwife, pharmacist and architect

Each Member State automatically recognises certificates of training giving access to professional activities as a doctor, nurse responsible for general care, dental practitioner, veterinary surgeon, midwife, pharmacist and architect, covered by Annex V to the directive.

The directive also adopts the principle of automatic recognition for medical and dental specialisations common to at least two Member States under existing law, but restricts future additions to the directive of new medical specialisations – eligible for automatic recognition – to those that are common to at least two-fifths of the Member States.

For the purposes of equivalence in qualifications, the directive sets minimum training conditions for the following professions:

(i) **Doctor**: basic medical training precedes specialist medical training or the training of general practitioners.

- *Basic medical training*: admission to basic medical training shall be contingent upon possession of a diploma or certificate providing access to universities or equivalent institutes which provide higher education and shall comprise a total of at least six years of study or 5,500 hours of theoretical and practical training provided by, or under the supervision of, a university.

- *Specialist medical training*: admission to specialist medical training shall be contingent upon completion of six years of study in basic medical training and comprise full-time theoretical and practical training at a university or other recognised centre for a minimum duration which is not less than the duration referred to by the directive in Annex V, point 5.1.3 (such as, for example, five years for the specialisation in general surgery).

- *Training of general practitioners*: admission to general medical training shall be contingent upon completion of six years of study in basic medical training and comprise full-time practical training in an approved hospital, for a minimum duration of two years for any training of general practitioners leading to the award of evidence of formal qualifications issued before 1 January 2006, and of three years for certificates of training issued after that date.

(ii) **Nurse responsible for general care**: admission to training for nurses responsible for general care shall be contingent upon completion of general education of ten years, as attested by a diploma or other recognised certificate, shall comprise at least three years of study or 4,600 hours of theoretical and clinical training on a full-time basis, and shall include at least the programme described in Annex V, point 5.2.1.

(iii) **Dental practitioner**: admission to training as a dental practitioner presupposes possession of a diploma or certificate giving access, for the studies in question, to universities or higher institutes of an equivalent level, and shall comprise a total of at least five years of full-time theoretical and practical study, comprising at least the programme described in Annex V, point 5.3.1.

(iv) **Veterinary surgeon**: admission to veterinary training shall be contingent upon possession of a diploma or certificate entitling the holder to enter, for the studies in question, university establishments or institutes of higher education of an equivalent level, and shall comprise a total of at least five years of full-time theoretical and practical study at a university or other recognised higher institute, covering at least the study programme referred to in Annex V, point 5.4.1.

(v) **Midwife**: access to training as a midwife shall be contingent upon the following routes:

- completion of at least the first ten years of general school education. In this case, it entails specific full-time training as a midwife comprising at least three years of theoretical and practical study covering at least the programme described in Annex V, point 5.5.1; or
- possession of evidence of formal qualifications as a nurse responsible for general care. In this case, it entails in total at least a specific full-time training as a midwife of 18 months' duration, covering at least the study programme described in Annex V, point 5.5.1.

(vi) **Pharmacist**: admission to a course of training as a pharmacist shall be contingent upon possession of a diploma or certificate giving access, for the studies in question, to universities or higher institutes of an equivalent level, and shall include training of at least five years' duration, including at least four years of full-time theoretical and practical training at a university and a six-month traineeship in a pharmacy which is open to the public or in a hospital.

(vii) **Architect**: admission to a course of training as an architect shall be contingent upon possession of a diploma or certificate giving access, for the studies in question, to universities or higher institutes of an equivalent level, and shall comprise a total of at least four years of full-time study or six years of study, at least three years of which are on a full-time basis. For certain qualifications, Germany derogates from the conditions for the training of architects.

The directive extends the possibility for Member States to authorise part-time training for all of these professions, provided that the overall duration, level and quality of such training is not lower than that of continuous full-time training.

With the exception of the professions of doctor and architect, the directive provides a minimum programme of subjects to follow, which leaves room for the Member States to draw up more detailed study programmes. These lists of subjects which appear in Annex V can be amended to the extent required to adapt them to scientific and technical progress. Following the professional training they have received, aspiring doctors, nurses, dentists, veterinary surgeons, midwives, pharmacists and architects will possess a training qualification which has been issued by the competent bodies in the Member States bearing the titles described in Annex V and will enable them to practise their profession in any Member State. Without prejudice to the provisions relating to established rights, the Member States shall make access to, and pursuit of, the professional activities of doctor, nurse, dentist, veterinary surgeon, midwife and pharmacist subject to possession of one of the qualifications listed in the corresponding annexes which give guarantees relating to the acquisition by the party concerned of the knowledge and aptitudes referred to in Arts 24, 31, 34, 38, 40 and 44.

Without prejudice to the specific established rights granted to the professions concerned, and particularly to general practitioners and architects (Annex VI), if the evidence of medical training (which provides access to the professional activities of doctors with basic training and specialised doctors, nurses responsible for general care, dental practitioners, specialised dental practitioners, veterinary surgeons, midwives and pharmacists) held by nationals of Member States does not satisfy all the training requirements described, each Member State shall recognise as sufficient proof certificates of training issued by those Member States in so far as they attest successful completion of training which began before the reference dates laid down in Annex V.

Articles 50–52: procedure for the mutual recognition of professional qualifications

Articles 50–51 provide that an individual application must be submitted to the competent authority in the host Member State, accompanied by certain documents and certificates as listed in the directive (see Annex VII). According to the directive, the competent authorities will have one month to acknowledge receipt of an application and to draw attention to any missing documents. A decision has to be taken within three months of the date on which the application was received in full. Reasons have to be given for any rejection. A rejection, or a failure to take a decision by the deadline, may be contested in the national courts.

Member State nationals shall be able to use the title conferred on them, and possibly an abbreviated form thereof, as well as the professional title of the corresponding host Member State. If a profession is regulated in the host Member State by an association or organisation (see Annex I), Member State nationals must be able to become members of that organisation or association in order to be able to use the title (Art 52).

Article 57: knowledge of languages

Member States may require migrants to have the knowledge of languages necessary for practising the profession. This provision must be applied proportionately, which rules out the systematic imposition of language tests before a professional activity can be practised. It should be noted that any evaluation of language skills is separate from the recognition of professional qualifications. It must take place after recognition, when actual access to the profession in question is sought (Art 53).

Articles 56–60: administrative cooperation and other provisions

In order to facilitate the application of the above provisions, the directive seeks close collaboration between the competent authorities in the host Member State and the home Member State, and the introduction of the following provisions:

(i)   each Member State shall designate a coordinator to facilitate the uniform application of the directive (Art 56);

(ii) each Member State shall designate contact points which will have the task of providing citizens with such information as is necessary concerning the recognition of professional qualifications and to assist them in enforcing their rights, particularly through contact with the competent authorities to rule on requests for recognition (Art 57);

(iii) the nomination of Member States' representatives to the Committee on the recognition of professional qualifications. This committee, which is chaired by the Commission representative, is to assist the Commission within the limits of the enforcement powers conferred on it by the directive (Art 58);

(iv) the Commission shall consult with experts from the professional groups in an appropriate manner (Art 59).

Every two years, the Member States shall send a report to the Commission on the application of the system. If the application of one of the provisions of the directive presents major difficulties in a particular area, the Commission shall examine those difficulties in collaboration with the Member State concerned (Art 60(1)).

As from 20 October 2007, every five years the Commission will draw up a report on the implementation of the directive (Art 60(2)).

Directive 2013/55: amendments to Directive 2005/36

Directive 2013/55 has amended Directive 2005/36 with updated conditions and procedures. These amendments had to be implemented by 18 January 2016. The amendments, which are intended to make the process of professional recognition easier for migrant professionals, include the following:

- The introduction of a 'professional card' for interested professions.
- Increased use of online tools (including the Internal Market Information (IMI) system).
- Recognition for traineeships and the possibility of 'partial access' in some cases.
- Updates to the details surrounding the training for the 'sectoral' professions: doctors, dentists, nurses, midwives, pharmacists, architects and veterinary surgeons.
- An 'alert mechanism' to let all relevant authorities know when health professionals, or those working with children, are banned from practising.
- NCPs will in future be termed 'Assistance Centres' to emphasise the role of providing tailored, informed advice and guidance on the process of professional recognition.

A consolidated version of Directive 2005/36 is available at:

> http://ec.europa.eu/growth/single-market/services/qualifications/
> policy-developments/legislation

Other qualifications

In the case of a qualification which does not fall within the scope of Directive 2005/36, the basic rules (developed through the case law of the Court of Justice) will continue to apply with regard to the recognition and investigation of the equivalence of the qualification. In such a case, the person seeking to establish himself in another Member State is relying directly on Art 49 TFEU. It is therefore necessary to review the case law of the Court of Justice:

Thieffry v Conseil de l'Ordre des Avocats à la Cour de Paris (Case 71/76)

A Belgian national had obtained a doctorate in law in Belgium. He practised as an advocate in Brussels (Belgium) for a number of years. His qualifications were recognised by a French university as *equivalent* to a degree in French law. He obtained a certificate stating that he was academically qualified for the profession of *avocat*. However, the French Bar refused him admission to the training stage solely on the ground that he did not have a degree in French law.

The Court held that if the applicant had already obtained what was recognised (professionally and academically) as an **equivalent qualification** and had **satisfied the necessary training requirements** then the French Bar would not have been justified in excluding him from admission solely because he did not have a French law degree. The fact that no directives had been adopted under what is now Art 53 TFEU (previously Art 47 EC Treaty) was irrelevant.

This was taken a stage further by the Court of Justice in the following case:

UNECTEF v Heylens (Case 222/86)

Heylens was a Belgian national who held a Belgian football trainer's diploma. He was taken on as the trainer of a French football team. He applied for recognition of his diploma as equivalent to the French diploma. His application was refused. He continued to practise as a trainer and was prosecuted by the French football trainers' union (UNECTEF). The French court referred the case to the Court of Justice under what is now Art 267 TFEU (previously Art 234 EC Treaty) for a preliminary ruling, questioning the compatibility of the French system with Union law. The Court of Justice held as follows:

10. In the absence of harmonisation of the conditions of access to a particular occupation, the Member States are entitled to lay down the knowledge and qualifications needed in order to pursue it and to require the production of a diploma certifying that the holder has the relevant knowledge and qualifications.

    . . .

13. Since it has to reconcile the requirement as to the qualifications necessary in order to pursue a particular occupation with the requirements of the free movement of workers, **the procedure for the recognition of equivalence must enable the national authorities to assure themselves, on an objective basis, that the foreign diploma certifies that its holder has the knowledge and qualifications which are, if not identical, at least equivalent to those certified by the national diploma. That assessment of the equivalence of the foreign diploma must be effected exclusively in the light of the level of knowledge and qualifications which its holder can be assumed to possess in the light of that diploma, having regard to the nature and duration of the studies and practical training which the diploma certifies that he has carried out.** [emphasis added]

In the above case, the Court of Justice held that the assessment of equivalence of a foreign diploma must be effected exclusively in the light of 'the level of knowledge and qualifications which its holder can be assumed to possess in the light of that diploma', having regard to 'the nature and duration of the studies and practical training which the diploma certifies that he has carried out'. This was further amplified by the Court of Justice in the following case:

Vlassopoulou v Ministerium für Justiz, Bundes- und Europaangelegenheiten Baden-Württemberg (Case C-340/89)

The applicant was a Greek who had obtained a Greek law degree and who had been admitted to the Athens Bar (in Greece). Most of her professional practice had been undertaken in Germany and involved the application of German law. She applied for admission to the German Bar. Her application was rejected on the ground that she lacked the necessary qualifications. The case came before the German Federal Supreme Court, who referred the matter to the Court of Justice to determine whether it was permissible to refuse admission for this reason. The Court of Justice held as follows:

15. It must be stated in this regard that, even if applied without any discrimination on the basis of nationality, national requirements concerning qualifications may have the effect of hindering nationals of the other Member States in the exercise of their right of establishment guaranteed to them by . . . [Article 49 TFEU]. That could be the case if the national rules in question took no account of the knowledge and qualifications already acquired by the person concerned in another Member State.

16. Consequently, a Member State which receives a request to admit a person to a profession to which access, under national law, depends upon the possession of a diploma or a professional qualification must take into consideration the diplomas, certificates and other evidence of qualifications which the person concerned has acquired in order to exercise the same profession in another Member State by making comparison between the specialised knowledge and abilities certified by those diplomas and the knowledge and qualifications required by the national rules. [emphasis added]

In the above case, the Court of Justice held that national authorities are required to consider any education or training received by that person which is indicated by the qualification, and to contrast that with the knowledge and skills required by the domestic qualification. If they are *equivalent* then the Member State *must* recognise the qualification. If they are not considered equivalent, then they must go on to consider the 'knowledge or training received by the applicant through study or experience'; this may be sufficient to make up for what was lacking in the formal qualification (paras 19–20).

A number of subsequent cases have confirmed this approach:

Colegio Oficial de Agentes de la Propriedad Inmobiliara v *Aguirre, Newman and Others* (Case C-104/91)

Newman was prosecuted for practising as an estate agent in Spain without being a member of the Colegio. He had applied for membership but had received no response. He was a member of the Royal Institute of Chartered Surveyors in the UK. It should be noted that the prosecution took place before 4 January 1991, the date by which Directive 89/48 should have been implemented in Member States. Directive 89/48 has since been repealed and replaced by Directive 2005/36; see above. The Spanish court referred to the Court of Justice the question of how far the Colegio was obliged to take into account the defendant's UK qualifications.

The Court held that, in the absence of harmonisation of the conditions of access to a particular profession, Member States were entitled to lay down the knowledge and qualifications needed in order to pursue it and to require the production of a diploma certifying that the holder had the relevant knowledge and qualifications. In this case, the Member State was required to carry out a comparative examination of professional qualifications, taking into account the differences between the national legal systems concerned.

If the comparison showed that the knowledge and qualifications corresponded to the national provisions of the host Member State, then it was bound to accept their equivalence. If, on the other hand, the examination revealed only partial equivalence, the host Member State had the right to require the person concerned to demonstrate that he had acquired the additional knowledge and qualifications needed. The host Member State was under an obligation to give full reasons when it determined a lack of equivalence. This was to enable the person to take steps to remedy the deficiency or, if he disagreed with the decision, to challenge it in a court of law (*UNECTEF v Heylens* (Case 222/86); *Vlassopoulou* (Case C-340/89)).

Fernandez de Bobadilla v *Museo Nacional del Prado and Others* (Case C-234/97)

Ms Fernandez de Bobadilla (F) was a Spanish national. She obtained a BA in History of Art from an American university, following which she obtained a postgraduate degree in fine arts and restoration from a UK university. For the following three years, F worked for the

Prado (in Madrid, Spain) as a restorer of works of art under a temporary contract. She also worked for other studios and museums.

The Prado is attached to Spain's Ministry of Culture, and a collective agreement entered into provided that the post of restorer would be available only to persons who possessed a specified qualification. This did not include the qualifications F had obtained.

F applied to have her qualifications recognised as equivalent to those specified in the collective agreement, but she was told that she would need to take additional examinations to demonstrate that she had sufficient knowledge. She did not take these examinations.

The Prado subsequently advertised a permanent vacancy as a restorer of works of art. F applied but her application was rejected because she did not possess one of the specified qualifications. F argued that this infringed her free movement rights.

The case came before the Court of Justice, and the Court stated that if the general Directives 89/48 or 92/51 (which have since been repealed and replaced by Directive 2005/36) did not apply then:

28. . . . Community [i.e. Union] law does not in principle preclude a public body in a Member State from restricting access to a post to candidates holding a qualification awarded by an educational establishment in that Member State or any other foreign qualification officially recognised by the competent authorities of that Member State. However, where the qualification was awarded in another Member State, the procedure for granting it official recognition must comply with the requirements of Community [i.e. Union] law.

29. The Court has already had occasion to set out, *inter alia*, in Case C-340/89 *Vlassopoulou* [1991] ECR I-2357, the conditions with which the competent authorities of a Member State must comply when they receive a request to admit a person to a profession to which entry under national law depends on the possession of a diploma or professional qualification. . . .

31. It is clear from paragraph 16 of the judgment in *Vlassopoulou* that the competent authorities of the host Member State must take into consideration the diplomas, certificates and other evidence of qualifications which the person concerned has acquired in order to practise that profession in another Member State by comparing the specialised knowledge and abilities certified by those diplomas with the knowledge and qualifications required by the national rules.

32. If the comparative examination of diplomas results in the finding that the knowledge and qualifications certified by the diploma awarded in another Member State correspond to those required by the national provisions, the competent authorities of the host Member State must recognise that diploma as fulfilling the requirements laid down by its national provisions. If, on the other hand, the comparison reveals that the knowledge and qualifications certified by the foreign diploma and those required by the national provisions correspond only partially, the competent authorities are entitled to require the person concerned to show that he has acquired the knowledge and qualifications which are lacking (judgment in *Vlassopoulou*, cited above, paragraph 19).

33. In that regard, the competent national authorities must assess whether the knowledge acquired by the candidate, either during a course of study or by way of practical experience, is sufficient to show possession of knowledge which is lacking (judgment in *Vlassopoulou*, cited above, paragraph 20).

34. **Where no general procedure for official recognition has been laid down at national level by the host Member State, or where that procedure does not comply with the requirements of Community [i.e. Union] law as set out in paragraphs 29–33 of this judgment, it is for the public body seeking to fill the post itself to investigate whether the diploma obtained by the candidate in another Member State, together, where appropriate, with practical experience, is to be regarded as equivalent to the qualification required.** [emphasis added]

In the above case, the Court of Justice was undecided as to whether or not the general Directives 89/48 and 92/51 applied and therefore it determined the case on the basis that these two directives did not apply (these two directives have since been repealed and replaced by Directive 2005/36; see above). The Court reaffirmed its previous case law at paras 29–33 and stated at para 34 that it was the responsibility of the public body seeking to fill the vacancy to determine whether the foreign qualification and/or experience of the candidate were such as to afford equivalence to the qualifications specified (see also *Morgenbesser* (Case C-313/01)).

This line of reasoning was followed by the Court of Justice in the following case:

Hugo Fernando Hocsman v *Ministre de l'Emploi et de la Solidarité* (Case C-238/98)

Hocsman held a diploma of doctor of medicine awarded in 1976 by a university in Argentina. He acquired Spanish nationality in 1986, and became a French citizen in 1998. During 1980 the Spanish authorities recognised Hocsman's Argentine qualification as equivalent to the Spanish university degree in medicine and surgery, which allowed him to practise medicine in Spain and train there as a specialist. Due to the fact that he was not a Spanish national at the time of his specialist training, the qualification he was subsequently awarded (specialist in urology) was an academic title. When he became a Spanish national in 1986 he obtained authorisation to practise as a specialist in urology.

In 1990 he entered France and held various urology posts. He applied to be registered to practise general medicine, but in 1997 the French authorities rejected his application on the ground that his Argentine qualification did not entitle him to practise general medicine in France. Hocsman issued proceedings in a French court to have that decision annulled.

Although there was a harmonising directive which applied to medicine, Hocsman's Argentine qualification was not covered. The French court referred the case to the Court of Justice pursuant to the former Art 234 EC Treaty (now Art 267 TFEU) and asked, *inter alia*, whether a person could rely on the former Art 43 EC Treaty (now Art 49 TFEU) where there was a directive covering the relevant profession. The Court of Justice held as follows:

The object of such [harmonising or coordinating] directives is, as appears from . . . [Article 53(1) TFEU], to make it easier for persons to take up and pursue activities as self-employed persons, and hence to make the existing possibilities of taking up those activities easier for nationals of other Member States . . .

The function of directives which lay down common rules and criteria for mutual recognition of diplomas is thus to introduce a system in which Member States are obliged to accept the equivalence of certain diplomas and cannot require the persons concerned to comply with requirements other than those laid down in the relevant directives.

Where the requirements such as those set out in Directive 93/16 [which gives Community [i.e. Union] recognition to specified medical training diplomas] are satisfied, mutual recognition of the diplomas in question renders superfluous their recognition under the principle referred to [i.e. as the Court held in *Haim* (see below), that in order to verify whether a training period requirement prescribed by the national rules is satisfied, the competent national authorities must take into account the professional experience of the person concerned, including that which he has acquired in another Member State]. However, that principle unquestionably remains relevant in situations not covered by such directives, as in Dr Hocsman's case.

In the above case, the Court of Justice held that even though there was a harmonising directive covering medical training diplomas, Hocsman could still rely directly on what is now Art 49 TFEU. In this instance, the principles espoused by the Court in its previous case law have to be applied to ascertain if Hocsman's qualifications and experience are sufficient to warrant recognition of his professional qualifications.

In the following case, the Court of Justice made it clear that where a qualification was not mentioned in one of the harmonising directives, then in accordance with the Court's previous case law there is a requirement for a comparative examination of the education and training received by the applicant:

Conseil National de l'Ordre des Architectes v Nicholas Dreesen (Case C-31/00)

Dreesen (a Belgian national) had a German engineering diploma, and had been employed for various architect firms in Belgium for 25 years. He applied to a Provincial Council within Belgium to have his name entered on the register of that association so that he could practise as a self-employed architect. This was refused because the qualification he had was not specified in Directive 85/384 (a harmonising directive which applied to architects; this directive has since been repealed and replaced by Directive 2005/36). The case came before the Court of Justice, which held as follows:

> Article 43 EC [now Art 49 TFEU] is to be interpreted as meaning that where a Community [i.e. Union] national applies to the competent authorities of a Member State for authorisation to practise a profession, access to which depends, under national legislation, on the possession of a diploma or professional qualification or on periods of practical experience, those authorities are required to take into consideration all of the diplomas, certificates and other evidence of formal qualifications of the person concerned, and his relevant experience, with the knowledge and qualifications required by the national legislation, **even where a directive on the mutual recognition of diplomas has been adopted for the profession concerned, but where application of the directive does not result in automatic recognition of the applicant's qualification or qualifications.** [emphasis added]

The following case builds upon the previous two cases:

Nasiopoulos v Ipourgos Igias kai Pronoias (Case C-575/11)

Nasiopoulos was a Greek national. After a training period of two- and- a- half years which he completed in Germany, he obtained a qualification entitling him to exercise, in Germany, the profession of medical masseur-hydrotherapist ('Masseur und medizinischer Bademeister').

That profession was not regulated in Greece. The nearest profession was that of physiotherapist, for which the minimum training was three years. For that reason, the Greek Ministry of Health rejected the application made by Nasiopoulos for access in Greece to the profession of physiotherapist.

The Simvoulio tis Epikratias (Council of State, Greece) referred the case to the Court of Justice to determine whether the principle of freedom of establishment allowed national legislation which excluded partial access to the profession of physiotherapist to be granted to a national of a Member State who had obtained, in another Member State, a qualification, such as that of masseur-hydrotherapist, which authorised him to carry out, in that second Member State (i.e. Germany), some of the activities coming under the profession of physiotherapist.

The Court stated that freedom of establishment had to be exercised according to the conditions defined by the host country for its own nationals. As the conditions for access to the profession of physiotherapist had not been harmonised at Union level, the Member States remained competent to define the conditions for access, while respecting the basic freedoms guaranteed by the Treaty.

The Court considered that the exclusion of any partial access to a regulated profession was liable to hinder or make less attractive the exercise of freedom of establishment and could only be justified by overriding reasons relating to the public interest, for example, consumer protection and health protection, without going beyond what was necessary to achieve those objectives.

Consumers had to be protected from the risk that they would be misled as to the scope of the qualifications associated with the profession of physiotherapist. To that end, less restrictive means than the exclusion from partial access to the profession could be applied: for example, the obligation to use the professional title of origin both in the language in which it was awarded and in its original form, and in the official language of the host Member State.

Moreover, **the protection of public health required a particular vigilance**. Nonetheless, the profession of physiotherapist and that of masseur came within the paramedical sector. The provision of the services consisted merely of the implementation of a therapy pre-scribed, as a general rule, by a doctor who chose the masseur-hydrotherapist and acted in close liaison with him, each depending on and cooperating with the other.

The Court concluded that exclusion from partial access to the profession of physio-therapist went beyond what was necessary for consumer protection and protection of public health.

The Court stated that where, in the Member State of origin and the host Member State, the two professions could be regarded as comparable, any shortcomings in the professional's education or training in relation to that required in the host Member State could be made up for through the application of compensation measures. How-ever, where the differences between the fields of activity were so great that in reality the professional should follow a full programme of education and training in order to pursue, in another Member State, the activities for which he was qualified, this was a factor which was liable to discourage him from pursuing those activities in the host Member State.

It was for the national authorities and, in particular, the competent courts in the host Member State (in this case Greece) to determine, in each specific case, to what extent the content of the education and training required in that state was different from that obtained in the state where the training was given (in this case Germany).

The Court indicated that one of the decisive issues to be considered at the outset by the national authorities was whether the activity of masseur-hydrotherapist could, objec-tively, be separated from the rest of the activities covered by the corresponding profes-sion in the host state.

Thus, where, in the state in which the training was given (Germany) the profession of masseur-hydrotherapist could be pursued independently or autonomously, the dissuasive effect as regard the freedom of establishment caused by the preclusion of any possibility of partial recognition of that qualification in the host state (Greece) could not be justified by the fear of potential harm to recipients of services.

Non-EU qualifications

As with most of the Treaty provisions on the free movement of persons, neither the specific harmonising directives nor the two general directives (which have been repealed and replaced by Directive 2005/36) cover non-EU nationals. The issue of whether they apply to qualifications obtained outside the EU was the issue in the following case:

Tawil-Albertini v *Ministre des Affairs Sociales* (Case C-154/93)

The applicant was a French national. He obtained a dental qualification in Lebanon. This qualification was later recognised in Belgium as equivalent to the Belgian dentistry qualification. He subsequently applied to the French authorities to practise in France, but his application was refused. The qualifications listed in the specific Council Directive 78/686 (which has been repealed and replaced by Directive 2005/36) on the mutual recognition of dental qualifications did not include any qualification obtained outside the EU. However, because his qualification had been recognised as equivalent to the Belgian diploma, and the Belgian diploma was included in the directive, he argued that his qualification was also covered by the directive.

The Court of Justice held that the mutual recognition of qualifications in dentistry was based upon minimum specific levels of competence agreed between all the Member States. Even though one Member State accepted a qualification as equivalent to its own standards it did not follow that this would bind all the other Member States. Only the qualifications listed in the specific directive were guaranteed equivalent. Obviously, if he had obtained work experience within Belgium then, according to the decision in *Hocsman*, above, that experience would have been required to be taken into consideration, relying directly on the former Art 43 EC Treaty (now Art 49 TFEU) rather than the directive.

The following case was referred to in the Court's judgment in **Hocsman** (see above):

Haim v *Kassenzahnärztliche Vereinigung Nordrhein* (Case C-319/92)

The applicant did not hold one of the qualifications specified in Council Directive 78/686 (which has been repealed and replaced by Directive 2005/36), but had nevertheless been authorised to practise as a dentist in Germany. He applied to work on a social security scheme in Germany, but was told that he would have to complete a further two-year training period.

He argued that his experience working for eight years as a dentist in Belgium should be taken into account. The Court of Justice cited the *Vlassopoulou* case (above) and ruled in his favour:

28. The competent national authority, in order to verify whether the training period requirement prescribed by the national rules is met, must take into account the professional experience of the plaintiff in the main proceedings, including that which he has acquired during his appointment as a dental practitioner of a social security scheme in another Member State.

In each of the above cases, the applicants had obtained non-EU qualifications. In the **Haim** case, the Court of Justice held that experience within the EU must be taken into account if the Member State recognised the qualification which had been obtained from outside the EU. However, nationals of non-Member States who are established in the EU have no rights of recognition or permission to practise under Union law. This is so even if they have obtained their professional qualification in one of the Member States and such qualification is listed in one of the earlier specific directives.

The *Tawil-Albertini* case (see above) can be contrasted with the following case:

Tennah-Durez (Case C-110/01)

Tennah-Durez carried out part of his doctor's training in Algeria. This training was subsequently recognised in Belgium (which awarded the diploma), and Tennah-Durez sought to have his diploma recognised in France.

The Court of Justice began by stating that the former Directive 93/16 (which has been repealed and replaced by Directive 2005/36) established automatic and unconditional recognition of certain diplomas, requiring Member States to acknowledge their equivalence without being able to demand that the persons concerned comply with conditions other than those laid down. It went on to draw a distinction between that system and the system laid down by the former Directive 89/48 (which has been repealed and replaced by Directive 2005/36), where recognition was not automatic but allowed Member States to require the person concerned to fulfil additional requirements, including a period of adaptation.

Concerning the extent to which medical training may consist of training received in a non-member country, the Court held that the directive did not require all or any particular part of that training to be provided at a university of a Member State or under the supervision of such a university, and that neither did the general scheme of the directive preclude medical training leading to a diploma, certificate or other evidence of a medical qualification eligible for automatic recognition from being received *partly* outside the EU. According to the Court, what mattered was not where the training had been provided but whether it complied with the qualitative and quantitative training requirements laid down by the former Directive 93/16. Moreover, responsibility for ensuring that the training requirements, both qualitative and quantitative, laid down by the former Directive 93/16 were fully complied with fell wholly on the competent authority of the Member State awarding the diploma. A diploma thus awarded amounted to a 'doctor's passport', enabling the holder to work as a doctor throughout the EU without the professional qualification attested to by the diploma being open to challenge in the host Member State except in specific circumstances laid down by Union law.

Consequently, provided the competent authority in the Member State awarding the diploma was in a position to validate medical training received in a third country (i.e. non-Member State) and to conclude on that basis that the training duly complied with the training requirements laid down by the former Directive 93/16, that training could be taken into account in deciding whether to award a doctor's diploma. In that respect, the proportion of the training carried out in a third country, and in particular the fact that the major part of the training was received in such a country, was immaterial. In the first place, the former Directive 93/16 contained no reference or even allusion to such a criterion. Moreover, a requirement for training to have been received mainly within the EU would undermine legal certainty, since such a concept was open to several interpretations.

The Court concluded that the training in question could consist, and even mainly consist, of training received in a third country, provided the competent authority of the Member State awarding the diploma was in a position to validate the training and to conclude on that basis that it duly served to meet the requirements for the training of doctors laid down by the former directive.

As for the extent to which national authorities were bound by a certificate confirming that the diploma conformed with the requirements of the former directive, the Court held that the system of automatic and unconditional recognition would be seriously jeopardised if it was open to Member States at their discretion to question the merits of a decision taken by the competent institution of another Member State to award the diploma. However, where new evidence cast serious doubt on the authenticity of the diploma presented, or as to its conformity with the applicable legislation, it was legitimate for Member States to require from the competent institution of the Member State which awarded the diploma confirmation of its authenticity.

The difference between the *Tawil-Albertini* case and that of *Tennah-Durez* was that in the former case the actual qualification was obtained outside the EU, whereas in the latter case the qualification was obtained within the EU, but some training, which contributed to the qualification, had been undertaken outside the EU. The qualification in the former case did not come within the scope of Union law, whereas the qualification in the latter case did.

The internal situation

From the wording of Art 49 TFEU there would appear to be a limitation in that it cannot be relied upon by a person seeking to establish himself in the Member State of his nationality (although see *Neri* (Case C-153/02), below). One obvious way in which a national may be disadvantaged is where he obtains a qualification in another Member State and then seeks to have it recognised in his own Member State.

In *Knoors* v *Secretary of State for Economic Affairs* (Case 115/78) the Court of Justice held that what is now Art 49 TFEU could be relied upon in a person's home Member State in respect of a qualification he had obtained in another Member State. However, later case law of the Court suggested that there were limitations to this. It held that the existence of a directive recognising the foreign qualification was essential. Article 49 TFEU of itself could not assist nationals established in the Member State of their nationality:

Ministère Public v *Auer* (Case 136/78)

A French citizen obtained a veterinary qualification in Italy. He was not permitted to practise in France, the Italian qualification not being considered to be equivalent. There was no Union directive in force at the time. The Court of Justice held as follows:

> 20. ... [Article 49 TFEU] concerns only – and can concern only – in each Member State the nationals of other Member States, those of the host Member State coming already, by definition, under the rules in question.

Following the Court of Justice's judgment in the above case, the Council adopted Directives 78/1026 and 78/1027 (both of which have been repealed and replaced by Directive 2005/36) which governed veterinary qualifications, thus recognising the qualification Auer had obtained. Generally, directives do not distinguish between nationals of the Member State in question. The case came before the Court of Justice for a second time, but on this occasion Auer was able to rely upon the directives (see *Auer* v *Ministère Public* (Case 271/82)).

Most situations involving a *regulated profession* will be covered by Directive 2005/36 (as was the case under the former Directives 89/48 and 92/51) and therefore reliance solely on Art 49 TFEU will not be necessary. Accordingly, the national may rely upon the relevant directive in the Member State of his nationality with regard to qualifications and training obtained in another Member State.

However, in the following case, the Court of Justice has cast doubt on whether or not *Auer* (Case 136/78) was correctly decided:

Fernandez de Bobadilla v *Museo Nacional del Prado and Others* (Case C-234/97)

The facts of this case have been considered above. The Court of Justice held as follows:

30. In contrast to **Vlassopoulou**, this case concerns a Spanish national seeking to practise her profession in Spain. However, if a national of a Member State, owing to the fact that he has lawfully resided in the territory of another Member State and has acquired a professional qualification there, finds himself with regard to his State of origin in a situation which may be assimilated to that of a migrant worker, he must also be entitled to enjoy the rights and freedoms guaranteed by the Treaty (see, to that effect, Case C-19/92 **Kraus** [1993] ECR I-1663, paragraphs 15 and 16).

In the above case, the Court of Justice was undecided whether or not the former Directives 89/48 and 92/51 (both of which have been repealed and replaced by Directive 2005/36) applied, and therefore it decided the case on the basis that they did not. It held that even if there was no directive applicable to the test of equivalence of her qualifications, she could rely upon the general principles of Union law.

The above applies only where there is some 'Union element'. In the **Bobadilla** case, the Union element was the completion of an educational course and training in another Member State. If there is no Union element present then this will constitute a wholly internal situation, and Union law will not provide a remedy (see **Nino and Others** (Cases 54 and 91/88 and 14/89)).

In the following case, the Court of Justice was faced with a different issue:

Neri (Case C-153/02)

An Italian administrative practice prevented the recognition of post-secondary university diplomas issued by a British university in circumstances where the courses were delivered in Italy by an educational establishment operating in the form of a capital company in accordance with an agreement between the two establishments.

The Court of Justice held that the Italian refusal to recognise the diplomas was incompatible with the former Art 43 EC Treaty (now Art 49 TFEU). In the view of the Court, the former Art 43 EC Treaty (now Art 49 TFEU) required the elimination of restrictions on freedom of establishment, whether they prohibited the exercise of that freedom, impeded it or rendered it less attractive.

The Court stated that non-recognition in Italy of degrees likely to facilitate the access of students to the employment market was likely to deter students from attending courses and thus seriously hinder the pursuit by the educational establishment concerned of its economic activity in that Member State.

Moreover, inasmuch as non-recognition of diplomas related solely to degrees awarded to Italian nationals, it did not appear suitable for attaining the objective of ensuring high standards of university education. Similarly, precluding any examination and, consequently, any possibility of recognition of degrees did not comply with the requirement of proportionality and went beyond what was necessary to ensure the objective pursued. It could not therefore be justified.

Summary

Now you have read this chapter you should be able to:

- Identify the provisions of the TFEU which apply to the free movement of providers and recipients of services and the freedom of establishment.
- Explain how Art 56 TFEU on the free movement of providers and recipients of services is applied by the European Court of Justice, and to ascertain the circumstances in which restrictions to such free movement may be objectively justified.
- Explain the provisions of Directive 2006/123 (the 'Services Directive').
- Explain how Art 54 TFEU has been applied by the European Court of Justice to remove obstacles to the freedom of establishment.
- Understand the circumstances in which Directive 2004/38 confers a general right of residence.
- Identify and explain the provisions of Directive 2004/38 which abolish restrictions on movement and residence.
- Discuss the conditions which apply pursuant to Directive 2004/38 with regard to an EU citizen who seeks to remain within a Member State having pursued a self-employed activity there.
- Explain how Art 18 TFEU and Art 24, Directive 2004/38 establish the right of equal treatment for persons who exercise their Union law rights of establishment.
- Understand how Art 18 TFEU and Art 24, Directive 2004/38 establish the right of equal treatment for persons who exercise their free movement rights as providers and recipients of services.
- Explain how Art 49 TFEU is applied in respect of qualifications and training.
- Assess the impact which the former harmonisation directives and the two general directives have had on Art 49 TFEU, and explain the changes which have been made to this system by Directive 2005/36.

Further reading

Textbooks

Barnard, C. (2013) *The Substantive Law of the EU: The Four Freedoms* (4th edn), Oxford University Press, Chapters 10 and 11.

Craig, P. and De Burca, G. (2011) *EU Law: Text, Cases and Materials* (5th edn), Oxford University Press, Chapter 22.

Foster, N. (2015) *Foster on EU Law* (5th edn), Oxford University Press, Chapter 9.

Steiner, J. and Woods, L. (2014) *EU Law* (12th edn), Oxford University Press, Chapters 22 and 24.

Weatherill, S. (2014) *Cases and Materials on EU Law* (11th edn), Oxford University Press, Chapter 14.

Journal articles

Apps, K., 'Damages claims against trade unions after Viking and Laval' (2009) 34 EL Rev 141.

Barnard, C., 'Unravelling the Services Directive' (2008) 45 CML Rev 323.

Dawes, A. and Struckmann, K., 'Rien ne va plus? Mutual recognition and the free movement of services in the gambling sector after the Santa Casa judgment' (2010) 35 EL Rev 236.

Doukas, D., 'In a bet there is a fool and a state monopoly: Are the odds stacked against cross-border gambling?' (2011) 36 EL Rev 243.

Johnston, A. and Syrpis, P., 'Regulatory competition in European company law after Cartesio' (2009) 34 EL Rev 378.

Kilpatrick, C., 'Laval's regulatory conundrum: Collective standard-setting and the Court's new approach to posted workers' (2009) 34 EL Rev 844.

Kocharov, A., 'What intra-Community mobility for third-country nationals?' (2008) 33 EL Rev 913.

Papadopoulos, T., 'EU regulatory approaches to cross-border mergers: Exercising the right of establishment' (2011) 36 EL Rev 71.

Prechal, S. and De Vries, S., 'Seamless web of judicial protection in the internal market' (2009) 34 EL Rev 5.

Ross, M., 'A healthy approach to services of general economic interest? The BUPA judgment of the Court of First Instance' (2009) 34 EL Rev 127.

Szydlo, M., 'Contracts beyond the scope of the EC procurement directives – who is bound by the requirement for transparency?' (2009) 34 EL Rev 720.

Van den Gronden, J. and De Waele, H., 'All's well that bends well? The constitutional dimension to the Services Directive' (2010) 6 ECL Rev 397.

Van der Mei, A.P., 'Cross-border access to healthcare and entitlement to complementary "Vanbraekel reimbursement"' (2011) 36 EL Rev 431.

Van Riemsdijk, M., 'Obstacles to the free movement of professionals: Mutual recognition of professional qualifications in the European Union' (2013) 15 EJML 47.

14

Social security

Objectives

At the end of this chapter you should understand:

1. How Art 48 TFEU, and Regulations 883/2004 and 987/2009 (previously Regulations 1408/71 and 574/72) facilitate the free movement of workers and the self-employed.

2. The range of persons who come within the scope of Regulations 883/2004 and 987/2009.

3. How the principle of equal treatment is applied in the context of Regulation 883/2004.

4. The principles of Art 48 TFEU as built upon by the former Regulation 1408/71 and the case law of the Court of Justice, and how such are relevant to Regulation 883/2004, in particular with regard to:

   - the aggregation of contributions and periods of contribution;
   - the exportability of benefits;
   - the prevention of overlapping benefits;
   - the types of benefit covered;
   - the double-function test.

5. The difference between social assistance and social advantages, and the availability of such within the UK.

Introduction to social security

Objective 1

A contributory social security scheme is similar to an insurance policy but, in this case, the policy is provided by the state. Membership to the scheme may be based upon periods of insurance, employment, self-employment or residency. Members of the scheme have the right to claim benefits in accordance with the scheme's conditions. An example of a contributory social security scheme is the state retirement pension. All Member States have contributory social security systems, but they vary greatly in the quantity and quality of the benefits they provide. This is, potentially, a major barrier to the mobility of the employed and self-employed (as well as those who are not 'economically active'). A person moving to another Member State may suffer the double disadvantage of losing out on the contributions to his own national insurance scheme, with a consequent loss of benefits in his home state, and he may also find that he is not entitled to benefits in the host Member State because he has not contributed sufficiently or for long enough. The founders of the Union were clearly aware of this difficulty and provision was made to deal with it in what is now Art 48 TFEU (previously Art 42 EC Treaty). This facilitates the adoption of such measures in the field of social security as are necessary to provide freedom of movement for workers. To this end it shall make arrangements to secure for employed and self-employed migrant workers and their dependants:

- aggregation, for the purpose of acquiring and retaining the right to social security benefits and of calculating the amount of such benefits, of all periods taken into account under the laws of the several Member States;
- payment of social security benefits to persons resident in the territories of Member States.

Article 48 TFEU is thus aimed at enabling the migrant worker to take his accrued rights with him, in the sense that his contributions and period of contribution in his home state will be taken into account in the host Member State (and will also entitle his benefit payments to be made in the host Member State), and his contributions in the host Member State will be taken into account in calculating his level of benefits when he returns to his home state. Given the variation in level and type of contribution in each Member State, and the dissimilarity of social security schemes, this is a complex task. It must, however, be emphasised that the scheme is not intended to equalise the level of social security benefits throughout the Union. It is simply directed at ensuring that the migrant worker obtains, as far as possible, equal treatment within local social security schemes, and does not lose out in relation to entitlements due from his home state. The Court of Justice has declared that, when applying national social security law to migrant workers, the host Member State should interpret its own legislation in the light of the aims of Arts 45–48 TFEU (previously Arts 39–42 EC Treaty). It should, as far as possible, avoid interpreting its own legislation in such a way as to discourage migrant workers from exercising their rights to freedom of movement (*Van Munster* (Case C-165/91)).

As a result of the large discrepancies between national social security schemes, this area of Union law has been highly productive in terms of litigation and the case law is considerable and complicated. This chapter will do no more than outline the general principles and provide some examples of their interpretation by the Court of Justice and their application in the UK.

Prior to 1 May 2010, the Union rules which gave effect to the principles laid down in Art 48 TFEU were found in Regulations 1408/71 and 574/72 (as amended by Regulations 2001/83 and 1247/92). Regulation 1408/71 contained the substantive provisions. Regulation 574/72 dealt with the procedures for the operation and interrelation of national social security schemes. Regulation 1247/92 limited the availability of national welfare provisions.

On 1 May 2010, Regulation 883/2004 (as subsequently amended) repealed and replaced Regulation 1408/71. On the same date, Regulation 987/2009 repealed and replaced Regulation 574/72. Regulation 883/2004 contains the substantive provisions, and Regulation 987/2009 contains the implementing provisions.

Details of all Union legislation relevant to social security (social protection) can be accessed through the 'Employment and Social Policy' section of the EUR-Lex website:

http://eur-lex.europa.eu/browse/summaries.html

The scope of Regulation 883/2004 is now examined.

The beneficiaries of Regulation 883/2004

Objective 2

Article 2, Regulation 883/2004 provides that:

1 This Regulation shall apply to nationals of a Member State, stateless persons and refugees residing in a Member State who are or who have been subject to the legislation of one or more Member States, as well as to the members of their families and to their survivors.

2 It shall also apply to the survivors of persons who have been subject to the legislation of one or more Member States, irrespective of the nationality of such persons, where their survivors are nationals of a Member State or stateless persons or refugees residing in one of the Member States.

Its scope is wider than under the former Regulation 1408/71, which only covered EU citizens who were employed or self-employed and who were, or who had been, subject to social security legislation in more than one of the Member States. Their families were also covered, together with any survivors of the worker or self-employed person after his death, provided that they were, at some stage, covered by the social security legislation of more than one Member State (Arts 1 and 2, Regulation 1408/71). The former Regulation 1408/71 also applied to refugees, stateless persons, and their families.

Regulation 883/2004 seeks to simplify and clarify the Union rules governing the coordination of the Member States' social security systems. It now includes persons who are not economically active within its scope, the rationale being to facilitate the free movement of *all* EU citizens, irrespective of their economic status. This complements the broader aims of Directive 2004/38, which establishes rights of entry and residence for all EU citizens (see Chapter 11).

In any event, the Court of Justice had already broadened the scope of the former Art 42 EC Treaty (now Art 48 TFEU) and the former Regulation 1408/71 by stipulating that the determining factor was not the economic status of the claimant, but membership of a national social security scheme. Thus, a person who travelled to another Member State, not in the capacity of a worker, could still come within the scope of the former Regulation 1408/71. In *Hoekstra (née Unger)* (Case 75/63), a person subject to the Netherlands' social security legislation who fell ill during a visit to her parents in Germany was entitled to claim the cost of treatment received in Germany on her return to the Netherlands. Similarly, in *Hessische Knappschaft v Maison Singer et Fils* (Case 44/65), a German worker was killed in a road accident while on holiday in France. It was argued that the rights arising under the former Art 42 EC Treaty (now Art 48 TFEU) were intended to promote the free movement of workers, not holidaymakers, but the Court of Justice rejected this argument. It held that nothing in the former Art 42 EC Treaty (now Art 48 TFEU) required the concept of workers to be limited strictly to that of migrant workers as such. In *Brack v Insurance Officer* (Case 17/76), the Court of Justice held that the term 'employed persons' must be applied taking into account the objectives and spirit of the former Regulation 1408/71 and the former Arts 39 to 42 EC Treaty (now Arts 45 to 48 TFEU) on which it was based. The claimant had been covered by the UK social security scheme, first as an employed person and then in a self-employed capacity. He had gone to France for health reasons, but had fallen seriously ill there. The Court held that he retained the status of an employed/self-employed person for the purpose of the former Art 1(a)(ii), Regulation 1408/71 during his stay in France.

As stated above, under Regulation 883/2004 this point is now otiose because it applies to all EU citizens irrespective of their economic status.

Family members

Unlike the provisions relating to the exercise of free movement rights for workers and the self-employed under Directive 2004/38 (see Chapters 12 and 13), the scope of family membership is initially left to the Member State concerned. Under Art 1(i)(1), Regulation 883/2004 'a member of the family' is stated to be: 'any person defined or recognised as a member of the family or designated as a member of the household by the legislation under which benefits are provided'. With regard to sickness benefits, maternity benefits and equivalent paternity benefits, the scope of a member of the family is slightly different: 'any person defined or recognised as a member of the family or designated as a member of the household by the legislation *of the Member State in which he resides*' (emphasis added).

Article 1(i)(2), Regulation 883/2004 provides that if the relevant Member State's legislation does not make a distinction between the members of the family and other persons to whom it is applicable, then a member of the family shall be the beneficiary's 'spouse, minor children, and dependent children who have reached the age of majority'. Article 1(i)(3), Regulation 883/2004 further provides that if the relevant Member State's legislation only recognises a member of the family or member of the household if 'he lives in the same household' as the beneficiary, this requirement is automatically satisfied if the person in question is 'mainly dependent' on the beneficiary.

Equality of treatment

Objective 3

The beneficiaries of Regulation 883/2004 'shall enjoy the same benefits and be subject to the same obligations under the legislation of any Member State as the nationals thereof' except where the regulation provides otherwise (Art 4). This is essentially identical to the former Art 3(1), Regulation 1408/71. The effect of Art 4, Regulation 883/2004 (and the former Art 3(1), Regulation 1408/71) is to prohibit direct or indirect discrimination. In *Commission v Belgium* (Case C-326/90), the Court of Justice held that the Belgian authorities had breached the former Art 3(1), Regulation 1408/71 by maintaining a requirement of a period of residence on Belgian territory which workers from other Member States subject to Belgian legislation had to fulfil in order to qualify for the grant of allowances for handicapped people, the guaranteed income for the elderly and the payment of the minimum subsistence allowance (minimex). An even more direct form of discrimination occurred in the following case:

Palermo (Case 237/78)

Under the French Social Security Code, an allowance was payable to French women of at least 65 years of age and without sufficient means, who were married and who had brought up at least five dependent children of French nationality during a period of at least nine years before their sixteenth birthday. The applicant, an Italian woman, submitted a claim for this allowance. The French authorities did not insist on the nationality requirement in the case of the applicant herself, but refused the benefit because five of the seven children were Italian and not French. The case came before the Court of Justice.

The Court of Justice held that payment of a benefit could not be made conditional on the nationality of the claimant or her children, provided that both she and the children held the nationality of a Member State.

Discrimination may occur in relation not only to entitlement to social security benefits but also to contributions. In *Allué and Coonan* (Case 33/88) a number of EU nationals employed as university teachers were obliged, as a consequence of Italian legislation, to pay their own social security contributions, whereas in the case of the ordinary salaried employees of the university, this burden was largely carried by the employer. The Court of Justice held that the practice violated the former Art 3(1), Regulation 1408/71. The Court of Justice has also said that a system of calculation of social security contributions that works less favourably in relation to trainee workers coming from another Member State in comparison to workers who come under the national educational system is unlawful because it is also discriminatory (*URSSAGF* v *Société à Responsabilité Limitée Hostellerie Le Manoir* (Case C-27/91)).

Another aspect of equality of treatment in Regulation 883/2004 (and in the former Regulation 1408/71) is specifically dealt with in relation to mobility and the receipt of benefits. Article 7, Regulation 883/2004 (previously Art 10(1), Regulation 1408/71) provides:

> Unless otherwise provided for by this Regulation, cash benefits payable under the legislation of one or more Member States or under this Regulation shall not be subject to any reduction, amendment, suspension, withdrawal or confiscation on account of the fact that the beneficiary or the members of his/her family reside in a Member State other than that in which the institution responsible for providing benefits is situated.

The effect of Art 7 is that a beneficiary who has, for example, contributed to a national insurance scheme in one Member State will be entitled to have any accrued benefit paid to him at the full rate, should he choose to move to another Member State.

This 'principle of equality' is also reflected in Directive 79/7, under which there is a prohibition against any kind of discrimination on the ground of sex (Art 4(1)). The principle applies in relation to access to social security schemes, the obligation to contribute and the calculation of contributions, and the calculation of benefits. This directive applies both to migrant workers and their families and to domestic claimants for social security who do not leave their own state. The equality requirement is, however, limited to schemes which relate to sickness, invalidity, old-age, accidents at work and occupational diseases, unemployment and social assistance, so far as the social assistance is intended to supplement or replace one of the schemes included. The directive does not, for example, cover housing benefits (*R* v *Secretary of State for Social Security, ex parte Smithson* (Case C-243/90)). However, where a benefit is linked to employment (e.g. child tax credit and working tax credit in the UK – which are being progressively replaced by Universal Credit – which are intended to bring a family's wages up to a minimum level) the position is different. The Court of Justice has held that benefits of this kind are concerned with improving access to employment. They are therefore subject to the prohibitions against discrimination in employment as provided for in Directive 76/207 (*Meyers* v *Adjudication Officer* (Case C-116/94)).

The principles of Article 48 TFEU

Objective 4

The principles underlying Art 48 TFEU (previously Art 42 EC Treaty) have been elaborated by the former Regulation 1408/71 and by decisions of the Court of Justice.

1. Aggregation of contributions and periods of contribution

The Court of Justice has held on a number of occasions that all the provisions of the former Regulation 1408/71 are to be interpreted in the light of the former Art 42 EC Treaty (now Art 48 TFEU); see, for example, *Reichling* v *INAMI* (Case C-406/93). The purpose of Art 48

TFEU is to facilitate freedom of movement for workers by securing for migrant workers and their dependants 'aggregation, for the purpose of acquiring and retaining the right to benefit and of calculating the amount of benefit of all periods taken into account under the laws of the several countries' (Art 48 TFEU).

Article 6, Regulation 883/2004 contains specific provisions on aggregation:

Unless otherwise provided for by this Regulation, the competent institution of a Member State whose legislation makes:

- the acquisition, retention, duration or recovery of the right to benefits;
- the coverage of legislation; or
- the access to or the exemption from compulsory, optional continued or voluntary insurance

conditional upon the completion of periods of insurance, employment, self-employment or residence shall, to the extent necessary, take into account periods of insurance, employment, self-employment or residence completed under the legislation of any other Member State as though they were periods completed under the legislation which it applies.

The former Art 18(b), Regulation 1408/71 contained similar provisions on aggregation, but only in relation to specified benefits.

Reichling, above, for example, concerned the way in which the amount of invalidity benefit to which the claimant was entitled should be calculated under the former Art 46(2)(a), Regulation 1408/71. The legislation of the state where he claimed the benefit required the amount to be calculated on the basis of the amount of his remuneration which he last received in that state. He was not, in fact, working in that state when the invalidity occurred. The Court of Justice held that the competent institution of the state in which he made the claim must calculate it on the basis of the remuneration he received in the state where he last worked. In *Paraschi v Handelsversicherungsanstalt Württemberg* (Case C-349/87), the failure of the host Member State to take account of the circumstances of the claimant in the state of origin in calculating the qualifying period for a benefit was held to constitute discrimination in breach of both the former Art 39(2) EC Treaty (now Art 45(2) TFEU) and the aggregation provisions of the former Art 42 EC Treaty (now Art 48 TFEU).

2. Exportability of benefits

Exportability is often more expressively described as 'the portability principle'. It requires that the right to receive a benefit, usually from the state of origin, attaches to an EU citizen as he travels around the EU, irrespective of national boundaries. It also enables individuals to have benefits remitted to dependants who live in other Member States. It does not, however, apply to all types of benefit. Under the former Regulation 1408/71, as a general rule it only applied to those payable on a long-term basis. The former Art 10(1), Regulation 1408/71 provided that the following benefits were exportable: unemployment, invalidity, old-age or survivors' cash benefits, pensions for accidents at work or occupational diseases, death grants and lump sum benefits granted in case of remarriage of a surviving spouse. Unemployment benefit was, however, exportable only for three months after the individual had left the home territory (Art 69(1)(c), Regulation 1408/71). Other benefits which were linked to the above could also be exportable. In *Re an Emigré to the Canary Islands* [1994] 1 CMLR 717, for example, the UK Social Security Commissioners decided that a constant attendance allowance that was payable to a recipient of an invalidity allowance should be treated in the same way, and be payable to the claimant who had emigrated from the UK to the Canary Islands.

Regulation 883/2004 now provides that all cash benefits are exportable, other than 'special non-contributory cash benefits' which satisfy the conditions set out in Art 70(2), Regulation 883/2004, and which are specifically listed in Annex X. Article 70, Regulation 883/2004 provides as follows:

1 This Article shall apply to special non-contributory cash benefits which are provided under legislation which, because of its personal scope, objectives and/or conditions for entitlement, has characteristics both of the social security legislation referred to in Article 3(1) and of social assistance.

2 For the purposes of this Chapter, 'special non-contributory cash benefits' means those which:
   (a) are intended to provide either:
      (i) supplementary, substitute or ancillary cover against the risks covered by the branches of social security referred to in Article 3(1), and which guarantee the persons concerned a minimum subsistence income having regard to the economic and social situation in the Member State concerned; or
      (ii) solely specific protection for the disabled, closely linked to the said person's social environment in the Member State concerned, and
   (b) where the financing exclusively derives from compulsory taxation intended to cover general public expenditure and the conditions for providing and for calculating the benefits are not dependent on any contribution in respect of the beneficiary. However, benefits provided to supplement a contributory benefit shall not be considered to be contributory benefits for this reason alone, and
   (c) are listed in Annex X.

3 Article 7 and the other Chapters of this Title shall not apply to the benefits referred to in paragraph 2 of this Article.

4 The benefits referred to in paragraph 2 shall be provided exclusively in the Member State in which the persons concerned reside, in accordance with its legislation. Such benefits shall be provided by and at the expense of the institution of the place of residence.

With regard to unemployment benefits, although they remain exportable for a period of up to three months, Member States now have the discretion to increase this for a period of up to six months (Art 64(1)(c), Regulation 883/2004).

As stated above, certain non-contributory cash benefits which are non-exportable are listed in Annex X to Regulation 883/2004. In the original Regulation, Annex X simply stated: 'The content of this Annex shall be determined by the European Parliament and by the Council in accordance with the Treaty as soon as possible and at the latest before the date of application of this Regulation as referred to in Article 91'. Regulation 988/2009 subsequently determined the content of Annex X, and made the necessary amendments to Regulation 883/2004. With regard to the UK, Annex X to Regulation 883/2004 (as subsequently amended) provides that the following constitute special non-contributory cash benefits, and will therefore not be exportable:

(a) State Pension Credit (State Pension Credit Act 2002 and State Pension Credit Act (Northern Ireland) 2002);
(b) Income-based allowances for jobseekers (Jobseekers Act 1995 and Jobseekers (Northern Ireland) Order 1995);
(c) . . .
(d) Disability Living Allowance mobility component (Social Security Contributions and Benefits Act 1992 and Social Security Contributions and Benefits (Northern Ireland) Act 1992);
(e) Employment and Support Allowance Income-related (Welfare Reform Act 2007 and Welfare Reform Act (Northern Ireland) 2007).

3. Prevention of overlapping benefits

The concept of overlapping benefits is closely related to exportability. It is intended to prevent a beneficiary of an exportable benefit from receiving it from both his country of origin and the state in which he resides.

Article 10, Regulation 883/2004 (previously Art 12(1), Regulation 1408/71) provides that:

> Unless otherwise specified, this Regulation shall neither confer nor maintain the right to several benefits of the same kind for one and the same period of compulsory insurance.

The Regulation makes special provision for certain types of benefit, for example: long-term care benefits (Art 34(1), Regulation 883/2004); invalidity, old-age and survivors' benefits (Art 14(3), Regulation 883/2004). It also contains rules relating to the overlapping of 'benefits of the same kind' (Art 54, Regulation 883/2004) and to 'benefits of a different kind' (Art 55, Regulation 883/2004).

Whether or not two benefits are of the same kind and do, in fact, overlap is a matter of interpretation of the national legislation by the national court (**Union Nationale des Mutualités Socialistes v Aldo Del Grosso** (Case C-325/93)).

4. The types of benefit covered

Article 3(1), Regulation 883/2004 provides that:

> This Regulation shall apply to all legislation concerning the following branches of social security:
>
> (a) sickness benefits;
> (b) maternity and equivalent paternity benefits;
> (c) invalidity benefits;
> (d) old-age benefits;
> (e) survivors' benefits;
> (f) benefits in respect of accidents at work and occupational diseases;
> (g) death grants;
> (h) unemployment benefits;
> (i) pre-retirement benefits;
> (j) family benefits.

This is substantially the same as the former Art 4(1), Regulation 1408/71 with two exceptions: 'equivalent paternity benefits' and 'pre-retirement benefits' have both been added to the new provision. Article 3(2), Regulation 883/2004 specifically provides that the Regulation will apply to 'general and special social security schemes, whether contributory or non-contributory' unless otherwise provided for in Annex XI. With regard to the UK, Annex XI lists a number of social security schemes which are therefore excluded from the scope of the Regulation.

Not all benefits are covered by the Regulation. Article 3(5), Regulation 883/2004 expressly excludes two types:

1 social and medical assistance; or

2 benefits in relation to which a Member State assumes the liability for damages to persons and provides for compensation, such as those for victims of war and military action or their consequences; victims of crime, assassination or terrorist acts; victims of damage occasioned by agents of the Member State in the course of their duties; or victims who have suffered a disadvantage for political or religious reasons or for reasons of descent.

The effect of these exclusions is that beneficiaries in other Member States will not be entitled to the benefits listed in Art 3(1), except where they are linked to other benefits to which they are entitled under the **'double-function test'** (see below).

The Regulation does not provide any criteria for differentiating between 'social security' and 'social assistance'. Within the context of the former Art 4(4), Regulation 1408/71 (which also excluded 'social assistance' benefits from its scope), the Court of Justice has held that benefits must satisfy two criteria to come within the scope of a 'social security' benefit:

(i) the legislation granting the benefit must place claimants in a legally defined position as a result of which they have an absolute right to benefits as opposed to a conditional right dependent upon the exercise of a discretionary power in their favour;

(ii) the benefit must cover one of the risks referred to in the former Art 4(1), Regulation 1408/71 (now Art 3(1), Regulation 883/2004).

The characteristic feature of social assistance is that it is discretionary and will be payable according to some nationally defined criteria indicating need. In the UK, for example, a payment such as the contribution-based jobseeker's allowance is dependent on contributions and other qualifying criteria. Once they are established, there is, as a general rule, an entitlement to payment. Payment of income-based jobseeker's allowance (which is being progressively replaced by Universal Credit) will depend on an assessment of means, and may be reduced or withheld in certain circumstances, even when the criteria are satisfied (e.g. if a claimant refuses to accept suitable employment). Under Directive 2004/38, a claim for social assistance by an economically self-sufficient EU citizen will be indicative that the EU citizen no longer has a right of residence under that directive.

The Commission, reflecting the jurisprudence of the Court of Justice, has laid down the following criteria for identifying social assistance (within the context of the former Art 4(4), Regulation 1408/71):

- The benefit must be designed to alleviate a manifest condition of need in the person concerned, established after a proper investigation into his resources and bearing in mind the standard of living in the country of residence. If cash benefits are concerned, the amount must be set, case-by-case, on the basis of the individual situation and means of livelihood of the person concerned.

- The award of benefit should not be subject to any condition as to the length of employment or length of residence.

- The fact that a benefit is non-contributory does not determine its nature as a social assistance benefit or exempt it from the rules laid down in the former Regulation 1408/71 (now Regulation 883/2004). In the same way, the fact that a benefit is linked to a means test is not sufficient in itself to give it the nature of a social assistance benefit.

> [Commentary on the former Regulation 1408/71 in *Compendium of Community [i.e. Union] Provisions on Social Security* (1980) European Commission, para 4084, p. 235]

Although the Court of Justice has emphasised that the list of benefits enumerated in the former Art 4(1), Regulation 1408/71 is exhaustive (see **Scrivner and Cole v Centre Public d'Aide Sociale de Chastre** (Case 122/84)), some benefits may, according to the circumstances, qualify as both social assistance and social security under the 'double-function' test.

5. The double-function test

Although the Court of Justice held in **Scrivner and Cole** that discretionary social assistance-type benefits would fall outside the scope of the regulation, as a result of the exclusion contained in the former Art 4(4), Regulation 1408/71 (now Art 3(5), Regulation 883/2004), it tended to be generous in its interpretation of the scope of Regulation 1408/71. The discretionary element which the Court established as the primary differentiation between social security and social assistance did not exclude many benefits (which might not, at first sight, appear to be social security benefits) from being accepted as coming within the scope of the regulation (*Inzirillo* (Case 63/76); *Vigier* (Case 70/80); *Palermo* (Case 237/78)). However, following *Scrivner and Cole*, in which the Court of Justice emphasised the exhaustive nature of the list in the former Art 4(1), Regulation 1408/71 (now Art 3(1), Regulation 883/2004) the opportunities for claiming benefits not listed in Art 3(1), Regulation 883/2004 as social security benefits seemed to have diminished. In *Scrivner and Cole*, the Court turned to the 'social advantages' route in the former Art 7(2), Regulation 1612/68 (now Art 7(2), Regulation 492/2011) as an alternative basis for entitlement (see below, and Chapter 12).

> The scope of 'social advantages' under Art 7(2), Regulation 492/2011 is considered at pages 393–406.

However, the advantage to the claimant if a benefit can be brought within the scope of Regulation 883/2004 through an application of the 'double-function test' is that the benefit will be 'exportable'. In contrast, 'social advantages' (see below) are available only in the host Member State and are only available to those who have the status of EU worker or who are members of the EU worker's family. The 'double-function' test was established by the Court of Justice in the following case (in the context of the former Regulation 1408/71):

Frilli (Case 1/72)

> The Court of Justice held that even a means-tested discretionary payment could become 'social security' rather than 'social assistance' where it was used to *supplement* a contributory old-age benefit. Thus, a supplement which, when it stood alone, might be considered to be 'social assistance', could come within the scope of the regulation if it could be regarded as a supplement to one of the listed benefits.

In *Giletti* (Cases 379–381/85), the Court of Justice held that Union social security benefits could include supplements to inadequate old-age, widows' and invalidity pensions. The problem of classification with regard to non-contributory benefits was partly alleviated as a result of the extension of the scope of the former Regulation 1247/92 to cover a wide range of non-contributory social security benefits. Regulation 883/2004 also applies to non-contributory social security schemes (Art 3(2)).

Social assistance and social advantages

> Objective 5

The exclusion of social and medical assistance from the scope of the original Regulation 1408/71 was, potentially, a major obstacle to social mobility, but it reflected the anxiety of Member States about 'social tourism'. Once EU citizenship (and Directive 2004/38) conferred a right to live anywhere in the Union, it seemed arguable that EU citizens, like citizens of the nation- states, should be able to do so regardless of means. This argument, as H.C. Taschner (a Commission official) observed:

> . . . overlooks the fact that the social security systems of Member States still differ enormously, and any effort to harmonise these systems is met with formidable resistance, mainly by those Member States that have highly developed social security systems financed by their taxpayers . . . the fear of an uncontrolled flow of persons seeking residence for no other reason than to become beneficiaries of better social security than at home was, and is, completely justified . . .
>
> (Taschner, 1993)

Although the former Regulation 1408/71 excluded social assistance (as does its replacement: Regulation 883/2004), the narrow definition given to that term and the generous interpretation of the listed benefits, in the ways described above, did somewhat diminish the problems caused by that exclusion. Where 'social assistance' payments could not, by the double-function test, be linked to a social security benefit, the Court of Justice developed the scope of social advantages under the former Art 7(2), Regulation 1612/68 (now Art 7(2), Regulation 492/2011) to plug the gap. The scope of social advantages has already been examined in some detail in Chapter 12, but something needs to be said about Art 7(2), Regulation 492/2011 (previously Art 7(2), Regulation 1612/68) in the context of social assistance.

In the following case, the Court of Justice had to consider the relationship between 'social assistance', which is excluded from the application of the former Regulation 1408/71 by Art 4(4) (and is similarly excluded under the current Art 3(5), Regulation 883/2004), and 'social advantages' under Art 7(2), Regulation 492/2011 (previously Art 7(2), Regulation 1612/68):

Scrivner and Cole v *Centre Public d'Aide Sociale de Chastre* (Case 122/84)

Mr and Mrs Scrivner settled in Belgium in 1978 with their six children. In June 1982 Mr Scrivner left his employment 'for personal reasons'. It is not stated in the report what they were, but the Court of Justice seems to have assumed that they were not such as to make Mr Scrivner 'voluntarily unemployed' and therefore deprive him of his worker status (see *Raulin* (Case C-357/89), para 22). Mr Scrivner and his family were refused payment of minimex (a grant to provide the minimum means of subsistence) because it was available only to those who had been resident in Belgium for at least five years. The claimants argued that the benefit fell within the former Regulation 1408/71, and that they should, therefore, be protected from discrimination under the former Art 3(1), Regulation 1408/71. The question was referred to the Court of Justice under what is now Art 267 TFEU. The Court – on this occasion adopting a more restrictive approach – held that minimex did not fall within the scope of the Regulation:

> The Court has stated in a number of decisions that the distinction between benefits which are excluded from the scope of [the former] Regulation 1408/71 and benefits which come within it rests entirely on factors relating to each benefit, in particular its purpose and the condition for its grant, and not whether the national legislation describes the benefit as a social security benefit or not. (para 11)

The list of benefits contained in the former Art 4(1), Regulation 1408/71 (now Art 3(1), Regulation 883/2004) is exhaustive. In the above case, the Court of Justice therefore held that a branch of social security not mentioned in the list does not fall within that category 'even if it confers upon individuals a legally defined position entitling them to benefits'. Furthermore, minimex 'adopts "need" as an essential criterion for its application and *does not make any stipulations as to periods of work, contribution or affiliation to any particular social security body covering a specific risk*' (para 13, emphasis added). The Court was, however, prepared to accept that minimex was a social advantage under the former Art 7(2), Regulation 1612/68 (now Art 7(2), Regulation 492/2011) and found that it could be seen to be an advantage granted to national workers 'primarily because of their objective status as workers or by virtue of the mere fact of their residence on the national territory'. In so deciding, the Court drew on the analogy of the guaranteed old people's income in *Castelli* v *ONPTS* (Case 261/83), which the Court had also found to be a social advantage under the former Art 7(2), Regulation 1612/68 (now Art 7(2), Regulation 492/2011).

Self-employed persons are not entitled to receive subsistence payments or social assistance as a social advantage, because Art 7(2), Regulation 492/2011 (previously Art 7(2), Regulation 1612/68) is applicable only to EU workers and their families. However, the distinction between having equal access to facilities to enable a person to pursue a business or a profession and equal access to benefits is not always clear. In *Commission v Italy* (Case 63/86), the Court of Justice held that denial of housing aid to a self-employed person claiming under the former Arts 43 and 49 EC Treaty (now Arts 49 and 56 TFEU) was unlawful as an 'obstacle to the pursuit of the occupation itself' (para 16).

Regulation 883/2004: the substantive provisions

As discussed above, on 1 May 2010, Regulation 883/2004 (as subsequently amended) repealed and replaced Regulation 1408/71. On the same date, Regulation 987/2009 repealed and replaced Regulation 574/72. Regulation 883/2004 contains the substantive provisions, and Regulation 987/2009 contains the implementing provisions. Regulation 883/2004 streamlines and updates the previous rules in Regulation 1408/71. Although it has been considered above, a review of its substantive provisions now follows.

The principal changes

Regulation 883/2004 rationalises the concepts, rules and procedures concerning the coordination of the Member States' social security systems. The principal changes made to the provisions under the former Regulation 1408/71 are as follows:

- enhancement of the insured's rights by extending the personal and material scope;
- extension of the scope to all Member State nationals covered by the social security legislation of a Member State and not just those who are economically active;
- increase in the number of social security branches subject to the coordination regime so as to include pre-retirement legislation;
- right to unemployment benefits for unemployed persons who go to another Member State to seek work (for a period of three months, up to a maximum of six months);
- reinforcement of the general principle of equal treatment;
- reinforcement of the right to export social security benefits;
- introduction of the principle of good administration.

General provisions

All persons residing in the territory of a Member State are subject to the same obligations and enjoy the same benefits under the legislation of any Member State as the nationals of that state. The general principle of equal treatment is widened in the framework of Regulation 883/2004. Under the former Regulation 1408/71, the principle was applicable to persons residing in the territory of a Member State; this prior condition of residence on the territory of a Member State is no longer required.

Scope

Regulation 883/2004 applies to all Member State nationals who are or who have been covered by the social security legislation of one of the Member States, as well as to the members of their family and their survivors. Non-active persons are now protected by the coordination rules.

The provisions of Regulation 883/2004 apply to all the traditional branches of social security (sickness, maternity, accidents at work, occupational diseases, invalidity benefits, unemployment benefits, family benefits, retirement and pre-retirement benefits, and death grants). The scope of the Regulation has been extended to cover statutory pre-retirement schemes, which means that the beneficiaries of such schemes have a guarantee that benefits will be paid, will be covered for health care and will receive family benefits even if they reside in another Member State. This is a new feature of this Regulation.

Regulation 883/2004 extends the principle of exportation of benefits acquired to all cash benefits other than the specified exceptions.

The Regulation also recognises the principle of the aggregation of periods, pursuant to which periods of insurance, employment or residence completed under the legislation of a Member State are taken into account in all the other Member States. This means that a Member State must take into account, for the purpose of the acquisition of the right to benefits, periods of insurance, employment, self-employment or residence in another Member State.

Determination of the applicable legislation

The insured person is subject to the legislation of a single Member State only. The Member State concerned is the one in which he pursues a gainful activity. Title II of the Regulation contains particular rules, such as rules for civil servants who are subject to the legislation of the Member State to which the administration employing them is subject, or for persons who are employed or self-employed in several Member States.

Persons who are normally employed in two or more Member States are subject to the legislation of the Member State of residence if they pursue a substantial part of their activity in that Member State. If they do not pursue a substantial part of their activities in the Member State of residence they are subject to the legislation of the Member State in whose territory the registered office or place of business of their employer is situated. In the case of self-employment, a person is subject to the legislation of the Member State of residence if he pursues a substantial part of his activity in that Member State. If the person does not reside in one of the Member States in which he pursues a substantial part of his activity, he is subject to the legislation of the Member State in which the centre of interest of his activities is situated.

Special provisions applying to different categories of benefits

Regulation 883/2004 allows all EU citizens, regardless of whether they are employees, self-employed workers, civil servants, students, pensioners or non-active persons, to keep their social security benefit entitlements when they move within the EU.

Sickness, maternity and paternity benefits

A person (and his family) affiliated in a Member State but who resides in another Member State is entitled to benefits in kind provided by the institution of the place of residence at the expense of the competent institution of the Member State. If this person is staying in the Member State of affiliation for any reason, he is fully entitled to benefits in kind in that state. However, specific provisions apply to members of the family of frontier workers.

An insured person who stays in a Member State other than the one in which he is affiliated or in which he resides is entitled to benefits in kind required on medical grounds during the stay, taking account of the nature of the benefits and the expected duration of the stay. Regulation 883/2004 no longer restricts medical benefits to emergency treatment. These benefits are provided by the Member State in which the person is staying. However, cash benefits are paid by the Member State of affiliation.

The members of the family of a pensioner who reside in a Member State other than the Member State in which the pensioner resides are also entitled to cash benefits provided by the institution of their place of residence.

As regards cash benefits, individuals and members of their family living or staying in a Member State other than the competent Member State are entitled to cash benefits paid by the competent institution (i.e. the institution with which the person concerned is insured at the time when an application for benefits is made).

Regulation 883/2004 introduces two measures for retired frontier workers:

- retired frontier workers are entitled to medical treatment without restriction in the last Member State in which they worked in so far as this is a continuation of treatment which began in that Member State;
- persons who have been frontier workers for two years during the five years preceding their retirement or invalidity may continue to receive health care without restriction in the last Member State in which they worked, provided the Member States concerned have opted for this.

Benefits for accidents at work and occupational diseases

The victim of an accident at work or occupational disease staying or residing in a Member State other than the competent state is entitled to any special benefits in kind provided by the scheme covering accidents at work and occupational diseases. These benefits are provided by the institution of the place of stay or residence in accordance with the provisions of the legislation which it administers as though he was insured pursuant to such legislation.

As regards the costs of transporting the victim of an accident at work or occupational disease, the competent institution of a Member State whose legislation provides for meeting the costs of transporting a victim shall meet such costs to the corresponding place in the territory of another Member State where the victim resides. The institution must have previously reached agreement on this form of transport, except in the case of frontier workers.

Death grants

When an insured person or member of his family dies in a Member State other than the competent Member State, death is deemed to have occurred in the competent Member State. Hence the competent institution must provide the death grants payable under the national legislation even if the person entitled resides in another Member State.

Invalidity benefits

As regards invalidity benefits, Member States apply one of two types of legislation (see Annex VI to the Regulation). Member States with Type A legislation are those in which the amount of the benefit is independent of the duration of periods of insurance or residence and which are expressly included in Annex VI, while the other Member States are considered as Type B.

Old-age and survivors' pensions

All Member States in which a person has been insured must pay an old-age pension when the insured person reaches the age of retirement.

The competent institution must take into consideration all the periods completed under the legislation of all other Member States, both in the case of general systems and special systems. However, if the Member State makes the granting of certain benefits conditional upon the periods of insurance having been completed only in a specific activity as an employed or self-employed person, the competent institution of that Member State only needs to take into account periods completed under the legislation of other Member States if they have been completed under a corresponding scheme.

The Regulation also contains rules concerning the way in which the competent institutions calculate benefits and establishes rules to prevent overlapping.

A person receiving benefits under the legislations of different Member States whose amount is less than the minimum provided for in the legislation of the Member State of residence is entitled to a supplementary pension from the institution of the Member State of residence.

The Regulation provides a special scheme for civil servants.

Unemployment benefits

As regards unemployment benefits, the competent institution of a Member State must take into account the periods of insurance, employment or self-employment completed under the legislation of any other Member State as though they were completed under the legislation it applies.

Regulation 883/2004 contains two provisions linked to unemployment benefits:

1   the exportation of unemployment benefits to another Member State when a person goes there in order to seek work;

2   the right to unemployment benefits for workers who, during their last job, resided in a Member State other than the competent state.

As regards unemployment benefits paid in another Member State while seeking work, an unemployed person may move to another Member State in order to seek work while retaining entitlement to benefits for three months. The competent state may extend this to a total of six months. If the unemployed person does not return on or before the expiry of this period he loses all entitlement to benefits.

As regards the entitlement to unemployment benefits for workers who, during their last employment, resided in a Member State other than the competent state, the new Regulation allows unemployed frontier workers to make themselves available to the employment services of the state in which they pursued their last activity. This rule may make it easier for workers to find work.

Pre-retirement

Statutory pre-retirement schemes are now included in the scope of Regulation 883/2004, guaranteeing equal treatment and the possibility of exporting pre-retirement benefits, as well as granting family benefits and health care to the persons concerned.

Statutory pre-retirement schemes exist only in a very small number of Member States and therefore the Regulation excludes the rule concerning the aggregation of periods for the acquisition of entitlement to pre-retirement benefits.

Family benefits

A person is entitled to family benefits in a competent Member State, including for members of his family residing in another Member State, as if they were residing in the former Member State.

In the case of overlapping benefits, family benefits are provided in line with the priority rules set out in the Regulation.

The Regulation puts an end to the distinction in the former Regulation 1408/71 between pensioners and orphans as opposed to other categories of insured persons, i.e. the distinction between family benefits and family allowances no longer applies and the same range of family benefits will be granted to all, including pensioners and persons responsible for orphans, just like workers and unemployed persons.

Special non-contributory cash benefits

Contrary to the general rule, non-contributory cash benefits are not exportable if they are listed in Annex X and if they satisfy certain criteria laid down in the Regulation. These criteria apply to all Member States, with the result that similar benefits will be treated in the same way.

Coordination instruments in social security systems

The Regulation introduces the principle of good administration. The institutions must respond to all queries within a reasonable period of time and must in this connection provide the persons concerned with any information required for exercising the rights conferred on them by the Regulation. In the event of difficulties in the interpretation or application of the Regulation, the institutions involved must contact one another in order to find a solution for the person concerned.

The Regulation contains a number of mechanisms designed to guarantee smooth functioning and enhanced cooperation between Member States and institutions in the field of social security, for example:

- an Administrative Commission, responsible for handling any question of interpretation arising from the provisions of the Regulation or any accord or agreement concluded in the framework of the Regulation;
- a Technical Commission within the Administrative Commission, responsible for assembling technical documents, studies and the associated activities;
- an Audit Board which will perform the calculations needed in connection with the decisions taken by the Administrative Commission;
- an Advisory Committee, responsible for preparing opinions and proposals for the Administrative Commission.

The Administrative Commission consists of a government representative from each of the Member States and a representative of the European Commission who participates in the meetings in an advisory capacity. The aim is to foster cooperation and coordination between the Member States and the Commission.

The full text of Regulation 883/2004 (including a consolidated version of the Regulations as subsequently amended) is available through the 'Employment and Social Policy' section of the EUR-Lex website:

http://eur-lex.europa.eu/browse/summaries.html

Social security and social assistance in the UK

The UK's Department for Work and Pensions has a website where information on social security benefits for EU citizens is available:

http://www.gov.uk/dwp

Social security

With the exception of pre-retirement benefits, the full range of benefits falling within Art 3(1), Regulation 883/2004 is available in the UK. The terms on which these benefits are available are complicated, but it is possible to match a number of contributory and non-contributory benefits which will be available to EU citizens, assuming that the qualifying provisions under both UK and Union law are met.

The UK benefits falling within Art 3(1) include: the contribution-based jobseeker's allowance, statutory sick pay and sickness benefit, maternity and paternity allowances, benefits relating to invalidity and disability, widows' benefits, retirement pensions, industrial injuries benefits and benefits for children. In *Re an Emigré to the Canary Islands* [1994] 1 CMLR 717, the Social Security Commissioner held that attendance allowance was equivalent to invalidity benefit, and should therefore, as a benefit payable under the former Regulation 1408/71 (which was repealed and replaced by Regulation 883/2004), continue to be paid to a claimant after he has moved to another Member State. In *Snares v Adjudication Officer* (Case C-20/96), however, disability living allowance was held by the Court of Justice to have been validly refused to a UK citizen in Tenerife because it was a non-exportable benefit.

Social assistance

Within the UK, income support, income-based jobseeker's allowance, child tax credit and working tax credit are calculated according to need (i.e. they are means-tested). These benefits, which are being progressively replaced by Universal Credit, would therefore appear to fall outside the social security criteria (see above). In relation to the former family credit (which, from April 2003, was replaced by two new tax credits: child tax credit and working tax credit), the Court of Justice stated, in relation to the form of family credit payable in Northern Ireland, that it was a Union social security benefit (*Hughes* (Case C-78/91)).

This position should now be viewed in the light of Regulation 883/2004, which provides that all cash benefits are exportable, other than 'special non-contributory cash benefits' which satisfy the conditions set out in Art 70(2), Regulation 883/2004, and which are specifically listed in Annex X. With regard to the UK, Annex X to Regulation 883/2004 (as amended by Regulation 988/2009) provides that the following are special non-contributory cash benefits, and will therefore not be exportable:

(a) State Pension Credit (State Pension Credit Act 2002 and State Pension Credit Act (Northern Ireland) 2002);

(b) Income-based allowances for jobseekers (Jobseekers Act 1995 and Jobseekers (Northern Ireland) Order 1995);

(c) . . .

(d) Disability Living Allowance mobility component (Social Security Contributions and Benefits Act 1992 and Social Security Contributions and Benefits (Northern Ireland) Act 1992);

(e) Employment and Support Allowance Income-related (Welfare Reform Act 2007 and Welfare Reform Act (Northern Ireland) 2007).

It should be remembered that, even if an entitlement to the above benefits does not arise as a social security benefit, there can be no doubt that all those benefits should be paid to an EU worker as a 'social advantage' under Art 7(2), Regulation 492/2011 (see Chapter 12). The fact that the benefit is included in Annex X to Regulation 883/2004 will have no bearing on the availability of the benefit as a 'social advantage'.

Income-related benefits

UK law is more generous than it is required to be in relation to income-related benefits. As discussed above, except where it is supplementing a social security benefit listed in Art 3(1), Regulation 883/2004, it does not have to be paid to an individual who has not yet acquired EU worker status. The Court of Justice decided in **Lebon** (Case 316/85) that work-seekers, as opposed to workers, were not entitled to the social advantages conferred by the former Art 7(2), Regulation 1612/68 (now Art 7(2), Regulation 492/2011). However, income-related benefits may constitute a social advantage for a person who has, for example, worked but lost his job involuntarily and thus retains his EU worker status (see Chapter 12).

In the UK, prior to 1 May 2004 a claimant was required to satisfy the 'habitual residence test' to be eligible for income support, income-based jobseeker's allowance, state pension credit, housing benefit and council tax benefit ('income-related benefits', which are being progressively replaced by Universal Credit). This test was introduced to prevent 'benefit tourism' by people who came to the UK from abroad and immediately claimed benefits. Its purpose was to ensure that income-related benefits were paid to people with reasonably close ties to the UK and an intention to settle within the UK.

The test was amended on 1 May 2004 when the Social Security (Habitual Residence) Amendment Regulations 2004 came into force. The modified test provided that no person would be treated as habitually resident in the Common Travel Area (the United Kingdom, the Channel Islands, the Isle of Man and the Republic of Ireland) if he did not have a 'right to reside' within the UK. Therefore, anyone without a right to reside could not qualify for the income-related benefits.

The 'right to reside' requirement was added to prevent those who did not have a right to reside in the UK from becoming a burden on the UK's social assistance system by being able to claim income-related benefits. This requirement strengthened the test against such abuse of the benefits system by people who were not in work and who came to the UK to live. At the time, economically inactive EU citizens did not have a right to reside within the UK unless they were self-sufficient.

As well as consolidating existing Union legislation concerning rights of residence, Directive 2004/38 created a new 'right to reside' (see Chapter 11). Article 6, Directive 2004/38 provides a new 'right to reside' for all EU citizens and their family members for the first three months of their stay in the UK, without any conditions or formalities other than the requirement to hold a valid identity card or passport.

Therefore, if the UK's 'right to reside' requirement had not been amended after 30 April 2006 (the date Directive 2004/38 had to be implemented), EU citizens and their family members who were not economically active could have become eligible for income-related benefits, if they were considered to be habitually resident and met the other conditions of entitlement on the basis of this general right of residence.

Article 24(2), Directive 2004/38 provides that Member States do not have to confer entitlement to social assistance on EU citizens during the first three months of residence unless they are workers, self-employed persons, persons who retain such status and their family members. Therefore the UK's various income-related benefit regulations were amended by the Social Security (Persons from Abroad) Amendment Regulations 2006 (SI 2006/1026), to ensure that EU citizens who reside solely on the basis of Art 6, Directive 2004/38 (or equivalent Home Office regulations) are not given a right to income-related benefits just because they have a right to reside. This ensures that the present policy in relation to economically inactive EU citizens continues.

Under Art 24(2), Directive 2004/38 there is no obligation on Member States to confer social assistance during any period when an EU citizen is seeking employment and has a genuine chance of being engaged. Nevertheless, prior to 1 January 2014, the UK's Social Security (Persons from Abroad) Amendment Regulations 2006 provided that EU work-seekers who had a right to reside under Art 45 TFEU (previously Art 39 EC Treaty) and who were habitually resident would, provided they satisfied the other conditions of entitlement, be eligible for income-based jobseeker's allowance. An EU work-seeker on income-based jobseeker's allowance was also eligible for housing benefit and council tax benefit. However, for other benefits an EU work-seeker with a right to reside under Art 45 TFEU (or equivalent Home Office regulations) would not, under these Regulations, have satisfied the 'right to reside' aspect of the habitual residence test. From 1 January 2014, the UK's Jobseeker's Allowance (Habitual Residence) Amendment Regulations 2013 removed the eligibility of an EU work-seeker to claim income-based jobseeker's allowance (which is being progressively replaced by Universal Credit).

The relationship between claims to benefit and the exercise of free movement rights in the UK is examined further in Chapter 16.

Summary

Now you have read this chapter you should be able to:

- Explain how Art 48 TFEU and Regulations 883/2004 and 987/2009 facilitate the free movement of workers and the self-employed.

- Understand the range of persons who come within the scope of Regulations 883/2004 and 987/2009.

- Explain how the principle of equal treatment is applied in the context of Regulation 883/2004.

- Describe the principles of Art 48 TFEU as built upon by the former Regulation 1408/71 and the case law of the Court of Justice, and how such are relevant to Regulation 883/2004, in particular with regard to:
  - the aggregation of contributions and periods of contribution;
  - the exportability of benefits;
  - the prevention of overlapping benefits;

- the types of benefit covered;
- the double-function test.

● Evaluate the difference between social assistance and social advantages, and the availability of such within the UK.

References

Taschner, H.C. (1993) 'Free movement of students, retired persons and other European citizens', in Schermers, H. (ed.) *Free Movement of Persons in Europe: Legal Problems and Experiences*, Martinus Nijhoff.

Further reading

Textbooks

Craig, P. and De Burca, G. (2011) *EU Law: Text, Cases and Materials* (5th edn), Oxford University Press, Chapters 21 to 23.

Steiner, J. and Woods, L. (2014) *EU Law* (12th edn), Oxford University Press, Chapter 23.

Journal article

Fahey, E., 'Interpretive legitimacy and the distinction between "social assistance" and "work seekers allowance": Comment on Case C-22/08 and C-23/08 Vatsouras and Koupatantze' (2009) 34 EL Rev 93.

15

Limitations on the Free Movement of Persons

Objectives

At the end of this chapter you should understand:

1. The provisions of the TFEU and Directive 2004/38 which provide for derogations from the freedom of movement and residence provisions, on the grounds of public policy, public security and public health.

2. The procedural protection afforded by Directive 2004/38 to EU citizens who are exercising their free movement rights.

3. The relationship between the **Convention for the Implementation of the Schengen Agreement (CISA)** and Directive 2004/38.

The TFEU and Directive 2004/38

Objective
1

See pages 327–347 for a detailed discussion of Directive 2004/38.

All the Treaty provisions conferring free movement rights, as discussed in Chapters 11–13, are subject to the power of national derogation on the grounds of public policy, public security and public health: Arts 45(3), 52(1) and 62 TFEU (previously Arts 39(3), 46(1) and 55 EC Treaty) and Art 27(1), Directive 2004/38 (previously Art 10, Directive 68/360 and Art 8, Directive 73/148).

Directives 64/221 (see below), 68/360 and 73/148 have all been repealed and replaced by Directive 2004/38. Directive 2004/38 had to be transposed into national law by 30 April 2006. The directive establishes the right of EU citizens and their family members to enter and reside freely within the Member States, subject to certain conditions, and in some cases to specified time limitations (see Chapters 11–13 for a discussion of the substantive rights of entry and residence). This is subject to Art 27(1), which provides that:

> Subject to the provisions of this Chapter [Chapter VI: Restrictions on the Right of Entry and the Right of Residence on Grounds of Public Policy, Public Security or Public Health], Member States may restrict the freedom of movement and residence of Union citizens and their family members, irrespective of nationality, on grounds of public policy, public security or public health. These grounds shall not be invoked to serve economic ends.

There is no Union definition of any of these three grounds, although Art 27(2) provides some guidance with regard to public policy and public security. This guidance was developed by the Court of Justice through its application of Art 27(1)'s predecessor: Art 3(1), Directive 64/221. Article 27(2), Directive 2004/38 provides that:

> Measures taken on grounds of public policy or public security shall comply with the principle of proportionality and shall be based exclusively on the personal conduct of the individual concerned. Previous criminal convictions shall not in themselves constitute grounds for taking such measures.
>
> The personal conduct of the individual concerned must represent a genuine, present and sufficiently serious threat affecting one of the fundamental interests of society. Justifications that are isolated from the particulars of the case or that rely on considerations of general prevention shall not be accepted.

Directive 2004/38 is intended, first, to limit the extent to which Member States are entitled to restrict the right of free movement and, second, to provide minimum standards of procedural protection for the individuals affected when Member States take such restrictive action. The scope of both aspects of the directive is now examined.

Public policy and public security

Directive 2004/38 does not attempt to define 'public policy'. It is a term that is also found in relation to permitted restrictions on the import and export of goods under Art 36 TFEU; see Chapter 18. Member States are free to determine the scope of public policy in their territory, which may be different in each Member State. It is, for example, permissible for Ireland to prohibit abortions on its territory, and equally acceptable under Union law for the UK to permit them. It would, however, probably not be compatible with Union law for a person to be prevented from receiving information in Ireland issued by an abortion clinic in the UK or from going to the UK to have an abortion. In the following case, the Court of Justice stated that abortion constituted a service within the scope of what is now Art 57 TFEU:

Society for the Protection of the Unborn Child Ireland Ltd v *Grogan*
(Case C-159/90)

> The Court of Justice held that medical termination of pregnancy, performed in accordance with the law of the state where it was carried out, constituted a service within the scope of the former Art 50 EC Treaty (now Art 57 TFEU).

In *Attorney-General* v *X and Others* [1992] 2 CMLR 277, decided by the Supreme Court of the Republic of Ireland, the Irish Court held that a woman who wished to go to the UK for an abortion had 'an unenumerated constitutional right to travel' under Irish law, and did not, therefore, need to rely on her Union right to travel to receive a service. Different public policy requirements in different states may result in the quite lawful prohibition of cross-border services, even where they are legitimate in one of the states concerned, provided that the prohibition is proportionate to the risk and provided it is applied equally in the receiving state to local citizens and EU citizens alike (*HM Customs and Excise Commissioners* v *Schindler* (Case C-275/92)). 'Public policy' and 'public security' are used interchangeably, and they seem to be regarded by the Court of Justice as overlapping concepts. However, although the Court of Justice accepted in ***Van Duyn*** (Case 41/74) that 'the concept of public policy may vary from one country to another and from one period to another and it is, therefore, necessary ... to allow the competent national authorities an area of discretion within the limits imposed by the Treaty', in more recent years it has tended to emphasise the limitations imposed by Union law and the need for equality of treatment between local nationals and EU citizens and their families (***Commission v Germany, Re Housing of Migrant Workers*** (Case 249/86), paras 18 and 19). An attempt to prevent an EU citizen from having access to a service relating to fertility treatment not available on policy grounds in the UK was held by the English Court of Appeal to be disproportionate and, therefore, unlawful (***R v Human Fertilisation and Embryology Authority, ex parte DB*** [1997] 2 WLR 806). It may well be that the Court of Justice would hold that, while the state has a broad discretion as to what services it controls on public policy grounds within its own frontiers, it would be disproportionate to prevent a citizen from receiving such services in other Member States where they are lawful.

Objective justification

Similar to the free movement of workers, if a restriction on the freedom to provide services is found to exist, the Member State can seek to justify it on grounds of public policy, public security or public health (Art 52 TFEU; previously Art 46 EC Treaty). The following case concerns Germany's successful argument that the restriction in question was objectively justified on grounds of public policy:

Omega (Case C-36/02)

Omega was a company established under German law. Omega operated a sports centre in Bonn (Germany) for the practice of a 'laser sport'. This laser sport was inspired by the film *Star Wars* and it used modern laser technology. The laser sport featured machine-gun-type laser targeting devices and sensory tags installed either in the firing corridors within the sports centres or on the jackets worn by players. The police authority took the view that games for entertainment featuring simulated killing were contrary to human dignity and thus constituted a danger to public order, so they issued a prohibition order against the company, requiring it to cease operating equipment intended for firing on human targets. Following dismissal of its administrative complaint and appeals brought against that administrative measure of the police authority, Omega brought an appeal on a point of law (Revision) before the Bundesverwaltungsgericht (Federal Administrative Court).

In support of its appeal, Omega submitted, *inter alia*, that the contested order infringed the freedom to provide services under the former Art 49 EC Treaty (now Art 56 TFEU) because the sports centre in question had to use equipment and technology supplied by a UK company. The Bundesverwaltungsgericht acknowledged in this regard that, while the commercial exploitation of a 'killing game' did indeed, as the lower court had ruled, constitute an affront to human dignity contrary to the Grundgesetz (German Basic Law), its prohibition infringed the freedom to provide services guaranteed under the former Art 49 EC Treaty (now Art 56 TFEU). It decided to ask the Court of Justice, by way of a reference under the former Art 234 EC Treaty (now Art 267 TFEU), whether, *inter alia*, the prohibition of a commercial activity that was at variance with the fundamental values enshrined in Germany's national constitution was compatible with the former Art 49 EC Treaty (now Art 56 TFEU).

The Court of Justice held that, by prohibiting Omega from operating the laser sport within its sports centre in accordance with the model developed by a UK company and lawfully marketed by that company in the UK, the contested order affected the freedom to provide services which the former Art 49 EC Treaty (now Art 56 TFEU) guarantees both to providers and to the persons receiving those services who are established in another Member State. However, the Court stated that both the Union and its Member States are required to respect fundamental rights. The protection of those rights is a legitimate interest which could, in principle, justify a derogation from the obligations imposed by Union law, even under a fundamental freedom guaranteed by the Treaty such as the freedom to provide services. However, measures which restricted the freedom to provide services could be justified on public policy grounds only if they were necessary for the protection of the interests they were intended to guarantee and only in so far as those objectives could not be attained by less restrictive measures.

Nonetheless, the need for, and proportionality of, the provisions adopted could not be excluded merely because one Member State had chosen a system of protection different from that adopted by another state. In other words, Germany could prohibit that which the UK authorised, if it could be established that the measure imposing the prohibition was both necessary and proportionate. The Court observed that this was the situation in this case. In the first place, the prohibition of the commercial exploitation of games involving the simulation of acts of violence against persons corresponded to the level of protection of human dignity which the national constitution sought to guarantee within Germany. Second, by prohibiting only the variant of the laser game the object of which was to fire on human targets, the contested order did not go beyond what was necessary in order to attain the objective pursued. For those reasons, the Court concluded, the order could not be regarded as a measure unjustifiably undermining the freedom to provide services.

The discretion retained by Member States in identifying the areas of public policy which may result in the restriction of free movement rights has been substantially limited by Directive 2004/38.

Scope of Directive 2004/38

The provisions of Directive 2004/38 are considered in detail at pages 327–347.

Directive 2004/38 establishes the right of entry, residence and permanent residence for EU citizens and their family members. These provisions are considered in detail in Chapters 11–13, but to summarise:

- Article 6 provides a right of residence for a period of up to three months for all EU citizens and their family members without any conditions or formalities other than the requirement to hold a valid identity card or passport. In the case of non-EU family members, they must hold a valid passport.

- Article 7 provides a right of residence for a period exceeding three months for EU citizens and their family members, but this is limited to three categories:
  - workers and the self-employed;
  - the economically self-sufficient; i.e. those with sufficient resources not to become a burden on the social assistance system of the host Member State and who have comprehensive sickness insurance cover in the host Member State;
  - students who are following a course of study, including vocational training, at a public or private institution which is accredited or financed by the host Member State. The student must have comprehensive sickness insurance and assure the

Member State that they have sufficient resources for themselves and their family members to ensure that they do not become a burden on the social assistance system of the host Member State during their stay.

● Article 16 provides a right of permanent residence to EU citizens (including EU family members) who have legally resided in the host Member State for a continuous period of five years. Non-EU family members also have the right to permanent residence provided they have legally resided with the EU citizen in the host Member State for a continuous period of five years.

As stated above, these rights of residence may be restricted on the grounds of public policy, public security or public health (Art 27(1), Directive 2004/38). Member States may decide, in some cases, that an individual, although an EU citizen, is not exercising the extended right of residence conferred by Art 7, Directive 2004/38. This is a decision taken on the facts of the case. The Court of Justice has, on a number of occasions (in the context of the former Directive 64/221, which was repealed and replaced by Directive 2004/38), declared that whether or not a person is an EU worker or a recipient of services is to be determined according to principles laid down by Union law (see, e.g., **Levin v Staatsecretaris van Justitie** (Case 53/81), para 11). In **Commission v The Netherlands** (Case C-68/89), the Court of Justice held that this was a decision which could not be made by the national authorities at the point of entry, but had to be determined subsequently on the basis of activities undertaken by the individual. It seems likely that a decision, say, that an individual is not economically active and is not economically self-sufficient to fall within the residual right of residence under Art 7(1)(b), Directive 2004/38, will not be a decision made on public policy or public security grounds. In any event, Art 14(3), Directive 2004/38 provides that expulsion shall not be an automatic consequence if an EU citizen or his family members have recourse to the host Member State's social assistance system. Article 14(4) further provides that (other than in accordance with the provisions relating to restrictions on the right of entry and residence on grounds of public policy, public security or public health) an expulsion order cannot be issued against an EU citizen or his family members if:

● the EU citizen is a worker or self-employed person in the host Member State; or

● the EU citizen entered the host Member State to seek employment and provided he can supply evidence that he is continuing to seek work and has a genuine chance of being employed.

Article 27(2), Directive 2004/38 provides that 'Measures taken on grounds of public policy or public security shall comply with the principle of proportionality and shall be based exclusively on the personal conduct of the individual concerned'. Although Member States have a wide discretion in determining the type of 'personal conduct' which may form the basis for action, the Court of Justice has laid down a number of criteria by which such national restrictions must be judged. In the first place, the Court of Justice has stated that the action of Member States must be assessed in the light of the European Convention on Human Rights, as illustrated in the following case:

Rutili v Minister of the Interior (Case 36/75)

An Italian national working in France had, following political and trade union activity, been confined by a ministerial order to certain areas of France. He challenged this restriction and the case was referred to the Court of Justice under what is now Art 267 TFEU. The Court of Justice held that:

> The concept of public policy must, in the Community [i.e. Union] context and where, in particular, it is used as a justification for derogating from the fundamental principles of equality of treatment and freedom of movement of workers, be interpreted strictly, so that its scope cannot be interpreted unilaterally by each Member State without being subject to control by the institutions of the Community [i.e. Union]. Accordingly, **restrictions cannot be imposed on the right of a national of any Member State to enter the territory of another Member State, to stay there and to move within it unless his presence constitutes a genuine and sufficiently serious threat to public policy** . . . Nor, under Article 8 of Regulation 1612/68, which ensures equality of treatment as regards membership of trades unions and the exercise of rights attached thereto, may the reservation relating to public policy be invoked on grounds arising from the exercise of those rights. Taken as a whole, these limitations placed on the powers of Member States in respect of control of aliens are a specific manifestation of the more general principle, enshrined in Articles 8, 9, 10 and 11 of the Convention for the Protection of Human Rights . . . which provide in identical terms, that no restrictions in the interests of national security or public safety shall be placed on the rights secured by the above-quoted articles other than such as are necessary for the protection of those interests 'in a democratic society'. [emphasis added]

In the above case the Court of Justice held that free movement rights entailed a right of entry and residence in the *whole* territory of the host Member State, and the restrictions imposed could not be justified in the case of EU nationals who were exercising their free movement rights unless they were also applicable in similar circumstances to nationals of the host Member State. The Court further held that the conduct must be both 'personal' and 'a genuine and serious threat' to public policy. This requirement has now been incorporated into Directive 2004/38, which provides that: 'The personal conduct of the individual concerned must represent a genuine, present and sufficiently serious threat affecting one of the fundamental interests of society' (Art 27(2)). The concepts of 'personal conduct' and 'genuine and serious threat to public policy' were explored by the Court of Justice in the following case:

Van Duyn v *Home Office* (Case 41/74)

Yvonne Van Duyn, a Netherlands' national, was a member of the Church of Scientology. She wished to enter the UK to work for the organisation. The UK government had decided in 1968 that membership of the church was 'socially harmful', but had not taken any steps to ban or restrict the activities which it carried out at its headquarters in East Grinstead, Sussex. Other Netherlands' nationals who wished to work for the organisation had, however, been excluded before the UK became a member of the EU (*Schmidt* v *Home Office* [1969] 2 Ch 149). Ms Van Duyn was refused entry on the grounds that her membership of the organisation constituted a threat to public policy. She challenged the refusal on the grounds that membership of an organisation could not be 'personal conduct' within the scope of the former Art 3(1), Directive 64/221 (now Art 27(2), Directive 2004/38). The case was referred to the Court of Justice, which held as follows:

> Although a person's past associations cannot, in general, justify a decision refusing him the right to move freely within the Community [i.e. Union], it is nevertheless the case that **present association**, which reflects participation in the activities of the body or of the organisation as well as identification with its aims and designs, **may be considered a voluntary act of the person concerned** and, consequently, as part of his personal conduct within the meaning of the provision cited. (para 17) [emphasis added]

The Court of Justice held that membership of an organisation could constitute 'personal conduct'. As to whether such an organisation could be regarded as a threat to public policy when no action had been taken against it and when it operated without restriction in the UK, the Court of Justice stated that:

> The particular circumstances justifying recourse to the concept of public policy may vary from one country to another and from one period to another ... It follows from the above that where the competent authorities of a Member State have clearly defined their standpoint as regards the activities of a particular organisation and where, considering it to be socially harmful, they have taken administrative measures to counteract their activities the Member State cannot be required, before it can rely on the concept of public policy, to make such activities unlawful, if recourse to such a measure is not thought appropriate in the circumstances. (paras 18 and 19) [emphasis added]

The above decision was somewhat anomalous. At para 19, the Court of Justice stated that a Member State *may* be justified in taking action preventing an EU citizen from participating in an activity which is considered to be socially harmful, provided it has 'taken administrative measures to counteract these activities' among its own citizens. In this case, the UK government had simply made a statement in Parliament expressing strong disapproval of the activities of the Church of Scientology. It did not seek to ban the church from operating in the UK, and it declared that there was no power to do so.

This decision seemed to provide that Member States were justified in excluding or expelling EU citizens for belonging to an organisation engaged in activities which were both 'a serious threat to public policy' and, at the same time, were not thought by the host Member State to be serious enough to merit even the mildest criminal sanctions when the citizens of the host Member State were engaged in the same activities. While membership of an organisation committed to activities which clearly breach the criminal law, such as a terrorist organisation, would seem to fall squarely within the concept of 'personal conduct constituting a serious threat to public policy' (see, e.g., *Astrid Proll (No. 2)* [1988] 2 CMLR 387, IAT), membership of an organisation enjoying the full protection of the law would hardly seem to fall within the same category. Neither would such a decision seem to be compatible with the rights to freedom of thought, conscience and religion, and freedom of expression enshrined in Arts 9 and 10 of the European Convention on Human Rights, which should, as the Court of Justice made clear in *Rutili* (above), inform all decisions made by Member States in relation to the exercise of free movement rights.

The wide discretion which the Court seemed to accept that Member States enjoyed in *Van Duyn* in relation to the type of prohibited conduct was subsequently limited by the Court of Justice in the following case:

Adoui and Cornuaille v *Belgian State* (Cases 115 and 116/81)

The applicants in this case were French nationals who worked in a Belgian café with a somewhat dubious reputation (hostesses/prostitutes worked there). They were refused residency in Belgium on public policy grounds. The case was referred to the Court of Justice because 'prostitution as such is not prohibited by Belgian legislation, although the law does prohibit certain incidental activities, such as the exploitation of prostitution by third parties and various forms of incitement to debauchery' (para 6). On this occasion the

Court emphasised the need for equality of treatment, as far as possible, between nationals and non-nationals exercising Union rights. Having pointed out that Member States cannot exclude or expel their own nationals, the Court of Justice stated that:

> Although that difference of treatment, which bears upon the nature of the measures available, must therefore be allowed, it must nevertheless be stressed that, in a Member State, the authority empowered to adopt [public policy/public security] measures must not base the exercise of its powers on assessment of certain conduct which would have the effect of applying an arbitrary distinction to the detriment of nationals of other Member States ... Although Community [i.e. Union] law does not impose upon the Member States a uniform scale of values as regards the assessment of conduct which may be considered as contrary to public policy, **it should nevertheless be stated that conduct may not be considered as being of a sufficiently serious nature to justify restrictions on the admission to or residence within the territory of a Member State of a national of another Member State in a case where the former Member State does not adopt, with respect to the same conduct on the part of its own nationals, repressive measures or other genuine and effective measures intended to combat such conduct.** (paras 7 and 8) [emphasis added]

Had the above test been imposed in the **Van Duyn** case, it is unlikely that the outcome would have been the same because, although the UK government had 'clearly defined its standpoint' on the Church of Scientology, it had, in fact, taken no 'repressive or other genuine and effective measures to combat it'. This approach, reflecting both a standard of equality of treatment and proportionality of response, is also to be found in decisions of the Court of Justice in relation to measures taken by national authorities restricting the importation of goods, where reliance is placed on the 'public morality' derogation permitted by Art 36 TFEU; see *Conegate Ltd* v *Customs and Excise Commissioners* (Case 121/85), and Chapter 18.

See pages 611–613 for a consideration of the 'public morality' derogation pursuant to Art 36 TFEU.

In order for action to be justified, 'personal conduct' must relate exclusively to the individual on whom the restriction is imposed, as illustrated in the following case:

Bonsignore v *Oberstadtdirektor der Stadt Köln* (Case 67/74)

Bonsignore, an Italian national working in Germany, had been found guilty of causing the death of his brother by the negligent handling of a firearm. Following his conviction, he was ordered by the German Aliens Authority to be deported. It was accepted by the German Aliens Authority that there was little likelihood of the commission of further offences by the defendant. They were, however, seeking to use the deportation for its deterrent effect 'which the deportation of an alien found in illegal possession of a firearm would have in immigrant circles having regard to the resurgence of violence in large urban areas' (para 4). The matter was referred to the Court of Justice. Advocate General Mayras emphasised, in his Opinion, that 'it is not permissible for a Community [i.e. Union] worker, even when convicted of a criminal offence, to be made into a "scapegoat" in order to deter other aliens from acting in the same way ... the concept of personal conduct must be examined not only in the light of the offences committed but also in view of the "potential criminality" of the offender'. The Court of Justice agreed with this view and held that the former Art 3(1), Directive 64/221 (now Art 27(2), Directive 2004/38) means that action taken against an individual on public policy or public security grounds 'cannot be justified on grounds extraneous to the individual case', and thus deportation as a deterrent or as a general preventive measure is prohibited.

In the above case, the Court of Justice held that action taken against an individual on public policy or public security grounds 'cannot be justified on grounds extraneous to the individual case', and thus deportation as a deterrent or as a general preventive measure is prohibited. This prohibition is now incorporated in Directive 2004/38, which provides that: 'Justifications that are isolated from the particulars of the case or that rely on considerations of general prevention shall not be accepted'.

The following case concerned the legality of a travel restriction imposed by a Member State on one of its own citizens:

Ministerul Administrației și Internelor – Direcția Generală De Pașapoarte Bucurebti v Jipa (Case C-33/07)

Jipa (a Romanian citizen) left Romania on 10 September 2006 to travel to Belgium. On account of his 'illegal residence' in that Member State, he was repatriated to Romania on 26 November 2006, by virtue of a readmission agreement signed by the two countries (Romania only joined the EU on 1 January 2007).

The Ministerul Administrației și Internelor – Direcția Generală de Pașapoarte București (Ministry of Administration and Home Affairs – Directorate General for Passports, Bucharest) applied to the Tribunalul Dâmbovița for a measure prohibiting Jipa from travelling to Belgium for a period of up to three years.

In those circumstances, the Tribunalul Dâmbovița referred the case to the Court of Justice, pursuant to the former Art 234 EC Treaty (now Art 267 TFEU) to determine whether Union law, in particular Directive 2004/38, precluded Romanian legislation which allowed the right of a national of a Member State to travel to another Member State to be restricted, in particular on the ground that he had previously been repatriated from the latter Member State on account of his 'illegal residence' there.

The Court of Justice stated that, as a Romanian national, Jipa enjoyed the status of an EU citizen and could therefore rely on the rights pertaining to that status, in particular the right to move and reside freely within the territory of the Member States, including against his Member State of origin. The Court noted that the right of freedom of movement includes both the right for EU citizens in possession of a valid identity card or passport to enter a Member State other than the one of origin and the right to leave the state of origin.

That right is not unconditional and may be subject to limitations and conditions imposed by the Treaty, in particular on grounds of public policy or public security. The Court stated that the Member States are competent to determine the requirements of public policy and public security in accordance with their national needs. However, in the Union context, those requirements must be interpreted strictly, so that their scope cannot be determined unilaterally by each Member State without any control by the Union institutions.

The Court added that such restrictions imply in particular that, **in order to be justified, measures taken on grounds of public policy or public security must be based exclusively on the personal conduct of the individual concerned, and justifications that are isolated from the particulars of the case in question or that rely on considerations of general prevention cannot be accepted. The Court stated that a measure limiting freedom of movement must be adopted in the light of considerations pertaining to the protection of public policy or public security in the Member State imposing the measure. Thus the measure cannot be based exclusively on reasons advanced by another Member State to justify a decision to remove an EU citizen from the territory of the latter Member State. That consideration does not however rule out the possibility of such reasons being taken** into account in the context of the assessment which the competent national authorities undertake for the purpose of adopting the measure restricting freedom of movement.

The Court, while stating that it is for the national court to make the necessary checks, observed that, in the present case, the Romanian authorities seemed to rely solely on the repatriation measure, with no specific assessment of Jipa's personal conduct and no reference to any threat that he might constitute to public policy or public security.

The Court concluded that Union law did not preclude national legislation that allows the right of a national of a Member State to travel to another Member State to be restricted, in particular on account of his 'illegal residence' there, provided that certain requirements are met: (i) the personal conduct of that national must constitute a genuine, present and sufficiently serious threat to one of the fundamental interests of society; and (ii) it is necessary that the restrictive measure envisaged be appropriate to ensure the achievement of the objective it pursues and not go beyond what is necessary to attain it.

The Court added that it was for the national court to establish whether that is so in the case before it.

The effect of criminal convictions

Previous criminal convictions shall not 'in themselves constitute grounds' for exclusion or expulsion on grounds of public policy or public security (Art 27(2), Directive 2004/38). In the following case, the Court of Justice was asked by Marlborough Street Magistrates' Court in London:

> Whether the wording of Art 3(2) of Directive 64/221 [now Art 27(2), Directive 2004/38], namely that previous criminal convictions shall not 'in themselves' constitute grounds for the taking of measures based on public policy or public security, means that previous criminal convictions are solely relevant in so far as they manifest a present or future propensity to act in a manner contrary to public policy or public security; alternatively, the meaning to be attached to 'in themselves' in Art 3(2) of Directive 64/221 [now Art 27(2), Directive 2004/38].

R v Bouchereau (Case 30/77)

In its reply to the magistrates' questions, the Court of Justice stated that the former Art 3(2), Directive 64/221 (now Art 27(2), Directive 2004/38):

> . . . must be understood as requiring the national authorities to carry out a specific appraisal from the point of view of the interests inherent in protecting requirements of public policy which does not necessarily coincide with the appraisals which formed the basis of the criminal conviction.
>
> The existence of a previous criminal conviction can, therefore, only be taken into account in so far as the circumstances which gave rise to that conviction are evidence of personal conduct constituting a present threat to the requirements of public policy.
>
> Although, in general, a finding that such a threat exists implies the existence in the individual concerned of a propensity to act in the same way in the future, it is possible that past conduct alone may constitute such a threat to the requirements of public policy. [emphasis added]

It would seem from this judgment that what the national authorities making the decision relating to an EU citizen should be looking for is an indication of whether or not the person concerned is likely to be a present or future threat; i.e. is there a likelihood of reoffending? That would seem to be the purpose of the assessment, despite Advocate General Warner having referred to 'circumstances when cases do arise, exceptionally, where the personal conduct of the alien has been such that, while not necessarily evincing any clear propensity on his part, has caused such deep revulsion that public policy requires his departure' ([1977] ECR 1999 at 2022). There is no indication, however, that the Court of Justice agreed with Advocate General Warner in this regard, and indeed, it had agreed with Advocate General Mayras in an earlier case when he warned against the use of deportation to mollify public opinion: 'one cannot avoid the impression that the deportation of a foreign worker, even a national of the Common Market [i.e. Union], satisfies the feeling of hostility, sometimes verging on xenophobia, which the commission of an offence by an alien generally causes or revives in the indigenous population' (*Bonsignore*, above). As stated above, Art 27(2), Directive 2004/38 now incorporates these principles developed by the Court of Justice. Article 27(2) provides that:

> . . . The personal conduct of the individual concerned must represent a genuine, present and sufficiently serious threat affecting one of the fundamental interests of society. Justifications that are isolated from the particulars of the case or that rely on considerations of general prevention shall not be accepted.

Article 27(2), Directive 2004/38 therefore prohibits Member States from making a decision on the basis of public reaction to an offence. Setting aside the frequent misreporting of the circumstances of offences in the press, which may well provoke a quite inappropriate response, the requirement in Art 27(2) is that decisions which are 'isolated from the particulars of the case or that rely on considerations of general prevention' shall not be acceptable. This clearly excludes Member States from taking into account such extraneous factors as the public response to an offence.

In *Bouchereau*, the Court of Justice stated that 'past conduct alone may constitute . . . a threat to the requirements of public policy'. A 'threat' must indicate that something may happen. A reasonable interpretation of this exceptional circumstance in which past conduct constitutes a future threat might be where the offence itself indicates some kind of mental or other disorder importing the risk of recurrent offending. As is seen in the case below, however, the authorities will have to decide at the time when the decision is taken, by making an assessment, whether the individual still constitutes a threat at the time when the exclusion or expulsion is given effect, 'as the factors to be taken into account, particularly those concerning his conduct, are likely to change in the course of time' (*R v Secretary of State for the Home Department, ex parte Santillo* (Case 131/79), para 18).

The following case concerned an EU citizen who was expelled from another Member State for life:

Donatella Calfa (Case C-348/96)

Ms Calfa, an Italian national, was charged with the possession and use of prohibited drugs while staying as a tourist in Crete (Greece). She was found guilty and sentenced to three months' imprisonment and ordered to be expelled for life from Greek territory, in accordance with national law. The national court was under an obligation to order her expulsion for life (unless there were compelling reasons, in particular family reasons). She would be able to return to Greece only after a period of three years, provided that the Minister of Justice exercised his discretion to grant approval.

Ms Calfa contested that the expulsion for life breached her Union law rights to travel to Greece as a tourist (i.e. as the recipient of services in accordance with what is now Art 56 TFEU (previously Art 49 EC Treaty)). The Greek authorities argued that she could be expelled in accordance with the public policy derogation. The Greek court referred the case to the Court of Justice under what is now Art 267 TFEU, seeking guidance on whether the penalty was compatible with Union law. The Court of Justice held as follows:

17. Although in principle criminal legislation is a matter for which the Member States are responsible, the Court has consistently held that Community [i.e. Union] law sets certain limits to their power, and such legislation may not restrict the fundamental freedoms guaranteed by Community [i.e. Union] law . . .

18. In the present case, the penalty of expulsion for life from the territory, which is applicable to the nationals of other Member States in the event of conviction for obtaining and being in possession of drugs for their own use, clearly constitutes an obstacle to the freedom to provide services recognised in . . . [Article 56 TFEU], since it is the very negation of that freedom. This would also be true for the other fundamental freedoms laid down in . . . [Article 45 TFEU (free movement of workers) and Article 49 TFEU (right of establishment)] . . . and referred to by the national court.

19. It is nonetheless necessary to consider whether such a penalty could be justified by the public policy exception provided for in *inter alia* . . . [Article 52 TFEU], which is relied upon by the Member State in question.

20. . . . [Article 52 TFEU] permits Member States to adopt, with respect to nationals of other Member States, and in particular on the grounds of public policy, measures which they cannot apply to their own nationals, inasmuch as they have no authority to expel the latter from the territory or to deny them access thereto . . .

21. **Under the Court's case law, the concept of public policy may be relied upon in the event of a genuine and sufficiently serious threat to the requirements of public policy affecting one of the fundamental interests of society** (see Case 30/77 *Bouchereau* [1977] ECR 1999, para 35).

22. In this respect, **it must be accepted that a Member State may consider that the use of drugs constitutes a danger for society such as to justify special measures against foreign nationals who contravene its laws on drugs, in order to maintain public order.**

23. However, as the Court has repeatedly stated, the public policy exception, like all derogations from a fundamental principle of the Treaty, must be interpreted restrictively.

24. In that regard, Directive 64/221 [which has been repealed and replaced by Directive 2004/38], Article 1(1) of which provides that the directive is to apply to *inter alia* any national of a Member State who travels to another Member State as a recipient of services, sets certain limits on the right of Member States to expel foreign nationals on the grounds of public policy. Article 3 of that directive [now Art 27, Directive 2004/38] states that measures taken on the grounds of public policy or of public security that have the effect of restricting the residence of a national of another Member State must be based exclusively on the personal conduct of the individual concerned. In addition, previous criminal convictions cannot in themselves constitute grounds for the taking of such measures. **It follows that the existence of a previous criminal conviction can, therefore, only be taken into account in so far as the circumstances which gave rise to that conviction are evidence of personal conduct constituting a present threat to the requirements of public policy** (*Bouchereau*, para 28).

25. It follows that an expulsion order could be made against a Community [i.e. Union] national such as Ms Calfa only if, besides her having committed an offence under

drugs laws, her personal conduct created a genuine and sufficiently serious threat affecting one of the fundamental interests of society.

26. In the present case, the legislation at issue in the main proceedings requires nationals of other Member States found guilty, on the national territory in which that legislation applies, of an offence under the drugs laws, to be expelled for life from that territory, unless compelling reasons, in particular family reasons, justify the continued residence in the country. The penalty can be revoked only by a decision taken at the discretion of the Minister for Justice after a period of three years.

27. Therefore, expulsion for life automatically follows a criminal conviction, without any account being taken of the personal conduct of the offender or the danger which that person represents for the requirements of public policy.

28. It follows that the conditions for the application of the public policy exception provided for in Directive 64/221 [which has been repealed and replaced by Directive 2004/38], as interpreted by the Court of Justice, are not fulfilled and that **the public policy exception cannot be successfully relied upon to justify a restriction on the freedom to provide services, such as that imposed by the legislation at issue in the main proceedings.**

29. In view of the foregoing considerations, the answer to be given to the national court's questions must be that . . . [Articles 45, 49 and 56 TFEU] and Article 3 of Directive 64/221 [now Art 27, Directive 2004/38] preclude legislation which, with certain exceptions, in particular where there are family reasons, requires a Member State's courts to order the expulsion for life from its territory of nationals of other Member States found guilty on that territory of the offences of obtaining and being in possession of drugs for their own personal use. [emphasis added]

In the above case, at paras 21 and 22 the Court of Justice reiterated the principles developed in its previous case law. At para 22, the Court accepted that in order to maintain public order a Member State could consider possession of drugs to constitute a danger to the public which could therefore justify special measures being taken against foreigners who breached its anti-drug laws. Having said that, the Court at para 25 stated that an EU citizen could only be expelled if it was shown that, in addition to breaching the anti-drug laws, their personal conduct 'created a genuine and sufficiently serious threat affecting one of the fundamental interests of society' (as stated above this is now incorporated in Art 27(2), Directive 2004/38). In any event, the Court held at para 28 that expulsion for life was not compatible with the Treaty provisions or the former Directive 64/221 (now Directive 2004/38). This was the case even though there was the possibility of review of that decision after three years. A mandatory ban on readmission would therefore not be compatible with Union law, because an EU citizen could only be prevented from exercising his free movement rights if he constitutes a genuine and sufficient threat (present or future, *not past*) to one of the fundamental interests of society.

This is confirmed by Directive 2004/38 which provides that persons excluded from a Member State on grounds of public policy or public security can apply for the exclusion order to be lifted after a reasonable period, and in any event after a maximum of three years, by putting forward arguments to establish that there has been a material change in the circumstances which justified the decision ordering their exclusion (Art 32(1)). The Member State concerned is required to reach a decision on such application within six months of its submission (Art 32(1)). The person applying for the lifting of the exclusion order does not have a right of entry into the Member State concerned while the application is being considered (Art 32(2)).

The following case was decided by the English Court of Appeal, applying the former Directives 73/148 and 64/221 (both of which have been repealed and replaced by Directive 2004/38):

Gough and Smith and Others v *Chief Constable of Derbyshire, Miller* v *Leeds Magistrates Court, Lilley* v *Director of Public Prosecutions* [2002] EWCA CIV 351

Gough had been convicted of violent offences in 1998 and Smith in 1990. In addition, both had been the subject of a 'profile' prepared by the police that indicated repeated involvement in or near incidents of violence at or around football matches. Upon conviction, banning orders for two years were made against them under s 14A, Football Spectators Act 1989 as amended by the Football (Disorder) Act 2000. Their appeal to the Divisional Court was dismissed and they appealed to the Court of Appeal. The Court of Appeal did not exercise its discretion to refer the case to the Court of Justice pursuant to the former Art 234 EC Treaty (now Art 267 TFEU).

Gough and Smith contended that, *inter alia*:

1 The banning orders derogated from the positive rights on freedom of movement and freedom to leave their home country which were conferred on them by the former Arts 1 and 2, Directive 73/148 (now Directive 2004/38) because it was not permissible to justify a banning order on public policy grounds; alternatively no such grounds were made out on the evidence;
2 The Football (Disorder) Act 2000 was contrary to Union law and therefore inapplicable in so far as it imposed mandatory restrictions on free movement within the Union which were based on criteria that were not provided for or permitted by Union legislation;
3 It was contrary to the Union law principle of proportionality to ban an individual from travelling anywhere within the Union even if the relevant match or tournament was not taking place within the Union.

The Court of Appeal held that:

1 It was entirely satisfied that there was a public policy exception to the former Art 2, Directive 73/148 (now Directive 2004/38). There was no absolute right to leave your home country.
2 Although at first glance it might appear disproportionate to ban all foreign travel, the court was satisfied that such a reaction was unsound. Banning orders were only to be imposed where there were strong grounds for concluding that the individual had a propensity for taking part in football hooliganism. It was proportionate that those who had shown such a propensity should be subject to a scheme that restricted their ability to indulge in it.

Accordingly the Court of Appeal upheld the banning orders and dismissed the appeal.

Directive 2004/38: additional provisions

There are a number of additional provisions within Directive 2004/38 which are of relevance to public policy and public security (and which were not included in the former Directive 64/221).

Article 27(3) provides that in order to ascertain whether the person concerned represents a danger to public policy or public security, the host Member State, if it considers it essential, may request the Member State of origin or other Member States to provide information concerning any previous police record the person concerned may have. The request is to be made by the host Member State:

(i)   when issuing the registration certificate; or
(ii) if there is no registration system, no later than three months from the date of the person's arrival in the host Member State or date the person reported his presence in the host Member State as provided for in Art 5(5); or
(iii) when issuing the residence card.

Such enquiries must not be made as a matter of routine. The Member State consulted should provide its reply within two months (see Chapters 11–13 for commentary on the issue of registration certificates and residence cards).

A person who is expelled from a Member State on grounds of public policy, public security or public health shall have the right to re-enter the Member State which issued him with a passport or identity card, even if the document is no longer valid, or if the nationality of the holder is in dispute (Art 27(4)).

Article 28(1) provides that before taking an expulsion decision on grounds of public policy or public security, the host Member State must assess a number of factors, such as: the period for which the individual concerned has been resident; his age; state of health; family and economic situation; degree of social and cultural integration in the host Member State; and the extent of his links with the country of origin. If an EU citizen or his family members have acquired the right of permanent residence, an expulsion decision can only be made on serious grounds of public policy or public security (Art 28(2); see Chapters 11–13 for commentary on the right of permanent residence). In addition, an expulsion decision may not be taken against an EU citizen or his family members who have resided in the host Member State for ten years or if he is a minor, unless the decision is based on imperative grounds of public security, and, in the case of a minor, provided that expulsion is necessary for the best interests of the child (Art 28(3)). The following case concerned the application of these provisions:

I v Oberbürgermeisterin der Stadt Remscheid (Case C-348/09)

Mr I, an Italian national, had lived in Germany since 1987. He was single and had no children. He never gained a school-leaving certificate or professional qualification and had been employed in Germany only occasionally.

In 2006, the Landgericht Köln (Regional Court, Cologne) sentenced Mr I to a term of imprisonment of seven years and six months for the sexual assault, sexual coercion and rape of a young girl, who was eight years old when the offences commenced. The acts which gave rise to the conviction took place between 1990 and 2001. Mr I, who had been in custody since 2006, was due to complete his sentence in July 2013.

By decision of 6 May 2008, the German authorities determined that Mr I had lost the right of entry and residence under German law, on grounds relating in particular to the serious nature of the offences committed and the risk of reoffending, and ordered him to leave Germany, failing which he would be deported to Italy. Mr I brought an action against the expulsion decision.

The Oberverwaltungsgericht für das Land Nordrhein-Westfalen (Higher Administrative Court of North Rhine-Westphalia), before which an appeal was brought, referred the case to the Court of Justice to ask the Court for an interpretation of the term 'imperative grounds of public security', which may justify the expulsion of an EU citizen who has been resident in the host Member State for more than ten years.

The Court of Justice stated that it had already held (in *Tsakouridis* (Case C-145/09)) that the fight against crime in connection with dealings in narcotics as part of an organised group was capable of being covered by the concept of 'imperative grounds of public security'.

The Court further stated that the concept of 'imperative grounds of public security' presupposed not only the existence of a threat to public security, but also that such a threat was of a particularly high degree of seriousness, as reflected by the use of the words 'imperative grounds'.

Member States essentially retain the freedom to determine the requirements of public security in accordance with their national needs – which can vary from one Member State to another and from one era to another – particularly as justification for a derogation from the fundamental principle of free movement of persons. However, those requirements must be interpreted strictly, so that their scope could not be determined unilaterally by each Member State without any control by EU institutions.

The Court pointed out that, in order to determine whether offences such as those committed by Mr I may be covered by the concept of 'imperative grounds of public security', account had to be taken of the fact that the sexual exploitation of children is one of the areas of particularly serious crime with a cross-border dimension for which express provision is made in the Treaty (Art 83(1) TFEU) and in which the EU legislature may intervene.

According to the Court, it is open to the Member States to regard criminal offences such as those referred to in Art 83 TFEU as constituting a particularly serious threat to one of the fundamental interests of society, which might pose a direct threat to the calm and physical security of the population and thus be covered by the concept of 'imperative grounds of public security'. However, such offences may justify an expulsion measure only if the manner in which they were committed discloses particularly serious characteristics, which is a matter for the national court to determine on the basis of an individual examination of the particular case before it.

However, should the national court find that, according to the particular values of the legal order of the Member State in which it has jurisdiction, offences such as those committed by Mr I pose a direct threat to the calm and physical security of the population, this should not necessarily lead to the expulsion of the person concerned.

Under EU law, the issue of any expulsion measure is conditional on the requirement that the personal conduct of the individual concerned must represent a genuine, present threat affecting one of the fundamental interests of society or of the host Member State, which implies, in general, the existence in the individual concerned of a propensity to act in the same way in the future.

Moreover, where an expulsion measure has been adopted as a penalty or legal consequence of a custodial penalty, but is enforced more than two years after it was issued, the Member States must check that the individual concerned is currently and genuinely a threat to public security and assess whether there has been any material change in the circumstances since the expulsion order was issued.

Lastly, the Court pointed out that, before taking an expulsion decision on grounds of public policy or public security, the host Member State must take account of considerations such as: how long the individual concerned has resided on its territory; his age; state of health; family and economic situation; social and cultural integration into that State; and the extent of his links with the country of origin.

An expulsion order cannot be issued by a Member State as a penalty or legal consequence of a custodial penalty, unless the requirements of Arts 27–29 (see above) are complied with (Art 33(1)). As stated by the Court of Justice in the above case, where an expulsion order is issued under this provision, and where it is enforced more than two years after it was issued, the Member State is required to check that the individual concerned is a current and genuine threat to public policy or public security, and the Member State shall assess whether there has been any material change in circumstances since the expulsion order was issued (Art 33(2)).

Public health

The former Art 4, Directive 64/221 permitted the exclusion of EU citizens and their families if they were suffering from one of the diseases listed in the annex to the directive. The list included diseases subject to quarantine under WHO regulations: tuberculosis in an active state, syphilis, and other infectious diseases subject to notification under the legislation of the host Member State. There was a separate category of diseases and disabilities which might threaten public policy and public security. These were: drug addiction, profound mental disturbance and manifest conditions of psychotic disturbance with agitation, delirium, hallucinations or confusion.

The former Art 4, Directive 64/221 has been repealed and replaced by Art 29, Directive 2004/38. Under Art 29(1), Directive 2004/38 the only diseases which can justify restricting the right of entry and residence on the ground of public health, are:

(i)   those with epidemic potential as defined by the relevant instruments of the WHO;

(ii) other infectious diseases or other contagious parasitic diseases if they are subject to protection provisions applying to nationals of the host Member State.

It is not permissible to carry out routine medical examinations for any of these conditions, as to do so would impose an additional requirement on entry which is prohibited by Art 29(1), Directive 2004/38; see *Commission* v *Netherlands* (Case C-68/89). Nor would it be open to a state to require production of medical or other certificates to confirm that individuals are free from infection, as this would constitute a further restriction. A medical examination would, however, be lawful if a person was manifesting obvious symptoms of sickness which might indicate that he was suffering from one of the conditions listed in Art 29(1), Directive 2004/38. Article 29(3), Directive 2004/38 provides that a Member State can require the person concerned to undergo a medical examination, which must be provided free of charge, if there are serious indications that a medical examination is necessary; such medical examination must not be carried out as a matter of routine. Article 29(2), Directive 2004/38 provides that diseases occurring after a three-month period from the date of arrival shall not constitute grounds for expulsion from the host Member State.

Although the following case is not concerned with the free movement of persons (as suggested by the title to this chapter) it is nevertheless concerned with the derogation from the Treaty provisions on the ground of public health, in relation to the free movement of services:

Konsumentombudsmannen (KO) v Gourmet International Products AB (GIP) (Case C-405/98)

The Court of Justice held that the Treaty provisions on freedom to provide services pre-cluded a prohibition on the advertising of alcoholic beverages because it had a particu-lar effect on the cross-border supply of advertising space, given the international nature of the advertising market in the category of products to which the prohibition related, and thereby constituted a restriction on the freedom to provide services within the mean-ing of the former Art 49 EC Treaty (now Art 56 TFEU).

The Court, however, held that such a restriction may be justified by the protection of public health, which is a ground of general interest recognised by the former Art 46 EC Treaty (now Art 52 TFEU), which is applicable to the provision of services in accordance with the former Art 55 EC Treaty (now Art 62 TFEU). The Court stated that it was for the national court to determine whether, in the circumstances of law and fact which character-ise the situation in the Member State concerned, the prohibition on advertising at issue in the main proceedings met the condition of proportionality required in order for the dero-gation from the freedom to provide services to be justified.

Procedural protection

Objective 2

The former Arts 5 to 9, Directive 64/221 were intended to ensure that when action was taken against EU citizens or others exercising their Union free movement rights, such action was taken in accordance with minimum standards of due process. Articles 30–33, Directive 2004/38 have replaced the former Arts 5 to 9, Directive 64/221. The provisions of Arts 30–33, Directive 2004/38 are now considered.

Article 30(1) provides that the person concerned by a decision refusing leave to enter or reside in a Member State on the ground of public policy, public security or public health must be notified in writing of that decision, in such a way that they are able to comprehend its content and the implications for them. The grounds for the decision must be given pre-cisely and in full, unless this is contrary to the interests of state security (Art 30(2)), and the person concerned must be informed of the appeal procedures available to them (Art 30(3)). Except in cases of urgency, the subject of such decision must be allowed at least one month in which to leave the Member State (Art 30(3)).

Article 31 sets out the procedural safeguards which apply if a decision is taken against a person's right of entry and residence on the grounds of public policy, public security or public health. Article 31 provides as follows:

1 The persons concerned shall have access to judicial and, where appropriate, administrative redress procedures in the host Member State to appeal against or seek review of any deci-sion taken against them on the grounds of public policy, public security or public health.

2 Where the application for appeal against or judicial review of the expulsion decision is accompanied by an application for an interim order to suspend enforcement of that deci-sion, actual removal from the territory may not take place until such time as the decision on the interim order has been taken, except:
   – where the expulsion decision is based on a previous judicial decision; or
   – where the persons concerned have had previous access to judicial review; or
   – where the expulsion decision is based on imperative grounds of public security under Article 28(3).

3 The redress procedures shall allow for an examination of the legality of the decision, as well as of the facts and circumstances on which the proposed measure is based. They shall ensure that the decision is not disproportionate, particularly in view of the requirements laid down in Article 28.

4 Member States may exclude the individual concerned from their territory pending the redress procedure, but they may not prevent the individual from submitting his/her defence in person, except when his/her appearance may cause serious troubles to public policy or public security or when the appeal or judicial review concerns a denial of entry to the territory.

An individual excluded from a Member State on grounds of public policy or public security can apply for the exclusion order to be lifted after a reasonable period, and in any event after a maximum of three years, by putting forward arguments to establish that there has been a material change in the circumstances which justified the decision ordering his exclusion (Art 32(1)). The Member State concerned is required to reach a decision on such application within six months of its submission (Art 32(1)). The person applying for the lifting of the exclusion order does not have a right of entry into the Member State concerned while the application is being considered (Art 32(2)).

An expulsion order cannot be issued by a Member State as a penalty or legal consequence of a custodial penalty, unless the requirements of Arts 27–29 (see above) are complied with (Art 33(1)). Where an expulsion order is issued under this provision, and where it is enforced more than two years after it was issued, the Member State is required to check that the individual concerned is a current and genuine threat to public policy or public security, and the Member State shall assess whether there has been any material change in circumstances since the expulsion order was issued (Art 33(2)).

The giving of sufficient reasons

The former Arts 5 and 6, Directive 64/221 provided that to enable an effective judicial challenge to be mounted, it was important that adequate reasons were given to a person who was excluded or expelled on public policy or public security grounds. The reasons would need to address the relevant aspects of public policy or public security on which the decision was based:

Rutili v *Minister of the Interior* (Case 36/75)

The Court of Justice held that:

> . . . this requirement means that the state concerned must, when notifying an individual of a restrictive measure adopted in his case, give him a precise and comprehensive statement of the grounds for the decision, to enable him to take effective steps to prepare his defence. (para 39)

As stated above, Directive 2004/38 now provides that the person concerned by a decision refusing leave to enter or reside in a Member State on the ground of public policy, public security or public health must be notified in writing of that decision, in such a way that they are able to comprehend its content and the implications for them. The grounds for the decision must be given precisely and in full, unless this is contrary to the interests of state security (Art 30(2)).

To be 'in full' (or 'comprehensive'), the statement will have to indicate the way in which a person continues to constitute a threat to public policy or public security. In determining whether or not to act against an individual, national authorities must 'carry out a specific appraisal from the point of view of the interests inherent in protecting the requirements of public policy' (*R v Bouchereau* (Case 30/77), para 27). It is the result of that appraisal that the authorities must communicate to the individual against whom they have decided to act. If the communication does not meet these requirements then it will invalidate the decision (*R v Secretary of State for the Home Department, ex parte Dannenberg* [1984] 2 CMLR 456 (CA)).

Although Art 30(2), Directive 2004/38 provides that an individual need not be given the reasons for a decision if this is contrary to the interests of the security of the state involved, it would probably not satisfy the Union's principle of effective judicial control if the authority does not at least provide some justification as to why the giving of reasons would threaten national security. The Court of Justice, in *Johnston v RUC* (Case 222/84), held that the mere issue of a certificate by the authorities to the effect that the disclosure of information would be prejudicial to national security was not sufficient without some indication of why this should be the case. Although the decision was given in the context of the need for an effective judicial process in the former Art 6, Directive 76/207, the Court emphasised that it was part of a broader principle of effective judicial control ([1986] ECR 1651 at p. 1663). However, the English Court of Appeal, in *R v Secretary of State for the Home Department, ex parte Gallagher* [1994] 3 CMLR 295, thought that a recital of the relevant section of the Prevention of Terrorism (Temporary Provisions) Act 1989 as the basis of an exclusion from the UK, without more, would meet the requirements of the former Art 6, Directive 64/221 (*per* Steyn LJ at p. 307). This case should be contrasted with that of *Tinnelly & Sons Ltd and McElduff v UK* (1998) 27 EHRR 269. In this case, the European Court of Human Rights, in relation to religious discrimination in Northern Ireland, refused to accept that such an '*ipse dixit* of the Executive' would satisfy Art 6 of the European Convention on Human Rights.

The Schengen Agreement and Directive 2004/38

Objective 3

Where an EU citizen travels within the EU in order to exercise the rights conferred on him by the EU Treaties, his spouse (or registered partner under Directive 2004/38), who is a national of a third country (i.e. a non-Member State), is covered to a large extent by the regulations and directives on freedom of movement for persons.

Although Member States may require such a spouse/registered partner to have an entry visa, they must accord him every facility in order to obtain it. Article 27(1), Directive 2004/38 (previously Art 2, Directive 64/221) also enables Member States to refuse entry into their territory to nationals of other Member States or their spouses who are third country nationals, on grounds of public policy or public security.

The Schengen Agreement is explained further at pages 364–369.

The Schengen Agreement and its implementing convention (CISA) have been incorporated into the framework of the EU (see Chapter 11). The CISA enabled checks at internal borders between the signatory states to be abolished and a single external border to be created. Common rules on visas, right to asylum, and control at external borders were adopted in order to facilitate freedom of movement for persons in the signatory states without disrupting public policy. An information system (SIS) was set up so that national authorities could exchange data on the identity of persons and the description of wanted property.

Under the CISA, the assessment of whether circumstances existed which justified the entry of an alert in the SIS for an alien, came within the competence of the state which issued that alert, and that state was responsible for the data it entered into the SIS. The state which issued the alert was the only state authorised to add to, correct or delete that data. The other contracting states were obliged to refuse entry or a visa to an alien for whom an alert had been issued for the purposes of refusing him entry.

The following case considers the relationship between the CISA and Union law on the free movement of persons, including the former Directive 64/221. Although Directive 64/221 has been repealed by Directive 2004/38, the following case remains relevant; Art 38(3), Directive 2004/38 stipulates that 'References made to the repealed provisions and Directives shall be construed as being made to this Directive':

Commission v Spain (Case 07/06)

This was the first time that the Court of Justice explained the relationship between the convention implementing the Schengen convention (CISA) and Union law on the free movement of persons. In this case, the European Commission brought proceedings against Spain before the Court of Justice, following complaints from two Algerian nationals (i.e. non-EU citizens), Farid and Bouchair, who were the spouses of Spanish nationals, living in Dublin and London, respectively.

The Spanish authorities had refused them entry into the Schengen Area simply because Germany had placed them on the SIS list of persons to be refused entry.

The Court of Justice explained, first of all, the relationship between the CISA and Union law on freedom of movement for persons.

It observed that **the Schengen Protocol confirms that the provisions of the Schengen *acquis* are applicable only if and in so far as they are compatible with Union law.** Closer cooperation in the Schengen field had to be conducted within the legal and institutional framework of the EU and with respect for the Treaties.

It followed that **the compliance of an administrative practice with the provisions of the CISA may justify the conduct of the competent national authorities only in so far as the application of the relevant provisions is compatible with the Union rules governing freedom of movement for persons.**

The Court stated that the concept of public policy within the meaning of the former Directive 64/221 (now Directive 2004/38) did not correspond to that in the CISA.

The directive states that measures taken on grounds of public policy or public security are to be based exclusively on the personal conduct of the individual concerned, so that previous criminal convictions are not in themselves to constitute grounds for the taking of such measures. The Court has always emphasised that the public policy exception is a derogation from the fundamental principle of freedom of movement for persons, which must be interpreted strictly. Reliance by a national authority on the concept of public policy presupposes a genuine and sufficiently serious threat affecting one of the fundamental interests of society.

However, circumstances such as a penalty involving deprivation of liberty of at least one year or a measure based on a failure to comply with national regulations on the entry or residence of aliens may provide a basis for the entry of an alert in the SIS for the purpose of refusing entry on grounds of public policy, irrespective of any specific assessment of the threat represented by the person concerned. Entry into the Schengen Area or the issue of a visa for that purpose cannot, in principle, be granted to an alien for whom an alert has been issued for the purposes of refusing entry.

The Court therefore held that a national of a third country who is the spouse of a Member State national, risks being deprived of the protection provided for by the former Directive 64/221 (now Directive 2004/38) where an alert has been issued for the purposes of refusing him entry. It observed that in a 1996 declaration the contracting states undertook not to issue an alert for the purposes of refusing entry in respect of a person covered by Union law unless the conditions required by that law are fulfilled. That means that a contracting state may issue an alert for such a person only after establishing that his presence constitutes a genuine, present and sufficiently serious threat affecting one of the fundamental interests of society within the meaning of the former Directive 64/221 (now Directive 2004/38).

Furthermore, a Member State that consults the SIS must be able to establish, before refusing entry into the Schengen Area to the person concerned, that his presence in that area constitutes such a threat. The Court recalled, in that connection, that the Schengen system had the means to answer requests for information made by national authorities faced with difficulties in enforcing an alert.

Therefore, the Court found against Spain on the ground that the Spanish authorities refused entry to Farid and Bouchair without having first verified whether their presence constituted a genuine, present and sufficiently serious threat affecting one of the fundamental interests of society.

Summary

Now you have read this chapter you should be able to:

- Identify the provisions of the TFEU and Directive 2004/38 which provide for derogations from the freedom of movement and residence provisions, on the grounds of public policy, public security and public health.

- Explain the procedural protection afforded by Directive 2004/38 to EU citizens who exercise their free movement rights.

- Describe the relationship between the Convention Implementing the Schengen Agreement (CISA) and Directive 2004/38.

Further reading

Textbooks

Barnard, C. (2013) *The Substantive Law of the EU: The Four Freedoms* (4th edn), Oxford University Press, Chapter 13.

Craig, P. and De Burca, G. (2011) *EU Law: Text, Cases and Materials* (5th edn), Oxford University Press, Chapter 21.

Foster, N. (2015) *Foster on EU Law* (5th edn), Oxford University Press, Chapter 9.

Steiner, J. and Woods, L. (2014) *EU Law* (12th edn), Oxford University Press, Chapter 25.

Weatherill, S. (2014) *Cases and Materials on EU Law* (11th edn), Oxford University Press, Chapter 13.

16

Free movement rights in the United Kingdom

Objectives

At the end of this chapter you should understand:

1. How EU free movement rights have been implemented within the UK, in particular through the Immigration (European Economic Area) Regulations 2006.

Introduction to free movement rights in the United Kingdom

Objective
1

For a full discussion of the Schengen Agreement see pages 364–369 and 533–535.

The maintenance of strict immigration controls at the ports and airports of the UK has characterised UK immigration policy since the First World War. Even after the effective date for the creation of the internal market at the beginning of 1993 had passed, the UK government continued to maintain the need for strict frontier controls and nationality checks on all passengers coming from within the Union. As discussed in Chapter 11, the UK (and Ireland) do not participate in the Schengen Agreement. This was an agreement reached outside the EU between the other 13 pre-2004 Member States, which removed most controls over individuals at the land frontiers of those states.

Successive UK governments have used the port control system to give effect to Union law and in some areas, such as registration with the police under the Immigration (Registration with the Police) Regulations 1972 (SI 1972/1758), as amended, EU nationals benefit from a more relaxed regime. Union law permits such registration, although not as a condition of residence (***Watson and Belmann*** (Case 118/75)); and now see Arts 5(5) and 8(1), Directive 2004/38. The more relaxed internal system reflects a less intrusive policy of internal controls when compared to mainland Europe. In most continental Member States, immigration controls have, for a great many years, been of a post-entry type, involving registration and identity cards, because borders with other Member States were largely unpoliced except at road crossing points. The effect of the UK's island geography, however, has placed the emphasis on the entry process and the granting or refusing of leave (i.e. permission) at the point of entry.

The distinct position of those exercising Union free movement rights was finally addressed, more than 20 years after UK entry, by the Immigration (European Economic

536

Area) Order 1994, which came into effect in July 1994 (SI 1994/1895). The Order was made under s 2(2), European Communities Act 1972 and was intended to implement the free movement rights conferred by all the directives relating to entry and residence. Although this was its intention, there were a number of areas where the 1994 Order was deficient.

The 1994 Order was repealed by the Immigration (European Economic Area) Order 2000 (the EEA Order 2000, SI 2000/2326). The EEA Order 2000, which came into force on 2 October 2000, re-enacted, with amendments, the provisions of the 1994 Order. It applied to workers, self-employed persons, providers and recipients of services, self-sufficient persons, retired persons (who had pursued an activity as an employed or self-employed person) and students. The EEA Order 2000 created free-standing rights of appeal which (in contrast to the position under the 1994 Order) were no longer dependent upon rights of appeal arising under the statutory provisions which applied to persons not claiming rights under Union law. The EEA Order 2000 copied out many of the provisions of the various directives and regulations and was a far better attempt than its predecessor at complying with Union law.

As discussed in Chapters 11–13, Directive 2004/38 (which relates to an EU citizen's right of entry and residence in a Member State of which they are not a national) had to be transposed into national law by 30 April 2006. The UK's EEA Order 2000 was repealed and replaced by the Immigration (European Economic Area) Regulations 2006 (the EEA Regulations 2006 (SI 2006/1003)). These Regulations, which came into force on 30 April 2006, transpose Directive 2004/38 into UK law. The Regulations have been subsequently amended, most recently by the Immigration (European Economic Area) (Amendment) Regulations 2015 (SI 2015/694). The provisions of the Regulations, as amended, are discussed further below.

See pages 327–347 for a review of the main provisions of Directive 2004/38.

Scope of the Immigration (European Economic Area) Regulations 2006

Nationality of beneficiaries

The European Economic Area is explained further at pages 8 and 54.

The EEA Regulations 2006 apply to all 'EEA Nationals', i.e. to all nationals of states who were parties to the European Economic Area Agreement of 1992, which was incorporated into UK law by the European Economic Area Act 1993. It therefore applies to all the Member States of the EU together with Iceland, Liechtenstein and Norway, except the UK (Regulation 2(1)). As with the EEA Order 2000, UK citizens are excluded because they already have an unqualified right of entry and residence under UK law (s 1, Immigration Act 1971). This is unfortunate because Union law confers certain rights on EU citizens which are more beneficial to UK citizens than the provisions of national law. The EEA Regulations 2006 also apply to Switzerland, even though it is not party to the European Economic Area Agreement of 1992 (Regulation 2(1)). The UK's rationale for including Switzerland within the scope of the EEA Regulations 2006 is to avoid having to apply a slightly different free movement regime to Swiss nationals and their family members. Operationally, the UK government has stated that it would be very difficult to run two EEA regimes conferring very similar rights, and in any event Swiss nationals constitute a very small percentage of the Home Office's overall caseload (Explanatory Memorandum to the EEA Regulations 2006).

Other nationalities may benefit from more limited free movement rights under Union law. These include employees of companies based in other Member States but which carry on economic activities here (***Van der Elst v OMI*** (Case C-43/93); and see Chapter 13), and nationals of states which have association agreements with the Union (***Kziber v ONEM*** (Case C-18/90); see Chapter 11). These are not covered by the EEA Regulations 2006, and the beneficiaries will have to rely upon the direct effect of the relevant provisions of the Treaties.

See pages 274–292 and 303–305 for a discussion of the principle of direct effect.

Family rights

Regulation 7(1), EEA Regulations 2006 provides that the following persons shall be treated as the family members of the EEA national:

(a) his spouse or his civil partner;

(b) direct descendants of his, his spouse or his civil partner who are –
   (i) under 21; or
   (ii) dependants of his, his spouse or his civil partner;

(c) dependent direct relatives in his ascending line or that of his spouse or his civil partner;

This definition of family member mirrors that in Art 2(1), Directive 2004/38. Article 3(2), Directive 2004/38 extends its scope to other family members who should have their entry and residence 'facilitated'. Regulation 8(1), EEA Regulations 2006, refers to these other family members as 'extended family members', stating that '"extended family member" means a person who is not a family member of an EEA national under Regulation 7(1)(a), (b) or (c) and who satisfies the conditions in paragraph (2), (3), (4) or (5)', i.e.:

(2) A person satisfies the condition in this paragraph if the person is a relative of an EEA national, his spouse or his civil partner and –
   (a) the person is residing in a country other than the United Kingdom and is dependent upon the EEA national or is a member of his household;
   (b) the person satisfied the condition in paragraph (a) and is accompanying the EEA national to the United Kingdom or wishes to join him there; or
   (c) the person satisfied the condition in paragraph (a), has joined the EEA national in the United Kingdom and continues to be dependent upon him or to be a member of his household.

(3) A person satisfies the condition in this paragraph if the person is a relative of an EEA national or his spouse or his civil partner and, on serious health grounds, strictly requires the personal care of the EEA national, his spouse or his civil partner.

(4) A person satisfies the condition in this paragraph if the person is a relative of an EEA national and would meet the requirements in the immigration rules (other than those relating to entry clearance) for indefinite leave to enter or remain in the United Kingdom as a dependent relative of the EEA national were the EEA national a person present and settled in the United Kingdom.

(5) A person satisfies the condition in this paragraph if the person is the partner of an EEA national (other than a civil partner) and can prove to the decision maker that he is in a durable relationship with the EEA national.

While the directive states that such 'extended family members' should have their entry 'facilitated', the EEA Regulations 2006 provide that 'a person who is an extended family member and has been issued with an EEA family permit, a registration certificate or a residence card shall be treated as the family member of the relevant EEA national for as long as he continues to satisfy the conditions in regulation 8(2), (3), (4) or (5) in relation to the EEA national and the permit, certificate or card has not ceased to be valid or been revoked' (Regulation 7(3)). Thus, under the EEA Regulations 2006, 'extended family members' will be treated exactly the same as 'family members' once they have been issued with the family permit, registration certificate or residence card. However, a family permit will only be issued to extended family members if, *inter alia*, 'in all the circumstances, it appears to the entry clearance officer appropriate to issue the EEA family permit' (Regulation 12(2)(c)); and in the case of registration certificates and cards if, *inter alia*, 'in all the circumstances, it appears to the Secretary of State appropriate to issue . . . [the registration certificate or card]' (Regulations 16(5)(b) and 17(4)(b)). Where an application is received by an extended family member, the entry clearance officer or Secretary of State (as appropriate) shall 'undertake an extensive examination of the personal circumstances of the applicant and if he refuses the application shall give reasons justifying the refusal unless this is contrary to the interests of national security' (Regulations 12(3), 16(6) and 17(5)).

The term 'spouse' in the EEA Regulations 2006 does not include 'a party to a marriage of convenience' (Regulation 2(1)). This exclusion, which was also included in the EEA Order 2000, takes advantage of Art 35, Directive 2004/38 which provides that:

> Member States may adopt the necessary measures to refuse, terminate or withdraw the right conferred by the Directive in the case of abuse of rights or fraud, such as marriages of convenience . . .

Entry

All UK ports and airports now have a route for UK, EU and EEA nationals (which for the purposes of the EEA Regulation 2006 includes Switzerland), and those arriving through the Channel Tunnel are examined in transit. Examination is generally confined to ensuring that a person is an EU citizen or a national of an EEA state, and any EU citizen or EEA national should be admitted simply on production of a valid national identity card or passport issued by an EEA state (Regulation 11(1)). In the case of family members who are not themselves EU citizens or EEA nationals, they will have to produce a valid passport (an identity card is not acceptable) and either an EEA family permit, a residence card or a permanent residence card (Regulation 11(2)). The family permit, residence card and permanent residence card are issued pursuant to the EEA Regulations 2006 (Regulations 12, 17 and 18, see below).

If the person does not produce on arrival one of the specified documents, before refusing the person admission to the UK the immigration officer must give the person concerned every reasonable opportunity to: (i) obtain the document; or (ii) have it brought to him within a reasonable period of time; or (iii) prove by other means that he has a right of entry under the Regulations (Regulation 11(4)).

Regulation 19, EEA Regulations 2006 provides that a person can be denied admission: (i) on grounds of public policy, public security or public health (see below); or (ii) if at the time of his arrival he is a family member of an EEA national *unless*: (a) he is accompanying the EEA national or joining him in the UK; and (b) the EEA national has the right to reside in the UK under the Regulations.

The following case concerned the application of Regulation 19, where permission to enter the UK was refused on the ground of public security:

ZZ v Secretary of State for the Home Department (Case C-300/11)

In the UK, administrative decisions refusing entry into national territory that are adopted on the basis of information whose disclosure would be liable to prejudice national security may be contested before the Special Immigration Appeals Commission ('SIAC'). In proceedings before SIAC, neither the person who has contested such a decision nor his own lawyers have access to the information upon which the decision was based when its disclosure would be contrary to the public interest. However, in such a case, a special advocate, who has access to that information, is appointed to represent the interests of the person concerned before SIAC. The special advocate cannot communicate with the person concerned about matters connected with the proceedings once material the Secretary of State (the competent UK authority) objects to being disclosed has been served on the special advocate. The special advocate may, however, request directions from SIAC authorising such communication.

ZZ had dual French and Algerian nationality. He had been married since 1990 to a British national, with whom he had eight children. ZZ resided lawfully in the UK from 1990 to 2005. However, in August 2005, after he had left the UK, the Secretary of State cancelled his right of residence on the ground that his presence was not conducive to the public good. In September 2006, ZZ travelled to the UK, where a decision refusing him entry was taken by the Secretary of State.

ZZ appealed to SIAC against the decision refusing entry. In those proceedings he was able to have consultations with his two special advocates on the public evidence only.

SIAC dismissed ZZ's appeal, and gave a 'closed judgment' with exhaustive grounds and an 'open judgment' with summary grounds. Only the 'open judgment' was provided to ZZ. It was apparent from the 'open judgment' that SIAC was satisfied, for reasons explained in the 'closed judgment', that ZZ was involved in activities of the Armed Islamic Group (GIA) network and in terrorist activities in 1995 and 1996.

ZZ appealed against SIAC's judgment to the Court of Appeal (England and Wales), which referred the case to the Court of Justice to ascertain to what extent SIAC was obliged to inform the person concerned of the public security grounds which constituted the basis of a decision refusing entry.

The Court of Justice stated that **under Directive 2004/38 the person concerned had to be notified in writing of a decision refusing entry, and in such a way that he was able to comprehend its content and the implications for him. In addition, he had to be informed, precisely and in full, of the public policy or public security grounds which constituted the basis of the decision, unless this was contrary to the interests of state security.**

In that context, the Court of Justice explained that Member States were required to provide effective judicial review of the merits of both the decision refusing entry and the reasons regarding state security invoked in order not to inform the person concerned of the grounds on which that decision was based. The court entrusted with review of the legality of the decision refusing entry had to be able to examine all the grounds and evidence underlying that decision. The court also had to be entrusted with verifying whether the reasons connected with state security stood in the way of disclosure of those grounds and that evidence.

In this connection, the Court of Justice stated that the competent national authority had to prove that state security would in fact be compromised by precise and full disclosure of the grounds to the person concerned. Consequently, **there was no presumption that the reasons invoked by a national authority in order to refuse disclosure of those grounds existed and were valid.**

If, accordingly, the court concluded that state security did not stand in the way of precise and full disclosure of the grounds on which a decision refusing entry was based, it gave the competent national authority the opportunity to disclose the missing grounds and evidence to the person concerned. However, if that authority did not authorise their disclosure, the court should proceed to examine the legality of such a decision on the sole basis of the grounds and evidence which had been disclosed.

Conversely, if it turned out that state security stood in the way of disclosure of the grounds to the person concerned, judicial review of the legality of the decision refusing entry had to be carried out in a procedure which struck an appropriate balance between the requirements flowing from state security and the requirements of the right to effective judicial protection, whilst limiting any interference with the exercise of that right to that which was strictly necessary.

That procedure had to ensure, to the greatest possible extent, that the adversarial principle was complied with, in order to enable the person concerned to contest the grounds on which the decision in question was based and to make submissions on the evidence relating to the decision and, therefore, to put forward an effective defence. In particular, the person concerned had to be informed of the essence of the grounds on which a decision refusing entry was based, as the necessary protection of state security could not have the effect of denying him his right to be heard and, therefore, of rendering his right of redress ineffective.

The Court of Justice also pointed out that the weighing up of the right to effective judicial protection against the necessity to protect the security of the state concerned was not applicable in the same way to the evidence underlying the grounds that were adduced before the national court. In certain cases, disclosure of that evidence was liable to compromise state security in a direct and specific manner, in that it could, in particular, endanger the life, health or freedom of persons or reveal the methods of investigation specifically used by the national security authorities and thus seriously impede, or even prevent, future performance of the tasks of those authorities.

Finally, the Court of Justice stated that the UK court had the task of: (i) ensuring that the person concerned was informed of the essence of the grounds which constituted the basis of the decision in question in a manner which took due account of the necessary confidentiality of the evidence; and (ii) drawing the appropriate conclusions from any failure to comply with that obligation to inform him.

Residence

Under the EEA Regulations 2006, a person who is admitted to or acquires a right to reside in the UK under the Regulations *shall not* require 'leave' (i.e. permission) to remain in the UK under the Immigration Act 1971 during any period in which he has a right to reside under the Regulations, but any person *shall* require leave under the 1971 Act during any period in which he does not have such a right (Para 1, Schedule 2). Additionally, where a person has leave to enter or remain under the 1971 Act which is subject to conditions, and that person also has a right to reside under the Regulations, those conditions shall not have effect for as long as the person has that right to reside (Para 1, Schedule 2).

General right of residence for up to three months

As has previously been discussed in Chapters 11–13, Directive 2004/38 introduces an initial general right of residence for up to three months for EU nationals and their family members provided they have a valid identity card or passport (or a passport in the case of non-EU family members), and do not become an unreasonable burden on the social assistance system of the host Member State (Arts 6(1) and 14(1)). This is reflected in the EEA Regulations 2006 (Regulation 13).

EU citizens qualifying for the general right of residence or the right of permanent residence and the members of their family benefit from equal treatment with host-country nationals in the areas covered by the Treaty (Art 24(1), Directive 2004/38). However, for the first three months of residence, or while the EU citizen is exercising his right to reside while seeking work under Art 14(4)(b), Directive 2004/38, the host Member State is not obliged to grant entitlement to social assistance to persons other than employed or self-employed workers and the members of their family (Art 24(2), Directive 2004/38). The EEA Regulations 2006 do not implement Art 24, Directive 2004/38, because this is dealt with by other legislation.

As discussed in Chapter 14, except where income-related benefits are supplementing a social security benefit listed in Art 3(1), Regulation 883/2004, they do not have to be paid to an individual who has not yet acquired EU worker status. The Court of Justice decided in *Lebon* (Case 316/85) that work-seekers, as opposed to workers, were not entitled to the social advantages conferred by the former Art 7(2), Regulation 1612/68 (now Art 7(2) Regulation 492/2011). However, income-related benefits may constitute a social advantage for a person who has, for example, worked but lost his job involuntarily and thus retains his EU worker status (see Chapter 12).

In the UK, prior to 1 May 2004 a claimant was required to satisfy the 'habitual residence test' to be eligible for income support, income-based jobseeker's allowance, state pension credit, housing benefit and council tax benefit ('income-related benefits', which are being progressively replaced by Universal Credit). This test was introduced to prevent 'benefit tourism' by people who came to the UK from abroad and immediately claimed benefits. Its purpose was to ensure that income-related benefits were paid to people with reasonably close ties to the UK and an intention to settle within the UK.

This test was amended on 1 May 2004 when the Social Security (Habitual Residence) Amendment Regulations 2004 came into force. The modified test provided that no person would be treated as habitually resident in the Common Travel Area (the United Kingdom, the Channel Islands, the Isle of Man and the Republic of Ireland) if he did not have a 'right to reside' within the UK. Therefore, anyone without a right to reside could not qualify for the income-related benefits.

The 'right to reside' requirement was added to prevent those who did not have a right to reside in the UK from becoming a burden on the UK's social assistance system by being able to claim income-related benefits. This requirement strengthened the test against such abuse of the benefits system by people who were not in work and who came to the UK to live. At the time, economically inactive EU citizens did not have a right to reside within the UK unless they were self-sufficient.

If this 'right to reside' requirement had not been amended after 30 April 2006 (the date Directive 2004/38 had to be implemented), EU citizens and their family members who were not economically active could have become eligible for income-related benefits, if they were considered to be habitually resident and met the other conditions of entitlement on the basis of this general right of residence in Art 6, Directive 2004/38.

Article 24(2), Directive 2004/38 provides that Member States do not have to confer entitlement to social assistance on EU citizens during the first three months of residence unless they are workers, self-employed persons, persons who retain such status and their family members. Therefore the UK's various income-related benefit regulations were amended by the Social Security (Persons from Abroad) Amendment Regulations 2006 (SI 2006/1026),

The scope of social advantages conferred by Art 7(2), Regulation 492/2011, is discussed at pages 393–406.

to ensure that EU citizens who reside solely on the basis of Art 6, Directive 2004/38 (or equivalent Home Office regulations) are not given a right to income-related benefits just because they have a right to reside. This ensures that the present policy in relation to economically inactive EU citizens continues.

Under Art 24(2), Directive 2004/38 there is no obligation on Member States to confer social assistance during any period when an EU citizen is seeking employment and has a genuine chance of being engaged. Nevertheless, prior to 1 January 2014, the UK's Social Security (Persons from Abroad) Amendment Regulations 2006 provided that EU work-seekers who had a right to reside under Art 45 TFEU (previously Art 39 EC Treaty) and who were habitually resident would, provided they satisfied the other conditions of entitlement, be eligible for income-based jobseeker's allowance. An EU work-seeker on income-based jobseeker's allowance was also eligible to claim housing benefit and council tax benefit. However, for other benefits an EU work-seeker with a right to reside under Art 45 TFEU (or equivalent Home Office regulations) would not, under these Regulations, have satisfied the 'right to reside' aspect of the habitual residence test. From 1 January 2014, the UK's Jobseeker's Allowance (Habitual Residence) Amendment Regulations 2013 removed the eligibility of an EU work-seeker to claim income-based jobseeker's allowance (which is being progressively replaced by Universal Credit).

Right of residence for more than three months

Regulation 14(1), EEA Regulations 2006 implements Art 7, Directive 2004/38. Regulation 14(1) provides that a 'qualified person' is entitled to reside in the UK for so long as he remains a 'qualified person'. A family member of a qualified person residing in the UK under Regulation 14(1) or the family member of an EEA national with a permanent right of residence under Regulation 15 (see below) is entitled to reside in the UK for so long as he remains a family member of the qualified person or EEA national (Regulation 14(2)). This extended right of residence, for a period exceeding three months, depends upon the EEA national coming within the scope of 'qualified person'. 'Qualified person' is defined by Regulation 6(1) as a person who is an EEA national and in the UK as:

(a) a jobseeker;

(b) a worker;

(c) a self-employed person;

(d) a self-sufficient person; or

(e) a student.

Each of these categories of qualified person is further defined by the Regulations:

(a) jobseeker means, *inter alia*:
  (i) a person who enters the UK in order to seek employment and who can provide evidence that he is seeking employment and has a genuine chance of being engaged (Regulation 6(4)); or
  (ii) a person who is in the UK seeking employment, immediately after enjoying a right to reside as a qualified person under Regulation 6(1)(b)-(e) and who can provide evidence that he is seeking employment and has a genuine chance of being engaged (Regulation 6(4)).

(b) worker means a worker within the meaning of Art 45 TFEU (Regulation 4(1)(a));

(c) self-employed person means a person who establishes himself in order to pursue an activity as a self-employed person in accordance with Art 49 TFEU (Regulation 4(1)(b));

   (d) self-sufficient person means a person who –
      (i)   has sufficient resources not to become a burden on the social assistance system of the UK during his period of residence;
      (ii) has comprehensive sickness insurance cover in the UK (Regulation 4(1)(c));

   (e) student means a person who –
      (i)   is enrolled at a public or private establishment, which is recognised by the Secretary of State as an accredited establishment or which is financed from public funds, for the principal purpose of following a course of study, including vocational training;
      (ii) has comprehensive sickness insurance cover in the UK;
      (iii) assures the Secretary of State, by means of a declaration, or by such equivalent means as the person may choose, that he has sufficient resources not to become a burden on the social assistance system of the UK during his period of residence (Regulation 4(1)(d)).

The above accurately implements the provisions of Art 7(1), Directive 2004/38 relating to those persons who have the right of extended residence. With regard to a self-sufficient person and a student, Regulation 4(4) provides that their resources shall be considered to be sufficient if, *inter alia*, 'they exceed the maximum level of resources which a United Kingdom national and his family members may possess if he is to become eligible for social assistance under the United Kingdom benefit system'.

The right of extended residence applies to the EEA national and his family members (and extended family members, see above). However, in the case of a student, the right of extended residence to his family members will be limited to the student's spouse or civil partner and to the dependent children of the student or of his spouse or civil partner (Regulation 7(2)). The right of extended residence to a student's 'extended family members' is also limited by Regulation 7(4).

Regulation 6(2) provides that a person who is no longer working shall be treated as a worker for the purpose of Regulation 6(1)(b) if:

   (a) he is temporarily unable to work as the result of an illness or accident (Regulation 6(2)(a));

   (b) he is in duly recorded involuntary unemployment after having been employed in the United Kingdom provided that –
      (i)   he has registered as a jobseeker with the relevant employment office;
      (ii) he has been unemployed for no more than six months;
      (iii) he can provide evidence that he is seeking employment in the United Kingdom and has a genuine chance of being engaged (Regulation 6(2)(b));

   (c) he is involuntarily unemployed and has embarked on vocational training (Regulation 6(2)(c)); or

   (d) he has voluntarily ceased working and embarked on vocational training that is related to his previous employment (Regulation 6(2)(d)).

A person who is no longer in self-employment shall not cease to be treated as a self-employed person if he is temporarily unable to pursue his activity as a self-employed person as a result of an illness or accident (Regulation 6(3)).

Regulation 10 sets out the circumstances in which a family member will retain the right of residence, where the EEA national dies or leaves the UK, or where the EEA national and his spouse or civil partner terminate their marriage or civil partnership. This provision implements Arts 12–13, Directive 2004/38.

Regulation 16(1) provides for the issuing of a *registration certificate* to a qualified person on application and production of: (i) a valid identity card or passport issued by an EEA state; and (ii) proof that he is a qualified person (Regulation 16(1)). Regulation 16 also provides for the issuing of a *registration certificate* to EEA family members (Regulation 16(3)) and to EEA extended family members (Regulation 16(5)). Regulation 17 provides for the issuing of a *residence card* to non-EEA family members (Regulation 17(1)) and to non-EEA extended family members (Regulation 17(4)).

EU citizens qualifying for the right of residence or the right of permanent residence and the members of their family benefit from equal treatment with host-country nationals in the areas covered by the Treaty (Art 24(1), Directive 2004/38). Host Member States are not required to provide maintenance aid (i.e. student grants or student loans) to persons with a right of residence who have come to the country in question to study (Art 24(2), Directive 2004/38). The EEA Regulations 2006 do not implement Art 24, Directive 2004/38.

Permanent right of residence

Regulation 15(1), EEA Regulations 2006 implements Art 16, Directive 2004/38. Regulation 15(1) sets out the persons who are entitled to reside in the UK permanently:

(a) an EEA national who has resided in the United Kingdom in accordance with these Regulations for a continuous period of five years;

(b) a family member of an EEA national who is not himself an EEA national but who has resided in the United Kingdom with the EEA national in accordance with these Regulations for a continuous period of five years;

(c) a worker or self-employed person who has ceased activity;

(d) the family member of a worker or self-employed person who has ceased activity;

(e) a person who was the family member of a worker or self-employed person where –
   (i) the worker or self-employed person has died;
   (ii) the family member resided with him immediately before his death;
   (iii) the worker or self-employed person had resided continuously in the United Kingdom for at least the two years immediately before his death or the death was the result of an accident at work or an occupational disease;

(f) a person who –
   (i) has resided in the United Kingdom in accordance with these Regulations for a continuous period of five years;
   (ii) was, at the end of that period, a family member who has retained the right of residence.

Regulation 15(1)(c) refers to a worker or self-employed person who has 'ceased activity'. This is defined by Regulation 5:

1 In these Regulations, 'worker or self-employed person who has ceased activity' means an EEA national who satisfies the conditions in paragraph (2), (3), (4) or (5).

2 A person satisfies the conditions in this paragraph if he –
   (a) terminates his activity as a worker or self-employed person and –
      (i) has reached the age at which he is entitled to a state pension on the date on which he terminates his activity; or
      (ii) in the case of a worker, ceases working to take early retirement;
   (b) pursued his activity as a worker or self-employed person in the United Kingdom for at least twelve months prior to the termination;

     (c)   resided in the United Kingdom continuously for more than three years prior to the termination.

3 A person satisfies the conditions in this paragraph if –
    (a)   he terminates his activity in the United Kingdom as a worker or self-employed person as a result of a permanent incapacity to work;
    (b)   either –
        (i)   he resided in the United Kingdom continuously for more than two years prior to the termination; or
        (ii) the incapacity is the result of an accident at work or an occupational disease that entitles him to a pension payable in full or in part by an institution in the United Kingdom.

4 A person satisfies the conditions in this paragraph if –
    (a)   he is active as a worker or self-employed person in an EEA State but retains his place of residence in the United Kingdom, to which he returns as a rule at least once a week;
    (b)   prior to becoming so active in that EEA State, he had been continuously resident and continuously active as a worker or self-employed person in the United Kingdom for at least three years.

5 A person who satisfies the condition in paragraph (4)(a) but not the condition in paragraph (4)(b) shall, for the purposes of paragraphs (2) and (3), be treated as being active and resident in the United Kingdom during any period in which he is working or self-employed in the EEA State.

6 The conditions in paragraphs (2) and (3) as to length of residence and activity as a worker or self-employed person shall not apply in relation to a person whose spouse or civil partner is a British citizen.

7 Subject to regulations 6(2), 7A(3) or 7B(3), For the purposes of this regulation –
    (a)   periods of inactivity for reasons not of the person's own making;
    (b)   periods of inactivity due to illness or accident;
    (c)   in the case of a worker, periods of involuntary unemployment duly recorded by the relevant employment office, shall be treated as periods of activity as a worker or self-employed person, as the case may be.

Regulation 3(2) provides that continuity of residence shall not be affected by: –
    (a)   periods of absence from the United Kingdom which do not exceed six months in total in any year;
    (b)   periods of absence from the United Kingdom on military service; or
    (c)   any one absence from the United Kingdom not exceeding twelve months for an important reason such as pregnancy and childbirth, serious illness, study or vocational training or an overseas posting.

Once the right of permanent residence has been acquired, it will only be lost through absence from the UK for a period exceeding two consecutive years (Regulation 15(2)). This is subject to Regulation 19(3)(b), which provides for the exclusion of a person on the grounds of public policy, public security or public health. Regulation 18 provides for the issuing of a document certifying permanent residence to qualifying EAA nationals and a permanent residence card to qualifying non-EEA nationals.

    EU citizens qualifying for the right of residence or the right of permanent residence and the members of their family benefit from equal treatment with host-country nationals in the areas covered by the Treaty (Art 24(1), Directive 2004/38). The EEA Regulations 2006 do not implement Art 24, Directive 2004/38.

Exclusion and removal

European Union citizens and EEA nationals may be removed from the UK on ceasing to have a right of residence as a qualified person, or if the removal is justified on public policy, public security or public health grounds (Regulation 19(3)). Regulations 22 to 24 contain procedural provisions relating to persons who claim admission under the Regulations, and who are refused admission or are being removed.

The EEA Regulations 2006 accurately transpose the provisions of Directive 2004/38 relating to exclusion and removal.

The effect of claims to social assistance

Many EU citizens will, after they have worked and gained worker status, be entitled to benefits such as 'social advantages' under Art 7(2), Regulation 492/2011 (previously Art 7(2), Regulation 1612/68) or, in some cases, under Regulation 883/2004 (see Chapters 12 and 14). Expulsions on the ground of public policy, public security or public health are contrary to Art 27(1), Directive 2004/38, if they are taken 'to service economic ends'. This prohibition is reflected in Regulation 21(2), EEA Regulations 2006, which provides that decisions taken on grounds of public policy, public security or public health 'may not be taken to serve economic ends'. Nevertheless, there remains an important link between claims to public funds and the rights of residence of EU citizens. The link may operate in two separate, but related, ways: (i) by denying the financial support which an EU citizen may require when he has insufficient resources to maintain himself; and (ii) by providing evidence that he cannot support himself without recourse to social assistance.

Regulation 13(3) provides that during the initial right of residence (i.e. for a period up to three months), an EEA national or his family members who become an unreasonable burden on the social assistance system of the UK shall cease to have the right to reside under the Regulations. However, Regulation 19(4) provides that a person must not be removed as the *automatic consequence* of having recourse to the UK's social assistance system.

For the first three months of residence, or while the EU citizen is exercising his right to reside while seeking work under Art 14(4)(b), Directive 2004/38, the host Member State is not obliged to grant entitlement to social assistance to persons other than employed or self-employed workers and the members of their family (Art 24(2), Directive 2004/38). Although the EEA Regulations 2006 do not implement Art 24, as discussed above the UK's Jobseeker's Allowance (Habitual Residence) Amendment Regulations removed the eligibility of an EU work-seeker to claim income-based jobseeker's allowance during this initial three-month period. This came into effect on 1 January 2014.

Prima facie, an economically self-sufficient person or student will have a right to remain as long as he satisfies the relevant requirements of Directive 2004/38. He cannot, however, look to the UK's welfare system for any kind of assistance, unless it is for social security benefits to which he may be entitled under Regulation 883/2004 (see Chapter 14). Income support, housing benefit and council tax benefit (which are being progressively replaced by Universal Credit), for example, are conditional upon proof by a claimant who is a national of an EEA state or an EU citizen that he has a 'right to reside' within the UK (Social

Security (Persons from Abroad) Amendment Regulations 2006). However, as discussed above, EU citizens who reside solely on the basis of Art 6, Directive 2004/38 are not given a right to such benefits just because they have a right to reside.

The social assistance system may also jeopardise a person's right to remain where there is evidence that he is no longer economically self-sufficient. The residence rights conferred on self-sufficient persons and students are conditional upon the beneficiaries not becoming a burden on the social assistance system of the host Member State. A claim to income support, housing benefit or council tax benefit, for example, is almost certain to fail. The details of the claim would then be forwarded to the Home Office and, if the individual is not a worker or a self-employed person, or otherwise entitled to remain under the EEA Regulations 2006, then he could be required to leave under Regulation 19(3)(a) as someone who 'ceases to have a right to reside under these Regulations'.

Deportations

In the UK, deportations are carried out by the Home Secretary either on his own initiative or following a recommendation of the courts at the time when a sentence is imposed on an offender (ss 3(5) and 6, Immigration Act 1971). The Home Secretary has a general power to deport a foreign national where he 'deems his deportation to be conducive to the public good' (s 3(5)(b), Immigration Act 1971). It was on this basis that deportations of EU citizens have previously been carried out, although both the Home Secretary and the courts have been obliged to make decisions on whether or not to deport or recommend deportation within the limits laid down by Directive 2004/38. The Union criteria are much narrower than those allowed under UK immigration law, and the EEA Regulations 2006 lay down both the circumstances for removal and deportation, and the Union criteria.

In *R v Secretary of State for the Home Department, ex parte Marchon* [1993] 2 CMLR 132, the appellant, a Portuguese national, who had been a general practitioner, was convicted of dealing in drugs. He was sentenced to a long term of imprisonment but not recommended for deportation by the trial court. The Home Secretary, nonetheless, issued notice of an intention to deport him. The English Court of Appeal upheld the decision on the ground that 'the offence merits deportation . . . it involves a disregard of the basic or fundamental tenets of society' (Dillon LJ). Concurring, Beldam LJ added that there should be no hint that society was prepared to tolerate the importation of, and dealing in, drugs: 'I say this *not simply because refusal to do so would act as a deterrent to others but rather because it serves to emphasise the grave and present danger from this threat*' [emphasis added]. While the decision may be compliant with Union law, the reasons for the decision are surprising, not least because there is a clear intention by the English court to take deterrent or general preventive action because of a concern about offences of this type. Such an approach obviously conflicts with the decision of the Court of Justice in *Bonsignore*, see Chapter 15. Now, it would also conflict with Regulation 21(5), EEA Regulations 2006 which provides that a decision taken on the grounds of public policy or public security shall be taken in accordance with the following principles:

(a) the decision must comply with the principle of proportionality;

(b) the decision must be based exclusively on the personal conduct of the person concerned;

(c) the personal conduct of the person concerned must represent a genuine, present and sufficiently serious threat affecting one of the fundamental interests of society;

(d) matters isolated from the particulars of the case or which relate to considerations of general prevention do not justify the decision;

(e) a person's previous criminal convictions do not in themselves justify the decision.

The following case concerned an application of Regulation 21(5), EEA Regulations 2006:

LC v Secretary of State for the Home Department (unreported: Appeal Number IA/13107/2006)

This case was decided by the UK's Asylum and Immigration Tribunal on 16 March 2007. It concerned the scope of Directive 2004/38 and the UK's implementing Regulations (Immigration (European Economic Area) Regulations 2006) with regard to the derogations from Union law provisions on free movement of persons on the grounds of public policy and public security.

LC, an EU citizen, was convicted in 1996 of the murder of Philip Lawrence. He was sentenced to be detained during Her Majesty's pleasure; a minimum period of 12 years' detention was laid down, and therefore he was eligible for release on parole in 2008.

In a letter to LC dated 7 March 2007, the Secretary of State concluded that LC had not obtained a right to permanent residence in the UK in accordance with the EEA Regulations 2006, and concluded that his removal from the UK was justified on the grounds of public policy or public security. It was this decision which was being contested by LC.

The tribunal held that the Secretary of State had not shown that the decision to deport was proportionate, or that the decision complied with the other requirements of Regulation 21(5), EEA Regulations 2006. Furthermore, the tribunal stated that Regulation 21(6) had not been properly considered. Regulation 21(6) provides that:

Before taking the relevant decision on the grounds of public policy or public security in relation to a person who is resident in the United Kingdom the decision maker must take account of considerations such as the age, state of health, family and economic situation of the person, the person's length of residence in the United Kingdom, the person's social and cultural integration in the United Kingdom and the extent of the person's links with his country of origin.

Procedural safeguards

Regulations 25 to 29 and Schedule 1, EEA Regulations 2006 set out the appeal rights in relation to decisions taken under the Regulations.

Summary

Now you have read this chapter you should be able to:

● Explain how Union free movement rights have been implemented within the UK, in particular through the Immigration (European Economic Area) Regulations 2006, with particular reference to:
  ○ nationality of the beneficiaries;
  ○ family rights;

- entry;
- residence (including the general right of residence for up to three months and tended right of residence for more than three months);
- permanent right of residence;
- exclusion and removal;
- the effect of claims to social assistance;
- deportations; and
- procedural safeguards.

Further reading

Textbook

Macdonald, I. and Webber, F. (2014) *Macdonald's Immigration Law and Practice* (9th edn), Butterworths.

Journal articles

de Mars, S., 'Economically inactive EU migrants and the United Kingdom's National Health Service: Unreasonable burdens without real links?' (2014) 39 EL Rev 770.

Shaw, J. and Miller, N., 'When legal worlds collide: An exploration of what happens when EU free movement law meets UK immigration law' (2013) 38 EL Rev 137.

Part 3

The free movement of goods

customs duty and explain the problems of ...

17

Customs duties and internal taxation

Objectives

At the end of this chapter you should understand:

1. The different ways in which the free movement of goods can be hindered and made more difficult.
2. How to differentiate between a customs duty and a charge having an equivalent effect to a customs duty and explain the provisions of the TFEU which regulate them.
3. The provisions of the TFEU which apply to internal taxation.
4. The different approach applied to internal taxation levied on goods which are similar compared to that where the effect of the internal tax affords an indirect protection to domestically produced goods.

Introduction to the free movement of goods

Objective 1

The European Union set as one of its central tasks the creation of an internal market characterised by the abolition, as between Member States, of obstacles to the free movement of goods, persons, services and capital. The Union bound itself, in Art 28(1) TFEU (previously Art 23(1) EC Treaty), to the maintenance of 'a **customs union** which shall cover all trade in goods and which shall involve the prohibition between Member States of customs duties on imports and exports and of all charges having equivalent effect, and the adoption of a common customs tariff in their relations with third countries'; a third country is a country which is not a member of the EU (i.e. a non-Member State). The object of this provision is to create not only an internal free trade area within the Union, where there are no duties imposed on goods when they cross an internal border, but also a customs union where there is a common external tariff. Goods entering the Union from a third country (i.e. a non-Member State) are subject to the same external tariff, irrespective of where they enter the Union. Once all import formalities have been complied with and duties and charges have been paid, goods – on crossing the external border from non-Member States of the Union – are regarded as being in 'free circulation' and are to be treated like any other goods produced within the Union (Art 28(2) TFEU (previously Art 23(2) EC Treaty)). Benefits are intended to accrue to producers in the opening up of new markets, the possibility of larger and hence cheaper product runs, and to consumers in the form of greatly increased choice in products at lower prices.

Tariff barriers between Member States have long since been removed. Border controls on goods were swept away by the Single European Act 1986. Much still remains to be done, however, to achieve a single undivided market in products such as exists, for example, between England, Scotland, Wales and Northern Ireland. The problems that still persist arise largely as a result of invisible barriers in the shape of different product and other standards, and a whole range of national measures aimed at consumer and environmental protection. Until these different standards are harmonised it would be very difficult for, say, a French manufacturer of a bicycle to make a product which he knows with confidence he will be allowed to sell to in excess of 500 million consumers living within the 28 Member States of the EU. In the long-term, these problems are being addressed by the creation of EU-wide standards through the approval of harmonising directives for a huge range of products (see Chapter 18). Until this massive task is achieved, however, producers will have to rely upon Arts 34 and 35 TFEU (previously Arts 28 and 29 EC Treaty), and the intervention of the Court of Justice, to ensure that national rules do not have the effect of excluding their products (see Chapter 18). Although it also remains one of the objectives of the TFEU to harmonise rates of indirect taxation (Art 113 TFEU (previously Art 93 EC Treaty)), little progress has been made in this area, and obstacles to the creation of a genuine undivided market continue to be caused by different rates of tax and other charges levied on goods by the Member States. The TFEU attempts to address these problems by the provisions of Arts 28 and 30 TFEU (previously Arts 23 and 25 EC Treaty), which prohibit customs duties on imports and exports and all charges having equivalent effect, and the prohibition of discriminatory internal taxation pursuant to Art 110 TFEU (previously Art 90 EC Treaty).

Considered first within this Chapter are Arts 28 and 30 TFEU, which relate to customs duties and charges having an equivalent effect. This is followed by a consideration of Art 110 TFEU which relates to discriminatory internal taxation. Articles 34–36 TFEU, which relate to quantitative restrictions and measures having an equivalent effect to quantitative restrictions, are considered in Chapter 18.

Articles 28 and 30 TFEU: the elimination of border charges and fiscal barriers

Objective 2

Article 28(1) TFEU (which is practically unchanged from the former Art 23(1) EC Treaty) provides as follows:

> The Union shall comprise a customs union which shall cover all trade in goods and which shall involve the prohibition between Member States of customs duties on imports and exports and of all charges having equivalent effect, and the adoption of a common customs tariff in their relations with third countries.

See page 566 for a flowchart which illustrates the application of Art 30 TFEU.

Article 30 TFEU (which is identical to the former Art 25 EC Treaty) provides as follows:

> Customs duties on imports and exports and charges having equivalent effect shall be prohibited between Member States. This prohibition shall also apply to customs duties of a fiscal nature.

The principle of direct effect is explained at pages 274–292 and 303–305.

Article 30 TFEU is directly effective (see, e.g., ***Van Gend en Loos* v *Nederlandse Administratie der Belastingen*** (Case 26/62)).

The case law of the Court of Justice with regard to these Treaty provisions is considered below.

Scope of the term 'goods'

The scope of the term 'goods' was explained by the Court of Justice in the following case:

Commission v *Italy* (Case 7/68)

Italy imposed a tax on the export of articles of an 'artistic, historical, archaeological or ethnographic nature'. The Commission took infraction proceedings against Italy pursuant to what is now Art 258 TFEU (previously Art 226 EC Treaty) alleging this tax was in breach of what is now Art 30 TFEU (previously Art 25 EC Treaty). Italy argued, *inter alia*, that the tax was being levied on 'cultural articles' which were being exported and such articles should not be regarded as goods. This argument was rejected by the Court of Justice, which held as follows:

> Under . . . [Art 30 TFEU] the Community [i.e. Union] is based on a customs union 'which shall cover all trade in goods'. By goods, within the meaning of that provision, **there must be understood products which can be valued in money and which are capable, as such, of forming the subject of commercial transactions.**
>
> The articles covered by the Italian law, whatever may be the characteristics which distinguish them from other types of merchandise, nevertheless resemble the latter, inasmuch as they can be valued in money and so be the subject of commercial transactions. That view corresponds with the scheme of the Italian law itself, which fixes the tax in question in proportion to the value of the articles concerned. [emphasis added]

In the above case, the Court of Justice held that goods, for the purpose of what are now Arts 28 and 30 TFEU, will consist of 'products which can be valued in money and which are capable . . . of forming the subject of commercial transactions'. The scope of 'goods' will therefore be very wide. In the following case, the Court of Justice was faced with a more difficult question:

Jägerskiöld v *Gustafsson* (Case C-97/98)

On 29 May 1997 Gustafsson (G) fished with a spinning rod in waters belonging to Jägerskiöld (J) in the township of Kimoto in Finland. Two days earlier, on 27 May 1997, G had paid a fishing licence fee, as required by Finnish law, to enable him to practise that type of fishing even in private waters. J brought an action before the national court for a declaration that G could not, without his permission, fish with a rod in his waters, notwithstanding the fact that G had paid the fishing licence fee. In support of his action, J argued that the Finnish law, on which the right to fish with a rod was based, was contrary to the rules of the Treaty concerning, *inter alia*, the free movement of goods. The Court of Justice held as follows:

> The Court has already defined goods, for the purposes of . . . [Art 28 TFEU] . . . as products which can be valued in money and which are capable, as such, of forming the subject of commercial transactions.

> J contends that fishing rights and fishing permits derived from them constitute 'goods' within the meaning of that case law, in so far as they can be valued in money terms and may be transferred to other persons as it is expressly provided for by [Finnish law] . . .
>
> As is clear from Council Directive 88/361/EEC of 24 June 1998, the Treaty provisions on the free movement of capital cover, in particular, operations relating to shares, bonds and other securities which, like fishing rights or fishing permits, can be valued in money and may be the subject of market transactions.
>
> Similarly, the organisation of lotteries does not constitute an activity relating to 'goods', even if such an activity is coupled with the distribution of advertising material and lottery tickets, but must be regarded as a provision of 'services' within the meaning of the Treaty. In that activity, the provision of services in question are those provided by the lottery organiser in letting ticket buyers participate in the lottery against payment of the price of the lottery tickets.
>
> The same applies to the grant of fishing rights and the issue of fishing permits. **The activity consisting of making fishing waters available to third parties, for consideration and upon certain conditions, so that they can fish there constitutes a provision of services which is covered by . . . [Art 56 TFEU] if it has a cross-frontier character. The fact that those rights or those permits are set down in documents which, as such, may be the subject of trade is not sufficient to bring them within the scope of the provisions of the Treaty relating to the free movement of goods.** [emphasis added]

In the above case, the Court of Justice held that the granting of fishing rights and the issuing of fishing permits could be valued in money and were capable of forming the subject of commercial transactions. However, they were not a tangible product; they constituted an intangible benefit even if those rights were set out in a document. The granting of fishing rights and the issuing of fishing permits could not therefore be considered to be 'goods', although they could constitute a service which would be regulated by what is now Art 56 TFEU (previously Art 49 EC Treaty); see Chapter 13.

Goods from third countries

Article 28(2) TFEU (which is practically unchanged from the former Art 23(2) EC Treaty) provides as follows:

> The provisions of Article 30 and of Chapter 2 of this Title shall apply to products originating in Member States and to products coming from third countries which are in free circulation in Member States.

Article 29 TFEU (which is identical to the former Art 24 EC Treaty) provides as follows:

> Products coming from a third country shall be considered to be in free circulation in a Member State if the import formalities have been complied with and any customs duties or charges having equivalent effect which are payable have been levied in that Member State, and if they have not benefited from a total or partial drawback of such duties or charges.

These provisions provide that once goods have lawfully entered the Union from a third country (i.e. a non-Member State), with all import formalities complied with and duties and charges paid, the provisions of Art 30 TFEU will apply to such goods (the provisions of Arts 34-36 TFEU will also apply; see Chapter 18).

Duties and equivalent charges: the effect, not the purpose

Whether or not Art 30 TFEU will apply depends upon the *effect* of the duty or charge. It is irrelevant *why* the Member State imposed the duty/charge (i.e. *purpose* is irrelevant). A reconsideration of the **Italian Art** case, which concerned what is now Art 30 TFEU, will serve to illustrate this:

Commission v Italy (Case 7/68)

Italy imposed a tax on the export of articles of an 'artistic, historical, archaeological or ethno-graphic nature'. The Commission took infraction proceedings against Italy, alleging this tax was in breach of what is now Art 30 TFEU (previously Art 25 EC Treaty). Italy argued, *inter alia*, that the purpose of the tax in question was not to raise revenue, but was designed to protect the artistic heritage of the country. This argument was rejected by the Court of Justice, which held as follows:

> In the opinion of the Commission the tax in dispute constitutes a tax having an effect equivalent to a customs duty on exports and therefore the tax should have been abolished, under . . . Article [30 TFEU], no later than the end of the first stage of the common market [i.e. internal market], that is to say, from 1 January 1962. The defendant argues that the disputed tax does not come within the category, as it has its own particular purpose which is to ensure the protection and safety of the artistic, historic and archaeological heritage which exists in the national territory. Consequently, the tax does not in any respect have a fiscal nature, and its contribution to the budget is insignificant.
>
> . . . [Article 30 TFEU] prohibits the collection in dealings between Member States of any customs duty on exports and of any charge having an equivalent effect, that is to say, any charge which, by altering the price of an article exported, has the same restrictive effect on the free circulation of that article as a customs duty. **This provision makes no distinction based on the purpose of the duties and charges the abolition of which it requires.**
>
> It is not necessary to analyse the concept of the nature of fiscal systems on which the defendant bases its argument upon this point, for the provisions of the section of the Treaty concerning the elimination of customs duties between the Member States exclude the retention of customs duties and charges having equivalent effect without distinguishing between those which are and those which are not of a fiscal nature.
>
> **The disputed tax falls within . . . [Article 30 TFEU] by reason of the fact that export trade in the goods in question is hindered by the pecuniary burden which it imposes on the price of the exported articles.** [emphasis added]

The above case demonstrates that it is the *effect* of the tax and not its *purpose* which is of prime importance. To have decided otherwise would have considerably weakened the effect of the current Arts 28 and 30 TFEU, the aim of which is to remove fiscal barriers from the borders of Member States which would otherwise hinder the free movement of goods. In the above case, Italy had argued that it had a legitimate reason for imposing the export tax (i.e. the protection of its artistic, historic and archaeological heritage), which should be recognised by the Court as a sufficient reason for it to declare that the tax fell outside the scope of the Treaty. If the Italian argument had been accepted by the Court, then the Court would have had to adjudicate in the future on what other legitimate reasons were sufficient to take them outside the Treaty (and thus afford a defence to an otherwise defaulting Member State). In rejecting the Italian argument, and confirming that the reason for the charge is irrelevant, the Court has made a significant impact on removing the financial frontiers which could otherwise have remained in a disguised form and thus impacted upon the free movement of goods. This was made explicitly clear by the Court of Justice in the following case:

Commission v *Italy* (Case 24/68)

The Court of Justice held as follows:

6. . . . the purpose of the abolition of customs barriers is not merely to eliminate their protective nature, as the Treaty sought on the contrary to give general scope and effect to the rule on the elimination of customs duties and charges having equivalent effect, in order to ensure the free movement of goods.
7. It follows from the system as a whole and from the general and absolute nature of the prohibition on any customs duty applicable to goods moving between Member States that customs duties are prohibited independently of any consideration of the purpose for which they were introduced and the destination of the revenue obtained therefrom.

The justification for this prohibition is based on the fact that any pecuniary charge, however small, imposed on goods by reason of the fact that they cross a frontier constitutes an obstacle to the movement of such goods. [emphasis added]

This is further illustrated in the following case:

Sociaal Fonds voor de Diamantarbeiders v *Sa Ch. Brachfeld & Sons* (Joined Cases 2 and 3/69)

It was argued that a small levy imposed under Belgian law on imported diamonds could not be in breach of what is now Art 28 TFEU (previously Art 23 EC Treaty) and Art 25 TFEU (previously Art 25 EC Treaty) because: (i) it had no protectionist purpose because Belgium did not produce diamonds; and (ii) the levy's purpose was to provide social security benefits for Belgian diamond workers. The Court of Justice explained the rationale for the sweeping nature of these provisions:

In prohibiting the imposition of customs duties, the Treaty does not distinguish between goods according to whether or not they enter into competition with the products of the importing country. Thus, the purpose of the abolition of customs barriers is not merely to eliminate their protective nature, as the Treaty sought on the contrary to give general scope and effect to the rule on elimination of customs duties and charges having equivalent effect in order to ensure the free movement of goods. It follows from the system as a whole and from the general and absolute nature of the prohibition of any customs duty applicable to goods moving between Member States that customs duties are prohibited independently of any consideration of the purpose for which they were introduced and the destination of the revenue obtained therefrom. **The justification for this prohibition is based on the fact that any pecuniary charge – however small – imposed on goods by reason of the fact that they cross a frontier constitutes an obstacle to the movement of such goods.** [emphasis added]

Charges having an equivalent effect to a customs duty

Article 30 TFEU prohibits not only customs duties but also *charges having an equivalent effect* to a customs duty (**CEEs**). If this phrase had been omitted, Member States could quite easily have avoided the prohibition. The scope of CEEs was considered by the Court of Justice in the following case:

Commission v *Italy* (Case 24/68)

Italy imposed a levy on goods which were exported to other Member States to finance the collecting of statistical data relating to trade patterns. The Commission challenged the legality of such a charge pursuant to its powers under what is now Art 258 TFEU (previously Art 226 EC Treaty). The Court of Justice held as follows:

8. The extension of the prohibition of customs duties to charges having an equivalent effect is intended to supplement the prohibition against obstacles to trade created by such duties by increasing its efficiency.

    The use of these two complementary concepts thus tends, in trade between Member States, to avoid the imposition of any pecuniary charge on goods circulating within the Community [i.e. Union] by virtue of the fact that they cross a national border.

9. Thus, in order to ascribe to a charge an effect equivalent to a customs duty, it is important to consider this effect in the light of the objectives of the Treaty, in the Parts, Titles and Chapters in which . . . [Articles 28 and 30 TFEU] are to be found, particularly in relation to the free movement of goods.

    Consequently, **any pecuniary charge, however small and whatever its designation and mode of application, which is imposed unilaterally on domestic or foreign goods by reason of the fact that they cross a frontier, and which is not a customs duty in the strict sense, constitutes a charge having equivalent effect within the meaning of . . . [Articles 28 and 30 TFEU], even if it is not imposed for the benefit of the State, is not discriminatory or protective in effect and if the product on which the charge is imposed is not in competition with any domestic product.**

10. It follows from all the provisions referred to and from their relationship with the other provisions of the Treaty that the prohibition of new customs duties or charges having equivalent effect, linked to the principle of the free movement of goods, constitutes a fundamental rule which, without prejudice to the other provisions of the Treaty, does not permit of any exceptions. [emphasis added]

In the above case the Court of Justice gave CEEs a broad scope (at para 9). Article 30 TFEU prohibits both customs duties and CEEs and the Court has strictly interpreted this provision, allowing very few exceptions. But are there any exceptions?

Provision of a service: exception to the general rule

In principle the Court of Justice has accepted that where the charge imposed is merely payment for a service which the Member State has rendered *directly* to the importer, then the charge should not be regarded as a CEE provided the charge levied is in proportion to the service provided. This is illustrated in the following case:

Commission v Belgium (Case 132/82)

Union rules allowed imported goods to be given customs clearance at public warehouses located inside a Member State rather than at the frontier. Belgium levied storage charges on goods which were stored temporarily at such warehouses at the request of the trader concerned. Charges were also levied on imported goods which simply attended the warehouse for customs clearance and were not in fact stored there. The Commission initiated infraction proceedings against Belgium, arguing that these charges were in breach of what are now Arts 28 and 30 TFEU (previously Arts 23 and 25 EC Treaty). The Court of Justice held as follows:

8. It is appropriate to recall, in the first place, that according to the established case law of the Court, any pecuniary charge, however small and whatever its designation and mode of application, which is imposed unilaterally on the goods by reason of the fact that they cross a frontier and which is not a customs duty in the strict sense, constitutes a charge having equivalent effect within the meaning of . . . [Articles 28 and 30 TFEU], even if it is not levied by the State. **The position is different only if the charge in question is the consideration for a service actually rendered to the importer and is of an amount commensurate with that service, when the charge concerned, as in this case, is payable exclusively on imported products.**

9. The prohibition of charges having an effect equivalent to customs duties, laid down in provisions of the Treaty, is justified on the ground that pecuniary charges imposed by reason or on the occasion of the crossing of the frontier represent an obstacle to the free movement of goods.

10. It is in the light of those principles that the question whether the disputed storage charges may be classified as charges having an effect equivalent to customs duties must be assessed. It should therefore be noted, in the first place, that the placing of imported goods in temporary storage in the special stores of public warehouses clearly represents a service rendered to traders. A decision to deposit the goods there can indeed be taken only at the request of the trader concerned and then ensures their storage without payment of duties, until the trader has decided how they are to be dealt with. Moreover the Commission does not dispute that the placing of goods in temporary storage may legally give rise to the payment of charges commensurate with the service thus rendered.

11. However, it appears . . . that the storage charges are payable equally when the goods are presented at the public warehouse solely for the completion of customs formalities, even though they have been exempted from storage and the importer has not requested that they be put in temporary storage.

12. Admittedly the Belgian Government claims that even in that case a service is rendered to the importer. It is always open to the latter to avoid payment of the disputed charges by choosing to have his goods cleared through customs at the frontier, where such a procedure is free. Moreover, by using a public warehouse, the importer is enabled to have the goods declared through customs near the places for which his products are bound and he is therefore relieved of the necessity of himself either having at his own disposal premises suitable for their clearance or having recourse to private premises, the use of which is more expensive than that of the public warehouses. It is therefore legitimate, in the Belgian Government's view, to impose a charge commensurate with that service.

13. That argument cannot however be accepted. Whilst it is true that the use of a public warehouse in the interior of the country offers certain advantages to importers it seems clear first of all that such advantages are linked solely with the completion of customs formalities which, whatever the place, is always compulsory. It should moreover be noted that such advantages result from the scheme of Community [i.e. Union] transit

introduced . . . in order to increase the fluidity of the movement of goods and to facilitate transport within the Community [i.e. Union]. There can therefore be no question of levying any charges for customs clearance facilities accorded in the interests of the common market [i.e. internal market].

14. It follows from the foregoing, that **when payment of storage charges is demanded solely in connection with the completion of customs formalities, it cannot be regarded as the consideration for a service actually rendered to the importer.**

15. **Consequently, it must be declared that, by levying storage charges on goods which originate in a Member State or are in free circulation, and which are imported into Belgium, and presented merely for the completion of customs formalities at a special store, the Kingdom of Belgium has failed to fulfil its obligations under . . . [Articles 28 and 30 TFEU].** [emphasis added]

In the above case, the Court of Justice held that the charge will not constitute a CEE 'if the charge in question is the consideration for a service actually rendered to the importer and is of an amount commensurate with that service' (para 8). Belgium made provision for customs formalities to be completed in-country as an alternative to at the border. Public warehouses were provided at the in-country customs posts. These warehouses provided temporary storage facilities for the goods while the customs formalities were completed. The importer had the option to store his goods in the warehouses for an extended period. In both instances, Belgium charged for the storage of the goods. In the first instance, Belgium was in breach of the Treaty provisions, because the charge for the service was solely connected with the completion of customs formalities. It could not be regarded as the consideration for a service actually rendered to the importer. However, in the latter instance, if the importer chose to store his goods in the warehouse for an extended period, this would constitute a service actually rendered to the importer. Belgium could therefore charge for this service provided the charge did not exceed the actual costs incurred by Belgium in providing this service. It was accepted by the Court that charges levied in relation to private premises did not fall to be considered within the former Arts 23 and 25 EC Treaty (now Arts 28 and 30 TFEU) (para 12); these provisions only apply to the state.

It is clear that an argument that the charge is consideration for a service actually rendered to the importer will be closely scrutinised by the Court. In its actual decisions, the Court has shown considerable reluctance in accepting that a particular charge falls outside Art 30 TFEU. In *Ford España v Spain* (Case 170/88), the Court of Justice said that even if a specific benefit to the person or body paying the charge can be identified, the state imposing the charge will still fall foul of what is now Art 30 TFEU if it cannot be shown that the sum demanded is proportionate to the cost of supplying the benefit. In this case, Ford received a demand for 0.165 per cent of the declared value of cars and other goods imported into Spain. The Spanish government maintained that the sum related to services rendered in connection with clearing the goods through customs. The Court held that, even if a specific benefit conferred on Ford could be shown, the flat-rate way in which the charge was calculated was evidently not fixed according to the cost of the alleged service and was, therefore, a breach of what is now Art 30 TFEU.

Commission v Italy, which was considered above, further illustrates the Court's reluctance to find that a charge falls outside the remit of what is now Art 30 TFEU:

Commission v *Italy* (Case 24/68)

The Italian government had argued that a charge which was imposed at the border constituted consideration for the collection of statistical information. It was argued that this information would provide importers with trade patterns and therefore give them a better competitive position in the Italian market. The Court of Justice held as follows:

15. The Italian Government further maintains that the disputed charge constitutes the consideration for a service rendered and as such cannot be designated as a charge having equivalent effect.

    According to the Italian Government the object of the statistics in question is to determine precisely the actual movements of goods and, consequently, changes in the state of the market. It claims that the exactness of the information thus supplied affords importers a better competitive position in the Italian market whilst exporters enjoy a similar advantage abroad and that the special advantages which dealers obtain from the survey justifies their paying for this public service and moreover demonstrates that the disputed charge is in the nature of a *quid pro quo*.

16. **The statistical information in question is beneficial to the economy as a whole and *inter alia* to the relevant administrative authorities.**

    Even if the competitive position of importers and exporters were to be particularly improved as a result, the statistics still constitute an advantage so general, and so difficult to assess, that the disputed charge cannot be regarded as the consideration for a specific benefit actually conferred.

17. It appears from the above mentioned considerations that in so far as the disputed charge is levied on exports it is contrary to . . . [Article 30 TFEU]. [emphasis added]

In the above case, the Court of Justice held that the service (i.e. provision of statistics) was not *directly* rendered to the importers/exporters because it was 'beneficial to the economy as a whole and *inter alia* to the relevant administrative authorities' (para 16). Even where it is more direct, the Court may still be reluctant to rule that the charge is consideration for the service rendered:

Bresciani v *Amministrazione Italiana delle Finanze* (Case 87/75)

The Italian authorities imposed a charge for compulsory veterinary and public health inspections carried out on the importation of raw cowhides. The case was referred by the national court pursuant to what is now Art 267 TFEU (previously Art 234 EC Treaty) for a preliminary ruling on the question of whether the charge for the inspection constituted a CEE. The Court of Justice held as follows:

6. The national court requests that the three following considerations be taken into account:

    First, the fact that the charge is proportionate to the quantity of the goods and not to their value distinguishes a duty of the type at issue from charges which fall within the prohibition under . . . [Article 30 TFEU]. Second, a pecuniary charge of the type at issue is no more than the consideration required from individuals who, through their own action in importing products of animal origin, cause a service to be rendered. In the third place, although there may be differences in the method and time of its application, the duty at issue is also levied on similar products of domestic origin.

    . . .

8. The justification for the obligation progressively to abolish customs duties is based on the fact that any pecuniary charge, however small, imposed on goods by reason of the fact that they cross a frontier constitutes an obstacle to the free movement of goods.

   The obligation progressively to abolish customs duties is supplemented by the obligation to abolish charges having equivalent effect in order to prevent the fundamental principle of the free movement of goods within the common market [i.e. internal market] from being circumvented by the imposition of pecuniary charges of various kinds by a Member State.

   The use of these two complementary concepts thus tends, in trade between Member States, to avoid the imposition of any pecuniary charge on goods circulating within the Community [i.e. Union] by virtue of the fact that they cross a national frontier.

9. Consequently, any pecuniary charge, whatever its designation and mode of application, which is unilaterally imposed on goods imported from another Member State by reason of the fact that they cross a frontier, constitutes a charge having an effect equivalent to a customs duty. In appraising a duty of the type at issue it is, consequently, of no importance that it is proportionate to the quantity of the imported goods and not their value.

10. Nor, in determining the effects of the duty on the free movement of goods, is it of any importance that a duty of the type at issue is proportionate to the costs of a compulsory public health inspection carried out on entry of the goods. **The activity of the administration of the State intended to maintain a public health inspection system imposed in the general interest cannot be regarded as a service rendered to the importer such as to justify the imposition of a pecuniary charge. If, accordingly, public health inspections are still justified at the end of the transitional period, the costs which they occasion must be met by the general public which, as a whole, benefits from the free movement of Community [i.e. Union] goods.** [emphasis added]

In the above case, at para 10, the Court of Justice held that a public health inspection system was imposed to benefit the general public, and therefore was not a service rendered *directly* to the importer. It was there for the benefit of the general public and therefore it was the general public who would have to meet the costs incurred by the state in carrying out those inspections.

Even where Union law *permits* an inspection to be undertaken by the state, the national authorities cannot recover the cost from the importers (see *Commission v Belgium* (Case 314/82)).

However, if Union law *requires* an inspection to be carried out, the costs of such an inspection *may* be recoverable and will not be caught by the provisions of Art 30 TFEU. This was decided by the Court of Justice in the following case:

Commission v Germany (Case 18/87)

German regional authorities charged certain fees on live animals when they were imported into Germany. These charges were to cover the cost of inspections undertaken pursuant to Directive 81/389. The question before the Court of Justice was whether such charges constituted CEEs and were therefore prohibited. The Court of Justice held as follows:

5. It should be observed in the first place that, as the Court has held on a number of occasions, the justification for the prohibition of customs duties and any charges having an equivalent effect lies in the fact that any pecuniary charge, however small, imposed on goods by reason of the fact that they cross a frontier, constitutes an obstacle to the

movement of goods which is aggravated by the resulting administrative formalities. It follows that any pecuniary charge, whatever its designation and mode of application, which is imposed unilaterally on goods by reason of the fact that they cross a frontier and is not a customs duty in the strict sense constitutes a charge having an equivalent effect to a customs duty within the meaning of . . . [Articles 28 and 30 TFEU].

6. However, the Court has held that such a charge escapes that classification if it relates to a general system of internal dues applied systematically and in accordance with the same criteria to domestic products and imported goods alike (judgment of 31 May 1979 in Case 132/78 *Denkavit v France* [1979] ECR 1923), if it constitutes payment for a service in fact rendered to the economic operator of a sum in proportion to the service (judgment of 9 November 1983 in Case 158/82 *Commission v Denmark* [1983] ECR 3573), or again, subject to certain conditions, if it attaches to inspections carried out to fulfil obligations imposed by Community [i.e. Union] law (judgment of 25 January 1977 in Case 46/76 *Bauhuis v Netherlands* [1977] ECR 5).

7. The contested fee, which is payable on importation and transit, cannot be regarded as relating to a general system of internal dues. Nor does it constitute payment for a service rendered to the operator, because this condition is satisfied only if the operator in question obtains a definite specific benefit (see judgment of 1 July 1969 in Case 24/68 *Commission v Italy* [1969] ECR 193), which is not the case if the inspection serves to guarantee, in the public interest, the health and life of animals in international transport (see judgment of 20 March 1984 in Case 314/82 *Commission v Belgium* [1984] ECR 1543).

8. Since the contested fee was charged in connection with inspections carried out pursuant to Community [i.e. Union] provision, it should be noted that according to the case law of the Court (judgment of 25 January 1977 in *Bauhuis*, cited above; judgment of 12 July 1977 *Commission v Netherlands* [1977] ECR 1355; judgment of 31 January 1984 in Case 1/83 *IFG v Freistaat Bayern* [1984] ECR 349) such fees may not be classified as charges having an equivalent effect to a **customs duty** if the following conditions are satisfied:

   (a) they do not exceed the actual costs of the inspections in connection with which they are charged;
   (b) the inspections in question are obligatory and uniform for all the products concerned in the Community [i.e. Union];
   (c) they are prescribed by Community [i.e. Union] law in the general interest of the Community [i.e. Union];
   (d) they promote the free movement of goods, in particular by neutralising obstacles which could arise from unilateral measures of inspection adopted in accordance with . . . [Article 36 TFEU].

9. In this instance these conditions are satisfied by the contested fee. In the first place it has not been contested that it does not exceed the real cost of the inspection in connection with which it is charged.

10. Moreover, all the Member States of transit and destination are required, under, *inter alia*, Article 2(1) of Directive 81/389/EEC, cited above, to carry out the veterinary inspections in question when the animals are brought into their territories, and therefore the inspections are obligatory and uniform for all the animals concerned in the Community [i.e. Union].

11. Those inspections are prescribed by Directive 81/389/EEC, which establishes the measures necessary for the implementation of Council Directive 77/489/EEC of 18 July 1977 on the protection of animals during international transport, with a view to the protection

of live animals, an objective which is pursued in the general interest of the Community [i.e. Union] and not a specific interest of individual states.

12. Finally, it appears from the preambles to the two abovementioned directives that they are intended to harmonise the laws of the Member States regarding the protection of animals in international transport in order to eliminate technical barriers resulting from disparities in the national laws (see third, fourth and fifth recitals in the preamble to Directive 77/489/EEC and the third recital in the preamble to Directive 81/389/EEC). In addition, failing such harmonisation, each Member State was entitled to maintain or introduce, under the conditions laid down in . . . [Article 36 TFEU], measures restricting trade which were justified on grounds of the protection of the health and life of animals. It follows that the standardisation of the inspections in question is such as to promote the free movement of goods.

13. The Commission has claimed, however, that the contested fee is to be regarded as a charge having equivalent effect to a customs duty because, in so far as fees of this type have not been harmonised, such harmonisation, moreover, being unattainable in practice, their negative effect on the free movement of goods could not be compensated or, consequently, justified by the positive effects of the Community [i.e. Union] standardisation of inspections.

14. In this respect, it should be noted that since the fee in question is intended solely as the financially and economically justified compensation for an obligation imposed in equal measure on all the Member States by Community [i.e. Union] law, it cannot be regarded as equivalent to a customs duty; nor, consequently, can it fall within the ambit of the prohibition laid down in . . . [Articles 28 and 30 TFEU]. [emphasis added]

In the above case, the Court of Justice held that an inspection fee levied on imported goods is valid under Union law, provided the four conditions laid down in para 8 above are satisfied. Two of the four conditions which are particularly important are that: (i) the inspection must be mandatory (i.e. compulsory) under Union law; and (ii) the inspection fee levied must not exceed the actual costs incurred by the Member State in carrying out the inspection. This judgment was subsequently applied by the Court in *Bauhuis* v *Netherlands* (Case 46/76), where there was a challenge to a fee imposed by The Netherlands' government for veterinary inspections of pigs imported into The Netherlands. Some of the checks were carried out to meet rules of national law, while others were made to meet the requirements of a Union directive. The Court held that, where such checks are mandatory under Union law and are part of the process of ensuring the free movement of goods, they are permitted under what is now Art 30 TFEU. The fee must, however, be proportionate to the actual cost of the inspection. In *Commission* v *Netherlands* (Case 89/76), the question arose as to the compatibility with what is now Art 30 TFEU, of plant inspections carried out under the International Plant Protection Convention 1951. This Convention was not a source of Union law, but it was binding in international law on those states which were signatories to it. It was designed to liberalise trade by replacing different checks in signatory states by a single check on which all states were able to rely. The Court drew a parallel with *Bauhuis*, and held that the charges imposed did not breach what is now Art 30 TFEU.

Figure 17.1 consists of a flowchart setting out the application of Art 30 TFEU.

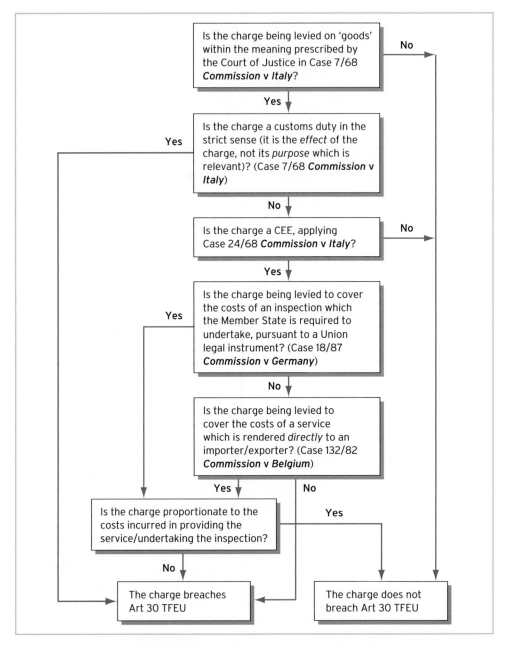

Figure 17.1 Article 30 TFEU: customs duties and charges having an equivalent effect

Customs duty or internal taxation?

Objective 3

Most charges which have been held to breach the prohibition in Arts 28 and 30 TFEU have been those levied directly on imported or exported goods. Charges which are levied indiscriminately on home-produced *and* imported goods will not, generally, breach Art 30 TFEU and will be lawful, provided they do not conflict with the prohibition in

Art 110 TFEU (previously Art 90 EC Treaty) against discriminatory internal taxation (see below). A breach of Arts 28 or 30 TFEU may occur if the charge on the imported product is not imposed in the same way and determined according to the same criteria as the domestic product. In **Marimex v Italian Finance Administration** (Case 29/72), a veterinary inspection tax imposed on imported meat to ensure that it complied with national health standards was also imposed on domestic meat, but the inspections were conducted by different bodies applying different standards.

Where the charge is in the nature of a tax, care must be taken to determine whether it is in fact a charge in the nature of a customs duty or CEE, or a provision of internal taxation. If it is a customs duty or CEE, it is unlawful in its entirety. If it is a provision of internal taxation, it is unlawful only to the extent that it is discriminatory against imported goods or protective of domestically produced goods (**IGAV v ENCC** (Case 94/74)). The difficulty of distinguishing between customs duties or CEEs on the one hand, and internal taxation on the other, is illustrated in the following case:

Capolongo v Azienda Agricola (Case 77/72)

A charge ostensibly levied on both imported and domestic products was claimed to be used to promote domestic products. The Court of Justice emphasised that the same charge could not be both a customs duty or CEE, and a provision of internal taxation. It held that where a charge is levied both on imports and on domestic products, it can, nevertheless, constitute a charge equivalent to a customs duty when it is intended exclusively to support activities which specifically benefit the taxed domestic product.

In **IGAV v ENCC** (above), the Court of Justice held that this was also the case where the domestic tax was remitted on the domestic product 'wholly or in part'. The Court of Justice later modified its position in the following case:

Fratelli Cucchi (Case 77/76)

The Court of Justice held that apparent internal taxation can only constitute a charge equivalent to a customs duty (i.e. a CEE): 'if it has the sole purpose of financing activities for the specific advantage of the taxed domestic product; if the taxed product and the domestic product benefiting from it are the same; and if the charges imposed on the domestic product are made good in full'.

A much more probable conclusion is that a tax on imported and domestic products which gives a partial benefit to the taxed domestic product will constitute discriminatory internal taxation, contrary to Art 110 TFEU, on the basis that it indirectly imposes a heavier burden on products from other Member States than on domestic products (**Commission v Italy** (Case 73/79)).

However, the Court of Justice did not follow this approach in the following case:

Haahr Petroleum Ltd v Abenra Havn (Case C-90/94)

The claimant challenged a Danish law under which the port of Abenra and others charged an import surcharge of 40 per cent, which was levied in addition to duties on all imported goods loaded or unloaded within Danish commercial ports or in the deep-water approach channel to those ports. On a reference to the Court of Justice, the Court held that the charges formed part of a general system of internal taxes payable for the use of commercial ports and facilities. It had been argued by the Danish government that the charge levied was lawful under what is now Art 30 TFEU (previously Art 25 EC Treaty) because it constituted a charge for a service actually rendered to traders, and could not therefore also fall foul of the prohibition against discriminatory taxation under what is now Art 110 TFEU (previously Art 90 EC Treaty). Without accepting that the charge might be lawful under what is now Art 30 TFEU, the Court held that even if this was the case, it did not mean that the charge also escaped the prohibition against discriminatory taxation under what is now Art 110 TFEU.

Article 110 TFEU: discriminatory and protectionist internal taxation

Objective 4

See page 581 for a flowchart which illustrates the application of Art 110 TFEU.

See pages 274–292 and 303–305 for a discussion of the principle of direct effect.

In the absence of a harmonised Union tax system, the Member States are entitled to take such measures as are necessary to make that system effective, even, it would seem, at the expense of fundamental rights under the Treaty, such as the right of establishment (*R v HM Treasury, ex parte Daily Mail* (Case 81/87)). Article 113 TFEU (previously Art 93 EC Treaty) provides for the enactment of measures to harmonise legislation on turnover taxes, excise duties and other forms of indirect taxation, but because such legislation can only be adopted by the Council of Ministers acting unanimously there has been little movement. Until a fully harmonised Union tax regime is achieved, however, Member States retain their national prerogative in relation to internal taxation. This principle of national autonomy gives way to another fundamental principle, that of free movement of goods. Article 110 TFEU (which is identical to the former Art 90 EC Treaty) provides that:

No Member State shall impose, directly or indirectly, on the products of other Member States any internal taxation of any kind in excess of that imposed directly or indirectly on similar domestic products.

Furthermore, no Member State shall impose on the products of other Member States any internal taxation of such a nature as to afford indirect protection to other products.

Article 110 TFEU is directly effective (see *Alfons Lütticke GmbH v Hauptzollamt Saarlouis* (Case 57/65)).

Goods from third countries

As Art 110 TFEU refers to 'products of other Member States' it might well be thought that discriminatory or protectionist taxation levied on goods coming from another Member State was permissible provided those goods originated from outside the Union. Unlike the provisions relating to the free movement of goods in Part Three, Title II, TFEU (i.e. Arts 28–37 TFEU) which relate both to products originating in the Union and 'to products coming from third countries [i.e. non-Member States] which are in free circulation in Member States', there is no such application to the non-discriminatory tax rules (Art 28(2) TFEU). The Court therefore at first held that Member States were entitled to impose discriminatory or protectionist taxes on third-country products circulating freely in the Union, provided such taxation was compatible with any concessions made to that state in any association or other agreement (*Hansen v Hauptzollamt Flensburg* (Case 148/77)).

It modified its position, however, in **Co-Frutta** (Case 193/85). In this case, which involved Italian taxation of bananas imported through other Member States, the Court of Justice accepted that the Common Customs Tariff and the Common Commercial Policy were intended to ensure a uniform treatment of goods imported from third countries and the facilitation of the free movement of such goods once they had been legitimately imported into one of the Member States.

The purpose of Article 110 TFEU

As discussed above, Arts 28–30 TFEU are designed to prevent financial measures from being imposed as a result of a product *crossing a frontier*. The financial measure does not necessarily have to be protectionist in nature; however, it often is. *Protectionist* means that the measure imposed has the effect of protecting domestic products from competition by foreign goods.

Articles 28–30 TFEU would be of little use if a Member State could impose taxes on foreign products (but not on the rival domestic product) once they were inside their territory; because the tax was not levied at the frontier it would not be caught by Arts 28–30 TFEU. Article 110 TFEU seeks to prevent this where a discriminatory or protectionist charge is levied on the imported product but not on the domestic product. The purpose of Art 110 TFEU (previously Art 90 EC Treaty) was set out by the Court of Justice in the following case:

Commission v Denmark (Case 171/78)

The Court of Justice held as follows:

> The . . . provisions supplement, within the system of the Treaty, the provisions on the abolition of customs duties and charges having equivalent effect. **Their aim is to ensure the free movement of goods between the Member States in normal conditions of competition by the elimination of all forms of protection which result from the application of internal taxation which discriminates against products from other Member States.** As the Commission has correctly stated . . . [Article 110 TFEU] must guarantee the complete neutrality of internal taxation as regards competition between domestic products and imported products. [emphasis added]

Article 110 TFEU is aimed at two distinct, but sometimes overlapping, national taxation practices: (i) the taxing of the same or similar imported and home-produced products in a different way (Art 110(1) TFEU); and (ii) the taxing of different but competing imported and home-produced products in such a way as to afford protection to the home-produced product (Art 110(2) TFEU). The two key concepts are therefore similarity and product competition (**Commission v France** (Case 168/78)). These two concepts are now considered further.

Article 110(1) TFEU: similar products

Article 110(1) TFEU (previously Art 90(1) EC Treaty) is a reference to Art 110, para 1, TFEU, which provides that:

> No Member State shall impose, directly or indirectly, on the products of other Member States any internal taxation of any kind in excess of that imposed directly or indirectly on similar domestic products.

Article 110(1) TFEU does not require a Member State to adopt a particular system of internal taxation, just that whatever system is adopted must be applied without discrimination to similar imported products: i.e. it prohibits the imposition of internal taxes on products from other Member States which are greater than those levied on *similar* domestic products. Therefore, once the imported and domestic products are considered to be *similar*, Art 110(1) TFEU will apply.

In *Commission v France* (Case 168/78), the Court of Justice considered the concept of *similar products* in the context of the former Art 90(1) EC Treaty (now Art 110(1) TFEU). The Court of Justice, at para 5, stated that it was necessary to consider as *similar*, products which have:

similar characteristics and meet the same needs from the point of view of consumers.

This was subsequently applied by the Court of Justice in the following case:

John Walker v Ministeriet For Skatter (Case 243/84)

The issue before the Court of Justice was whether liqueur fruit wine was *similar* to whisky for the purposes of what is now Art 110(1) TFEU (previously Art 90(1) EC Treaty). The Court analysed the **objective characteristics of the products**, including their alcoholic contents, methods of production and consumer perceptions as to the nature of the products. The Court held that they were *not* similar. They had different alcoholic contents and different manufacturing processes (whisky was distilled rather than fermented). Any scrutiny of the tax therefore had to be considered under what is now Art 110(2) TFEU (previously Art 90(2) EC Treaty).

The Court of Justice was required to assess the similarity of alcoholic beverages in the following case:

FG Roders BV EA v Inspecteur der Inverrechten en Accijnzen (Joined Cases C-367 And 377/93)

Importers of French wine, Spanish sherry and Italian vermouth challenged the higher rates of excise duty that were charged on those products, as compared to fruit wines produced in the Benelux countries (i.e. Belgium, The Netherlands and Luxembourg). The Court of Justice decided that fruit wines and grape wines were similar. They are made from the same kind of agricultural products, and by the same process of natural fermentation. Both beverages possess the same kind of organoleptic properties, in particular taste and alcoholic strength, and meet the same needs of consumers, since they can be consumed for the same purposes, namely to quench thirst, to refresh, and to accompany meals.

Product similarity was also at issue in the following case:

Commission v Italy (Case 184/85)

The issue of product similarity related to different types of fruit. Italy levied a consumption tax on bananas which amounted to about half their import price. The tax was not levied on other fruit (e.g. apples, pears, plums). Italy produced large amounts of fruit, other than bananas, which it imported from France. The Commission took action against Italy, alleging the tax infringed what is now Art 110 TFEU (previously Art 90 EC Treaty). The Court of Justice first considered whether bananas and other fruit were *similar* for the purpose of what is now Art 110(1) TFEU (previously Art 90(1) EC Treaty). The Court held that they were *not* similar, taking into account the objective characteristics of the products. Any further examination of the tax had to proceed under what is now Art 110(2) TFEU (previously Art 90(2) EC Treaty); see below.

If goods are *similar* under Art 110(1) TFEU then the tax will be unlawful if it is discriminatory. This discrimination can be either direct or indirect.

Direct discrimination

Different rates and methods of taxation applied to similar imported or domestic products are usually easily recognisable. For this reason direct discrimination of this kind is rare.

In *Lütticke GmbH v Hauptzollamt Saarlouis* (Case 57/65), an internal tax was levied on imported dried milk but not on domestically produced dried milk. The tax was directly discriminatory and breached what is now Art 110(1) TFEU (previously Art 90(1) EC Treaty).

In *Bobie Getränkvertrieb v Hauptzollamt Aachen-Nord* (Case 127/75), a German beer tax imposed a sliding scale on home-produced beer, varying between DM 12 and 15 per hectolitre, according to the size of the brewery (**DM** (i.e. **Deutsche Mark**) was Germany's national currency before Germany adopted the euro). Imported beers had a flat-rate tax of DM 14.40 levied upon them. The Court of Justice held that the tax was discriminatory, because small foreign breweries could not avail themselves of the low rate (DM 12) available to small domestic breweries.

The method for the collection of the tax may also involve discrimination, even if the criteria for its payment do not. In *Commission v Ireland* (Case 55/79), the Court of Justice held an Irish tax incompatible with what is now Art 110 TFEU. The tax was payable according to the same criteria, irrespective of the origin of the goods. However, domestic producers were permitted several weeks' grace to pay the tax, while importers had to pay immediately on importation.

Indirect discrimination

Indirectly discriminatory internal taxation will be similarly caught by Art 110(1) TFEU. On the face of it, an internal tax rule may not differentiate between domestic and imported goods, but the actual effect of the tax may place a greater burden on the imported goods. An example of this is illustrated in the following case:

Humblot v *Directeur des Services Fiscaux* (Case 112/84)

France imposed two different types of annual car tax. The key threshold between the two was the power rating (or fiscal horsepower) of the car. Below 16 CV the tax increased gradually in proportion to the car's fiscal horsepower, up to a maximum of 1,100 **francs** (the franc was France's national currency before France adopted the euro). Above 16 CV a flat-rate tax of 5,000 francs was imposed. The way in which the fiscal horsepower was calculated was complex. It took into consideration: the number of cylinders; the bore in centimetres; the stroke in centimetres; and the rotation speed in revolutions per second. The result of applying this calculation was that no French car was given a fiscal horsepower rating above 16 CV. Therefore, only imported vehicles were subject to the higher flat-rate tax. The effect of the fiscal horsepower calculation was such that a foreign car of similar characteristics to a French car (e.g. same engine size, similar specifications, etc.) would fall within a higher rating and therefore attract a higher level of annual tax.

Humblot was charged 5,000 francs on his imported car, which had been given a fiscal horsepower rating of 36 CV. He claimed the tax breached what is now Art 110 TFEU (previously Art 90 EC Treaty) and sought a refund. As discussed above, Art 110 TFEU is directly effective. The French court referred questions to the Court of Justice under what is now Art 267 TFEU (previously Art 234 EC Treaty). The Court of Justice held as follows:

12. It is appropriate in the first place to stress that as Community [i.e. Union] law stands at present the Member States are at liberty to subject products such as cars to a system of road tax which increases progressively in amount depending on an objective criterion, such as the power rating for tax purposes, which may be determined in various ways.

13. Such a system of domestic taxation is, however, compatible with . . . [Article 110 TFEU] only in so far as it is free from any discriminatory or protective effect.

14. That is not true of a system like the one at issue in the main proceedings. Under that system there are two distinct taxes: a differential tax which increases progressively and is charged on cars not exceeding a given power rating for tax purposes and a fixed tax on cars exceeding that rating which is almost five times as high as the highest band of the differential tax. Although the system embodies no formal distinction based on the origin of the products it manifestly exhibits discriminatory or protective features contrary to . . . [Article 110 TFEU], since the power rating determining liability to the special tax has been fixed at a level such that only imported cars, in particular from other Member States, are subject to the special tax whereas all cars of domestic manufacture are liable to the distinctly more advantageous differential tax.

15. In the absence of considerations relating to the amount of the special tax, consumers seeking comparable cars as regards such matters as size, comfort, actual power, maintenance costs, durability, fuel consumption and price would naturally choose from among cars above and below the critical power rating laid down by French law. However, liability to the special tax entails a much larger increase in taxation than passing from one category of car to another in a system of progressive taxation embodying balanced differentials like the system on which the differential tax is based. **The resultant additional taxation is liable to cancel out the advantages which certain cars imported from other Member States might have in consumers' eyes over comparable cars of domestic manufacture, particularly since the special tax continues to be payable for years. In that respect the special tax reduces the amount of competition to which cars of domestic manufacture are subject and hence is contrary to the principle of neutrality with which domestic taxation must comply.**

16. In the light of the foregoing considerations the questions raised by the national court for a preliminary ruling should be answered as follows: . . . [Article 110 TFEU] prohibits the charging on cars exceeding a given power rating for tax purposes of a special fixed tax the amount of which is several times the highest amount of the progressive tax payable on cars of less than the said power rating for tax purposes, where the only cars subject to the special tax are imported, in particular from other Member States. [emphasis added]

Following the above judgment, France amended its legislation, but the Court of Justice was required to adjudicate on the amended legislation's compatibility with what is now Art 110 TFEU on numerous occasions. See, for example:

● *Feldain* v *Services Fiscaux du Département du Haut-Rhin* (Case 433/85);
● *Deville* v *Administration des Impôts* (Case 240/87);

- *Jacquier* v *Directeur Général des Impôts* (Case C-113/94);
- *Yves Tarantik* v *Direction des Services Fiscaux de Seine-et-Marne* (Case C-421/97)

A further example of indirect discrimination is illustrated in the following case:

Haahr Petroleum Ltd v Abenra Havn (Case C-90/94)

A lower rate of harbour tax was levied on goods which were unloaded in harbours which originated in inland waterways, compared to goods unloaded in harbours which originated in deep-water channels. The Court of Justice stated as follows:

> A criterion for the charging of higher taxation which by definition can never be fulfilled by similar domestic products cannot be considered to be compatible with the prohibition of discrimination laid down in . . . [Article 110 TFEU]. Such a system has the effect of excluding domestic products in advance from the heaviest taxation. Likewise, the Court has held that such differential taxation is incompatible with Community [i.e. Union] law if the products most heavily taxed are, by their very nature, imported products.

In the above case, goods unloaded at harbours in inland waterways were overwhelmingly the product of the home state, and goods unloaded at harbours originating in deep-water channels were imported. The higher taxation levied on goods unloaded at harbours originating in deep-water channels was indirectly discriminatory, and was therefore contrary to Art 110(1) TFEU.

Objective justification: a defence to indirect discrimination

While direct discrimination will never be justifiable, tax rules of a Member State which tend to favour the domestic product may be held not to breach Art 110(1) TFEU if there is some *objective justification* for the conduct complained of. This objective justification must be acceptable to the Court. If accepted it will prevent Art 110(1) TFEU from being applied too harshly, as illustrated in the following case:

Chemial Farmaceutici v Daf Spa (Case 140/79)

Italian internal taxation of *synthetic* ethyl alcohol was higher than taxation of *fermented* ethyl alcohol. The products were interchangeable in use. Italy produced very little of the higher taxed synthetic product, and therefore the tax system had a harsher impact upon importers. The rationale for the tax policy was to encourage the manufacture of the fermented product (the raw material of which was agricultural products), thus preserving the petroleum ingredients used to make the synthetic product for other more economically important purposes. The Court considered the legitimacy of this policy choice. The Court of Justice held as follows:

> 13. . . . the different taxation of synthetic alcohol and of alcohol produced by fermentation in Italy is the result of an economic policy decision to favour the manufacture of alcohol from agricultural products and, correspondingly, to restrain the processing into alcohol of ethylene, a derivative of petroleum, in order to reserve that raw material for other more important economic uses. It accordingly constitutes a legitimate choice of economic policy to which effect is given by fiscal means. The implementation of that policy

> does not lead to any discrimination since although it results in discouraging imports of synthetic alcohol into Italy, it also has the consequence of hampering the development in Italy itself of production of alcohol from ethylene, that production being technically perfectly possible.
>
> 14. As the Court has stated on many occasions, particularly in the judgments cited by the Italian Government, in its present stage of development Community [i.e. Union] law does not restrict the freedom of each Member State to lay down tax arrangements which differentiate between certain products on the basis of objective criteria, such as the nature of the raw materials used or the production processes employed. Such differentiation is compatible with Community [i.e. Union] law if it pursues economic policy objectives which are themselves compatible with the requirements of the Treaty and its secondary law and if the detailed rules are such as to avoid any form of discrimination, direct or indirect, in regard to imports from other Member States or any form of protection of competing domestic products.
>
> 15. Differential taxation such as that which exists in Italy for denatured synthetic alcohol on the one hand and denatured alcohol obtained by fermentation on the other satisfies these requirements. It appears in fact that the system of taxation pursues an objective of legitimate industrial policy in that it is such as to promote the distillation of agricultural products as against the manufacture of alcohol from petroleum derivatives. That choice does not conflict with the rules of Community [i.e. Union] law or the requirements of a policy decided within the framework of the Community [i.e. Union].
>
> 16. The detailed provisions of the legislation at issue before the national court cannot be considered as discriminatory since, on the one hand, it is not disputed that imports from other Member States of alcohol obtained by fermentation qualify for the same tax treatment as Italian alcohol produced by fermentation, and on the other hand, although the rate of tax prescribed for synthetic alcohol results in restraining the importation of synthetic alcohol originating in other Member States, it has an equivalent economic effect in the national territory in that it also hampers the establishment of profitable production of the same product by Italian industry. [emphasis added]

In the above case, the Court of Justice stated at para 16 that there was no *actual* discrimination, direct or indirect, because the tax would deter not only importers of the affected product but also national producers, even though there was very little domestic production of the affected product. The tax was applicable to both imported and domestic products, so it could only have the potential for being indirectly discriminatory (i.e. if the tax had a greater impact on the imported product than on the domestic product). If there is no actual discrimination then the tax is *per se* (i.e. automatically) outside Art 110 TFEU. However, in this case the Court, in finding that there was no actual discrimination, was no doubt strongly influenced by the *reason* for the imposition of the tax (i.e. 'legitimate choice of economic policy', see para 13). It is therefore considered that this case provides scope for a defence to an internal tax that is indirectly discriminatory. The defence will apply where the measure can be objectively justified; in this case on the ground that the imposition of the tax constituted a 'legitimate choice of economic policy'. Although the Court did not expressly state it constituted a defence, it was influenced by the reason when deciding not to impose a strict application of the former Art 90 EC Treaty (now Art 110 TFEU).

Similarly, in the course of what are now Art 258 TFEU (previously Art 226 EC Treaty) proceedings brought by the Commission against France, the Court of Justice held that a more favourable tax rate applied to natural sweet wine as compared to ordinary table wine was justified. The purpose of the tax was to assist the economy of areas that were heavily reliant on such wines, which were produced in difficult circumstances (***Commission v France*** (Case 196/85)). Where such tax relief is applied, it must be operated indiscriminately, even where there is a legitimate and defensible objective. Thus, it has been held that an importer of spirits into Germany was entitled to take advantage of tax relief available, *inter alia*, in respect of spirits made by small businesses and collective farms. The Court of Justice accepted that such tax concessions could meet legitimate economic and social purposes, but the former Art 90 EC Treaty (now Art 110 TFEU) required that such preferential systems must be extended without discrimination to spirits coming from other Member States (***Hansen v Hauptzollamt Flensburg*** (Case 148/77)).

Article 110(1) and (2) TFEU: the relationship

As discussed above, Art 110(1) TFEU prohibits the imposition of internal taxes on products from other Member States which are greater than those levied on *similar* domestic products. Therefore, once the imported and domestic products can be considered to be *similar*, Art 110(1) TFEU will apply and the taxes must be *equalised*.

Article 110(2) TFEU (previously Art 90(2) EC Treaty) refers to Art 110, para 2, TFEU, which provides that:

> Furthermore, no Member State shall impose on the products of other Member States any internal taxation of such a nature as to afford indirect protection to other products.

Article 110(2) TFEU applies to other products which are not *similar*, but the effect of the tax is to afford *indirect protection* to some other domestic products: i.e. products which are not similar but which may otherwise be in competition with each other. For example, wine and beer may not be considered to be similar; however, they may be in competition with one another. One question which needs to be addressed when considering whether the products are in competition with one another, is whether the two products have a **cross-elasticity** of demand; are the products interchangeable? Having established a competitive relationship between the two products, if the tax on wine is greater than that on beer, it could deter beer drinkers from switching to wine. If the Member State which has adopted this tax policy is a major producer of beer but produces only small amounts of wine, the vast majority of it being imported, the tax policy could afford an indirect protection to its domestic beer producers.

The Court of Justice considered the scope of what is now Art 110(1) and (2) TFEU in the following case:

Commission v France (Case 168/78)

France had higher tax rates for spirits which were based upon grain (e.g. whisky, rum, gin, vodka) than those based upon wine or fruit (e.g. cognac, armagnac). France produced very little of the more heavily taxed grain-based spirits, but was a major producer of the wine and fruit-based spirits. The Commission took infraction proceedings against France pursuant to what is now Art 258 TFEU (previously Art 226 EC), alleging the tax breached what is now Art 110 TFEU (previously Art 90 EC Treaty). The Court of Justice held as follows:

4. [Article 110 TFEU] supplements within the system of the Treaty, the provisions on the abolition of customs duties and charges having equivalent effect [i.e. Articles 28 and 30 TFEU]. Their aim is to ensure free movement of goods between the Member States

in normal conditions of competition by the elimination of all forms of protection which result from the application of internal taxation which discriminates against products from other Member States. As the Commission has correctly stated . . . [Article 110 TFEU] must guarantee the complete neutrality of internal taxation as regards competition between domestic products and imported products.

5. The first paragraph of . . . [Article 110 TFEU], which is based on a comparison of the tax burdens imposed on domestic products and imported products which may be classified as 'similar', is the basic rule in this respect. This provision, as the Court has had occasion to emphasise in its judgment of 10 October 1978 in Case 148/77, *H Hansenjun & O. C. Balle GmbH & Co. v Hauptzollamt Flensburg* [1978] ECR 1787, must be interpreted widely so as to cover all taxation procedures which conflict with the principle of the equality of treatment of domestic products and imported products; it is therefore necessary to interpret the concept of 'similar products' with sufficient flexibility. The Court specified in the judgment of 17 February 1976 in the *REWE* case (Case 45/75 [1976] ECR 181) that it is necessary to consider as similar products which have 'similar characteristics and meet the same needs from the point of view of consumers'. It is therefore necessary to determine the scope of the first paragraph of . . . [Article 110] on the basis not of the criterion of the strictly identical nature of the products but on that of their similar and comparable use.

6. The function of the second paragraph of . . . [Article 110] is to cover, in addition, all forms of indirect tax protection in the case of products which, without being similar within the meaning of the first paragraph, are nevertheless in competition, even partial, indirect or potential, with certain products of the importing country. The Court has already emphasised certain aspects of that provision in its judgment of 4 April 1968 in Case 27/67 *Firma Fink-Frucht GmbH v Hauptzollamt München-Landsbergerstrasse* [1968] ECR 223, in which it stated that for the purposes of the application of the second paragraph of . . . [Article 110] it is sufficient for the imported product to be in competition with the protected domestic production by reason of one of several economic uses to which it may be put, even though the condition of similarity for the purposes of the first paragraph of . . . [Article 110] is not fulfilled.

7. Whilst the criterion indicated in the first paragraph of . . . [Article 110] consists in the comparison of tax burdens, whether in terms of the rate, the mode of assessment or other detailed rules for the application thereof, in view of the difficulty of making sufficiently precise comparisons between the products in question, the second paragraph of that article is based upon a more general criterion, in other words the protective nature of the system on internal taxation. [emphasis added]

The above case was decided on the basis that there had been an infringement of what is now Art 110 TFEU (previously Art 90 EC Treaty) without a detailed examination of the paragraphs separately. The reason why the Court of Justice was not unduly worried whether the infringement was based on the first or second paragraph of what is now Art 110 TFEU (previously Art 90 EC Treaty) was explained by the Court as follows:

12. Two conclusions follow from this analysis of the market in spirits. First, there is, in the case of spirits considered as a whole, an indeterminate number of beverages which must be classified as 'similar products' within the meaning of the first paragraph of . . . [Article 110], although it may be difficult to decide this in specific cases, in view of the nature of the factors implied by distinguishing criteria such as flavour and consumer habits. Secondly, even in cases in which it is impossible to recognise a sufficient degree of similarity between the products concerned, there are nevertheless, in the case of all spirits, common characteristics which are sufficiently pronounced to accept that in all cases there is at least partial or potential competition. It follows that the application of the second paragraph of . . . [Article 110] may come into consideration in cases in which

the relationship of similarity between the specific varieties of spirits remains doubtful or contested.

13. It appears from the foregoing that . . . [Article 110], taken as a whole, may apply without distinction to all the products concerned. It is sufficient therefore to examine whether the application of a given national tax system is discriminatory or, as the case may be, protective, in other words whether there is a difference in the rate or the detailed rules for levying the tax and whether that difference is likely to favour a given national production.

. . .

39. The Court deems it unnecessary for the purposes of solving this dispute to give a ruling on the question whether or not the spirituous beverages concerned are wholly or partially similar products within the meaning of the first paragraph of . . . [Article 110] when it is impossible reasonably to contest that without exception they are in at least partial competition with the domestic products to which the application refers and that it is impossible to deny the protective nature of the French tax system within the second paragraph of . . . [Article 110].

40. In fact, as indicated above, spirits obtained from cereals have, as products obtained from distillation, sufficient characteristics in common with other spirits to constitute at least in certain circumstances an alternative choice for consumers . . .

41. As the competitive and substitution relationships between the beverages in question are such, the protective nature of the tax system criticised by the Commission is clear. A characteristic of that system is in fact that an essential part of domestic production, . . . spirits obtained from wine and fruit, come within the most favourable tax category whereas at least two types of product, almost all of which are imported from other Member States, are subject to higher taxation under the 'manufacturing tax'.

In the above case, the Court of Justice considered that classification into the first or second paragraph of what is now Art 110 TFEU was difficult (para 12). It also stated that the end result would be the same. At para 39 the Court concluded that the tax would fail, notwithstanding that the spirits were not similar, because they were to some degree in competition with one another and the tax was protective. The Court therefore got around the problem of classification.

However, this failure by the Court creates a problem for the defaulting Member State which will need to take remedial action to remedy the breach. If the tax is in breach of Art 110(1) TFEU, the tax must be equalised. However, if the tax is in breach of Art 110(2) TFEU, the *protective effect* must be eliminated; this does not necessarily require the tax to be equalised. The concept of *protective effect* is considered below, but suffice to note at this stage that in its later judgments the Court has distinguished between the two paragraphs.

Article 110(2) TFEU: protective effect

One of the early 'alcohol' cases brought by the Commission was against the UK with regard to the discriminatory taxation of wine in comparison with beer (***Commission v UK*** (Case 170/78)). There is quite clearly a greater difference between the objective characteristics of beer and wine than there is between two spirits. Beer and wine were not considered to be *similar* within the meaning of what is now Art 110(1) TFEU and therefore the Court of Justice proceeded under what is now Art 110(2) TFEU. This case provides an insight into how the Court of Justice approaches the application of Art 110(2) TFEU:

Commission v *UK* (Case 170/78)

The UK levied a tax on certain wines, which was about five times that levied on beer in terms of 'volume'. The tax on wine represented about 38 per cent of its sale price compared to 25 per cent for beer. The UK produced vast amounts of beer, but very little wine. The Commission took infraction proceedings against the UK pursuant to what is now Art 258 TFEU (previously Art 226 EC Treaty) claiming the differential UK tax breached what is now Art 110(2) TFEU (previously Art 90(2) EC Treaty). Following an adjournment while further evidence was gathered relating to the competitive relationship between beer and wine, the Court held as follows:

8. As regards the question of competition between wine and beer, the Court considered that, to a certain extent at least, the two beverages in question were capable of meeting identical needs, so that it had to be acknowledged that there was a degree of substitution for one another. It pointed out that, for the purpose of measuring the possible degree of substitution, attention should not be confined to consumer habits in a Member State or in a given region. Those habits, which were essentially variable in time and space, could not be considered immutable; the tax policy of a Member State must not therefore crystallise given consumer habits so as to consolidate an advantage acquired by national industries concerned to respond to them.

9. The Court nonetheless recognised that, in view of the substantial differences between wine and beer, it was difficult to compare the manufacturing processes and the natural properties of those beverages, as the Government of the UK had rightly observed. For that reason, the Court requested the parties to provide additional information with a view to dispelling the doubts which existed concerning the nature of the competitive relationship between the two products.

    . . .

11. The Italian Government contended in that connection that it was inappropriate to compare beer with wines of average alcoholic strength or, *a fortiori*, with wines of greater alcoholic strength. In its opinion, it was the lightest wines with an alcoholic strength in the region of 9, that is to say the most popular and cheapest wines, which were genuinely in competition with beer. It therefore took the view that those wines should be chosen for purposes of comparison where it was a question of measuring the incidence of taxation on the basis of either alcoholic strength or the price of the products.

12. The Court considers that observation by the Italian Government to be pertinent. **In view of the substantial differences in the quality and, therefore, in the price of wines, the decisive competitive relationship between beer, a popular and widely consumed beverage, and wine must be established by reference to those wines which are the most accessible to the public at large, that is to say, generally speaking the lightest and cheapest varieties. Accordingly, that is the appropriate basis for making fiscal comparisons by reference to the alcoholic strength or to the price of the two beverages.**

    . . .

19. It is not disputed that comparison of the taxation of beer and wine by reference to the volume of the two beverages reveals that wine is taxed more heavily than beer in both relative and real terms. Not only was the taxation of wine increased substantially in relation to the taxation of beer when the UK replaced customs duty with excise duty . . . but it is also clear that during the years to which those proceedings relate, namely 1976 and 1977, the taxation of wine was, on average, five times higher, by reference to volume, than the taxation of beer; in other words wine was subject to an additional tax of 400% in round figures.

20. As regards the criterion for comparison based on alcoholic strength . . .
21. In the light of the indices which the Court has already accepted, it is clear that in the UK during the period in question wine bore a tax burden which, by reference to alcoholic strength, was more than twice as heavy as that borne by beer, that is to say an additional tax burden of at least 100%.
22. As regards the criterion of the incidence of taxation on the price net of tax, the Court experienced considerable difficulty in forming an opinion, in view of the disparate nature of the information provided by the parties.

    . . .

26. After considering the information provided by the parties, the Court has come to the conclusion that, if a comparison is made on the basis of those wines which are cheaper than the types of wine selected by the UK and of which several varieties are sold in significant quantities on the UK market, it becomes apparent that precisely those wines which, in view of their price, are most directly in competition with domestic beer pro-duction are subject to a considerably higher tax burden.
27. **It is clear, therefore, following the detailed inquiry conducted by the Court – whatever criterion for comparison is used, there being no need to express a preference for one or the other – that the UK's tax system has the effect of subjecting wine imported from other Member States to an additional burden so as to afford protection to domestic beer production, inasmuch as beer production constitutes the most relevant reference criterion from the point of view of competition.** Since such protection is most marked in the case of the most popular wines, the effect of the UK tax system is to stamp wine with the hallmarks of a luxury product which, in view of the tax burden which it bears, can scarcely constitute in the eyes of the consumer a genuine alternative to the typically produced domestic beverage.
28. It follows from the foregoing considerations that, by levying excise duty on still light wines made from fresh grapes at a higher rate, in relative terms, than on beer, the UK has failed to fulfil its obligations under the second paragraph of . . . [Article 110 TFEU]. [emphasis added]

In the above case, the Court of Justice carried out a two-stage process to determine whether the UK had breached what is now Art 110(2) TFEU:

1 The Court sought to establish some competitive relationship between the two products to ascertain if Art 110(2) TFEU could be applicable at all (paras 8–12). In considering this issue, the Court took account of the extent to which the goods were substitutable for each other; i.e. whether they had a high or low degree of cross-elasticity. In consider-ing whether or not the goods are substitutable, the Court will ignore current consumer perceptions, because such perceptions can change over a period of time. Indeed, the consumer may be affected because of the differential tax on the two products. This may deter the consumer from purchasing the more heavily taxed product. At para 27, the Court declared that the UK's taxation of cheap wine was to stamp it with the hallmark of a luxury product. If there is a competitive relationship between the two products the Court will also examine the nature of this competition. In this case the nature of the competition was held to be between beer and the cheaper, lighter wines (rather than the more expensive, heavier wines).

2 Having established a competitive relationship between the two products, the Court will ascertain whether the tax system is in fact protective of the domestically produced

goods. In this case it was quite clear that the differential rates had a protective effect on beer. Tax on wine was greater than that levied on beer in the following proportions: (i) 400 per cent by reference to 'volume'; and (ii) 100 per cent by reference to 'alcoholic strength'. However, the difference in the level of taxation may not be that great. The Court may therefore be faced with a much more difficult task. Much will depend on the degree of cross-elasticity between the two products. If this is low then a small tax differential will probably make no difference, whereas if it is high, the level of taxation may be of critical importance to the consumer. Alternatively, although the differential rate of tax between the two products may be high in percentage terms, it may only form a very low proportion of the final selling price. For example, in the UK beer and wine case, if the tax on beer had been 2p per litre compared to 8p per litre on wine then, by volume, the tax on wine is 400 per cent greater than that on beer. However, the level of tax is low with respect to the final selling price of the products and therefore the level of taxation is unlikely to have a protective effect on domestic beer producers (i.e. the tax difference alone would be unlikely to deter a beer drinker from switching to wine).

This two-stage process can be seen in the following two cases:

FG Roders BV and Others v Inspecteur der Invoerrechten en Accijnzen (Joined Cases C-367 and 377/93)

The Court of Justice conceded that fruit wine produced in the Benelux countries was not similar to imported sherry, madeira, vermouth and champagne. However, the Court recognised that these products might, nevertheless, be in competition with fruit wine, and the differential tax structure might, therefore, favour home-produced fruit wine. The Court observed that the existence of a competitive relationship between the products had to be considered to establish whether or not there was a breach of what is now Art 110(2) TFEU. The essential question was whether the charge imposed was of such a kind as to have the effect, on the market in question, of reducing potential consumption of the imported products. The national court that has to make the final decision must have regard to the difference between the selling prices of the products in question and the impact of that difference on the consumer's choice, as well as to changes in the consumption of those products.

Commission v Italy (Case 184/85)

The facts of this case were considered above. The Court of Justice decided that bananas were not similar to other fruit and therefore the former Art 90(1) EC Treaty (now Art 110(1) TFEU) did not apply. However, the Court decided that there was a competitive relationship between bananas and other fruit, and went on to consider whether the Italian consumption tax levied on bananas, but not on other home-grown fruit, had a protective effect. It held that it did have a protective effect, because the tax levied on bananas was almost half their import price, while no tax was levied on almost all Italian-grown fruit. This was clear evidence of protectionism, contrary to the former Art 90(2) EC Treaty (now Art 110(2) TFEU).

However, as stated above, the fact that there is a tax differential between domestic and imported goods will not automatically result in protectionism being established, as illustrated in the following case:

Commission v Belgium (Case 356/85)

Belgium levied a tax on beer, which was produced in Belgium, and a tax on wine, which was mostly imported. There was a 6 per cent difference in the tax levied, wine being taxed more heavily. The Court of Justice held that this did not have a protective effect because the cost of the two products differed substantially, and therefore a relatively minor difference in the tax rates would not serve to protect the Belgian beer producers.

The fact that tax is imposed on a product which is not produced in the importing state and for which there is no domestic equivalent may well mean that there is no breach of Art 110 TFEU, as there will be no similar product in relation to which discrimination can be alleged for which the home market can be protected (*Fink-Frucht v HZA München-Landsbergerstrasse* (Case 27/67)).

Figure 17.2 consists of a flowchart setting out the application of Art 110 TFEU.

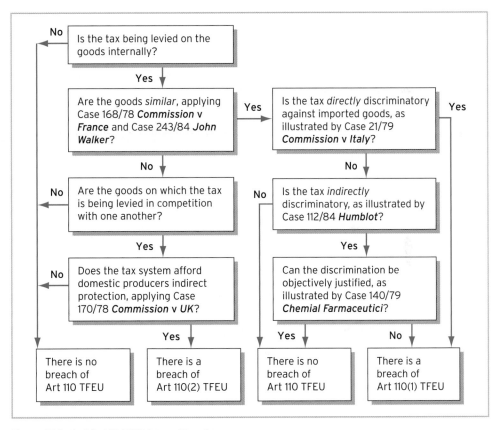

Figure 17.2 Article 110 TFEU: internal taxation

Summary

Now you have read this chapter you should be able to:

● Identify the ways in which the free movement of goods can be hindered and made more difficult.

- Understand how to differentiate between a customs duty and a charge having an equivalent effect to a customs duty and explain the provisions of Arts 28 and 30 TFEU which regulate such duties and charges.
- Explain the provisions of Art 110 TFEU which apply to internal taxation.
- Understand how internal taxation which is levied on goods which are similar (pursuant to Art 110(1) TFEU) is treated differently from the situation where the effect of the internal taxation affords an indirect protection to domestically produced goods (pursuant to Art 110(2) TFEU).

Further reading

Textbooks

Barnard, C. (2013) *The Substantive Law of the EU: The Four Freedoms* (4th edn), Oxford University Press, Chapters 2 and 3.

Craig, P. and De Burca, G. (2011) *EU Law: Text, Cases and Materials* (5th edn), Oxford University Press, Chapter 18.

Foster, N. (2015) *Foster on EU Law* (5th edn), Oxford University Press, Chapter 8.

Steiner, J. and Woods, L. (2014) *EU Law* (12th edn), Oxford University Press, Chapters 15 to 18.

Weatherill, S. (2014) *Cases and Materials on EU Law* (11th edn), Oxford University Press, Chapters 9 and 10.

Journal article

Tryfonidou, A., 'Further steps on the road to convergence among the market freedoms' (2010) 35 EL Rev 36.

18

The elimination of quantitative restrictions and measures having an equivalent effect

Objectives

At the end of this chapter you should understand:

1. The purpose and effect of Arts 34–36 TFEU.

2. How to distinguish between a quantitative restriction and a measure having an effect equivalent to a quantitative restriction.

3. The difference between a distinctly applicable measure and an indistinctly applicable measure.

4. How the law relating to indistinctly applicable measures is applied, how to differentiate between rules of dual-burden and those of equal-burden, and how to apply the *Keck* judgment.

5. The circumstances in which a Member State may rely upon Art 36 TFEU to defend a distinctly or indistinctly applicable measure.

6. How the *Cassis* rule of reason can be relied upon by a Member State to justify an indistinctly applicable measure.

An introduction to Articles 34–36 TFEU

Objective 1

At page 644 there is a flowchart which illustrates the application of Arts 34–36 TFEU.

The elimination of any restrictions on the free movement of goods is central to the creation of an internal market in the Member States of the Union, and this is one of the main objectives of the Union (Art 3 TEU (previously Art 3(1)(a) EC Treaty)). Article 34 TFEU (which is worded identically to the previous Art 28 EC Treaty) provides that:

> Quantitative **restrictions on imports** and all measures having equivalent effect shall be **prohibited** between Member States. [emphasis added]

The prohibition of restrictions on *imports* in Art 34 TFEU is reflected by a matching prohibition on *export* restrictions in Art 35 TFEU (previously Art 29 EC Treaty). Both prohibitions are, however, qualified by the right of Member States to impose limited restrictions on trade, if they can *justify* them under the criteria laid down in Art 36 TFEU (previously Art 30 EC Treaty), or in some cases under the *Cassis* rule of reason (see below). Articles 34–36 TFEU attempt to strike a balance between achieving a genuine free and competitive market in goods on the one hand, and the recognition of the need, in some circumstances, to protect essential public interests on the other. The process of harmonising national standards of consumer and environmental protection, through a programme of stand-ardising directives for goods throughout the Union, is part of a programme to reduce the need for such national exceptions to the general Union right of free movement of goods. Much of the jurisprudence of the Court of Justice has been devoted to consideration of the extent to which such national measures infringe the relevant provisions of the Treaty or fall within the permitted derogations.

Articles 34 and 35 TFEU adopt the same approach as has been adopted for the prohibi-tions set out in Arts 28 and 30 TFEU (previously Arts 23 and 25 EC Treaty); see Chapter 17. They are aimed at measures which are clearly directed at imports from, and exports to, other Member States, but they also prohibit measures which have the same effect as such restric-tions, even though there may be no intention by the Member State imposing them to have that effect. Articles 34 and 35 TFEU are directly effective. Any state measure breaching them can give rise to a claim in damages against the Member State concerned, provided that the criteria laid down by the Court of Justice in *Brasserie du Pêcheur* (Case C-46/93) in rela-tion to imports and *R v Ministry of Agriculture Fisheries and Food, ex parte Hedley Lomas Ireland Ltd* (Case C-5/94) in relation to exports can be met (see Chapter 9). Articles 34 and 35 TFEU are directed at the state. Therefore they cannot be used by private individuals against each other. They may, however, be used by individuals as a defence in civil proceed-ings where the national law is alleged to breach Arts 34 or 35 TFEU (*Vereinigte Familiapress Zeitungsverlags und Vertriebs GmbH v Heinrich Bauer Verlag* (Case C-368/95)).

See pages 272–292 and 303–305 for an explanation of the principle of direct effect and pages 292–300 for an explanation of the principle of state liability.

The prohibition on restrictions affects all types of products, including agricultural pro-duce, and it applies not only to goods which originate in the Member States but also to goods which come from third countries (i.e. non-Member States) and which are in free cir-culation in a Member State. Such goods are in free circulation when they have crossed the Common External Tariff wall, with all import formalities complied with and duties and charges paid (Art 29 TFEU; see Chapter 17).

For the purpose of Arts 34–36 TFEU, the Court of Justice has held that 'goods' are 'man-ufactured material objects' (*Cinéthèque* (Cases 60 and 61/84)). The term is wide enough to include not only plants, vegetables, fruit and livestock and a whole variety of animal products (*Société Civile Agricole* (Case C-323/93)), but also even covers generated electric-ity (*Commission v Netherlands* (Case C-157/94)). The context in which an item is applied may, however, result in it being regarded not as a product in itself subject to the provisions of Arts 34–36 TFEU, but as an incident to the provision of a service, and thus subject to Art 56 TFEU (previously Art 49 EC Treaty); *HM Customs and Excise Commissioners v Schindler* (Case C-275/92), para 23. Coins and banknotes or bearer cheques are not 'goods', as their transfer is subject to the rules on transfer of capital under Art 63 TFEU (previously Art 56 EC Treaty); *Aldo Bordessa and Others* (Joined Cases C-358 and 416/93). However, in *R v Thompson* (Case 7/78), the Court of Justice held that old gold coins were 'goods' because they were not a normal means of payment.

Articles 34–36 TFEU are considered in greater detail throughout the remainder of this chapter.

State measures

Articles 34 and 35 TFEU are directed at the governments of Member States. They apply only to measures adopted by the state and not measures taken by private parties. However, the provisions of Art 34 TFEU have also been held by the Court of Justice to be binding on the institutions of the Union. The Court has expressed the view that it would have been prepared to strike down a Council Regulation requiring Member States to gather information from importers and exporters, had it been satisfied that the regulation imposed a disproportionately heavy burden on the free movement of goods (*Rene Kieffer and Romain Thill* (Case C-114/96)).

The prohibition of customs duties and discriminatory internal taxes imposed by Member States has already been considered in Chapter 17. Articles 34–36 TFEU form part of a larger strategy to free up trade and to prevent Member States from adopting both overt and covert protectionist policies. The same strategy also includes the regulation of state monopolies of a commercial character under Art 37 TFEU (previously Art 31 EC Treaty) and state aids to nationalised industries under Arts 107–108 TFEU (previously Arts 87–88 EC Treaty); see Chapter 19. It underlies Union legislation on public procurement, which is intended to prevent the governments of Member States from favouring national contractors in the award of public works contracts. For that reason, attempts by a private undertaking to persuade consumers to buy national products in, say, a 'Buy UK' advertising campaign will not breach Art 34 TFEU, although such a campaign would infringe Art 34 if promoted by a public, or publicly sponsored, body (*Apple and Pear Development Council v K.J. Lewis Ltd* (Case 222/82), see below).

So what exactly constitutes a *state* measure for the purposes of Arts 34 and 35 TFEU? This question was considered by the Court of Justice in the following case:

Commission v *Ireland* (Case 249/81)

The Irish government embarked upon a 'Buy Irish' campaign. In 1978, the Irish government introduced a three-year programme to help promote Irish products. The campaign was launched by a speech delivered by the Irish Minister for Industry, Commerce and Energy. A number of measures were adopted, of which two were carried out: (i) the encouragement of the use of a 'Buy Irish' symbol for goods made in Ireland; and (ii) the organisation of a publicity campaign by the Irish Goods Council in favour of Irish products, designed to encourage consumers to buy Irish products.

The Commission brought proceedings under what is now Art 258 TFEU (previously Art 226 EC Treaty), against the Irish government, alleging the campaign was a measure equivalent to a quantitative restriction and therefore in breach of what is now Art 34 TFEU (previously Art 28 EC Treaty). Ireland defended the action on the ground it had never adopted 'measures' for the purpose of what is now Art 34 TFEU; it was the Irish Goods Council. It argued that any financial assistance it had given to the Council should be judged under what are now Arts 107–108 TFEU (previously Arts 92–93 EC Treaty), relating to aids granted by states, and not under what is now Art 34 TFEU. The members of the Irish Goods Council were appointed by the Irish government and it was funded in proportions of 6:1 by the government and private industry, respectively. The initial question to be considered by the Court of Justice was whether or not the campaign constituted a *measure* undertaken *by the state*. The Court of Justice held as follows:

15. It is thus apparent that the Irish Government appoints the members of the Management Committee of the Irish Goods Council, grants it public subsidies which cover the greater part of its expenses and, finally, defines the aims and the broad outline of the campaign conducted by that institution to promote the sale and purchase of Irish products. In the circumstances the Irish Government cannot rely on the fact that the campaign was conducted by a private company in order to escape any liability it may have under the provisions of the Treaty.

...

21. The Irish Government maintains that the prohibition against measures having an effect equivalent to quantitative restrictions in . . . [Article 34 TFEU] is concerned only with 'measures', that is to say, binding provisions emanating from a public authority. However, no such provision has been adopted by the Irish Government, which has confined itself to giving moral support and financial aid to the activities pursued by the Irish industries.

. . .

23. . . . the campaign is a reflection of the Irish Government's considered intention to substitute domestic products for imported products on the Irish market and thereby check the flow of imports from other Member States. It must be remembered here that a representative of the Irish Government stated when the campaign was launched that it was a carefully thought-out set of initiatives constituting an integrated programme for promoting domestic products; that the Irish Goods Council was set up at the initiative of the Irish Government a few months later; and that the task of implementing the integrated programme as it was envisaged by the Government was entrusted, or left, to that Council.

. . .

28. Such a practice cannot escape the prohibition laid down by . . . [Article 34 TFEU] solely because it is not based on decisions which are binding upon undertakings. Even measures adopted by the government of a Member State which do not have binding effect may be capable of influencing the conduct of traders and consumers in that state and thus of frustrating the aims of the Community [i.e. Union].

In the above case, the Court of Justice considered the involvement of the Irish government with the Irish Goods Council at para 15. At paras 21 and 28, the Court rebutted the Irish argument that only formally binding measures are caught by what is now Art 34 TFEU.

The principle established in the above case was developed further by the Court of Justice in the following case:

Apple and Pear Development Council v *K.J. Lewis Ltd* (Case 222/82)

There was a statutory obligation on the growers of fruit to pay a levy to the Development Council. This statutory underpinning was sufficient to bring it within the scope of a state entity for the purposes of what is now Art 34 TFEU (previously Art 28 EC Treaty). As the Court of Justice stated:

. . . a body such as the Development Council, which is set up by the government of a Member State and is financed by a charge imposed on growers, cannot under Community [i.e. Union] law enjoy the same freedom as regards the methods of advertising used as that enjoyed by producers themselves or producers' associations of a voluntary character.

The Court of Justice stated that what is now Art 34 TFEU imposed on the Development Council 'a duty not to engage in any advertising intended to discourage the purchase of products from other Member States or to disparage those products in the eyes of consumers. Nor must it advise consumers to purchase domestic products solely by reason of their national origin' (para 18).

Similarly, in the following case:

R v *Royal Pharmaceutical Society, Ex Parte Api* (Cases 266 and 267/87)

The Royal Pharmaceutical Society was an independent body which had the responsibility for the regulation of standards among UK pharmacists. In order to practise, a pharmacist had to appear on the Society's register. The Society had certain statutory functions under the Pharmacy Act 1954. The Court of Justice held that the Society had a sufficient measure of state support or 'statutory underpinning' to constitute it a state entity for the purposes of what is now Art 34 TFEU (previously Art 28 EC Treaty). Accordingly, the Society was bound by what is now Art 34 TFEU. The Court therefore held that rules of the society, which required pharmacists to supply, under a prescription, only a named branded drug, were *prima facie* in breach of what is now Art 34 TFEU.

It is, of course, not only the state and public bodies which may, either directly or indirectly, seek to exclude foreign competition. Articles 34–36 TFEU must also be considered in the light of Arts 101 and 102 TFEU (previously Arts 81 and 82 EC Treaty), which play an important part in preventing national cartels and national monopolies from using private economic power to keep goods from other Member States from entering national markets (see Chapters 20 and 21). Where the private body enjoys a monopoly conferred on it by the state, which enables it to restrict the import of foreign products by virtue of that monopoly, there may be an overlap between Arts 34 and 102 TFEU. In such circumstances, the state may be liable for maintaining a situation which has the effect of excluding products from other Member States in breach of Art 34 TFEU, or an unlawful state monopoly in breach of Art 37 TFEU; *Harry Franzen* (Case C-189/95) and *Société Civile Agricole v Coopérative d'Elevage de la Mayenne* (Case C-323/93), and see also Chapter 19.

If the measure has been adopted by the state, the next issue to be determined, within the context of Art 34 TFEU, is whether the measure constitutes a **quantitative restriction (QR)** or a **measure having equivalent effect to a quantitative restriction (MEQR)**.

Quantitative restrictions (QRs)

Objective
2

Direct restrictions, such as quotas and bans on certain products of other Member States, were abolished or phased out in the early days of the Union and during transitional periods following the admission of new Member States. The concept of 'quantitative restrictions' (QR) is straightforward enough: in *Geddo v Ente Nazionale Risi* (Case 2/73), the Court of Justice stated that:

> The prohibition on quantitative restrictions covers measures which amount to a total or partial restraint of, according to the circumstances, imports, exports, or goods in transit.

The concept of quantitative restrictions therefore applies to an outright ban (e.g. a French ban on UK beef) or the imposition of a quota (e.g. a numerical restriction on the number of vehicles which can be imported into Spain each year from Germany). The following case provides a rare example of a quantitative restriction which is, *prima facie*, in breach of the former Art 28 EC Treaty (now Art 34 TFEU):

Klas Rosengren and Others v Riksåklagaren (Case C-170/04)

Under the Swedish Law on alcohol, retail sales of alcoholic beverages in Sweden were carried out under a monopoly held by Systembolaget. Only Systembolaget and wholesalers authorised by the state could import alcoholic beverages. Private individuals were prohibited from importing alcoholic beverages. That prohibition meant that a person wishing to import alcohol from other Member States had to do so exclusively through Systembolaget. Systembolaget was required to obtain any alcoholic beverage on request at the consumer's expense, provided that it saw no objection to doing so.

> Rosengren and several other Swedish nationals ordered, by correspondence, cases of bottles of Spanish wine. The wine was imported into Sweden, without being declared to customs, by a private transporter. The wine was then confiscated by the customs authorities at Göteborg (in Sweden). Criminal proceedings were brought against Mr Rosengren and other individuals for unlawful importation of alcoholic beverages. The Högsta domstolen (Swedish Supreme Court), dealing with the case at final instance, asked the Court of Justice, pursuant to a reference for a preliminary ruling pursuant to the former Art 234 EC Treaty (now Art 267 TFEU), whether the provisions of the Swedish legislation were compatible with Union law, in particular with the former Art 28 EC Treaty (now Art 34 TFEU).
>
> **The Court of Justice held that the fact that Systembolaget may refuse an order from a consumer to import alcoholic beverages amounts to a quantitative restriction on imports.**
>
> Furthermore, the Court stated that consumers, when making use of the services of Systembolaget to secure the importation of alcoholic beverages, faced a variety of inconveniences with which they would not be faced if they imported the beverages themselves. Above all, independently of administrative or logistical questions, it appeared that for all importations the price demanded of the purchaser included, in addition to the cost of the beverages invoiced by the supplier, the reimbursement of administrative and transport costs paid by Systembolaget and a margin of 17 per cent which, in principle, the purchaser would not have had to pay if he had directly imported those goods himself.
>
> Consequently, **the Court of Justice held that the fact that private individuals were prohibited from importing alcoholic beverages amounted to a quantitative restriction on the free movement of goods, contrary to the former Art 28 EC Treaty (now Art 34 TFEU).**

Some national prohibitions do survive, such as the prohibition on the importation of obscene materials into the UK under the Customs Consolidation Act 1876. It was argued by the UK government in *R v Henn and Darby* (Case 34/79) that a ban on the import of pornographic material under the Act was not a quantitative restriction under what is now Art 34 TFEU. The Court of Justice disagreed, in a reference pursuant to what is now Art 267 TFEU (previously Art 234 EC Treaty). It held that what is now Art 34 TFEU 'includes such a prohibition on imports in as much as this is the most extreme form of restriction'. The reference in Art 34 TFEU to 'quantitative restrictions' was to be read in the light of what is now Art 36 TFEU, which refers also to 'prohibitions' on imports. In the event, the Court held that the prohibition in this case was justified under what is now Art 36 TFEU. That aspect of the case is discussed below.

Although a quantitative restriction is readily recognisable, measures having an equivalent effect to quantitative restrictions on imports have proved much more elusive and have resulted in a large, and growing, jurisprudence on the subject by the Court of Justice.

Measures having equivalent effect to quantitative restrictions (MEQRs)

The *Dassonville* formula

In addition to prohibiting quantitative restrictions, Art 34 TFEU also prohibits 'measures having [an] equivalent effect' to quantitative restrictions (**MEQRs**). In the following case, the Court of Justice considered the scope of what is now Art 34 TFEU in relation to MEQRs, and provided a very useful definition (referred to as the *Dassonville* formula) of exactly what constitutes an MEQR:

Procureur Du Roi v *Dassonville* (Case 8/74)

A Belgian importer of Scotch whisky was prosecuted for selling whisky with false certificates of origin. He had imported the whisky from France and it had been difficult to obtain the certificates from the producers. He argued that the Belgian law infringed what is now Art 34 TFEU (previously Art 28 EC Treaty), in that it made the importation of whisky from anywhere other than the state of origin more difficult. The Belgian court referred the case to the Court of Justice under what is now Art 267 TFEU (previously Art 234 EC Treaty). The Court of Justice held as follows:

2. By the first question it is asked whether a national provision prohibiting the import of goods bearing a designation of origin where such goods are not accompanied by an official document issued by the government of the exporting country certifying their right to such designation constitutes a measure having an effect equivalent to a quantitative restriction within the meaning of . . . [Article 34 TFEU].

3. This question was raised within the context of criminal proceedings instituted in Belgium against traders who duly acquired a consignment of Scotch whisky in free circulation in France and imported it into Belgium without being in possession of a certificate of origin from the UK customs authorities, thereby infringing Belgian rules.

4. It emerges from the file and from the oral proceedings that a trader, wishing to import into Belgium Scotch whisky which is already in free circulation in France, can obtain such a certificate only with great difficulty, unlike the importer who imports directly from the producer country.

5. **All trading rules enacted by Member States which are capable of hindering, directly or indirectly, actually or potentially, intra-Community [i.e. intra-Union] trade are to be considered as measures having an effect equivalent to quantitative restrictions.**

. . .

9. Consequently, the requirement by a Member State of a certificate of authenticity which is less easily obtainable by importers of an authentic product which has been put into free circulation in a regular manner in another Member State than by importers of the same product coming directly from the country of origin constitutes a measure having an effect equivalent to a quantitative restriction as prohibited by the Treaty. [emphasis added]

It is clear from the Court of Justice's definition of an MEQR at para 5 of the above case that the crucial element in proving the existence of an MEQR is its *effect*; a discriminatory *intent* is not required. This is a very broad definition (the ***Dassonville*** formula) which, as is discussed below, indicates a determination by the Court of Justice to ensure that very few measures will be permitted to hinder the free movement of goods between Member States.

Directive 70/50

Directive 70/50, issued in December 1969, was intended to provide guidance on the kind of acts and activities which constituted 'measures' infringing what is now Art 34 TFEU, and which were in existence when the original Treaty came into force. It was formally only of application during the Member States' transitional period, yet it has been very influential in representing the Commission's view of the scope of Art 34 TFEU. It is still on occasion referred to by the Court of Justice. Although many measures will have been made since that time, and will be outside the directive's scope, it still has value in identifying prohibited acts or conduct.

Article 2, Directive 70/50 covers measures 'other than those applicable equally to domestic or imported products, which hinder imports which could otherwise take place, including measures which make importation more difficult or costly than the disposal of domestic products'. Article 2 is thus concerned with national measures which apply specifically to, or affect only, imported goods. These are often referred to as 'distinctly applicable measures', because they explicitly *distinguish* between imported and domestically produced goods (see below). Article 2, Directive 70/50 contains a non-exhaustive list of the sort of measures applied to imported goods which would constitute MEQRs. They include:

- the laying down of minimum and maximum sale prices;
- the fixing of less favourable prices for imported than for domestically produced goods;
- the exclusion of prices for imported goods which reflect importation costs;
- the making of access to markets in the importing state dependent upon having an agent there;
- the laying down of conditions of payment in respect of imported products only, or the subjection of imported goods to conditions which are different from those laid down for domestic products and are more difficult to satisfy;
- requiring, for imported goods only, the giving of guarantees or the making of payment on account;
- subjecting only imported products to conditions in respect of shape, size, weight, composition, presentation and identification, or subjecting imported products to conditions which are different from those for domestic products and more difficult to satisfy;
- hindering the purchase by individuals of imported products only, or encouraging, requiring or giving preference to the purchase of domestic products only;
- the total or partial preclusion of the use of national facilities or equipment in respect of imported products only, or the total or partial confinement of such facilities to national producers;
- the prohibition or limitation of publicity in respect of imported products only, or the total or partial restriction of publicity to home-produced products.

The above list is indicative of the sort of national measures which will constitute MEQRs, but the ability of Member States to introduce measures which are either intended to protect, or will have the effect of protecting, domestically produced goods can neither be anticipated nor underestimated. The Court has laid down a number of general principles about measures which specifically affect imported goods and which constitute MEQRs. Each national measure will have to be assessed against these principles as and when the measure comes before a national court or the Court of Justice.

Article 3, Directive 70/50 also refers to measures which are applied to both domestic and imported goods which may, nonetheless, have the effect of impeding imports. These are referred to as 'indistinctly applicable measures' (see below).

Distinctly applicable measures are now considered in further detail, followed by indistinctly applicable measures.

Distinctly applicable measures

Objective
3

Distinctly applicable measures, as stated above, are measures which are applied only to imported or exported goods; the measure is not applied to domestically produced goods.

Hence the reason for them being referred to as 'distinctly applicable measures', i.e. measures which explicitly *distinguish* between domestic and foreign goods.

There are many examples where the Court of Justice has struck down national rules which apply only to imported or exported goods. Some specific categories are now considered further.

Import and export restrictions

The *Dassonville* formula is set out at pages 588–589.

In *International Fruit Company* v *Produktschap voor Groenten en Fruit (No. 2)* (Cases 51–54/71), the Court of Justice held that import or export licences are caught by what are now Arts 34 and 35 TFEU because, applying *Dassonville*, such a measure is 'capable of hindering, directly or indirectly, actually or potentially, intra-Community [i.e. intra-Union] trade'. The necessity to apply for a licence before goods can be imported into a Member State, or exported out of a Member State, has a threefold impact: (i) until the licence application has been processed, goods cannot be imported or exported (and therefore this in effect constitutes a ban); (ii) the application could be rejected; and (iii) the very fact of having to apply for a licence will require additional paperwork to be completed by the importer or exporter. Completing the paperwork will cost time and money, and this additional cost will have to be accounted for when determining the price of the goods. Increasing the cost of the goods could decrease their competitiveness with domestically produced goods, and therefore the measure is capable of affecting trade within the Union.

In *Commission* v *Italy* (Case 154/85), Italy had procedures and data requirements which applied only to the importation of cars, which meant that their registration was longer, more complicated and more expensive, compared to the registration of domestic cars. The Court of Justice held that such procedures and requirements were prohibited under what is now Art 34 TFEU.

In *Rewe-Zentralfinanz* v *Landwirtschaftskammer* (Case 4/75), phyto-sanitary inspections on imported apples contravened what is now Art 34 TFEU because there were no similar inspections of domestically grown apples. The Court of Justice stressed the fact that border inspections made imports more difficult and costly.

In *Procureur de la République Besançon* v *Bouhelier* (Case 53/76), the same approach was applied to discriminatory export rules. This case concerned a French rule which imposed quality checks on watches for export, but there was no similar inspection of those intended for the domestic market. The Court of Justice held such inspections contravened what is now Art 35 TFEU.

In the following case, the Court of Justice held that a *failure to act* by a Member State could constitute an infringement of what is now Art 34 TFEU:

Commission v *France* (Case C-265/95)

Fruit and vegetables imported into France from other Member States were targeted by French farmers, who would obstruct their passage, preventing them from reaching their final destination. For more than a decade, the Commission had received complaints concerning the inactivity of the French authorities in the face of violent acts by the French farmers. From April to July 1993, that campaign was directed particularly at strawberries originating in Spain. In August and September 1993, tomatoes from Belgium were treated in the same way. In 1994, the same type of action, involving threats against shopping centres and destruction of goods and means of transport, was directed against Spanish strawberries in particular. On 20 April 1995, further serious incidents occurred in the south-west of France, in the course of which agricultural products from Spain were destroyed. On 3 June 1995, three lorries transporting fruit and vegetables from Spain were the subject of acts of violence in the south of France, without any intervention by the police.

At the beginning of July 1995, Italian and Spanish fruit was once again destroyed by French farmers. Further serious incidents of the same type occurred in 1996 and 1997. It was not denied by France that when such incidents occurred the French police were either not present on the spot, despite the fact that in certain cases the competent authorities had been warned of the imminence of demonstration by the French farmers, or they simply failed to intervene, even where the police far outnumbered the French farmers. As regards the numerous acts of vandalism committed between April and August 1993, the French authorities could cite only a single case of criminal prosecution.

The Commission took action against France, arguing that its failure to act impeded the free movement of goods imported from other Member States and constituted a breach of what is now Art 34 TFEU (previously Art 28 EC Treaty). The Court of Justice held as follows:

> In the light of all the foregoing factors, the Court, while not discounting the difficulties faced by the competent authorities in dealing with situations of the type in question in this case, cannot but find that, having regard to the frequency and seriousness of the incidents cited by the Commission, the measures adopted by the French Government were manifestly inadequate to ensure freedom of intra-Community [i.e. intra-Union] trade in agricultural products on its territory by preventing and effectively dissuading the perpetrators of the offences in question from committing and repeating them.
>
> Although it is not impossible that the threat of serious disruption to public order may, in appropriate cases, justify non-intervention by the police, that argument can, on any view, be put forward only with respect to a specific incident and not, as in this case, in a general way covering all the incidents cited by the Commission . . .
>
> It must be concluded that in the present case the French Government has manifestly and persistently abstained from adopting appropriate and adequate measures to put an end to the acts of vandalism which jeopardise the free movement on its territory of certain agricultural products originating in other Member States and to prevent the recurrence of such acts . . .
>
> By failing to adopt all necessary and proportionate measures in order to prevent the free movement of fruit and vegetables from being obstructed by actions by private individuals, the French Republic has failed to fulfil its obligations under . . . [Article 34 TFEU].

The above case can be contrasted with the following case:

Schmidberger (Case C-112/00)

A demonstration in Austria resulted in the complete closure of a major transit route for a continuous period of almost 30 hours. The Court of Justice stated that a failure to ban such a demonstration is capable of restricting intra-Union trade in goods and must therefore be regarded as constituting a measure of equivalent effect to a quantitative restriction which is *prima facie* incompatible with the obligations arising from the former Arts 28 and 29 EC Treaty (now Arts 34 and 35 TFEU), read together with the former Art 10 EC Treaty (now Art 4(3) TEU), unless that failure to ban can be objectively justified.

The *Schmidberger* case can be distinguished from that of **Commission v France** (see above) in that *Schmidberger* concerned an **indistinctly applicable measure** (because the demonstration would affect both domestic and imported goods), whereas **Commission v France** concerned a **distinctly applicable measure** (because only imported goods were being targeted). *Schmidberger* will be considered below in the context of indistinctly applicable measures, but suffice to note here that the Court of Justice held that the failure to ban the demonstration was objectively justified (primarily to respect the fundamental rights of the demonstrators' freedom of expression and freedom of assembly, which are enshrined in and guaranteed by the European Convention on Human Rights and the Austrian Constitution). Of interest is that the Court of Justice pointed out differences between the facts of *Schmidberger* and those of *Commission v France*. The Court stated that in the latter case, France had failed to adopt all necessary and proportionate measures in order to prevent the free movement of fruit and vegetables from being obstructed by the actions of private individuals, such as the interception of lorries and the destruction of their loads, violence against lorry drivers and other threats. The Court found that in *Schmidberger*, unlike in *Commission v France*: (i) the demonstration at issue took place following authorisation; (ii) the obstacle to the free movement of goods resulting from that demonstration was limited; (iii) the purpose of that public demonstration was not to restrict trade in goods of a particular type or from a particular source; (iv) various administrative and supporting measures were taken by the competent authorities in order to limit as far as possible the disruption to road traffic; (v) the isolated incident in question did not give rise to a general climate of insecurity such as to have a dissuasive effect on intra-Union trade flows as a whole; and (vi) taking account of the Member States' wide margin of discretion, the competent national authorities were entitled to consider that an outright ban on the demonstration at issue would have constituted unacceptable interference with the fundamental rights of the demonstrators to gather and express peacefully their opinion in public.

Promotion of domestic goods

A Member State may promote or favour a domestic product to the detriment of competing imports, but this may be caught by Art 34 TFEU (previously Art 28 EC Treaty). An obvious example of this is where a Member State engages in a campaign to persuade consumers to purchase domestic rather than imported products. This is illustrated in the following case:

Commission v Ireland (Case 249/81)

The Irish government (through the Irish Goods Council) embarked upon a 'Buy Irish' campaign. The aim of the campaign was to achieve 'a switch from imports to Irish products equivalent to 3 per cent of total consumer spending'. The campaign was 'a carefully thought-out set of initiatives that add up to an integrated programme for promoting Irish goods, with specific proposals to involve the producer, distributor and consumer'. A number of measures were adopted, of which two were carried out: (i) the encouragement of the use of a 'Buy Irish' symbol for goods made in Ireland; and (ii) the organisation of a publicity campaign by the Irish Goods Council in favour of Irish products, designed to encourage consumers to buy Irish products. The Commission brought proceedings against the Irish government pursuant to what is now Art 258 TFEU (previously Art 226 EC Treaty), alleging the campaign was an MEQR. The Court of Justice held as follows:

22. The Irish Government goes on to emphasise that the campaign has had no restrictive effect on imports since the proportion of Irish goods to all goods sold on the Irish market fell from 49.2 per cent in 1977 to 43.4 per cent in 1980.

      . . .

25. Whilst it may be true that the two elements of the programme which have continued in effect, namely the advertising campaign and the use of the 'Guaranteed Irish' symbol,

have not had any significant success in winning over the Irish market to domestic products, it is not possible to overlook the fact that, regardless of their efficacy, those two activities form part of a government programme which is designed to achieve the substitution of domestic products for imported products and is liable to affect the volume of trade between Member States.

. . .

27. In the circumstances the two activities in question amount to the establishment of a national practice, introduced by the Irish Government and prosecuted with its assistance, the potential effect of which on imports from other Member States is comparable to that resulting from government measures of a binding nature.

. . .

29. That is the case where, as in this instance, such a restrictive practice represents the implementation of a programme defined by the government which affects the national economy as a whole and which is intended to check the flow of trade between Member States by encouraging the purchase of domestic products, by means of an advertising campaign on a national scale and the organisation of special procedures applicable solely to domestic products, and where those activities are attributed as a whole to the government and are pursued in an organised fashion throughout the national territory.

30. Ireland has therefore failed to fulfil its obligations under the Treaty by organising a campaign to promote the sale and purchase of Irish goods within its territory.

The Court of Justice's reasoning in the above case illustrates that, as concerns what is now Art 34 TFEU, the Court is more interested in *substance* than *form*. At para 25, the Court rejected the argument that because the campaign appeared to fail the Union law should be unconcerned with it. There is no need to prove that trade between Member States has *actually* been affected by the measure. Applying the **Dassonville** formula all that is necessary is for there to be the *possibility* of such an effect.

See pages 588–589 for an explanation of the *Dassonville* formula.

The Court of Justice remains very ready to assume that different treatment of imported goods may result in a reduced volume of sales. ***Lucien Ortscheit GmbH v Eurim-Pharm GmbH*** (Case C-320/93) concerned a German law prohibiting the advertising of foreign medicinal products which had not been authorised for sale in Germany but which could, nonetheless, still be imported into Germany. The German law was held to fall within the scope of what is now Art 34 TFEU because it did not have the same effect on the marketing of medicinal products from other Member States as on the marketing of national medicinal products. The Court added that the prohibition of advertising might restrict the volume of imports of medicinal products not authorised in Germany, because it deprived pharmacists and doctors of a source of information on the existence and availability of such products. It was, therefore, equivalent to a quantitative restriction.

In ***Commission v Germany*** (Case 12/74), the Court of Justice stated that it may be possible for origin-marking to be acceptable, where it implies a certain quality in the goods, that they were made from certain materials or by a particular form of manufacturing, or where the origin indicates a special place in the folklore or tradition of the particular region in question. However, this exception will be treated with caution by the Court, as illustrated in the following case:

Commission v Ireland (Case 113/80)

This case concerned Irish legislation which required imported articles of jewellery depicting motifs or possessing characteristics which suggested they were souvenirs of Ireland (e.g. an Irish character, event or scene; a wolfhound; a round tower or a shamrock) to bear an indication of their country of origin or the word 'foreign'. The Court of Justice held as follows:

1. By an application lodged at the Court Registry on 28 April 1980, the Commission instituted proceedings under . . . [Article 258 TFEU], for a declaration that Ireland had failed to fulfil its obligations under . . . [Article 34 TFEU] by requiring that the imported goods falling within the scope of the Merchandise Marks (Restrictions on Sale of Imported Jewellery) Order 1971 (SI No 306) . . . and the Merchandise Marks (Restriction on Importation of Jewellery) Order 1971 (SI No 307) . . . bear an indication of origin or the word 'foreign'.

2. According to the explanatory notes thereto, SI No 306 (hereinafter referred to as 'the Sale Order') prohibits the sale or exposure for sale of imported articles of jewellery depicting motifs or possessing characteristics which suggest that they are souvenirs of Ireland, for example an Irish character, event or scene, wolfhound, round tower, shamrock etc. and SI No 307 (hereinafter referred to as 'the Importation Order') prohibits the importation of such articles unless, in either case, they bear an indication of their country of origin or the word 'foreign'.

3. The articles concerned are listed in a schedule to each order. However, in order to come within the scope of the orders the article must be made of precious metal or rolled precious metal or of base metal, including polished or plated articles suitable for setting.

4. In the Commission's opinion, the restrictions on the free movement of the goods covered by the two orders constitute measures having an effect equivalent to quantitative restrictions on imports, contrary to the provisions of . . . [Article 34 TFEU]; it also observes that according to Article 2(3)(f) of Directive 70/50/EEC . . . 'measures which lower the value of an imported product, in particular by causing a reduction in its intrinsic value, or increase its costs' must be regarded as measures having an effect equivalent to quantitative restrictions, contrary to . . . [Article 34 TFEU].

   . . .

17. Thus by granting souvenirs imported from other Member States access to the domestic market solely on condition that they bear a statement of origin, whilst no such statement is required in the case of domestic products, the provisions contained in the Sale Order and the Importation Order indisputably constitute a discriminatory measure.

18. The conclusion to be drawn therefore is that by requiring all souvenirs and articles of jewellery imported from other Member States which are covered by the Sale Order and the Importation Order to bear an indication of origin or the word 'foreign', the Irish rules constitute a measure having equivalent effect within the meaning of . . . [Article 34 TFEU]. Ireland has consequently failed to fulfil its obligations under the article. [emphasis added]

However, not all measures which promote domestic goods will be caught by Art 34 TFEU, as illustrated in the following case:

Apple and Pear Development Council v K.J. Lewis Ltd (Case 222/82)

The Apple and Pear Development Council was set up by the UK government. It was financed by a mandatory charge imposed on UK fruit growers (the charge was calculated as a sum per hectare of land). Part of the Council's role was to market the goods. It brought actions against certain fruit growers who refused to pay the charge. The actions were defended on the basis that the charges were contrary to what is now Art 34 TFEU (previously Art 28 EC Treaty). The Court of Justice reiterated its decision in the above case, and then continued as follows:

> 18. . . . such a body [as the Council] is under a duty not to engage in any advertising intended to discourage the purchase of products of other Member States or to disparage those products in the eyes of consumers. Nor must it advise consumers to purchase domestic products solely by reason of their national origin.
>
> 19. On the other hand . . . [Article 34 TFEU] does not prevent such a body from drawing attention, in its publicity, to the specific qualities of fruit grown in the Member State in question or from organising campaigns to promote the sale of certain varieties, mentioning their particular properties, even if those varieties are typical of national production.

The above case provides that it is permissible for the government of a Member State to promote, for example, varieties of apples. The French may promote Golden Delicious apples, and may draw attention to the particular qualities of the apples. However, such promotion may overstep the boundary if the advertising is intended to discourage the purchase of imported products. This will be a fine line to draw in practice.

Two forms of national favour have been considered: (i) a national campaign to purchase domestic goods; and (ii) origin-marking. A third form, towards which the Court of Justice is equally harsh, occurs in the field of public procurement (i.e. public service contracts). In the following case, the Court of Justice held that a Member State which reserved a proportion of its public supplies to products which were made in a particular depressed region of the country automatically contravened what is now Art 34 TFEU because the measure impeded imports:

Du Pont De Nemours Italiana Spa v *Unità Sanitaria Locale No. 2 Di Cascara* (Case C-21/88)

The Court of Justice held as follows:

> 11. It must be pointed out . . . that such a system, which favours goods processed in a particular region of a Member State, prevents the authorities and public bodies concerned from procuring some of the supplies they need from undertakings situated in other Member States. Accordingly, it must be held that products originating in other Member States suffer discrimination in comparison with products manufactured in the Member State in question, with the result that the normal course of intra-Community [i.e. intra-Union] trade is hindered.
>
> 12. That conclusion is not affected by the fact that the restrictive effects of a preferential system of the kind at issue are borne in the same measure both by products manufactured by undertakings from the Member State in question which are not situated in the region covered by the preferential system and by products manufactured by undertakings established in other Member States.
>
> 13. . . . the fact remains that all the products benefiting by the preferential system are domestic products.

Similarly, in **Campus Oil Ltd v Minister for Industry and Energy** (Case 72/83), Ireland had placed an obligation on importers to buy a certain proportion of their oil supplies (35 per cent) from Ireland's only state-owned refinery, at prices fixed by the government. The Court of Justice held that this was clearly discriminatory and breached what is now Art 34 TFEU.

Price-fixing regulations

Another way in which a Member State can treat imports less favourably than domestic products is by fixing prices to make it more difficult for an importer to market his goods within that Member State. If price- fixing is applied only to the imported product, then clearly it will be caught by Art 34 TFEU; e.g. a minimum price for imported apples at £10 per kg.

Indistinctly applicable measures

Objective
4

Article 3, Directive 70/50 (see above) covers measures which affect both home-produced and imported products, but which have a harsher impact on imported products. The measures do not explicitly distinguish between goods according to their origin, and are therefore referred to as 'indistinctly applicable measures'. Specifically, Art 3 refers to measures relating to the marketing of products dealing with shape, size, weight, composition, presentation or identification 'which are equally applicable to domestic and imported products where the restrictive effect of such measures on the free movement of goods exceeds the effects intrinsic to trade rules'. This will be the case where the restrictive effects on the free movement of goods are out of proportion to their purpose and where the same objective can be attained by other means which are less of a hindrance to trade (i.e. an application of the 'proportionality test'). These criteria have been crucial in the development of the jurisprudence of the Court of Justice in relation to national measures which appear, at least, to apply indiscriminately to both imported and home-produced goods.

In the following case, the Court of Justice laid down an important principle on whether such national provisions could constitute MEQRs:

Rewe-Zentrale Ag v *Bundesmonopolverwaltung Für Branntwein* (Case 120/78)

The applicant wished to import the liqueur 'Cassis de Dijon' into Germany from France; for this reason the case is usually referred to as the *Cassis* case. The relevant German authorities refused to allow the importation because the French liqueur was not of sufficient alcoholic strength to be marketed in Germany. Under German law, liqueurs had to have an alcoholic strength of 25 per cent, whereas that of the French liqueur was between 15 per cent and 20 per cent. The importer challenged the decision on the basis that the rule infringed what is now Art 34 TFEU (previously Art 28 EC Treaty). The case was referred to the Court of Justice under what is now Art 267 TFEU (previously Art 234 EC Treaty). The Court accepted that, in the absence of any common rules in the Union relating to the production and marketing of alcohol, it was up to Member States to regulate these activities in their own territories. However, the Court held as follows:

14. . . . It . . . appears that the unilateral requirement imposed by the rules of a Member State of a minimum alcohol content for the purposes of the sale of alcoholic beverages constitutes an obstacle to trade which is incompatible with the provisions of . . . [Article 34 TFEU].

There is therefore no valid reason why, provided that they have been lawfully produced and marketed in one of the Member States, alcoholic beverages should not be introduced into any other Member State; the sale of such products may not be subject to a legal prohibition on the marketing of beverages with an alcohol content lower than the limits set by national rules. [emphasis added]

The above case reaffirms para 5 of the Court's judgment in *Dassonville* (see above). It is made clear that Art 34 TFEU can apply to indistinctly applicable rules, which apply equally to domestic and imported goods, but which nevertheless inhibit trade between Member States because the rules applied are different from those which apply in the product's country of origin. This imposes a *dual burden* on the foreign producer. The domestic producer will already comply with domestic laws and will therefore not be further disadvantaged, whereas the foreign producer will have to change the method of production to comply with the laws of the importing Member State, thus inhibiting intra-Union trade. In the above case the German producers of liqueurs would already be complying with the German law that requires the alcoholic content to be at least 25 per cent. In contrast, the French producers would have had to change their manufacturing processes in order to satisfy this requirement, thus increasing their costs and decreasing any competitive (e.g. financial) advantage French liqueurs might otherwise have had over German liqueurs. An additional point to be aware of is that other Member States could have different regulations: e.g. Denmark could have had a law requiring liqueurs to have a maximum alcoholic content of 10 per cent. French liqueur producers would therefore have had to employ different manufacturing processes for the respective Member States.

The rule of mutual recognition

The first *Cassis* principle, referred to as 'the **rule of mutual recognition**', is set out by the Court of Justice at para 14: once goods have been lawfully marketed in one Member State, they should be free to be marketed in any other Member State without restriction. Derogations from this general principle are considered below.

Examples of indistinctly applicable measures

Following *Cassis*, there have been a number of cases applying the rule of mutual recognition to a wide variety of different measures. Some examples follow:

Origin-marking

Commission v UK (Case 207/83)

UK legislation required that certain goods which were sold in retail markets had to be marked with their country of origin. The Commission took infraction proceedings against the UK under what is now Art 258 TFEU (previously Art 226 EC Treaty), claiming this requirement was in breach of what is now Art 34 TFEU (previously Art 28 EC Treaty) in that it constituted an MEQR. French manufacturers had complained that goods for the UK market had to be origin-marked, which increased production costs. The Commission also argued that such origin-marking encouraged consumers to exercise their prejudices in favour of national products and was likely to reduce the sale of Union-produced goods. The UK government defended the origin-marking order on the grounds that the origin details gave important information to the consumer about the nature and quality of the product, and that the requirement of origin-marking was non-discriminatory because it applied to both domestic and imported products. Considering the second of the UK's arguments (i.e. that the measure applied equally to imported and national products), the Court of Justice stated as follows:

> 17. ... it has to be recognised that the purpose of indications of origin or origin-marking is to enable consumers to distinguish between domestic and imported products and this

> enables them to assert any prejudices which they may have against foreign products. As the Court has had occasion to emphasise in various contexts, the Treaty, by establishing a common market [i.e. internal market] and progressively approximating the economic policies of the Member States, seeks to unite national markets in a single market, the origin-marking requirement not only makes the marketing in a Member State of goods produced in other Member States in the sectors in question more difficult; it also has the effect of slowing down economic interpenetration in the Community [i.e. Union] by handicapping the sale of goods produced as a result of a division of labour between Member States.
>
> 18. It follows from those considerations that the UK provisions in question are liable to have the effect of increasing the production costs of imported goods and making it more difficult to sell them on the UK market. [emphasis added]

In the above case, the Court of Justice was not persuaded that origin-marking was a necessary consumer protection measure. It agreed with the Commission that it encouraged the exercise of national prejudices and therefore, applying the *Dassonville* formula, the measure was capable of affecting intra-Union trade. Any distinctive national quality of the goods could be highlighted by individual retailers, but should not be the subject of national legislation.

See pages 588–589 for an explanation of the *Dassonville* formula.

National quality standard

Commission v *Ireland* (Case 45/87)

> The Commission brought an action against the Irish government under what is now Art 258 TFEU (previously Art 226 EC Treaty), for allowing a specification relating to a water supply contract which, it alleged, breached what is now Art 34 TFEU (previously Art 28 EC Treaty). The water supply contract was being commissioned by a local authority in Ireland (Dundalk Council). The specification stipulated that the water pipes had to be certified as complying with Irish Standard 188. Only one manufacturer, located in Ireland, made pipes which complied with this standard. This was an indistinctly applicable measure because the requirement applied to all pipes whether Irish or imported. One of the bids was based on the use of pipes not conforming to this standard, although it did comply with international standards. Dundalk Council refused to consider the bid for that reason. The question before the Court of Justice was whether this specification constituted a barrier to the importation of pipes for this contract. The Court held as follows:
>
> 19. . . . it must first be pointed out that the inclusion of such a clause (as 4.29) in an invitation to tender may cause economic operators who produce or utilise pipes equivalent to pipes certified with Irish standards to refrain from tendering.
>
> 20. It further appears from the documents in the case that only one undertaking has been certified by the IRIS to IS 188:1975 to apply the Irish Standard Mark to pipes of the type required for the purposes of the public works contract at issue. That undertaking is located in Ireland. Consequently, the inclusion of Clause 4.29 had the effect of restricting the supply of the pipes needed for the Dundalk scheme to Irish manufacturers alone.
>
> 21. The Irish Government maintains that it is necessary to specify the standards to which materials must be manufactured, particularly in a case such as this where the pipes utilised must suit the existing network. Compliance with another standard, even an international standard such as ISO 160:1980, would not suffice to eliminate technical difficulties.

> 22. That technical argument cannot be accepted. The Commission's complaint does not relate to compliance with technical requirements but the refusal of the Irish authorities to verify whether those requirements are satisfied where the manufacturer of the materials has not been certified by the IRIS to IS 188. By incorporating in the notice in question the words 'or equivalent' after the reference to the Irish standard, as provided for by Directive 71/305 where it is applicable, the Irish authorities could have verified compliance with the technical conditions without from the outset restricting the contract to tenderers proposing to utilise Irish materials.

In the above case, the Court of Justice held that while it was perfectly reasonable to specify the quality of pipes to be used for the transmission of drinking water, the attainment of that objective could as well have been achieved by allowing the use of pipes which had been produced abroad to a standard which was *equivalent* to the Irish standard.

In the above categories of case, the Court of Justice considered the *effect* of the national practice, rather than its legal form. This is quite clear in the following category.

Administrative practices

Commission v *France* (Case 21/84)

The Commission alleged that France had violated what is now Art 34 TFEU (previously Art 28 EC Treaty) by delaying a request to approve postal franking machines from other Member States. This was an indistinctly applicable measure because approval was required for both the domestic and imported machines. However, administrative practices resulted in the approval of foreign machines being delayed. A UK manufacturer had failed to secure the approval of the French authorities, despite repeated applications, and even after France had repealed an earlier law which explicitly stated a preference for domestic machines. The Court of Justice held as follows:

11. The fact that a law or regulation such as that requiring prior approval for the marketing of postal franking machines conforms in formal terms to . . . [Article 34 TFEU] is not sufficient to discharge a Member State of its obligation under that provision. Under the cloak of a general provision permitting the approval of machines imported from other Member States, the administration might very well adopt a systematically unfavourable attitude towards imported machines, either by allowing considerable delay in replying to applications for approval or in carrying out the examination procedure, or by refusing approval on the grounds of various alleged technical faults for which no detailed explanations are given or which prove to be inaccurate.
12. The prohibition on measures having an effect equivalent to quantitative restrictions would lose much of its useful effect if it did not cover protectionist or discriminatory practices of that type.
13. It must however be noted that for an administrative practice to constitute a measure prohibited under . . . [Article 34 TFEU] that practice must show a certain degree of consistency and generality. That generality must be assessed differently according to whether the market concerned is one on which there are numerous traders or whether it is a market, such as that in postal franking machines, on which only a few undertakings are active. In the latter case, a national administration's treatment of a single undertaking may constitute a measure incompatible with . . . [Article 34 TFEU].
14. In the light of those principles it is clear from the facts of the case that the conduct of the French postal administration constitutes an impediment to imports contrary to . . . [Article 34 TFEU].

15. It must therefore be concluded that by refusing without proper justification to approve postal franking machines from another Member State, the French Republic has failed to fulfil its obligations under . . . [Article 34 TFEU].

In the above case, the Court of Justice held that a law which on the face of it does not breach what is now Art 34 TFEU, could result in a breach if the method of its application results in imported goods being treated more harshly.

Price-fixing regulations

Article 34 TFEU can also prohibit price-fixing regulations which apply to both imported and domestic goods, as was declared by the Court of Justice in the following case:

Openbaar Ministerie v *Van Tiggele* (Case 82/77)

The Netherlands' legislation provided for minimum selling prices for certain spirits. A seller sold spirits for less than this minimum and was prosecuted. In his defence he argued that the legislation breached what is now Art 34 TFEU (previously Art 28 EC Treaty) and should therefore be inapplicable. The question referred to the Court of Justice was whether this minimum price constituted an MEQR within what is now Art 34 TFEU. The Court of Justice held as follows:

12. For the purposes of this prohibition it is sufficient that the measures in question are likely to hinder, directly or indirectly, actually or potentially, imports between Member States.
13. Whilst national price-control rules applicable without distinction to domestic products and imported products cannot in general produce such an effect they may do so in certain specific cases.
14. Thus imports may be impeded in particular when a national authority fixes prices or profit margins at such a level that imported products are placed at a disadvantage in relation to identical domestic products either because they cannot profitably be marketed in the conditions laid down or because the competitive advantage conferred by lower cost prices is cancelled out.

In the above case, the Court of Justice held that on the facts the Netherlands' law did contravene what is now Art 34 TFEU. As a matter of Union law, price-fixing schemes must give the importer the opportunity to benefit from any competitive advantage the imported goods may possess (e.g., by the setting of a lower price than the competing domestic product), or to take account of any disadvantage they may possess (e.g., by setting a higher price). Schemes which exclude the importer's ability to achieve such flexibility are capable of violating Art 34 TFEU (although see the *Keck* case below).

Differentiation between dual-burden and equal-burden rules

Cassis, and many cases after it, concerned **dual-burden rules**. This would be the case where, for example, one Member State imposed certain rules relating to the manufacture of goods (e.g. margarine must be packaged in cube-shaped containers) and these rules applied equally to domestic and imported goods, even though the exporting producer would have had to comply with the relevant trade rules of his own Member State. This is said to place a dual burden on the exporting producer. *Cassis* would render such rules incompatible with

Art 34 TFEU unless they could be saved by one of the mandatory requirements (or Art 36 TFEU); see below.

Equal-burden rules, by contrast, again apply to all goods (domestic and imported); they regulate trade in some manner, but do not have a protectionist effect. Even though they may have an impact on the overall volume of trade, the impact is equal as between the sale of domestic products and imported products.

Whereas dual-burden rules have been held to fall within Art 34 TFEU, there was some confusion as to whether equal-burden rules should also fall within Art 34, subject to the *rule of reason* defence (and Art 36 TFEU); see below.

Equal-burden rules: outside Article 34 TFEU

In a number of cases the Court of Justice held that rules which did not relate to the *characteristics* of the product and did not impose a dual burden on the importer, but only concerned the *conditions* under which the product was to be sold, were outside the remit of what is now Art 34 TFEU; see, e.g., *Oebel* (Case 155/80), which concerned a national rule prohibiting the delivery of bakery products to consumers and retailers during the night, and *Quietlynn Ltd* v *Southend-on-Sea Borough Council* (Case C-23/89), which concerned a UK law restricting the sale of lawful sex products to shops that had been licensed by the local authority.

Equal-burden rules: within Article 34 TFEU

In other cases, however, the Court of Justice held that such rules would come within the scope of what is now Art 34 TFEU. The Court would then seek to exclude them from the effect of what is now Art 34 TFEU by applying the *rule of reason* or the defences under what is now Art 36 TFEU; see below. In *Cinéthèque SA* v *Fédération Nationale des Cinémas Français* (Cases 60 and 61/84), French legislation prohibited the selling or hiring of film videos during the first year of the film receiving its performance certificate. The objective was to encourage people to go and watch the film at the cinema. The effect was that both domestic and imported films could not be sold during that first year. A distributor of videos relied on what is now Art 34 TFEU before French courts to challenge the law as a trade barrier. The Court of Justice held that although 'its effect is not to favour national production as against the production of other Member States . . . the application of such a system may create barriers to intra-Community [i.e. intra-Union] trade in video-cassettes'. In those circumstances it held that there was a *prima facie* breach of what is now Art 34 TFEU.

The difficult question of whether equal-burden cases fell within what is now Art 34 TFEU was the issue in a series of UK Sunday trading cases which came before the Court of Justice. In *Torfaen Borough Council* v *B&Q plc* (Case 145/88), B&Q was prosecuted for violation of Sunday trading laws, which prohibited retail shops from selling goods on Sundays, subject to certain exceptions. B&Q claimed that these laws constituted an MEQR. The effect of the laws was to reduce turnover, but imported goods were in the same position as domestic goods; the reduction in turnover affected all goods equally. Nevertheless, the Court of Justice held that this constituted a *prima facie* breach of what is now Art 34 TFEU.

The *Keck* judgment

This confused state of affairs was totally unhelpful as the Court of Justice was inconsistent in its approach in dealing with equal-burden rules. In the following case, the Court recognised that it was time to clear up some of the confusion and to adopt a *general rule* which would apply in these circumstances:

Criminal Proceedings Against Keck and Mithouard (Cases C-267 and 268/91)

The defendants (Keck and Mithouard) were prosecuted in a French court for having resold goods at a loss, a practice which was forbidden under French law. In their defence they pleaded, *inter alia*, that this rule constituted an MEQR and was unlawful under what is now Art 34 TFEU (previously Art 28 EC Treaty). The case was referred to the Court of Justice under what is now Art 267 TFEU (previously Art 234 EC Treaty). The Court of Justice held as follows:

11. By virtue of . . . [Article 34 TFEU], quantitative restrictions on imports and all measures having equivalent effect are prohibited between Member States. The Court has consistently held that any measure which is capable of directly or indirectly, actually or potentially, hindering intra-Community [i.e. intra-Union] trade constitutes a measure having equivalent effect to a quantitative restriction.

12. It is not the purpose of national legislation imposing a general prohibition on resales at a loss to regulate trade in goods between Member States.

13. Such legislation may, admittedly, restrict the volume of sales, and hence the volume of sales of products from other Member States, in so far as it deprives traders of a method of sales promotion. But the question remains whether such a possibility is sufficient to characterise the legislation in question as a measure having equivalent effect to a quantitative restriction on imports.

14. In view of the increasing tendency of traders to invoke . . . [Article 34 TFEU] as a means of challenging any rules whose effect is to limit commercial freedom even where such rules are not aimed at products from other Member States, **the Court considers it necessary to re-examine and clarify its case law on this matter.**

15. In *'Cassis de Dijon'* . . . it was held that, in the absence of harmonisation of legislation, measures of equivalent effect prohibited by . . . [Article 34 TFEU] include obstacles to the free movement of goods where they are the consequence of applying rules that lay down requirements to be met by such goods (such as requirements as to designation, form, size, weight, composition, presentation, labelling, packaging) to goods from other Member States where they are lawfully manufactured and marketed, even if those rules apply without distinction to all products unless their application can be justified by a public-interest objective taking precedence over the free movement of goods.

16. **However, contrary to what has previously been decided, the application to products from other Member States of national provisions restricting or prohibiting certain selling arrangements is not such as to hinder directly or indirectly, actually or potentially, trade between Member States within the meaning of the *Dassonville* judgment . . . provided that those provisions apply to all affected traders operating within the national territory and provided that they affect in the same manner, in law and fact, the marketing of domestic products and of those from other Member States.**

17. Where those conditions are fulfilled, the application of such rules to the sale of products from another Member State is not by nature such as to prevent their access to the market or to impede access any more than it impedes the access of domestic products. Such rules therefore fall outside the scope of . . . [Article 34 TFEU].

18. Accordingly, the reply to be given to the national court is that . . . [Article 34 TFEU] is to be interpreted as not applying to legislation of a Member State imposing a general prohibition on resale at a loss. [emphasis added]

In the above case, the Court of Justice established a general rule to be applied in all cases involving equal-burden rules. The Court distinguished between *rules which relate to the goods themselves* in terms of packaging, composition, size, etc. (para 15), which clearly fall within the *Cassis* doctrine, and *rules relating to selling arrangements* (para 16), which do not fall within what is now Art 34 TFEU *provided* the conditions set out in the second part of para 16 are met.

The reason why rules which fall within para 16 are outside the scope of Art 34 TFEU is that their *purpose* is not to regulate trade as such (para 12) and because their *effect and nature* do not prevent access to the market, or at least they do not make it any more difficult for imported products to penetrate the market than national products (para 17). They impose an equal- burden on both domestic products and imported products. However, if the conditions set out in para 16 are not met, then the rule would come within the scope of Art 34 TFEU. The para 16 conditions are:

- the provisions of the rule apply to all traders operating within the national territory;
- they affect in the same manner, in law and in fact, the marketing of domestic goods and imports.

Provided these two conditions are met, then a rule which relates to selling arrangements will not come within the scope of Art 34 TFEU.

Commenting on the Court's judgment in *Keck*, Advocate General Jacobs has observed:

> It seems to me . . . that the *Dassonville* formula was indeed too broad – and illustrates the dangers in taking as a starting point a very broad proposition which subsequently has to be whittled down – but that the main body of the Court's case law on . . . [Art 34 TFEU] was wholly satisfactory and that to introduce at this stage a notion of discrimination may raise more problems than it solves.
>
> (*The European Advocate* (1994/1995) 2, 4)

Post-Keck case law

'Selling arrangements' will not breach Art 34 TFEU provided they are non-discriminatory. This means that they must affect, in the same way, in law and in fact, the marketing of domestic goods and goods from other Member States. If they do not affect the marketing of domestically produced and imported goods in the same way and are liable substantially to restrict access to the national market, then they will breach Art 34 TFEU. 'Selling arrangements' can cover a multitude of activities. The expression includes price restrictions, as in *Keck* itself, or any other national rules which govern the way products or services are sold or advertised.

The rule in *Keck* has been applied to a number of cases relating to the marketing of goods, as illustrated below:

Criminal Proceedings Against Tankstation 'T Heukske Vof v JBE Boermans (Cases C-401 and 402/92)

National rules provided for the compulsory closure of petrol stations. The Court of Justice applied the *Keck* general rule and held that the rules did not fall within what is now Art 34 TFEU (previously Art 28 EC Treaty) because they related to selling arrangements which applied equally to all traders without distinguishing between origin. It was an equal-burden rule, affecting domestic traders and importers equally. The Court stated as follows:

> Those conditions [in *Keck*] are fulfilled [in this case]. The rules in question relate to the times and places at which the goods in question may be sold to consumers. However, they apply to all relevant traders without distinguishing between the origin of the products in question and do not affect the marketing of products from other Member States in a manner different from that in which they affect domestic products.

In *Hunermund* (Case C-292/92) there was a prohibition by the German pharmacists' association, preventing its members from advertising popular medicines outside their premises. The Court of Justice ruled that this was a 'selling arrangement' within the meaning of *Keck*, and consequently the former Art 28 EC Treaty (now Art 34 TFEU) did not apply. Two years later, in *Leclerc-Siplec* (Case C-412/93), the Court of Justice considered a French law which prevented Leclerc-Siplec from advertising unleaded petrol imported by them and sold in their supermarkets. The law applied to all advertisers, irrespective of the source of their product. The Court acknowledged that 'the prohibition may . . . restrict the volume of sales, and hence of products from other Member States, in so far as it deprives distributors of a particular form of advertising for their goods'. It held that this was a 'selling arrangement' which affected the sale of all such goods equally, and what is now Art 34 TFEU did not therefore apply.

In *Morellato* (Case C-416/00), Italian legislation prohibited the sale of bread which had been prepared by completing the baking of partly baked bread, if that bread had not been packaged by the retailer prior to its sale. In considering the question, the Court of Justice first had to determine whether such requirements constituted 'selling arrangements' which are not likely to hinder trade between Member States within the meaning of its judgment in *Keck*. The Court held that in this case the requirement for prior packaging laid down in the legislation at issue did not make it necessary to alter the product because it only related to the marketing of the bread which resulted from the final baking of pre-baked bread. The Court held that in principle such a requirement would fall outside the scope of what is now Art 34 TFEU provided that it did not in reality constitute discrimination against imported products.

In the following two cases, the Court of Justice held that the measures in question imposed a *dual burden* on the manufacturer and were therefore, *prima facie*, in breach of what is now Art 34 TFEU:

Mars (Case C-470/93)

The manufacturers challenged a national law in Germany which prohibited the selling of Mars bars marked '110 per cent' (as part of a Europe-wide selling campaign). The Court of Justice held that these requirements related to the presentation, labelling and packaging of the product lawfully manufactured and marketed in another Member State. The prohibition imposed a dual burden on the manufacturer and was therefore, *prima facie*, in breach of what is now Art 34 TFEU (previously Art 28 EC Treaty).

Vereinigte Familiapresse (Case C-368/95)

A German newspaper publisher was selling newspapers in the German and Austrian markets in which readers were offered the opportunity to take part in games with prizes. This practice breached the Austrian Unfair Competition Act 1992. A competitor tried to stop the imported German papers and the case was referred to the Court of Justice. The Court rejected the Austrian argument that this was merely a 'selling arrangement', as it affected the content of the newspaper and its access to the Austrian market. Potentially, therefore, it breached what is now Art 34 TFEU (previously Art 28 EC Treaty). The Court of Justice held as follows:

> 11. The Court finds that, even though the relevant national legislation is directed against a method of sales promotion, in this case it bears on the actual content of the products, in so far as the competitions in question form an integral part of the magazine in which

they appear. As a result, the national legislation in question as applied to the facts of the case is not concerned with a selling arrangement within the meaning of the judgment in *Keck* . . .

12. Moreover, since it requires traders established in other Member States to alter the contents of the periodical, the prohibition at issue impairs access of the products concerned to the market of the Member State of importation and consequently hinders free movement of goods. It therefore constitutes in principle a measure having equivalent effect within the meaning of . . . [Article 34 TFEU].

As discussed above, in the *Keck* case one of the conditions which has to be satisfied in order to remove a rule relating to 'selling arrangements' from the scope of Art 34 TFEU is that the rule affects in the same manner, in law and in fact, the marketing of domestic goods and imports. This was considered by the Court of Justice in the following case:

Konsumentombudsmannen (Ko) v *Gourmet International Products Ab (Gip)* (Case C-405/98)

A Swedish law prohibited the advertising of alcoholic beverages in periodicals. It was argued that this breached the former Art 28 EC Treaty (now Art 34 TFEU). The Court of Justice stated that, if national provisions restricting or prohibiting certain selling arrangements are to avoid being caught by the former Art 28 EC Treaty (now Art 34 TFEU), they must not be of such a kind as to prevent access to the market by products from another Member State or to impede access any more than they impede the access of domestic products. The Court held that, in the case of products like alcoholic beverages, the consumption of which is linked to traditional social practices and to local habits and customs, a prohibition of all advertising directed at consumers in the form of advertisements in the press is liable to impede access to the market by products from other Member States more than it impedes access by domestic products. Hence the Court held that the prohibition came within the scope of the former Art 28 EC Treaty (now Art 34 TFEU), despite being concerned with selling arrangements. This was because the *Keck* condition that 'the rule affected in the same manner, in law and in fact, the marketing of domestic goods and imports' was not satisfied.

This condition was also at issue in the following two cases:

Deutscher Apothekerverband (Case C-322/01)

Germany prohibited the import and retail sale of medicinal products by mail order or over the internet. As regards medicinal products which had received authorisation under the provisions of Directive 65/65, the Court of Justice considered the relevance of the actual or potential effect of the German restriction on intra-Union trade to assess whether it was consistent with those provisions. The Court held that the requirement that it must affect in the same manner, in law and in fact, the marketing of both domestic products and those from other Member States, was not fulfilled here. The prohibition at issue was more of an obstacle to pharmacies outside Germany than to those within it. Although there was little doubt that, as a result of the prohibition, pharmacies in Germany did not use the extra or alternative method of gaining access to the German market consisting of end consumers of medicinal products, they were still able to sell the products in their dispensaries. However, for pharmacies not established in Germany, mail order and the internet would provide a more significant way to gain direct access to the German market. The prohibition would therefore have a greater impact on pharmacies established outside German territory and could impede access to the market for products from other Member States more than it impedes access for domestic products. The Court of Justice therefore held that the prohibition was a measure having an effect equivalent to a quantitative restriction, in breach of the former Art 28 EC Treaty (now Art 34 TFEU).

Ker-Optika Bt v *Ántsz Dél-Dunántúli Regionális Intézete* (Case C-108/09)

Under Hungarian legislation, the selling of contact lenses required a specialist shop with a minimum area of 18 square metres or premises separated from the workshop. Further, for sales of those products, the services of an optometrist or an ophthalmologist qualified in the field of contact lenses had to be used.

The Hungarian firm Ker-Optika sold contact lenses through its internet site. The Hungarian health authorities prohibited it from pursuing that activity on the ground that, in Hungary, those products could not be sold through the internet.

Ker-Optika brought action challenging that prohibition and the Baranya Megyei Bíróság (the district court of Baranya, Hungary), which heard the case, referred the case to the Court of Justice for a preliminary ruling. It asked whether Union law precluded the Hungarian legislation which authorised the selling of contact lenses only in shops which specialised in the sale of medical devices and which, consequently, prohibited the selling of contact lenses through the internet.

The Court of Justice stated that the prohibition on selling contact lenses through the internet applied to contact lenses from other Member States which were sold by mail order and delivered to customers living in Hungary. The Court stated that this prohibition deprived traders from other Member States of a particularly effective means of selling those products and thus significantly impeded the access of those traders to the Hungarian market. Consequently, that legislation constituted an obstacle to the free movement of goods in the Union.

Article 35 TFEU: exports

Most of the cases considered so far have involved national restrictions, or measures equivalent to restrictions, on *imports*. As discussed above, Art 35 TFEU (previously Art 29 EC Treaty) applies in much the same way as Art 34 TFEU, in that it prohibits quantitative restrictions and MEQRs, but in relation to *exports* rather than *imports*. The principles applicable to restrictions on exports are, broadly, the same. ***Procureur de la République* v *Bouhelier*** (Case 53/76) provides an example of a case involving the application of Art 35 TFEU. In this case, a quality control charge was only imposed on exports and not on goods sold on the domestic market. The Court of Justice held that this was a measure equivalent to a quantitative restriction on exports. However, the Court of Justice appears to look for some element of discrimination, either formal or material, in the case of exports. It emphasised that aspect in the following case:

Groenveld (Case 15/79)

The Court of Justice held as follows:

[Article 35(1) TFEU] concerns national measures which have as their specific object or effect the restrictions of patterns of exports and thereby the establishment of a difference in treatment between the domestic trade of a Member State and its export trade in such a way as to provide a particular advantage for national production of the domestic market of the state in question at the expense of the production or of the trade of other Member States. This is not so in the case of a prohibition like that in question which is applied objectively to the production of goods of a certain kind without drawing a distinction depending on whether such goods are intended for the national market or for export. (para 7)

Whether or not there is discrimination is a matter of both national law and practice. Clearly, therefore, a national law requiring producers to deliver poultry offal to their local authority has been held, necessarily, to involve a ban on exports (***Nertsvoederfabriek Nederland*** (Case 118/86)). However, legislation applied to all producers of cheese in The Netherlands, affecting its content and quality – which put Netherlands' producers at a disadvantage in comparison to foreign producers who did not have to produce their cheese to the same standards – was held by the Court of Justice not to be a measure equivalent to a quantitative restriction on exports, although it made exporting more difficult for Netherlands' producers (***Jongeneel Kaas BV* v *Netherlands*** (Case 237/82)). In this case the Court demonstrated its willingness to tolerate measures which, although not actually discriminating against exports, had an adverse effect on domestic producers, which it would not have been prepared to tolerate in relation to imports.

Article 36 TFEU: defences to distinctly and indistinctly applicable measures

Objective 5

Article 36 TFEU (which is worded identically to the former Art 30 EC Treaty) permits Member States to derogate from their obligation to ensure the free movement of goods. Article 36 TFEU provides that:

The provisions of Articles 34 and 35 shall not preclude prohibitions or restrictions on imports, exports or goods in transit justified on grounds of public morality, public policy or public security; the protection of health and life of humans, animals and plants; the protection of national treasures possessing artistic, historic or archaeological value; or the protection of industrial and commercial property. Such prohibitions or restrictions shall not, however, constitute a means of arbitrary discrimination or a disguised restriction on trade between Member States.

These derogations comprise an *exhaustive* list and are interpreted strictly by the Court of Justice. Article 36 TFEU is most often pleaded by Member States in defence of distinctly applicable measures (***Commission* v *Ireland*** (Case 113/80)). Article 36 TFEU is, however, equally applicable to indistinctly applicable measures, as decided by the Court of Justice in the following case:

Wurmser (Case 25/88)

The Court of Justice held as follows:

> A measure which, in regard both to domestic products and imported products, imposes an obligation to verify conformity [with the rules in force on that market] on the person who first places the product on the market is, in principle, applicable without distinction to both categories of products. It may, therefore, be justified under . . . [Article 36 TFEU] and under . . . [Article 34 TFEU]] as interpreted by the Court [in the *Cassis* case].

As the exceptions contained in Art 36 TFEU are treated as exhaustive, national measures not falling clearly within its terms are rejected by the Court.

The Art 36 TFEU exceptions can be advanced to justify national measures only in the absence of any relevant Union-wide provisions aimed at harmonising the legislation protecting the interest which the national measure seeks to protect:

Lucien Ortscheit Gmbh v *Eurim-Pharm Gmbh* (Case C-320/93)

German legislation prohibited the advertising of foreign drugs which had not been authorised for use in the German market, but which could, under certain conditions, be imported into Germany. The Court of Justice was in no doubt that the measure was distinctly applicable and equivalent to a quantitative restriction. It noted, however, that the health and life of humans ranks foremost among the interests protected by what is now Art 36 TFEU (previously Art 30 EC Treaty), and at the present stage of harmonisation there was no procedure for Union authorisation or mutual recognition of national authorisations. In those circumstances, it was for Member States, within the limits imposed by the Treaty, to decide what degree of protection they intend to ensure. In the circumstances, the Court was satisfied that the German measures were justified under what is now Art 36 TFEU.

However, if there is relevant Union legislation, there will be no scope for national measures that are incompatible with it, and Art 36 TFEU cannot be relied upon to justify the measure. The Court reiterated its position in the following case:

R v *Ministry Of Agriculture, Fisheries and Food, Ex Parte Compassion in World Farming Ltd* (Case C-1/96)

The applicants had attempted to argue that the Minister was entitled to ignore the effect of a new Council directive on the treatment of farm animals in transit, and stop the export of live animals in reliance on what is now Art 36 TFEU (previously Art 30 EC Treaty), as the directive did not conform to an international convention on the humane treatment of animals. The Court of Justice rejected this argument, insisting that what is now Art 36 TFEU could not be used to justify a national prohibition, because the directive was intended to deal exhaustively with the situation.

Similarly in the following case:

Société Agricole De La Crespelle (Case C-323/93)

French rules conferred a monopoly on a number of regional bovine insemination centres and, effectively, created a restrictive regime for the importation of bovine semen from other Member States. The Court of Justice was satisfied that the restrictive regime amounted to an MEQR, but could it be justified under what is now Art 36 TFEU (previously Art 30 EC Treaty)? The Court decided that it could not be:

> The Court has consistently held that where . . . Community [i.e. Union] Directives provide for the harmonisation of the measures necessary to ensure, *inter alia*, the protection of animal and human health and established Community [i.e. Union] procedures to check that they were observed, invoking . . . [Article 36 TFEU] is no longer justified and the appropriate checks have to be carried out and protective measures adopted within the framework of the directive.

The above rule applies where the Union has introduced a consistent and exhaustive set of measures to cover the type of importation in question (***Commission v Italy (Re Authorisation for Importation of Plants)*** (Case C-296/92)). However, it does not preclude restrictions on imports where these are specifically authorised by the directive (***The State v Vitaret and Chambron*** [1995] 1 CMLR 185 (this case was decided by the French Cour de Cassation, *not* the Court of Justice)).

Where Art 36 TFEU can be advanced as a justification for national measures, it is for the national government relying on it to provide evidence to support the grounds justifying its actions. This principle of casting the evidential burden upon the Member State taking the action applies not only in relation to the national measure itself, but also in relation to individual cases in which that national measure is applied. This is illustrated in the following case:

Officier Van Justitie v Sandoz BV (Case 174/82)

Sandoz wished to sell confectionery in the Netherlands to which vitamin supplements had been added. The confectionery was freely sold in Belgium and Germany. The Netherlands' authorities refused permission for it to be sold, on the grounds that the vitamins were a risk to health. The case was referred to the Court of Justice under what is now Art 267 TFEU (previously Art 234 EC Treaty). The Court was in no doubt that the measure breached what is now Art 34 TFEU (previously Art 28 EC Treaty), but in the absence of Union harmonising measures on the kinds of additives which were acceptable, it was permissible under what is now Art 36 TFEU (previously Art 30 EC Treaty) for the Member State to determine the kind and extent of protection to be given. However, the Court of Justice held that the state had first to establish the existence of a risk:

> In as much as the question arises as to where the onus of proof lies when there is a request for authorisation [to market a foodstuff] . . . it must be remembered that . . . [Article 36 TFEU] creates an exception, which must be strictly interpreted, to the rule of free movement of goods within the Community [i.e. Union] which is one of the fundamental principles of the Common Market [i.e. internal market]. **It is therefore for the national authorities who rely on that provision in order to adopt a measure restricting intra-Community [i.e. intra-Union] trade to check in each instance that the measure contemplated satisfies the criteria of that provision** . . . Community [i.e. Union] law does not permit national rules which subject authorisation to market to proof by the importer that the product in question is not harmful to health. (paras 22, 24) [emphasis added]

Where action may be justified under Art 36 TFEU, measures taken by Member States will still have to meet two fundamental Union criteria: (i) there must be no arbitrary discrimination between imported and domestic products; and (ii) any national measures must be proportionate to any risk and must not restrict trade any more than is necessary to protect the legitimate public interests recognised by Art 36 TFEU. The operation of these principles is discussed further below in the context of case law of the Court of Justice relating to the specific Art 36 TFEU exceptions.

Public morality

The concept of public morality will vary widely from state to state and is not expanded upon in Art 36 TFEU or in any secondary legislation. The Court has, for example, refused to rule that termination of pregnancy is intrinsically immoral and cannot constitute a service under Art 56 TFEU (previously Art 49 EC Treaty), because it is lawfully carried out in several Member States (*Society for the Protection of the Unborn Child v Grogan* (Case C-159/90)). In *HM Customs and Excise Commissioners v Schindler and Others* (Case C-275/92) the Court of Justice observed, with regard to gambling, that 'Even if the morality of lotteries is at least questionable, it is not for the Court to substitute its assessment for that of the legislature where that activity is practised legally' (para 32). The Court may, however, have to assess whether or not national rules are applied proportionately and without discrimination (see Chapter 13). The issue first came before the Court of Justice in relation to what is now Art 36 TFEU in a reference from the UK's House of Lords, pursuant to what is now Art 267 TFEU (previously Art 234 EC Treaty):

R v Henn and Darby (Case 34/79)

The defendants were convicted of being 'knowingly concerned in the fraudulent evasion of the prohibition of the importation of indecent or obscene articles' contrary to s 42, Customs Consolidation Act 1876 and s 304, Customs and Excise Act 1952. The articles involved in the charges formed part of a consignment of several boxes of obscene films and magazines which had been brought into the UK in 1975 on a lorry travelling on a ferry from Rotterdam (Holland). The six films and magazines referred to in the charges were all of Danish origin.

The House of Lords (the judicial functions of which are now exercised by the Supreme Court) referred a number of questions to the Court of Justice. The first question related to whether a law of a Member State prohibiting the importation of pornographic articles is a quantitative restriction. The Court was in no doubt that it was, because a prohibition on imports is 'the most extreme form of restriction' (para 12). However, the Court of Justice emphasised that Member States were free to take such action in appropriate circumstances:

In principle, it is for each Member State to determine in accordance with its own scale of values and in the form selected by it the requirements of public morality in its territory. In any event, it cannot be disputed that the statutory provisions applied by the UK in regard to the importation of articles having an indecent or obscene character come within the powers reserved to the Member States by the first sentence of Article 36 [now Art 30].

The House of Lords was also concerned to know whether the fact that the prohibition imposed on the importation of pornography was different in scope from that imposed by the criminal law on the possession and publication of such material in the UK constituted a means of arbitrary discrimination or a disguised restriction on trade between Member States.

In particular, there were differences in treatment of the possession and publication of pornography in different parts of the UK, and there were circumstances in which, under the Obscene Publications Act 1959, possession and publication may not be a criminal offence. The defences available in those circumstances had no application to the Customs and Excise Acts under which the defendants were prosecuted. The Court of Justice was satisfied that the differences, such as they were, were not significant:

> Whatever may be the differences between the laws on this subject in force in the different constituent parts of the UK, and notwithstanding the fact that they contain certain exceptions of limited scope, these laws, taken as a whole, have as their purpose the prohibition, or at least the restraining, of the manufacture and marketing of publications or articles of an indecent or obscene character. **In these circumstances it is permissible to conclude, on a comprehensive view, that there is no lawful trade in such goods in the UK.** A prohibition on imports which may in certain respects be more strict than some of the laws applied within the UK cannot, therefore, be regarded as amounting to a measure designed to give indirect protection to some national product or aimed at creating arbitrary discrimination. (para 21) [emphasis added]

In the above case, the Court of Justice held that although there were 'certain exceptions' with regard to the trade of pornographic material in the UK, these exceptions were 'of limited scope'. The Court therefore concluded that 'there is no lawful trade in such goods in the UK'. This is similar to the application of the *de minimis* rule in English law. The Court in this case decided that because the degree of regulation within the UK was so extensive, the incidental trade of pornographic goods within the UK was on such a small scale that it could effectively be ignored.

The following case is another example of goods being seized by HM Customs and Excise under s 42, Customs Consolidation Act 1876:

Conegate Ltd v *HM Customs and Excise* (Case 121/85)

The seized goods consisted of inflatable sex dolls and other erotic articles. The importers argued that the situation was different to that in *Henn and Darby* because sex dolls, although not permitted to be publicly displayed, could be lawfully sold throughout the UK. The Court of Justice agreed:

15. . . . Although Community [i.e. Union] law leaves the Member States free to make their own assessments of the indecent or obscene character of certain articles, it must be pointed out that the fact that the goods cause offence cannot be regarded as sufficiently serious to justify restrictions on the free movement of goods where the Member State concerned does not adopt, with respect to the same goods manufactured or marketed within its territory, penal measures or other serious or effective measures intended to prevent the distribution of such goods in its territory.

16. It follows that a Member State may not rely on grounds of public morality in order to prohibit the importation of goods from other Member States when its legislation contains no prohibition on the manufacture or marketing of the same goods in its territory. [emphasis added]

The *Adoui* case is fully discussed at pages 520–521.

There is a striking similarity in the language used by the Court of Justice in the above case to that employed by it, with regard to the free movement of workers, in *Adoui and Cornuaille* v *Belgium* (Cases 115 and 116/81); see Chapter 15. That case concerned the scope of the public policy exception in the former Art 39(3) EC Treaty (now Art 45(3) TFEU). In *Adoui*, the Court of Justice held that a Member State could not take action under the public policy exception against an EU citizen unless it took some kind of 'repressive measures' against its own nationals for engaging in the same conduct on which the exclusion is based. A similar concept of equality of treatment underlies the requirement that the Member State excluding the goods on the ground of public morality must take 'penal measures or other serious or effective measures' in relation to the same kind of goods produced on its own territory.

Public policy and public security

Very few attempts have been made by national governments to justify restrictive measures on these grounds. Public policy was, however, successfully advanced by the UK government in the following case:

R v Thompson and Others (Case 7/78)

The defendants traded in coins, some of which were old UK gold coins that were no longer legal tender. They were convicted in England of being knowingly concerned in the fraudulent evasion of the prohibition on importation of gold coins into the UK. They argued, on appeal, that the provisions under which they had been convicted breached what are now Arts 34 and 35 TFEU (previously Arts 28 and 29 EC Treaty). The UK government defended the legislation on the ground that it was an important aspect of public policy to protect the national coinage and the Court of Justice agreed. It held that a ban on destroying old coinage with a view to it being melted down or destroyed in another Member State was justified on grounds of public policy under what is now Art 36 TFEU (previously Art 30 EC Treaty) because it was based on the need to protect the right to mint coinage, which is traditionally regarded as involving the fundamental interests of the state.

In the following case, the French government argued before the Court of Justice that national rules fixing retail selling prices for fuel were justified on grounds of public order and public security, which would arise in relation to retailers affected by unrestrained competition:

Cullet (Case 231/83)

The Advocate General warned against the dangers of responding to public agitation:

The acceptance of civil disturbance as a justification for encroachments upon the free movement of goods would . . . have unacceptably drastic consequences. If road-blocks and other effective weapons of interest groups which feel threatened by the importation and sale at competitive prices of certain cheap products or services, or by immigrant workers or foreign businesses, were accepted as justification, the existence of the four freedoms of the Treaty could no longer be relied upon. Private interest groups would then, in the place of the Treaty and Community [i.e. Union] (and, within the limits laid down in the Treaty), determine the scope of those freedoms. In such cases, the concept of public policy requires, rather, effective action on the part of the authorities to deal with the disturbances. (para 5.3)

The Court of Justice was equally sceptical about the incapacity of the French authorities in the face of rampaging fuel retailers on the streets of France. It remarked:

In that regard, it is sufficient to state that the French Government has not shown that it would be unable, using the means at its disposal, to deal with the consequences which an amendment of the rules in question . . . would have upon public order and security. (paras 32, 33)

In response to attempts by animal welfare groups to block the export of live animals, the issue was seen by Simon Brown LJ, expressly adopting the Advocate General's Opinion in *Cullet*, above, as a straightforward issue of the rule of law, both Union and national (*R v Coventry City Council, ex parte Phoenix Aviation* [1995] 3 All ER 37 at 67; and see also *R v Chief Constable of Sussex, ex parte International Trader's Ferry Ltd* [1995] 4 All ER 364). Although the English Court of Appeal did not uphold the decision of the Divisional Court, the Court of Justice has since reiterated that Member States cannot prevent the import or export of products because of the 'views or behaviour of a section of the Community [i.e. Union]'. A failure to act, where persistent obstruction by private groups has been drawn to the attention of the authorities, will represent a breach of the Member State's obligation to uphold the law of the Union and will not be justified by Art 36 TFEU; *Commission v France* (Case C-265/95).

The Irish government had more success with the public security argument in the following case:

Campus Oil v Ministry for Industry and Energy (Case 72/83)

Irish legislation required importers of petroleum products to purchase up to 35 per cent of their requirements from Ireland's state-owned refinery at prices fixed by the Minister. There was no doubt that the requirement breached what is now Art 34 TFEU (previously Art 28 EC Treaty). The government, however, argued that the measure was necessary on the ground that the importance of oil for the maintenance of the life of the country made it essential to maintain fuel capacity in Ireland. The system it had adopted was the only means by which a fuel reserve could be built up. The Court of Justice agreed that petroleum products were of fundamental importance to the country's existence, as they were needed for the country's institutions, vital services and the survival of its inhabitants. The Court therefore accepted the public security justification. It did, however, warn the Irish government that the purchasing obligation could be continued only if there was no less restrictive measure which was capable of achieving the same objective; nor should the quantities covered by the scheme exceed the minimum supply requirements without which the public security of the state would be affected. The scheme had, in other words, to be proportionate to the anticipated risk.

Public health

The same principle of proportionality has been prominent in the many decisions of the Court of Justice in which Member States have sought to rely on the exception relating to the health of humans, animals and plants. In this context, Art 36 TFEU attempts to strike a balance between the interests involved in the creation of the internal market and the protection of health, and the Court is particularly careful to determine whether or not a measure is, in fact, a disguised form of protectionism. To be capable of justification as a health measure, it must form part of 'a seriously considered health policy'. This was lacking in the following case:

Commission v UK (RE Imports of Poultry Meat) (Case 40/82)

In September 1981, the UK banned the import of turkeys from France (and some other Member States). There was evidence before the Court of Justice that, in the two years before the ban, there had been a steep rise in turkey imports for the Christmas market from France and other Member States. This had been followed by a chorus of complaints about unfair competition from UK poultry producers. The imposition of a sudden ban on the import of French turkeys was, ostensibly, because of the risk of the outbreak of New-castle Disease, a serious poultry infection. There had, however, been no recent outbreak in France, and the main object of the UK government's ostensible concern was imports of turkeys into France from Eastern European countries where there was a more serious risk. The Court was unconvinced by the UK justification:

> Certain established facts suggest that the real aim of the 1981 measure was to block, for commercial and economic reasons, imports of poultry products from other Member States, in particular from France. The UK government had been subject to pressure from UK poultry producers to block these imports. It hurriedly introduced its new policy with the result that French Christmas turkeys were excluded from the UK market for the 1981 season . . . The deduction must be made that the 1981 measures did not form part of a seriously considered health policy.
>
> Taken together, these facts are sufficient to establish that the 1981 measures constitute a disguised restriction on imports of poultry products from other Member States, in particular from France, unless it can be shown that, for reasons of animal health, the only possibility open to the UK was to apply the strict measures which are at issue in this case and that, therefore, the methods prescribed by the 1981 measures . . . were not more restrictive than was necessary for the protection of poultry flocks in Great Britain.

In the above case, the Court of Justice was satisfied that, on the evidence, there were much less restrictive methods available that were appropriate to the degree of risk. The UK had, therefore, breached what is now Art 34 TFEU. Subsequently, this successful action by the Commission led to a claim in the UK courts by an importer affected by the ban (***Bourgoin* v *Ministry of Agriculture, Fisheries and Food (MAFF)*** [1986] QB 716; see Chapter 10).

Many of the cases in which the health exception is raised turn on whether there is, in fact, any risk at all. The perception of risk may, quite genuinely, be different in different Member States. The Court of Justice will have to assess on the best available scientific evidence: (i) whether there is a risk to health; and (ii) if there is such a risk, whether the Member State taking the restrictive measures has responded appropriately. In ***Commission v France*** (Case 216/84), for example, French legislation prohibited the marketing of milk substitutes. The French government attempted to justify the prohibition on two grounds: (i) milk substitutes had a lower nutritional value; and (ii) milk substitutes were harmful to some people. The Court of Justice rejected both arguments. The fact that milk substitutes had a lower nutritional value than milk products hardly constituted a health risk when consumers had so many other food products to choose from. Milk products themselves could pose a risk to some individuals with certain allergies or suffering from certain diseases. Labelling would provide consumers with the necessary information to enable them to make a properly informed choice.

Milk also figured in ***Commission v UK (Re UHT Milk)*** (Case 124/81). In this case, the Commission brought proceedings against the UK under what is now Art 258 TFEU (pre-viously Art 226 EC Treaty) for imposing a requirement that UHT milk should be marketed only by approved dairies or distributors. The government argued that this was necessary to ensure that milk was free from bacterial or viral infections. The effect of the restric-tion was that all imported milk had to be repackaged and re-treated. The Court of Justice rejected these measures as inappropriate and unnecessary. There was evidence that milk in all Member States was of similar quality and subject to equivalent controls. The restric-tion was, therefore, unjustified. The Court of Justice has also held that German legislation, which prohibited the import from other Member States of meat products manufactured from meat not coming from the country of manufacture of the finished product, could not be justified on health grounds as there was no reason to believe that the risk of contamination increased simply because the fresh meat crossed a Union frontier (**Commission v Germany** (Case 153/78)).

Although the Court of Justice has held that the fact that testing has occurred in the country of origin should give rise to a presumption that the imported goods are safe to use, this is not the universal rule (**De Peijper** (Case 104/75); **Frans-Nederlandse** (Case 272/80)). In particular, differences in approach to food additives or medical products may justify additional testing by the importing Member State before authorisation to market the goods is given, as illustrated in the following case:

Officier Van Justitie v Sandoz BV (Case 174/82)

There was uncertainty about the point at which a large intake of vitamin additives in food could become harmful. The Court of Justice held that the importing Member State was entitled to carry out tests on the food before it was put on the market:

> Community [i.e. Union] law permits national rules prohibiting without prior authorisation the marketing of foodstuffs lawfully marketed in another Member State to which vitamins have been added, provided that the marketing is authorised when the addition of vitamins meets a real need, especially a technical or nutritional one. (para 20)

The position is similar for medical products. The Court of Justice has held that Member States are entitled, at the present stage of harmonisation and in the absence of a procedure for Union authorisation or mutual recognition of national authorisation, to exclude from other Member States medical products which have not been authorised by the competent national authorities (**Lucien Ortscheit GmbH v Eurim-Pharm GmbH** (Case C-320/93)). See also the cases below, discussed under the 'Public health' subsection of 'The mandatory requirement defence: "the rule of reason"'.

Protection of industrial and commercial property

Industrial and commercial property rights are valuable rights relating to the protection and distribution of goods and services. Such rights are protected by patents, trade marks, copyrights and similar mechanisms. Each Member State has devised its own system for protecting the investment, creativity and innovation which has gone into a new product or system. The period of protection may vary widely between Member States and between different kinds of industrial property rights. In the UK, for example, the exclusive rights enjoyed under a patent endure for 20 years, indefinitely for trade marks, and the author's lifetime plus 70 years for copyright. As each form of industrial property is defined under national law, it would seem *prima facie* not to be a matter within Union competence and, indeed, Art 345 TFEU (previously Art 295 EC Treaty) appears to emphasise the exclusive competence of each Member State in this matter:

> The Treaties shall in no way prejudice the rules in Member States governing the system of property ownership.

However, it is clear that a restrictive approach taken by the owners of industrial property rights could have a very significant effect on the free movement of goods. The different national rules on such property rights could be used, effectively, to partition the market for those products on a national basis, and prevent the achievement of one of the Union's primary aims. The Court of Justice has, therefore, drawn a distinction between rules affecting the ownership of such rights and their exercise. It has declared that the protection given to the different systems of property ownership in different Member States by the former Art 295 EC Treaty (now Art 345 TFEU) does not allow national legislatures to adopt measures relating to industrial and commercial property which would adversely affect the principle of free movement of goods within the internal market (**Spain v Council** (Case C-350/92)). It has also emphasised that this exception under what is now Art 36 TFEU cannot 'constitute a means of arbitrary discrimination or a disguised restriction on trade between Member States'. National rules protecting patents and copyrights must therefore operate without discrimination. This is illustrated in the following case:

Collins v Imtrat (Case C-92/92)

> The performer Phil Collins attempted to bring proceedings to stop the distribution in Germany of pirated tapes and illegal recordings taken at his concerts. Under German law, such relief was available only to German nationals. The Court of Justice held that, although Member States were still free to determine the nature and extent of protection provided by national copyright rules, such rules should be applied without discrimination.

On this basis it has also held that there is a breach of what is now Art 34 TFEU when national rules require that a patent be exploited only on the territory where the patent is granted and which prohibit or restrict its development elsewhere, so that the patented goods may not be manufactured elsewhere and imported into the patent-granting Member State (**Commission v Italy** (Case C-235/89); **Commission v UK** (Case C-30/90)). There is a parallel here to the prohibition of discrimination in the acquisition of real property rights by those attempting to establish themselves under Art 49 TFEU (previously Art 43 EC Treaty); **Steinhauser v City of Biarritz** (Case 197/84); **Commission v Italy (Re Housing Aid)** (Case 63/86) – see Chapter 13.

The Court has tried to allow the property exception to operate only in relation to the essential core of property rights, although what those are in each case is sometimes difficult to determine. The following case illustrates the Court of Justice's approach in the case of a patent:

Centrafarm v Winthrop BV (Cases 15 and 16/74)

> The Court of Justice stated that:
>
> > . . . [Article 36 TFEU] in fact only admits of derogations from the free movement of goods where such derogations are justified for the purpose of safeguarding rights which constitute the specific subject matter of this property. In relation to patents, the specific subject matter of the industrial property is the guarantee that the patentee, to reward the creative effort of the inventor, has the exclusive right to use an invention with a view to manufacturing industrial products and putting them into circulation for the first time, either directly or by the grant of licences to third parties, as well as the right to oppose infringements.

This exclusive right is enjoyed in the Member State in which the goods are patented. The patentee, under the Art 36 TFEU exception, can exclude goods which breach his patent (this also applies to copyright owners; see **Donner** (Case C-5/11)). However, once the patented (or copyrighted) goods are circulated in another Member State, either by him or with his consent, his right to exclude those goods as the patentee is then said to be exhausted. The following case demonstrates this principle:

Centrafarm v Winthrop BV (Cases 15 and 16/74)

Sterling Drug Inc. held patents relating to a drug called Negram in the UK and the Netherlands. In both countries the drug was marketed either by Sterling Drug itself, or by companies which it had licensed to do so. Centrafarm, an independent Netherlands' company, bought supplies of the drug in both the UK and Germany, where it was much cheaper, and resold it in the Netherlands. Sterling Drug and its subsidiaries invoked their respective patent and trade mark rights before the Netherlands' courts to prevent Negram being marketed in the Netherlands by Centrafarm. The Netherlands' court referred a number of questions to the Court of Justice under what is now Art 267 TFEU (previously Art 234 EC Treaty). The Court described the limits of national patent rights in this context:

> An obstacle to the free movement of goods may arise out of the existence, within national legislation concerning industrial and commercial property, of provisions laying down that a patentee's right is not exhausted when the product protected by the patent is marketed in another Member State, with the result that the patentee can prevent importation of the product into his own Member State when it has been marketed in another Member State. Whereas an obstacle to the free movement of goods of this kind may be justified on the ground of the protection of industrial property where such protection is invoked against a product coming from a Member State where it is not patentable and has been manufactured by third parties without the consent of the patentee and in cases where there exist patents, the original proprietors of which are legally and economically independent, a derogation from the principle of the free movement of goods is not, however, justified where the product has been put onto the market in a legal manner, by the patentee himself or with his consent, in the Member State from which it has been imported, in particular in the case of a proprietor of parallel patents. (paras 10 and 11)

The 'exhaustion of rights' principle has been applied by the Court of Justice with regard not only to patent rights, but also to trade marks, copyright and industrial design. It defined the proprietorial interest in relation to trade marks in the same case:

Centrafarm v Winthrop BV (Cases 15 and 16/74)

The Court of Justice stated that:

> The specific subject matter of the industrial property is the guarantee that the owner of the trade mark has the exclusive right to use that trade mark for the purpose of putting products protected by the trade mark into circulation for the first time, and is therefore intended to protect him against any competitor wishing to take advantage of the status and reputation of the trade mark by selling products illegally bearing the trade mark.

Crucial to the application of the 'exhaustion of rights' principle is the meaning of 'consent' in this context. Consent is assumed where the owner markets the goods himself, where he does so through a subsidiary company, or where the owner and the undertaking responsible for the first marketing are under common control. The limits of consent were explored in the following case:

Pharmon B v Hoechst AG (Case 19/84)

Hoechst owned a patent in Germany for the manufacture of a drug called Frusemide. Hoechst also owned parallel patents in the Netherlands and the UK. Frusemide was not manufactured by Hoechst or any of its subsidiaries in the UK. In the UK it was manufactured by an independent company called DDSA under a compulsory licence granted under UK legislation. A compulsory licence does not require the consent of the owner of the patent, but royalties on sales are paid to him. The litigation in this case arose out of imports from the UK placed on The Netherlands' market by Pharmon. Because UK prices for the drug were much lower, Pharmon stood to make a considerable profit at Hoechst BV's expense. Could Hoechst resist Pharmon's marketing in The Netherlands? The question turned on whether the compulsory licensing and payment of royalties to Hoechst amounted to 'consent'. The Court of Justice, in a reference pursuant to what is now Art 267 TFEU (previously Art 234 EC Treaty), did not think that it did:

> It is necessary to point out that where, as in this instance, the competent authorities of a Member State grant a third party a compulsory licence which allows him to carry out manufacturing and marketing operations which the patentee would normally have the right to prevent, the patentee cannot be deemed to have consented to the operation of that third party. Such a measure deprives the patent proprietor of his right to determine freely the conditions under which he markets his products. (para 25)

The Court of Justice went further in the following case:

Iht Internationale Heiztechnik GMBH v Ideal-Standard GMBH (Case C-11/93)

The Court of Justice held that action by an assignee under contract (as opposed to a subsidiary in another Member State) could not be regarded as carried out with 'consent' of the assignor in relation to the use of a trade mark on goods imported into another Member State, and the import could be restrained under the property justification in what is now Art 36 TFEU (previously Art 30 EC Treaty).

The above decision is surprising because it could be said that the assignment itself included a right to deal generally with the trade mark and the assignment would therefore exhaust the rights of the assignor. The Court of Justice, however, stressed that the free movement of the goods would undermine the essential function of the trade mark. Consumers would no longer be able to identify, for certain, the origin of the marked goods, and the proprietor of the trade mark could be held responsible for the poor quality of the goods for which he is in no way accountable. In this case, at least, the Court's concern for the proprietorial interest of the patentee seems to have outweighed its concern to secure the free movement of goods.

The importance of consent can be seen in two apparently similar cases involving copyright. In **Musik Vertrieb Membran GmbH v GEMA** (Case 55/80) the Court of Justice held that the performing rights society GEMA could not rely on its German copyright in sound recordings to prevent **parallel imports** of records from the UK which had been put on the market there with its consent. In **EMI Electrola v Patricia** (Case 341/87), the claimants owned the production and distribution rights in Germany of the musical works of Cliff Richard. The defendants sold records of Cliff Richard's songs in Germany which had been imported from Denmark, where the copyright protection had expired. The claimants applied for an order from the German courts to exclude these imports. The defendants resisted on the ground that such an order would breach what is now Art 34 TFEU, as the records were in lawful circulation within Denmark. The Court of Justice, in a reference pursuant to what is now Art 267 TFEU (previously Art 234 EC Treaty), did not agree. Lawful circulation was not equivalent to consent. The Court distinguished the *GEMA* case on the ground that the marketing in Denmark was due to the expiry of the protection period in another Member State, and not to the consent of the copyright owner or his licensee. This was an aspect of ownership and the different rights of copyright owners in different Member States. The problems caused by these difficulties would continue unless these rules were harmonised for the whole Union.

Harmonisation of industrial property rights

The Commission has two principal aims in this field. The first is that each Member State should employ, as far as possible, the same substantive industrial property rules. The second is that intellectual property monopolies should run the length and breadth of the Union, irrespective of the country of their origin. Some progress has been made towards achieving both these aims. There are broadly similar rules in Member States governing criteria for patentability and the patent term. Registration is, however, undertaken according to different rules in different states. In 2012, Member States and the European Parliament agreed on a 'patent package' comprising a legislative initiative consisting of two Regulations and an international Agreement, which lay the foundations for the creation of unitary patent protection across the Union. The patent package was adopted by 25 of the then 27 Member States (Italy and Spain did not adopt the package; Croatia adopted the patent package following its membership of the Union on 1 July 2013). Following the adoption of the two Regulations in December 2012, the contracting Member States proceeded with the signature and ratification of the Agreement on a Unified Patent Court. This is the third and last component of the patent package which establishes a single and specialised patent jurisdiction. When the Agreement and the Regulations entered into force in early 2014, it introduced a European patent with unitary effect. This will ensure uniform protection for an invention across the participating Member States on a one-stop shop basis, providing significant cost advantages and reduced administrative burdens.

A harmonising directive on copyright (Directive 2001/29) was adopted on 22 May 2001, with an implementation date of 22 December 2002.

With regard to trade marks and designs, the Trade Mark Approximation Directive 89/104 (which has been codified as 2008/95) lays down principles common to the Union's national or regional trade mark systems. In addition, the Community Trade Mark Regulation 40/94 (which has been codified as 207/2009) provides for a single standard of registrability for a trade mark which grants protection to its proprietor throughout the Union. Both have been implemented in the UK by the Trade Marks Act 1994.

On 27 March 2013, the European Commission presented a package of initiatives to make trade mark registration systems all over the Union more cost effective, speedier, reliable and predictable. The proposed reform will improve conditions for businesses to innovate and to benefit from more effective trade mark protection against counterfeits, including fake goods in transit through the EU's territory. As regards fees, the Commission is proposing a principle of 'one-class-per-fee' that will apply both for Community trade mark applications and for national trade mark applications. This will enable any business to apply for trade mark protection according to their actual business needs, at a cost that covers those individual needs only. Under the current system, the fee for registering a trade mark allows for the registration of up to three product classes. Under the revised system, a trade mark can be registered for only one product class. So at Union level, businesses will pay substantially less when they seek to obtain protection for one class of product only. The proposed revision will:

- streamline and harmonise registration procedures, including at Member State level, taking the Community trade mark system as a benchmark;
- modernise the existing provisions and increase legal certainty by amending outdated provisions, removing ambiguities, clarifying trade mark rights in terms of their scope and limitations and incorporating extensive case law of the Court of Justice;
- improve the means to fight against counterfeit goods in transit through the EU's territory;
- facilitate cooperation between the Member States' offices and the EU trade mark agency – the Office for Harmonisation in the Internal Market (OHIM) – in order to promote convergence of their practices and the development of common tools.

The proposed package contains the following:

- recast of the Trade Mark Approximation Directive 89/104 approximating the laws of the Member States relating to trade marks (this directive has been codified as 2008/95);
- revision of the Community Trade Mark Regulation 40/94 on the Community trade mark (this directive has been codified as 207/2009).

The relationship between the Trade Mark Directive and the Court's existing case law on the protection of intellectual property rights and the scope of the former Art 30 EC Treaty (now Art 36 TFEU) was considered by the Court in **Bristol Myers Squibb** (Joined Cases C-427, 429 and 436/93). This case concerned the repackaging of goods, but the principles involved covered a much wider area of intellectual property law. Repackaging of trademarked products presents a particular problem in reconciling the fundamental principle of free movement of goods with the Treaty's guarantee of protection of intellectual property rights. The problem of repackaging is particularly acute in relation to pharmaceutical products, where prices vary widely throughout the Union. The wide price differentials are, largely, because the pricing of medical products in each Member State is regulated through state health service provisions. Traders can exploit the price differentials by buying goods in a low-price state and then selling them in a high-price market for a figure which undercuts the recommended retail price in that state. The usual practice, in these cases, is for the goods to be repackaged to meet the requirements of the importing Member State. The manufacturer will frequently attempt to prevent these parallel imports on the basis that the repackaging infringes its trade mark. The Court of Justice rejected these attempts at restraining imports and effectively partitioning the market. In **Hoffman La Roche v Centrafarm** (Case 102/77), the Court declared that the trade mark owner could not resist repackaging if: (i) his marketing system contributed to the artificial partitioning of the market; (ii) the repackaging could not adversely affect the original condition of the product; (iii) he received prior notice of the marketing of the repackaged product; and (iv) the identity of the repackager was stated on the new packaging. The issue in **Bristol Myers Squibb** (Cases C-427, 429 and 436/93) was, essentially, whether, and if so, how far, the existing case law was still relevant after the coming into effect of the Trade Mark Directive 89/104. Article 7, Directive 89/104 gives legislative recognition to the idea of exhaustion of rights which, as was seen in relation to all intellectual property rights, prevents the owners of a trade mark or patent from developing separate markets for their products in each Member State (see ***Centrafarm* v *Winthrop BV*** (Cases 15 and 16/74), above). The Court stressed that, as Directive 89/104 was a harmonising measure, it had to be interpreted in the light of the Treaty rules on the free movement of goods. On that basis, it specifically reiterated the four conditions set out in ***Hoffman La Roche*** (above) and affirmed that they continued to apply. However, although the directive had to be read in the light of what is now Art 36 TFEU (previously Art 30 EC Treaty), it did not allow the repackager to treat the goods (including the way they were advertised) in such a way as to damage their market 'image'. In ***Parfums Christian Dior SA* v *Evora BV*** (Case C-337/95), the subject matter of the repackaging was high-prestige perfume. The Court held that Art 7, Directive 89/104 allowed the owner of the trade mark to take steps to ensure that the presentation and advertising 'did not affect the value of the trade mark by detracting from the allure and prestigious image of the goods in question and from their aura of luxury'; also see ***Copad SA* v *Christian Dior couture SA, Société industrielle lingerie (SIL)*** (Case C-59/08).

Union legislation on intellectual property rights is likely never to be exhaustive, as modern technology continues to develop new products which raise new issues. There is an inevitable time lag between the evolution of the new product and the Union's response. The exception covering intellectual property rights in Art 36 TFEU, and the Court's jurisprudence on the subject, will therefore continue to be important.

Article 36 TFEU and the UK's implementation of the free movement of goods

This interpretative obligation (referred to as the principle of indirect effect) is considered further at pages 273–274 and pages 300–303.

The implementation of Arts 34 and 35 TFEU and the Union's harmonising measures in the UK has involved a major legislative programme to give effect to the Union directives that were intended to complete the internal market by 1 January 1993. In terms of primary legislation, this involved measures of a general kind, such as the Customs and Excise Management Act 1979, which imposed a general obligation on the UK customs authorities 'for the purpose of implementing Community [i.e. Union] obligations . . . [to] co-operate with other customs services . . . to give effect . . . to any Community [i.e. Union] requirement or practice as to the movement of goods between countries'. More specific Acts of Parliament were passed to implement major directives, such as the Product Liability Directive 85/374, which was put into effect by the Consumer Protection Act 1987. Other specific legislation was enacted to put decisions of the Court of Justice into effect. For example, the Importation of Milk Act 1983 was enacted to comply with the judgment in ***Commission* v *UK (Re UHT Milk)*** (Case 124/81); see above. In implementing the law relating to the free movement of goods, as with other Union provisions, the UK has, essentially, four options:

- where the requirements of a directive are already met in national law, no specific action may be necessary;
- where there is existing UK legislation, by creating the power to make appropriate national regulations;
- by delegated legislation under s 2(2), European Communities Act 1972;
- through primary legislation.

Where legislation is enacted to implement a directive, it must give precise effect to the directive. It was thought by many writers that the Product Liability Directive, which created liability for the manufacturers of defective goods, had not been effectively implemented by the Consumer Protection Act 1987. The Commission brought proceedings against the UK before the Court of Justice. This was because the Act provided a defence to manufacturers based on the state of knowledge existing at the time the goods were put into circulation in circumstances in which, the Commission argued, a manufacturer might escape liability by demonstrating that he had not been negligent if he was unaware of any potential risk. The directive itself imposed strict liability. The Court of Justice refused to accept the Commission's interpretation of the Act, and noted that there was 'nothing . . . to suggest that the courts of the UK, if called upon to interpret [the Consumer Protection Act] would not do so in the light of the wording and the purposes of the Directive' (***Commission v UK*** (Case C-300/95)).

The *Cassis* rule of reason: defences to indistinctly applicable measures

Objective 6

The *Cassis* case was considered above. In *Cassis* the Court of Justice held that the former Art 28 EC Treaty (now Art 34 TFEU) applies to indistinctly applicable measures (i.e. measures which apply to *both* imported and domestic products) which impact upon the free movement of intra-Union trade. The first *Cassis* principle (the rule of mutual recognition) was discussed, which provides that once goods have been lawfully marketed in one Member State they should be free to be marketed in any other Member State without restriction. However, this is subject to the second principle, the 'rule of reason', or the '**mandatory requirements defence**':

Rewe-Zentrale AG v Bundesmonopolverwaltung Für Branntwein (Case 120/78)

In the *Cassis* case, the applicant wished to import the liqueur 'Cassis de Dijon' into Germany from France. The relevant German authorities refused to allow the importation because the French liqueur was not of sufficient alcoholic strength to be marketed in Germany. Under German law, liqueurs had to have an alcoholic strength of 25 per cent, whereas that of the French liqueur was between 15 per cent and 20 per cent. The applicant argued that this rule was an MEQR, since it prevented the French version of the drink being marketed in Germany. The Court of Justice held as follows:

8. In the absence of common rules relating to the production and marketing of alcohol . . . it is for the Member States to regulate all matters relating to the production and marketing of alcohol and alcoholic beverages on their own territory.

   Obstacles to movement within the Community [i.e. Union] resulting from disparities between the national laws relating to the marketing of the products in question must be accepted in so far as those provisions may be recognised as being necessary in order to satisfy mandatory requirements relating in particular to the effectiveness of fiscal supervision, the protection of public health, the fairness of commercial transactions and the defence of the consumer.

9. The Government of the Federal Republic of Germany, intervening in the proceedings, put forward various arguments which, in its view, justify the application of the provisions relating to the minimum alcohol content of alcoholic beverages, adducing considerations relating on the one hand to the protection of public health and on the other to the protection of the consumer against unfair commercial practices.

10. As regards the protection of public health the German Government states that the purpose of the fixing of minimum alcohol contents by national legislation is to avoid the proliferation of alcoholic beverages with a low alcohol content, since, in its view, such products may more easily induce a tolerance towards alcohol than more highly alcoholic beverages.

11. Such considerations are not decisive since the consumer can obtain on the market an extremely wide range of weakly or moderately alcoholic products and furthermore a large proportion of alcoholic beverages with a high alcohol content freely sold on the German market is generally consumed in diluted form.

12. The German Government also claims that the fixing of a lower limit for the alcohol content of certain liqueurs is designed to protect the consumer against unfair practices on the part of producers and distributors of alcoholic beverages.

    This argument is based on the consideration that the lowering of the alcohol content secures a competitive advantage in relation to beverages with a higher alcohol content, since alcohol constitutes by far the most expensive constituent of beverages by reason of the high rate of tax to which it is subject.

    Furthermore, according to the German Government, to allow alcoholic products into free circulation wherever, as regards their alcohol content, they comply with the rules laid down in the country of production would have the effect of imposing as a common standard within the Community [i.e. Union] the lowest alcohol content permitted in any of the Member States, and even of rendering any requirements in this field inoperative since a lower limit of this nature is foreign to the rules of several Member States.

13. As the Commission rightly observed, the fixing of limits to the alcohol content of beverages may lead to the standardisation of products placed on the market and of their designations, in the interests of a greater transparency of commercial transactions and offers for sale to the public. However, this line of argument cannot be taken so far as to regard the mandatory fixing of minimum alcohol contents as being an essential guarantee of the fairness of commercial transactions, since **it is a simple matter to ensure that suitable information is conveyed to the purchaser by requiring the display of an indication of origin and of the alcohol content on the packaging of products.**

14. It is clear from the foregoing that the requirements relating to the minimum alcohol content of alcoholic beverages do not serve a purpose which is in the general interest and such as to take precedence over the requirements of the free movement of goods, which constitutes one of the fundamental rules of the Community [i.e. Union].

    In practice, the principal effect of requirements of this nature is to promote alcoholic beverages having a high alcohol content by excluding from the national market products of other Member States which do not answer that description.

    It therefore appears that the unilateral requirement imposed by the rules of a Member State of a minimum alcohol content for the purposes of the sale of alcoholic beverages constitutes an obstacle to trade which is incompatible with the provisions of . . . [Article 34 TFEU].

    There is therefore no valid reason why, provided that they have been lawfully produced and marketed in one of the Member States, alcoholic beverages should not be introduced into any other Member State; the sale of such products may not be subject to a legal prohibition on the marketing of beverages with an alcohol content lower than the limits set by national rules. [emphasis added]

Paragraph 8 of the above judgment contains the second *Cassis* principle, which is commonly referred to as the 'rule of reason':

. . . Obstacles to movement within the Community [i.e. Union] resulting from disparities between the national laws relating to the marketing of the products in question must be accepted in so far as those provisions may be recognised as being necessary in order to satisfy mandatory requirements relating in particular to the effectiveness of fiscal supervision, the protection of public health, the fairness of commercial transactions and the defence of the consumer.

There are four grounds listed which may prevent a rule from being caught by Art 34 TFEU:

- fiscal supervision;
- public health;
- fairness of commercial transactions;
- protection of the consumer.

This list is not exhaustive, and it has been expanded by the Court of Justice in subsequent cases; see below. Any measure which satisfies the *rule of reason* will not be caught by Art 34 TFEU. This is separate and distinct from the Art 36 TFEU derogations (considered above).

The Member State is placed upon the defensive. After asserting the right of the state to regulate, the Court provides that such indistinct rules which interfere with the free movement of goods will be lawful only in so far as they are justified under one of the heads of the rule of reason.

The mandatory requirement defence: 'the rule of reason'

As discussed above, Art 36 TFEU provides a defence to rules otherwise caught by Art 34 TFEU. Although this defence can apply to both distinctly and indistinctly applicable measures, the Court has applied Art 36 TFEU very strictly so that a Member State cannot breach the principle of free movement of goods very easily. However, the Court has recognised that an indistinctly applicable rule which in some way restricts trade may be defended under the *Cassis* rule of reason.

The fact that the rule of reason applies only to an indistinctly applicable measure has been made clear by the Court of Justice on a number of occasions (see, for example, *Italian State* v *Gilli and Andres* (Case 788/79)). The Court held that it was only where national rules applied without distinction to both national and imported products that they could be justified using the mandatory requirements derived from *Cassis*.

In the following case, the Court of Justice held that the rule of reason applied only to indistinctly applicable measures:

Commission v *Ireland* (Case 113/80)

When considering the nature of a distinctly applicable measure, the Irish government, as part of its defence, argued that the distinctly applicable measure could be saved because it satisfied the *Cassis* rule of reason. This was rejected by the Court of Justice which held as follows:

5. The Irish Government does not dispute the restrictive effects of these orders on the free movement of goods. However, it contends that the disputed measures are justified in the interests of consumer protection and of fairness in commercial transactions between producers.

. . .

10. In this respect, the Court has repeatedly affirmed (in the judgments of 20 February 1979 in Case 120/78 *Rewe* [1979] ECR 649, 26 June 1980 in Case 788/79 *Gilli and Andres*

> [1980] ECR 2071, 19 February 1981 in Case 130/80 *Kelderman* [1981] ECR 527) that 'in the absence of common rules relating to the production and marketing of the product in question it is for Member States to regulate all matters relating to its production, distribution and consumption on their own territory subject, however, to the condition that those rules do not present an obstacle . . . to intra-Community [i.e. intra-Union] trade' and that 'it is only where national rules, which apply without discrimination to both domestic and imported products, may be justified as being necessary in order to satisfy imperative requirements relating in particular to . . . the fairness of commercial transactions and the defence of the consumer that they may constitute an exception to the requirements arising under . . . [Article 34 TFEU]'.
>
> 11. The orders concerned in the present case are not measures which are applicable to domestic products and to imported products without distinction but rather a set of rules which apply only to imported products and are therefore discriminatory in nature, with the result that the measures in issue are not covered by the decisions cited above which relate exclusively to provisions that regulate in a uniform manner the marketing of domestic products and imported products. [emphasis added]

As discussed above, the Court of Justice set out a list of mandatory requirements in the *Cassis* case:

> 8. . . . Obstacles to movement within the Community [i.e. Union] resulting from disparities between the national laws relating to the marketing of the products in question must be accepted in so far as those provisions may be recognised as being necessary in order to satisfy mandatory requirements **relating in particular to the effectiveness of fiscal supervision, the protection of public health, the fairness of commercial transactions and the defence of the consumer.** [emphasis added]

This list is not exhaustive (note the use of the words 'relating in particular to . . . '). The Court has added others to that list. Some of the specific mandatory requirements are now considered.

Consumer protection

Commission v *Germany* (Case 178/84)

> The Commission instituted what are now Art 258 TFEU (previously Art 226 EC Treaty) proceedings against Germany, alleging a breach of what is now Art 34 TFEU (previously Art 28 EC Treaty). Germany prohibited the marketing, on its territory, of beer lawfully produced and marketed in other Member States if the beer failed to comply with the provisions of the *Biersteuergesetz* of 1952 (Beer Duty Act 1952). There were two provisions the Commission wished to challenge. The first one was that the name 'Bier' could only be used for products brewed using malted barley, hops, yeast and water alone. The use of other ingredients such as maize did not prohibit the product being marketed, but it could not be called 'Bier'. The German government sought to defend its law on the basis that it was necessary to protect the German consumer who associated the label 'Bier' with beverages made exclusively from the stated ingredients. The Court of Justice ruled that the law was a barrier to free trade and then considered whether it was necessary to protect consumers:
>
> 31. The German Government's argument that section 10 of the Biersteuergesetz is essential in order to protect German consumers because, in their minds, the designation 'Bier' is inseparably linked to the beverage manufactured solely from the ingredients laid down in section 9 of the Biersteuergesetz must be rejected.

32. Firstly, consumers' conceptions which vary from one Member State to the other are also likely to evolve in the course of time within a Member State. The establishment of the Common Market [i.e. internal market] is, it should be added, one of the factors that may play a major contributory role in that development. Whereas rules protecting consumers against misleading practices enable such a development to be taken into account, legislation of the kind contained in section 10 of the Biersteuergesetz prevents it from taking place. As the Court has already held in another context (Case 170/78 *Commission* v *UK*), the legislation of a Member State must not 'crystallise given consumer habits so as to consolidate an advantage acquired by national industries concerned to comply with them'.

33. Secondly, in the other Member States of the Community [i.e. Union] the designations corresponding to the German designation 'Bier' are generic designations for a fermented beverage manufactured from barley, whether malted barley on its own or with the addition of rice or maize. The same approach is taken in Community [i.e. Union] law as can be seen from heading 22.03 of the Common Customs Tariff. The German legislature itself utilises the designation 'Bier' in that way in section 9(7) and (8) of the Biersteuergesetz in order to refer to beverages not complying with the manufacturing rules laid down in section 9(1) and (2).

34. The German designation 'Bier' and its equivalents in the languages of the other Member States may therefore not be restricted to beers manufactured in accordance with the rules in force in the Federal Republic of Germany.

35. **It is admittedly legitimate to seek to enable consumers who attribute specific qualities to beers manufactured from particular raw materials to make their choice in the light of that consideration. However, as the Court has already emphasised (Case 193/80 *Commission* v *Italy*) that possibility may be ensured by means which do not prevent the importation of products which have been lawfully manufactured and marketed in other Member States and, in particular, 'by the compulsory affixing of suitable labels giving the nature of the product sold'.** By indicating the raw materials utilised in the manufacture of beer 'such a course would enable the consumer to make his choice in full knowledge of the facts and would guarantee transparency in trading and in offers to the public'. It must be added that such a system of mandatory consumer information must not entail negative assessments for beers not complying with the requirements of section 9 of the Biersteuergesetz. [emphasis added]

In the above case, the Court of Justice held that the German law breached what is now Art 34 TFEU. Although there were some arguments in favour of Germany's 'consumer protection' claim, the Court looked at whether the action taken was necessary, or whether action which was less restrictive of intra-Union trade could have been taken (i.e. an application of the proportionality test). At para 35 the Court held that consumer interests could be met through better labelling rather than an outright ban.

Other cases have followed this approach. In ***De Kikvorsch Groothandel-Import-Export BV*** (Case 94/82), the Court of Justice again rejected a restrictive rule which was a barrier to free movement on the ground that better labelling could achieve the objective sought – protection of the consumer. A similar result was achieved in the following case:

Ministère Public v *Deserbais* (Case 286/86)

French legislation restricted the use of the name 'Edam' to cheese with a minimum fat content of 40 per cent. Mr Deserbais imported cheese into France from Germany, where it was lawfully produced with a fat content of 34.3 per cent. He marketed the cheese in France as 'Edam' cheese and was prosecuted. In his defence he argued that French law was not applicable because it contravened what is now Art 34 TFEU (previously Art 28 EC Treaty). The matter was referred to the Court of Justice under what is now Art 267 TFEU (previously Art 234 EC Treaty) for a preliminary ruling. The Court held as follows:

10. The national court starts from the premise that the cheese in question, containing 34 per cent fat, has been lawfully and traditionally produced in the Federal Republic of Germany under the name 'Edam' in accordance with the laws and regulations applicable to it there, and that consumers' attention is adequately drawn to that fact by the labelling.

11. It must also be stated that at the present stage of development of Community [i.e. Union] law there are no common rules governing the various types of cheeses in the Community [i.e. Union]. Accordingly, it cannot be stated in principle that a Member State may not lay down rules making the use by national producers of a name for a cheese subject to the observance of a traditional minimum fat content.

12. However, it would be incompatible with . . . [Article 34 TFEU] and the objectives of a common market [i.e. internal market] to apply such rules to imported cheeses of the same type where those cheeses have been lawfully produced and marketed in another Member State under the same generic name but with a different minimum fat content. **The Member State into which they are imported cannot prevent the importation and marketing of such cheeses where adequate information for the consumer is ensured.**

13. The question may arise whether the same rule must be applied where a product presented under a particular name is so different, as regards its composition or production, from the products generally known by that name in the Community [i.e. Union] that it cannot be regarded as falling within the same category. However, no situation of that kind arises in the circumstances described by the national court in this case . . . [Article 34 TFEU] must be interpreted as precluding a Member State from applying national legislation making the right to use the trade name of a type of cheese subject to the observance of a minimum fat content to products of the same type imported from another Member State when those products have been lawfully manufactured and marketed under that name in that Member State and consumers are provided with proper information. [emphasis added]

In the above case, the Court of Justice held that France's indistinctly applicable rule was a restriction on trade in relation to cheese which had been lawfully produced and marketed in Germany. It was therefore in breach of what is now Art 34 TFEU, unless the rule could be justified under one of the heads of the rule of reason (in this case, defence of the consumer). The Court held that the consumer could be provided with adequate information about the fat content of the different 'Edam' cheeses and therefore the rule was not justified under the rule of reason. However, the Court acknowledged in para 13 that a product may be so different (as regards composition or production) from products generally known by that name in the importing country that it could not be considered to fall within the same category.

A similar issue relating to a restriction on the use of a particular name for certain goods was considered by the Court of Justice in the following case:

Commission v Spain (Case C-12/00) and *Commission v Italy* (Case C-14/00)

Spanish and Italian legislation prohibited cocoa and chocolate products to which vegetable fats other than cocoa butter had been added from being marketed under the name 'chocolate', and required them to be marketed using the term 'chocolate substitute'. As regards the applicability of the former Art 28 EC Treaty (now Art 34 TFEU) to the prohibition laid down by the legislation at issue, the Court of Justice observed that such legislation was likely to impede trade between Member States. It compelled the traders concerned to adjust the presentation of their products according to the place where they were to be marketed and consequently to incur additional packaging costs and adversely affect the consumer's perception of the products. The inclusion in the label of a neutral and objective statement informing consumers of the presence in the product of vegetable fats other than cocoa butter would be sufficient to ensure that consumers are given correct information. The Court concluded that the Spanish and Italian legislation which required the sales name of those products to be changed did not appear to be necessary to satisfy the overriding requirement of consumer protection and that the legislation at issue was incompatible with the former Art 28 EC Treaty (now Art 34 TFEU).

The proportionality test was once again applied by the Court of Justice in the following case, resulting in Italy being prevented from relying on the 'consumer protection' defence:

Italian State v *Gilli and Andres* (Case 788/79)

Italian law required that vinegar had to be made from the fermentation of wine. Importers of apple vinegar from Germany into Italy were prosecuted for fraud. The importers relied on what is now Art 34 TFEU (previously Art 28 EC Treaty) as a defence. There were no Union harmonisation rules on the issue. The Court of Justice adopted the *Cassis* reasoning and said that in the absence of harmonisation measures, a Member State could regulate the production and marketing of products within its territory, provided that such regulation did not constitute an obstacle, actually or potentially, to the free movement of intra-Union trade. This rule did hinder the free movement of goods and therefore it could be saved only if it could be justified under one of the heads of the rule of reason. The Court held that it could not be justified because once again the consumer could be protected by proper labelling of the products and in this case there was no danger to health.

The same approach was adopted by the Court of Justice in the following case:

Walter Rau Lebensmittelwerke v *DE Smedt PVBA* (Case 261/81)

The claimants manufactured margarine and complained that a Belgian law, under which margarine had to be sold in Belgium in cube-shaped packs to distinguish it from butter, infringed what is now Art 34 TFEU (previously Art 28 EC Treaty). The Court of Justice, in a reference for a preliminary ruling under what is now Art 267 TFEU (previously Art 234 EC Treaty), agreed. Although the rule applied to all margarine sold in Belgium, foreign manufacturers wishing to import margarine into Belgium would have to establish a special production and packaging line for the Belgian market, which would increase their production costs. There was no consumer protection reason for the packaging requirement. The true nature of the product could just as well be conveyed to the consumer by effective labelling.

The Treaty specifically requires Union harmonising measures on the free movement of goods to contribute to the protection of the health, safety and economic interests of consumers, in addition to 'promoting their right to information, education and to organise themselves in order to safeguard their interests' (Art 169 TFEU (previously Art 153 EC

Treaty)). In the absence of a Union harmonising measure, where possible it is preferable for national measures to require the disclosure of stipulated information to consumers rather than an outright prohibition against sale. However, labelling requirements themselves may not escape Art 34 TFEU, as illustrated in the following case:

Fietje (Case 27/80)

The Court of Justice stated:

10. Although the extension to imported products of an obligation to use a certain name on the label does not wholly preclude the importation into the Member State concerned of products originating in other Member States or in free circulation in those States it may nonetheless make their marketing more difficult, especially in the case of parallel imports. As the Netherlands Government itself admits in its observations, such an extension of that obligation is thus capable of impeding, at least indirectly, trade between Member States. It is therefore necessary to consider whether it may be justified on the ground of public interest in consumer protection which, according to observations of the Netherlands Government and according to 'Warenwet' [i.e. The Netherlands' Commodities Act], underlies the rules in question.

11. If the national rules relating to a given product include the obligation to use a description that is sufficiently precise to inform the purchaser of the nature of the product and to enable it to be distinguished from products with which it may be confused, it may well be necessary, in order to give consumers effective protection, to extend this obligation to imported products also, even in such a way as to make necessary the alteration of the original labels of some of these products. At the level of Community [i.e. Union] legislation, this possibility is recognised in several directives on the approximation of the laws of the Member States relating to certain foodstuffs as well as by Council Directive 79/112/EEC of 18 December 1978 on the approximation of the laws of the Member States relating to the labelling, presentation and advertising of foodstuffs for sale to the ultimate consumer (*Official Journal* 1979, L33, p. 1).

12. However, there is no longer any need for such protection if the details given on the original label of the imported product have as their content information on the nature of the product and that content includes at least the same information, and is just as capable of being understood by consumers in the importing State, as the description prescribed by the rules of that State. In the context of . . . [Article 267 TFEU], the making of findings of fact necessary in order to establish whether there is such equivalence is a matter for the national court. [emphasis added]

In the above case, the Court of Justice held that a labelling requirement (that a specific name had to appear on the label) may render it more difficult for an importer to market goods in another Member State and therefore it would come within the scope of what is now Art 34 TFEU unless justified (e.g. on the ground of consumer protection). The Court held the labelling requirement would not be justified if the necessary information required by the Member State of import was included on the original label (but not the specific name) and this was just as capable of being understood by consumers. This theme was continued in the following case:

Neeltje v *Houtwipper* (Case C-293/93)

The issue in this case concerned the compatibility with the former Art 28 EC Treaty (now Art 34 TFEU) of national legislation requiring the hallmarking of precious metals offered for sale. All such metals in the Netherlands, both domestic and imported, had to be hallmarked to show the content of precious metals. The measure thus appeared to be indistinctly applicable, but in practice it meant that it rendered the import of precious metals into the Netherlands more difficult and costly, because importers would have to have their products reassayed and date-stamped to indicate the year of manufacture in accordance with the Netherlands' hallmarking law. In practice, therefore, the importers of precious metals were at a disadvantage. Although the Court of Justice accepted that hallmarking of precious metals was a mandatory requirement designed to ensure effective protection of consumers and the promotion of fair trading, it held that the way in which the system operated breached the former Art 28 EC Treaty (now Art 34 TFEU):

> A Member State cannot require a fresh hallmark be affixed to products imported from another Member State in which they have been lawfully marketed and hallmarked in accordance with the legislation of that state, where the information provided by that hallmark, in whatever form, is equivalent to that prescribed by the Member State of importation and intelligible to consumers of that state.

Fairness of commercial transactions

This overlaps with the previous mandatory requirement, and both may be pleaded in the alternative. In the *Cassis* case, Germany argued, *inter alia*, that the rule that liqueurs must contain a minimum alcohol content of 25 per cent was justified under the rule of reason on the ground of fairness of commercial transactions. It was argued that French Cassis, with a lower alcohol content, gained an unfair competitive advantage because tax on alcohol content constituted the greatest proportion of the cost of the product. A liqueur with a lower alcohol content would be taxed at a lower rate and therefore its selling price would be less than those liqueurs with a higher alcohol content (which would be subjected to a higher level of taxation). This argument was rejected by the Court of Justice.

Public health

Public health is included in both Art 36 TFEU and the list of mandatory requirements. When faced with a rule which is being defended by the imposing Member State on the ground of public health, the Court may not be overly concerned with whether it falls to be considered under Art 36 TFEU or the *Cassis* rule of reason, as illustrated in the following case:

Commission v *Germany* (Case 178/84)

This case, which has been considered above, concerned a German rule which banned using the name 'Bier' unless the beverage in question was made from certain prescribed ingredients. The Commission was also concerned with a provision under the German Foodstuffs Act 1974, which banned the marketing of beer which contained additives. It was accepted that this indistinctly applicable rule constituted a barrier to intra-Union trade, because it banned beer which was lawfully produced and marketed in other Member States where such beer contained additives. The question before the Court of Justice was whether this rule could be justified under what is now Art 36 TFEU (previously Art 30 EC Treaty) on public health grounds:

41. The Court has consistently held (in particular in Case 174/82 *Criminal Proceedings Against Sandoz BV*) that 'in so far as there are uncertainties at the present state of scientific research it is for the Member States, in the absence of harmonisation, to decide

what degree of protection of the health and life of humans they intend to assure, having regard to the requirements of the free movement of goods within the Community [i.e. Union]'.

42. As may also be seen from the decision of the Court (and especially the *Sandoz* case, cited above, in Case 247/84, *Motte*, and in Case 308/84, *Ministère Public* v *Muller*), in such circumstances Community [i.e. Union] law does not preclude the adoption by Member States of legislation whereby the use of additives is subjected to prior authorisation granted by a measure of general application for specific additives, in respect of all products, for certain products only or for certain uses. Such legislation meets a genuine need of health policy, namely that of restricting the uncontrolled consumption of food additives.

43. However, the application to imported products of prohibitions on marketing products containing additives which are authorised in the Member State of production but prohibited in the Member State of importation is permissible only in so far as it complies with the requirements of . . . [Article 36 TFEU] as it has been interpreted by the Court.

44. **It must be borne in mind, in the first place, that in its judgments in *Sandoz*, *Motte* and *Muller*, the Court inferred from the principle of proportionality underlying the last sentence of . . . [Article 36 TFEU] that prohibitions on the marketing of products containing additives authorised in the Member State of production but prohibited in the Member State of importation must be restricted to what is actually necessary to secure the protection of public health. The Court also concluded that the use of a specific additive which is authorised in another Member State must be authorised in the case of a product imported from that Member State where, in view, on the one hand, of the findings of international scientific research, and in particular the work of the Community's [i.e. Union's] Scientific Committee for Food, the Codex Alimentarius Committee of the Food and Agriculture Organisation of the United Nations (FAO) and the World Health Organisation and, on the other, of the eating habits prevailing in the importing Member State, the additive in question does not present a risk to public health and meets a real need, especially a technical one.**

45. Secondly, it should be remembered that, as the Court held in *Muller*, by virtue of the principle of proportionality, traders must also be able to apply, under a procedure which is easily accessible to them and can be concluded within a reasonable time, for the use of specific additives to be authorised by a measure of general application . . . [emphasis added]

The Court of Justice proceeded to state that the German rule prohibited all additives and there was no procedure whereby a trader could obtain authorisation to use a specific additive. Additives were allowed in other beverages. It was argued by the German government that if the beer was manufactured in accordance with German law (i.e. s 9 of the Biersteuergesetz) additives would not be needed. The Court continued:

51. It must be emphasised that the mere reference to the fact that beer can be manufactured without additives if it is made from only the raw materials prescribed in the Federal Republic of Germany does not suffice to preclude the possibility that some additives may meet a technological need. Such an interpretation of the concept of technological need, which results in favouring national production methods, constitutes a disguised means of restricting trade between Member States.

52. The concept of technological need must be assessed in the light of the raw materials utilised and bearing in mind the assessment made by the authorities of the Member States where the product was lawfully manufactured and marketed. Account must also be taken of the findings of international scientific research and in particular the work of the Community's [i.e. Union's] Scientific Committee for Food, the Codex Alimentarius Committee of the FAO and the World Health Organisation.

> 53. Consequently, in so far as the German rules on additives in beer entail a general ban on additives, their application to beers imported from other Member States is contrary to the requirements of Community [i.e. Union] law as laid down in the case law of the Court, since that prohibition is contrary to the principle of proportionality and is therefore not covered by . . . [Article 36 TFEU].

In the above case, the Court of Justice held that the German law breached what is now Art 34 TFEU because it was not proportionate. Although individual Member States have a margin of discretion in deciding what level of protection to provide to consumers, the Court, in determining whether such national measures are proportionate, will take into account the extent of current knowledge, particularly when assessing national provisions to protect the health of consumers. This is illustrated in the following case:

Proceedings against M Debus (Cases C-13 and 113/91)

> The defendant was prosecuted for importing and marketing in Italy, beer containing sulphur dioxide in a quantity permitted by the relevant French legislation but higher than that permitted in Italy. The defendant contested the prosecution on the basis that the Italian legislation breached what is now Art 34 TFEU (previously Art 28 EC Treaty). The case was referred to the Court of Justice under what is now Art 267 TFEU (previously Art 234 EC Treaty). The Court had little difficulty in finding that the Italian rules led to 'a general and absolute prohibition of all beers containing more than 20 mg of sulphur dioxide per litre without any exception whatsoever'. There was uncontested evidence that the level of sulphur dioxide prohibited was far less than that found to constitute a risk by the WHO. It was an indistinctly applicable measure. The Court did not accept that, as there were other methods of preserving beer, the importing Member State was entitled to determine the method to be used, 'since such an interpretation of the concept of technological requirement, which leads to preference for domestic production methods, constituted a means of imposing a disguised restriction on trade between Member States' (see also *Sandoz BV* (Case 174/82); *Deserbais* (Case 286/86)).

In the following case, the Court of Justice was required to address the issue of prior authorisation in the context of application of the public health mandatory requirement (although the Court considered this defence under what is now Art 36 TFEU rather than the *Cassis* rule of reason, the principle is, nevertheless, exactly the same):

Greenham v ABEL (Case C-95/01)

> The question before the Court of Justice concerned whether the former Arts 28 and 30 EC Treaty (now Arts 34 and 36 TFEU) must be interpreted as meaning that they preclude a Member State from prohibiting the marketing (without prior authorisation) of foodstuffs which have been lawfully marketed in another Member State, if nutrients such as vitamins or minerals have been added to the foodstuff, other than those whose use has been declared lawful in the first Member State. The Court held that the former Arts 28 and 30 EC Treaty (now Arts 34 and 36 TFEU) do not preclude a Member State from prohibiting the marketing of such foodstuffs, but this is subject to the following conditions:
>
> ● the prior authorisation procedure must be readily accessible and capable of being completed within a reasonable time;

- if an application for prior authorisation is refused, there must be a right to challenge this refusal before the courts;
- a refusal to authorise marketing must be based on a detailed assessment of the risk to public health, based on the most reliable scientific data available and the most recent results of international research.

Applying these conditions in *Commission v France* (Case C-24/00), the Court of Justice held that France was unable to rely on the public health defence and was in breach of what is now Art 34 TFEU. France had failed to: (i) provide a procedure for including nutrients on the list of authorised substances which was accessible, transparent, and could be completed within a reasonable time; and (ii) justify refusals on the basis of a detailed assessment of the genuine risk to public health.

The following case concerned food supplements which contained certain vitamins and/or minerals, and their automatic classification as medicinal products:

Commission v Germany (Case C-387/99) and *Commission v Austria* (Case C-150/00)

The Commission had received a number of complaints against the administrative practice in Germany and Austria of automatically classifying as medicinal products, preparations which were based on certain vitamins and/or minerals and which were lawfully marketed as food supplements in the Member State from which they were imported, where those substances were present in amounts exceeding the recommended daily intake (Case C-150/00) or exceeded it by three times (Case C-387/99). The Commission brought action before the Court of Justice against Germany and Austria for infringement of the former Art 28 EC Treaty (now Art 34 TFEU).

In support of those actions, the Commission argued essentially that the classification of each vitamin or mineral as a medicinal product had to be carried out case-by-case, having regard to the pharmacological properties that it was recognised as having in the present state of scientific knowledge. The harmfulness of vitamins and minerals varied.

The Commission argued that a single general and abstract approach for all those substances went beyond what was necessary for achieving the objective of the protection of health laid down in the former Art 30 EC Treaty (now Art 36 TFEU), so that that approach was not proportionate. The barrier to the free movement of goods resulting from the contested practices could not therefore be justified, even though it pursued a legitimate aim.

The Court of Justice, upholding the Commission's argument, held that to determine whether vitamin preparations or preparations containing minerals should be classified as medicinal products within the meaning of Directive 65/65 on proprietary medicinal products, the national authorities, acting under the control of the Court, must work on a case-by-case basis, having regard to the characteristics of those preparations, in particular: (i) their composition; (ii) their pharmacological properties; (iii) the manner in which they are used; (iv) the extent of their distribution; (v) their familiarity to consumers; and (vi) the risks their use may entail. Classification as a medicinal product of a vitamin preparation or a preparation containing minerals which was based solely on the recommended daily amount of the nutrient it contains, did not fully satisfy the requirement for a classification on the basis of the pharmacological properties of each preparation. Even though it was true that the concentration of vitamins or minerals above which a preparation was classified as a medicinal product varied according to the vitamin or mineral in question, it did not necessarily follow that all preparations containing more than once, or three times, the recommended daily intake of one of those substances came within the definition of a medicinal product for the purposes of Directive 65/65.

The Court stated that in those circumstances it was clear that the contested practices created a barrier to trade, as such preparations lawfully marketed or produced in other Member States as food supplements could not be marketed in Germany or Austria until they had been subject to the marketing authorisation procedure for medicinal products.

The Court held that this barrier could not be justified on the basis of the former Art 30 EC Treaty (now Art 36 TFEU). While Member States are afforded a certain discretion with regard to the protection of public health, the means used must be proportionate to the objective pursued, which it must not be possible to attain by measures less restrictive of intra-Union trade. In this respect, stated the Court, the systematic nature of the contested practices did not make it possible to identify and assess a real risk to public health, which required a detailed assessment on a case-by-case basis of the effects the addition of the vitamins and minerals in question could entail. A preparation that would not pose a real risk to public health thus also required a marketing authorisation as a medicinal product. In the light of those considerations, the Court held that Germany and Austria had failed to fulfil their obligations under the former Art 28 EC Treaty (now Art 34 TFEU).

The above case involved indistinctly applicable measures, because the restrictions applied to both domestic and imported goods. The Court of Justice decided the case with reference to the former Art 30 EC Treaty (now Art 36 TFEU) derogation rather than under the *Cassis* rule of reason. The end result is nevertheless the same.

The following case concerned Germany's prohibition on the import and retail sale of medicinal products by mail order or over the internet:

Deutscher Apothekerverband (Case C-322/01)

The Court of Justice held that the prohibition was a measure having an effect equivalent to a quantitative restriction for the purposes of the former Art 28 EC Treaty (now Art 34 TFEU), because although it related to selling arrangements within the context of the Court's *Keck* judgment, the prohibition did not affect in the same manner, in law and in fact, the marketing of both domestic products and those from other Member States (see above). The Court then considered whether the prohibition could be justified under the former Art 30 EC Treaty (now Art 36 TFEU). Similar to the case considered above (*Commission v Germany* (Case C-387/99) and *Commission v Austria* (Case C-150/00)), it was irrelevant that Court considered the case under the former Art 30 EC Treaty (now Art 36 TFEU) rather than under the mandatory requirements defence. The Court held that the only plausible arguments were those relating to the need to: (i) provide individual advice to the customer and to ensure his protection when he is supplied with medicines; (ii) check that prescriptions are genuine; and (iii) guarantee that medicinal products are widely available and sufficient to meet requirements. None of those reasons could provide a valid basis for the absolute prohibition on the sale by mail order of non-prescription medicines, because the 'virtual' pharmacy provided customers with an identical or better level of service than traditional pharmacies. Conversely, for prescription medicines, such control could be justified in view of the greater risks which those medicines may present and the system of fixed prices which applied to them and which formed part of the German health system. The need to be able to check effectively and responsibly the authenticity of doctors' prescriptions and to ensure that the medicine was handed over either to the customer himself, or to a person to whom its collection had been entrusted by the customer, was such as to justify a prohibition on mail order sales. The former Art 30 EC Treaty (now Art 36 TFEU) may, therefore, be relied on to justify such a prohibition. The Court stated that the same arguments applied where medicinal products were imported into a Member State in which they were authorised, having been previously obtained by a pharmacy in another Member State from a wholesaler in the importing Member State.

As regards the compatibility with Union law of prohibitions on advertising of medicines sold by mail order, the Court declared that such prohibitions could not be justified for medicines which could only be supplied by pharmacies but which were not subject to prescription.

Other mandatory requirements

As stated above, the *Cassis* list is not exhaustive. The list was left open so that it could be added to by the Court of Justice as its case law developed. The Court has accepted a wide range of national measures, many of them going well beyond either those which are designed to protect consumers or the specific exceptions permitted to Member States under Art 36 TFEU:

Commission v *Denmark* (Case 302/86)

The Commission challenged a Danish law under which all containers for beer and soft drinks must be returnable. This constituted a *prima facie* barrier because foreign manufacturers would not be geared up to selling drinks in such containers and would have to take special steps to do so, in order to supply the Danish market. Citing the case of *Walter Rau* (above), the Court of Justice recognised that the rule constituted an obstacle to trade. Was it, however, a mandatory requirement? The Court accepted that protection of the environment is one of the Union's 'essential objectives', which may justify certain limitations to the principle of the free movement of goods (see, now, Art 3(3) TEU). Those limitations must not, however, 'go beyond the inevitable restrictions which are justified by the pursuit of the objective of environmental protection'. It was therefore necessary to examine whether all the restrictions which the contested rules imposed on the free movement of goods were necessary to achieve the objectives pursued by those rules.

In *Commission* v *Germany* (Case C-463/01) and *Radlberger Getränke and S. Spitz* (Case C-309/02), the Court of Justice reconfirmed that indistinctly applicable measures could be justified on environmental protection grounds, provided that the measures taken are proportionate to the objective pursued. The following case concerned an indistinctly applicable measure which the Member State in question (Austria) sought to justify on environmental grounds (protection of the health of humans, animals and plants):

Commission v *Austria* (Case C-320/03)

A regulation adopted by the First Minister of the Tyrol on 27 May 2003 limited transport on the A12 motorway in Austria. That regulation prohibited lorries of more than 7.5 tonnes carrying certain goods, such as waste, stone, soil, motor vehicles, timber and cereals, from being driven on a 46 km section of the A12 motorway. The aim of the contested regulation was to improve air quality so as to ensure lasting protection of human, animal and plant health.

The Court of Justice, hearing an infringement action brought by the Commission, found that by adopting the contested regulation Austria had failed to fulfil its obligations under the former Arts 28 and 29 EC Treaty (now Arts 34 and 35 TFEU).

The sectoral prohibition on road transport obstructed the free movement of goods, in particular their free transit, and was therefore to be regarded as constituting a measure having equivalent effect to a quantitative restriction which was incompatible with the former Arts 28 and 29 EC Treaty (now Arts 34 and 35 TFEU) and which could not moreover be justified by overriding requirements relating to protection of the environment because it was disproportionate.

The Court held that before adopting a measure as radical as a ban, the Austrian authorities were under a duty to examine carefully the possibility of using measures less restrictive to the free movement of goods, and discount them only if their inadequacy, in relation to the objective pursued, was clearly established. More particularly, given the declared objective of transferring transportation of the goods concerned from road to rail, those authorities were required to ensure that there was sufficient and appropriate rail capacity to allow such a transfer before deciding to implement a measure such as that laid down by the Tyrolean regulation. The Court observed that it had not been conclusively established that the Austrian authorities, in preparing the contested regulation, sufficiently studied the question whether the aim of reducing pollutant emissions could be achieved by other means less restrictive to the free movement of goods and whether there actually was a realistic alternative for the transportation of the affected goods by other means of transport or by other road routes. Moreover, the Court considered that a transition period of only two months between the date on which the contested regulation was adopted and the date fixed by the Austrian authorities for implementation of the sectoral-traffic ban was clearly insufficient to reasonably allow the operators concerned to adapt to the new circumstances.

Following the above judgment, the Austrian authorities gradually implemented new measures to ensure that the limit value for nitrogen dioxide set by the directives was complied with. Those measures included a 100 km/h speed restriction on a section of the A12 motorway, which was later replaced by a variable speed limit and a traffic prohibition for certain classes of lorry. As air quality on the A12 motorway did not improve, the Austrian authorities adopted a traffic prohibition for lorries over 7.5 tonnes carrying certain goods on a section of the motorway, this time of approximately 84 km. They took the view that those goods, largely identical to those covered by the prohibition introduced in 2003, should be transported in Austrian territory by more environment-friendly modes of transport such as rail. The Commission considered that this new sectoral traffic prohibition was likewise an unjustified obstacle to the principle of the free movement of goods and it brought an action before the Court of Justice, asking the Court to declare that there was an infringement:

Commission v *Austria* (Case C-28/09)

The Court of Justice stated that the Member States are obliged to ensure that the limit value of nitrogen dioxide set by the directives is not exceeded in their territory. In this context the directives authorised the Member States to take the necessary measures for compliance with the limit value. However, while the Member States have discretion in adopting those measures, they must exercise that discretion consistently with the rules of Union law, including the principle of the free movement of goods.

The Court held that the sectoral traffic prohibition was an obstacle to the transport of certain goods by road. Such a measure was a restriction of the free movement of those goods. Similarly, the Court emphasised that the existence of alternative solutions for the transport of those goods, such as rail transport or the use of other motorways, did not negate the existence of a restriction. By forcing the undertakings concerned to seek viable alternative solutions for the transport of the goods in question, the sectoral traffic prohibition was liable to have a substantial effect on the transit of goods between northern Europe and northern Italy.

The Court then stated that **a restriction of the free movement of goods may be justified if it is a measure that is appropriate and necessary for attaining an objective in the public interest such as protection of the environment.** The Court observed that the Austrian regulations actually contributed to the protection of the environment, as they made it possible to reduce emissions of atmospheric pollutants and bring about an improvement in air quality. The contested prohibition was thus a measure that was appropriate for achieving the objective in the public interest.

The Court then examined whether that objective could have been attained by less restrictive measures. As the Court stated in its Case C-320/03 judgment, the Member States must, before adopting a measure so radical as a total traffic ban on a section of motorway constituting a vital route between certain of those states, examine carefully the possibility of using measures less restrictive of freedom of movement, and discount them only if their inappropriateness to the objective pursued was clearly established.

In this respect, and with regard to the Commission's suggestion that the traffic prohibition for lorries in certain classes could be extended to lorries in other classes, the Court considered that those standards reliably reflected actual emissions of vehicles as regards nitrogen oxides. In the Court's view, it had not been established that such an extension would not have been able to contribute to the objective sought as effectively as the implementation of the sectoral traffic prohibition.

With regard to the possibility of replacing the variable speed limit by a permanent 100 km/h speed limit, the Court did not accept the Austrian Government's argument that a permanent speed limit would not be observed in practice by road users. Austria could not rely on the average speed actually measured in the zone in question, namely 103 km/h, for assessing the effect of introducing a permanent 100 km/h speed limit. On the contrary, it was obliged to ensure that the limit was actually complied with, by adopting compulsory measures, with penalties if need be.

In those circumstances, the Court found that the solution suggested by the Commission offered a potential for reducing nitrogen dioxide emissions which was not sufficiently taken into account by Austria. Consequently, **the Court held that, by adopting a sectoral traffic prohibition without sufficiently examining the possibility of having recourse to other less restrictive measures, Austria had disproportionately restricted the free movement of goods.**

The Court of Justice has shown a willingness to accept that restrictions aimed at protecting national, cultural and social values could constitute a mandatory requirement, as illustrated in the following case:

Cinéthèque (Cases 60 and 61/84)

The Court of Justice upheld a non-discriminatory French rule prohibiting the sale or hire of videos of films within a year of their first showing at a cinema. Although the rule had the effect of restricting the import of videos from other Member States, the Court held that the restriction was justified and not, therefore, in breach of what is now Art 34 TFEU (previously Art 28 EC Treaty). The Court accepted that the protection of the French cinema was a legitimate objective, presumably (although it was not stated) as a means of protecting national culture.

The above case can, perhaps, be compared to a case involving the free movement of workers. In **Groener v Minister for Education** (Case 379/87) the Court of Justice accepted a requirement of a knowledge of the Irish language imposed on a Netherlands' teacher seeking employment in Ireland, although it was not needed for the subject she was to teach. The Court did so in recognition of the clear national policy of maintaining and promoting the language as a means of promoting national identity and culture (see Chapter 12).

In the following case, the Court of Justice accepted as a mandatory requirement national rules intended to protect the character of Sunday, and the limitation of workers' hours on that day, provided that national legislation did not go further than was necessary to achieve those legitimate aims:

Torfaen Borough Council v *B&Q Plc* (Case 145/88)

The Court of Justice laid down some general principles applicable to national restrictions on activities of this kind:

> It is therefore necessary in a case such as this to consider first of all whether the rules such as those at issue pursue an aim which is justified with regard to Community [i.e. Union] law. As far as that question is concerned, the Court has already stated in its judgment of 14 July 1981 in *Oebel* (Case 155/80) that national rules governing hours of work, delivery and sale in the bread and confectionery industry constitute a legitimate part of economic and social policy, consistent with the objectives of public interest pursued by the Treaty.
>
> The same consideration must apply as regards national rules governing the opening hours of retail premises. Such rules reflect certain political and economic choices in so far as their purpose is to ensure that working and non-working hours are so arranged as to accord with national or regional socio-cultural characteristics, and that, in the present state of Community [i.e. Union] law, is a matter for the Member States. Furthermore, such rules are not designed to govern the patterns of trade between Member States.

See pages 602–607 for a discussion of the *Keck* judgment.

It should be noted that **Cinéthèque** and **Torfaen Borough Council** have been overturned following the Court's judgment in **Keck** (see above) because they would be outside the scope of Art 34 TFEU *per se*, with no necessity to rely upon the defence of objective justification. However, this aspect of these two judgments is undoubtedly still good law.

In **Schmidberger** (Case C-112/00), considered below, Austria had failed to ban a demonstration which resulted in the complete closure of a major transit route for almost 30 hours on end. The Court of Justice stated that a failure to ban such a demonstration is capable of restricting intra-Union trade in goods and must therefore be regarded as constituting a measure of equivalent effect to a quantitative restriction. Such a measure is *prima facie* incompatible with the obligations arising from what are now Arts 34 and 35 TFEU, read together with what is now Art 4(3) TEU (previously Art 10 EC Treaty), unless that failure to ban can be objectively justified. This case differed from that of **Commission v France** (C-265/95), see above, in that **Schmidberger** concerned an indistinctly applicable measure (because the demonstration would affect both domestic and imported goods), whereas **Commission v France** concerned a distinctly applicable measure (because only imported goods were being targeted). The Court of Justice was then required to determine whether Austria could objectively justify its failure to ban the demonstration:

Schmidberger (Case C-112/00)

In assessing whether there was any objective justification, the Court of Justice took account of the objective pursued by the Austrian authorities in authorising the demonstration in question and held that it was to respect the fundamental rights of the demonstrators to freedom of expression and freedom of assembly, which are enshrined in and guaranteed by the European Convention on Human Rights and the Austrian Constitution. Given that fundamental rights form an integral part of the general principles of law which the Court ensures are observed, their protection is a legitimate interest which, in principle, justifies a restriction of the obligations imposed by Union law. This is the case even under a fundamental freedom guaranteed by the Treaty such as the free movement of goods.

The Court went on to say that the question of whether the facts before the referring court are consistent with respect for fundamental rights raises the question of the need to reconcile the requirements of the protection of fundamental rights in the Union with those arising from a fundamental freedom enshrined in the Treaty; i.e. the question of the respective scope of the freedom of expression and freedom of assembly and of the free movement of goods, given that they are both subject to restrictions justified by public interest objectives.

In considering whether the restrictions on intra-Union trade are proportionate in the light of the objective pursued, that is the protection of fundamental rights, the Court pointed out differences between the facts of this case and those of *Commission v France*.

In the latter case, the Court of Justice held that France had failed to fulfil its obligations under the former Art 28 EC Treaty (now Art 34 TFEU) by failing to adopt all necessary and proportionate measures in order to prevent the free movement of fruit and vegetables from being obstructed by actions of private individuals, such as the interception of lorries transporting such products and the destruction of their loads, violence against lorry drivers and other threats.

The Court of Justice found that, in the present case, unlike in *Commission v France*: (i) the demonstration at issue took place following authorisation; (ii) the obstacle to the free movement of goods resulting from that demonstration was limited; (iii) the purpose of that public demonstration was not to restrict trade in goods of a particular type or from a particular source; (iv) various administrative and supporting measures were taken by the competent authorities in order to limit as far as possible the disruption to road traffic; (v) the isolated incident in question did not give rise to a general climate of insecurity such as to have a dissuasive effect on intra-Union trade flows as a whole; and (vi) taking account of the Member States' wide margin of discretion, in this case the competent national authorities were entitled to consider that an outright ban on the demonstration at issue would have constituted unacceptable interference with the fundamental rights of the demonstrators to gather and express peacefully their opinion in public.

The imposition of stricter conditions concerning both the site and the duration of the demonstration in question could have been perceived as an excessive restriction, depriving the action of a substantial part of its scope. According to the Court, although an action of that type usually entails inconvenience for non-participants, such inconvenience may in principle be tolerated provided that the objective pursued is essentially the public and lawful demonstration of an opinion.

The Court concluded that the fact that the Austrian authorities did not, in the circumstances, ban the demonstration was not such as to render the failure incompatible with the former Arts 28 and 29 EC Treaty (now Arts 34 and 35 TFEU). In so deciding, the

Court decided that the fundamental rights of the demonstrators to freedom of expression and freedom of assembly, which are enshrined in and guaranteed by the European Convention on Human Rights, was a legitimate interest which, in principle, justified a restriction of the obligations imposed by Union law.

Overcoming barriers created by differing national standards

The relationship between harmonising directives and Articles 34–36 TFEU

Much of the jurisprudence of the Court of Justice relating to MEQRs concerns national measures enacted, ostensibly at least, for the protection of consumers or to promote other national concerns. It was apparent from the inception of the Union that such national provisions, including an enormously diverse range of standards, could be effectively tackled only by creating a Union-wide minimum standard binding on all Member States. In that way producers could have the advantage of large product runs, without having to go to the additional expense of having to tailor their products to the standards set in each Member State. Consumers could have a wider range of products at a lower cost. Article 115 TFEU (previously Art 94 EC Treaty) is included specifically for this purpose. Article 115 TFEU empowers the Commission to propose directives for the approximation of national legislation on matters which directly affect the establishment or functioning of the internal market. However, such proposals can only be adopted by the Council of Ministers acting *unanimously*.

Considerable difficulties were encountered in this harmonising process, not least because some Member States, not unnaturally, wished to ensure that their own high national standards were reflected in the Union standard. Member States were unwilling to accept a standard that represented the lowest common denominator. Procedures for agreeing common standards were time-consuming and cumbersome. There had to be unanimous agreement and therefore the opportunity for procrastination was great. The standards adopted were, in some cases, technically obsolete by the time they came into effect and the cost, in terms of lost intra-Union trade, was high.

Where, however, a common standard has been reached and the appropriate directive adopted, there is no further scope for national measures in the same field, and attempts to justify them either as mandatory requirements or under the specific exceptions in Art 36 TFEU will be rejected. In *Commission v Germany (Re Compound Feedingstuffs)* (Case 28/84), the Commission brought proceedings against the German government because, the Commission contended, Council directives adopted in 1970, 1974 and 1979 constituted a complete and exhaustive set of rules covering the whole field of production and marketing of compound animal feedstuffs. The Court of Justice agreed and consequently held that German rules on the minimum and maximum levels of certain ingredients could not apply (see also *Société Civile Agricole v Coopérative d'Elevage du Département de la Mayenne* (Case C-323/93)).

The current approach to harmonisation

The *Cassis* case gave a new impetus to the harmonisation process. It led to a declaration by the Commission that it would concentrate on steps for the harmonisation of national laws which could still affect intra-Union trade and which would have to be justified, in the absence of harmonisation, if at all, as mandatory requirements under the first *Cassis* principle or under one of the specific exceptions provided for in Art 36 TFEU. It also led to a Council Resolution of 7 May 1985 on a different approach to technical harmonisation and standards. The resolution established four fundamental principles on which this approach would be based:

1 Legislative harmonisation is limited to adoption, by means of directives based on what is now Art 115 TFEU, of the essential safety requirements (or other requirements in the general interest) with which products put on the market must conform, and which should therefore enjoy free movement throughout the Union.

2 The task of drawing up the technical specifications needed for the production and placing on the market of products conforming to the essential requirements established by the directives, while taking into account the current stage of technology, is entrusted to organisations competent in the standardisation area.

3 These technical specifications are not mandatory and maintain their status of voluntary standards.

4 National authorities are obliged to recognise that products manufactured in conformity with harmonised standards (or, provisionally, with national standards) are presumed to conform to the 'essential requirements' established by the directive. This signifies that the producer has the choice of not manufacturing in conformity with the standards, but that in this event he has an obligation to prove that his products conform to the essential requirements of the directive. In order that this system may operate it is necessary to ensure:
   - on the one hand that the standards offer a guarantee of quality with regard to the 'essential requirements' established by the directives;
   - on the other hand that the public authorities keep intact their responsibility for the protection of safety (or other requirements envisaged) on their territory.

There is a clear link between the resolution and the *Cassis* principles, which is most apparent in the above four fundamental principles. This approach established a clear break with the past. Instead of attempting to create a detailed technical specification for a 'Euro-product', which was a difficult and lengthy task, new directives would only set minimum safety and other standards which could be satisfied in a number of different ways in Member States, including different manufacturing methods. The emphasis was now on broad performance standards rather than compliance with detailed technical specifications. Once a Union directive has been adopted under this approach, and after the date for implementation has passed, performance is verified at Union level under a process monitored by the Commission. Where a directive has been adopted, Member States are obliged to assume that products purporting to conform to the essential requirements do, in fact, do so. Until new directives are adopted establishing Union-wide standards in other products, Member States should recognise (under the *Cassis* 'mutual recognition' principle) that those products meet appropriate essential requirements, unless there are indications that they do not.

Besides the adoption of a broader approach to essential requirements, agreement between Union institutions was further facilitated by the addition of the former Art 95 EC Treaty by the Single European Act. The former Art 95 EC Treaty has now been replaced by Art 114 TFEU. Under Art 114 TFEU, the Council now needs only to agree on a *qualified majority* basis 'measures for the approximation of the provisions laid down by law, regulation or administrative action in Member States which have as their object the establishment and functioning of the internal market'. Member States may seek approval from the Commission to derogate from the terms of a measure adopted pursuant to Art 114 TFEU if 'it deems it necessary to maintain national provisions on grounds of major needs referred to in Article 36, or relating to the protection of the environment or the working environment' (Article 114(4) TFEU). Article 114 TFEU (the wording of which is practically unchanged from the previous Art 95 EC Treaty) provides as follows:

(4) If, after the adoption of a harmonisation measure by the European Parliament and the Council, by the Council or by the Commission, a Member State deems it necessary to maintain national provisions on grounds of major needs referred to in Article 36, or relating to the protection of the environment or the working environment, it shall notify the Commission of these provisions as well as the grounds for maintaining them.

. . .

(6) The Commission shall, within six months of the notification as referred to in paragraphs 4 and 5, approve or reject the national provisions involved after having verified whether or not they are a means of arbitrary discrimination or a disguised restriction on trade between Member States and whether or not they shall constitute an obstacle to the functioning of the internal market.

. . .

(9) By way of derogation from the procedures laid down in Articles 258 and 259, the Commission and any Member State may bring the matter directly before the Court of Justice of the European Union if it considers that another Member State is making improper use of the powers provided for in this Article.

Between 1984 and 1990, over 800 European product standards were adopted, which was three times as many as in the previous 20 years. Since 1986, when a target of more than 300 directives was set to lay the foundations for the internal market on 1 January 1993, very few national provisions were approved under the exception contained in the former Art 95 EC Treaty (now Art 114 TFEU). It remains, however, a valuable safety valve to deal with national concerns over specific products. Overall, the new approach is widely regarded as having had considerable success in reducing national legal and technical barriers and in moving the Union towards a genuine internal market.

Figure 18.1 consists of a flowchart setting out the application of Arts 34 and 36 TFEU.

Summary

Now you have read this chapter you should be able to:

- Explain the purpose and effect of Arts 34–36 TFEU which relate to the elimination of quantitative restrictions and measures having an effect equivalent to a quantitative restriction.

- Distinguish between a quantitative restriction and a measure having an effect equivalent to a quantitative restriction.

- Explain the difference between a distinctly applicable measure and an indistinctly applicable measure.

- Understand how the law relating to indistinctly applicable measures is applied by the Court of Justice.

Figure 18.1   Articles 34 and 36 TFEU: quantitative restrictions and measures having an equivalent effect

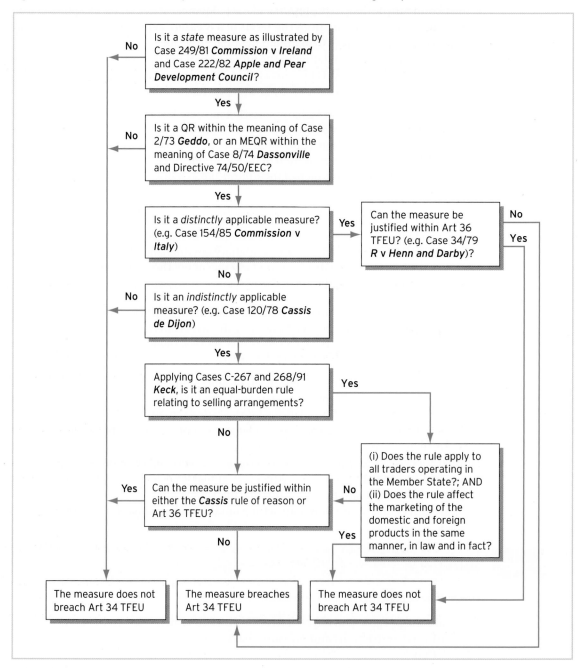

- Explain how to differentiate between rules of dual -burden and those of equal-burden, and how to apply the Court of Justice's *Keck* judgment.
- Explain the circumstances in which a Member State may rely upon Art 36 TFEU to justify a distinctly or indistinctly applicable measure.
- Understand how the *Cassis* rule of reason (established by the Court of Justice) can be relied upon by a Member State to justify an indistinctly applicable measure.

Further reading

Textbooks

Barnard, C. (2013) *The Substantive Law of the EU: The Four Freedoms* (4th edn), Oxford University Press, Chapters 4 to 6.

Craig, P. and De Burca, G. (2011) *EU Law: Text, Cases and Materials* (5th edn), Oxford University Press, Chapter 19.

Foster, N. (2015) *Foster on EU Law* (5th edn), Oxford University Press, Chapter 8.

Steiner, J. and Woods, L. (2014) *EU Law* (12th edn), Oxford University Press, Chapters 18 and 19.

Weatherill, S. (2014) *Cases and Materials on EU Law* (11th edn), Oxford University Press, Chapters 11 and 12.

Journal articles

Dawes, A., 'A freedom reborn? The new yet unclear scope of Art 29 EC' (2009) 34 EL Rev 639.

Favale, M., 'Fine-tuning European copyright law to strike a balance between the rights of owners and users' (2008) 33 EL Rev 687.

Lazowski, A., 'Withdrawal from the European Union and alternatives to membership' (2012) 37 EL Rev.

Lianos, I., 'In memoriam Keck: The reformation of the EU law on the free movement of goods' (2015) 40 EL Rev 225.

MacMaolain, C., 'Waiter! There's a beetle in my soup. Yes sir, that's E120: Disparities between actual individual behaviour and regulating food labelling for the average consumer in EU law' (2008) 45 CML Rev 1147.

Prechal, S. and De Vries, S., 'Seamless web of judicial protection in the internal market' (2009) 34 EL Rev 5.

Spaventa, E., 'Leaving Keck behind? The free movement of goods after the rulings in Commission v Italy and Mickelsson and Roos' (2009) 34 EL Rev 914.

Tryfonidou, A., 'Further steps on the road to convergence among the market freedoms' (2010) 35 EL Rev 36.

Van Harten, H. and Nauta, T., 'Towards horizontal direct effect for the free movement of goods? Comment on Fra.bo' (2013) 38 EL Rev 677.

Wenneras, P. and Moen, K.B., 'Selling arrangements, keeping Keck' (2010) 35 EL Rev 387.

Wilsher, D., 'Does Keck discrimination make any sense? An assessment of the non-discrimination principle within the European single market' (2008) 33 EL Rev 3.

Part 4

Union competition law

19

State monopolies and state aid

Objectives

At the end of this chapter you should understand:

1. How Arts 37, 102 and 106 TFEU are applied by the Commission and Court of Justice of the European Union (which includes the General Court) to regulate state monopolies.

2. How Arts 107 and 108 TFEU are applied by the Commission and Court of Justice of the European Union to regulate state aid.

3. The nature and scope of the block exemption regulations adopted pursuant to Art 109 TFEU, which concern the application of Arts 107 and 108 TFEU.

4. The provisions of Regulations 659/1999 and 794/2004 which lay down the general procedural rules relating to state aid and the application of Art 108 TFEU.

Introduction to state monopolies and state aid

When the Union was formed, state ownership of major utilities played an important part in the economic and social policies of the founding states. It continues to do so, although state ownership is now less favoured, and subsidies and direct or indirect regulation of private undertakings providing important services have become more common. In the UK during the 1980s (while Margaret Thatcher was Prime Minister), state ownership of gas, electricity, water and telecommunications was abandoned in favour of private ownership. State intervention will continue to provide a safety net to industries in decline or facing sudden crises, and to support undertakings providing important public services (such as gas, electricity, water, etc.). During the global 'credit crunch' of 2008, and the impending worldwide recession, EU states intervened to provide financial support to the banking sector. In some instances this comprised full state control (e.g. the UK government nationalised the Northern Rock Bank). Although intervention in these activities by the state may well breach the Union's commitment to the internal market, in which goods and services compete on an equal basis, the Union's own support for agriculture and agricultural products, and its regional and social funds, demonstrate an equal commitment to social, educational, health and cultural objectives supported by Union intervention. The TFEU (and the former EC Treaty) seeks to strike a balance between state intervention and the operation of the market. In Member States, the position of public ownership is, like private ownership, protected by Art 345 TFEU (previously Art 295 EC Treaty). The balance between public and private ownership is a matter for national policy, but state ownership is subject to similar constraints to private ownership. The title to that ownership is a matter of state policy, but the exercise of ownership rights, if it affects trade between Member States, is governed by Union law. The Court of Justice has increasingly seen state intervention as a process that is *prima facie* likely to interfere with the establishing and functioning of the Union's internal market, and has shown a tendency to interpret provisions of Union law allowing state monopolies and subsidies (i.e. state aid) in a restrictive manner, accepting only those seen as necessary to achieve certain clearly defined aims.

The provisions of Union law regulating state monopolies are considered first, followed by the law regulating state aid.

State monopolies

Objective
1

The position with regard to state monopolies is dealt with by Art 37 TFEU (previously Art 31 EC Treaty). Article 37 TFEU (which is practically unchanged from the former Art 31 EC Treaty) provides as follows:

1 Member States shall adjust any State monopolies of a commercial character so as to ensure that no discrimination regarding the conditions under which goods are procured and marketed exists between nationals of Member States.

   The provisions of this Article shall apply to any body through which a Member State, in law or in fact, either directly or indirectly supervises, determines or appreciably influences imports or exports between Member States. These provisions shall likewise apply to monopolies delegated by the State to others.

2 Member States shall refrain from introducing any new measure which is contrary to the principles laid down in paragraph 1 or which restricts the scope of the articles dealing with the prohibition of customs duties and quantitative restrictions between Member States.

3 If a State monopoly of a commercial character has rules which are designed to make it easier to dispose of agricultural products or obtain for them the best return, steps should be taken in applying the rules contained in this Article to ensure equivalent safeguards for the employment and standard of living of the producers concerned.

Article 37 TFEU must be read in conjunction with Art 106 TFEU (previously Art 86 EC Treaty). Article 37 is concerned with the procurement and marketing of goods while Art 106 is concerned with services. Article 106 TFEU (which is practically unchanged from the former Art 86 EC Treaty) provides as follows:

1 In the case of public undertakings and undertakings to which Member States grant special or exclusive rights, Member States shall neither enact nor maintain in force any measure contrary to the rules contained in the Treaties, in particular to those rules provided for in Article 18 and Articles 101 to 109.

2 Undertakings entrusted with the operation of services of general economic interest or having the character of a revenue-producing monopoly shall be subject to the rules contained in the Treaties, in particular to the rules on competition, in so far as the application

of such rules does not obstruct the performance, in law or in fact, of the particular tasks assigned to them. The development of trade must not be affected to such an extent as would be contrary to the interests of the Union.

3 The Commission shall ensure the application of the provisions of this Article and shall, where necessary, address appropriate directives or decisions to Member States.

Article 106(3) TFEU requires the Commission to enforce Art 106 by addressing, where necessary, appropriate directives or decisions to Member States.

State monopolies of a commercial character

The nature of 'state monopolies of a commercial character' referred to in Art 37 TFEU was considered by the Court of Justice in the following case:

Costa v ENEL (CASE 6/64)

This case concerned the compatibility with Union law of the nationalisation of the Italian electricity industry. The Court of Justice held that:

One must consider . . . carefully paragraph (1) of . . . [Article 37 TFEU]. This prevents the creation not indeed of all national monopolies but only of those that present 'a commercial character' and even of these, insofar as they tend to introduce the discrimination aforesaid. It follows, therefore, that **to come within the terms of the prohibition of this Article, national monopolies and bodies must on the one hand have as objects transactions in commercial products capable of competition and exchanges between Member States; and on the other hand play a leading part in such exchanges.** [emphasis added]

Whether or not a state monopoly exists is a matter of law and fact.

Article 37 TFEU: directly effective

See pages 274–292 and 303–305 for an explanation of direct effect.

A claimant who proves the existence of a breach of Art 37 TFEU and loss caused by that breach may obtain an award of damages, as the provision is directly effective (**Hansen v Hauptzollamt Flensburg** (Case 91/78)).

Compatibility with Union law

The operation of a body enjoying a state monopoly may involve: (i) potential restrictions on the importation of goods into a Member State, thus breaching Art 34 TFEU (previously Art 28 EC Treaty); (ii) discrimination by such a body in relation to the provision of such goods and services; and (iii) the abuse of a monopoly position. An example of the interplay of these provisions was considered by the Court of Justice in the following case:

Société Civile Agricole de la Crespelle v Coopérative d'Elevage de la Mayenne (CASE C-323/93)

Under French law, certain approved bovine insemination centres were granted exclusive rights within a defined area. Breeders established in those areas were, effectively, obliged to use their services. Such licensed centres enjoyed what the Court of Justice described as 'a contiguous series of monopolies territorially limited but together covering the entire territory of a Member State'.

> The Court held, first, that the mere creation of such a dominant position by the granting of an exclusive right within the meaning of the former Art 86(1) EC Treaty (now Art 106(1) TFEU) was not as such incompatible with the former Art 82 EC Treaty (now Art 102 TFEU); see Chapter 21. A Member State contravened the prohibitions contained in those two provisions only if, in merely exercising the exclusive right granted to it, the undertaking in question could not avoid abusing its dominant position. An undertaking abused its dominant position where it had an administrative monopoly and charged fees for its services which were disproportionate to the economic value of the services provided. Secondly, the Court held that national rules, which required importers of bovine semen from a Member State to deliver it only to an approved insemination or production centre, were in breach of the former Art 28 EC Treaty (now Art 34 TFEU), but were in the circumstances saved by the former Art 30 EC Treaty (now Art 36 TFEU) as necessary for the protection of animal health (see Chapter 18).

Although the point was not specifically dealt with in this case, the Court of Justice has held that an exclusive right, *inter alia*, to import particular goods falls within the scope of Art 37 TFEU (**Manghera** (Case 59/75)).

In the following case, the Court of Justice had to consider the extent to which the German state alcohol monopoly was compatible with what is now Art 37 TFEU:

Hansen v Hauptzollamt Flensburg (CASE 91/78)

> The Court of Justice held, first, that what is now Art 37 TFEU (previously Art 31 EC Treaty) remains applicable wherever the exercise by a state monopoly of its exclusive rights entails a discrimination or restriction prohibited by that article. Secondly, that what is now Art 37 TFEU prohibits a monopoly's right to purchase and resell national alcohol from being exercised so as to undercut imported products with publicly subsidised domestic products.

While Art 106(2) TFEU recognises that publicly owned undertakings can carry on revenue-producing economic activities, it specifically prohibits their operation in a way which would constitute an abuse of a monopoly position or which would distort the operation of the market. However, the public body is allowed to derogate from these rules, in so far as it is actually necessary to carry out the tasks assigned to it. This issue was considered by the Court of First Instance ((CFI), which has now been renamed the General Court) in the following case:

FFSA and Others v Commission (CASE T-106/96)

> The 'task', in this case, was the maintenance of uneconomic postal services in rural areas. A body of insurers had unsuccessfully complained to the European Commission that the French Post Office was being unlawfully subsidised, contrary to the former Art 87(1) EC Treaty (now Art 107(1) TFEU). The CFI (now the General Court) upheld the Commission's decision. Following the decision of the Court of Justice in **Corbeau** (Case 320/91), the CFI held that the postal monopoly was necessary to enable the Post Office to subsidise the regional development of the postal service. It was only lawful, however, if 'the sole purpose of the aid was to offset the additional costs incurred' and 'the grant of the aid is necessary for the undertaking to perform its public service obligations under conditions of economic equilibrium'.

A similar issue arose in the following case, which concerned a dispute between an undertaking and a German administrative body, in relation to a refusal by the German administrative body to renew authorisation for the provision of patient transport services by ambulance:

Ambulanz Glöckner (CASE C-475/99)

The German court was uncertain whether reasons which related to the pursuit of a task of general economic interest were sufficient to justify the exclusion of all competition for that type of service. The German court referred a series of questions to the Court of Justice pursuant to the former Art 234 EC Treaty (now Art 267 TFEU).

The Court of Justice found that the German legislation conferred on medical aid organisations a special or exclusive right within the meaning of the former Art 86(1) EC Treaty (now Art 106(1) TFEU), which was therefore applicable in this case. With regard to the former Art 86(1) EC Treaty (now Art 106(1) TFEU), in conjunction with the former Art 82 EC Treaty (now Art 102 TFEU; see Chapter 21), the Court found, in its analysis of the relevant market, that patient transport was a service which was distinct from that of emergency transport, and that the *Land* of Rhineland-Palatinate (Germany) constituted a substantial part of the internal market, given its surface area and population. The Court nevertheless left it to the national court to determine the geographical extent of the market and to determine whether a dominant position was being occupied. According to the Court, there was potentially an **abuse of a dominant position** in that the legislation of the *Land* reserved to certain medical aid organisations an ancillary transport activity which could be carried on by independent operators. Finally, the Court concluded that such legislation could be justified under the former Art 86(2) EC Treaty (now Art 106(2) TFEU) if the legislation did not bar the grant of an authorisation to independent operators, where the authorised medical aid organisations were unable to satisfy demand existing in the area of medical transport services.

In the following case, the Court of Justice dismissed an action brought by Portugal for annulment of a Commission decision relating to the former Art 86 EC Treaty (now Art 106 TFEU):

Portugal v Commission (CASE C-163/99)

In the contested decision, the Commission had found that the Portuguese legislation which provided for a system of discounts on landing charges that were applied according to the origin of the flight was incompatible with the former Art 86(1) EC Treaty (now Art 106(1) TFEU), in conjunction with the former Art 82 EC Treaty (now Art 102 TFEU – see Chapter 21). Portugal pleaded, *inter alia*, breach of the principle of proportionality. However, the Court of Justice held that the decision was not disproportionate, having regard to the wide discretion enjoyed by the Commission under the former Art 86(3) EC Treaty (now Art 106(3) TFEU). Portugal also contended that there had been no abuse of a dominant position with regard to discounts granted on the basis of the number of landings. The Court stated, however, that the system of discounts appeared to favour certain airlines, in the present case the national airlines.

The following case concerned an action brought by a trade association of companies offering express courier services, against a Commission decision declaring that the logistical and commercial assistance given by the French Post Office (La Poste) to a private company to which it had entrusted the management of its express courier service did not constitute state aid:

Chronopost, La Poste and French Republic (Joined Cases C-83/01 P, C-93/01 P and C-94/01 P)

In its judgment in **Ufex and Others** (Case T-613/97), the CFI (now the General Court) had annulled the Commission's decision that the assistance given by the French Post Office did not constitute state aid, on the ground that the Commission should have examined whether the 'full costs' took account of the factors which an undertaking acting under normal market conditions should have taken into consideration when fixing the remuneration for the services provided.

Hearing the case on appeal, the Court of Justice considered at the outset that the assessment by the CFI had failed to take account of the fact that an undertaking such as La Poste was in a situation very different from that of a private undertaking acting under normal market conditions. La Poste had to acquire substantial infrastructures and resources to enable it to carry out its task of providing a service of general economic interest within the meaning of the former Art 86 EC Treaty (now Art 106 TFEU), even in sparsely populated areas where the tariffs did not cover the cost of providing the service in question. The creation and maintenance of the basic postal network were not in line with a purely commercial approach. The Court held that the provision of logistical and commercial assistance was inseparably linked to that network, because it consisted precisely in making available that network which had no equivalent on the market.

The Court of Justice therefore concluded that, in the absence of any possibility of comparing the situation of La Poste with that of a private group of undertakings not operating in a reserved sector, 'normal market conditions', which are necessarily hypothetical, allowing it to be determined whether the provision by a public undertaking of logistical and commercial assistance to its private-law subsidiary was capable of constituting state aid, had to be assessed by reference to the objective and verifiable elements which were available. The costs borne by La Poste in providing such assistance could constitute such objective and verifiable elements. On that basis, there could be no question of state aid to the subsidiary if: (i) it was established that the price charged properly covered all the additional variable costs incurred in providing the logistical and commercial assistance, an appropriate contribution to the fixed costs arising from use of the postal network and an adequate return on the capital investment in so far as it was used for the subsidiary's competitive activity; and (ii) there was nothing to suggest that those factors had been underestimated or fixed in an arbitrary fashion.

State undertakings and the need for transparency

Where an undertaking is state-owned, or directly or indirectly controlled by the state, it is subject to the provisions of Directive 80/723. This directive (the Transparency Directive) was made under the former Art 86(3) EC Treaty (now Art 106(3) TFEU) and requires that financial relations between public authorities and public undertakings are transparent. 'Transparency' in this context means transparency to the Commission (Art 5, Directive 80/723). The particular matters requiring disclosure are the amount of public funds made available directly by public authorities to the public undertakings concerned, or through intermediaries, and the uses to which such public funds are put (Art 1, Directive 80/723).

The extent and nature of such support may well be of concern to the Commission in determining whether or not unlawful state aids have been provided.

Directive 80/723 was amended by Directive 2000/52, the main provisions of which had an implementation date of 31 July 2001. The aim of the amending directive is to achieve the basic objective of transparency by laying down rules requiring specified undertakings to maintain separate accounts relating to the different activities which they carry on. This is considered to be 'the most efficient means by which fair and effective application of the rules on competition to [public and private undertakings granted special or exclusive rights or entrusted with the operation of services of general economic interest . . .] can be assured' (Preamble, Directive 2000/52). The obligation of maintaining separate accounts does not apply to undertakings whose activities are limited to the provision of services of general economic interest and which do not operate activities outside the scope of services of general economic interest, unless such undertakings receive state aid (see below).

Directive 80/723 was further amended by Directive 2005/81, which had an implementation date of 19 December 2006. This amendment was in response to the Court of Justice's decision in ***Altmark Trans GmbH and Regierungspräsidium Magdeburg v Nahverkehrsgesellschaft Altmark GmbH*** (Case C-280/00) in which the Court held that, under certain conditions, public service compensation does not constitute state aid within the meaning of the former Art 87(1) EC Treaty (now Art 107(1) TFEU). This case, which is considered below, would have had an impact with regard to the obligation to maintain separate accounts where an undertaking providing 'services of general economic interest', and operating no activities outside the scope of such services, receives state aid. The amendments made by Directive 2005/81 provide that irrespective of the legal classification of public service compensation under Art 107(1) TFEU, the obligation to maintain separate accounts applies to all undertakings receiving such compensation if they also carry on activities outside the scope of 'services of general economic interest' (Art 1, Directive 2005/81). It is only by maintaining separate accounts that the costs imputable to 'services of general economic interest' can be identified and the correct amount of compensation calculated (Preamble, Directive 2005/81).

State aid

Objective 2

There is no absolute prohibition of state aid in the Treaty. Rather, that the prohibitions are directed against the use of state aid in ways that are 'incompatible with the internal market'.

Article 107(1) TFEU (which is practically unchanged from the former Art 87(1) EC Treaty) provides as follows:

> Save as otherwise provided in the Treaties, any aid granted by a Member State or through State resources in any form whatsoever which distorts or threatens to distort competition by favouring certain undertakings or the production of certain goods shall, in so far as it affects trade between Member States, be incompatible with the internal market.

Article 107(1) TFEU is not concerned with how state aid is granted. It is directed at aid granted by the state or derived from state resources, which either distorts or may distort competition, by favouring certain undertakings resulting in an impact on trade between Member States.

The scope of 'state aid'

'State aid' has a wide scope including, but not confined to, state subsidies, as determined by the Court of Justice in the following case:

Steenkolenmijnen v HA (CASE 30/59)

The Court of Justice held that:

> The concept of an aid is . . . wider than that of a subsidy because it embraces not only positive benefits, such as subsidies themselves, but also interventions which, in various forms, mitigate the charges which are normally included in the budget of an undertaking and which would without, therefore, being subsidies in the strict sense of the word, be similar in character and have the same effect.

State aid may come in a large number of different guises and has been held to include: exemption from duties and taxes; exemption from parafiscal charges; preferential interest rates; guarantees of loans on especially favourable terms; making land or buildings available either for nothing or on especially favourable terms; provision of goods, services or personnel on preferential terms; indemnities against operating losses; and the purchase of a company's shares which is in financial difficulties (***Intermills v Commission*** (Case 323/82); ***Spain v Commission*** (Joined Cases C-278–280/92); ***Commission v Sytraval*** (Case C-367/95)).

Despite the wide scope of state aid favoured by the Commission, the Court has tended to insist that if it is to be regarded as state aid it must constitute a government measure 'involving a charge on the public account' of the state concerned (***Sloman Neptun*** (Case C-72/91); ***Kirsammer Hack*** (Case C-189/91)). This was not, however, the view of the Advocates General in both cases. Both decisions have been the subject of criticism for allowing too much scope for states to give unfair competitive advantages to undertakings in their territories by such devices as relaxing environmental and planning controls, or by making various beneficial administrative concessions (Slotboom, 1995).

The following case related to the free movement of goods, but also had a state aid dimension:

Preussen Elektra (CASE C-379/98)

A German court was unsure as to the compatibility with Union law of German legislation which obliged electricity supply undertakings to purchase the electricity produced in their area of supply from renewable energy sources, and to pay for it in accordance with a statutory minimum price. The national court sought a preliminary ruling on the interpretation of the former Arts 28 and 87 EC Treaty (now Arts 34 and 107 TFEU). The Court of Justice held that there was no breach of the former Art 28 EC Treaty (now Art 34 TFEU) which relates to the free movement of goods (see Chapter 18).

From the point of view of state aid, the main issue was whether legislation such as the German legislation could be categorised as state aid. The Court of Justice pointed out that the concept of state aid has been defined by it as covering 'advantages granted directly or indirectly through state resources'. It then stated that 'the distinction made in . . . [Art 107(1) TFEU] between "aid granted by a Member State" and aid granted "through state resources" does not signify that all advantages granted by a state, whether financed through state resources or not, constitute aid but is intended merely to bring within that definition both advantages which are granted directly by the state and those granted by a public or private body designated or established by the state' (para 58).

In the case in point, the Court found that the obligation imposed on private electricity supply undertakings to purchase electricity produced from renewable energy sources at fixed minimum prices, did not involve any direct or indirect transfer of state resources to undertakings which produce that type of electricity. Accordingly, there was no state aid for the purposes of the former Art 87 EC Treaty (now Art 107 TFEU). The Court also rejected the Commission's argument that in order to preserve the effectiveness of the state aid rules, read in conjunction with the former Art 10 EC Treaty (now Art 4(3) TEU), which requires that Member States ensure that the obligations set out within the Treaties are fulfilled, it is necessary for the concept of state aid to be interpreted in such a way as to include support measures which are decided upon by the state but which are financed by private undertakings.

The Court held that the Treaty articles concerning state aid refer directly to measures emanating from the Member States. The former Art 10 EC Treaty (now Art 4(3) TEU) cannot be used to extend the scope of the former Art 87 EC Treaty (now Art 107 TFEU) to include conduct by states which does not fall within it.

The following case concerned the question of whether state aid covers public subsidies to allow the operation of regular urban, suburban or regional transport services:

Altmark Trans and Regierungspräsidium Magdeburg (CASE C-280/00)

The Court of Justice first examined whether the condition that trade between Member States had to be affected was met. The Court emphasised that the latter did not depend on the local or regional character of the transport services supplied or on the scale of the field of activity concerned. Referring to its case law describing state aid as an advantage granted to a beneficiary undertaking which the latter would not have obtained under normal market conditions, the Court emphasised that public subsidies such as those referred to above are not caught by the former Art 87(1) EC Treaty (now Art 107(1) TFEU) where such subsidies are to be regarded as compensation for the services provided by the recipient undertakings in order to discharge public service obligations.

The Court of Justice set out four conditions which had to be met for such compensation to be regarded as being present:

1 the recipient undertaking must be actually required to discharge public service obligations and those obligations must have been clearly defined;
2 the parameters on the basis of which the compensation is calculated must have been established beforehand in an objective and transparent manner;
3 the compensation must not exceed what is necessary to cover all or part of the costs incurred in discharging the public service obligations, taking into account the relevant receipts and a reasonable profit for discharging those obligations;
4 where the undertaking which is to discharge public service obligations is not chosen in a public procurement procedure, the level of compensation needed must have been determined on the basis of an analysis of the costs which a typical undertaking, well run and adequately provided with means of transport so as to be able to meet the necessary public service requirements, would have incurred in discharging those obligations, taking into account the relevant receipts and a reasonable profit for discharging the obligations.

The following case, decided by the General Court, further considered the scope of state aid:

France and Others v *Commission* (Joined Cases T-425/04, T-444/04, T-450/04 and T-456/04)

France Télécom SA (FT) was established in 1991 in the form of a public law corporation, and had been a public limited company since 1996. Since October 1997, FT has been quoted on the stock exchange. At the time when the disputed Commission decision was adopted, FT was a group active in the provision of telecommunications networks and services. In France, that group was active in particular in the fixed telephony sector, and through its subsidiary companies in the sectors of mobile telephony, the internet, data transmission and other information services. In 2002, the French state's holding in FT amounted to 56.45 per cent of its share capital.

On 31 December 2001, FT showed a net debt in its published accounts for the year 2001 of 63.5 billion euros and a loss of 8.3 billion euros.

On 30 June 2002, FT's net debt reached 69.69 billion euros, which included 48.9 billion euros of bonded debt repayable during the years 2003 to 2005.

In the light of FT's financial situation, the French Minister for the Economy stated in an interview published on 12 July 2002 in a French daily newspaper that: '. . . the shareholder State will act as a prudent investor and were FT to encounter difficulties, we would take the appropriate measures . . . I repeat that were FT to face funding problems, which is not the case today, the State would take the necessary decisions in order to overcome them'. That statement was followed by further public statements aimed essentially at assuring FT that it had the support of the French authorities.

On 4 December 2002, the French state published an announcement of a proposal for a shareholder loan which it was considering making to FT. That proposal would have opened a 9 billion euro credit line in the form of a loan contract. The contractual offer for the loan was sent to FT on 20 December 2002. The offer was neither accepted nor acted on by FT.

By decision of 2 August 2004, the Commission concluded that, placed in the context of the statements made since July 2002, the shareholder loan granted by France to FT in December 2002 in the form of a 9 billion euro credit line constituted state aid incompatible with Union law.

Action was brought before the General Court, seeking annulment of the Commission's decision.

The General Court noted that, in order for a measure to be classified as state aid: (i) it must entail a financial advantage; and (ii) that advantage must come directly or indirectly from state resources.

After analysing the statements of the French authorities made from July 2002 onwards, the Court held that those statements did confer a financial advantage on FT.

When taken together, those statements had a decisive influence on the reaction of the ratings agencies and that reaction was later instrumental in improving FT's image in the eyes of investors and creditors. They were decisive for the conduct of the financial market players who subsequently participated in FT's refinancing. Thus, the positive and stabilising effect on FT's rating, which was a direct consequence of the statements, necessarily resulted in a financial advantage being granted to FT.

However, the Court held that this financial advantage did not entail any transfer of state resources. On account of their open, imprecise and conditional nature the statements made from July 2002 onwards could not be construed as a state guarantee or be interpreted as containing an irrevocable commitment to provide specific financial assistance to FT.

A specific, unconditional and irrevocable commitment of public resources by France would have required those statements to set out clearly: (i) the exact sums to be invested, or the specific debts to be guaranteed, or a predefined financial framework, such as a credit line up to a certain amount; and (ii) the conditions for granting the assistance envisaged. The statements made from July 2002 onwards were silent on those issues.

The Court also noted that it was only by publishing the announcement of the shareholder loan proposal on 4 December 2002 that France made clear to the public the financial assistance which it was considering granting to FT. That financial assistance consisted in opening a 9 billion euro credit line in the form of a loan contract, the contractual offer for which was never accepted or acted on by FT.

Like the statements made from July 2002 onwards, that announcement granted an advantage to FT in that it played a role in enhancing the confidence of the financial markets and in improving the conditions of FT's refinancing. However, the Commission failed to prove that the announcement in itself entailed a transfer of state resources.

The Court rejected the Commission's argument that the shareholder loan proposal was the realisation of France's earlier statements, as the Commission failed to prove that France had considered granting specific financial assistance of that kind as early as July 2002. It was not until December 2002 that France formed the view that the economic conditions for such financial assistance had been fulfilled, which confirmed that there was a significant break in the series of events at that stage.

In the light of that break in the series of events the Commission was not entitled to establish a link between: (i) a possible commitment of state resources; and (ii) advantages granted by earlier measures, i.e. the statements made from July 2002 onwards.

Therefore, even if it was open to the Commission to take account of all the events which led up to and influenced the final decision by France in December 2002 to support FT through a shareholder loan, it failed to prove that there was a transfer of state resources related to that advantage.

Consequently, the Court annulled the Commission's decision.

State aid which is *per se* compatible under Article 107(2) TFEU

Some types of aid are, *per se*, deemed to be compatible under Art 107(2) TFEU (previously Art 87(2) EC Treaty). Article 107(2) TFEU provides as follows:

The following shall be compatible with the internal market:

(a) aid having a social character, granted to individual consumers, provided that such aid is granted without discrimination related to the origin of the products concerned;

(b) aid to make good the damage caused by natural disasters or exceptional occurrences;

(c) aid granted to the economy of certain areas of the Federal Republic of Germany affected by the division of Germany, in so far as such aid is required in order to compensate for the economic disadvantages caused by that division. Five years after the entry into force of the Treaty of Lisbon, the Council, acting on a proposal from the Commission, may adopt a decision repealing this point.

An example of aid of the kind referred to in (a) would be sales of basic food products such as bread, pasta and butter at a low, fixed price. In these cases, the wholesaler might be compensated by the state for the loss of his profit. The proviso would, however, require that such support would be equally available to imported and home-produced products. The aid referred to in (b) is self-explanatory. The aid to which Germany is entitled under (c) was introduced because following reunification considerable difficulties were suffered by the Eastern territories of the Federal Republic of Germany, and these were partly due to the original division. This justified state subsidies being granted to the Eastern industries to bring them up to Western standards, provided that the aid given was no more than necessary to achieve that purpose. The Commission is of the view that this provision is no longer necessary and may therefore be repealed.

State aid which is potentially justifiable under Article 107(3) TFEU

Other types of aid are seen as potentially justifiable. Under Art 107(3) TFEU (previously Art 87(3) EC Treaty), there are five categories of aid listed as being potentially justifiable. Before a Member State commences or alters any of the aid projects falling within categories (a) to (e) below, it must inform the Commission in sufficient time to enable it to submit its comments (Art 108(3) TFEU (previously Art 88(3) EC Treaty)). The Commission has the power to block the project or require its amendment (Arts 108(2) and (3) TFEU (previously Arts 88(2) and (3) EC Treaty)). Article 107(3) TFEU (which is practically unchanged from the former Art 87(3) EC Treaty) provides as follows:

The following may be considered to be compatible with the internal market:

(a) aid to promote the economic development of areas where the standard of living is abnormally low or where there is serious underemployment, and of the regions referred to in Article 349, in view of their structural, economic and social situation;

(b) aid to promote the execution of an important project of common European interest or to remedy a serious disturbance in the economy of a Member State;

(c) aid to facilitate the development of certain economic activities or of certain economic areas, where such aid does not adversely affect trading conditions to an extent contrary to the common interest;

(d) aid to promote culture and heritage conservation where such aid does not affect trading conditions and competition in the Union to an extent that is contrary to the common interest;

(e) such other categories of aid as may be specified by decision of the Council on a proposal from the Commission.

Each of the five categories of state aid which are potentially justifiable, set out within Art 107(3) TFEU, are now considered.

The promotion of economic development of areas of low income or high underemployment (Article 107(3)(a) TFEU)

The Commission's criteria to determine whether or not an aid scheme should be approved received the support of the Court of Justice in the following case:

Philip Morris v *Commission* (CASE 730/79)

The Court of Justice held that, first, the aid must promote or further a project that is in the Union interest as a whole. Aid which therefore promotes a national interest is unacceptable. Second, the aid must be necessary for promoting the first objective. Finally, the way in which the aid is provided must be proportional to the legitimate object, and must not be likely to affect trade between Member States and distort competition.

In this case, the Netherlands government proposed to grant the applicant capital assistance to enable it to increase cigarette production so that it would account for nearly 50 per cent of cigarette production in the Netherlands. Eighty per cent of that production would be exported to other Member States. There was the possibility that aid could have an effect, therefore, on trade between Member States. Philip Morris argued that the former Art 87(3) EC Treaty (now Art 107(3) TFEU) only required that the investment plan be compatible with the objectives set out in paragraphs (a), (b) and (c). It did not have to be shown that the aid would contribute to the attainment of one of those legitimate objectives. The development of cigarette manufacture was to take place in Bergen-op-Zoom, where underemployment was high and the per capita income was lower than the national average in the rest of the Netherlands. The company maintained that the Commission had been wrong to compare underemployment and income, not with that prevailing elsewhere in the Netherlands, but with that elsewhere in the Union.

The Court of Justice rejected the argument that trade with other Member States was not likely to be distorted:

> When State financial aid strengthens the position of an undertaking compared with other undertakings competing in intra-Community [i.e. intra-Union] trade, the latter must be regarded as affected by that aid. In this case the aid which the Netherlands government proposed to grant was for an undertaking organised for international trade and this is proved by the high percentage of its production which it intends to export to other Member States. The aid in question was to help enlarge its production capacity and consequently to increase its capacity to maintain the flow of trade including that between Member States. On the other hand the aid is said to have reduced the cost of converting the production facilities and has thereby given the applicant a competitive advantage over manufacturers who have completed or intend to complete at their own expense a similar increase in the productive capacity of their plant.

The Court also refused to accept the company's argument that it was legitimate to look at underemployment and income levels only in the Netherlands, and that the Commission had been wrong to take a broader view of all the circumstances:

> These arguments put forward by the applicant cannot be upheld. It should be borne in mind that the Commission has a discretion the exercise of which involves economic and social assessments which must be made in a Community [i.e. Union] context. That is the context in which the Commission has with good reason assessed the standard of living and serious underemployment in the Bergen-op-Zoom area, not with reference to the national average in the Netherlands but in relation to the Community [i.e. Union] level . . . The Commission could very well take the view, as it did, that the investment to be effected in this case was not 'an important project of Common European interest' . . . since the proposed aid would have permitted the transfer to the Netherlands of an investment which could be effected in other Member States in a less favourable economic situation than that of the Netherlands, where the national level of unemployment is one of the lowest in the Community [i.e. Union].

Although the Court of Justice has held that decisions of the kind in the above case involve the making of complicated economic assessments with which the Court will not readily interfere, when the Commission purports to be acting according to a stated economic policy, its decisions must be compatible with that policy (*Spain* v *Commission* (above)).

The Commission issued guidelines on national regional aid outlining the circumstances in which aid would be considered to be in the interest of the Union (OJ 1998 C

74/9, as amended in OJ 2000 C 258/5). These guidelines covered the period 2000 to 2006. Further guidelines were issued in 2002 governing regional aid for large investment projects (OJ 2002 C 70/8, as amended in OJ 2003 C 263/3).

In view of important political and economic developments within the Union since the initial guidelines were issued in 1998 (including Union enlargement on 1 May 2004, the accession of Bulgaria and Romania on 1 January 2007, the accession of Croatia on 1 July 2013 and the accelerated process of integration following the introduction of the single currency), a comprehensive review of national regional aid was undertaken. As a result of this review, new guidelines on national regional aid were issued to cover the period 2007 to 2013 (OJ 2006 C 54/13) and subsequently extended until 30 June 2014. New guidelines came into force on 1 July 2014 to cover the period through to 2020. These guidelines are available at:

http://ec.europa.eu/competition/state_aid/regional_aid/regional_aid.html

Although these guidelines do not have legal force, they will undoubtedly be taken into account by the Court of Justice.

The promotion of the execution of a project of common European interest or to remedy a serious economic disturbance (Article 107(3)(b) TFEU)

The sort of projects which have been approved by the Commission under this head are mostly ones in which there is cross-Union cooperation in some technological or environmental project. In this connection, see for example the following case:

Exécutif Régional Wallon and Glaverbel v Commission (CASE 62/87)

The Court of Justice held that there will be no common European interest in a scheme 'unless it forms part of a transnational European programme supported jointly by a number of governments of the Member States, or arises from concerted action by a number of Member States to combat a common threat such as environmental pollution'. As a result, the Court found that a scheme under which modernisation aid was granted to Glaverbel, who were manufacturers of glass in Belgium, was not an important project of European interest, because it was not part of a transnational programme.

The following case had a 'common interest objective' and therefore the state aid in question came within the scope of Art 107(3) TFEU (Art 107(3)(b) and/or Art 107(3)(c)):

Mediaset SpA v Commission (CASE T-177/07)

The digital switchover of television signals began in Italy in 2001, with November 2012 set as the statutory deadline by which switchover had to be completed. The Finance Law 2004 made provision for a state subsidy of 150 euros to be granted to every user who purchased or rented equipment for the reception of TV signals transmitted using digital *terrestrial* technology (i.e. the subsidy did not apply to digital *satellite* technology). In 2005, that aid was refinanced, but the subsidy was reduced to 70 euros. The spending limit of the subsidy for each year was 110 million euros.

Following complaints filed by satellite broadcasters, the Commission initiated a formal investigation procedure. In 2007, the Commission found that the subsidy constituted state aid to digital terrestrial broadcasters offering pay-TV services (in particular, pay-per-view services) and digital cable pay-TV operators (Decision 2007/374/EC). The Commission took the view that **the transition from analogue to digital TV broadcasting was a common interest objective and came within the scope of justifiable state aid pursuant to Art 107(3) TFEU. However, the subsidy was disproportionate and did not prevent unnecessary distortions of competition.** Because the measure at issue did not apply to digital satellite decoders, it was not technologically neutral. The decision ordered Italy to recover the aid from the beneficiaries, together with interest.

Mediaset SpA, a digital terrestrial programmes broadcaster, brought the present action seeking to have that decision annulled.

The General Court (previously the Court of First Instance) **dismissed the action in its entirety.**

The Court confirmed that the measure enabled cable operators and digital terrestrial broadcasters, such as Mediaset, **to benefit, as compared with satellite broadcasters, from an advantage.** In order to be entitled to the subsidy it was necessary to purchase or rent equipment for the reception of digital *terrestrial* TV signals. A consumer who opted for equipment exclusively for the reception of digital *satellite* TV signals could not benefit from the subsidy. Consequently, the subsidy did not meet the requirement of technological neutrality. Furthermore, the measure created an incentive for consumers to switch from the analogue to the digital terrestrial mode and, at the same time, enabled digital terrestrial broadcasters to consolidate their position on the market in terms of brand image and customer retention. The automatic price reduction prompted by the subsidy was also liable to affect the choice of consumers mindful of costs.

The Court held that the measure, the direct beneficiaries of which were the final consumers, constituted an indirect advantage for operators on the digital TV market, such as Mediaset. The Treaty prohibits state aid without drawing a distinction as to whether the related advantages are granted directly or indirectly. Furthermore, an advantage granted directly to certain natural or legal persons who are not necessarily undertakings may constitute an indirect advantage, hence state aid, for other natural or legal persons who are undertakings.

The Court further held that the selective nature of the measure resulted in a distortion of competition between digital terrestrial broadcasters and satellite broadcasters. Even though all the satellite broadcasters could have benefited from the measure by offering 'hybrid' decoders (which are both terrestrial and satellite), that would have exposed them to extra costs to pass on to consumers in the selling price.

Mediaset claimed that the aim of the subsidy was to address a market failure where, owing to a problem of coordination between operators, there was a barrier to the development of digital broadcasting. In that regard, the Court considered that by driving incumbent broadcasters to develop new commercial strategies, the mandatory nature of the date laid down for switchover was enough to resolve that problem and the subsidy was therefore unnecessary. **In any event, even if the measure had been necessary and proportionate to the objective of addressing the market failures, the fact remains that such a factor could not have justified the exclusion of satellite broadcasters from the benefit of that measure.**

Aid to facilitate the development of certain economic activities or certain economic areas (Article 107(3)(c) TFEU)

In its *First Report on State Aids in the European Community [i.e. Union]* published in 1989, the Commission reported a very large increase in the preceding ten years of cases notified and investigated under what is now Art 107 TFEU (previously Art 87 EC Treaty). A survey in the report indicated that over 108 billion **European Currency Units (ECUs)** was given in aid each year over that period, the majority of which went to manufacturing companies pursuant to what is now Art 107(3)(c) TFEU (previously Art 87(3)(c) EC Treaty). In its *18th Report on Competition Policy*, published the same year, the Commission described its approach to applications made by Member States for approval of state aids in relation to the regional aspect of what is now Art 107(3)(c) TFEU:

> Regions falling under . . . [Art 107(3)(c) TFEU] are those with more general development problems in relation to the national as well as the Community [i.e. Union] situation. Often they suffer from the decline of traditional industries and are frequently located in the more central prosperous parts of the Community [i.e. Union]. In its . . . [Art 107(3)(c) TFEU] method, the Commission has established a system which takes account of national regional problems and places them into a Community [i.e. Union] context.

The Commission has, in the context of Art 107(3)(c) TFEU, operated on the basis of two primary indicators. The first is income (as measured by gross domestic product or gross value added) and the second is structural unemployment. In this context (unlike that with regard to the criteria applicable to Art 107(3)(a) TFEU, above), the assessment of conditions is made in the national and the Union context. The better the position of the Member State in which the region is located in relation to the Union as a whole, the wider must be the disparity between the region concerned and the state as a whole, in order to justify the aid. Broadly, regions seeking aid must, in relative terms, be worse off than regions in poorer Member States before aid is approved by the Commission. In addition, for approval of the Commission to be secured, any aid proposal must be linked to a major restructuring of the sector of the industry concerned. It should not be used either simply to 'prop up' an ailing concern, or to allow an undertaking to gain an unfair competitive advantage (*Spain v Commission* (Case C-42/93)). In 1998, the Commission approved a research and development grant to Rolls-Royce by the UK government to develop a new generation of aero engines in Derby. The grant was authorised under what are now Arts 107(3)(c) and 174 TFEU (previously Arts 87(3)(c) and 158 EC Treaty); Art 174 TFEU relates to the reduction of disparities between different regions. The Commission also took account of the need to enable the Union to compete in the worldwide aviation market (*Competition Policy Newsletter* (1998) No. 2, p. 85).

The promotion of heritage conservation (Article 107(3)(d) TFEU)

This provision was added by the Treaty on European Union, and must be read in the light of Art 167(2) TFEU (previously Art 151(2) EC Treaty), which provides that:

> Action by the Union shall be aimed at encouraging cooperation between Member States and, if necessary, supporting and supplementing their action in . . . conservation and safeguarding of cultural heritage of European significance.

Heritage conservation is closely linked to the promotion of tourism, the right of access to which is a primary service under Art 56 TFEU (previously Art 49 EC Treaty); see *Luisi and Carbone* (Case 286/82) and Chapter 13. It is also linked to the obligation of the Union, in Title XIII TFEU (which relates to culture), to contribute to 'the flowering of the cultures of the Member States' (Art 167(1) TFEU (previously Art 151(1) EC Treaty)). The Union is also obliged 'to respect and to promote the diversity of its cultures' (Art 167(4) TFEU (previously Art 151(4) EC Treaty)). This is intended to provide specific authorisation for the kind of aid approved by the Commission in the past to sustain the Greek film industry (Decision 89/441, OJ 1989 L 208/3).

Specific state aids approved by the Council (Article 107(3)(e) TFEU)

A number of directives have been made under the former Art 87(3)(e) EC Treaty (now Art 107(3)(e) TFEU), including Directive 90/684 on state aid to shipbuilding. Under the directive, state aid could be deemed to be compatible with the internal market if it related to shipbuilding and ship conversion, which was granted as development assistance to a developing country. The Commission had to verify the development content of the proposal in accordance with criteria laid down by an **OECD** Working Party. In October 1991, the German government notified the Commission of its intention to grant aid to mainland China in the form of aid credit for three container vessels to be operated by a state-owned Chinese trading company, Cosco. The Commission informed Germany that the proposed aid could not be regarded as 'genuine development aid . . . and is therefore incompatible with the common market [i.e. internal market]'. It declared that it was not satisfied that the aid was any more than 'an operating aid to the German shipyards . . . rather than a genuine aid to a developing country'. This decision was challenged by the German government in an action to annul the decision under what is now Art 263 TFEU (previously Art 230 EC Treaty). The Court of Justice upheld the Commission's decision. The directive conferred a discretion on the Commission which was required to satisfy itself that the aid complied with the OECD criteria. It also had to verify the particular development content of the project. It decided that Cosco was not a company which needed development aid in order to contribute to the general development of China. It was entitled to come to that decision and was well within its discretion to do so.

Block exemptions

Objective
3

Under Art 109 TFEU (previously Art 89 EC Treaty) the Council can adopt regulations which concern the application of Arts 107 and 108 TFEU. Pursuant to the former Art 89 EC Treaty (now Art 109 TFEU), the Council adopted Regulation 994/98, the purpose of which is to facilitate the operation of the state aid system. It provides for a block exemption system to be used for certain categories of aid. This regulation has been amended by Regulation 733/2013 as part of the Commission's modernisation measures. Pursuant to this regulation (as amended), the Commission has adopted the following regulations:

- Regulation 651/2014, the General Block Exemption Regulation, which declares certain categories of aid compatible with the internal market in the application of Arts 107 and 108 TFEU.
- Regulation 1407/2013 on the application of Arts 107 and 108 TFEU to *de minimis* aid.

These two regulations are available at:

> http://ec.europa.eu/competition/state_aid/legislation/block.html

The Commission's role of monitoring the grant of state aid

Objective
4

The Commission has a general obligation to keep all systems of state aid under review, both those which are *prima facie* lawful under Art 107(2) TFEU and those which have been approved under the Commission's discretionary powers under Art 107(3) TFEU, to ensure that both continue to be operated in a way that is compatible with the internal market. It is the Commission which has to decide whether any kind of state aid is compatible with

Union law, except for those types of aid which have been given specific clearance by the Council under Art 107(3)(e) TFEU.

To enable it to assess whether or not any new aid scheme is permitted under Art 107 TFEU, there is a clearance procedure which must be followed by Member States. Under Art 108(3) TFEU:

> The Commission shall be informed, in sufficient time to enable it to submit its comments, of any plans to grant or alter aid. If it considers that any such plan is not compatible with the internal market having regard to Article 107, it shall without delay initiate the procedure provided for in paragraph 2. The Member State concerned shall not put its proposed measures into effect until this procedure has resulted in a final decision.

The Commission is required to decide relatively quickly if a proposed measure is justified under Art 107 TFEU. In *Germany* v *Commission* (Case 84/82), the Court declared that two months should suffice for this purpose. If at the end of that time the Commission has not defined its attitude towards the proposal, the Member State that has made the proposal could go ahead with it, but should notify the Commission of its intention to do so.

If the Commission decides that the proposed state aid is incompatible with the Treaty, or if aid which has previously been approved by it is being misused, it can inform the state concerned that the aid scheme should be abolished or altered within a timescale fixed by the Commission, and that the aid, together with interest, should be recovered by the state (*Commission* v *Italy* (Case C-348/93)). Failure to comply could result in that state being brought before the Court of Justice (Art 108(2) TFEU). This occurred in the following case:

Commission v *Greece* (CASE C-415/03)

The Court of Justice observed that the only defence available to a Member State in opposing an application by the Commission under the former Art 88(2) EC Treaty (now Art 108(2) TFEU) for a declaration that it has failed to fulfil its Treaty obligations is to plead that it was absolutely impossible for it properly to implement the decision ordering recovery of the aid in question. The condition that it is absolutely impossible to implement a decision is not fulfilled where the defendant government merely informs the Commission of the legal, political or practical difficulties involved in implementing the decision, without taking any real step to recover the aid from the undertakings concerned, and without proposing to the Commission any alternative arrangements for implementing the decision which could enable those difficulties to be overcome. Where the implementation of such a decision encounters no more than a number of difficulties at national level, the Commission and the Member State concerned must respect the principle underlying the former Art 10 EC Treaty (now Art 4(3) TEU), which imposes a duty of genuine cooperation on the Member States and the Union institutions to work together in good faith with a view to overcoming difficulties while fully observing the Treaty provisions, in particular the provisions on state aid.

The Court also stated that, in an action concerning the failure to implement a decision on state aid which has not been referred to the Court by the Member State to which it was addressed, the latter is not justified in challenging the lawfulness of that decision.

The Court also observed that no provision of Union law requires the Commission, when ordering the recovery of aid declared incompatible with the internal market, to fix the exact amount of the aid to be recovered. It is sufficient for the Commission's decision to include information enabling its recipient to work out itself, without too much difficulty, that amount.

The Commission may confine itself to declaring that there is an obligation to repay the aid in question and leave it to the national authorities to calculate the exact amounts to be repaid. The operative part of a Commission decision on state aid is inextricably linked to the statement of reasons for it. When the decision has to be interpreted, account must be taken of the reasons which led to its adoption. Therefore, the amounts to be repaid pursuant to the decision can be established by reading its operative part in conjunction with the relevant grounds.

Although it is not specifically provided for in Art 107 TFEU, the Court of Justice has accepted that any aid which has been unlawfully paid may also be recovered by the Commission (***Commission v Germany*** (Case 70/72)).

Even though the aid may have been accepted by an undertaking in good faith, without any reason to believe that it had been paid in breach of Union law, that innocent receipt cannot found a legitimate expectation that the aid may be retained. The effect of doing so could be fatal to the effective operation of Arts 107 and 108 TFEU, as the Court of Justice stated in the following case:

Commission v Germany (CASE C-5/89)

The Court of Justice held as follows:

A Member State whose authorities have granted aid contrary to the procedural rules laid down in . . . Article 108 TFEU] may not rely on the legitimate expectations of recipients in order to justify a failure to comply with the obligation to take the steps necessary to implement a Commission decision instructing it to recover the aid. If it could do so . . . [Articles 107 and 108 TFEU] would be set at nought, since national authorities would thus be able to rely on their own unlawful conduct in order to deprive decisions taken by the Commission under provisions of the Treaty of their effectiveness.

In ***Land Rheinland-Pfalz v Alcan Deutschland GmbH*** (Case C-24/95) the Court of Justice also made it clear that repayment had to be made even if it would be unlawful under state time-limit rules.

The obligation to recover aid declared incompatible with the internal market was examined by the CFI (now the General Court) in ***ESF Elbe-Stahlwerke Feralpi v Commission*** (Case T-6/99). In this case, the CFI held that the principle of legitimate expectation precluded the Commission from ordering the recovery of aid when, according to information from third parties, it considered its compatibility with the internal market in coal and steel *several years after approval of the aid concerned*, and held it incompatible with that market.

It is not only the Commission which will have an interest in the payment of state aids. Rival companies may also feel threatened by the actual or proposed distribution of state support and may wish to challenge a decision of the Commission approving it:

ASPEC and AAC v Commission (CASE T-435/93)

Aid had been approved by the Commission under what are now Arts 107 and 108 TFEU (previously Arts 87 and 88 EC Treaty) in relation to the production of starch in the Mezzogiorno area of Italy. This would have had the consequence of increasing production by 7 per cent at Union level and of establishing a production level in Italy alone which would have exceeded the previous total production capacity of that country. The challengers would have been seriously affected by the decision and the CFI (now the General Court) recognised that they had a sufficient interest to mount a challenge under what is now Art 263 TFEU (previously Art 230 EC Treaty); see Chapter 8.

Although the Court has previously held that the Commission enjoys a wide discretion in granting approval, its reasoning must be consistent with its declared policy, and it must adopt proper procedures when adopting its decision (see *Spain v Commission* (above)). In *ASPEC and AAC* (see above), the decision had never actually been taken by the full Commission but, in breach of its own procedures, had been delegated to Ray MacSharry, the then Agriculture Commissioner, on the eve of the Commission's annual holiday. The decision to approve the aid was, accordingly, annulled by the Court.

Damages can be awarded against the government of a Member State that has granted competition-distorting state aids without having notified these to the Commission for review (*Fédération Nationale du Commerce v France* (Case 354/90)).

In the following case, the Court of Justice was required to interpret the last sentence of the former Art 88(3) EC Treaty (now Art 108(3) TFEU). This provided the Court with an opportunity to confirm, and provide clarification of, a number of points on the role of national courts in the implementation of the system of monitoring state aid, particularly in a situation involving aid that is illegal on the ground that it is granted in breach of the obligation to notify aid laid down in that provision but is subsequently declared compatible with the internal market by a Commission decision:

Transalpine Ölleitung in Österreich (CASE C-368/04)

In accordance with a consistent line of decisions, the Court held that the last sentence of the former Art 88(3) EC Treaty (now Art 108(3) TFEU) must be interpreted as meaning that it is for the national courts to safeguard the rights of individuals against possible disregard, by the national authorities, of the prohibition on putting aid into effect before the Commission has adopted a decision authorising that aid. The Court emphasised, as it had done shortly beforehand in *Air Liquide Industries Belgium* (Joined Cases C-393/04 and C-41/05), that in doing so the national courts must take the Union interest fully into consideration, which precludes them from adopting a measure which would have the sole effect of extending the circle of recipients of the aid.

The Court also recalled that a Commission decision declaring aid that has not been notified compatible with the internal market does not have the effect of regularising *ex post facto* implementing measures which, at the time of their adoption, were invalid because they had been taken in disregard of the prohibition laid down in the last sentence of the former Art 88(3) EC Treaty (now Art 108(3) TFEU). The Court stated that otherwise the direct effect of that provision would be impaired and the interests of individuals, which are to be protected by national courts, would be disregarded.

The Court stated that in that regard, it is little consequence that the Commission decision states that its assessment of the aid in question relates to a period preceding the adoption of the decision or that an application for reimbursement is made before or after adoption of the decision declaring the aid compatible with the internal market, as that application relates to the unlawful situation resulting from the lack of notification.

Finally, the Court held that, depending on what is possible under national law including the available remedies, a national court may be: (i) called upon to order recovery of unlawful aid from its recipients, even if that aid has subsequently been declared compatible with the internal market by the Commission; or (ii) required to rule on an application for compensation for the damage caused by reason of the unlawful nature of such a measure.

Regulation 659/1999

Regulation 659/1999 was adopted by the Council on 22 March 1999 and lays down detailed rules for the application of Art 108 TFEU. This regulation has been amended by Regulation 734/2013 as part of the Commission's modernisation measures. The aim of the regulation (as amended) is to improve transparency and legal certainty by codifying and clarifying the procedural rules relating to state aid; these procedural rules have been discussed above. The regulation sets out procedures regarding the following:

- notified aid;
- unlawful aid;
- misuse of aid;
- existing aid schemes.

It also sets out the rights of interested parties and codifies monitoring mechanisms through a system of annual reports and on-site monitoring. This regulation has been implemented by Regulation 794/2004 (which has been amended by Regulation 372/2014 as part of the Commission's modernisation measures).

Regulations 659/1999 and 794/2004 (and the amending regulations) are available at:

http://ec.europa.eu/competition/state_aid/legislation/rules.html

Summary

Now you have read this chapter you should be able to:

- Explain how Arts 37, 102 and 106 TFEU are applied by the Commission and the Court of Justice of the European Union (which includes the General Court) to regulate state monopolies.
- Outline the provisions of Directive 80/723 (the Transparency Directive) which requires transparency of financial relations between public authorities and undertakings.
- Explain how Arts 107 and 108 TFEU are applied by the Commission and the Court of Justice of the European Union to regulate state aid.
- Outline the types of aid which are *per se* compatible with Art 107(1) TFEU.
- Understand and describe the types of aid which may be potentially justifiable pursuant to Art 107(3) TFEU.
- Describe and evaluate the nature and scope of the block exemption regulations adopted pursuant to Art 109 TFEU, which concern the application of Arts 107 and 108 TFEU.
- Outline the provisions of Regulations 659/1999 and 794/2004 which lay down the general procedural rules relating to state aid and the application of Art 108 TFEU.

Reference

Slotboom, M., 'State aid in community law: A broad or a narrow definition?' (1995) 20 EL Rev 289.

Further reading

Textbooks

Craig, P. and De Burca, G. (2011) *EU Law: Text, Cases* and *Materials* (5th edn), Oxford University Press, Chapter 28.

Steiner, J. and Woods, L. (2014) *EU Law* (12th edn), Oxford University Press, Chapters 28 and 29.

Journal articles

Braun, J-D. and Kühling, J., 'Article 87 EC and the Community courts: From revolution to evolution' (2008) 45 CML Rev 485.

Gilliams, H., 'Stress testing the regulator: Review of state aid to financial institutions after the collapse of Lehman' (2011) 36 EL Rev 3.

Giraud, A., 'A study of the notion of legitimate expectations in state aid recovery proceedings: "Abandon all hope, ye who enter here"?' (2008) 45 CML Rev 1399.

Graves, R., 'Autonomous regions, taxation and EC state-aid rules' (2009) 34 EL Rev 779.

Heuninokx, B., 'Defence procurement: The most effective way to grant illegal state aid and get away with it . . . or is it?' (2009) 46 CML Rev 191.

Kurks, B., 'Can general measures be . . . selective? Some thoughts on the interpretation of a state aid definition' (2008) 45 CML Rev 159.

Nebbia, P., 'Do the rules on state aids have a life of their own? National procedural autonomy and effectiveness in the Lucchini case' (2008) 33 EL Rev 427.

Ross, M., 'A healthy approach to services of general economic interest? The BUPA judgment of the Court of First Instance' (2009) 34 EL Rev 127.

20

Cartels and restrictive agreements: Article 101 TFEU

Objectives

At the end of this chapter you should understand:

1. The scope of Union competition law and policy.

2. The scope of Art 101(1) TFEU, which prohibits agreements which restrict competition.

3. How to apply the Art 101(3) TFEU criteria, which provide exemption from the prohibition under Art 101(1) TFEU and the procedural changes made to the application of Art 101(3) TFEU by Regulation 1/2003.

Competition law and policy

Objective 1

In its *First Report on Competition Policy* the Commission emphasised the value of effective competition in the Union. Competition is the best stimulant of economic activity, because it guarantees the widest possible freedom of action to all. An active competition policy, pursued in accordance with the provisions of the Treaties, makes it easier for the supply and demand structures to continually adjust to technological development. Through the interplay of decentralised decision-making machinery, competition enables enterprises continuously to improve their efficiency, which is essential for the steady improvement of living standards and employment prospects within the Member States. From this point of view, competition policy is an essential means for satisfying to a great extent the individual and collective needs of society.

Competition is not, however, regarded as an end in itself. It is one of the most important means by which a genuinely integrated market is achieved. Articles 101 and 102 TFEU (previously Arts 81 and 82 EC Treaty) match Arts 34 and 35 TFEU (previously Arts 28 and 29 EC Treaty), in the sense that the latter are aimed at measures taken by Member State governments which have the effect of restricting the free movement of goods (see Chapter 18), while the former are concerned with restrictive and abusive practices by undertakings which have the effect of excluding or restricting goods or services from Member States. The distinction between state and private undertaking in this context is not, of course, absolute. States may run commercial monopolies and private undertakings, and may secure an unfair competitive advantage by injections of state capital and other state aids. Both practices are subject to restriction under the Treaty and have been considered in Chapter 19. Large private business corporations, some of which have a higher annual turnover than the gross domestic product of many small states, dominate major sectors of the EU's economy. Abusive practices by such businesses may have more impact on cross-border trade than the actions of smaller Member State governments. Paradoxically, to create a genuinely free and competitive market, some restrictions are essential to ensure that the largest actors in the marketplace do not distort the working of the market to their own advantage and to the disadvantage of competitors and consumers. The primary objective, therefore, of Union competition policy has been market integration. A secondary one has been a form of equity or equality of competition, an aspect of 'the level playing field' to which many businesses aspire in the Union. The third aspect of competition policy is that espoused by the Commission in its First Report – the promotion of efficiency. Increasingly, this is viewed in the wider trading context of North and South America, the Pacific Rim, China and India.

Competition law, more than any other area of Union law, is informed by economic factors. Conduct which may be lawful in one context, may be unlawful in another. The behaviour of business actors will have to be assessed in the light of prevailing economic circumstances, and the way in which particular markets may react. The pricing policy of a company which has a monopoly will be the subject of acute interest to consumers, whereas overpricing by a company in a highly competitive market will rapidly be corrected by the effect on that company of consumers taking their custom elsewhere. The behaviour of business undertakings in relation to competition law and policy must always, therefore, be viewed in the context of such matters as degrees of concentration and the relevance of market power, the importance of entry barriers, and actual and potential competition.

Union competition policy, taking the objectives discussed above into account, is directed towards three types of anti-competitive activity:

1 restrictive trading agreements between otherwise independent business undertakings, which may affect trade between Member States and which distort competition within the internal market (Art 101 TFEU (previously Art 81 EC Treaty)); considered further within this chapter;

2 abusive, anti-competitive practices of large undertakings, which dominate markets for goods or services which affect trade between Member States (Art 102 TFEU (previously Art 82 EC Treaty)); considered further within Chapter 21;

3 major mergers of undertakings resulting in positions of market dominance in the Union (Merger Regulation 139/2004, which replaced Regulation 4064/89); considered further within Chapter 21.

Each of these types of anti-competitive practice is subject to regulation and control by the Commission, and the national competition authorities and courts of the Member States. The powers of the Commission, and the national competition authorities and courts of the Member States, and the way in which these powers are interpreted and applied, are considered in Chapter 22. The primary law on which the regulation of anti-competitive practices is based is considered within this chapter and the next.

Over the past few years there have been major changes to the regulation and control of these anti-competitive practices. These changes have been implemented primarily through secondary Union instruments. In addition, in some instances, the Commission has issued guidelines on the application of the anti-competitive measures. The aim of these guidelines is to assist industry in making the regulation and control processes more transparent. These changes are discussed throughout this and the next two chapters, where relevant.

Current primary and secondary competition legislation, including the guidelines, are available at:

http://ec.europa.eu/competition/antitrust/legislation/legislation.html

Article 101 TFEU

Objective 2

Article 101 TFEU is directed against cooperation between companies that operate in an anti-competitive way. Article 101(1) TFEU (which is substantially the same as the former Art 81(1) EC Treaty) provides as follows:

> The following shall be prohibited as incompatible with the internal market: all agreements between undertakings, decisions by associations of undertakings and **concerted practices** which may affect trade between Member States and which have as their object or effect the prevention, restriction or distortion of competition within the internal market . . .

A number of examples of the type of agreements covered by Art 101(1) TFEU are provided in Art 101(1)(a)–(e), i.e. those which:

(a) directly or indirectly fix purchase or selling prices or any other trading conditions;

(b) limit or control production, markets, technical development, or investment;

(c) share markets or sources of supply;

(d) apply dissimilar conditions to equivalent transactions with other trading parties, thereby placing them at a competitive disadvantage;

(e) make the conclusion of contracts subject to acceptance by the other parties of supplementary obligations which, by their nature or according to commercial usage, have no connection with the subject of such contracts.

Article 101(2) TFEU provides that any agreement or decision prohibited by Art 101(1) shall be automatically void. Although the list in Art 101(1)(a)–(e) is not exhaustive, it is indicative of the kind of practices which will breach the prohibition. It is primarily aimed at 'horizontal' cooperation between nominally competing companies; the classic cartel. It is also designed to deal with restrictive agreements between manufacturers, wholesalers and retailers (i.e. **vertical restrictive agreements**) which also affect the availability of goods and services, and the terms on which they are supplied. The Commission remains free to identify other agreements or practices which are operated in an anti-competitive way. There are, in addition, a number of agreements, decisions and practices which may be declared *not* to breach the prohibition in Art 101(1). These are listed in Art 101(3) TFEU (which is practically unchanged from the former Art 81(3) EC Treaty):

> The provisions of paragraph 1 may, however, be declared inapplicable in the case of:
>
> – any agreement or category of agreements between undertakings,
> – any decision or category of decisions by associations of undertakings,
> – any concerted practice or category of concerted practices,
>
> which contributes to improving the production or distribution of goods or to promoting technical or economic progress, while allowing consumers a fair share of the resulting benefit, and which does not:

(a) impose on the undertakings concerned restrictions which are not indispensable to the attainment of these objectives;

(b) afford such undertakings the possibility of eliminating competition in respect of a substantial part of the products in question.

Prior to 1 May 2004, the Commission was solely empowered to apply the former Art 81(3) EC Treaty (now Art 101(3) TFEU). However, Regulation 1/2003 now provides that the former Art 81(3) EC Treaty (now Art 101(3) TFEU) can be applied by the national competition authorities and the courts of the Member States (Arts 5 and 6, Regulation 1/2003; see below and Chapter 22).

Undertakings

The term 'undertaking' includes every kind of natural or legal person engaged in economic or commercial activity; it must be established in order to make a profit. The Court has often had to consider the nature of 'undertakings' to which Arts 101 and 102 TFEU are applicable, as illustrated in the following four cases:

Poucet v Assurances Générales De France (Case C-159/91)

Complaints had been made alleging anti-competitive restrictions on market access for 'consumers' of social insurance 'services'. The Court of Justice decided that regional social security organisations were not 'undertakings'. The Court distinguished between bodies pursuing economic activities as such, and those activities which are based upon a principle of solidarity and which are pursued entirely without an intention to make a profit.

Aok Bundesverband and Others (Joined Cases C-264/01, C-306/01, C-354/01 and C-355/01)

Several questions on the interpretation of the former Arts 81, 82 and 86 EC Treaty (now Arts 101, 102 and 106 TFEU) were referred to the Court of Justice for a preliminary ruling by the Oberlandesgericht Düsseldorf (Higher Regional Court, Düsseldorf, Germany) and the Bundesgerichtshof (Federal Court of Justice, Germany). The cases concerned disputes between: (i) associations of sickness and health insurance funds; and (ii) pharmaceutical companies, concerning the fixed maximum amounts payable by sickness funds towards the cost of medicinal products and treatment materials which had been established by the German legislature.

The Oberlandesgericht Düsseldorf and the Bundesgerichtshof essentially asked the Court of Justice whether the competition rules laid down by the Treaty precluded groups of sickness funds, such as the fund associations, from determining fixed maximum amounts corresponding to the upper limit of the price of medicinal products whose cost is borne by the sickness funds.

The Court adopted the solution set out in its *Poucet* case law, to the effect that the concept of an undertaking, within the context of Union competition law, does not cover bodies entrusted with the management of statutory health insurance and old-age insurance schemes which pursue an exclusively social objective and do not engage in economic activity. The Court took the view in *Poucet* that this was the position with regard to sickness funds, which, even though the legislature had given them a degree of latitude in setting contribution rates in order to promote sound management, were compelled by law to offer to their members essentially identical obligatory benefits which do not depend on the amount of the contributions. The Court of Justice accordingly ruled in the present cases that 'in determining the fixed maximum amounts, the fund associations merely perform a task for management of the German social security system which is imposed upon them by legislation and they do not act as undertakings engaging in economic activity' (para 64). The former Arts 81 and 82 EC Treaty (now Arts 101 and 102 TFEU) were therefore not applicable to such measures.

SAT v *Eurocontrol* (Case C-364/92)

The Court of Justice concluded that Eurocontrol, a body set up by treaty to recover fees payable by airlines for traffic control services, was not an 'undertaking'. It undertook the tasks assigned to it in the public interest with a view to assuring the maintenance and improvement of air transport. There was not a sufficient economic element in the work of Eurocontrol, which could not be held responsible for the amounts which it collected. The fees payable had been established by the states which were parties to the treaty by which it was established.

Diego Cali v *SEPG* (Case C-343/95)

The Court of Justice held that a body established under national law to collect harbour dues in the port of Genoa (intended to cover the cost of anti-pollution measures) was not an 'undertaking' within the meaning of what are now Arts 101 and 102 TFEU (previously Arts 81 and 82 EC Treaty). The body performed 'a task in the public interest, which forms part of the essential functions of the states as regards protection of the environment in maritime areas'.

The fact that a body is state-owned or state-financed and provides a service usually provided by the state does not prevent it from being an 'undertaking' within what are now Arts 101 and 102 TFEU if it is providing services 'of general economic interest' (*Job Centre Coop* (Case C-55/96)).

Rules of professional conduct

The issue before the Court of First Instance ((CFI, now renamed the General Court) in the following case was whether the rules which regulate the exercise of a liberal profession fall within the scope of the former Art 81 EC Treaty (now Art 101 TFEU):

Institut Des Mandataires Agréés v *Commission* (Case T-144/99)

The CFI (now the General Court) decided that rules which regulate the exercise of a liberal profession cannot be considered to fall as a matter of principle outside the scope of the former Art 81(1) EC Treaty (now Art 101(1) TFEU) merely because they are classified as 'rules of professional conduct' by the competent bodies. It follows that an examination on a case-by-case basis is essential in order to assess the validity of such rules under that provision of the Treaty, in particular by taking account of their impact on the freedom of action of the members of the profession and on its organisation and also on the recipients of the services in question. In this case that approach yielded real results because the CFI

> confirmed, on one point, the Commission's finding that a simple prohibition, under a code of conduct, of comparative advertising between professional representatives restricts competition in that it limits the ability of more efficient professional representatives to develop their services. This has the consequence, *inter alia*, that the clientele of each professional representative is crystallised within a national market.

In **Wouters and Others v Algemene Raad van de Nederlandse Orde van Advocaten** (Case C-309/99) the Court of Justice held that a regulation concerning partnerships between members of the Bar and other professionals, adopted by a body such as the Bar of The Netherlands, was to be treated as a decision adopted by an association of undertakings within the meaning of the former Art 81(1) EC Treaty (now Art 101(1) TFEU). The Court of Justice further held that the regulation in question did not breach the former Art 81(1) EC Treaty because, although its effect was to restrict competition, the Bar of The Netherlands could reasonably have considered that the regulation was necessary for the proper practice of the legal profession within the Netherlands.

Sporting bodies

The following case concerned the issue of whether or not a sporting body (in this case the International Olympic Committee (IOC)) was subject to Union competition law. With regard to the free movement of workers and freedom to provide services, the Court of Justice has previously held that sport is subject to Union law only in so far as it constitutes an economic activity. Therefore, for example, rules which limit the number of professional players who are nationals of other Member States are in breach of the provisions relating to the free movement of workers (see, for example, **Bosman** (Case C-415/93), and Chapter 11). In the following case, the CFI (now the General Court) extended this rationale to Union competition law and decided that, because the IOC was not engaged in an economic activity, with regard to the rules in question, it was not subject to Union competition law. However, the Court of Justice decided otherwise:

Meca-Medina and Majcen v Commission (Case C-519/04P)

The two applicants were athletes who competed in long-distance swimming events. They had been suspended under the Olympic Movement's Anti-Doping Code after testing positive for Nandrolone. They had claimed before the Commission that the IOC's anti-doping rules infringed the Union rules on competition (and the free movement of services). They lodged a complaint with the Commission. The Commission rejected the complaint and the two athletes made an application to the CFI (now the General Court) for the Commission's decision to be annulled. The CFI upheld the decision (in Case T-313/02).

The CFI stated that, according to the settled case law of the Court of Justice, sport is subject to Union law only in so far as it constitutes an economic activity within the meaning of Union law. The provisions of the Treaty on free movement of workers and services apply to the rules adopted in the field of sport which concern the economic aspect which sporting activity can present. That applies, in particular, to the rules providing for the payment of fees for the transfer of professional players between clubs (transfer clauses) or limiting the number of professional players who are nationals of other Member States those clubs may field in matches. Conversely, Union law does not extend to what are purely sporting rules which for that reason have nothing to do with economic activity, like the rules on the composition of national teams or rules fixing: for example, the length of matches or the number of players on the field.

After noting that the Court of Justice had not, in cases concerning the former Art 39 EC Treaty on the free movement of workers (now Art 45 TFEU) and the former Art 49 EC Treaty on the freedom to provide services (now Art 56 TFEU), had to rule on whether sporting rules are subject to the Treaty provisions on competition, the CFI considered that the principles identified in respect of free movement of workers and services are equally valid as regards the provisions of the Treaty relating to competition and that the opposite is also true. According to the CFI, it followed that purely sporting legislation did not come under either the Union provisions on free movement of persons and services or the provisions on competition.

The applicants appealed to the Court of Justice, seeking: (i) the setting aside of the CFI's judgment; and (ii) annulment of the Commission's decision.

The Court of Justice reiterated that sport is subject to Union law in so far as it constitutes an economic activity, but that the provisions of the Treaty on freedom of movement for persons and freedom to provide services do not affect rules concerning questions which are of purely sporting interest and, as such, have nothing to do with economic activity.

The Court of Justice stated that if, by contrast, those rules do not constitute restrictions on freedom of movement because they concern questions of purely sporting interest and, as such, have nothing to do with economic activity, that fact means neither that the sporting activity in question necessarily falls outside the scope of the provisions of Union competition law nor that the rules do not satisfy the specific requirements of those provisions.

By adopting the opposite approach, without first determining whether those rules fulfilled the specific requirements of Union competition law, the Court of Justice held that the CFI erred in law. The Court of Justice set aside the judgment of the CFI.

The Court of Justice then went on to rule on the application for annulment of the Commission's decision. As regards the compatibility of the rules at issue, with the rules on competition the Court of Justice stated that the penal nature of the rules at issue, and the magnitude of the penalties applicable if they are breached, are capable of producing adverse effects on competition. In order to escape the prohibition on distortion of competition laid down by the Treaty, the restrictions imposed by those rules must be limited to what is necessary to ensure the proper conduct of competitive sport.

Rules of that kind could indeed prove excessive as a result of: (i) the way in which the dividing line is drawn between circumstances which amount to doping in respect of which penalties may be imposed and those which do not; and (ii) the severity of those penalties. With regard to the threshold beyond which the presence of Nandrolone in an athlete's body was presumed to indicate doping, the Court stated that it did not appear that this presumption was excessive – it did not go beyond what was necessary in order to ensure that sporting events took place and functioned properly.

As the applicants had not pleaded that the penalties that were applicable and were imposed in the present case were excessive, the Court of Justice held that it had not been established that the anti-doping rules at issue were disproportionate. Consequently, the Court of Justice dismissed the action for annulment of the Commission's decision.

The following case was decided by the CFI prior to the Court of Justice's judgment in the above case:

PIAU v Commission (Case T-193/02)

The CFI (now the General Court) once again made it clear that Union competition rules can, in certain circumstances, apply in the area of sport. In this case, the Commission had rejected, on grounds of lack of Union interest, a complaint by the applicant challenging the Fédération Internationale de Football Association (FIFA) Players' Agents Regulations. In its judgment, the CFI held that football clubs and the national associations grouping them together are undertakings and associations of undertakings respectively, within the meaning of Union competition law. Consequently, FIFA, which brings together national associations, itself constitutes an association of undertakings within the meaning of the former Art 81 EC Treaty (now Art 101 TFEU). On the basis of that initial finding, the CFI held that the Players' Agents Regulations constituted a decision by an association of undertakings. The purpose of the occupation of players' agent was to introduce, on a regular basis, and for a fee, a player to a club with a view to employment, or to introduce two clubs to one another with a view to concluding a transfer contract. It was therefore an economic activity involving the provision of services, which did not fall within the scope of the specific nature of sport, as defined by the case law.

Piau's appeal to the Court of Justice was dismissed (Case C-171/05P).

While the CFI's approach may be inconsistent with that of the Court of Justice in *Meca-Medina and Majcen v Commission*, the CFI's decision (that FIFA's Players' Agents Regulations come within the scope of Union competition law) is undoubtedly correct.

Agreements, decisions and concerted practices

Article 101 TFEU is applicable only if there is an 'agreement', a 'decision by an association of undertakings' or a 'concerted practice'. Each of these is considered further.

Agreement

Agreements are not confined to binding contracts of whatever kind, but include understandings and 'gentlemen's agreements' (*ACF Chemiefarma v Commission* (Case 41/69)). The type of loose arrangement that may fall foul of Art 101(1) TFEU is demonstrated by the facts of the following case:

BMW Belgium v Commission (Case 32/78)

An attempt was made by BMW's subsidiary in Belgium to discourage car dealers there from selling BMW cars to other Member States. BMW dealers in Belgium had received a circular from BMW Belgium urging them not to engage in such sales. They were asked to indicate assent to this policy by signing and returning a copy of the circular. It was made clear that this was not a contractual document, but the Court nonetheless held that it was an 'agreement' under what is now Art 101(1) TFEU (previously Art 81(1) EC Treaty).

The scope of 'agreement' was considered by the CFI (now the General Court) in the following case:

Tréfilenrope Sarl v Commission (Case T-148/89)

The CFI (now the General Court) declared that:

> For there to be an agreement within the meaning of . . . [Article 101(1) TFEU], it is sufficient for the undertakings in question to have expressed their joint intention to conduct themselves in the market in a particular way.

In *Volkswagen* v *Commission* (Case T-62/98), the CFI (now the General Court) partially dismissed the action for annulment of the Commission's decision imposing a fine on Volkswagen for infringement of what is now Art 101 TFEU. Volkswagen appealed the CFI's decision to the Court of Justice:

Volkswagen v Commission (Case C-338/00)

The Court of Justice considered that the CFI (now the General Court) had correctly applied the case law, whereby:

> . . . a call by a motor vehicle manufacturer to its authorised dealers is not a unilateral act which falls outside the scope of what is now Art 101(1) TFEU (previously Art 81(1) EC Treaty) but is an agreement within the meaning of that provision if it forms part of a set of continuous business relations governed by a general agreement drawn up in advance.

The implementation of a policy of supply quotas by a motor manufacturer on dealers with a view to blocking re-exports, constitutes not a unilateral measure but an agreement within the meaning of that provision. In this case, in order to impose that policy, the manufacturer used clauses of the dealership agreement, such as those enabling supplies to dealers to be limited, and thereby influenced the commercial conduct of those dealers.

The 'agreement' does not have to be voluntary. In *Community* v *Volkswagen AG and Others* (Case IV/35.733), the Commission concluded that there existed an 'agreement' between Volkswagen and its dealers in Italy where they complied with instructions (reinforced by heavy pressure from Volkswagen) not to sell to purchasers from outside Italy.

Decision by an association of undertakings

The most common type of decision at which Art 101(1) TFEU is aimed is that of a trade association which lays down standards for the activities of its members. Standardisation of pricing or the way in which a service may be supplied may well fall foul of the provisions of Art 101 TFEU. Even an agreement to supply information about sales by competitors, although it is concerned with neither prices nor any anti-competitive arrangement, has been held to fall within Art 101 TFEU, as it could enable the dominant suppliers to adopt strategies to resist market penetration by those competitors (*Fiatagri UK Ltd* v *Commission* (Case T-34/92)). The body concerned does not, however, have to be engaged in commercial activity itself, as illustrated in the following case:

Nv Iaz International Belgium and Others v Commission (Case 96/82)

Two Belgian Royal Decrees provided that washing machines and dishwashers could be connected to the main water supply only if they satisfied Belgian standards. For the purpose of monitoring the conformity of washing machines or dishwashers with those Belgian standards, the manufacturers and sole importers of electrical appliances affiliated to certain trade organisations made an agreement with the national association of water suppliers (the ANSEAU–NAVEWA agreement). Under this agreement, all appliances put into commercial distribution had to bear a label issued by a designated trade organisation. The Commission made a decision that certain provisions of the agreement infringed what is now Art 101(1) TFEU (previously Art 81(1) EC Treaty). In its view, the offending provisions excluded the possibility for importers other than the sole importers to obtain a conformity check for the washing machines and dishwashers they imported into Belgium under conditions which did not discriminate against them. ANSEAU attempted to argue that the agreement did not fall within what is now Art 101(1) TFEU as its member undertakings were not legally bound by the agreement and since ANSEAU did not itself carry on any kind of economic activity. The Court of Justice rejected both arguments:

> . . . [Article 101(1) TFEU] also applies to associations of undertakings in so far as their own activities or those of the undertakings affiliated to them are calculated to produce the results which it aims to suppress . . . A recommendation, even if it has no binding effect, cannot escape . . . [Article 101(1) TFEU] where compliance with the recommendation by the undertakings to which it is addressed has an appreciable influence in the market in question.

However, the Court of Justice has recognised that there is a limit to the application of Art 101 TFEU where the nominees of trade organisations concerned with the fixing of prices were genuinely independent of their parent bodies:

Germany v Delta Schiffahrts und Speditionsgesellschaft GmbH (Case C-153/93)

Shippers and inland waterway ship operators were both represented on freight commissions which fixed inland waterway freight charges. These commissions set the relevant charges, which were approved by the Federal Minister of Transport and were then compulsory. A shipper challenged these charges as being contrary to what is now Art 101 TFEU (previously Art 81 EC Treaty) and the case was referred to the Court of Justice under what is now Art 267 TFEU (previously Art 234 EC Treaty). The Court held that what is now Art 101 TFEU did not preclude rules of a Member State from providing that tariffs for commercial inland waterways traffic might be fixed by the freight commissions comprised of individuals recommended by the businesses concerned, provided that they were genuinely independent of those businesses and provided that the public authority retained a power to override their decisions.

Concerted practice

'Concerted practice' refers to some type of coordinated action which, although it may fall short of an agreement, knowingly substitutes practical cooperation for competition. This is illustrated in the following case:

ICI v Commission (Case 48/69)

ICI was among a number of businesses producing aniline dyestuffs in Italy. It was the first to impose a price increase, but was shortly followed by other producers of similar products, accounting for more than 80 per cent of the market. A similar pattern of price increases had taken place among the ten major producers of aniline dyestuffs who dominated the dyestuffs market in the Union. The Commission concluded from the circumstances that there had been a 'concerted practice' between the undertakings, and imposed fines on them. The undertakings challenged the Commission's decision, arguing that the price increases merely reflected parallel behaviour in an oligopolistic market where each producer followed the price leader. An **oligopoly** is a market in which a small number of suppliers supply the preponderant portion of demand. The Court of Justice considered the circumstances and the nature of a concerted practice in the context of what is now Art 101 TFEU (previously Art 81 EC Treaty):

> . . . [Article 101 TFEU] draws a distinction between the concept of 'concerted practices' and that of 'agreements between undertakings' or of 'decisions of associations'; the object is to bring within the prohibition of that Article a form of coordination between undertakings which, without having reached the stage where an agreement properly so called has been concluded, knowingly substitutes practical cooperation between them for the risks of competition.
>
> By its very nature, then, a concerted practice does not have all the elements of a contract but may *inter alia* arise out of coordination which becomes apparent from the behaviour of the participants. Although parallel behaviour may not by itself be identified with a concerted practice, it may, however, amount to strong evidence of such a practice if it leads to conditions of competition which do not correspond to the normal conditions of the market, having regard to the nature of the products, the size and number of the undertakings and the volume of the said market. (paras 64 to 66)

In the above case, the Court of Justice went on to decide that there was evidence of a concerted practice that breached what is now Art 101 TFEU. Concertation is difficult to prove, and the mere fact of parallel price increases is not conclusive. There must be 'a firm, precise and consistent body of evidence' on concertation to justify such a finding (*Åhlström Osakeyhito* v *Commission* (Joined Cases C-89, 104, 114, 116, 117 and 125–129/85)). In the following case, the Court of Justice held that a single meeting between companies *may* constitute a 'concerted practice':

T-Mobile Netherlands BV and Others v *Raad van bestuur van der Nederlandse Mededingingsautoriteit* (Case C-8/08)

In 2001, five operators in the Netherlands had their own mobile telephone network. Representatives of the five operators held a meeting on 13 June 2001. At that meeting they discussed, *inter alia*, the reduction of standard dealer remunerations for post-paid subscriptions, which was to take effect on or about 1 September 2001.

By decision of 30 December 2002, the Netherlands competition authority found that the five operators had concluded an agreement with each other or had entered into a concerted practice. Taking the view that such conduct restricted competition to an appreciable extent and was thus prohibited under national law, the authority imposed fines on those undertakings. They challenged that decision.

The case went to appeal before the Administrative Court for Trade and Industry, which referred the case to the Court of Justice for clarification about the concept of concerted practice, and in particular:

(i) the criteria to be applied when assessing whether a concerted practice pursues an anti-competitive object;
(ii) to state whether the national court considering whether there is a concerted practice is obliged to apply the presumption of a causal connection established in the Court's case law on that matter;
(iii) to determine whether that presumption is applicable even where the concerted practice has its roots in participation by the undertakings concerned at a single meeting.

The criteria to be applied in determining whether a concerted practice pursues an anti-competitive object

The Court observed that the criteria laid down in the Court's case law for the purpose of determining whether conduct has as its object or effect the prevention, restriction or distortion of competition are applicable irrespective of whether the case entails an agreement, a decision or a concerted practice. With regard to the definition of a concerted practice, the Court stated that such a practice is a form of coordination between undertakings by which, without it having been taken to the stage where an agreement properly so-called has been concluded, practical cooperation between them is knowingly substituted for the risks of competition.

The Court pointed out that it had already provided a number of criteria on the basis of which it was possible to ascertain whether a concerted practice is anti-competitive, which included, in particular:

(i) the details of the arrangements on which it is based;
(ii) the objectives it is intended to attain;
(iii) its economic and legal context.

In order for a concerted practice to be regarded as having an anti-competitive object, it is sufficient that it has the potential to have a negative impact on competition. In other words, it must simply be capable in an individual case, having regard to the specific legal and economic context, of resulting in the prevention, restriction or distortion of competition within the internal market.

Moreover, the Court stated that a concerted practice may be regarded as having an anti-competitive object even though the practice has no direct effect on the price paid by end-users but relates simply to the remuneration paid to dealers for concluding post-paid subscription agreements.

Finally the Court stated that any exchange of information between competitors pursues an anti-competitive object if it is capable of removing uncertainties as to the anticipated conduct of the participating undertakings, including where, as in the present case, the conduct relates to the reduction in the standard commission paid to dealers. The Court stated that it is for the referring court to determine whether the information exchanged at the meeting held on 13 June 2001 was capable of removing such uncertainties.

Whether the national court is under an obligation to apply the presumption of a causal connection established in the Court's case law

The Court stated that the concept of a concerted practice implies, in addition to the participating undertakings concerting with each other, subsequent conduct on the market and a relationship of cause and effect between the two. In that context, the Court has established in its case law a presumption of a causal connection, according to which the undertakings taking part in the concerted action and remaining active on the market are presumed to take account of the information exchanged with their competitors in determining their conduct on that market.

The Court stated that since any interpretation of Union law provided by the Court is binding on all the national courts and tribunals of the Member States, the national court is obliged to apply that presumption of a causal connection.

Whether the presumption of a causal connection is to be applied in cases in which the concerted action is the result of a meeting on a single occasion

The Court pointed out that, depending on the structure of the market, the possibility cannot be ruled out that a meeting on a single occasion between competitors may, in principle, constitute a sufficient basis for the participating undertakings to concert their market conduct. If the undertakings concerned establish a cartel with a complex system of concerted actions in relation to a multiplicity of aspects of their market conduct, regular meetings over a long period may be necessary. If, on the other hand, as in the present case, the objective of the exercise is only to concert action on a selective basis with reference simply to one parameter of competition, a single meeting between competitors may constitute a sufficient basis on which to implement the anti-competitive object the participating undertakings aim to achieve.

In those circumstances, what matters is whether the meeting or meetings which took place afforded them the opportunity to take account of the information exchanged with their competitors in order to determine their conduct on the market in question and knowingly substitute practical cooperation between them for the risks of competition. Where it can be established that such undertakings successfully concerted with one another and remained active on the market, they may justifiably be called upon to adduce evidence that the concerted action did not have any effect on their conduct on the market in question.

The Court of Justice held that in so far as the undertaking participating in the concerted action remains active on the market in question, there is a presumption of a causal connection between the concerted practice and the conduct of the undertaking on that market, even if the concerted action is the result of a meeting held by the participating undertakings on a single occasion.

An agreement between undertakings

As discussed above, the concept of an 'undertaking' is wide, and it includes all legal and natural persons involved in economic or commercial activity, such as companies, sole traders and state-owned public utilities. Undertakings may be engaged in the manufacture, sale or distribution of products or the provision of services and may comprise several companies which are owned or controlled by another one. There must be an agreement or concerted practice by two or more such undertakings, as stated by the Court of Justice in the following case:

Viho Europe BV v Commission (Case T-102/92)

The Court of Justice stated that there will be no agreement between 'undertakings' where it is within:

> . . . one economic unit within which subsidiaries do not enjoy real autonomy in determining their course of action in the market. Where, as in this case, the subsidiary, although having a separate legal personality, does not freely determine its conduct on the market but carries out instructions given to it directly or indirectly by the parent company by which it is wholly controlled, . . . [Article 101(1) TFEU] does not apply to the relationship between the subsidiary and the parent company with which it forms an economic unit.

The substantive requirements of Article 101 TFEU

Having established the kind of agreement or arrangement which, potentially, may breach Art 101 TFEU, what is the content of such a deal that will infringe Art 101 TFEU? Not all agreements that affect trading relations between undertakings will breach Art 101. Clearly, the exemption provided under Art 101(3) recognises that the potentially restrictive effect of some agreements may be outweighed by their beneficial effect. Before an assessment can be made of the grounds for exemption, however, it is necessary to isolate the constituent elements in Art 101 which will enable an offending agreement to be identified.

An agreement which may affect trade between Member States

Article 101(1)(a)–(e) TFEU, see above, provides a non-exhaustive list of the sort of agreements which will *prima facie* breach Art 101 TFEU, but they must be set within a Union context. The type of conduct at which Art 101 is primarily aimed is the conclusion of agreements or concerted practices between apparently competing producers or distributors who agree to give each other a 'free run' in specific national territories. Such horizontal agreements (e.g. between producer and producer; or between distributor and distributor) clearly continue to partition what should be a single market on a national basis, and attempt to defeat one of the primary aims of the Union. In *Suiker Unie* **v** *Commission* (Case 40/73), for example, sugar producers agreed to keep out of one another's territories; and in *ACF Chemiefarma* **v** *Commission* (Case 41/69) the undertakings concerned agreed (in a 'gentlemen's agreement') to share out domestic markets and to fix common prices of synthetic quinidine. Clearly, in these cases trade is affected and the effect of these horizontal agreements is to deny consumers the benefit of competitive products from other Member States.

The possible effect on trade between Member States received careful examination by the Court of Justice in relation to a vertical agreement (e.g. between producer and distributor) in the following landmark case:

Consten and Grundig v *Commission* (Case 56/64)

As part of its international distribution network, the German manufacturer of electrical equipment (Grundig) came to an agreement with the French distributor (Consten) by which Consten was appointed as Grundig's sole representative in France, Corsica and the Saarland. This is referred to as **'absolute territorial protection'**; Grundig products could only be distributed in these three countries by Consten. Under that agreement Consten was authorised to use Grundig's name and trade mark, and Consten duly registered the Grundig trade mark 'GINT' in France. Consten then brought proceedings for infringement of a trade mark against a French company, UNEF, which had attempted to sell, in France, Grundig products which it had bought in Germany. Such goods are referred to as 'parallel imports' (i.e. goods which are purchased in one Member State and imported into another Member State). The Commission, after an investigation, decided that the Consten–Grundig agreement breached what is now Art 101 TFEU (previously Art 81 EC Treaty), and Grundig and Consten applied to the Court of Justice for annulment of that decision under what is now Art 263(2) TFEU (previously Art 230(2) EC Treaty). The applicants argued that the Commission had relied on a mistaken interpretation of the concept of an agreement which may affect trade between Member States, and had not shown that such trade would have been greater without the disputed agreement. The Court of Justice rejected the argument:

> The concept of an agreement 'which may affect trade between Member States' is intended to define, in the law governing cartels, the boundary between the areas respectively covered by Community [i.e. Union] law and national law. It is only to the extent to which the agreement may affect trade between Member States that the deterioration in competition caused by the agreement falls under the prohibition of Community [i.e. Union] law contained in . . . [Article 101 TFEU]; otherwise it escapes the prohibition. In this connection, what is particularly important is whether the agreement is capable of constituting a threat, either direct or indirect, actual or potential, to freedom of trade between Member States in a manner which might harm the attainment of the objectives of a single market between States. Thus the fact that an agreement encourages an increase, even a large one, in the volume of trade between states is not sufficient to exclude the possibility that the agreement may 'affect'

> such trade in the above mentioned manner. In the present case, the contract between Grundig and Consten, on the one hand by preventing undertakings other than Consten from importing Grundig products into France, and on the other hand by prohibiting Consten from re-exporting those products to other countries of the common market [i.e. internal market], indisputably affects trade between Member States.

In the above case, the Court of Justice stated that it was not necessary to wait to see if trade was in fact affected by the way in which the agreement was intended to operate. The Court said that 'there is no need to take into account the concrete effects of an agreement *once it appears that it has as its object the prevention, restriction or distortion of competition*' (emphasis added).

The effect of the ***Consten and Grundig*** decision is that Art 101 TFEU applies not only to competing undertakings on a horizontal level, but also to vertical agreements between companies which are not themselves competing with each other but which aim to exclude competitors from the market (as stated above, this provides the competitor with 'absolute territorial protection'), provided that the agreement is one that affects trade between Member States. Article 101 TFEU can catch such vertical supply agreements as affecting trade between Member States, even if they are not in any way concerned to affect trade outside one Member State. Trade may, however, in fact be affected if the agreement, taken in the context of trading conditions in that state, is likely to affect trade into that state. This situation is most likely to occur in relation to 'sole-supply' agreements between producers and retailers, as illustrated in the following case:

Brasserie de Haecht SA v Wilkin (No. 1) (Case 23/67)

> The proprietor of a café in Belgium obtained a loan from a Belgian brewery on the basis that he would obtain supplies of beverages exclusively from the brewery. The legality of the agreement in the context of what is now Art 101(1) TFEU (previously Art 81(1) EC Treaty) was raised in subsequent proceedings and referred by the Belgian court to the Court of Justice under what is now Art 267 TFEU (previously Art 234 EC Treaty). The Court held that the validity of the agreement under what is now Art 101 TFEU had to take into account not only the scope and effect of the agreement itself, but also the trading conditions in the state in which it was made. The agreement, when viewed in isolation, as Advocate General Roemer observed in the case, did not 'seem to be prejudicial to the common market [i.e. internal market] in any way . . . On the other hand it is possible for such an effect to occur as the result of the combined operation of all the beer distribution agreements in a Member State'. The Court agreed, and said:
>
> > . . . [Article 101(1) TFEU] implies that regard must be had to such effects in the context in which they occur, that is to say in the economic and legal context of such agreements, decisions and practices and where they might combine with others to have a cumulative effect on competition. In fact, it would be pointless to consider an agreement, decision or practice by reason of its effects if those effects were to be taken distinct from the market in which they are seen to operate and could only be examined apart from the body of effects, whether convergent or not surrounding their implementation.

The problem of restrictions of competition generated by the cumulative effect of similar vertical agreements was dealt with in depth by the CFI (now the General Court) in the following case:

Roberts v *Commission* (Case T-25/99)

The operators of a pub in the UK complained to the Commission that the lease used by the local brewery, Greene King, from which, as tenants, they were subject to an obligation to obtain beer, was contrary to the former Art 81(1) EC Treaty (now Art 101(1) TFEU). The Commission rejected their complaint on the ground that the standard lease used by Greene King did not fall within the scope of the former Art 81 EC Treaty (now Art 101 TFEU). The action which they brought before the CFI (now the General Court) sought the annulment of that decision. The CFI stated that the contested decision correctly defined the relevant market as that of the distribution of beer in establishments selling alcoholic beverages for consumption on the premises. The CFI then considered whether the Commission was right to find that Greene King's network of agreements, consisting of leases with a purchasing obligation concluded between that brewery and its tenants, did not make a significant contribution to the **foreclosure** of the relevant market, so that the agreements were not caught by the prohibition in the former Art 81(1) EC Treaty (now Art 101(1) TFEU). The CFI endorsed the Commission's conclusion.

In that connection the CFI stated, first, that in order to assess whether a standard beer supply agreement contributes to the cumulative effect of closing off the market produced by all such agreements, it is necessary to take into consideration the position of the contracting parties in the market. The contribution also depends on the duration of the agreements. If it is manifestly excessive in relation to the average duration of agreements generally concluded in the relevant market, the individual agreement falls under the prohibition laid down in the former Art 81(1) EC Treaty (now Art 101(1) TFEU). A brewery holding a relatively small share of the market, which ties its sales outlets for many years, may contribute to foreclosure (i.e. closing off) of the market as significantly as a brewery with a comparatively strong position in the market which regularly frees its outlets at frequent intervals. In this case neither the market share of the brewer nor the duration of the beer supply contracts were held to contribute significantly to the foreclosure of the market.

The CFI then went on to consider whether a network of agreements of a wholesaling brewery, here Greene King, which does not in itself significantly contribute to the foreclosure of the market, may be linked to networks of agreements of supplying breweries, which do contribute significantly to such foreclosure, and may thus fall within the scope of the former Art 81(1) EC Treaty (now Art 101(1) TFEU). Two conditions must be satisfied in that regard:

1 First, it must be considered whether the beer supply agreements concluded between the wholesaling brewery and the supplying breweries, known as 'upstream' agreements, may be regarded as forming part of the supplying breweries' networks of agreements. That condition is satisfied if the upstream agreements contain terms which may be analysed as a purchasing obligation (commitment to purchase minimum quantities, stocking obligations or non-competition obligations).

2 Second, for not only the 'upstream' agreements but also the agreements concluded between the wholesaling brewery and the establishments tied to it (the 'downstream' agreements) to be attributed to the supplying breweries' networks of agreements, it is also necessary for the agreements between the supplying breweries and the wholesaling brewery to be so restrictive that access to the wholesaling brewery's network of 'downstream' agreements is no longer possible, or at least very difficult, for other breweries. If the restrictive effect of the 'upstream' agreements is limited, other breweries are able to conclude supply agreements with the wholesaling brewery and so enter the latter's network of 'downstream' agreements. They are therefore in a position to have access to all the establishments in that network without it being necessary to conclude

separate agreements with each outlet. The existence of a network of 'downstream' agreements thus constitutes a factor which can promote penetration of the market by other breweries.

Concluding its analysis, the CFI held that the Commission did not make a manifest error of assessment in concluding in the contested decision (point 106) that Greene King's network of 'downstream' agreements could not be attributed to those of the supplying breweries which had concluded beer supply agreements with Greene King.

In the following case, the CFI considered whether what is now Art 101(1) TFEU was breached where an organisation set recommended prices for equipment hire, and also prohibited the hiring of such equipment to non-members:

Stichting Certificatie Kraanhuurbedrijf (SCK) and FNK and Another v Commission (Joined Cases T-213/95 and T-18/96)

FNK, an organisation of crane owners and hirers in the Netherlands which purported to maintain the quality of cranes hired out, published recommended prices for hire and prohibited members from hiring cranes from anyone except its members. The Commission declared that these practices were in breach of what is now Art 101(1) TFEU (previously Art 81(1) EC Treaty). SCK challenged the decision, arguing that, because its membership covered only 37 per cent of the market, the system of recommended hiring charges and restrictions on hiring could not affect trade between Member States. The CFI (now the General Court) rejected this argument, stating that:

. . . even if the market share of FNK members was 'only' 37 per cent or 40 per cent of The Netherlands market, the applicants were large enough and had sufficient economic power for their practices . . . to be capable of having an appreciable effect on trade between Member States.

The 'context within Member States' may also have to take account of the actions of undertakings outside the Union, where those actions have an effect within Member States. This is illustrated in the following case:

Åhlström Osakeyhito v Commission (Re Wood Pulp) (Joined Cases C-89, 104, 116, 117 and 125–129/85)

Concerted action by forestry undertakings in Finland, Sweden and Canada was said to have had an effect on wood pulp prices in the Union. At the time, Finland and Sweden were not members of the EU. The undertakings submitted that what is now Art 101 TFEU (previously Art 81 EC Treaty) did not extend to regulate conduct restricting competition outside the Union merely because it had economic repercussions within it. The Court disagreed, holding that where wood pulp producers established outside the Union sell directly to purchasers established in the Union and engage in price competition in order to win orders from those customers, this constitutes competition within the internal market. Where those producers concert on the prices to be charged to their customers in the Union and put that concertation into effect by selling at prices which are actually coordinated, they are taking part in concertation which has the object and effect of restricting competition within the internal market within the meaning of what is now Art 101 TFEU.

Block Exemption Regulation 330/2010

Although Art 101 TFEU applies to vertical agreements, a large number of such agreements will be exempted by Regulation 330/2010. Regulation 330/2010, which is discussed further below, is a block exemption regulation governing vertical supply and distribution agreements. It replaced Regulation 2790/1999.

Commission notices: horizontal and vertical anti-competitive activities

As stated above, Art 101(1) TFEU applies to both horizontal and vertical anti-competitive activities. The Commission has issued two notices providing non-binding guidelines concerning: (i) vertical restraints; and (ii) horizontal cooperation agreements.

The Guidelines on Vertical Restraints (OJ 2010 C 130/01) are stated to be without prejudice to the case law of the General Court and the Court of Justice of the European Union in relation to the application of Art 101 TFEU to vertical agreements (para 1(4)). The Commission's aim in issuing these guidelines is to 'help companies conduct their own assessment of vertical agreements under the EU's competition rules' (para 1(3)). The guidelines are structured as follows:

- Section II describes vertical agreements which generally fall outside Art 101(1) TFEU;
- Section III comments on the application of the Block Exemption Regulation 330/2010 on the application of Art 101(3) TFEU to categories of vertical agreements and concerted practices (see below);
- Section IV describes the principles concerning the withdrawal of the block exemption and the disapplication of the Block Exemption Regulation;
- Section V addresses market definition and market share calculation issues;
- Section VI describes the general framework of analysis and the enforcement policy of the Commission in individual cases concerning vertical agreements (see below and Chapter 22).

The guidelines are available at:

http://ec.europa.eu/competition/antitrust/legislation/vertical.html

The Guidelines on Horizontal Cooperation Agreements (OJ 2011 C 11/01) are stated to be without prejudice to the case law of the Court of Justice in relation to the application of Art 101 TFEU to such agreements (para 17). Paragraph 7 of the Guidelines provides that:

Given the potentially large number of types and combinations of horizontal cooperation and market circumstances in which they operate, it is difficult to provide specific answers for every possible scenario. These guidelines will nevertheless assist businesses in assessing the compatibility of an individual cooperation agreement with Article 101. Those criteria do not, however, constitute a "checklist" which can be applied mechanically. Each case must be assessed on the basis of its own facts, which may require a flexible application of these guidelines.

Chapters 2–7 of the guidelines are concerned with specific types of agreement. Practical examples are included of situations where Art 101 TFEU would apply and where it would not. The specific types of agreement covered are as follows:

- information exchange (Chapter 2, paras 55–110);
- agreements on research and development (Chapter 3, paras 111–149);

- production agreements (Chapter 4, paras 150–193);
- purchasing agreements (Chapter 5, paras 194–224);
- commercialisation agreements (Chapter 6, paras 225–256);
- agreement on standardisation (Chapter 7, paras 258–335).

The guidelines are available at:

http://ec.europa.eu/competition/antitrust/legislation/horizontal.html

The object or effect of distorting competition

Article 101 TFEU prohibits both conduct which is *intended* to affect trade between Member States, and conduct which, although not based upon any such intention, in fact has, or is *likely* to have, such an effect. There is no need for both elements to be present; they are alternative, not cumulative (***Ferriere Nord SpA v Commission*** (Case C-219/95P)). As seen in ***Consten and Grundig*** (above), there will be a breach of Art 101 TFEU even if an agreement is likely to increase trade between Member States. Unlike Art 34 TFEU (previously Art 28 EC Treaty), Art 101 TFEU is not aimed at restrictions on trade between Member States as such, but at the use of restrictive agreements to partition markets and to distort the flow of trade which would normally take place in a genuinely open market. The Court of Justice stated the underlying principle of what is now Art 101 TFEU in the following case:

Züchner v *Bayerische Vereinsbank Ag* (Case 172/80)

The Court of Justice held that:

A basic principle of the . . . [Union] competition rules is that each trader must determine independently the policy which he intends to adopt on the common market [i.e. internal market] and the conditions which he intends to offer to his customers. This does not prevent the traders adapting themselves intelligently to the existing or anticipated conduct of their competitors; it does, however, strictly preclude any direct or indirect contact between such traders the object or effect of which is to create conditions of competition which do not correspond to the normal conditions of the relevant market, in the light of the nature of the products or services offered, the size and number of the undertakings and the size of the market.

In cases where there is an attempt to rig the market by price-fixing and market-sharing agreements, there is no problem in concluding that the object of any agreement or concerted action is the prevention, restriction or distortion of competition. Difficulties arise in identifying situations where, although there is no such attempt at market distortion, the effect of an agreement may have the same, probably unintended, outcome. The intention of a sole-supply agreement may, for example, be that the supplier is repaid money that he may have lent the retailer and, at the same time, is guaranteed an outlet for his goods. A network of such sole-supply agreements across a Member State, even if concluded between a large number of different suppliers and retailers, may have the effect of denying penetration of that market to producers in other Member States of the goods which are subject to the agreements. This was the basis of the Court's reasoning in the ***Brasserie de Haecht*** case in relation to 'tied-houses' supplied by breweries in Belgium (see above).

In analysing the object and effect of an agreement, the Court will look first to its content and then to its effect. Even if its terms do not indicate an intention to restrict or distort competition, its operation may have that effect. Factors such as the percentage of the market affected and the duration and terms of the agreements will all have to be assessed, as illustrated in the following case:

Langnese-Iglo GmbH v Commission (Case T-7/93)

The CFI (now the General Court) found that the applicant held more than 30 per cent of the market share of ice-cream sold through shops. These outlets were protected by a series of exclusive purchasing agreements under which the retailers bound themselves to sell only the applicant's ice-cream for two-and-a-half years and to use the freezer cabinets supplied by the applicant only for the applicant's products. The CFI concluded that, in view of the strong position occupied by the applicant in the relevant market and, in particular, its market share, the agreements contributed significantly to the closing -off of the market.

A network of sole-supply agreements across a Member State will, however, not automatically be regarded as providing an insurmountable barrier to market penetration from other Member States. In **Stergios Delimitis v Henninger Bräu** (Case C-234/89) the Court of Justice emphasised that it was important to look at the state of the market in question to determine 'whether there are real concrete possibilities for a new competitor to penetrate the bundle of contracts' (para 21). An exclusive supply agreement may even, in some circumstances, assist in opening up competition:

Société Technique Minière v Maschinenbau Ulm GmbH (Case 56/65)

Maschinenbau Ulm (MU) granted Société Technique Minière (STM) the exclusive right to sell its earth-moving equipment in France, on condition that STM did not sell competing machinery. The validity of the agreement was disputed in a French court, which referred the issue to the Court of Justice for a preliminary ruling. The Commission argued in the proceedings that the agreement in question breached what is now Art 101 TFEU (previously Art 81 EC Treaty).

The Court did not agree. It described the two stages two stages which were necessary to determine whether or not what is now Art 101 TFEU was infringed. 'Object or effect' in this context are alternative, not cumulative. It was first necessary to look at the precise purpose of the agreement, in the economic context in which it was to be applied. An intention to interfere with competition in the way prohibited by what is now Art 101 TFEU was to be deduced, if at all, from the clauses of the agreement itself. If those clauses indicated an intention to restrict competition, the fact that the involvement of one of the participants had a negligible effect on competition was irrelevant (*Usines Gustave Boël SA v Commission* (Case T-142/89)). If the agreement disclosed no such intention, or an effect on competition that was not 'sufficiently deleterious', the consequences of the agreement would then have to be considered.

A consideration of those consequences would include, in the case of an exclusive sale agreement: (i) the nature and quantity, limited or otherwise, of the products covered by the agreement; (ii) the position and importance of the grantor and the concessionaire on the market for the product concerned; (iii) the isolated nature of the disputed agreement or, alternatively, its position in a series of agreements; and (iv) the severity of the clauses intended to protect the exclusive dealership or, alternatively, the opportunities allowed for other commercial competitors in the same products by way of parallel re-exportation and importation.

In this case the Court also took into account the fact that there was an attempt at market penetration in another Member State, and it doubted whether there was an interference with competition if the agreement 'was really necessary for the penetration of a new area by an undertaking'.

The *Société Technique Minière* case can be distinguished from the *Consten and Grundig* case (see above) because in the latter case the agreement prohibited parallel imports (i.e. Consten had the sole right to distribute Grundig products in the specified Member State) whereas in the former case, the agreement did *not* prohibit parallel imports. The Consten and Grundig agreement was, *prima facie*, more restrictive of competition than the Société Technique Minière agreement.

The *Société Technique Minière* case not only defined the relationship between the intention and the consequences of an agreement, but also introduced the concept of *de minimis* in the context of promoting the desirable objective of market penetration (see below). In other words, a distributor of a new product in another Member State may need some protection in order to launch the product in that state. Essentially, the Court recognised that a balance needs to be struck between the legal control of agreements which appear, on their face, to be restrictive of competition, but which may, in fact, assist in promoting market integration and product distribution. Thus, the limited restrictive effect of an agreement may be outweighed by its more beneficial long-term consequences. This has been described as a 'rule of reason'. As long as an agreement does not have as its object the restriction of competition, its anti-competitive effect may be outweighed by its ultimate competitive advantages. The apparently conflicting priorities contained within this rule of reason were considered by the Court of Justice in the following case:

Nungesser v Commission (Case 258/78)

Within a written agreement there was an attempt to protect techniques of cultivating new types of maize. The agreement conferring exclusive rights to the technique on Nungesser was challenged by the Commission, which concluded that its terms must, inevitably, breach what is now Art 101 TFEU (previously Art 81 EC Treaty). The Court of Justice disagreed with the Commission's approach. It decided that some protection for the licensee of the new technique for hybrid maize seeds was a necessary precondition for penetration of the German market by INRA, the developers of the technique:

> The exclusive licence which forms the subject-matter of the contested decision concerns the cultivation and marketing of hybrid maize seeds which were developed by INRA after years of research and experimentation and were unknown to German farmers at the time when the cooperation between INRA and the applicants was taking shape . . . In the case of a licence of breeders' rights over hybrid maize seeds newly developed in one Member State, an undertaking established in another Member State which was not certain that it would encounter competition from other licensees for the territory granted to it, or from the owner of the right himself, might be deterred from accepting the risk of cultivating and marketing that product; such a result would be damaging to the dissemination of new technology and would prejudice competition in the Community [i.e. Union] between the new product and similar existing products. (paras 55 and 56)

Given that the launching of the new seed and cultivation technique called for some protection for the licensee, did that mean that total protection of the production and distribution of the seed was justified? The Court of Justice would not go so far, citing its view in *Consten and Grundig* that absolute territorial protection, granted to a licensee in order to enable parallel imports to be controlled and prevented, results in the artificial maintenance of separate national markets, in breach of the Treaty. It would, however, countenance the grant of an open exclusive licence, under which the grantor himself would not compete with the licensee in Germany and would not license anyone else there to do so. Such a licence should not, however, contain an assurance by the grantor that he would protect the licensee from parallel imports, by preventing licensees in other Member States from exporting to Germany.

A limited approval by the Court of Justice has also been given to apparently restrictive franchise agreements, provided that the restrictions are no more than those which are strictly necessary to ensure that the know-how and assistance provided by the franchisee do not benefit competitors, or which establish the control necessary for maintaining the identity and reputation of the network identified by the common name or symbol. However, provisions which share markets between the franchisor and the franchisee, or between franchisees, do breach Art 101 TFEU (***Pronuptia de Paris GmbH*** v ***Pronuptia de Paris Irmgaard Schillgalis*** (Case 161/84)).

Despite what appeared to be the emergence of a 'rule of reason', such a rule has been firmly rejected by the CFI (now the General Court). In the following case (which concerned an action for annulment of a Commission decision) the applicant companies submitted that the application of a 'rule of reason' would have shown that the former Art 81(1) EC Treaty (now Art 101(1) TFEU) did not apply to an exclusivity clause and to a clause relating to the special-interest channels agreed on when Télévision par Satellite (TPS) was set up, with the result that those two clauses should not have been examined under the former Art 81(1) EC Treaty (now Art 101(1) TFEU):

M6 and Others v *Commission* (Case T-112/99)

The CFI stated that the existence of a general 'rule of reason' in the application of the former Art 81(1) EC Treaty (now Art 101(1) TFEU) could not be upheld. The former Art 81(1) EC Treaty (now Art 101(1) TFEU) expressly provides for the possibility of exempting agreements that restrict competition if they satisfy a number of conditions, in particular if they are indispensable to the attainment of certain objectives and do not afford undertakings the possibility of eliminating competition in respect of a substantial part of the products in question. It is only in the precise framework of that provision (rather than through the application of a general 'rule of reason') that the pro and anti-competitive aspects of a restriction may be weighed. Otherwise the former Art 81(3) EC Treaty (now Art 101(3) TFEU) would lose much of its effectiveness.

Citing certain judgments in which the Court of Justice and the CFI favoured a more flexible interpretation of the prohibition laid down in the former Art 81(1) EC Treaty (now Art 101(1) TFEU), the CFI nonetheless took the view that those judgments could not be interpreted as establishing the existence of a rule of reason in Union competition law. They are part of a broader trend in the case law according to which it is not necessary to hold, wholly abstractly and without drawing any distinction, that any agreement restricting the freedom of action of one or more of the parties is necessarily caught by the prohibition laid down in the former Art 81(1) EC Treaty. In assessing the applicability of that article to an agreement, account should be taken of the actual conditions in which it functions, in particular the economic and legal context in which the undertakings operate, the nature of the products or services covered by the agreement and the actual operation and structure of the market concerned.

Commission guidelines on the 'effect on trade concept' contained in Articles 101 and 102 TFEU

Guidelines on the 'effect on trade concept' which is contained in Arts 101 and 102 TFEU, were adopted by the Commission on 30 March 2004 (OJ 2004 C 101/81) as part of the 'Modernisation Package', which included the adoption of Regulation 1/2003 (see above and Chapter 22).

De minimis presumption

There is a *de minimis* **presumption** by the Commission, which was originally contained in a notice issued in 1986 and which was amended in 1994 (OJ 1986 C 231/2, as amended by OJ 1994 C 368/20)). The amended 1984 notice was replaced by the Commission in 1997 (OJ 1997 C 372/13) which itself was replaced in 2001 (OJ 2001 C 368/13).

The Commission issued the current *de minimums* notice in 2014 (OJ 2014 C 57/01). Paragraph 8 of this notice provides as follows:

8. The Commission holds the view that agreements between undertakings which may affect trade between Member States and which may have as their effect the prevention, restriction or distortion of competition within the internal market, do not appreciably restrict competition within the meaning of Article 101(1) of the Treaty:
   (a) if the aggregate market share held by the parties to the agreement does not exceed 10% on any of the relevant markets affected by the agreement, where the agreement is made between undertakings which are actual or potential competitors on any of those markets (agreements between competitors); or
   (b) if the market share held by each of the parties to the agreement does not exceed 15% on any of the relevant markets affected by the agreement, where the agreement is made between undertakings which are not actual or potential competitors on any of those markets (agreements between non-competitors).

The list of agreements likely to breach Article 101(1) TFEU

Article 101(1) TFEU contains a list, in paragraphs (a)–(e), of the kind of agreements which will be prohibited (see above). The cases examined so far range far beyond those described in that list, and it provides no more than a guide as to the sort of agreements which will fall foul of the prohibition. However, with the help of the list and the case law of the Court of Justice, it is possible to draw some conclusions as to the type of agreement which may breach Art 101 TFEU. A list indicative of the types of offending agreements could include:

- exclusive distribution agreements;
- exclusive purchasing agreements;
- exclusive licences of intellectual property rights (such as patents, copyright and trade marks);
- selective distribution agreements;
- franchise agreements;

- research and development agreements;
- joint ventures on development;
- joint sale and buying agencies;
- information-sharing agreements.

Each of these types of agreement has been held at some time or other to be actually or potentially in breach of what is now Art 101 TFEU. If they are found to breach Art 101(1) TFEU, they are, by Art 101(2) TFEU, automatically void. The effect of this finding is that they cannot, for example, form the basis of a claim or a defence in contract in national courts. What is now Art 101 TFEU (previously Art 81 EC Treaty) was used in this way in both the *Brasserie de Haecht* and the *Société Technique Minière* cases (see above). In many cases, the Court is obliged to give an indication, on the basis of the facts in the relevant market (as found by the Commission), and after weighing up all the relevant circumstances, of whether the agreement actually breaches the prohibition. If it does breach Art 101(1) TFEU, there always remains the possibility that it may be exempt under Art 101(3) TFEU.

Exemption under Article 101(3) TFEU

Objective 3

The object of Art 101(3) TFEU (previously Art 81(3) EC Treaty), set out at the beginning of this chapter, is to provide criteria for exemption from the prohibition under Art 101(1) TFEU on agreements which restrict competition. Essentially, exemption may apply in cases where the anti-competitive effects of an agreement or concerted practice are outweighed by the economic benefit to consumers or the public at large. Prior to 1 May 2004, exemption could result either from an individual decision of the Commission pursuant to Regulation 17/62, or as a consequence of an agreement falling within a type to which a block or group exemption had been granted (see below). In order to obtain an exemption, undertakings which entered into restrictive agreements had to either make a formal application to the Commission pursuant to Regulation 17/62, or draft their agreements to comply with one of the block or group exemption regulations which had been specifically drawn up by the Commission. In the latter instance, if the agreement complied with one of the regulations, it would automatically obtain exemption without the necessity for a formal application to the Commission.

On 1 May 2004, Regulation 1/2003 came into force, replacing Regulation 17/62 which was repealed. The new regulation is considered in detail in Chapter 22. Article 1(2), Regulation 1/2003 provides that:

> Agreements, decisions and concerted practices caught by . . . [Article 101(1) TFEU] which satisfy the conditions of . . . [Article 101(3) TFEU] shall not be prohibited, **no prior decision to that effect being required**. [emphasis added]

This is a major change. While the block or group exemption regulations will continue to apply, undertakings which cannot take advantage of such a regulation no longer need the prior approval of the Commission in order to be able to rely upon the Art 101(3) TFEU exemption. The rationale for this change is set out in the preamble to Regulation 1/2003:

> (2) . . . there is a need to rethink the arrangements for applying the exception from the prohibition on agreements, which restrict competition, laid down in . . . [Article 101(3) TFEU]. Under . . . [Article 83(2)(b) TFEU], account must be taken in this regard of the need to ensure effective supervision, on the one hand, and to simplify administration to the greatest possible extent, on the other.

(3) The centralised scheme set up by Regulation No. 17 no longer secures a balance between those two objectives. It hampers application of the Community [i.e. Union] competition rules by the courts and competition authorities of the Member States, and the system of notification it involves prevents the Commission from concentrating its resources on curbing the most serious infringements. It also imposes considerable costs on undertakings.

From 1 May 2004, not only was the Commission empowered to apply the former Art 81(3) EC Treaty (and now, Art 101(3) TFEU), but also the national competition authorities and the courts of the Member States were likewise empowered (Arts 5 and 6, Regulation 1/2003).

Comfort letters and guidance letters

As stated above, prior to 1 May 2004 each agreement had to be notified to the Commission and exemption obtained under the procedure established for that purpose under Arts 4, 19 and 21, Regulation 17/62. Exemptions would only be granted for specific periods, and conditions could be attached; the exemption could be renewed or revoked. Delays of two or three years could ensue following an application, hence the need for reform. The Commission was required to give a fully reasoned decision in each case, and therefore the Commission tended to try to avoid formal decisions, which were normally reserved for what were considered to be important cases. In other cases a 'comfort letter' was issued after informal meetings with the parties concerned stating that, in the Commission's view, the agreement which had been notified did not infringe the former Art 81(1) EC Treaty (now Art 101(1) TFEU) at all or was of a type which fell within an exempt category. The file would then be closed, although it could be reopened if the legal, material or factual circumstances changed. The parties were then entitled to rely upon the letter and enjoy a legitimate expectation that the Commission would take no further action. Comfort letters only had a limited legal status and, because they were not 'decisions', they could not be challenged in Art 263 TFEU (previously Art 230 EC Treaty) proceedings before the Court of Justice (*SA Lancôme* v *ETOS BV ('Perfumes')* (Case 99/79)). Nor were opinions expressed in such letters 'binding on the national courts but constitute a factor which the latter may take into account in examining whether or not the agreements are in accordance with the provisions of . . . [Article 101 TFEU]'. The reliance which the parties could place on a comfort letter depended very much on the circumstances in which the letter was issued remaining the same. Any change in those circumstances, or any misrepresentation, could result in the reopening of the file (*Langnese-Iglo* v *Commission* (Case T-7/93)).

From 1 May 2004, the Commission no longer issued comfort letters, because from that date there was no longer a requirement to notify the Commission of an agreement in order for the Commission to decide whether or not the exemption set out in Art 101(3) TFEU applies. However, in very limited circumstances the Commission is empowered to issue a 'guidance letter'. To support the new procedural regime brought in by Regulation 1/2003, the Commission issued a non-legally enforceable Notice: 'Informal Guidance relating to novel questions concerning . . . [Arts 101 and 102 TFEU] that arise in individual cases (guidance letters)' (OJ 2004 C 101/78). In cases which give rise to genuine uncertainty because they present novel or unresolved questions for the application of Arts 101 and 102 TFEU, individual undertakings may seek informal guidance from the Commission (para 5 of the Guidance). If it is considered appropriate, the Commission may provide such guidance in a written statement, referred to as a 'guidance letter'. However, a guidance letter may only be issued by the Commission if the following cumulative conditions apply:

(a) The substantive assessment of an agreement or practice with regard to . . . [Articles 101 and 102 TFEU], poses a question of application of the law for which there is no clarification in the existing . . . [Union] legal framework including the case law of the . . . [Union] Courts, nor publicly available general guidance or precedent in decision-making practice or previous guidance letters.

(b) A *prima facie* evaluation of the specificities and background of the case suggests that the clarification of the novel question through a guidance letter is useful, taking into account the following elements:
  – the economic importance from the point of view of the consumer of the goods or services concerned by the agreement or practice; and/or
  – the extent to which the agreement or practice corresponds or is liable to correspond to more widely spread economic usage in the marketplace; and/or
  – the extent of the investments linked to the transaction in relation to the size of the companies concerned and the extent to which the transaction relates to a structural operation such as the creation of a non-full function joint venture.

(c) It is possible to issue a guidance letter on the basis of the information provided, i.e. no further fact-finding is required. (para 8 of the Guidance)

Furthermore, the Commission will not consider a request for a guidance letter in either of the following circumstances:

  – the questions raised in the request are identical or similar to issues raised in a case pending before the . . . [Court of Justice of the European Union]; or
  – the agreement or practice to which the request refers is subject to proceedings pending with the Commission, a Member State court or Member State competition authority. (para 9 of the Guidance)

Paragraph 10 of the Guidance provides that the Commission will not consider hypothetical questions and 'will not issue guidance letters on agreements or practices that are no longer being implemented by the parties. Undertakings may however present a request for a guidance letter to the Commission in relation to questions raised by an agreement or practice that they envisage, i.e. before the implementation of that agreement or practice. In this case the transaction must have reached a sufficiently advanced stage for a request to be considered'.

Article 101(3) TFEU: the four conditions

Whether the Art 101(3) TFEU exemption can be relied upon will depend on four conditions being satisfied:

1 The agreement must contribute to the improvement of the production or distribution of goods, or the promotion of technical or economic progress.

2 The agreement must allow consumers a fair share of the resulting benefit.

3 The agreement must not impose upon the undertakings concerned restrictions which are not indispensable to the attainment of the above objects.

4 The agreement should not provide the undertakings with the possibility of eliminating competition in respect of a substantial part of the product in question.

These are all linked conditions which must, in each case, be satisfied (Commission Decision 73/323 *Prym-Werke*).

Besides meeting the formal requirements as set out in the four conditions above, application of Art 101(3) TFEU will also be examined in the light of the Commission's broader policy objectives in relation to agreements between undertakings. The Commission's aim is to encourage those agreements which favour the introduction of new technology resulting in better production methods, economies of scale, the faster or more effective development of new products or the process of change in older industries. Agreements which are highly unlikely to secure exemption are price-fixing agreements, agreements limiting production or controlling markets, or agreements aimed at retaining dominance in a national market. An example of an application that met both the specific and general criteria can be seen in *Prym-Werke* [1973] CMLR D250, [1981] 2 CMLR 217 (see also the *ACEC/Berliet* decision [1968] CMLR D35; *Re Vacuum Interrupters (No. 2)* [1981] 2 CMLR 217):

Prym-Werke [1973] CMLR D250, [1981] 2 CMLR 217

Prym agreed to give up making needles and instead to buy them from Beka, who agreed to supply Prym. Beka could then specialise in needle production. The Commission explained the approach it had adopted in its decision:

> The concentration of manufacturing agreed on by Prym and Beka has, from the point of view of the improvement of production, favourable effects analogous to those of specialisation; it causes an increase of at least 50 per cent in the quantity of needles to be manufactured at the European factory, which makes it possible to make more intensive use of the existing plant and to introduce production line manufacture.

The following case, which was considered above, concerned regulations which had been adopted by FIFA to regulate the agents of professional football players (the 'Players' Agents Regulations'). FIFA brings together national football associations from throughout the world. Regulations adopted by FIFA are applied by all the national football associations:

Piau v *Commission* (Case T-193/02)

The FIFA Players' Agents Regulations required agents to hold a licence. The Commission had held that the compulsory nature of this licence requirement might be justified under the former Art 81(3) EC Treaty (now Art 101(3) TFEU).

In its judgment, the CFI (now the General Court) pointed out that the requirement to hold a licence in order to carry on the occupation of players' agent was a barrier to access to that economic activity and affected competition. Accordingly, it could be accepted only in so far as the conditions set out in the former Art 81(3) EC Treaty (now Art 101(3) TFEU) were met.

The CFI found that the Commission had not made a manifest error of assessment in taking the view that the restrictions stemming from the compulsory nature of the licence might benefit from such an exemption. The following circumstances justified the action taken by FIFA: (i) the need to raise professional and ethical standards for the occupation of players' agent in order to protect players; (ii) the fact that competition was not eliminated by the licence system; (iii) the virtual absence of any national rules; and (iv) the lack of any collective organisation for players' agents.

The sort of agreement which will not be exempt under Art 101(3) TFEU was considered by the CFI in the following case:

SPO v Commission (Case T-29/92)

The applicants were a group of associations of building contractors in the Netherlands. Since 1952 they had adopted a body of rules which concerned the organisation of competition. The rules were intended to 'promote and administer orderly competition, to prevent improper conduct in price tendering and to promote the formation of economically justified prices'. From 1980, these rules became binding on all contractors belonging to the member associations of the SPO.

In 1988 the SPO notified its amended rules with a view, *inter alia*, to obtain an exemption under what is now Art 101(3) TFEU (previously Art 81(3) EC Treaty). The Commission rejected the application for exemption and found the SPO rules in breach of what is now Art 101(1) TFEU (previously Art 81(1) EC Treaty).

The CFI (now the General Court) upheld this decision. It had no hesitation in finding that the provision of information to SPO by contractors submitting tenders for contracts which enabled other contractors to adjust their commercial behaviour and their prices amounted to unlawful concertation in the Netherlands' building market, affecting not just contractors from the Netherlands but contractors wishing to tender from other Member States. It therefore breached what is now Art 101(1) TFEU.

The CFI, applying the four conditions for exemption, also found the rules wanting. The applicants had argued that an open tendering system would necessarily lead to ruinous competition, which would ultimately have adverse repercussions on contract awarders. The CFI observed drily that it was impossible to distinguish between normal competition and ruinous competition as, potentially, any competition is ruinous for the least efficient undertakings. That is why, by taking action to counteract what they regard as ruinous competition, the applicants necessarily restrict competition and therefore deprive consumers of its benefits.

Commission guidelines on the application of Article 101(3) TFEU

Guidelines on the application of Art 101(3) TFEU were adopted by the Commission on 30 March 2004 (OJ 2004 C 101/97) as part of the 'Modernisation Package' which included the adoption of Regulation 1/2003; see above and Chapter 22. In order to promote coherent application and provide guidance to businesses, the detailed guidelines set out the methodology for the application of Art 101(3) TFEU. These guidelines do not replace, but complement, the guidance already available in Commission guidelines on particular types of agreements, in particular the guidelines on horizontal cooperation agreements and the guidelines on vertical restraints (see above). The guidelines are available at:

http://europa.eu/legislation_summaries/competition/firms/index_en.htm

Block exemptions

The four conditions for exemption (see above) are reflected in the Block Exemption Regulations. Block exemptions came about as a result of the huge burden placed on the Commission by the requirement in the former Regulation 17/62 to investigate each application before delivering a decision. As discussed above, this requirement no longer applies following the adoption of Regulation 1/2003 and the repeal of Regulation 17/62. While the Block Exemption Regulations will remain, Art 29, Regulation 1/2003 provides that they may be withdrawn in a particular case by the Commission or a national competition authority. Article 29, Regulation 1/2003 provides as follows:

1 Where the Commission, empowered by a Council Regulation . . . to apply . . . [Article 101(3) TFEU] by regulation, has declared . . . [Article 101(1) TFEU] inapplicable to certain categories of agreements, decisions by associations of undertakings or concerted practices, it may, acting on its own initiative or on a complaint, withdraw the benefit of such an exemption Regulation when it finds that in any particular case an agreement, decision or concerted practice to which the exemption Regulation applies has certain effects which are incompatible with . . . [Article 101(3) TFEU].

2 Where, in any particular case, agreements, decisions by associations of undertakings or concerted practices to which a Commission Regulation referred to in paragraph 1 applies have effects which are incompatible with . . . [Article 101(3) TFEU] in the territory of a Member State, or in a part thereof, which has all the characteristics of a distinct geographic market, the competition authority of that Member State may withdraw the benefit of the Regulation in question in respect of that territory.

The value of block exemptions is that undertakings can make their own assessment as to whether or not the agreement to which they are a party falls within the terms of an apparently relevant block exemption regulation. If the agreement is clearly within it, they may treat it as *prima facie* valid and enforceable. The Commission (and the national competition authorities and courts of the Member States) remain free to decide that agreements which purport to fall within an existing block exemption do in fact fall outside it, and to take the necessary action against the participants.

A number of block exemption regulations have been issued, some of which have been amended or replaced by subsequent regulations. Examples of block exemption regulations which are currently in force include:

- Technology Transfer Regulation 316/2014 (OJ 2014 L 93/03);
- Insurance Sector Agreements Regulation 267/2010 (OJ 2010 L 83/01);
- Vertical Supply and Distribution Agreements Regulation 330/2010 (OJ 2010 L 102/01);
- Motor Vehicle Distribution Regulation 461/2010 (OJ 2010 L 129/52);
- Research and Development Agreements Regulation 1217/2010 (OJ 2010 L 335/36);
- Specialisation Agreements Regulation 1218/2010 (OJ 2010 L 335/43).

The pattern of block exemption regulations is similar. They reflect both the content of Art 101(3) TFEU and the decisions of the Court of Justice in relation to individual applications concerning the activities covered by the regulation. However, the regulations have moved away from the approach of listing clauses in an agreement which would be exempted from Art 101(1) TFEU, and instead place a greater emphasis on defining the categories of agreements which are exempted up to a certain level of market power and on specifying the restrictions or clauses which are not to be contained in such agreements.

The fact that an agreement falls within the terms of a block exemption regulation does not confer immunity under Art 101(1) TFEU on everything purported to be done under that agreement. If, for example, the operation of the agreement in practice excludes parallel imports, the effect of the agreement would still be to restrict competition (***Automobiles Peugeot SA* v *Commission*** (Case C-322/93P)). On this basis, the Commission decided that the former Regulation 123/85 (block exemption regulation on selective distribution in the motor vehicle sector) did not allow Volkswagen to prohibit its dealers in Italy from selling to consumers and motor agencies outside Italy (***Community* v *Volkswagen AG and***

Others (Case IV/35.733) (1998)). The decision demonstrates the way in which an agreement, ostensibly lawful as within the block exemption, can work to the disadvantage of customers and lead to the partitioning of the market.

Block Exemption Regulation 330/2010

As discussed above, although Art 101 TFEU applies to vertical agreements, a large number of such agreements will be exempted by Regulation 330/2010. Regulation 330/2010 is a block exemption regulation which applies to vertical supply and distribution agreements. It replaced Regulation 2790/1999. The following summary of Regulation 330/2010 was published on www.europa.eu:

> Article 101(1) of the Treaty on the Functioning of the European Union (TFEU) (ex-Article 81(1) of the Treaty Establishing the European Community (TEC)) prohibits agreements that may affect trade between European Union (EU) countries and which prevent, restrict or distort competition. Agreements which create sufficient benefits to outweigh the anti-competitive effects are exempt from this prohibition under Article 101(3) TFEU (ex-Article 81(3) TEC).
>
> Vertical agreements are agreements for the sale and purchase of goods or services which are entered into between companies operating at different levels of the production or distribution chain. Distribution agreements between manufacturers and wholesalers or retailers are typical examples of vertical agreements. Vertical agreements which simply determine the price and quantity for a specific sale and purchase transaction do not normally restrict competition. However, a restriction of competition may occur if the agreement contains restraints on the supplier or the buyer, for instance an obligation on the buyer not to purchase competing brands. These **vertical restraints** may not only have negative effects, but also positive effects. They may, for instance, help a manufacturer to enter a new market, or avoid the situation whereby one distributor 'free rides' on the promotional efforts of another distributor, or allow a supplier to depreciate an investment made for a particular client.
>
> Whether a vertical agreement actually restricts competition and whether in that case the benefits outweigh the anti-competitive effects will often depend on the market structure. In principle, this requires an individual assessment. However, the Commission has adopted this Regulation (EU) No. 330/2010, the **Block Exemption Regulation** (the BER), which provides a safe harbour for most vertical agreements. The BER renders, by block exemption, the prohibition of Article 101(1) TFEU inapplicable to vertical agreements which fulfil certain requirements. The Commission has also published guidelines on vertical restraints. These describe the approach taken towards vertical agreements not covered by the BER.

Requirements for application of the Block Exemption Regulation

The BER contains certain requirements that must be fulfilled before a particular vertical agreement is exempt from the prohibition of Article 101(1) TFEU. The first requirement is that the agreement does not contain any of the **hardcore restrictions** set out in the BER. The second requirement concerns a **market share cap** of 30% for both suppliers and buyers. Thirdly, the BER contains conditions relating to three **specific restrictions**.

Hardcore restrictions

This BER contains five hardcore restrictions that lead to the exclusion of the whole agreement from the benefit of the BER, even if the market shares of the supplier and buyer are below 30%. Hardcore restrictions are considered to be severe restrictions of competition because of the likely harm they cause to consumers. In most cases they will be prohibited and it is considered unlikely that vertical agreements containing such hardcore restrictions fulfil the conditions of Article 101(3) TFEU.

The **first hardcore restriction** concerns resale price maintenance: suppliers are not allowed to fix the (minimum) price at which distributors can resell their products.

The **second hardcore restriction** concerns restrictions concerning the territory into which or the customers to whom the buyer may sell. This hardcore restriction relates to market partitioning by territory or by customer. Distributors must remain free to decide where and to whom they sell. The BER contains exceptions to this rule, which, for instance, enable companies to operate an exclusive distribution system or a selective distribution system.

The **third and fourth hardcore restrictions** concern selective distribution. Firstly, selected distributors, while being prohibited to sell to unauthorised distributors, cannot be restricted in the end-users to whom they may sell. Secondly, the appointed distributors must remain free to sell or purchase the contract goods to or from other appointed distributors within the network.

The **fifth hardcore restriction** concerns the supply of spare parts. An agreement between a manufacturer of spare parts and a buyer which incorporates these parts into its own products may not prevent or restrict sales by the manufacturer of these spare parts to end-users, independent repairers or service providers.

The 30% market share cap

A vertical agreement is covered by this BER if both the supplier and the buyer of the goods or services do not have a market share exceeding 30%. For the supplier, it is its market share on the relevant supply market, i.e. the market on which it sells the goods or services, that is decisive for the application of the block exemption. For the buyer, it is its market share on the relevant purchase market, i.e. the market on which it purchases the goods or services, which is decisive for the application of the BER.

The excluded restrictions

This regulation applies to all vertical restraints other than the abovementioned hardcore restraints. However, it does impose specific conditions on three vertical restraints:

- non-compete obligations during the contract;
- non-compete obligations after termination of the contract;
- the exclusion of specific brands in a selective distribution system.
- When the conditions are not fulfilled, these vertical restraints are excluded from the exemption by the BER. However, the BER continues to apply to the remaining part of the vertical agreement if that part is severable (i.e. can operate independently) from the non-exempted vertical restraints.

Source: http://europa.eu/legislation_summaries/competition/firms/cc0006_en.htm

Summary

Now you have read this chapter you should be able to:

- Outline the scope of Union competition law and policy.
- Understand and describe how Art 101(1) TFEU operates to prohibit agreements which restrict competition.
- Explain the conditions which apply whereby agreements, decisions and practices which come within the scope of Art 101(3) TFEU may be exempted from the prohibition under Art 101(1) TFEU.

- Outline and evaluate the procedural changes made to the application of Art 101(3) TFEU by Regulation 1/2003.

Further reading

Textbooks

Craig, P. and De Burca, G. (2011) *EU Law: Text, Cases and Materials* (5th edn), Oxford University Press, Chapter 26.

Foster, N. (2015) *Foster on EU Law* (5th edn), Oxford University Press, Chapter 10.

Steiner, J. and Woods, L. (2014) *EU Law* (12th edn), Oxford University Press, Chapter 29.

Weatherill, S. (2014) *Cases and Materials on EU Law* (11th edn), Oxford University Press, Chapter 16.

Journal articles

Aresu, A., 'Optimal contract reformation as a new approach to private antitrust damages in cartel cases' (2010) 35 EL Rev 349.

Brouwer, O.W., Goydner, J. and Mes, D., 'Developments in EC competition law in 2007: An overview' (2008) 45 CML Rev 1167.

Cengiz, F., 'Multi-level governance in competition policy: The European Competition Network' (2010) 35 EL Rev 660.

Graham, C., 'Methods for determining whether an agreement restricts competition: Comment on Allianz Hungaria' (2013) 38 EL Rev 542.

Harding, C., 'Capturing the cartel's friends: Cartel facilitation and the idea of joint criminal enterprise' (2009) 34 EL Rev 298.

Lianos, I., 'Collusion in vertical relations under Art 81 EC' (2008) 45 CML Rev 1027.

Petrucci, C., 'Parallel trade of pharmaceutical products: The ECJ finally speaks – comment on GlaxoSmithKline' (2010) 35 EL Rev 275.

Tsouloufas, G., 'Limiting pharmaceutical parallel trade in the European Union: Regulatory and economic justifications' (2011) 36 EL Rev 385.

21

Abuse of a dominant position and mergers: Article 102 TFEU

Objectives

At the end of this chapter you should understand:

1. How Art 102 TFEU is applied to prevent the abuse of a dominant position.
2. The relationship between Arts 101(1) and 102 TFEU with regard to collective dominance.
3. How Art 102 TFEU and Regulation 139/2004 are applied to regulate mergers which may produce a degree of market control and distortion of competition which is detrimental to the effective operation of the internal market.

Introduction

Article 102 TFEU, which is practically identical to the former Art 82 EC Treaty, provides as follows:

> Any abuse by one or more undertakings of a dominant position within the internal market or in a substantial part of it shall be prohibited as incompatible with the internal market in so far as it may affect trade between Member States.
>   Such abuse may, in particular, consist in:

> (a) directly or indirectly imposing unfair purchase or selling prices or other unfair trading conditions;
> (b) limiting production, markets or technical development to the prejudice of consumers;
> (c) applying dissimilar conditions to equivalent transactions with other trading parties, thereby placing them at a competitive disadvantage;
> (d) making the conclusion of contracts subject to acceptance by the other parties of supplementary obligations which, by their nature or according to commercial usage, have no connection with the subject of such contracts.

There are three key elements in Art 102 TFEU. There must be:

- a dominant position;
- an abuse of that position;
- the abuse must affect trade between Member States.

Whereas Art 101 TFEU is directed at cooperation between nominally competing businesses, which has the effect of diminishing or distorting competition (see Chapter 20), Art 102 TFEU is aimed at the position and conduct of one undertaking. Essentially, Art 102 TFEU is not concerned with the *fact* of monopoly power in the Union, but with *abuse* of that monopoly or dominant position. To determine whether or not that has occurred, each of these three key elements mentioned will be analysed and applied to the relevant circumstances.

Article 102 TFEU: a dominant position

Objective 1

The concept of dominance must be viewed in the context of the relevant market for the goods or services produced or distributed by the undertaking, the conduct of which is in question. In the following case, the Court of Justice defined 'a dominant position':

United Brands Co v *Commission* (Case 27/76)

The Court of Justice stated that a dominant position, within the context of what is now Art 102 TFEU (previously Art 82 EC Treaty), is:

> A position of economic strength enjoyed by an undertaking which enables it to hinder the maintenance of effective competition on the relevant market by allowing it to behave to an appreciable extent independently of its competitors and customers and ultimately of consumers. (para 65)

To determine whether or not an undertaking is 'dominant' it is necessary to look at the relevant product market. The following case is a useful example for this exercise:

United Brands Co v *Commission* (Case 27/76)

United Brands Co (UBC), at the time of the Commission's investigation, was a **conglomerate** which handled 40 per cent of the EU's banana trade. In some Member States (the Benelux countries, Germany, Denmark and Ireland) its share of the banana market was much greater. The Commission accordingly contended that UBC enjoyed a dominant position in the banana market which, on the facts, it was abusing. UBC challenged the decision on a number of grounds. It argued that it did not enjoy a dominant position in the *fruit market*, and that this was the proper context for the examination of its position. To support this argument, UBC stated that bananas compete with other fresh fruit in the same shops, on the same shelves, at prices which can be compared and satisfying the same needs (i.e. consumption as a dessert or between meals). The Commission also contended that there is a demand for bananas which is distinct from the demand for other fresh fruit, especially as the banana is a very important part of the diet of certain sections of the Union, especially the very young and the very old. The specific qualities of the banana influence customer preference and induce him not readily to accept other fruits as a substitute. The Court of Justice accepted the Commission's argument that the relevant market was in bananas, and not in fruit generally:

> For the banana to be regarded as forming a market which is sufficiently differentiated from other fruit markets, it must be possible for it to be singled out by such special features distinguishing it from other fruits that it is only to a limited extent exchangeable with them and is only exposed to their competition in a way that is hardly perceptible.

> The ripening of bananas takes place the whole year round without any season having to be taken into account. Throughout the year production exceeds demand and can satisfy it at any time. Owing to this particular feature the banana is a privileged fruit and its production and marketing can be adapted to the seasonal fluctuations of other fresh fruit which are known and can be computed. There is no unavoidable seasonal substitution since the consumer can obtain this fruit all the year round . . . It follows from these considerations that a very large number of consumers having a constant need for bananas are not noticeably or even appreciably enticed away from the consumption of this product by the arrival of other fresh fruit on the market and that even the seasonal peak periods only affect it for a limited period of time and to a very limited extent from the point of view of substitutability.
>
> Consequently the banana market is a market which is sufficiently distinct from the other fresh fruit markets. (paras 22–26, and 34–35)

In the above case, the most noticeable feature of this part of the judgment is the way in which the Court focused on *product substitution* as a primary determinant in isolating bananas as a separate market. There are two kinds of substitutability: (i) demand-side substitutability; and (ii) **supply-side substitutability**.

Demand-side substitutability

Demand-side substitutability determines which products compete with each other from the perspective of the consumer. The Commission normally refers to the criteria of price, quality and intended use as the determining factors. In the *UBC* case the relatively constant price and lack of seasonal variation, and the suitability and intended use for children and the elderly meant that other fruits could not be readily substituted for bananas. This test can result in a very narrow market definition, as illustrated in the following case:

Hugin Kassaregister AB v *Commission* (Case 22/78)

The Commission found Hugin to be in breach of what is now Art 102 TFEU (previously Art 82 EC Treaty) because of its refusal to supply spare parts for Hugin cash registers to Liptons. It defined the relevant product market as consisting of spare parts for Hugin machines required by independent repairers. Hugin rejected this finding as too narrow. It insisted that the relevant market was the very competitive cash register market. The Court of Justice, however, accepted the Commission's market definition in relation to the independent repairers of Hugin machines:

> The role of those undertakings [the repairers] on the market is that of businesses which require spare parts for their various activities. They need such parts in order to provide services for cash register users in the form of maintenance and repairs and for the reconditioning of used machines intended for re-sale or renting out . . . It is, moreover, established that there is a specific demand for Hugin spare parts, since those spare parts are not interchangeable with spare parts for cash registers of other makes. (para 7)

The Court of Justice has accepted that there was dominance in an equally narrow market of information on the content of BBC and RTE television programmes in *RTE and ITP* v *Commission* (Cases C-241/91 and C-242/91P). Subsequently, in *Deutsche Bahn AG* v *Commission* (Case T-229/94), the Court of First Instance ((CFI) now renamed the General Court) held that there was a *distinct sub-market* in the carriage of maritime containers by rail and, in assessing dominance, the Commission was justified in not taking into account other services provided by rail transport operators, road hauliers and inland waterway operators.

Supply-side substitutability

Supply-side substitutability is concerned with the ability of a manufacturer to switch his production system from product A to product B, and therefore constitutes a test of whether the manufacturer of product A is a rival to the manufacturer of product B:

Tetra-Pak International SA v Commission (Case T-83/91)

The Court of Justice rejected Tetra-Pak's argument that there were separate markets for: (i) aseptic cartons and the related packing machinery; and (ii) non-aseptic cartons and packaging machinery, because of the relative ease with which the manufacturer could switch from one to the other.

Europemballage and Continental Can v Commission (Case 6/72)

The issue involved packaging containers and the scope of the market. The Court of Justice held that, in order to be regarded as constituting a distinct market, the products must be individualised, not only by the mere fact that they are used in packing certain products, but also by the peculiar characteristics of production which make them specifically suitable for this purpose:

Consequently, a dominant position on the market for light metal containers for fish and meat cannot be decisive, as long as it has not been proved that competitors from other sectors of the market for light metal containers are not in a position to enter this market, by a simple adaptation, with sufficient strength to create a serious counterweight.

Whether or not supply-side substitutability exists is a matter of fact to be investigated by the Commission, as illustrated in the following case:

Istituto Chemioterapico Italiano SPA and Commercial Solvents Corporation v Commission (Cases 6 and 7/73)

An American company, CSC, and its Italian subsidiary, cut off supplies of aminobutanol to another Italian company, Zoja. Aminobutanol is an effective and cheap raw material used in the production of ethambutol, a drug used for treating tuberculosis. The Commission alleged that CSC had an almost worldwide monopoly in aminobutanol, and was considering manufacturing ethambutol in Italy, through its subsidiary there. There were other drugs for the treatment of tuberculosis, which were based on different but less effective raw materials. The Court of Justice decided that the relevant product market was the supply of aminobutanol, and not the production of ethambutol. It could not accept that Zoja could readily adapt its production facilities to other raw materials for the manufacture of ethambutol. Only if other materials could be substituted without difficulty could they be regarded as acceptable substitutes.

The geographical market

In order to decide whether or not the dominant position is held in a substantial part of the internal market, it is necessary to look not only at the geographical extent of the market in question but also at: (i) the economic importance of the area as defined; (ii) the pattern and volume of the production and consumption of the relevant product; and (iii) the habits of producers and consumers in that area. An area can be defined by factors which promote its geographical isolation. Factors tending to emphasise that isolation might be lack of transport facilities, or the cost of transportation relative to the value of a product, giving an unchallengeable advantage to local producers. The transport cost factor was held in *Suiker Unie* v *Commission* (Case 40/73) to be very significant in defining the geographical market. Conversely, in *Tetra-Pak International SA* v *Commission* (Case T-83/91) the CFI (now the General Court) supported the Commission's finding that the geographical market consisted of the whole of the Union because, *inter alia*, the very low cost of transport for cartons and machines meant they could easily and readily be transported between states. Sometimes the geographical market can be readily identified as lying within the borders of a Member State. In *NV Nederlandsche Banden-Industrie Michelin* v *Commission* (Case 322/81) the Court of Justice found that tyre companies operated in the Netherlands' market through local subsidiaries, to which local dealers looked for their supplies. It therefore upheld the decision of the Commission to regard the Netherlands as the area in which the competition facing NBIM was located.

Another factor identifying a separate geographical market is its homogeneity. Article 9(7) of the EU Merger Regulation 139/2004 (which replaced Regulation 4064/89) recognises this factor:

> The geographical reference market shall consist of the area in which the undertakings concerned are involved in the supply and demand of products and services, in which the conditions of competition are sufficiently homogenous and which can be distinguished from neighbouring areas because, in particular, conditions of competition are appreciably different in those areas. This assessment should take account in particular of the nature and characteristics of the products or services concerned, of the existence of entry barriers or of consumer preferences, of appreciable differences of the undertakings' market shares between the area concerned and neighbouring areas or of substantial price differences.

These features were significant in the *United Brands* case when the Court of Justice considered the geographical market:

United Brands Co v *Commission* (Case 27/76)

With regard to the banana market throughout the Union, the Commission identified three states which had distinctive rules for the import and sale of bananas: (i) Italy, which operated a national system of quota restrictions; (ii) the UK, which had a system of Commonwealth preference; and (iii) France, which had a similar preferential system favouring the African francophone states. Only the then remaining six Member States had a completely free market in bananas. The Commission therefore excluded France, Italy and the UK from the analysis and the other six states were identified as the relevant geographical market. The Court of Justice supported this finding on the basis that:

> . . . although the applicable tariff provisions and transport costs are of necessity different but not discriminatory . . . and . . . the conditions of competition are the same for all . . . [t]hese six states form an area which is sufficiently homogenous to be considered in its entirety' (paras 52 and 53).

The Court of Justice went so far, in a case involving the application of Regulation 4064/89 (which was replaced in 2004 by the EU Merger Regulation 139/2004), as to hold that, for the purposes of the production of potash and rocksalt, the whole Union, apart from Germany, was 'sufficiently homogenous to be regarded overall as a separate geographical market' (*France* v *Commission* (Joined Cases C-68/94 and C-30/95)).

Dominance in fact

Besides the ability to operate independently of its rivals, another indicator of dominance is the extent of market share. The larger this is, the more likely, and well-founded, will be an acceptance of dominance. In *Hoffman La Roche* v *Commission* (Case 85/76), the company's market shares over a three-year period of 75 to 87 per cent were held to be so large that they were, in themselves, evidence of a dominant position. Similarly, in *Tetra-Pak*, the company's 90 per cent share of the market in aseptic cartons and the relevant packaging machines made it 'an inevitable partner for packers and guaranteed it the freedom of conduct characteristic of a dominant position'. However, in *United Brands*, a market share of between 40 and 45 per cent did not 'permit the conclusion that UBC automatically controls the market'.

Besides market share, there are a number of other factors indicative of actual dominance of the market. These will include ownership of, or ready access to, massive financial resources. In addition, a firm's ability to establish and maintain a lead in product development or technical services may well contribute to the maintenance of a dominant position. The process of using financial resources or a technical advantage to maintain a dominant position could also constitute an abuse of that position.

Article 102 TFEU: abuse of a dominant position

Article 102(a)–(d) TFEU provides a non-exhaustive list of the sort of conduct which will constitute an abuse of a dominant position, primarily concerned with unfair trading practices (such as imposing unfair purchase or selling prices), restricting production to create an artificial shortage, and discriminating unfairly between different trading partners. It was originally thought that the former Art 82 EC Treaty (now Art 102 TFEU) applied exclusively to practices which constituted an abuse of market power, rather than to activities intended to gain or maintain dominance. However, in *Continental Can* ((Case 6/72); see below), the Court of Justice rejected such a narrow interpretation of the former Art 82 EC Treaty (now Art 102 TFEU) and declared that 'the provision is not only aimed at practices which may cause damage to consumers directly, but also at those which are detrimental to them through their impact on an effective competitive structure . . .'.

In the *Continental Can* case, the conduct complained of was an agreement by Continental Can to buy a competitor in the food packaging market that would, in the Commission's view, have enabled it to achieve absolute dominance in its sector of the market. The Court of Justice accepted, in principle, that this sort of conduct could breach the former Art 82 EC Treaty (now Art 102 TFEU), but decided, on the facts of the case, that the Commission had chosen the wrong relevant product market.

It should, however, be noted that gaining or maintaining dominance is not *per se* in breach of Art 102 TFEU, as illustrated in the following case:

Gottrub Klim Grovvareforening v *Dansk Landbrugs Grovvaresel*
(Case C-250/92)

> The Court of Justice held that the conduct of a cooperative of growers that dominated the market of purchasers for certain agricultural supplies was not in breach of what is now Art 102 TFEU (previously Art 82 EC Treaty). The cooperative had strengthened its own statutes to reduce competition from members who had left the cooperative. The Court held that:
>
> > . . . neither the creation nor the strengthening of a dominant position is in itself contrary to . . . [Article 102 TFEU] . . . The activities of cooperative purchasing organisations may actually encourage more effective competition on some markets, provided that the rules binding members do no more than is necessary to ensure that the cooperative functions properly and maintains its contractual power in relation to producers.

What is important is the effect of achieving or maintaining dominance. The Court of Justice explored this concept further in the following case:

Hoffman La Roche v *Commission* (Case 85/76)

> The Court of Justice stated that:
>
> > The concept of abuse is an objective concept relating to the behaviour of an undertaking in a dominant position where, as a result of the very presence of the undertaking in question, the degree of competition is weakened and which, through recourse to methods different from those which condition normal competition in products and services on the basis of the transactions of commercial operators, has the effect of hindering the maintenance of the degree of competition still existing in the market or the growth of that competition.

Specific abuses

Article 102 TFEU contains a number of examples of the type of conduct by an undertaking in a dominant position which constitutes an abuse. The list is indicative and not exhaustive, but it provides a useful starting point for an examination of abusive practices.

The imposition of unfair purchase or selling prices

The most obvious abuse by a supplier in a monopoly position is the imposition of extortionate prices on consumers. There is an element of subjectivity in any assessment of what is a fair price, but in **United Brands** the Court of Justice declared that a price is excessive if 'it has no reasonable relation to the economic value of the product supplied'. In determining the economic value, it is necessary to take into account the difference between the costs actually incurred and the price charged. A price may also be excessive if it is not attributable to ordinary market conditions. In **Tetra-Pak**, the CFI (now the General Court) found that the very great disparity in charges between the prices paid by Italian purchasers and those paid elsewhere in the Union could not be explained by additional market or transport costs in Italy, but were derived simply from Tetra-Pak's dominance in that country. The prices charged in Italy were, essentially, discriminatory.

In relation to prices for services, an undertaking would be abusing its dominant position if it charged fees which were disproportionate to the economic value of the service provided. In *Société Civile Agricole de la Crespelle* v *Coopérative d'Elevage de la Mayenne* (Case C-323/93), artificial insemination centres providing bovine semen, which enjoyed a virtual monopoly under national legislation in each region of France, were held by the Court of Justice to be abusing their position if they were to charge additional costs over and above those actually incurred in obtaining and conserving semen imported from other Member States. The Commission has applied this decision to price-fixing for dock-work in a series of local port monopolies established by national law throughout Italy (*Re Italian Ports Employment Policy: The Italian Community* v *Italy* (Case 97/94)).

Unnaturally low prices may also amount to an abuse, where they are intended to drive an actual or potential competitor from the market. This practice is normally called 'predatory pricing' and this was the issue in the following case:

AKZO Chemie BV v Commission (Case C-62/86)

The Commission found that AKZO occupied a dominant position in the market for flour additives and for organic peroxides used in the making of plastics. Another company, ECS, which was already in the flour additives market, was seeking to enter the peroxide for plastics market in the UK. The Commission found that AKZO had made direct threats to ECS, had systematically offered and supplied flour additives to ECS's customers at abnormally low prices and had also offered them products at below cost price which it did not normally supply. The Court of Justice repeated its previously stated position that what is now Art 102 TFEU (previously Art 82 EC Treaty) prohibits a dominant undertaking from eliminating a competitor and thus reinforcing its position by means other than competition on merit. In that sense, not all price competition can be regarded as legitimate:

> Prices lower than the average total costs by which a dominant undertaking seeks to eliminate a competitor must be regarded as an abuse. A dominant undertaking has no interest in offering such prices except to eliminate its competitors in order then to raise its prices again on the basis of its monopolistic position, since every sale involves it in a loss, namely all the fixed costs and at least a part of the variable costs relating to the unit produced.

Exclusive supply

It is not uncommon for suppliers to give discounts to customers who place large orders with them, and indeed there is nothing wrong, in principle, with such arrangements. But if the discount is tied to a requirement that the trader purchase all or a very large part of his supplies from the dominant undertaking, the arrangement may very well fall foul of Art 102 TFEU:

Hoffman La Roche (Case 85/76)

The investigation by the Commission revealed that the company, which was the largest producer of pharmaceuticals in the world, occupied a dominant position in markets for a number of vitamin products. It sold these products on the basis that customers were bound by an exclusive or preferential purchasing commitment in favour of the company for all or a large proportion of their requirements. This was achieved either by an express exclusive purchase agreement, or as a result of 'fidelity rebates'. The Court of Justice rejected these arrangements, as the discounts did not reflect any real cost saving as a result of a bulk purchase (i.e. transport, storage, etc.) but were a direct attempt to 'buy' the exclusive custom of the purchaser.

Michelin v Commission (Case 322/81)

Michelin gave target bonuses to its dealers according to their marketing efforts. Dealers were not given a clear indication of the basis on which such bonuses were calculated. The Commission found that the system had the effect of ensuring that the dealers remained attached to Michelin in the hope of receiving the often unknown, but hoped-for, bonuses. The Court of Justice accepted the Commission's finding and ruled that discounts had to be justified by a benefit conferred on the supplier which reduced the supplier's costs and enabled the supplier to pass on the benefit in terms of reduced prices. Across-the-board discounts on a range of products are also an abuse, because they make it more difficult for other suppliers who may not have a similar range of products to compete for an opportunity to supply.

Tied sales

Article 102(d) TFEU prohibits 'making the conclusion of contracts subject to acceptance by the other parties of supplementary obligations which, by their nature or according to commercial usage, have no connection with the subject of such contracts'. Typically, this applies to an arrangement under which the supplier requires the trader to purchase its requirements of a second product (the 'tied' product) as a condition of being able to buy a first product (the 'tying' product):

Tetra-Pak (Case T-83/91)

The Commission had found that Tetra-Pak held approximately 90 per cent of, *inter alia*, the market of machines for making aseptic cartons for liquids. Purchasers of such machines were required to obtain their supplies of cartons exclusively from Tetra-Pak or from a supplier designated by it. The CFI (now the General Court) declared:

> It is clear that the tied-sale clauses [in the agreements with purchasers] . . . went beyond their ostensible purpose and are intended to strengthen Tetra-Pak's dominant position by reinforcing its customers' economic dependence on it. Those clauses are therefore wholly unreasonable in the context of protecting public health and also go beyond the recognised right of an undertaking in a dominant position to protect its commercial interests. Whether considered in isolation or together, they were unfair.

Refusal to supply

Whether or not a dominant undertaking's refusal to supply another undertaking is an abuse or not will be very much a matter of fact, depending on the circumstances of the refusal and the previous dealings of the parties, as illustrated in the following two cases:

Commercial Solvents Corporation v Commission (Cases 6 and 7/73)

Commercial Solvents Corporation had decided to discontinue sales of aminobutanol to another manufacturer, Zoja, because it wanted to manufacture aminobutanol's derivative, ethambutol, itself. The Court of Justice held that the decision to manufacture ethambutol itself did not justify a refusal to supply the raw material to a potential rival. To do so would effectively eliminate one of the principal manufacturers of ethambutol in the Union. There may, however, be objectively justifiable reasons for not supplying a commodity.

BP v *Commission* (Case 77/77)

BP refused to sell oil to an intermittent purchaser during the oil crisis in the early 1970s. There was, effectively, an oil embargo of Western Europe and BP had drawn up a list of regular customers whom it would continue to supply, and others whom it would not, or would supply only as and when it was able. The Court of Justice held that, in such a supply crisis, a refusal to supply was justified. There must, however, be an objective justification for a refusal.

In the following case, the issue was the nature of the banana market and a number of alleged abuses by UBC (see above):

United Brands v *Commission* (Case 27/76)

One of the alleged abuses was a refusal to supply certain, hitherto regular, customers. One of these, Olesen, had participated in an advertising campaign run by one of UBC's rivals, and it was this participation that UBC sought to 'punish'. The Court of Justice rejected this attempted justification of a refusal to supply:

> Although it is true, as the applicant points out, that the fact that an undertaking is in a dominant position cannot disentitle it from protecting its own commercial interests if they are attacked, and that such an undertaking must be conceded the right to take such reasonable steps as it deems appropriate to protect its said interests, such behaviour cannot be countenanced if its actual purpose is to strengthen this dominant position and abuse it.
>
> Even if the possibility of a counter-attack is acceptable, that attack must still be proportionate to the threat taking into account the economic strength of the undertakings confronting each other.
>
> The sanction consisting of a refusal to supply by an undertaking in a dominant position was in excess of what might, if such a situation were to arise, reasonably be contemplated as a sanction for conduct similar to that for which UBC blamed Olesen.

Another example of a refusal to supply being used to retain dominance in a market occurred in the following case (the Commission's decision was not challenged before the Court of Justice):

British Brass Band Instruments v *Boosey and Hawkes* [1988] 4 CMLR 67

Boosey and Hawkes produced and sold brass band instruments within the UK. The Commission found that they dominated 90 per cent of the UK's brass band instrument market. The BBBI wished to import and distribute brass band instruments originating in other parts of the Union. Boosey and Hawkes refused to continue to supply the BBBI with UK instruments until it desisted in its importation and sale of continental brass band instruments. The Commission found that the discontinuance of supply was abusive.

The following case concerned the refusal by an undertaking in a dominant position to grant a licence (i.e. permission) to use a piece of computer software (referred to as a 'brick structure') which was protected by an intellectual property right:

IMS Health (Case C-418/01)

The case involved a dispute between two companies specialising in market studies in the pharmaceutical products and healthcare sectors, which centred on the claim by one of them that it was entitled to use a 'brick structure' developed by the other for the provision of data on regional sales of pharmaceutical products in Germany. The Court of Justice held that:

30. . . . for the purposes of examining whether the refusal by an undertaking in a dominant position to grant a licence for a brick structure protected by an intellectual property right which it owns is abusive, the degree of participation by users in the development of that structure and the outlay, particularly in terms of cost, on the part of potential users in order to purchase studies on regional sales of pharmaceutical products presented on the basis of an alternative structure are factors which must be taken into consideration in order to determine whether the protected structure is indispensable to the marketing of studies of that kind.

. . .

52. . . . the refusal by an undertaking which holds a dominant position and owns an intellectual property right in a brick structure indispensable to the presentation of regional sales data on pharmaceutical products in a Member State to grant a licence to use that structure to another undertaking which also wishes to provide such data in the same Member State, constitutes an abuse of a dominant position within the meaning of . . . [Art 102 TFEU] where the following conditions are fulfilled:
    (i) the undertaking which requested the licence intends to offer, on the market for the supply of the data in question, new products or services not offered by the owner of the intellectual property right and for which there is a potential consumer demand;
    (ii) the refusal is not justified by objective considerations;
    (iii) the refusal is such as to reserve to the owner of the intellectual property right the market for the supply of data on sales of pharmaceutical products in the Member State concerned by eliminating all competition on that market. [emphasis added]

Where an undertaking has a monopoly of information, a refusal to supply that information to a potential publisher of television programmes can constitute a refusal to supply under Art 102(b) TFEU (**RTE & ITP v Commission** (Cases C-241/91P and C-242/91P)).

The following case concerned the refusal to supply medicinal products – a potential breach of the former Art 82(b) EC Treaty (now Art 102(b) TFEU). In this case, the dominant company (the supplier of the medicinal products) argued that its refusal to supply was justified in order to prevent parallel exports of the medicinal products to Member States where the selling prices were higher:

Sot. Lélos kai Sia EE and Others v Glaxosmithkline AEVE Farmakeftikon Proïonton (Cases C-468/06 to C-478/06)

GlaxoSmithKline AEVE (GSK AEVE) is the Greek subsidiary of GlaxoSmithKline plc (GSK plc), a pharmaceuticals research and manufacturing company established in the United Kingdom. It imports, warehouses and distributes pharmaceutical products of the GSK group in Greece. As such, it holds the marketing authorisation in Greece for certain prescription-only medicines.

In November 2000 GSK AEVE stopped meeting the orders of the Greek wholesalers who buy the medicines in question for distribution in Greece and export to other Member States. The company cited a shortage of the products at issue, for which it denied responsibility, and it began itself to distribute those medicines to Greek hospitals and pharmacies.

In February 2001, taking the view that the supply of medicines on the Greek market had to some extent normalised and that stocks had been reconstituted, GSK AEVE started once more to supply the wholesalers with limited quantities of the medicinal products.

The wholesalers brought an action claiming that the sales policy of GSK AEVE and GSK plc in respect of those medicinal products constituted an abuse of the dominant position which those companies held on the markets for the medicinal products in question. The Athens Court of Appeal referred questions to the Court of Justice on the compatibility of these practices with the former Art 82 EC Treaty (now Art 102 TFEU).

The Court observed, first, that any abuse by an undertaking of its dominant position is prohibited as incompatible with the internal market in so far as it may affect trade between Member States. Such abuse may, in particular, consist in limiting production, markets or technical development to the prejudice of consumers.

The Court stated that, in this case, by refusing to meet the Greek wholesalers' orders, GSK AEVE aimed to limit parallel exports by those wholesalers to the markets of other Member States in which the selling prices of the medicines in dispute are higher.

The Court went on to consider whether, in the pharmaceuticals sector, there were particular circumstances which might, generally, justify a refusal to meet orders.

First, the Court pointed out that parallel exports of medicinal products from a Member State where the prices are low, to other Member States in which the prices are higher, open up in principle an alternative source of supply to buyers of the medicines in those latter states at lower prices than those applied on the same market by the pharmaceuticals companies. It therefore could not be argued that the parallel exports were of only minimal benefit to the final consumers.

The Court then analysed the possible effect of state regulation of the prices of medicines on the assessment of whether the refusal to supply is an abuse. The Court observed that the control exercised by Member States over the selling prices or the reimbursement of medicines does not entirely remove the prices of those products from the law of supply and demand. Although the degree of price regulation in the pharmaceuticals sector could not therefore preclude the Union rules on competition from applying, in the case of Member States with a system of price regulation, state intervention was one of the factors liable to create opportunities for parallel trade. The Union rules on competition are not capable of being interpreted in such a way that, in order to defend its own commercial interests, the only choice left for a pharmaceuticals company in a dominant position was not to place its medicines on the market at all in a Member State where the prices of those products were set at a relatively low level.

It followed that, **even if the degree of regulation regarding the price of medicines could not prevent a refusal by a pharmaceuticals company in a dominant position to meet orders sent to it by wholesalers involved in parallel exports from constituting an abuse, such a company must nevertheless be in a position to take steps that are reasonable and in proportion to the need to protect its own commercial interests. In order to assess whether such steps are reasonable and proportionate, it must be ascertained whether the orders of the wholesalers are out of the ordinary.**

Finally, the Court examined the impact of state regulation on the supply of medicinal products, and more particularly the argument put forward by GSK AEVE that undertakings that engage in parallel exports are not subject to the same obligations regarding distribution and warehousing as the pharmaceuticals companies and are therefore liable to disrupt the planning of production and distribution of medicines.

In that connection, the Court observed that, in cases where parallel trade would effectively lead to a shortage of medicines on a given national market, it would not be for the undertakings holding a dominant position but for the national authorities to resolve the situation, by taking appropriate and proportionate steps. However, a producer of pharmaceutical products must be in a position to protect its own commercial interests if it is confronted with orders that are out of the ordinary in terms of quantity.

The Court stated that it was for the national court to ascertain whether the orders are ordinary in the light of both the previous business relations between the pharmaceuticals company and the wholesalers concerned and the size of the orders in relation to the requirements of the market in the Member State concerned.

It concluded that an undertaking occupying a dominant position on the relevant market for medicinal products which, in order to put a stop to parallel exports, refuses to meet ordinary orders is abusing its dominant position.

In the above case, the Court of Justice provided some protection for pharmaceutical companies who refused to supply medicinal products because of the danger of parallel exports. A refusal to meet 'ordinary orders' (i.e. orders which would be consumed within that particular Member State, and not exported to other Member States where the products enjoyed a higher selling price) would constitute an abuse of a dominant position, contrary to Art 102 TFEU. However, a pharmaceuticals company could legitimately refuse to supply orders for medicinal products which are 'out of the ordinary' in order to prevent parallel exports; i.e. such a refusal would *not* constitute an abuse of a dominant position.

Other abusive practices

The ingenuity of undertakings seeking to extend their dominance and to exclude competitors makes it impossible to provide a full account of abusive practices. The following case provides some examples of practices which have been deemed to be abusive:

Tetra-Pak International SA v Commission (Case T-83/91)

Besides the tying agreements and excessive and predatory pricing which have already been considered, Tetra-Pak was also found by the Commission to have engaged in the following abusive practices: buying back competitors' machines with a view to withdrawing them from the market; obtaining an undertaking from one of the dairies with which it did business not to use two machines it had acquired from competitors of Tetra-Pak; eliminating in Italy all Resolvo aseptic packaging machines developed by a rival company; and finally, appropriating advertising media by obtaining an exclusive rights agreement with an Italian milk industry journal under which Tetra-Pak's rivals would not be allowed to advertise in the journal.

Article 102 TFEU: affecting trade between Member States

See pages 684–693 for further discussion of the 'effect on trade' concept within the context of Art 101 TFEU.

As with Art 101 TFEU, there must be some effect on trade between Member States for Art 102 TFEU to apply. To satisfy this condition, it is not necessary that the effect on trade should be of a particular kind. Typically, it would meet the requirement if the effect of the conduct would be to partition markets in the Union. This is illustrated in the following case:

Greenwich Film Production v *SACEM* (Case 22/79)

SACEM (Société des Auteurs, Compositeurs et Editeurs de Musique) was an association formed to collect royalties arising out of the performance of artistic and other works in France and elsewhere. SACEM demanded payment of royalties arising out of the performance of music in films distributed in France. Greenwich argued that SACEM effectively had a monopoly of such rights in France and was abusing its position. SACEM contended, *inter alia*, that even if this was so, it did not affect trade between Member States. The Court of Justice, however, accepted that there might be some effect. It recognised that in certain Member States organisations such as SACEM were entrusted by composers to supervise performances of their work and to collect royalties. It held that it is possible in those circumstances that 'the activities of such associations may be conducted in such a way that their effect is to partition the common market [i.e. internal market] and thereby restrict the freedom to provide services which constitutes one of the objectives of the Treaty'.

This partitioning of the internal market will not arise where the activities are exclusively directed at part of a Member State:

Hugin v *Commission* (Case 22/78)

The Commission had found that Hugin, the Swedish manufacturers of cash registers, had refused to supply spare parts of their machines to a London-based firm, Liptons. Liptons serviced, repaired and reconditioned such machines. Their business was essentially local, and they did no work outside the UK. The Court of Justice concluded that the abuse did not have the effect of preventing Liptons from carrying out their servicing in other Member States or affect the trade in parts between Member States, because those requiring the parts would normally obtain them direct from the manufacturers in Sweden. At the time Sweden was in neither the European Union nor the European Economic Area.

Commission guidelines on the 'effect on trade concept' contained in Articles 101 and 102 TFEU

Guidelines on the 'effect on trade concept' which is contained in Arts 101 and 102 TFEU were adopted by the Commission on 30 March 2004 (OJ 2004 C 101/81) as part of the 'Modernisation Package' which included the adoption of Regulation 1/2003 (see above and Chapter 22). The guidelines are available at:

http://europa.eu/legislation_summaries/competition/firms/

Relationship between Articles 101(1) and 102 TFEU: collective dominance?

Objective 2

See Chapter 20 for a detailed discussion of Art 101 TFEU.

It is clear that many undertakings in a dominant position will endeavour to reinforce that position by various kinds of loyalty, tying and other agreements. Such agreements in themselves may infringe Art 101(1) TFEU, or they may also constitute forms of abusive behaviour which breach Art 102 TFEU. Agreements between a parent company and subsidiaries may not breach Art 101 TFEU because their action is seen as the action of one and the same entity (*VIHO Europe BV* v *Commission* (C-73/95P)). In such circumstances, the agreement between a parent company and subsidiaries may, where it is intended to drive out or exclude a competitor from the market, constitute an abuse of a dominant position. In *Istituto Chemioterapico Italiano and Commercial Solvents Corporation* v *Commission* (Cases 6 and 7/73), see above, it was CSC, the controlling company, which had instructed its subsidiary ICI not to supply aminobutanol to Zoja.

An agreement between several undertakings, each of which has a powerful position in a particular market, may come close to creating dominance which may then be subject to abuse by them. Article 102 TFEU, indeed, refers to abuse by 'one or more undertakings'. However, the undertakings involved are more likely to be penalised for a breach of Art 101(1) TFEU than a breach of Art 102 TFEU (Commission decision on *Italian Flat Glass* [1990] 4 CMLR 535). The nearest the Court has come to accepting a breach of Art 102 TFEU where there is a linkage of several undertakings was in the case of an actual or proposed merger of those undertakings (see, e.g., *Continental Can* (Case 6/72)). Tacit collusion between major undertakings comprising, in effect, a tight oligopoly, may be difficult for the Commission to deal with:

Hoffman La Roche (Case 85/76)

The Court of Justice declared (in response to Advocate General Lenz's observation that there was a problem in knowing where a collective monopoly ends and an oligopoly begins):

> A dominant position must also be distinguished from parallel courses of conduct which are peculiar to oligopolies in that in an oligopoly the courses of conduct interact, while in the case of an undertaking occupying a dominant position the conduct of the undertaking which derives profits from that position is to a great extent determined unilaterally.

In the absence of clear evidence, a concerted practice breaching Art 101(1) TFEU may not be demonstrable. If that is the case then, *a fortiori*, an abuse by connected undertakings cannot be shown to breach Art 102 TFEU. Evidence of some judicial movement in relation to the concept of collective dominance came first when the CFI (now the General Court) considered the Commission's decision in *Italian Flat Glass* v *Commission* (Joined Cases T-68, 77 and 78/89). The CFI held that what is now Art 102 TFEU (previously Art 82 EC Treaty) was capable of applying to independent firms which, because of the economic links between them, held a collective dominant position on the relevant market. Nevertheless, on the facts of the case, it decided that there was insufficient evidence to support a finding of collective dominance. However, in *Compagnie Maritime Belge* (Joined Cases T-24–26 and 28/93), the CFI held that the members of a shipping conference had abused the collective dominant position they held as a result of close relations between them. The

Court of Justice had already, by then, accepted in principle that what is now Art 102 TFEU was capable of applying to collective dominance (***DIP and Others* v *Comune di Bassano del Grappa*** (Joined Cases C-140–142/94)). The basis of these decisions is the fact that Art 102 TFEU applies to 'one or more undertakings'. Originally, this may have been intended to refer only to a primary undertaking and its subsidiaries, as in ***VIHO* v *Commission*** (Case C-73/95P), but the difficulty of proving the existence of a concerted practice in the former Art 81(1) EC Treaty (now Art 101(1) TFEU) seems to have led the Court to take a more sympathetic view of collective dominance, in order to bring the activities within the former Art 82 EC Treaty (now Art 102 TFEU), and to bridge the apparent gap between the former Arts 81 and 82 EC Treaty (now Arts 101 and 102 TFEU).

Mergers

Objective 3

A merger takes place when two or more undertakings which were formerly independent are brought under common control. As a result of the decision of the Court of Justice in ***Continental Can*** (see above), it was clear that a merger between undertakings could, in appropriate circumstances, breach Art 102 TFEU. What those circumstances were became the subject, after prolonged discussions, of a Council regulation on mergers (Council Regulation 4064/89 on the control of concentrations between undertakings). Under the regulation, the Commission was given sole competence to take decisions with regard to 'concentrations with a Community [i.e. Union] dimension'. Regulation 4064/89 was replaced in 2004 by the EU Merger Regulation 139/2004.

Such concentrations may be viewed from two perspectives. On the one hand, the combined economic strengths of fully merged undertakings, or the cooperation between undertakings which have partly merged, may produce a degree of market control and distortion of competition that is detrimental to the effective operation of the market. On the other hand, the merger may produce economies of scale, and result in the creation of an undertaking whose size and strength may enable it to compete effectively on world markets. In considering the effect of a merger under the EU Merger Regulation 139/2004, the Commission has to strike a balance between competing objectives.

Article 2(1), Regulation 139/2004 requires the Commission to make an appraisal of the proposed merger, taking into account:

(a) the need to maintain and develop effective competition within the common market [i.e. internal market] in view of, among other things, the structure of all the markets concerned and the actual or potential competition from undertakings located either within or outwith the Community [i.e. Union];

(b) the market position of the undertakings concerned and their economic and financial power, the alternatives available to suppliers and users, their access to suppliers or markets, any legal and other barriers to entry, supply and demand trends for the relevant goods and services, the interests of the intermediate and ultimate consumers, and the development of technical and economic progress provided that it is to the consumers' advantage and does not form an obstacle to competition.

Article 2(2), Regulation 139/2004 provides that a concentration which '*would not* significantly impede effective competition in the common market [i.e. internal market] or in a substantial part of it, in particular as a result of the creation or strengthening of a dominant position shall be declared *compatible* with the common market [i.e. internal market]' (emphasis added). Article 2(3), Regulation 139/2004 contains the corollary provision that a concentration which '*would* significantly impede effective competition in the common market [i.e. internal market] or in a substantial part of it, in particular as a result of the creation or strengthening of a dominant position shall be declared *incompatible* with the common market [i.e. internal market]' (emphasis added). The declaration of compatibility or incompatibility is made by the Commission in the form of a decision (Art 8, Regulation 139/2004).

The Union dimension of a merger is achieved when the aggregate worldwide turnover of all the undertakings concerned is more than 5,000 million euros and the aggregate Union-wide turnover of each of at least two of the undertakings involved is more than 250 million euros, unless each of the undertakings concerned achieves more than two-thirds of its aggregate Union-wide turnover in one and the same Member State (Art 1(2), Regulation 139/2004).

Regulation 139/2004 provides that where a concentration does not meet the above thresholds, it will still have a Union dimension where:

(a) the combined aggregate worldwide turnover of all the undertakings concerned is more than 2,500 million euros;

(b) in each of at least three Member States, the combined aggregate turnover of all the undertakings concerned is more than 100 million euros;

(c) in each of at least three Member States included for the purpose of point (b), the aggregate turnover of each of at least two of the undertakings concerned is more than 25 million euros;

(d) the aggregate Community-wide [i.e. Union-wide] turnover of each of at least two of the undertakings concerned is more than 100 million euros;

unless each of the undertakings concerned achieves more than two-thirds of its aggregate Community-wide [i.e. Union-wide] turnover within one and the same Member State.

Regulation 139/2004, and its predecessor Regulation 4064/89, have not, to date, constituted much of a barrier to mergers. The vast majority of mergers notified to the Commission have obtained clearance. The Commission seems to see mergers as a way of reducing national control of undertakings and promoting the strength of large Union undertakings on the world market. Less attention appears to be paid to the possible adverse effects on consumers in the Union. One case where the Commission denied clearance, *Aérospatiale-Alenia/de Haviland* [1992] 4 CMLR M2, on the grounds that the merger would have had an unacceptable impact on customers' freedom of choice and the balance of competition in the Union, was widely criticised by governments, many with clear political interests in a different outcome than that resulting from the decision.

In *France* v *Commission* (Cases C-68/94 and C-30/95), the Court of Justice gave the previous Merger Regulation 4064/89 a new cutting edge, holding that it applied to a situation of collective dominance which fell short of an actual merger (see Editorial (1998) 23 EL Rev 199, 'Collective dominance: Trump card or joker?'). Under the current EU Merger Regulation 139/2004, cooperative aspects of joint ventures by undertakings which fall within the turnover threshold will have to be notified to the Commission and assessed for compatibility with Arts 101(1) and 101(3) TFEU (Art 2(4), Regulation 139/2004).

The CFI (now the General Court) gave a ground-breaking judgment when it overturned the Commission's decision to block the takeover of UK holiday company First Choice by Airtours:

Airtours Plc v *Commission* (Case T-342/99)

It was the first time that the CFI (now the General Court) had overturned a Commission decision to block a takeover. In its reasoning, the CFI concluded that the Commission had failed to prove satisfactorily that the proposed merger would establish a position of collective dominance. According to Art 2(3), Regulation 4064/89 (which has been replaced by Regulation 139/2004), a concentration that 'creates or reinforces a dominant position as a result of which effective competition would be significantly impeded in the common market [i.e. internal market] or in a substantial part of it' is to be declared incompatible with the internal market. This had not been shown in this particular case and the Commission's decision was annulled.

Article 2(3), Regulation 139/2004 has substantially re-enacted Art 2(3), Regulation 4064/89. The CFI could therefore have reached a similar decision in the *Airtours* case if it had been required to apply Art 2(3), Regulation 139/2004 rather than Art 2(3) of the earlier regulation.

In the following case the CFI annulled the Commission's decision authorising a proposed concentration between Bertelsmann and Sony, whereby the two companies would merge their global recorded music activities (with the exclusion of Sony's activities in Japan) into three new companies operated together under the name Sony BMG:

Independent Music Publishers and Labels Association (Impala) v *Commission* (Case T-464/04)

On 24 May 2004, the Commission informed the notifying parties that it had reached the provisional conclusion that the concentration was incompatible with Union law, as, in particular, it would reinforce a collective dominant position on the market for recorded music. However, after hearing the parties, the Commission on 18 July 2004 declared the concentration to be compatible with the internal market.

On 3 December 2004, Impala, an international association whose members are 2,500 independent music production companies and which had participated in the procedure before the Commission, applied to the CFI (now the General Court) for annulment of that decision.

The CFI observed that, according to the Commission's decision, the absence of a collective dominant position on the market for recorded music might be inferred from the heterogeneity of the product concerned, from the lack of transparency of the market and from the absence of retaliatory measures between the five largest companies.

However, the CFI found that the theory that promotional discounts have the effect of reducing the transparency of the market, to the point of preventing the existence of a collective dominant position, was not supported by a statement of reasons of the requisite legal standard and was vitiated by a manifest error of assessment. The elements on which that argument was founded were incomplete and did not include all the relevant data that ought to have been taken into account by the Commission. They were therefore not capable of supporting the conclusions drawn from them.

The CFI further pointed out that the Commission relied on the absence of evidence that retaliatory measures had been used in the past, whereas, according to case law, the mere existence of effective deterrent mechanisms is sufficient, as where the companies comply with the common policy there is no need to have recourse to sanctions. In that context, the CFI stated that the decision and the case file revealed that such credible and effective deterrent measures appeared to exist, in particular the possibility of sanctioning a deviating record company by excluding it from compilations. In addition, even if the appropriate test in that regard was to consist of determining whether retaliatory measures had been exercised in the past, the Commission's examination was inadequate. At the hearing it was not in a position to indicate the slightest step that it had completed or undertaken for that purpose.

As those two grounds constituted the essential grounds on which the Commission concluded that there was no collective dominant position, each of those errors would in itself constitute sufficient reason to annul the decision.

Furthermore, as regards the possible creation of a collective dominant position after the concentration, the CFI criticised the Commission for having carried out an extremely cursory examination and for having presented in the decision only a few superficial and formal observations on that point.

The CFI considered that the Commission could not rely, without making an error, on the lack of transparency of the market or on the absence of evidence that retaliatory measures had been used in the past in order to conclude that the concentration did not entail a risk that a collective dominant position would be created.

Summary

Now you have read this chapter you should be able to:

- Explain how Art 102 TFEU operates to prevent the abuse of a dominant position, describing:
  - what is meant by a dominant position (distinguishing between demand-side substitutability and supply-side substitutability);
  - in what circumstances such a dominant position will be deemed to be abused;
  - how such abuse must affect trade between Member States.
- Describe and evaluate the relationship between Arts 101(1) and 102 TFEU with regard to collective dominance.
- Understand and explain how Art 102 TFEU and Regulation 139/2004 are applied to regulate mergers which may produce a degree of market control and distortion of competition which is detrimental to the effective operation of the internal market.

Reference

Editorial, 'Collective dominance: Trump card or joker?' (1998) 23 EL Rev 199.

Further reading

Textbooks

Craig, P. and De Burca, G. (2011) *EU Law: Text, Cases and Materials* (5th edn), Oxford University Press, Chapter 27.

Foster, N. (2015) *Foster on EU Law* (5th edn), Oxford University Press, Chapter 10.

Steiner, J. and Woods, L. (2014) *EU Law* (12th edn), Oxford University Press, Chapter 29.

Weatherill, S. (2014) *Cases and Materials on EC Law* (11th edn), Oxford University Press, Chapter 16.

Journal articles

Akman, P., 'The role of intent in the EU case law on abuse of dominance' (2014) 39 EL Rev 316.

Andreangeli, A., 'Interoperability as an "essential facility" in the Microsoft case – encouraging competition or stifling innovation?' (2009) 34 EL Rev 584.

Brisimi, V., 'Abuse of a dominant position and public policy justifications: A question of attribution' (2013) 24 EBL Rev 261.

Brouwer, O.W., Goydner, J. and Mes, D., 'Developments in EC competition law in 2007: An overview' (2008) 45 CML Rev 1167.

Cengiz, F., 'Multi-level governance in competition policy: The European Competition Network' (2010) 35 EL Rev 660.

Papadopoulos, T., 'EU regulatory approaches to cross-border mergers: Exercising the right of establishment' (2011) 36 EL Rev 71.

Prechal, S. and De Vries, S., 'Seamless web of judicial protection in the internal market' (2009) 34 EL Rev 5.

Tsouloufas, G., 'Limiting pharmaceutical parallel trade in the European Union: Regulatory and economic justifications' (2011) 36 EL Rev 385.

Wang, W. and Rudanko, M., 'EU merger remedies and competition concerns: An empirical assessment' (2012) 18 ELJ 555.

Witt, A.C., 'The Commission's guidance paper on abusive exclusionary conduct – more radical than it appears?' (2010) 35 EL Rev 214.

22

Enforcement of Union competition law: powers and procedures

At the end of this chapter you should understand:

1. How the rules of Union competition law have been implemented by Regulation 1/2003 and Regulation 773/2004 and the nature and scope of the ten Commission Notices issued to support these regulations.

2. The Commission's role in initiating an action for an apparent breach of Arts 101 or 102 TFEU.

3. What applications (if any) can be made by a party to a possible infringement of Arts 101 or 102 TFEU.

4. The nature and scope of the Commission's powers of investigation and a party's right to a hearing.

5. The nature and scope of the Commission's powers to make decisions, and the power to impose fines and periodic penalty payments.

6. The relationship between the Commission, and the national competition authorities and courts of the Member States.

7. The role of national competition authorities and courts of the Member States in the enforcement of Arts 101 and 102 TFEU.

8. The relationship between Union and national competition law.

9. How Union competition law is implemented and enforced in the UK.

Introduction

Objective 1

The European Commission has a general duty, imposed on it by Art 105(1) TFEU (previously Art 85(1) EC Treaty), to 'ensure the application of the principles laid down in Articles 101 and 102'. Article 105(1) TFEU requires that:

> On application by a Member State or on its own initiative, and in cooperation with the competent authorities in the Member States, who shall give it their assistance, the Commission shall investigate cases of suspected infringement of these principles. If it finds that there has been an infringement, it shall propose appropriate measures to bring it to an end.

Under Art 105(2) TFEU (previously Art 85(2) EC Treaty), if the infringement is not brought to an end, the Commission is required to record details of the infringement in a reasoned decision and to authorise Member States to take the necessary measures to remedy the situation.

Article 105 TFEU enables the Commission to make the appropriate decision, but it does not confer specific investigative powers, define the investigative process or prescribe any means of enforcement by the Commission. These powers and duties were initially conferred on the Commission by Regulation 17/62 and, with the exception of transport (which was subject to a special process under Regulation 141/62), they applied to all investigations by the Commission.

Regulation 1/2003

On 1 May 2004, the same day the Union was enlarged from 15 to 25 Member States, Regulation 17/62 was replaced by Regulation 1/2003 (OJ 2003 L 1/1). This new Regulation creates the conditions for a greater involvement of national competition authorities and courts by making Arts 101 and 102 TFEU (previously Arts 81 and 82 EC Treaty) directly applicable in their entirety (see Chapters 20 and 21). The Regulation also covers transport and therefore the former Regulation 141/62 was repealed. One further regulation has been adopted:

● Regulation 773/2004 relates to the conduct of proceedings by the Commission pursuant to Arts 101 and 102 TFEU (OJ 2004 L 123/18).

The Commission has also issued ten notices (which are not legally binding):

1 Commission Notice on the definition of relevant market for the purpose of Union competition law (OJ 1997 C 372/5).

2 Commission Notice on cooperation within the Network of Competition Authorities (OJ 2004 C 101/43).

3 Commission Notice on the cooperation between the Commission and national courts in the application of Arts 101 and 102 TFEU (OJ 2004 C 101/54).

4 Commission Notice on the handling of complaints by the Commission under Arts 101 and 102 TFEU (OJ 2004 C 101/65).

5 Commission Notice on informal guidance relating to novel questions concerning Arts 101 and 102 TFEU that arise in individual cases (guidance letters) (OJ 2004 C 101/78); see Chapter 20.

6 Commission Notice: Guidelines on the effect on trade concept contained in Arts 101 and 102 TFEU (OJ 2004 C 101/81); see Chapters 20 and 21.

7 Commission Notice: Guidelines on the application of Art 101(3) TFEU (OJ 2004 C 101/118); see Chapter 20.

8 Commission Notice on the rules for access to the Commission file in cases pursuant to Arts 101 and 102 TFEU (OJ 2005 C 325/7).

9 Commission Notice: Guidelines on the method of setting fines imposed pursuant to Article 23(2)(a), Regulation 1/2003 (OJ 2006 C 210/2).

10 Commission Notice on immunity from fines and reduction of fines in cartel cases (OJ 2006 C 298/17).

The two regulations and ten notices are available in full-text format at:

http://europa.eu/legislation_summaries/competition/firms

In the sections that follow, there is a discussion of the application of Union competition law under Regulation 1/2003.

Initiating action by the Commission and the Member States

Objective 2

Where an apparent breach of Arts 101 or 102 TFEU has come to the notice of the Commission through, for example, a question by a member of the European Parliament, or a report in the press, the Commission can, under the general power conferred on it by Art 105 TFEU, commence an investigation. Article 17, Regulation 1/2003 sets out the powers of the Commission to investigate a particular sector of the economy or particular type of agreement across various sectors 'where the trend of trade between Member States, the rigidity of prices or other circumstances suggest that competition may be restricted or distorted within the common market [i.e. internal market]'. Article 5, Regulation 1/2003 empowers the competition authorities of the Member States to apply Arts 101 and 102 TFEU in individual cases, and the national laws relating to investigation will apply. While the competition authorities of the Member States had previously had the power to apply the former Arts 81(1) and 82 EC Treaty (now Arts 101(1) and 102 TFEU), for the first time they are empowered to apply the exception from the prohibition on agreements which restrict competition as laid down in Art 101(3) TFEU (see Chapter 20).

Complaints by a natural or legal person

Regulation 1/2003

Under Regulation 1/2003, a complaint may be lodged with either the Commission (Art 7) or the competition authorities of the Member States (Art 5). Article 6 provides that national courts are also required to safeguard the rights of individuals through an application of Arts 101 and 102 TFEU. Article 13 provides for the suspension or termination of proceedings:

1 Where competition authorities of two or more Member States have received a complaint or are acting on their own initiative under . . . [Articles 101 or 102 TFEU] against the same agreement, decision of an association or practice, the fact that one authority is dealing with the case shall be sufficient grounds for the others to suspend the proceedings before them or to reject the complaint. The Commission may likewise reject a complaint on the ground that a competition authority of a Member State is dealing with the case.

2 Where a competition authority of a Member State or the Commission has received a complaint against an agreement, decision of an association or practice which has already been dealt with by another competition authority, it may reject it.

The following case concerned an application of Art 13(1), Regulation 1/2003. For the first time the General Court ruled on the Commission's rejection of a complaint on the ground that the competition authority of a Member State was already dealing with the case:

Si.mobil telekomunikacijske storitve v *Commission* (Case T-201/11)

Si.mobil telekomunikacijske storitve is a Slovenian company which operates in the mobile telephone sector and is wholly owned by Telekom Austria Group. Mobitel telekomunikacijske storitve was the historical operator of the mobile telephone market in Slovenia before being taken over by Telekom Slovenije, a company in which the Slovenian State has a majority shareholding.

In 2009, Si.mobil lodged a complaint with the Commission criticising Mobitel's alleged strategy of ousting its competitors on the retail mobile telephone market and the wholesale mobile access and call origination services market. By decision of 2011 (Decision C (2011) 355 Final) the Commission rejected Si.mobil's complaint on the ground that, as regards the retail mobile telephone market, the Slovenian competition authority was already dealing with the case and that, as regards the wholesale mobile access and call origination services market, there was not a sufficient degree of EU interest in conducting a further investigation of the case.

The General Court upheld the rejection of Si.mobil's complaint. The Court applied for the first time Art 13(1), Regulation 1/2003 (and Recital 18 of the Regulation) in order to ensure that cases are dealt with by the most appropriate authorities within the European Competition Network.

With regard to the retail mobile telephone market, the Court stated that, under EU law, the Commission may reject a complaint where a competition authority of a Member State is already dealing with the case. For that purpose, the Commission must be satisfied, on the one hand, that a competition authority of a Member State is dealing with the case that has been referred to the Commission (first condition) and, on the other, that the case relates to the same agreement, decision of an association, or practice (second condition). Provided those two conditions are fulfilled, EU law does not lay down any rules on the allocation of powers as between the Commission and the competition authorities of the Member States, so that Si.mobil did not have a right to have the case dealt with by the Commission.

As regards the first condition, the Court found that, as the Slovenian competition authority was already actively dealing with the case, the Commission was not required to carry out an assessment as to whether the approach adopted by that authority was well founded. As regards the second condition, the Court reached the same conclusion as that of the Commission, namely that the procedure before the Slovenian competition authority concerned the same infringements, on the same market and within the same timeframe as those referred to on the retail market in the complaint submitted to the Commission by Si.mobil.

With regard to the wholesale mobile access and call origination services market, the Court rejected Si.mobil's arguments, sharing the Commission's view that there was not a sufficient degree of EU interest in conducting a further investigation of the case.

Regulation 773/2004

Article 33, Regulation 1/2003 specifically empowers the Commission to adopt measures relating to, *inter alia*, 'the form, content, and other details of complaints lodged pursuant to Article 7 and the procedure for rejecting complaints'. Pursuant to this power, Regulation 773/2004 has been adopted. Chapter IV of this Regulation deals with the handling of complaints:

CHAPTER IV
HANDLING OF COMPLAINTS
Article 5
Admissibility of complaints

1 Natural and legal persons shall show a legitimate interest in order to be entitled to lodge a complaint for the purposes of Article 7 of Regulation (EC) No 1/2003. Such complaints shall contain the information required by Form C, as set out in the Annex. The Commission may dispense with this obligation as regards part of the information, including documents, required by Form C.

2 Three paper copies as well as, if possible, an electronic copy of the complaint shall be submitted to the Commission. The complainant shall also submit a non-confidential version of the complaint, if confidentiality is claimed for any part of the complaint.

3 Complaints shall be submitted in one of the official languages of the Community [i.e. Union].

Article 6
Participation of complainants in proceedings

1 Where the Commission issues a statement of objections relating to a matter in respect of which it has received a complaint, it shall provide the complainant with a copy of the non-confidential version of the statement of objections and set a time-limit within which the complainant may make known its views in writing.

2 The Commission may, where appropriate, afford complainants the opportunity of expressing their views at the oral hearing of the parties to which a statement of objections has been issued, if complainants so request in their written comments.

Article 7
Rejection of complaints

1 Where the Commission considers that on the basis of the information in its possession there are insufficient grounds for acting on a complaint, it shall inform the complainant of its reasons and set a time-limit within which the complainant may make known its views in writing. The Commission shall not be obliged to take into account any further written submission received after the expiry of that time-limit.

2 If the complainant makes known its views within the time-limit set by the Commission and the written submissions made by the complainant do not lead to a different assessment of the complaint, the Commission shall reject the complaint by decision.

3 If the complainant fails to make known its views within the time-limit set by the Commission, the complaint shall be deemed to have been withdrawn.

Article 8
Access to information

1 Where the Commission has informed the complainant of its intention to reject a complaint pursuant to Article 7(1) the complainant may request access to the documents on which the Commission bases its provisional assessment. For this purpose, the complainant may however not have access to business secrets and other confidential information belonging to other parties involved in the proceedings.

2 The documents to which the complainant has had access in the context of proceedings conducted by the Commission under . . . [Articles 101 and 102 TFEU] may only be used by the complainant for the purposes of judicial or administrative proceedings for the application of those Treaty provisions.

Article 9

Rejections of complaints pursuant to Article 13 of Regulation (EC) No 1/2003

Where the Commission rejects a complaint pursuant to Article 13 of Regulation (EC) No 1/2003, it shall inform the complainant without delay of the national competition authority which is dealing or has already dealt with the case.

Article 5(1), Regulation 773/2004 provides that natural and legal persons who can show a legitimate interest are entitled to lodge a complaint. The complaint must be submitted in a standard format using a specific form (Art 5(1)). Following a complaint being submitted, if the Commission issues a 'statement of objections' to the party being complained about, the Commission will provide the complainant with a copy of the non-confidential version of the statement, and invite the complainant to submit written comments within a specified time-limit (Art 6(1)). There will subsequently be an oral hearing of the party against which a statement of objections has been issued. If the complainant requested in his written comments to express his views at this hearing, then he will be allowed to do so (Art 6(2)).

The Commission is entitled to reject a complaint if, on the basis of information in its possession, it considers there are insufficient grounds for acting on a complaint. In this instance, before rejecting the complaint, the Commission will inform the complainant of its view, and invite the complainant to submit written comments within the specified time-limit (Art 7(1)). If the complainant submits such written comments within the time-limit, and these comments do not lead to the Commission coming to a different conclusion, then the Commission will reject the complaint (Art 7(2)). If the complainant fails to submit any written comments then the complaint will be deemed to have been withdrawn (Art 7(3)). Under Art 8, if the Commission informs the complainant of its intention to reject a complaint, the complainant has a limited right of access to documents (Art 9).

If the Commission rejects a complaint pursuant to Art 13, Regulation 1/2003 (see above), the Commission will inform the complainant, without delay, of the national competition authority which is dealing with the case (Art 9).

Commission notice on the handling of complaints by the Commission under Articles 101 and 102 TFEU

As stated above, during 2004 the Commission issued a detailed notice on the handling of complaints by the Commission under the former Arts 81 and 82 EC Treaty (now Arts 101 and 102 TFEU) (OJ 2004 C 101/65). This notice is divided into three sections:

I   introduction and subject matter of the notice;
II   different possibilities for lodging complaints about suspected infringements of Arts 101 and 102 TFEU;
III the Commission's handling of complaints pursuant to Art 7(2), Regulation 1/2003.

The notice recognises that Regulation 1/2003 establishes a system of parallel competence for the application of Arts 101 and 102 TFEU by the Commission, and the national competition authorities and courts of the Member States (para 1). It further recognises that the Commission's action can be focused on the investigation of serious infringements of Arts 101 and 102 TFEU (para 2). There are two ways in which a complaint can be made to the Commission: (i) formally, pursuant to Art 7(2), Regulation 1/2003 (see above); or (ii) informally, for example, through the Commission's website (para 4). Part II of the notice (paras 7–25) gives indications about the choice between complaining to the Commission and bringing a lawsuit before a national court. Moreover, it recalls the principles related to the work-sharing between the Commission and the national competition authorities in the enforcement system established by Regulation 1/2003 that are explained in the 'Notice on cooperation within the network of competition authorities'.

Part III of the notice (paras 26–81) contains detailed provisions relating to:

- making a complaint pursuant to Art 7(2), Regulation 1/2003;
- assessment of complaints by the Commission;
- the Commission's procedures when dealing with complaints.

Part III is particularly informative and therefore it is set out in full (although the footnotes have been omitted):

III. THE COMMISSION'S HANDLING OF COMPLAINTS PURSUANT TO ARTICLE 7(2) OF REGULATION 1/2003
A. GENERAL

26. According to Article 7(2) of Regulation 1/2003 natural or legal persons that can show a legitimate interest are entitled to lodge a complaint to ask the Commission to find an infringement of . . . [Articles 101 and 102 TFEU] and to require that the infringement be brought to an end in accordance with Article 7(1) of Regulation 1/2003. The present part of this Notice explains the requirements applicable to complaints based on Article 7(2) of Regulation 1/2003, their assessment and the procedure followed by the Commission.

27. The Commission, unlike civil courts, whose task is to safeguard the individual rights of private persons, is an administrative authority that must act in the public interest. It is an inherent feature of the Commission's task as public enforcer that it has a margin of discretion to set priorities in its enforcement activity.

28. The Commission is entitled to give different degrees of priority to complaints made to it and may refer to the Community [i.e. Union] interest presented by a case as a criterion of priority. The Commission may reject a complaint when it considers that the case does not display a sufficient Community [i.e. Union] interest to justify further investigation. Where the Commission rejects a complaint, the complainant is entitled to a decision of the Commission without prejudice to Article 7(3) of Regulation 773/2004.

B. MAKING A COMPLAINT PURSUANT TO ARTICLE 7(2) OF REGULATION 1/2003
(a) Complaint form

29. A complaint pursuant to Article 7(2) of Regulation 1/2003 can only be made about an alleged infringement of . . . [Articles 101 and 102 TFEU] with a view to the Commission taking action under Article 7(1) of Regulation 1/2003. A complaint under Article 7(2) of Regulation 1/2003 has to comply with Form C mentioned in Article 5(1) of Regulation 773/2004 and annexed to that Regulation.

30. . . . The complaint must be submitted in three paper copies as well as, if possible, an electronic copy. In addition, the complainant must provide a non-confidential version of the complaint (Article 5(2) of Regulation 773/2004). Electronic transmission to the Commission is possible via the website indicated, the paper copies should be sent to the following address:
Commission Européenne/Europese Commissie
Competition DG B–1049
Bruxelles/Brussels

31. Form C requires complainants to submit comprehensive information in relation to their complaint. They should also provide copies of relevant supporting documentation reasonably available to them and, to the extent possible, provide indications as to where relevant information and documents that are unavailable to them could be obtained by the Commission. In particular cases, the Commission may dispense with the obligation to provide information in relation to part of the information required by Form C (Article 5(1) of Regulation 773/2004). The Commission holds the view that this possibility can in particular play a role to facilitate complaints by consumer associations where they, in the context of an otherwise substantiated complaint, do not have access to specific pieces of information from the sphere of the undertakings complained of.

32. Correspondence to the Commission that does not comply with the requirements of Article 5 of Regulation 773/2004 and therefore does not constitute a complaint within the meaning of Article 7(2) of Regulation 1/2003 will be considered by the Commission as general information that, where it is useful, may lead to an own-initiative investigation (cf. point 4 above).

(b) Legitimate interest

33. The status of formal complainant under Article 7(2) of Regulation 1/2003 is reserved to legal and natural persons who can show a legitimate interest. Member States are deemed to have a legitimate interest for all complaints they choose to lodge.

34. In the past practice of the Commission, the condition of legitimate interest was not often a matter of doubt as most complainants were in a position of being directly and adversely affected by the alleged infringement. However, there are situations where the condition of a 'legitimate interest' in Article 7(2) requires further analysis to conclude that it is fulfilled. Useful guidance can best be provided by a non-exhaustive set of examples.

35. The Court of First Instance [now renamed the General Court] has held that an association of undertakings may claim a legitimate interest in lodging a complaint regarding conduct concerning its members, even if it is not directly concerned, as an undertaking operating in the relevant market, by the conduct complained of, provided that, first, it is entitled to represent the interests of its members and, secondly, the conduct complained of is liable to adversely affect the interests of its members. Conversely, the Commission has been found to be entitled not to pursue the complaint of an association of undertakings whose members were not involved in the type of business transactions complained of.

36. From this case law, it can be inferred that undertakings (themselves or through associations that are entitled to represent their interests) can claim a legitimate interest where they are operating in the relevant market or where the conduct complained of is liable to directly and adversely affect their interests. This confirms the established practice of the Commission which has accepted that a legitimate interest can, for instance, be claimed by the parties to the agreement or practice which is the subject of the complaint, by competitors whose interests have allegedly been damaged by the behaviour complained of or by undertakings excluded from a distribution system.

37. Consumer associations can equally lodge complaints with the Commission. The Commission moreover holds the view that individual consumers whose economic interests are directly and adversely affected insofar as they are the buyers of goods or services that are the object of an infringement can be in a position to show a legitimate interest.

38. However, the Commission does not consider as a legitimate interest within the meaning of Article 7(2) the interest of persons or organisations that wish to come forward on general interest considerations without showing that they or their members are liable to be directly and adversely affected by the infringement (*pro bono publico*).

39. Local or regional public authorities may be able to show a legitimate interest in their capacity as buyers or users of goods or services affected by the conduct complained of. Conversely, they cannot be considered as showing a legitimate interest within the meaning of Article 7(2) of Regulation 1/2003 to the extent that they bring to the attention of the Commission alleged infringements *pro bono publico*.

40. Complainants have to demonstrate their legitimate interest. Where a natural or legal person lodging a complaint is unable to demonstrate a legitimate interest, the Commission is entitled, without prejudice to its right to initiate proceedings of its own initiative, not to pursue the complaint. The Commission may ascertain whether this condition is met at any stage of the investigation.

C. ASSESSMENT OF COMPLAINTS

(a) Community [i.e. Union] interest

41. Under the settled case law of the Community [i.e. Union] Courts, the Commission is not required to conduct an investigation in each case or, *a fortiori*, to take a decision within the meaning of . . . [Article 288 TFEU] on the existence or non-existence of an infringement of . . . [Articles 101 or 102 TFEU], but is entitled to give differing degrees of priority to the complaints brought before it and refer to the Community [i.e. Union] interest in order to determine the degree of priority to be applied to the various complaints it receives. The position is different only if the complaint falls within the exclusive competence of the Commission.

42. The Commission must however examine carefully the factual and legal elements brought to its attention by the complainant in order to assess the Community [i.e. Union] interest in further investigation of a case.

43. The assessment of the Community [i.e. Union] interest raised by a complaint depends on the circumstances of each individual case. Accordingly, the number of criteria of assessment to which the Commission may refer is not limited, nor is the Commission required to have recourse exclusively to certain criteria. As the factual and legal circumstances may differ considerably from case to case, it is permissible to apply new criteria which had not before been considered. Where appropriate, the Commission may give priority to a single criterion for assessing the Community [i.e. Union] interest.

44. Among the criteria which have been held relevant in the case law for the assessment of the Community [i.e. Union] interest in the (further) investigation of a case are the following:

    - The Commission can reject a complaint on the ground that the complainant can bring an action to assert its rights before national courts.
    - The Commission may not regard certain situations as excluded in principle from its purview under the task entrusted to it by the Treaty but is required to assess in each case how serious the alleged infringements are and how persistent their consequences are. This means in particular that it must take into account the duration and the extent of the infringements complained of and their effect on the competition situation in the Community [i.e. Union].
    - The Commission may have to balance the significance of the alleged infringement as regards the functioning of the common market [i.e. internal market], the probability of establishing the existence of the infringement and the scope of the investigation required in order to fulfil its task of ensuring that . . . [Articles 101 and 102 TFEU] are complied with.
    - While the Commission's discretion does not depend on how advanced the investigation of a case is, the stage of the investigation forms part of the circumstances of the case which the Commission may have to take into consideration.

    – The Commission may decide that it is not appropriate to investigate a complaint where the practices in question have ceased. However, for this purpose, the Commission will have to ascertain whether anticompetitive effects persist and if the seriousness of the infringements or the persistence of their effects does not give the complaint a Community [i.e. Union] interest.

    – The Commission may also decide that it is not appropriate to investigate a complaint where the undertakings concerned agree to change their conduct in such a way that it can consider that there is no longer a sufficient Community [i.e. Union] interest to intervene.

45. Where it forms the view that a case does not display sufficient Community [i.e. Union] interest to justify (further) investigation, the Commission may reject the complaint on that ground. Such a decision can be taken either before commencing an investigation or after taking investigative measures. However, the Commission is not obliged to set aside a complaint for lack of Community [i.e. Union] interest.

(b) Assessment under . . . [Articles 101 and 102 TFEU]

46. The examination of a complaint under . . . [Articles 101 and 102 TFEU] involves two aspects, one relating to the facts to be established to prove an infringement of . . . [Articles 101 and 102 TFEU] and the other relating to the legal assessment of the conduct complained of.

47. Where the complaint, while complying with the requirements of Article 5 of Regulation 773/2004 and Form C, does not sufficiently substantiate the allegations put forward, it may be rejected on that ground. In order to reject a complaint on the ground that the conduct complained of does not infringe the . . . [Union] competition rules or does not fall within their scope of application, the Commission is not obliged to take into account circumstances that have not been brought to its attention by the complainant and that it could only have uncovered by the investigation of the case.

48. The criteria for the legal assessment of agreements or practices under . . . [Articles 101 and 102 TFEU] cannot be dealt with exhaustively in the present Notice. However, potential complainants should refer to the extensive guidance available from the Commission, in addition to other sources and in particular the case law of the Community [i.e. Union] Courts and the case practice of the Commission. Four specific issues are mentioned in the following points with indications on where to find further guidance.

49. Agreements and practices fall within the scope of application of . . . [Articles 101 and 102 TFEU] where they are capable of affecting trade between Member States. Where an agreement or practice does not fulfil this condition, national competition law may apply, but not . . . [Union] competition law. Extensive guidance on this subject can be found in the Notice on the effect on trade concept.

50. Agreements falling within the scope of . . . [Article 101 TFEU] may be agreements of minor importance which are deemed not to restrict competition appreciably. Guidance on this issue can be found in the Commission's *de minimis* Notice.

51. Agreements that fulfil the conditions of a block exemption regulation are deemed to satisfy the conditions of . . . [Article 101(3) TFEU]. For the Commission to withdraw the benefit of the block exemption pursuant to Article 29 of Regulation 1/2003, it must find that upon individual assessment an agreement to which the exemption regulation applies has certain effects which are incompatible with . . . [Article 101(3) TFEU].

52. Agreements that restrict competition within the meaning of . . . [Article 101(1) TFEU] may fulfil the conditions of . . . [Article 101(3) TFEU]. Pursuant to Article 1(2) of Regulation 1/2003 and without a prior administrative decision being required, such agreements are not prohibited. Guidance on the conditions to be fulfilled by an agreement pursuant to . . . [Article 101(3) TFEU] can be found in the Notice on . . . [Article 101(3) TFEU].

D. THE COMMISSION'S PROCEDURES WHEN DEALING WITH COMPLAINTS

(a) Overview

53. As recalled above, the Commission is not obliged to carry out an investigation on the basis of every complaint submitted with a view to establishing whether an infringement has been committed. However, the Commission is under a duty to consider carefully the factual and legal issues brought to its attention by the complainant, in order to assess whether those issues indicate conduct which is liable to infringe . . . [Articles 101 and 102 TFEU].

54. In the Commission's procedure for dealing with complaints, different stages can be distinguished.

55. During the first stage, following the submission of the complaint, the Commission examines the complaint and may collect further information in order to decide what action it will take on the complaint. That stage may include an informal exchange of views between the Commission and the complainant with a view to clarifying the factual and legal issues with which the complaint is concerned. In this stage, the Commission may give an initial reaction to the complainant allowing the complainant an opportunity to expand on his allegations in the light of that initial reaction.

56. In the second stage, the Commission may investigate the case further with a view to initiating proceedings pursuant to Article 7(1) of Regulation 1/2003 against the undertakings complained of. Where the Commission considers that there are insufficient grounds for acting on the complaint, it will inform the complainant of its reasons and offer the complainant the opportunity to submit any further comments within a time-limit which it fixes (Article 7(1) of Regulation 773/2004).

57. If the complainant fails to make known its views within the time-limit set by the Commission, the complaint is deemed to have been withdrawn (Article 7(3) of Regulation 773/2004). In all other cases, in the third stage of the procedure, the Commission takes cognisance of the observations submitted by the complainant and either initiates a procedure against the subject of the complaint or adopts a decision rejecting the complaint.

58. Where the Commission rejects a complaint pursuant to Article 13 of Regulation 1/2003 on the grounds that another authority is dealing or has dealt with the case, the Commission proceeds in accordance with Article 9 of Regulation 773/2004.

59. Throughout the procedure, complainants benefit from a range of rights as provided in particular in Articles 6 to 8 of Regulation 773/2004. However, proceedings of the Commission in competition cases do not constitute adversarial proceedings between the complainant on the one hand and the companies which are the subject of the investigation on the other hand. Accordingly, the procedural rights of complainants are less far-reaching than the right to a fair hearing of the companies which are the subject of an infringement procedure.

(b) Indicative time-limit for informing the complainant of the Commission's proposed action

60. The Commission is under an obligation to decide on complaints within a reasonable time. What is a reasonable duration depends on the circumstances of each case and in particular, its context, the various procedural steps followed by the Commission, the conduct of the parties in the course of the procedure, the complexity of the case and its importance for the various parties involved.

61. The Commission will in principle endeavour to inform complainants of the action that it proposes to take on a complaint within an indicative time frame of four months from the reception of the complaint. Thus, subject to the circumstances of the individual case and in particular the possible need to request complementary information from the

complainant or third parties, the Commission will in principle inform the complainant within four months whether or not it intends to investigate its case further. This time-limit does not constitute a binding statutory term.

62. Accordingly, within this four-month period, the Commission may communicate its proposed course of action to the complainant as an initial reaction within the first phase of the procedure (see point 55 above). The Commission may also, where the examination of the complaint has progressed to the second stage (see point 56 above), directly proceed to informing the complainant about its provisional assessment by a letter pursuant to Article 7(1) of Regulation 773/2004.

63. To ensure the most expeditious treatment of their complaint, it is desirable that complainants cooperate diligently in the procedures, for example by informing the Commission of new developments.

(c) Procedural rights of the complainant

64. Where the Commission addresses a statement of objections to the companies complained of pursuant to Article 10(1) of Regulation 773/2004, the complainant is entitled to receive a copy of this document from which business secrets and other confidential information of the companies concerned have been removed (non-confidential version of the statement of objections; cf. Article 6(1) of Regulation 773/2004). The complainant is invited to comment in writing on the statement of objections. A time-limit will be set for such written comments.

65. Furthermore, the Commission may, where appropriate, afford complainants the opportunity of expressing their views at the oral hearing of the parties to which a statement of objections has been addressed, if the complainants so request in their written comments.

66. Complainants may submit, of their own initiative or following a request by the Commission, documents that contain business secrets or other confidential information. Confidential information will be protected by the Commission. Under Article 16 of Regulation 773/2004, complainants are obliged to identify confidential information, give reasons why the information is considered confidential and submit a separate non-confidential version when they make their views known pursuant to Article 6(1) and 7(1) of Regulation 773/2004, as well as when they subsequently submit further information in the course of the same procedure. Moreover, the Commission may, in all other cases, request complainants which produce documents or statements to identify the documents or parts of the documents or statements which they consider to be confidential. It may in particular set a deadline for the complainant to specify why it considers a piece of information to be confidential and to provide a non-confidential version, including a concise description or non-confidential version of each piece of information deleted.

67. The qualification of information as confidential does not prevent the Commission from disclosing and using information where that is necessary to prove an infringement of . . . [Articles 101 or 102 TFEU]. Where business secrets and confidential information are necessary to prove an infringement, the Commission must assess for each individual document whether the need to disclose is greater than the harm which might result from disclosure.

68. Where the Commission takes the view that a complaint should not be further examined, because there is no sufficient Community [i.e. Union] interest in pursuing the case further or on other grounds, it will inform the complainant in the form of a letter which indicates its legal basis (Article 7(1) of Regulation 773/2004), sets out the reasons that have led the Commission to provisionally conclude in the sense indicated and provides the complainant with the opportunity to submit supplementary information or

observations within a time-limit set by the Commission. The Commission will also indicate the consequences of not replying pursuant to Article 7(3) of Regulation 773/2004, as explained below.

69. Pursuant to Article 8(1) of Regulation 773/2004, the complainant has the right to access the information on which the Commission bases its preliminary view. Such access is normally provided by annexing to the letter a copy of the relevant documents.

70. The time-limit for observations by the complainant on the letter pursuant to Article 7(1) of Regulation 773/2004 will be set in accordance with the circumstances of the case. It will not be shorter than four weeks (Article 17(2) of Regulation 773/2004). If the complainant does not respond within the time-limit set, the complaint is deemed to have been withdrawn pursuant to Article 7(3) of Regulation 773/2004. Complainants are also entitled to withdraw their complaint at any time if they so wish.

71. The complainant may request an extension of the time-limit for the provision of comments. Depending on the circumstances of the case, the Commission may grant such an extension.

72. In that case, where the complainant submits supplementary observations, the Commission takes cognisance of those observations. Where they are of such a nature as to make the Commission change its previous course of action, it may initiate a procedure against the companies complained of. In this procedure, the complainant has the procedural rights explained above.

73. Where the observations of the complainant do not alter the Commission's proposed course of action, it rejects the complaint by decision.

(d) The Commission decision rejecting a complaint

74. Where the Commission rejects a complaint by decision pursuant to Article 7(2) of Regulation 773/2004, it must state the reasons in accordance with . . . [Article 296 TFEU], i.e. in a way that is appropriate to the act at issue and takes into account the circumstances of each case.

75. The statement of reasons must disclose in a clear and unequivocal fashion the reasoning followed by the Commission in such a way as to enable the complainant to ascertain the reasons for the decision and to enable the competent Community [i.e. Union] Court to exercise its power of review. However, the Commission is not obliged to adopt a position on all the arguments relied on by the complainant in support of its complaint. It only needs to set out the facts and legal considerations which are of decisive importance in the context of the decision.

76. Where the Commission rejects a complaint in a case that also gives rise to a decision pursuant to Article 10 of Regulation 1/2003 (Finding of inapplicability of . . . [Articles 101 or 102 TFEU]) or Article 9 of Regulation 1/2003 (Commitments), the decision rejecting a complaint may refer to that other decision adopted on the basis of the provisions mentioned.

77. A decision to reject a complaint is subject to appeal before the Community Courts.

78. A decision rejecting a complaint prevents complainants from requiring the reopening of the investigation unless they put forward significant new evidence. Accordingly, further correspondence on the same alleged infringement by former complainants cannot be regarded as a new complaint unless significant new evidence is brought to the attention of the Commission. However, the Commission may re-open a file under appropriate circumstances.

79. A decision to reject a complaint does not definitively rule on the question of whether or not there is an infringement of . . . [Articles 101 or 102 TFEU], even where the Commission has assessed the facts on the basis of . . . [Articles 101 and 102 TFEU]. The assessments made by the Commission in a decision rejecting a complaint therefore do not prevent

a Member State court or competition authority from applying . . . [Articles 101 and 102 TFEU] to agreements and practices brought before it. The assessments made by the Commission in a decision rejecting a complaint constitute facts which Member States' courts or competition authorities may take into account in examining whether the agreements or conduct in question are in conformity with . . . [Articles 101 and 102 TFEU].

(e) Specific situations

80. According to Article 8 of Regulation 1/2003 the Commission may on its own initiative order interim measures where there is the risk of serious and irreparable damage to competition. Article 8 of Regulation 1/2003 makes it clear that interim measures cannot be applied for by complainants under Article 7(2) of Regulation 1/2003. Requests for interim measures by undertakings can be brought before Member States' courts which are well placed to decide on such measures.

81. Some persons may wish to inform the Commission about suspected infringements of . . . [Articles 101 or 102 TFEU] without having their identity revealed to the undertakings concerned by the allegations. These persons are welcome to contact the Commission. The Commission is bound to respect an informant's request for anonymity, unless the request to remain anonymous is manifestly unjustified.

Applications by parties to a possible infringement

Regulation 1/2003

Objective 3

Under the former Regulation 17/62, the Commission was spending a disproportionate amount of time in dealing with applications for negative clearance (with regard to what are now Arts 101(1) and 102 TFEU) and applications for exemption (with regard to what is now Art 101(3) TFEU). Regulation 1/2003 changed this dramatically, and undertakings are no longer able to make such applications to the Commission. The Commission is empowered to make a 'finding of inapplicability' pursuant to Art 10, Regulation 1/2003:

> Where the Community [i.e. Union] public interest relating to the application of . . . [Articles 101 and 102 TFEU] so requires, the Commission, acting on its own initiative, may by decision find that . . . [Article 101 TFEU] is not applicable to an agreement, a decision by an association of undertakings or a concerted practice, either because the conditions of . . . [Article 101(1) TFEU] are not fulfilled, or because the conditions of . . . [Article 101(3) TFEU] are satisfied.

The Commission may likewise make such a finding with reference to Art 102 TFEU.

Guidance letters

However, in very limited circumstances the Commission is empowered to issue a guidance letter. To support the new procedural regime brought in by Regulation 1/2003, the Commission has issued a non-legally enforceable notice: 'Informal Guidance relating to novel questions concerning . . . [Arts 101 and 102 TFEU] that arise in individual cases (guidance letters)' (OJ 2004 C 101/78). In cases which give rise to genuine uncertainty because they present novel or unresolved questions for the application of Arts 101 and 102 TFEU, individual undertakings may seek informal guidance from the Commission (para 5 of the Guidance). If it is considered appropriate, the Commission may provide such guidance in a written statement, referred to as a 'guidance letter'. However, a guidance letter may only be issued by the Commission if the following cumulative conditions apply:

1 The substantive assessment of an agreement or practice with regard to . . . [Articles 101 and/or 102 TFEU], poses a question of application of the law for which there is no clarification in the existing . . . [Union] legal framework including the case law of the Community [i.e. Union] Courts, nor publicly available general guidance or precedent in decision-making practice or previous guidance letters.

2 A *prima facie* evaluation of the specificities and background of the case suggests that the clarification of the novel question through a guidance letter is useful, taking into account the following elements:
   – the economic importance from the point of view of the consumer of the goods or services concerned by the agreement or practice; and/or
   – the extent to which the agreement or practice corresponds or is liable to correspond to more widely spread economic usage in the marketplace; and/or
   – the extent of the investments linked to the transaction in relation to the size of the companies concerned and the extent to which the transaction relates to a structural operation such as the creation of a non-full function joint venture.

3 It is possible to issue a guidance letter on the basis of the information provided, i.e. no further fact-finding is required. (para 8 of the Guidance)

Furthermore, the Commission will not consider a request for a guidance letter in either of the following circumstances:

   – the questions raised in the request are identical or similar to issues raised in a case pending before the . . . [Court of Justice of the European Union];
   – the agreement or practice to which the request refers is subject to proceedings pending with the Commission, a Member State court or Member State competition authority. (para 9 of the Guidance)

Paragraph 10 of the Guidance provides that the Commission will not consider hypothetical questions and:

   will not issue guidance letters on agreements or practices that are no longer being implemented by the parties. Undertakings may however present a request for a guidance letter to the Commission in relation to questions raised by an agreement or practice that they envisage, i.e. before the implementation of that agreement or practice. In this case the transaction must have reached a sufficiently advanced stage for a request to be considered.

The provision of information

Regulation 1/2003 has refined the procedural rules relating to the gathering of information, ensuring that such rules are compliant with the case law of the Court of Justice and the General Court which related to the former Regulation 17/62.

Article 18(6), Regulation 1/2003 provides the Commission with the power to request all necessary information from the governments and competition authorities of the Member States. The Commission may also, by simple request or decision, require undertakings or associations of undertakings to provide all necessary information (Art 18(1)). A copy will be sent to the relevant national competition authority (Art 18(5)). If the Commission seeks the information from an undertaking or association of undertakings by *simple request*, then the Commission shall:

● state the legal basis and the purpose of the request;

- specify what information is required;
- specify the time-limit within which the information must be provided;
- indicate the penalties provided for in Art 23, Regulation 1/2003 if incorrect or misleading information is supplied (Art 18(2), Regulation 1/2003).

If the Commission seeks the information from an undertaking or association of undertakings by *decision*, then in addition to the above, the Commission shall: (i) indicate or impose the penalties provided for in Art 24, Regulation 1/2003 (i.e. periodic penalty payments); and (ii) indicate the right to have the decision reviewed by the Court of Justice.

The preamble to Regulation 1/2003 provides that:

> The Commission should be empowered throughout the Community [i.e. Union] to require such information to be supplied as is necessary to detect any agreement, decision or concerted practice prohibited by . . . [Article 101 TFEU] or any abuse of a dominant position prohibited by . . . [Article 102 TFEU]. When complying with a decision of the Commission, **undertakings cannot be forced to admit that they have committed an infringement, but they are in any event obliged to answer factual questions and to provide documents, even if this information may be used to establish against them or against another undertaking the existence of an infringement.** (para 23) [emphasis added]

The emphasised words, although they do not appear in the main body of the Regulation, embrace the decisions of the Court of Justice and the General Court which related to the former Regulation 17/62.

Powers of investigation

Regulation 1/2003

Objective 4

Compared to the former Regulation 17/62, Regulation 1/2003 provides greater clarification of the Commission's powers of inspection, and also the role of the national competition authorities and courts of the Member States with regard to inspections.

The Regulation empowers the Commission to undertake such inspections as are necessary to detect any agreement, decision or concerted practice prohibited by Art 101 TFEU or any abuse of a dominant position prohibited by Art 102 TFEU. Article 20(1), Regulation 1/2003 provides that, in order to carry out the duties assigned to it by the Regulation, the Commission 'may conduct all necessary inspections of undertakings and associations of undertakings'. The competition authorities of the Member States are required to actively assist the Commission in the exercise of these powers, if the Commission makes a request for assistance (Art 20(5)). In addition, if an undertaking opposes an inspection 'the Member State concerned shall afford them [i.e. the inspectors] the necessary assistance, requesting where appropriate the assistance of the police or of an equivalent enforcement authority, so as to enable them to conduct their inspection' (Art 20(6)). Article 20(7) provides that if this assistance requires authorisation from a national court, then such authorisation must be applied for, and in any event authorisation may be applied for as a precautionary measure. Article 20(8) sets out the role of the national court when considering an application for authorisation under Art 20(7):

> Where authorisation as referred to in paragraph 7 is applied for, the national judicial authority shall control that the Commission decision is authentic and that the coercive measures envisaged are neither arbitrary nor excessive having regard to the subject matter of the inspection.

In its control of the proportionality of the coercive measures, the national judicial authority may ask the Commission, directly or through the Member State competition authority, for detailed explanations in particular on the grounds the Commission has for suspecting infringement of . . . [Articles 101 and 102 TFEU], as well as on the seriousness of the suspected infringement and on the nature of the involvement of the undertaking concerned. However, the national judicial authority may not call into question the necessity for the inspection nor demand that it be provided with the information in the Commission's file. The lawfulness of the Commission decision shall be subject to review only by the Court of Justice.

Detection of infringements of the competition rules is difficult. The former Art 14(1), Regulation 17/62 provided that officials authorised by the Commission were empowered to:

- examine the books and other business records;
- take copies of, or extracts from, the books and business records;
- ask for oral explanations on the spot;
- enter any premises, land, and means of transport of undertakings.

In order to protect competition effectively, the Commission's powers of investigation have been increased. Article 20(2), Regulation 1/2003 additionally empowers the Commission to interview any representative or member of staff of the relevant undertaking 'for explanations on facts or documents relating to the subject -matter and purpose of the inspection and to record the answers'. Article 20(2) also provides that in the course of an inspection, officials authorised by the Commission are empowered to affix seals to any business premises and books or records 'for the period and to the extent necessary for the inspection'.

Officials authorised by the Commission to act in relation to these powers of inspection are entitled to exercise them on production of an authorisation in writing, specifying the subject matter and purpose of the investigation and the penalties (under Art 23) for supplying incomplete books and other business records or where the answers to questions asked under Art 20(2) are incorrect or misleading (Art 20(3)). Undertakings are obliged to submit to investigations ordered by a decision of the Commission (Art 20(4)). In addition to the above information, the undertaking must also be informed of the date of the inspection, an indication of the periodical penalty payments which may be applied under Art 24, and of the undertaking's right to have the decision reviewed by the Court of Justice. In good time before the investigation the Commission has to inform the relevant authority in the host Member State (Art 20(3) and (4)).

In order to safeguard the effectiveness of inspections, Art 21 empowers officials and other persons authorised by the Commission to enter any premises where business records may be kept, including private homes. However, the exercise of this power is subject to the Commission adopting a decision, and the prior authorisation of the national court. Article 21, Regulation 1/2003 provides as follows:

1 If a reasonable suspicion exists that books or other records related to the business and to the subject matter of the inspection, which may be relevant to prove a serious violation of . . . [Articles 101 or 102 TFEU], are being kept in any other premises, land and means of transport, including the homes of directors, managers and other members of staff of the undertakings and associations of undertakings concerned, the Commission can by decision order an inspection to be conducted in such other premises, land and means of transport.

2 The decision shall specify the subject matter and purpose of the inspection, appoint the date on which it is to begin and indicate the right to have the decision reviewed by the

Court of Justice. It shall in particular state the reasons that have led the Commission to conclude that a suspicion in the sense of paragraph 1 exists. The Commission shall take such decisions after consulting the competition authority of the Member State in whose territory the inspection is to be conducted.

3 A decision adopted pursuant to paragraph 1 cannot be executed without prior authorisation from the national judicial authority of the Member State concerned. The national judicial authority shall control that the Commission decision is authentic and that the coercive measures envisaged are neither arbitrary nor excessive having regard in particular to the seriousness of the suspected infringement, to the importance of the evidence sought, to the involvement of the undertaking concerned and to the reasonable likelihood that business books and records relating to the subject matter of the inspection are kept in the premises for which the authorisation is requested. The national judicial authority may ask the Commission, directly or through the Member State competition authority, for detailed explanations on those elements which are necessary to allow its control of the proportionality of the coercive measures envisaged. However, the national judicial authority may not call into question the necessity for the inspection nor demand that it be provided with information in the Commission's file. The lawfulness of the Commission decision shall be subject to review only by the Court of Justice.

4 The officials and other accompanying persons authorised by the Commission to conduct an inspection ordered in accordance with paragraph 1 of this Article shall have the powers set out in Article 20(2)(a), (b) and (c). Article 20(5) and (6) shall apply *mutatis mutandis*.

In order to assist the competition authorities of the Member States to apply Arts 101 and 102 TFEU effectively, it was considered expedient to enable them to support one another (and the Commission) by carrying out inspections and other fact-finding measures. Article 22, Regulation 1/2003 provides as follows:

1 The competition authority of a Member State may in its own territory carry out any inspection or other fact-finding measure under its national law on behalf and for the account of the competition authority of another Member State in order to establish whether there has been an infringement of . . . [Articles 101 or 102 TFEU]. Any exchange and use of the information collected shall be carried out in accordance with Article 12.

2 At the request of the Commission, the competition authorities of the Member States shall undertake the inspections which the Commission considers to be necessary under Article 20(1) or which it has ordered by decision pursuant to Article 20(4). The officials of the competition authorities of the Member States who are responsible for conducting these inspections as well as those authorised or appointed by them shall exercise their powers in accordance with their national law.

If so requested by the Commission or by the competition authority of the Member State in whose territory the inspection is to be conducted, officials and other accompanying persons authorised by the Commission may assist the officials of the authority concerned.

There is an obligation that information obtained during the course of an investigation shall only be used for the purpose for which it was acquired (Art 28(1), Regulation 1/2003). Article 28(2), Regulation 1/2003 sets out the undertaking's right to professional secrecy.

Regulation 773/2004

Article 33(1), Regulation 1/2003 specifically empowers the Commission to adopt measures 'as may be appropriate in order to apply this Regulation'. As discussed above, Regulation 773/2004 was adopted pursuant to this power. Chapter III of this Regulation deals with investigations by the Commission, with regard to the power to take statements (Art 3) and ask questions during inspections (Art 4). The power to take statements is set out in Art 19, Regulation 1/2003:

1   In order to carry out the duties assigned to it by this Regulation, the Commission may interview any natural or legal person who consents to be interviewed for the purpose of collecting information relating to the subject-matter of an investigation.

2   Where an interview pursuant to paragraph 1 is conducted in the premises of an undertaking, the Commission shall inform the competition authority of the Member State in whose territory the interview takes place. If so requested by the competition authority of that Member State, its officials may assist the officials and other accompanying persons authorised by the Commission to conduct the interview.

With regard to the power to take statements, Art 3, Regulation 773/2004 provides that:

1   Where the Commission interviews a person with his consent in accordance with Article 19 of Regulation (EC) No 1/2003, it shall, at the beginning of the interview, state the legal basis and the purpose of the interview, and recall its voluntary nature. It shall also inform the person interviewed of its intention to make a record of the interview.

2   The interview may be conducted by any means including by telephone or electronic means.

3   The Commission may record the statements made by the persons interviewed in any form. A copy of any recording shall be made available to the person interviewed for approval. Where necessary, the Commission shall set a time-limit within which the person interviewed may communicate to it any correction to be made to the statement.

With regard to the power to ask questions, Art 4, Regulation 773/2004 provides that:

1   When, pursuant to Article 20(2)(e) of Regulation (EC) No 1/2003, officials or other accompanying persons authorised by the Commission ask representatives or members of staff of an undertaking or of an association of undertakings for explanations, the explanations given may be recorded in any form.

2   A copy of any recording made pursuant to paragraph 1 shall be made available to the undertaking or association of undertakings concerned after the inspection.

3   In cases where a member of staff of an undertaking or of an association of undertakings who is not or was not authorised by the undertaking or by the association of undertakings to provide explanations on behalf of the undertaking or association of undertakings has been asked for explanations, the Commission shall set a time-limit within which the undertaking or the association of undertakings may communicate to the Commission any rectification, amendment or supplement to the explanations given by such member of staff. The rectification, amendment or supplement shall be added to the explanations as recorded pursuant to paragraph 1.

The right to a hearing

Regulation 1/2003

Article 27, Regulation 1/2003 concerns the hearing of the parties, complainants and others. Article 27(1) provides that before the Commission makes a decision pursuant to: (i) Art 7 in relation to an infringement of Arts 101 or 102 TFEU; (ii) Art 8 in relation to interim measures; (iii) Art 23 in relation to fines; or (iv) Art 24(2) in relation to periodic penalty payments, the undertakings which are the subject of the proceedings shall be given the opportunity of being heard on the matters to which the Commission has taken objection. The rights of defence of the parties shall be fully respected in the proceedings (Art 27(2)). The parties will be entitled to have access to the Commission's file, subject to the 'legitimate interest of undertakings in the protection of their business secrets'; however, this right of access will not extend to confidential information and internal documents of either the Commission or the national competition authorities of the Member States (Art 27(2)). The Commission has issued a notice, clarifying both the extent and the exercise of the right of access to the Commission's file in cases pursuant to Arts 101 and 102 TFEU (OJ 2005 C 325/7).

The Commission has the right to hear any other natural or legal person, provided such a person shows a sufficient interest (Art 27(3)). The national competition authorities of the Member States may request the Commission to hear other natural or legal persons (Art 27(3)).

If the Commission intends adopting a decision pursuant to: (i) Art 9 with regard to commitments made by an undertaking, or (ii) Art 10 in relation to a finding of inapplicability, the Commission will publish a concise summary of the case and the main content of the commitments or the proposed course of action (Art 27(4)).

Regulation 773/2004

Chapter V (Arts 10–14), Regulation 773/2004 concerns the exercise of the right to be heard. Chapter V provides as follows:

CHAPTER V
EXERCISE OF THE RIGHT TO BE HEARD
Article 10
Statement of objections and reply
1   The Commission shall inform the parties concerned in writing of the objections raised against them. The statement of objections shall be notified to each of them.
2   The Commission shall, when notifying the statement of objections to the parties concerned, set a time-limit within which these parties may inform it in writing of their views. The Commission shall not be obliged to take into account written submissions received after the expiry of that time-limit.
3   The parties may, in their written submissions, set out all facts known to them which are relevant to their defence against the objections raised by the Commission. They shall attach any relevant documents as proof of the facts set out. They shall provide a paper original as well as an electronic copy or, where they do not provide an electronic copy, 28 paper copies of their submission and of the documents attached to it. They may propose that the Commission hear persons who may corroborate the facts set out in their submission.

Article 11
Right to be heard
1   The Commission shall give the parties to whom it has addressed a statement of objections the opportunity to be heard before consulting the Advisory Committee referred to in Article 14(1) of Regulation (EC) No 1/2003.
2   The Commission shall, in its decisions, deal only with objections in respect of which the parties referred to in paragraph 1 have been able to comment.

Article 12
Right to an oral hearing

The Commission shall give the parties to whom it has addressed a statement of objections the opportunity to develop their arguments at an oral hearing, if they so request in their written submissions.

Article 13
Hearing of other persons

1 If natural or legal persons other than those referred to in Articles 5 and 11 apply to be heard and show a sufficient interest, the Commission shall inform them in writing of the nature and subject matter of the procedure and shall set a time-limit within which they may make known their views in writing.
2 The Commission may, where appropriate, invite persons referred to in paragraph 1 to develop their arguments at the oral hearing of the parties to whom a statement of objections has been addressed, if the persons referred to in paragraph 1 so request in their written comments.
3 The Commission may invite any other person to express its views in writing and to attend the oral hearing of the parties to whom a statement of objections has been addressed. The Commission may also invite such persons to express their views at that oral hearing.

Article 14
Conduct of oral hearings

1 Hearings shall be conducted by a Hearing Officer in full independence.
2 The Commission shall invite the persons to be heard to attend the oral hearing on such date as it shall determine.
3 The Commission shall invite the competition authorities of the Member States to take part in the oral hearing. It may likewise invite officials and civil servants of other authorities of the Member States.
4 Persons invited to attend shall either appear in person or be represented by legal representatives or by representatives authorised by their constitution as appropriate. Undertakings and associations of undertakings may also be represented by a duly authorised agent appointed from among their permanent staff.
5 Persons heard by the Commission may be assisted by their lawyers or other qualified persons admitted by the Hearing Officer.
6 Oral hearings shall not be public. Each person may be heard separately or in the presence of other persons invited to attend, having regard to the legitimate interest of the undertakings in the protection of their business secrets and other confidential information.
7 The Hearing Officer may allow the parties to whom a statement of objections has been addressed, the complainants, other persons invited to the hearing, the Commission services and the authorities of the Member States to ask questions during the hearing.
8 The statements made by each person heard shall be recorded. Upon request, the recording of the hearing shall be made available to the persons who attended the hearing. Regard shall be had to the legitimate interest of the parties in the protection of their business secrets and other confidential information.

The decision

Objective
5

There is a general principle of Union law contained in Art 296 TFEU (previously Art 253 EC Treaty) that 'legal acts [which includes decisions] shall state the reasons on which they are based'. They should also be made by the Commission according to the proper procedure and according to the proper form. Failure to observe these principles may render the decision a nullity from the start:

Commission v BASF AG and Others (Case C-137/92P)

The CFI (now the General Court) had declared a Commission decision non-existent. The decision had declared that the applicants and others had infringed what is now Art 101 TFEU (previously Art 81 EC Treaty) in relation to the production of PVC (Commission Decision 89/190/EEC of 21 December 1988). The CFI had found that the original decision had been altered after it had been adopted by the Commissioners 'by persons who were clearly not Commissioners'. The CFI also found that the contested decision had been adopted only in its English, German and French versions, leaving it to the Commissioner then responsible for competition, Mr Sutherland, to adopt the text of the decision in the other official languages of the Union. The CFI noted that Mr Sutherland had no competence to do this and held that the measure was 'vitiated by particularly serious and manifest defects rendering it non-existent in law'.

The Commission appealed against this decision, and the appeal was allowed by the Court of Justice. The Court pointed out that, as a general rule, acts of the Union institutions are presumed to be lawful and productive of legal effects even if affected by irregularities, until such time as they are annulled or withdrawn. There was, however, an exception to that rule in relation to acts:

> . . . tainted by an irregularity whose gravity is so obvious that it cannot be tolerated by the Community [i.e. Union] legal order. [Such acts] . . . must be treated as having no legal effect, even provisional, that is to say that they must be regarded as legally non-existent. The purpose of this exception is to maintain a balance between two fundamental, but sometimes conflicting, requirements with which a legal order must comply, namely stability of legal relations and respect for legality.

The Court of Justice emphasised the collegiate nature of the Commission's decision-making process. It rejected the Commission's argument that in the decision-making process the college of Commissioners can confine itself to making clear its intention without having to become involved in the drafting and finalisation of the act giving effect to its intention. After the final form of the decision had been approved by the Commissioners as a body, only simple corrections of spelling and grammar could be made to the text. In the event, however, the Court of Justice thought that the CFI had gone too far in holding the decision to be non-existent. It was, however, annulled on the same procedural grounds on which the CFI decision had been based.

Under Art 7(1), Regulation 1/2003, if the Commission decides that there has been an infringement of Arts 101 or 102 TFEU, the Commission is empowered to adopt a decision ordering that the infringement be brought to an end. Article 24(1), Regulation 1/2003 empowers the Commission to impose a periodic penalty payment 'not exceeding 5% of the average daily turnover in the preceding business year per day and calculated from the date appointed by the decision' (Art 24(1)). This daily penalty is payable until the infringement is brought to an end. Fines can also be imposed on the undertaking (Art 23).

Judicial review of Commission decisions

Like any other legal act of the institutions, decisions made by the Commission in relation to alleged infringements, including findings of infringements and the imposition of fines and periodic penalty payments, are subject to judicial review. The General Court may review such acts under Art 263 TFEU (previously Art 230 EC Treaty); see Chapter 8. Decisions of the General Court can be appealed on a point of law to the Court of Justice. The General Court, when reviewing the legality of the decision of the Commission, has the power not only to quash any decision, but also to reduce or increase any fine or periodic penalty payment imposed by the Commission (Art 261 TFEU; Art 31, Regulation 1/2003).

Regulation 1/2003: interim measures, commitments and finding of inapplicability

Regulation 1/2003 provides for three other types of decision to be taken by the Commission. Article 8 empowers the Commission to adopt a decision ordering interim measures, provided it is an urgent case where there is a risk of 'serious and irreparable damage to competition' and provided that there is a *prima facie* finding of infringement. Article 9 provides that if the Commission intends to adopt a decision relating to an infringement of Arts 101 or 102 TFEU, and the undertaking concerned offers commitments to meet the Commission's concerns, then the Commission is empowered to adopt a decision making those commitments binding on the undertaking(s). Article 10 provides that if the Union public interest relating to the application of Arts 101 and 102 TFEU so requires, the Commission may adopt a decision finding that Art 101 TFEU is not applicable to a particular agreement, either because the Art 101(1) TFEU conditions are not fulfilled or because the conditions of Art 101(3) TFEU are satisfied. The Commission can also make such a decision with reference to Art 102 TFEU.

Fines and periodic penalty payments

Article 23, Regulation 1/2003 is concerned with the Commission's power to impose fines, and Art 24 with the power to impose periodic penalty payments. Article 23, Regulation 1/2003 provides that:

1 The Commission may by decision impose on undertakings and associations of undertakings fines not exceeding 1 per cent of the total turnover in the preceding business year where, intentionally or negligently:
   (a) they supply incorrect or misleading information in response to a request made pursuant to Article 17 or Article 18(2);
   (b) in response to a request made by decision adopted pursuant to Article 17 or Article 18(3), they supply incorrect, incomplete or misleading information or do not supply information within the required time-limit;
   (c) they produce the required books or other records related to the business in incomplete form during inspections under Article 20 or refuse to submit to inspections ordered by a decision adopted pursuant to Article 20(4);
   (d) in response to a question asked in accordance with Article 20(2)(e),
      – they give an incorrect or misleading answer,
      – they fail to rectify within a time-limit set by the Commission an incorrect, incomplete or misleading answer given by a member of staff, or
      – they fail or refuse to provide a complete answer on facts relating to the subject-matter and purpose of an inspection ordered by a decision adopted pursuant to Article 20(4);

     (e) seals affixed in accordance with Article 20(2)(d) by officials or other accompanying persons authorised by the Commission have been broken.

2 The Commission may by decision impose fines on undertakings and associations of undertakings where, either intentionally or negligently:

    (a) they infringe . . . [Articles 101 or 102 TFEU]; or

    (b) they contravene a decision ordering interim measures under Article 8; or

    (c) they fail to comply with a commitment made binding by a decision pursuant to Article 9.

For each undertaking and association of undertakings participating in the infringement, the fine shall not exceed 10 per cent of its total turnover in the preceding business year.

Where the infringement of an association relates to the activities of its members, the fine shall not exceed 10 per cent of the sum of the total turnover of each member active on the market affected by the infringement of the association.

3 In fixing the amount of the fine, regard shall be had both to the gravity and to the duration of the infringement.

4 When a fine is imposed on an association of undertakings taking account of the turnover of its members and the association is not solvent, the association is obliged to call for contributions from its members to cover the amount of the fine.

Where such contributions have not been made to the association within a time-limit fixed by the Commission, the Commission may require payment of the fine directly by any of the undertakings whose representatives were members of the decision-making bodies concerned of the association.

After the Commission has required payment under the second subparagraph, where necessary to ensure full payment of the fine, the Commission may require payment of the balance by any of the members of the association which were active on the market on which the infringement occurred.

However, the Commission shall not require payment under the second or the third subparagraph from undertakings which show that they have not implemented the infringing decision of the association and either were not aware of its existence or have actively distanced themselves from it before the Commission started investigating the case.

The financial liability of each undertaking in respect of the payment of the fine shall not exceed 10 per cent of its total turnover in the preceding business year.

5 Decisions taken pursuant to paragraphs 1 and 2 shall not be of a criminal law nature.

The following case came before the General Court and concerned a Commission Decision where an undertaking was fined pursuant to Art 23(1)(e), Regulation 1/2003:

E.ON Energie v Commission (Case T-141/08)

During an investigation into alleged anti-competitive practices on the German electricity market, the Commission carried out inspections at the Munich premises of E.ON Energie AG, a wholly owned subsidiary of E.ON AG. Being unable to complete the inspection in a single day, documents which had been selected for a more detailed examination were placed in a room made available to the Commission by E.ON Energie. The door to this room was locked and an official seal of the Commission was affixed to it. The key to the door was taken by the inspectors. Later, however, it became apparent that 20 other 'master keys', which would open the door to the room, were also in circulation.

The Commission's seals are plastic stickers. If they are removed they do not tear but the word 'VOID' irreversibly appears on its surface. When the inspection team returned to the premises on the morning of the second day, it was noticed that the word 'VOID' was visible on the seal that had been affixed the previous evening.

By a decision dated 30 January 2008, the Commission imposed a fine of 38 million euros on E.ON Energie for having broken the seal affixed during this inspection.

E.ON Energie brought an action before the General Court requesting that the Commission's decision be annulled, or at least that the fine be reduced.

The General Court rejected the application, ruling that the Commission was entitled in law to consider in the present case that, at the very least, the seal had been negligently broken. E.ON Energie was required to take all necessary measures to prevent any tampering with the seal, having been clearly informed of the significance of the seal and the consequences of any breach.

The General Court also ruled that the fine imposed on E.ON Energie, which amounted to approximately 0.14 per cent of its turnover, was not disproportionate to the infringement given the particularly serious nature of breaking a seal, the size of the company and the need to ensure a sufficiently dissuasive effect of the fine so as to ensure that it is not advantageous for a company to break a seal affixed by the Commission during its inspections.

Article 24, Regulation 1/2003 provides that:

1 The Commission may, by decision, impose on undertakings or associations of undertakings periodic penalty payments not exceeding 5 per cent of the average daily turnover in the preceding business year per day and calculated from the date appointed by the decision, in order to compel them:

   (a) to put an end to an infringement of . . . [Articles 101 or 102 TFEU], in accordance with a decision taken pursuant to Article 7;

   (b) to comply with a decision ordering interim measures taken pursuant to Article 8;

   (c) to comply with a commitment made binding by a decision pursuant to Article 9;

   (d) to supply complete and correct information which it has requested by decision taken pursuant to Article 17 or Article 18(3);

   (e) to submit to an inspection which it has ordered by decision taken pursuant to Article 20(4).

2 Where the undertakings or associations of undertakings have satisfied the obligation which the periodic penalty payment was intended to enforce, the Commission may fix the definitive amount of the periodic penalty payment at a figure lower than that which would arise under the original decision. Article 23(4) shall apply correspondingly.

Guidelines

The Guidelines on the method of setting fines imposed pursuant to Art 23(2)(a), Regulation 1/2003 seek to increase the deterrent effect of fines. Regulation 1/2003 (as with Council Regulation 17/62 before it) provides that companies may be fined up to 10 per cent of their total annual turnover. Within this limit, the Guidelines provide that fines may be based on up to 30 per cent of the company's annual sales to which the infringement relates, multiplied by the number of years of participation in the infringement. Moreover, a part of the fine – the so-called 'entry fee' – may be imposed irrespective of the duration of the infringement. Repeat offenders will also be fined more than in the past.

In order to deter companies from ever entering into seriously illegal conduct, the Commission may add to the amount as calculated above a sum equal to 15 per cent to 25 per cent of the yearly relevant sales, whatever the duration of the infringement. According to the Guidelines, such an 'entry fee' will be applied in cartel cases and may be applied in other types of anti-trust infringements. The mere fact that a company enters into a cartel could 'cost' it at least 15–25 per cent of its yearly turnover in the relevant product.

If an undertaking has been found to have been previously involved in one or more similar infringements, the Guidelines provide that each prior infringement will justify an increase of the fine by up to 100 per cent.

Leniency notice

The Commission has issued a Notice (Immunity from fines and reduction of fines in cartel cases (OJ 2006 C 298/17)). The policy of leniency is designed to encourage firms which are involved in cartels to inform the competition authorities of their involvement (a form of whistle-blowing), in return for total immunity or a reduction of the fines which would otherwise be imposed.

Relationship between the Commission, and the competition authorities and courts of the Member States

Objective 6

As discussed above and in Chapters 20 and 21, Regulation 1/2003 changed the role of the Commission, and the competition authorities and courts of the Member States with regard to the application of Arts 101 and 102 TFEU. Article 5, Regulation 1/2003 has empowered the competition authorities of the Member States to apply Arts 101 and 102 TFEU in their entirety; Art 6 has provided the same power to the courts of the Member States. This has had the most profound impact with regard to the application of Art 101(3) TFEU; see above and Chapter 20.

Article 35, Regulation 1/2003 provides that Member States will designate the competition authority or authorities (which could include the courts) responsible for the application of Arts 101 and 102 TFEU. The competition authorities must be able to effectively comply with the Regulation. Articles 11 and 12, Regulation 1/2003 are particularly relevant to the interaction between the Commission and national competition authorities. Article 11, Regulation 1/2003 provides as follows:

Cooperation between the Commission and the competition authorities of the Member States

1   The Commission and the competition authorities of the Member States shall apply the Community [i.e. Union] competition rules in close cooperation.

2   The Commission shall transmit to the competition authorities of the Member States copies of the most important documents it has collected with a view to applying Articles 7, 8, 9, 10 and Article 29(1). At the request of the competition authority of a Member State, the Commission shall provide it with a copy of other existing documents necessary for the assessment of the case.

3   The competition authorities of the Member States shall, when acting under . . . [Article 101 or Article 102 TFEU], inform the Commission in writing before or without delay after commencing the first formal investigative measure. This information may also be made available to the competition authorities of the other Member States.

4   No later than 30 days before the adoption of a decision requiring that an infringement be brought to an end, accepting commitments or withdrawing the benefit of a block exemption Regulation, the competition authorities of the Member States shall inform the Commission. To that effect, they shall provide the Commission with a summary of the

case, the envisaged decision or, in the absence thereof, any other document indicating the proposed course of action. This information may also be made available to the competition authorities of the other Member States. At the request of the Commission, the acting competition authority shall make available to the Commission other documents it holds which are necessary for the assessment of the case. The information supplied to the Commission may be made available to the competition authorities of the other Member States. National competition authorities may also exchange between themselves information necessary for the assessment of a case that they are dealing with under . . . [Article 101 or Article 102 TFEU].

5 The competition authorities of the Member States may consult the Commission on any case involving the application of Community [i.e. Union] law.

6 The initiation by the Commission of proceedings for the adoption of a decision under Chapter III shall relieve the competition authorities of the Member States of their competence to apply . . . [Articles 101 and 102 TFEU]. If a competition authority of a Member State is already acting on a case, the Commission shall only initiate proceedings after consulting with that national competition authority.

Article 12, Regulation 1/2003 provides as follows:

Exchange of information

1 For the purpose of applying . . . [Articles 101 and 102 TFEU] the Commission and the competition authorities of the Member States shall have the power to provide one another with and use in evidence any matter of fact or of law, including confidential information.

2 Information exchanged shall only be used in evidence for the purpose of applying . . . [Article 101 or Article 102 TFEU] and in respect of the subject-matter for which it was collected by the transmitting authority. However, where national competition law is applied in the same case and in parallel to Community [i.e. Union] competition law and does not lead to a different outcome, information exchanged under this Article may also be used for the application of national competition law.

3 Information exchanged pursuant to paragraph 1 can only be used in evidence to impose sanctions on natural persons where:
   – the law of the transmitting authority foresees sanctions of a similar kind in relation to an infringement of . . . [Article 101 or Article 102 TFEU] or, in the absence thereof,
   – the information has been collected in a way which respects the same level of protection of the rights of defence of natural persons as provided for under the national rules of the receiving authority. However, in this case, the information exchanged cannot be used by the receiving authority to impose custodial sanctions.

Article 14, Regulation 1/2003 establishes an Advisory Committee on Restrictive Practices and Dominant Positions, which the Commission is required to consult prior to the taking of any decision pursuant to:

- Art 7 in relation to an infringement of Arts 101 or 102 TFEU;
- Art 8 in relation to interim measures;
- Art 9 in relation to commitments;
- Art 10 in relation to findings of inapplicability;
- Art 23 in relation to fines;
- Art 24(2) in relation to periodic penalty payments;
- Art 29(1) in relation to the withdrawal of an exemption regulation in a particular case.

The Committee comprises representatives of the competition authorities of the Member States (Art 14(2)). There is provision for the consultation to take place by written procedure, subject to the right of any Member State requesting a meeting, in which case the Commission will convene a meeting (Art 14(4)). Article 14(5) provides that 'the Commission shall take the utmost account of the opinion delivered by the Advisory Committee. It shall advise the Committee of the manner in which its opinion has been taken into account'. A competition authority of a Member State can request the Commission to include on the agenda of the Advisory Committee a case that is being dealt with by another competition authority under Arts 101 and 102 TFEU. If a request is made then the Commission is obliged to put the case on the agenda, and it may also do so on its own initiative (Art 14(7)). The Advisory Committee does not issue an opinion with regard to such cases. The Committee can also discuss general issues of Union competition law (Art 14(7)).

Article 15, Regulation 1/2003 covers cooperation between the Commission and national courts. In a case before a national court which concerns the application of Arts 101 or 102 TFEU, the court can request the Commission to provide it with any information in the Commission's possession, and can also ask the Commission for an opinion on the application of Union competition law (Art 15(1)). This is additional to the power (or duty in some cases) to make an Art 267 TFEU (previously Art 234 EC Treaty) referral to the Court of Justice (see Chapter 6).

Member States are required to send the Commission without delay a copy of the written judgment of a national court which decides on the application of Arts 101 or 102 TFEU. A competition authority of a Member State can submit written observations to national courts of *their* Member State on issues relating to the application of Arts 101 or 102 TFEU, and they may also submit oral observations if the national court grants it permission (Art 15(3)). The same applies to the Commission with regard to the national courts of *all* the Member States (Art 15(3)).

The Commission has issued a non-legally binding 'Notice on the cooperation between the Commission and the courts of the EU Member States in the application of Arts 101 and 102 TFEU' (OJ 2004 C 101/54). This notice is available at:

http://europa.eu/legislation_summaries/competition/firms

The role of national competition authorities and courts in the enforcement of Union competition law

Objective 7

In the following case, the CFI (now the General Court) demonstrated some sympathy for the Commission's attempt to leave individual complaints which had a largely national dimension, although potentially affecting trade between Member States, to the courts of the state most affected:

Automec and Asia Motor France v Commission (Cases T-24 and 28/90)

Where the national court would be able to rule on the compatibility of a national distribution agreement for cars under what is now Art 101(1) TFEU (previously Art 81(1) EC Treaty) and provide the appropriate remedies if there was a breach, there was no need for Commission intervention. The CFI (now the General Court) therefore held that the Commission was not under an obligation to commence proceedings to determine whether or not a violation of Union law had occurred.

Similarly in the following case:

Tremblay v *Commission* (Case T-5/93)

The Commission had declined to investigate an alleged abuse of a monopoly position enjoyed by the Société des Auteurs, Compositeurs et Editeurs de Musique (SACEM) in relation to musical copyrights on the grounds, *inter alia*, that the effects of the alleged infringements outside France were limited and that several cases raising the same issues were pending before the French courts. The CFI (now the General Court) supported this approach:

> The fact that a national court or national competition authority is already dealing with a case concerning the compatibility of an agreement or practice with . . . [Articles 101 and 102 TFEU] is a factor which the Commission may take into account in evaluating the extent to which a case displays a Community [i.e. Union] interest . . . The Court considers that where the effects of the infringement alleged in a complaint are essentially confined to the territory of one Member State and where proceedings have been brought before the courts and competent administrative authorities of that Member State by the complainant against the body against which the complaint was made, the Commission is entitled to reject the complaint through lack of any sufficient Community [i.e. Union] interest, provided however that the rights of the complainant or its members can be adequately safeguarded, in particular by the national courts.

The principle of direct effect is discussed further at pages 274–292 and 303–305.

Articles 101(1) and 102 TFEU are both directly effective in national courts and can be used both offensively and defensively. As discussed above, Art 101(3) TFEU can now be applied by the national courts. The availability of remedies for private parties in national courts on the basis of Union competition rules arose from the decision of the Court of Justice in *BRT* v *SABAM* (Case 127/73). In this case, the Court held that a party could claim that an agreement was void under what is now Art 101(2) TFEU (previously Art 81(2) EC Treaty), that an injunction should be granted to enforce the competition rules, and that damages were payable for breach of the former Arts 101 or 102 TFEU.

The following case, which came before the Court of Justice, concerned the question of whether a party to a contract which was contrary to what is now Art 101 TFEU could rely on the breach of that provision before a national court to obtain compensation for any losses which resulted from the unlawful contractual clause:

Courage and Crehan (Case C-453/99)

The Court of Justice founded its judgment on its case law relating to the nature and effect of Union law, recalling *Van Gend en Loos* (Case 26/62), *Costa* (Case 6/64) and *Francovich and Bonifaci* (Joined Cases C-6/90 and C-9/90) (see Chapter 9), and on the basis that what is now Art 101 TFEU (previously Art 81 EC Treaty) constitutes 'a fundamental provision which is essential for the accomplishment of the tasks entrusted to the Community [i.e. Union] and, in particular, for the functioning of the internal market' (para 20).

The Court deduced from the nature of the Union legal order, the particularly important position of the competition rules in that order, and other more specific considerations that 'any individual can rely on a breach of . . . [Article 101(1) TFEU] before a national court even where he is a party to a contract that is liable to restrict or distort competition within the meaning of that provision' (para 24). That right entailed, *inter alia*, the right to seek compensation for the loss caused. Accordingly, there could not be any absolute bar to an action for damages being brought by one of the parties to a contract which violated what is now Art 101(1) TFEU (previously Art 81(1) EC Treaty). Moreover, the bringing of such actions strengthened the working of the Union competition rules and discouraged agreements or practices, which were frequently covert, that were liable to restrict or distort competition. However, if it was established that the party relying on the breach of what is now Art 101 TFEU was significantly responsible for the distortion of competition, Union law would not preclude a rule of national law barring him from relying on his own unlawful actions to obtain damages.

Regulation 1/2003

As previously discussed, Regulation 1/2003 has dramatically changed the way in which Arts 101 and 102 TFEU are now applied, following the empowerment of the national competition authorities and courts of the Member States to apply the two articles in their entirety.

The Commission has issued a 'Notice on cooperation within the Network of Competition Authorities' (OJ 2004 C 101/43). This notice is divided into five sections:

- Introduction.
- Division of work (which includes the principles of allocating cases to: a single competition authority, several competition authorities acting in parallel or the Commission; mechanisms of cooperation for the purpose of case allocation and assistance; and the position of undertakings).
- Consistent application of Union competition rules.
- The role and functioning of the Advisory Committee in the new system.
- Final remarks.

The notice is available at:

http://europa.eu/legislation_summaries/competition/firms

Relationship between Union and national competition law

Objective
8

Article 3, Regulation 1/2003 addresses the issue of the relationship between Arts 101 and 102 TFEU and national competition laws. Article 3 provides that:

1 Where the competition authorities of the Member States or national courts apply national competition law to agreements, decisions by associations of undertakings or concerted practices within the meaning of . . . [Article 101(1) TFEU] which may affect trade between Member States within the meaning of that provision, they shall also apply . . . [Article 101 TFEU] to such agreements, decisions or concerted practices. Where the competition authorities of the Member States or national courts apply national competition law to any abuse prohibited by . . . [Article 102 TFEU], they shall also apply . . . [Article 102 TFEU].

2 The application of national competition law may not lead to the prohibition of agreements, decisions by associations of undertakings or concerted practices which may affect trade between Member States but which do not restrict competition within the meaning

of . . . [Article 101(1) TFEU], or which fulfil the conditions of . . . [Article 101(3) TFEU] or which are covered by a Regulation for the application of . . . [Article 101(3) TFEU]. Member States shall not under this Regulation be precluded from adopting and applying on their territory stricter national laws which prohibit or sanction unilateral conduct engaged in by undertakings.

3 Without prejudice to general principles and other provisions of Community [i.e. Union] law, paragraphs 1 and 2 do not apply when the competition authorities and the courts of the Member States apply national merger control laws nor do they preclude the application of provisions of national law that predominantly pursue an objective different from that pursued by . . . [Articles 101 and 102 TFEU].

Article 16, Regulation 1/2003 provides that when national courts (or competition authorities) rule on agreements, decisions or practices under Arts 101 or 102 TFEU which are already the subject of a Commission decision, they cannot take decisions which run counter to the Commission's decision. National courts must also avoid giving decisions which would conflict with a decision contemplated by the Commission in proceedings it has initiated. In the latter situation, the national court could stay the proceedings until the Commission has reached its decision.

Enforcing Union competition law in UK courts

Objective
9

Article 101 TFEU is directly effective and therefore it may be used in UK courts both as a defence to a claim for breach of contract and, for example, as the basis for a claim that an unlawful agreement between competitors has damaged an undertaking that is not a party to that agreement (***MTV Europe* v *BMG Records (UK) Ltd*** [1995] CMLR 437; ***Society of Lloyds* v *Clementson*** [1995] 1 CMLR 693). The following case illustrates this point:

Cutsworth v Mansfield Inns [1986] 1 CMLR 1

Pursuant to an agreement, the claimants had for many years supplied coin-operated amusement machines to the tenants of more than 50 public houses. During 1985 the public houses were taken over by Mansfield Inns (the defendants). Not long after this, the defendants gave their tenants a list of suppliers of amusement machines from whom tenants were permitted to purchase. The claimants (who were not on that list) applied for an injunction to restrain the defendants from restricting their tenants from buying from them. They claimed that there was a seriously arguable case that the covenant in the licensees' tenancy agreement had the object or effect of distorting competition and potentially affected trade between Member States, contrary to what is now Art 101(1) TFEU (previously Art 81(1) EC Treaty). This argument was accepted by the national court and the injunction was granted (see also *Holleran and Evans* v *Daniel Thwaites plc* [1989] 2 CMLR 917).

It now seems clear that a declaration that an agreement breaches Art 101(1) TFEU will not be sufficient. Under Union law, the national court has to make an award of damages (***H.J. Banks and Co Ltd* v *British Coal Corporation*** (Case C-128/92)). Article 101 TFEU can also be used defensively. In ***Société Technique Minière* v *Maschinenbau Ulm*** (Case 56/65), the defendant distributors were held to be able to plead the invalidity of the distribution agreement in the national courts as a defence to a breach of contract (see also ***Brasserie de Haecht* v *Wilkin (No. 1)*** (Case 23/67)).

Article 102 TFEU can provide the basis for a claim for damages in the English courts as illustrated in the following case:

Garden Cottage Foods Ltd v *Milk Marketing Board* [1984] AC 130

An application was made for an interlocutory injunction to restrain the defendants from refusing to supply milk to the claimants. The refusal to supply was alleged by the claimants to be an abuse of a dominant position by the Board, and much of the case was concerned with whether or not it was appropriate, in the circumstances, to grant an interlocutory injunction. In determining this point, the House of Lords (the judicial functions of which are now exercised by the Supreme Court) had to consider whether or not an award of damages would be available if the claimants were successful in the substantive proceedings. Lord Diplock, who delivered the principal speech, thought that damages could be awarded under English law for a breach of what is now Art 102 TFEU (previously Art 82 EC Treaty):

> . . . [Art 102 TFEU] was held by the European Court of Justice in *Belgische Radio en Televisie* v *SV SABAM* (Case 127/73) to produce direct effects in relations between individuals and to create direct rights in respect of the individuals concerned which the national courts must protect. This decision of the European Court of Justice is to the effect that . . . [Art 102 TFEU] is one which s 3(1) of the European Communities Act 1972 requires your lordships to follow. The rights which the article confers upon citizens in the UK accordingly fall within s 2(1) of the Act. They are without further enactment to be given legal effect in the UK and enforced accordingly. A breach of the duty imposed by . . . [Art 102 TFEU] not to abuse a dominant position in the common market [i.e. internal market] or in a substantial part of it, can thus be categorised in English law as a breach of statutory duty that is imposed not only for the purpose of promoting the general economic prosperity of the common market [i.e. internal market] but also for the benefit of private individuals to whom loss or damage is caused by breach of that duty.

There is little case law on successful claims for damages for breach of Art 102 TFEU as a breach of statutory duty, but the principle has been applied in the English Divisional Court and affirmed in the Court of Appeal. In ***An Bord Bainne Co-operative Limited (The Irish Dairy Board)* v *The Milk Marketing Board*** [1984] 2 CMLR 584 CA, Neill J declared that the speeches of their Lordships in the ***Garden Cottage*** case provided 'compelling support for the proposition that contraventions of . . . [Union] regulations which have "direct effects" create rights in private law which national courts must protect'. Article 102 TFEU could also provide a defence to an action that, for example, an exclusive supply agreement was entered into by one party while being subject to abuse of a dominant position by another undertaking. Thus, the UK purchasers of Tetra-Pak drinks packaging machines who were required to buy only Tetra-Pak cartons for use in those machines would be free to buy other cartons and could use the breaches of what are now Arts 101 and 102 TFEU (previously Arts 81 and 82 EC Treaty) found by the CFI (now the General Court) as a defence to any action for breach of contract in UK courts (***Tetra-Pak International SA* v *Commission*** (Case T-83/91)).

Summary

Now you have read this chapter you should be able to:

- Explain how the rules of Union competition law are implemented by Regulations 1/2003 and 773/2004.

- Outline and describe the nature and scope of the ten Commission Notices which have been issued to support Regulations 1/2003 and 773/2004.

- Understand and evaluate the role of the Commission when it initiates an action for an alleged breach of Arts 101 or 102 TFEU.

- Outline the provisions of Regulation 1/2003 which provide for a complaint to be lodged with either the Commission or the competition authority of a Member State.

- Explain what applications can be made by a party where it is unclear whether the party is in breach of Arts 101 or 102 TFEU, specifically explaining the legal status of a guidance letter.

- Discuss the nature and scope of the Commission's powers of investigation and a party's right to a hearing.

- Understand and describe the nature and scope of the Commission's powers to make decisions, and the power to impose fines and periodic penalty payments.

- Explain and evaluate the relationship between the Commission on the one hand, and the national competition authorities and courts of the Member States on the other.

- Compare and contrast the respective enforcement roles undertaken by national competition authorities and the courts of the Member States pursuant to Arts 101 and 102 TFEU.

- Analyse the relationship between Union and national competition law.

- Explain how Union competition law is implemented and enforced in the UK.

Further reading

Textbooks

Craig, P. and De Burca, G. (2011) *EU Law: Text, Cases and Materials* (5th edn), Oxford University Press, Chapter 26.

Foster, N. (2015) *Foster on EU Law* (5th edn), Oxford University Press, Chapter 10.

Steiner, J. and Woods, L. (2014) *EU Law* (12th edn), Oxford University Press, Chapter 29.

Weatherill, S. (2014) *Cases and Materials on EU Law* (11th edn), Oxford University Press, Chapter 16.

Journal articles

Andreangeli, A., 'Private enforcement of the EU competition rules: The Commission wishes to "practice what it preaches" . . . but can it do so? Comment on Otis' (2014) 39 EL Rev 717.

Botta, M., 'Testing the decentralization of competition law enforcement: Comment on Toshiba' (2013) 38 EL Rev 107.

Cengiz, F., 'Multi-level governance in competition policy: The European Competition Network' (2010) 35 EL Rev 660.

Forrester, I.S., 'Due process in EC competition cases: A distinguished institution with flawed procedures' (2009) 34 EL Rev 817.

Forrester, I.S., 'A challenge for Europe's judges: The review of fines in competition cases' (2011) 36 EL Rev 185.

Lavrijssen, S., 'What role for national competition authorities in protecting non-competition interests after Lisbon?' (2010) 35 EL Rev 636.

Nascimbene, B., 'Fair trial and the rights of the defence in antitrust proceedings before the Commission: A need for reform?' (2013) 38 EL Rev 573.

Nebbia, P., 'Damages actions for the infringement of EC competition law: Compensation or deterrence' (2008) 33 EL Rev 23.

Glossary

A fortiori   Latin phrase which literally means 'from the stronger', but which is more often used to mean 'even more so' or 'with even stronger reason'.

Ab initio   Latin phrase which means 'from the beginning'. In a legal context it refers to something being the situation from the start, rather than from when the court declared it so.

Absolute territorial protection   Where a manufacturer of goods grants a business undertaking (e.g. a wholesaler or retailer) a sole licence for the sale/distribution of such goods within a particular Member State. Often this is in an attempt to prevent parallel imports. *See also* PARALLEL IMPORTS.

Abuse of a dominant position   A business undertaking which has a monopoly position in the market place, and uses that position (i.e. dominance) to affect trade between the Member States is referred to as the 'abuse of a dominant position'. Article 102 TFEU (previously Art 82 EC Treaty) prohibits the use (abuse) of a dominant position in this way. *See also* MONOPOLY.

Acquis   Derived from French, *acquis* (or *acquis communautaire*) is used in Union law to refer to the total body of Union law accumulated so far. The term is also used to refer to the laws adopted under the Schengen Agreement. In this context it is referred to as the *Schengen acquis*. *See also* SCHENGEN AGREEMENT.

Acts of the Union institutions   Article 288 TFEU (previously Art 249 EC Treaty) empowers the Union institutions to adopt regulations, directives, decisions, recommendations and opinions. These instruments are referred to as 'acts of the Union institutions'.

Advocate General   The Court of Justice is assisted by eight Advocates General (Art 252 TFEU (previously Art 222 EC Treaty)). The principal role of an Advocate General is to assist the Court

of Justice reach its judgment by delivering an Opinion in open court. The Opinion is not binding on the Court, although the Court usually follows the Opinion when reaching its judgment.

Aggregation of contributions   Article 48 TFEU (previously Art 42 EC Treaty) facilitates the Union's policy of free movement of workers by providing EU workers with the right to have their social security contributions and period of contribution in their home state recognised in the host Member State, and their contributions and length of service in the host Member State recognised in their home state when they return. This is referred to as 'aggregation of contributions'. *See also* DOUBLE-FUNCTION TEST; EXPORTABILITY OF BENEFITS.

Benelux Agreement   In 1948, Belgium, the Netherlands and Luxembourg established the Benelux customs union, which removed customs barriers between the three countries and also imposed a common customs tariff on goods entering the three countries from outside their national boundaries. In 1954, the free movement of capital was permitted between these three countries, followed by the free movement of labour in 1956. The agreement establishing these provisions is referred to as the 'Benelux Agreement'. *See also* BENELUX CUSTOMS UNION.

Benelux countries   Comprises Belgium, the Netherlands (also referred to as Holland) and Luxembourg. *See also* BENELUX AGREEMENT; BENELUX CUSTOMS UNION.

Benelux customs union   The Benelux customs union established the free movement of goods between the three Benelux countries (Belgium, The Netherlands and Luxembourg) from 1 January 1948. Customs barriers were removed and a common customs tariff was introduced for goods entering the customs union from outside the customs union. This developed in 1954 to include the free movement of capital, and developed further in 1956 to include the free movement of labour. *See also* BENELUX AGREEMENT.

Cartel An agreement between otherwise independent business undertakings, the aim of which is to protect their market share.

CEE Is the acronym for 'charge having an equivalent effect to a customs duty'. Articles 28 and 30 TFEU (previously Arts 23 and 25 EC Treaty) prohibit customs duties and CEEs. *See also* COMMON EXTERNAL TARIFF; CUSTOMS DUTY; CUSTOMS UNION.

CISA *See* CONVENTION FOR THE IMPLEMENTATION OF THE SCHENGEN AGREEMENT.

Co-decision procedure The founding treaties excluded the European Parliament from direct involvement in the legislative process. The European Parliament's greatest level of involvement in the legislative process was a right to be consulted in a few policy areas. Following the introduction of direct elections to the European Parliament in 1979 there was a call for the European Parliament to have a greater involvement in the legislative process. The cooperation procedure, set out in the former Art 252 EC Treaty, was introduced by the Single European Act (SEA). It empowered the European Parliament, in certain specified policy areas, to propose amendments to a legislative proposal. The cooperation procedure no longer exists following amendments made to the EC Treaty (now renamed the TFEU) by the Treaty of Lisbon. The co-decision procedure, which was set out in the former Art 251 EC Treaty, provided the European Parliament with a greater involvement in the legislative process. The co-decision procedure empowered the Parliament, in certain specified policy areas, to propose amendments and ultimately to veto the proposal. The legal base determines the legislative procedure to be used for the adoption of a particular instrument. Following amendments made to the EC Treaty (now renamed the TFEU) by the Treaty of Lisbon, the co-decision procedure no longer exists. It has been replaced by the 'ordinary legislative procedure' which applies in the vast majority of cases (Art 294 TFEU). The 'ordinary legislative procedure' is practically a carbon copy of the former co-decision procedure. *See also* COOPERATION PROCEDURE; LEGAL BASE;

ORDINARY LEGISLATIVE PROCEDURE; SPECIAL LEGISLATIVE PROCEDURE.

Committee of Permanent Representatives (COREPER) The Committee of Permanent Representatives, known by its French acronym COREPER, comprises senior national officials from the Member States of the EU, who are based in Brussels. The role of the Committee is to provide continuity during the inevitable absences of relevant ministers from the Council. *See also* COUNCIL; EUROPEAN COUNCIL.

Committee of the Regions The Committee of the Regions was established by the TEU as an advisory body. It is not a formal Union institution. The members of the Committee are representatives of regional and local bodies who either hold a regional or local authority electoral mandate or are politically accountable to an elected assembly (Art 300 TFEU (previously Art 263 EC Treaty)). Its main role is to deliver opinions on proposed legislation when consulted by the Council and to issue own-initiative opinions in appropriate cases. In a few policy areas (e.g. culture (Art 167(5) TFEU)), the legal base for a legislative proposal stipulates that the Committee must be consulted in relation to proposed measures. *See also* LEGAL BASE.

Common external tariff A customs union comprises an association of countries which prohibits customs duties and charges having an equivalent effect from being levied on goods as they cross the borders of the countries within the association. A common external tariff (i.e. a fixed customs duty) is applied to goods entering the customs union from a non-member country. *See also* CEE; CUSTOMS DUTY; CUSTOMS UNION.

Common market The common market was established by the European Economic Community (EEC) Treaty (subsequently renamed the European Community (EC) Treaty, and now renamed the TFEU). The common market is a free trade area founded upon the free movement of goods, persons, services and capital. Since 1 December 2009 (when the Treaty of Lisbon came into force) it is now referred to as the 'internal market' rather than the common market. *See also* EUROPEAN COMMUNITIES; EUROPEAN COMMUNITY; INTERNAL MARKET.

Complainant   Refers to a person who makes a complaint; also referred to as the applicant or plaintiff. It may also refer to a person who makes a claim in a court or tribunal against another person.

Concerted practice   Within the context of Art 101 TFEU (previously Art 81 EC Treaty), a concerted practice refers to some kind of coordinated action which, although it may fall short of an agreement, knowingly substitutes practical cooperation for competition. *See also* RESTRICTIVE AGREEMENT.

Conglomerate   One large business undertaking which consists of divisions of (quite often unrelated) businesses.

Constitutional Treaty   The (proposed) Constitutional Treaty was adopted by the Member States of the EU in 2004. This Treaty would have replaced all the existing EU treaties (e.g. EC Treaty, TEU). Before it could come into force it had to be ratified (i.e. approved) by each Member State, according to each Member State's constitutional requirements. In some Member States their constitution required approval by the electorate in a referendum. This was the situation in both France and The Netherlands, both of which rejected the Treaty in 2005. As a result, the (proposed) Constitutional Treaty did not come into force, and was subsequently abandoned. The Treaty of Lisbon which came into force on 1 December 2009 replaced the (proposed) Constitutional Treaty. *See also* TREATY OF LISBON.

Contextual interpretation   Contextual interpretation is used by courts to interpret legislation. If this method is employed, the provision being interpreted is placed within its context and interpreted in relation to the provisions of the legislation in question. This method of legislative interpretation, together with teleological interpretation, is extensively used by the Court of Justice of the European Union. *See also* HISTORICAL INTERPRETATION; LITERAL INTERPRETATION; TELEOLOGICAL INTERPRETATION.

Contra legem   Latin phrase which means 'against the law'.

Convention for the Implementation of the Schengen Agreement (CISA)   CISA is, as its title implies, the convention which implemented the Schengen Agreement. *See also* SCHENGEN AGREEMENT.

Cooperation procedure   The founding treaties excluded the European Parliament from direct involvement in the legislative process. The European Parliament's greatest level of involvement in the legislative process was a right to be consulted in a few policy areas. Following the introduction of direct elections to the European Parliament in 1979 there was a call for the European Parliament to have a greater involvement in the legislative process. The cooperation procedure, set out in the former Art 252 EC Treaty, was introduced by the SEA. It empowered the European Parliament, in certain specified policy areas, to propose amendments to a legislative proposal. Following amendments to the founding treaties by subsequent treaties (e.g. the TEU, ToN, ToA), the cooperation procedure was rarely used; the co-decision procedure was more commonly used. The legal base determines the legislative procedure which has to be used for the adoption of a particular instrument. Following amendments made to the EC Treaty (now renamed the TFEU) by the Treaty of Lisbon (which came into force on 1 December 2009), the cooperation procedure no longer exists. *See also* CO-DECISION PROCEDURE; LEGAL BASE; ORDINARY LEGISLATIVE PROCEDURE; SPECIAL LEGISLATIVE PROCEDURE.

COREPER   *See* COMMITTEE OF PERMANENT REPRESENTATIVES.

Corrigendum   Derived from Latin, a *corrigendum* is an error in printing. From time to time a *corrigendum* is published in the *Official Journal of the European Union* to correct errors in a previous edition of the journal.

Council   The Council is one of the Union institutions. It is also referred to as the Council of Ministers. The Council consists of a representative from each of the 28 Member States at ministerial level, who is authorised to bind the government of their Member State. *See also* COMMITTEE OF PERMANENT REPRESENTATIVES.

Court of Auditors   The Court of Auditors is not, strictly speaking, a court. Article 13(1) TEU (previously Art 7 EC Treaty) classifies the Court as a

Union institution. It is responsible for the external audit of the general budget of the European Union.

Cross-elasticity   Within the context of Art 110(2) TFEU (previously Art 90(2) EC Treaty), cross-elasticity refers to the degree to which goods are substitutable for each other (i.e. the readiness with which a consumer will switch between two competing products).

Customs duty   A customs duty is a state levy charged on goods at the border. Articles 28 and 30 TFEU (previously Arts 23 and 25 EC Treaty) prohibit customs duties. *See also* CEE; COMMON EXTERNAL TARIFF; CUSTOMS UNION.

Customs union   A customs union is an association of countries which prohibits customs duties and charges having an equivalent effect from being levied on goods as they cross the borders of the countries within the association. A common external tariff (i.e. a fixed customs duty) is applied to goods entering the customs union from a non-member country. Article 28 TFEU (previously Art 23 EC Treaty) establishes a customs union between the 28 Member States of the EU. *See also* CEE; CUSTOMS DUTY; COMMON EXTERNAL TARIFF.

De minimis   Latin phrase which, in a legal context, means matters which are not worthy of the law's attention. *See also* DE MINIMIS PRESUMPTION.

De minimis presumption   In Union competition law, there are a number of formalised *de minimis* presumptions, set out in Commission Notices. For example, the Notice on Agreements of Minor Importance (OJ 2001 C 368/13) stipulates the circumstances in which agreements between companies (particularly smaller companies) will not be in breach of Art 101 TFEU (previously Art 81 EC Treaty). *See also* DE MINIMIS.

Decision   A decision is a legally effective Union instrument. Article 288 TFEU (previously Art 249 EC Treaty) provides that a decision shall be binding in its entirety upon those to whom it is addressed.

Demand-side substitutability   Demand-side substitutability determines which products compete with each other from the perspective of the consumer (e.g. whether a consumer will switch from purchasing one product to another, e.g. from apples to bananas).

Democratic deficit   When the European Union was first founded the legislative process primarily only involved the European Commission (which initiated/proposed the legislation) and the Council (which adopted the proposed legislation). The European Parliament's greatest level of involvement in the legislative process was a right to be consulted in a few policy areas. When the Members of the European Parliament (MEPs) were directly elected for the first time in 1979, it was argued that its role within the legislative process should be enhanced. There was a 'democratic deficit' because the only directly elected Union institution had little or no involvement in the legislative process. Subsequent treaties (e.g. the SEA, TEU, ToN, ToA, ToL) amended the founding treaties to enhance the legislative role of the European Parliament, but ultimately the European Commission and the Council continue to dominate the legislative process. *See also* CO-DECISION PROCEDURE; COOPERATION PROCEDURE; ORDINARY LEGISLATIVE PROCEDURE; SPECIAL LEGISLATIVE PROCEDURE.

Derogation   A derogation is an exception to the general rule.

Deutsche Mark   The Deutsche Mark (DM) was Germany's national currency before Germany adopted the euro. *See also* EURO.

Direct effect   If a provision of Union law has direct effect, it can be enforced in national courts and tribunals overriding any inconsistent national provisions. In order to be capable of having direct effect, the provision of Union law must be sufficiently precise and unconditional (Case 26/62 *Van Gend en Loos*). *See also* HORIZONTAL DIRECT EFFECT; VERTICAL DIRECT EFFECT.

Directive   A directive is a legally effective Union instrument. Article 288 TFEU (previously Art 249 EC Treaty) provides that a directive shall be binding, as to the result to be achieved, upon each Member State to which it is addressed, but shall leave to the national authorities the choice of form and methods. This normally requires a Member State to adopt implementing legislation to incorporate the directive into the national legal system.

Distinctly applicable measure   Within the context of Arts 34 and 35 TFEU (previously Arts 28 and 29 EC Treaty), a distinctly applicable measure is a quantitative restriction (QR) or measure having an equivalent effect to a quantitative restriction (MEQR) which is applied only to imported or exported goods; i.e. the restriction is not applied to domestically produced goods. *See also* INDISTINCTLY APPLICABLE MEASURE; MEASURE HAVING AN EQUIVALENT EFFECT TO A QUANTITATIVE RESTRICTION; QUANTITATIVE RESTRICTION.

DM *See* DEUTSCHE MARK.

Double-function test Article 48 TFEU (previously Art 42 EC Treaty) facilitates the Union's policy of free movement of workers by providing EU workers with the right to have their social security contributions and period of contribution in their home state recognised in the host Member State, and their contributions and length of service in the host Member State recognised in their home state when they return. Article 3(5), Regulation 883/2004 (which replaced Art 4(4), Regulation 1408/71) excludes social-assistance-type benefits. However, the double-function test, established by the Court of Justice in Case 1/72 *Frilli* (within the context of the former Art 4(4), Regulation 1408/71) provides that even a means-tested discretionary payment could constitute 'social security' rather than 'social assistance', and thus come within the scope of the Regulation, if it could be regarded as a supplement to one of the benefits listed in the former Art 4(1), Regulation 1408/71 (which has been replaced by Art 3(1), Regulation 883/2004). *See also* AGGREGATION OF CONTRIBUTIONS; EXPORTABILITY OF BENEFITS.

Dual-burden rule Within the context of Arts 34 and 35 TFEU (previously Arts 28 and 29 EC Treaty), a dual-burden rule is one which imposes an additional burden on foreign producers and goods. *See also* EQUAL-BURDEN RULE. 18

EC *See* EUROPEAN COMMUNITY.

ECB *See* EUROPEAN CENTRAL BANK.

ECHR *See* EUROPEAN CONVENTION ON HUMAN RIGHTS.

Economic and Monetary Union (EMU) Economic and Monetary Union was established by the EC Treaty (which has been renamed the TFEU by the Treaty of Lisbon), following amendments made to it by the TEU. A timetable for the adoption of the single currency (the euro) was set out. The euro became legal tender in 12 of the 15 pre-2004 Member States on 1 January 2002. The UK, Denmark and Sweden opted out of the single currency. On 1 January 2007 Slovenia adopted the euro, followed by Southern Cyprus and Malta on 1 January 2008, Slovakia on 1 January 2009, Estonia on 1 January 2011, Latvia on 1 January 2014 and Lithuania on 1 January 2015. The euro has therefore replaced the national currency in 19 of the current 28 Member States. *See also* EURO; SINGLE EUROPEAN CURRENCY.

Economically self-sufficient An economically self-sufficient person is one who has sufficient financial resources not to be a burden on others. In the context of the Union's free movement of persons' policy, an economically self-sufficient person is one who does not have recourse to a state's social assistance scheme.

ECSC *See* EUROPEAN COAL AND STEEL COMMUNITY.

ECU *See* EUROPEAN CURRENCY UNIT.

EEA *See* EUROPEAN ECONOMIC AREA.

EEC *See* EUROPEAN ECONOMIC COMMUNITY.

EESC *See* EUROPEAN ECONOMIC AND SOCIAL COMMITTEE.

Effet utile French phrase which means 'useful effect'.

EFTA *See* EUROPEAN FREE TRADE ASSOCIATION.

EIB *See* EUROPEAN INVESTMENT BANK.

Ejusdem generis rule Latin phrase which is applied in the English legal system as an aid to legislative interpretation. The rule provides that if specific categories are followed by general words, then the general words are limited to the context of the specific categories. For example, if a UK Act of Parliament provided that a person had to apply for a licence if he owned a 'dog, cat or other animal', the rule would operate to limit the general words 'or other animal' to the context of the categories 'dog and cat'. The court could legitimately decide that 'or other animals' was limited to domestic pets.

EMU *See* ECONOMIC AND MONETARY UNION.

Equal-burden rule Within the context of Arts 34 and 35 TFEU (previously Arts 28 and 29 EC Treaty), an equal-burden rule is a rule which applies equally to domestic and foreign producers (and goods). *See also* DUAL-BURDEN RULE.

Equitable doctrine of estoppel To deny the assertion of a right. *See also* ESTOPPEL.

Estoppel To deny the assertion of a right. *See also* EQUITABLE DOCTRINE OF ESTOPPEL.

EU *See* EUROPEAN UNION.

Euratom *See* EUROPEAN ATOMIC ENERGY COMMUNITY.

Euro Following amendments made to the EC Treaty (now the TFEU) by the TEU, a timetable for the adoption of the Single European Currency (the euro) was established. The euro became legal tender in 12 of the 15 pre-2004 Member States on 1 January 2002. The UK, Denmark and Sweden opted out of the single currency. On 1 January 2007, Slovenia adopted the euro, followed by Southern Cyprus and Malta on 1 January 2008, Slovakia on 1 January 2009, Estonia on 1 January 2011, Latvia on 1 January 2014 and Lithuania on 1 January 2015. The euro has therefore replaced the national currency in 19 of the current 28 Member States. *See also* ECONOMIC AND MONETARY UNION; SINGLE EUROPEAN CURRENCY.

European Atomic Energy Community (Euratom) The European Atomic Energy Community came into existence on 1 July 1958. Euratom covers the research and development of nuclear energy within the EU.

European Central Bank (ECB) Article 13(1) TEU recognises the European Central Bank as one of the Union institutions. The ECB was set up as part of the progression towards the Single European Currency (the euro). *See also* EURO.

European Coal and Steel Community (ECSC) The ECSC came into existence on 23 July 1952 and ended on 23 July 2002. It regulated the control and production of coal and steel.

European Commission The European Commission is one of the Union institutions. There are 28 Commissioners (one from each of the 28 Member States). The Commission initiates/proposes Union legislation, acts as the watchdog of the EU to ensure Union law is being complied with, and has limited direct legislative powers.

European Communities Initially, the European Communities collectively comprised the following three Communities: European Coal and Steel Community (ECSC), European Economic Community (EEC) (later renamed EC) and European Atomic Energy Community (Euratom). The ECSC ended on 23 July 2002 and therefore the European Communities consisted of the EC and Euratom. When the Treaty of Lisbon came into force on 1 December 2009, the EC Treaty was renamed the Treaty on the Functioning of the European Union (TFEU). The Union replaced and succeeded the Community (Art 1 TEU). Throughout the TFEU, the word 'Community' has been replaced with the word 'Union'. The following terms are therefore no longer used: European *Community*; European *Communities*; or *Community* law. Reference is made solely to the European *Union* (or *Union*) and European *Union* law (or *Union* law). *See also* EUROPEAN ATOMIC ENERGY COMMUNITY; EUROPEAN COAL AND STEEL COMMUNITY; EUROPEAN COMMUNITY; EUROPEAN ECONOMIC COMMUNITY; EUROPEAN UNION; TREATY OF LISBON; TREATY ON EUROPEAN UNION.

European Community (EC) In 1957 the Treaty Establishing the European Economic Community (EEC Treaty) was adopted. The EEC Treaty came into force on 1 July 1958. Following subsequent amendments to the EEC Treaty, the EEC increasingly became concerned with, *inter alia*, social policy and political issues, departing from its predominantly economic roots. For this reason, the TEU renamed the EEC Treaty the 'Treaty Establishing the European Community' (EC Treaty). This change came into effect on 1 November 1993 when the TEU came into force. When the Treaty of Lisbon came into force on 1 December 2009, the EC Treaty was renamed the Treaty on the Functioning of the European Union (TFEU). The Union has replaced and succeeded the Community (Art 1 TEU). Throughout the TFEU, the word 'Community' has been replaced with the word 'Union'. The following terms are therefore no longer used: European *Community*; European *Communities*; or *Community* law. Reference is made solely to the European *Union* (or *Union*) and European *Union* law (or *Union* law). *See also* EUROPEAN ATOMIC ENERGY COMMUNITY; EUROPEAN COAL AND STEEL COMMUNITY; EUROPEAN COMMUNITIES; EUROPEAN ECONOMIC COMMUNITY; EUROPEAN UNION; TREATY OF LISBON; TREATY ON EUROPEAN UNION.

European Convention on Human Rights (ECHR)   The European Convention on Human Rights (ECHR) is a treaty entered into by a number of European countries. All 28 Member States of the EU have signed up to the ECHR. The ECHR requires signatory states to protect the human rights set out in the Convention (e.g. Art 8 ECHR protects family life, home and family correspondence). Although the ECHR is separate and distinct from the EU, when the Treaty of Lisbon came into force on 1 December 2009, Art 6(2) TEU was amended to provide that the Union will accede to the Convention, although it states that 'such accession shall not affect the Union's competences as defined in the Treaties'. This means that accession to the Convention will not extend the Union's powers and tasks; application of the Convention will be limited to those areas which come within the competence of the Union. Article 6(3) TEU now provides that the 'fundamental rights guaranteed by the European Convention on Human Rights and Fundamental Freedoms and as they result from the constitutional traditions common to the Member States, *shall constitute general principles of the Union's law*' [emphasis added]. This simply restates the position prior to the Treaty of Lisbon. However, once the Union accedes to the Convention, Union law will have to be interpreted and applied in accordance with the Convention, not simply as a 'general principle of the Union's law', but because: (i) the Convention is directly applicable to the Union; and (ii) the Union is required (in international law) to adhere to the Convention's provisions.

European Council   The European Council is recognised by Art 13(1) TEU as one of the Union institutions (prior to the Treaty of Lisbon it was not recognised as a Union institution). The European Council consists of the heads of government of the 28 Member States. Its role is to provide the Union with the necessary impetus for its development and to define its political directions and priorities (Art 15(1) TEU). The European Council meets at least twice a year, at meetings often referred to as 'European Summits'.

European Court of Human Rights   An aggrieved person whose human rights have been infringed by a state which is a signatory to the European Convention on Human Rights (ECHR) has a right to bring the case before the European Court of Human Rights. Decisions made by this court are not binding on national courts. This court is not a Union institution. *See also* EUROPEAN CONVENTION ON HUMAN RIGHTS.

European Currency Unit (ECU)   The European Currency Unit was used by the Member States for their internal accounting purposes, prior to the adoption of the euro. *See also* EURO.

European Economic and Social Committee (EESC)   The European Economic and Social Committee, originally known by its French acronym ECOSOC but now as the EESC, was established by the TEU as an advisory body. It is not a formal Union institution. The members of the Committee consist of 'representatives of organisations of employers, of the employed, and of other parties representative of civil society, notably in socioeconomic, civic, professional and cultural areas' (Art 300(2) TFEU (previously Art 257 EC Treaty)). Its main role is to deliver opinions on proposed legislation when consulted by the Council and to issue own-initiative opinions in appropriate cases. In a few policy areas (e.g. employment (Art 148(2) TFEU)), the legal base for a legislative proposal stipulates that the Committee must be consulted in relation to proposed legislation. *See also* LEGAL BASE.

European Economic Area (EEA)   On 2 May 1992, the then seven European Free Trade Association (EFTA) states, the EU and the Member States, signed an agreement to establish the European Economic Area (EEA). The EEA, which some initially saw as an alternative to full membership of the European Union, was intended to integrate the EFTA states *economically* into the Union without giving them a role in its institutions. The EEA gave the EFTA states access for their goods, persons, services and capital to the markets of the Union. Equally, the same facilities were granted by EFTA states in their territories to Member States of the EU. Only Switzerland refused to participate in the EEA, after a hostile national referendum. In this new trading area, all the *economic* rules of the EU apply, although the Member States of EFTA are not represented in any of the EU institutions and do not participate in the

EU's decision-making process. *See also* EUROPEAN FREE TRADE ASSOCIATION.

European Economic Community (EEC) The European Economic Community was created by the Treaty Establishing the European Economic Community. This Treaty (which is often referred to as the Treaty of Rome, because it was signed in Rome) came into force on 1 July 1958. The EEC created, *inter alia*, the common market (now referred to as the internal market). The EEC was renamed the European Community (EC) on 1 November 1993 by the Treaty on European Union (TEU). When the Treaty of Lisbon came into force on 1 December 2009, the EC Treaty was renamed the Treaty on the Functioning of the European Union (TFEU). The Union has replaced and succeeded the Community (Art 1 TEU). Throughout the TFEU, the word 'Community' has been replaced with the word 'Union'. The following terms are therefore no longer used: European *Community*; European *Communities*; or *Community* law. Reference is made solely to the European Union (or Union) and European Union law (or Union law). *See also* EUROPEAN ATOMIC ENERGY COMMUNITY; EUROPEAN COAL AND STEEL COMMUNITY; EUROPEAN COMMUNITIES; EUROPEAN COMMUNITY; EUROPEAN UNION; TREATY ON EUROPEAN UNION.

European Free Trade Association (EFTA) The European Free Trade Association was set up by non-Member States as an alternative to EU membership. EFTA established a free-trade area between the participating states (currently Iceland, Liechtenstein, Norway and Switzerland). *See also* EUROPEAN ECONOMIC AREA.

European Investment Bank The European Investment Bank (EIB) was established by Art 308 TFEU (previously Art 9 EC Treaty). It is not a Union institution within the scope of Art 13(1) TEU (previously Art 7 EC Treaty). The EIB is the European Union's long-term lending bank and the regional development bank for Europe. It makes grants and loans to projects which affect more than one Member State, where they cannot be funded sufficiently from within those Member States.

European Parliament The European Parliament is one of the Union institutions. Members of the European Parliament (MEPs) are directly elected to the Parliament. Direct elections took place for the first time in 1979.

European Union (EU) The European Union was established by the Treaty on European Union (TEU). Until 1 December 2009 the EU comprised three pillars: (i) the European Communities; (ii) Common Foreign and Security Policy; and (iii) Police and Judicial Cooperation in Criminal Matters. When the Treaty of Lisbon came into force on 1 December 2009, the Union replaced and succeeded the Community (Art 1 TEU), and the three pillars were merged (i.e. they no longer exist). *See also* EUROPEAN ATOMIC ENERGY COMMUNITY; EUROPEAN COAL AND STEEL COMMUNITY; EUROPEAN COMMUNITIES; EUROPEAN COMMUNITY; EUROPEAN ECONOMIC COMMUNITY; TREATY OF LISBON; TREATY ON EUROPEAN UNION.

European Union (EU) worker A worker who comes within the scope of the provisions of Union law relating to the free movement of workers is referred to as an 'EU worker'. An EU worker is defined as one who is engaged in a genuine and effective economic activity which is not on such a small scale as to be marginal or ancillary (Case 53/81 *Levin*). The Union law provisions only apply to an EU citizen who is working in a Member State other than that of his nationality.

Exportability of benefits Within the context of Art 48 TFEU (previously Art 42 EC Treaty) and Regulation 883/2004 (previously Regulation 1408/71), which establishes social security rights for EU workers, the right to receive a social security benefit, usually from the state of origin, attaches to an EU worker as he travels around the EU, irrespective of national boundaries. This is referred to as the 'exportability of benefits' and is also known as 'the portability principle'. *See also* AGGREGATION OF CONTRIBUTIONS; DOUBLE-FUNCTION TEST.

Fait accompli French phrase which means 'an accomplished and presumably irreversible deed or fact'.

Foreclosure Closing off the market.

Franc The franc was France's national currency before France adopted the euro. *See also* EURO.

Francovich damages Also referred to as the principle of state liability, **Francovich** damages were established by the Court of Justice in Cases

C-6 and 9/90 *Francovich*. This principle provides that if a person suffers damage because of a Member State's breach of Union law, the Member State is liable to the aggrieved person if: (i) the rule of Union law infringed is intended to confer rights on individuals; (ii) the breach is sufficiently serious; and (iii) there is a direct causal link between the breach of the rule and the damage sustained by the person (Cases C-46 and 48/93 *Brasserie du Pêcheur* and *Factortame*). *See also* STATE LIABILITY.

Fundamental rights   Fundamental rights are those which the Court of Justice has deemed are central to the European Union's policies. For example, the rights established by the free movement provisions of the TFEU have been classified by the Court of Justice as fundamental rights. Fundamental rights will be protected by the Court of Justice from interference, unless such interference is permitted by the Treaty.

Harmonising directive   A harmonising directive is one which establishes a set of common laws which apply throughout the Member States. *See also* RULE OF MUTUAL RECOGNITION.

Historical interpretation   Historical interpretation is used by courts to interpret legislation. If this method is employed, there is a consideration of the subjective intention of the author of the text of the legislation. This method may be equated with the English mischief rule of legislative interpretation, where the judge seeks to establish the legislative intent. This method of legislative interpretation is occasionally used by the Court of Justice of the European Union. *See also* CONTEXTUAL INTERPRETATION; LITERAL INTERPRETATION; TELEOLOGICAL INTERPRETATION.

Horizontal direct effect   A provision of Union law which is enforceable in national courts or tribunals against natural and legal persons, overriding any inconsistent national provisions, is said to have horizontal direct effect (Case 152/84 *Marshall* v *Southampton AHA*). Treaty articles and regulations are capable of having horizontal direct effect if the provision is sufficiently precise and unconditional (Case 26/62 *Van Gend en Loos*). Directives cannot have horizontal direct effect (Case 152/84 *Marshall* v *Southampton AHA*). *See also* DIRECT EFFECT; VERTICAL DIRECT EFFECT.

Horizontal restrictive agreement   A horizontal restrictive agreement is one where the parties to the agreement are competitors (e.g. an agreement between producers of a particular commodity).

In camera   Latin phrase which means 'in the chamber' but more commonly used to mean 'in secret'.

Indirect effect   National courts and tribunals are under an obligation to interpret national law in such a way that it avoids a conflict with Union law, if that is possible (Case C-106/89 *Marleasing*). This is referred to as the principle of indirect effect. *See also* DIRECT EFFECT; INTERPRETATIVE OBLIGATION; MARLEASING INTERPRETATIVE OBLIGATION.

Indistinctly applicable measure   Within the context of Arts 34 and 35 TFEU (previously Arts 28 and 29 EC Treaty), an indistinctly applicable measure is a QR or MEQR which is applied to all goods without distinction; i.e. the restriction is applied to both home-produced and foreign goods. *See also* DISTINCTLY APPLICABLE MEASURE; MEASURE HAVING AN EQUIVALENT EFFECT TO A QUANTITATIVE RESTRICTION; QUANTITATIVE RESTRICTION.

Infraction proceedings   Article 258 TFEU (previously Art 226 EC Treaty) empowers the Commission to take action against a Member State which is in breach of Union law. If the Member State fails to remedy the breach, ultimately the Commission can bring proceedings against the defaulting Member State before the Court of Justice. Such proceedings are referred to as infraction proceedings.

Intellectual property right   Intellectual property rights protect the product of one person's work (by hand or brain) against unauthorised use or exploitation by another. Such rights are protected by laws relating to, *inter alia*, copyright, patents and trade marks.

Inter alia   Latin phrase which means 'among other things'.

Inter partes   Latin phrase which means 'between the parties'.

Intergovernmental   Refers to non-legally binding cooperation between two or more countries.

Intergovernmental conference (IGC)   An intergovernmental conference is the title given to a meeting of the European Council which is primarily concerned with drafting a Treaty to amend the founding treaties (e.g. TFEU).

Interlocutory proceedings   When court or tribunal proceedings have been initiated, sometimes the court will need to make an order (for example) before it finally determines the case. Such an order is referred to as an interim order. Interlocutory proceedings occur during the course of the action (i.e. before the case is finally determined), when, for example, an interim order is required.

Internal market   The internal market is 'an area without internal frontiers in which the free movement of goods, persons, services and capital is ensured in accordance with the provisions of the Treaties' (Art 26(2) TFEU (previously Art 14 EC Treaty)). One of the aims of the SEA was to complete the European Union's internal market by 1 January 1993. *See also* COMMON MARKET

Interpretative obligation   National courts and tribunals are under an obligation to interpret national law in such a way that it avoids a conflict with Union law, if that is possible (Case C-106/89 *Marleasing*). This is known as the principle of indirect effect and is also referred to as the national court's interpretative obligation. *See also* DIRECT EFFECT; INDIRECT EFFECT; *MARLEASING* INTERPRETATIVE OBLIGATION.

Ioannina Declaration   Under a declaration made in March 1994 at the Ioannina Summit of the European Council, it was provided that where a decision is to be taken by a qualified majority, if a minority of Member States (which do not have sufficient votes to block the decision being adopted) indicate their intention to oppose the decision, the Council is required to do all in its power to reach, within a reasonable period of time, a satisfactory solution. This declaration is referred to as the Ioannina Declaration. On 1 December 2009 when the Treaty of Lisbon came into force (pursuant to a decision adopted by the Council) a revised 'Ioannina' compromise was adopted. *See also* QUALIFIED MAJORITY.

Ipse dixit   Latin phrase which means 'he himself said it', or, in a general context to emphasise that some assertion comes from some authority.

Judge-Rapporteur   In Union law and politics, Rapporteur refers to a person who is appointed by a deliberative body to investigate a particular issue, and to report back to that body. When a case is heard by the Court of Justice, a Judge-Rapporteur is appointed. The Court of Justice delivers a single judgment for each case (rather than each judge delivering separate judgments). It is the responsibility of the Judge-Rapporteur to draft the judgment, which will inform the discussions of all the other judges assigned to that case. A single judgment will then be agreed by the judges acting by simple majority.

Jurisdiction   Normally used to refer to the power of a court or tribunal to hear a case. With regard to the Court of Justice of the European Union (i.e. the Court of Justice, the General Court and the specialised courts), its jurisdiction (i.e. power) to hear cases derives from the treaties.

Jus cogens   Latin phrase which means 'fundamental rights of the human person'.

Legal base   The Treaty article under which a legislative instrument (e.g. regulation, directive or decision) is proposed is often referred to as the legal base (and is occasionally referred to as legal basis). The legal base will set out the legislative procedure which must be followed for the proposed instrument to be adopted. *See also* LEGAL BASIS.

Legal basis   The Treaty article under which a legislative instrument (e.g. regulation, directive or decision) is proposed is occasionally referred to as the legal basis (it is normally referred to as legal base). The legal basis will set out the legislative procedure which must be followed for the proposed instrument to be adopted. *See also* LEGAL BASE.

Legal certainty   In Case 70/81 *Kloppenburg*, the Court of Justice stated that Union legislation must be unequivocal and its application must be predictable for those who are subject to it. This is referred to as the principle of legal certainty. *See also* NON-RETROACTIVITY.

Legitimate expectation   The principle of legitimate expectation provides that assurances relied on in good faith should be honoured (Case 169/73 *Compagnie Continentale* v *Council*).

Literal interpretation   Literal interpretation is used by courts to interpret legislation. If this method is employed, words are given their natural, plain meaning. This method of legislative interpretation is widely used by courts in the English legal system, but it is rarely used by the Court of Justice of the European Union. *See also* CONTEXTUAL INTERPRETATION; HISTORICAL INTERPRETATION; TELEOLOGICAL INTERPRETATION.

Locus standi   Latin phrase which means 'a place of standing'. In a legal context it refers to an individual's right to be heard in a court or tribunal.

Luxembourg Accords   The Luxembourg Accords were the result of an impasse between France and the other Member States of the EU during 1965. France refused to attend meetings of the Council resulting in important decision-making within the Union grinding to a halt. The Luxembourg Accords were negotiated. The Accords are not legally enforceable and are rarely (if ever) relied on.

Mandatory requirements defence   In the context of Arts 34 and 35 TFEU (previously Arts 28 and 29 EC Treaty), the second *Cassis* principle (Case 120/78) established a rule of reason (also referred to as the 'mandatory requirements defence') which provides that obstacles to the free movement of goods within the Union resulting from disparities between the national laws relating to the marketing of the products in question, must be accepted in so far as those provisions may be recognised as being necessary in order to satisfy mandatory requirements relating to, in particular, the effectiveness of fiscal supervision, the protection of public health, the fairness of commercial transactions and the defence of the consumer. *See also* PROPORTIONALITY TEST; RULE OF MUTUAL RECOGNITION; RULE OF REASON.

Marleasing interpretative obligation   National courts and tribunals are under an obligation to interpret national law in such a way that it avoids a conflict with Union law, if that is possible (Case C-106/89 *Marleasing*). This is known as the principle of indirect effect and is also referred to as the national court's *Marleasing* interpretative obligation. *See also* DIRECT EFFECT; INDIRECT EFFECT; INTERPRETATIVE OBLIGATION.

Marshall Plan   Following the end of the Second World War, the USA provided financial assistance to Western European states to aid economic recovery. This aid was referred to as the Marshall Plan.

Measure having an equivalent effect to a quantitative restriction (MEQR)   In the context of Arts 34 and 35 TFEU (previously Arts 28 and 29 EC Treaty), a measure having an equivalent effect to a quantitative restriction includes 'all trading rules enacted by Member States which are capable of hindering, directly or indirectly, actually or potentially, intra-Community [i.e. intra-Union] trade' (Case 8/74 *Procureur du Roi v Dassonville*). This is also referred to as the *Dassonville* formula. *See also* DISTINCTLY APPLICABLE MEASURE; INDISTINCTLY APPLICABLE MEASURE; QUANTITATIVE RESTRICTION.

MEP   Member of the European Parliament. *See also* EUROPEAN PARLIAMENT.

MEQR   *See* MEASURE HAVING AN EQUIVALENT EFFECT TO A QUANTITATIVE RESTRICTION.

Merger   A merger occurs when two or more business undertakings join together to form one business undertaking.

Mischief rule   The mischief rule is a method of legislative interpretation, sometimes used by courts in the English legal system. When applying this rule, the judge seeks to establish the legislative intent.

Monopoly   A monopoly exists if a commodity or service is controlled solely (or primarily) by one business undertaking or the state. *See also* STATE MONOPOLY.

Mutatis mutandis   Latin phrase which means 'with those things changed which need to be changed' or 'with the appropriate changes'.

NATO   *See* NORTH ATLANTIC TREATY ORGANISATION.

Natural justice   Concept in Union law derived from the English legal system, and closely linked to the USA's 'due process'. The Court of Justice often refers to it as a duty to act fairly (Case 222/86 *UNECTEF v Heylens*).

Non-retroactivity   Means that any changes to the law (through legislation or case law) should not be applied retrospectively. To do otherwise would conflict with the principle of legal certainty. In Union law this principle is applied in particular with regard to legal provisions which impose criminal sanctions. *See also* LEGAL CERTAINTY.

North Atlantic Treaty Organisation (NATO)   NATO was founded in 1949, following the end of the Second World War. It is a defence organisation for North America and Europe.

Obiter dictum   Latin phrase which is often referred to simply as *obiter* and means 'a thing said in passing'. In a legal context it refers to an observation by a judge on a point of law which is not directly relevant to the case before the court. The point of law is neither required by the judge's decision nor does it serve as a precedent. However, it may be of persuasive authority. The plural, *obiter dicta*, may be used, for example, when reference is made to multiple *obiter* statements which are contained within a judgment.

Objective justification   Objective justification (or the rule of reason) is a common concept throughout much of the Union's substantive law. It is based on the premise that a restriction, which might otherwise breach Union law, will be permissible provided: (i) the reason for the restriction is for a legitimate public interest; and (ii) the restriction is proportionate (i.e. it does not go beyond what is necessary to protect the legitimate public interest). *See also* PROPORTIONALITY TEST; RULE OF REASON.

OECD   *See* ORGANISATION FOR ECONOMIC COOPERATION AND DEVELOPMENT (OECD).

Oligopoly   An oligopoly is a market in which a small number of suppliers supply the vast majority of demand.

Opinion   Article 288 TFEU (previously Art 249 EC Treaty) provides that an opinion is a non-legally enforceable Union instrument. It may have a persuasive element (i.e. it may be taken into account by the Court of Justice of the European Union when determining a case).

Ordinary legislative procedure   Article 288 TFEU provides that regulations, directives and decisions constitute 'legal acts' of the Union. Article 289(3) TFEU provides that 'legal acts [i.e. regulations, directives and decisions] adopted by *legislative procedure* shall constitute *legislative acts*' (emphasis added). There are two legislative procedures prescribed by the TFEU: (i) the 'ordinary legislative procedure' (Art 289(1) TFEU); and (ii) the 'special legislative procedure' (Art 289(2) TFEU). The ordinary legislative procedure applies in the vast majority of cases. This procedure is practically a carbon copy of the former co-decision procedure (Art 294 TFEU (previously Art 251 EC Treaty)). The ordinary legislative procedure empowers the Parliament to propose amendments and ultimately to veto the proposal. The legal base determines the legislative procedure which has to be used for the adoption of a particular instrument. *See also* CO-DECISION PROCEDURE; COOPERATION PROCEDURE; LEGAL BASE; SPECIAL LEGISLATIVE PROCEDURE.

Organisation for Economic Cooperation and Development (OECD)   The OECD is a group of 34 member countries which share a commitment to democratic government and the market economy. It has active relationships with around 70 other countries and economies, non-governmental organisations (NGOs) and civil society. It is not a Union institution.

Parallel imports   Parallel imports refers to the situation where goods which are sold in one Member State, are purchased at a lower cost in another Member State, and imported (for sale) into the first Member State.

Per   Latin word which means 'by means of' or 'according to'.

Pillars   The Treaty on European Union (TEU) established the European Union. The former Art A TEU provided that 'the Union shall be founded on the European Communities, supplemented by the policies and forms of cooperation established by this Treaty'. It followed from this that the EU was to be founded upon three pillars. Following amendments made to the TEU by the ToA, Art 1 TEU provided that the three pillars would comprise: (i) the European Communities (i.e. the EC and Euratom); (ii) Common Foreign and Security Policy (CFSP); and (iii) Police and Judicial Cooperation in Criminal Matters. When the Treaty of Lisbon came into force on 1 December 2009, the EC Treaty was renamed the Treaty on the Functioning of the European Union (TFEU). The Union replaced and succeeded the Community (Art 1 TEU). Throughout the TFEU, the word 'Community' was replaced with the word 'Union'. The three pillars of the European Union no longer exist.

Posted workers   A business which employs workers in one Member State may send their workers to another Member State. Such workers are referred to as posted workers (i.e. a worker 'posted' from one Member State to another).

Precedent   The doctrine of precedent (*stare decisis*; a Latin phrase which means 'let the decision stand'), provides that courts and tribunals are bound by points of law decided by courts higher up in the hierarchy, and sometimes they are bound by their own previous decisions. The doctrine does not apply to the Court of Justice. However, the Court of Justice normally follows its own previous decisions for the sake of legal certainty. *See also* RATIO DECIDENDI.

Preliminary ruling   Pursuant to Art 267 TFEU (previously Art 234 EC Treaty), a national court or tribunal may (and in certain circumstances it must) refer a case to the Court of Justice if the national court or tribunal considers such a referral is necessary in order for it to reach its decision. The national court or tribunal asks the Court of Justice questions relating to, *inter alia*: interpretation of the Treaties; or the interpretation or validity of regulations, directives or decisions. The Court of Justice answers those questions and sends the case back to the referring court or tribunal for it to give judgment. This procedure is referred to as the 'preliminary ruling' procedure.

Prima facie   Latin phrase which means 'at first sight'. In a legal context, '*prima facie* case' refers to evidence which will suffice to support the allegation, unless there is evidence which rebuts the allegation.

Pro forma   Latin phrase which means 'for form' or 'as a matter of form', i.e. prescribing a set form or procedure.

Procedural *ultra vires*   When a decision maker, who is exercising a power or discretion, fails to follow an essential procedural requirement (quite often set out in the enabling legislation), this is referred to as 'procedural *ultra vires*'. The exercise of the power or discretion in such circumstances is unlawful. *See also* SUBSTANTIVE *ULTRA VIRES; ULTRA VIRES*.

Product substitution   Product substitution determines which products compete with each other. *See also* DEMAND-SIDE SUBSTITUTION; SUPPLY-SIDE SUBSTITUTION.

Proportionality test   The proportionality test is imported into Union law from the German legal system. The test is applied to ensure that interference with Union law principles, rights, prohibitions, etc. must be no more than is necessary to achieve the stated objective, which itself must be justifiable in the public interest. *See also* OBJECTIVE JUSTIFICATION; RULE OF REASON.

Protectionism   A rule imposed by the state or a regulatory body, the aim of which is to protect domestic traders from competition by foreign traders, is referred to as 'protectionism'.

Protocol   Protocols are often annexed (i.e. attached) to EU treaties. With regard to the protocols annexed to the TEU and TFEU, Art 51 TEU (previously Art 311 EC Treaty) states that 'The protocols and annexes to the Treaties shall form an integral part thereof'. The UK's opt-out from the Single European Currency is set out in a protocol annexed to the TFEU.

QR   *See* QUANTITATIVE RESTRICTION.

Qualified majority   The legal base determines the legislative procedure which has to be used for the adoption of a particular instrument. If the legal base provides for the instrument to be adopted by the Council acting by a 'qualified majority', the votes are weighted according to the population size of the Member States.

Quantitative restriction (QR)   In the context of Arts 34 and 35 TFEU (previously Arts 28 and 29 EC Treaty), a quantitative restriction (QR) relates to measures which amount to a total or partial restraint of imports, exports or goods in transit (Case 2/73 ***Geddo***). *See also* DISTINCTLY APPLICABLE MEASURE; INDISTINCTLY APPLICABLE MEASURE; MEASURE HAVING AN EQUIVALENT EFFECT TO A QUANTITATIVE RESTRICTION.

Rapporteur   In Union law and politics, Rapporteur refers to a person who is appointed by a deliberative body (e.g. the European Parliament) to investigate a particular issue, and to report back to that body.

Ratification   Means 'approval'.

Ratio decidendi   Latin phrase which means the legal reason (or ground) for a judicial decision. It is the *ratio decidendi* (or *ratio*) of a case which will bind later courts under the system of precedent. *See also* PRECEDENT.

Recommendation Article 288 TFEU (previously Art 249 EC Treaty) provides that a recommendation is a non-legally enforceable Union instrument. It may have a persuasive element (i.e. it may be taken into account by the Court of Justice of the European Union when determining a case).

Regulation A regulation is a legally effective Union instrument. Article 288 TFEU (previously Art 249 EC Treaty) provides that a regulation shall be directly applicable. This means it is incorporated automatically into the national legal systems of the Member States.

Respondent A respondent is the person against whom a claim is made in a court or tribunal (also referred to as a defendant).

Restrictive agreement A restrictive agreement is an agreement between otherwise independent business undertakings the aim of which is to protect their market share, which may affect trade between the Member States, and which distorts competition within the internal market. Such agreements are prohibited by Art 101 TFEU (previously Art 81 EC Treaty).

Rule of mutual recognition The first *Cassis* principle (Case 120/78), referred to as the 'rule of mutual recognition', provides that once goods have been lawfully marketed in one Member State, they should be free to be marketed in any other Member State without restriction. *See also* MANDATORY REQUIREMENTS DEFENCE; RULE OF REASON.

Rule of reason The rule of reason (or objective justification) is a common concept throughout much of the Union's substantive law. It is based on the premise that a restriction, which might otherwise breach Union law, will be permissible provided: (i) the reason for the restriction is for a legitimate public interest; and (ii) the restriction is proportionate (i.e. it does not go beyond what is necessary to protect the legitimate public interest). In the context of Arts 34 and 35 TFEU (previously Arts 28 and 29 EC Treaty), the second *Cassis* principle (Case 120/78) established a rule of reason which provides that obstacles to the free movement of goods within the Union resulting from disparities

between the national laws relating to the marketing of the products in question must be accepted in so far as those provisions may be recognised as being necessary in order to satisfy mandatory requirements relating to, in particular, the effectiveness of fiscal supervision, the protection of public health, the fairness of commercial transactions and the defence of the consumer. *See also* MANDATORY REQUIREMENTS DEFENCE; OBJECTIVE JUSTIFICATION; PROPORTIONALITY TEST; RULE OF MUTUAL RECOGNITION.

Schengen Agreement The Schengen Agreement abolished the internal borders of the signatory states and created a single external border where immigration checks for the Schengen area are carried out in accordance with a single set of rules. Common rules regarding visas, asylum rights and checks at external borders were adopted to allow the free movement of persons within the signatory states without disturbing law and order. *See also* SCHENGEN INFORMATION SYSTEM.

Schengen Information System (SIS) The SIS is an information network which was set up to allow all border posts, police stations and consular agents from Schengen group Member States to access data on specific individuals or on vehicles or objects which have been lost or stolen. Member States supply the network through national networks (N-SIS) connected to a central system (C-SIS), and this is supplemented by a network known as SIRENE (Supplementary Information Request at the National Entry). The system was not designed to operate in more than 15 Member States. SIS-II is the new second-generation SIS. SIS-II has greater capacity, thus enabling all Member States to use the system. *See also* SCHENGEN AGREEMENT. 10

SEA *See* SINGLE EUROPEAN ACT.

Secondary legislation In Union law, secondary legislation refers to Union instruments which are adopted by the Union institutions, pursuant to powers contained within the treaties. Article 288 TFEU (previously Art 249 EC Treaty) provides that such instruments shall be in the form of regulations, directives or decisions.

Single European Act (SEA) The SEA came into force on 1 July 1987 and amended the founding Treaties (in particular the EC Treaty (now renamed TFEU)).

Single European Currency Following amendments made by the TEU to the EC Treaty (renamed the TFEU by the ToL), a timetable for the adoption of the Single European Currency (the euro) was established. The euro became legal tender in 12 of the 15 pre-2004 Member States on 1 January 2002. The UK, Denmark and Sweden opted out of the single currency. On 1 January 2007 Slovenia adopted the euro, followed by Southern Cyprus and Malta on 1 January 2008, Slovakia on 1 January 2009, Estonia on 1 January 2011, Latvia on 1 January 2014 and Lithuania on 1 January 2015. The euro has therefore replaced the national currency in 19 of the current 28 Member States. *See also* ECONOMIC AND MONETARY UNION; EURO.

SIS *See* SCHENGEN INFORMATION SYSTEM.

Social Chapter The Social Chapter was annexed to the TEU as a protocol, applying to all of the then Member States except the UK. The Social Chapter covers, *inter alia*, employee protection rights. Following the election of a Labour government in the UK on 1 May 1997, the UK no longer objected to the Social Chapter and therefore it was incorporated into the EC Treaty when the Treaty was amended by the ToA on 1 May 1999. The EC Treaty was renamed the TFEU when the ToL came into force on 1 December 2009.

Soft law Non-legally enforceable instruments which may aid the interpretation and/or application of Union law are referred to as 'soft law'. Soft law, in the EU context, includes recommendations and opinions.

Special legislative procedure Article 288 TFEU provides that regulations, directives and decisions constitute 'legal acts' of the Union. Article 289(3) TFEU provides that 'legal acts [i.e. regulations, directives and decisions] adopted by *legislative procedure* shall constitute *legislative acts*' (emphasis added). There are two legislative procedures prescribed by the TFEU: (i) the 'ordinary legislative procedure' (Art 289(1) TFEU); and (ii) the 'special legislative procedure' (Art 289(2) TFEU). The ordinary legislative procedure applies in the vast majority of cases. This procedure is practically a carbon copy of the former co-decision procedure (Art 294 TFEU (previously Art 251 EC Treaty)). The special legislative procedure refers to specific cases where the Treaties provide for the adoption of a regulation, directive or decision: (i) by the European Parliament with the Council's involvement; or (ii) by the Council with the participation of the European Parliament (Art 289(2) TFEU). The difference between the two is that the former will require the act to be adopted jointly by the Parliament and the Council, whereas the latter simply requires consultation with Parliament. The legal base will detail the exact role of each institution, together with the voting procedure (in the case of the Council, the voting procedure is qualified majority unless otherwise stated (Art 16(3) TEU)). *See also* CO-DECISION PROCEDURE; COOPERATION PROCEDURE; LEGAL BASE; ORDINARY LEGISLATIVE PROCEDURE.

Stare decisis Latin phrase which means 'let the decision stand'. In a legal context it refers to the doctrine of precedent. *See also* PRECEDENT.

State aid State aid is aid (financial or non-financial) which is granted by the state to a business undertaking. The compatibility of state aid with the internal market is governed by Art 107(1) TFEU (previously Art 87(1) EC Treaty).

State liability The principle of state liability, established by the Court of Justice in Cases C-6 and 9/90 *Francovich*, provides that if a person suffers damage because of a Member State's breach of Union law, the Member State is liable to the aggrieved person if: (i) the rule of Union law infringed is intended to confer rights on individuals; (ii) the breach is sufficiently serious; and (iii) there is a direct causal link between the breach of the rule and the damage sustained by the person (Cases C-46 and 48/93 *Brasserie du Pêcheur* and *Factortame*). *See also* FRANCOVICH DAMAGES.

State monopoly A state monopoly exists where a commodity or service is controlled solely by the state (e.g. nationalised utilities: gas, electricity, water, etc.). Article 37 TFEU (previously Art 31 EC Treaty) regulates state monopolies. *See also* MONOPOLY.

Subsidiarity The exercise of Union competences is governed by 'the principles of subsidiarity and proportionality' (Art 5(1) TEU). In those areas which do not fall within the Union's exclusive competence, the Union shall act 'only if and so far as the objectives of the proposed action cannot be sufficiently achieved by the Member States, either at central level or at regional and local level' (Art 5(3) TEU). This is referred to as the principle of subsidiarity. Article 5(1) TEU is complemented by a Protocol on the application of the two principles of subsidiarity and proportionality (Protocol No. 2 which is annexed to the TEU and TFEU), which incorporates an 'early-warning system' involving national parliaments in the monitoring of how subsidiarity is applied. National parliaments are informed of all new legislative initiatives and if at least one-third of them are of the view that a proposal infringes the principle of subsidiarity, the Commission will have to reconsider the proposal.

Substantive *ultra vires* When a decision-maker, who exercises a power or discretion, has no competence to exercise such power or discretion, this is referred to as 'substantive *ultra vires*'. The exercise of the power or discretion in such circumstances is unlawful. *See also* PROCEDURAL *ULTRA VIRES; ULTRA VIRES.*

Sui generis Latin phrase which means 'of its own kind' or 'in a class of its own'.

Supply-side substitutability Supply-side substitutability is concerned with the ability of a manufacturer to switch production from one product to another.

Teleological interpretation Teleological interpretation is used by courts to interpret legislation. If this method is employed when interpreting Union law, the provision will be interpreted in furtherance of the aims and objectives of the Union as a whole. This method of legislative interpretation, together with contextual interpretation, is extensively used by the Court of Justice of the European Union. *See also* CONTEXTUAL INTERPRETATION; HISTORICAL INTERPRETATION; LITERAL INTERPRETATION

TEU *See* TREATY ON EUROPEAN UNION.

TFEU *See* TREATY ON THE FUNCTIONING OF THE EUROPEAN UNION.

Third country Within Union law, third country is used to refer to a country which is not a member of the EU (i.e. a non-Member State).

Three pillars of the European Union The Treaty on European Union (TEU) established the European Union. The former Art A TEU provided

that 'the Union shall be founded on the European Communities, supplemented by the policies and forms of cooperation established by this Treaty'. It followed from this that the EU was to be founded upon three pillars. Following amendments made to the TEU by the ToA, Art 1 TEU provided that the three pillars would comprise: (i) the European Communities (i.e. the EC and Euratom); (ii) Common Foreign and Security Policy (CFSP); and (iii) Police and Judicial Cooperation in Criminal Matters. When the Treaty of Lisbon came into force on 1 December 2009, the EC Treaty was renamed the Treaty on the Functioning of the European Union (TFEU). The Union replaced and succeeded the Community (Art 1 TEU). Throughout the TFEU, the word 'Community' was replaced with the word 'Union'. The three pillars of the European Union no longer exist.

ToA *See* TREATY OF AMSTERDAM.

ToL *See* TREATY OF LISBON.

ToN *See* TREATY OF NICE.

Treaty A Treaty is an agreement between two or more countries. A treaty will not be legally enforceable unless this is provided for within the treaty. The TEU and TFEU incorporate enforcement mechanisms to ensure Member States comply with their Union law obligations. In addition, Union institutions were established to develop Union law through the adoption of Union instruments. A Court of Justice of the European Union was established to ensure uniform application of Union law throughout the Member States.

Treaty of Accession A Treaty of Accession is adopted by the Member States to provide for enlargement of the European Union. There was a Treaty of Accession to provide for Croatia's entry to the EU on 1 July 2013.

Treaty of Amsterdam (ToA) The Treaty of Amsterdam came into force on 1 May 1999 and amended the EC Treaty (now renamed the TFEU) and the TEU.

Treaty of Lisbon (ToL) The Treaty of Lisbon came into force on 1 December 2009. The EC Treaty has been renamed the Treaty on the Functioning of the European Union (TFEU). The articles within both the TEU and TFEU have been renumbered as part of a simplification exercise.

The ToL renumbering came into effect when the ToL itself came into force (1 December 2009). The Union has replaced and succeeded the Community (Art 1 TEU). Throughout the TFEU, the word 'Community' has been replaced with the word 'Union'. The following terms are therefore no longer used: European *Community*; European *Communities*; or *Community* law. Reference is made solely to the European *Union* (or *Union*) and European *Union* law (or *Union* law). The TEU and the TFEU now constitute the Treaties on which the Union is founded (Art 1 TEU).

Treaty of Nice (ToN)   The Treaty of Nice came into force on 1 February 2003 and amended the EC Treaty (now renamed the TFEU) and the TEU.

Treaty of Rome   The EEC Treaty is often referred to as the Treaty of Rome because it was signed in Rome on 25 March 1957. However, the Euratom Treaty was also signed in Rome at the same time. The EEC Treaty's official title is 'The Treaty Establishing the European Community', not the Treaty of Rome. The EEC Treaty was renamed the TFEU when the ToL came into force on 1 December 2009.

Treaty on European Union (TEU)   The Treaty on European Union came into force on 1 November 1993. The TEU amended the founding treaties, and also established the European Union. The TEU renamed the EEC the EC. Following the ToL coming into force on 1 December 2009 the term 'EC' is no longer used. *See also* EUROPEAN ATOMIC ENERGY COMMUNITY; EUROPEAN COAL AND STEEL COMMUNITY; EUROPEAN COMMUNITIES; EUROPEAN COMMUNITY; EUROPEAN ECONOMIC COMMUNITY; EUROPEAN UNION.

Treaty on the Functioning of the European Union (TFEU)   When the Treaty of Lisbon came into force on 1 December 2009, the EC Treaty was renamed the Treaty on the Functioning of the European Union (TFEU). The articles within the TFEU have been renumbered as part of a simplification exercise. The ToL renumbering came into effect when the ToL itself came into force (1 December 2009). The Union has replaced and succeeded the Community (Art 1 TEU). Throughout the TFEU, the word 'Community' has been replaced with the word 'Union'. The following terms are therefore no longer used: European *Community*; European *Communities*; or *Community* law. Reference is made solely to the European *Union* (or *Union*) and European *Union* law (or *Union* law). The TEU and the TFEU now constitute the Treaties on which the Union is founded (Art 1 TEU). *See also* TREATY OF LISBON.

Ultra vires   Latin phrase which means 'beyond the power' or 'without authority'. In a legal context it means an act which is in excess of that authorised by law, thus rendering the act invalid. *See also* PROCEDURAL *ULTRA VIRES*; SUBSTANTIVE *ULTRA VIRES*.

Undertaking   An undertaking is a business. In the English legal system this could refer to a sole trader, a partnership, or a company.

Vertical direct effect   A provision of Union law which is enforceable in national courts or tribunals against the state or emanation of the state, overriding any inconsistent national provisions, is said to have vertical direct effect (Case C-188/89 *Foster* v *British Gas*). Treaty articles, regulations and directives are capable of having vertical direct effect if the provision is sufficiently precise and unconditional (Case 26/62 *Van Gend en Loos*). *See also* DIRECT EFFECT; HORIZONTAL DIRECT EFFECT.

Vertical restrictive agreement   A vertical restrictive agreement refers to an agreement where the parties to the agreement are not in direct competition with each other (e.g. an agreement between a manufacturer and a retailer, or a wholesaler and a retailer).

Vis-à-vis   French phrase which means 'in comparison with' or 'in relation to'.

Index

787